— start/run   type in CMD   [Enter]
— type in Dos [commands] —> ping   IP add   - t

CONTENTS AT A GLANCE

Table of Contents

Part II   Operating System Technologies

7 1.0 Operating System Fundamentals   585

Part III   Final Review

Part IV   Appendixes

About the Author

Charles J. Brooks is currently the President of Marcraft International Corporation, located in Kennewick, Washington, and is in charge of research and development. He is the author of several books, including *Speech Synthesis, Pneumatic Instrumentation, The Complete Introductory Computer Course, Radio-Controlled Car Project Manual,* and *IBM PC Peripheral*

Troubleshooting and Repair. A former electronics instructor and technical writer with the National Education Corporation, Charles has taught and written on post-secondary EET curriculum, including introductory electronics, transistor theory, linear integrated circuits, basic digital theory, industrial electronics, microprocessors, and computer peripherals.

ABOUT THE TECHNICAL REVIEWERS

These reviewers contributed their considerable hands-on expertise to the entire development process for *A+ Certification Training Guide, Third Edition*. As the book was being written, these dedicated professionals reviewed all the material for technical content, organization, and flow. Their feedback was critical to ensuring that *A+ Certification Training Guide, Third Edition* fits our reader's need for the highest-quality technical information.

Brian Alley has been in the PC industry since 1985. He has worked as a contract consultant primarily at law enforcement agencies installing networks and custom software. Joining Boston University's Corporate Education Center in 1992 as a contract instructor, Mr. Alley developed the first PC Service and Support course. This involved writing training materials, labs, and course outlines for PC Service and Support.

Additionally, Mr. Alley taught several Novell NetWare courses, Data Communications, Network, and applications programs. In 1995 Mr. Alley joined BUCEC as a full-time staff instructor, becoming the lead instructor for PC Service and Support and the A+ Certification programs. In his role as lead instructor, Mr. Alley regularly reviews new training materials, writes new labs, and qualifies new instructors. He has been contracted by a major computer training material publisher to serve as Technical Editor for three books currently in print and is working on soon-to-be-published new materials for Network +. Mr. Alley, as an MCT and MCSE, is currently certified to teach more than 20 Microsoft courses, including Windows 95, Windows 98, Windows NT, Windows 2000, and network-related topics. He has served as a Subject Matter Expert for the 1995 A+ exam rewrite, and served as a Beta tester for A+, Network +, Windows 98, Windows 2000, and several other products. He has served on the A+ Advisory Committee and the Internet + Advisory Committee. He is currently A+, iNet+, Server+, and Network+ certified in addition to being an MCT, MCP, and MCSE.

Jerald A. Dively has been involved in computers and computer networks for five years. He was the Workgroup manager for the Department of the Air Force for six years. While there he was responsible for utilization and training for 90 workgroup managers. He has an AS Degree in Network Administration and Business Administration. He was a Systems Administrator at a major Air Force installation in Texas, where he was responsible for a network consisting of 1,100 clients. He has written a CCNA Test Preparation book for a major publishing company and has reviewed many computer books. He now works as a Network Administrator and Systems Integrator in Florida. He has received his MSCE, CCNA, CNA, CNST, A+, Networking +, CST and other certifications.

Dedication

Charles J. Brooks

Once again, I want to thank my wife, Robbie, for her support throughout another book campaign. Without her support and help, I'm sure there would be no books by Charles Brooks.

Acknowledgments

I want to thank many individuals for their efforts in preparing this book.

My staff at Marcraft has worked diligently to make certain that this is a quality product. I want to thank Cathy Boulay and Mike Hall for their artistic efforts, which are demonstrated throughout the book.

I also owe a big thanks to Paul Havens, Wanda Dawson, Evan Samaritano, Grigoriy Ter-oganov, Yu Wen Ho, and Caleb Sarka of my Technical Services and Development staffs for many things, including turning my hands-on procedure ideas into working lab explorations, for their review and proofreading skills, and for their test-bank compilation work. Thanks also to Tony Tonda for all his work preparing user-support materials for the project.

I want to thank Brian Alley of Boston University for his invaluable insight on this project and his friendship.

Also, I want to give a big thanks to Jerry Dively, my other Technical Reviewer, for his diligent efforts to point me in the right directions. Input and suggestions from both of you have been very helpful in refining this book into the great educational and certification tool that it is.

As always, everyone I have worked with at New Riders Publishing has made this a pleasant experience. Jeff Riley, Keith Cline, and Lori Lyons, thanks again for another great life experience. Let's do another one sometime.

Finally, I want to thank all the people who purchased the first or second editions of the book and cared enough to share their feedback with me. You may see one of your suggestions in this version. Good luck with the exam, but I hope you don't need it after using this book and CD.

Tell Us What You Think

As the reader of this book, you are the most important critic and commentator. We value your opinion and want to know what we're doing right, what we could do better, what areas you'd like to see us publish in, and any other words of wisdom you're willing to pass our way.

As the Executive Editor for the Web Development team at New Riders Publishing, I welcome your comments. You can fax, email, or write me directly to let me know what you did or didn't like about this book—as well as what we can do to make our books stronger.

Please note that I cannot help you with technical problems related to the topic of this book, and that due to the high volume of mail I receive, I might not be able to reply to every message.

When you write, please be sure to include this book's title and author as well as your name and phone or fax number. I will carefully review your comments and share them with the author and editors who worked on the book.

Fax: 317-581-4663

Email: stephanie.wall@newriders.com

Mail: Stephanie Wall
            Executive Editor
            New Riders Publishing
            201 West 103rd Street
            Indianapolis, IN 46290 USA

How to Use This Book

New Riders Publishing has made an effort in its Training Guide series to make the information as accessible as possible for the purposes of learning the certification material. Here, you have an opportunity to view the many instructional features that have been incorporated into the books to achieve that goal.

CHAPTER OPENER

Each chapter begins with a set of features designed to allow you to maximize study time for that material.

List of Objectives: Each chapter begins with a list of the objectives as stated by CompTIA.

Objective Explanations: Immediately following each objective is an explanation of it, providing context that defines it more meaningfully in relation to the exam. Because the objectives list can sometimes be vague, the objective explanations are designed to clarify any vagueness by relying on the authors' test-taking experience.

OBJECTIVES

This chapter helps you to prepare for the Core Hardware module of the A+ Certification examination by covering the following objectives within the "Domain 1.0: Installation, Configuration, and Upgrading" section.

1.1 Identify basic terms, concepts, and functions of system modules, including how each module should work during normal operation and during the boot process.

Examples of concepts and modules:

- System board
- Power supply
- Processor/CPU
- Memory
- Storage devices
- Monitor
- Modem
- Firmware
- BIOS
- CMOS
- LCD (portable systems)
- Ports
- PDA (Personal Digital Assistant)

▶ Every computer technician should be able to identify the major components of a typical personal computer (PC) system and be able to describe their functions.

CHAPTER 1

1.0 Installation, Configuration, and Upgrading

OUTLINE

Chapter Outline: Learning always gets a boost when you can see both the forest and the trees. To give you a visual image of how the topics in a chapter fit together, you will find a chapter outline at the beginning of each chapter. You will also be able to use this for easy reference when looking for a particular topic.

STUDY STRATEGIES

To prepare for the motherboard, processors, and memory objective of the Core Hardware exam:

▶ Read the objectives at the beginning of this chapter.

▶ Study the information in this chapter.

▶ Review the objectives listed earlier in this chapter.

▶ Perform any step-by-step procedures in the text.

▶ Answer the Review and Exam Questions at the end of the chapter and check your results.

▶ Use the ExamGear test engine on the CD that accompanies this book for additional review and exam questions concerning this material

▶ Review the Test Tips scattered throughout the chapter and make certain that you are comfortable with each point.

Study Strategies: Each topic presents its own learning challenge. To support you through this, New Riders has included strategies for how to best approach studying in order to retain the material in the chapter, particularly as it is addressed on the exam.

INSTRUCTIONAL FEATURES WITHIN THE CHAPTER

These books include a large amount and different kinds of information. The many different elements are designed to help you identify information by its purpose and importance to the exam and also to provide you with varied ways to learn the material. You will be able to determine how much attention to devote to certain elements, depending on what your goals are. By becoming familiar with the different presentations of information, you will know what information will be important to you as a test-taker and which information will be important to you as a practitioner.

> **WARNING**
>
> **Lethal Voltage Levels** You must exercise great caution when opening or working inside the monitor. The voltage levels present during operation are lethal. Electrical potentials as high as 25,000V are present inside the unit when it is operating.

> **TEST TIP**
>
> Memorize the values of lethal voltage associated with the inside of the CRT video monitor. The values given on tests may not be exactly the same as those stated in the textbook, but they will be in the same high range.

Warning: In using sophisticated information technology, there is always potential for mistakes or even catastrophes that can occur through improper application of the technology. Warnings appear in the margins to alert you to such potential problems.

Test Tip: Test Tips appear in the margins to provide specific exam-related advice. Such tips may address what material is covered (or not covered) on the exam, how it is covered, mnemonic devices, or particular quirks of that exam.

---

28   Part I   CORE HARDWARE SERVICE TECHNICIAN

provide an introductory course on common PC components that includes a brief discussion of the theory of their operation and the basic functions that each component supplies. These sections also present the standards that the industry has developed for these components.

PC Standards

Late in 1981, IBM entered the microcomputer market with the unveiling of their now famous *IBM Personal Computer* (PC). At the time of its introduction, the IBM PC was a drastic departure from the status quo of the microcomputer world.

The IBM PC employed an Intel 8088 16/8-bit microprocessor. (It processes data 16 bits at a time internally, but moves it around in 8-bit packages.) Relatively speaking, the IBM PC was fast, powerful, flexible, and priced within the range of most individuals. The general public soon became aware of the tremendous possibilities of the PC, and the microcomputer quickly advanced from a simple game machine to an office tool with a seemingly endless range of advanced personal and business applications. In 1983, IBM added a small hard disk drive to the PC and introduced the Extended Technology (PC-XT) version.

IBM elevated the PC market again when, in 1984, IBM introduced the *Advanced Technology PC (PC-AT)*. The AT used a true 16-bit microprocessor (which processes data 16 bits at a time internally and has a 16-bit external data bus) from Intel, called the 80286. The wider data bus increased the speed of the computer's operation, just because the 80286 could transfer and process twice as much data at a time as the 8088 could.

Many of the decisions made in designing the AT still influence the PC-compatible computer today. The AT architecture established industry standards for its

◆ Expansion bus

◆ System addressing

◆ Peripheral addressing

◆ System resource allocations

> **Reference Shelf**
>
> For more in-depth technical information about the 8088 microprocessor and its operation, refer to the "8088 Microprocessor" section of the Electronic Reference Shelf located on the CD that accompanies this book.

> **NOTE**
>
> **Industry Standard Architecture** The tremendous popularity of the original IBM PC-XT and PC-AT systems created a set of pseudo-standards for hardware and software compatibility. The AT architecture became so popular that it has become the *Industry Standard Architecture* (ISA). Most microcomputers are still both hardware- and software-compatible with the original A

Reference Shelf: These margin notes refer you to articles located in the electronic Reference Shelf provided on the CD. These articles provide in-depth technical information about a particular topic.

Note: Notes appear in the margins and contain various kinds of useful information, such as tips on the technology or administrative practices, historical background on terms and technologies, or side commentary on industry issues.

STEP BY STEP

1.1   Removing a System Board

1. Remove all external I/O systems.

2. Remove the system unit's outer cover.

3. Remove the option adapter cards.

4. Remove the cables from the system board.

5. Remove the system board.

Step by Step: Step by Steps are hands-on tutorial instructions that walk you through a particular task or function relevant to the exam objectives.

Chapter 1   1.0 INSTALLATION, CONFIGURATION, AND UPGRADING   207

FIGURE 1.139
Installing an external CD-R

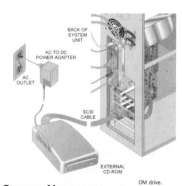

BACK OF
SYSTEM
UNIT

AC TO DC
POWER ADAPTER

AC
OUTLET

SCSI
CABLE

EXTERNAL
CD-ROM

OM drive.

Figure: Detailed figures help clarify your understanding of the text.

SYSTEM UPGRADING AND OPTIMIZING

▶ 1.8 Identify hardware methods of upgrading system performance, procedures for replacing basic subsystem components, unique components and when to use them.

The A+ Core Hardware objective 1.8 states that the test taker should be able to "identify hardware methods of upgrading system performance, procedures for replacing basic subsystem components, unique components and when to use them."

Examples include the following:

◆ Memory

◆ Hard drives

◆ Processors/CPU

◆ Upgrading BIOS

◆ When to upgrade BIOS

Objective Coverage Text: In the text before an exam objective is specifically addressed, you will notice the objective is listed to help call your attention to that particular material.

CHAPTER SUMMARY

This chapter has covered the fundamental hardware structures and components associated with PC-compatible systems. It has presented a mini-course on the basic organization and operation of the PC.

This chapter also has dealt expressly with the peculiar aspects of the portable computer systems. It has documented how portable units differ from conventional PC units. After completing the chapter, you should be able to identify the components of portable systems and describe how they differ from typical desktop components. You also should be able to identify their unique problems.

KEY TERMS

- Active-matrix display
- Adapter cards
- Advanced Power Management (APM)
- Advanced technology PC (PC-AT)

Chapter Summary: Before the Apply Your Knowledge section, you will find a chapter summary that wraps up the chapter and reviews what you should have learned.

Key Terms: A list of key terms appears at the end of each chapter. These are terms that you should be sure you know and are comfortable defining and understanding when you go in to take the exam.

EXTENSIVE REVIEW AND SELF-TEST OPTIONS

At the end of each chapter, along with some summary elements, you will find a section called "Apply Your Knowledge" that gives you several different methods with which to test your understanding of the material and review what you have learned.

RESOURCE URLS

www1.islandnet.com/~kpolsson/comphist.htm

www.levin.co.nz/pages/bios_survival/bios_sg.htm

http://webopedia.internet.com/term/m/motherboard.html

www.sysopt.com/bios.html

www.tomshardware.com/mainboard/99q1/990208/index.html

www.levin.co.nz/pages/bios_survival/bios_sg.htm

http://webopedia.internet.com/TERM/V/VESA.html

Resource URLs: Following the Key Terms is a list of helpful URLs you can check out.

APPLY YOUR KNOWLEDGE

Review Questions

1. Describe the major maintenance problem associated with notebook computers.

2. List the four subunits typically found inside the desktop system unit.

3. How can you avoid confusion between the DB-15M connectors for VGA and game port connections?

4. List three types of memory typically found on modern system boards.

5. Describe how data is stored on a magnetic disk.

6. List three power-management modes and describe how they differ.

7. What is the major procedural difference between installing a floppy drive and a hard drive?

8. What is the purpose of a docking station?

15. How is upgrading a system with a Flash BIOS different from upgrading a syste[m] standard ROM BIOS?

Exam Questions

1. What type of IC is the brain of the PC

   A. The ROM BIOS

   B. The ASIC device

   C. The memory controller

   D. The microprocessor

2. What function does the FDISK progra[m] perform?

   A. It removes lost allocation units fro[m] drive.

   B. It creates partitions on the physical

Review Questions: These open-ended, short-answer questions allow you to quickly assess your comprehension of what you just read in the chapter. Instead of asking you to choose from a list of options, these questions require you to state the correct answers in your own words. Although you will not experience these kinds of questions on the exam, these questions will indeed test your level of comprehension of key concepts.

Exam Questions: These questions reflect the kinds of multiple-choice questions that appear on the exams. Use them to become familiar with the exam question formats and to help you determine what you know and what you need to review or study more.

540   Part I   CORE HARDWARE SERVICE TECHNICIAN

APPLY YOUR KNOWLEDGE

Answers to Exam Questions

1. **C.** Dot-matrix printers have commonly been produced in 9-pin, 18-pin, and 24-pin versions. Currently, most dot-matrix printers use 24-pin printheads. For more information, see the section "Character Types."

2. **B.** A Hewlett-Packard laser cartridge contains the toner supply, a corona wire, the drum assembly, and the developing roller. Toner cartridges for other makes of laser printers may contain other components, or variations of these components. For more information, see the section "Component Variations."

3. **B.** The primary corona wire conditions the photosensitive drum by applying a uniform electrical charge to it after it has been cleaned. For more information, see the section "Laser-Printing Operations."

4. **A.** The printing process in a dot-matrix printer is mechanical and therefore, many things wear. The ink ribbon is the first place to look when print begins to degrade. This is the cheapest, easiest, and usually the only part that needs to be replaced when print quality diminishes. For more information, see the section "Ribbon Cartridges."

5. **A.** Adjusting the contrast control is the cheapest and easiest check to make when print quality diminishes in a laser printer. The toner supply is the second choice to check when print quality

comes into question. For more information, see the section "Print on Page Is Missing or Bad."

6. **D.** The Transfer corona wire applies a relatively positive charge to the paper so that it attracts the negatively charged toner particles. For more information, see the section "Laser-Printing Operations."

7. **C.** The six stages of the laser printing process, in order, are cleaning, conditioning, writing, developing, transferring, and fusing. For more information, see the section "Laser-Printer Components."

8. **B.** All dot-matrix printers consist of a power supply, an interface board, a paper-feed motor, a printhead mechanism, a printhead-positioning motor, and various sensors. They do not necessarily possess a tractor feed and they do not use ink cartridges. For more information, see the section "Dot-Matrix Printers."

9. **A.** Drop-on-demand ink delivery is used in consumer-oriented inkjet printers. This is used for the relatively low cost (when compared to the cost of continuous-stream ink-delivery systems). For more information, see the section "Inkjet Printers."

10. **D.** ALL paper is specified by weight expressed in terms of 500 22" × 17" sheets. (Envision four, standard 8.5" × 11" sheets organized to create the standard-weight sheet.) For more information, see the section "Paper Specifications."

Answers and Explanations: For each Review and Exam question, you will find thorough explanations located at the end of the section.

Introduction

A+ Certification Training Guide, Third Edition, is designed for those with the goal of certification as an A+ certified technician. It covers both the Core Hardware Service Technician (220-201) and Operating System Technologies (220-202) exams.

These exams measure essential competencies for a microcomputer hardware service technician with six months of on-the-job experience. You must demonstrate knowledge that would enable you to properly install, configure, upgrade, troubleshoot, and repair microcomputer hardware. This includes basic knowledge of desktop and portable systems, basic networking concepts, and printers. You also must demonstrate knowledge of safety and common preventive maintenance procedures.

This book is your one-stop shop. Everything you need to know to pass the exams is in here. You do not have to take a class in addition to buying this book to pass the exam. Depending on your personal study habits or learning style, however, you may benefit from buying this book *and* taking a class.

This book also can help advanced users and administrators who are not studying for the exam but are looking for a single-volume technical reference.

How This Book Helps You

This book provides a self-guided tour of all the areas covered by the Core Hardware Service Technician and Operating System Technologies exams and identifies the specific skills you need to achieve your A+ certification. You also will find the features that make New Riders' training guides so successful: clear organization,

helpful hints, tips, real-world examples, and step-by-step exercises. Specifically, this book is set up to help you in the following ways:

◆ **Organization**. This book is organized according to individual exam objectives. This book covers every objective that you need to know for the Core Hardware Service Technician and Operating System Technologies exams. The objectives are covered in the same order as they are listed by the certifying organization, CompTIA, to make it as easy as possible for you to learn the information. We also have attempted to make the information accessible in the following ways:

- This introduction includes the full list of exam topics and objectives.

- Each chapter begins with a list of the objectives to be covered.

- Each chapter also begins with an outline that provides an overview of the material and the page numbers of where you can find particular topics.

- Objectives are repeated within the text where the material most directly relevant to them is covered.

- Information on where the objectives are covered is also conveniently condensed on the tear card at the front of this book.

◆ **Instructional features**. This book has been designed to provide you with multiple ways to learn and reinforce the exam material. Following are some of the helpful methods:

- *Objective explanations*. As mentioned previously, each chapter begins with a list of the objectives covered in the chapter. In addition, immediately following each objective is an explanation in a context that defines it more meaningfully.

- *Study strategies.* The beginning of each chapter also includes strategies for studying and retaining the material in the chapter, particularly as it is addressed on the exam.

- *Test tips.* Exam tips appear in the margin to provide specific exam-related advice. Such tips may address what material is covered (or not covered) on the exam, how it is covered, mnemonic devices, and particular quirks of that exam.

- *Review breaks and summaries.* Crucial information is summarized at various points in the book in lists or tables. Each chapter ends with a summary as well.

- *Key terms.* A list of key terms appears at the end of each chapter. The key terms are also italicized the first time they appear in the text of the chapter.

- *Notes.* These appear in the margin and contain various kinds of useful information such as tips on technology or administrative practices, historical background on terms and technologies, or side commentary on industry issues.

- *Warnings.* When using sophisticated technology improperly, the potential for mistakes or even catastrophes to occur is ever-present. Warnings appear in the margin to alert you to such potential problems.

- *Step by Steps.* These are hands-on, tutorial instructions that lead you through a particular task or function relevant to the exam objectives.

- *Lab exercises.* There are 44 exercises or lab procedures included on the CD that accompanies this book, providing you with more opportunities for hands-on learning and reinforcement of the concepts.

◆ **Extensive practice test options**. This book provides numerous opportunities for you to assess your knowledge and to practice for the exam. The practice options include the following:

- *Review Questions.* These open-ended questions appear in the "Apply Your Knowledge" section at the end of each chapter. They enable you to quickly assess your comprehension of what you just read in the chapter. Answers to the questions are provided later in the section.

- *Exam Questions.* These questions also appear in the "Apply Your Knowledge" section. They reflect the kinds of multiple-choice questions that appear on the A+ exams. Use them to practice for the exam and to help you determine what you know and what you need to review or study further. Answers and explanations for them are provided.

- *Practice exam.* A practice exam is included in the "Final Review" section for each exam (as discussed later).

- *ExamGear.* The *ExamGear* software included on the CD that accompanies this book provides even more practice questions. You also can purchase more questions; these questions are already on the CD and merely need to be "unlocked" so that you can access them.

N O T E | **More About ExamGear** For a complete description of the New Riders *ExamGear* test engine, see Appendix D, "Using the *ExamGear Training Guide Edition* Software."

◆ **Final Review**. This part of the book provides the following three valuable tools that can help you prepare for the exam:

- *Fast Facts*. This condensed version of the information contained in the book will prove extremely useful for last-minute review.

- *Study and Exam Prep Tips*. Read this section early on to help you develop study strategies. It also provides valuable exam-day tips and information.

- *Practice Exam*. A full practice test for each of the exams is included. Questions are written in the styles used on the actual exams. Use it to assess your readiness for the real thing.

The book includes several valuable appendixes as well, including a glossary (Appendix A), an overview of the A+ certification program (Appendix B), a description of what is on the CD-ROM (Appendix C), and an explanation of the *ExamGear* test engine (Appendix D).

These and all the other book features mentioned previously will enable you to thoroughly prepare for the exam.

To register for the A+ exam, contact Marcraft at 800-441-6006. Special discounts are available for New Riders customers.

For more information about the exam or the certification process, contact Marcraft International or the CompTIA organization:

Marcraft International
Atten: A+ Certification
Exam Dept.
100 N. Morain St.
Kennewick, WA 99336
Tel: 800-441-6006
Fax: 509-374-1951
info@mic-inc.com
www.mic-inc.com

CompTIA Headquarters
450 E. 22nd St., Suite 230
Lombard, IL 60148-6158
Tel: 630-268-1818
Fax: 630-268-1834
info@comptia.org
www.comptia.org

A+ CORE HARDWARE SERVICE TECHNICIAN EXAMINATION BLUEPRINT

For A+ certification, you must pass both this examination and the A+ Operating System Technologies examination. As noted previously, the examination measures essential competencies for a microcomputer hardware service technician with six months of on-the-job experience.

N O T E | **Post-Beta Objectives** The objectives detailed in this section cover the A+ Core Hardware Service Technician exam blueprint. This document was produced after the final technical and psychometric review of the item pool following the beta-testing period. This document reflects the topics and technologies that appear as part of the A+ Core Hardware exam.

The objectives listed here represent CompTIA's outline of November 20, 2000. This certification exam went live on January 31, 2001, with a few cosmetic changes to the outline. (CompTIA made their changes two weeks before the test went live.) This should in no way affect the test taker's ability to study for and pass the exam because no additional material was added to the exam itself.

The skills and knowledge measured by the examination are derived from an industry-wide job-task analysis and validated through a worldwide survey of 5,000 A+ certified professionals. The results of the worldwide survey were used in weighting the domains and ensuring that the weighting is representative of the relative importance of that content to the job requirements of a service technician with six months of on-the-job experience. The results of the job-task analysis and survey can be found in the following report:

◆ CompTIA A+ Job Task Analysis (JTA) (November 2000)

This examination blueprint includes weighting, test objectives, and example content. Example topics and concepts are included to clarify the test objectives; do not construe these as a comprehensive list of the content of this examination.

The following table lists the domains measured by this examination and the approximate extent to which they are represented.

TABLE 1

DOMAIN REPRESENTATION

Domain	% of Examination (Approximately)
1.0 Installation, Configuration, and Upgrading	30%
2.0 Diagnosing and Troubleshooting	30%
3.0 Preventive Maintenance	5%
4.0 Motherboard/Processors/Memory	15%
5.0 Printers	10%
6.0 Basic Networking	10%
Total	100.00%

In terms of the exam itself, the examinee selects, from four response options, the one option that best completes the statement or answers the question. The exam directions read as follows:

> Read the statement or question and, from the response options, select only one letter that represents the most correct or best answer.

Distracters or wrong answers are response options that examinees with incomplete knowledge or skill would likely choose, but are generally plausible responses fitting into the content area.

The sections that follow outline the objectives for the exam and provide representative (but not necessarily complete) content areas that reflect each objective.

Domain 1.0 Installation, Configuration, and Upgrading

This domain requires the knowledge and skills required to identify, install, configure, and upgrade microcomputer modules and peripherals, following established basic procedures for system assembly and disassembly of field-replaceable modules. Elements include the ability to identify and configure IRQs, DMAs, I/O addresses, and set switches and jumpers.

Objectives and Representative Content

1.1   Identify basic terms, concepts, and functions of system modules, including how each module should work during normal operation and during the boot process.

Examples of concepts and modules include the following:

- System board
- Power supply
- Processor/CPU
- Memory
- Storage devices
- Monitor
- Modem
- Firmware
- BIOS
- CMOS
- LCD (portables)
- Ports
- PDAs

1.2   Identify basic procedures for adding and removing field replaceable modules for desktop and portable systems.

Examples of modules include the following:

- System board
- Storage device
- Power supply
- Processor/CPU
- Memory
- Input devices
- Hard drive
- Keyboard
- Video board
- Mouse
- Network Interface Card

Portable System Components

- AC adapters
- DC controllers
- LCD panel
- PC Card
- Pointing devices

1.3   Identify available IRQs, DMAs, and I/O addresses and procedures for configuring them for device installation and configuration.

Content may include the following:

- Standard IRQ settings
- Modems
- Floppy drive controllers
- Hard drive controllers
- USB port
- Infrared ports
- Hexadecimal/Addresses

1.4   Identify common peripheral ports, associated cabling and their connectors.

Content may include the following:

- Cable types
- Cable orientation
- Serial versus parallel
- Pin connections

Examples of types of connectors include the following:

- DB-9
- DB-25
- RJ-11
- RJ-45

- BNC
- PS2/MINI-DIN
- USB
- IEEE-1394

1.5 Identify proper procedures for installing and configuring IDE/EIDE devices.

Content may include the following:

- Master/slave
- Devices per channel
- Primary/Secondary

1.6 Identify proper procedures for installing and configuring SCSI devices.

Content may include the following:

- Address/termination conflicts
- Cabling
- Types (regular, wide, ultra-wide)
- Internal versus external
- Jumper block settings (binary equivalents)

1.7 Identify proper procedures for installing and configuring peripheral devices.

Content may include the following:

- Monitor/video card
- Modem
- USB peripherals and hubs
- IEEE-1284
- IEEE-1394
- External Storage

Portables

- Docking stations
- PC Cards
- Port replicators
- Infrared devices

1.8 Identify hardware methods of upgrading system performance, procedures for replacing basic and unique subsystem components and when to use them.

Content may include the following:

- Memory
- Hard drives
- CPU
- Upgrading BIOS
- When to upgrade

Portable Systems

- Battery
- Hard Drive
- Type I, II, III cards
- Memory

Domain 2.0 Diagnosing and Troubleshooting

This domain requires the ability to apply knowledge relating to diagnosing and troubleshooting common module problems and system malfunctions. This includes knowledge of the symptoms relating to common problems.

Objectives and Representative Content

2.1 Identify common symptoms and problems associated with each module and how to troubleshoot and isolate the problems.

Content may include the following:

- Processor/memory symptoms
- Mouse
- Floppy drive
- Parallel ports
- Hard drives
- CD-ROM
- DVD
- Sound card/audio
- Monitor/video
- Motherboards
- Modems
- BIOS
- USB
- NIC
- CMOS
- Power supply
- Slot covers
- POST audible/visual error codes
- Troubleshooting tools (multimeter)
- Large LBA, LBA
- Cables
- Keyboard
- Peripherals

2.2 Identify basic troubleshooting procedures and how to elicit problem symptoms from customers.

Content may include the following:

- Troubleshooting/isolation/problem determination procedures
- Determining whether hardware or software problem
- Gathering information from user regarding:
  - Customer environment
  - Symptoms/error codes
  - Situation when the problem occurred

Domain 3.0 Preventive Maintenance

This domain requires the knowledge of safety and preventive maintenance. With regard to safety, it includes the potential hazards to personnel and equipment when working with lasers, high-voltage equipment, ESD, and items that require special disposal procedures that comply with environmental guidelines. With regard to preventive maintenance, this includes knowledge of preventive maintenance products, procedures, environmental hazards, and precautions when working on microcomputer systems.

Objectives and Representative Content

3.1 Identify the purpose of various types of preventive maintenance products and procedures and when to use/perform them.

Content may include the following:

- Liquid cleaning compounds
- Types of materials to clean contacts and connections
- Non-static vacuums (chassis, power supplies, fans)

3.2   Identify issues, procedures and devices for protection within the computing environment, including people, hardware, and the surrounding workspace.

Content may include the following:

- UPS (uninterruptible power supply) and suppressors
- Determining the signs of power issues
- Proper methods of component storage for future use

Potential hazards and proper safety procedures:

- High-voltage equipment
- Power supply
- CRT

Special disposal procedures complying with environmental guidelines:

- Batteries
- CRTs
- Toner kits/cartridges
- Chemical solvents and cans
- MSDS (Material Safety Data Sheet)

ESD (electrostatic discharge)

- What ESD can do, how it may be apparent or hidden
- Common ESD protection devices
- Situations that could present a danger or hazard

Domain 4.0 Motherboard/ Processors/Memory

This domain requires knowledge of specific terminology and facts, along with ways and means of dealing with classifications, categories, and principles of motherboards, processors, and memory in microcomputer systems.

Objectives and Representative Content

4.1   Distinguish between the popular CPU chips in terms of their basic characteristics.

Content may include the following:

- Popular CPU chips (Intel, AMD, Cyrix)
- Characteristics:
  - Physical size
  - Voltage
  - Speeds
  - Onboard cache or not
  - Sockets
  - SEC (Single Edge Contact)

4.2   Identify the categories of RAM (Random Access Memory) terminology, their locations and physical characteristics.

Content may include the following:

- Terminology, including the following:
  - EDO RAM (Extended Data Output RAM)
  - DRAM (Dynamic Random Access Memory)
  - SRAM (Static RAM)
  - RIMM (Rambus Inline Memory Module 184-pin)
  - VRAM (Video RAM)

- SDRAM (Synchronous Dynamic RAM)
- WRAM (Windows Accelerator Card RAM)

- Locations and physical characteristics, including the following:

  - Memory bank
  - Memory chips (8-bit, 16-bit, and 32-bit)
  - SIMMS (Single In-line Memory Module)
  - DIMMS (Dual In-line Memory Module)
  - Parity chips versus non-parity chips

4.3 Identify the most popular type of motherboards, their components and their architecture (bus structures and power supplies).

Content may include the following:

- Types of motherboards:

  - AT (full and baby)
  - ATX

- Components, including the following:

  - Communication ports
  - SIMM AND DIMM
  - Processor sockets
  - External cache memory (Level 2)

- Bus architecture, including the following:

  - ISA
  - PCI
  - AGP
  - USB
  - VL-Bus

- Basic compatibility guidelines

  - IDE (ATA, ATAPI, ULTRA-DMA, EIDE)
  - SCSI (Wide, Fast, Ultra, LVD (Low Voltage Differential))

4.4 Identify the purpose of CMOS (Complementary Metal-Oxide Semiconductor), what it contains and how to change its basic parameters.

Examples of basic CMOS settings are as follows:

- Printer parallel port (uni/bidirectional, disable/enable, ECP, EPP)
- COM/serial port (memory address, interrupt request, disable)
- Floppy drive (enable/disable drive or boot, speed, density)
- Hard drive (size and drive type)
- Memory (parity, non-parity)
- Boot sequence
- Date/time
- Passwords
- Plug & Play BIOS

Domain 5.0 Printers

This domain requires knowledge of basic types of printers, basic concepts, printer components, how they work, how they print onto a page, paper path, care and service techniques, and common problems.

Objectives and Representative Content

5.1   Identify basic concepts, printer operations and printer components.

Content may include the following:

- Types of printers:
    - Laser
    - Inkjet
    - Dot matrix

- Types of printer connections and configurations:
    - Parallel
    - Network
    - USB
    - Infrared
    - Serial

5.2   Identify care and service techniques and common problems with primary printer types.

Content may include the following:

- Feed and output
- Errors
- Paper jam
- Print quality
- Safety precautions
- Preventive maintenance

Domain 6.0 Basic Networking

This domain requires knowledge of basic network concepts and terminology, ability to determine whether a computer is networked, knowledge of procedures for swapping and configuring network interface cards, and knowledge of the ramifications of repairs when a computer is networked.

Objectives and Representative Content

6.1   Identify basic networking concepts, including how a network works and the ramifications of repairs on the network.

Content may include the following:

- Installing and configuring network cards
- Network access
- Full-duplex, half-duplex
- Cabling (twisted pair, coaxial, fiber optic, RS-232)
- Ways to network a PC
- Physical network topographies
- Increasing bandwidth
- Loss of data
- Network slowdown
- Infrared
- Hardware protocols

A+ OPERATING SYSTEM TECHNOLOGIES EXAMINATION BLUEPRINT

In addition to passing the Core Hardware exam, you must pass the Operating System Technologies exam to receive your certification. You must demonstrate basic knowledge of Windows 9x and 2000 for installing, configuring, upgrading, troubleshooting, and repairing microcomputer systems.

> **NOTE**
>
> **Post-Beta Objectives** This is the A+ Operating Systems Technologies exam blueprint. This document was produced after the final technical and psychometric review of the item pool following the beta-testing period. This document is reflective of the topics and technologies that appear as part of the A+ Operating Systems Technologies exam.
>
> The objectives listed here represent CompTIA's outline of November 20, 2000. This certification exam went live on January 31, 2001 (with a few cosmetic changes to the outline). This should in no way affect the test taker's ability to study for and pass the exam because no additional material was added to the exam itself.

As with the Core Hardware exam, the skills and knowledge measured by this examination are derived from an industry-wide job-task analysis and validated through a worldwide survey of 5,000 A+ certified professionals. The results of the worldwide survey were used in weighting the domains and ensuring that the weighting is representative of the relative importance of that content to the job requirements of a service technician with six months on-the-job experience. The results of the job-task analysis and survey can be found in the following report:

◆ CompTIA A+ Job Task Analysis (JTA) (November 2000)

This examination blueprint includes weighting, test objectives, and example content. Example topics and concepts are included to clarify the test objectives; they should not be construed as a comprehensive listing of the content of this examination.

The following table lists the domains measured by this examination and the approximate extent to which they are represented.

TABLE 2

DOMAIN REPRESENTATION

Domain	% of Examination (Approximately)
1.0 OS Fundamentals	30%
2.0 Installation, Configuration and Upgrading	15%
3.0 Diagnosing and Troubleshooting	40%
4.0 Networks	15%
Total	100%

Domain 1.0 Operating System Fundamentals

This domain requires knowledge of Windows 9x and 2000 operating systems in terms of functions and structure, managing files and directories, and running programs.

Objectives and Representative Content

1.1 Identify the operating system's functions, structure and major system files to navigate the operating system and how to get needed technical information.

Content may include the following:

Major Operating System Functions

- Create folders
- Checking OS version

Major Operating System Components

- Explorer
- My Computer
- Control Panel

Contrasts Between Windows 9x and 2000

Major system files: (what they are, where they are located, how they are used, and what they contain)

- System, configuration, and user interface files
    - IO.SYS
    - BOOT.INI
    - WIN.COM
    - MSDOS.SYS
    - AUTOEXEC.BAT
    - CONFIG.SYS
    - COMMAND LINE PROMPT
- Memory management
    - Conventional
    - Extended/upper memory
    - High memory
    - Virtual memory
    - HIMEM.SYS
    - EMM386.EXE

- Windows 9x
    - IO.SYS
    - WIN.INI
    - USER.DAT
    - SYSEDIT
    - SYSTEM.INI
    - MSCONFIG (98)
    - COMMAND.COM
    - REGEDIT.EXE
    - SYSTEM.DAT
    - RUN COMMAND
    - COMMAND LINE PROMPT
- Windows 2000
    - Computer Management
    - BOOT.INI
    - REGEDT32
    - REGEDIT
    - RUN CMD
    - NTLDR
    - NTDETECT.COM
    - NTBOOTDD.SYS
- Command Prompt Procedures
    - DIR
    - ATTRIB
    - VER
    - MEM
    - SCANDISK
    - DEFRAG

- EDIT
- XCOPY
- COPY
- SETVER
- SCANREG

1.2   Identify basic concepts and procedures for creating, viewing and managing files, directories and disks. This includes procedures for changing file attributes and the ramifications of those changes (security issues, and so on).

Content may include the following:

- File attributes (Read Only, Hidden, System and Archive attributes)
- File naming conventions (most common extensions)
- Windows 2000 COMPRESS, ENCRYPT
- IDE/SCSI
- Internal/External
- Backup/Restore
- Partitioning/Formatting/File System
  - FAT
  - FAT16
  - FAT32
  - NTFS4
  - NTFS5
  - HPFS

Windows-based utilities

- ScanDisk
- Device Manager
- System Manager
- Computer Manager
- MSCONFIG.EXE
- REGEDIT.EXE
- REGEDT32.EXE
- ATTRIB.EXE
- EXTRACT.EXE
- DEFRAG.EXE
- EDIT.COM
- FDISK.COM
- SYSEDIT.EXE
- SCANREG
- WSCRIPT.EXE
- HWINFO.EXE
- ASD.EXE
- Cvt1.EXE

Domain 2.0 Installation, Configuration and Upgrading

This domain requires knowledge of installing, configuring, and upgrading Windows 9x and 2000. This includes knowledge of system boot sequences.

Objectives and Representative Content

2.1   Identify the procedures for installing Windows 9x and 2000, and bringing the software to a basic operational level.

Content may include the following:

- Start Up
- Partition
- Format drive
- Loading drivers
- Run appropriate setup utility

2.2   Identify steps to perform an operating system upgrade.

Content may include the following:

- Upgrading Windows 95 to Windows 98
- Upgrading Windows NT Workstation 4.0 to Windows 2000
- Replacing Windows 9x with Windows 2000
- Dual boot Windows 9x/NT4.0/2000

2.3   Identify the basic system boot sequences and boot methods, including the steps to create an emergency boot disk with utilities installed for Windows 9x, NT and 2000.

Content may include the following:

- Startup disk
- Safe mode
- MS-DOS mode
- NTLDR, BOOT.INI
- Files required to boot
- Creating Emergency Repair Disk

2.4   Identify procedures for loading/adding and configuring application device drivers, and the necessary software for certain devices.

Content may include the following:

- Windows 9x Plug & Play and Windows 2000
- Identify the procedures for installing and launching typical Windows and non-Windows applications

Procedures for setting up and configuring Windows printing subsystem

- Setting default printer
- Installing/Spool setting
- Network printing (with LAN admin)

Domain 3.0 Diagnosing and Troubleshooting

This domain requires the ability to apply knowledge to diagnose and troubleshoot common problems relating to Windows 9x and 2000. This includes understanding normal operation and symptoms relating to common problems.

Objectives and Representative Content

3.1   Recognize and interpret the meaning of common error codes and startup messages from the boot sequence, and identify steps to correct the problems.

Content may include the following:

- Safe mode
- No operating system found
- Error in CONFIG.SYS line XX
- Bad or missing COMMAND.COM
- HIMEM.SYS not loaded

- Missing or corrupt HIMEM.SYS

- SCSI

- Swap file

- NT boot issues

- Dr. Watson

- Failure to start GUI

- Windows Protection Error

- Event Viewer — Event log is full

- A device referenced in SYSTEM.INI, WIN.INI, Registry is not found

3.2   Recognize common problems and determine how to resolve them.

Content may include the following:

- Eliciting problem symptoms from customers

- Having customer reproduce error as part of the diagnostic process

- Identifying recent changes to the computer environment from the user

- Troubleshooting Windows-specific printing problems

    - Print spool is stalled

    - Incorrect/incompatible driver for print

    - Incorrect parameter

Other common problems

- General Protection Faults

- Illegal operation

- Invalid working directory

- System lock up

- Option (sound card, modem, input device) will not function

- Application will not start or load

- Cannot log on to network (option – NIC not functioning)

- TSR (Terminate Stay Resident) programs and virus

- Applications don't install

- Network connection

Viruses and virus types

- What they are

- Sources (floppy, emails, and so on)

- How to determine presence

Domain 4.0 Networks

This domain requires knowledge of network capabilities of Windows, and how to connect to networks, including what the Internet is about, its capabilities, basic concepts relating to Internet access, and generic procedures for system setup.

Objectives and Representative Content

4.1   Identify the networking capabilities of Windows including procedures for connecting to the network.

Content may include the following:

- Protocols

- IPCONFIG.EXE

- WINIPCFG.EXE

- Sharing disk drives

- Sharing print and file services

- Network type and network card
- Installing and configuring browsers
- Configure OS for network connection

4.2 Identify concepts and capabilities relating to the Internet and basic procedures for setting up a system for Internet access.

Content may include the following:

- ISP
- TCP/IP
- IPX/SPX
- NetBEUI
- E-mail
- PING.EXE
- HTML
- HTTP://
- FTP
- Domain names (Web sites)
- Dial-up networking
- TRACERT.EXE

HARDWARE AND SOFTWARE YOU WILL NEED

As a self-paced study guide, this book was designed with the expectation that you will use your computer as you follow along through the exercises. You also will want to use the *ExamGear* software and complete the

labs on the CD that accompanies this book. Your computer should meet the following criteria:

- ◆ 32-bit operating system (Windows 9x/2000 or NT 4.0)
- ◆ 10MB hard drive space
- ◆ 16MB RAM
- ◆ IE 4.01 or later
- ◆ 640 × 480 video resolution with 256 colors or more
- ◆ CD-ROM drive

ADVICE ON TAKING THE EXAM

More extensive tips are found in the "Final Review" section titled "Study and Exam Prep Tips," but keep this advice in mind as you study:

- ◆ **Read all the material.** Make sure your exam preparation is thorough. Do not just drop into the book and read around. Read through all the material. This book has included additional information not reflected in the objectives in an effort to give you the best possible preparation for the examination—and for the on-the-job experiences to come.
- ◆ **Do the Step by Steps.** This will provide you with another way of understanding the material as well as more information on how well you comprehend it.
- ◆ **Use the questions to assess your knowledge.** Do not just read the chapter content; use the questions to find out what you know and what you do not. Study some more, review, and then assess your knowledge again.

◆ **Review the exam objectives.** Develop your own questions and examples for each topic listed. If you can develop and answer several questions for each topic, you should not find it difficult to pass the exam.

NOTE

> **Exam-Taking Advice**   Although this book is designed to prepare you to take and pass the Core Hardware Service Technician and Operating System Technologies exams, there are no guarantees. Read this book, work through the questions and exercises, and when you feel confident, take the practice exam and additional exams using the *ExamGear* test engine. This should tell you whether you are ready for the real thing.
>
> When taking the actual certification exam, make sure you answer all the questions before your time limit expires. Do not spend too much time on any one question. If you are unsure, answer it as best as you can; then mark it for review after you have finished the rest of the questions.

Remember, the primary object is not to pass the exam—it is to understand the material. After you understand the material, passing the exam should be simple. Knowledge is a pyramid; to build upward, you need a solid foundation. This book and the CompTIA A+ certification program are designed to ensure that you have that solid foundation.

Good luck!

NEW RIDERS PUBLISHING

The staff of New Riders Publishing is committed to bringing you the very best in computer reference material. Each New Riders book is the result of months of work by authors and staff who research and refine the information contained within its covers.

As part of this commitment to you, the NRP reader, New Riders invites your input. Please let us know if you enjoy this book, if you have trouble with the information or examples presented, or if you have a suggestion for the next edition.

Please note, however, that New Riders staff cannot serve as a technical resource during your preparation for the A+ certification exams or for questions about software- or hardware-related problems. Please refer instead to the documentation that accompanies the products or to the applications' Help systems.

If you have a question or comment about any New Riders book, there are several ways to contact New Riders Publishing. We will respond to as many readers as we can. Your name, address, and phone number will never become part of a mailing list or be used for any purpose other than to help us continue to bring you the best books possible. You can write to us at the following address:

New Riders Publishing
Attn: Stephanie Wall, Executive Editor
201 W. 103rd Street
Indianapolis, IN 46290

If you prefer, you can fax New Riders Publishing at 317-581-4663.

You also can send email to New Riders at the following Internet address:

nrfeedback@newriders.com

NRP is an imprint of Pearson Education. To obtain a catalog or information, contact us at nrmedia@newriders.com. To purchase a New Riders book, call 1-800-428-5331.

Thank you for selecting *A+ Certification Training Guide, Third Edition*.

Core Hardware Service Technician

This chapter helps you to prepare for the Core Hardware module of the A+ Certification examination by covering the following objectives within the "Domain 1.0: Installation, Configuration, and Upgrading" section.

1.1 Identify basic terms, concepts, and functions of system modules, including how each module should work during normal operation and during the boot process.

Examples of concepts and modules:

- **System board**
- **Power supply**
- **Processor/CPU**
- **Memory**
- **Storage devices**
- **Monitor**
- **Modem**
- **Firmware**
- **BIOS**
- **CMOS**
- **LCD (portable systems)**
- **Ports**
- **PDA (Personal Digital Assistant)**

▶ Every computer technician should be able to identify the major components of a typical personal computer (PC) system and be able to describe their functions.

CHAPTER 1

1.0 Installation, Configuration, and Upgrading

1.2 Identify basic procedures for adding and removing field replaceable modules for both desktop and portable systems.

Examples of modules:

- System board
- Storage device
- Power supply
- Processor/CPU
- Memory
- Input devices
- Hard drive
- Keyboard
- Video board
- Mouse
- Network interface card (NIC)

Examples of portable system components:

- AC adapters
- DC controllers
- LCD panel
- PC Card
- Pointing devices

▶ Every technician should be aware of typical PC components that can be exchanged in the field. Technicians should be able to install, connect, and configure these components to upgrade or repair an existing system. They also should be aware of how these same components are fitted in portable systems.

1.3 Identify available IRQs, DMAs, and I/O addresses and procedures for configuring them for device installation.

Content may include the following:

- Standard IRQ settings

- Modems
- Floppy drive controllers
- Hard drive controllers
- USB port
- Infrared port
- Hexadecimal/addresses

▶ To successfully install hardware components in a PC, the technician must be able to determine what system resources are required for the component, what resource are available in the system, and how they may be allocated.

1.4 Identify common peripheral ports, associated cabling, and their connectors.

Content may include the following:

- Cable types
- Cable orientation
- Serial versus parallel
- Pin connections

Examples of types of connectors:

- DB-9
- DB-25
- RJ-11
- RJ-45
- BNC
- PS2/MINI-DIN
- USB
- IEEE-1394

▶ To successfully add peripheral devices to a PC system, the technician must be able to recognize what type of port the device requires, locate standard I/O port connections, and determine what type of cabling is required to successfully connect the port and the device.

1.5 Identify proper procedures for installing and configuring IDE/EIDE devices.

Content may include the following:

- **Master/slave**

- **Devices per channel**

- **Primary/secondary**

▶ The computer technician must be able to successfully install and configure an IDE drive.

1.6 Identify proper procedures for installing and configuring SCSI devices.

Content may include the following:

- **Address/Termination conflicts**

- **Cabling**

- **Types (for example, regular, wide, ultra-wide)**

- **Internal versus external**

- **Jumper block settings (binary equivalents)**

▶ The computer technician must be able to successfully install and configure devices that use a SCSI interface.

1.7 Identify proper procedures for installing and configuring peripheral devices.

Content may include the following:

- **Monitor/video card**

- **Modem**

- **USB peripherals and hubs**

- **IEEE-1284**

- **IEEE-1394**

- **External storage**

Examples of portable system components:

- **Docking stations**

- **PC Cards**

- **Port replicators**

- **Infrared devices**

▶ The computer technician must be able to successfully install and configure common PC peripheral devices and systems.

1.8 Identify hardware methods of upgrading system performance, procedures for replacing basic subsystem components, unique components and when to use them.

Content may include the following:

- **Memory**

- **Hard drives**

- **CPU**

- **Methods for upgrading BIOS**

- **When to upgrade BIOS**

Examples of portable system components:

- **Battery**

- **Hard drive**

- **Types I, II, III cards**

- **Memory**

▶ Computer technicians must be able to upgrade the system's BIOS as part of a system upgrade. They also should be able to optimize PC hardware to obtain the best performance possible for a given system configuration.

OUTLINE

OUTLINE

OUTLINE

STUDY STRATEGIES

To prepare for the Installation, Configuration, and Upgrading objective of the Core Hardware exam:

▶ Read the objectives at the beginning of this chapter.

▶ Study the information in this chapter.

▶ Review the objectives listed earlier in this chapter.

▶ Perform any step-by-step procedures in the text.

▶ Answer the Review and Exam Questions at the end of the chapter and check your results.

▶ Use the ExamGear test engine on the CD-ROM that accompanies this book for additional Review and Exam Questions concerning this material.

▶ Review the Test Tips scattered throughout the chapter and make certain that you are comfortable with each point.

INTRODUCTION

This section of the exam challenges the test taker to identify, install, configure, and upgrade microcomputer modules and peripherals, following established basic procedures for system assembly and disassembly of field replaceable modules. Test elements include the ability to identify and configure IRQs, DMAs, and I/O addresses, as well as to properly set configuration switches and jumpers. Questions from this domain represent 30% of the Core Hardware exam content.

BASIC TERMS AND CONCEPTS

▶ 1.1 Identify basic terms, concepts, and functions of system modules, including how each module should work during normal operation.

The A+ Core Hardware objective 1.1 states that the test taker should be able to "identify basic terms, concepts, and functions of system modules, including how each module should work during normal operation and during the boot process."

Examples of concepts and modules include the following:

- System board
- Power supply
- Processor/CPU
- Memory
- Storage devices
- Monitor
- Modem

- Firmware
- Boot process
- BIOS
- CMOS
- LCD (portable systems)
- Ports
- PDA (Personal Digital Assistant)

As with any group or industry, the PC world has produced a peculiar vocabulary to describe its products and their functions. As indicated by the A+ objective, the computer technician must be able to use that vocabulary to identify PC products and to understand how they work and what they do. The following sections of this chapter provide an introductory course on common PC components that includes a brief discussion of the theory of their operation and the basic functions that each component supplies. These sections also present the standards that the industry has developed for these components.

PC Standards

Late in 1981, IBM entered the microcomputer market with the unveiling of their now famous *IBM Personal Computer* (PC). At the time of its introduction, the IBM PC was a drastic departure from the status quo of the microcomputer world.

The IBM PC employed an Intel 8088 16/8-bit microprocessor. (It processes data 16 bits at a time internally, but moves it around in 8-bit packages.) Relatively speaking, the IBM PC was fast, powerful, flexible, and priced within the range of most individuals. The general public soon became aware of the tremendous possibilities of the PC, and the microcomputer quickly advanced from a simple game machine to an office tool with a seemingly endless range of advanced personal and business applications. In 1983, IBM added a small hard disk drive to the PC and introduced the Extended Technology (PC-XT) version.

IBM elevated the PC market again when, in 1984, IBM introduced the *Advanced Technology PC (PC-AT)*. The AT used a true 16-bit microprocessor (which processes data 16 bits at a time internally and has a 16-bit external data bus) from Intel, called the 80286. The wider data bus increased the speed of the computer's operation, just because the 80286 could transfer and process twice as much data at a time as the 8088 could.

Many of the decisions made in designing the AT still influence the PC-compatible computer today. The AT architecture established industry standards for its

◆ Expansion bus

◆ System addressing

◆ Peripheral addressing

◆ System resource allocations

Reference Shelf

For more in-depth technical information about the 8088 microprocessor and its operation, refer to the "8088 Microprocessor" section of the Electronic Reference Shelf located on the CD that accompanies this book.

NOTE

Industry Standard Architecture The tremendous popularity of the original IBM PC-XT and PC-AT systems created a set of pseudo standards for hardware and software compatibility. The AT architecture became so popular that it has become the *Industry Standard Architecture* (ISA). Most microcomputers are still both hardware- and software-compatible with the original AT design.

The majority of all microcomputers today are based on the AT design but incorporate newer microprocessors, expansion buses, and memory-management structures. For this reason, every computer technician should possess a thorough understanding of the architecture developed in these systems. This chapter provides an introduction to the basic ISA architecture and its most popular upgrade components. Other Core Hardware chapters provide extended discussions of these structures.

PC Systems

A typical PC system is depicted in Figure 1.1. The PC is called a system because it includes all the components required to have a functional computer:

◆ **Input devices.** Keyboard and mouse

◆ **Computer.** System unit

◆ **Output devices.** CRT monitor and character printer

Most PCs are modular by design, with allowances for adding or exchanging modules that conform the system so that it can carry out specific functions.

The system unit is the main portion of the microcomputer system and is the basis of any PC system arrangement.

The components surrounding it, referred to as *peripherals*, vary from system to system depending on what particular functions the system is supposed to serve. In the Figure 1.1, the keyboard, monitor, mouse, printer, and speakers are considered peripheral devices.

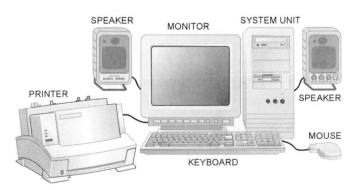

FIGURE 1.1
A typical PC system.

Cases

System units may be packaged in a number of standard case designs. Each design offers characteristics that adapt the system for different environments. The key characteristics for case design include mounting methods for components, ventilation characteristics, drive capacity, and footprint (desk space they take up).

Desktops

Figure 1.2 depicts typical PC cases. The most familiar PC case style is probably the desktop case design. These cases are designed to set horizontally on the desk (hence the name). Variations of the basic desktop design include narrow cases, referred to as baby AT cases, and short desktops, called low-profile cases.

Towers

Tower cases sit vertically on the floor beneath the desk. This case design came about to free up workspace on the desktop. Tower cases offer extended drive bay capacities that make them especially useful in file server applications where many disk, CD-ROM, and tape drive units may be desired. Although tower designs are convenient, their ventilation characteristics tend to be poor. *Adapter cards* are mounted horizontally in tower units and the heat produced by the lower cards must rise past the upper cards, adding to their heat build up. To compensate for this problem, most tower cases include a secondary fan unit to increase airflow through the case and thereby dissipate more heat.

Mini towers and mid towers are short towers designed to take up less vertical space. Internally, their design resembles a vertical desktop unit. They are considerably less expensive than the larger towers due to reduced materials needed to produce them. Unlike their taller relatives, mini towers do not provide abundant space for internal add-ons or disk drives. However, they do possess the shortcomings of full towers (such as heat build up). Mini towers exist more as a function of marketing than as a solution to some functional industry requirement.

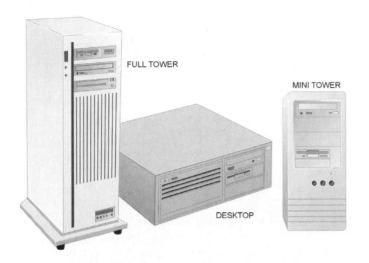

FIGURE 1.2
PC case styles

Portable Systems

To free the computer user from the desk, an array of *portable PCs* has been developed. These units package the system unit, input devices, and *output devices* into a single, lightweight package that can be carried along with the user. Portable systems have characteristics that differ considerably from the other PC designs.

The original portables were called luggables. Although smaller than desktop computers, they were not truly convenient to transport. The first portables included small, built-in CRT displays and detachable keyboards. Their batteries and CRT equipment made them extremely bulky and heavy to carry. Therefore, they never really had a major impact on the PC market. However, they set the stage for the development of future portable computer systems. Figure 1.3 shows examples of different portable computer designs.

With advancements in battery design and the advent of usable, large-screen, flat-panel displays, the first truly portable PCs, referred to as *laptops*, were introduced. These units featured all-in-one, AT-compatible PC boards. The system board included the I/O and video controller functions. Laptops featured built-in keyboards and hinged *liquid crystal display* (LCD) display panels that flipped up from the case for use. They also used an external *power supply* and a removable, rechargeable battery.

FIGURE 1.3
Portable computers.

The battery life of typical laptops was minimal and their size was still large enough to be inconvenient at times. However, the inclusion of LCD viewing screens and external power-supply/battery arrangements made them useful enough to spawn a healthy portable computer market. Even though these units could weigh in excess of seven pounds, the user could easily take work from the office to the home, or to a hotel room while traveling. Workers also could get work done at traditionally nonproductive times, such as on long automobile or airplane rides. An occasional game of computerized cards or golf was always at hand as well.

Continued advancements in IC and peripheral technology allowed PCs' circuitry to be reduced. This allowed portable sizes to be reduced further so that they could achieve sizes of 8.75" × 11" × 2.25" and smaller. Portables in this size range are referred to as *notebook computers*. The weight of a typical notebook dropped down to five or six pounds. Figure 1.4 depicts a typical notebook computer.

FIGURE 1.4
A notebook computer.

Even smaller subnotebook PCs have been created by moving the disk drives outside of the case and reducing the size of the display screen. These units tend to be slightly thinner than traditional notebooks and weigh in the neighborhood of three to four pounds.

Very small subnotebooks, referred to as *palmtop PCs*, were produced for a short time in the pre-Windows days. These units limited everything as far as possible to reach sizes of 7" × 4" × 1" and weights of one to two pounds. Subnotebooks have decreased in popularity as notebooks have continued to decrease in weight and cost.

Personal Digital Assistants

The palmtop market was diminished for some time because of the difficulty of running Windows on such small displays. Human ergonomics also come into play when dealing with smaller notebooks. The smaller display screens become difficult to see and keyboards become more difficult to use as the size of the keys decreases.

However, the market was revived by the introduction of palm tops as Personal Digital Assistants (PDAs). Figure 1.5 depicts a typical PDA. These handheld devices use a special stylus, referred to as a pen, to input data and selections instead of a keyboard or mouse. Basically, the PDA is an electronic time-management system that also may include computer applications such as word processors, spreadsheets, and databases.

The PDA's display is a touch-screen LCD that works in conjunction with a graphical user interface running on top of a specialized operating system. Some PDAs employ a highly modified, embedded (on a chip) version of the Microsoft Windows operating system called Windows CE as their operating system. These systems are particularly well suited for exchanging and synchronizing information with larger Windows-based systems.

Two items have made PDAs popular: their size and their capability to communicate with the user's desktop computer system. Early PDAs exchanged information with the full-sized computer through serial port connections. Newer models communicate with the user's desktop computer through infrared communications links or *docking stations.*

FIGURE 1.5
A Personal Digital Assistant (PDA).

Inside the System Unit

The components inside the system unit can be divided into four distinct subunits: a switching power supply, the disk drives, the system board, and the options adapter cards, as illustrated in Figure 1.6.

FIGURE 1.6
The components in a system unit.

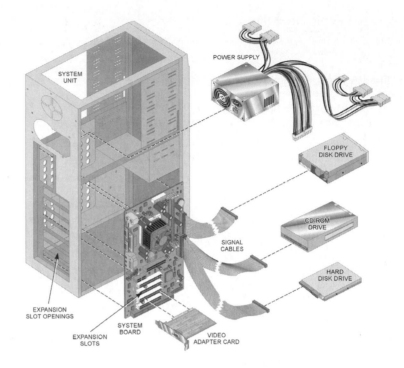

A typical system unit contains a single power-supply unit that converts commercial power into the various levels required by the different units in the system. The number and types of disk drives installed in a system varies according to the intended use of the system. However, a single *floppy disk drive* (FDD) unit, a single *hard disk drive* (HDD) unit, and a single *CD-ROM drive* are typically installed to handle the system's mass-storage requirements.

The *system board* is the center of the system. It contains the portions of the system that define its computing power and speed.

System boards also are referred to as motherboards, main boards, or planar boards. Plug-in *options adapter cards* (or just adapter cards) permit a wide array of peripheral equipment to be added to the basic PC system. The most frequently installed adapter cards in PC systems are *video adapter cards.* Older units also may include different types of *input/output (I/O)* adapter cards.

Adapter cards plug into *expansion slot* connectors located at the rear of the system board. Peripheral devices, such as printers and modems, normally connect to adapter cards through expansion slot openings in the rear of the system unit.

> **TEST TIP**
> Memorize the different names the industry uses for system boards.

> **TEST TIP**
> Know the names of all the components of a typical PC system and be able to identify them by sight.

Inside Portables

Portable computers have two ideal characteristics: compact and lightweight. Portable computer designers work constantly to decrease the size and power consumption of all the computer's components. Special low-power-consumption *integrated circuits* (ICs) and disk drives have been developed to extend their battery life. Likewise, their cases have been designed to be as small as possible while providing as many standard features as possible. Figure 1.7 shows the inside of a typical notebook computer.

Notice how the components are interconnected by the design. The system board is designed so that it wraps around other components whose form factors cannot be altered—such as the disk drive units. The components also tend to be layered in portable designs. Disk drives cover portions of the system board; the keyboard unit covers nearly everything. The internal battery may slide into a cutout area of the system board, or more likely, it may be located beneath the system board.

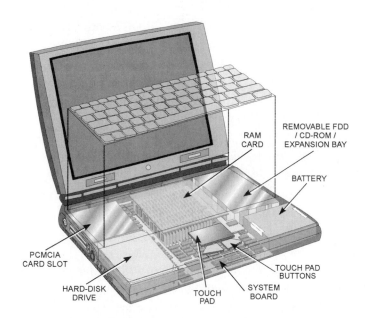

FIGURE 1.7
Inside a portable computer.

Portable Drawbacks

The continued minimization of the system comes at a cost. Most notably, the number of I/O ports, memory, and disk drive expansion capabilities are limited. In addition, there is no chance to use common, full-sized adapter cards that are inexpensive and easy to find.

NOTE

> **Portable Drawbacks**   From a service point of view, the greatest drawback of portable computers is that conventions and compatibility disappear.

One of the biggest problems for portable computers is heat buildup inside the case. Because conventional power supplies (and their fans) are not included in portable units, separate fans must be designed into portables to carry the heat out of the unit. The closeness of the portable's components and the small amount of free airspace inside their cases also adds to heat-related design problems.

The internal PC boards of the portable computer are designed to fit around the nuances of the portable case, and its components, rather than to match a standard design with standard spacing and connections. Therefore, interchangeability of parts with other machines or makers goes by the wayside. The only source of most portable computer parts, with the exception of *PC Cards* and disk drive units, is the original manufacturer. Even the battery case may be proprietary. If the battery dies, you must hope that the original maker has a supply of that particular model.

Access to the notebook's internal components is normally challenging. Each case design assembles and disassembles the unit in different ways. Even the simplest upgrade task can be difficult with a notebook computer. Although adding RAM and options to desktop and tower units is a relatively easy and straightforward process, the same tasks in notebook computers can be difficult.

In some notebooks, it is necessary to disassemble the two halves of the case and remove the keyboard to add RAM modules to the system. In other portables, the hinged display unit must be removed to disassemble the unit. After you are inside the notebook, you may find several of the components are hidden behind other units. Figure 1.8 demonstrates a relatively simple disassembly process for a notebook unit.

In this example, a panel in front of the keyboard can be removed to gain access to the notebook's internal user-serviceable components. Four screws along the front edge of the unit's lower body must be removed. Afterward, the LCD panel is opened and the front panel of the notebook's chassis is pulled up and away to expose a portion of the unit's interior.

To overcome the shortfalls of miniaturization, a wide variety of specialty items aimed at the portable computer market has emerged. Items such as small 2.5-inch hard disk drives have been developed expressly for use in portable computers. Other such items include small internal and *external modems*, special network adapters that

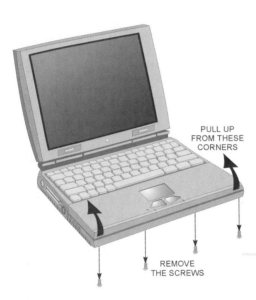

PULL UP
FROM THESE
CORNERS

REMOVE
THE SCREWS

FIGURE 1.8
Disassembling a notebook computer.

plug into *parallel printer ports*, docking stations (or ports), special carrying cases and briefcases, detachable keypads, clip-on or built-in *trackballs*, and touch-sensitive mouse pads.

In addition, a sequence of special, credit card–like adapter cards has been designed expressly for use with portable computers. These adapters are standardized through the Personal Computer Memory Card International Association (PCMCIA) and are commonly referred to as PC Cards. The different types of PCMCIA Cards are covered in greater detail later in this chapter.

Power Supplies

The system's power-supply unit provides electrical power for every component inside the system unit, as well as to the video display monitor.

It converts commercial electrical power received from a 120V AC, 60Hz (or 220V AC, 50Hz outside the United Stated) outlet into other levels required by the components of the system. In desktop and tower PCs, the power supply is the shiny metal box located at the rear of the system unit.

You need to be aware of two basic types of power supplies: traditional *AT power supplies* (designed to support AT-compatible system boards) and *ATX power supplies* (designed according to newer ATX design specifications). The AT power supply has two 6-pin system board power connectors (P8/P9), whereas ATX power supplies use a single 20-pin power connector. In the AT-compatible power supply, the cooling fan pulls air through the case from the front and exhausts it out the rear of the power-supply unit. Conversely, the ATX design pulls air in through the rear of the power-supply unit and blows it directly on the ATX system board.

The desktop/tower power supply produces four (or five) different levels of efficiently regulated DC voltage. These are +5V, –5V, +12V and –12V. (The ATX design also provides a +3.3V level to the system board.) The power-supply unit also provides the system's ground. The +5V level is used by the IC devices on the system board and adapter cards. The +3.3V level is used by the microprocessor. The 12V levels are typically used to power the motors used in hard and floppy disk drives.

System board power connectors provide the system board and the individual expansion slots with up to 1 ampere of current each. The basic four voltage levels are available for use through the system board's expansion slot connectors.

Several bundles of cable emerge from the power supply to provide power to the components of the system unit and to its peripherals. The power supply delivers power to the system board, and its expansion slots, through the system board power connectors. The ATX system board connector is a 20-pin keyed connector. Figure 1.9 shows the wiring configuration diagram of an ATX system board power connector. Notice that it is keyed so that it cannot be installed incorrectly.

FIGURE 1.9

The ATX system board power connector.

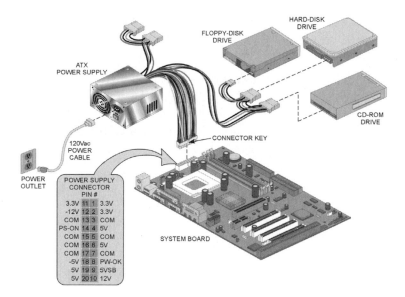

In AT-compatible power supplies, two 6-wire bundles are typically marked P8 and P9. The physical construction of these power connectors significantly differs from that of the other bundles. They are designed to be plugged into the system board's P1 and P2 power plugs, respectively, as depicted in Figure 1.10.

The P8/P9 connectors are normally keyed and numbered. However, their construction and appearance are identical. The voltage levels associated with each plug differ and *severe damage could result* to the computer by reversing them. The power connector labeled P8 should be plugged into the circuit board power connector labeled P1, whereas connector P9 should be plugged into the P2 connector next to it. A good rule of thumb to remember when attaching these two connectors to the system board is that the black wires in each bundle should be next to each other in the middle, as illustrated in Figure 1.10.

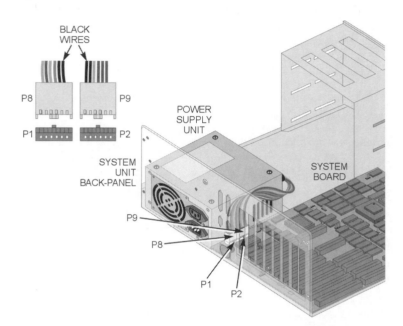

FIGURE 1.10
The P1/P2—P8/P9 connections.

The other power-supply bundles are used to supply power to optional systems, such as the disk and CD-ROM drives. These bundles provide a +5V and +12V DC supply, as shown in Figure 1.11. The larger connector is carried over from older PC/XT/AT designs, whereas the smaller connector has gained widespread usage with smaller form-factor disk drives. The +5V supply provides power for electronic components on the optional devices, whereas the +12V level is used for disk drive motors and other devices that require a higher voltage. In the ATX design, a special soft switch line is included that enables the system to shut itself off under control of the system software. This allows power-management components of the operating system software to manage the hardware's power usage. This concept is discussed further in the "Power Management" section later in this chapter. As Figure 1.11 illustrates, these connectors are keyed, so they must be plugged in correctly.

WARNING

Don't Switch the P8/P9 Connectors!   Although they look alike, the voltage levels of each plug differ. Reversing them can cause *severe damage*.

TEST TIP

Be aware that ATX power supplies can be shut off from the system itself.

FIGURE 1.11
Auxiliary power connectors.

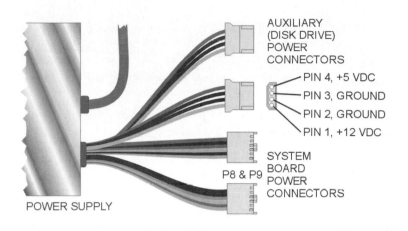

Power can be delivered to the monitor through a special plug in the rear of the AT-style power supply. This permits the monitor to be switched on and off via the system's power switch. In PC and XT units, the power switch was an integral part of the power supply and extended from its right side. In AT and ATX units, the On/Off switch is located on the front panel of the system unit and connected to the power supply by a cable. Figure 1.12 illustrates the typical power-supply connections found in a desktop or tower unit.

FIGURE 1.12
System power-supply connections.

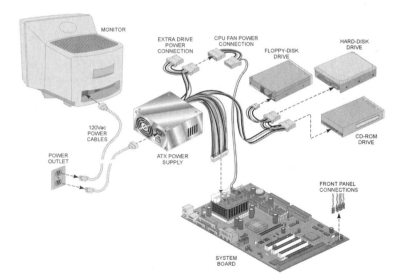

In the United States, a grounded, three-prong power cord provides the AC input voltage to the power supply. The smaller vertical blade in the connector is considered the hot, or phase, side of the connector. A small slide switch on the back of the unit permits the power supply to be switched over to operate on 220V AC input voltages found outside the United States. When the switch is set to the 220 position, the voltage supplied to the power supply's monitor outlet also is 220. In this position, it is usually necessary to exchange the power cord for one that has a plug suited to the country in which the computer is being used.

Power-supply units come in a variety of shapes and power ratings. The shapes of the power supplies are determined by the type of case in which they are designed to be used. The major difference between these two power-supply types is in their form factors. The ATX power supply is somewhat smaller in size than the AT-style power supply, and their hole patterns differ.

Another point that differentiates power supplies is their power (or wattage) rating. Typical power ratings include 150, 200, and 250-watt versions.

> **TEST TIP**
>
> Be aware that power supply's form factor and wattage ratings must be taken into account when ordering a replacement power supply for a system.

Portable Power Sources

Notebooks and other portables use a detachable, rechargeable battery and an external power supply, as illustrated in Figure 1.13. (Battery sizes vary from manufacturer to manufacturer.) They also employ power-saving circuits and ICs designed to lengthen the battery's useful time. The battery unit contains a recharging regulator circuit that enables the battery to recharge while it is being used with the external power supply. Like other hardware aspects of notebook computers, there are no standards for their power-supply units. Like other computer power-supply types, portable power supplies convert commercial AC voltage into a single DC voltage that the computer can use to power its components and use to recharge its batteries. From manufacturer to manufacturer, however, these power converters employ different connector types and possess different DC voltage and current-delivery capabilities. Therefore, a power supply from one notebook computer will not necessarily work with another portable model.

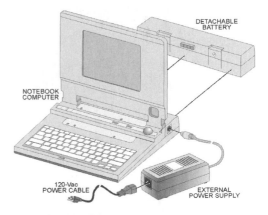

FIGURE 1.13
Laptop/notebook power supplies.

Because the premise of portable computers is mobility, it can be assumed that they should be able to run without being plugged into an AC outlet. The question for most portables is how long will it run without being plugged in. This is the point where portable designs lead the industry. They continuously push forward in three design areas:

◆ Better battery design

◆ Better power-consumption devices

◆ Better power management

Batteries

To be honest, the desktop world doesn't really pay much attention to power-conservation issues. Conversely, portable computer designers must deal with the fact that they are tied to a battery. Older portable designs included the battery as an external, detachable device, as depicted in the preceding figure. These units normally contained rows of nickel-cadmium (Ni-Cad) batteries wired together to provide the specified voltage and current capabilities for the portable. The housing was constructed to both hold the Ni-Cads and to attach to the portable case.

Typical Ni-Cad batteries offer operating times approaching two hours in some models. As with other devices that rely on Ni-Cads, computer battery packs constructed with this type of battery suffer from the charge/discharge cycle "memory-effect" problem associated with Ni-Cads. A full recharge for some Ni-Cad packs could take up to 24 hours to complete. For these reasons, Ni-Cad battery packs have all but disappeared from the portable computer market.

Newer portable designs have switched to nickel metal-hydride (Ni-MH), lithium-ion (Li-ion), or lithium-ion polymer batteries. These batteries are often housed in a plastic case that can be installed inside the portable's case, as illustrated in Figure 1.14. Other designs use plastic cases that attach to the outside of the portable case. These types of batteries typically provide up to two or three hours of operation. It is best to run the battery until the system produces a Battery Low warning message, indicator, or chime.

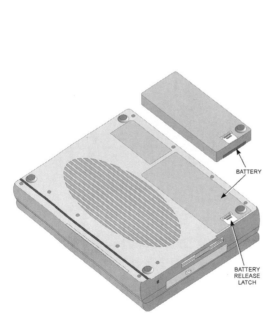

BATTERY

BATTERY
RELEASE
LATCH

FIGURE 1.14
Removable battery packs.

It should take about two to three hours to fully recharge the typical Ni-MH battery pack and about four to five hours for a Li-ion pack. The battery packs should always be fully recharged before using. When the AC adapter is used, a trickle charge is applied to the battery pack to keep it in a fully charged condition. The AC adapter should be used whenever possible to conserve the battery.

Power Consumption

As mentioned earlier, power-consumption consideration has been built in to most devices intended for use with portable computers. Many of the Pentium chipsets provide a *standby mode* that turns off selected components, such as the hard drive and display, until a system event, such as a keyboard entry or a mouse movement, occurs. An additional power-saving condition called *suspend mode* places the system in a shutdown condition except for its memory units.

An additional power-saving mode, known as *hibernate mode*, writes the contents of RAM memory to a hard drive file and completely shuts the system down. When the system is restarted, the feature reads the hibernated file back into memory and normal operation is restarted at the place it left off.

Power Management

Each sector of the portable computer market has worked to reduce power-consumption levels, including software suppliers. Advanced operating systems include power-management features that monitor the system's operation and turn off some high-power-consumption items when they are not in use (standby mode), and switch the system into a low-power-consumption *sleep mode* (suspend mode) if inactivity continues.

These modes are defined by a Microsoft/IBM standard, called the *Advanced Power Management* (APM) standard. The hardware producers refer to this condition as a *green mode*. The standard is actually implemented through the cooperation of the system's chipset devices and the operating system. Control of the APM system is provided through the BIOS' CMOS Setup utility, as described in Chapter 4, "4.0 Motherboard/Processors/Memory."

Most newer portable computers possess a number of automatic power-saving features to maximize battery life. Some can be controlled through the Power menu of the Advanced CMOS Setup utility. If the Hard Disk Timeout value is set to 3 minutes, the Standby Timeout to 5 minutes, and the Auto Suspend value is set to 10 minutes, the following activities occur:

1. The hard disk spins down after 3 minutes of inactivity.

2. After 2 additional minutes of inactivity, the system enters standby mode.

3. After 10 additional inactive minutes, the system stores the hibernation file on the hard drive and enters suspend mode.

Suspend mode also can be entered by pressing a key combination, for those times when the user must step away from the computer for a few minutes but does not want to shut down.

When the system suspends operation, the following events take place:

◆ The video screen is turned off.

◆ The CPU, DMA, clocks, and math coprocessor are powered down.

◆ All controllable peripheral devices are shut down.

The amount of time the unit can remain in suspend mode is determined by the remaining amount of battery power. For this reason, data should be saved to the hard drive before voluntarily going to suspend mode. Pressing the computer's power button returns the system to its preceding operational point.

System Boards

TEST TIP

Know the parts of a typical system board and make sure that you can identify these components (and variations of them) from a pictorial or photographic representation.

The system board is the center of the PC-compatible microcomputer system. It contains the circuitry that establishes the computing power and speed of the entire system. In particular, it contains the *microprocessor* and control devices that form the brains of the system. The major components of interest on a PC system board are the microprocessor, the system's primary memory sections (*read-only* [ROM], *random-access* [RAM], and *cache memory*), expansion slot connectors, and microprocessor support ICs that coordinate the operation of the system. Figure 1.15 depicts a typical system board layout.

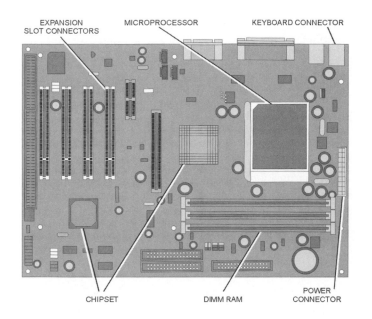

FIGURE 1.15
The parts of a typical system board.

Portable System Processor Boards

Figure 1.16 depicts a typical notebook system board. The first thing you should notice about it is its unusual shape. As noted earlier, system boards for portable computers are not designed to fit a standardized form factor. Instead, they are designed to fit around all the components that must be installed in the system. Therefore, system boards used in portable computers tend to be proprietary to the model for which model they are designed. Mounting-hole positions are determined by where they will best suit the placement of the other system components.

The second item to notice is that there are no "standard" expansion slots or adapter cards present on the portable's system board. These system board designs typically include the standard multi-I/O (MI/O) and video circuitry as an integral part of the board. They also provide the physical connections for the unit's parallel and serial I/O ports, as well as onboard connectors for the disk drives, display unit, and keyboard units.

The computer's external I/O connections, such as serial and parallel port connectors, are arranged on the system board so that they align with the corresponding openings in the portable case. It would be highly unlikely that a system board from another portable would match these openings. On the maintenance side, a blown parallel

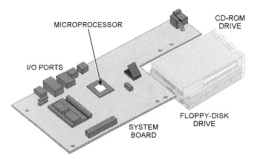

FIGURE 1.16
Typical notebook system board.

port circuit would require that the entire system board be replaced to correct the problem. In a desktop unit, a simple I/O card could be installed in an expansion slot to overcome such a situation.

Major Components

For orientation purposes, the end of the board where the keyboard connector, expansion slots, and power connectors are located on standard desktop and tower system boards is generally referred to as the rear of the board. The rear of the system board corresponds to the back of the system unit.

As mentioned earlier, the system board receives power from the power-supply unit through special power connectors. These connectors are often located along the right-rear corner of the system board so that they are near the power-supply unit. They also are keyed so that the power cord cannot be plugged in backward. On AT system boards, the power connectors are typically labeled as P1 and P2 and are always located directly beside each other. However, they are identical and can be reversed. Therefore, in an AT system the P8 and P9 power connectors should always be installed so that the black wires from each connector are together.

The system's keyboard connector is normally located along the back edge of the board as well. In most AT-compatible systems, the keyboard connector is a round, 5-pin DIN socket. ATX systems place a standard block of I/O connections along the back edge of the system board. The keyboard connector in an ATX system is typically a round, 6-pin mini-DIN (PS/2) socket.

Microprocessors

The microprocessor is the major component of any system board. It can be thought of as the "brains" of the computer system because it reads, interprets, and executes software instructions, and also carries out arithmetic and logical operations for the system.

The original PC and PC-XT computers were based on the 8/16-bit 8088 microprocessor from Intel. This microprocessor featured a 16-bit internal structure, an 8-bit data bus, and a 20-bit address bus. Its 20-bit address bus established the size of the PC's memory map at 1MB.

The IBM PC-AT system employed a 16-bit 80286 microprocessor. The 80286 remained compatible with the 8088 microprocessor used in the earlier PC and XT systems, while offering increased processing power and speed. The 80286 would run the same software that the 8088 did, but it would run it much faster.

The 80286 was much more than a fast 8088 microprocessor, however. Unlike the 8088, the 80286 microprocessor was designed to support multiuser and multitasking operations. In these types of operations, the computer appears to work on several tasks, or to serve several users, simultaneously. Of course, the microprocessor cannot actually work on more than one item at a time; the appearance of simultaneous operations is created by storing the parameters of one task, leaving the task, loading up the state of another task, and beginning operation on it.

The 80286's internal register set was identical to the register set of the 8088. However, it possessed an extended instruction set and a 24-bit address bus. The address bus enabled it to directly access up to 16MB of physical memory, and the extended instruction set provided two distinctly different addressing modes: real mode and virtual-protected mode.

In real-mode operation, the microprocessor emulates an 8088/86 microprocessor and can directly access only the first 1MB of RAM addresses in segments of 64KB. It also can work on only one task at a time. In this mode, the microprocessor produces addresses on its first 20 address pins only.

If software increments the 80286's addresses past 0FFFFFh in this mode, the address just rolls over to 000000h and the four highest address bits are not activated. Intel microprocessors default to this mode on startup and reset.

In protected mode, the microprocessor's upper address bits are enabled, and it can access physical memory addresses above the 1MB limit (up to 16MB for the 80286). If software increments the microprocessor's addresses past 0FFFFFh in protected mode, the address increments to 100000h.

Protected mode also can perform *virtual memory* operations. (Virtual memory is RAM that doesn't physically exist.) In these operations, the system treats an area of disk space as an extension of RAM memory. It uses this designated area to shift data from RAM memory to the disk (and vice versa) as required. This method enables the system to simulate large areas of RAM.

Reference Shelf

For more in-depth information about how microprocessor systems actually work, refer to the "How Microprocessors Work" section of the Electronic Reference Shelf located on the CD that accompanies this book.

Since the days of the original AT design, Intel introduced several different microprocessors for the PC market. These include devices such as the 80386DX and SX, the 80486DX and SX, the Pentium (80586), the Pentium Pro (80686), and Pentium II. Intel used the SX notation to define reduced function versions of exiting microprocessors. (That is, the 80486SX was a version of the 80486DX that had some functionality removed.) SX devices were normally created to produce price variations that kept the Intel product competitive with other devices.

Other IC manufacturers produce work-alike versions of the Intel processors that are referred to as clones. In response to clone microprocessor manufactures using the 80x86 nomenclature, Intel dropped their 80x86 numbering system after the 80486 and adopted the Pentium name so that they could copyright it.

All these microprocessors are backward compatible with the 8088— that is, programs written specifically for the 8088 can be executed by any of the other processors.

Microprocessor Packages

These ICs can take on a number of different package styles depending on their vintage and manufacturer.

The notches and dots on the various ICs are important keys when replacing a microprocessor. These notches and dots specify the location of the number 1 pin. This pin must be lined up with the pin-1 notch of the socket. The writing on the package is also significant. It contains the number that identifies the type of device in the package and normally includes a speed rating for the device.

The 8088 and 8086 microprocessors were housed in a 40-pin dual in-line package (DIP)–style package. Later XT versions employed a turbo speed function that allowed faster versions of the 8088 (8088-10 and 8088-12) to be used in systems that maintained speed compatibility with the 4.77MHz PC Bus expansion slot.

The 80286 was manufactured in a variety of 68-pin IC types including a ceramic leadless chip carrier (CLCC), a plastic leaded chip carrier (PLCC), and a pin grid array (PGA) package.

CLCC devices are designed to set inside sockets. Contacts along the side and bottom of the device make connection with spring-loaded contacts embedded in the socket. PLCC ICs have small pins that gull-wing out from the side of the chip and are soldered to the top of a PC board. PGA packages employ metal pins that protrude from the bottom of the chip. These pins are pressed into a corresponding flat socket that has been mounted on the PC board.

The 80386DX continued the evolution of the AT architecture and was produced in a 132-pin PGA package. A reduced-function 80386SX version was also produced in a 100-pin surface-mount IC package.

The 80486DX and first-generation Pentium microprocessors returned to 168-pin and 273-pin PGA packages. Figure 1.17 depicts these microprocessor packages.

Advanced Pentium processors use a variety of pin configurations, which are discussed in Chapter 4.

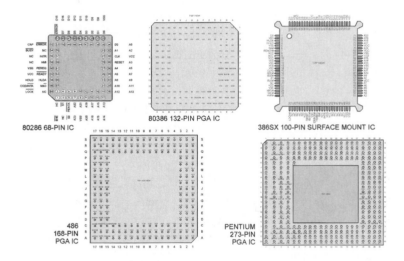

80286 68-PIN IC   80386 132-PIN PGA IC   386SX 100-PIN SURFACE MOUNT IC

486 168-PIN PGA IC   PENTIUM 273-PIN PGA IC

FIGURE 1.17
Microprocessors.

For mathematically intensive operations, some programs may shift portions of the work to special high-speed math coprocessors, if they are present in the system. These devices are specialized microprocessors that work in parallel with the main microprocessor, and extend its instruction set to speed up math and logic operations. They basically add large register sets to the microprocessor, along with additional arithmetic processing instructions. Some microprocessors—such as the 8088, 80286, 80386SX/DX, and 80486SX microprocessors—employed external coprocessors. More advanced devices, such as the 80486DX, and Pentium processors, have built-in coprocessors that are an integral part of the IC design.

Reference Shelf

For more in-depth technical information about how math coprocessors actually work, refer to the "Coprocessors" section of the Electronic Reference Shelf located on the CD that accompanies this book.

Mobile Microprocessors

The portable computer market is so large that it even influences the microprocessor and IC manufacturers. They produce special low-power-consumption microprocessors and chipsets just for portable computer systems. These power-saving IC devices are typically identified by an "SL" designation (that is, 80486SLC).

Powerful high-speed microprocessors, such as the Pentium microprocessors, produce large amounts of heat, even by desktop standards. Most of the portables currently on the market are based on Pentium devices. To minimize the heat buildup condition, Intel has produced a complete line of mobile Pentium processors for use in portable systems. Mobile devices differ from standard microprocessor devices in terms of their internal construction and their external packaging. In mobile microprocessors, both design aspects have been optimized to provide minimum size and power consumption, as well as maximum heat reduction.

Figure 1.18 depicts a mobile Pentium MMX processor. It is constructed using Intel's voltage-reduction technology, which enables the processor to run at lower core voltages (1.8–2.0V DC) and, thereby, consume less energy and generate less heat. The package style created for the mobile Pentium is referred to as a tape carrier package (TCP). The microprocessor chip is embedded in a polymide film (tape) that has been laminated with a copper foil. The leads of the IC are etched into the foil and attached to the processor.

FIGURE 1.18
The mobile Pentium.

The TCP arrangement makes the mobile package much smaller and lighter than the PGA and SPGA packages used with the standard Pentium devices. It also mounts directly to the PC board instead of plugging into a bulky, heavy socket. A special insertion machine cuts the strip of microprocessors into individual, 24mm units, as it is soldered to the system board. The system board furnishes a heat sink area beneath the processor that helps to dissipate heat. A layer of thermal conductive paste is applied to this connection prior to the soldering process to increase the heat transfer away from the processor. This design enables the full-featured Pentium processor to run at competitive speeds without additional heat sinks and fan modules. Figure 1.19 shows the cross section of the complete mobile Pentium attachment.

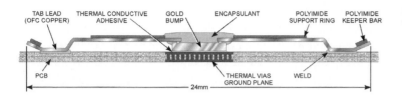

FIGURE 1.19
The mobile Pentium installation.

The attachment of the mobile microprocessor to a system board makes the arrangement permanent for all practical purposes. To allow for microprocessor upgrading, portable system boards often employ mobile processors mounted on plug-in daughter boards, or modules. Intel has produced two Pentium plug-in variations. It supplies mobile Pentiums on a 4" × 2.5" × 0.3" mobile module, referred to as an MMO. This module is attached to the system board via screws and plugs into it through a 280-pin connector. The other Intel module is a mini-cartridge for the Pentium II.

Primary Memory

All computers need a place to temporarily store information while other pieces of information are processed. In digital computers, information storage is normally conducted at two different levels: primary memory (made up of semiconductor RAM and ROM chips), and mass-storage memory (usually involving floppy and hard disk drives).

Most of the system's primary memory is located on the system board. Primary memory typically exists in two or three forms on the system board:

◆ **Read-only memory (ROM).** Contains the computer's permanent startup programs.

◆ **Random-access memory (RAM).** Quick enough to operate directly with the microprocessor and can be read from, and written to, as often as desired.

◆ **Cache memory.** A fast RAM system specially designed to hold information that the microprocessor is likely to use.

TEST TIP

Be aware of which memory types are volatile and what this means.

ROM devices store information in a permanent fashion and are used to hold programs and data that do not change. RAM devices retain only the information stored in them as long as electrical power is applied to the IC. Any interruption of power causes the contents of the memory to vanish. This is referred to as *volatile* memory. ROM, on the other hand, is nonvolatile.

Every system board contains one or two ROM ICs that hold the system's *basic input/output system* (BIOS) program. The BIOS program contains the basic instructions for communications between the microprocessor and the various input and output devices in the system. Until recently, this information was stored permanently inside the ROM chips, and could be changed only by replacing the chips.

Advancements in EEPROM technology have produced *Flash ROM* devices that allow new BIOS information to be written (downloaded) into the ROM to update it. This can be done from an update disk, or downloaded from another computer. Unlike RAM ICs, the contents of the Flash ROM remain after the power is removed from the chip. In either case, the upgraded BIOS must be compatible with the system board it is being used with and should be the latest version available.

The information in the BIOS represents all the intelligence that the computer possesses until it can load more information from another source, such as a hard or floppy disk. Taken together, the BIOS software (programming) and hardware (the ROM chip) are referred to as firmware. These ICs can be located anywhere on the system board, but they are usually easy to recognize due to their size and shape (typically 28-pin, socket-mounted DIP devices).

In older PC designs, such as XT and AT, the system's RAM memory was comprised of banks of discrete RAM ICs in DIP sockets. Intermediate clone designs placed groups of RAM ICs on small 30-pin daughter boards, referred to as single in-line pin (SIP) modules, that plugged into the system board vertically. This mounting method required less horizontal board space.

Further refinements of the RAM module produced snap-in *single in-line memory modules* (SIMMs) and *dual in-line memory modules* (DIMMs). Like the SIP, the SIMM and DIMM units mount vertically on the system board. Instead of using a pin-and-socket arrangement, however, both use special snap-in sockets that support the module firmly.

PCs are typically sold with less than their full RAM capacity. This enables users to purchase a less-expensive computer to fit their individual needs and yet retain the option to install more RAM if future applications call for it. Figure 1.20 depicts DIP, SIP, SIMM, and DIMM modules.

Chipsets

The first digital computers were giants that took up entire rooms and required several technicians and engineers to operate. They were constructed with vacuum tubes and their computing power was limited compared to modern computers. However, the advent of IC technology in 1964 launched a new era in compact electronic packaging. The much-smaller, low-power transistor replaced the vacuum tube and the size of the computer started to shrink.

The first ICs were relatively small devices that performed simple digital logic. These basic digital devices still exist and occupy a class of ICs referred to as small-scale integration (SSI) devices. SSI devices range up to 100 transistors per chip. As manufacturers improved techniques for creating ICs, the number of transistors on a chip grew and complex digital circuits were fabricated together. Eventually, large-scale integration (LSI) and very large-scale integration (VLSI) devices were produced. LSI devices contain between 3,000 and 100,000 electronic components, and VLSI devices exceed 100,000 elements.

Modern IC technology can produce millions of transistor circuits on a single small piece of silicon. Some VLSI devices contain complete computer modules.

These devices are commonly referred to as application-specific integrated circuits (ASICs). By connecting a few ASIC devices together on a printed circuit board, computers that once inhabited an entire room have shrunk to fit on the top of an ordinary work desk, and now, into the palm of the hand. Figure 1.21 shows various IC package types.

For the IC manufacturer, PC compatibility means designing chipsets that use the same basic memory map that was employed in the IBM PC-AT. (That is, the chipset's programmable registers, RAM, ROM, and other addresses had to be identical to those of the AT.) Therefore, instructions and data in the program would be interpreted, processed, and distributed the same way in both systems. In doing

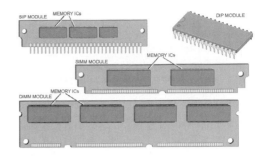

FIGURE 1.20
DIP, SIP, SIMM, and DIMM memory modules.

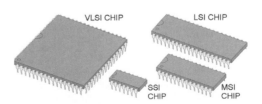

FIGURE 1.21
Integrated circuit packages.

Reference Shelf

For more in-depth information about IC devices and how they actually work, refer to the "Chips" section of the Electronic Reference Shelf located on the CD that accompanies this book.

so, the supporting chipset was decreased from eight major ICs and dozens of SSI devices to two or three VLSI chips and a handful of SSI devices.

In some highly integrated system boards, the only ICs that remain are the microprocessor, one or two *ROM BIOS* chips, a single chipset IC, and the system's memory modules.

Connectors and Jumpers

System boards possess a number of jumpers and connectors that you must be aware of. PC-compatible system boards include switches and jumper blocks (called BERG connectors, after the connector company that developed them) to select operating options such as processor speed, installed RAM size, and so forth. You may be required to alter these settings if you change a component or install a new module in the system.

Figure 1.22 illustrates the operation of typical configuration jumpers and switches. A metal clip in the cap of the jumper creates an electrical short between the pins it is installed across. When the cap is removed, the electrical connection also is removed and an electrically open condition is created.

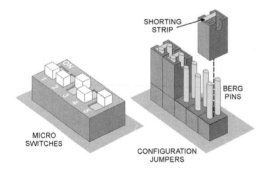

FIGURE 1.22
Jumpers and configuration switches.

System boards and I/O cards can use micro switches for configuration purposes. These micro switches are normally integrated into a DIP package, as illustrated in Figure 1.22. The switches can use a rocker or slide-switch mechanism to create the short or open condition. The switches are typically numbered sequentially and marked for On/Off positioning. Because the switches are small, they can just be marked with an On or Off, or with a 1 or 0.

It is usually necessary to consult the PC board's Installation Guide to locate and properly set configuration jumpers and switches. The Installation Guide typically provides the locations of all the board's configuration jumpers and switches. It also defines the possible configuration settings, along with corresponding switch, or jumper positions.

The system board is connected to the front panel's indicators and controls by BERG connectors. Over time, these connection points have become fairly standard between cases. The normal connections are the power LED, hard drive activity indicator, system reset switch, and system speaker. Older system boards may also include turbo led, turbo switch, and keylock switch connections to handle special high-speed operating modes and physical hardware-security locking devices. Figure 1.23 depicts a typical front-panel connector layout. It will be necessary to access these points when the system board is replaced or upgraded. Additional system board connectors that would have to be dealt with include the keyboard and power-supply connectors.

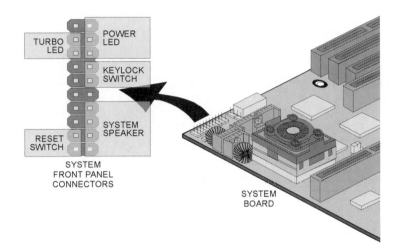

FIGURE 1.23
Typical system board connection points.

Configuration Settings

Each time the system is turned on, or reset, the BIOS program checks the system's configuration settings to determine the types of optional devices that may be included in the system.

Depending on the model of the computer, the configuration information may be read from hardware jumper or switch settings, from battery-powered RAM, or, in some cases, a combination of jumper and software settings. The PC, PC-XT, and their clones used hardware switches for configuration purposes. The original PC-AT featured a battery-powered RAM area that held some of the system's advanced configuration information. This configuration storage area became known as *CMOS RAM*.

Clone IC manufacturers quickly integrated the advanced software configuration function to their chipsets along with the system's real-time clock (RTC) function. The RTC function keeps track of time and date information for the system. Clone system board designers added a rechargeable, Ni-CAD battery to their system boards to maintain the information when the system was turned off.

NOTE

Plug and Play   Newer PCs can automatically reconfigure themselves for new options
that are installed. This feature is referred to as
Plug and Play (PnP) capability.

In newer systems, there are no rechargeable Ni-CAD batteries for
the CMOS storage. Instead, the CMOS storage area and RTC functions have been integrated with a 10-year nonreplaceable lithium cell
in an independent RTC IC module.

Because these configuration settings are the system's primary way to
get information about what options are installed, they must be set to
accurately reflect the actual options being used with the system. If
not, an error occurs. You should always suspect configuration problems if a machine fails to operate immediately after a new
component is installed. The CMOS configuration values
can be accessed for change by pressing the Ctrl and Delete keys (or
some other key combination) simultaneously during the boot-up
procedure.

In 1994, Microsoft and Intel teamed up to produce a set of system
specifications that would enable options added to the system to
automatically be configured for operation. Under this scenario, the
user is not involved in setting hardware jumpers or CMOS entries.
To accomplish this, the system's BIOS, expansion slots, and adapter
cards are designed in a manner so that they can be reconfigured
automatically by the system software.

During the startup process, the PnP BIOS looks through the system
for installed devices. Devices designed for PnP compatibility can tell
the BIOS what types of devices they are and how to communicate
with them. This information is stored in memory so that the system
can work with the device. PnP information is scattered throughout
the remainder of the text as it applies to the topic covered.

Expansion Slots

It would be expensive to design and build a computer that fit every
conceivable user application. With this in mind, computer designers
include standardized connectors that enable users to configure the
system to their particular computing needs.

Most PCs use standardized expansion slot connectors that enable
various types of peripheral devices to be attached to the system.
Optional I/O devices, or their interface boards, are plugged into
these slots to connect the devices to the system's address, data, and
control buses.

The system board communicates with various optional I/O and memory systems through adapter boards that plug into its expansion slots. These connectors are normally located along the left-rear portion of the system board so that the external devices they serve can access them through openings at the rear of the case.

Several different types of expansion slots are in use today. A particular system board may contain only one type of slot, or it may have a few of each type of expansion slot. Be aware that adapter cards are compatible with particular types of slots, so it is important to know which type of slot is being used. The major expansion slot types are

◆ 8-bit *PC-bus*

◆ 16-bit *AT-bus,* or *Industry Standard Architecture (ISA)* bus

◆ 32-bit *Extended ISA* (EISA) and *Microchannel Architecture* (MCA) buses

◆ *Video Electronics Standards Association* (VESA) and *Peripheral Component Interconnect* (PCI) local buses

Figure 1.24 depicts these expansion slots; they are discussed in detail in Chapter 4.

The PC-bus slot is the most famous example of an 8-bit expansion slot; and the AT-bus, or ISA bus, slot is the consummate 16-bit expansion bus. The 32-bit expansion buses include the MCA, the EISA, VESA, and PCI buses.

The PC bus was included in the original PC, PC-XT, and XT clone computers. The expansion bus in the IBM PC-AT and its clones became the *de facto* Industry Standard Architecture for 16-bit computers. The EISA bus was used in 80386- and 80486-based AT clone computers. The MCA bus was featured in some models of IBM's Personal System 2 (PS/2) line of computers.

The 32-bit VESA and PCI buses are typical included on 80486- and Pentium-based computers along with traditional ISA slots.

ADAPTER CARDS

The openness of the IBM PC, XT, and AT architectures, coupled with their overwhelming popularity, led companies to develop a wide assortment of expansion devices for them. Most of these devices communicate with the basic system through adapter cards

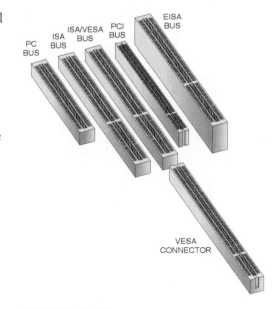

FIGURE 1.24
Expansion slot connectors.

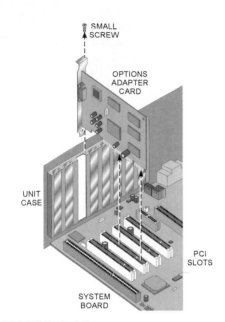

FIGURE 1.25

Plugging in a typical adapter card.

that plug into the expansion slots of the computer's main board, as illustrated in Figure 1.25. They typically contain the interfacing and controller circuitry for the peripheral. In some cases, however, the entire peripheral may be included on the adapter card.

This expansion approach enables a wide variety of peripheral devices to be added to the basic system to modify it for particular applications. Adapter cards permit less-expensive devices to be used with low-end system, such as a word processor, and yet still allow high-end, high-performance peripherals to be added to the same system to produce a more advanced computer system that can handle more demanding applications.

Three important characteristics are associated with any adapter card:

◆ Size

◆ Expansion slot connector style

◆ Function

Many companies have developed adapter cards and devices for different types of computer applications, including I/O controllers, disk drive controllers, video controllers, modems, and proprietary I/O devices (such as *scanners*).

The adapter cards in the original IBM PC were $13.2" \times 4.2"$. The PC normally came with a disk drive adapter card and a video card. These units were referred to as full-size adapter cards. They were so long that plastic guide rails were present at the front of the system unit to keep them from flexing due to system heating. A smaller ($6" \times 4.2"$) printer adapter card also was made available for the PC. This size card is referred to as a half-size card. When the AT appeared, the I/O cards became more powerful and taller ($13.2" \times 4.8"$).

The AT cards became the standard against which later I/O cards have been measured. Like system boards, adapter cards have developed into smaller, more powerful units. Most current adapter cards are two-thirds-size cards, half-size, or smaller cards. In addition, the height of the cards has been significantly reduced. Many adapters are only half the height, or less, of the original AT cards. Therefore, they are referred to as half-height cards.

The only real requirements for adapter cards now are that they fit securely in the expansion slot, cover the slot opening in the rear of the system unit, and provide standard connectors for the types of devices they serve. Figure 1.26 depicts various adapter card designs. In this example, all the cards employ an ISA edge connector. The same I/O functions and card sizes can be used to create cards for all the other expansion connector types.

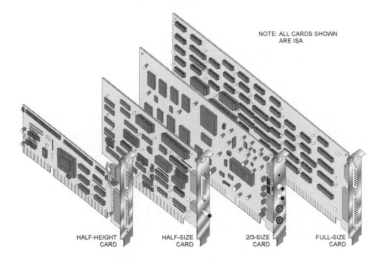

FIGURE 1.26
Adapter card designs.

Most early adapter cards employed hardware jumpers, or configuration switches, that enabled them to be configured specifically for the system they were being used in. The user had to set up the card for operation and solve any interrupt or memory-addressing conflicts that occurred. Such cards are referred to as *legacy cards*.

In newer PnP systems, adapter cards can identify themselves to the system during the startup process, along with supplying information about what type of device they are, how they are configured, and what resources they need access to. In addition, these cards must be able to be reconfigured by the system software if a conflict is detected between it and another system device.

Prior to the Pentium-based system boards, two types of adapter cards were traditionally supplied as standard equipment in most desktop and tower PC systems. These were a video adapter card and a MI/0 adapter card. In Pentium units, however, the MI/O functions have been built in to the system board. Similarly, both the video and I/O functions are an integral part of the system board in portable systems.

Video Adapter Cards

The video adapter card provides the interface between the system board and the display monitor.

The original IBM PCs and XTs offered two types of display adapters: a monochrome (single color) display adapter (MDA) and a color graphic adapter (CGA). Both of these units also included the system's first parallel printer port connector.

These initial units have been followed by a number of improved and enhanced video adapters and monitors. The most common type of video adapter card currently in use is the video graphic adapter (VGA) card like the one depicted in Figure 1.27. The system uses it to control video output operations.

Unlike most other computer components, the VGA video standard uses analog signals and circuitry rather than digital signals. The main component of most video adapter cards is an ASIC called the Integrated Video Controller IC. It is a microprocessor-like chip that oversees the operation of the entire adapter. It can access RAM and ROM memory units on the card. The video RAM chips hold the information that is to be displayed onscreen. Their size determines the card's video and color capacities.

In addition to offering vastly improved color-production capabilities, VGA provided superior resolution capabilities. Standard VGA resolution is defined as 720×400 pixels using 16 colors in text mode, and 640×480 pixels using 16 onscreen colors in graphics mode. However, improved-resolution VGA systems, referred to as *Super VGAs,* are now commonly available in formats of $1,024 \times 768$ with 256 colors, $1,024 \times 768$ with 16 colors, and 800×600 with 256 colors. The SVGA definition continues to expand, with video controller capabilities ranging up to $1,280 \times 1,024$ (with reduced color capabilities) currently available in the market.

IBM produced its own *eXtended Graphics Array* standard, called the XGA. This standard was capable of both 800×600 and $1,024 \times 768$ resolutions, but added a 132-column, 400-scan line resolution. Unfortunately, IBM based the original XGA on interlaced monitors, and therefore, never received a large following.

The maximum resolution/color capabilities of a particular VGA adapter ultimately depend on the amount of onboard memory the adapter has installed. The standard 640×480 display format, using

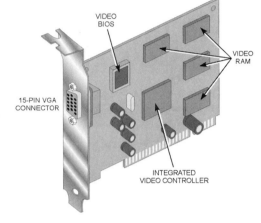

VIDEO
BIOS

VIDEO
RAM

15-PIN VGA
CONNECTOR

INTEGRATED
VIDEO CONTROLLER

FIGURE 1.27
A typical VGA card.

16 colors, requires nearly 256KB of video memory to operate (640 × 480 × 4/8 = 153,600 bytes). With 512KB of video memory installed, the resolution can be improved to 1,024 × 768, but only 16 colors are possible (1,024 ×768 × 4/8 = 393,216 bytes). To achieve full 1,024 × 768 resolution with 256 colors, the video memory has to be expanded to a full 1MB 1,024 × 768 × 8/8 = 786,432 bytes). Access to this memory is flexible.

Standard VGA monitors employ a 31.5KHz horizontal scanning rate, and Super VGA monitors use frequencies between 35 and 48KHz for their horizontal sync, depending on the vertical refresh rate of the adapter card. Standard VGA monitors repaint the screen (vertical refresh) at a frequency of 60 or 70Hz, and Super VGA vertical scanning occurs at frequencies of 56, 60, and 72Hz. Table 1.1 presents a summary of the different video standards.

TABLE 1.1

VIDEO STANDARDS

Standard	Mode	Resolution (hxv pixels)	A/N Display	A/N Character	Refresh Rate	Buffer Address
MDA	Alpha-Numberic (A/N)	720 × 348	80 × 25	7 × 9" 9 × 14"	50/60Hz	B0000-B7FFF B0000-B7FFF B0000-B7FFF
CGA	A/N graphics	640 × 200 160 × 100 320 × 200 640 × 200	80 × 25	7 × 7" 8 × 8"	60Hz	B8000-BBFFF
HGA	A/N Graphics	720 × 348	80 × 25	7 × 9" 9 × 14"	50Hz	B0000-B7FFF
EGA	A/N Graphics	640 × 350 640 × 350	80 × 25 80 × 43	7 × 9" 8 × 14"	60Hz	0A0000
VGA	Text Graphics	720 × 400 640 × 480	80 × 25 80 × 43	9 × 16"	60 or 70Hz	0A0000-BFFFF
SVGA	Text Graphics	1,280 × 1,024 1,024 × 768 800 × 600	80 × 25 80 × 43	9 × 16"	50, 60, or 72Hz	0A0000-BFFFF
XGA	Text Graphics	1,024 × 768 800 × 600	132 × 25	9 × 16" 8 × 16"	44/70Hz	0A0000-BFFFF

The adapter also has a video BIOS ROM that is similar to the ROM BIOS on the system board. This BIOS acts as an extension of the system BIOS and is located between address C0000h and C7FFFh. It is used to store firmware routines that are specific only to video functions.

As Table 1.1 hows, a typical VGA card can support up to as many as 27 distinct modes of operation. These modes cover various character-box sizes and resolution selections. They also include two different ways to store screen data in the video memory. The first method is the A/N (Alpha-Numeric) mode, which is used for text operations. The second method is an All Points Addressable (APA) mode, which is normally used for graphics applications.

The video controller also contains the video DAC (digital-to-analog converter) that converts digital data in the controller into the analog signal used to drive the display. The video output connector is a three-row, DB-15 female connector used with analog VGA displays.

Other Adapter Cards

Although the MI/O card has largely disappeared and the video display adapter card is typically the only adapter card required in the system, many other I/O functions can be added to the system through adapter cards. Some of the most popular I/O cards in modern Pentium systems include the following:

◆ **Modem cards.** Used to carry out data communications through telephone lines

◆ **Local area network cards.** Used to connect the local computer to a group of other computers so that they can share data and resources

◆ **Sound cards.** Used to provide high-quality audio output to the computer system

Figure 1.28 shows samples of these cards and their connections. Although they represent the most popular options added to computer systems, many other I/O devices can be plugged into an expansion slot to enhance the operation of the system.

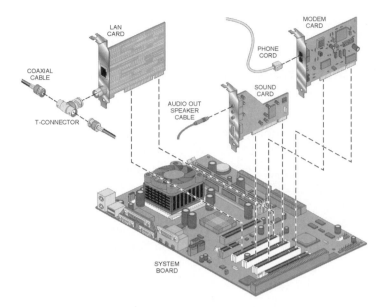

FIGURE 1.28
Typical I/O cards.

STORAGE DEVICES

Programs and data disappear from the system's RAM when the computer is turned off. In addition, IC RAM devices tend to be too expensive to construct large memories that can hold multiple programs and large amounts of data. Therefore, storage systems that can be used for long-term data storage are desirable as a second level of memory.

With this in mind, a number of secondary memory technologies have been developed to extend the computer's memory capabilities and store data on a more permanent basis. These systems tend to be too slow to be used directly with the computer's microprocessor. The secondary memory unit holds the information and transfers it in batches to the computer's faster internal memory when requested.

From the beginning, most secondary memory systems have involved storing binary information in the form of magnetic charges on moving magnetic surfaces.

Magnetic storage remains popular because of three factors:

◆ Low cost-per-bit of storage.

◆ Intrinsically nonvolatile nature.

◆ It has successfully evolved upward in capacity.

The major magnetic storage mediums are floppy disks, hard disks, and tape.

In magnetic disk systems, information is stored as magnetized spots arranged in concentric circles around the disk. These circles are referred to as *tracks* and are numbered, beginning with 0, from the outside edge inward. The number of tracks may range from 40 up to 2,048, depending on the type of disk and drive being used.

In hard disk drives, multiple disks are stacked together on a common spindle. The corresponding tracks of each surface are logically arranged to form a cylinder. (That is, all the track-0 tracks are taken together to form cylinder-0.)

Because the tracks at the outer edge of the disk are longer than those at its center, each track is divided into an equal number of equal-sized blocks called *sectors*. This arrangement is used so that the logic circuitry for processing data going to, or coming from the disk can be as simple as possible. The number of sectors on a track can range from 8 to more than 60, depending on the disk and drive type and the operating system software used to format it.

As an example, a typical IBM floppy disk will have 40 or 80 tracks per surface, with each track divided into 8, 9, or 18 sectors each. In a PC-compatible system, each sector holds 512 bytes of data. Figure 1.29 shows the organizational structure of a typical magnetic disk.

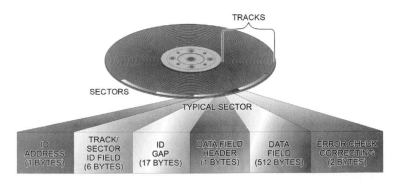

FIGURE 1.29
The organizational structure of a magnetic disk.

In magnetic tape systems, data is stored in sequential tracks along the length of the tape, as depicted in Figure 1.30. Each track is divided into equal-sized blocks. The blocks are separated by small gaps of unrecorded space. Multiple tracks can be recorded across the width of the tape. Using multiple read/write heads, the tracks can be read simultaneously as the tape moves forward. The tracks also can be read in a serpentine (a back and forth weaving) manner, using a single read/write head.

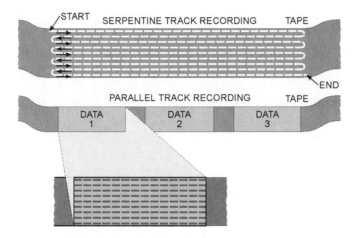

FIGURE 1.30
Formats for storing data on magnetic tape.

Although it is possible to directly access any of the sectors on a magnetic disk, the sections on the tape can be accessed only in a linear order. To access the information in block 32 of the tape, the previous 31 blocks must pass through the drive.

Tape generally represents a cheaper storage option, but its inherent slowness, due to its sequential nature, makes it less desirable than rotating magnetic disks. The disks offer much quicker access to large blocks of data, at a cost that is still affordable to most users.

DISK DRIVES

The system unit normally comes from the manufacturer with a *floppy disk drive* (FDD), a *hard disk drive* (HDD), and a *CD-ROM drive* installed, as illustrated in Figure 1.31.

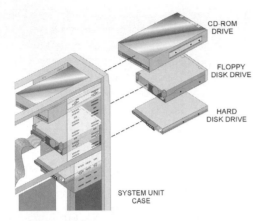

FIGURE 1.31
The disk drives of a typical system.

The system's disk drive capacity is not usually limited to the standard units installed. In most cases, the system cabinet is designed to hold additional disk drive units. These units can normally be a mixture of 3.5-inch or 5.25-inch drive units and include floppy disk, hard disk, CD-ROM, rewritable CD (CD-RW), or digital video (DVD) drive types. Although three FDD units could physically be installed in most systems, the typical floppy drive controller supports only two drives.

One or more HDD units can be installed in the system unit, along with the floppy drive(s). The system should normally be set up to recognize a single hard disk unit in the system as the C: drive. However, a single, physical hard disk drive can be *partitioned* (divided) into two or more volumes that the system recognizes as *logical drives* C:, D:, and so on. Hard drive partitioning is discussed in much greater detail later in this chapter in the section "Logical and Physical Drives."

Floppy Disk Drives

The most widely used data storage systems in PCs are floppy disk drive units. These units store information in the form of tiny, magnetized spots on small flexible disks that can be removed from the drive unit. After the information is written on the disk, it theoretically remains there until the disk is magnetically erased or written over. The information remains on the disk even if it is removed from the disk drive or if power is removed from the system. Whenever the information is required by the system, it can be obtained by inserting the disk back into the drive and causing the software to read it from the disk.

NOTE

Data Vanish   Over long periods of time, such as 10 years or so, data will disappear from a magnetic disk.

The disks are relatively inexpensive and are easy to transport and store. In addition, they can easily be removed and replaced if they become full. Figure 1.32 depicts a typical floppy disk drive unit.

The standard floppy disk drive for 8088-based machines was the 5.25-inch, full-height and half-height drive. These drives used disks capable of storing 368,640 bytes (referred to as 360KB of information. The term half-height was used to describe drive units that were half as tall as the full-height drive units used with the original IBM PC. Smaller 3.5-inch half-height drives, capable of storing 720KB (737,280 bytes) of information, also were used with 8088-based computers.

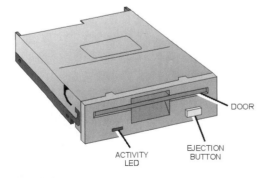

FIGURE 1.32
A typical floppy disk drive unit.

The PC AT and its compatibles originally used high-density, 5.25-inch drives that could hold more than 1,200,000 bytes (1.2MB) of information. In newer machines, high-density, 3.5-inch floppy drives, capable of holding 1.44MB (1,474,560 bytes), are the norm.

The typical floppy disk, depicted in Figure 1.33, is a flexible, 3.5-inch diameter mylar disk that has been coated with a ferro-magnetic material. It is encased in protective, hard plastic envelope that contains a low-friction liner that removes dust and contaminants from the disk as it turns within the envelope. Typical floppy drives turn the disk at 300 or 360rpm and the drive's R/W heads ride directly on the disk surface. Information is written to or read from the disk as it spins inside the envelope. The small light-emitting diode (LED) on the front of the disk drive unit lights up whenever either of these operations is in progress.

The drive's read/write heads access the disk surface through a spring-loaded metal cover, which the drive unit moves out of the way. The drive spindle turns the disk by engaging a keyed metal wafer attached to the underneath side of the disk. A small, sliding tab in the left-front corner of the envelope performs a write-protect function for the disk. If the tab covers the opening, the disk may be written to. If the opening is clear, however, the disk is said to be write-protected, and the drive does not write information on the disk.

Current PC systems use a type of floppy disk referred to as double-sided, high density (DS-HD). This means that the disk can be used on both sides, and that advanced magnetic recording techniques may be used to effectively double or triple the storage capacity previously available using older recording techniques. These disks can hold 1.44MB of information using the Microsoft operating systems.

This type of floppy disk drive also can operate with an older a type of floppy disk that is referred to as a double-sided, double-density (DS-DD) disk. This notation indicates that the disks are constructed so that they can be used on both sides, and that they can support recording techniques that double the storage capacity available with older recording techniques.

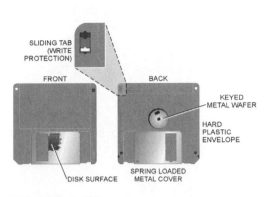

FIGURE 1.33
Floppy disks.

Hard Disk Drives

The system's data storage potential is extended considerably by the high-speed, high-capacity hard disk drive units like the one shown in Figure 1.34. These units store much more information than

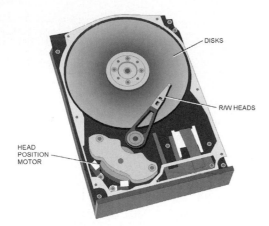

FIGURE 1.34

Inside a hard disk drive.

floppy disks. Modern hard drives can have storage capacities ranging up to several tens of gigabytes. Hard drives also differ from floppy disk units in that they use rigid disks that are permanently sealed in a nonremovable, vacuum-tight portion of the drive unit.

The disks have historically been aluminum platters coated with a nickel-cobalt or ferro-magnetic material. Newer disk drives use ceramic platters. These platters are not as prone to mechanical expansion at high speeds as aluminum disks. Expansion of the disk caused by high rotational speeds leads to data corruption on the disk. Two or more platters are usually mounted on a common spindle, with spacers between them, to allow data to be recorded on both sides of each disk. The drive's read/write mechanism is sealed inside a dust-free compartment along with the disks.

Modern hard disk drives come in sizes of 5.25-, 3.5-, and 2.5-inch diameters. Of these sizes, the 3.5-inch versions are the most popular due to their association with personal and business desktop computers. Although popular for many years, 5.25-inch hard drives are quickly disappearing from the marketplace. Conversely, the popularity of the 2.5-inch drives is growing with the rising popularity of laptop and notebook-size computers. Hard drives ranging into the gigabytes of storage are available for these machines.

Hard disk drives normally used with PCs typically contain between one and five disks that are permanently mounted inside a sealed enclosure, along with the R/W head mechanisms. There is one R/W head for each disk surface. The platters are typically turned at a speed of 5,400rpm. This high rotational speed creates a thin cushion of air around the disk surface that causes the R/W heads to fly just above the disk.

The flying R/W heads glide over the disks at a height of approximately 50 micro inches. This may seem like an unimportant measurement until you consider the size of a common dust particle or a human hair.

Figure 1.35 depicts this relationship. If the R/W head should strike one of these contaminants as the disk spins at high speed, the head would be lofted into the air and then crash into the disk surface, damaging the R/W head and/or the disk surface. This is known as a head crash, or as *head-to-disk interference* (HDI). To avoid this, hard disks are encased in the sealed protective housing. It is important to realize that at no time should the disk housing be opened to the atmosphere. Repairs to hard disk drives are performed in special repair facilities having ultra-clean rooms. In these rooms, even particles the size of those in Figure 1.35 have been removed from the air.

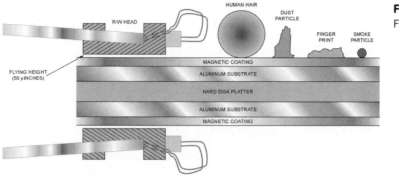

FIGURE 1.35
Flying R/W heads.

The rigid structure of the hard disk allows its tracks to be placed close together. This, in turn, makes its storage capacity very high. Typical hard disks may have between 315 and 2,048 tracks on each side of each platter. As mentioned earlier, the term *cylinders* refers to the collection of all the tracks possessing the same number on different sides of the disks (that is, track0/side0, track0/side1, track0/side2, and so on). Each track on the hard drive is divided into between 17 and 65 equal-size sectors, depending on the diameter of the disk. Sectors generally contain 512 bytes. The high speed at which the hard disk revolves also provides very rapid data transfer rates. On a typical 100MB, 3.5-inch hard disk, there are 1,002 cylinders (tracks per side) divided into 32 sectors.

The major differences between floppy and hard disk drives are storage capacity, data transfer rates, and cost.

Drive Arrays

As applications pushed storage capacity requirements past available drive sizes, it became logical to combine several drives together to hold all the data produced. In a desktop unit, this can be as simple as adding an additional physical drive to the system. *Wide area* and *local area networks* (WANs and LANs) connect computers together so that their resources (including disk drives) can be shared. If you

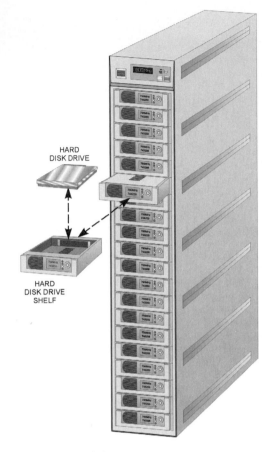

HARD
DISK DRIVE

HARD
DISK DRIVE
SHELF

FIGURE 1.36
A drive array stack.

extend this idea of sharing disk drives to include several different drive units operating under a single controller, you have a *drive array*. Figure 1.36 depicts a drive array.

Actually, drive arrays have evolved in response to storage requirements for LANs. These are particularly useful in client/server networks, where the data for the network tends to be centrally located and shared by all the users around the network.

In the cases of multiple drives within a unit, and drives scattered around a network, all the drives assume a different letter designation. In a drive array, the stack of drives can be made to appear as a single, large hard drive. The drives are operated in parallel so that they can deliver data to the controller in a parallel format. If the controller is simultaneously handling 8 bits of data from 8 drives, the system sees the speed of the transfer as being 8 times faster. This technique of using the drives in a parallel array is referred to as a *striped drive array*.

It is also possible to just use a small drive array as a data backup system. In this case, referred to as a *mirrored drive array*, the drives are each supplied with the same data. In the event that the data from one drive is corrupted, or one of the drives fails, the data is still safe. Of course, a mirrored drive array requires at least two hard drives to store one set of information. Both types of arrays are created through a blend of specialized connection hardware (a RAID controller) and control software.

RAID Systems

The most common drive arrays are *redundant arrays of inexpensive disks* (RAID) systems. There are many levels of RAID technology specifications given by the RAID Advisory Board.

The RAID Advisory Board designated the classic striped array described earlier as RAID level 0 (RAID 0—striped disk array without fault tolerance). Likewise, the mirrored drive array described earlier is labeled RAID 1. The following list describes each level:

◆ **RAID 1** (mirroring and duplexing) is a redundancy scheme that uses two equal-sized drives, where both drives hold the same information. Each drive serves as a backup for the other. Figure 1.37 illustrates the operation of a mirrored array used in a RAID 1 application.

Duplicate information is stored on both drives. When the file is retrieved from the array, the controller reads alternate sectors from each drive. This effectively reduces the data read time by half. If each hard drive is controlled by its own controller the process is referred to as disk duplexing.

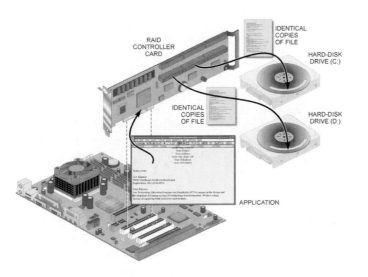

FIGURE 1.37
Operation of a mirrored array.

◆ **RAID 2** (data striping with error recovery) strategy interleaves data on parallel drives, as described in Figure 1.38. Bits or blocks of data are interleaved across the disks in the array. The speed afforded by collecting data from the disks in a parallel format is the biggest feature of the system. In large arrays, complete bytes, words, or double-words can be written to, and read from, the array simultaneously.

The RAID 2 specification uses multiple disks for error-detection and correction functions. Depending on the error-detection and correction algorithms used, large portions of the array are used for nondata storage overhead. Of course, the reliability of the data being delivered to the system is excellent, and there is no need for time-consuming corrective read operations when an error is detected. Arrays dealing with large systems may use between three and seven drives for error-correction purposes. Because of the high hardware overhead, RAID 2 systems are not normally used with microcomputer systems.

FIGURE 1.38

Interleaved data on parallel drives.

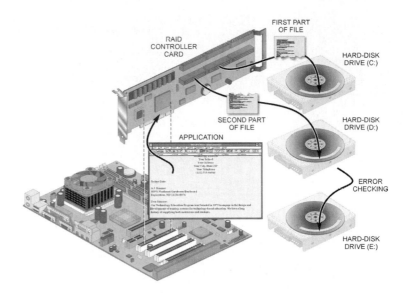

When the array is used in this manner, a complex error-detection and correction algorithm is normally employed. The controller contains circuitry based on the algorithm that detects, locates, and corrects the error without retransmitting any data. This is a quick and efficient method of error-detection and correction.

In Figure 1.38, the data block being sent to the array is broken apart and distributed to the drives in the array. The data word already has a parity bit added to it. The controller generates parity for the block, and stores it on the error-detection drive. When the controller reads the data back from the array, it regenerates the error-check character, and compares it to the one written on the error-check drive. By comparing the error-check character to the rewritten one, the controller can detect the error in the data field and determine which bit within the field is incorrect. With this information in hand, the controller can just correct that bit as it is processed.

◆ In a **RAID 3** (parallel transfer with parity striping) arrangement, the drives of the array operate in parallel like a RAID 2 system. However, only parity checking is used for error detection and correction—requiring only one additional drive. If an error occurs, the controller reads the array again to verify the error. This method of error correction is ineffecient and time consuming.

◆ A **RAID 4** (independent data disks with shared parity disk) controller interleaves sectors across the drives in the array. This creates the appearance of one very large drive. The RAID 4 format is generally used for smaller drive arrays, but also can be used for larger arrays. Only one parity-checking drive is allotted for error control. The information on the parity drive is updated after reading the data drives. This creates an extra write activity for each data read operation performed.

◆ The **RAID 5** scheme (independent data disks with distributed parity blocks) alters the RAID 4 specification by allowing the parity function to rotate through the different drives. Under this system, error checking and correction is the function of all the drives. If a single drive fails, the system can regenerate its data from the parity information on the other drives. RAID 5 is usually the most popular RAID system because it can be used on small arrays, with a high level of error recovery built in.

CD-ROM

Soon after the *compact disc* (CD) became popular for storing audio signals on optical material, the benefits of storing computer information in this manner became apparent. The term *disc* is used rather than *disk* to differentiate between magnetic disks and optical discs. With a CD, data is written digitally on a light-sensitive material by a powerful, highly focused laser beam.

The writing laser is pulsed with the modulated data to be stored on the disc. When the laser is pulsed, a microscopic blister is burned into the optical material, causing it to reflect light differently from the material around it. The blistered areas are referred to as pits, and the areas between them are called lands. Figure 1.39 illustrates the writing of data on the optical disc.

The recorded data is read from the disc by scanning it with a lower power, continuous laser beam. The laser diode emits the highly focused, narrow beam that is reflected back from the disc. The reflected beam passes through a prism, and is bent 90 degrees, where it is picked up by the diode detector and converted into an electrical signal. Only the light reflected from a land on the disc is picked up by the detector. Light that strikes a pit is scattered and is not detected. The lower power level used for reading the disc ensures that the optical material is not affected during the read operation.

FIGURE 1.39
Writing on a CD-ROM drive.

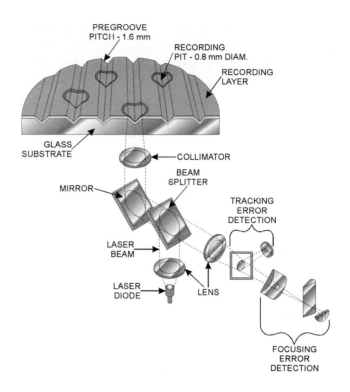

With an audio CD, the digital data retrieved from the disc is passed through a digital-to-analog converter circuit to reproduce the audio sound wave. This is not required for digital computer systems, however, because the information is already in a form acceptable to the computer. Therefore, CD players designed for use in computer systems are referred to as CD-ROM drives, to differentiate them from audio CD players. Otherwise, the mechanics of operation are very similar between the two devices. The ROM designation refers to the fact that most of the drives available are read-only.

CD-ROM Discs

A typical CD-ROM disc is 4.7 inches in diameter, and consists of three major parts:

◆ Acrylic substrate

◆ Aluminized, mirror-finished data surface

◆ Lacquer coating

The scanning laser beam comes up through the disc, strikes the aluminized data surface, and is reflected back. Because no physical contact occurs between the reading mechanism and the disc, the disc never wears out (one of the main advantages of the CD system). The blisters on the data surface are typically just under 1 micrometer in length, and the tracks are 1.6 micrometers apart. The data is encoded by the length and spacing of the blisters, and the lands between them. Figure 1.40 illustrates this concept.

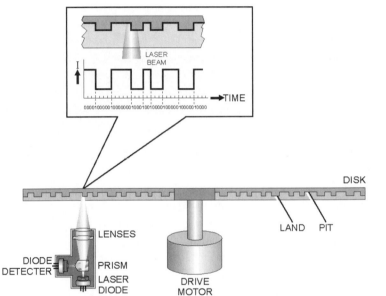

FIGURE 1.40
Encoding data on a CD-ROM.

The information on a compact disc is stored in one continuous spiral track, unlike floppy disks (where the data is stored in multiple, concentric tracks). The CD storage format still divides the data into separate sectors. However, the sectors of a CD-ROM disc are physically the same size. The disc spins counter-clockwise, and slows down as the laser diode emitter/detector unit approaches the outside of the disc.

It begins spinning at approximately 500rpm at the inner edge of the disc, and slows down to about 200rpm at the outer edge of the disc.

The spindle motor controls the speed of the disc so that the track always passes the laser at between 3.95 and 4.6 feet per second. Therefore, CD-ROM drives must have a variable-speed spindle motor, and cannot just be turned on and off like a floppy drive's spindle motor. The variable speed of the drive enables the disc to contain more sectors, thereby giving it a much larger storage capacity. In fact, the average storage capacity of a CD-ROM disc is about 680MB. For reference purposes, consider that this amount of storage corresponds to over 472 HD-DS floppy disks.

CD-ROM Drives

CD-ROM drives that operate at the speed of a conventional audio CD player are called single-speed (1×) drives. Advanced drives that spin twice, and three times as fast as the typical CD player are referred to as double-speed (2×) drives, triple-speed (3×) drives, and so forth. Single-speed drives transfer data at a rate of 150KB per second. Double-speed drive transfers occur at 300KB per second, and so on. Most manufacturers are now focusing on 50× and 52× drives.

CD-ROM drives can play audio CDs. However, a CD player cannot produce any output from the CD-ROM disc. CDs are classified by a color-coding system that corresponds to their intended use. CDs that contains digital data intended for use in a computer are referred to as Yellow Book CDs. Red Book CDs refer to those formatted to contain digital music. Orange Book refers to the standard for CDs that are used in WORM drives. Green Book CDs are used with interactive CD systems, and Blue Book CDs are those associated with laser-disc systems.

CD Writers

Another type of CD drive is classified as Write Once, Read Many (WORM) drive. As the acronym implies, these drives enable users to write information to the disk once, and then retrieve this information as you would with a CD-ROM drive. With WORM drives, after information is stored on a disk, the data cannot be changed or deleted.

CD writer technology has developed to the point where it is inexpensive enough to be added to a typical PC system. CD writers record data on blank *CD-Recordable* (CD-R) discs. A CD-R is a WORM media that is generally available in 120mm and 80mm sizes. The drives are constructed using a typical 5.25-inch half-height drive form factor. This form factor is convenient in that it fits into a typical PC drive bay. CD-R technology has continued to evolve into a recordable, ReWritable compact disc referred to as a CD-RW disc. These discs can be recorded, erased, and rewritten in the same fashion as floppy disks.

The physical construction of the CD-R disc differs considerably from the CD-ROM disc. The writable disc is constructed as illustrated in Figure 1.41. The CD-R disc is created by coating a transparent polycarbonate substrate with an opaque polymer dye. The dye is covered with a thin layer of gold and topped with a protective lacquer layer and a label. The CD-R writing mechanism is not as strong as that of a commercial CD-ROM duplicator. Instead of burning pits into the substrate of the disc, the CD-writer uses a lower power laser to discolor the dye material.

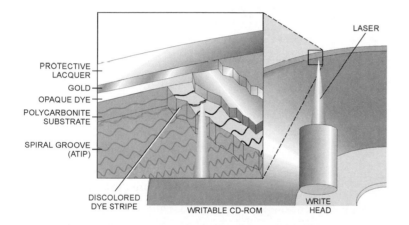

FIGURE 1.41
Writable CD-R disc.

The CD-R disc format is identical to that of a CD-ROM and information written on it can be read by a typical CD-ROM drive. The spiral-track formation and sectoring are the same as that used with CD-ROM discs. In addition, the CD writer can produce recordings in the standard CD book formats (that is, Red, Yellow, Orange, and Green).

During the write operation, the CD writer uses a medium-intensity laser to write the data on the thermally sensitive media. The laser light is applied to the bottom side of the disc. It passes through the substrate to the reflective layer and is reflected back through the substrate. The light continues through the drive's optics system until it reaches the laser detector.

When the polymer is exposed to the light of the writing laser, it heats up and becomes transparent. This exposes the reflective gold layer beneath the polymer. During read back, the reflective layer reflects more light than the polymer material does. The transitions between lighter and darker areas of the disc are used to encode the data.

CD writers can typically write to the CD-R at either 2× or 4× CD speeds. These settings have nothing to do with playback speeds. CD-RW drives are specified in a *Record* x *Write-once* x *Rewrite* speed format (that is, a 32 × 8 × 4 CD-RW can read at 32×, write at 8× and rewrite at 4× speeds).

CD-ROM Interfaces

With as many speed choices as there are, there also are five choices of architectures for CD-ROM drives, as follows:

◆ SCSI interfaces

◆ IDE/EIDE interfaces

◆ USB interfaces

◆ IEEE-1394 interfaces

◆ Proprietary interfaces

Because both the SCSI and IDE interfaces are system-level interfaces, most of their controller circuitry is actually located on the drives. In pre-Pentium systems, the SCSI and IDE drives employed *host adapter cards* that plugged into the system board's expansion slots. In the Pentium environment, the IDE host adapter function has been integrated into the system board. The IDE interface connectors are located on the system board.

SCSI systems continue to use host adapter cards as their interface connectors. The host adapter provides a BERG pin connector for the system's internal SCSI ribbon cable. There are many versions of the SCSI standard, however, and several types of SCSI connecting cables. An internal SCSI CD-ROM drive must be capable of connecting to the type of SCSI cable being used. The SCSI interface, using a Centronics-type connector, is the most widely used way to connect external CD-ROM drives to systems. There also are two versions of the IDE interface: the original IDE specification and a newer, *Enhanced IDE* (EIDE) standard. The EIDE interface has been redefined to allow faster transfer rates, as well as the handling of more storage capacity. It also can be used to control drive units such as a tape or CD-ROM. The EIDE interface is often described as an *AT Attachment Packet Interconnect* (ATAPI) or a Fast ATA (Fast AT Attachment) interface. All these standards are described in detail later in this chapter.

The controllers for proprietary interfaces are often included with the drive, or with a *sound card*. To gain full advantage of a CD-ROM, it's becoming essential to have a sound card. Many sound cards include a CD-ROM drive interface, or controller. However, these controllers may not be IDE or SCSI compatible. They often contain proprietary interfaces that work only with a few CD-ROM models.

Tape Drives

Tape-drive units are another popular type of information storage system. These units can store large amounts of data on small tape cartridges, similar to the one depicted in Figure 1.42.

When storing large amounts of data, tapes tend to be more economic than other magnetic media. Access to information stored on tape tends to be very slow, however; unlike disks, tape operates in a linear fashion. The tape transport must run all the tape past the drive's R/W heads to access data that is physically stored at the end of the tape.

Therefore, tape drives are generally used to store large amounts of information that do not need to be accessed often, or quickly. Such applications include making backup copies of programs and data. This type of data security is a necessity with records such as business transactions, payroll, artwork, and so on.

Data backup has easily become the most widely used tape application. With the large amounts of information that can be stored on a hard disk drive, a disk crash is a very serious problem. If the drive crashes, all the information stored on the disk can be destroyed. This can easily add up to billions of pieces of information. Therefore, an inexpensive method of storing data away from the hard drive is desirable.

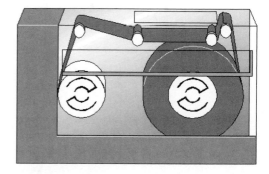

FIGURE 1.42
A tape cartridge.

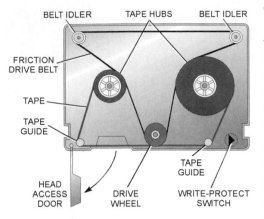

FIGURE 1.43
A 1/4" tape cartridge.

Tape Standards

As more users employed tape as a backup media, standards for tape systems were formed. The most widely used tape standard is the quarter-inch cartridge (QIC) standard. This standard calls for a tape cartridge like the one depicted in Figure 1.43. Its physical dimensions are 6" × 4" × 5/8". The cartridge has a head access door in the front that swings open when it is inserted in the drive unit.

Unlike audio-cassette tapes, cartridge tapes are not driven by capstans that extend through their tape spools. Instead, they employ a belt drive system that loops through the cartridge, and turns both spools synchronously. The belt is driven by a rubber drive wheel, which, in turn, is driven by the capstan. This design provides smoother, more precise operation than the audio-cassette tape is capable of.

The R/W heads magnetize the tape as it passes by, in much the same manner as described for other magnetic storage media. The data is placed on the tape serially as it moves past the head. The tape is organized into sectors of data, separated by intergap blocks. The data can be applied in parallel tracks (using multiple R/W heads), in a continuous stream of data (streaming tape systems), or in a serpentine manner, where the data is applied to the tape in one direction for odd tracks, and in the other direction for even tracks.

Magnetic tape must be formatted before use, just like a disk. In the formatting process, the controller marks the tape off into sectors. In addition, it establishes a file allocation table in its header, similar to that of a floppy or hard disk. The header also contains a bad-sector table to prevent defective areas of the tape from being used. Some of the tape is devoted to the error-detection and correction information that must be used with tape systems.

Cartridge tapes were referred to as DC-6000-style tapes. Their model numbers would normally include a reference to their tape capacity as the last digits (that is, DC-6200 would be a 200MB tape). As the cartridge tape industry matured, manufacturers came together to establish standards for tape formats and labeling. In the process, the DC-6000 number has been replaced in discussions about capacity and format.

For the most part, a series of QIC numbers have been used to describe different tape cartridges. Table 1.2 provides a sample list of QIC standard numbers.

| TABLE 1.2 | | | |

QIC SPECIFICATIONS

Specification	Tracks	Capacity	Cartridge
QIC-02	9	60MB	DC-3000
QIC-24	9	60MB	DC-6000
QIC-40	20	40MB	DC-2000
QIC-80	32	80MB	DC-2000
QIC-100	12/24	100MB	DC-2000
QIC-150	18	250MB	DC-6000
QIC-1000	30	1.0GB	DC-6000
QIC-1350	30	1.35GB	DC-6000
QIC-2100	30	2.1GB	DC-6000

A minicartridge version of the quarter-inch tape cartridge, with dimensions of 3-1/4" × 2-1/2" × 5/8", has been developed to provide a more compact form factor to fit in 3-1/2" drive bays. The internal operation of the cartridge has remained the same, but the amount of tape inside has been reduced. The reduced amount of tape in the cartridge is offset by the use of more advanced data-encoding schemes that store more data on less tape. Minicartridges are referred to as DC-2000-style cartridges. Like the DC-6000 tapes, the DC-2000 model numbers normally include a reference to their tape capacity as the last digits.

A number of QIC tape standards have developed over time. The original QIC standard was QIC-40. This standard called for a unit that could be connected to a floppy disk drive interface so that it acted like a large B: drive. It specified a 20-track format, with each track consisting of 68 segments, having 29 sectors of 1024 bytes each. This format provided 40MB of data storage. The specification treated the tape's sectors like the sectors of a floppy disk, in that they were organized into files.

An updated QIC-80 specification was developed to replace the QIC-40 standard. Advanced R/W head structures allow the QIC-80 to place 32 tracks on the tape rather than 20. Coupled together with improved data-per-inch storage capabilities, the total capacity of the cartridge was boosted to 80MB. The QIC-80 systems included data-compression software that could effectively double the capacity of the drive from its stated value.

The QIC-80 standard has been superseded by the QIC-500M format, which allows for up to 500MB of data to be stored on the cartridge. Newer standards for tape drives continue to emerge. Specifications that depart from the floppy disk drive interface, and use the IDE or SCSI interfaces, are producing data storage potentials into the multiple gigabyte ranges.

Newer digital tape standards have appeared in the PC market as the need to back up larger blocks of data has increased. The most noteworthy of these are the Digital Audio Tape (DAT) and the Digital Linear Tape (DLT) formats.

The DAT format borrows helical scan techniques from video tape recording to large blocks of information in a small length of tape. The system uses a dual, read-after-write recording head to place data on the tape at angles. The first write head records data on the tape in stripes that run at an angle to the motion of the tape. The angled recording acts to minimize the linear space required for the data. The follow-after read head reads the data back to verified that it has been recorded correctly.

The second write head records additional data over the stripes of the first data. The second data is written at an angle to the first data, using an opposite polarity-encoding method. The second read head follows behind and verifies that the second data has been recorded accurately.

DAT tapes can store up to 24GB of compressed data, depending on the data format used. There are three digital data storage (DDS) formats in use:

◆ **DDS-1.** 2GB uncompressed/4GB compressed

◆ **DDS-2.** 4GB uncompressed/8GB compressed

◆ **DDS-3.** 12GB uncompressed/24GB compressed

DLT tape drives provide reliable, high-speed, high-capacity tape backup functions. DLT drives use multiple parallel tracks and high-speed data-streaming techniques to provide fast backup operations with capacities in excess of 70GB.

PERIPHERALS

Peripherals are devices and systems added to the basic system to extend its capabilities. These devices and systems can be divided into three general categories: input systems, output systems, and memory systems.

Most peripheral devices interact with the basic system through adapter cards that plug into the system board's expansion slots. The peripheral devices connect to the adapter cards through expansion slot openings in back of the system unit.

The standard peripherals associated with PCs are the *keyboard* and the *CRT monitor*. With the rapid growth of GUI-oriented software, the mouse has become a common input peripheral as well. The next most common peripheral has to be the character printer. These peripherals are used to produce hard-copy output on paper. Many other types of peripheral equipment are routinely added to the basic system. As long as there are open expansion slots, or other standard I/O connectors, it is possible to add compatible devices to the system.

I/O Connections

Figure 1.44 illustrates external connections for a basic AT-style system configuration.

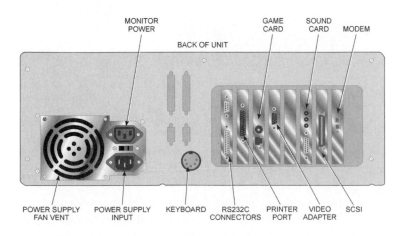

FIGURE 1.44
External connections.

The power-supply unit provides three points of interest at the system's back panel. The first is the female power receptacle, which can be used to provide power to IBM PC-compatible monitors. Next to the monitor power receptacle is the power supply's input connector. The detachable power cord plugs into this socket. Beside the power connector is the power supply's fan vent. In a small opening near the power-supply openings is the circular, 5-pin DIN connector for connecting a keyboard to the system.

Across the remainder of the back panel are 8 expansion-slot openings. Typical interface connections found in a basic system include two RS-232C connectors, a parallel printer port connector, and a game adapter connector. In this illustration, the game port connector is located above the parallel port connector. On other systems, the locations of the various connectors may vary. The last connector on the back panel is the video adapter's monitor connector. This example features a VGA-compatible, 3-row, 15-pin RGB color-output port connector.

Figure 1.45 illustrates typical connectors found on the back of an ATX-style system.

FIGURE 1.45
ATX back-panel connections.

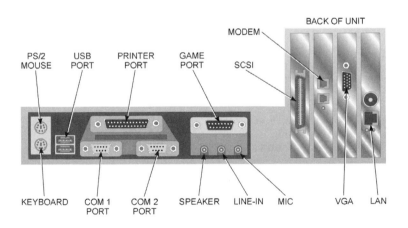

On the ATX back panel, many of the system board–related I/O functions have been grouped into a standardized block of connections as illustrated. The panel features two 6-pin PS/2 mini-DIN connectors. The lower connector is for the keyboard, whereas the upper connector is intended for use with a PS/2 serial mouse. Because these connectors are physically identical, it is relatively easy to confuse them. Just to the right of the keyboard and mouse ports are two USB connectors for attaching USB devices to the system.

The master I/O block contains two DB-9M COMM port connectors for use with serial devices and a DB-25F parallel port connector for SPP, EPP, and ECP parallel devices. This board also features a game port and built-in audio connections. The DB-15F connector is the standard for the PC game port and is used to attach joysticks and other game-playing devices. The audio block features standard RCA jacks for the microphone, audio-in, and speaker connections.

In the expansion slots, located to the right of the ATX I/O block, you will see a DB-15F VGA video connector, a 50-pin Centronic SCSI bus connector, two RJ-11 jacks for an *internal modem* (one is for the phone line; the other is used to attach a traditional telephone handset), and an RJ-45/BNC combination for making LAN connections with the system's network interface card (NIC). The DB-15F connector used with VGA video devices uses a 3-row pin arrangement to differentiate it from the 2-row DB-15F connector specified for the game port. This prevents them from being confused with each other. With the NIC card, the RJ-45 jack is used with unshielded twisted pair (UTP) LAN cabling, whereas the British Naval Connector (BNC) connector is provided for coaxial cable connections. Network cabling is discussed in more detail in Chapter 6, "6.0 Basic Networking."

Table 1.3 summarizes the types of connectors typically found on the back panel of a system unit, along with their connector and pin-count information.

TABLE 1.3

TYPICAL I/O PORTS

Port	AT	ATX
Keyboard	5-pin DIN	PS/2 6-pin mini-DIN
Mouse	xxxxxxx	PS/2 6-pin mini-DIN
COM1	DB-9M	DB-9M
COM2	DB-25M	DB-9M
LPT	DB-25F	DB-25F
VGA	DB-15F (3)	DB-15F (3)
Game	DB-15F (2)	DB-15F (2)
Modem	RJ-11	RJ-11

continues

TABLE 1.3	*continued*	

TYPICAL I/O PORTS

Port	*AT*	*ATX*
LAN	BNC/RJ-45	BNC/RJ-45
Sound	RCA jacks	RCA jacks
SCSI	Centronics 50-pin	Centronic 50-pin

Portable I/O Connections

The I/O ports included in most notebook computers consist of a single parallel port, a single serial port, an external VGA monitor connector, an external keyboard connector, and a docking port expansion bus. Some models can be found with a second serial port connector, but they are not common. Figure 1.46 shows the port connections associated with most portable systems. This example places the connectors on the back of the unit, just as they would be in a typical desktop. Other units may place some of these connectors on each side of the unit instead. High-end portables may include an array of other connectors, such as external microphone and speaker jacks. Some connectors may be hidden behind hinged doors for protection. These doors normally snap closed.

FIGURE 1.46

Notebook back-panel connections.

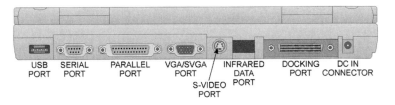

Input Devices

Figure 1.47 depicts common input devices. These devices include keyboards, mice, joysticks, scanners, and trackballs. Most PCs use a detachable alphanumeric keyboard that is connected to the system by a 6-foot coiled cable. This cable plugs into a round 5-pin DIN connector located on the rear of the system board. The connector is keyed so that it cannot be misaligned. Unlike other I/O devices, the keyboard requires no interface adapter card. Its interface circuitry is generally built directly in to the system's main board.

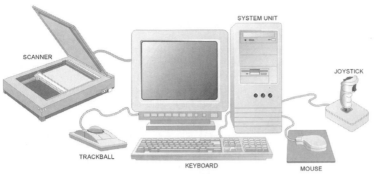

FIGURE 1.47
Typical input devices.

Keyboards

The keyboard most widely used with desktop and tower units is a detachable, low-profile, 101/102-key model (depicted in Figure 1.48). These units are designed to provide the user with a high degree of mobility and functionality. The key tops are slightly concave to provide a comfortable "feel" for the typist. In addition, the key makes a noticeable tap when it bottoms out during a keystroke.

FIGURE 1.48
An alphanumeric keyboard.

Most AT-style detachable keyboards use a round, half-inch, 5-pin DIN connector to plug into the PC's system board. The connection is most often made through a round opening in the rear of the system unit's case. In some case designs, a front-mounted 5-pin plug-in is included. The front-mounted connector is routed to the system board through an extension cable.

With the IBM PS/2 line, a smaller (quarter-inch) 6-pin mini-DIN connector was adopted. Other PC compatibles use a modular, 6-pin AMP connector to interface the keyboard to the system. The ATX design specification adopted this type of connector as their standard for keyboard connections. Figure 1.49 shows the various connection schemes used with detachable keyboards.

Although many newer peripheral devices can safely be unplugged and reattached to the system while it is powered up, this is not so with the standard keyboard. Plugging the keyboard into the system while power is applied may cause the system board to fail due to the power surge and electrostatic discharge (ESD) that may occur between it and the keyboard.

> **TEST TIP**
>
> Be aware that plugging hot-swappable devices such as the keyboard into the system while it is turned on can damage parts of the system.

FIGURE 1.49
Connection schemes for detachable keyboards.

> **Reference Shelf**
>
> For more in-depth information about how keyboards work, refer to the "How Keyboards Work" section of the Electronic Reference Shelf located on the CD that accompanies this book.

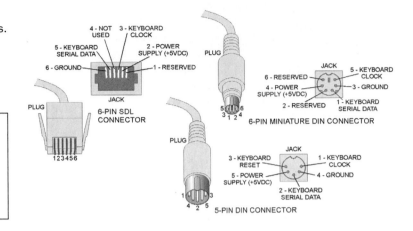

Portable Keyboards

The most widely used notebook keyboard is the 84-key version. The keys are slightly smaller and shorter than those found in full-size keyboards. A number of keys or key functions may be combined or deleted from a notebook keyboard. Figure 1.50 shows a typical notebook keyboard.

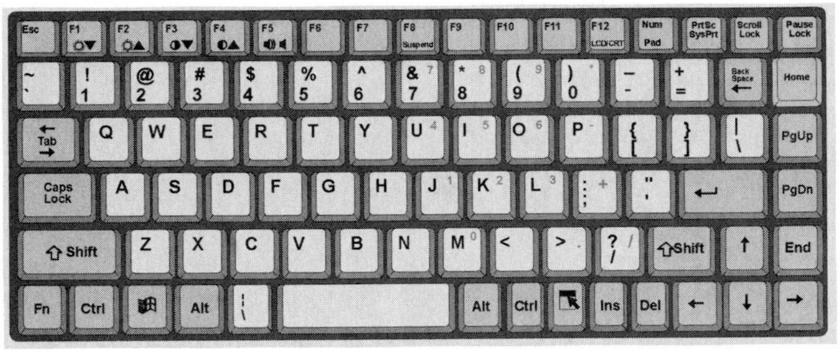

FIGURE 1.50
An 84-key notebook keyboard.

Because portable keyboards tend to be more compact than the detachable models used with desktop units, many of their keys are typically given dual or triple functions. The portable keyboard normally contains an F*n* function key. This key activates special functions in the portable, such as display brightness and contrast. Other common F*n* functions include suspend-mode activation and LCD/external-CRT device selection.

Newer keyboard models also may include left and right Windows keys (*WinKeys*), and an application key, as identified in Figure 1.51. The WinKeys are located next to the Alt keys and provide specialized

Windows functions, as described in Table 1.4. Similarly, the application key is located near the right WinKey, or the Ctrl key, and provides context-sensitive help for most applications.

FIGURE 1.51
Win and application keys.

TABLE 1.4

WINKEY DEFINITIONS

Winkey	Definition
WIN/E	Start Windows Explorer
WIN/F	Start Find Files or Folders
Ctrl/WIN/F	Find the computer
WIN/M	Minimize All
Shift/WIN/M	Undo Minimize All
WIN/R	Display Run dialog box
WIN/F1	Start Help
WIN/Tab	Move through taskbar objects
WIN/Break	Show System Properties dialog box

Pointing Devices

Mice, joysticks, trackballs, and light pens belong to a category of input devices called *pointing devices.* They are all small, handheld input devices that enable the user to interact with the system by moving a cursor or some other screen image around the display screen to choose options from an onscreen menu instead of typing commands from a keyboard. Because pointing devices make it easier to interact with the computer than other types of input devices, they are, therefore, friendlier to the user.

The most widely used pointing device is the mouse. Mice are handheld devices that produce input data by being moved across a surface, such as a desktop. The mouse has become a standard input device for most systems because of the popularity of GUI-based software.

The *trackball mouse* detects positional changes through the movement of a rolling trackball that it rides on. As the mouse moves across the surface, the mouse circuitry detects the movement of the trackball and creates pulses that the system converts into positional information.

Mice may have one, two, or three buttons that can be pressed in different combinations to interact with software running in the system. When the cursor is positioned onscreen, one or more of the mouse buttons can be "clicked" to execute an operation or select a variable from the screen. Specialized graphics software enables the user to operate the mouse as a drawing instrument.

A newer mouse design, referred to as wheel mice, includes a small thumb wheel built in to the top of the mouse between the buttons. This wheel enables the user to efficiently scroll up and down the video screen without using scrollbars or arrows.

Some scrolling functions, such as click-and-drag text highlighting in a word processor, can be awkward when the text extends off the bottom of the screen. In faster computers, the automatic scroll functions in some software packages will take off at the bottom of the screen and scroll several pages before stopping. The wheel in the mouse is designed to control this type of action. Additional software drivers must be installed to handle the additional wheel functions for the mouse.

Historically, most mice have been serial mice. These devices communicate serially with the system. Serial mice plug into a 9-pin or a 25-pin male D-shell connector on the back of the system unit and employ an RS-232C interface. In older systems, a 25-pin–to–9-pin adapter may be required to physically connect the mouse to the unit. Newer mice, referred to as PS/2 mice, are serial mice designed to plug into the 6-pin mini-DIN connector included in the ATX design standard.

Joysticks are popular input devices used primarily with computer video games. However, they also can provide a convenient computer/human interface for a number of other applications. These peripherals are X-Y positioning devices with a gimbal (handle) that can be moved forward, backward, left, right, or at any angular combination of these basic directions to move a cursor or other screen element across a video display. Buttons on the joystick can be used in the same manner as buttons on a mouse. Joysticks are normally connected to the 2-row, 15-pin female D-shell game port connector at the back of the system unit.

Scanners

Scanners convert pictures, line art, photographs, and text into electronic signals that can be processed by software packages such as desktop publishers and graphic design programs. These programs, in turn, can display the image on the video display or can print it out on a graphics printer.

Scanners basically come in two types: handheld scanners and flatbed scanners. Handheld scanners tend to be less expensive than flatbed scanners due to less-complex mechanics. However, handheld scanners also tend to produce lower quality images than flatbed scanners. These types normally require two passes to scan an entire page-sized image, but flatbed scanners can pick up the complete image in one pass. The handheld scanner can be used to scan images from large documents or from irregular surfaces, but they depend on the steadiness of the user for their accuracy.

Scanners also can be classified by the types of images they can reproduce. Some scanners can differentiate only between different levels of light and dark. These scanners are called grayscale scanners. Color scanners, on the other hand, include additional hardware that helps them distinguish from among different colors.

Handheld Scanners

The handheld scanner depicted in Figure 1.52 operates by being pulled across an image. The user begins the scanning process by pressing the Scan button and then moving the scanner body across the image. An LED in the scanner projects light on the image as the scanner moves. As the light passes over darker and lighter areas of the page, varying levels of light are reflected back to a focusing lens.

FIGURE 1.52
Inside a handheld scanner.

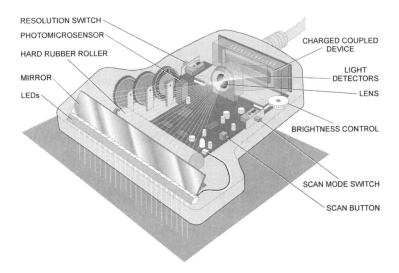

RESOLUTION SWITCH
PHOTOMICROSENSOR
HARD RUBBER ROLLER
MIRROR
LEDs
CHARGED COUPLED DEVICE
LIGHT DETECTORS
LENS
BRIGHTNESS CONTROL
SCAN MODE SWITCH
SCAN BUTTON

The lens focuses the reflected light stream onto a charge-coupled device (CCD), which converts the intensity of the light into a proportional voltage signal. The CCD is the same type of device used in the lens of a typical handheld video recorder. The voltage level produced corresponds to black, gray, and white light levels.

The color of the light source used in the scanner also affects how the human eye perceives the output. When scans of color material are made, the color of the scanning light used may not produce brightness levels compatible with how the human eye perceives it. This is true in both color and grayscale output. The two most common scanner light source colors are red and green. The green light produces output that looks much closer to the way the eye perceives it than the red light can. For line art and text scans, the color of the light source is not important.

NOTE

Older hand scanners provided scanning resolutions up to 300 dots per inch (dpi). Common scanning resolutions are 600dpi and 1,200dpi. Newer color hand scanners can produce 24-bit, high-resolution (3,200dpi) image editing with 16 million colors.

As the scanner moves across the surface, a wide rubber roller turns a series of gears, which in turn rotate a perforated disk. A light shines through the slots in the disk as it turns and strikes an optical sensor on the other side of the disk. This arrangement produces pulses as the spokes interrupt the light stream. The pulses are used to coordinate the transmission of the digitized image values with the movement of the scanner. Each time a line of image data is transmitted to the adapter card, the scanner's buffer is cleared and it begins gathering a new line of image data. The software included with most scanners provides the user with at least a limited capability to manipulate the image after it has been scanned. Because of the limited width of most hand scanners, the software also provides for integrating two consecutive scans to form a complete picture.

Flatbed Scanners

Flatbed scanners differ from handheld units. With flatbed scanners, the scanner body remains stationary as a scan head moves past the paper (see Figure 1.53). The paper is placed face down on the scanner's glass window. The light source from the scanning mechanism is projected up through the glass and onto the paper. The lighter areas of the page reflect more light than the darker areas do.

A precision positioning motor moves the scan head below the paper. As the head moves, light reflected from the paper is captured and channeled through a series of mirrors. The mirrors pivot to focus the reflected light on a light-sensitive diode. The diode converts the reflected light intensity into a corresponding digital value.

A normal scanner resolution is 300 dots (or pixels) per inch. Newer flatbed scanners can achieve resolutions up to 4,800dpi. At these resolutions, each dot corresponds to about 1/90,000 of an inch. The higher the selected scanning resolution, the slower the computer and printer performance, because of the increased amount of data that must be processed.

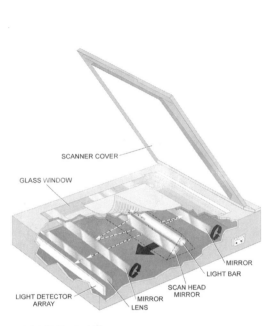

FIGURE 1.53
A flatbed scanner.

The digitized information is routed to the scanner adapter card in one of the PC's expansion slots. In main memory, the graphic information is stored in a format that can be manipulated by graphic design software.

Grayscale scanners can differentiate between varying levels of gray on the page. This capability is stated in shades. A good-quality grayscale scanner can differentiate between 256 levels of gray. Color scanners, on the other hand, use three passes to scan an image. Each scan passes the light through a different color filter to separate them from each other. The red, blue, and green filters create three different electronic images that can be integrated to form a complete picture. For intermediate colors, varying levels of the three colors are blended to create the desired shade.

As with the handheld scanners, many flatbed scanners use a proprietary adapter card and cable to communicate with the system. However, a number of SCSI-interfaced scanners are available. One of the most common problems with installing scanners involves finding a vacant expansion slot for the adapter card. This was particularly true with earlier Pentium boards that used a mixture of ISA and local bus slots. To overcome this problem, scanners are now being produced that operate through the system's enhanced EPP and ECP parallel ports. In these units, the printer plugs into the scanner, which, in turn, connects to the port. In older units, such as PCs and XTs, the limited number of available *interrupt request* lines often became a problem.

Output Devices

Figure 1.54 depicts common output devices. The most widely used output device for PCs is the *cathode ray tube* (CRT) video display monitor. The most widely used display device for current PCs is the VGA color monitor. The monitor's *signal cable* connects to a 3-row, 15-pin D-shell connector at the back of the system unit. A power cord supplies 120V AC power to the monitor from a conventional power outlet or from a special connector on the back of the AT-style power-supply unit.

FIGURE 1.54
Typical output devices.

After the monitor, the next most often added output device is the character printer. These peripherals are used to produce hard-copy output on paper. They convert text and graphics data from the computer into print on a page.

Video Displays

Desktop and tower units normally use a color CRT display monitor, similar to the one shown in Figure 1.55, as standard video output equipment. The PC and PC/XT and PC-AT often used monochrome (single-color) monitors. They could also use color monitors by just adding a color video adapter card and monitor. The color CRT monitor is sometimes referred to as an RGB monitor, because the three primary colors that make a color CRT are red, green, and blue.

The monitor can either be plugged into a commercial, three-prong power receptacle or into the special receptacle provided through the power supply at the rear of the unit. This option depends on the type of power cord provided by the manufacturer. A special adapter is cable available to match a standard 120V AC plug to this power-supply receptacle. The signal cable (connected to the video adapter card) permits the monitor to be positioned away from the system unit if desired.

FIGURE 1.55
The CRT display monitor.

SIGNAL CABLE

POWER CABLE

TILT / SWIVEL BASE

DISPLAY CONTROLS

POWER LIGHT

FIGURE 1.55
The CRT display monitor.

The display's normal external controls are brightness and contrast. These controls are located in different positions on the monitor depending on its manufacturer. There is also a power On/Off switch on the monitor. Its location varies from model to model as well. If the monitor receives power through the system unit's power supply, the monitor's power switch can be set to On and the monitor will turn on and off along with the system.

Basic CRT Operations

A CRT is an evacuated glass tube with an electron gun in its neck, and a fluorescent-coated surface opposite the electron gun, A typical CRT is depicted in Figure 1.56. When activated, the electron gun emits a stream of electrons that strike the fluorescent coating on the inside of the screen, causing an illuminated dot to be produced.

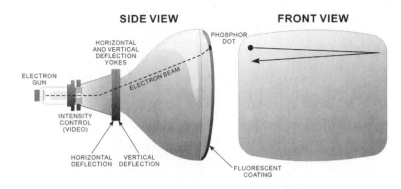

FIGURE 1.56
A cathode ray tube.

The sweeping electron beam begins at the upper-left corner of the screen and moves across its face to the upper-right corner, leaving a line across the screen. This is called a raster line. Upon reaching the right side of the screen, the trace is blanked out, and the electron beam is repositioned to the left side of the screen, one line below from the first trace (horizontal retrace). At this point, the horizontal sweep begins producing the second display line on the screen. The scanning continues until the horizontal sweeps reach the bottom of the screen, as shown in Figure 1.57. At that point, the electron beam is blanked again and returned to the upper-left corner of the screen (vertical retrace), completing one field.

As the beam moves across the screen, it leaves an illuminated trace, which requires a given amount of time to dissipate. The amount of time depends on the characteristics of the fluorescent coating and is referred to as persistence. Video information is introduced to the picture by varying the voltage applied to the electron gun as it scans the screen. The human eye perceives only the "picture" because of the blanking of the retrace lines and the frequency at which the entire process is performed.

The video adapter's cathode ray tube controller (CRTC) circuitry develops the video signals, and the horizontal (HSYNC) and vertical (VSYNC) synchronization signals for the CRT. Typically, a horizontal sweep requires about 63 microseconds to complete, whereas a complete field requires approximately 1/60 of a second, or 1/30 of a second per frame. The *National Television Standards Committee* (NTSC) specifies 525 lines per frame, composed of two fields of 262.5 lines, for television pictures. The two fields, one containing the even-numbered lines, and the other containing the odd-numbered lines, are interlaced to produce smooth, flickerless images.

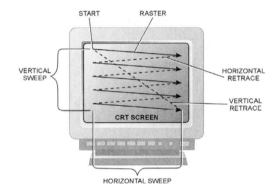

FIGURE 1.57
Raster scan video.

This method of creating display images is referred to as interlaced scanning, and is primarily used with television. Most computer monitors use *noninterlaced scanning* methods.

In text-mode operations, the most common monitor arrangement calls for 25 lines of text, with 80 characters per line. This requires that the top row of up to 80 character blocks be serialized during the first horizontal trace of the CRT. Afterward, the second line of 80 character blocks is serialized for the second horizontal trace. This serialization is repeated until all the horizontal traces have been made.

After a line, or a page, of text has been displayed on the screen, it must be rewritten periodically to prevent it from fading away. For the rewrite to be performed fast enough to avoid display flicker, the contents of the display are stored in a special memory, called the screen memory. This memory is typically located on the video adapter card. However, some newer systems use sections of the system's onboard memory for the video screen memory function. In the example of 25 lines of text at 80 characters per line, the memory must be able to hold at least 2000 bytes of screen data for a single display.

The 80 × 25 format previously discussed is for alphanumeric text mode. When the adapter is in text mode, it typically requires at least 2 bytes of screen memory for each character position on the screen. The first byte is for the ASCII code of the character itself, and the second byte is used to specify the screen attributes of the character and its cell. Under this scenario, the screen memory must be capable of holding at least 4000 bytes. The attribute byte specifies how the character is to be displayed. Common attributes include underlining, blinking, and the color of a text character for the color displays.

Color Monitors

The monitor discussing so far is referred to as a monochrome monitor, because it can display only shades of a single phosphor color. A color monitor, on the other hand, employs a combination of three, color phosphors (red, blue, and green), arranged in adjacent trios of dots or bars, called *pixels* or pels (an abbreviation for pixels). By using a different electron gun for each element of the trio, the individual elements can be made to glow at different levels to produce almost any color desired. The electron guns scan the front of a screen in unison, in the same fashion described earlier for a monochrome CRT. Color CRTs add a metal grid in front of the phosphor coating called a *shadow mask*. It ensures that an electron gun assigned to one color does not strike a dot of another color. The basic construction of a color CRT is shown in Figure 1.58.

Screen Resolution

The quality of the image produced on the screen is a function of two factors: the speed at which the image is retraced on the screen, and the number of pixels on the screen. The more pixels on a given screen size, the higher the image quality. This quantity is called resolution, and is often expressed in an X-by-Y format. Using this format, the quality of the image is still determined by how big the viewing area is. (That is, an 800×600 resolution on a 14-inch monitor produces much better quality than the same number of pixels spread across a 27-inch monitor.)

Resolution can be expressed as a function of how close pixels can be grouped together on the screen. This form of resolution is expressed in terms of dot pitch. A monitor with a .28 dot pitch has pixels that are located .28mm apart. In monochrome monitors, dot pitch is measured from center to center of each pixel. In a color monitor, the pitch is measured from the center of one dot trio to the center of the next trio.

Portable Display Types

Notebook and laptop computers use non-CRT displays, such as LCD and gas-plasma panels. These display systems are well suited to the portability needs of portable computers. They are much lighter and more compact than CRT monitors and require much less electrical energy to operate. Both types of display units can be operated from batteries.

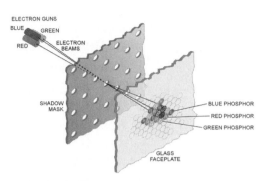

FIGURE 1.58
Color CRT construction.

Reference Shelf

For more in-depth information about how monitors work, refer to the Electronic Reference Shelf located on the CD that accompanies this book.

TEST TIP

Be able to explain the definition of dot pitch.

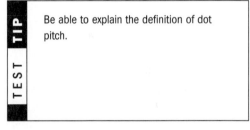

Reference Shelf

For more in-depth information about how CRT monitors and computer video systems actually work, refer to the "How Video Displays Work" section of the Electronic Reference Shelf located on the CD that accompanies this book.

TEST TIP

Know that notebook display panels are powered by low-voltage DC power sources, such as a battery or converter.

NOTE

Liquid Crystal Displays The most common flat-panel displays used with portable PCs are LCDs. They are relatively thin, flat, lightweight, and require very little power to operate. In addition to reduced weight and improved portability, these displays offer better reliability and longer life than CRT units.

Portable computers continue to gain popularity because the user can travel with them. This has been made possible by the development of different, flat-panel display technologies. Early attempts at developing portable microcomputers used small CRTs that minimized the size of the unit. However, these units quickly gained the label of luggables, because of their weight. The high-voltage circuitry required to operate a CRT device is heavy by nature (so could be reduced only slightly).

Liquid Crystal Displays

The LCD, illustrated in Figure 1.59, is constructed by placing thermotropic liquid crystal material between two sheets of glass. A set of electrodes is attached to each sheet of glass. Horizontal (row) electrodes are attached to one glass plate; vertical (column) electrodes are fitted to the other plate. These electrodes are transparent and let light pass through. A picture element, or pixel, is created in the liquid crystal material at each spot where a row and a column electrode intersect. A special plate called a *polarizer* is added to the outside of each glass plate. There is one polarizer on the front, and one on the back of the display.

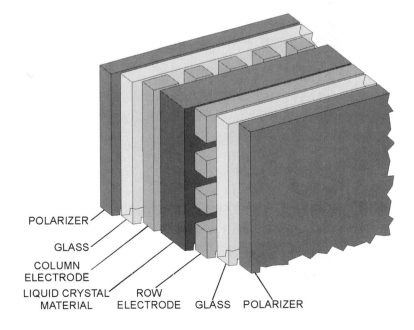

FIGURE 1.59
LCD construction.

The display is designed so that when the pixel is off, the molecules of the liquid crystal twist from one edge of the material to the other, as depicted in Figure 1.60. The spiral effect created by the twist polarizes light and prevents it from passing through the display. When an electric field is created between a row and column electrode, the molecules move, lining up perpendicular to the front of the display. This allows light to pass through the display, producing a single dot onscreen.

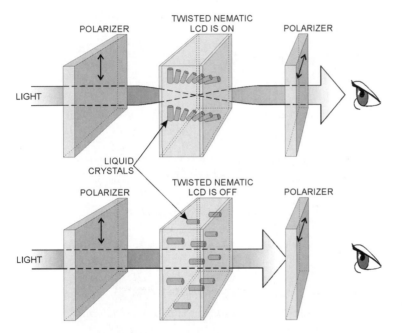

FIGURE 1.60
LCD operation.

Depending on the orientation of the polarizers, the energized pixels can be made to look like a dark spot on a light screen, or a light dot on a dark screen. In most notebook computers, the display is lit from behind the panel. This is referred to as back lighting. Some units are constructed so that the display can be removed from the body of the computer and used with an overhead projector, to display computer output on a wall or large screen.

Because no current passes through the display to light the pixels, the power consumption of LCD displays is very low. The screen is scanned using IC multiplexers and drivers to activate the panel's row and column electrodes. The scanning circuitry addresses each row sequentially, column by column. Although the column electrode is activated for a short portion of each horizontal scan, the pixels appear to be continuously lit because the scanning rate is so high. The electrodes can be controlled (turned on and off) using standard time-to-live (TTL) voltage levels. This translates into less control circuitry required to operate the panel. LCDs using this type of construction are referred to as dual-scan, or passive-matrix displays. Advanced passive-matrix technologies are referred to as color supertwist nematic (CSTN) and double-layer super-twist nematic (DSTN) displays.

An improved LCD approach is similar in design to the passive-matrix designs, except that it adds a transistor at each of the matrix' row-column junctions to improve switching times. This technology produces an LCD display type referred to as an *active-matrix display*. In these displays, a small current is sent to the transistor through the row-column lines. The energized transistor conducts a larger current, which, in turn, is used to activate the pixel seen onscreen. The active matrix is produced by using thin film transistor (TFT) arrays to create between one and four transistors for each pixel on a flexible, transparent film. TFT displays tend to be brighter and sharper than dual-scan displays. They also tend to require more power to operate, however, and to be more expensive.

Color LCD displays are created by adding a three-color filter to the panel. Each pixel in the display corresponds to a red, blue, or green dot on the filter. Activating a pixel behind a blue dot on the filter produces a blue dot onscreen. Like color CRT displays, the dot color on the screen of the color LCD panel is established by controlling the relative intensities of a three-dot (RGB) pixel cluster.

The construction of LCD displays prevents them from providing multiple-resolution options like an adapter-driven CRT display can. The resolution of the LCD display is dictated by the construction of the LCD panel.

The life and usefulness of the portable's LCD panel can be extended through proper care and handling. The screen should be cleaned periodically with a glass cleaner and a soft, lint-free cloth. Spray the cleaner on the cloth and then wipe the screen. Never spray the cleaner directly on the screen. Also, avoid scratching the surface of the screen. It is relatively easy to damage the front polarizer of the display. Take care to remove any liquid droplets from the screen because they can cause permanent staining. After cleaning, allow 30 minutes for complete drying.

The screen should be shielded from bright sunlight and heat sources. Moving the computer from a cooler location to a hot location can cause damaging moisture to condense inside the housing (including the display). It should also be kept away from ultra-violet light sources and extremely cold temperatures. The liquid crystals can freeze in extremely cold weather. A freeze/thaw cycle may damage the display and cause it to be unusable.

Other Peripherals

Character printers are the other most widely used peripheral devices. Most printers communicate with the system through a parallel interface. Parallel printers are connected to the 25-pin female D-shell connector at the rear of the system.

Many printers use serial interfacing so that they can be located farther from the computer. Serial-interface versions normally plug into a 9-pin or 25-pin male D-shell connector. Most often, the serial printer is connected to the 25-pin connector that has been set up as the system's second serial port. The first serial port is typically set up with the 9-pin connector and handles the mouse connection. Figure 1.61 depicts common peripheral connections.

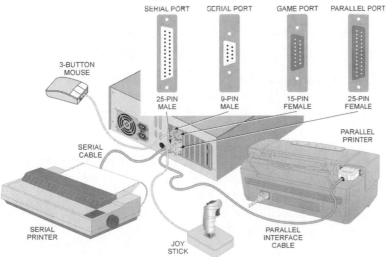

FIGURE 1.61
Typical peripheral connectors.

Modems

Generally, the most difficult aspect of connecting peripheral equipment to a computer is obtaining the proper interfacing and cabling.

If the peripheral is located some distance away from the computer (more than 100 feet, for example), they cannot be connected together by just using a longer cable. As the connecting cable gets longer, its natural resistance and distributive capacitance tend to distort digital signals until they are no longer digital. This loss of signal strength is referred to as attenuation.

To overcome this signal deterioration, a device called a *modem* (short for modulator/demodulator) is used to convert the parallel, digital signals of the computer, into serial, analog signals, which are better suited for transmission over wire. A modem allows a computer to communicate with other computers through telephone lines, as depicted in Figure 1.62.

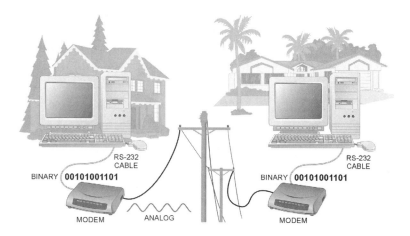

FIGURE 1.62
Modem communications.

In its simplest form, a modem consists of two major blocks, a modulator and a demodulator. The modulator is a transmitter that converts the parallel/digital computer data into a serial/analog format for transmission. The demodulator is the receiver that accepts the serial/analog transmission format and converts it into a parallel/digital format usable by the computer, or peripheral.

When a modem is used to send signals in only one direction, it is operating in simplex mode. Modems capable of both transmitting and receiving data are divided into two groups, based on their mode of operation. In *half-duplex mode,* modems exchange data, but only in one direction at a time, as illustrated in Figure 1.63. Multiplexing the send and receive signal frequencies allow both modems to send and receive data simultaneously. This mode of operation is known as *full-duplex mode.*

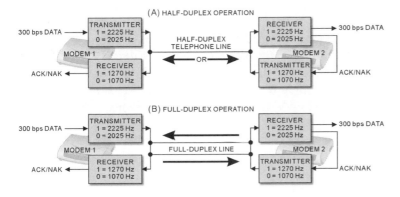

FIGURE 1.63
Half-duplex and full-duplex communications.

As the distance between terminals increases, it soon becomes impractical to use dedicated cabling to carry data. Fortunately, there is already a very extensive communications network in existence: the public telephone network. Unfortunately, the phone lines were designed to carry analog voice signals rather than digital data. The design of the public phone system limits the frequency at which data can be transmitted over these lines.

Modems are generally classified by their *baud rate.* Baud rate is used to describe the number of signal changes that occur per second, during the transfer of data. Because signal changes are the quantity actually being limited by the telephone lines, the baud rate is the determining factor. Most modems encode data into different transmission formats so that a number of data bits can be represented by a single signal change. In this way, the bit rate can be high, whereas the baud rate is still low. As an example, a modem using an industry-standard v.34bis communication format can transmit data at up to 28,800bps with a baud rate of just 4,800. Common bit rates for telecommunications include 2,400, 9,600, 14,400, 28,800, 33,600, and 56,000 bits per second. To complete a successful connection at maximum speed, the other party involved must have a compatible modem, capable of using the same baud rate.

TEST TIP

Be able to state the difference between simplex, half-duplex, and full-duplex transmissions; and as you move through the text, be able to identify which types of communications systems use each type.

A modem can be either an internal or an external device, as illustrated in Figure 1.64. An internal modem is installed in one of the computer's expansion slots, and has its own interfacing circuitry. The external modem is usually a box that resides outside the system unit and is connected to one of the computer's *serial ports* by an RS-232 serial cable. These units depend on the interfacing circuitry of the computer's serial ports. Most PC-compatible computers contain two serial port connections. External modems also require a separate power source.

In both cases, the modem typically connects to the telephone line through a standard 4-pin RJ-11 telephone jack. The RJ designation stands for *registered jack*. A second RJ-11 jack in the modem allows an additional telephone to be connected to the line for voice usage. A still smaller 4-pin RJ-12 connector is used to connect the telephone handset to the telephone base. Be aware that an RJ-14 jack looks exactly like the RJ-11, but that it defines two lines to allow for advanced telephone features such as caller ID and call waiting.

Reference Shelf

For more in-depth technical information about how modems really work, refer to the "How Modems Work" section of the Electronic Reference Shelf located on the CD that accompanies this book.

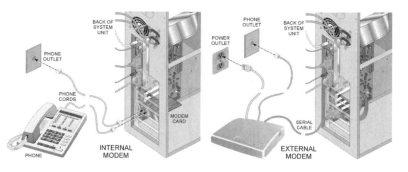

FIGURE 1.64
Internal and external modems.

Sound Cards

The sound-producing capabilities of early PCs was practically nonexistent. They included a single, small speaker that was used to produce beep-coded error messages. Even though programs could be written to produce a wide array of sounds from this speaker, the quality of the sound was never any better than the limitations imposed by its small size.

Figure 1.65 depicts a typical audio-digitizer (A/D) system. A microphone converts sound waves from the air into an encoded, analog electrical signal. The analog signal is applied to the audio input of the sound card. On the card, the signal is applied to an A/D converter circuit, which changes the signal into corresponding digital values.

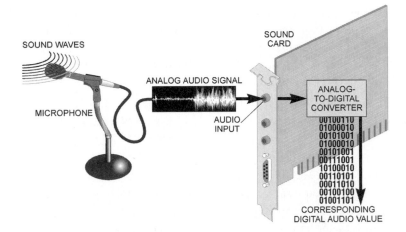

FIGURE 1.65
A typical audio-digitizer system.

The sound card takes samples of the analog waveform at predetermined intervals and converts them into corresponding digital values. Therefore, the digital values approximate the instantaneous values of the sound wave.

The fidelity (the measure of how closely the original sound can be reproduced) of the digital samples depends on two factors: the accuracy of the samples taken, and the rate at which the samples are taken. The accuracy of the sample is determined by the resolution capabilities of the A/D converter. Resolution is the capability to differentiate between values. If the value of the analog waveform is 15.55 microvolts at a given point, how close can that value be approximated with a digital value?

The resolution of an A/D converter is determined by the number of digital output bits it can produce. For example, an 8-bit A/D converter can represent up to 256 (2^8) different values. On the other hand, a 16-bit A/D converter can represent up to 65,536 (2^{16}) different amplitudes. The more often the samples are taken, the more accurately the original waveform can be reproduced.

Playback of the digitized audio signal is accomplished by applying the digital signals to a D/A converter at the same rate the samples were taken. When the audio files are called for, the sound card's software driver sends commands to the audio output controller on the sound card. The digitized samples are applied to the audio output IC, and converted back into the analog signal.

Reference Shelf

For more in-depth technical information about sound cards and other multimedia devices and systems, refer to the "How Multimedia Works" section of the Electronic Reference Shelf located on the CD that accompanies this book.

The analog signal is applied to an audio preamplifier that boosts the power of the signal and sends it to an RCA, or mini jack. This signal is still too weak to drive conventional speakers. It can be applied to an additional amplifier, however, or to a set of speakers that have an additional amplifier built in to them.

A CD-quality audio signal requires a minimum of 16-bit samples, taken at approximately 44KHz. If you calculate the disk space required to store all the 16-bit samples collected in one minute of audio at this rate, the major consideration factor associated with using digitized audio becomes clear ($16 \times 44,000 \times 60 \times 8 = 5.28MB$). If you want stereo sound, this will double to a whopping 10.56MB. Therefore, CD-quality audio is not commonly used in multimedia productions. The audio-sampling rate used in multimedia titles is generally determined by the producer. Another alternative is to limit the digitized audio used in a product to short clips.

SOFTWARE

After the system's components are connected together and their power connectors have been plugged into a receptacle, the system is ready for operation. However, one thing is still missing: the software. Without good software to oversee its operation, the most sophisticated computer hardware is worthless.

The following three general classes of software are discussed in this section:

◆ System software

◆ Applications software

◆ Games and learning software

The bulk of the software discussed in this book deals with the system software category, because this type of software requires more technical skills to manipulate and, therefore, most often involves the service person.

System Software

The system software category consists of special programs used by the system itself to control the computer's operation. Two classic examples of this type of software are the system's *basic input/output system* (BIOS) program and the *disk operating system* (DOS). These programs, described in Figure 1.66, control the operation of the other classes of software. The BIOS is located in a ROM IC device on the system board. Therefore, it is commonly referred to as ROM BIOS. The DOS software is normally located on a magnetic disk.

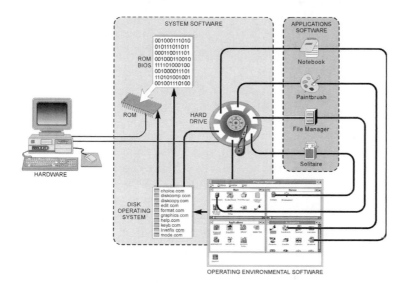

FIGURE 1.66
System software.

Basic Input/Output Systems

When a PC is turned on, the entire system is reset to a predetermined starting condition. From this state, it begins carrying out software instructions from its BIOS program. This small program is permanently stored in the ROM memory ICs located on the system board. The information stored in these chips is all the inherent intelligence that the system has to begin with.

A system's BIOS program is one of the keys to its compatibility. To be IBM PC compatible, for example, the computer's BIOS must perform the same basic functions that the IBM PC's BIOS does.

Because the IBM BIOS software is copyrighted, however, the compatible's software must accomplish the same results that the original did, but it must do it in some different way.

During the execution of the BIOS firmware routines, three major sets of operations are performed. First, the BIOS performs a series of diagnostic tests (called *Power-On Self-Tests* or POST) on the system, to verify that it is operating correctly.

If any of the system's components are malfunctioning, the tests cause an error-message code to display on the monitor screen, and/or an audio code to be output through the system's speaker.

The BIOS program also places starting values in the system's various programmable devices. These intelligent devices regulate the operation of different portions of the computer's hardware. This process is called initialization. When the system is first started, for example, the BIOS moves the starting address and mode information into the DMA controller. Likewise, the locations of the computer's interrupt handler programs are written into the interrupt controller. This process is repeated for several of the microprocessor support devices so that they have the information they need to begin operation.

Finally, the BIOS checks the system for a special program that it can use to load other programs into RAM. This program is called the *Master Boot Record*. The boot record program contains information that allows the system to load a much more powerful control program, called the disk operating system, into RAM memory. After the operating system has been loaded into the computer's memory, the BIOS gives it control over the system. From this point, the operating system oversees the operation of the system.

This operation is referred to as *booting up* the system. If the computer is started from the off condition, the process is referred to as a *cold boot*. If the system is restarted from the on condition, the process is called a *reset*, or a *warm boot*.

The boot-up process may take several seconds to perform depending on the configuration of the system. If a warm boot is performed, or if the POST tests have been disabled, the amount of time required to get the system into operation decreases. The three components of the boot-up process are illustrated in Figures 1.67, 1.68, and 1.69.

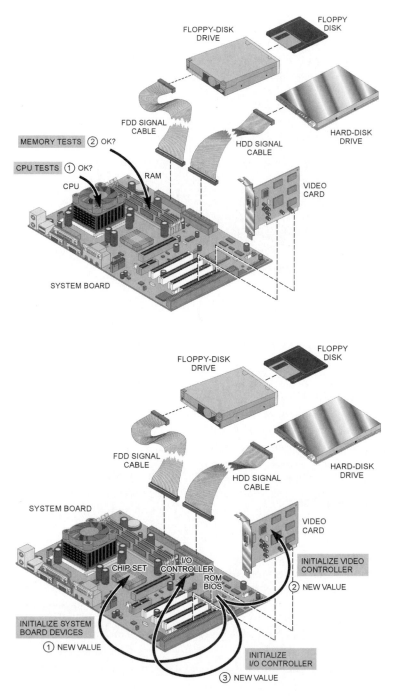

FIGURE 1.67
The steps of a boot up: phase one.

FIGURE 1.68
The steps of a boot up: phase two.

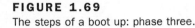

FIGURE 1.69
The steps of a boot up: phase three.

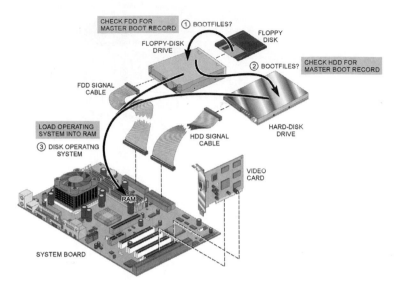

In the first phase of the operation, the BIOS tests the microprocessor (1) and the system's RAM memory (2). In the second phase, it furnishes starting information to the system's microprocessor support devices (1), video adapter card (2), and disk drive adapter card (3). Finally, the BIOS searches through the system in a predetermined sequence for a Master Boot Record to turn over control of the computer to. In this case, it checks the floppy disk drive first (1) and the hard disk drive second (2). If a boot record is found in either location, the BIOS will move it onto the computer's RAM memory and turn over control to it (3).

BIOS Services

While the system is operating, the BIOS continues to perform several important functions. It contains routines that the operating system calls on to carry out basic services. These services include providing BIOS interrupt calls (software interrupt routines) for such operations as printer, video, and disk drive accesses.

BIOS interrupt calls form the logical backbone of the system's operation. The BIOS and DOS are constantly handing control of the system back and forth between themselves as normal system functions are carried out. Figure 1.70 illustrates this relationship. These exchanges are responsible for most of the drawbacks of the DOS-based PC system. Advanced operating systems implement better methods of handling system functions just to avoid handing control over to the BIOS interrupts.

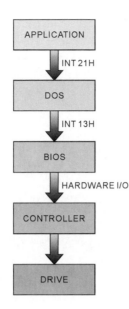

FIGURE 1.70
The DOS/BIOS relationship.

Some older PCs cannot support newer hardware because their BIOS do not support the new item. In this situation, it is usually necessary to load a software driver program to support the device. Another possibility is to replace the BIOS with an improved version. This operation is not performed often because an upgraded BIOS must be compatible with the older chipset.

Operating Systems

Operating systems are programs designed to control the operation of a computer system. As a group, they are easily some of the most complex programs devised.

Every portion of the system must be controlled and coordinated so that the millions of operations that occur every second are carried out correctly and on time. In addition, it is the job of the operating system to make the complexity of the PC as invisible as possible to the user.

Likewise, the operating system acts as an intermediary between nearly as complex software applications, and the hardware they run on. Finally, the operating system accepts commands from the computer user and carries them out to perform some desired operation.

A *disk operating system (DOS)* is a collection of programs used to control overall computer operation in a disk-based system. These programs work in the background to enable the user of the computer to input characters from the keyboard, to define a file structure for storing records, or to output data to a monitor or printer. The DOS is responsible for finding and organizing your data and applications on the disk.

The disk operating system can be divided into three distinct sections:

◆ **Boot files.** Take over control of the system from the ROM BIOS during startup

◆ **File-management files.** Enable the system to manage information within itself

◆ **Utility files.** Enable the user to manage system resources, troubleshoot the system, and configure the system

The operating system acts as a bridge between the application programs and the computer, as described in Figure 1.71. These applications programs enable the user to create files of data pertaining to certain applications such as word processing, remote data communications, business processing, and user programming languages.

FIGURE 1.71

The position of DOS in the computer system.

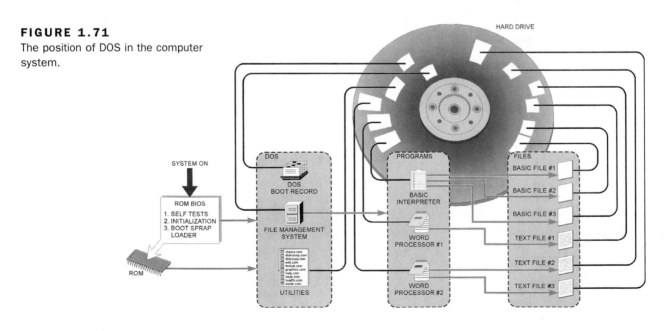

Graphical User Interfaces

Another form of operating environment, referred to as a *graphical user interface* (GUI), has gained widespread popularity in recent years. GUIs, like the Windows desktop depicted in Figure 1.72, employ a graphics display to represent procedures and programs that can be executed by the computer. These programs routinely use small pictures, called *icons*, to represent different programs. The advantage of using a GUI is that the user doesn't have to remember complicated commands to execute a program.

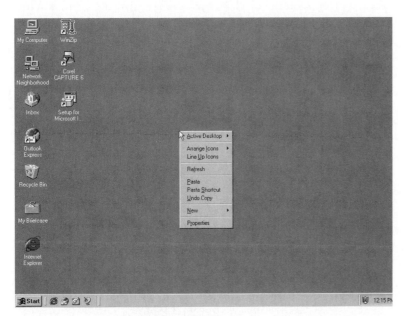

FIGURE 1.72
A graphical user interface (GUI) screen.

CMOS Setup Utilities

Just prior to completing the boot-up process, PCs and PC-XTs check a set of configuration switches on the system board to determine what types of options were installed in the system. On newer systems, the configuration information is stored on the system board in a battery-powered storage area called the CMOS RAM. Newer BIOS enable users to have access to this configuration information through their setup utility.

When the computer is set up for the first time, or when new options are added to the system, it is necessary to run the CMOS Configuration Setup utility. The values input through this utility are stored in the system's CMOS configuration registers. These registers are examined each time the system is booted up to tell the computer what types of devices are installed.

While performing its normal tests and boot-up functions, the BIOS program displays an active RAM memory count as it is being tested. Immediately following the RAM test count, the BIOS program places a prompt on the display to tell the user that the CMOS Setup utility can be accessed by pressing a special key or a key combination. Typical keys and key combinations include the Delete key, the Esc key, the F2 function key, the Ctrl and Esc keys, and the Ctrl+Alt+Esc key combination.

The keys, or key combinations, used to access the setup menus vary from one BIOS manufacturer to another. If the proper keys are not pressed within a predetermined amount of time, the BIOS program will continue with the boot-up process. If the keys are pressed during this time, however, the boot-up routine will be put on hold and the program will display a CMOS Setup Selection screen, similar to the one depicted in Figure 1.73.

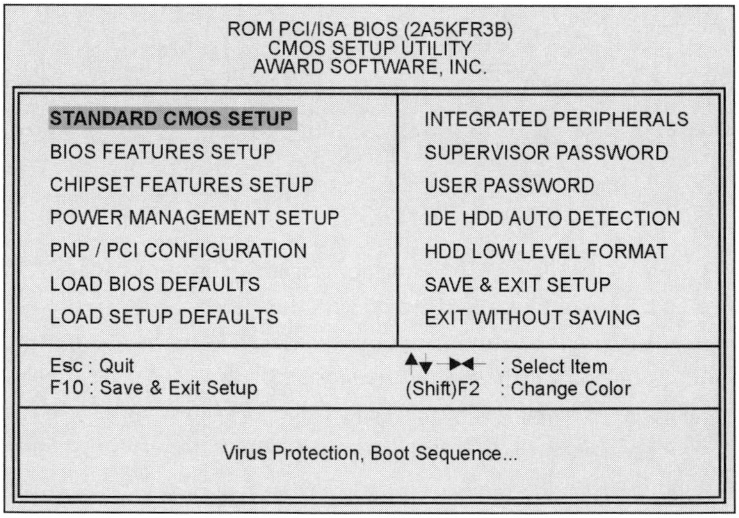

```
                    ROM PCI/ISA BIOS (2A5KFR3B)
                        CMOS SETUP UTILITY
                        AWARD SOFTWARE, INC.
 ┌──────────────────────────────────┬──────────────────────────────────┐
 │  STANDARD CMOS SETUP              │  INTEGRATED PERIPHERALS           │
 │  BIOS FEATURES SETUP              │  SUPERVISOR PASSWORD              │
 │  CHIPSET FEATURES SETUP           │  USER PASSWORD                    │
 │  POWER MANAGEMENT SETUP           │  IDE HDD AUTO DETECTION           │
 │  PNP / PCI CONFIGURATION          │  HDD LOW LEVEL FORMAT             │
 │  LOAD BIOS DEFAULTS               │  SAVE & EXIT SETUP                │
 │  LOAD SETUP DEFAULTS              │  EXIT WITHOUT SAVING              │
 ├──────────────────────────────────┴──────────────────────────────────┤
 │  Esc : Quit                       ↑↓ ►◄─  : Select Item               │
 │  F10 : Save & Exit Setup         (Shift)F2  : Change Color            │
 ├───────────────────────────────────────────────────────────────────── │
 │              Virus Protection, Boot Sequence...                       │
 └───────────────────────────────────────────────────────────────────────┘
```

FIGURE 1.73
A CMOS Setup Selection screen.

Every chipset variation has a specific BIOS designed for it. Therefore, there are functions specific to the design of system boards using that chipset. The example screen in Figure 1.73 serves as the main menu for entering and exiting the CMOS Setup utility and for moving between its configuration pages.

A typical Configuration Setup screen is shown in Figure 1.74. Through this screen, the user enters the desired configuration values into the CMOS registers. The cursor on the screen can be moved from item to item using the keyboard's cursor control keys.

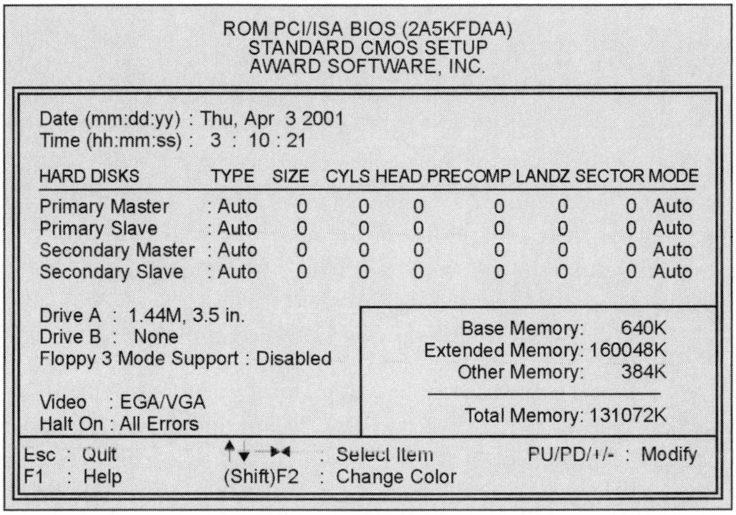

FIGURE 1.74
The CMOS Configuration Setup screen.

When the cursor is positioned on top of a desired option, the PgUp and PgDn cursor keys can be used to change its value. When all the proper options have been configured, pressing the Esc key causes the routine to exit the Setup screen, update any changes made, and resume the boot-up process.

Advanced CMOS Utilities

Depending on the maker of the BIOS, advanced CMOS Configuration screens, such as Chipset and BIOS Features Setup screens, may be provided to extend the user's control over the configuration of the system. A relatively simple BIOS Features screen is illustrated in Figure 1.75. In this example, several boot-up options can be enabled in CMOS, such as the boot drive sequence and password enabling.

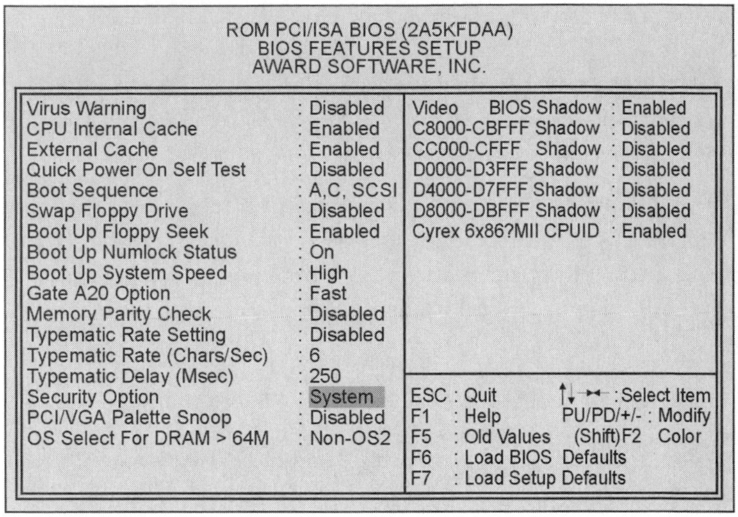

FIGURE 1.75
A BIOS Features Setup screen.

```
                    ROM PCI/ISA BIOS (2A5KFDAA)
                         BIOS FEATURES SETUP
                         AWARD SOFTWARE, INC.

 Virus Warning              : Disabled    Video    BIOS Shadow : Enabled
 CPU Internal Cache         : Enabled     C8000-CBFFF Shadow  : Disabled
 External Cache             : Enabled     CC000-CFFF  Shadow  : Disabled
 Quick Power On Self Test   : Disabled    D0000-D3FFF Shadow  : Disabled
 Boot Sequence              : A,C, SCSI   D4000-D7FFF Shadow  : Disabled
 Swap Floppy Drive          : Disabled    D8000-DBFFF Shadow  : Disabled
 Boot Up Floppy Seek        : Enabled     Cyrex 6x86?MII CPUID : Enabled
 Boot Up Numlock Status     : On
 Boot Up System Speed       : High
 Gate A20 Option            : Fast
 Memory Parity Check        : Disabled
 Typematic Rate Setting     : Disabled
 Typematic Rate (Chars/Sec) : 6
 Typematic Delay (Msec)     : 250
 Security Option            : System      ESC : Quit         ↑↓ ←→ :Select Item
 PCI/VGA Palette Snoop      : Disabled    F1  : Help      PU/PD/+/- : Modify
 OS Select For DRAM > 64M   : Non-OS2     F5  : Old Values    (Shift)F2  Color
                                          F6  : Load BIOS  Defaults
                                          F7  : Load Setup Defaults
```

The boot-up sequence allows the system to boot up without checking all the drives in order. This setting may need to be adjusted to include the A: floppy disk drive if it becomes impossible to boot to the hard drive.

The password setting prevents users without the password from accessing the system. If the system has an unknown password, it will be necessary to clear the CMOS. Most system boards have a jumper block that can be shorted to reset the CMOS to its default settings. If this option is used, it will be necessary to reenter the original configuration information.

On Pentium-based system boards, the hardware configuration jumpers and switches used to enable various memory and I/O functions have been replaced by BIOS-enabling settings. These settings usually include enabling the disk drives, keyboard, and video options, as well as the onboard serial and parallel ports.

In addition, the user can turn certain sections of the system's RAM on or off for shadowing purposes, as well as establish parity or non-parity memory operation.

ADDING AND REMOVING FRU MODULES

▶   1.2 Identify basic procedures for adding and removing field replaceable modules for both desktop and portable systems.

The A+ Core Hardware objective 1.2 states that the test taker should be able to "identify basic procedures for adding and removing field replaceable modules."

Examples of modules include the following:

◆   System board

◆   Storage devices

◆   Power supply

◆   Processor/CPU

◆   Memory

◆   Input devices

◆   Hard drive

◆   Keyboard

◆   Video board

◆   Mouse

◆   Network interface card (NIC)

Portable system components include the following:

◆   AC adapters

◆   DC controllers

◆   LCD panel

◆   PC Card

◆   Pointing devices

As the A+ objective points out, every technician should be aware of typical PC components that can be exchanged in the field. They should be able to install, connect, and configure these components to upgrade or repair an existing system. The following sections of this chapter present standard procedures for installing and removing typical field replaceable units (FRUs).

System Boards

System boards are generally removed for one of two possible reasons. Either the system board has failed and needs to be replaced or the user wants to install a new system board with better features. In either case, it is necessary to remove the current system board and replace it. The removal procedure can be defined in five steps, as described in Step by Step 1.1.

STEP BY STEP

1.1 Removing a System Board

1. Remove all external I/O systems.

2. Remove the system unit's outer cover.

3. Remove the option adapter cards.

4. Remove the cables from the system board.

5. Remove the system board.

To replace a system board, it is necessary to disconnect several cables from the old system board and reconnect them to the new system board. The easiest way to handle this is to use tape (preferably masking tape) to mark the wires and their connection points (on the new system board) before removing any wires from the old system board.

Removing External I/O Systems

Unplug all power cords from the commercial outlet. Remove all peripherals from the system unit. Disconnect the mouse, keyboard, and monitor signal cable from the rear of the unit. Finally, disconnect the monitor power cord from the system (or the outlet). Figure 1.76 illustrates the system unit's back-panel connections.

Removing the System Unit's Outer Cover

Unplug the 120V AC power cord from the system unit. Determine which type of case you are working on. If the case is a desktop model, does the cover slide off the chassis in a forward direction, bringing the front panel with it, or does it raise off of the chassis from the rear? If the back lip of the outer cover folds over the edge of the back panel, the lid raises up from the back, after the retaining screws are removed. If the retaining screws go through the back panel without passing through the lip, the outer cover will slide forward after the retaining screws have been removed.

Determine the number of screws that hold the outer cover to the chassis. (Do not confuse the power-supply retaining screws with those holding the back panel.) The power-supply unit requires four screws. Check for screws along the lower edges of the outer cover that would hold it to the sides of the chassis. Remove the screws that hold the cover to the chassis. Store the screws properly.

Remove the system unit's outer cover, as illustrated in Figure 1.77, and set it aside. Slide the case forward. Tilt the case upward from the front and remove it from the unit. Or, lift the back edge of the outer cover to approximately 45 degrees, and then slide it toward the rear of the chassis.

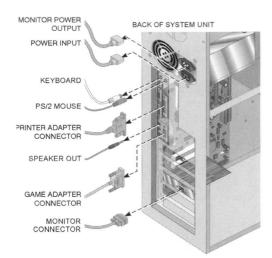

FIGURE 1.76
System unit back-panel connections.

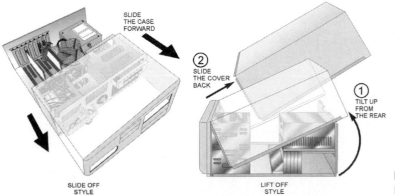

FIGURE 1.77
Removing the case.

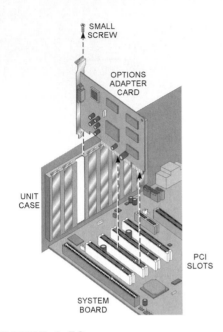

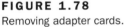

FIGURE 1.78
Removing adapter cards.

Removing Adapter Cards

A wide variety of peripheral devices are used with PC-compatible systems. Many of these devices communicate with the main system through options adapter cards that fit into expansion slot connectors on the system board.

Remove the retaining screws that secure the adapter cards to the system unit's back panel. Remove the adapter cards from the expansion slots. It is a good practice to place adapter cards back into the same slots they were removed from, if possible. Store the screws properly. Figure 1.78 shows how to perform this procedure.

If the system employs an MI/O card, disconnect the floppy drive signal cable (smaller signal cable) and the hard drive signal cable (larger signal cable) from the card. Also disconnect any I/O port connections from the card before removing it from the expansion slot.

Removing the Cables from the System Board

The Pentium system board provides the interface connections for the system's disk drives. The disk drive signal cables must be removed in order to exchange the system board. Although the FDD and IDE connectors are different sizes, there have been instances in which individuals have forced the 34-pin FDD cable onto the 40-pin IDE connector. The main consideration when removing the disk drive cables from the system board is their locations and orientation. Some system boards furnish keyed FDD and IDE connections so that they cannot be plugged in backward. However, this is not true for all system boards. Also, it is easy to reverse the primary and secondary IDE connections because they are identical. It also is possible to confuse the 80-wire/40-pin EIDE cable used in some advanced IDE interfaces with the standard 40-wire/40-pin IDE cable used with other IDE devices.

The system board provides an operator interface through a set of front-panel indicator lights and switches. These indicators and switches connect to the system board by BERG connectors, as depicted in Figure 1.79.

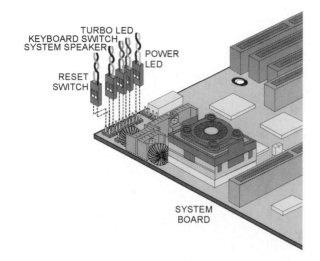

FIGURE 1.79
Front-panel connections.

The front-panel connectors must be removed to exchange the system board for a new one. Because it is quite easy to get these connections reversed, make sure that you mark them for identification purposes before removing them from their connection points. Record the color and function of each connection. Trace each wire back to its front-panel connection to determine what its purpose is. This will ensure that they are reinstalled correctly after the exchange has been completed.

Disconnect the power-supply connections from the system board as well.

Removing the System Board

Verify the positions of all jumper and switch settings on the old system board. Record these settings and verify their meanings before removing the board from the system. This may require the use of the board's User Manual, if available. Remove the grounding screw (or screws) that secures the system board to the chassis. Store the screw(s) properly.

In a desktop unit, slide the system board toward the left (as you face the front of the unit) to free its plastic feet from the slots in the floor of the system unit. Tilt the left edge of the board up, and then lift it straight up and out of the system unit, as illustrated in Figure 1.80.

FIGURE 1.80
Removing the system board from a desktop case.

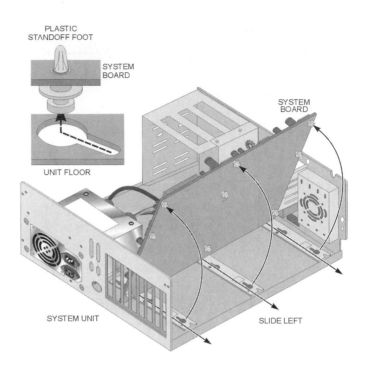

In a tower unit, slide the system board toward the bottom of the system unit to free its plastic feet from the slots in the side panel. Tilt the bottom edge of the board away from the unit and pull it straight out of the chassis, as shown in Figure 1.81.

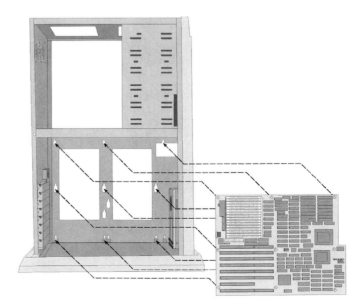

FIGURE 1.81
Removing the system board from a tower case.

System Board Devices

A few serviceable devices reside on the system board, including the following:

◆ The microprocessor

◆ The system RAM modules

◆ Specialized support ICs

Like the system board itself, there are really only two possible reasons for replacing any of these devices: to replace a failed unit or to upgrade the unit.

Microprocessors

PC manufacturers mount microprocessors in sockets so that they can be easily replaced. This enables a failed microprocessor to just be exchanged with a working unit. More often, however, the microprocessor is replaced with an improved version to upgrade the speed or performance of the system.

The notches and dots on the various ICs are important keys when replacing a microprocessor. They specify the location of the IC's number 1 pin. This pin must be lined up with the pin-1 notch of the socket for proper insertion. In older systems, the microprocessors had to be forcibly removed from the socket using an IC extractor tool. As the typical microprocessor's pin count increased, special zero insertion force (ZIF) sockets were designed that allowed the microprocessor to be set in the socket without force and then be clamped in place. An arm-activated clamping mechanism in the socket shifts to the side, locking the pins in place. A ZIF socket and microprocessor arrangement is depicted in Figure 1.82.

To release the microprocessor from the socket, the lever arm beside the socket must be pressed down and away from the socket. When it comes free from the socket, the arm raises up to release the pressure on the microprocessor's pins.

A notch and dot in one corner of the CPU marks the position of the processor's number 1 pin. The dot and notch should be located at the free end of the socket's locking lever for proper installation. Both the CPU and the socket have one corner that does not have a pin (or pinhole) in it. This feature prevents the CPU from being incorrectly inserted into the socket.

FIGURE 1.82
A microprocessor and ZIF socket.

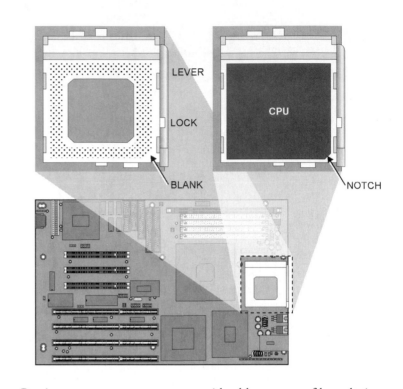

Pentium processors generate a considerable amount of heat during normal operation. To prevent this heat from reaching a destructive level for the device, all Pentiums require that a CPU cooling fan and heat sink unit be installed on the microprocessor. These units are available in glue-on and snap-on models. A special heat-conducting grease is typically used with snap-on heat sinks to provide good thermal transfer between the microprocessor and the heat sink. Power for the fans is normally obtained from one of the system's options power connectors or from a special jumper block on the system board. These items must be installed before operating the microprocessor.

Pentium microprocessors come in a number of speed ratings and many use a dual-processor voltage arrangement. In addition, the processor unit may be a Pentium clone unit manufactured by some company other than Intel. The microprocessor's supply voltage is controlled by a voltage regulator module (VRM) on the system board. Jumpers on the system board are used to establish the proper +3V and CPU core voltage settings for the particular type of microprocessor being installed in the system.

All Pentium processors operate from one of four external clock frequencies: 50MHz, 60MHz, 66MHz, or 100MHz. Their advertised speed ratings are derived from internal clock multiplier circuitry. System board jumpers also are used to establish the external/internal clock ratio for the microprocessor, as well as its external bus frequency.

Memory Modules

Modern system boards typically provide rows of single in-line memory module (SIMM) sockets and one or two, dual in-line memory module (DIMM) sockets. These sockets accept small, piggyback memory modules that can contain various combinations of DRAM devices. Both SIMMs and DIMMs use edge connectors that snap into a retainer on the system board. The SIMMs used on Pentium boards are typically 72-pin SIMMs; the DIMM socket accepts 168-pin DIMM units.

The SIMM modules can be inserted only in one direction because of a plastic safety tab at one end of the SIMM slot. The notched end of the SIMM module must be inserted into this end. To install a SIMM module, insert the module into the slot at a 45-degree angle, making sure that all the contacts are aligned with the slot. Rock the module into a vertical position so that it snaps into place and the plastic guides go through the SIMM's mounting holes. The metal clip should lock into place. To release the SIMM module, gently push the metal clips outward and rotate the module out of the slot. The DIMM module just slides vertically into the socket and is locked in place by a tab at each end. Figure 1.83 illustrates these processes.

On most Pentium system boards, the SIMM sockets are organized so that slots 1 and 2 make up bank-0, and slots 2 and 3 form bank-1. Each bank can be filled with single-sided (32-bit) SIMMs or double-sided (64-bit) SIMMs. The system can be operated with only bank-0 full. It also will operate with both banks full. However, it cannot be operated with a portion of any banks filled. (A bank in use must be full.)

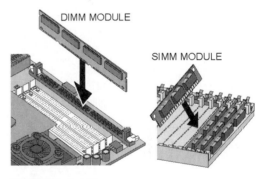

FIGURE 1.83
Installing SIMM and DIMM modules.

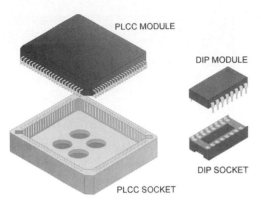

FIGURE 1.84
Socket-mounted ICs.

Support ICs

In many system board designs, the ROM BIOS is installed in a DIP socket, as illustrated in Figure 1.84. This permits the BIOS to be upgraded by replacing the IC device in the socket. Many Pentium-class system boards have advanced BIOS devices that can be flashed (rewritten electrically) and still hold the information stored in them when the power is removed. In these cases, the BIOS device is likely to be a surface-mounted device that is permanently soldered to the system board. However, other Pentium-class system boards have shifted the BIOS into a Plastic Leadless Chip Carrier (PLCC) socket.

Other parts of the system's chipset can be mounted in sockets to permit them to be exchanged for improved parts, or to be repaired easily. Devices called IC extractors should be used to remove most ICs from their sockets. They are designed to remove devices with a minimum amount of stress on the PC board and to remove the device without bending its pins. You also should be careful when inserting an IC device into a socket to make certain that you do not bend one of the device's pins, or misalign the pins in the socket. Protective antistatic devices should be used when handling ICs to ensure that they are not damaged by electrostatic discharges from your body. These discharges and protective measures are discussed in more detail in Chapter 3, "3.0 Preventive Maintenance."

Power Supplies

Figure 1.85 illustrates the typical power-supply connections in a PC. To exchange the power supply, all its connections to the system must be removed. Step by Step 1.2 details the steps necessary to remove a power supply.

STEP BY STEP

1.2 Removing a Power Supply

1. Disconnect the exterior power connections from the system unit.

   a. Unplug the power cord from the commercial receptacle.

   b. In an AT-class system, disconnect the monitor's power cord from the power supply.

2. Disconnect the interior power connections.

    a. Disconnect the power-supply connections from the system board.

    b. Disconnect the power-supply connector from the floppy disk drive.

    c. Disconnect the power-supply connector from the hard disk drive.

    d. Disconnect the power-supply connector from the CD-ROM drive.

    e. Disconnect the power-supply connector to the front-panel switch (if used in your case style).

3. Remove the power-supply unit from the system.

    a. Remove the four retaining screws that secure the power-supply unit to the rear of the system unit. (Note that, in some AT style cases, an additional pair of screws is used along the front edge of the power supply to secure it to the metal bracket it is mounted on.)

    b. Store the screws properly.

    c. Remove the power supply from the system unit by lifting it out of the unit.

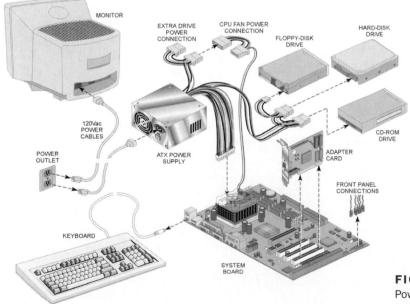

FIGURE 1.85
Power-supply connections.

Input Devices

With the exception of the keyboard, the steps associated with installing input devices are similar to those of installing other I/O devices. The keyboard differs in that its installation procedure normally consists of just plugging it into the keyboard connector.

Some input devices, such as the mouse, are so widely used that they plug into a one of the system's standard I/O ports. In the case of the mouse, it is almost standard procedure to plug it into either the PS/2 mouse port or the 9-pin serial port on the back of the unit.

In most cases, the port will have an enabling jumper that controls its use and a configuration jumper that establishes the port value and addressing of the physical connector. The I/O port-enabling function may also be controlled through the CMOS Setup utility's Peripherals Configuration screen.

Other input devices may require that a proprietary adapter card be installed in the system to manage them. This card may have a jumper or switches that need to set to configure the adapter for the system. PnP device installation does not normally require physical configuration steps.

In DOS systems, the input device may have software that needs to be configured to work with the host system. In Windows systems, the device's driver software must to be installed before it can function within the operating system.

Mice

As mentioned earlier, the mouse usually plugs into the 9-pin serial port, or a 6-pin PS/2 mini-DIN connector on the back of the system unit. This points out one of the major points to consider when choosing a new mouse for an upgrade of an existing system, or a replacement for a defective mouse: the type of connector required to attach it to the system. The only other steps are to ensure that the port's hardware is properly selected and enabled, and that the mouse's driver software is installed. Step by Step 1.3 details the actions needed to install a serial mouse.

TEST TIP

Be aware that the mouse connector type is an important consideration in selecting a mouse for use.

STEP BY STEP

1.3   Installing a Serial Mouse

1. Configure the serial port for operation with the mouse.

    a. Remove the system unit cover.

    b. Locate the serial port adapter function in the system (that is, on the system board or an I/O card).

    c. If a ribbon cable is used between the adapter and the D-shell connector, ensure that pin 1 of the cable lines up with pin 1 of the adapter, as illustrated in Figure 1.86.

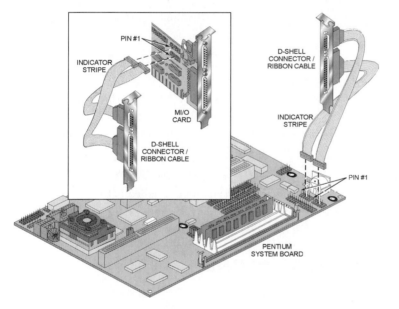

FIGURE 1.86
Cable alignment.

    d. Refer to the system documentation to locate any port-enable jumpers on the MI/O card or system board.

    e. Ensure that the enable jumper is in the Enable position.

    f. Locate the Serial Port COM Selection jumper (if present).

continues

continued

    g. Ensure that the COM Port selection jumper is in the COM1 position.

    h. Start the system.

    i. When prompted, enter the CMOS Setup utility.

    j. Check for any enabling settings in the Extended CMOS screens.

    k. Turn the system off.

2. Attach the mouse to the system.

    a. Plug the mouse connector into the DB9M connector.

3. Configure the mouse software.

    a. In a DOS system, create a C:\mouse directory and copy the mouse support files into it.

    b. Edit the AUTOEXEC.BAT file so that the mouse driver is loaded each time the system is booted up.

    c. In a Windows system, check the IRQ, COM port, and base-address settings for the serial port the mouse is attached to.

    d. Check the Control Panel to verify that the mouse driver is loaded and correct.

Installing Sound Cards

Installing a sound card is similar to installing any other adapter card. Refer to the card's User Guide to determine what hardware configuration settings may need to be made before inserting the card into the system. It also may be beneficial to run a diagnostic software package to check the system's available resources before configuring the card.

After the hardware configuration is complete, just install the card in one of the system's vacant expansion slots and secure it to the back panel of the system unit. Plug the microphone and speakers into the proper jacks on the card's back plate. With the card installed in the system, load its software drivers according to the directions in the User Guide.

Figure 1.87 depicts the connectors located on the back of a typical sound card.

Most sound cards support microphones through stereo RCA jacks. A very similar speaker jack also is normally present on the back of the card. Depending on the card, the jack may be designed for mono or stereo output. An onboard volume control wheel also may protrude through the card's back plate.

A typical Sound Blaster-compatible I/O address range used by sound cards is 220h through 22Fh. Alternative address ranges include 230–23Fh, 240–24Fh, and 250–25Fh. Typically, the sound card uses IRQ channel 7 as the default. DMA channel 1 is typically used as well.

Some sound cards contain game port adapter circuitry for attaching joysticks to the sound card. The game port circuitry must conform to the (201h) I/O addressing specifications to remain compatible with the IBM standard. Likewise, the sound card will use an IBM-compatible 15-pin, 2-row female D-shell connector for the game port connection. Advanced sound cards may also include a MIDI port connection.

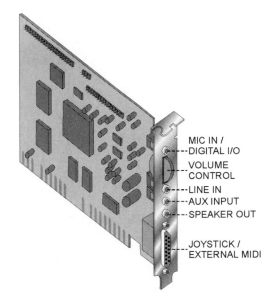

FIGURE 1.87
Sound card connections.

Installing Storage Devices

For installation purposes, storage devices fall into one of two categories: internal and external. Internal devices are typically mounted in the system unit's drive bays. External devices normally connect to options adapter cards installed in the system board's expansion slots. Although internal devices typically derive their power from the system unit's power supply, external storage devices tend to employ separate, external power-supply units.

Most internal storage devices conform to traditional disk drive form factors. Therefore, the hardware installation procedures for most storage devices are the same.

To install a storage device in a disk drive bay, disconnect the system's power cord from the back of the unit. Slide the device into one of the system unit's open drive bays, and install two screws on each side to secure the unit to the disk drive cage. If the unit is a 3-1/2" drive, and it is being installed into a 5-1/4" drive bay, you need to fit the drive with a universal mounting kit. These kits attach to the drive and extend its form factor so that it fits correctly in the 5-1/4" half-height space.

Connect the device's signal cable to the proper interface header on the system board (or on an I/O card). Then connect the signal cable to the storage device. Use caution when connecting the disk drives to the adapter. Make certain that the pin 1 indicator stripe on the cable aligns with the pin 1 position of the connectors on both the storage device and its controller. Figure 1.88 depicts proper connection of a signal cable. Finally, connect one of the power supply's optional power connectors to the storage device.

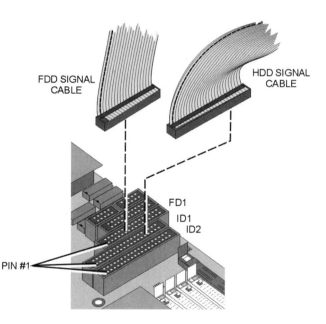

FIGURE 1.88
Connecting a drive's signal cable.

FDD Installation

The FDD installation procedure follows the sample procedure describe earlier. Just slide the FDD into one of the system unit's open drive bays, install two screws on each side to secure the drive to the system unit, and connect the signal and power cords to the drive. Figure 1.89 illustrates the steps required to install the floppy disk drive.

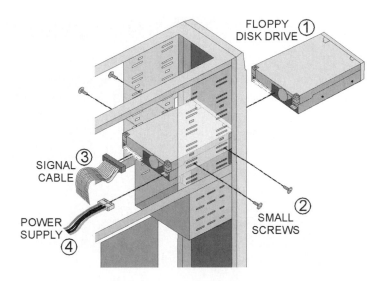

FLOPPY DISK DRIVE ①

SIGNAL CABLE ③

POWER SUPPLY ④

SMALL SCREWS ②

FIGURE 1.89
Installing a floppy disk drive.

The PC-compatible FDD unit uses a 34-pin signal cable. The FDD signal cable is designed to accommodate two FDD units, as illustrated in Figure 1.90. If the drive is the only floppy drive in the system, or intended to operate as the A: drive, connect it to the connector at the end of the cable. If it is being installed as a B: drive, attach it to the connector toward the center of the cable. A small twist should exist in part of the cable between the A: and B: drive connectors. This twist is what ultimately designated the A: and B: drives. On older floppy disk drives, the cable connected to an edge connector on the drive's printed circuit board. With newer units, the connection is made to a BERG connector.

On Pentium and other types of all-in-one system boards, look for an FDD-enabling jumper and make certain that it is set correctly for the FDD installed. In newer systems, the FDD-enabling function also may be set in the Advanced CMOS Setup screen.

Reinstall the system unit's power cord and boot up the computer. As the system boots, move into the CMOS Setup utility and configure the CMOS for the type of FDD installed.

TEST TIP

Know what makes a floppy drive an A: or B: drive in a PC system.

FIGURE 1.90
Connecting floppy drives.

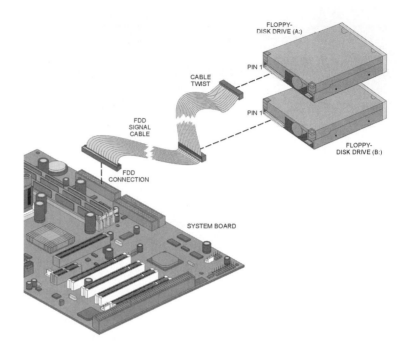

FIGURE 1.90
Connecting floppy drives.

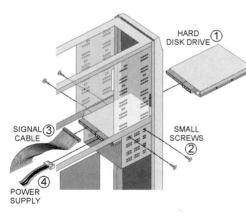

FIGURE 1.91
Securing the drive unit.

HDD Installation

The HDD hardware installation process is similar to that of other storage devices, as illustrated in Figure 1.91. However, the configuration and preparation of a typical hard disk drive is more involved than that of a floppy disk drive. It is a good idea to confirm the IDE drive's master/*slave*/single, or the SCSI drive's ID configuration setting before installing the unit in the drive bay. If a replacement HDD is being installed for repair or upgrading purposes, the data on the original drive should be backed up to some other media before replacing it, if possible.

After completing the hardware-installation process, the drive needs to be configured and formatted. Unlike floppy drives, which basically come in four accepted formats, hard disk drives are created in a wide variety of storage capacities. When the drive is created, its surface is electronically blank. To prepare the disk for use by the system, four levels of preparation must take place. The order of these steps is as follows in Step by Step 1.4.

STEP BY STEP

1.4   Preparing a Hard Drive for Use by the System

1. Set up the CMOS configuration for the drive.

2. Low-level format the drive.

3. Partition the drive.

4. High-level format the drive.

The system's CMOS Setup holds the HDD's configuration settings. As with other I/O devices, these settings must be set correctly for the type of drive being installed. Newer BIOS versions possess *autodetection* capabilities that enable them to find and identify the drives in the system. If the BIOS does not support autodetection, however, it will be necessary to move into the CMOS Configuration Setup utility and identify the drive type being installed.

The Hard Disk C: Type entry is typically located in the CMOS Setup utility's main screen. Just move to the entry and scroll through the HDD selections until an entry is found that matches the type of you are installing. In some cases, such as with SCSI drives, it will be necessary for the CMOS Configuration entry be set to None Installed before the drive will operate correctly. Store this parameter in the CMOS Configuration file by following the directions given on the menu screen.

A low-level format routine marks off the disk into cylinders and sectors and defines their placement on the disk. In older device-level drive types (such as ST-506 and ESDI drives), the user was required to perform the low-level format routine using debug commands or vendor-specific disk-management software.

System-level HDD interfaces, such as IDE and SCSI drives, come with automatic low-level formatting routines already performed. Therefore, no low-level formatted needs to be performed before they can be partitioned and high-level formatted. Doing so will not produce physical damage, but it may cause the loss of prerecorded bad track and sector information, as well as alignment information used to control the R/W heads for proper alignment over the tracks. If this occurs, you must normally send the drive to the manufacturer to restore this information to the disk.

Logical and Physical Drives

Before a *high-level format* can be performed, the drive must be partitioned. The disk-management capabilities of the oldest versions of MS-DOS (2.x, 3.x) imposed a limit on the size of a drive at 32MB. As HDD technology steadily increased, however, the capacities of the physical drives eventually passed this limit. Fortunately, operating systems can partition, or divide, large physical drives into multiple logical drives. Each logical drive is identified by a different drive letter (such as C, D, E, and so on).

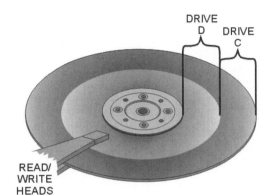

FIGURE 1.92
Partitions on an HDD.

Figure 1.92 illustrates the concept of creating multiple logical drives on a single hard drive. This is normally done for purposes of organization and increased access speeds. However, drives also can be partitioned to permit multiple operating systems to exist on the same physical drive.

Basically, DOS provides for two partitions on an HDD unit. The first partition, or the *primary partition*, must exist as the C: drive. The system files must be located in this partition, and the partition must be set to Active for the system to boot up from the drive. The active partition is the logical drive that the system will boot to.

After the primary partition is established and properly configured, an additional partition, referred to as an *extended partition*, is also permitted. However, the extended partition can be further subdivided into 23 logical drives (the letters in the alphabet minus a, b, and c). The extended partition cannot be deleted if logical drives have been defined within it.

On a partitioned drive, only one logical drive can be active at a time. When the system check the MBR of the physical disk during the boot process, it also checks to see which partition on the disk has been marked as active and then boots to the partition boot record located in that logical drive. This arrangement enables a single physical disk to hold different operating systems to which the system can boot.

In LANs and WANs, the concept of logical drives is carried a step further. A particular hard disk drive may be a logical drive in a large system of drives along a peer-to-peer network. On the other hand, a very large centralized drive may be used to create several logical drives for a server/client type of network. LANs are covered in detail in both Chapter 6, "6.0 Basic Networking," and in Chapter 10, "4.0 Networks."

The partitioning program for MS-DOS and Windows 9x is named *FDISK*. The FDISK utility in MS-DOS version 4.0 raised the maximum size of a logical drive to 128MB, and version 5.0 raised it to 528MB. The FDISK utility in Windows 9x provided upgraded support for very large hard drives. The original version of Windows 95 set a size limit for logical drives at 2GB. The FDISK version in the upgraded OSR2 version of Windows 95 extended the maximum partition size to 8GB.

In Windows NT, the partitioning process should be performed through the Disk Administrator utility. Windows 2000 replaces this utility with a graphical version called *Disk Management*. Disk Administrator/Management performs the same basic functions as the FDISK utility; however, it also can provide many additional functions associated with enterprise computing systems. When activated, the Disk Administrator/Manager will show you the basic layout of the system's disks, including the following:

◆ The size of each disk

◆ The size and file system type used in each logical drive

◆ The size and location of any unformatted (free) space on the drive

The Disk Administrator enables you to create both traditional primary and extended partitions as FAT or NTFS. It also can be used to create four types of volumes:

◆ Volume sets

◆ Striped sets

◆ Mirrored sets

◆ Striped sets with parity

These types of volumes are used in the RAID systems described earlier in this chapter.

Even though newer operating system versions provide for partitions larger than 528MB, there is another factor that limits the size of disk partitions: the BIOS. The standard BIOS has a 504MB capacity limit. To overcome this, newer BIOS include an enhanced mode that use *logical block addressing* (LBA) techniques to enable the larger partition sizes available through DOS and Windows to be used.

This technique—known as *enhanced cylinder, heads, sectors* (ECHS)—effectively increases the number of R/W heads the system can recognize from 16 to 256. The parameters of 1,024 cylinders, 63 sectors/track, and 512 bytes/sector remain unchanged.

The high-level format procedure is performed by the operating system and creates logical structures on the disk that tell the system what files are on the disk and where they can be found. In MS-DOS and Windows 9x systems, the format process creates a blank *file allocation table* (FAT) and root directory structure on the disk. In the case of Windows NT and Windows 2000 systems, the format operation may produce FATs and root directories, or it may produce more flexible master file table (MFT) structures. Chapter 7, "1.0 Operating System Fundamentals," provides more detailed information about the organization of disks, including FATs, MFTs, and directory structures.

Installing CD-ROM Drives

Before installing an internal CD-ROM drive, confirm its master/slave/single, or SCSI ID configuration setting. Afterward, install the CD-ROM unit in one of the drive bays, connect the power and signal cables, and load the CD-ROM driver software. Due to their widespread use with portable systems, the procedure for installing external CD-ROM drives is presented later in this chapter.

Figure 1.93 illustrates the installation of an internal CD-ROM drive. If the interface type differs from that of the HDD, you must install a controller card in an expansion slot. Finally, refer to the User Manual for information regarding any necessary jumper or switch settings.

To connect the drive to the system, connect the CD-ROM drive to the HDD signal cable, observing proper orientation. Connect the audio cable to the drive and to the sound card's CD input connection (if a sound card is installed).

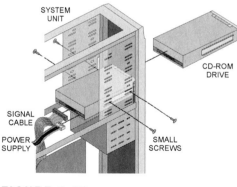

FIGURE 1.93
Installing an internal CD-ROM drive.

Configuring CD-ROM Drives

As previously indicated, the CD-ROM drive must be properly configured for the system it is being installed in. In an IDE system, the master/slave setting must be confirmed. In a SCSI system, the ID setting must be correct. In a SCSI system, the only requirement is that a valid ID setting is configured. In an IDE system, however, some thought may be required as to how to configure the drive.

In a single HDD system, the CD-ROM drive is normally set up as the slave drive on the primary interface. In a two-HDD system, however, the CD-ROM drive would most likely be configured as the master or single drive on the secondary interface. If the system also contains a sound card with a built-in IDE interface, it should be disabled to prevent it from interfering with the primary or secondary interfaces.

After the hardware is installed, it is necessary to install its software drivers. Consult the User Guide for instructions on software installation. Typically, all that is required is to insert the OEM driver disk in the floppy drive and follow the manufacturer's directions for installing the drivers. If the drive fails to operate at this point, reboot the system using single-step verification and check the information on the various boot screens for error messages associated with the CD-ROM drive.

If the installation is in a Windows 3.x-based system, use the Windows Write program to check the AUTOEXEC.BAT and CONFIG.SYS files for updated information. *Microsoft CD Extension* (MSCDEX) driver is used to provide access to the system's CD-ROM drives. It must be loaded from the CONFIG.SYS file using a **DEVICE=** or **DEVICEHIGH** command. This driver assigns the logical drive letters to all CD-ROM drives in the system along with a unique driver signature (name). The signature is used to differentiate one CD-ROM drive from another in the system.

TEST TIP
Remember what type of device the MSCDEX file is used with and where it should be located.

In Windows 9x, an advanced CD-ROM driver called *CD-ROM File System* (CDFS) has been implemented to provide protected-mode operation of the drive. Windows 9x retains the MSCDEX files for real-mode operation. If Windows 9x detects that the CDFS has taken over control of the CD-ROM on its initial boot up, it will REM the MSCDEX lines in the AUTOEXEC.BAT file.

The performance of the system's CD-based operations can be improved in a Windows 9x system by implementing a supplemental CD-ROM cache. This cache enables the system to store pages of information cached from the CD in RAM memory. As you already know, RAM access is always faster than accessing any other computer structure. More is said about optimizing the CD-ROM drive in Chapter 7, in the section "Memory Management."

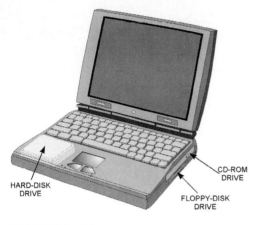

FIGURE 1.94
Portable disk drives.

Portable Drives

Smaller 2.5" form-factor hard drives, low-profile 3.5" floppy drives, and combination FDD/CD-ROM drives have been developed to address the portable computer market's need for compact devices. Older portables included one FDD and one HDD as standard equipment. Newer models tend to include a CD-ROM drive and an HDD as standard internal units. Figure 1.94 shows the placement of drives in a high-end notebook unit that includes one of each drive type.

Newer portable models include swappable drive bays that enable the combination of internal drives in the unit to be changed as dictated by the work being performed. In some units, a disk drive that is not needed for a particular task can be removed and replaced by an extra battery.

Three basic considerations should be observed when replacing disk drives in a portable: its physical size and layout, its power consumption, and whether the BIOS supports it.

Portable Memory

In compact computers, memory and memory-expansion hardware standards do not exist. Some designs use standard SIMM or DIMM modules for RAM; others use proprietary memory modules. Still other designs rely on memory card modules for additional RAM. The key to upgrading or replacing RAM in a portable can be found in its User Manual. Only memory modules recommended by the portable manufacturer should be installed, and only in the configurations suggested.

Portable I/O

Personal computer users are creatures of habit as much as anyone else. Therefore, as they moved toward portable computers, they wanted the types of features they had come to expect from their larger desktops and towers. These features typically include an alphanumeric keyboard, a video display, and a pointing device.

Most portables offer standard connectors to enable full-size keyboards and VGA monitors to be plugged in, as shown in Figure 1.95. The VGA connector is usually the standard 15-pin D-shell type; the external keyboard connector is generally the 6-pin mini-DIN (PS/2) type. When an external keyboard is plugged in, the built-in keyboard is disabled. The portable's software may allow both or either display to remain active while the external monitor is connected.

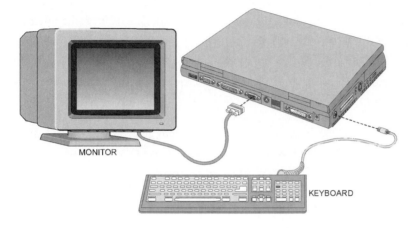

FIGURE 1.95
Attaching standard I/O devices.

Trackballs

In some applications, such as notebook computers, it is desirable to have a pointing device that does not require a surface to be moved across. The *trackball* can be thought of as an inverted mouse that permits the user to directly manipulate it. Trackballs, like the one depicted in Figure 1.96, can be separate units that sit on a desk or clip onto the side of the computer. Like the mouse, a trackball connects to the PS/2 mouse connector, or to one of the system's serial ports. In many laptop and notebook computers, trackballs are built directly in to the system housing and connected directly to its I/O circuitry. In keeping with the mouse function, trackballs can come with between one and three buttons.

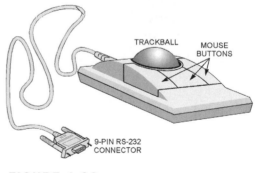

FIGURE 1.96
A trackball unit.

Touch Pads

Hewlett-Packard introduced the first *touch-screen monitor* screen in 1983. These screens divide the display into rows and columns that correspond to x and y coordinates onscreen. This technology has been adapted to notebook computers in the form of *touch pad* pointing devices, like the one illustrated in Figure 1.97. This pointing device normally takes the place of the mouse as the pointing device in the system. The user controls the screen cursor by moving a finger across the pad surface. Small buttons are included near the pad to duplicate the action of the mouse buttons. With some touch pads, single- and double-clicking can be simulated by tapping a finger on the pad.

The touch pad contains a grid of electric conductors that organize it in a row and column format, as described in Figure 1.98. When the user presses the touch pad, the protective layer over the grid flexes and causes the capacitance between the two grids within the pad to change. This produces a signal change that is detected by the touch pad controller at one x-grid line and one y-grid line. The controller converts the signal generated between the two strips into an approximate x/y position on the video display.

The human fingertip is broad and does not normally provide a fine-enough pointing device to select precise points onscreen. Therefore, accurately locating a small item onscreen can be difficult due to the relative size of the fingertip. The touch pad software designers have created drivers that take this possibility into account and compensate for it.

Touch pads are available as built-in units in some portables; others are designed as add-ons to existing units. These units clip onto the body of the computer, or sit on a desktop, and plug into the PS/2 mouse port or one of the system's serial ports, just as a mouse or trackball does.

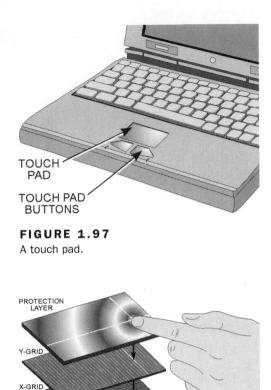

FIGURE 1.97
A touch pad.

FIGURE 1.98
Inside a touch pad.

SYSTEM RESOURCES

▶ 1.3 Identify available IRQs, DMAs, and I/O addresses and procedures for configuring them for device installation and configuration.

The A+ Core Hardware objective 1.3 states that the test taker should be able to "identify available IRQs, DMAs, and I/O addresses with procedures for configuring them for device installation."

Examples include the following:

◆ Standard IRQ settings

◆ Modems

◆ Floppy drives

◆ Hard drives

◆ USB ports

◆ Infrared ports

An IBM-compatible PC system is a very flexible tool because it can be configured to perform so many tasks. By selecting appropriate hardware and software options, the same basic system can be customized to be an inventory-management business machine, a multimedia-development system, or a simple game machine. As this A+ objective indicates, the computer technician must be able to determine what system resources are required for the component, what resource are available in the system, and how they may be allocated to successfully install hardware components in a PC. The following sections describe various standard I/O methods and peripheral connection schemes used to attach options to a PC system.

Input/Output

In addition to the millions of possible memory locations in a PC, typically thousands of addresses are set aside for I/O devices in a system. For any device to operate with the system's microprocessor, it must have an address (or group of addresses) where the system can find it.

Referring to the computer system depicted in Figure 1.99, it can be seen that external I/O devices connect to the computer's bus systems through interfacing circuits. The job of the interfacing circuits is to make the peripherals compatible with the system.

FIGURE 1.99
Basic input/output organization.

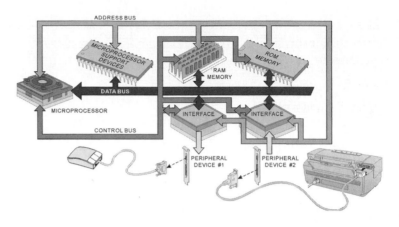

Interface Circuits Interface circuits (ICs) are necessary because the characteristics of most peripherals differ greatly from those of the basic computer. Most interface circuits in the PC-compatible world have been integrated into application-specific ICs.

The microcomputer is a completely solid-state, digital electronic device that uses parallel words of a given length and adheres to basic digital logic levels. However, computer peripherals generally tend to be more mechanical and analog in nature. Conversely, humans are analog in nature.

The computer's input and output units allow it to communicate with the outside world. The input units contain all the circuitry necessary to accept data and programs from peripheral input devices such as keyboards, light pens, mice, joysticks, and so on, and convert the information into a form that is usable by the microprocessor. The input unit can be used to enter programs and data into the memory unit before execution, or it can be used to enter data directly to the microprocessor during execution.

The output units contain all the circuitry necessary to transform data from the computer's language into a form that is more convenient for the outside world. Most often that is in the form of alphanumeric characters, which are convenient for humans. Common output devices include video display monitors, audio speakers, and character printers. Figure 1.100 depicts several common I/O devices associated with PCs.

Some computer peripherals do double duty as both input and output units. These devices are collectively referred to as I/O devices and include secondary storage devices such as hard disk drives, floppy disk drives, and magnetic tape drives, as well as modems. In these devices, the form that data takes is not for the convenience of human beings, but the form most suitable to carry out the function of the device.

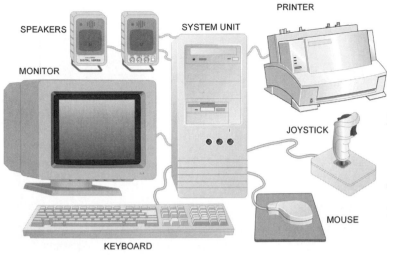

FIGURE 1.100
Common I/O devices used with PCs.

Moving Data

The most frequent operation performed in a computer is the movement of information from one location to another. This information is moved in the form of words. Basically, computer words can be transferred in two modes: parallel mode and serial mode. In parallel transfers, an entire word is transferred from location A to location B by a set of parallel conductors at one instant. In serial mode, the bits of the word are transmitted along a single conductor, one bit at a time. Serial transfers require more time to accomplish than parallel transfers because a clock cycle must be used for each bit transferred.

A parallel transfer requires only one clock pulse to complete. Figure 1.101 depicts examples of both parallel and serial transfers. Because speed is normally of the utmost importance in computer operations, all data movements within the computer are conducted in parallel, as shown in (a). But when information is being transferred between the computer and its peripherals (or another computer), conditions may dictate that the transfer be carried out in serial mode, as shown in (b).

Peripherals can use parallel or serial transmission modes between themselves and the system board. Parallel buses are generally used for high-speed devices, such as disk drives and some printers. Conversely, serial transmission is used with remotely located devices or with devices whose operation is more compatible with serial data flow, such as monitors, modems, certain input devices, and some printers.

FIGURE 1.101
Parallel and serial data transfers.

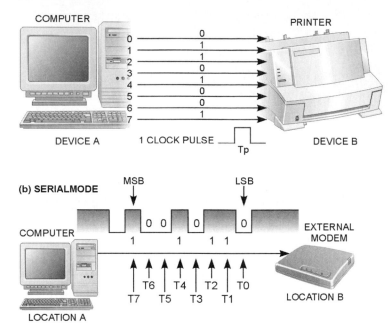

(a) PARALLEL MODE

COMPUTER

PRINTER

DEVICE A   1 CLOCK PULSE T_p DEVICE B

(b) SERIALMODE

MSB   LSB

COMPUTER

EXTERNAL MODEM

T7 T6 T5 T4 T3 T2 T1 T0

LOCATION A

LOCATION B

Initiating I/O Transfers

During a program's execution, the microprocessor constantly reads from or writes to memory locations. The program also can call on the microprocessor to read from or write to one of the system's I/O devices. Regardless of how the peripheral is connected to the system (serial or parallel), one of four methods can be used to initiate data transfer between the system and the peripheral, as follows:

◆ **Polling** is where the microprocessor examines the status of the peripheral under program control.

◆ **Programmed I/O** is where the microprocessor alerts the designated peripheral by applying its address to the system's address bus.

◆ **Interrupt-driven I/O** is where the peripheral alerts the microprocessor that it is ready to transfer data.

◆ **DMA** is where the intelligent peripheral assumes control of the system's buses to conduct direct transfers with primary memory.

Polling and Programmed I/O

Both *polling* and programmed I/O represent software approaches to data transfer; interrupt-driven and DMA transfers, on the other hand, are basically hardware approaches.

In the polling method, the software periodically checks with the system's I/O devices to determine whether any device is ready to conduct a data transfer. If so, it begins reading or writing data to the corresponding I/O port. The polling method is advantageous in that it is easy to implement and reconfigure because the program controls the entire sequence of events during the transfer. Polling is often inconvenient, however, because the microprocessor must be totally involved in the polling routine and cannot perform other functions.

The programmed I/O method calls for the microprocessor to alert the desired peripheral of an I/O operation by issuing its address to the address bus. The peripheral can delay the transfer by asserting its busy line. If the microprocessor receives a busy signal from the peripheral, it continues to perform other tasks, but periodically checks the device until the busy signal is replaced by a ready signal.

To establish an orderly flow of data during the transfer, a number of handshakes may occur between the peripheral and the system. This prevents the microprocessor from sending or requesting data at a faster rate than the peripheral can handle. In both methods, the main system resource that is used is the microprocessor's time.

Interrupts

In the course of normal operations, the various I/O devices attached to a PC, such as the keyboard and disk drives, require servicing from the system's microprocessor. Although I/O devices may be treated like memory locations, there is one big difference between the two: I/O devices generally have the capability to interrupt the microprocessor while it is executing a program. The I/O device does this by issuing an interrupt request (IRQ) input signal to the microprocessor. Each device in a PC-compatible system that is capable of interrupting the microprocessor must be assigned its own, unique IRQ number. The system uses this number to identify which device is in need of service.

If the microprocessor is responding to INT signals and a peripheral device issues an interrupt request on an IRQ line, the microprocessor will finish executing its current instruction and issue an interrupt acknowledge (INTA) signal on the control bus. The microprocessor suspends its normal operation and stores the contents of its internal registers in a special storage area referred to as the stack.

The interrupting device responds by sending the starting address of a special program, called the interrupt service routine, to the microprocessor. The microprocessor uses the interrupt service routine to service the interrupting device. After it finishes servicing the interrupting device, the contents of the stack are restored to their original locations, and the microprocessor returns to the original program at the point where the interrupt occurred. If two interrupt signals occur at the same instant, the interrupt that has the highest priority is serviced first.

A programmable interrupt controller, and its relationship to the system's microprocessor, is illustrated in Figure 1.102. The interrupt controller accepts prioritized IRQ signals from up to eight peripheral devices on IRQ lines 0 through 7. When one of the peripherals desires to communicate with the microprocessor, it sends an IRQ to the interrupt controller. The controller responds by sending an INT signal to the microprocessor. If two interrupt requests are received at the same instance, the interrupt controller accepts the one which has the higher priority and acts on it first. The priority order is highest for the device connected to the IRQ-0 line and descends in order, with the IRQ-7 input given the lowest priority.

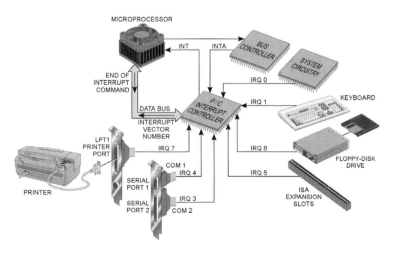

FIGURE 1.102
A programmable interrupt controller operation.

Of the 16 interrupt channels (IRQ0 through IRQ15) available, 3 are generally used inside the system board's chipset. Therefore, they do not have external IRQ pins. The other 13 IRQ inputs are available to the system for user-definable interrupt functions. Each IRQ input is assigned a priority level. IRQ0 is the highest, and IRQ15 is the lowest. The internally connected channels are as follows:

Channel 0 (IRQ0) Timer/Counter interrupt is OK.

Channel 1 (IRQ1) Keyboard buffer full.

Channel 2 (IRQ2) Cascaded to INTC2.

Channel 8 (IRQ8) Real-time clock interrupt.

Channel 9 (IRQ9) Cascade between INTC1 and INTC2.

Channel 13 (IRQ13) Math coprocessor interrupt.

Table 1.5 shows the designations for the various interrupt levels in the system.

Two system board–related conditions cause a *nonmaskable interrupt* (NMI) signal to be sent to the microprocessor. The first condition occurs when an active IO Channel Check (IOCHCK) signal is received from an adapter card located in one of the board's expansion slots. The other event that causes an NMI signal to be generated is the occurrence of a Parity Check (PCK) error in the system's DRAM memory.

> **Reference Shelf**
>
> For more in-depth information about how interrupt requests actually work, refer to the "How Interrupts Work" section of the Electronic Reference Shelf located on the CD that accompanies this book.

TABLE 1.5

SYSTEM INTERRUPT LEVELS

Interrupt	Description
NMI	I/O Channel Check or Parity Check error
	INTC1
IRQ0	Time-of-Day Tick
IRQ1	Keyboard Buffer Full
IRQ2	Cascade from INTC2
IRQ3	Serial Port 2
IRQ4	Serial Port 1
IRQ5	Parallel Port 2

continues

Interrupt	Description
TABLE 1.5	*continued*
IRQ6	FDD Controller
IRQ7	Parallel Port 1
	INTC2
IRQ8	Real-Time Clock
IRQ9	Cascade to INTC1
IRQ10	Spare
IRQ11	Spare
IRQ12	Spare
IRQ13	Coprocessor
IRQ14	Primary IDE Controller
IRQ15	Secondary IDE Controller

Direct Memory Access

Another difference between memory and some intelligent, high-speed I/O devices is that the I/O device may have the capability to perform data transfers (read and write operations) on their own. This type of operation is called *direct memory access* (DMA). DMA generally involves a high-speed I/O device taking over the system's buses to perform read and write operations with the primary memory, without the intervention of the system microprocessor.

When the peripheral device has data ready to be transferred, it sends a DMA request (DREQ) signal to a special IC device called a DMA controller, which in turn, sends a hold input signal to the microprocessor. The microprocessor finishes executing the instruction it is currently working on and places its address and data pins in a high-impedance state (floating), effectively disconnecting the microprocessor from the buses. At this time, the microprocessor issues a buses available (BA) or hold acknowledge (HLDA) signal to the DMA controller. The DMA controller, in turn, issues a DMA acknowledge (DACK) to the peripheral and the necessary R/W and enable signals for the data transfer to begin. The key to DMA operations is that the DMA controller has been designed specifically to transfer data bytes faster than the microprocessor can.

The PC-compatible DMA subsystem provides an AT-compatible PC with 4 channels for 8-bit DMA transfers (DMA1) and 3 channels (DMA2) for 16-bit DMA transfers. The DMA1 channels are used to carry out DMA transfers between 8-bit options adapters and 8- or 16-bit memory locations. These 8-bit transfers are conducted in 64KB blocks and can be performed throughout the system's address space. The DMA2 channels (channels 5, 6, and 7) are used only with 16-bit devices and can transfer only words in 128KB blocks. The first 16-bit DMA channel (DMA channel 4) is used internally to cascade the two DMA controllers together. Table 1.6 describes the system's DMA channel designations.

TABLE 1.6

SYSTEM'S DMA CHANNEL DESIGNATIONS

Channel	Function	Controller	Page Register Address
CH0	Spare	1	0087
CH1	SDLC (Network)	1	0083
CH2	FDD Controller	1	0082
CH3	Spare	1	0081
CH4	Cascade to Cntr 1	2	none
CH5	Spare	2	008B
CH6	Spare	2	0089
CH7	Spare	2	008A

Reference Shelf

For more in-depth information about how DMA operations actually work, refer to the "How DMA Works" section of the Electronic Reference Shelf located on the CD that accompanies this book.

Onboard I/O

When dealing with a PC-compatible, you must contend with two forms of I/O: the system board's onboard I/O, and peripheral devices that interact with the system through its expansion slots.

In a PC-compatible system, certain I/O addresses are associated with intelligent devices on the system board, such as the interrupt and DMA controllers, timer counter channels, and keyboard controller. Other system I/O ports and their interfaces are located on optional plug-in cards. These easily installed options give the system a high degree of flexibility in adapting to a wide variety of peripheral devices.

Most of the I/O functions associated with PC-compatible systems have become so standardized that IC manufacturers produce them in single-chip ASIC formats. Figure 1.103 illustrates an ASIC for standard AT-compatible system board functions.

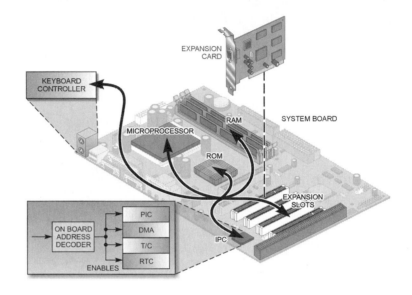

FIGURE 1.103
Onboard I/O.

Certain I/O connections have become standards associated with PC compatibles. These include the system's parallel printer ports, RS-232 serial ports, and the game port. Figure 1.104 depicts an M/IO ASIC for standard peripheral control.

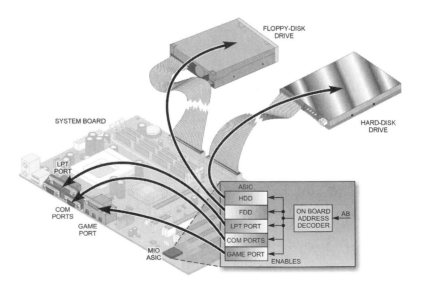

FIGURE 1.104
System I/O methods.

In both cases, the I/O controllers integrated into the ASIC are responsible for matching signal levels and *protocols* between the system and the I/O device.

The system treats its onboard intelligent devices as I/O addresses. The onboard address decoder, similar to the one displayed in Figure 1.105, converts addresses from the address bus into enabling bits for the system's intelligent devices. These addresses are included in the overall I/O addressing map of the system.

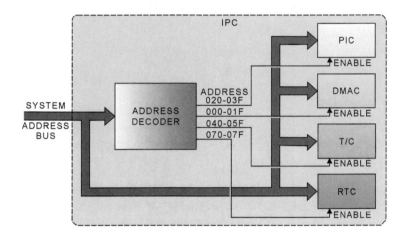

FIGURE 1.105
Onboard address decoding.

The various I/O port addresses listed in Table 1.7 are used by standard I/O adapters in the PC-compatible system. Notice that these addresses are redundant with those stated for the system's interrupt vectors given in Table 1.8. This method of addressing is referred to as redundant addressing. Figure 1.106 illustrates how a system address is routed through the system to an I/O port location.

TABLE 1.7

I/O PORT ADDRESSES

Hex Address	Device	Usage
000-01F	DMA Controller	System
020-03F	Interrupt Controller	System
040-05F	Timer/Counter	System
060-06F	Keyboard Controller	System

continues

TABLE 1.7	continued	
Hex Address	**Device**	**Usage**
070-07F	Real-Time Clock, NMI Mask	System
080-09F	DMA Page Register	System
0A0-0BF	Interrupt Controller	System
0F0	Clear Math Coprocessor Busy	System
0F1	Reset Math Coprocessor	System
0F8-0FF	Math Coprocessor	System
170-177	Second IDE Interface	I/O
1F0-1F8	First IDE Interface	I/O
200-207	Game Port	I/O
278-27F	Parallel Printer Port 2	I/O
2E8-2EF	Serial Port 4	I/O
2F8-2FF	Serial Port 2	I/O
370-375	Second FDD Controller	I/O
378-37F	Parallel Printer Port 1	I/O
3B0-3BF	MGA,VGA Video/First Printer Port	I/O
3C0-3CF	VGA Video	I/O
3D0-3DF	CGA,VGA Video	I/O
3E8-3EF	Serial Port 3	I/O
3F0-3F7	FDD Controller	I/O
3F8-3FF	Serial Port 1	I/O
FF80-FF9F	USB Controller	I/O

TEST TIP

Memorize the I/O port addresses for the first and second IDE controller.

TABLE 1.8	

SYSTEM MEMORY MAP

Address	Function
0-3FF	Interrupt vectors
400-47F	ROM-BIOS RAM
480-5FF	Basic and special system function RAM

Address	*Function*
600-9FFFF	Program memory
0A0000-0AFFFF	VGA/EGA display memory
0B0000-0B0FFF	Monochrome display adapter memory
0B8000-0BFFFF	Color graphics adapter memory
0C0000-0C7FFF	VGA/SVGA BIOS
0C8000-0CBFFF	EIDE/SCSI ROM (also older HDD types)
0D0000-0D7FFF	Spare ROM
0D8000-0DFFFF	LAN adapter ROM
0E0000-0E7FFF	Spare ROM
0E8000-0EFFFF	Spare ROM
0F0000-0F3FFF	Spare ROM
0F4000-0F7FFF	Spare ROM
0F8000-0FBFFF	Spare ROM
0FC000-0FDFFF	ROM BIOS
0FE000-0FFFFF	ROM BIOS

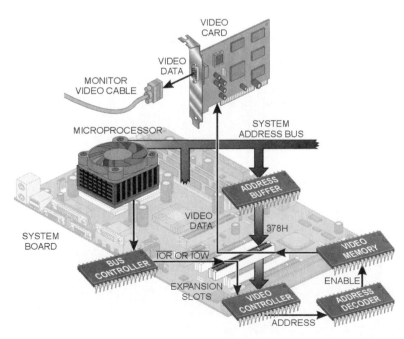

FIGURE 1.106
Address routing to an I/O port.

Hexadecimal Addresses

Addresses in PC systems are always referred to by their hexadecimal value. The reason for this is that digital computers are built on components that work only with two logic levels: On/Off, High/Low (1/0). This corresponds directly to the Base2 or binary numbering system. In the binary system, each piece of information represents a binary digit, or bit.

The power of the digital computer lies in how it groups bits of information into words. The basic word length in PCs is the 8-bit word called a byte. Some computers can handle data as 16, 32, and 64-bit words. With the byte as the basic data unit, it is easier for humans to speak of computer numbers in the base16 or hexadecimal (hex) numbering system. In this system, groups of 4 bits can be represented directly by a single hex character (that is, 1001 base2 = 09 base16). For human representation, the values in the numbering system run from 0 to 9 and then from A through F, as illustrated in Table 1.9.

TABLE 1.9

BINARY, DECIMAL, AND HEXADECIMAL NUMBERS

Decimal (10)	Binary (2)	Hexadecimal (16)
0	0000	0
1	0001	1
2	0010	2
3	0011	3
4	0100	4
5	0101	5
6	0110	6
7	0111	7
8	1000	8
9	1001	9
10	1010	A
11	1011	B
12	1100	C
13	1101	D

Decimal (10)	Binary (2)	Hexadecimal (16)
14	1110	E
15	1111	F
16	10000	10

Although this may seem a littler inconvenient for those of you not familiar with binary and hexadecimal systems, it is much easier to convey the number 3F8h to someone than it is 001111111000. The real difficulty of reconciling a hexadecimal value comes when you try to convert binary or hexadecimal values to the decimal (base10) number system you are familiar with.

> **Reference Shelf**
>
> For more in-depth information about computer-related numbering systems, refer to the "Bits, Bytes, and Computer Words" section of the Electronic Reference Shelf located on the CD that accompanies this book.

PERIPHERALS AND PORTS

▶   1.4 Identify common peripheral ports, associated cabling, and their connectors.

The A+ Core Hardware objective 1.4 states that the test taker should be able to "identify common peripheral ports, associated cabling, and their connectors.

Examples include the following:

◆ Cable types

◆ Cable orientation

◆ Serial verses parallel

◆ Pin connections

Examples of connector types include the following:

◆ DB-9

◆ DB-25

◆ RJ-11

◆ BNC

◆ RJ-45

◆ PS2/Mini-DIN

◆ USB

◆ IEEE-1394

As mentioned earlier, a wide variety of peripheral devices can be added to a PC-compatible system. Most of these devices are designed to employ some type of PC-compatible I/O connection method. As this A+ objective indicates, the computer technician must be able to recognize what type of port the device requires, locate standard I/O port connections, and determine what type of cabling is required to successfully connect the port and the device, to successfully add peripheral devices to a PC system. The following sections of the chapter describe standardized I/O ports and connections found in a PC-compatible system.

Standard I/O Ports

Although many different ways have been developed to connect devices to the PC-compatible system, the following three ports have been standard since the original PCs were introduced:

◆ The IBM versions of the Centronics parallel port

◆ The RS-232C serial port

◆ The game port

Figure 1.107 shows typical connectors found on the PC's back panel.

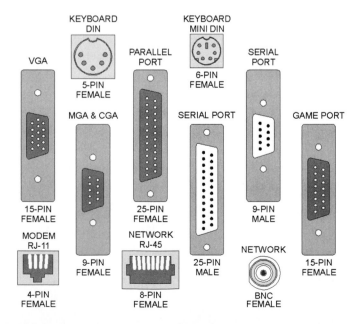

FIGURE 1.107
Typical I/O port connectors.

Parallel Ports

Parallel ports have been a staple of the PC system since the original PCs were introduced. They are most widely used to connect printers to computers.

In many instances, parallel ports are referred to as parallel printer ports. Because of the parallel port's capability to quickly transfer bytes of data in a parallel mode, it has been adopted to interface a number of other peripheral devices to the computer. These devices include X-Y plotters; fast computer-to-computer transfer systems; high-speed, high-volume, removable disk backup systems; and optical scanners.

The Centronics Standard

Figure 1.108 shows a typical parallel printer connection, using the IBM version of the Centronics standard. This interface enables the computer to pass information to the printer, 8 bits at a time, across the 8 data lines. The other lines in the connection carry control signals (handshaking signals) back and forth between the computer and the printer.

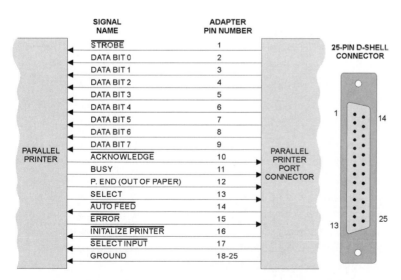

FIGURE 1.108
Parallel port connector and signals.

The original Centronics interface used a 36-pin D-shell connector at the adapter and a 36-pin Centronics connector at the printer end. The IBM version of the interface, which became known as the Standard Parallel Printer (SPP) port specification, reduced the pin count to 25 at the computer end of the connection.

In the SPP specification, the data strobe line is used by the computer to signal the printer that a character is available on the data lines. The printer reads the character from the data lines into its buffer, to be printed at the printer's convenience. If, for some reason, the printer cannot accept the character from the data lines, such as being out of paper or its buffer being full, the printer sends a "busy" signal to the computer on the busy line, telling the computer not to send any more data.

After the peripheral device has read the data word from the data lines, it pulses the acknowledge (AC*K*) line to tell the computer it is ready to accept another data word, so long as the busy line is not asserted. The printer also uses the select line (SLCT) to let the computer know that data can be sent to it. In the event that the SLCT signal is not present, the computer cannot send the printer any data.

In addition to the lines discussed here, the Centronics standard calls for additional printer-related control lines, which include paper end (PE), auto feed (AUTO-FD), error, initialize printer (INIT), and select input (SLCT-IN). Not all printers use the complete standard and all its control lines. In many instances, only a few of the lines are used, and nonstandard pin numbers and connector types also may be used.

TEST TIP
Know the recommended length of a standard parallel printer cable.

When the port is used in SPP mode, all the printer port's signals are transmitted between the adapter card and the printer at standard digital logic levels. This means that the signals can deteriorate quickly with long lengths of cable. The cable length used for the parallel printer should be kept to less than 10 feet. If longer lengths are needed, the cable should have a low-capacitance value. The cable should also be shielded, to minimize *electromagnetic field interference* (EFI). EFI is unwanted radio interference that can escape from improperly shielded cases and peripherals.

LPT Handles

Microsoft operating systems keep track of the system's installed printer ports by assigning them the logical device names (handles) LPT1, LPT2, and LPT3. Whenever the system boots up, DOS searches the hardware for parallel ports installed at hex addresses 3BCh, 378h, and 278h, consecutively.

If a printer port is found at 3BCh, DOS assigns it the title of LPT1. If no printer port is found at 3BCh, but there is one at 378h, however, DOS assigns LPT1 to the latter address. Likewise, a system that has printer ports at physical addresses 378h and 278h would have LPT1 assigned at 378h, and LPT2 at location 278h.

The address of the printer port can normally be changed to respond as LPT1, LPT2, or LPT3, depending on the setting of address-selection jumpers. The printer port also can be disabled completely through these jumper settings.

The interrupt level of the printer port may be set at a number of different levels by changing its configuration jumpers, or CMOS-enabling setting. Normal interrupt request settings for printer ports in a PC-compatible system are IRQ5 or IRQ7. IRQ7 is normally assigned to the LPT1 printer port, whereas IRQ5 typically serves the LPT2 port, if installed.

Although the data pins of the parallel printer port are defined as output pins, Figure 1.108 illustrates that they are actually bidirectional. However, some less-expensive ports may not have the electronics built in to them to handle the input function. This is not important for most printer operations, so many users won't notice.

However, newer *enhanced parallel port* (EPP) and extended capabilities port (ECP) ports can be converted between unidirectional and bidirectional operation through the CMOS Setup screen. If a bidirectional port is being used to support an I/O device, such as a local area network adapter or a high-capacity storage device, this feature would need to be checked at both a hardware and software level.

The parallel cable also should be checked to see that it complies with the IEEE-1284 standard for use with bidirectional parallel ports. Using a traditional SPP cable could cause the device to operate erratically or fail completely.

TEST TIP

Memorize the system resources that the PC typically assigns to parallel ports.

TEST TIP

As you study the I/O ports in this chapter, be aware of which ports provide bidirectional, half-duplex, and full-duplex operation.

Reference Shelf

For more in-depth technical information about how parallel ports actually work, refer to the "How a Parallel Printer Port Works" section of the Electronic Reference Shelf located on the CD that accompanies this book.

Serial Ports

As the distance between the computer and a peripheral reaches a certain point (10 feet), it becomes less practical to send data as parallel words. An alternative way to send data is to break the parallel words into their individual bits and transmit them one at a time in a serial bit stream over a single conductor.

In this manner, the number of conductors connecting the computer and the peripheral is reduced from eight or more data lines, and any number of control lines, to one (or two) communication lines, a ground line, and maybe a few control lines. Therefore, when a peripheral device must be located at some distance from the computer, the cost of connecting equipment is reduced by using serial communication techniques.

Serial Transmission Modes

The biggest problem encountered when sending data serially is keeping the transmitted data bit timing synchronized between the two devices.

Two methods are used to provide the proper timing for serial transfers: the data bits can be sent synchronously (in conjunction with a synchronizing clock pulse), or asynchronously (without an accompanying clock pulse).

When data is transmitted synchronously, the bits of a word, or a character, are synchronized by a common clock signal, which is applied to both the transmitting and receiving shift registers. The two
registers are initialized before data transmission begins, when the transmitting circuitry sends a predefined bit pattern, which the receiver recognizes as the initialization command. After this, receiving circuitry processes the incoming bit stream by counting clock pulses and dividing the bit stream into words of a predetermined length. If the receiver misses a bit for any reason, all the words that follow are processed erroneously.

When data is transferred asynchronously, the receiving system is not synchronized with the sending system. In asynchronous communications, the transmission depends on the capability of two separate clocks, running at the same frequency, to remain synchronized for a short period of time. The transmitted material is sent character by character (usually in ASCII format), with the beginning and end of each character framed by character start and stop bits. Between these marks, the bits of the character are sent at a constant rate, but the time interval between characters may be irregular, as illustrated in Figure 1.109.

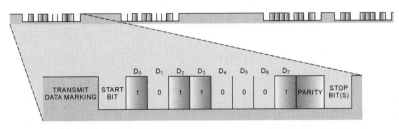

FIGURE 1.109
Asynchronous transmission.

Over a given period of time, synchronous communications are much faster than asynchronous methods. This is due to the extra number of bits required to send each character asynchronously. PC serial ports and analog modems use asynchronous communications methods; digital modems and local area network adapters use synchronous methods. Although asynchronous transfer methods have been the standard for serial ports in the PC industry and synchronous ports were typically used in specialized applications, most of the newer ports and buses include a high-speed synchronous mode as a standard option.

Serial Interface ICs

Like the single-chip parallel ports, IC manufacturers have developed a number of single-chip devices that perform all the functions necessary for serial transfers to occur. These serial port ICs are referred to as *universal asynchronous receiver/transmitters* (UARTs). Synchronous devices are usually called USARTs (universal synchronous/asynchronous receiver/transmitters).

Not only do these devices provide the parallel-to-serial and serial-to-parallel conversions required for serial communications, they also handle the parallel interface required with the computer's bus, and all the control functions associated with the transmission.

For more in-depth technical information about how a serial port actually work, refer to the "How a Serial Port Works" section of the Electronic Reference Shelf located on the CD that accompanies this book.

UARTs

The original PC serial port adapters featured 8250 UARTs with programmable baud rates from 50 to 9600 baud, a fully programmable interrupt system, and variable character lengths (5-, 6-, 7-, or 8-bit characters). In addition, the adapter added and removed start, stop, and parity bits, had false start bit detection, line break detection and generation, and possessed built-in diagnostics capabilities. As modems became faster and faster, upgraded UARTs were included, or integrated, to keep up.

Notable advanced UART versions include the 16450 and 16550. The 16450 is the 16-bit improvement of the 8250; the 16550 is a high-performance UART, with an onboard 16-byte buffer. The buffer allows the UART to store, or transmit, a string of data without interrupting the system's microprocessor to handle them. This provides the 16550 with an impressive speed advantage over previous UARTs. These advanced UARTs allow serial ports to reach data transmission rates of up to 115Kbps. Although some features have changed between these UARTs, and although they are sometimes integrated directly into an integrated I/O chip, they must still adhere to the basic 8250 structure to remain PC compatible.

Serial Interface Connections

Because of the popularity of asynchronous serial data transmissions and the number of devices that use them, such as printers and modems, standardized serial bit signals and connection schemes have been developed to simplify the connecting of serial devices to computers. The most popular of these serial interface standards is the Electronic Industry Association (EIA) RS-232C interface standard.

Basically, the IBM version of the RS-232C standard calls for a 25-pin male D-type connector, as depicted in Figure 1.110. It also designates certain pins for data transmission and receiving, along with a number of control lines. The standard was developed to cover a wide variety of peripheral devices, and therefore, not all the lines are used in any given application. Normally, only 9 of the pins are active for a given application. The other lines are used for secondary, or backup, lines and grounds. Different device manufacturers may use various combinations of the RS-232C lines, even for peripherals of the same type.

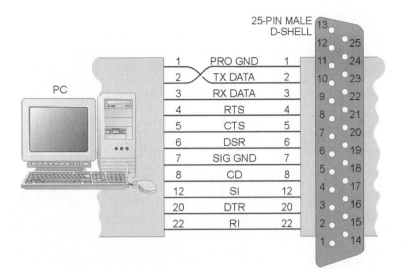

FIGURE 1.110
RS-232C.connector.

In addition to defining the type of connector to be used, and the use of its individual pins, the RS-232 standard also establishes acceptable voltage levels for the signals on its pins. These levels are generally converted to and from standard digital logic level signals that can produce a maximum baud rate of 20000 baud over distances of less than 50 feet.

> **TEST TIP**
> Know the maximum recommended length of an RS-232 cable.

Advanced Serial Standards

With the advent of the mouse as a common input device, a 9-pin male D-shell version of the RS-232 serial port became common. This version is commonly used as the COM1 serial port for the mouse in Windows-based systems. Figure 1.111 depicts the 9-pin version of the interface being used to connect a serial printer.

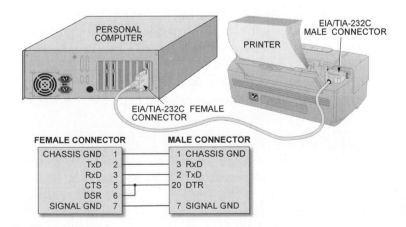

FIGURE 1.111
RS-232C 9-pin serial printer connection.

The exchanging of pins 2 and 3 between the two devices forms the basis of the *null modem*. Because the device in Figure 1.111 is a serial printer, pins 5 and 6 of the DTE equipment are tied to the DTR pin of the DCE equipment.

The character bit stream is transmitted to the printer on the line designated as the transmit data line (TXD) at the computer connector and receive data line (RXD) at the printer connector. A reciprocal line (TXD at the printer connector and RXD at the computer connector) also is used in the printer interface. Because data does not flow from the printer to the computer, this line basically informs the computer that a printer is connected to the interface, turned on, and ready to receive data (much like the select line in the Centronics interface standard).

The flow of data to the printer is moderated by the data set ready (DSR) line at the computer connector, and data terminal ready (DTR) line at the printer connector. The printer uses this line in much the same manner as the busy line of the Centronics interface. When the buffer is full, the printer signals on this line to tell the computer to not send any more data. More complex serial interfacing may include a line called the clear to send (CTS) line at the computer connector and ready to send (RTS) line at the printer connector, and its reciprocal line, where the identifications are reversed.

At the printer's end of the cable, another UART receives the serial bit stream, removes the start and stop bits, checks the parity bit for transmission errors, and reassembles the character data into parallel form.

Because the movement of data is asynchronous using the UART, an agreement must be established between the computer's UART and the printer's UART, concerning the speed at which characters will be sent. The baud rate of the UART is generally set by software. On the other hand, the printer's baud rate is usually designated by a set of DIP switches in the printer. Common transmission rates used with serial printers are 300, 1200, 2400, and 9600 bits per second (bps). One of the most common problems associated with getting a serial interface to work is mismatched baud rate.

Since the adoption of the RS-232C standard, the EIA has also adopted two more improved serial standards: the RS-422 and RS-423, which are enhancements of the RS-232C standard.

The RS-422 uses twisted-pair transmission lines and differential line signals to provide a high degree of noise immunity for transmitted data. The RS-423 standard uses coaxial cable to provide extended transmission distances and higher data transfer rates.

Serial Cables

Although the information in Figure 1.110 shows a designation for nearly every pin in the RS-232 connection (except 11, 18, and 25), many of the pins are not actually used in most serial cables. Figure 1.112 illustrates the basic 25-pin to 25-pin variation of the RS-232 serial cable. In this example, the connection depicted is a straight through-cabling scheme associated with PCs and PC XTs.

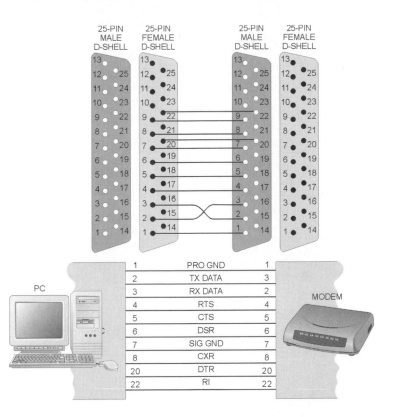

FIGURE 1.112
A 25-pin to 25-pin RS-232 cable.

Since the advent of the PC AT, the system's first serial port has typically been implemented in a 9-pin male D-shell connector on the DTE. Figure 1.113 depicts a typical 9-pin to 25-pin connection scheme. Notice the crossover wiring technique employed for the TXD/RXD lines displayed in this example. This type of connection became popular with the 9-pin PC AT serial port.

FIGURE 1.113
A 9-pin to 25-pin RS-232 cable.

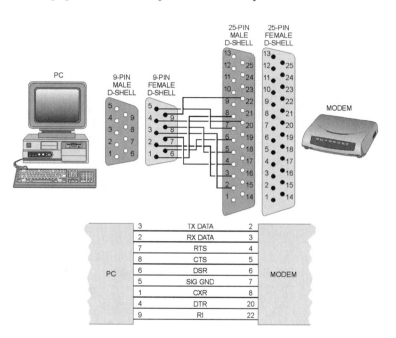

PC		MODEM
3	TX DATA	2
2	RX DATA	3
7	RTS	4
8	CTS	5
6	DSR	6
5	SIG GND	7
1	CXR	8
4	DTR	20
9	RI	22

In cases where the serial ports are located close enough to each other, a null modem connection can be implemented. A null modem connection allows the two serial ports to communicate directly without using modems. A typical null modem connection scheme is illustrated in Figure 1.114. Notice that, unlike the unidirectional serial printer connection, the null modem connection scheme crosses pins 4 and 5 between the DTE and DCE to facilitate two-way communications.

In any event, it should be apparent from the previous trio of figures that all serial cables are not created equal. Incorrect serial cabling can be a major problem when attaching third-party communication equipment to the computer. Read the DCE User Manual carefully to make certain the correct pins are being connected together.

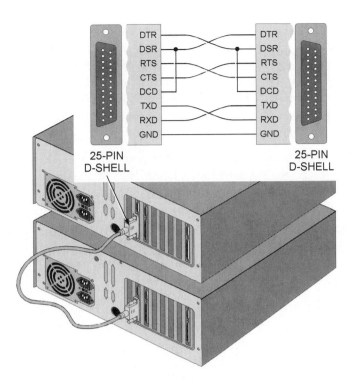

FIGURE 1.114
A null modem cable.

DOS Serial Port Names

As with parallel ports, DOS assigns COM port designations to the system's serial ports during boot up. COM port designations are normally COM1 and COM2 in most systems, but they can be extended to COM3 and COM4 in advanced systems.

Either RS-232 port can be designated as COM1, COM2, COM3, or COM4, so long as both ports are not assigned to the same COM port number. In most PCs, COM1 is assigned as port address hex 3F8h and uses IRQ channel 4. The COM2 port is typically assigned port address hex 2F8h and IRQ3. Likewise, COM3 uses IRQ4 and is assigned an I/O address of 3E8h; COM4 usually resides at 2E8 and uses IRQ3.

> **TEST TIP**
>
> Know the system addresses and other resources that a PC-compatible system uses for serial ports. It may be easy to remember that IBM set up these standards so that the odd-numbered COM ports use the even-numbered IRQ channel, and vice versa.

Game Ports

The game control adapter enables two *joysticks* to be used with the system. The adapter converts resistive input values into relative joystick positions. This adapter also can function as a general-purpose I/O converter, featuring four analog and four digital input points.

This interface is simple and straightforward, combining elementary hardware and software techniques. When the game software issues the game port's address (201h) along with an I/O Write signal, a group of timers in the port are triggered into action. Each timer output remains active for a length of time, proportional to the resistive input value of the joystick. As each timer times out according to its own resistive input, its output returns to an inactive state.

The game software periodically polls the port's address, along with an I/O Read signal, to determine whether any of the outputs have timed out. A software counter keeps track of the number of times the port has been polled before each timer times out. The number of polling cycles performed before a timer times out is directly proportional to the resistive setting of its joystick. The game software converts this value into screen-positioning information.

The input to the game port is generally a pair of resistive joysticks. Joysticks are defined as having two variable resistances, each of which should be variable between 0 and 100k ohms. Joysticks can have one or two normally open fire buttons. The order of fire buttons should correspond with that of the resistive elements (A and B or A, B, C, and D). The wiring structure for the 15-pin female D-shell connector is shown in Figure 1.115.

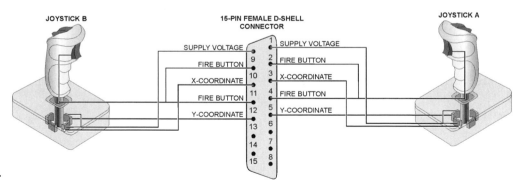

FIGURE 1.115
Game port connections.

Universal Serial Bus

A new serial interface scheme, called the *Universal Serial Bus* (USB), has been developed to provide a fast, flexible way to attach up to 127 peripheral devices to the computer. The USB provides a connection format designed to replace the system's traditional serial and parallel port connections.

USB peripherals can be daisy-chained, or networked together using connection hubs that enable the bus to branch out through additional port connections. A practical USB desktop connection scheme is presented in Figure 1.116.

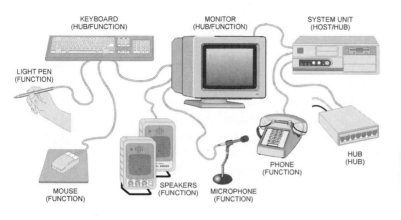

FIGURE 1.116
USB desktop connection scheme.

In this example, some of the peripheral devices are just devices, whereas others serve as both devices and connection hubs. The system provides a USB host connection that serves as the main USB connection.

USB devices can be added to or removed from the system while it is powered up and fully operational. This is referred to as hot swapping or hot plugging the device. The PnP capabilities of the system will detect the presence (or absence) of the device and configure it for operation.

> **TEST TIP**
> Remember how many devices can be attached to a single USB port.

> **TEST TIP**
> Be aware that USB devices can be plugged in and removed while power is applied and remember what this is called.

USB Cabling and Connectors

USB transfers are conducted over a four-wire cable, as illustrated in Figure 1.117. The signal travels over a pair of twisted wires (D+ and D–) in a 90-ohm cable. The differential signal and twisted-pair wiring provide minimum signal deterioration over distances and high-noise immunity.

A Vbus and ground (GND) wire also are present. The Vbus is the +5V DC power cord. The interface provides power to the peripheral attached to it. The root hub provides power directly from the host system to those devices directly connected to it. Hubs also supply power to the devices connected to them. Even though the interface supplies power to the USB devices, they are permitted to have their own power sources if necessary.

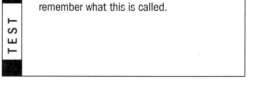

FIGURE 1.117
The USB cable.

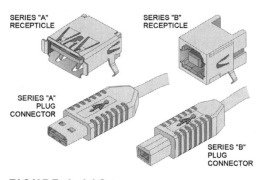

FIGURE 1.118
USB connectors.

In these instances, the device must be designed specifically to avoid interference with the power-distribution scheme of the bus. The USB host's power-management software can apply power to devices when needed and suspend power to it when not required.

The USB specification defines two types of plugs: Series A and Series B. Series A connectors are used for devices where the USB cable connection is permanently attached to devices at one end. Examples of these devices include keyboards, mice, and hubs. Conversely, the Series B plugs and jacks are designed for devices that require detachable cabling (printers, scanners, and modems, for example). Both are four-contact plugs and sockets embedded in plastic connectors, as shown in Figure 1.118. The sockets can be implemented in vertical, right-angle, and panel-mounted variations. The icon used to represent a USB connector is depicted by the centers of the A and B "plug connectors" in Figure 1.118.

The connectors for both series are keyed so that they cannot be plugged in backward. All hubs and functions possess a single, permanently attached cable with a Series B connector at its end. The connectors are designed so that the Series A and Series B connections cannot be interchanged.

IEEE-1394 Firewire Bus

While the USB specification was being refined for the computer industry, a similar serial interface bus was being developed for the consumer products market. Apple Computers and Texas Instruments worked together with the IEEE to produce the Firewire (or IEEE-1394) specification. The new bus offers a very fast option for connecting consumer electronics devices, such as camcorders and DVDs to the computer system.

The Firewire bus is similar to USB in that devices can be daisy-chained to the computer using a single connector and host adapter. It requires a single IRQ channel, an I/O address range, and a single DMA channel to operate. Firewire also can use the high-speed isochronous transfer mode described for USB to support data transfer rates up to 400Mbps. This actually makes the Firewire bus superior to the USB bus. Its high-speed capabilities make Firewire well suited for handling components, such as video and audio devices, which require real-time, high-speed data transfer rates.

A single IEEE-1394 connection can be used to connect up to 63 devices to a single port. However, up to 1,023 Firewire buses can be interconnected. PCs most commonly use a PCI expansion card to provide the Firewire interface. Whereas AV equipment typically employs 4-pin 1394 connectors, computers normally use a 6-pin connector, with a 4-pin to 6-pin converter. The maximum segment length for an IEEE-394 connection is 4.5m (14 ft.).

Figure 1.119 depicts the Firewire connector and plug most commonly used with PCs.

The IEEE-1394 cable is composed of two twisted-pair conductors similar to those used in the LANs described later in this chapter. Like USB, it supports both PnP and hot swapping of components. It also provides power to the peripheral devices through one pair of the twisted conductors in the interface cable.

Firewire operates in peer-to-peer mode and is supported in both the Windows 9x and Windows NT/2000 operating systems. Both operating systems support advanced Firewire operations by including support for three critical 1394-related specifications: OHCI, IEC 61883, and SBP-2. The Open Host Controller Interface (OHCI) standard defines the way Firewire interfaces to a PC. The IEC 61883 standard defines the details for controlling specific audio-video devices over the IEEE-1394 bus. The Serial Bus Protocol - 2 (SBP-2) specification defines standard ways of encapsulating device commands over 1394 and is essential for DVD players, printers, scanners, and other devices. The Home AV Interoperability (HAVi) standard is another layer of protocols for the Firewire specification. This standard is directed at making Firewire devices PnP capable in networks where no PC host is present.

A proposed version of the IEEE-1394 standard (titled P1394b) provides an additional electrical signaling method that permits data transmission speeds of 800Mbps and greater. The new version of the standard also supports new transport media including glass and plastic optical fiber, as well as Category 5 copper cable. With the new media comes extended distances (for instance, 100 meters over Cat5).

Infrared Ports

The Infrared Data Association (IrDA) has produced a wireless peripheral connection standard based on infrared light technology, similar to that used in consumer remote-control devices. Many

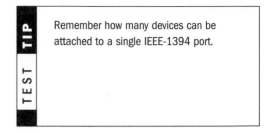

TEST TIP

Remember how many devices can be attached to a single IEEE-1394 port.

RECEPTACLE CONNECTOR

CABLE PLUG

FIGURE 1.119
Firewire plugs and connectors.

system board designs include an IrDA-compliant port standard to provide wireless communications with devices such as character printers, PDAs, and notebook computers. Figure 1.120 illustrates an IrDA-connected printer port. The same technology has been employed to carry out transfers between computer communications devices such as modems and LAN cards.

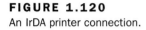

FIGURE 1.120
An IrDA printer connection.

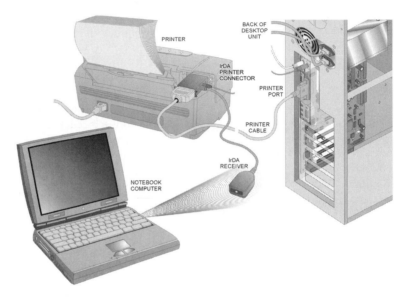

The IrDA standard specifies four protocols that are used with different types of devices:

◆ **IrLPT.** Used with character printers to provide a high-speed wireless interface between the computer and the printer.

◆ **IrDA-SIR.** The Standard infrared protocol used to provide a standard serial port interface with transfer rates ranging up to 115Kbps.

◆ **IrDA-FIR.** The Fast infrared protocol used to provide a high-speed serial port interface with transfer rates ranging up to 4Mbps.

◆ **IrTran-P.** Used to provide a digital image transfer standard for communications with digital image capture devices.

These protocols specify communication ranges up to 2 meters (6 feet), but most specifications usually state 1 meter as the maximum range. All IrDA transfers are carried out in half-duplex mode and must have a clear line of sight between the transmitter and receiver.

The receiver must be situated within 15 degrees of center with the line of transmission.

The Windows operating system supports the use of infrared devices. The properties of installed IrDA devices can be viewed through the Device Manager. Likewise, connections to another IrDA computer can be established through the Windows Network Dialup Connections applet. By installing a Point-to-Point Protocol (PPP) or an IrDA LAN protocol through this applet, you can conduct wireless communications with other computers without a modem or network card.

> **TEST TIP**
>
> Remember that the IrLPT port is a new, high-speed printer interface that can be used to print from a wide array of computing devices.

INSTALLING AND CONFIGURING DISK DRIVES

▶ 1.5 Identify proper procedures for installing and configuring IDE/EIDE devices.

▶ 1.6 Identify proper procedures for installing and configuring SCSI devices.

The A+ Core Hardware objective 1.5 states that the test taker should be able to "identify proper procedures for installing and configuring IDE/EIDE devices."

Examples include the following:

◆ Master/slave

◆ Devices per channel

The A+ Core Hardware objective 1.6 states that the test taker should be able to "identify proper procedures for installing and configuring SCSI devices."

Topics include the following:

◆ Address/termination conflicts

◆ Cabling

◆ Types (standard, wide, fast, ultra-wide)

◆ Internal versus external

◆ Switch and jumper settings

Hard disk drives are the mainstays of mass data storage in PC-compatible systems. In modern PC systems, IDE and SCSI drives are most commonly used. Therefore, the computer technician must be able to successfully install and configure both IDE and SCSI drives, as well as other devices that employ IDE and SCSI interfaces. The following sections cover the characteristics of these two interfaces, including standard variations and common connector types associated with each.

Integrated Drive Electronics Interface

The Integrated Drive Electronics (IDE) interface is a system-level interface. It is also referred to as an *AT Attachment* (ATA) interface. The IDE interface places most of the controller electronics on the drive unit. Therefore, data travels in parallel between the computer and the drive unit. The controller circuitry on the drive handles all the parallel-to-serial and serial-to-parallel conversions. This allows the interface to be independent of the host computer design.

An IDE drive stores low-level formatting information on itself. This information is placed on the drive by its manufacturer, and is used by the controller for alignment and sector sizing of the drive. The IDE controller extracts the raw data (format and actual data information) coming from the R/W heads and converts it into signal that can be applied to the computer's buses.

The standard IDE interface uses a single 40-pin cable to connect the hard drives to the adapter card or system board. Its signal cable arrangement is depicted in Figure 1.121. Some systems that employ system-level interfaces, such as an IDE interface, employed an adapter card called a host adapter rather than a controller card. These cards are referred to as host adapters rather than controller cards because they have no intelligent control devices on them. They just offer physical extensions of the system buses to the I/O device. It should be apparent from Figure 1.121 that the IDE host adapter is simple because most of the interface signals originate directly from the system's extended bus lines.

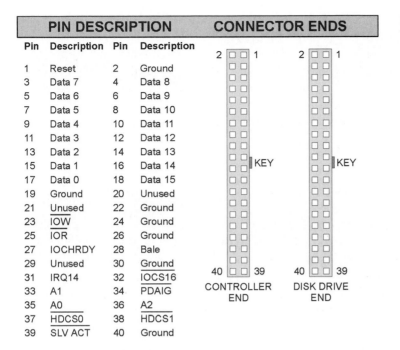

PIN DESCRIPTION				CONNECTOR ENDS
Pin	Description	Pin	Description	
1	Reset	2	Ground	
3	Data 7	4	Data 8	
5	Data 6	6	Data 9	
7	Data 5	8	Data 10	
9	Data 4	10	Data 11	
11	Data 3	12	Data 12	
13	Data 2	14	Data 13	
15	Data 1	16	Data 14	
17	Data 0	18	Data 15	
19	Ground	20	Unused	
21	Unused	22	Ground	
23	IOW	24	Ground	
25	IOR	26	Ground	
27	IOCHRDY	28	Bale	
29	Unused	30	Ground	
31	IRQ14	32	IOCS16	
33	A1	34	PDAIG	
35	A0	36	A2	
37	HDCS0	38	HDCS1	
39	SLV ACT	40	Ground	

FIGURE 1.121
The IDE signal cable.

Configuring IDE Drives

The host adapter basically serves three functions. These include providing the select signals to differentiate between a single drive system, or the master and slave drives. It also provides the three least significant address bits (A0–A2) and the interface reset signal. The HDCS0 signal is used to enable the master drive, and the HDCS1 signal is used to enable the slave drive. The relationship between the host adapter, the system buses, and the IDE interfaces are described in Figure 1.122.

Most IDE drives come from the manufacturer configured for operation as a single drive, or as the master drive in a multidrive system. To install the drive as a second (or slave) drive, it is usually necessary to install, remove, or to move a jumper block, as illustrated in Figure 1.123. Some hosts disable the interface's Cable Select pin for slave drives. With these types of hosts, it is necessary to install a jumper for the Cable Select option on the drive. Consult the system's User Manual to see whether it supports this function.

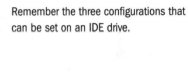

TEST TIP

Remember the three configurations that can be set on an IDE drive.

FIGURE 1.122

The host adapter, system buses, and IDE interface.

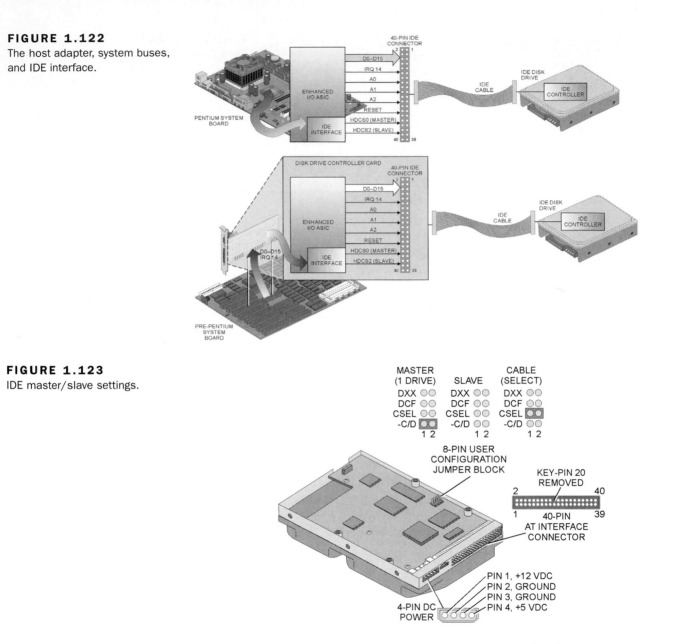

FIGURE 1.123

IDE master/slave settings.

In the MS-DOS system, the primary partitions of multiple IDE hard drives are assigned the first logical drive identifiers. If an IDE drive is partitioned into two logical drives, the system identifies them as the C: drive and the D: drive. If a second IDE drive is added as a slave drive with two additional logical drives, it reassigns the partitions on the first drive to be logical drives C: and E:, and the partitions on the slave drive become D: and F:.

Advanced EIDE Specifications

As mentioned previously in this chapter, updated IDE specifications have been developed that enable more than two drives to exist on the interface. This new specification is called Enhanced IDE (EIDE), or the ATA-2 interface, and permits up to four IDE devices to operate in a single system. Under this specification, the host supplies two IDE interfaces that can handle a master and a slave device in a daisy-chained configuration. The first interface is the primary IDE interface and is typically labeled IDE1. Likewise, the second IDE interface is the secondary IDE interface and is usually marked as IDE2, as illustrated in Figure 1.124.

Actually, the update covers more than just increasing the number of drives that can be accommodated. It also provides for improved IDE drivers, known as the AT Attachment Packet Interface (ATAPI), for use with CD-ROM drives, as well as new DMA data transfer methods.

In addition to the new DMA transfer modes, the fastest IDE enhancements—referred to as Ultra DMA (UDMA), ATA-4/Ultra ATA 66, and Ultra ATA 100—extend the high data throughput capabilities of the bus by increasing the number of conductors in the IDE signal cable to 80. Although the number of wires has doubled, the IDE connector has remained compatible with the 40-pin IDE connection; but each pin has been provided with its own ground conductor in the cable.

This fact becomes important when you install a newer EIDE drive in a system. If you use an older 40-wire IDE cable with a newer UDMA drive, the performance of the drive will be severely limited.

The IDE/EIDE interface has been the standard PC disk drive interface for some time. The IDE controller structure is an integrated portion of most PC system boards. This structure includes BIOS and chipset support for the IDE version the board will support, as well as the IDE host connector. For this reason, you should refer to Chapter 4 for additional information about advanced IDE bus specifications.

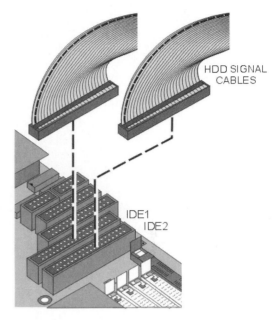

FIGURE 1.124
IDE1 and IDE2 identification.

TEST TIP

Remember that IDE bus driver support is built in to the BIOS of system boards that have integrated IDE host adapters.

Small Computer System Interface

The *Small Computer System Interface* (SCSI, often referred to as "scuzzy") standard, like the IDE concept, provides a true system-level interface for the drive. Nearly all the drive's controller electronics are located on the peripheral device. As with the IDE host adapter, the duties of the *SCSI host adapter* are reduced to mostly physical connection functions, along with some signal-compatibility handling.

Using this arrangement, data arrives at the system interface in a form that is already usable by the host computer. This can be seen through the SCSI interface description in Figure 1.125. Note that the original SCSI interface described in Figure 1.125 makes provisions only for 8-bit parallel data transfers.

PIN DESCRIPTION				CONNECTOR ENDS
Pin	**Description**	**Pin**	**Description**	
1	Ground	2	Data 0	
3	Ground	4	Data 1	
5	Ground	6	Data 2	
7	Ground	8	Data 3	
9	Ground	10	Data 4	
11	Ground	12	Data 5	
13	Ground	14	Data 6	
15	Ground	16	Data 7	
17	Ground	18	Data Parity (Odd)	
19	Ground	20	Ground	
21	Ground	22	Ground	
23	Ground	24	Ground	
25	No Connection	26	No Connection	
27	Ground	28	Ground	
29	Ground	30	Ground	
31	Ground	32	Attention	
33	Ground	34	Ground	
35	Ground	36	Busy	
37	Ground	38	ACK	
39	Ground	40	Reset	
41	Ground	42	Message	
43	Ground	44	Select	
45	Ground	46	C/D	
47	Ground	48	Request	
49	Ground	50	I/O	

CONTROLLER END   DISK-DRIVE END

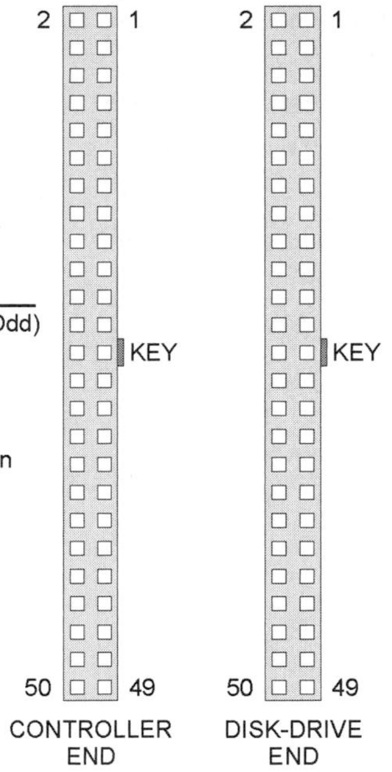

FIGURE 1.125
The SCSI interface connection.

The SCSI interface can be used to connect diverse types of peripherals to the system. As an example, a SCSI chain could connect a controller to a hard drive, a CD-ROM drive, a high-speed tape drive, a scanner, and a printer. Additional SCSI devices are added to the system by daisy-chaining them together. The input of the second device is attached to the SCSI output of the first device, and so forth.

SCSI Cables and Connectors

The SCSI standard has been implemented using a number of cable types. In PC-compatible systems, the SCSI interface uses a 50-pin signal cable arrangement. Internally, the cable is a 50-pin flat-ribbon cable. However, a 50-pin, shielded cable with Centronics-like connectors is used for external SCSI connections. The 50-pin SCSI connections are referred to as A-cables.

Advanced SCSI specification have created additional cabling specifications. A 50-conductor alternative cable, using 50-pin D-shell connectors has been added to the A-cable specification for SCSI-2 devices. A second cable type, referred to as B-cable, was added to the SCSI-2 specification to provide 16- and 32-bit parallel data transfers. However, this arrangement employed multiple connectors at each end of the cable and never received widespread acceptance in the market. A revised 68-pin P-cable format, using D-shell connectors, was introduced to support 16-bit transfers in the *SCSI-3* specification. A 68-pin Q-cable version also was adopted in SCSI for 32-bit transfers. The P and Q cables must be used in parallel to conduct 32-bit transfers.

For some PS/2 models, IBM used a special 60-pin Centronics-like connector for their SCSI connections. The version of the SCSI interface used in the Apple Macintosh employs a variation of the standard that features a proprietary, miniature 25-pin D-shell connector.

These cabling variations create a hardware incompatibility between different SCSI devices. Likewise, some SCSI devices just do not work with each other due to software incompatibilities.

In addition, SCSI devices can be classified as internal or as external devices. An internal SCSI device has no power supply of its own and, therefore, must be connected to one of the system's option's power connectors. On the other hand, external SCSI devices come with built-in or plug-in power supplies that need to be connected to a commercial AC outlet. Therefore, when choosing a SCSI device, always inquire about compatibility between it and any other SCSI devices installed in the system.

Figure 1.126 depicts both a 25-pin D-shell and a 50-pin Centronics-type SCSI connector used for external connections. Inside the computer, the SCSI specification uses a 50-pin ribbon cable with BERG pin connectors.

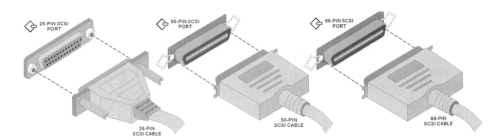

FIGURE 1.126
SCSI connectors.

SCSI Addressing

The SCSI specification permits up to eight SCSI devices to be connected together. The SCSI port can be daisy-chained to allow up to six external peripherals to be connected to the system. To connect multiple SCSI devices to a SCSI host, all the devices, except the last one, must have two SCSI connectors: one for SCSI-In, and one for SCSI-Out. Which connector is which does not matter. If the device has only one SCSI connector, however, it must be connected to the end of the chain.

It is possible to use multiple SCSI host adapters within a single system to increase the number of devices that can be used. The system's first SCSI controller can handle up to 7 devices; the additional SCSI controller can boost the system to support up to 14 SCSI devices.

Each SCSI device in a chain must have a unique ID number assigned to it. Even though there are a total of eight possible SCSI ID numbers for each controller, only six are available for use with external devices. Most SCSI controller cards are set to SCSI-7 by default from their manufacturers. Historically, many manufacturers have classified the first internal hard drive as SCSI-0. In other cases, most notably IBM, the manufacturer routinely uses ID 2 for the first SCSI hard drive and ID 6 for the host adapter. In most newer systems, it typically does not matter which devices are set to which ID settings. If two SCSI devices in a system are set to the same ID number, however, one or both of them will appear invisible to the system. The priority levels assigned to SCSI devices are determined by their ID number, with the highest numbered device receiving the highest priority.

With older SCSI devices, address settings were established through jumpers on the host adapter card. Each device had a SCSI number selection switch, or a set of configuration jumpers for establishing its ID number. Figure 1.127 illustrates a three-jumper configuration block that can be used to establish the SCSI ID number. In Figure 1.127, an open jumper pair can be counted as a binary 0, whereas a shorted pair represents a binary 1. With a three-pair jumper block, it is possible to represent the numbers 0 through 7. In PnP systems, the BIOS configures the device addresses using information obtained directly from the SCSI host adapter during the boot-up process.

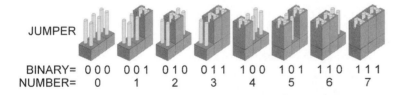

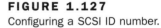

FIGURE 1.127
Configuring a SCSI ID number.

Unlike other HDD types, SCSI hard drives are not configured as part of the system's CMOS Setup function. This is due to the fact that DOS and Windows 3.x never included support for SCSI devices. Therefore, SCSI drivers must be loaded during boot up before the system can communicate with the drive. However, Windows 9x does offer SCSI support. SCSI drives also require no low-level formatting. Therefore, the second thing you do when installing a SCSI drive is partition it.

SCSI Termination

The SCSI daisy chain must be terminated with a resistor network pack at both ends. Single-connector SCSI devices are normally terminated internally. If not, a SCSI terminator cable (containing a built-in resistor pack) must be installed at the end of the chain.

TEST TIP

Be aware of how SCSI ID priorities are set.

SCSI termination is a major cause of SCSI-related problems. Poor terminations cause a variety of different system problems, including the following:

◆ Failed system startups

◆ Hard drive crashes

◆ Random system failures

SCSI Specifications

Maximum recommended length for a complete standard SCSI chain is 20 feet (6 meters). Unless the cables are heavily shielded, however, they become susceptible to data corruption caused by induced noise. Therefore, a maximum single SCSI segment of less than 3 feet (1 meter) is recommended. Do not forget the length of the internal cabling when dealing with SCSI cable distances. You can realistically count on about 3 feet of internal cable, so reduce the maximum total length of the chain to about 15 feet (4.5 meters).

An updated SCSI specification was developed by the ANSI committee to double the number of data lines in the standard interface. It also adds balanced, dual-line drivers that enable much faster data transfer speeds to be used. This implementation is referred to as Wide SCSI-2. The specification expands the SCSI specification into a 16/32-bit bus standard and increased the cable and connector specification to 68 pins.

An additional improvement increased the synchronous data transfer option for the interface from 5Mbps to 10Mbps. This implementation became known as *Fast SCSI-2*. Under this system, the system and the I/O device conduct nondata message, command, and status operations in 8-bit asynchronous mode. After agreeing on a larger, or faster, file transfer format, they conduct transfers using an agreed-upon word size and transmission mode. The increased speed of the Fast SCSI specification reduced the maximum length of the SCSI chain to about 10 feet. Fast SCSI-2 connections use 50-pin connectors.

A third version brought together both improvements and became known as *Wide Fast SCSI-2*. This version of the standard doubles the bus size to 16 bits and employs the faster transfer methods to provide a maximum bus speed of 20MBps supporting a chain of up to 15 additional devices.

A newer update, referred to as Ultra SCSI, makes provisions for a special high-speed serial transfer mode and special communications media, such as fiber-optic cabling. This update has been combined with both Wide and Fast revisions to produce the following:

◆ Ultra SCSI

◆ Ultra2 SCSI

◆ Wide Ultra SCSI

◆ Wide Ultra2 SCSI

◆ Wide Ultra3 SCSI

The addition of the Wide specification doubles the bus width and number of devices that can be serviced by the interface. Likewise, the Ultra designation indicates a speed increase because of improved technology. Combining the two technologies will yield a 4× increase in data throughput. (For instance, Wide-Ultra SCSI = 40MBps compared to Ultra SCSI = 20MBps and Wide and Fast SCSI = 10MBps.)

The latest SCSI specification, referred to as Ultra 320 SCSI, boosts the maximum bus speed to 320MBps, using a 16-bit bus and supporting up to 15 external devices. The Ultra 320 SCSI connection employs a special 80-pin single connector attachment (SCA) connector.

The increased speed capabilities of the SCSI interfaces make them attractive for intensive applications such as large file servers for networks and for multimedia video stations. However, the EIDE interface is generally more widely used due to its lower cost and nearly equal performance. Table 1.10 contrasts the specifications of the SCSI and IDE interfaces.

> **TEST TIP**
>
> Know the number of devices that can be attached to an IDE, EIDE, and standard SCSI interfaces.

TABLE 1.10

SCSI/IDE SPECIFICATIONS

Interface	Bus Size	Number of Devices	Async. Speed	Sync Speed
IDE	16 bits	2	4MBps	-
EIDE (ATA-2)	16 bits	4	4MBps	16MBps
SCSI (SCSI-1)	8 bits	7	2MBps	5MBps
Wide SCSI (SCSI-2)	8/16 bits	15	2MBps	5MBps
Fast SCSI (SCSI-2)	8/16 bits	7	2MBps	5/10MBps
Wide Fast SCSI	8/16 bits	15	2MBps	10/20MBps
Ultra SCSI	8 bits	7	2MBps	10/20MBps
Wide Ultra SCSI	16 bits	15	2MBps	10/20/40MBps
Ultra2 SCSI	8 bits	7	2MBps	10/20/40MBps
Wide Ultra2 SCSI	16 bits	15	2MBps	10/20/40/80MBps
Wide Ultra3 SCSI	16 bits	15	2MBps	10/20/40/160MBps
Ultra 320 SCSI	16 bits	15	2MBps	10/20/40/320MBps

INSTALLING AND CONFIGURING PERIPHERAL DEVICES

▶ 1.7 Identify proper procedures for installing and configuring peripheral devices.

The A+ Core Hardware objective 1.7 states that the test taker should be able to "identify proper procedures for installing and configuring peripheral devices."

Topics include the following:

◆ Monitor/video card

◆ Modem

◆ USB peripherals and hubs

◆ IEEE-1284

◆ IEEE-1394

◆ External storage

Examples of portable system components:

◆ Docking stations

◆ PC Cards

◆ Port replicators

◆ Infrared devices

In addition to installing hard drives and peripheral devices that connect to standard I/O ports, technicians must be able to successfully install and configure peripheral devices (or systems) that connect to the system in other ways—such as through the system's expansion slots. The following sections deal with installing the system's video output components, internal and external modems, and alternative data storage systems.

Video/Monitor Systems

The video display system is one of the easiest systems to add to the computer. The components associated with the video display are depicted in Figure 1.128. The video adapter card typically plugs into one of the system's expansion slots. The monitor's signal cable plugs into the video adapter card. The monitor's power cord can be plugged into a commercial wall outlet, or it can be attached to the special power outlet provided by the power-supply unit. Using this outlet allows the monitor to be turned on and off along with the system unit.

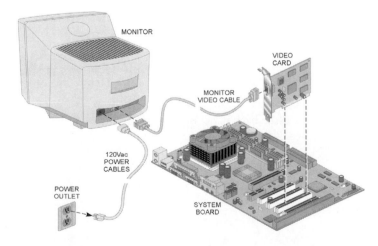

FIGURE 1.128
Video system components.

In a command-prompt mode, such as one of the Windows 9x or Windows 2000 safe-mode options, the video display should come up in text mode with no further effort. If the Windows operating system is being used, the video adapter's driver must be loaded before Windows can be loaded and run.

Modems

The steps for installing a modem vary somewhat depending on whether it is an internal or external device. The steps for both procedures are covered in Step by Step 1.5 and Step by Step 1.6.

STEP BY STEP

1.5 Installing an Internal Modem

1. Prepare the system for installation.
   a. Turn the system off.
   b. Remove the cover from system unit.
   c. Locate a compatible empty expansion slot.
   d. Remove the expansion slot cover from the rear of the system unit.

2. Configure the modem's IRQ and COM settings.
   a. Refer to modem's User Manual regarding any IRQ and COM jumper or switch settings.
   b. Record the card's default IRQ and COM settings.
   c. Set the modem's configuration jumpers to operate the modem as COM2.

3. Install the modem card in the system.
   a. Install the modem card in the expansion slot.
   b. Reinstall the screw to secure the modem card to the back panel of the system unit.

c. Connect the phone line to the appropriate connector on the modem, as shown in Figure 1.129.

d. Connect the other end of the phone line to the commercial phone jack.

4. Disable any competing COM ports.

a. Disable COM2 on the MI/O adapter.

5. Finish the hardware installation.

a. Replace the system unit cover.

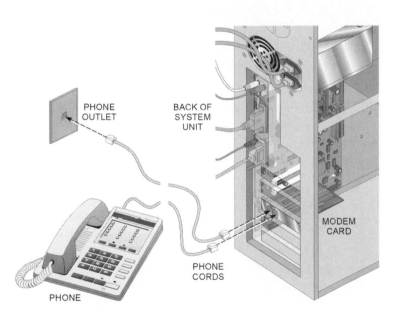

FIGURE 1.129
Installing an internal modem.

It is necessary to disable the COM2 port because the system looks to see how many COM ports are available when it boots up. Even if no device is connected to a COM port, the computer knows the port is there. By disabling this setting, possible interrupt conflict problems are avoided. In addition, some communication software will assign a COM port to an empty serial port. By disabling the port, software that assigns empty COM ports will not see the port at all, and therefore, no conflict will occur.

STEP BY STEP

1.6 Installing an External Modem

1. Make the modem connections.

   a. Connect the serial cable to the 25-pin serial port at the rear of the system.

   b. Connect the opposite end of the cable to the RS-232 connector of the external modem unit.

   c. Connect the phone line to the appropriate connector on the modem.

   d. Connect the other end of the phone line to the phone system jack.

   e. Optionally, connect the phone to the appropriate connector on the modem.

   f. Verify that the power switch or power supply is turned off.

   g. Connect the power supply to the external modem unit.

   h. Verify this connection arrangement in Figure 1.130.

2. Enable the system's internal support circuitry.

   a. Remove the cover from system unit.

   b. Enable COM2 on the system board or MI/O adapter.

   c. Replace the system unit cover.

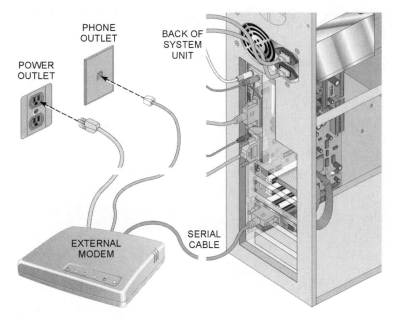

FIGURE 1.130
Installing an external modem.

Modem Configuration

The parameters for control of the modem, or its supporting COM port, must be established in software. The character frame must be established along with the port's baud rate and flow-control information. The method of controlling the flow of information between the two devices must be agreed to by both devices for the transfer to be successful.

Examine the communications software being used to drive the modem to determine which elements need to be configured (see Step by Step 1.7).

STEP BY STEP

1.7 Configuring the Modem

1. Install and configure the communications software package.

    a. Locate the modem's communication software.

    b. Locate the software documentation.

    c. Locate the installation instructions inside the manual.

    d. Follow the instructions in the manual and on the screen to install the software.

    e. Configure the software to match the system's hardware settings.

2. Set up Windows COM ports and character-frame information.

    a. Establish the baud rate, character frame, and flow-control information in the Windows Control Panel.

    b. Set up the IRQ, COM port, and base-address settings in the Control Panel for the COM port the modem is using.

Communications Software

All modems require software to control the communication session. This software is typically included with the purchase of the modem and must be configured to operate in the system the modem will be used in.

At the fundamental instruction level, most modem software employs a set of commands known as the *Hayes-compatible command set*. This set of commands is named after the Hayes Microcomputer Products company that first defined them.

In the Hayes command structure, the operation of the modem shifts back and forth between a command mode and a communications mode. In the command mode, the modem exchanges commands and status information with the host system's microprocessor. In communications mode, the modem facilitates sending and receiving data, between the local system and a remote system. A short guard period between communications mode and command mode allows the system to switch smoothly, without interrupting a data transmission.

Protocols

To maintain an orderly flow of information between the computer and the modem, and between the modem and another modem, a *protocol*, or set of rules governing the transfer of information, must be in place. All the participants in the "conversation" must use the same protocols to communicate.

The following two distinct classes of protocols are in widespread use with modems today:

◆ Hardware-oriented protocols

◆ Control-code-oriented protocols

Hardware-Oriented Protocols

Hardware-oriented protocols are tied to the use of particular interface pins to control data flow. As far as standalone modems are concerned, the most basic hardware standard is the RS-232C serial interface standard. Within the realm of the RS-232 standard, however, a proliferation of communication methods exist.

The RS-232C standard begins by identifying communication equipment using two categories:

◆ Data Terminal Equipment (DTE), usually a computer

◆ Data Communication Equipment (DCE), usually a modem

The term DTE refers to any equipment that has data processing as its main purpose. On the other hand, any communication equipment that changes data during transmission is referred to as DCE. Figure 1.131 illustrates typical DTE/DCE relationship.

FIGURE 1.131

The DTE/DCE relationship.

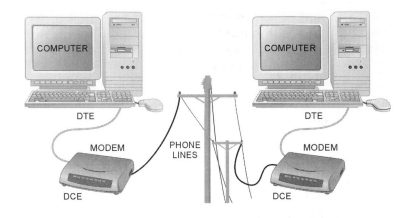

In its most basic form, the RS-232C interface makes provision for full-duplex operating mode through its Transmitted Data (TXD) and Received data (RXD) pins. Normally, data passes from the DTE to the DCE on the TXD line, and from the DCE to the DTE on the RXD line, although these two pins can sometimes be reversed.

The two most common forms of hardware protocols are DTR and RTS, named after the interface's Data Terminal Ready and Request To Send pins. These lines are toggled on and off to control when to send, and not send, data. The DTE uses the RTS pin to inform the DCE that it is ready to send data.

The DCE uses a trio of reciprocal lines signal the DTE: Clear to Send (CTS), Data Set Ready (DSR), and Data Carrier Detect (DCD). It uses the CTS line to inform the DTE that it is ready to accept data. The modem uses the DSR line to notify the DTE that it is connected to the phone line.

Control-Code-Oriented Protocols

Most data flow control is performed using the control-code class of protocols. Of this class of protocols, three types are in widespread use:

◆ XON/XOFF

◆ ACK/NAK

◆ ETX/ACK

In these protocols, control codes are sent across the data lines to control data flow, as opposed to using separate control lines.

The XON/XOFF protocol, where *X* represents two special control characters, is a relatively simple concept used to regulate data flow. This control is necessary to prevent buffer memories from overfilling. When data overflows the buffer, the result is usually an error code. The XON/XOFF protocol uses special control characters to start, and stop, data flow.

The ACK/NAK and ETX/ACK protocols are considered to be *high-level protocols* because they require special interface programs called *device drivers* to be installed. In both cases, these protocols use special control characters, and escape-code sequences, to provide functions such as data transmission integrity, flow control, requests for retransmission, and so forth.

The ACK/NAK protocol derives its title from the ASCII control characters for ACKnowledge, and Not ACKnowledge. It uses these characters to provide a means of error correction for transmitted data. Basically, the ACK/NAK protocol expects a block of data to be preceded by a Start-Of-Text (STX) character, and to be followed by both an End-Of-Text (ETX) character and an error-checking code, as depicted in Figure 1.132. At the receiving end, the Block Check Character (BCC) is checked for errors. Depending on the outcome of the check, either an ACK signal will be returned, indicating a successful transmission, or a NAK signal, indicating an error has occurred. If a NAK signal is returned, the transmitting device responds by retransmitting the entire block.

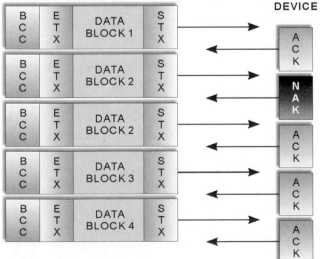

FIGURE 1.132
ACK/NAK transmission.

The ETX/ACK protocol is somewhat simpler than ACK/NAK, in that no character check is performed. If the receiving device does not return an ACK signal within a predetermined length of time, the sending device assumes an error or malfunction has occurred and retransmits the character block.

Error-Correcting Protocols

Several error-correcting file transfer protocols have been developed for modem communications packages. Some of the more common protocols include the following:

- ◆ Xmodem
- ◆ Ymodem
- ◆ Zmodem
- ◆ Kermit

> **TEST TIP**
> Know the fundamental difference between parity error checking and error-checking and error-correcting protocols.

These protocols use extensive error-detection schemes to maintain the validity of the data as its being transmitted. Error-detecting and error-correcting protocols generate more exotic error-detection algorithms, such as checksum and cyclic redundancy checks (CRCs), to identify, locate, and possibly correct data errors.

Compression Protocols

Advanced communication protocols use *data-compression techniques* to reduce the volume of data that must be transmitted. Each protocol involves a mathematical algorithm that reads the data and converts it into encoded words. The modem at the receiving end must use the same algorithm to decode the words and restore them to their original form.

Some modem compression standards reach ratios as high as 4:1. The major standards for modem data compression have come from a company named Microcom and from the Comite Consultatif International Telegraphique et Telephonique (CCITT) worldwide standards organization. The Microcom Networking Protocol level7 (MNP7) standard can produce 3:1 compression ratios, and the CCITT v.42bis standard reaches 4:1.

The CCITT standards are identified by a v.xx nomenclature. The original CCITT standard was the v.22 protocol that established transfers at 1,200bps using 600 baud. The v.22bis standard followed providing 2,400bps transfers at 600 baud. The v.32 protocol increased the bps rate to 4,800 and 9,600.

The CCITT standards also include an error-correction and a data-compression protocol. The v.42 standard is the error-correction protocol, and the v.42bis protocol is the CCITT equivalent of the MNP5 and MNP7 protocols. Both protocols run as modules along with the v.32 and v.32bis protocols to provide additional transmission speed.

The MNP Microcom standards began with protocols MNP2 through MNP4. These standards dealt with error-correction protocols. The MNP5 and MNP7 standards followed as the first data-compression protocols. The MNP10 standard introduced the first adverse channel-enhancement protocol. This type of protocol is designed to provide maximum performance for modems used in typically poor-connection applications, such as cellular phones. It features multiple connection attempts and automatically adjusted transmission rates. Like the advanced CCITT protocols, the MNP10 protocol module runs along with a v.42 protocol to maximize the data-transmission rate. Newer CCITT and MNP protocols provide modems with 56Kbps transmission capabilities.

During a special training period conducted at lower speeds, the modem tests the integrity of the transmission medium. The modem then negotiates with the remote modem to determine the maximum transfer rate for the existing line conditions.

Character Framing

Within a particular protocol, a number of parameters must be agreed upon before an efficient exchange of information can occur. Chief among these parameters are character type and character framing. Basically, character type refers to the character set, or alphabet, understood by the devices. Depending on the systems, the character set may be an 8-bit, ASCII line code; a 7-bit, ASCII code (with an error-checking bit); or an EBCDIC code.

Character framing refers to the total number of the bits used to transmit a character. This includes the length of the coded character and the number and type of overhead bits required for transmitting it. A common character-framing scheme calls for a start bit, 7 data bits, an odd-parity bit, and a stop bit, as depicted in Figure 1.133. An additional bit is often added to the frame for error-checking purposes.

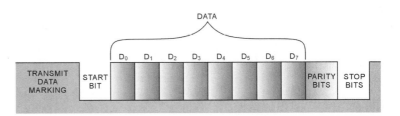

FIGURE 1.133
Asynchronous character format.

Although this is a typical character-framing technique, it is not universal throughout the industry. The problem here is one of device comprehension. The local unit may be using a 10-bit character frame consisting of a start bit, 7 data bits, an odd-parity bit, and a stop bit. If the remote system is using something besides 7-bit, odd-parity ASCII, with one stop bit, however, the response from it would be unintelligible as anything written in English. The composition of the character frame must be the same at both the sending and receiving ends of the transmission.

Peripheral Storage Devices

As mentioned earlier, external storage devices normally connect to options adapter cards installed in the system board's expansion slots. They also tend to employ separate, external power-supply units.

Several newer storage technologies, such as removable hard drive media, have been designed to take advantage of enhanced parallel port specifications of modern systems. These devices can be connected directly into the system's parallel port, or can be connected through another device that is connected to the port. The device's installation software is used to configure it for use in the system. To install an external storage device, see Step by Step 1.8.

STEP BY STEP

1.8 Installing External Storage Devices

1. Configure the device for operation.

    a. Refer to the device's User Manual for information regarding any IRQ and COM jumper or switch settings.

    b. Record the card's default IRQ and COM settings.

    c. Set the device's configuration jumpers to operate at the default setting.

2. Install the device's adapter card (if necessary).

    a. Turn the system off.

    b. Remove the cover from system unit.

    c. Locate a compatible empty expansion slot.

    d. Remove the expansion slot cover from the rear of the system unit.

    e. Install the adapter card in the expansion slot.

    f. Reinstall the screw to secure the card to the back panel of the system unit.

3. Make the device's external connections.

    a. Connect the device's signal cable to the appropriate connector at the rear of the system.

    b. Connect the opposite end of the cable to the device.

    c. Verify that the power switch or power supply is turned off.

    d. Connect the power supply to the external storage unit.

4. Configure the device's software.

    a. Turn the system on.

    b. Check the CMOS setup to ensure that the port setting is correct.

    c. Run the device's installation routine.

Configuring Advanced Ports

Most *device drivers* new I/O port and bus types (for instance, USB, IEEE-1394, PCMCIA, and IrDA) feature *hot insertion* and removal, as well as PnP operation. The devices that use these ports and buses are designed to be plugged in and removed as needed. Installing these ports or their devices is nearly a hands-off operation.

While the operation of the USB and Firewire buses actually resembles that of local area networking architectures (covered in Chapter 6), in complexity and capabilities, they are much easier to implement.

Installing one of these devices normally involves the following steps:

1. Enable the USB or Firewire resources in the CMOS Setup screen, as illustrated in Figure 1.134. In some cases, this involves enabling the port and reserving an IRQ resource for the device.

2. Plug the device into an open USB or Firewire connector.

3. Wait for the operating system to recognize the device and configure it through the PnP process.

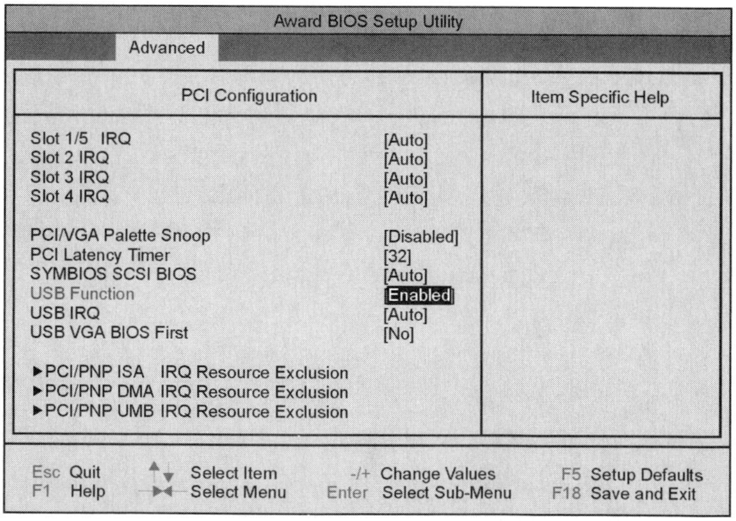

```
                        Award BIOS Setup Utility
         Advanced

              PCI Configuration                    Item Specific Help

  Slot 1/5  IRQ                    [Auto]
  Slot 2 IRQ                       [Auto]
  Slot 3 IRQ                       [Auto]
  Slot 4 IRQ                       [Auto]

  PCI/VGA Palette Snoop            [Disabled]
  PCI Latency Timer                [32]
  SYMBIOS SCSI BIOS                [Auto]
  USB Function                     [Enabled]
  USB IRQ                          [Auto]
  USB VGA BIOS First               [No]

  ▶PCI/PNP ISA   IRQ Resource Exclusion
  ▶PCI/PNP DMA IRQ Resource Exclusion
  ▶PCI/PNP UMB IRQ Resource Exclusion

  Esc  Quit        ▲▼  Select Item      -/+  Change Values      F5  Setup Defaults
  F1   Help        ◄►  Select Menu    Enter  Select Sub-Menu    F18 Save and Exit
```

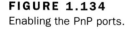

FIGURE 1.134
Enabling the PnP ports.

In the case of the Microsoft Windows 2000 operating system, the operating system detects the presence of the USB or Firewire device and starts its Found New Hardware Wizard program, depicted in Figure 1.135, to guide you through the installation process. Just follow the instructions provided by the wizard to set up the new device; there is no need to shut down or turn off the computer. You can find more information about the USB and Firewire ports in Chapter 4.

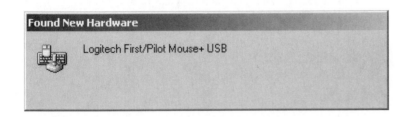

FIGURE 1.135
The Windows Found New Hardware Wizard.

Installing an IrDA device in an infrared-enable system is even easier. When an IrDA device is installed in the system, a Wireless Link icon appears in the Windows Control Panel, as depicted in Figure 1.136. When another IrDA device comes within range of the host port, the icon appears on the Windows desktop and in the taskbar. In the case of an IrDA printer, a printer icon appears in the Printer folder.

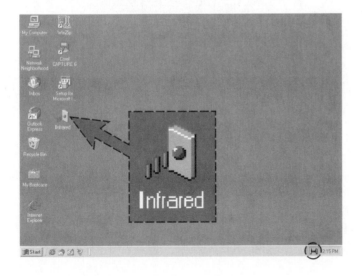

FIGURE 1.136
The Windows Wireless Link icon.

PORTABLE PERIPHERALS

The basic portable should contain all the devices that the user needs to do work while away from the office. Users have become accustomed to using additional items with their computers, however. For this reason, portable computers typically offer a full range of I/O port types. In addition, the portable computer manufacturers have produced an extensive array of products that can be added to a basic portable system to enhance its performance.

Docking Stations

A docking station, or docking port, is a specialized structure that allows the notebook unit to be inserted into it. When the notebook is inside, the docking port extends its expansion bus so that it can be used with a collection of desktop devices, such as an AC power source, a full-sized keyboard and CRT monitor, as well as modems, mice, and standard PC port connectors. Figure 1.137 depicts a typical docking station.

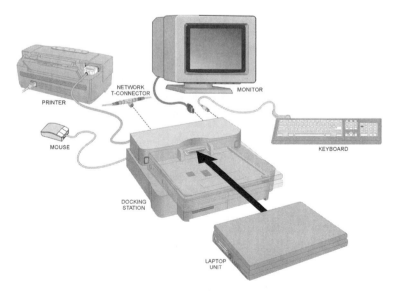

FIGURE 1.137
A docking station.

The notebook and the docking station communicate with each other through a special docking port connector in the rear of the notebook. When the notebook is inserted into the docking station, the extension bus in the docking station plugs into the expansion connector in the notebook. Most docking stations provide standard PC expansion slots so that non-notebook peripheral devices, such as network adapters and sound cards, can be used with the system.

When the notebook is in the docking station, its normal I/O devices (keyboard, display, and pointing device) are disabled and the docking station's peripherals take over.

For the most part, docking stations are proprietary to the portable for which they were designed to work. The docking port connection in the docking station must correctly align with the connector in the notebook. The notebook unit also must fit correctly within the docking station opening. Because there are no standards for these systems, the chances of two different manufacturers locating the connectors and/or designing the same case outline are very remote.

External Drive Units

The first laptops and notebooks incorporated the traditional single floppy drive and single hard drive concept that was typical in most desktop units. As CD-ROM drives and discs became the norm for new operating systems and software packages, however, a dilemma was created. There is just not enough room in most notebook computers for three, normal-size drive units. Even with reduced-size drives, the size limitations of most portables require that one of the three major drives be external.

External FDDs

Typically, the first item to be left out of a new notebook design is the internal floppy drive. So much of the latest software is distributed on CD-ROM that those drives now have preference in newer designs. Even so, because so many applications still use floppy disks, an external FDD is almost always an add-on option for a new notebook. Because large volumes of software are still available on floppy disks (and so many users have cherished data stored on floppy disks), an additional unit usually makes sense.

The external floppy comes as a complete unit with an external housing and a signal cable. As with other external devices, it requires an independent power source, such as an AC adapter pack. The external floppy drive's signal cable generally connects to a special FDD connector, such as the one shown in Figure 1.138.

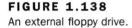

FIGURE 1.138
An external floppy drive.

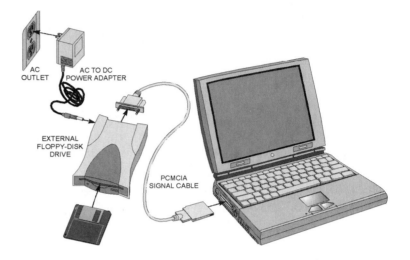

External CD-ROM Drives

Prior to the CD-ROM drive becoming an accepted part of the notebook PC, some manufacturers produced external CD-ROM drives for use with these machines. They are still available as add-ons to all types of PCs. External CD-ROM drives typically connect to a SCSI host adapter or to an enhanced parallel port. The latter connection requires a fully functional, bidirectional parallel port and a special software device driver.

Figure 1.139 illustrates the installation of an external SCSI CD-ROM drive. Because the drive is external, connecting the CD-ROM unit to the system usually involves just connecting a couple of cables together. First, connect the CD-ROM's power supply to the external drive unit. Before making this connection, verify that the power switch, or power supply, is turned off. Connect the signal cable to the computer. Finally, connect the opposite end of the cable to the external CD-ROM unit. Complete the installation by installing the CD-ROM driver software on the system's hard disk drive.

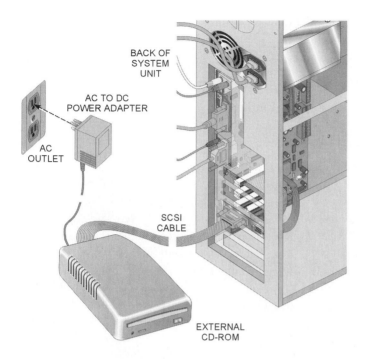

FIGURE 1.139
Installing an external CD-ROM drive.

BACK OF
SYSTEM
UNIT

AC TO DC
POWER ADAPTER

AC
OUTLET

SCSI
CABLE

EXTERNAL
CD-ROM

System Upgrading and Optimizing

▶ 1.8 Identify hardware methods of upgrading system performance, procedures for replacing basic subsystem components, unique components and when to use them.

The A+ Core Hardware objective 1.8 states that the test taker should be able to "identify hardware methods of upgrading system performance, procedures for replacing basic subsystem components, unique components and when to use them."

Examples include the following:

◆ Memory

◆ Hard drives

◆ Processors/CPU

◆ Upgrading BIOS

◆ When to upgrade BIOS

Examples of portable system components:

◆ Battery

◆ Hard drive

◆ Type I, II, III cards

◆ Memory

The modular design of the PC-compatible system enables portions of the system to be upgraded, as new or better, components become available, or as the system's application changes. As this A+ objective points out, computer technicians must be able to upgrade the system's BIOS as part of a system upgrade. Technicians also should be able to optimize PC hardware to obtain the best performance possible for a given system configuration. The following sections cover upgradeable components found in common PC systems, including information about when and how to upgrade them.

System Board Upgrading

There are typically five serviceable components on the system board. These include the following:

◆ The microprocessor

◆ The RAM modules

◆ The CMOS backup battery

◆ The ROM BIOS IC(s)

◆ The cache memory

Of the five items listed, three—the microprocessor, the RAM modules, and the cache memory—can be exchanged to increase the performance of the system. These devices are normally mounted in sockets to make replacing or upgrading them an easy task.

Take great care when exchanging these parts to avoid damage to the ICs from electrostatic discharge (ESD). ESD prevention is covered in detail in Chapter 3. In addition, take care during the extraction and replacement of the ICs to avoid misalignment and bent pins. Make sure to correctly align the IC's pin 1 with the socket's pin 1 position.

As mentioned earlier in this chapter, microprocessor manufacturers have devised upgrade versions for virtually every type of microprocessor in the market. It is also common for clone microprocessors to be pin-for-pin compatible with older Intel socket designs. This strategy enables the end user to realize a speed increase by upgrading, along with an increase in processing power.

Upgrading the processor is a fairly easy operation after gaining access to the system board. Just remove the microprocessor from its socket and replace it with the upgrade. Set the system's Voltage and Bus Ratio configuration jumpers to the correct settings for the processor being installed. You can find these settings in the system board's Installation Manual.

Two items must be observed when changing the microprocessor:

◆ Make sure the replacement microprocessor is hardware compatible with the original; otherwise, the system board will not support the new microprocessor type.

◆ Make certain to properly orient the new processor in the socket so that its pin 1 matches the socket's pin 1.

The physical upgrade also should be accompanied by a logical upgrade. When the microprocessor is upgraded, the BIOS should also be upgraded. In newer system boards, this can be accomplished by flashing (electrically altering) the information in the BIOS with the latest compatibility firmware. If the BIOS does not possess the Flash option, and does not support the new microprocessor, it will be necessary to obtain an updated BIOS IC from the manufacturer that is compatible with the new processor and the system board's chipset. Make certain to record your CMOS configuration information before flashing or changing the BIOS device. This permits you to reinstall those settings on the updated BIOS.

TEST TIP	Know what precautions to take before upgrading the system's BIOS.

Upgrading system board memory also is a fairly simple process. Having more RAM onboard allows the system to access more data from extended or expanded memory, without having to access the disk drive. This speeds up system operation considerably. Normally, upgrading memory just amounts to installing new memory modules in vacant SIMM or DIMM slots. If the slots are already populated, you must remove them to install faster or higher capacity modules.

Consult the system board's User Guide to determine what speed the memory devices must be rated for. You should be aware that RAM and other memory devices are rated in access time rather than clock speed. Therefore, a –70 nanosecond (ns) RAM device is faster than an –80 nanosecond device. The guide should also be checked for any memory configuration settings that must be made to accept the new memory capacity.

If the system has socketed cache memory, some additional performance can be gained by optimizing the cache. Upgrading the cache on these system boards normally only requires that additional cache ICs be installed in vacant sockets. If the sockets are full but the system's cache size is less than maximum, it will be necessary to remove the existing cache chips and replace them with faster, higher capacity devices. Make sure to observe the pin 1 alignment as well as check the system board's User Guide for any configuration jumper changes.

Before upgrading the system board's FRU units, check the cost of the proposed component upgrade against the cost of upgrading the system board itself. In many cases, the RAM from the original board can be used on a newer, faster model that should include a more advanced microprocessor. Before finalizing the choice to install a new system board, however, make sure that the current adapters, software, and peripherals will function properly with the updated board. If not, the cost of upgrading may be unexpectedly higher than just replacing an FRU component.

HDD Upgrading

One of the key components in keeping the system up-to-date is the hard disk drive. Software manufacturers continue to produce larger and larger programs. In addition, the types of programs found on the typical PC are expanding. Many newer programs place high demands on the hard drive to feed information, such as large graphics files or digitized voice and video, to the system for processing.

Invariably, the system begins to produce error messages that say that the hard drive is full. The first line of action is to use software disk utilities to optimize the organization of the drive. These utilities, such as Check Disk, *ScanDisk*, and Defrag are covered in detail in Chapter 9, "3.0 Diagnosing and Troubleshooting." The second step is to remove unnecessary programs and files from the hard drive. Programs and information that is rarely, or never, used should be moved to an archival media, such as removable disks or tape.

In any event, there may come a time when it is necessary to determine whether the hard drive needs to be replaced to optimize the performance of the system. One guideline suggests that the drive should be replaced if the percentage of unused disk space drops below 20%.

Another reason to consider upgrading the HDD involves its capability to deliver information to the system. If the system is constantly waiting for information from the hard drive, replacing it should be considered as an option. Not all system slowdowns are connected to the HDD, but many are. Remember that the HDD is the mechanical part of the memory system; everything else is electronic.

As with the storage space issue, HDD speed can be optimized through software configurations, such as a disk cache. After it is optimized in this manner, however, any further speed increases must be accomplished by upgrading the hardware.

When considering an HDD upgrade, determine what the real system needs are for the hard drive. Multimedia-intensive applications can place heavy performance demands on the hard disk drive to operate correctly. Moving large image, audio, and video files into RAM on demand requires high performance from the drive. Critical HDD specifications associated with disk drive performance include the following:

◆ **Access time.** The average time, expressed in milliseconds, required to position the drive's R/W heads over a specified track/cylinder and reach a specified sector on the track

◆ **Track seek time.** The amount of time required for the drive's R/W heads to move between cylinders and settle over a particular track following the **Seek** command being issued by the system

◆ **Data transfer rate.** The speed, expressed in megabytes per second (MBps), at which data is transferred between the system and the drive

These factors should be checked thoroughly when upgrading an HDD unit for speed-critical applications. In contemporary systems, the choice of hard drives for high-performance applications alternates back and forth between IDE/EIDE drives and SCSI drives. The EIDE drives are competitive and relatively easy to install; the high-end SCSI specifications offers additional performance, but require additional setup effort and an additional host adapter card.

Before upgrading the HDD unit, make certain that the existing drive is providing all the performance that it can. Check for SMARTDRV or VCACHE arrangements at the software configuration level and optimize them if possible. Also, determine how much performance increase can be gained through other upgrading efforts (check the "System Board Upgrading" section earlier in this chapter) before changing the hard drive.

If the drive is being upgraded substantially, such as from a 500MB IDE drive to a 10GB EIDE drive, check the capabilities of the system's ROM BIOS. If the BIOS does not support LBA or ECHS enhancements, the drive capacity of even the largest hard drive will be limited to 528MB.

Finally, determine how much longer the unit in question is likely to be used before being replaced. If the decision to upgrade the HDD stands, ultimately, the best advice is to get the biggest, fastest hard drive possible. Don't forget to look at the fact that a different I/O bus architecture may add to the performance increase.

TEST TIP

Be aware that the BIOS may be a size-limiting factor in disk drive partition sizes.

Portable System Upgrading

As more and more desktop users began to use laptop and notebook computers, they demanded that additional peripheral systems be included. With the limited space inside these units, it became clear that a new way to install options would need to be developed.

Portable I/O

In the early days of laptop and notebook computers, manufacturers included proprietary expansion connections for adding such devices as fax/modems, additional memory, and additional storage devices.

Of course, these devices tended to be expensive because they were proprietary to a single vendor. In addition, they were not useful as the user upgraded to newer or more powerful units.

In 1989, the Personal Computer Memory Card International Association (PCMCIA) developed the *PCMCIA bus* standard that was primarily intended to accommodate the needs of the space-conscious notebook and subnotebook computer markets. A small form-factor expansion-card format, referred to as the PC Card standard, was adopted for use as well. This format was derived from earlier proprietary laptop/notebook memory-card designs. Over time, the entire standard has come to be called the PC Card standard. This is somewhat easier to say than PCMCIA.

PC Cards

The PCMCIA bus standard is based on the 68-pin JEIDA connector, depicted in Figure 1.140. The figure also lists the definitions of the connector's 68 pins.

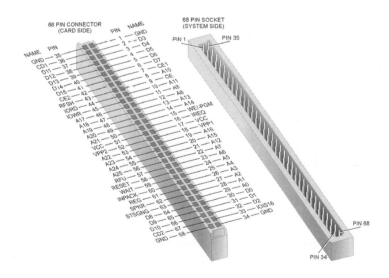

FIGURE 1.140
PCMCIA connector standard.

The interface is designed so that cards can be inserted into the unit while it is turned on (hot insertion). Although the PC Card connection scheme was never intended for use with full-sized units, its design is compatible with all the other bus types. As a matter of fact, PC Card adapters are available for use in desktop and tower units. These slots are often designed so that they can be mounted in a standard disk drive bay of a desktop case.

The PC Card standard defines a methodology for software programmers to write standard drivers for PC Card devices. The standard is referred to as *socket services* and provides for a software head to identify the type of card being used, its capabilities, and its requirements. Although the card's software driver can be executed directly on the card (instead of moving it into RAM for execution), the system's PC Card enablers must be loaded before the card can be activated. This is referred to as execute-in-place mode. In addition, PC Cards can use the same file-allocation system used by floppy and hard disk drives. This also makes it easier for programmers to write code for PCMCIA devices.

PC Card Types

Three types of PCMCIA adapters currently exist. The PCMCIA Type I cards, introduced in 1990, are 3.3mm thick and work as memory-expansion units.

In 1991, the PCMCIA Type II cards were introduced. They are 5mm thick and support virtually any traditional expansion function, except removable hard drive units. Type II slots are backward compatible, so Type I cards will work in them.

Currently, PCMCIA Type III cards are being produced. These cards are 10.5mm thick and are intended primarily for use with removable hard drives. Both Type I and Type II cards can be used in a Type III slot.

All three card types adhere to a form factor of 2.12" × 3.37" and use a 68-pin, slide-in socket arrangement. They can be used with 8-bit or 16-bit data bus machines and operate on +5V or +3.3V supplies. The design of the cards allows them to be installed in the computer while it is turned on and running. Figure 1.141 shows the three types of PCMCIA cards.

PC Card versions of most adapter types are available. Even PC Card hard drives (with disks the size of a quarter) can be found. Other common PC Card adapters include fax/modems, SCSI adapters, network adapters, and IDE host adapters. The PCMCIA standard

TEST TIP

Memorize the physical sizes of the three card standards. Also, know what applications each type of card is capable of.

actually allows for up to 255 adapters, each capable of working with up to 16 cards. If a system implemented the standard to its extreme, it could, theoretically, work with more than 4,000 PC Cards installed. Most portable designs include only 2 PC Card slots.

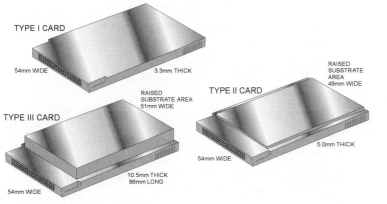

FIGURE 1.141
PCMCIA cards.

Networking Portables

When the portable computer returns to the office, there is usually a gap between what is on the portable and what is on the desktop machine. One alternative is to use a docking station to allow the notebook to function as both a portable and as a desktop system. The other alternative is to make the portable computer network ready so that it can plug into the network in the office.

There are PC Card network adapters that can be used with a network socket device to enable the portable to be connected into the office network. The socket device has internal circuitry that prevents the open network connection from adversely affecting the network when the portable is removed. Some network adapters use the system's parallel port and a pocket LAN adapter to connect portables to the network. The LAN adapter actually works between the network, the computer, and its printer, as described in Figure 1.142.

FIGURE 1.142
Networking portables.

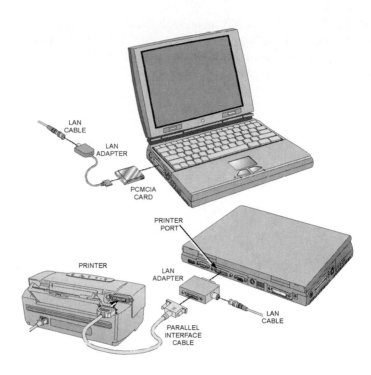

CHAPTER SUMMARY

This chapter has covered the fundamental hardware structures and components associated with PC-compatible systems. It has presented a mini-course on the basic organization and operation of the PC.

This chapter also has dealt expressly with the peculiar aspects of the portable computer systems. It has documented how portable units differ from conventional PC units. After completing the chapter, you should be able to identify the components of portable systems and describe how they differ from typical desktop components. You also should be able to identify their unique problems.

You should be able to identify the major components of a typical PC system and describe the function of each component. In addition, you should be able to install, connect, and configure common computer hardware components to form a working system. Finally, you should be able to describe the different levels of system software associated with a PC.

KEY TERMS

- Active-matrix display
- Adapter cards
- Advanced Power Management (APM)
- Advanced technology PC (PC-AT)
- AT Attachment (ATA)
- AT Attachment Packet Interface (ATAPI)
- AT command set
- AT power supplies

At this point, review the objectives listed at the beginning of the chapter to be certain that you understand the information associated with each one and that you can perform each item listed there. Afterward, answer the Review and Exam Questions that follow to verify your knowledge of the information.

- AT-bus
- ATX power supplies
- Autodetection
- Basic input/output system (BIOS)
- Baud rate
- Booting up
- Bus mice
- Cache memory
- Cathode ray tube (CRT)
- CDFS (CD-ROM file system)
- CD-Recordable (CD-R) disc
- CD-ROM drive
- Centronics parallel port
- Character printer
- CMOS RAM
- Cold boot
- Compact disc (CD)
- CRT monitor
- Cylinders
- Data-compression techniques
- Device drivers
- Direct memory access (DMA)
- Disk Management
- Disk operating system (DOS)
- Docking station
- Drive array
- Dual in-line memory modules (DIMMs)

continues

continued

- Electromagnetic field interference (EFI)
- Enhanced Centronic parallel (ECP)
- Enhanced cylinder, heads, sectors (ECHS)
- Enhanced IDE (EIDE)
- Enhanced parallel port (EPP)
- Expansion slots
- eXtended Graphics Array (XGA)
- Extended ISA (EISA)
- Extended partition
- External modem
- Fast SCSI-2
- FDISK
- File allocation table (FAT)
- Flash ROM
- Floppy disk drive (FDD)
- Full-duplex mode
- Graphical user interface (GUI)
- Green mode
- Half-duplex mode
- Hard disk drive (HDD)
- Hayes-compatible command set
- Head-to-disk interference (HDI)
- Hibernate mode
- High-level format
- High-level protocols
- Host adapter cards
- Hot insertion
- I/O devices
- IBM Personal Computer (PC)
- Industry Standard Architecture (ISA)
- Input/Output (I/O)
- Integrated circuit (IC)
- Internal modem
- Interrupt request (IRQ)
- Joysticks
- Keyboard
- Laptops
- Legacy cards
- Liquid crystal displays (LCDs)
- Local area networks (LANs)
- Logical block addressing (LBA)
- Logical drives
- Master Boot Record
- Microchannel Architecture (MCA)
- Microprocessor
- Microsoft CD Extension (MSCDEX)
- Mirrored drive array
- Modem
- National Television Standards Committee (NTSC)
- Noninterlaced scanning
- Nonmaskable interrupts (NMI)
- Notebook computers
- null modem
- Operating systems
- Options adapter cards
- Output devices
- Palmtop PCs
- Parallel printer port
- Partition
- Passive-matrix displays
- PC Cards
- PC-bus
- PCMCIA bus
- Peripheral Component Interconnect (PCI)
- Peripherals
- Pixel
- Pixels
- Plug and Play (PnP)
- Pointing devices
- Polarizer
- Polling
- Portable PCs
- Power supply

- Power-On Self-Tests (POST)
- Primary partition
- Protocol
- Random access memory (RAM)
- Read-only memory (ROM)
- Redundant arrays of inexpensive disks (RAID)
- ROM BIOS
- RS-232C serial port
- ScanDisk
- Scanners
- SCSI host adapter
- SCSI-3
- Sectors
- Serial ports
- Shadow mask
- Signal cable
- Single in-line memory modules (SIMMs)
- Slave
- Sleep mode
- Small Computer System Interface (SCSI)
- Socket services
- Sound card
- Standby mode
- Striped drive array
- Super VGA
- Suspend mode
- System board
- Touch pad
- Touch-screen monitor
- Trackball
- Trackball mouse
- Tracks
- Ultra-wide SCSI
- Universal asynchronous receiver/transmitters (UARTs)
- Video adapter card
- Video Electronics Standards Association (VESA)
- Video Graphic Array (VGA)
- Volatile
- Warm boot
- Wide area networks (WANs)
- Wide SCSI-2
- Wide-Fast SCSI-2
- WinKeys

Resource URLs

www1.islandnet.com/~kpolsson/comphist.htm

www.levin.co.nz/pages/bios_survival/bios_sg.htm

http://webopedia.internet.com/term/m/motherboard.html

www.sysopt.com/bios.html

www.tomshardware.com/mainboard/99q1/990208/index.html

www.levin.co.nz/pages/bios_survival/bios_sg.htm

http://webopedia.internet.com/TERM/V/VESA.html

http://webopedia.internet.com/TERM/P/PCI.html

http://webopedia.internet.com/TERM/X/XGA.html

www.acnc.com/raid.html

http://webopedia.internet.com/TERM/h/hard_disk_drive.html

http://webopedia.internet.com/TERM/f/floppy_drive.html

www.pcguide.com/ref/fdd/

www.pctechguide.com/15tape.htm

http://webopedia.internet.com/TERM/k/keyboard.html

www.pctechguide.com/06crtmon.htm

http://webopedia.internet.com/TERM/m/modem.html

www.pctechguide.com/11sound.htm

www.levin.co.nz/bios_sg.htm

webopedia.internet.com/TERM/B/BIOS.html

www.cs.uregina.ca/~bayko/cpu.html

www.intel.com/education/mpuworks/

www.kingston.com/tools/umg/default.asp

www5.tomshardware.com/guides/ram.html

www.epson.com/cam_scan/scanners/scan_glossary/index.html

www.driverzone.com/drivers/mscdex/

www.computerhope.com/mscdex.htm

www.whatis.com/lba.htm

http://burks.bton.ac.uk/burks/foldoc/61/30.htm

http://webopedia.internet.com/TERM/I/IRQ.html

www.pcguide.com/ref/mbsys/res/

www.fapo.com/ecpmode.htm

www.fapo.com/eppmode.htm

www.starkelectronic.com/czp33a.htm

www.connectworld.net/c2.html

www.eia.org

http://desperado.blinncol.edu/newcisc/1301/notes/slides/chapter8

www.whatis.com/ide.htm

www.scsita.org

www.paralan.com/sediff.html

http://chac.sco.com/HW_modem/CTOC-modem.intro.html

www.svi.org/projects/pcday/manual/section_8.htm

http://hatbox.do.losrios.cc.ca.us/%7Efichera/WIN95/006/sld023.htm

www.ami.com

www.phoenix.com

http://www6.tomshardware.com/guides/storage/index-01.html

http://rama.bl.pg.gda.pl/~slawcok/mirror/pcmech/sysopt.htm

http://support.neccsdeast.com/products/versa/p/docs/sec4c.htm

http://webopedia.internet.com/Types_of_Computers/Notebook_Computers/notebook_computer.html

www.pc-card.com/pccardstandard.htm

http://webopedia.internet.com/Types_of_Computers/Notebook_Computers/docking_station.html

http://webopedia.internet.com/TERM/L/LCD.html

APPLY YOUR KNOWLEDGE

Review Questions

1. Describe the major maintenance problem associated with notebook computers.

2. List the four subunits typically found inside the desktop system unit.

3. How can you avoid confusion between the DB-15M connectors for VGA and game port connections?

4. List three types of memory typically found on modern system boards.

5. Describe how data is stored on a magnetic disk.

6. List three power-management modes and describe how they differ.

7. What is the major procedural difference between installing a floppy drive and a hard drive?

8. What is the purpose of a docking station?

9. Describe the differences between the two types of drive-array applications.

10. Which type of RAM modules are typically used in a portable PC?

11. When connecting an AT power supply to a system board, what precaution should be taken?

12. What does EFI stand for and why is it associated with a microcomputer system?

13. What do the terms SIMM and DIMM stand for, and what kind of devices are they?

14. Describe two ways to connect a portable computer to a network.

15. How is upgrading a system with a Flash ROM BIOS different from upgrading a system with a standard ROM BIOS?

Exam Questions

1. What type of IC is the brain of the PC system?

   A. The ROM BIOS

   B. The ASIC device

   C. The memory controller

   D. The microprocessor

2. What function does the FDISK program perform?

   A. It removes lost allocation units from the drive.

   B. It creates partitions on the physical disk.

   C. It provides the low-level format for the drive.

   D. It provides the high-level format for the drive.

3. Where would you normally expect to encounter a PCMCIA card?

   a. In an ISA expansion slot

   b. In a serial port

   c. In a notebook computer

   d. In an MCA expansion slot

4. Where is the system's BIOS program located?

   A. ROM ICs located on the system board

   B. In the CMOS chip

APPLY YOUR KNOWLEDGE

C. In the keyboard encoder

D. In the microprocessor's L2 cache

5. How many floppy drives can a typical FDC controller handle? How are these drives identified to the system?

   A. The normal FDC controller can control two floppy disk drives that the system sees as Drives A: and B:.

   B. The normal FDC controller can control four floppy disk drives that the system sees as Drives A:, B:, C:, and D:.

   C. The normal FDC controller can control one floppy disk drive that the system sees as Drive A:.

   D. The normal FDC controller can control two floppy disk drives that the system sees as Drives A: and an assigned drive name.

6. What type of port is indicated by the presence of a 9-pin male connector on the back panel of the computer?

   A. A parallel printer port

   B. A game port

   C. A serial communications port

   D. A VGA port

7. To which type of communications products do Hayes-compatible commands pertain?

   A. Hubs

   B. Network adapter cards

   C. Routers

   D. Modems

8. Where is the MI/O function normally found in a Pentium system?

   A. On the multi-I/O card

   B. On the system board

   C. On the video card

   D. On the SCSI adapter card

9. A Type I PCMCIA card is _____ thick.

   A. 3.3mm

   B. 5.0mm

   C. 7.5mm

   D. 10.5mm

10. Which function can be performed by a Type III PCMCIA card but not by Type I or Type II cards?

    A. Removable HDD functions

    B. Memory-expansion functions

    C. Serial port functions

    D. Parallel port functions

Answers to Review Questions

1. Nonstandard printed circuit boards, proprietary battery-case designs, and difficult internal structure creating difficult access to many parts of the system. For more information, see the section "Portable Drawbacks."

APPLY YOUR KNOWLEDGE

2. The components inside the system unit can be divided into four distinct subunits: a switching power supply, the disk drives, the system board, and the options adapter cards. For more information, see the section "Inside the System Unit."

3. The pins of this game port's 15-pin D-shell are arranged differently from those in the 15-pin VGA connector. In the VGA connector, the pins are arranged in 3 rows; the pins in the game port are arranged in 2 rows. For more information, see the section "I/O Connections."

4. ROM, RAM, and cache memory. For more information, see the section "Primary Memory."

5. Data is stored on the disk in the form of positively and negatively charged spots. The spots are encoded to represent bits. The bits are formed into bytes that are stored in sectors along the tracks of the disk. For more information, see the section "Storage Devices."

6. Standby mode, suspend mode, and hibernate mode. Standby mode turns off selected system components until a system event occurs. Suspend mode places the system in a shutdown condition except for its memory units. Hibernate mode writes the contents of RAM memory to a hard drive file and completely shuts the system down. For more information, see the section "Power Consumption."

7. The HDD's type and operating parameter information must be installed in the CMOS setup. The HDD unit must be partitioned and formatted before it can be used. For more information, see sections "FDD Installation" and "HDD Installation."

8. A docking station is a specialized structure that the portable is inserted into to extend its expansion bus so that a collection of desktop devices can be used with it. For more information, see the section "Docking Stations."

9. The first drive array type is used as a data backup method. The second type of drive array uses multiple drives to store large amounts of data in a manner that provides high reliability and recoverability. For more information, see the section "RAID Systems."

10. Only the RAM types suggested in the User Manual should be used to upgrade or repair a portable computer. For more information, see the section "Portable Memory."

11. That the black wires from the P8 and P9 connectors are side by side. For more information, see the section "Power Supplies."

12. Electromagnetic field interference. This is unwanted radio interference that can escape from an improperly shielded case. For more information, see the section "The Centronics Standard."

13. SIMM stands for single in-line memory module; SIPP stands for single in-line pin package. Both devices are types of RAM memory modules. For more information, see the section "Primary Memory."

14. A PC Card network adapter can be used, or a parallel port–based pocket LAN adapter can be used. For more information, see the section "Networking Portables."

15. The Flash ROM feature allows new information to be transferred into the ROM chip from the system. With a standard ROM BIOS, either the IC must be replaced or the entire system board must be replaced. For more information, see the section "Primary Memory."

Answers to Exam Questions

1. **D.** The microprocessor "thinks" for the computer by processing instructions and data for the system. The BIOS just stores the system's native intelligence; the other devices provide support for the microprocessor. For more information, see the subsection "System Boards" under the section "PC Systems."

2. **B.** The FDISK utility performs the system's disk-partitioning functions. The low-level format is a function of the BIOS and the drive manufacturer. The Check Disk and ScanDisk utilities are used to identify and remove lost clusters from a disk. For more information, see the section "Logical and Physical Drives."

3. **C.** Although available for standard desktop and tower-style PCs, PCMCIA cards were developed primarily for notebook and laptop computers. For more information, see the section "PC Cards."

4. **A.** The BIOS is always located in the ROM BIOS IC on the system board. The information in the BIOS is used to initialize the contents of the keyboard controller. The BIOS does check the battery-powered information stored in the CMOS area for configuration settings. The L2 cache is used by the microprocessor to hold temporary information during the operation of the system. For more information, see the section "Primary Memory."

5. **A.** In the original IBM PC, the system was designed to accommodate up to four FDD units. When the PC-XT came along with an HDD included, however, the standard became two FDD units identified as A: and B: drives. The A: and B: status was determined by how they connected to the FDD signal cable. For more information, see the section "Other Adapter Cards."

6. **C.** The 9-pin male D-shell connector in a PC system indicates a serial connection. The parallel port uses a 25-pin female D-shell connector at the computer; the game port employs a female 15-pin, 2-row female D-shell; and the VGA adapter uses a 15-pin, 3-row female D-shell connector. For more information, see the section "I/O Connections."

7. **D.** Hayes-compatible AT commands are the industry standards for modem control. The other components may be programmable devices, but they have no connection to the Hayes/AT standard. For more information, see the section "Communications Software."

8. **B.** In pre-Pentium systems, the M/IO functions were located on adapter cards that plugged into the system board's expansion slots. By the time Pentium systems began to appear, the basic MI/O functions were accepted standards that IC makers had integrated into a single ASIC. This made it very convenient to add directly into the new system board designs. By doing so, only a single adapter card was required to create a basic PC-compatible Pentium system. For more information, see the section "Adapter Cards."

9. **A.** The Type I card is 3.3mm thick. For more information, see the section "PC Card Types."

10. **A.** By definition, only a Type III PC Card can be used for removable disk drive functions. For more information, see the section "PC Card Types."

This chapter helps you to prepare for the Core Hardware module of the A+ Certification examination by covering the following objectives within the "Domain 2.0: Diagnosing and Troubleshooting" section.

2.1 Identify common symptoms and problems associated with each module and how to troubleshoot and isolate the problems. Content may include the following:

- **Processor/memory symptoms**
- **Mouse**
- **Floppy drive failures**
- **Parallel ports**
- **Hard drives**
- **Sound card/audio**
- **Monitor/video**
- **Motherboards**
- **Modems**
- **BIOS**
- **USB**
- **CMOS**
- **Power supply**
- **Slot covers**
- **POST audible/visual error codes**
- **Troubleshooting tools (for example, multimeter)**
- **Large LBA, LBA**

▶ One of the primary responsibilities of every PC technician is to diagnose and troubleshoot computer problems.

CHAPTER 2

2.0 Diagnosing and Troubleshooting

2.2 Identify basic troubleshooting procedures and good practices for eliciting problem symptoms from customers. Content may include the following:

- **Troubleshooting/isolation/problem determination procedures**

- **Determining whether problem is hardware or software related**

- **Gathering information from user, such as the following:**

  - **Customer environment**

  - **Symptoms/error codes**

  - **Situation when the problem occurred**

▶ Every technician should be able to effectively acquire information from the customer concerning the nature of a problem and then practice basic troubleshooting methods.

STUDY STRATEGIES

To prepare for the "Diagnosing and Troubleshooting" section of the Core Hardware exam:

▶ Read the objectives at the beginning of this chapter.

▶ Study the information in this chapter.

▶ Review the objectives listed earlier in this chapter.

▶ Perform any step-by-step procedures in the text.

▶ Answer the Review and Exam Questions at the end of the chapter and check your results.

▶ Use the ExamGear test engine on the CD that accompanies this book for additional Review and Exam Questions concerning this material.

▶ Review the Test Tips scattered throughout the chapter and make certain that you are comfortable with each point.

INTRODUCTION

This domain requires the test taker to apply knowledge that relates to diagnosing and troubleshooting common module problems and system malfunctions, including knowledge of the symptoms that relate to common problems. Questions from this domain account for 25% of the Core Hardware test.

For flow and clarity, this chapter is organized just a bit differently from the objectives in the exam blueprint. It begins with material listed under objective 2.2 and then covers the material for objective 2.1.

BASIC TROUBLESHOOTING TECHNIQUES

▶ 2.2 Identify basic troubleshooting procedures and good practices for eliciting problem symptoms from customers.

The A+ Core Hardware objective 2.2 states that the test taker should be able to "identify basic troubleshooting procedures and good practices for eliciting problem symptoms from customers."

One of the most important aspects of troubleshooting anything is the gathering of information about the problem at hand and the symptoms it is showing. One of the best sources for this type of information is the computer user. As this A+ objective states, the computer technician should be able to effectively acquire information from the customer (user) concerning the nature of a problem and then be able to practice basic troubleshooting methods to isolate and repair the problem. To this end, the following sections of the chapter address these topics. A place to start this discussion is with your tools and workspace.

Workspace

The first order of business when working on any type of electronic equipment is to prepare a proper work area.

You need a clear, flat workspace on which to rest the device. Make sure that your workspace is large enough to accommodate the work piece. Confirm that you have an adequate number of power receptacles to handle all the equipment you may need. Try to locate your workspace in a low-traffic area.

Good lighting is a prerequisite for the work area because the technician must be able to see small details, such as part numbers, cracked circuit foils, and solder splashes. An adjustable lamp with a shade is preferable. Fluorescent lighting is particularly desirable. In addition, a magnifying glass helps to read small part numbers.

Organizational Aids

Because some troubleshooting problems may require more than one session, it is a good idea to have some organizational aids in-hand before you begin to disassemble any piece of equipment. The following list identifies some of the organizational aids you need:

◆ A parts organizer to keep track of small parts, such as screws and connectors, you may remove from the device. This organizer need not be extravagant. A handful of paper cups or clear plastic sandwich bags will do nicely.

◆ A roll of athletic or masking tape. You can use the tape to make tags and labels to help identify parts, where they go, and how they are connected in the circuit. Take the time to write notes and stick them on your parts organizers, circuit boards, cables you remove from the system, and so forth.

◆ A small note pad or notebook to keep track of your assembly/troubleshooting steps.

Diagnostic and Repair Tools

Obviously, anyone who wants to work on any type of equipment must have the proper tools for the task. The following sections discuss the tools and equipment associated with the testing and repair of digital systems.

Hand Tools

The well-prepared technician's tool kit should contain a wide range of both flat-blade and Phillips-head screwdriver sizes. At a minimum, it should have a small jeweler's and a medium-size flat-blade screwdriver, along with a medium-size Phillips screwdriver. In addition, you may want to include a small set of miniature nut drivers, a set of Torx *drivers*, and a special nonconductive screwdriver-like device called an alignment tool.

You also need a couple of pairs of needle-nose pliers. These pliers are available in a number of sizes. You need at least one pair with a sturdy, blunt nose and one with a longer, more tapered nose. You also might want to get a pair that has a cutting edge built in to its jaws. You may perform this same function with a different type of pliers called diagonals, or cross-cuts. Many technicians carry a pair of surgical forceps in addition to their other pliers.

Another common set of tools associated with computer repair are IC pullers, or IC extractors. These tools come in various styles, as illustrated in Figure 2.1, and are used to remove ICs from sockets. Socket-mounted ICs are not as common on modern PC boards as they were in the past. Potential failures associated with the mechanical connections between sockets and chips, coupled with the industry's reliance on surface-mount soldering techniques, have led to far fewer socket-mounted chips. However, on some occasions, such as upgrading a ROM BIOS chip, the IC puller comes in handy.

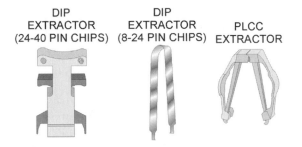

DIP
EXTRACTOR
(24-40 PIN CHIPS)

DIP
EXTRACTOR
(8-24 PIN CHIPS)

PLCC
EXTRACTOR

FIGURE 2.1
IC pullers.

Figure 2.2 depicts hand tools commonly associated with micro-computer repair.

FIGURE 2.2
Hand tools.

Using a Multimeter

A number of test instruments can help you to isolate problems. One of the most basic pieces of electronic troubleshooting equipment is the multimeter. These test instruments are available in both analog and digital read-out form and can be used to directly measure values of *voltage* (V), *current*, in milliamperes (mA) or amperes (A), and resistance, in ohms. Therefore, these devices are referred to as *VOMs* (volt-ohm-milliammeters) for analog types, or *DMMs* (digital *multimeters*) for digital types. Figure 2.3 depicts a digital multimeter.

With a little finesse, you can use this device to check diodes, transistors, capacitors, motor windings, relays, and coils. This particular DMM contains facilities built in to the meter to test transistors and diodes. These facilities are in addition to its standard functions of current, voltage, and resistance measurement.

The first step in using the multimeter to perform tests is to select the proper function. For the most part, you never need to use the current functions of the multimeter when working with computer systems. However, the voltage and resistance functions can be very valuable tools.

In computer and peripheral troubleshooting, fully 99% of the tests made are DC voltage readings. These measurements most often involve checking the DC side of the power-supply unit. You can make these readings between ground and one of the expansion-slot pins, or at the system board power-supply connector. It is also common to check the voltage level across a system board capacitor to verify that the system is receiving power. The voltage across most of the capacitors on the system board is 5V (DC). The DC voltages that can normally be expected in a PC-compatible system are +12V, +5V, −5V, and −12V. The actual values for these reading may vary by 5% in either direction.

The *DC voltage function* is used to take measurements in live DC circuits. It should be connected in parallel with the device being checked. This could mean connecting the reference lead (black lead) to a ground point and the measuring lead (red lead) to a test point to take a measurement, as illustrated in Figure 2.4.

As an approximate value is detected, you can decrease the range setting to achieve a more accurate reading. Most meters allow for over-voltage protection. However, it is still a good safety practice to decrease the range of the meter after you have achieved an initial value.

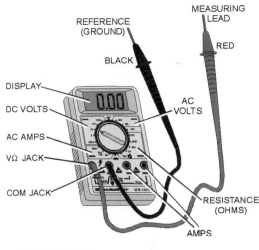

FIGURE 2.3
Digital multimeter.

W A R N I N G	**Setting the Meter** It is normal practice to first set the meter to its highest voltage range to make certain that the voltage level being measured does not damage the meter.

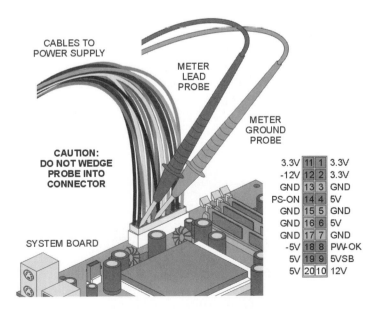

FIGURE 2.4
DC voltage check.

The second most popular test is the *resistance*, or *continuity test*.

Failure to turn off the power when making resistance checks can cause serious damage to the meter and can pose a potential risk to the user. Resistance checks also require that you electrically isolate the component being tested from the system. For most circuit components, this means desoldering at least one end from the board.

The resistance check is very useful in isolating some types of problems in the system. One of the main uses of the resistance function is to test fuses. You must disconnect at least one end of the fuse from the system. You should set the meter on the 1k ohm resistance setting. If the fuse is good, the meter should read near 0 ohms. If it is bad, the meter reads infinite. The resistance function also is useful in checking for cables and connectors. By removing the cable from the system and connecting a meter lead to each end, you can check the cable's continuity conductor by conductor to verify its integrity. You also use the resistance function to test the system's speaker. To check the speaker, just disconnect the speaker from the system and connect a meter lead to each end. If the speaker is good, the meter should read near 8 ohms. If the speaker is defective, the resistance reading should be 0 or infinite.

Only a couple of situations involve using the *AC voltage function* for checking microcomputer systems. The primary use of this function is to check the commercial power being applied to the power-supply unit. As with any measurement, it is important to select the correct measurement range. However, the lethal voltage levels associated with the supply power call for additional caution when making such measurements. The second application for the AC voltage function is to measure ripple voltage from the DC output side of the power-supply unit. This particular operation is very rarely performed in field-service situations.

Information Gathering

Gather information from the user regarding the environment the system is being used in, any symptoms or error codes produced by the system, and the situations that existed when the failure occurred. Ask the user to list the procedures that led to the malfunction. This communication can help you narrow a problem down to a particular section of the computer. It does no good to check the video display when the user is having trouble using the disk drive.

Finally, observe the symptoms of a malfunction to verify the problem for yourself. After you have identified a problem, try to associate the malfunction with a section of the system responsible for that operation.

Environment

Take note of the environment that the equipment is being used in and how heavy its usage is. If the system is located in a particularly dirty area, or an area given to other environmental extremes, it may need to be cleaned and serviced more frequently than if it were in a clean office environment. The same proves true for systems subjected to heavy or continuous use. In an industrial environment, check with the management to see whether any office or industry maintenance standards for servicing apply.

Finally, use simple observation of the wear and tear on the equipment to gauge the need for additional or spot maintenance steps. Look for signs of extended use (such as frayed cords, missing slot covers, keyboards with letters worn off, and so on) to spot potential problems resulting from age or usage.

Symptoms/Error Codes

Most PCs have reasonably good built-in self-tests that are run each time the computer is powered up. These tests can prove very beneficial in detecting hardware-oriented problems within the system.

Some PCs issue numerically coded error messages on the display when errors occur. Conversely, other PCs display a written description of the error. Tables 2.1 and 2.2 define the error messages and beep codes produced by a particular BIOS version from American Megatrends. The error messages and codes will vary among different BIOS manufacturers and from version to version.

NOTE

Careful Observation The most important thing to do when checking a malfunctioning device is to be observant. Begin by talking to the person who reported the problem. You can obtain many clues from this person. Careful listening also is a good way to eliminate the user as a possible cause of the problems. Part of the technician's job is to determine whether the user could be the source of the problem—either trying to do things with the system that it cannot do, or not understanding how some part of it is supposed to work.

TEST TIP

Be well aware that the user is one of the most common sources of PC problems. In most situations, your first troubleshooting step should be to talk to the user.

NOTE

Error Messages Formats Whenever a self-test failure or *setup* mismatch is encountered, the BIOS may indicate the error through a blank screen, or a visual error message on the video display, or through an audio response (*beep codes*) produced by the system's speaker.

TABLE 2.1	
VISUAL DISPLAY ERROR MESSAGES	

System-Halted Errors

Error Message	Problem Indicated or Action Needed
CMOS INOPERATIONAL	Failure of CMOS shutdown register test.
8042 GATE A20 ERROR	Error getting into protected mode.
INVALID SWITCH MEMORY FAILURE	Real/protected-mode change over error.
DMA ERROR	DMA controller failed page register test.
DMA #1 ERROR	DMA device #1 failure.
DMA #2 ERROR	DMA device #2 failure.

Nonfatal Errors—with Setup Option

CMOS BATTERY LOW	Failure of CMOS battery or CMOS checksum test.
CMOS SYSTEM OPTION NOT SET	Failure of CMOS battery or CMOS checksum test.
CMOS CHECKSUM FAILURE	CMOS battery low or CMOS checksum test failure.
CMOS DISPLAY MISMATCH	Failure of display-type verification.
CMOS MEMORY SIZE MISMATCH	System configuration and setup failure.
CMOS TIMER AND DATE NOT SET	System configuration and setup failure in timer circuitry.

Nonfatal Errors—without Setup Option

CH-X TIMER ERROR	Channel X (2, 1, or 0) timer failure.
KEYBOARD ERROR	Keyboard test failure.
KB/INTERFACE ERROR	Keyboard test failure.
DISPLAY SWITCH SETTING NOT PROPER	Failure to verify display type.
KEYBOARD IS LOCKED	Unlock it.
FDD CONTROLLER ERROR	Failure to verify floppy disk setup by System Configuration file.
HDD CONTROLLER FAILURE	Failure to verify hard disk setup by System Configuration file.
C:DRIVE ERROR	Hard disk setup failure.
D:DRIVE ERROR	Hard disk setup failure.

TABLE 2.2

BEEP CODE MESSAGES

Number of Beeps	*Problem Indicated*
1	DRAM refresh failure
2	RAM failure (base640KB)
3	System timer failure
5	Microprocessor failure
6	Keyboard controller failure
7	Virtual-mode exception failure
9	ROM BIOS checksum failure
1 long, 2 short	Video controller failure
1 long, 3 short	Conventional and extended test failure
1 long, 8 short	Display test failure

Initial Troubleshooting Steps

As a general rule, you can reduce the majority of all equipment problems to the simplest things you can think of. The problem is, most people don't think of them. Successful troubleshooting results from careful observation, deductive reasoning, and an organized approach to solving problems. These techniques apply to the repair of any type of defective equipment.

Effective troubleshooting of electronic equipment is a matter of combining good knowledge of the equipment and its operation with good testing techniques and deductive reasoning skills. In general, the process of troubleshooting microprocessor-based equipment begins at the outside of the system and moves inward. First, always try the system to see what symptoms you produce. Second, you must isolate the problem to either software- or hardware-related problems. Finally, you should isolate the problem to a section of the hardware or software.

NOTE

Check the Outside   Check all externally accessible switch settings.

NOTE

Document Things   Take time to document the problem, including all the tests you perform and their outcomes. Your memory is never as good as you think it is, especially in stressful situations such as with a down computer. This recorded information can prevent you from making repetitive steps that waste time and may cause confusion. This information also proves very helpful when you move on to more detailed tests or measurements. Also, label all cables and connectors prior to removing them. This will assist you in reconnecting things as you progress through the troubleshooting process.

NOTE

Observing Boot Up   Carefully observing the steps of a boot-up procedure can reveal a great deal about the nature of problems in a system. Faulty areas can be included or excluded from possible causes of errors during the boot-up process.

Performing the Visual Inspection

If no prior knowledge of the type of malfunction exists, you should proceed by performing a careful visual inspection of the system. Check the outside of the system first. Look for loose or disconnected cables. Consult all the external front-panel lights. If no lights display, check the power outlet, the plugs and power cords, as well as any power switches that may affect the operation of the system. You also might want to check the commercial power-distribution system's fuses or circuit breakers to confirm their functionality.

If part of the system is active, try to localize the problem by systematically removing peripheral devices from the system. Try swapping suspected devices with known good parts from another computer of the same type. Try to revive the system, or its defective portion, by restarting it several times. As a matter of fact, you should try to restart the system after performing each correctional step.

For example, check all system jumper settings to see that they are set correctly for the actual configuration of the system. In Pentium-based systems, check the BIOS advanced CMOS configuration screens for enabling settings that may not be correct. Also, make certain that any peripheral devices in the system, such as printers or *modems*, are set up correctly.

Consult any additional user or operations manuals liberally. Indeed, many of the computers and peripheral systems on the market, such as printers, have some level of self-diagnostics built in to them. Generally, these diagnostics programs produce coded error messages. The key to recognizing and using these error messages is usually found in the device's User Manual. In addition, the User Manual may contain probable cause and suggested remedy information, and/or specialized tests to isolate specific problems.

Watching the Boot-Up Procedure

The observable actions of a working system's cold-boot procedure are listed as follows, in their order of occurrence:

1. When power is applied, the power-supply fan activates.
2. The keyboard lights flash as the rest of the system components are being reset.
3. A BIOS message displays on the monitor.
4. A memory test flickers on the monitor.

5. The floppy disk drive access light comes on briefly.

6. The hard disk drive access light comes on briefly.

7. The system beeps, indicating that it has completed its Power-On Self-Tests and initialization process..

8. The floppy disk drive access light comes on briefly before switching to the hard drive. At this point in the process, the BIOS is looking for additional instructions (boot information), first from the floppy drive and then from the hard drive (assuming that the CMOS setup is configured for this sequence).

9. For Windows machines, the Starting Windows message appears onscreen.

> **TEST TIP**
>
> Memorize the order of the series of observable events that occur during the normal (DOS) boot up.

If a section of the computer is defective, you will observe just some (or possibly none) of these events. By knowing the sections of the computer involved in each step, you can suspect a particular section of causing the problem if the system does not advance past that step. For instance, it is illogical to replace the floppy disk drive (step 5) when a memory test (step 4) has not been displayed on the monitor.

When a failure occurs, you can eliminate components as a possible cause by observing the number of steps that the system completes in the preceding list. You can eliminate those subsystems associated with steps successfully completed. Focus your efforts only on those sections responsible for the symptom. When that symptom is cleared, the computer should progress to another step. However, another unrelated symptom may appear further down the list. You should deal with this symptom in the same manner. Always focus on diagnosing the present symptom and eventually all the symptoms will disappear.

Determining Hardware/Software/ Configuration Problems

It should be obvious that a functional computer system is composed of two major parts: the system's hardware and the software that controls it. These two elements are so closely related that it is often difficult to determine which part might be the cause of a given problem. Therefore, one of the earliest steps in troubleshooting a computer problem (or any other programmable system problem) is to determine whether the problem is due to a hardware failure or to faulty programming.

In PCs, you can use a significant event that occurs during the boot-up process as a key to begin separating hardware problems from software problems: the single beep that most PCs produce between the end of the POST and the beginning of the boot-up process (step 7 in the preceding list).

Errors that occur, or are displayed, before this beep indicate that a hardware problem of some type exists. This conclusion should be easy to understand because up to this time, only the BIOS and the basic system hardware have been active. The operating system side of the system does not come into play until after the beep occurs.

If the system produces an error message (such as `The System Has Detected Unstable RAM at Location` *x*) or a beep code before the beep, for example, the system has found a problem with the RAM hardware. In this case, a bad memory device is indicated.

You can still group errors that occur before the beep into two distinct categories:

◆ Configuration errors

◆ Hardware failures

> **T E S T   T I P**
>
> **Configuration Problems**   You can trace the majority of all problems that occur in computer systems back to configuration settings.

A special category of problems tends to occur whenever a new hardware option is added to the system, or when the system is used for the very first time. These problems are called *configuration problems*, or setup problems, and result from mismatches between the system's programmed configuration, held in CMOS memory, and the actual equipment installed in the system.

This mismatch also can be between the system's CMOS configuration settings and the option's hardware jumper or switch settings.

It is normally necessary to run the system's CMOS setup utility in the following three situations:

◆ When the system is first constructed.

◆ If it becomes necessary to replace the CMOS backup battery on the system board.

◆ Whenever a new or different option is added to the system (such as a hard drive, floppy drive, or video display), it may be necessary to run the Setup utility (although see the note "CMOS Setup Utility and Plug and Play").

Configuration problems occur with some software packages when first installed. The user must enter certain parameters into the program to match its capabilities to the actual configuration of the system. These configuration settings are established through the startup software in the ROM BIOS. If these configuration parameters are set incorrectly, the software cannot direct the system's hardware properly and an error occurs.

When you are installing new hardware or software options, be aware of the possibility of this type of error. If you encounter configuration (or setup) errors, refer to the installation instructions found in the new component's User Manual. Table 2.3 lists typical configuration error codes and messages produced when various types of configuration mismatches are incurred.

NOTE

CMOS Setup Utility and Plug and Play In most newer systems, the BIOS and operating system use Plug and Play (PnP) techniques to detect new hardware that has been installed in the system. These components work together with the device to allocate system resources for the device. In some situations, the PnP logic will not be able to resolve all the system's resource needs and a configuration error will occur. In these cases, the user must manually resolve the configuration problem.

TABLE 2.3

COMMON CONFIGURATION ERROR CODES

Configuration Error Message	Meaning
CMOS System Option Not Set	Failure of CMOS battery or CMOS checksum test
CMOS Display Mismatch	Failure of display-type verification
CMOS Memory Size Mismatch	System configuration and setup failure
Press F1 to Continue	Invalid configuration information

TEST TIP

Know the situations that cause a Press F1 to Continue error message to display.

If you cannot confirm a configuration problem, the problem most likely is a defective component. The most widely used repair method involves substituting known good components for suspected bad components. Other alternatives for isolating and correcting a hardware failure that appears before the boot up depend on how much of the system is operable.

These alternatives include running a diagnostic program to test the system's components, and using a POST card to determine what problems a system may have. Several diagnostic software packages enable you to test system components. However, these diagnostic tools require that certain major blocks of the system be operational. The POST card is a device that plugs into the system's expansion slots and reads the information moving through the system's buses. It is used when not enough of the system is running to support any other type of diagnostic tool. Both of these options are discussed in greater detail later in this chapter.

After the beep, the system begins looking for and loading the operating system. Errors that occur between the beep and the presentation of the operating system's user interface (command prompt or GUI) generally have three possible sources:

◆ Hardware failure (physical problem with the boot drive)

◆ Corrupted or missing boot files

◆ Corrupted or missing operating system files

You can read more about the process of sorting out these potential problems in Chapter 9, "3.0 Diagnosing and Troubleshooting." In these cases, checking the drive hardware is generally the last step of the troubleshooting process. Unless some specific symptom indicates otherwise, the missing or corrupted boot and operating system files are checked first.

Software Diagnostics

Many companies produce disk-based diagnostic routines that check the system by running predetermined tests on different areas of its hardware. The diagnostic package evaluates the response from each test and attempts to produce a status report for all the system's major components. Like the computer's self-test, these packages produce visual and beep-coded error messages. Figure 2.5 shows the main menu of a typical self-booting software diagnostic.

This menu is the gateway to information about the system's makeup and configuration, as well as the entryway to the program's Advanced Diagnostic Test functions. You can find utilities for performing low-level formats on older hard drive types and for managing SCSI interface devices through this menu. Additionally, options to print or show test results are available here, as is the exit point from the program.

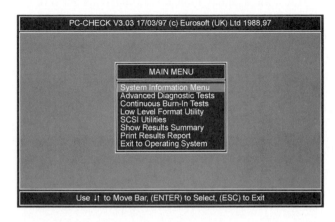

FIGURE 2.5
The main menu.

The most common software troubleshooting packages test the system's memory, microprocessor, keyboard, display monitor, and the disk drive's speed. If at least the system's CPU, disk drive, and clock circuits are working, you may be able to use one of these special software-troubleshooting packages to help localize system failures. They can prove especially helpful when trying to track down, non-heat-related intermittent problems.

The first option in the sample diagnostic package is the System Information menu. As described in Figure 2.6, this option provides access to the system's main functional blocks. The menu's IRQ Information, I/O Port Information, and Device Drivers options are valuable aids in locating configuration conflicts.

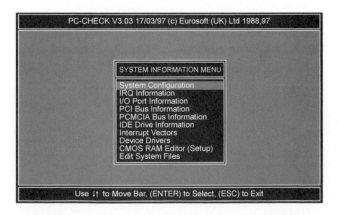

FIGURE 2.6
The System Information menu.

The Advanced Diagnostics Tests selection from the main menu performs extended tests in 13 system areas. These tests, listed in Figure 2.7, contain several lower-level tests that you can select from submenus. Error notices and diagnostic comments appear on the display in the form of overlay boxes. In addition to these fundamental software tests, this diagnostic includes tests for multimedia-related devices such as CD-ROMs. The CD-ROM tests cover both access time and transfer performance. Both of these values affect the multimedia performance of the system. The multimedia tests also check the system's speaker and sound card capabilities.

FIGURE 2.7
The advanced diagnostics tests.

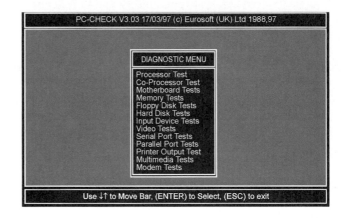

If a diagnostic program indicates that multiple items should be replaced, replace the units one at a time until the unit starts up. Then, replace any units removed prior to the one that caused the system to start. This process ensures that there were not multiple bad parts. If you have replaced all the parts, and the unit still does not function properly, the diagnostic software is suspect.

For enterprises that repair computers, or build computers from parts, diagnostic programs that perform continuous *burn-in* tests are a valuable tool. After the system has been built or repaired, this program runs continuous tests on the system for an extended burn-in period, without intervention from a technician or operator.

The tests performed are similar to the selection from the main menu. However, these tests are normally used for reliability testing rather than general troubleshooting. Different parts of the system can be selected for the burn-in tests. Because the burn-in tests are meant to be run unattended, the user must be careful to select only tests that apply to hardware that actually exists. The diagnostic keeps track of how many times each test has been run and how often it failed during the designated burn-in period. This information displays on the monitor, as depicted in Figure 2.8.

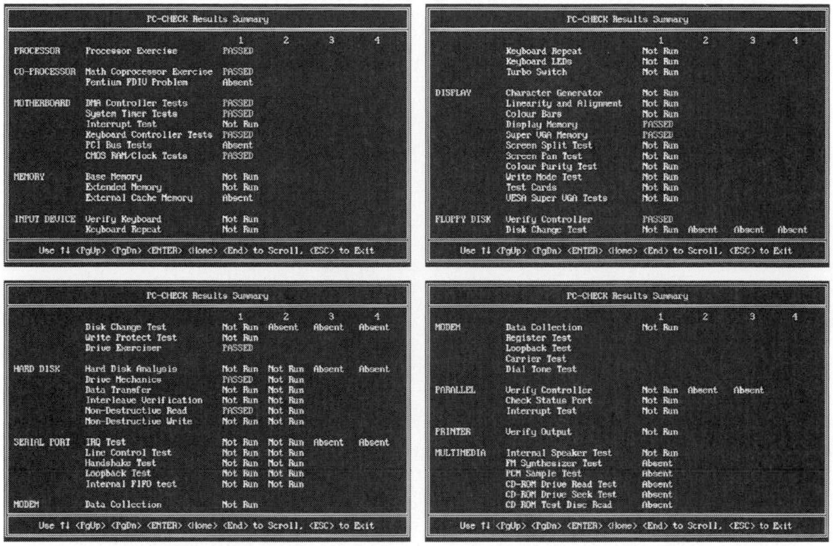

FIGURE 2.8
The burn-in test report.

Using POST Cards

Most BIOS program chips do not have an extensive set of onboard diagnostics built in to them. Therefore, several companies produce *POST cards* and diagnostic software to aid in hardware troubleshooting. A POST card is a diagnostic device that plugs into the system's expansion slot and tests the operation of the system as it boots up. These cards can be as simple as interrupt and DMA channel monitors, or as complex as full-fledged ROM BIOS diagnostic packages that carry out extensive tests on the system.

POST cards are normally used when the system appears to be dead, or when the system cannot read from a floppy or hard drive. The firmware tests on the card replace the normal BIOS functions and send the system into a set of tests. The value of the card lies in the fact that the tests can be carried out without the system resorting to software diagnostics located on the hard disk or in a floppy drive.

The POST tests located in most BIOS chips will report two types of errors: fatal and nonfatal. If the POST encounters a fatal error, it stops the system. The error code posted on the indicator corresponds to the defective operation. If the POST card encounters a nonfatal

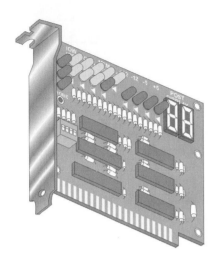

FIGURE 2.9
A typical POST card.

error, however, it notes the error and continues through the initial-ization routine to activate as many additional system resources as possible. When these types of errors are encountered, the POST card must be observed carefully, because the error code on its indicator must be coordinated with the timing of the error message or beep code produced by the BIOS routines.

Simple POST cards come with a set of light-emitting diodes (LEDs) on them that produce coded error signals when a problem is encountered. Other cards produce beep codes and seven-segment LED readouts of the error code. Figure 2.9. depicts a typical XT/AT-compatible POST card.

Hardware Troubleshooting

Unfortunately, most software diagnostics packages do not lead to specific components that have failed. Indeed, you might not even be able to use a software package to isolate faults if major components of the system are inoperative. If you have eliminated software and configuration problems, you need to pull out the test equipment and check the system's internal hardware for proper operation under controlled conditions.

Turn off the power and remove any peripheral devices from the system one at a time. Make sure to restore the power and retry the system after you remove each peripheral. If you have removed all the peripherals and the problem persists, you must troubleshoot the basic components of the system. This troubleshooting usually involves checking the components inside the system unit.

Performing Quick Tests

After you have removed the cover of the system unit, perform a care-ful visual inspection of its interior. Look for signs of overheating, such as charred components or wires. When electronic components overheat, they produce a noticeable odor, so you may be able to do some troubleshooting with your nose. If you do find an overheated component, especially a resistor, don't assume that you can clear up the problem by just replacing the burnt component. Many times when a component fails, it causes another component to fail.

WARNING

Ground Yourself Because there may be *metal-oxide semiconductor* (MOS) devices on the board, you want to ground yourself before performing this test. You can do so by touching an exposed portion of the unit's chassis, such as the top of the power supply.

You can make a very quick check of the system's integrated circuits (ICs) by just touching the tops of the chips with your finger to see whether they are hot.

If the system has power applied to it, all the ICs should be warm. Some will be warmer than others by nature; if a chip burns your finger, however, it is probably bad and needs to be replaced. Just replacing the chip might not clear up your problem, however. Instead, you may end up with two dead chips (the original and the replacement). The original chip may have been wiped out by some other problem in the system. For this reason, you should use this quick test only to localize problems.

Other items to check include components and internal connections that may have come loose. Check for foreign objects that may have fallen through the device's air vents. Remove any dust buildup that might have accumulated, and then retry the system.

Field-Replaceable Unit Troubleshooting

Field-replaceable units (FRUs) are the portions of the system that you can conveniently replace in the field. Figure 2.10 depicts typical microcomputer FRUs. FRU troubleshooting involves isolating a problem within one section of the system. A section consists of one device such as a keyboard, video display, video adapter card, I/O adapter card, system board, disk drive, printer, and so on. These are typically components that can simply be exchanged for a replacement on site and require no actual repair work.

This is the level of troubleshooting most often performed on PCs. Due to the relative low cost of computer components, it is normally not practical to troubleshoot failed components to the IC level. The cost of using a technician to diagnose the problem further, and repair it, can quickly exceed the cost of the new replacement unit.

When exchanging system components, be sure to replace the device being removed with one of exactly the same type. Just because two components have the same function *does not* mean that they can be substituted for each other. (For example, an EGA video adapter card cannot just be used to replace a monochrome adapter card without making other modifications to the system.) Interchanging similar parts is possible in some cases and not in others. Whether two components can be exchanged depends on the particular modules.

TEST TIP

Know which devices in a typical PC system are FRU devices.

NOTE

Exchanging FRU Components   When a hardware error has been indicated, start troubleshooting the problem by exchanging components (cards, drives, and so on) with known good ones.

FIGURE 2.10
The typical FRUs of a microcomputer system.

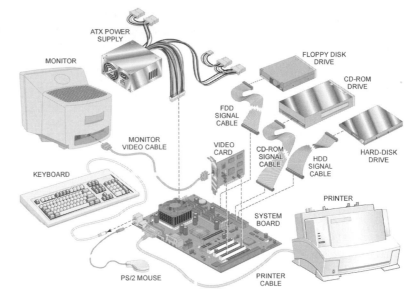

Assume that only a single component has failed. The odds against more than one component failing at the same time are extremely high. At the point where the system's operation is restored, it can reasonably be assumed that at least the last component removed was defective.

If a diagnostic tool indicates that multiple components have failed, use the one-at-time exchange method, starting with the first component indicated, to isolate the original source of the problem. Test the system between each component exchange and work backward through the exchanged components after the system has started to function again.

If it is necessary to disconnect cables or connectors from boards, take the time to mark the cables *and* their connection points so that they are easy to identify later. The simplest way to mark cables is to place identification marks on tape (masking or athletic) and then attach the tape to the cables and connection points.

Match the markings on the cable with the markings at its connection point. At many connection points, the color of the wire connected to a certain pin may be important. When placing the identifying marks on the tape, you may want to note the color arrangement of the wires being disconnected so that you can be sure to get them back in their proper places after you have swapped the component.

Always check cabling connections after plugging them in. Look for missed connections, bent pins, and so on. Also, check the routing of cables. Try to establish connections that do not place unnecessary strain on the cable. Route cables away from ICs as much as possible. Some ICs, such as microprocessors, can become quite hot, so hot that they and may eventually damage cables. Avoid routing cables near cooling fans as well because they produce high levels of EMI that can be introduced into the signal cables as electrical noise.

It is often helpful to just reseat (remove and reinstall) connections and adapter cards in the expansion slots when a problem occurs. *Corrosion* may build up on the computer's connection points and cause a poor electrical contact to occur. By reseating the connection, the contact problem often disappears.

Working backward, one at a time, through any components that have been removed from the system, enables you to make certain that only one failure occurred in the machine. If the system fails after installing a new card, check the card's default configuration settings against those of the devices already installed in the system.

NOTE **Write It Down** Make certain to take the time to document the symptoms associated with the problem, including all the tests you make and any changes that occur during the tests. This information can keep you from making repetitive steps.

NOTE **Work Backward** After you have isolated the problem, and the computer boots up and runs correctly, work backward through the troubleshooting routines, reinstalling any original boards and other components removed during the troubleshooting process.

Isolating Undefined Problems

Effective troubleshooting is a process of observing symptoms and applying logic to isolate and repair the cause as quickly and efficiently as possible. If the FRU troubleshooting system were taken to its most extreme, it would be logical to expect that anyone could repair a computer by just exchanging all the parts one at a time until the system started working.

Although this is technically possible, it is also highly unlikely to occur. In addition, such a scenario would not be efficient or cost effective to carry out. Therefore, technicians use symptoms and tools to provide effective troubleshooting.

Other problems, however, may just refuse to be classified under a particular symptom. If a multiple-component failure occurs, or if one failure causes a second failure to occur, the symptoms produced by the computer may not point to any particular cause. Secondary problems may also hide the symptoms of the real failure. These types of failures, which do not point to a clear-cut component in the system, are referred to as undefined problems.

Even in these cases, the technician should use the symptoms presented to isolate the problem to an area of the system for checking. Normally, symptoms can be divided into three sections: *configuration problems, boot-up problems*, and *operational problems.*

The system's configuration settings are normally checked first. It is important to observe the system's symptoms to determine in which part of the system's operation the fault occurs. Error messages typically associated with configuration problems include the following:

◆ CMOS Display Type Mismatch

◆ CMOS Memory Size Mismatch

◆ CMOS Battery State Low

◆ CMOS Checksum Failure

◆ CMOS System Options Not Set

◆ CMOS Time and Date Not Set

These errors occur and are reported before the single beep tone is produced at the end of the POST routines.

After the beep tone has been produced in the startup sequence, the system shifts over to the process of booting up. Typical error messages associated with boot-up problems include the following:

◆ General Failure Error Reading Drive *x*

◆ Bad or Missing Command Interpreter

◆ Non-System Disk or Disk Error

◆ Bad File Allocation Table

Configuration problems and boot-up problems can both be caused by a hardware or operational problem. If no configuration settings are incorrect, but the symptoms are present, a hardware problem is indicated as the cause of the problem. Procedures for diagnosing and troubleshooting problems associated with typical PC hardware components are presented throughout section "2.1 Symptoms and Troubleshooting" later in this chapter.

Conversely, boot-up problems are typically associated with the operating system. Steps for isolating and correcting operating system problems are presented in Chapter 9.

The Shotgun Approach

At rare times, it is best to just begin with some logical starting point and work through the entire system until you cure the problem. One such method, referred to as the shotgun method, divides the system into logical sections to quickly isolate the cause of the problem to an area.

The system may be made up of the basic computer, monitor, and keyboard, or it may be a highly developed combination of equipment, involving the basic computer and a group of peripherals. For troubleshooting purposes, you should divide the system into logically related subsections.

The first division naturally falls between the components that make up the basic system and other devices. The basic system consists of the system unit, the keyboard, and the video display monitor. Other devices consist of components that are optional as far as the system's operation is concerned. You can remove these items from the system without changing its basic operation. They include such things as printers, mouse devices, digitizing tablets, hard disk drives, tape drives, scanners, and so on.

When a problem occurs, you should first remove the optional items from the system. By doing so, you divide the system in half and can determine whether the problem exists in one of the computer's main components or in one of its options.

The second logical division falls between the internal and external options. When you have no idea what the problem is, you should test all external devices before removing the outer cover to check internal devices.

Inside the system unit, the next dividing point exists between the system board and all the internal options. The first items to be removed from the system are the options adapters, except for the disk drive and video controller cards. You should check these cards only if the system still won't work properly with the other options adapters removed.

The next components to exchange are the floppy drives and the power-supply unit, in that order. The system board is the last logical and most difficult component to exchange. Therefore, it should be the last component in the system to be exchanged.

SYMPTOMS AND TROUBLESHOOTING

▶ 2.1 Identify common symptoms and problems associated with each module and how to troubleshoot and isolate the problems.

The A+ Core Hardware objective 2.1 states that the test taker should be able to "identify common symptoms and problems associated with each module and how to troubleshoot and isolate the problems."

One of the primary responsibilities of every PC technician is to diagnose and troubleshoot computer problems. As this A+ objective points out, the technician should be able to identify common symptoms associated with computer components, and to use those symptoms to effectively troubleshoot and repair the problem. Numerous sources of problems and symptoms are discussed here, beginning with those that relate to the power supply.

Isolating Power-Supply Problems

Typical symptoms associated with power-supply failures include the following:

◆ No indicator lights visible, with no disk drive action, and no display onscreen. Nothing works; the system is dead.

◆ The On/Off indicator lights are visible, but there is no disk drive action and no display on the monitor screen. The system fan may or may not run.

◆ The system produces a continuous beep tone.

The power-supply unit is one of the few components in the system that is connected to virtually every other component in the system. Therefore, it can affect all the other components if it fails. Figure 2.11 illustrates the interconnections of the power-supply unit with the other components in the system.

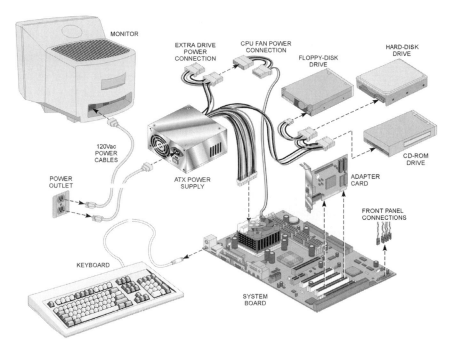

FIGURE 2.11
Power-supply interconnections.

When tracking down power-supply problems, remember that in addition to the obvious power connections shown in the diagram, the power supply also delivers power to other components through the system board. These include: (1) all the options adapter cards (through the expansion-slot connectors); and (2) the keyboard (through the keyboard connector). Power-supply problems can cause symptoms to occur in all these areas, and problems in any of these areas can affect the operation of the power supply.

Checking a Dead System

Special consideration must be taken when a system is inoperable. In a totally inoperable system, there are no symptoms to give clues where to begin the isolation process. In addition, it is impossible to use troubleshooting software or other system aids to help isolate the problem.

The following discussion covers a standard method of troubleshooting dead microprocessor-based equipment. The first step in troubleshooting any dead system is to visually inspect the system. Check for unseated cards, loose cables, or foreign objects within the system unit.

When the system exhibits no signs of life—including the absence of lights—the best place to start looking for the problem is at the power supply. The operation of this unit affects virtually every part of the system. Also, the absence of any lights working usually indicates that no power is being supplied to the system by the power supply.

1. Begin by checking the external connections of the power supply. This is the first step in checking any electrical equipment that shows no signs of life.

2. Confirm that the power-supply cord is plugged into a functioning outlet.

3. Check the position of the On/Off switch.

4. Examine the power cord for good connection at the rear of the unit.

5. Check the setting of the 110/220 switch setting on the outside of the power supply. The normal setting for equipment used in the United States is 110.

6. Check the power at the commercial receptacle using a voltmeter, or by plugging in a lamp (or other 110V device) into the outlet.

If power is reaching the power supply and nothing is happening, the next step in isolating the cause of the problem is to determine which component is causing the problem. The most likely cause of the problems in a totally dead system is the power supply itself. However, be aware that in an ATX system, if the cable that connects the system board to the power switch has become loose, the power supply will appear dead. Use a voltmeter to check for the proper voltages at one of the system's option's power connectors. (All system voltages should be present at these connectors.) If any voltage is missing, check the power supply by substitution.

If the power supply is not the reason the system is dead, one of the other components must be overloading the power supply. Under such conditions, it is normal for the system to trip the breaker, or to blow the fuse, in the commercial power system. You must sort out which component is affecting the power supply. Remove the peripheral devices so that only the basic system needs to be checked.

TEST TIP

Remember the first step of checking out electrical equipment that appears dead.

Divide the system into basic and optional sections for testing.
Remove all external options from the system and restart the system.
If the system begins to work, troubleshoot the optional portions of
the system.

Finally, divide the basic system into optional and basic components.
Remove all optional adapter cards from their expansion slots and
restart the system. If the system begins to work, troubleshoot the
various options' adapters by reinstalling them one at a time until the
system fails again.

> **WARNING**
>
> **Turn It Off First!**   Before changing any
> board or connection, always turn the sys-
> tem off first. In an ATX-style system, you
> should also disconnect the power cable
> from the power supply. This is necessary
> because even with the power switch off,
> there are still some levels of voltages
> applied to the system board in these units.

Other Power-Supply Problems

If the front-panel lights are on and the power-supply fan is running,
but no other system action is occurring, you should consider the
power supply as one of the most likely sources of such a problem.

The presence of the lights and the fan operation indicate that power
is reaching the system and that at least some portion of the power
supply is functional. This type of symptom results from the following two likely possibilities:

◆ A portion of the power supply has failed, or is being over-
loaded. One or more of the basic voltages supplied by the
power supply is missing while the others are still present.

◆ A key component on the system board has failed, preventing it
from processing, even though the system has power. A defective capacitor across the power input of the system board can
completely prevent it from operating.

Check the power supply by substitution. If the power supply is not
the cause of the dead system, one of the other components must be
overloading that portion of the power supply. You must sort out
which component is causing the problem.

System Board Troubleshooting

Troubleshooting problems related to the system board can be difficult to solve because of the system board's relative complexity. So
many system functions rely at least partially on the system board
that certain symptoms can be masked by other symptoms.

As with any troubleshooting procedure, begin by observing the symptoms produced by boot up and operation. Observe the steps that lead to the failure and determine under what conditions the system failed. Were any unusual operations in progress? Note any error messages or beep codes.

Try any obvious steps, such as adjusting brightness controls on a dim monitor or checking for loose connections on peripheral equipment. Retry the system several times to observe the symptoms clearly. Take time to document the problem—write it down.

Refer to the User Manuals for the system board and peripheral units to check for configuration problems. Examine the CMOS setup entries for configuration problems. In Pentium systems, also check the advanced CMOS setup parameters to make certain that all the appropriate system board–enabling settings have been made.

If possible, run a software diagnostics package to narrow the possible causes. Remember that the microprocessor, RAM modules, ROM BIOS, CMOS battery, and possibly cache ICs are typically replaceable units on the system board. If enough of the system is running to perform tests on these units, you can replace them. If symptoms suggest that one or more of these devices may be defective, you can exchange them with a known good unit of the same type.

If the diagnostics program indicates a number of possible bad components, replace them one at a time until you isolate the bad unit. Then insert any possible good units back into the system and check them. You also should consider the possibility of bad software when multiple FRU problems are indicated.

System Board Symptoms

So much of the system's operation is based on the system board that it can have several different types of symptoms. Typical symptoms associated with system board hardware failures include the following:

◆ The On/Off indicator lights are visible, the display is visible on the monitor screen, but there is no disk drive action and no boot up.

◆ The On/Off indicator lights are visible, the hard drive spins up, but the system appears dead and there is no boot up.

◆ The system locks up during normal operation.

◆ The system produces a beep code with 1, 2, 3, 5, 7, or 9 beeps.

◆ The system produces a beep code of 1 long and 3 short beeps.

◆ The system will not hold date and time.

◆ An `8042 Gate A20 Error` message displays—error getting into protected mode.

◆ An `Invalid Switch Memory Failure` message displays.

◆ A `DMA Error` message displays—DMA controller failed page register test.

◆ A `CMOS Battery Low` message displays, indicating failure of CMOS battery or CMOS checksum test.

◆ A `CMOS System Option Not Set` message displays, indicating failure of CMOS battery or CMOS checksum test.

◆ A `CMOS Checksum Failure` message displays, indicating CMOS battery low or CMOS checksum test failure.

◆ A 201 error code displays, indicating a RAM failure.

◆ A parity check error message displays, indicating a RAM error.

TEST TIP	Memorize standard IBM error code numbers.

Typical symptoms associated with system board setup failures include the following:

◆ A `CMOS Inoperational` message displays, indicating failure of CMOS shutdown register.

◆ A `Display Switch Setting Not Proper` message displays—failure to verify display type.

◆ A `CMOS Display Mismatch` message displays—failure of display-type verification.

◆ A `CMOS Memory Size Mismatch` message displays—system configuration and setup failure.

◆ A `CMOS Time & Date Not Set` message displays—system configuration and setup failure.

◆ An IBM-compatible error code displays, indicating that a configuration problem has occurred.

Typical symptoms associated with system board I/O failures include the following:

◆ Speaker doesn't work during operation. The rest of the system works, but no sounds are produced through the speaker.

◆ Keyboard does not function after being replaced with a known good unit.

Most of the hardware problems that occur with computers, outside of those already described, involve the system board. Because the system board is the center of virtually all the computer's operations, it is only natural that you must check it at some point in most troubleshooting efforts. The system board normally marks the end of any of the various troubleshooting schemes given for different system components. It occupies this position for two reasons. First, the system board supports most of the other system components, either directly or indirectly. Second, it is the system component that requires the most effort to replace and test.

Other System Board Problems

In addition to containing the circuitry that directs all the system's operations, the system board contains a number of other circuits on which the rest of the system's components depend. These include the system's DRAM memory (which all software programs use) and the system's data, address, and signal buses. The part of the buses you are most familiar with are the expansion slots.

Problems with key system board components produce symptoms similar to those described for a bad power supply. Both the microprocessor and the ROM BIOS can be sources of such problems. You should check both by substitution when dead system symptoms are encountered but the power supply is good.

Because all the system's options adapter cards connect to the buses through the expansion slots, failure of any component attached to one of the slots can prevent information movement between other components along the bus. In this case, you must remove the offending component from the bus before any operation can proceed.

You can add a number of other optional devices to the system just by installing an appropriate adapter card in one of the system board's expansion slots and then connecting the option to it. Figure 2.12 illustrates the flow of information between the system board and a typical connection port (a parallel printer port) located on an option's adapter card.

An often overlooked output device is the system's speaker. Unlike other I/O devices, all the circuitry that controls the speaker is contained on the system board. Therefore, the speaker should fail for only a few reasons, including the speaker itself is defective, the speaker circuitry on the system board is defective, the speaker is unplugged from the system board, or the software is failing to drive the speaker circuits.

The easiest time to detect a speaker problem is during the boot-up process. The system may use the speaker to produce different sounds at various points in this process. However, the most direct way to check a speaker is to check across its leads using the resistance function of a digital multimeter. The DMM should read approximately 8 ohms for most speakers used with PCs. Figure 2.13 depicts a system's typical speaker-related components.

The keyboard is another I/O device supported directly from the system board. When examining keyboard problems, there are only three items to check: the keyboard, the system board, and the keyboard driver software. The most basic way to determine keyboard problems is to watch the keyboard's NumLock and ScrollLock lights during the boot-up process. These lights should flash when the system attempts to initialize the keyboard.

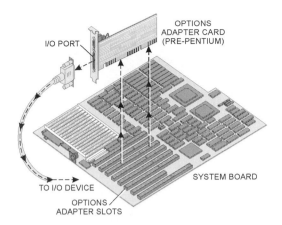

FIGURE 2.12
Moving information to an I/O port.

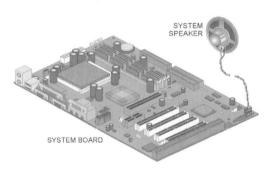

FIGURE 2.13
Speaker-related components.

Configuration Checks

Observe the boot-up RAM count to see that it is correct for the amount of physical RAM actually installed in the system. If not, swap RAM devices around to see whether the count changes. Use logical rotation of the RAM devices to locate the defective part.

Normally, the only time a configuration problem occurs is when the system is being set up for the first time, or when a new option is installed. The other condition that causes a configuration problem involves the system board's CMOS backup battery. If the battery fails, or has been changed, the contents of the CMOS setup will be lost. After replacing the battery, it is always necessary to run the CMOS setup utility to reconfigure the system.

The values stored in CMOS must accurately reflect the configuration of the system; otherwise, an error occurs. You can access these values for change by pressing a predetermined key combination during the boot-up procedure.

In Pentium-based systems, check the advanced CMOS configuration and enabling settings in the BIOS and Chipset Features screens. These settings, illustrated in Figure 2.14, usually include the disk drives, keyboard, and video options, as well as onboard serial and parallel ports.

In addition, the user can turn on or off certain sections of the system's RAM for shadowing purposes and establish parity or nonparity memory operations.

Incorrectly set BIOS-enabling parameters cause the corresponding hardware to fail. Therefore, check the enabling functions of the advanced CMOS settings as a part of every hardware configuration troubleshooting procedure.

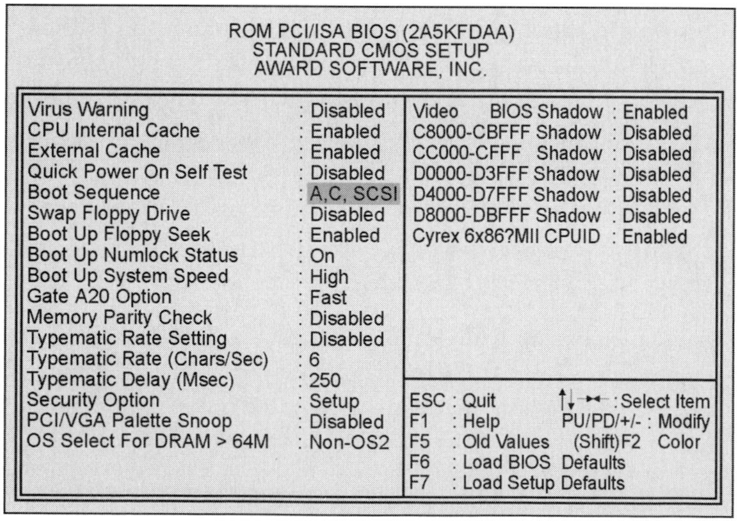

FIGURE 2.14
BIOS-enabling settings.

```
                    ROM PCI/ISA BIOS (2A5KFDAA)
                       STANDARD CMOS SETUP
                       AWARD SOFTWARE, INC.

  Virus Warning            : Disabled    Video     BIOS Shadow  : Enabled
  CPU Internal Cache       : Enabled     C8000-CBFFF Shadow  : Disabled
  External Cache           : Enabled     CC000-CFFF  Shadow  : Disabled
  Quick Power On Self Test : Disabled    D0000-D3FFF Shadow  : Disabled
  Boot Sequence            : A,C, SCSI   D4000-D7FFF Shadow  : Disabled
  Swap Floppy Drive        : Disabled    D8000-DBFFF Shadow  : Disabled
  Boot Up Floppy Seek      : Enabled     Cyrex 6x86?MII CPUID : Enabled
  Boot Up Numlock Status   : On
  Boot Up System Speed     : High
  Gate A20 Option          : Fast
  Memory Parity Check      : Disabled
  Typematic Rate Setting   : Disabled
  Typematic Rate (Chars/Sec) : 6
  Typematic Delay (Msec)   : 250
  Security Option          : Setup       ESC : Quit      ↑↓→← :Select Item
  PCI/VGA Palette Snoop    : Disabled    F1  : Help       PU/PD/+/- : Modify
  OS Select For DRAM > 64M : Non-OS2     F5  : Old Values  (Shift)F2  Color
                                         F6  : Load BIOS Defaults
                                         F7  : Load Setup Defaults
```

The complexity of modern system boards has created a huge number of configuration options for the CMOS, as reflected in the complexity of their advanced CMOS configuration screens. It is very easy to place the system in a condition where it cannot respond. Because the problem is at the BIOS level, it may be difficult to get back into the CMOS to correct the problem. Therefore, system designers have included a couple of options to safeguard the system from this condition.

In some BIOS, holding down the Del key throughout the startup erases the CMOS contents and starts from scratch. Jumpers that can be set to start the contents from a bare-essentials setting may also be placed on the system board. In either case, you must rebuild any advanced features in the CMOS configuration afterward.

Newer system boards have an autoconfiguration mode that takes over most of the setup decisions. This option works well in the majority of applications. Its settings produce an efficient, basic level of operation for standard devices in the system. However, they do not optimize the performance of the system. To do that, you must turn off the autoconfiguration feature and insert desired parameters into the configuration table. There are typically two options for the autoconfiguration function: Autoconfigure with Power-On Defaults and Autoconfigure with BIOS Defaults.

Using power-on defaults for autoconfiguration loads the most conservative options possible into the system from the BIOS. This is the most effective way to detect BIOS-related system problems. These settings replace any user-entered configuration information in the CMOS setup registers. Any turbo-speed mode is disabled, all memory caching is turned off, and all wait states are set to maximum. This allows the most basic part of the system to start up. If these default values fail to get the system to boot up, it is an indication of hardware problems (such as incorrect jumper settings or bad hardware components).

Using autoconfiguration with BIOS defaults provides a little more flexibility than the power-on option. If you have entered an improper configuration setting and cannot determine which setting is causing the problem, this option is suggested. Like the power-on option, this selection replaces the entered configuration settings with a new set of parameters from the BIOS. Choosing this option will likely get you back into the CMOS setup screen so that you can track down the problem. It also is the recommended starting point for optimizing the system's operation.

The many configuration options available in a modern BIOS requires the user to have a good deal of knowledge about the particular function being configured. Therefore, an extended discussion of the advanced CMOS setup options cannot be conducted at this point. However, such information is covered along with the system component it relates to as the book moves through various system components.

CMOS setup utilities may also offer a wide array of exit options. One common mistake in working with CMOS configuration settings is that of not saving the new settings before exiting. When this happens, the new settings are not stored, and so the old settings are still in place when the system reboots.

Software Checks

Boot up the system and start the selected diagnostic program if possible. Try to use a diagnostic program that deals with the system board components. It should include memory, microprocessor, interrupt, and DMA tests.

Run the program's *System Board Tests* function and perform the equivalent of the All Tests function. These types of tests are particularly good for detecting memory errors, as well as interrupt and DMA conflicts. Note all the errors indicated by the tests. If a single type of error is indicated, you might be able to take some corrective actions, such as replacing a memory module or reconfiguring interrupt/DMA settings, without replacing the system board. If more complex system board problems are indicated, however, exit the diagnostic program and use the following hardware checks and installation/removal procedure to troubleshoot and replace the system board.

You can use the DOS **MEM** command (MEM.EXE) to view the system's memory-utilization scheme. It displays both the programs currently loaded into memory, and the system's free memory areas. You can use the **/C** switch with the **MEM** command as a valuable

---

NOTE

Hardware Conflicts and the CMOS

Typically, if the boot-up process reaches the point where the system's CMOS configuration information displays onscreen, you can safely assume that no hardware configuration conflicts exist in the system's basic components. After this point in the boot-up process, the system begins loading drivers for optional devices and additional memory. If the error occurs after the CMOS screen displays and before the boot-up tone, you must clean-boot the system and single-step through the remainder of the boot-up sequence.

tool to sort out TSR conflicts in upper memory. Likewise, you can add a **/D** switch to the **MEM** command to view detailed information about memory usage. This switch gives very detailed information about all items stored in memory.

Hardware Checks

If the system's CMOS configuration setup appears to be correct and a system board hardware problem is suspected, you probably need to exchange the system board for a working unit. Because most of the system must be dismantled to exchange it, however, a few items are worth checking before doing so.

Check the system board for signs of physical problems, such as loose cables and devices. If nothing is apparently wrong, check the power-supply voltage levels on the system board. Check for +5V and +12V (DC) on the system board, as illustrated in Figure 2.15. If these voltages are missing, turn off the system, disconnect power to all disk drives, and swap the power-supply unit with a known good one.

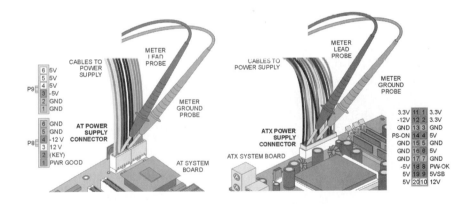

FIGURE 2.15
The system board voltage check location.

Onboard FRU Devices

Finally, consider checking the FRU devices present on the board. Normally, a few serviceable items on the system board might be checked by substitution before doing so. These include the RAM modules, the microprocessor (and its cooling fan), the ROM BIOS chip(s), and the system battery.

RAM

The system board's memory is a very serviceable part of the system. RAM failures basically fall into two major categories and create two different types of failures. The first category of memory errors, called *soft-memory errors,* are caused by infrequent and random glitches in the operation of applications and the system. You can clear these events just by restarting the system. However, the other category of RAM failures are referred to as *hard-memory errors.* These are permanent physical failures that generate NMI errors in the system and require that the memory units be checked by substitution.

You can swap the RAM modules out in a one-at-a-time manner, to isolate defective modules. These modules are also swapped out when a system upgrade is being performed. The burn-in tests in most diagnostic packages can prove helpful in locating borderline RAM modules.

Take care when swapping RAM into a system for troubleshooting purposes to make sure that the new RAM is the correct type of RAM for the system and that it meets the system's bus speed rating. Also, make sure that the replacement RAM is consistent with the installed RAM. Mixing RAM types and speeds can cause the system to lock up and produce hard memory errors.

Microprocessor

In the case of the microprocessor, the system may issue a slow, single beep, with no display or other I/O operation. This indicates that an internal error has disabled a portion of the processor's internal circuitry (usually the internal cache). Internal problems also may allow the microprocessor to begin processing, but then fail as it attempts operations. Such a problem results in the system continuously counting RAM during the boot up process. It also may lock up while counting RAM. In either case, the only way to remedy the problem is to replace the microprocessor.

If the system consistently locks up after being on for a few minutes, this is a good indication that the microprocessor's fan is not running or that some other heat buildup problem is occurring. You also should check the microprocessor if its fan has not been running, but the power is on. This situation may indicate that the microprocessor has been without adequate ventilation and has overheated. When this happens, you must replace the fan unit and the microprocessor. Check to make certain that the new fan works correctly; otherwise, a second microprocessor will be damaged.

You can easily exchange the microprocessor on most system boards. Only the 80386SX is a soldered-in device, so it presents more of a challenge to exchange (and is not likely worth the expense involved). However, the fact that most microprocessors, as well as the BIOS chips, are mounted in sockets brings up another point. These items should be pulled and reseated in their sockets, if they seem to be a possible cause of problems. Sockets are convenient for repair and upgrade purposes, but they also can attract corrosion between the pins of the device, and those of the socket. Over time, the corrosion may become so bad that the electrical connection becomes too poor for the device to operate properly.

ROM

Like the microprocessor, a bad or damaged ROM BIOS typically stops the system dead. When you encounter a dead system board, examine the BIOS chip(s) for physical damage. If these devices overheat, it is typical for them to crack or blow a large piece out of the top of the IC package. Another symptom of a damaged BIOS is indicated by the boot up moving into the CMOS configuration, but never returning to the boot-up sequence. In any case, you must replace the defective BIOS with a version that matches the chipset used by the system.

Battery

Corrosion also can affect the system clock over time. If a system refuses to maintain time and date information after the backup battery has been replaced, check the contacts of the holder for corrosion. Two types of batteries are commonly used for CMOS backup: *Nickel-Cadmium* (Ni-Cad) and *lithium batteries*. Of the two, Ni-Cads have historically been the most favored. Conversely, lithium batteries are gaining respect due to their long-life capabilities when installed in systems designed to recharge lithium batteries. However, lithium battery life is noticeably short when they are installed in systems designed for the higher current drain Ni-Cads. Therefore, you should always use the correct type of battery to replace a system board battery.

TEST TIP

Know the effects on the system of heat buildup and microprocessor fan failures.

Exchanging the System Board

If there is any uncertainty about the system board being the source of the problem, use the isolation step presented in the "Isolating Undefined Problems" section earlier in this chapter to isolate the fault down to the system board.

Reduce the system to its basic components. If it still refuses to boot up, remove the basic adapter cards one by one and restart the system.

If possible, back up the contents of the system's hard drive to some other media before removing the system board. Also, record the CMOS configuration settings, along with the settings of all jumpers and switches, before exchanging the system board.

If the system still won't boot up, remove the video and disk drive controller cards from the system board's expansion slots. Disconnect the system board from the power-supply unit and the system board/front-panel connections. Take care to mark any connection removed from the system board, and its connection point, to ensure proper reconnection. Exchange the system board with a known good one. Reconnect all the power-supply and front-panel connections to the system board. Reinstall the video and disk drive controller cards in the expansion slots and try to reboot the system.

Reconfigure the system board to operate with the installed peripherals. Reseat the video and disk drive controller cards in the system unit. Reset the CMOS setup to match the installed peripherals and turn on the system.

When the system boots up, reinstall any options removed from the system and replace the system unit's outer cover. Return the system to full service and service the defective system board. If the system still does not boot up, retest all the system components one at a time until you find a cause. Check the small things such as cable connections and key switches carefully.

Troubleshooting Keyboard Problems

Most of the circuitry associated with the computer's keyboard is contained in the keyboard itself. However, some keyboard interface circuitry is located on the system board. Therefore, the steps required to isolate keyboard problems are usually confined to the keyboard, its connecting cable, and the system board.

This arrangement makes isolating keyboard problems relatively easy. Just check the keyboard and the system board. Figure 2.16 depicts the components associated with the keyboard.

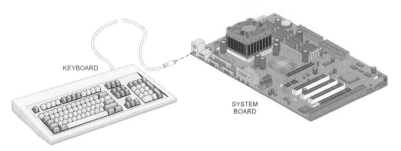

FIGURE 2.16
Keyboard-related components.

Keyboard Symptoms

Typical symptoms associated with keyboard failures include the following:

◆ No characters appear onscreen when entered from the keyboard.

◆ Some keys work, whereas others do not work.

◆ A `Keyboard Is Locked—Unlock It` error displays.

◆ A `Keyboard Error—Keyboard Test Failure` error displays.

◆ A `KB/Interface Error—Keyboard Test Failure` error displays.

◆ An error code of 6 short beeps is produced during boot up.

◆ Wrong characters display.

◆ An IBM-compatible 301 error code displays.

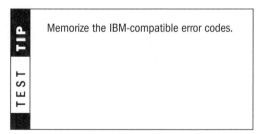

TEST TIP

Memorize the IBM-compatible error codes.

Basic Keyboard Checks

Keyboard information is stored in the CMOS setup memory, and must accurately reflect the configuration of the system; otherwise, an error occurs. In most CMOS screens, the setup information includes keyboard enabling, NumLock key condition at startup, typematic rate, and typematic delay. The typematic information applies to the keyboard's capability to repeat characters when the key is held down. The typematic rate determines how quickly characters are repeated, and the delay time defines the amount of time the key can be held before typematic action occurs. A typical typematic rate setting is 6 characters per second; the delay is normally set at 250 milliseconds.

As with other components, the only time a configuration problem is likely to occur is when the system is being set up for the first time or when a new option is installed. The other condition that causes a configuration problem involves the system board's CMOS backup battery. If the battery fails, or has been changed, the contents of the CMOS setup will be lost. After replacing the battery, you must always run the setup utility to reconfigure the system.

Turn on the system and observe the BIOS screens as the system boots up. Note the Keyboard Type listed in the BIOS summary table. If possible, run a selected diagnostic program to test the keyboard. Run the program's Keyboard Tests function, and perform the equivalent of the All Tests function if available. These tests are normally very good at testing the keyboard for general operation and sticking keys.

The keys of the keyboard can wear out over time. This may result in keys that do not make good contact (no character is produced when the key is pushed) or one that remains in contact (sticks) even when pressure is removed. The stuck key will produce an error message when the system detects it. However, it has no way of detecting an open key. If you detect a stuck key, or keys, you can desolder and replace the individual key switches with a good key from a manufacturer or a similar keyboard. However, the amount of time spent repairing a keyboard quickly drives the cost of the repair beyond the cost of a new unit.

If the keyboard produces odd characters on the display, check the Windows keyboard settings in the Control Panel's Device Manager. If the keyboard is not installed, or is incorrect, install the correct keyboard type. Also, make certain that you have the correct language setting specified under the Control Panel's keyboard icon.

Keyboard Hardware Checks

If you suspect a hardware problem, you must first isolate the keyboard as the definite source of the problem (a fairly easy task). Because the keyboard is external to the system unit, detachable, and inexpensive, begin by exchanging the keyboard with a known good keyboard.

If the new keyboard works correctly, return the system to full service and service the defective keyboard appropriately. Remove the back cover from the keyboard and check for the presence of a fuse in the

+5V (DC) supply and check it for continuity. Disconnecting or plugging in a keyboard with this type of fuse while power is on can cause it to fail. If the fuse is present, just replace it with a fuse of the same type and rating.

If the system still won't boot up, recheck the CMOS setup to make sure that the keyboard is enabled. Check the keyboard cabling for continuity. And, finally, check the video display system (monitor and adapter card) to make sure that it is functional.

If replacing the keyboard does not correct the problem, and no configuration or software reason is apparent, the next step is to troubleshoot the keyboard receiver section of the system board. On most modern system boards, this ultimately involves replacing the system board with another one. Refer to the system board removal and installation instructions in the section titled "1.2 Adding and Removing FRU Modules," in Chapter 1, "1.0 Installation, Configuration, and Upgrading," to carry out this task.

After you have removed the system unit's cover, examine the keyboard connector on the system board. Also, look for auxiliary BERG connectors for the keyboard. Make certain that no item is shorting the pins of this connector together. Check for enable/disable jumpers for the keyboard on the system board.

Troubleshooting Mouse Problems

The levels of mouse troubleshooting move from configuration problems to software problems—including command line, Windows, and applications—to hardware problems.

Maintenance of the mouse is fairly simple. Most of the problems with mice involve the trackball. As the mouse is moved across the table, the trackball picks up dirt or lint, which can hinder the movement of the trackball, typically evident by the cursor periodically freezing and jumping onscreen. On most mice, you can remove the trackball from the mouse by a latching mechanism on its bottom. Twisting the latch counter-clockwise enables you to remove the trackball. Then you can clean dirt out of the mouse.

TEST TIP

Be aware that standard 5-pin DIN and PS/2 mini-DIN keyboards cannot be hot swapped and that doing so can cause damage to the keyboard and system board.

TEST TIP

Be aware of the condition that causes the cursor to jump and freeze on the display.

Basic Mouse Checks

When the mouse does not work in a Windows system, restart it and move into safe mode by pressing the F5 function key when the Starting Windows message displays. This action starts the operating system with the most basic mouse driver available.

If the mouse will not operate in safe mode, restart the system and check the CMOS Setup screen during boot up for the presence of the serial port that the mouse is connected to.

If the mouse works in safe mode, click the Mouse icon in the Control Panel to check its configuration and settings. Follow this by checking the port configuration in Windows Control Panel. Consult the Device Manager entry under the Control Panel's System icon. Select the Ports option, click the COM*x* Properties option in the menu, and click Resources. Make certain that the selected IRQ and address range match that of the port.

Click on the Mouse entry in the Device Manager and double-click its driver to obtain the Mouse Properties page depicted in Figure 2.17. Move to the Resources tab as illustrated and check the IRQ and *base address settings* for the mouse in Windows. Compare these settings to the actual configuration settings of the hardware. If they differ, change the IRQ or base address setting in Windows to match those of the installed hardware.

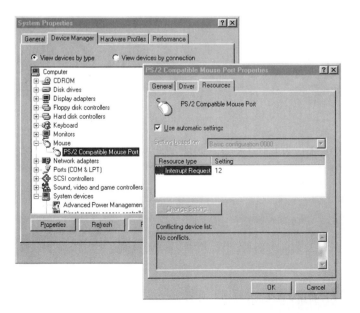

FIGURE 2.17
Mouse properties.

If the correct driver is not available in the Windows list, place the manufacturer's driver disk in the floppy drive and load it using the Other Mouse (requires disk from OEM) option. If the OEM driver fails to operate the mouse in Windows, contact the mouse manufacturer for an updated Windows driver. Windows normally supports only mice on COM1 and COM2. If several serial devices are being used in the system, you might have to establish alternative *IRQ settings* for COM3 and COM4.

In older systems, check the directory structure of the system for a Mouse directory. Also, check for AUTOEXEC.BAT and CONFIG.SYS files that may contain conflicting device drivers. Two common driver files may be present: the MOUSE.COM file called for in the AUTOEXEC.BAT file; and the MOUSE.SYS file referenced in the CONFIG.SYS file. If these files are present and have mouse lines that do not begin with a REM statement, they could be overriding the settings in the operating system. In particular, look for a **DEVICE=** command associated with the mouse.

Mouse Hardware Checks

If the 2/3 button switch and driver setup is correct, you must divide the port circuitry in half. For most systems, this involves isolating the mouse from the serial port. Just replace the mouse to test its electronics.

If the replacement mouse works, the original mouse is probably defective. If the electronics are not working properly, few options are available for servicing the mouse. It may need a cleaning, or a new trackball. However, the low cost of a typical mouse generally makes it a throwaway item if simple cleaning does not fix it.

If the new mouse does not work either, chances are very high that the mouse's electronics are working properly. In this case, the driver software, or port hardware, must be the cause of the problem.

Troubleshooting Joystick Problems

As with other input devices, there are three levels of possible problems with a joystick: configuration, software, and hardware.

Attempt to run the joystick with a DOS-based program. If the joystick does not work at the DOS level, check the game port's hardware configuration settings. Compare the hardware settings to that of any software using the game port. Try to swap the suspect joystick for a known good one.

Windows 9x contains a joystick icon in the Start/Settings/Control Panel window. Figure 2.18 shows the contents of the Windows 9x Joystick Properties dialog box. The Joystick icon is not loaded into the Control Panel window if the system does not detect a game port during installation. If the port is detected during boot up, but no joystick device is found, the window says that the joystick is not connected correctly.

FIGURE 2.18

The Joystick Properties dialog box.

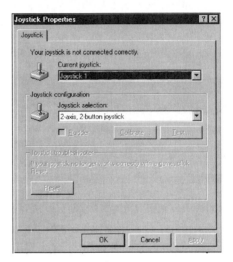

The Joystick Properties dialog box is used to select different numbers of joysticks (1–16) that can be used. It shows the currently selected joystick type, and allows other devices to be selected. The default joystick setting is a two-axis, two-button device. You also can select None, or Custom, joystick types. Other selections include two-axis four-button joysticks, and two-button game pads, as well as specialized flight *yoke assemblies* and flight stick assemblies.

The Joystick Properties dialog box also contains a button to calibrate the joystick's position. This button allows the zero-position of the stick to be set for the center of the screen. The Test button allows the movement of the stick and its button operation to be checked, as directed by the test program. Windows 95 also allows for a rudder device to be added to the system. The Joystick Troubleshooter section contains a Reset button to reinitialize the game port. This function is normally used if the stick stops responding to the program.

Troubleshooting Video

Figure 2.19 depicts the components associated with the video display. It may be most practical to think of the video information as starting out on the system board. In reality, the keyboard, one of the disk drives, or some other I/O device, may be the actual originating point for the information. In any case, information intended for the video display monitor moves from the system board, to the video adapter card, by way of the system board's expansion slots. The adapter card also obtains power for its operation from these expansion slots. Finally, the information is applied to the monitor through the video signal cable.

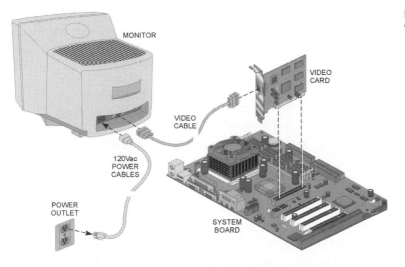

FIGURE 2.19
Video-related components.

Basically, three levels of troubleshooting apply to video problems: the DOS level, the Windows level and the hardware level. At the DOS level, you have two considerations: configuration problems and hardware problems.

In the case of hardware problems, the components associated with video problems include the video adapter card, and the monitor. To a lesser degree, the system board, and optional adapter cards, such as

FIGURE 2.20
Video failures.

sound and scanner cards, can cause video problems. Figure 2.20 illustrates some of the typical symptoms produced by video display failures.

Other common symptoms associated with display problems include the following:

◆ No display.

◆ Wrong characters displayed onscreen.

◆ Diagonal lines onscreen (no horizontal control).

◆ Display scrolls (no vertical control).

◆ An error code of 1 long and 6 short beeps is produced by the system.

◆ A `Display Switch Setting Not Proper—Failure to Verify Display Type` error displays.

◆ A `CMOS Display Mismatch—Failure to Verify Display Type` error displays.

◆ An error code of 1 long and 2 short beeps indicates a display adapter problem.

The following sections cover the digital portion of the video system. Troubleshooting the actual monitor is discussed immediately following the video adapter troubleshooting sections. Only experienced technicians should participate in troubleshooting internal monitor problems because of the very high voltages present there.

Basic Video Checks

While booting up the system to the DOS prompt, observe the BIOS video type information displayed on the monitor. The values stored in this CMOS memory must accurately reflect the type of monitor installed in the system; otherwise, an error occurs. You can access these values for change by pressing the Ctrl and Del keys (or some other key combination) simultaneously, during the boot-up procedure.

Reboot the system and run a diagnostic software program, if possible. Try to use a diagnostic program that conducts a bank of tests on the video components. Run the program's Video Tests function and perform the equivalent of the All Tests function.

Note all the errors indicated by the tests. If a single type of error is indicated, you might be able to take some corrective actions. If more complex system board problems are indicated, however, exit the diagnostic program and use the troubleshooting information in the "Hardware Checks" section of this chapter to locate and repair the video problem.

Windows 9x Video Checks

You can gain access to the Windows video information by double-clicking the Control Panel's Display icon. From the Display page, there are a series of file folder tabs at the top of the screen. Of particular interest is the Settings tab. Under this tab, the Change Display Type button provides access to both the adapter type and monitor type settings.

In the Adapter type window, information about the adapter's manufacturer, version number, and current driver files is given. Pressing the Change button beside this window brings a listing of available drivers to select from. You also can use the Have Disk button with an OEM disk to install video drivers not included in the list. You also can alter the manner in which the list displays by choosing the Show Compatible Devices or the Show All Devices options.

In the Monitor type window, there is an option list for both manufacturers and models. You also can use this function with the Have Disk button to establish OEM settings for the monitor.

You can access additional Windows video information under the Control Panel's System icon. Inside the *System Properties* page, click the *Device Manager* and select the Display Adapters option from the list. Double-click the monitor icon that appears as a branch.

The adapter's Properties page pops up onscreen. From this page, the Driver tab reveals the driver file in use. Selecting the Resources tab displays the video adapter's register address ranges and the video memory address range, as described in Figure 2.21. You can manipulate these settings manually by clicking the Change Setting button. You also can obtain information about the monitor through the System icon.

FIGURE 2.21
Video adapter resources.

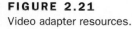

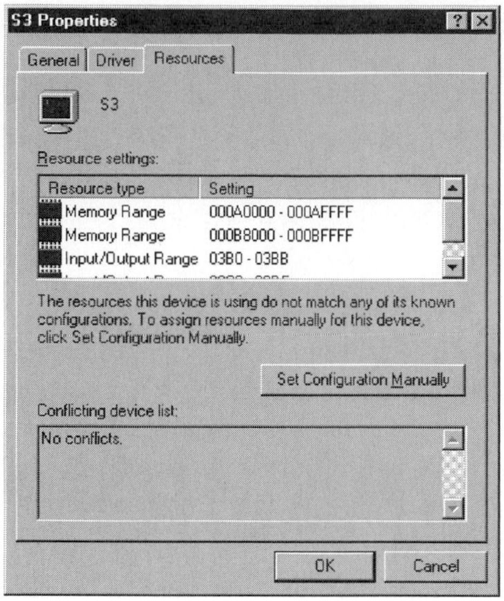

The first step when isolating Windows video problems involves checking the video drivers. Check for the drivers in the locations specified in the previous paragraphs. If the video driver from the list is not correct, reload the correct driver. If the problem persists, reinstall Windows.

If the Windows video problem prevents you from seeing the driver, restart the system, press the F8 function key when the Starting Windows message appears, and select Safe Mode. This should load Windows with the standard 640 × 480 × 16–color VGA driver (the most fundamental driver available for VGA monitors), and should furnish a starting point for installing the correct driver for the monitor being used.

If the problem reappears when a higher resolution driver is selected, refer to the Color Palette box under the Control Panel's Display option/Settings tab, and try minimum color settings. If the problem goes away, contact the *Microsoft Download Service* (MSDL) or the adapter card maker for a new, compatible video driver. If the problem remains, reinstall the driver from the Windows 9x distribution disk or CD. If the video is distorted or rolling, try an alternative video driver from the list.

Video Hardware Checks

If you suspect a video display hardware problem, the first task is to check the monitor's On/Off switch to see that it is in the On position. Also, check the monitor's power cord to see that it is either plugged into the power-supply's monitor outlet, or into an active 120V (AC) commercial outlet. Also check the monitor's intensity and contrast controls to make certain that they are not turned down.

The next step is to determine which of the video-related components is involved. On most monitors, you can do this by just removing the video signal cable from the adapter card. If a raster appears onscreen with the signal cable removed, the problem is probably a system problem, and the monitor is good. If the monitor is an EPA-certified Energy Star–compliant monitor, this test may not work. Monitors that possess this power-saving feature revert to a low-power mode when they do not receive a signal change for a given period of time.

With the system off, remove any multimedia-related cards such as VGA-to-TV converter cards and video capture cards. Try to reboot the system.

If the system boots up, and the display is correct with these options removed, you can safely assume that one of them is the cause of the problem. To verify which device is causing the problem, reinstall them, one at a time, until the problem reappears. The last device reinstalled before the problem reappeared is defective.

Replace this item and continue reinstalling options, one at a time, until all the options have been reinstalled.

If the display is still wrong or missing, check the components associated with the video display monitor. Start by disconnecting the monitor's signal cable from the video controller card at the rear of the system unit, and its power cord from the power-supply connector, or the 120V (AC) outlet. Then, exchange the monitor for a known good one of the same type (that is, VGA for VGA). If the system boots up and the video display is correct, return the system to full service and service the defective monitor as indicated.

If the display is still not correct, exchange the video controller card with a known good one of the same type. Remove the system unit's outer cover. Disconnect the monitor's signal cable from the video controller card. Swap the video controller card with a known good one of the same type. Reconnect the monitor's signal cable to the new video controller card and reboot the system.

Other symptoms that point to the video adapter card include a shaky video display and a high-pitched squeal from the monitor or system unit.

If the system boots up and the video display is correct, replace the system unit's outer cover, return the system to full service, and service the defective video controller appropriately. If the system still does not perform properly, the source of the problem may be in the system board.

Troubleshooting Monitors

All the circuitry discussed so far is part of the computer or its video adapter unit. The circuitry inside the monitor is responsible for accepting, amplifying, and routing the video and synchronizing information to the CRT's electron guns and the deflection coils.

Figure 2.22 shows the components located inside a typical CRT color monitor. Of particular interest is the high-voltage anode that connects the tube to the high-voltage sections of the signal-processing board. This is a very dangerous connection that is not to be touched.

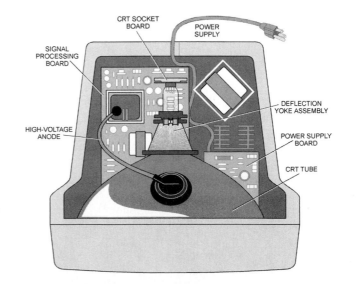

FIGURE 2.22
Inside the CRT monitor.

Operation of a monitor with the cover removed poses a shock hazard from the power supply. Therefore, anyone unfamiliar with the safety precautions associated with high-voltage equipment should not attempt servicing.

The high-voltage levels do not necessarily disappear because the power to the monitor is turned off. Like television sets, monitors have circuitry capable of storing high-voltage potentials long after power has been removed. Always discharge the anode of the picture tube to the receiver chassis before handling the CRT tube. Due to the high voltage levels, you should never wear antistatic grounding straps when working inside the monitor.

An additional hazard associated with handling CRTs is that the tube is fragile. Take extra care to prevent the neck of the tube from striking any surface. Never lift the tube by the neck—especially when removing or replacing a CRT tube in the chassis. If the picture tube's envelope is cracked or ruptured, the inrush of air will cause a high-velocity *implosion*, and the glass will fly in all directions. Therefore, you should always wear protective goggles when handling picture tubes.

Color monitors produce a relatively high level of *X-radiation*. The CRT tube is designed to limit X-radiation at its specified operating voltage. If a replacement CRT tube is being installed, make certain to replace it with one of the same type, and with suffix numbers that are the same. You can obtain this information from the chassis schematic diagram inside the monitor's housing.

Diagnosing Monitor Problems

The first step in isolating the monitor as the cause of the problem is to exchange it for a known good one. If the replacement works, the problem must be located in the monitor.

Like the keyboard, the monitor is easy to swap because it is external and involves only two cables. If the problem produces a blank display, disconnect the monitor's signal cable from its video adapter card. If a raster appears, a video card problem is indicated.

Check obvious items first. Examine the power cord to see that it is plugged in. Check to see that the monitor's power switch is in the On position. Check the external settings to see that the brightness and contrast settings are not turned off.

WARNING

Lethal Voltage Levels   You must exercise great caution when opening or working inside the monitor. The voltage levels present during operation are lethal. Electrical potentials as high as 25,000V are present inside the unit when it is operating.

TEST TIP

Memorize the values of lethal voltage associated with the inside of the CRT video monitor. The values given on tests may not be exactly the same as those stated in the textbook, but they will be in the same high range.

Troubleshooting Floppy Disk Drives

Typical symptoms associated with floppy disk drive (FDD) failures during boot up include the following:

◆ FDD errors are encountered during boot up.

◆ The front-panel indicator lights are visible, and the display is present on the monitor screen, but there is no disk drive action and no boot up.

◆ An IBM-compatible 6xx (that is, 601) error code displays.

◆ An FDD Controller Error message displays, indicating a failure to verify the FDD setup by the System Configuration file.

◆ The FDD activity light stays on constantly, indicating that the FDD signal cable is reversed.

Additional FDD error messages commonly encountered during normal system operation include the following:

◆ Disk Drive Read Error messages.

◆ Disk Drive Write Error messages.

◆ Disk Drive Seek Error messages.

◆ No Boot Record Found message, indicating that the system files in the disk's boot sector are missing or have become corrupt.

◆ The system stops working while reading a disk, indicating that the contents of the disk have become contaminated.

◆ The drive displays the same directory listing for every disk inserted in the drive, indicating that the FDD's disk-change detector or signal line is not functional.

Figure 2.23 depicts the components associated with the system's floppy disk drives. All of these items can impact the operation of the floppy disk drive.

NOTE

Causes of Floppy Disk Problems   A number of things can cause improper floppy disk drive operation or disk drive failure. These items include the use of unformatted disks, incorrectly inserted disks, damaged disks, erased disks, loose cables, drive failure, adapter failure, system board failure, or a bad or loose power connector.

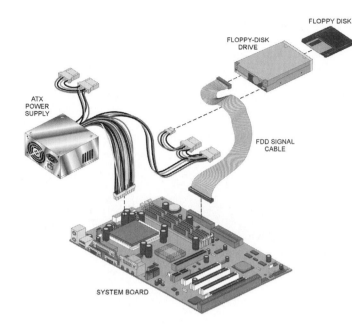

FLOPPY DISK

FLOPPY-DISK DRIVE

ATX POWER SUPPLY

FDD SIGNAL CABLE

SYSTEM BOARD

FIGURE 2.23
FDD-related components.

Information is written to, and read from, the floppy disks by the floppy disk drive unit. This unit moves information and control signals back and forth between the disk drive controller and the surface of the disks. The information moves between the controller and the drive through a flat, ribbon cable. The small printed circuit board, located on the drive unit, is called the analog control board. It is responsible for turning the digital information received from the adapter card into magnetic information that can be stored on the surface of the disk, and vice versa.

FDD Configuration Checks

Normally, the only time a configuration problem occurs is when the system is being set up for the first time, or when a new option is installed. The other condition that causes a configuration problem involves the system board's CMOS backup battery. If the battery fails, or has been changed, the contents of the CMOS setup will be lost. After replacing the battery, you must always run the CMOS setup utility to reconfigure the system.

NOTE **Levels of Troubleshooting**   Basically three levels of troubleshooting apply to FDD problems: configuration, the software level, and the hardware level. No *Windows-level troubleshooting* applies to floppy disk drives.

While booting up the system to the DOS prompt, observe the BIOS FDD type information displayed on the monitor. Note the types of FDDs that the BIOS believes are installed in the system. With newer BIOS, you must examine the advanced CMOS setup to check the boot-up order. In these BIOS, you can set the boot order so that the FDD is never examined during startup.

The values stored in this CMOS memory must accurately reflect the type, and number, of FDDs installed in the system; otherwise, an error occurs. You can access these values for change during the boot-up procedure.

Basic FDD Checks

If the FDD configuration information is correct, and a floppy disk drive problem is suspected, the first task is to make certain that the system won't boot up from the floppy disk drive if a disk with a known good boot file is in the drive. Try the boot disk in a different computer to see whether it works on that machine. If not, there is a problem with the files on the disk. If the disk boots up the other computer, you must troubleshoot the floppy disk drive system.

If possible, run a diagnostic software program from the hard drive or a B: floppy disk drive. Try to use a diagnostic program that conducts a bank of tests on the FDD's components. Run the program's FDD Tests, and perform the equivalent of the All Tests function.

From the command-prompt level, it is also very easy to test the operation of the drive using a simple batch program. At the command prompt, type **COPY CON:FDDTEST.BAT**, and press the Enter key. On the first line, type the DOS **DIR** command. On the second line, type **FDDTEST**. Finally, press the F6 function key to exit, and save the program to the hard disk drive.

You can execute this test program from the command prompt just by typing its name. When invoked, it exercises the drive's R/W head-positioning motors and read channel-signal processing circuitry. At the same time, the signal cable and the FDC circuitry are tested.

FDD Hardware Checks

If you do not find any configuration or enabling problems, you must troubleshoot the hardware components associated with the floppy disk drives. These components consist of the drives, the signal cable, and the FDC controller. The controller may be located on an adapter card or integrated into the system board. Begin the process by exchanging the suspect floppy disk drive with another one of the same type.

If the system has a second floppy disk drive, turn off the computer and exchange its connection to the floppy disk drive's signal cable so that it becomes the A: drive. Try to reboot the system using this other floppy disk drive as the A: drive.

Also, check the floppy disk drive's signal cable for proper connection at both ends. In many systems, the pin-1 designation is difficult to see. Reversing the signal cable causes the FDD activity light to stay on continuously. The reversed signal cable will also erase the Master Boot Record from the disk, making it non-bootable. Because this is a real possibility, you should always use an expendable backup copy of the boot disk for troubleshooting FDD problems.

Insert the bootable disk in the new A: drive and turn on the system. If the system boots up, reinstall any options removed and replace the system unit's outer cover. Return the system to full service and repair the defective floppy disk drive accordingly.

If the system still refuses to boot up, turn it off, and exchange the disk drive controller card (if present) with a known good one. Disconnect the disk drive's signal cable from the controller card and swap the controller card with a known good one of the same type. Make certain to mark the cable and its connection point to ensure proper reconnection after the exchange. Reconnect the signal cable to the FDD controller.

Try to reboot the system with the new disk drive controller card installed. If the controller is built in to the system board, it may be easier to test the drive and signal cable in another machine than to remove the system board. If the system boots up, reinstall any options removed and replace the system unit's outer cover. Return the system to full service and return the defective controller card.

If the system still will not boot up, or perform FDD operations correctly, check the disk drive cables for proper connection at both ends. If necessary, exchange the signal cable with a known good one. Finally, exchange the system board with a known good one.

Troubleshooting Hard Disk Drives

Typical symptoms associated with hard disk drive (HDD) failures include the following:

◆ The computer does not boot up when turned on.

◆ The computer boots up to a system disk in the A: drive, but not to the hard drive, indicating that the system files on the HDD are missing or have become corrupt.

◆ No motor sounds are produced by the HDD while the computer is running. (In desktop units, the HDD should always run when power is applied to the system—this also applies to portables because of their advanced power-saving features.)

◆ An IBM-compatible 17xx error code is produced on the monitor screen.

◆ An HDD Controller Failure message displays, indicating a failure to verify hard disk setup by system configuration file error.

◆ A C: or D: Fixed Disk Drive Error message displays, indicating a hard disk CMOS setup failure.

◆ An Invalid Media Type message displays, indicating the controller cannot find a recognizable track/sector pattern on the drive.

◆ A No Boot Record Found, a Non-System Disk or Disk Error, or an Invalid System Disk message displays, indicating that the system boot files are not located in the root directory of the drive.

◆ The video display is active, but the HDD's activity light remains on and no boot up occurs, indicating that the HDD's CMOS configuration information is incorrect.

◆ An Out of Disk Space message displays, indicating that the amount of space on the disk is insufficient to carry out the desired operation.

◆ A `Missing Operating System`, a `Hard Drive Boot Failure`, or an `Invalid Drive or Drive Specification` message displays, indicating that the disk's Master Boot Record is missing or has become corrupt.

◆ A `No ROM BASIC—System Halted`, or `ROM BASIC Interpreter Not Found` message displays, followed by the system stopping, indicating that no Master Boot Record was found in the system. This message is produced only by PCs, XTs, and some clones.

◆ A `Current Drive No Longer Valid` message displays, indicating that the HDD's CMOS configuration information is incorrect or has become corrupt.

Figure 2.24 depicts the relationship between the hard disk drive and the rest of the system. It also illustrates the control and signal paths through the system.

The system board is a logical extension of the components that make up the HDD system. Unless the HDD controller is integrated into it, however, the system board is typically the least likely cause of HDD problems.

TEST TIP

Be able to describe the conditions indicated by Invalid Drive or Drive Specification, Missing Operating System, and the Hard Drive Boot Failure error messages.

NOTE

Hard Drive Systems Hard drive systems are very much like floppy drive systems in structure: They have a controller, one or more signal cables, a power cord, and a drive unit. The troubleshooting procedure typically moves from setup and configuration, to formatting, and finally to the hardware component-isolation process.

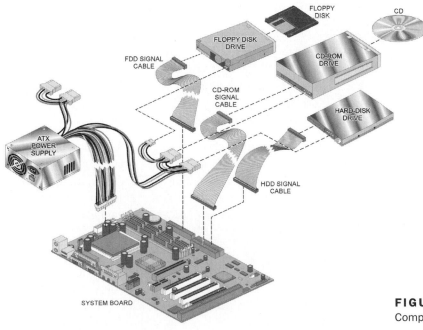

FIGURE 2.24
Components related to the hard disk drive.

Notice that unlike a floppy drive, there is no Windows component to check with a hard disk drive. Windows relies on the system's DOS/BIOS structure to handle HDD operations.

HDD Configuration Checks

While booting up the system, observe the BIOS's HDD type information displayed on the monitor. Note the type of HDD(s) that the BIOS believes is installed in the system. The values stored in this CMOS memory must accurately reflect the actual HDD(s) format installed in the system; otherwise, an error occurs. Possible error messages associated with HDD configuration problems include the `Drive Mismatch Error` message and the `Invalid Media Type` message. You can access these values for change by pressing the Ctrl and Del keys (or some other key combination) simultaneously, during the boot-up procedure.

If the HDD is used with a system board–mounted controller, check for the presence of an HDD-enabling jumper on the system board. Make certain that it is set to enable the drive, if present. Check the drive to make sure that it is properly terminated. Every drive type requires a termination block somewhere in the interface. On system-level drives, check the Master/Slave jumper setting to make sure that it is set properly for the drive's logical position in the system.

If you have more than one device attached to a single interface cable, make sure that they are of the same type. (For instance, all are EIDE devices or all are ATA100 devices.) Mixing device types will create a situation in which the system cannot provide the different types of control information each device needs. The drives are incompatible and you may not be able to access either device.

If the drive is a SCSI drive, check to see that its ID has been set correctly and that the SCSI chain has been terminated correctly. Either of these errors results in the system not being able to see the drive. Also, check the CMOS Setup utility to make sure that SCSI support has been enabled, along with large SCSI drive support.

TEST TIP

Know that there can only be one master drive selection on each IDE channel.

TEST TIP

Be aware that mixing drive types on a single signal cable can disable both devices.

TEST TIP

Know that in newer systems, SCSI drive support and large drive support are both enabled in the BIOS.

Basic HDD Checks

If the HDD configuration information is correct and you suspect a hard disk drive problem, the first task is to determine how extensive the HDD problem is. Place a *clean boot disk* in the A: drive and try to boot the system. Then, execute a DOS DIR command to access the C: drive. If the system can see the contents of the drive, the boot files have been lost or corrupted, but the architecture of the disk is intact.

Modify the DOS **DIR** command with an **/AH** or **/AS** switch (that is, **DIR C: /AH** or **DIR C: /AS**) to look in the root directory for the system files and the COMMAND.COM file. It is common to receive a Disk Boot Failure message onscreen, if this type of situation occurs. The No (or Missing) ROM BASIC Interpreter message may also be produced by this condition.

If the clean boot disk has a copy of the FDISK program on it, attempt to restore the drive's Master Boot Record (including its partition information) by typing the following:

A>FDISK /MBR

Providing that the hard disk can be accessed with the DIR command, type and enter the following command at the DOS prompt (with the clean boot disk still in the A: drive):

SYS C:

This command copies the IO.SYS, MSDOS.SYS, and COMMAND.COM system files from the DOS disk to the hard disk drive. Turn off the system, remove the DOS disk from the A: drive, and try to reboot the system from the hard drive.

If the system boots up properly, check to see that the operating system commands are functioning properly. Also, check to see that all installed software programs function properly. Recheck the installation instructions of any program that does not function properly. Reinstall the software program if necessary.

> **TEST TIP**
>
> Know how and when to use the **FDISK /MBR** and **SYS C:** commands.

Actually, three conditions produce a Bad or Missing COMMAND.COM error message. These conditions include the following:

◆ The first condition occurs when the COMMAND.COM file cannot be found on the hard drive (because it has become corrupted), and no bootable disk is present in the A: drive.

◆ The COMMAND.COM file is not located in the hard drive's root directory. This message is likely when installing a brand new hard drive or a new DOS version.

◆ The message also occurs if the user inadvertently erases the COMMAND.COM file from the root directory of the hard drive.

If the system cannot see the drive after booting to the floppy disk drive, an Invalid Drive message or an Invalid Drive Specification message should be returned in response to any attempt to access the drive. Under these conditions, you must examine the complete HDD system. Use the FDISK utility to partition the drive. Next, use the **FORMAT /S** command to make the disk bootable. Any data that was on the drive will be lost in the formatting process, but it was already gone because the system could not see the drive.

Attempt to run a diagnostic software program, if possible. Try to use a diagnostic program that conducts a bank of tests on the HDD's components. Run the program's HDD Tests, and perform the equivalent of the All Tests function.

HDD Hardware Checks

If you cannot access the hard disk drive, and its configuration settings are correct, you must troubleshoot the hardware components associated with the hard disk drive. As previously indicated, these components include the drive, its signal cable, and the HDC. Like the FDC from the floppy disk drive, the HDC can be mounted on an adapter card, or it can be integrated into the system board. Normally, you must remove the outer cover from the computer to troubleshoot these components.

In a pre-Pentium system, the easiest component to check is the controller card that holds the HDD interface circuitry. Exchange the controller card with a known good one of the same type. Make certain to mark all the card's control/signal cables before disconnecting them. Also, identify their connection points and direction. Your markings help to ensure their proper reinstallation. Reconnect the disk drive signal cables to the new controller card.

Try to reboot the system from the hard drive. If the system boots up properly, check to see that all the DOS commands (DIR, COPY, and so on) are working properly. Also, check the operation of all the hard disk's software programs to make sure they are still functioning correctly. Reinstall any program that does not function properly.

If the system still won't boot up, recheck the system configuration setup to see that it matches the actual configuration of the HDD. Record the HDD values from the setup so that they are available if a replacement drive needs to be installed.

The next logical step may seem to be to replace the hard drive unit. However, it is quite possible that the hard drive may not have any real damage. It may just have lost track of where it was, and now it cannot find its starting point. In this case, the most attractive option is to reformat the hard disk. This action gives the hard drive a new starting point to work from. Unfortunately, it also destroys anything that you had on the disk before. At the very least, attempting to reformat the drive before you replace it may save the expense of buying a new hard disk drive that is not needed. Make certain to use the /S modifier, or repeat the SYS C: operation with the FORMAT command, to restore the system files to the hard drive.

If not, check the HDD signal cable for proper connection at both ends. Exchange the signal cable(s) for a known good one. Check the HDD Drive Select jumper and Master/Slave/Single jumper settings to make sure they are set correctly, as illustrated in Figure 2.25. Check to see whether the system might be using the *Cable Select* option also depicted in the figure. This setting requires a special *CSEL* signal cable designed to determine the master/slave arrangements for multiple IDE drives. Exchange the HDD power connector with another one from the power supply, to make certain that it is not a source of problems.

FIGURE 2.25
IDE master/slave settings.

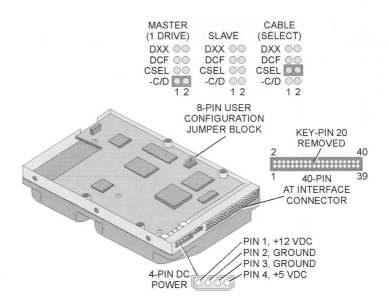

If the reformatting procedure is not successful, or the system still won't boot from the hard drive, you must replace the hard disk drive unit with a working one. Disconnect the signal, control, and power cords from the HDD unit, and exchange it with a known good one of the same type. Reconnect the signal, control, and power cords to the replacement HDD unit.

If a similar computer is being used as a source of test parts, take great care in removing the HDD from its original computer and reinstalling it in the defective computer. With pre-system-level interfaces (IDE/SCSI), such as an MFM drive, it is advisable, and common practice, to swap both the disk drive and the controller card together.

Try to reboot the system from the new hard drive. If no boot up occurs, reformat the new drive. Make sure that any information on the replacement drive has been backed up on floppy disks, or tape, before removing it from its original system.

If the system still won't boot up with a different HDD, swap the hard disk drive's signal/control cables with known good ones. Make certain to mark the cables for identification purposes so that they will be reinstalled properly. Also, use a different power connector from the power-supply unit to make certain that the current connector is not a source of the problems.

Check the system's configuration setup to see that it matches the actual configuration of the new HDD. Check to see that all installed software programs function properly.

If the system reboots from the replacement drive without reformatting, replace the drive (either with the one you have just installed or with a new one). Also, try reinstalling the original disk drive controller card to see whether it works with the new drive.

If the system still boots up and operates properly, reinstall any options removed from the system. Replace the system unit's outer cover and return the system to full service. Reboot the system and reinstall all software programs to the new hard disk drive. (See the Installation Guide from the software manufacturer.) Return the system to full service and return the defective controller card appropriately.

Troubleshooting CD-ROM Drives

The troubleshooting steps for a *CD-ROM drive* are almost identical to those of an HDD system. The connections and data paths are very similar. Basically, four levels of troubleshooting apply to CD-ROM problems: configuration level, the DOS level, the Windows level, and the hardware level. Figure 2.26 shows the parts and drivers associated with CD-ROMs.

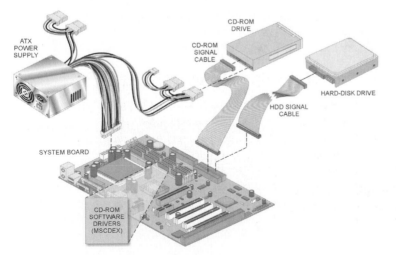

FIGURE 2.26
Components and drivers associated with CD-ROMs.

Basic CD-ROM Checks

Because the CD-ROM does not appear in the CMOS configuration information, reboot the system and observe the boot-up information that scrolls up the screen. In particular, look for error messages associated with the CD-ROM drive (such as an MSCDEX *XXX* error.

The simplest point to test the operation of the CD-ROM drive is in the DOS environment. For the CD-ROM drive to work at this level, its drivers must be referenced in the CONFIG.SYS and AUTOEXEC.BAT files. The Microsoft driver for CD-ROMs is the Microsoft CD-ROM Extensions (MSCDEX) file.

Check the CONFIG.SYS file for a CD-ROM DEVICE= line similar to the following:

```
DEVICE=C:\CDROM\ATAPI.SYS /D:MSCD001
```

This statement loads the ATAPI Enhanced IDE interface to support an IDE CD-ROM device that the system will know as MSCD001.

Then, check the AUTOEXEC.BAT for a statement that looks like the following:

```
C:\DOS\MSCDEX /D:MSCD001 /L:E /M:12
```

This line loads the Microsoft CD-ROM driver into the system and defines its operating parameters. In this case, the switch modifiers set up the drive for the E: drive as the upper possibility for CD-ROM drive letters, EMS memory mode enabled, and 12-sector buffers. The /D:MSCD001 designation identifies the drive as the MSCS001 drive defined in the CONFIG.SYS file.

These statements define the CD-ROM drive for the system and make it usable under DOS. Most CD-ROMs come with installation programs that automatically write these lines into your AUTOEXEC.BAT and CONFIG.SYS files correctly. If you have any question about their validity, run the drive's installation program and allow it to reinstall these statements.

If the MSCDEX *XXX* error appears in the DOS environment, check for the MSCDEX statement in the AUTOEXEC.BAT file.

Many of the software diagnostic packages available include test functions for CD-ROM drives. Try to choose a diagnostic package that includes a good variety of CD-ROM test functions. Run the program's CD-ROM function from the Multimedia selection menu. Select the equivalent of the program's Run All Tests option.

Use a diagnostic program to check the IRQ and I/O address settings for possible conflicts with other devices. If the settings differ from those established by the hardware jumpers on the controller, change the settings so that they both match each other, and so that they do not conflict with other devices.

Windows Checks

In Windows, you can access the CD-ROM through the CD icon in the desktop's My Computer icon. The CD-ROM drive's information is contained in the Control Panel's System icon. The properties of the installed drive are located under the Settings tab. Figure 2.27 shows a typical set of CD-ROM specifications in Windows.

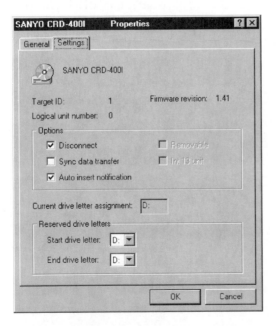

FIGURE 2.27
Control Panel/Device Manager/Settings.

Check the system for AUTOEXEC.BAT and CONFIG.SYS files that could contain updated information. To do this, open the Wordpad program from the Windows Accessories listing, check the AUTOEXEC.BAT file for the following line:

> REM C:\XXX\MSCDEX

Then check the CONFIG.SYS file for this line:

> REM Device=C:\XXX\XXX /D:MSCDXXX

If the correct drivers are not installed, load the correct driver, or contact the CD-ROM manufacturer for the correct Windows driver.

CD-ROM Hardware Checks

If the configuration and software checks do not remedy the CD-ROM problem, you must troubleshoot the CD-ROM-related hardware. Basically, the hardware consists of the CD-ROM drive, the signal cable, the power cord, and the controller. The controller may be mounted on a host adapter card or, in a Pentium system, on the system board. For external drives, you also need to check the plug-in power adapter.

In most systems, the CD-ROM drive shares a controller or host adapter with the hard disk drive. Therefore, if the hard drive is working and the CD-ROM drive is not, the likelihood that the problem is in the CD-ROM drive is very high.

Before entering the system unit, check for simple user problems. Is there a CD in the drive? Is the label side of the disk facing upward? Is the disk a CD-ROM or some other type of CD? If the CD-ROM drive is inoperable and there is a CD locked inside, insert a straightened paper clip into the tray-release access hole (which is usually located beside the ejection button). This action releases the spring-loaded tray and pops out the disc.

If no simple reasons for the problem are apparent, begin by exchanging the CD-ROM drive with a known good one of the same type. For external units, just disconnect the drive from the power and signal cords, and then substitute the new drive for it. With internal units, you must remove the system unit's outer cover and disconnect

TEST TIP

Know how to retrieve a CD from a disabled CD-ROM drive.

the signal and power cords from the drive. Remove the screws that secure the drive in the drive bay. Install the replacement unit and attempt to access it.

If the new drive does not work, check the CD-ROM drive's signal cable for proper connection at both ends. Exchange the signal cable for a known good one.

If the drive still refuses to operate, turn off the system and exchange the controller card (if present) with a known good one. In Pentium systems, the controller is mounted on the system board. In other systems, the controller is normally mounted on an MI/O card. Disconnect the disk drive's signal cable from the controller card and swap the card with a known good one of the same type. If the controller is built in to the system board, it may be easier to test the drive and signal cable in another machine than to remove the system board. Make certain to mark the cable and its connection points to ensure proper reconnection after the exchange.

If the controller is built in to the system board and becomes defective, it is still possible to install an IDE host adapter card in an expansion slot and use it without replacing the system board. This action also can be taken to upgrade older IDE systems to EIDE systems so that they can use additional IDE devices. The onboard IDE controller may need to be disabled before the system will address the new host adapter version.

> **TEST TIP**
>
> Remember that card-mounted IDE host adapters can be used to repair system boards with defective onboard IDE controllers and to upgrade older IDE systems.

Reconnect the signal cable to the controller and try to reboot the system with the new controller card installed. If the system boots up, reinstall any options removed and replace the system unit's outer cover. Return the system to full service and service the defective controller card as appropriate.

If the drive still refuses to work, check to see whether the CD-ROM drive has been properly terminated. Exchange the CD-ROM's power connector with another one to make sure that it is not a cause of problems. Finally, exchange the system board with a known good one.

Troubleshooting Port Problems

Three basic levels of testing apply to troubleshooting port problems: the DOS level, the Windows level, and the hardware level.

Before concentrating on any of these levels, troubleshooting should begin by observing the symptoms produced by operation of the port. Observe the steps that lead to the failure. Determine under what conditions the port failed. Was a new peripheral device installed in the system? Were any unusual operations in progress? Note any error messages or beep codes. Use the troubleshooting hints that follow to isolate the parallel, serial, or game port circuitry as the source of the problem. Retry the system several times to observe the symptoms clearly. Take the time to document the problem.

Figure 2.28 illustrates the components involved in the operation of the serial, parallel, and game ports. Failures in these devices tend to end with poor or no operation of the peripheral. Generally, there are only four possible causes for a problem with a device connected to an I/O port:

◆ The port is defective.

◆ The software is not configured properly for the port.

◆ The connecting signal cable is bad.

◆ The attached device is not functional.

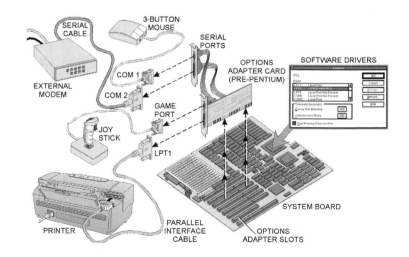

FIGURE 2.28
Components associated with I/O ports.

Port Problem Symptoms

Typical symptoms associated with serial, parallel, or game port failures include the following:

◆ A 199, 432, or 90x IBM-compatible error code displays on
the monitor (printer port).

◆ Online light is on, but no characters are printed by the printer.

◆ An 110x IBM-compatible error code displays on the monitor
(serial port).

◆ A Device Not Found error message displays, or you have an
unreliable connection.

◆ Input device does not work on the game port.

As you can see from the symptoms list, I/O ports do not tend to
generate many error messages onscreen.

Port Hardware Checks

In the area of hardware, only a few items pertain to the system's
ports: the port connector, signal cabling between the port circuitry
and the connector in some units, the port circuitry itself, and the
system board. As mentioned earlier, you can find the port circuitry
on video cards in some older units, on specialized I/O cards in other
units, and on the system board in newer units. In any of these situations, some configuration settings must be correct.

Check the board containing the I/O port circuitry and its User
Guide for configuration information, which normally involves LPT,
COM, and IRQ settings. Occasionally, you must set up hexadecimal
addressing for the port addresses; however, this is becoming rare.

For example, a modern parallel port must be enabled and set to the
proper protocol type to operate advanced peripherals.

For typical printer operations, the setting can normally be set to
Standard Parallel Port (SPP) mode. However, devices that use the
port in a bidirectional manner need to be set to EPP or ECP mode
for proper operation. In both cases, the protocol must be set properly for both the port and the device to carry out communications.

NOTE

**Checking Ports on Newer Pentium-Based
Systems**   With newer Pentium systems, you
must check the advanced CMOS setup to
determine whether the port in question has
been enabled, and, if so, has it been enabled
correctly.

Figure 2.29 illustrates the movement of data to the parallel port mounted on an AT system board. On an ATX-style board, the standard I/O port connectors are mounted directly on the system board and extend from the rear of the system unit. No connecting cables are needed.

FIGURE 2.29
Moving information through an AT-style I/O port.

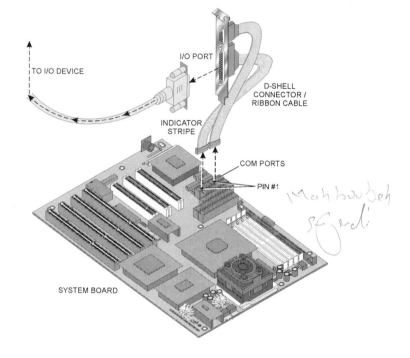

It is helpful to single-step through the boot up to read the port assignments in the boot-up window. If serial or parallel port problems are occurring, the CMOS configuration window is the first place to look. If the system does not detect the presence of the port hardware at this stage, none of the more advanced levels will find it either. If values for any of the physical ports installed in the system do not appear in this window, check for improper port configuration jumpers or switches.

Because the unit has not loaded DOS at the time the configuration window appears, DOS and Windows cannot be sources of port problems at this time. If all jumpers and configuration settings for the ports appear correct, assume that a hardware problem exists. Diagnose the hardware port problem to a section of the system (in this case, the board containing the port).

Basic Port Checks

If possible, run a software diagnostic package to narrow the possible problem causes. This is not normally a problem because port failures do not generally affect the main components of the system. Try to use a diagnostic program that deals with the system board components. It should include parallel- and serial-port tests, as well as a game-port test if possible.

Run the program's Port Tests function and perform the equivalent of the All Tests function. Note all the errors indicated by the tests. If a hardware error is indicated, such as those already mentioned, you might be able to take some corrective actions, such as resetting or reconfiguring LPT, COM, or IRQ settings, without replacing the unit containing the port hardware. If more complex port problems are indicated, however, exit the diagnostic program and replace the port hardware.

Basic Parallel Ports

Software diagnostic packages normally ask you to place a loopback test plug in the parallel port connector to run tests on the port. The *loopback plugs* simulate a printer device by redirecting output signals from the port into port input pins. Figure 2.30 describes the signal-rerouting scheme used in a parallel port loopback plug.

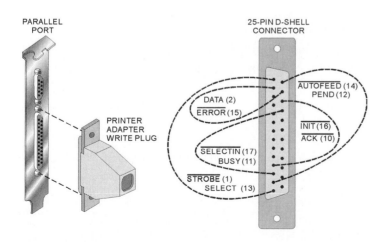

FIGURE 2.30
Parallel port loopback connections.

You can use a live printer with the port for testing purposes, but this action elevates the possibility that problems can be injected into the troubleshooting process by the printer.

If the software diagnostic program does not provide enough information to solve the problem, attempt to print to the first parallel port from the DOS level. To do this, type **COPY AUTOEXEC .BAT LPT1:** at the DOS prompt, and press the Enter key.

If the file is not successfully printed, at the C:\>> command prompt, type **EDIT AUTOEXEC.BAT**. Check the file for a SET TEMP = command. If the command is not present, add a **SET TEMP** statement to the AUTOEXEC.BAT file. At the C:\>> DOS prompt, type **EDIT AUTOEXEC.BAT**. Create a blank line in the file and type **SET TEMP=C:\WINDOWS\TEMP** into it. Save the updated file to disk and reboot the system. Make sure to check the **SET TEMP=** line for blank spaces at the end of the line.

Is there a printer switch box between the computer and the printer? If so, remove the print-sharing equipment, connect the computer directly to the printer, and try to print from the command-prompt level as previously described.

Check the free space on the HDD. Remove any unnecessary files to clear space on the HDD and defragment the drive, as described in Chapter 9.

Basic Serial Ports

As with parallel ports, diagnostic packages typically ask you to place a *loopback test plug* in the serial port connector to run tests on the port. Use the diagnostic program to determine whether any IRQ or addressing conflicts exist between the serial port and other installed options. The serial loopback plug is physically connected differently from a parallel loopback plug so that it can simulate the operation of a serial device. Figure 2.31 describes the signal-rerouting scheme used in a serial port loopback plug.

You can use a live serial device with the port for testing purposes but, like the printer, this elevates the possibility that nonport problems can be injected into the troubleshooting process.

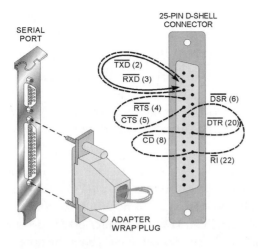

FIGURE 2.31
Serial port loopback connections.

If the software diagnostic program does not provide enough information to solve the problem, attempt to print to the serial port from the DOS level. To do this, type **DIR > COM***x* at the DOS prompt. The value of *x* is equal to the COM port being printed to.

Windows 9x Checks

You can reach the I/O port functions in Windows 9x through two avenues. You can access port information through the desktop's Start/Settings buttons. You also can reach this information through the My Computer icon on the desktop. Printer port information can be viewed through the Printers icon; serial port information is accessed through the System/Device Manager entries under the Control Panel icon.

Windows 9x Parallel Ports

Isolate the problem to the Windows 9x program by attempting to print from a non-Windows environment. Restart the computer in MS-DOS mode, and attempt to print a batch file from the command prompt.

If the system prints from DOS, but not from Windows 9x, check to see whether the Print option from the application's File menu is *unavailable* (gray). If so, check the My Computer/Printers window for correct parallel port settings. Make certain that the correct printer driver is selected for the printer being used. If no printer (or the wrong printer type) is selected, use the *Add Printer Wizard* to install and set up the desired printer.

The system's printer configuration information is also available through the Device Manager tab under the System icon in the Control Panel. Check this location for printer port setting information. Also, check the definition of the printer under the Control Panel's Printer icon.

Windows 9x comes with an online tool, called *Print Troubleshooter*, to help solve printing problems. To use the Print Troubleshooter, click the Troubleshooting entry in the Windows 9x Help system, as illustrated in Figure 2.32. Press F1 to enter the Help system. The Troubleshooter asks a series of questions about the printing setup. After you have answered all of its questions, the Troubleshooter returns a list of recommendations for fixing the problem.

If the conclusions of the troubleshooter do not clear up the problem, try printing a document to a file. This enables you to separate the printing software from the port hardware. If the document successfully prints to a file, use the DOS COPY command to copy the file to the printer port. The format for doing this is as follows:

Copy /b *filename.prn* lpt1:

If the document prints to the file, but does not print out on the printer, the hardware setup and circuitry are causing the problem.

Continue troubleshooting the port by checking the printer driver to ensure that it is the correct driver and version number. Click the Printer icon and select the Properties entry from the menu. Click the Details tab to view the driver's name. Click the About entry under the Device Options tab to verify the driver's version number.

Click the printer port in question (under the Printer icon) to open the Print Manager screen. Check the Print Manager for errors that have occurred and that might be holding up the printing of jobs that follow it. If an error is hanging up the print function, highlight the offending job and remove it from the print spool by clicking the Delete Document entry of the Document menu.

FIGURE 2.32
Accessing Windows 9x Troubleshooting Help.

Windows 9x Serial Ports

Information on the system's serial ports is contained in three areas under the Device Manager. These are the Resources entry, the Driver entry, and the Port Settings entry. The Resources entry displays port address ranges and IRQ assignments. The Driver entry displays the names of the installed device drivers and their locations. The Port Settings entry, depicted in Figure 2.33, contains speed and character frame information for the serial ports. The Advanced entry under Port Settings enables you to adjust the transmit and receive buffer speeds for better operation.

Check under the Windows 9x Control Panel/System/Device Manager window for correct serial port settings.

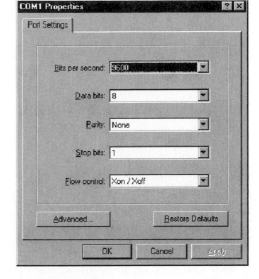

FIGURE 2.33
Port Settings entry.

STEP BY STEP

2.1 Checking for the Correct Serial Port Settings Under Windows 9x

1. Click the Port Settings option to see the setup for the ports. Most serial printers use settings of 9600 Baud, No Parity, 8 Bits, 1 Stop Bit, and *Hardware Handshaking (Xon-Xoff)*.

2. Click the Resources button to determine the IRQ setup for the port.

3. Check the User Manual to document the correct settings for the device using the port in question.

USB Port Checks

Because nearly any type of peripheral device can be added to the PC through the USB port, the range of symptoms associated with USB device can include all the symptoms listed for peripheral devices in this chapter. Therefore, problems associated with USB ports can be addressed in three general areas:

◆ The USB hardware device

◆ The USB controller

◆ The USB drivers

The first step in troubleshooting USB problems is to check the CMOS setup screens to make sure that the USB function is enabled there. If the USB function is enabled in BIOS, check in the Windows Control Panel/System/Device Manager to make certain that the USB controller appears there. In Windows 2000, the USB controller should be listed under the Universal Serial Bus Controllers entry, or in the Human Interface Devices entry (using the default Devices by Type setting).

If the controller does not appear in Device Manager, or a yellow warning icon appears next to the controller, the system's BIOS may be outdated. Contact the BIOS manufacturer for an updated copy of the BIOS.

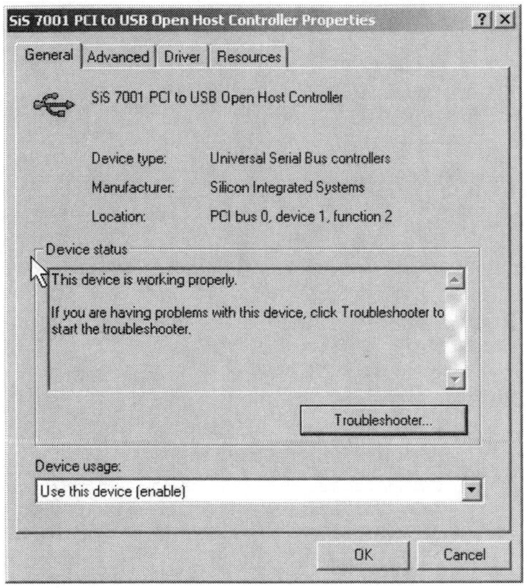

If the controller is present in the Device Manager, right-click the USB controller entry and click the Properties tab. If there are any problems, a message appears in the Device Status window, depicted in Figure 2.34, describing any problems and suggesting what action to take.

If the BIOS and controller settings appear to be correct, the next items to check are the USB port drivers. These ports have a separate entry in the Device Manager that you can access by clicking the Universal Serial Bus Controllers option, right-clicking the USB Root Hub entry, and then clicking the Properties tab.

If a USB device does not install itself automatically, you may have conflicting drivers loaded for that device and you may need to remove them.

FIGURE 2.34
The USB Controller Properties page.

STEP BY STEP

2.2 Removing Potentially Conflicting USB Drivers

1. Disconnect any USB devices connected to the system and start the system in safe mode.

2. Under Windows 2000, you are asked about which operating system to use. Use the up- and down-arrow keys to highlight Windows 2000 Professional or Windows 2000 Server, and then press Enter.

3. If alert messages appear, read each alert and then click the
    OK button to close it.

    Open the Device Manager, click the USB device, and
    then click the Remove option.

4. Your particular USB device may be listed under the
    Universal Serial Bus Controller, Other Devices, Unknown
    Devices, or a particular device category (such as the
    Modem entry if the device is a USB modem).

    Click the Start menu, select the Shut Down option fol-
    lowed by the Restart entry, and then click the OK button.

5. Connect the USB device directly to the USB port on your
    computer. If the system does not autodetect the device,
    you must install the drivers manually. You may need
    drivers from the device manufacturer to perform this
    installation.

> **NOTE**
>
> **Authority Needed**   To use the Windows
> 2000 Device Manager utility to troubleshoot
> USB problems, you must be logged on as an
> administrator, or as a member of the
> Administrators group.

Troubleshooting Scanners

The driver software that comes with the scanner must be configured
to match the settings on its adapter card. The adapter card settings
are normally established through hardware jumpers. Check the
scanner software's setup screen to confirm the settings.

Most scanners have three important configuration parameters to
consider: the I/O address, the IRQ setting, and the DMA channel
setting.

Typical I/O address settings for the scanner adapter are 150h to
151h (default), 170h to 171h, 350h to 351h, or 370h to 371h.
Typical IRQ settings are 10 (default) 3, 5, and 11. Likewise, typical
DMA channel settings are channel 5 (default), 1, 3, or 7. Figure
2.35 shows the components associated with scanners.

FIGURE 2.35
Scanner-related components.

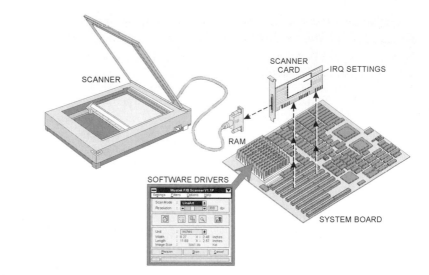

Generally, IRQ conflicts with network and sound cards tend to be the biggest problem associated with scanners. Typical symptoms associated with IRQ conflicts include the following:

◆ The image onscreen appears misaligned.

◆ The scanning function appears to be activated and the scanner light comes on, but no image is produced onscreen.

In these cases, a good software diagnostic package can be quite helpful in spotting and correcting the conflicts.

The scanning function appears to be activated and the scanner light comes on symptom also can apply to the DMA channel of the interface card conflicting with the DMA setting of another card. Select another DMA channel for the card and software.

If the scanner light does not come on when trying to scan, there are two possible causes of the problem. First, the system may not meet minimum system requirements for the particular scanner being used. If this is the case, research the minimum system requirements of the scanner to make sure that it can be used with the system. If the system requirements are not met, either return the scanner to the supplier, or upgrade the system to meet the minimum specifications for the scanner. The second possible cause of the problem is that the I/O address setting conflicts with another card in the computer. Try other address settings on the adapter card, and in the software.

If the problem seems to be a hardware problem, make the checks described in the "Performing Quick Tests" section earlier in this chapter. Make sure the power to the scanner is plugged in and turned on. Exchange the signal cable for a new one, if available. Refer to the User Guide for troubleshooting hints.

Troubleshooting Tape Drives

Because the fundamentals of recording on tape are so similar to those used with magnetic disks, the troubleshooting process is also very similar.

The tape itself can be a source of several problems. Common points to check with the tape include the following:

NOTE

Tape Drive Components   The basic components associated with the tape drive include the tape drive, the signal cable, the power connection, the controller, and the tape drive's operating software.

◆ Is the tape formatted correctly for use with the drive in question?

◆ Is the tape inserted securely in the drive?

◆ Is the tape write-protected?

◆ Is the tape broken or off the reel in the cartridge?

As cartridge tapes are pulled back and forth, their mylar base can become stretched over time. This action can cause the tape's format to fail before the tape actually wears out. To remedy this, you should retention the tape periodically using the software's retention utility. Cartridge tapes are typically good for about 150 hours of operation. If the number of tape errors begins to increase dramatically before this time, try reformatting the tape to restore its integrity. After the 150-hour point, just replace the tape.

If the tape is physically okay and properly formatted, the next easiest thing to check is the tape software. Check the software Setup and Configuration settings to make sure they are correct for any hardware settings. Refer to the tape drive's User Guide for a list of system requirements, and check the system to make sure they are being met.

If any configuration jumpers or switches are present on the controller, verify that they are set correctly for the installation. Also, run a diagnostic program to check for resource conflicts that may be preventing the drive from operating (such as IRQ and base memory addressing).

The software provided with most tape drives includes some error-messaging capabilities. Observe the system and note any tape-related error messages it produces. Consult the User Manual for error-message definitions and corrective suggestions. Check for error logs that the software may keep. You can view these logs to determine what errors have been occurring in the system.

Because many tape drives are used in networked and multiuser environments, another problem occurs when you are not properly logged in, or enabled to work with files being backed up or restored. In these situations, the operating system may not allow the tape drive to access secured files, or any files, because the correct clearances have not been met. Consult the network administrator for proper password and security clearances. See Chapter 10, "4.0 Networks," for more information about the network environment.

Reinstall the drive's software and reconfigure it. Go through the installation process carefully, paying close attention to any user-selected variables and configuration information requested by the program.

If you suspect hardware problems, begin by cleaning the drive's R/W heads. Consult the User Guide for cleaning instructions, or use the process described in Chapter 3, "3.0 Preventive Maintenance," for manual cleaning of floppy drive R/W heads. The R/W heads should be cleaned after about 20 backups or restores. Also, try to use a different tape to see whether it works. Make certain that it is properly formatted for operation. It should also be a clean tape, if possible, to avoid exposing any critical information to potential corruption.

If cleaning does not restore the drive to proper operation, continue by checking the power and signal cables for good connection and proper orientation.

Because matching tape drives are not common at a single location, checking the drive by substitution should be considered as a last step. Check the User Guide for any additional testing information and call the drive manufacturer's technical service number for assistance, before replacing the drive.

Troubleshooting Modems

A section on troubleshooting modems has to be subdivided into two segments:

◆ External modems

◆ Internal modems

In the case of an internal modem, you check it out in the same basic sequence as any other I/O card. First, check the modem's hardware and software configuration, check the system for conflicts, and check for correct drivers. Improper software setup is the most common cause of modems not working when they are first installed. Inspect any cabling connections to see that they are made correctly and functioning properly, and test the modem's hardware by substitution. If an external modem is being checked, it must be treated as an external peripheral, with the serial port being treated as a separate I/O port. Figure 2.36 shows the components associated with internal and external modems.

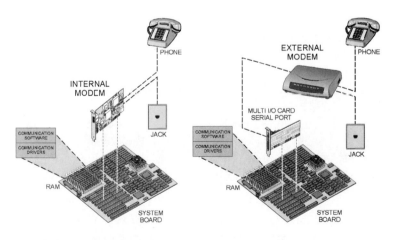

FIGURE 2.36
Internal and external modem components.

Modem Problem Symptoms

Typical symptoms associated with modem failures include the following:

◆ No response from the modem.

◆ Modem does not dial out.

◆ Modem does not connect after number has been dialed.

◆ Modem does not transmit after making connection with remote unit.

- ◆ Cannot get modem installed properly for operation.
- ◆ Garbled messages transmitted.
- ◆ Cannot terminate a communication session.
- ◆ Cannot transfer files.

COM Port Conflicts

As stated earlier, every COM port on a PC requires an IRQ line to signal the processor for attention. In most PC systems, two COM ports share the same IRQ line. The IRQ4 line works for COM1 and COM3, and the IRQ3 line works for COM2 and COM4. This is common in PC compatibles. The technician must make sure that two devices are not set up to use the same IRQ channel.

If more than one device is connected to the same IRQ line, a conflict occurs, because it is not likely that the interrupt handler software can service both devices.

If a mouse is set for COM1 and a modem is set for COM3, for example, neither device can communicate effectively with the system, because COM1 and COM3 both use IRQ4. Both the mouse and the modem may be interrupting the microprocessor at the same time. The same is true if two devices are connected to IRQ3, because COM2 and COM4 use this IRQ. Therefore, the first step to take when installing a modem is to check the system to see how its interrupts and COM ports are allocated. You can alleviate this particular interrupt conflict by using a bus mouse rather than a serial mouse, thus freeing up a COM port.

To install a non-PnP device on a specific COM port (for instance, COM2), you must first disable that port in the system's CMOS settings to avoid a device conflict. If not, the system may try to allocate that resource to some other device, because it has no way of knowing that the non-PNP device requires it.

Use a software diagnostic package to obtain information about the serial port's base I/O port address. A typical value for this setting is 02E8h. Also, obtain the modem's IRQ setting. This setting is typically IRQ=3. Other common modem settings are as follows:

COM1 with IRQ=4, 5, or 7
COM2 with IRQ=3, 5, or 7

COM3 with IRQ=4, 5, or 7

COM4 with IRQ=3, 5, or 7

Take care when using IRQ5 or IRQ7 with the modem. These interrupt channels are typically reserved for LPT1 (IRQ7) and LPT2
(IRQ5). The arrangements in the preceding list assume that IRQ3
and IRQ4 are already taken. It also assumes that at least one of the
LPT interrupts is not being used by a printer.

Be aware that the system may conflict with non-PNP devices for resources if it is not informed they are have been reserved.

Basic Modem Checks

Many of the software diagnostic packages available include a utility
for testing modems. If such a program is available, run the equivalent of its Run All Tests entry to test the modem. If all the configuration settings are correct, attempt to run the modem's DOS-based
communications package to test the modem's operation.

In Windows 9x, you can find the modem configuration information
in the Control Panel under the Modems icon. Under the icon are
two tabs: the General tab and the Diagnostics tab. The Properties
button in the General window provides Port and Maximum-Speed
settings. The Connection tab provides character-framing information, as illustrated in Figure 2.37. The Connection tab's Advanced
button provides error and flow-control settings, as well as modulation type.

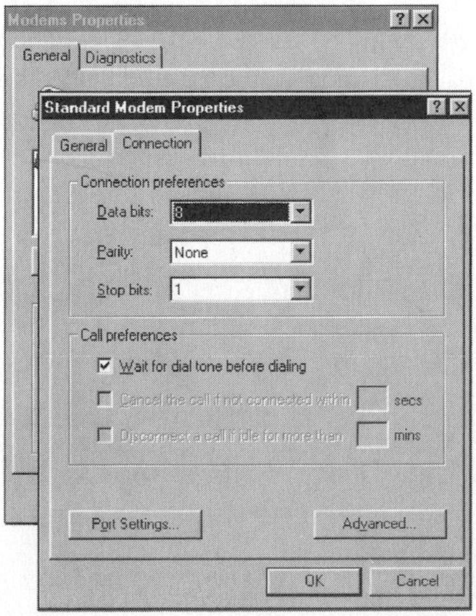

FIGURE 2.37
The Connection tab of the Standard Modem Properties dialog box.

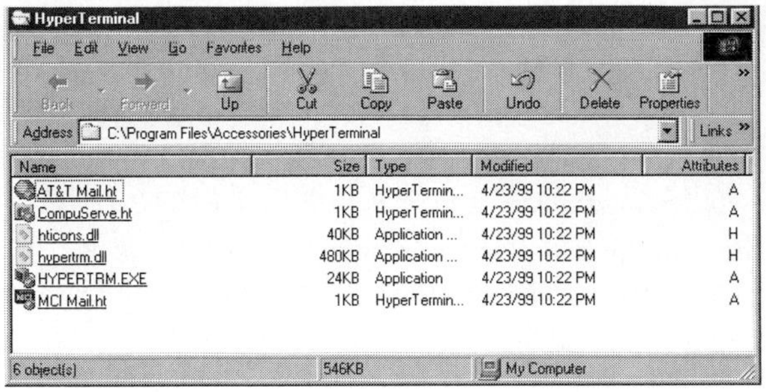

FIGURE 2.38

The Diagnostics tab of the Modem Properties dialog box.

The Diagnostics tab's dialog box, depicted in Figure 2.38, provides access to the modem's driver and additional information. The PnP feature reads the modem card and returns its information to the screen, as demonstrated in the figure.

Windows 9x provides fundamental troubleshooting information for wide area networking through its system of Help screens. Just select Help from the Control Panel's toolbar, and click the topic that you are troubleshooting.

Communications Software

All modems require software to control the communication session. This software is typically included with the purchase of the modem. At the fundamental instruction level, most modems use a set of commands known as the Hayes-compatible command set.

This set of commands is named after the Hayes Microcomputer Products company that first defined them. The command set is based on a group of instructions that begin with a pair of attention characters, followed by command words. Because the attention characters are an integral part of every Hayes command, the command set is often referred to as the AT command set.

In the Hayes command structure, the operation of the modem shifts back and forth between a command mode (local mode) and a communications mode (remote mode). In the command mode, the modem exchanges commands and status information with the host system's microprocessor. In communications mode, the modem facilitates sending and receiving data between the local system and a remote system. A short guard period between communications mode and command mode allows the system to switch smoothly without interrupting a data transmission.

AT Command Set

Hayes-compatible **AT** commands are entered at the command line using an AT*Xn* format. The *Xn* nomenclature identifies the type of command being given (*X*) and the particular function to be used (*n*). Except for **ATA**, **ATDn**, and **ATZn** commands, the AT sequence can be followed by any number of commands. The **ATA** command forces the modem to immediately pick up the phone line (even if it does not ring). The **Dn** commands are dialing instructions, and the **Zn** commands reset the modem by loading new default initialization information into it. Table 2.4 provides a summary of the Hayes-compatible AT command set.

TABLE 2.4

AT COMMAND SET SUMMARY

Command	Function
A/	Re-execute command
A	Go off-hook and attempt to answer a call
B0	Select V.22 connection at 1200bps
B1	Select Bell 212A connection at 1200bps
C1	Return OK message
Dn	Dial modifier (see Dial Modifier)
E0	Turn off command echo
E1	Turn on command echo
F0	Select auto-detect mode (equivalent to N1)
F1	Select V.21 of Bell 103
F2	Reserved
F3	Select V.23 line modulation
F4	Select V.22 or Bell 212A 1200bps line speed
F5	Select V.22bis 7200 line modulation
F6	Select V.32bis or V.32 4800 line modulation
F7	Select V.32bis 7200 line modulation

continues

TABLE 2.4	*continued*

AT COMMAND SET SUMMARY

Command	Functions
F8	Select V.32bis or V.32 9600 modulation
F9	Select V.32bis 12000 line modulation
F10	Select V.32bis 14400 line modulation
H0	Initiate a hang-up sequence
H1	If on-hook, go off-hook and enter command mode
I0	Report product code
I1	Report computed checksum
I2	Report OK
I3	Report firmware revision, model, and interface type
I4	Report response
I5	Report the country code parameter
I6	Report modem data pump model and code revision
L0	Set low speaker volume
L1	Set low speaker volume
L2	Set medium speaker volume
L3	Set high speaker volume
M0	Turn off speaker
M1	Turn speaker on during handshaking, and turn speaker off while receiving carrier
M2	Turn speaker on during handshaking and while receiving carrier
M3	Turn speaker off during dialing and receiving carrier, and turn speaker on during answering
N0	Turn off Automode detection
N1	Turn on Automode detection
O0	Go online

Command	*Functions*
O1	Go online and initiate a retrain sequence
P	Force pulse dialing
Q0	Allow result codes to PC
Q1	Inhibit result codes to PC
Sn	Select S-Register as default
Sn?	Return the value of S-Register n
=v	Set default S-Register to value v
?	Return the value of default S-Register
T	Force DTMF dialing
V0	Report short form (terse) result codes
V1	Report long form (verbose) result codes
W0	Report PC speed in EC mode
W1	Report line speed, EC protocol, and PC speed
W2	Report modem speed in EC mode
X0	Report basic progress result codes, OK, CONNECT, RING, NO CARRIER (also for busy, if enabled, and dial tone not detected), NO ANSWER, and ERROR
X1	Report basic call progress result codes and connection speeds such as OK, CONNECT, RING, NO CARRIER (also for busy, in enabled, and dial tone not detected), NO ANSWER, CONNECT XXXX, and ERROR
X2	Report basic call progress result codes and connection speeds such as OK, CONNECT, RING, NO CARRIER (also for busy, in enabled, and dial tone not detected), NO ANSWER, CONNECT XXXX, and ERROR
X3	Report basic call progress result codes and connection rate such as OK, CONNECT, RING, NO CARRIER, NO ANSWER, CONNECT XXXX, BUSY, and ERROR

After a command has been entered at the command line, the modem attempts to execute the command and then returns a result code to the screen. Table 2.5 describes the command result codes.

TABLE 2.5

COMMAND RESULT CODES

Code	Message	Result
0	OK	The OK code is returned by the modem to acknowledge execution of a command line.
1	CONNECT	The modem sends this result code when line speed is 300bps.
2	RING	The modem sends this result code when incoming ringing is detected on the line.
3	NO CARRIER	The carrier is not detected within the time limit, or the carrier is lost.
4	ERROR	The modem could not process the command line (entry error).
5	CONNECT 1200	The modem detected a carrier at 1200bps.
6	NO DIAL TONE	The modem could not detect a dial tone when dialing.
7	BUSY	The modem detected a busy signal.
8	NO ANSWER	The modem never detected silence (@ command only).
9	CONNECT 0600	The modem sends this result code when line speed is 7200bps.
10	CONNECT 2400	The modem detected a carrier at 2400bps.
11	CONNECT 4800	Connection is established at 4800bps.
12	CONNECT 9600	Connection is established at 9600bps.
13	CONNECT 7200	The modem sends this result code when the line speed is 7200bps.
14	CONNECT 12000	Connection is established at 12000bps.
15	CONNECT 14400	Connection is established at 14400bps.
17	CONNECT 38400	Connection is established at 38400bps.
18	CONNECT 57600	Connection is established at 57600bps.
22	CONNECT 75TX/ 1200RX	The modem sends this result code when establishing a V.23 Originate.
23	CONNECT 1200TX/ 75RX	The modem sends this result code when establishing a V.23 answer.
24	DELAYED	The modem returns this result code when a call fails to connect and is considered delayed.

Code	Message	Result
32	BLACKLISTED	The modem returns this result code when a f/call fails to connect and is considered blacklisted.
40	CARRIER 300	The carrier is detected at 300bps.
44	CARRIER 1200/75	The modem sends this result code when V.23 backward channel carrier is detected.
45	CARRIER 75/1200	The modem sends this result code when V.23 forward channel carrier is detected.
46	CARRIER 1200	The carrier is detected at 1200bps.
47	CARRIER 2400	The carrier is detected at 2400bps.
48	CARRIER 4800	The modem sends this result code when either the high or low channel carrier in V.22bis modem has been detected.
49	CARRIER 7200	The carrier is detected at 7200bps.
50	CARRIER 9600	The carrier is detected at 9600bps.
51	CARRIER 12000	The carrier is detected at 12000bps.
52	CARRIER 14400	The carrier is detected at 14400bps.
66	COMPRESSION: CLASS 5	MNP Class 5 is active CLASS 5.
67	COMPRESSION: V.42bis	COMPRESSION: V.42bis is active V.42bis.
69	COMPRESSION: NONE	No data compression signals NONE.
70	PROTOCOL: NONE	No error correction is enabled.
77	PROTOCOL: LAPM	V.42 LAP-M error correction is enabled.
80	PROTOCOL: ALT	MNP Class 4 error correction is enabled.

Specialized fax and voice software programs also are included, if the modem has these capabilities. Most communication software packages include an electronic phonebook to hold frequently dialed numbers. Other features include the use of a variety of different software protocols. Common protocols included at this level include Xmodem, Ymodem, and Zmodem. Both the originating and answering modems must agree on the same protocol, baud rate, and data length for the session to succeed.

To communicate with other computers, some information about how the communication will proceed is needed. In particular, it is necessary to match the protocol of the remote unit, as well as its parity, character framing, and baud rate settings. With older modems, this may involve a telephone call to the other computer user. In the case of online services, the information comes with the introductory package the user receives when joining the service.

The Windows program contains an application called *Hyper Terminal* that can be used to control the operation of the system's modem with Telnet services. HyperTerminal is capable of operating with several different modem configurations. This flexibility enables it to conduct transfers with a wide variety of other computer systems on the Internet, such as UNIX and Linux, without worrying about operating system differences. Using HyperTerminal with Telnet to access other locations is much quicker than browsing Web sites with a graphical browser. The HyperTerminal New Connections window, shown in Figure 2.39 provides the options for configuring the communications settings. This program can be accessed through the Start/Programs/Accessories/Communications path in Windows 98.

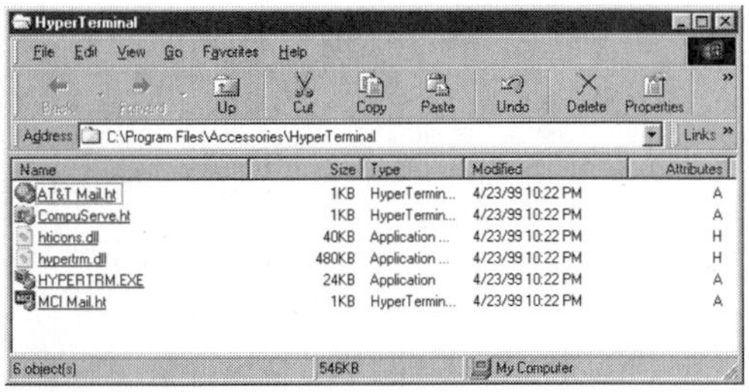

FIGURE 2.39
HyperTerminal.

Using the AT Command Set

At the command line, type **ATZ** to reset the modem and enter the command mode using the Hayes-compatible command set. You should receive a 0, or OK response, if the command was processed.

If no result code is returned to the screen, check the modem's configuration and setup again for conflicts. Also, check the Speed setting of the *communications software* to make sure it is compatible with that of the modem. On the other hand, a returned OK code indicates that the modem and the computer are communicating properly.

You can use other AT-compatible commands to check the modem at the DOS level. The *ATL2* command sets the modem's output volume to medium, to make sure that it is not set too low to be heard. If the modem dials, but cannot connect to a remote station, check the modem's Speed and DTR settings. Change the DTR setting by entering **AT&Dn**. When

n = 0	The modem ignores the DTR line.
n = 1	The modem goes to async command state when the DTR line goes off.

n = 2   A DTR off condition switches the modem to the off-hook state and back into the command mode.

n = 3   When the DTR line switches to off the modem gets initialized.

The modem's User Guide should contain the complete AT command set. Some of the commands and features listed may not work with your particular modem.

If the modem connects, but cannot communicate, check the character-framing parameter of the receiving modem, and set the local modem to match. Also, match the terminal emulation of the local unit to that of the remote unit. ANSI terminal emulation is the most common. Finally, match the file transfer protocol to the other modem.

A number of things can occur to prevent the modem from going into the online state. An intelligent modem waits a specified length of time, after pickup, before it starts dialing. This wait allows the phone system time to apply a dial tone to the line. After the number has been dialed, the modem waits for the ringback from the telephone company. (This is what you hear when you are making a call.)

When the ringing stops, indicating that the call has gone through, the modem waits a specified length of time for an answer tone (carrier) from the receiving modem. If the carrier is not detected within the allotted time, the originating modem begins automatic disconnect procedures. If a busy signal is detected, the originating modem also hangs up, or refers to a second number.

During the data transfer, both modems monitor the signal level of the carrier to prevent the transfer of false data, due to signal deterioration. If the carrier signal strength drops below some predetermined threshold level, or is lost for a given length of time, one or both modems initiate automatic disconnect procedures.

Use the *ATDT*70* command to disable call waiting, if the transmission is frequently garbled. The +++ command will interrupt any activity the modem is engaged in, and bring it to the command mode.

TEST TIP

Be familiar with the basic Hayes AT communication codes.

Modem Hardware Checks

Most serial ports and modems can perform self-tests on their circuitry.

Modems actually have the capability to perform three different kinds of self-diagnostic tests:

◆ The local digital loopback test

◆ The local analog loopback test

◆ The remote digital loopback test

In a *local digital loopback test*, data is looped through the registers of the port's UART. When testing the RS-232 port itself, a device called a loopback plug (or wrap-plug) channels the output data directly back into the received data input, and only the port is tested.

Many modems can extend this test by looping the data through the local modem, and back to the computer (the *local analog loopback test*). Some modems can even loop back data to a remote computer through its modem (the *remote digital loopback test*). In this manner, the entire transmit and receive path can be validated, including the communication line (that is, the telephone line). One of the most overlooked causes of transmission problems is the telephone line itself. A noisy line can easily cause garbled data to be output from the modem. Figure 2.40 illustrates adapter, analog, and digital loopback tests.

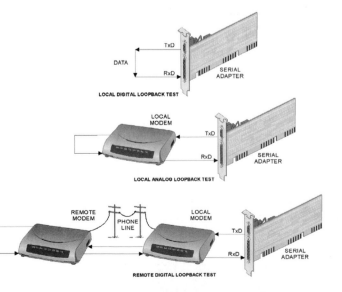

FIGURE 2.40
Loopback tests.

If transmission errors occur frequently, you should use the various loopback tests to locate the source of the problem. Begin by running the remote digital loopback test. If the test runs successfully, the problem is likely to be located in the remote computer.

If the test fails, run the local digital loopback test with self-tests. If the test results are positive, the problem may be located in the local computer. On the other hand, you should run the local analog loopback test if the local digital test fails.

If the local analog test fails, the problem is located in the local modem. If the local analog test is successful, and problems are occurring, you should run the local analog test on the remote computer. The outcome of this test should pinpoint the problem to the remote computer or the remote modem.

If the modem is an internal unit, you can test its hardware by exchanging it with a known good unit. If the telephone line operates correctly with a normal handset, only the modem, its configuration, or the communications software can be causes of problems. If the modem's software and configuration settings appear correct and problems are occurring, the modem hardware is experiencing a problem and it will be necessary to exchange the modem card for a known good one.

With an external modem, you can use the front-panel lights as diagnostic tools to monitor its operation. You can monitor the progress of a call, and its handling, along with any errors that may occur.

Figure 2.41 depicts the front-panel lights of a typical external modem.

The Modem Ready (MR), Terminal Ready (TR), and Auto Answer (AA) lights are preparatory lights that indicate that the modem is plugged in, powered on, ready to run, and prepared to answer an incoming call. The MR light becomes active when power is applied to the modem and the modem is ready to operate. The TR light becomes active when the host computer's communication software and the modem contact each other. The AA light just indicates that the Auto Answer function has been turned on.

The *Off-Hook* (OH), *Ring Indicator* (RI), and *Carrier Detect* (CD) lights indicate the modem's online condition. The OH light indicates that the modem has connected to the phone line. This action

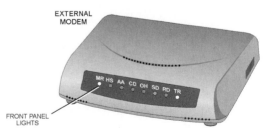

FIGURE 2.41
Modem front-panel indicators.

can occur when the modem is receiving a call, or when it is commanded to place a call. The RI light becomes active when the modem detects an incoming ring signal. The CD light activates when the modem detects a carrier signal from a remote modem. As long as this light is on, the modem can send and receive data from the remote unit. If the CD light will not activate with a known good modem, a problem with the data communication equipment exists.

The final three lights indicate the status of a call in progress. The Send Data (SD) light flickers when the modem transmits data to the remote unit, and the Received Data (RD) light flickers when the modem receives data from the remote unit. The High Speed (HS) light becomes active when the modem is conducting transfers at its highest possible rate. If an external modem will not operate at its highest rated potential, check the specification for the UART on the adapter card to make certain that it is capable of operating at that speed.

Troubleshooting Sound Cards

Some very basic components are involved in the audio output of most computer systems: a sound card, some speakers, the audio-related software, and the host computer system. Several software diagnostic packages enable you to test sound card operation.

Most sound cards perform two separate functions. The first is to play sound files; the second is to record them. You might need to troubleshoot problems for either function.

Sound Card Configuration Checks

If sound problems are occurring in the multimedia system, two of the first things to check are the hardware and audio software configuration settings. Refer to the sound card manufacturer's documentation for proper hardware settings. These items usually include checking the card's jumper settings for IRQ and I/O address settings. With more PnP cards on the market, software configuration of IRQ and I/O addressing is becoming more common.

In the past, sound cards have been notorious for interrupt conflict problems with other devices. Because these conflicts typically exist between peripheral devices, they may not appear during boot up. If the sound card operates correctly except when a printing operation is in progress, for example, an IRQ conflict probably exists between the sound card and the printer port. Similar symptoms would be produced for tape backup operations if the tape drive and the sound card were configured to use the same IRQ channel. Use a software diagnostic program to check the system for interrupt conflicts.

Checking the system for resource conflicts in Windows is relatively easy. Access the Control Panel and select the System icon. From this point, click the Device Manager and select the Sound, video, and game controller option. If the system detects any conflicts, it places an exclamation point within a circle on the selected option.

From the Device Manager, choose the proper sound card driver from the list and move into its Resource window. The page's main window displays all the resources the driver is using for the card. The Conflicting Device list window provides information about any conflicting resource that the system has detected in conjunction with the sound card.

If the Windows PnP function is operating properly, you should be able to remove the driver from the system, reboot the computer, and allow the operating system to redetect the sound card and assign new resources to it.

Sound Card Software Checks

Many diagnostic packages offer testing features for sound cards and other multimedia-related components. Sound card problems should not prevent the system from loading a software diagnostic, so run the All Tests equivalent in the multimedia section of the diagnostic package. Also, run checks to see whether addressing (IRQ or DMA) conflicts are causing a problem. If they are, reconfigure the system's components to remove the conflicts.

Is the software application running a DOS version? If so, it may not be able to output audio under Windows. You can use the Windows *Sound Recorder* to check the operation of WAV files under Windows. WAV is a Microsoft specification for audio files and is one of the most popular file formats for use with audio files. The Sound

Recorder utility can be accessed through the Start/Programs/ Accessories path under the Multimedia entry in Windows 95 or the Entertainment entry in Windows 98. If the audio file will not play from the Sound Recorder, make sure the Sound Recorder is working by attempting to play audio files that have played on the system before. If the files play from the Sound Recorder, examine the other application that was attempting to play the file for proper installation and setup.

If the Sound Recorder will not play audio files through the sound card, check to see that the multimedia icon is installed in the Control Panel, and available through the Start/Programs/Accessories path. Also check the Control Panel's Device Manager to see that the correct audio driver is installed, and that its settings match those called for by the sound card manufacturer. If the drivers are missing, or wrong, add them to the system through the Control Panels' Add/Remove Hardware wizard.

If the driver is not installed, or is incorrect, add the correct driver from the Available Drivers list. If the correct driver is not available, reinstall it from the card's OEM disk or obtain it from the card's manufacturer.

Reference Shelf

For more in-depth technical information about multimedia systems and the MIDI sound standard, refer to the "Multimedia" section of the Electronic Reference Shelf located on the CD that accompanies this book.

Professional music users like to work with a special file and equipment standard for music known as MIDI. Windows is capable of handling and playing MIDI files through its MIDI Player utility located under the Start/Programs/Accessories path. Like the Sound Recorder utility, the MIDI Player is located under the Multimedia entry in Windows 95, or the Entertainment entry in Windows 98. If the Windows Media Player will not play MIDI files, look in the System/Device Manager section of the Control Panel to see that the MIDI driver is set up properly. Check to see whether more than one MIDI device is connected. If so, disconnect the other MIDI devices.

Sound Card Hardware Checks

Figure 2.42 depicts the system's sound card–related components. Provided that the sound card's configuration is properly set, and the software configuration matches it, the sound card and speakers will need to be checked out if problems exist. Most of these checks are very simple. They include checking to see that the speakers are plugged into the speaker port. It is not uncommon for the speakers to be mistakenly plugged into the card's MIC (microphone) port.

Likewise, if the sound card will not record sound, make certain that the microphone is installed in the proper jack (not the speaker jack), and that it is turned on. Check the amount of disk space on the drive, to ensure that there is enough to hold the file being produced.

In the case of stereo speaker systems, it is possible to place the speakers on the wrong sides. This will produce a problem when you try to adjust the balance between them. Increasing the volume on the right speaker will instead increase the output of the left speaker. The obvious cure for this problem is to physically switch the positions of the speakers.

TEST TIP

Know how to correct a balance problem that occurs with add-on stereo speakers.

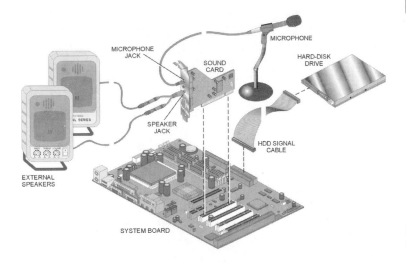

FIGURE 2.42
Sound card–related components.

If the system will not produce sound, troubleshoot the audio output portion of the system. Do the speakers require an external power supply? If so, is it connected, and are the speakers turned on? If the speakers use batteries for their power source, check them to see that they are installed, and good. Check the speakers' volume setting to make certain they are not turned down.

Troubleshooting General Multimedia Problems

Typical symptoms associated with multimedia failures include the following:

◆ Sound not working.

◆ The system will not capture video.

◆ Software cannot access the CD-ROM.

◆ The system will not play video.

Figure 2.43 depicts various multimedia support systems. These systems include a sound card, a CD-ROM drive, external speakers, and a video capture card. Most or all of these devices are included in any particular multimedia system. These types of equipment typically push the performance of the system, and therefore they require the most services from technicians (especially during setup and configuration).

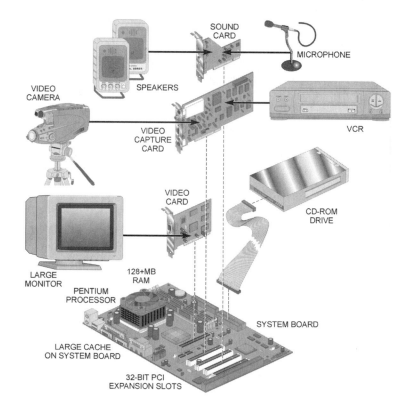

FIGURE 2.43
Multimedia components.

One of the major points to be aware of when building or upgrading a multimedia PC is the interrupt channel usage of the system. It is important that all the devices have access to unique, acceptable interrupt request lines. To ensure this, the technician should map out the system's IRQ capabilities with the number and level of interrupts needed by the different devices being installed. In some instances, it also is necessary to map the DMA capabilities of the system to the number of available DMA channels. IRQ and DMA availability and utilization is covered in detail in Chapter 4, "4.0 Motherboard/Processors/Memory."

The wide variety of I/O systems that come together to create a true multimedia machine can quickly use up all the available I/O slots on most system boards, especially in Pentium systems (where the expansion slots are often a mix of ISA and PCI buses). This lack of available slots sometimes leads to problems getting I/O cards with the correct mix of bus connectors.

> **Reference Shelf**
>
> For more in-depth technical information about multimedia systems, refer to the "Multimedia" section of the Electronic Reference Shelf located on the CD that accompanies this book.

CHAPTER SUMMARY

This chapter has covered fundamental troubleshooting tools and techniques. The first half of the chapter presented the basic tools and investigative techniques used to troubleshoot computer systems. It dealt with the early steps of computer problem solving, including differentiating hardware versus software problems and identifying configuration problems. The final portion of this section focused on software diagnostic packages and their use. Upon completion of this material, you should be able to identify basic troubleshooting procedures and good practices for eliciting problem symptoms from customers.

The second half of the chapter presented typical symptoms and standard troubleshooting procedures for various system components. It included FRU troubleshooting procedures that included software, configuration, and hardware segments for each device. The procedures for most of the devices included related troubleshooting information associated with command prompt and Windows level problems. After completing the chapter, you should be able to identify common symptoms and problems associated with each module and how to troubleshoot and isolate the problems.

KEY TERMS

- Add Printer Wizard
- AT&Dn
- ATDT*70
- ATL2
- ATZ
- Bad or missing COMMAND.COM
- Base address settings
- Beep codes
- Boot-up problems
- CD-ROM drive
- Clean boot disk

continues

continued

At this point, review the objectives listed at the beginning of the chapter to be certain that you understand and can perform each item listed there. Afterward, answer the Review Questions that follow to verify your knowledge of the information.

- Communications software
- Configuration problems
- Continuity test
- Corrosion
- Device drivers
- Device Manager
- Disk Boot Failure message
- DMMs (digital multimeters)
- Drive Mismatch Error message
- FDISK /MBR
- Field-replaceable units (FRUs)
- Hard-memory errors
- Hardware handshaking
- Hardware problems
- Implosion hazard
- Invalid Media Type message
- IRQ setting
- Joystick Properties dialog box
- Local analog loopback test
- Local digital loopback test
- Loopback plug
- MEM command (MEM.EXE)
- Microsoft Download Service (MSDL)
- Modem
- Metal-oxide semiconductor (MOS)

- Nickel-Cadmium (Ni-Cad) battery
- Operational problems
- POST cards

- Remote digital loopback test
- Setup utility
- Soft-memory errors
- Standard Parallel Port (SPP)

- System Properties page
- VOMs (volt-ohm-milliammeters)
- Xon-Xoff

RESOURCE URLS

www.pctusa.com/pcerror.htm

www.sysopt.com/biosbmc.html

www.sysopt.com/post.html

www.pctestpro.com/demo.htm

www.windsortech.com/

Note that these preceding two sites are included to show some of the types of diagnostic tools available in the industry. We have no experience with the free downloadable demo software available from these locations.

www.pcguide.com/ts/gen/index.htm

http://november.dtc.net/HW_config/hwconfigC.tshoot.html

http://citabria.westmont.edu/tech/hardware.html

www.co.umist.ac.uk/~ch/psinfo/psinfo.2.0568.html

www.pcguide.com/ts/x/comp/mbsys/index.htm

http://desperado.blinncol.edu/newcisc/1301/notes/vii.htm

www.anselm.edu/homepage/ptaglini/kbmouse.html

www.colosys.net/computeraid/t6.htm

http://amptech.com/tech/floppy.htm#question

continues

continued

http://amptech.com/tech/hdd.htm

www.pctusa.com/ide.htm

http://desperado.blinncol.edu/newcisc/1301/notes/vii.htm

http://rama.bl.pg.gda.pl/~slawcok/mirror/pcmech/tsprinter.htm

www.pumatech.com/techsupp/troubleshoot/hyprtrm_port.html

www.plustekusa.com/technicalsupport/troubleshoot.html

Note that the preceding site contains information about a specific set of products. However, its troubleshooting information is somewhat universal in nature.

http://desperado.blinncol.edu/newcisc/1301/notes/slides/chapter8/tsld066.htm

http://comminfo.com/pages/tips.htm

http://rama.bl.pg.gda.pl/~slawcok/mirror/pcmech/tsmodem.htm

http://amptech.com/tech/modem.htm

www.gravis.com/support/faq_sound/index.html

http://amptech.com/tech/soundmain.htm

http://amptech.com/tech/video1-1.htm

http://plop.phys.cwru.edu/repairfaq/REPAIR/F_monfaq.html

http://ftp.unina.it/pub/electronics/repairfaq/REPAIR/F_crtfaq.html

APPLY YOUR KNOWLEDGE

Review Questions

1. If the system issues a single beep and the C:\> prompt appears onscreen, what condition is indicated?

2. List the FDD-related hardware components that should be checked when you suspect floppy disk problems.

3. List three situations that normally require the CMOS setup routines to be run.

4. What type of problem is indicated by a Press F1 to Continue message during boot up?

5. What is the recommended way to use a digital multimeter to check voltage in a computer system?

6. If the system functions correctly after all the optional equipment has been removed, what action should you take next?

7. If you are replacing components one at a time and the system suddenly begins working properly, what can you assume?

8. List three items commonly tested using the resistance function of a multimeter.

9. What action should you take first, when you suspect a software failure?

10. What resistance reading is normally expected from a fuse if it is functional?

11. If you were measuring across a capacitor on the system board with a DMM, what voltage reading would you normally expect to see from a DMM?

12. Which noncomputer possibility should you eliminate early in the troubleshooting process?

13. What range should you set the voltage function of a DMM to for an initial measurement?

14. When would you normally use a POST card?

15. Where are loopback plugs used?

Exam Questions

1. If an error occurs before the single beep tone in the boot-up sequence, what type of failure is probable?

   A. The problem is probably associated with the operating system.

   B. The BIOS code has become corrupted.

   C. A setup or configuration problem.

   D. The problem is hardware related.

2. If an error occurs after the single beep in the boot-up process, what type of problem is likely?

   A. The problem is probably associated with the operating system.

   B. The BIOS code has become corrupted.

   C. A setup or configuration problem.

   D. The problem is hardware related.

3. If the system refuses to boot up after a new component is installed, what type of problem is normally assumed?

   A. The problem is probably associated with the operating system.

   B. The BIOS code has become corrupted.

   C. A setup or configuration problem has occurred.

   D. A hardware-related problem has occurred.

APPLY YOUR KNOWLEDGE

4. What component has the capability to affect the operation of all the other sections of the computer system?

   A. The power supply

   B. The ROM BIOS

   C. The microprocessor

   D. The system board

5. What function and reading would be appropriate for checking a system's speaker?

   A. Infinity

   B. Near 0 ohms

   C. 4 ohms

   D. 8 ohms

6. What type of problem does a continuous beep tone from the system indicate?

   A. A power-supply failure

   B. An undefined problem

   C. A configuration problem

   D. A boot-up problem

7. If a system appears to be completely dead, what item should logically be checked first?

   A. The system board

   B. The microprocessor

   C. The hard disk drive

   D. The power supply

8. The `Bad File Allocation Table` error message indicates what type of problem?

   A. An operating system problem

   B. A runtime problem

   C. A configuration problem

   D. A boot-up problem

9. If a CMOS `Display Type Mismatch` message appears onscreen, what type of error is indicated?

   A. An operating system problem

   B. A runtime error

   C. A setup or configuration problem

   D. A boot-up failure

10. Which of the following is not normally considered an FRU?

    A. A system board

    B. A floppy disk drive

    C. A power supply

    D. A video controller IC

Answers to Review Questions

1. The system has successfully booted up to the operating system prompt. For more information, see the section "Isolating Undefined Problems."

2. The floppy disk, the floppy drive, the FDD signal cable, the FDC controller (MI/O or system board), and the FDD's power connector. For more information, see the section "Troubleshooting Floppy Disk Drives."

3. When installing a new system, after replacing the CMOS backup battery, and when a new option is installed in the system. For more information, see the section "Determining Hardware/Software/Configuration Problems."

APPLY YOUR KNOWLEDGE

4. The system has encountered invalid configuration information during the boot-up process. Either the configuration has been set incorrectly, or the hardware was unable to confirm the configuration settings. For more information, see the section "Determining Hardware/Software/Configuration Problems."

5. The leads of the meter should be placed so that the meter is in parallel with the device being checked. The tests must be performed while power is applied to the component. For more information, see the section "Using a Multimeter."

6. Reinstall the removed components one at a time until the problem reappears. The last component returned to the system is at least partially responsible for the problem. However, other removed components must be reinstalled to confirm that only one was bad. For more information, see the section "Field-Replaceable Unit Troubleshooting."

7. That at least the last component reinstalled is defective. For more information, see the section "Field-Replaceable Unit Troubleshooting."

8. Fuses, speakers, and the continuity of connecting cables. For more information, see the section "Using a Multimeter."

9. Test the hardware with software that has been known to operate correctly in the past. For more information, see the section "Determining Hardware/Software/Configuration Problems."

10. 0 ohms. For more information, see the section "Using a Multimeter."

11. 5V (DC). For more information, see the section "Using a Multimeter."

12. The operator. For more information, see the section "Initial Troubleshooting Steps."

13. The highest range possible. For more information, see the section "Using a Multimeter."

14. POST cards are normally used when the system appears to be dead, or when the system cannot read from a floppy or hard drive. For more information, see the section "Using POST Cards."

15. Loopback plugs are used to test parallel and serial ports. They simulate the presence of a parallel printer or a serial device. For more information, see the section "Modem Hardware Checks."

Answers to Exam Questions

1. **D.** A hardware problem has occurred. Before this beep, the system is sorting out, testing, and configuring its hardware. After the beep, it begins to boot up the system and software configuration issues are taken into account. Recall that BIOS code is firmware and is, therefore, not likely to become defective. For more information, see the section "Isolating Undefined Problems."

2. **A.** After the beep in the startup sequence, the system performs the boot-up routine to hand off control to the operating system. For more information, see the section "Isolating Undefined Problems."

3. **C.** When a new component is installed and the system will not run properly, a configuration (or setup) problem is usually indicated. Either a configuration setting on the new device has conflicted with that of another device over some system resource, or the system may just not be

able to identify the settings for the new device. In PnP systems, the BIOS and operating system are supposed to be able to establish the configuration settings for the new device through the hardware detection process. In some cases, the PnP effort will not resolve the conflict and the user will need to manually sort out the problem. For more information, see the section "Determining Hardware/Software/Configuration Problems."

4. **A.** The power-supply unit affects most of the system's components directly, and the rest (such as adapter cards and peripherals) it affects indirectly. Therefore, symptoms caused by power-supply problems can appear anywhere. For more information, see the section "Isolating Power-Supply Problems."

5. **D.** Most PC speakers are rated for 8 ohms of resistance. This is the reading that should be found across a speaker that has been disconnected from the system. For more information, see the section "Using a Multimeter."

6. **A.** A power-supply problem creates a continuous beep tone in closely compatible PC systems. For more information, see the section "Isolating Power-Supply Problems."

7. **D.** If the system appears to be completely dead, the power-supply unit (or its commercial supply) are the most likely culprits. Failure of other system components generally leaves some appearance of life in the system (fan running, front-panel light on, and so forth). For more information, see the section "Checking a Dead System."

8. **D.** The FAT on the system's boot disk is checked during the boot-up process. Therefore, if any problems occur with this table, they will produce the `Bad File Allocation Table` error message at that time. For more information, see the section "Checking a Dead System."

9. **C.** A `Display Type Mismatch` error occurs during the system configuration checks, when the system is checking to make sure that the list of components it has in CMOS actually matches what it finds in the system. For more information, see the section "Isolating Undefined Problems."

10. **D.** In modern PCs, integrated circuits are not considered replaceable units, much less FRUs. Most ICs in PCs are large, surface-mounted devices that require complex equipment to remove. The time and expense of identifying and replacing a defective IC far outweighs any reason for replacing it. For more information, see the section "Field-Replaceable Unit Troubleshooting."

This chapter helps you to prepare for the Core Hardware module of the A+ Certification examination by covering the following objectives within the "Preventive Maintenance" section.

3.1. Identify the purpose of various types of preventive maintenance products and procedures, and when to use/perform them.

Content may include the following:

- **Liquid cleaning compounds**

- **Types of materials to clean contacts and connections**

- **Vacuum-out systems, power supplies, and fans**

▶ An important part of most computer service jobs is providing preventive maintenance for computer equipment, or teaching users the proper steps to care for their equipment.

3.2. Identify procedures and devices for protection within the computing environment, including people, technology, and the ecosystem.

Content may include the following:

- **UPSs (uninterruptible power supplies) and suppressors**

- **Determining the signs of power issues**

- **Proper methods of storage of components for future use**

Potential hazards and proper safety procedures relating to lasers.

Content may include the following:

- **High-voltage equipment**

- **Power supply**

- **CRTs**

CHAPTER 3

3.0 Preventive Maintenance

Special disposal procedures complying with environmental guidelines.

- **Batteries**

- **CRTs**

- **Toner kits/cartridges**

- **Chemical solvents and cans**

- **MSDS (Material Safety Data Sheet)**

ESD (electrostatic discharge) precautions and procedures.

- **What ESD can do as well as how it may be apparent or hidden**

- **Common ESD protection devices**

- **Situations that could present a danger or hazard**

▶ Computer technicians should be aware of potential environmental hazards and know how to prevent them from becoming a problem.

▶ Safety is an issue in every profession. Technicians should be aware of the potential hazards associated with certain areas of the computer and with certain types of peripheral equipment.

▶ Concerns for the world environment are at their highest. Many of the materials used in the construction of computer-related equipment can be harmful. Also, many of the products used to service computer equipment can have an adverse effect on the environment. Therefore, the technician should be aware of requirements associated with the disposal of this equipment and these materials.

▶ PC repair personnel should be aware of the causes and damaging effects of ESD so that they can prevent its occurrence.

To prepare for the Preventive Maintenance objective of the Core Hardware exam:

▶ Read the objectives at the beginning of this chapter.

▶ Study the information in this chapter.

▶ Review the objectives listed earlier in this chapter.

▶ Perform any step-by-step procedures in the text.

▶ Use the ExamGear test engine on the CD that accompanies this book for additional Review and Exam Questions concerning this material.

▶ Review the Test Tips scattered throughout the chapter and make certain that you are comfortable with each point.

INTRODUCTION

This domain requires the test taker to show knowledge of safety and preventive maintenance. With regard to safety, it includes the potential hazards to personnel and equipment when working with lasers, high-voltage equipment, ESD, and items that require special disposal procedures that comply with environmental guidelines.

With regard to preventive maintenance, this includes knowledge of preventive maintenance products, procedures, environmental hazards, and precautions when working on microcomputer systems. Questions from this domain account for 5% of the Core Hardware test.

PREVENTIVE MAINTENANCE

▶ 3.1 Identify the purpose of various types of preventive maintenance products and procedures, and when to use/perform them.

The A+ Core Hardware objective 3.1 states that the test taker should be able to "identify the purpose of various types of preventive maintenance products and procedures, and when to use/perform them."

It has long been known that one of the best ways to fix problems with complex systems is to prevent them before they happen. This is the concept behind preventive maintenance procedures. Breakdowns never occur at convenient times. By planning for a few minutes of nonproductive activities, hours of repair and recovery work can be avoided.

Cleaning

Cleaning is a major part of keeping a computer system healthy. Therefore, the technician's tool kit also should contain a collection of cleaning supplies. Along with hand tools, it needs a lint-free, soft cloth (chamois) for cleaning the plastic outer surfaces of the system.

To clean outer surfaces, just use a soap-and-water solution, followed by a clear water rinse. Take care to make sure that none of the liquid splashes or drips into the inner parts of the system. A damp cloth is easily the best general-purpose cleaning tool for use with computer equipment.

Follow the cleaning by applying an antistatic spray or *antistatic solution* to prevent the buildup of static charges on the components of the system. A solution composed of 10 parts water and 1 part common household fabric softener makes an effective and economical antistatic solution. To remove dust from the inside of cabinets, a small paintbrush is handy.

Another common problem is the buildup of oxidation, or corrosion, at electrical contact points. These buildups occur on electrical connectors and contacts, and can reduce the flow of electricity through the connection. You can follow some simple steps to keep corrosion from becoming a problem. The easiest way to prevent corrosion is to observe the correct handling procedures for printed circuit boards and cables, as shown in Figure 3.1. Never touch the electrical contact points with your skin, because the moisture on your body can start corrosive action.

Even with proper handling, some corrosion may occur over time. You can remove this *oxidation buildup* in a number of ways. The oxide buildup can be sanded off with emery cloth, rubbed off with a common pencil eraser or special solvent-wipe, or dissolved with an electrical-contact cleaner spray. Socketed devices should be reseated (removed and reinstalled to establish a new electrical connection) as a part of an anticorrosion cleaning. However, they should be handled according to the *metal-oxide semiconductor* (MOS) handling guidelines in this chapter to make certain that no static discharge damage occurs.

If you use the emery cloth or rubber eraser to clean your contacts, always rub toward the outer edge of the board or connector to prevent damage to the contacts. Rubbing the edge may lift the foil from the PC board. Printed circuit board connectors are typically very thin. Therefore, rub hard enough to remove only the oxide layer. Also, take time to clean up any dust or rubber contamination generated by the cleaning effort.

Cleaning other internal components, such as disk drive read/write (R/W) heads, can be performed using lint-free foam swabs and isopropyl alcohol or methanol. It is important that the cleaning

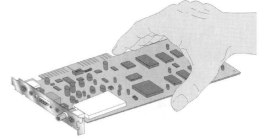

FIGURE 3.1
How to handle a PC board.

solution be one that dries without leaving residue. The following tools and equipment are recommended for a well-prepared computer-repair toolbox:

◆ Assorted flat-blade screwdrivers

◆ Assorted Phillips screwdrivers

◆ Assorted small nut drivers

◆ Assorted small torx bit drivers

◆ Needle-nose pliers

◆ Diagonal pliers

◆ Contact cleaner

◆ Foam swabs

◆ Tweezers

◆ Cleaning supplies

◆ Magnifying glass

◆ Clip leads

◆ IC extractors

Preventive Maintenance Procedures

The environment around a computer system, and the manner in which the computer is used, determines greatly how many problems it will have. Occasionally dedicating a few moments of care to the computer can extend its *mean time between failures* (MTBF) period considerably. This activity, involving maintenance not normally associated with a breakdown, is called *preventive maintenance* (PM).

The following sections describe PM measures for the various areas of the system.

As with any electronic device, computers are susceptible to failures caused by dust buildup, rough handling, and extreme temperatures.

Over time, dust builds up on everything it can gain access to. Many computer components generate static electrical charges that attract dust particles. In the case of electronic equipment, dust forms an

TEST TIP

Know what environmental conditions, or activities, are most likely to lead to equipment failures.

insulating blanket that traps heat next to active devices and can cause them to overheat. Excessive heat can cause premature aging and failure. The best dust protection is a dust-tight enclosure. However, computer components tend to have less than dust-tight seals. Power-supply and microprocessor fans pull air from outside through the system unit.

Another access point for dust is uncovered expansion slot openings. Missing expansion slot covers adversely affect the system in two ways. First, the missing cover permits dust to accumulate in the system, forming the insulating blanket that causes component overheating. Second, the heat problem is complicated further by the fact that the missing slot cover interrupts the designed airflow patterns inside the case, causing components to overheat due to missing or inadequate airflow.

> **TEST TIP**
> Be aware of the effect that missing expansion slot covers have on the operation of the system unit.

Smoke is a more dangerous cousin of dust. Like dust particles, smoke collects on all exposed surfaces. The residue of smoke particles is sticky and will cling to the surface. In addition to contributing to the heat buildup problem, smoke residue is particularly destructive to moving parts such as floppy disks, fan motors, and so forth.

Dust buildup inside system components can be taken care of with a soft brush. A static-free vacuum also can be used to remove dust from inside cases and keyboards. Be sure to use a static-free vacuum, because normal vacuums are natural static generators. The static-free vacuum has special grounding to remove the static buildup it generates. Dust covers also are helpful in holding down dust problems. These covers are just placed over the equipment when not in use and removed when the device is needed.

> **TEST TIP**
> Know that computer vacuums have special grounding to dissipate static buildup that can damage computer devices.

Rough handling is either a matter of neglect or a lack of knowledge about how equipment should be handled. Therefore, overcoming rough-handling problems requires that technicians be aware of proper handling techniques for sensitive devices, such as hard disk drives and monitors, and that they adjust their component-handling practices to compensate.

Identifying and controlling heat buildup problems can require some effort and planning. Microcomputers are designed to run at normal room temperatures. If the ambient temperature rises above about 85°F, heat buildup can become a problem. High humidity also can lead to heat-related problems.

To combat heat problems, make sure that the area around the system is uncluttered so that free airflow around the system can be maintained. Make sure the power supply's fan is operational. If not, replace the power-supply unit. Likewise, be sure that the microprocessor fan is plugged in and operational. It is very easy for a high-speed microprocessor to fry if its fan fails. A good rule of thumb is to install a fan on any microprocessor running above 33MHz.

If heat buildup still exists, make sure that the outer cover is secured firmly to the machine and that all the expansion slot covers are in place. These items can disrupt the designed airflow characteristics of the case. Finally, add an additional case fan to draw more air through the system unit.

Protecting Monitors

The PM associated with video display monitors basically consists of periodic cleaning, dusting, and good, common-sense practices around the monitor. The monitor's screen and cabinet should be dusted frequently and cleaned periodically. Dust and smoke particles can build up very quickly around the monitor's screen, because of the presence of static charges on its face. When cleaning the screen, use caution to avoid scratching its surface and, in the case of antiglare screens, to preserve its glare-reduction features.

Avoid aerosol sprays, solvents, and commercial cleaners because they can damage the screen and cabinet. The simple cleaning solution, described earlier, also is fine for cleaning the monitor. Make sure that the monitor's power cord is disconnected from any power source before washing. The monitor's screen should be dried with a soft cloth after rinsing.

The monitor should not be left on for extended periods with the same image displayed onscreen. Over a period of time, the image will become permanently "burned" into the screen. If it is necessary to display the same information onscreen for a long period of time, turn the intensity level of the monitor down or install a *screen saver program* to alter the screen image periodically.

Inside the monitor's housing are very dangerous voltage levels (in excess of 25,000 volts; more than enough to kill or badly injure someone). Therefore, you should remove the monitor's outer cabinet only if you are fully qualified to work on CRT-based units. Even if the monitor has been turned off and unplugged for a year, it may still hold enough electrical potential to be deadly. Figure 3.2 shows the areas of the monitor that should be avoided (if you must work inside its housing).

Video display monitors often include a tilt/swivel base that enables the users to position it at whatever angle is most comfortable. This offers additional relief from eyestrain by preventing the users from viewing the display at an angle. Viewing the screen at an angle causes the eyes to focus separately, which places strain on the eye muscles.

Protecting Hard Disk Drives

Hard disk drives do not require much preventive maintenance, because the R/W heads and disks are enclosed in sealed, dust-tight compartments. However, you can do some things to optimize the performance and life span of hard disk systems. Rough handling is responsible for more hard disk drive damage than any other factor.

Never move the drive while you can hear its disk spinning. The disk is most vulnerable during startup and shutdown, when the heads are not fully flying. Even a small jolt during these times can cause a great deal of damage to both the platters and the R/W heads. If the drive must be moved, a waiting period of one full minute should be allotted after turning off the system.

If the drive is to be transported, or shipped, make sure to pack it properly. The forces exerted on the drive during shipment may be great enough to cause the R/W heads to slap against the disk surfaces, causing damage to both. Pack the drive unit in an oversized box, with *antistatic foam* all around the drive. You also may pack the drive in a box-within-a-box configuration, once again using foam as a cushion. Figure 3.3 illustrates this concept.

At no time should the hard drive's housing, which protects the platters, be removed in open air. The drive's disks and R/W heads are sealed in the airtight housing under a vacuum. The contaminants floating in normal air will virtually ruin the drive. If the drive malfunctions, the electronic circuitry and connections may be tested; but when it comes to repairs within the disk chamber, factory service or a professional service facility with a proper clean room is a must!

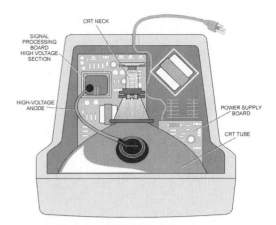

FIGURE 3.2
Caution areas inside the monitor.

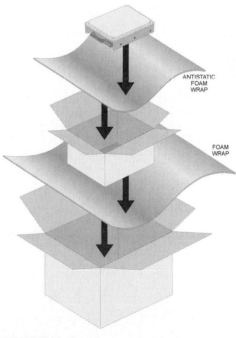

FIGURE 3.3
Proper packing of a hard drive for shipment.

To recover quickly from hardware failures, operator mistakes, and acts of nature, some form of software backup is essential with a hard disk system. The most common backup for larger systems is high-speed, streaming tape cartridges, which can automatically back up the contents of the entire disk drive on magnetic tape. In the event of data loss on the disk, a full reinstall from the tape is possible in a matter of a few minutes.

Backups also may be kept on disks. However, the volume of data stored on modern hard disks would require a tremendous number of floppy disks to back up. The floppy disks also would need to be stored. Other high-volume disk-based devices, such as optical drives and removable hard drives, have become attractive ways to back up the contents of large hard drives. CD-R and CD-RW drives provide an attractive option for storing limited amounts (680MB) of critical data. Their high capacities allow large amounts of information to be written on a single disc. The major drawback of using a CD-R disc is that after the disc has been written to, it cannot be erased or reused. Figure 3.4 depicts various backup methods. In any case, failure to maintain backups will eventually result in a great deal of grief when the system goes down because of a hardware or software failure.

Copies of the system backup should be stored in a convenient, but secure place. In the case of secure system backups, such as client/server networks, the backup copies should be stored where the network administrators can have access to them, but not the general public (for instance, in a locked file cabinet). Left unsecured, these copies could be used by someone without authority to gain access the system, or to its data. Even Emergency Repair Disks associated with Windows NT and Windows 2000 should be stored in a secure location. These disks also can be used by people other than administrators to gain access to information in client/server networks. Many companies maintain a copy of their backup away from the main site. This is done for protection in case of disasters such as fire.

The operation of hard drives can slow down with general use. Files stored on the drive may be erased and moved, causing parts of them to be scattered around the drive. This is referred to as file fragmentation and causes the drive to reposition the R/W heads more often during read and write operations, thereby requiring more time to complete the process.

TEST TIP

Be aware of the precautions that should be employed with storing system backups.

FIGURE 3.4
Data backup systems.

A number of hard disk drive software utilities are designed to optimize and maintain the operation of the hard disk drive. They should be used as part of a regular preventive maintenance program. The primary HDD utilities are the Check Disk, ScanDisk, Defrag, Backup, and antivirus utilities that have been available with different version of DOS and Windows since early MS-DOS versions. These are discussed in more detail in the Chapter 7, "1.0 Operating System Fundamentals," and in Chapter 9, "3.0 Diagnosing and Troubleshooting."

Protecting Floppy Disk Drives

Unlike hard disk drives, floppy drives are at least partially open to the atmosphere, and they may be handled on a regular basis. This opens the floppy disk drive to a number of maintenance concerns not found in hard disk drives. Also, the removable disks are subject to extremes in temperature, exposure to magnetic and electromagnetic fields, bending, and airborne particles that can lead to information loss.

The mechanical mechanisms of the floppy drive should never be positioned by hand. The weighted drive spindle and the track-zero sensor may be accessible with the drive's outer cover removed. Moving these mechanisms by hand can cause the R/W heads to drag across the disk, damaging the heads and disk surfaces.

Protecting Disks

Because the disk stores information in the form of magnetized spots on its surface, it is only natural that external magnetic fields will have an adverse effect on the stored data. Never bring disks near magnetic-field-producing devices, such as CRT monitors, television sets, or power supplies. They also should never be placed on or near appliances such as refrigerators, freezers, vacuum cleaners, and other equipment containing motors. Any of these can alter the information stored on the disk.

Proper positioning of the drive, and proper connection of peripheral interface cables, helps to minimize noise and *radio frequency interference* (RFI). RFI can cause the drive to operate improperly. Magnetic fields generated by power supplies and monitors can interfere with the magnetic recording on the disk. The drive and signal cables should be positioned away from these magnetic-field sources. Never bring magnets near the drive unit.

Another major cause of floppy disk failures is surface contamination. Several preventive measures minimize disk contamination and lengthen the life expectancy of your disks. Although the disk is enclosed in a protective case, whose liner sweeps contaminants from its surface, enough dust particles can collect to overpower the liner over time. Take care to never touch the exposed surfaces of the disk. Store disks in their protective envelopes and keep your computer area as clean and free from dust as possible.

There should be no smoking around the computer. Residues from tobacco smoke are a problem for floppy disk drives because they tend to build up on the exposed surfaces of both the disks and the drive. These deposits are detrimental to both the drive and the disk, because they gum up the close-tolerance mechanics of the drive and cause scratching to occur on the disk surface and the faces of the

R/W heads. This makes the heads less effective in reading and writing information to and from the disk and eventually leads to failure of the disk and the drive.

Additional ways to protect your disks include storing them in a cool, dry, clean environment, out of direct sunlight. Excessive temperature causes the disk and its jacket to warp. Take care when inserting the disk into the drive so as not to damage its jacket or the drive's internal mechanisms.

Maintaining the Floppy Drive

So far, each preventive action has involved the disk. Users can perform two procedures on the disk drive to ward off bigger maintenance problems: routine cleaning of the R/W heads (to remove oxide buildup), and periodic disk drive speed tests and adjustments when necessary.

Cleaning R/W heads removes residue and oxide buildup from the face of the head to ensure accurate transfer of data from the head to the disk. Two accepted methods may be used to clean the heads: special *head-cleaning disks*, and manual cleaning of the heads.

Head-cleaning disks are convenient to use, but some precautions must be taken when using them. There are, basically, two types of cleaning disks: dry (abrasive) disks, and wet (chemical) disks. Abrasive head-cleaning disks remove buildup as the disk spins in the drive. This is similar to using sandpaper to remove paint from a surface. These disks can be damaging to the head if used for too long of a time.

The dry disk must be left in the drive just long enough to remove the buildup on the head, but not long enough to scratch the head surface. Because of the difficulties of timing this operation, manufacturers have developed nonabrasive, cloth-covered disks that are used with a solvent solution. Depending on the type of kit you purchase, the disk may be premoistened or may come with a separate solvent solution that must be applied to the disk before cleaning, as illustrated in Figure 3.5.

The opportunity for abrasion of the head still exists with this type of cleaning disk. However, it is not as great as with the dry disks. Consult the instructions that come with the cleaning kit for proper usage and cleaning-time duration.

NOTE

Floppy Disks Wear Out The fact that the R/W heads ride directly on the floppy disk surface produces a certain amount of contamination and wear on the disk and heads. During read and write operations, the abrasion between the heads and disk cause some of the oxide coating on the disk to be transferred to the head. This makes the head less effective in reading and writing operations, and eventually leads to the failure of the disk.

FIGURE 3.5
FDD cleaning disks.

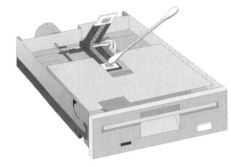

FIGURE 3.6
Cleaning the R/W heads.

A somewhat more complicated way to clean R/W heads is to clean them manually, as depicted in Figure 3.6. This operation involves removing the cover of the drive, gaining access to the R/W heads, and cleaning them manually with a swab that has been dipped in alcohol. Although this may appear to be a lot of work compared to the cleaning disk, manual cleaning is much safer for the drive. This is particularly true when combined with other cleaning, oiling, and inspection work. Together, these steps provide an excellent preventive maintenance program that should ensure effective, long-term operation of the drive.

The cleaning solution can be isopropyl alcohol, methanol, or some other solvent that does not leave a residue when it dries. Common cotton swabs are not recommended for use in manual cleaning because they tend to shed fibers. These fibers can contaminate the drive and, in certain circumstances, damage the R/W heads. Instead, cellular foam swabs or lint-free cloths are recommended for manual head cleaning. Using either cleaning method, the interval of time between head cleanings depends on several factors, such as the relative cleanliness of your computer area and how often you use your disk drive. A good practice is to clean the heads after 40 hours of disk drive operation. If read/write errors begin to appear before this time elapses, more frequent cleaning, or the use of higher quality disks, may be required.

Protecting Input Devices

Input peripherals generally require very little in the way of preventive maintenance. An occasional dusting and cleaning should be all that's really required.

You should, however, keep a few common-sense items in mind when using input devices; these should prevent damage to the device and ensure its longevity.

The keyboard's electronic circuitry is open to the atmosphere and should be vacuumed, as described in Figure 3.7, when you are cleaning around your computer area. Dust buildup on the keyboard circuitry can cause its ICs to fail due to overheating. To remove dirt and dust particles from inside the keyboard, disassemble the keyboard and carefully brush particles away from the board with a soft brush. A lint-free swab can be used to clean between the keys. Take care not to snag any exposed parts with the brush or swab. To minimize dust collection in the keyboard, cover your keyboard when not in use.

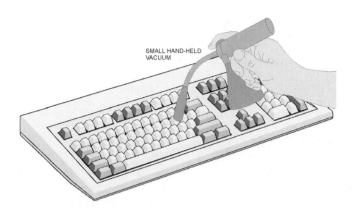

Never set keyboards or pointing devices on top of the monitor or near the edge of the desk where they may fall off. To prevent excessive wear on special keys, avoid applications and game programs that use keys in a repetitive manner. For these applications, use an appropriate pointing device, such as a mouse or joystick, for input.

When using a mouse, keep its workspace clear, dry, and free from dust. Remove and clean the trackball periodically. Use a lint-free swab to clean the X and Y trackball rollers inside the mouse, as described in Figure 3.8.

As with detachable keyboards, keep the connecting cables of all pointing devices out of harm's way.

Scheduling Preventive Maintenance

There is no perfect PM schedule; however, the following is a reasonable schedule that can be used to effectively maintain most computer equipment. The schedule is written from the point of view of a personal computer. Because this is an outside maintenance perspective, some of the steps need to be shared with the daily users. As a matter of fact, the users carry out most of the daily and weekly PM activities.

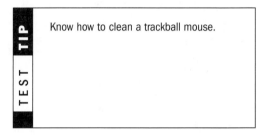

TEST TIP
Remember that dust can settle into the keyboard through the cracks between the keys.

FIGURE 3.7
Cleaning the keyboard.

TEST TIP
Know how to clean a trackball mouse.

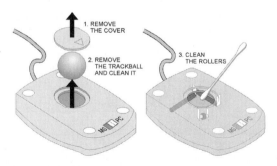

FIGURE 3.8
Cleaning the rollers in a trackball mouse.

Daily Activities

Back up important data from the unit. This can be done by using floppy disks, backup tape, another network drive, or some other backup media. Check computer ventilation to make sure that papers and other desk clutter are not cutting off airflow to the unit. Check for other sources of heat buildup around the computer and its peripherals. These sources include the following:

◆ Direct sunlight from an outside window

◆ Locations of portable heaters in the winter

◆ Papers/books piled up around the equipment

Weekly Activities

Clean the outside of the computer and its peripheral equipment. Wipe the outsides of the equipment with a damp cloth. The cloth can be slightly soapy. Wipe dry with an antistatic cloth. Clean the display screen using a damp cloth with the antistatic solution described earlier in this chapter. An antistatic spray also can be used for static-buildup prevention.

Run **CHKDSK/F** on all hard drives to locate and remove any lost clusters from the drives. This utility is available in all the Microsoft operating systems including Windows 9x, Windows NT, and Windows 2000. The **CHKDSK** command must be run from the command prompt in all versions. Run a current virus-check program to check for hard drive infection. Back up any revised data files on the hard drive. Inspect the peripherals (mice, keyboard, and so on) and clean them if needed.

Monthly Activities

Clean the inside of the system. Use a long-nozzle vacuum cleaner attachment to remove dust from the inside of the unit. Wipe the nozzle with antistatic solution before vacuuming. A soft brush also can be used to remove dust from the system unit.

Clean the inside of the printer using the same equipment and techniques as those used with the system unit. Check system connections for corrosion, pitting, or discoloration. Wipe the surface of any peripheral card's edge connectors with a lubricating oil, to protect it from atmospheric contamination.

Vacuum the keyboard. Clean the X and Y rollers in the trackball mouse using a lint-free swab and a noncoating cleaning solution.

Defragment the system's hard drive using the Defrag utility. Remove unnecessary temporary (TMP) files from the hard drive. Check software and hardware manufacturers for product updates that can remove problems and improve system operation. Back up the entire hard disk drive.

Semi-Annual Activities

Every six months, perform an extensive PM check. Apply an antistatic wash to the entire computer/peripheral work area. Wipe down books, desktop, and other workspace surfaces with antistatic solution. Disconnect power and signal cords and cables from the system's devices and reseat them. Clean the inside of the printer. Run the printer's self-tests.

Use a software diagnostic package to check each section of the system. Run all system tests available, looking for any hint of pending problems.

Annual Activities

Reformat the hard drive by backing up its contents and performing a high-level format. If the drive is an MFM, RLL, or ESDI drive, a low-level format also should be performed annually. Reinstall all the application software from original media and reinstall all user files from the backup system. Check all floppy disks in the work area with a current *antivirus program*.

Clean the R/W heads in the floppy drive using a lint-free swab. Cotton swabs have fibers that can hang up in the ceramic insert of the head and damage it. Perform the steps outlined in the "Monthly Activities" and "Semi-Annual Activities" sections.

Although this is a good model PM schedule, it is not the definitive schedule. Before establishing a firm schedule, consider several other points, including any manufacturers' guidelines for maintaining the equipment. Read the User Manuals of the various system components and work their suggested maintenance steps into the model.

Over time, adjust the steps and frequency of the plan to effectively cope with any environmental or usage variations. After all, the objective is not to complete the schedule on time, it is to keep the equipment running and profitable.

SYSTEM PROTECTION

▶ 3.2 Identify procedures and devices for protecting against environmental hazards.

The A+ Core Hardware objective 3.2 states that the test taker should be able to "identify procedures and devices for protecting against environmental hazards."

As this A+ objective indicates, computer technicians should be aware of potential environmental hazards and know how to prevent them from becoming a problem. A good place to start checking for environmental hazards is from the incoming power source. The following sections deal with power-line issues and solutions.

Power-Line Protection

Typical power-supply variations fall into two categories:

◆ **Transients.** An overvoltage condition; sags are undervoltage conditions. Overvoltage conditions can be classified as *spikes* (measured in nanoseconds) or as *surges* (measured in milliseconds).

◆ **Sags.** Sags can include *voltage sags* and *brownouts*. A voltage sag typically lasts only a few milliseconds; a brownout can last for a protracted period of time.

The effects of these power-supply variations are often hard to identify as power issues. Brownouts and power failures are easy to spot because of their duration. However, faster acting disturbances can cause symptoms not easily traced to the power source. Spikes can be damaging to electronic equipment, damaging devices such as hard drives and modems. Other occurrences will just cause data loss. Sags may cause the system to suddenly reboot because it thinks the power has been turned off. These disturbances are relatively easy to detect because they typically cause lights in the room to flicker.

NOTE

Avoid Power Variations Digital systems tend to be sensitive to power variations and losses. Even a very short loss of electrical power can shut a digital computer down, resulting in a loss of any current information that has not been saved to a mass-storage device.

TEST TIP

Be aware of how undervoltage and overvoltage situations are categorized (that is, time lengths).

In general, if several components go bad in a short period of time, or if components go bad more often than usual at a given location, these are good indicators of power-related issues. Likewise, machines that crash randomly and often could be experiencing power issues. If "dirty" power problems are suspected, a voltage-monitoring device should be placed in the power circuit and left for an extended period of time. These devices observe the incoming power over time and produce a problem indicator if significant variations occur.

Surge Suppressors

Inexpensive *power-line filters*, called *surge suppressors*, are good for cleaning up dirty commercial power. These units passively filter the incoming power signal to smooth out variations. You must consider two factors when choosing a surge suppresser:

◆ Clamping speed

◆ Clamping voltage

These units protect the system from damage, up to a specified point. However, large variations, such as surges created when power is restored after an outage, can still cause considerable data loss and damage. In the case of startup surges, making sure that the system is turned off, or even disconnected from the power source, until after the power is restored is one option. In the case of a complete shutdown, or a significant sag, the best protection from losing programs and data is an *uninterruptible power supply* (UPS).

> **TEST TIP**
>
> Know what type of devices will protect systems from minor power sags and power surges.

> **TEST TIP**
>
> Know what type of device prevents power interruptions that can corrupt data.

Uninterruptible Power Supplies

Uninterruptible power supplies are battery-based systems that monitor the incoming power and kick in when unacceptable variations occur in the power source. The term UPS is frequently used to describe two different types of power backup systems.

The first is a *standby power system*, and the second is a truly uninterruptible power system. Figure 3.9 depicts a typical UPS system.

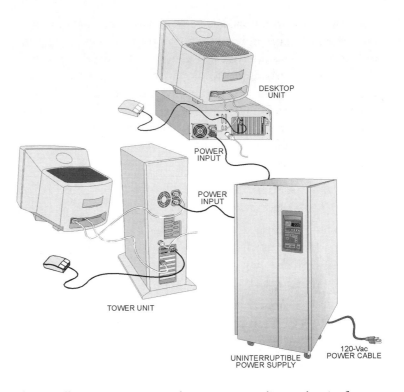

FIGURE 3.9
UPS systems.

The standby system monitors the power input line and waits for a significant variation to occur. The batteries in this unit are held out of the power loop and draw only enough current from the AC source to stay recharged. When an interruption occurs, the UPS senses it and switches the output of the batteries into an inverter circuit that converts the DC output of the batteries into an AC current, and voltage, that resembles the commercial power supply. This power signal is typically applied to the computer within 10 milliseconds.

The uninterruptible systems do not keep the batteries offline. Instead, the batteries and converters are always actively attached to the output of UPS. When an interruption in the supply occurs, no switching of the output is required. The battery/inverter section just continues under its own power. Figure 3.10 shows how a UPS connects into a system.

Standby systems do not generally provide a high level of protection from sags and spikes. They do, however, include additional circuitry to minimize such variations. Conversely, an uninterruptible system is an extremely good power-conditioning system. Because it always sits between the commercial power and the computer, it can supply a constant power supply to the system.

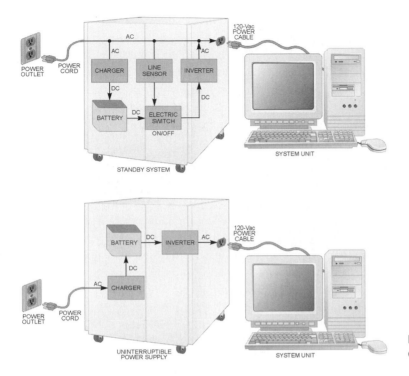

FIGURE 3.10
Connecting the UPS in the system.

When dealing with either type of UPS system, the most important rating to be aware of is its *volt-ampere (VA) rating*. The VA rating indicates the capability of the UPS system to deliver both voltage (V) and current (A) to the computer, simultaneously. This rating differs from the device's *wattage rating*, and the two should not be used interchangeably.

The wattage power rating is a factor of multiplying the voltage and current use, at any particular time, to arrive at a power-consumption value. The VA rating is used in AC systems because peak voltage and current elements do not occur at the same instant. This condition is referred to as being out-of-phase with each other, and makes it slightly more difficult to calculate power requirements. In general, always make sure that the UPS system has a higher wattage capability than the computer requires, and likewise, that the VA rating of the UPS is higher than that required by the computer.

High-power-consumption peripheral devices, such as laser printers, should not be connected directly to the UPS. These devices can overload the UPS and cause data loss.

The other significant specification for UPS systems is the length of time they can supply power. Because the UPS is a battery-powered device, it uses an *ampere-hour rating*. This is the same time notation system used for automobile batteries and other battery-powered systems. The rating is obtained by multiplying a given current drain from the battery, for a given amount of time. (That is, a battery capable of sustaining 1.5 amps of output current for 1 hour would be rated at 1.5 amp-hours.)

The primary mission of the UPS is to keep the system running when a power failure occurs (usually, long enough to conduct an orderly shutdown of the system). Because it is a battery-based system, it cannot keep the system running indefinitely. For this reason, you should not connect nonessential, power-hungry peripheral devices, such as a laser printer, to the UPS supply. If the power goes out, it is highly unlikely that you will really have to print something before shutting the system down. If the UPS is being used to keep a critical system in operation during the power outage, the high current drain of the laser printer would severely reduce the length of time that the UPS could keep the system running.

TEST TIP

Remember that nonessential peripheral devices should not be connected to UPS supplies.

Protection During Storage

The best storage option for most computer equipment is the original manufacturer's box. These boxes are designed specifically to store and transport the device safely. They include form-fitting protective foam to protect the device from shock hazards. The device is normally wrapped in a protective *antistatic bag* or wrapper to defeat the effects of ESD.

Printed circuit boards are normally shipped on a thin piece of antistatic foam. The board is typically placed solder-side down on the foam. Both the foam and the board are placed in an antistatic bag and then into a storage box.

Hard disk drives are usually placed directly into a static bag and then placed in a thick foam box. The foam box is then inserted into a storage carton. FDDs typically receive less padding than HDD units do.

Monitors, printers, scanners, and other peripheral equipment should be stored in their original boxes, using their original packing foam and protective storage bag. The contours in the packing foam of these devices are not generally compatible from model to model or device to device. If the original boxes and packing materials are not available, make sure to use sturdy cartons and cushion the equipment well on all sides before shipping.

All electronic devices should be stored in dry, cool areas away from heat sources and direct sunlight. Low-traffic areas also are preferable for storage because there is less chance of incidental damage from people and/or equipment passing by.

> **TEST TIP**
>
> Know that the best device for transporting computer equipment is the original manufacturer's packaging, including the antistatic foam and bags used to pack it.

Hazards and Safety Procedures

▶ 3.2 Identify the potential hazards and proper safety procedures relating to lasers.

A subsection of the A+ Core Hardware objective 3.2 states that the test taker should be able to identify "the potential hazards and proper safety procedures relating to lasers" and high-voltage equipment.

This discussion starts with safety procedures when dealing with high-voltage areas of the computer. Note the following:

◆ Lasers can cause blindness.

◆ High-voltage equipment (such as the power supply and CRT) can cause electrocution.

Avoiding High-Voltage Hazards

Most IBM compatibles have only two potentially dangerous areas. One of these is inside of the CRT display; the other is inside the power-supply unit. Both of these areas contain lethal voltage levels. Both of these areas reside in self-contained units, however, and you will normally not be required to open either unit.

> **TEST TIP**
>
> Be aware of the voltage levels present inside a CRT cabinet.

As a matter of fact, you should never enter the interior of a CRT cabinet unless you have been trained specifically to work with this type of equipment. The tube itself is dangerous if accidentally cracked. In addition, extremely high voltage levels (in excess of 25,000 volts) can be present inside the CRT housing, even up to a year after electrical power has been removed from the unit.

Never open the power-supply unit either. Some portions of the circuitry inside the power supply carry extremely high voltage levels and have very high current capabilities.

Generally, no open shock hazards are present inside the system unit. However, you should not reach inside the computer while power is applied to the unit. Jewelry and other metallic objects do pose an electrical threat, even with the relatively low voltage present in the system unit.

Never have liquids around energized electrical equipment. It is a good idea to keep food and drinks away from all computer equipment at all times. Before cleaning around the computer with liquids, make certain to unplug all power connections to the system, and its peripherals. When cleaning external computer cabinets with liquid cleaners, take care to prevent any of the solution from dripping or spilling into the equipment.

Do not defeat the safety feature of three-prong power plugs by using two-prong adapters. The equipment ground of a power cord should never be defeated or removed. This plug connects the computer chassis to an earth ground through the power system. This provides a reference point for all the system's devices to operate from and supplies protection for personnel from electrical shock. In defeating the ground plug, a very important level of protection is removed from the equipment.

Periodically examine the power cords of the computer and peripherals for cracked or damaged insulation. Replace worn or damaged power cords promptly. Never allow anything to rest on a power cord. Run power cords and connecting cables safely out of the way so that they do not become trip or catch hazards. Remove all power cords associated with the computer and its peripherals from the power outlet during thunder or lightning storms.

Do not apply liquid or aerosol cleaners directly to computer equipment. Spray cleaners on a cloth and then apply the cloth to the equipment. Freon-propelled sprays should not be used on computer equipment, because they can produce destructive electrostatic charges.

Check equipment vents to see that they are clear and have ample airspace to allow heat to escape from the cabinet. Never block these vents, and never insert or drop objects into them.

Avoiding Laser and Burn Hazards

Laser printers contain many hazardous areas. The laser light can be damaging to the human eye. In addition, there are multiple high-voltage areas in the typical laser printer and a high-temperature area to contend with.

The technician is normally protected from these areas by interlock switches built in to the unit. It is often necessary to bypass these interlocks, however, to isolate problems. When doing so, proper precautions must be observed, such as avoiding the laser light, being aware of the high temperatures in the fuser area, and taking proper precautions with the high-voltage areas of the unit. The laser light is a hazard to eyesight, the fuser area is a burn hazard, and the power supplies are shock hazards. More information about these areas of laser printers is presented in Chapter 5, "5.0 Printers."

Another potential burn hazard is the printhead mechanism of a dot-matrix printer. During normal operation, it can become hot enough to be a burn hazard if touched.

Because computers have the potential to produce these kinds of injuries, it is good practice to have a well-stocked first-aid kit in the work area. In addition, a *Class-C fire extinguisher* should be on hand. Class-C extinguishers are the type specified for use around electrical equipment. You can probably imagine the consequences of applying a water-based fire extinguisher to a fire with live electrical equipment around. The class, or classes, that the fire extinguisher is rated for are typically marked on its side.

You may think that there's not much chance for a fire to occur with computer equipment, but this is not so. Just let a capacitor from a system board blow up and have a small piece land in a pile of packing materials in the work area. It becomes a fire!

This covers the major safety precautions and considerations that you need to be aware of while working on computer equipment. Most of all, use common sense and sound safety practices around all electrical equipment.

> **TEST TIP**
> Know the areas of the computer system that are dangerous for personnel and how to prevent injury from these areas.

> **TEST TIP**
> Remember the type of fire extinguisher that must be used with electrical systems, such as a PC.

DISPOSAL PROCEDURES

▶ 3.2 Identify items that require special disposal procedures complying with environmental guidelines.

A subsection of the A+ Core Hardware objective 3.2 states that the test taker should be able to identify "items that require "special disposal procedures complying with environmental guidelines."

As with any mechanical device, a computer eventually becomes obsolete in the application for which it was originally intended. Newer machines, with improved features, arise to replace earlier models. And slowly, but surely, components fail and get replaced. Then comes the question: What do I do with the old stuff? Can it just be placed in the garbage bin so that it is hauled to the landfill and buried?

In today's world of environmental consciousness, you might not think so. After all, computers and peripherals contain some environmentally unfriendly materials.

Most computer components contain some level of *hazardous substances*. Printed circuit boards consist of plastics, precious metals, fiberglass, arsenic, silicon, gallium, and lead. CRTs contain glass, metal, plastics, lead, barium, and rare earth metals. Batteries from portable systems can contain lead, cadmium, lithium, alkaline manganese, and mercury.

Although all these materials can be classified as hazardous materials, so far there are no widespread regulations when it comes to placing them in the landfill. Conversely, local regulations concerning acceptable disposal methods for computer-related components should always be checked before disposing of any electronic equipment.

Laser-printer toner cartridges can be refilled and recycled. This should be done only in draft-mode operations, however, where very good resolution is not required. Ink cartridges from inkjet printers also can be refilled and reused. Like laser cartridges, they can be very messy to refill and often do not function as well as new cartridges do. In many cases, the manufacturer of the product will have a policy of accepting spent cartridges.

TEST TIP

Remember that toner cartridges from a laser printer should be recycled.

For both batteries and cartridges, the desired method of disposal is *recycling*. It should not be too difficult to find a drop site that recycles these products. On the other hand, even nonhazardous Subtitle D dump sites can handle the hardware components if need be. Subtitle D dump sites are nonhazardous solid-waste dump sites that have been designed to meet EPA standards set for this classification. These sites are designed to hold hazardous materials safely.

Fortunately, several charitable organizations around the country take in old computer systems and refurbish them for various applications. Contact your local chamber of commerce for information about such organizations. On the Internet, you also can find several computer disposal organizations that take old units and redistribute them. In addition, a few companies will dispose of your old computer components in an "environmentally friendly" manner—for a fee.

In addition to the computer parts that provide hazardous materials, many of the cleaning substances used on computer equipment can be classified as hazardous materials. When it comes to disposing of the chemical solvents used to clean computers the containers they come in, it will normally be necessary to clear these items with the local waste-management agencies before disposing of them. Many dump sites will not handle free liquids. Free liquids are substances that can pass through a standard paint filter. If the liquid passes through the filter, it is a free liquid and cannot be disposed of in the landfill. Therefore, solvents and other liquid cleaning materials must be properly categorized and disposed of at an appropriate type of disposal center.

All hazardous materials are required to have *Material Safety Data Sheets* (MSDS) that accompany them when they change hands. They also are required to be on hand in areas where hazardous materials are stored and commonly used. The MSDS contains information about the following:

- ◆ What the material is
- ◆ Its hazardous ingredients
- ◆ Its physical properties
- ◆ Fire and explosion data
- ◆ Reactivity data
- ◆ Spill or leak procedures

TEST TIP

Remember that the proper disposal method for batteries is to recycle them.

- Health-hazard information
- Any special-protection information
- Any special-precaution information

The supplier of the hazardous material must provide this information sheet. If you supply this material to a third party, you also must supply the MSDS for the material. The real reason for the sheets is to inform workers and management about hazards associated with the product and how to handle the product safely. It also provides instructions about what to do if an accident occurs involving the material. For this reason, employees should know where the MSDSs are stored in their work area.

ELECTROSTATIC DISCHARGE

▶ 3.2 Identify ESD (electrostatic discharge) precautions and procedures, including the use of ESD protection devices.

A subsection of the A+ Core Hardware objective 3.2 states that the test taker should be able to identify "ESD (electrostatic discharge) precautions and procedures."

The first way to avoid *electrostatic discharge* (ESD) is to be able to identify when and why it occurs.

Identifying and Avoiding Electrostatic Discharge

Static can easily discharge through digital computer equipment. The electronic devices used to construct digital equipment are particularly susceptible to damage from ESD. As a matter of fact, ESD is the most damaging form of electrical interference associated with digital equipment.

The following are the most common causes of ESD:

- Moving people
- Low humidity (hot and dry conditions)
- Improper grounding

TEST TIP

Remember what the acronym ESD stands for.

NOTE

What Is an ESD Electrostatic discharges are the most severe form of *electromagnet interference* (EMI). The human body can build up static charges that range up to 25,000 volts. These buildups can discharge very rapidly into an electrically grounded body or device. Placing a 25,000V surge through any electronic device is potentially damaging to it.

- ◆ Unshielded cables
- ◆ Poor connections
- ◆ Moving machines

Elementary school teachers demonstrate the principles of static to their students by rubbing different materials together. When people move, the clothes they are wearing rub together and can produce large amounts of electrostatic charge on their bodies. Walking across carpeting can create charges in excess of 1,000 volts. Motors in electrical devices, such as vacuum cleaners and refrigerators, generate high levels of ESD.

ESD is most likely to occur during periods of low humidity. If the relative humidity is below 50%, static charges can accumulate easily. ESD generally does not occur when the humidity is above 50%. Anytime the charge reaches around 10,000 volts, it is likely to discharge to grounded metal parts.

Although ESD will not hurt humans, it will destroy certain electronic devices. The high-voltage pulse can burn out the inputs of many IC devices. This damage may not appear instantly. It can build up over time and cause the device to fail. Electronic logic devices, constructed from MOS materials, are particularly susceptible to ESD. The following section describes the special handling techniques that should be observed when working with equipment containing MOS devices.

IN THE FIELD

HIGH VOLTAGE, LOW RISK TO HUMANS

You may be a little confused by the warning about the lethal 25,000 volts present inside the monitor and the statement that the 10,000 to 25,000 volts of ESD are not harmful to humans. The reason for this is the difference in current-delivering capabilities created by the voltage. For example, the circuitry in the monitor and the power supply is capable of delivering amps of current, whereas the current-producing capabilities of the electrostatic charge are less than a thousandth of that. Therefore, the 120V AC, 1-amp current produced by the power-supply unit is lethal, whereas the 25,000V DC, microamp current produced by ESD is not.

TEST TIP
Memorize the conditions that make ESD more likely to occur.

TEST TIP
Be aware that compressed air can be used to blow dust out of components and that it does not create ESD.

TEST TIP
Memorize conditions and actions that produce electrostatic discharge.

TEST TIP
Remember that the current capabilities of electrical devices establish the potential danger levels associated with working around them.

MOS-Handling Techniques

In general, MOS devices are sensitive to voltage spikes and static-electricity discharges. This can cause many problems when you have to replace MOS devices, especially *complementary-symmetry metal-oxide semiconductor* (CMOS) devices. The level of static electricity present on your body is high enough to destroy the inputs of a CMOS device if you touch its pins with your fingers.

To minimize the chances of damaging MOS devices during handling, special procedures have been developed to protect them from static shock. ICs are generally shipped and stored in special conductive-plastic tubes or trays. You may want to store MOS devices in these tubes, or you may just ensure their safety by inserting the IC's leads into aluminum foil or antistatic (conductive) foam—not styrofoam. PC boards containing static-sensitive devices are normally shipped in special antistatic bags. These bags are good for storing ICs and other computer components that may be damaged by ESD. They also are the best way to transport PC boards with static-sensitive components.

Professional service technicians employ a number of precautionary steps when they are working on systems that may contain MOS devices. These technicians normally use a *grounding strap*, like the one depicted in Figure 3.11. These antistatic devices may be placed around the wrists or ankle to *ground* the technician to the system being worked on. These straps release any static present on the technician's body and pass it harmlessly to ground potential.

Antistatic straps should never be worn while working on higher voltage components, such as monitors and power-supply units. Some technicians wrap a copper wire around their wrist or ankle and connect it to the ground side of an outlet. This is not a safe practice, because the resistive feature of a true wrist strap is missing. As an alternative, most technician's work areas include *antistatic mats* made out of rubber or other antistatic materials that they stand on while working on the equipment. This is particularly helpful in carpeted work areas, because carpeting can be a major source of ESD buildup. Some antistatic mats have ground connections that should be connected to the safety ground of an AC power outlet.

TEST TIP

Know when not to wear an antistatic wrist strap.

To avoid damaging static-sensitive devices, the following procedures will help to minimize the chances of destructive static discharges:

◆ Because computers and peripheral systems may contain a number of static-sensitive devices, before touching any components inside the system, touch an exposed part of the chassis or the power-supply housing with your finger, as illustrated in Figure 3.12. Grounding yourself in this manner ensures that any static charge present on your body is removed. Use this technique before handling a circuit board or component. Of course, be aware that this technique works safely only if the power cord is attached to a grounded power outlet. The ground plug on a standard power cord is the best tool for overcoming ESD problems.

◆ Do not remove ICs from their protective tubes (or foam packages) until you are ready to use them. If you remove a circuit board or component containing static-sensitive devices from the system, place it on a conductive surface, such as a sheet of aluminum foil.

◆ If you must replace a defective IC, use a soldering iron with a grounded tip to extract the defective IC and while soldering the new IC in place. Some of the ICs in computers and peripherals are not soldered to the printed circuit board. Instead, an IC socket is soldered to the board, and the IC is just inserted into the socket. This allows for easy replacement of these ICs.

In the event that you must replace a hard-soldered IC, you may want to install an IC socket along with the chip. Be aware that normal operating vibrations and *temperature cycling* can degrade the electrical connections between ICs and sockets over time. This gradual deterioration of electrical contact between chips and sockets is referred to as chip creep. It is a good practice to reseat any socket-mounted devices when handling a printed circuit board. Before removing the IC from its protective container, touch the container to the power supply of the unit in which it is to be inserted.

◆ Some devices used to remove solder from circuit boards and chips can cause high static discharges that may damage the good devices on the board. The device in question is referred to as a solder-sucker, and is available in antistatic versions for use with MOS devices.

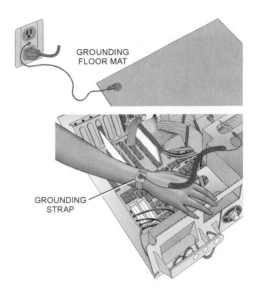

FIGURE 3.11
Typical antistatic devices.

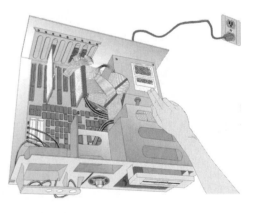

FIGURE 3.12
Discharging through the power-supply unit.

TEST TIP

Be aware of the effects that temperature cycling can have on socket-mounted devices.

◆ Use antistatic sprays or solutions on floors, carpets, desks, and computer equipment. An antistatic spray or solution, applied with a soft cloth, is an effective deterrent to static.

◆ Install static-free carpeting in the work area. You also can install an antistatic floor mat as well. Install a conductive table-top to carry away static from the work area. Use antistatic table mats.

◆ Use a room humidifier to keep the humidity level above 50% in the work area. Figure 3.13 summarizes proper IC handling procedures.

FIGURE 3.13
Antistatic precautions.

Understanding Grounds

The movement of the electrical current along a conductor requires a path for the current to return to its source. In early telegraph systems and even modern power-transmission systems, the earth provides a return path and, hypothetically, produces an electrical reference point of absolute zero. Figure 3.14 depicts this type of ground.

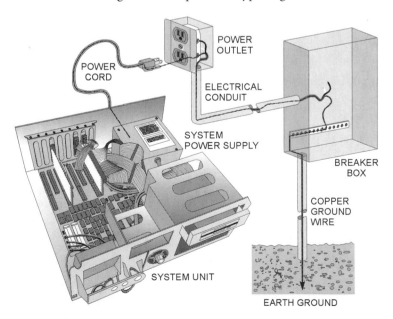

FIGURE 3.14
Power-transmission system.

Many electronic circuits use an actual conductor as a return path. This type of ground is referred to as a *signal ground*. Electronic devices also may contain a third form of ground called *chassis ground*, or *protective ground*. In any event, ground still remains the reference point from which most electrical signals are measured. In the case of troubleshooting computer components, measurements referenced to ground may be made from the system unit's chassis.

The other measurement reference is the signal ground point, on the printed circuit board, where the test is being performed. This point is not too difficult to find in a circuit board full of ICs, because most DIP-style chips use the highest numbered pin for the positive supply voltage and the last pin on the pin-1 side of the chip as the ground pin. Figure 3.15 depicts this type of ground. Some caution should be used with this assumption, because not all ICs use this pin for ground. If you examine a number of ICs and connectors on the board, however, you should be able to trace the ground foil and use it as a reference.

N O T E

What Are Grounds The term *ground* is often a source of confusion for novices, because it actually encompasses a collection of terms. Generically, ground is just any point from which electrical measurements are referenced. However, the original definition of ground actually referred to the ground. This ground is called *earth ground*.

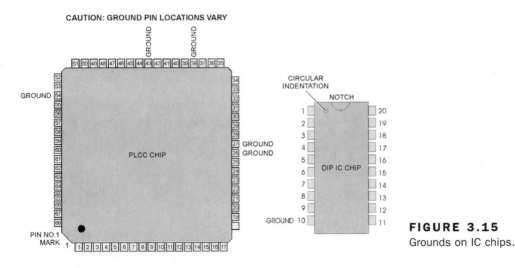

FIGURE 3.15
Grounds on IC chips.

TEST TIP

Remember that ESD is destructive and EMI is not.

TEST TIP

Know the best protection for a computer system during an electrical storm.

Grounding is an important aspect of limiting EMI in computer systems. Left unchecked, EMI can distort images on the video display, interfere with commercial communication equipment (such as radios and televisions), and corrupt data on floppy disks. In addition, EMI can cause signal deterioration and loss caused by improper cable routing. If a signal cable is bundled with a power cord, radiation from the power cord may be induced into the signal cable, affecting the signals that pass through it. Good grounding routes the induced EMI signals away from logic circuitry and toward ground potential, preventing it from disrupting normal operations. Unlike ESD, which is destructive, the effects of EMI can be corrected without damage.

Because the computer system is connected to an actual earth ground, it should always be turned off and disconnected from the wall outlet during electrical storms. This includes the computer and all its peripherals. The electrical pathway through the computer equipment can be very inviting to lightning on its way to earth ground. The extremely high electrical potential of a lightning strike is more than any computer can withstand.

CHAPTER SUMMARY

The focus of this chapter was to present important points for inclusion in preventive maintenance programs associated with personal computer systems. The first section of the chapter dealt with typical cleaning chores. It also featured preventive maintenance procedures for the system's different components. A suggested PM schedule also was presented. This is time-proven information and should always be shared freely with customers.

The second major section of the chapter focused on environmental hazards that affect the operation of computer equipment. The majority of this section dealt with problems that revolve around fluctuations in the computer's in-coming power line. Different types of universal power supplies were discussed, along with other power-line conditioning devices. The remainder of the section discussed proper storage methods for computer components.

Potentially hazardous areas of the computer and its peripherals were presented in the third major section of the chapter. Although not an intrinsically unsafe environment, some areas of a computer system can be harmful if approached unawares.

CHAPTER SUMMARY

Disposal of old and defective equipment and cleaning materials was discussed in the fourth section of the chapter. MSDS records were also introduced.

The final section of the chapter described the danger and causes of electrostatic discharges and provided information about how to eliminate them.

At this point, review the objectives listed at the beginning of the chapter to be certain that you understand the information associated with each one and that you can perform each item listed there. Afterward, answer the Review Questions that follow to verify your knowledge of the information.

KEY TERMS

- Ampere-hour rating
- Antistatic bags
- Antistatic foam
- Antistatic mats
- Antistatic solution
- Antivirus program
- Brownouts
- Chassis ground
- Class-C fire extinguisher
- Complementary-symmetry metal oxide semiconductor (CMOS)
- Earth ground
- Electromagnetic interference (EMI)
- Electrostatic discharges (ESD)
- Ground
- Grounding strap
- Hazardous substances
- Head-cleaning disks
- Material Safety Data Sheets (MSDS)
- Mean time between failures (MTBF)
- Metal oxide semiconductor (MOS)
- Oxidation buildup

continued

- Power-line filters
- Preventive maintenance (PM)
- Protective ground
- Radio frequency interference (RFI)
- Recycling
- Screen saver program
- Signal ground
- Spikes
- Standby power system
- Surge Suppressors
- Surges
- Temperature cycling
- Transients
- Uninterruptible Power Supply (UPS)
- Voltage sags
- Volt-ampere (VA) rating
- Wattage rating

URL RESOURCES

www.halloa.com.tw/

http://suttondesigns.com/upssizing.htm#CLONES

www.powerprotector.com/scripts/gc_page.exe?F=F&K=protect

www.hei.com/heco/esafe.htm

http://kerr.arborlink.com/computers/disposal.html

http://kerr.arborlink.com/computers/recycle.html

www.borg.com/~eosesd/eos19.htm

www.netlabs.net/hp/echase/

APPLY YOUR KNOWLEDGE

At this point, review the objectives listed at the beginning of the chapter to be certain that you understand the information associated with each one and that you can perform each item listed there. Afterward, answer the Review and Exam Questions that follow to verify your knowledge of the information.

Review Questions

1. List the two most dangerous areas of a typical microcomputer system, and describe why they are so dangerous.

2. Name three devices used to minimize ESD in the repair area.

3. The best general-purpose cleaning tool for computer equipment is _____.

4. List at least three environmental conditions that can adversely affect microcomputer equipment.

5. A short undervoltage condition, lasting milliseconds, is called _____.

6. Are there any restrictions on disposing of a spent toner cartridge?

7. Which type of IC device is most likely to be damaged by ESD?

8. Can an effective ESD strap be constructed by just wrapping a grounded bare wire around your wrist?

9. What is the most effective way to deal with EMI problems?

10. The best way to protect computer equipment from a thunderstorm is to _____.

11. The best way to transport electronic devices is _____.

12. Will a surge suppresser prevent electrical damage from occurring to a system board?

13. List computer-related PM items that should be performed annually.

14. Name two characteristics that should be checked carefully before purchasing a UPS for a given computer system.

15. Describe the normal duration of a voltage spike.

Exam Questions

1. What is the most common cause of ESD in microcomputer systems?

   A. Moving people

   B. High humidity

   C. Rubber mats

   D. Grounded power-supply cables

2. Where would it be inappropriate to use an ESD wrist strap?

   A. While working on hard disk drives

   B. While working on system boards

   C. While working on CRT video monitors

   D. While working on printers

3. What is the best substance for cleaning the plastic surfaces of a computer system?

   A. A water and fabric softener solution

   B. A water and ammonia solution

   C. A water and bleach solution

   D. A hydrogen tetrachloride solution

APPLY YOUR KNOWLEDGE

4. The most effective grounding system for a micro-computer is _____.

   A. An ESD wrist or ankle strap

   B. The safety ground plug at a commercial AC receptacle

   C. The ground plane of the system board

   D. The chassis ground provided by brass standoffs

5. A short overvoltage occurrence (nanoseconds) is called _____.

   A. A spike

   B. A surge

   C. A brownout

   D. A sag

6. ESD is most likely to occur during periods of _____.

   A. Low humidity

   B. High humidity

   C. Medium humidity

   D. Rain

7. What is the best way to clean a keyboard?

   A. Spray with an antistatic solution

   B. Blow with compressed air

   C. Vacuum and clean with a damp cloth

   D. Wash with soap and water

8. What type of backup device is typically used to store large banks of information for an extended period of time?

   A. A floppy disk

   B. A tape drive

   C. A hard drive

   D. A CD-ROM drive

9. The best protection against power-failure data loss is _____.

   A. A tape backup

   B. A surge suppresser

   C. A UPS

   D. A line filter

10. Define a voltage sag.

   A. An overvoltage condition that lasts for a few milliseconds

   B. An undervoltage condition that lasts for an extended period

   C. An overvoltage condition that lasts for an extended period

   D. An undervoltage condition that lasts for a few milliseconds

Answers to Review Questions

1. The inside of the monitor and the inside of the power supply. Both units house potentially dangerous voltage levels inside their housings. For more information, see the section "Avoiding High-Voltage Hazards."

2. An antistatic wrist strap, rubber antistatic mats, and a humidifier. For more information, see the section "MOS-Handling Techniques."

3. A damp cloth is the best general-purpose cleaning tool. For more information, see the section "Cleaning."

4. Smoke, dust, temperatures above 85°F, and on/off cycles. For more information, see the section "Preventive Maintenance Procedures."

5. A sag. For more information, see the section "Power-Line Protection."

6. No, not currently. However, it is economical to recycle toner cartridges unless the output from the printer has to be of very high quality. For more information, see the section "Disposal Procedures."

7. MOS devices in general, and CMOS devices in particular, are most likely to be affected by ESD damage. For more information, see the section "MOS-Handling Techniques."

8. No. True ESD protection devices have resistive elements built in to them to protect the user (human) from shock hazards. For more information, see the section "MOS-Handling Techniques."

9. The best protection against EMI problems is good grounding. For more information, see the section "Understanding Grounds."

10. Unplug it and all of its peripherals from the power outlet so that there is no path for the lightening to follow. For more information, see the section "Understanding Grounds."

11. To place them in an antistatic bag. For more information, see the section "MOS-Handling Techniques."

12. A surge suppresser can protect an electrical device only from power damage up to a point. If the ratings of the suppresser are exceeded, the device it is guarding could be damaged. For more information, see the section "Power-Line Protection."

13. Reformat the hard drive, reinstall all the application software, check all floppy disks, clean the R/W heads in the floppy drive, and then perform the monthly and semi-annual activities outlined in this chapter. For more information, see the section "Annual Activities."

14. Ampere-hour rating and wattage rating. For more information, see the section "Uninterruptible Power Supplies."

15. Nanoseconds. For more information, see the section "Power-Line Protection."

Answers to Exam Questions

1. **A.** People moving around are the number-one source of ESD. Clothing rubbing against other materials or the body can create it, as can moving across certain types of carpet. ESD is more likely to happen in times of low humidity. Rubber mats and grounded conductors are the best way to prevent and safely remove ESD. For more information, see the section "Electrostatic Discharge."

2. **C.** Due to the dangerous voltage levels present inside the monitor, it is not a place to be wearing a conductive strap attached to your body. It may be dangerous to wear an antistatic strap in some areas of a printer. However, they are generally thought of as safe for such devices. For more information, see the section "MOS-Handling Techniques."

3. **A.** A water and fabric softener solution applied with a soft cloth is the best tool for cleaning the plastic surfaces of the system, as well as the monitor face. The antistatic properties of the fabric

APPLY YOUR KNOWLEDGE

softener removes static buildup from the surfaces in addition to removing dust and dirt. For more information, see the section "Cleaning."

4. **B.** The ground lead of a commercial three-prong power receptacle generally provides the best grounding source available, because it is tied to the true (earth) ground. The commercial power system provides a well-planned grounding system. For more information, see the section "Understanding Grounds."

5. **A.** A power surge lasts for periods ranging into the nanosecond range. Shorter overvoltage occurrences are called spikes. Brownouts and sags are undervoltage conditions. For more information, see the section "Power-Line Protection."

6. **A.** Low humidity raises the likelihood that ESD will occur. The other conditions decrease the likelihood of ESD. For more information, see the section "Electrostatic Discharge."

7. **C.** The keyboard can be vacuumed to remove dust and debris from inside the unit, and should be wiped with a damp cloth to clean the outside. Blowing dust out of the keyboard with low-power-compressed air bottles is acceptable, but liquids should never be used on electronic equipment except when applied with a cloth. For more information, see the section "Protecting Input Devices."

8. **B.** Tape drives are routinely used for storage due to their low-cost-per-bit storage capabilities and their nonvolatile nature. Although CD-Rs are gaining ground as storage devices, they are not yet widely used for this purpose. For more information, see the section "Protecting Hard Disk Drives."

9. **C.** The UPS is the best protection against losing data when power interruptions occur. Surge suppressors and line filters can protect against small power variations, but cannot handle sustained power-line problems. Tape drives offer the best protection for data that has been backed up to a storage media, but cannot protect data that has been entered since the last backup. For more information, see the section "Power-Line Protection."

10. **D.** A voltage sag is an undervoltage condition that lasts for a few milliseconds. Sags that last for a sustained period of time are referred to as brownouts. For more information, see the section "Power-Line Protection."

This chapter helps you to prepare for the Core Hardware module of the A+ Certification examination by covering the following objectives within the "Domain 4.0: Motherboard/Processors/Memory" section.

4.1 Distinguish between the popular CPU chips in terms of their basic characteristics.

Content may include the following:

- **Popular CPU chips (Pentium class and higher)**

- **Characteristics**

- **Physical size**

- **Voltage**

- **Speeds**

- **Onboard cache or not**

- **Sockets**

- **SEC (Single Edge Contact)**

▶ Computer technicians are often asked to upgrade existing systems with new devices, such as the microprocessor. Therefore, every technician should be aware of the characteristics of possible CPU upgrades and be able to determine whether a particular upgrade is physically possible and worthwhile.

4.2 Identify the categories of RAM (Random Access Memory) terminology, their locations, and physical characteristics.

Content may include the following:

Terminology:

- **EDO RAM (Extended Data Output RAM)**

- **DRAM (Dynamic RAM)**

- **SRAM (Static RAM)**

- **RIMM (Rambus Inline Memory Module 184 Pin)**

- **VRAM (Video RAM)**

CHAPTER 4

4.0 Motherboard/ Processors/Memory

- **SDRAM (synchronous dynamic RAM)**

- **WRAM (Windows accelerator card RAM)**

Locations and physical characteristics:

- **Memory bank**

- **Memory chips (8 bit, 16 bit, and 32 bit)**

- **SIMMs (single in-line memory module)**

- **DIMMs (dual in-line memory module)**

- **Parity chips versus non-parity chips**

▶ Similar to the CPU, every technician should be aware of the characteristics of different RAM devices and be able to determine whether a particular device is suited to a given application and whether it physically fits the system in question.

4.3   Identify the most popular type of motherboards, their components, and their architecture (for example, bus structures and power supplies).

Content may include the following:

- **Types of motherboards:**

  - **AT (full and baby)**

  - **ATX**

- **Motherboard components:**

  - **Communication ports**

  - **SIMM and DIMM**

  - **Processor sockets**

  - **External cache memory (Level 2)**

- **Bus architecture:**

  - **ISA**

  - **PCI**

  - **AGP**

  - **USB (Universal Serial Bus)**

  - **VESA local bus (VL bus)**

- **Basic compatibility guidelines**

- **IDE (ATA, ATAPI, ULTRA-DMA, EIDE)**

- **SCSI (Wide, Fast, Ultra, LVD (Low Voltage Differential)**

▶ Computer technicians should be aware of the differences between different types of system boards in the marketplace. This will enable them to make intelligent choices about upgrading or exchanging system boards.

4.4   Identify the purpose of CMOS (complementary metal-oxide semiconductor), what it contains, and how to change its basic

parameters.

Example basic CMOS settings include the following:

- **Printer parallel port: unidirectional, bidirectional, disable/enable, ECP, EPP**

- **COM/serial port: memory address, interrupt request, disable**

- **Hard drive: size and drive type**

- **Floppy drive: enable/disable drive or boot, speed, density**

- **Boot sequence**

- **Memory: parity, non-parity**

- **Date/Time**

- **Passwords**

- **Plug & Play BIOS**

▶ The configuration of every AT-compatible PC system is controlled by its CMOS Setup utility. Therefore, every technician should be aware of the contents of typical CMOS utilities and be able to properly manipulate the parameters they contain to achieve a fully functional unit and to optimize its performance.

To prepare for the motherboard, processors, and memory objective of the Core Hardware exam:

▶ Read the objectives at the beginning of this chapter.

▶ Study the information in this chapter.

▶ Review the objectives listed earlier in this chapter.

▶ Perform any step-by-step procedures in the text.

▶ Answer the Review and Exam Questions at the end of the chapter and check your results.

▶ Use the ExamGear test engine on the CD that accompanies this book for additional review and exam questions concerning this material

▶ Review the Test Tips scattered throughout the chapter and make certain that you are comfortable with each point.

INTRODUCTION

This domain requires the test taker to demonstrate knowledge of specific terminology, facts, ways, and means of dealing with classifications, categories, and principles of motherboards, processors, and memory in microcomputer systems. Questions from this domain account for 15% of the Core Hardware test.

For purposes of progressive information flow, this chapter is organized just a bit differently from the objectives in the exam blueprint. It begins with objective 4.3 and then covers objectives 4.1, 4.2, and 4.4, respectively.

MOTHERBOARDS

▶ 4.3 Identify the most popular type of motherboards, their components, and their architecture (for example, bus structures and power supplies).

The A+ Core Hardware Objective 4.3 states that the test taker should be able to "identify the most popular type of motherboards, their components, and their architecture (for example, bus structures and power supplies)."

The system board is the main component in a PC-compatible microcomputer system. As this A+ objective indicates, technicians must be aware of the characteristics of different types of system boards. This will enable them to make intelligent choices about repairing, upgrading, or exchanging system boards.

The following sections deal with the various types of system boards that have commonly been used in PC systems. This discussion starts by covering system board evolution.

System Board Evolution

The system board contains the components that form the basis of the computer system. Even though the system board's physical structure has changed over time, its logical structure has remained

NOTE

Changing the Guard   System boards fundamentally change for four reasons: new industry form factors, new microprocessor designs, new expansion slot types, and reduced chip counts. Reduced chip counts are typically the result of improved microprocessor support chipsets.

relatively constant. Since the original PC, the system board has contained the microprocessor, its support devices, the system's primary memory units, and the expansion slot connectors. Figure 4.1 depicts a typical system board layout.

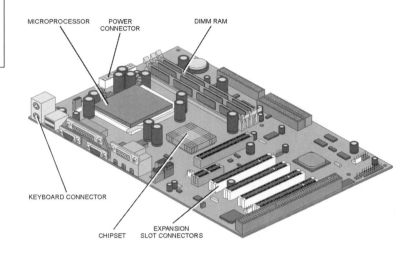

MICROPROCESSOR   POWER CONNECTOR   DIMM RAM

KEYBOARD CONNECTOR

CHIPSET   EXPANSION SLOT CONNECTORS

FIGURE 4.1
A typical system board layout.

System Board Form Factors

It should be evident that all system boards are not alike. The term *form factor* is used to refer to the physical size and shape of a device. When used in conjunction with system boards, however, it also refers to their case style and power-supply compatibility, as well as to their I/O connection placement schemes. These factors come into play when assembling a new system from components, as well as in repair and upgrade situations in which the system board is being replaced.

The original IBM PC form factor established the industry standard for the PC, PC-XT, and PC-AT clone system boards. While IBM produced a large AT format board, the industry soon returned to the PC-XT/Baby AT form factor. Within the parameters of this form factor several variations of the AT-class system board have been produced. Currently, technicians must deal with primarily only two system board form factors: the older AT system boards, and newer *ATX system boards*. Although the AT class of system boards has been around for a long time, the ATX class currently dominates the new computer market.

ATX System Boards

The newest system board designation is the *ATX form factor* developed by Intel for Pentium-based systems. This specification is an evolution of the older *Baby AT form factor* that moves the standard I/O functions to the system board.

The ATX specification basically rotates the Baby AT form factor by 90 degrees, relocates the power-supply connection, and moves the microprocessor and memory modules away from the expansion slots.

Figure 4.2 depicts a Pentium-based, ATX system board that directly supports the FDD, HDD, serial, and parallel ports. The board is 12" (305mm) wide and 9.6" (244mm) long. A revised, mini-ATX specification allows for 11.2"-by-8.2" system boards. The hole patterns for the ATX and *mini-ATX system boards* require a case that can accommodate the new boards. Although ATX shares most of its mounting-hole pattern with the Baby AT specification, it does not match exactly.

NOTE

The Changing Face of System Boards
Chipset-based system boards and I/O cards tend to change often as IC manufacturers continue to integrate higher levels of circuitry into their devices.

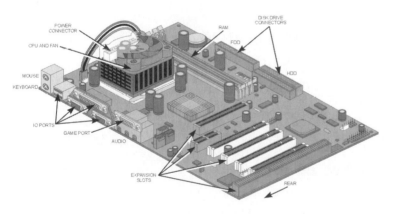

FIGURE 4.2
An ATX Pentium system board.

The power-supply orientation enables a single fan to be used to cool the system. This provides reduced cost, reduced system noise, and improved reliability. The relocated microprocessor and memory modules allow full-length cards to be used in the expansion slots while providing easy upgrading of the microprocessor, RAM, and I/O cards.

The fully implemented ATX format also contains specifications for the power-supply and I/O connector placements. In particular, the ATX specification for the power-supply connection calls for a single, 20-pin power cord between the system board and the power-supply unit rather than the typical P8/P9 cabling.

As illustrated in Figure 4.3, the new cable adds a +3.3V DC supply to the traditional +/– 12V DC and +/–5V DC supplies. A software-activated power switch also can be implemented through the ATX power-connector specification. The PS-ON and 5VSB (5V Standby) signals can be controlled by the operating system to perform automatic system shutdowns.

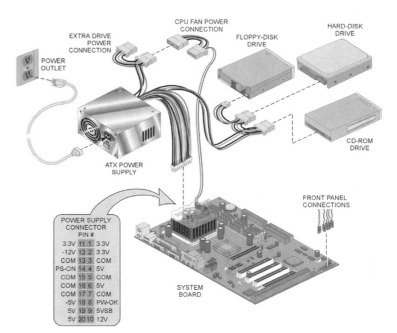

FIGURE 4.3
An ATX power-supply connector.

AT System Boards

The forerunner of the ATX system board was a derivative of the Industry Standard Architecture system board developed for the IBM PC-AT. The original *PC-AT system board* measured 30.5 × 33 centimeters.

As the PC-AT design became the de facto industry standard, printed circuit board manufacturers began to combine portions of the AT design into larger IC devices to reduce the size of their system boards. These chipset-based system boards were quickly reduced to match that of the original PC and *PC-XT system boards* (22cm × 33cm). This permitted the new 80286 boards to be installed in the smaller XT-style cases. This particular system board size, depicted in Figure 4.4, is referred to as a Baby AT system board.

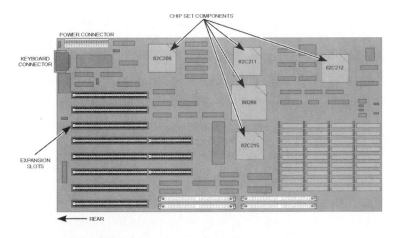

FIGURE 4.4
Baby AT system board.

System Board Compatibility

Obviously, the first consideration when installing or replacing a system board is whether it will physically fit and work with the other system components. In both of these situations, the following basic compatibility issues must dealt with:

◆ The system board's form factor

◆ The case form factor

◆ The power-supply connection type

System boards of different types have different mounting-hole patterns. Obviously the hole patterns of the replacement system board must match that of the case. If not, the replacement board cannot be installed or grounded properly.

Standard PC, PC-XT, and Baby AT system boards share the same mounting-hole patterns and can be exchanged with each other. However, the original PC-AT and ATX system boards have different hole-pattern specifications. Most case manufacturers provide a variety of hole patterns in their designs to permit as many system board form factors as possible to be used with their cases.

Some clone system boards do not observe standard sizes (only compatible standoff spacing). If the case has a power supply that mounts in the floor of the unit, there may not be enough open width in the case to accommodate an extra-wide system board. The same can be said for a full-height disk drive bay. If the disk drive bay reaches from the floor of the case to its top, there will be no room for a wide system board to fit under it.

In addition to the mounting-hole alignment issue, the case openings for expansion slots and port connections must be compatible with those of the system board.

Various types of keyboard connectors have been used in different types of systems. In Chapter 1, "1.0 Installation, Configuration, and Upgrading," Figure 1.49 demonstrated the most common connectors used with PC keyboards: 6-pin mini-DINs, 5-pin DINs, and RJ-11 plugs and jacks. PC-XT- and AT-compatible systems have historically used the 5-pin DIN connector. However, the 6-pin mini-DIN is used with ATX systems. All three types of connectors have been used in noncompliant clone systems. If this is not taken into account when selecting a replacement board, additional expense may be incurred through the need to purchase an additional keyboard with the proper connector type.

Likewise, expansion slot placement may vary somewhat between different form factors. The bad alignment created by this situation can make it difficult to install I/O cards in some systems. Similarly, I/O connectors mounted directly on the backs of some system boards may not line up with any openings in other case styles.

Expansion Slot Considerations

The types of adapter cards used in the system are another issue when replacing a system board. Make sure the new board has enough of the correct types of expansion slots to handle all the I/O cards that must be reinstalled. There is some upward compatibility between *PC-bus*, ISA, *Extended ISA* (EISA), and VESA cards. Some PC-bus cards can be installed in ISA, EISA, and VESA slots—most cannot, however, because of a small skirt on the bottom of the card that conflicts with the ISA extension portion of the slot. Both the EISA and VESA slots can accommodate ISA cards. Be aware that these relationships are not backward compatible. MCA and PCI are not compatible with the other bus types.

Some *low-profile* (LTX) cases are designed to be used with backplanes. In these units, the I/O cards are mounted horizontally on a backplane card that extends from an expansion slot on the motherboard. This arrangement produces a very low-profile desktop case style. The expansion slots in the back panel of the cases are horizontal as well. Therefore, standard system board/adapter card arrangements will not fit.

Power-Supply Considerations

Power-supply size, orientation, and connectors present another compatibility consideration. For example, an AT power supply cannot be installed in an ATX case. Because the AT bolt pattern differs from the ATX bolt pattern, it cannot be properly secured and grounded in the ATX case. Also, the single power connector from the ATX power supply will not connect to an AT system board's dual (P8/P9) power connector. Finally, ATX fans blow air into the case from the rear; AT power supplies pull it through the case from the front.

Major Components

The original IBM PC used a six-chip chipset to support the 8088 microprocessor. These devices included the following intelligent support devices:

- ◆ An 8284 clock generator
- ◆ An 8288 bus controller
- ◆ An 8255 parallel peripheral interface (PPI)
- ◆ An 8259 programmable interrupt controller (PIC)
- ◆ An 8237 DMA controller (DMAC)
- ◆ An 8253 programmable interval timer (PIT)
- ◆ An 8042 intelligent keyboard controller

The clock generator and bus controller ICs assisted the microprocessor with system clock and control-bus functions. The PPI chip handled system configuration and onboard addressing functions for the system's intelligent devices.

The interrupt controller provided the system with eight channels of programmable interrupt capabilities. The 8237 DMA controller provided four channels of high-speed DMA data-transfer service for the system. The 8253 was used to produce three programmable timer channel outputs to drive the system's time-of-day clock, DRAM refresh signal, and system-speaker output signal. Figure 4.5 depicts the PC/XT interrupt and DMA controller functions.

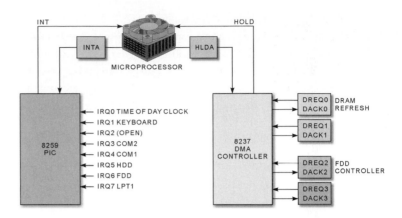

FIGURE 4.5

PC/XT interrupt and DMA controller functions.

When the IBM PC-AT came to the market, it brought an upgraded chipset that expanded the capabilities of the system. IBM improved the basic 8284 and 8288 devices by upgrading them to 82284 and 82288 versions. Likewise, the keyboard controller and the three-channel timer/counter were updated in the AT.

The PC-AT's interrupt and DMA channel capabilities were both nearly doubled by cascading two of each device together. (Actually, the usable channel counts only rose to 15 and 7, respectively.) In each case, one IC is the master device and the other is the slave device. One channel of each master device was used to accept input from the slave device. Therefore, that channel was not available for use by the system.

As an example, the output of the secondary interrupt controller is cascaded through the IRQ2 input of the master controller. In this way, the system sees all the devices attached to the secondary controller as IRQ2. A priority resolver sorts out which interrupt from the slave controller is causing the interrupt. The PC-AT interrupt and DMA controller functions, described in Figure 4.6, still form the basis for all PC-compatible architectures.

Because the second interrupt controller is cascaded through the first controller, the system sees the priority of the IRQ lines as described in Table 4.1. The table also indicates the area of usage for each IRQ line.

> **TEST TIP**
>
> Remember how many total IRQ and DMA channels are involved in the PC/XT and PC-AT systems.

> **TEST TIP**
>
> Know the standard assignment for each IRQ channel in an ISA compatible PC system.

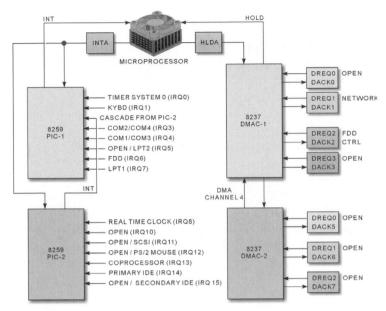

FIGURE 4.6
PC-AT interrupt and DMA controller functions.

TABLE 4.1

IRQ PRIORITIES

AT Priority	Use
IRQ0	System Board
IRQ1	System Board
IRQ2	System Board
IRQ8	System Board
IRQ9	I/O
IRQ10	I/O
IRQ11	I/O
IRQ12	I/O - System Board
IRQ13	System Board
IRQ14	I/O
IRQ15	I/O
IRQ3	I/O
IRQ4	I/O
IRQ5	I/O
IRQ6	I/O
IRQ7	I/O

TEST TIP

Remember which IRQ channel is used by the system's real-time clock (RTC) .

Chipsets

IC manufacturers produce chipset packages that system board designers can use to support different microprocessors and standardized functions. Although microprocessors have always had supporting chipsets supplied by their manufacturers, third-party chipsets began to appear when the AT architecture became the pseudo-standard for PC compatible computers. Since then, IC manufacturers have tended to create chipsets for any complex circuitry that becomes a standard.

The original system board chipsets combined the major PC- and AT-compatible structures into larger integrated circuits. In particular, many IC makers produced single ICs that perform the AT interrupt, DMA, timer/counter, and real-time clock functions. These ICs also contained the address decoding and timing circuitry to support those functions.

Because chipset-based system boards require much fewer small- and medium-sized discrete devices to produce, printed circuit board manufacturers have been able to design much smaller PC boards.

As VLSI chip technology improves, IC manufacturers continue to integrate higher levels of circuitry into their chips. All the functions of the four-chip chipset system board of Figure 4.4 are duplicated using the two-chip chipset depicted in Figure 4.7. The high level of circuit concentration in this chipset allows the size of the system board to be reduced even further. It is approximately half the length of a standard Baby AT system board; therefore, this size system board is referred to as a half-size system board.

By combining larger blocks of circuitry into fewer ICs, a price-reduction spiral is created. Fewer ICs on the board leads to reduced manufacturing costs to produce the board. The material cost of the board is decreased due to its smaller physical size. The component cost is decreased because it is cheaper to buy a few VLSI chips than several SSI or MSI devices. Finally, the assembly cost is less because only a few items must be mounted on the board.

Reduced board costs create lower computer prices, which in turn create greater consumer demand for the computers. Increased demand for the computers, and therefore the chipsets, acts to further push down the prices of all the computer components.

It is normal to consider the ROM BIOS as an integral part of any chipset model because it is designed to support the register structure of a particular chipset. Therefore, replacing a ROM BIOS chip on a system board is not as simple as placing another ROM BIOS IC in the socket. The replacement BIOS must be correct for the chipset being used on the system board.

Pentium Chipsets

Several IC manufacturers have developed chipsets to support the Pentium processor and its clones. Most of these designs feature a three-chip chipset that supports a combination PCI/ISA bus architecture. Figure 4.8 depicts a generic chipset arrangement for this type of system board.

The typical Pentium chipset consists of a memory controller (called the north bridge), a PCI-to-ISA host bridge (referred to as the south bridge), and an enhanced I/O controller. The memory controller provides the interface between the system's microprocessor, its various memory sections, and the PCI bus. In turn, the host bridge provides the interface between the PCI bus, the IDE bus, and the ISA bus. The enhanced I/O chip interfaces the standard PC peripherals (LPT, COM, and FDD interfaces) to the ISA bus.

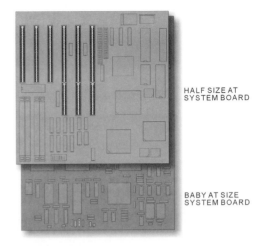

HALF SIZE AT SYSTEM BOARD

BABY AT SIZE SYSTEM BOARD

FIGURE 4.7
A half-size system board.

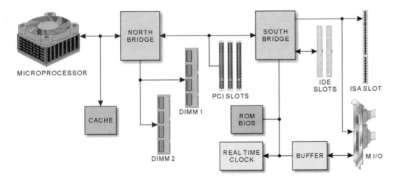

FIGURE 4.8
Typical Pentium chipset.

This typical chipset arrangement may vary for a couple of reasons. The first reason is to include a specialized function, such as an AGP or USB interface. The second reason is to accommodate changes in bus specifications.

System Bus Speeds

Microprocessor and chipset manufacturers are continually developing products to speed up the operation of the system. One method of doing this is to speed up the movement of data across the systems data buses. Looking at the arrangement described in Figure 4.8, you should note that the buses operating directly with the microprocessor and north bridge are running at one speed, whereas the PCI bus is running at a different speed, and the ISA/MIO devices are running at still another speed. The chipset devices are responsible for coordinating the movement of signals and data between these different buses.

The buses between the microprocessor and the north bridge are referred to as the front side bus (FSB), whereas the PCI and ISA buses are referred to as the backside buses (BSB). Historically, the Pentium processors have operated at many speeds between 50MHz and 1.1GHz. At the same time, the front side buses have been operating at 66MHz, 100MHz, and 133MHz. Likewise, the PCI bus has operated at standard speeds of 33MHz, 44MHz, and 66MHz. Although the speeds of these buses have been improved, the speed of operation for the ISA bus has remained constant at 8MHz.

Using an example of a current Pentium system board, the processor may run at 1.1GHz internally, whereas the front side bus runs at 133MHz, the PCI bus runs at 44.3MHz, the IDE bus runs at 100MHz, and the ISA bus runs at 8MHz.

> **TEST TIP**
> Know which processors can be used with which system board bus speeds.

Expansion Bus Architectures

Whereas the system's buses run to all the devices on the system board, the system's expansion slots provide the connecting point for those buses and most of its I/O devices. Interface cards communicate with the system through the extended microprocessor buses in these slots.

As mentioned in Chapter 1, expansion slots basically come in three formats: 8-bit, 16-bit, and 32-bit data buses. The PC-bus slot is the most famous example of an 8-bit expansion slot; the ISA slot is the consummate 16-bit expansion bus. The 32-bit expansion buses include the MCA bus, the EISA bus, the VESA bus, and the PCI bus. This discussion covers the 8-bit expansion slots first.

PC-Bus Expansion Slots

The 8-bit expansion slots in the original PC, PC-XT, and their compatibles became the de facto industry connection standard for 8-bit systems. It was dubbed the PC-bus standard.

The PC-bus expansion slot connector, illustrated in Figure 4.9, featured an 8-bit, bidirectional data bus and 20 address lines for the I/O channel. It also provided six interrupt channels, control signals for memory and I/O read or write operations, clock and timing signals, and three channels of DMA control lines. In addition, the bus offered memory-refresh timing signals, and an I/O channel-check line for peripheral problems, as well as power and ground lines for the adapters that plug into the bus.

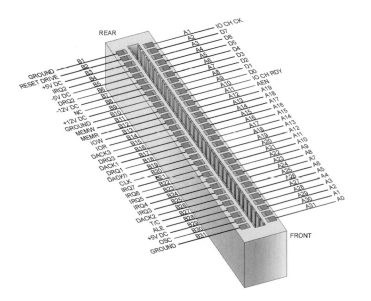

FIGURE 4.9
An 8-bit PC bus expansion slot.

ISA Expansion Slots

The overwhelming popularity of the IBM-PC AT established it as the 16-bit standard to which all other PC-compatible equipment is compared. Originally, this bus was called the *AT bus*. However, its widespread acceptance earned it the *Industry Standard Architecture* (ISA) title it now carries. As a matter of fact, the ISA slot is the most common expansion slot used with microcomputers. Even in units that have newer, faster 32-bit expansion slots, it is not uncommon to find one or more ISA slots.

This bus specification originally appeared on the 16-bit, 80286-based PC-AT system board. Its 16-bit data bus improved the performance of the system by enabling twice as much data to pass through the slot at a time. It also made transfers with 16-bit microprocessors a single-step operation. Although the ISA bus ran at microprocessor-compatible speeds up to 10 or 12MHz, incompatibility with slower I/O cards caused manufacturers to settle for running the bus at 8 or 8.33MHz in newer designs.

Figure 4.10 describes an ISA-compatible expansion slot connector. These expansion slots actually exist in two parts: the slightly altered, 62-pin I/O connector, similar to the standard PC-Bus connector; and a 36-pin auxiliary connector.

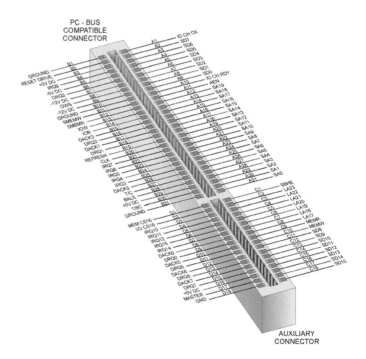

FIGURE 4.10
A 16-bit ISA expansion slot.

It provides twice as many interrupt and DMA channels as the PC-bus specification. This made it possible to connect more peripheral devices to ISA systems. To maintain compatibility with older adapter cards, the transfer speed for the ISA bus was limited to the same speed as that of the older PC bus.

32-Bit Architectures

As 32-bit microprocessors gained popularity, the shortcomings and restrictions of the 16-bit ISA bus became noticeable. Obviously, the ISA bus could not support the full, 32-bit capabilities of micro-processors such as the 80386DX, the 80486DX, and the Pentium. In addition, the physical organization of the signal lines in the ISA bus produced unacceptable levels of *radio frequency interference* (RFI) as the bus speed increased. These factors caused designers to search for a new bus system to take advantage of the 32-bit bus and the faster operation of the processors.

Two legitimate 32-bit bus standards were developed to meet these challenges. They were the *Extended Industry Standard Architecture* (EISA) bus, which, as its name implies, was an extension of the existing ISA standard bus, and an IBM-sponsored bus standard called *Micro Channel Architecture* (MCA).

Although both 32-bit designs were revolutionary and competed for the market, both have passed from the scene. In both cases, market demand did not support these designs and they were eventually replaced by other more acceptable standards.

Local Bus Designs

To speed up the operation of their systems, system board manufac-turers began to add proprietary bus designs to their board to increase the speed and bandwidth for transfers between the microprocessor and a few selected peripherals. This was accomplished by creating special, local buses, between the devices that would enable the peripherals to operate at speeds close to that of the microprocessor.

When these designs began to appear, the peripherals that could be used in them were typically only available from the original system board manufacturer. The industry soon realized the benefits of such designs and the need for "standards." Currently, most Pentium sys-tem boards include a combination of ISA, AGP, and PCI expansion slots.

Both local bus specifications include slot-addressing capabilities and reserve memory space to permit PnP reconfiguration of each device installed in the system. Unfortunately, system boards that use these expansion slots normally have a few ISA-compatible slots also. This feature can seriously disrupt the PnP concept because no identification or reconfiguration capabilities were designed into the ISA bus specification.

Due to industry moves away from anything related to ISA cards, the PCI bus has become the dominant force in system board designs. Each generation of PCI designs has provided fewer and fewer ISA buses. Current designs include three or four PCI slots, an AGP slot, and may include a single ISA connector for compatibility purposes (or none at all).

PCI Local Bus

The *peripheral component interconnect* (PCI) local bus was developed jointly by IBM, Intel, DEC, NCR, and Compaq. Its design incorporates three elements: a low-cost, high-performance local bus; an automatic configuration of installed expansion cards (PnP); and the capability to expand with the introduction of new microprocessors and peripherals. The data-transfer performance of the PCI local bus is 132MBps using a 32-bit bus and 264MBps using a 64-bit bus. This is accomplished even though the bus has a maximum clock frequency of 33MHz.

The PCI peripheral device has 256 bytes of onboard memory to hold information as to what type of device it is. The peripheral device can be classified as a controller for a mass-storage device, a network interface, a display, or other hardware. The configuration space also contains control, status, and latency timer values. The latency timer register on the device determines the length of time that the device can control the bus for bus-mastering operations.

Figure 4.11 illustrates the structure of a system based on PCI local bus chipset components.

In PC-compatible systems, the PCI bus normally coexists with an ISA bus. The PCI portion of the bus structure functions as a mezzanine bus between the ISA bus and the microprocessor's main bus system. The figure also depicts a PCI-to-ISA bridge that enables ISA adapters to be used in the PCI system. Other bridge devices also can accommodate either EISA or MCA adapters.

TEST TIP

Remember which expansion slot types are most prevalent on a modern system board.

NOTE

The Host Bridge The main component in the PCI-based system is the PCI bus controller, called the host bridge. This device monitors the microprocessor's address bus to determine whether addresses are intended for devices on the system board, in a PCI slot, or in one of the system board's other expansion slots.

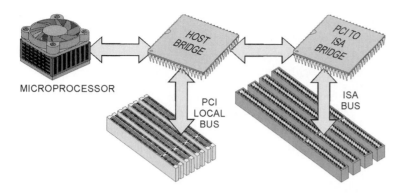

FIGURE 4.11
PCI bus structure.

The host bridge routes 32-bit PCI data directly to the PCI expansion slots through the local bus. These transfers occur at speeds compatible with the microprocessor. However, it must route non-PCI data to the PCI-to-ISA bridge that converts it into a format compatible with the ISA expansion slot. In the case of ISA slots, the data is converted from 32-bits to the 16-bit ISA format. These transfers occur at typical ISA bus speeds.

Figure 4.12 shows the pin-out of a PCI connector. The PCI bus specification uses multiplexed address and data lines to conserve the pins of the basic 124-pin PCI connector. Within this connector are signals for control, interrupt, cache support, error reporting, and arbitration.

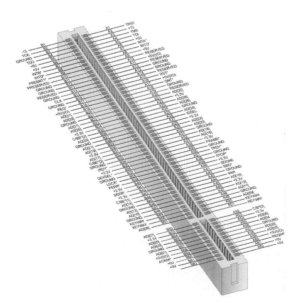

FIGURE 4.12
PCI slot pin-out.

The PCI bus employs 32-bit address and data buses. Its specification also defines 64-bit multiplexed address, however, and data buses for use with 64-bit processors such as the Pentium. Its clock (CLK) line was originally defined for a maximum frequency of 33MHz and a 132MBps transfer rate, but it can be used with microprocessors operating at higher clock frequencies (66MHz under the PCI 2.1 specification).

The request (REQ) and grant (GNT) lines provide arbitration conventions for bus-mastering operations. The arbitration logic is contained in the host bridge. To enable faster access, a bus master can request use of the bus while the current bus cycle is in progress. When the current bus cycle ends, the master can immediately begin to transfer data, assuming the request has been granted.

PCI Configuration

The PCI standard is part of the PnP hardware standard. As such, the system's BIOS and system software must support the PCI standard. Although the PCI function is self-configuring, many of its settings can be viewed and altered through the CMOS Setup utility. Figure 4.13 depicts sample PCI PnP configuration information obtained from a typical system.

```
                   ROM PCI/ISA BIOS (P155TVP4)
                        PNP AND PCI SETUP
                       AWARD SOFTWARE, INC.

Slot  1  (Right) IRQ    : Auto          DMA  1  Used By ISA       : No/ICU
Slot  2  IRQ            : Auto          DMA  3  Used By ISA       : No/ICU
Slot  3  IRQ            : Auto          DMA  5  Used By ISA       : No/ICU
Slot  4  IRQ            : Auto
PCI  Latency Timer      : 32 PCI Clock  ISA MEM Block BASE        : No/ICU

                                        NCR SCSI BIOS             : Auto
IRQ  3   Used By ISA   : No/ICU         USB Function              : Disabled
IRQ  4   Used By ISA   : No/ICU
IRQ  5   Used By ISA   : No/ICU
IRQ  6   Used By ISA   : No/ICU
IRQ  7   Used By ISA   : No/ICU
IRQ  8   Used By ISA   : No/ICU
IRQ  9   Used By ISA   : No/ICU
IRQ  10  Used By ISA   : No/ICU
IRQ  11  Used By ISA   : No/ICU
IRQ  12  Used By ISA   : No/ICU         ESC  : Quit         ↑↓←→      : Select Item
IRQ  13  Used By ISA   : No/ICU         F1   : Help         PU/PD/+/- : Modify
IRQ  14  Used By ISA   : No/ICU         F5   : Old Values   (Shift) F2 : Color
IRQ  15  Used By ISA   : No/ICU         F6   : Load BIOS Defaults
                                        F7   : Load Setup Defaults
```

FIGURE 4.13
PCI configuration settings.

During a portion of the boot up known as the detection phase, the PnP-compatible BIOS checks the system for devices installed in the expansion slots to see what types they are, how they are configured, and which slots they are in. For PnP-compatible I/O cards, this information is held in a ROM device on the adapter card.

The BIOS reads the information from all the cards and then assigns each adapter a handle (logical name) in the *PnP registry*. It then stores the configuration information for the various adapters in the registry as well. This process is described in Figure 4.14. Next, the BIOS checks the adapter information against the system's basic configuration for *resource conflicts*. After evaluating the requirements of the cards and the system's resources, the PnP routine assigns system resources to the cards as required.

Because the PnP process has no method for reconfiguring legacy devices during the resource assignment phase, it begins by assigning resources, such as IRQ assignments, to legacy devices before servicing the system's PnP devices.

Likewise, if the BIOS detects the presence of a new device during the detection phase, it will disable the resource settings for its existing cards, checks to see what resources are required and available, and then reallocates the system's resources as necessary.

TEST TIP

Know which system resources the PnP system must assign first and why.

TEST TIP

Know the process the PnP system employs to allocate resources to a new device in an existing system.

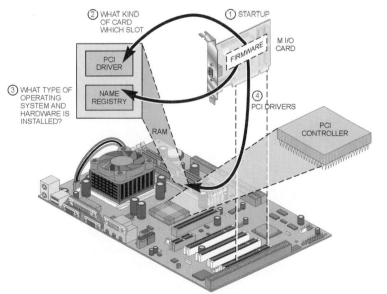

FIGURE 4.14
PCI information acquisition.

Depending on the CMOS settings available with a particular PCI chipset, the startup procedure may be set up to configure and activate all the PnP devices at startup. With other chipsets, it also may be possible to check all cards, but only enable those actually needed for startup. Some CMOS routines may contain several user-definable PCI configuration settings. Typically, these settings should be left in default positions. The rare occasion for changing a PCI setting occurs when directed to do so by a product's Installation Guide.

Systems may theoretically contain an unlimited number of PCI slots. A maximum of four slots are normally included on a system board, however, due to signal loading considerations. The PCI bus includes four internal interrupt lines (INTa through INTd, or INT1 through INT4) that allow each PCI slot to activate up to four different interrupts. PCI interrupts should not be confused with the system's IRQ channels, although they can be associated with them if required by a particular device. In these cases, IRQ9 and IRQ10 are normally used.

VESA Local Bus

The *VESA* local bus was developed by the *Video Electronics Standards Association*. This local bus specification, also referred to as the VL bus, was originally developed to provide a local bus connection to a video adapter. Its functionality has since been defined for use with other adapter types, however, such as drive controllers and network interfaces.

Figure 4.15 illustrates the flow of information through the VL bus–based computer. It also indicates data-transfer priority levels.

Like the PCI bus, the VL-bus controller monitors the microprocessor's bus to determine what type of operation is being performed, and where the address is located in the system.

The highest level of activity occurs between the microprocessor and the system's cache memory unit. The second level of priority exists between the microprocessor and the system's DRAM memory unit. The third priority level is between the microprocessor and the VL-bus controller. The final priority level exists between the VL-bus controller and the non-VESA bus controller.

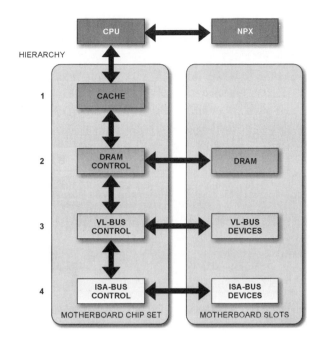

FIGURE 4.15
VL-bus block diagram.

VL-bus data is passed to the VESA slots on the local bus in 32-bit format at VL-bus speeds. The VL-bus controller passes non-VESA data to the ISA bus controller to be applied to the ISA expansion slots. These transfers are carried out in 16-bit ISA format, at ISA-compatible speeds.

The VL-bus also defines the operation of devices connected to the bus and classifies them as either local bus controller, local bus master, or local bus target. The local bus controller arbitrates requests for use of the bus between the microprocessor and local bus masters. A local bus master is any device, such as a SCSI controller, that can initiate data transfers on the VL bus. A local bus target is any device capable of answering only requests for a data transfer. The data transfer can be either a read or a write operation. Figure 4.16 depicts the VESA connector.

The VL bus defines a local bus that was originally designed for use with 80386 or 80486 microprocessors. It can operate at up to 66MHz if the VL-bus device is built directly on the system board. If the VL-bus devices are installed into an expansion slot, however, the maximum frequency allowed is 50MHz.

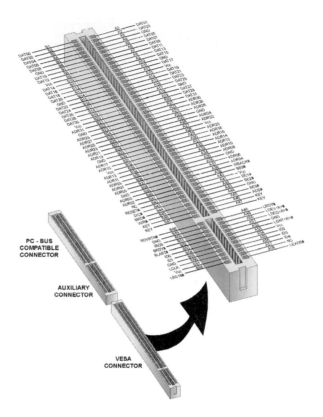

FIGURE 4.16
The VESA local bus slot.

Newer revisions of the VESA bus standard multiplex the address and data buses to provide 64-bit buses for use with the Pentium and future generation microprocessors. These revisions allow for a 32-bit adapter to operate in a 64-bit slot, or vice versa.

AGP Slots

Newer Pentium systems include an advanced accelerated graphics port (AGP) interface for video graphics. The AGP interface is a variation of the PCI bus design that has been modified to handle the intense data throughput associated with 3-D graphics.

The AGP specification was introduced by Intel to provide a 32-bit video channel that runs at 66MHz in basic 1× video mode. The standard also supports two high-speed modes that include a 2× (5.33MBps) and a 4× (1.07GBps) mode.

The AGP standard provides for a direct channel between the AGP graphic controller and the system's main memory, instead of using the expansion buses for video data. This removes the video data traffic from the PCI buses. The speed provided by this direct link permits video data to be stored in system RAM rather than in special video memory.

Figure 4.17 shows the standard AGP slot connector used with desktop system boards. The system board typically supports a single slot that is supported by a Pentium/AGP-compliant chipset. System boards designed for portable systems and single-board systems may incorporate the AGP function directly into the board without using a slot connector.

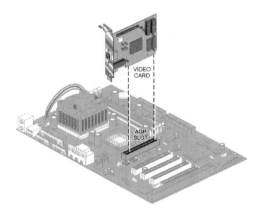

FIGURE 4.17
An AGP slot.

Audio Modem Risers

Intel has developed a new audio/modem standard for system board designs. This standard includes an expansion slot connection, called the audio/modem riser (AMR), and a companion expansion card format, known as the mobile daughter card (MDC). These components are depicted in Figure 4.18.

The design specification separates the analog and digital functions of audio (sound card) and modem devices. The analog portion of the function is placed on the MDC riser card, whereas the digital functions are maintained on the system board. This permits the system board to be certified without passing through the extended FCC and international telecom certification process attached with modem certifications. Only the MDC needs to pass the FCC certification process.

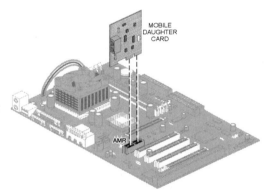

FIGURE 4.18
Audio/modem riser components.

The contents of the MDC basically consist of an analog audio coder/decoder (codec) or a modem circuit. The digital functions performed by the system board are a function of software rather than a hardware device such as a UART. The system microprocessor basically performs the UART functions under the control of the audio or modem software. This relationship makes the AMR device much less expensive but places additional overhead on the operation of the microprocessor.

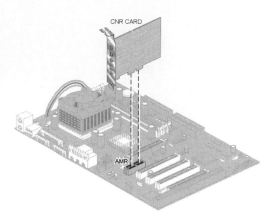

FIGURE 4.19
Communication and networking riser card.

AMR slots are already being replaced in Pentium systems by a new design called the communications and networking riser (CNR) card, depicted in Figure 4.19. This specification improves on the AMR specification by including support for advanced V.90 analog modems, multichannel audio, telephone-based dial-up networking, and *USB devices*, as well as 10/100 Ethernet-based LAN adapters.

Table 4.2 compares the capabilities of the various bus types commonly found in personal computers. It is quite apparent that the data-transfer rates possible with each new version increase dramatically. The reason this is significant is that the expansion bus is a speed-limiting factor for many of the system's operations. Every peripheral access made through the expansion slots requires the entire computer to slow down to the operating speed of the bus.

| TABLE 4.2 |

EXPANSION BUS SPECIFICATIONS

Bus Type	Transfer Rate	Data Bits	Address Bits	DMA Channels	INT Channels
PC Bus	1MBps	8	20	4	6
ISA	8MBps	16	24	8	11
VESA	150/275MBps	32/64	32	None	1
PCI 2	132/264MBps	32/64	32	None	3
PCI 2.1	264/528MBps	32/64	32	None	3
AGP	266/533/1,070MBps	32	32	None	3

I/O Connections

As mentioned in Chapter 1, pre-Pentium computers typically employed a multi-I/O (MI/O) adapter card to provide standardized AT-compatible I/O connections. However, the chipsets used to construct Pentium-based system boards move these I/O functions to the system board by including the ports' interfaces and controllers in the chipset.

Pentium AT Ports

The typical Pentium chipset integrates the circuitry for all the traditional MI/O functions, except the game port, into one or two VLSI chips. Figure 4.20 illustrates a sample arrangement for the AT-style Pentium system board's standard I/O connectors (ports).

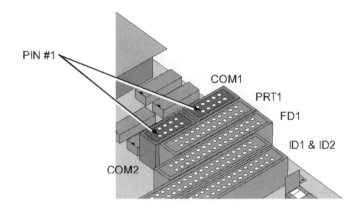

FIGURE 4.20
Pentium system board I/O connections.

The Pentium chipset normally provides a single, programmable parallel printer port, which allows a wide range of printers and other parallel devices to be connected to the system. Parallel I/O devices plug into a DB-25F connector located on an expansion slot cover. This port is connected to the system board at the 26-pin BERG pin block PRT1.

The last of the system board's I/O adapter functions are the RS-232C serial/asynchronous interface-port connections—COM1 and COM2. These ports support serial communications for serial I/O devices, such as mice and modems. A ribbon cable connects the system board's COM1 connector to a DB-9M connector located on one of the unit's slot covers. This serial port is typically the system's first serial port and is normally the mouse connector.

Another ribbon cable connects the system board's COM2 connection to a DB-25F connector on one of the expansion slot covers. This connector serves as the second logical serial port.

Separate hardware jumpers on the system board are typically used to configure the interrupt levels for the first and second serial ports (COM1 and COM2). Take care when setting these jumpers because the two serial ports cannot share the same COM-port designation. Figure 4.21 illustrates the proper connection of the parallel and serial port ribbon cables to the AT style system board.

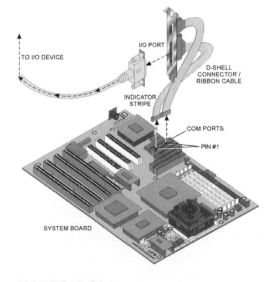

FIGURE 4.21
AT-style parallel and serial port connections.

Pentium ATX Ports

On ATX-compliant system boards, the M/IO port connections have been moved to a vertical stack form factor located at the rear of the board. Figure 4.22 depicts the standard arrangement of the I/O port connections in an ATX system.

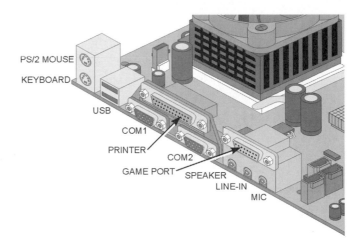

FIGURE 4.22
ATX I/O connections.

The ATX specification employs two 6-pin mini-DIN connectors (also referred to as PS/2 connectors) for the mouse and keyboard. Of course, the fact that both connections use the same type of connector can lead to problems if they are reversed. The standard also provides for two USB port connections, a DB-25F D-shell parallel printer port connector, two RS-232 serial COM ports implemented in a pair of DB-9M D-shell connectors, a DB-15F D-shell game port, and an RCA audio port. Unlike the AT-style integrated I/O connections, these port connections require no system board connecting cables that can become defective.

> **TEST TIP**
> Be aware that the use of the 6-pin mini-DIN in ATX systems can cause confusion between the keyboard and PS/2 mouse connection.

> **TEST TIP**
> Memorize the number of devices that can be attached to a USB port.

Universal Serial Bus

Chapter 1 presented the Universal Serial Bus (USB) standard as a way to daisy-chain peripherals together using a high-speed I/O bus. In that example, peripheral devices could plug into each other extending the bus to service up to 127 devices. The resulting connection architecture forms a tiered-star configuration, like the one depicted in Figure 4.23.

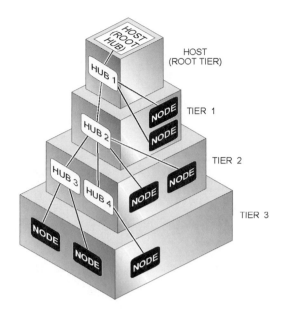

HOST
(ROOT TIER)

TIER 1

TIER 2

TIER 3

FIGURE 4.23
Universal Serial Bus architecture.

The USB system is composed of a *USB host* and *USB devices*. The devices category consists of *hubs* and nodes. In any system, there is one USB host. This unit contains the interface that provides the USB *host controller*. The controller is actually a combination of USB hardware, firmware, and software.

Hubs are devices that provide additional connection points for other USB devices. A special hub, called the *root hub*, is an integral part of the host system and provides one or more attachment points for USB devices.

Many of the newer AT and ATX system boards feature built-in USB host ports. In the AT-style boards, the port is furnished as part of a BERG pin connection, as illustrated in Figure 4.24. The ports are converted to standard connectors through an additional back-panel cable set that mounts in an open back-panel slot. On the other hand, ATX boards feature a pair of USB port connectors as part of the ATX port connection block, as illustrated in the figure. There are also PCI card-mounted USB ports that can be added to the system to enable even more USB devices to be attached to the system. These host ports function as the system's root hub.

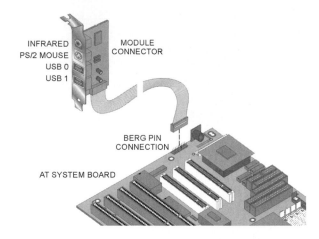

INFRARED
PS/2 MOUSE
USB 0
USB 1

MODULE
CONNECTOR

BERG PIN
CONNECTION

AT SYSTEM BOARD

FIGURE 4.24
Implementing USB ports.

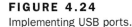

TEST TIP

Know the length limits for full- and low-speed USB devices. It should help you to remember that the low-speed distance is actually shorter than the high-speed length.

In the case of built-in USB ports, the operation of the port connections is controlled by settings in the system board's CMOS Setup utility. In most cases, it will be necessary to access the PCI Configuration screen in the system's CMOS Setup utility, enable the USB function, and assign the ports IRQ channels to use. If no USB device is being used with the system, the IRQ allocation should be set to NA, to free up the IRQ line for use by other devices.

It is evident that some of the components of the system serve as both a USB device and as a USB hub (that is, the keyboard and monitor). In these devices, the package holds the components of the function, and also provides an embedded hub to which other functions can be connected. These devices are referred to as compound devices.

Although the tiered architecture described in Figure 4.23 approaches the complexity and capabilities of the LAN architectures covered in Chapter 6, "6:0 Basic Networking," the overhead for managing the port is much easier to implement. As mentioned in Chapter 1, USB devices can be added to or removed from the system while it is fully operational. In reality, this means that the USB organizational structure is modified any time a device is added to or removed from the system.

USB devices are rated as full-speed and low-speed devices based on their communications capabilities. The length limit for a cable serving a full speed device is 16 feet 5 inches (5 meters). Likewise, the length limit for cables used between low-speed devices is 9 feet 10 inches (3 meters).

USB Data Transfers

Unlike traditional serial interfaces that transmit framed characters one at a time, data moves across the USB in the form of data packets. Packet sizes vary with the type of transmission being carried out. However, they are typically 8, 16, 32, or 64 bytes in length. All transmissions require that 2 or 3 packets of information be exchanged between the host, the source location, and the destination location.

All data transfers are conducted between the host and an endpoint device. The flow of data can occur in either direction. USB transactions begin when the host controller sends a token packet that contains information about the type of transaction to take place, the direction of the transmission, the address of the designated USB device, and an endpoint number. If the device is the source of the transaction, it either places a data packet on the bus or informs the host that it has no data to send. If the host is the source, it just places the data packet on the bus.

In either case, the destination returns a handshake packet if the transfer was successful. If an error is detected in the transfer, a not acknowledge (NACK) packet is generated. Figure 4.25 demonstrates the USB's four-packet formats: token packet, the start-of-frame (SOF) packet, the data packet, and the handshake packet.

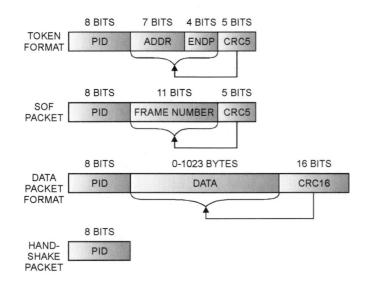

FIGURE 4.25
USB packet formats.

Each type of packet begins with an 8-bit *packet ID* (*PID*) section. The SOF packet adds an 11-bit frame-number section and a 5-bit *cyclic redundancy check* (CRC) error-checking code section. In the data packet, a variable-length data section replaces the frame-number section, and the CRC frame is enlarged to 16 bits. The data section can range up to 1023 bytes in length. The handshake packet just consists of a PID byte.

The USB management software dynamically tracks what devices are attached to the bus and where they are. This process of identifying and numbering bus devices is known as bus enumerating. The USB specification allows a hot-swap peripheral connection that does not require the system to be shut down. The system automatically detects peripherals and configures the proper driver. Instead of just detecting and charting devices at startup in a PnP style, the USB continuously monitors the bus and updates the list whenever a device is added to or removed from it.

The USB specification allows for the following four types of transfers to be conducted:

◆ **Control transfers** are used by the system to configure devices at startup or time of connection. Other software can use control transfers to perform other device specific operations.

◆ **Bulk data transfers** are used to service devices that can handle large batches of data (scanners and printers, for example). Bulk transfers are typically made up of large bursts of sequential data. The system arranges for bulk transfers to be conducted when the bus has plenty of capacity to carry out the transfer.

◆ **Interrupt transfers** are small, spontaneous transfers from a device that are used to announce events, provide input coordinate information, or transfer characters.

◆ **Isochronous transfers** involve large streams of data. This format is used to move continuous, real-time data streams such as voice or video. Data delivery rates are predetermined and correspond to the sampling rate of the device.

TEST TIP

Be aware of the USB high-speed data-streaming mode.

Onboard Disk Drive Connections

Along with the I/O port connections, Pentium system boards moved the hard and floppy disk drive controller functions and interface connections to the system board, as illustrated in Figure 4.26. As is the case with most Pentium-based system boards, this example provides the system's IDE host adapter and floppy disk drive controller interface connections.

The FDC portion of the chipset can control two floppy disk drives whose signal cable connects to the system board at the 34-pin BERG block (labeled FD1 in Figure 4.26). As with any disk drive connections, take care when connecting the floppy disk drive signal cable to the system board; pin 1 of the connector must line up with the signal cable's indicator stripe.

The IDE host adapter portion of the chipset is normally capable of controlling up to four hard disk or CD-ROM drives. These adapters furnish two complete IDE channels: IDE1 and IDE2. Each channel can handle one master and one slave device. The hard drives and CD-ROM drives are connected to the system board's IDE connectors by 40-conductor ribbon cables at connectors ID1 or ID2.

The primary partition of the drive attached to the ID1 connector will be designated as logical C: drive. If a second drive is attached to ID1 as a slave, its primary partition will be designated as logical D: drive. If there is an additional partition on the first drive, it will be designated as the E: drive. The hierarchy of assigning logical drive designations in the IDE interface calls for primary partitions to be assigned sequentially from ID1 master, ID1 slave, ID2 master, to ID2 slave. This is followed by assigning extended partitions for each drive in the same order.

The hard drives are connected in much the same manner as the floppy drives. The first hard drive is connected to the end of the cable farthest away from the ID1 or ID2 connector. Observe the same cable orientation that was used for connecting the floppy disk drives when connecting the cable to the FD1 connector for the hard drives. Figure 4.27 provides an example of the alignment of the FDD and HDD cables on the system board.

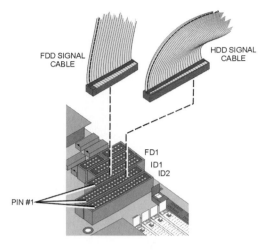

FIGURE 4.26
Pentium board disk drive connections.

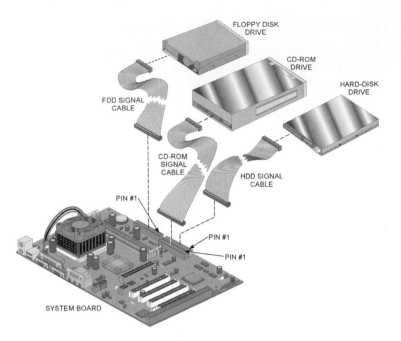

FIGURE 4.27
HDD and FDD system board connections.

As discussed in Chapter 1, there are a variety of IDE-related specifications. The initial IDE standard was the IDE/ATA specification. IDE and ATA are the same standard. It supported a maximum throughout of 8.3MBps through the 40-pin IDE signal cable.

The second IDE standard includes the ATA-2/EIDE/ATAPI specifications. (The ATAPI standard is a derivative of the ATA-2 standard.) This specification provides maximum throughput of 16.7MBps through the 40-pin IDE signal cable.

The ATA standards provide for different programmed I/O (PIO) modes that offer higher performance capabilities, as illustrated in Table 4.3. Most IDE devices are now capable of operating in modes 3 or 4. However, the IDE port must be attached to the PCI bus to use these modes. Some system boards only place the IDE1 connection on this bus, although the IDE2 connection is a function of the ISA bus. In these cases, devices installed on the IDE2 connector are capable of only mode-2 operation.

TABLE 4.3

ATA PIO MODES

PIO Mode	Transfer	ATA Version
0	3.3MBps	ATA-1
1	5.2MBps	ATA-1
2	8.3MBps	ATA-1
3	11.1MBps	ATA-1
4	16.6MBps	ATA-1
4	33.3MBps	ATA-3/Ultra DMA 33
4	66.6MBps	ATA-4/Ultra DMA 66
4	100MBps	ATA 100

An additional development of the ATA standard has provided the ATA-3/Ultra ATA 33 specification that boosts throughput between the IDE device and the system to 33.3MBps. This standard still employs the 40-pin IDE signal cable. It relies on the system to support the 33.3MBps burst-mode transfer operation through the Ultra DMA (UDMA) protocol.

Newer IDE enhancements called ATA-4/Ultra ATA 66 and Ultra ATA 100 provide even higher data throughput by doubling the number of conductors in the IDE signal cable. The IDE connector has remained compatible with the 40-pin IDE connection, but each pin has been provided with its own ground conductor in the cable. The Ultra ATA 66 specification provides 66MBps while the Ultra ATA 100 connection will provide 100MBps.

TEST TIP	Remember how the Ultra ATA 66 interface cable can be identified.

Both Ultra ATA versions support 33.3MBps data rates when used with a standard 40-pin/40-conductor IDE signal cable. Therefore, Ultra ATA 66 and 100 devices can still be used with systems that do not support the new IDE standards.

These operating modes must be configured correctly through the system's CMOS Setup utility. These settings are discussed in the "Chipset Features Setup Functions" section later in this chapter.

> **TEST TIP**
>
> Be aware of the types of expansion slots for which SCSI cards are typically available.

There is no industry-accepted equivalent for onboard SCSI adapters. Although a few such system board designs are available, they are not standard boards and have probably been created to fill the specific needs of a particular application. Therefore, SCSI devices require that a SCSI host adapter card be installed in most systems. SCSI host adapters are typically available for use with ISA, EISA, and PCI bus interfaces.

MICROPROCESSORS

▶ 4.1 Distinguish between the popular CPU chips in terms of their basic characteristics.

The A+ Core Hardware objective 4.1 states that the test taker should be able to "distinguish between the popular CPU chips in terms of their basic characteristics."

The successful technician must be aware of the capabilities of the different microprocessors that are available for use in a system. They must know what impact placing a particular microprocessor in an existing system may have on its operation. They also must be able to identify the type of processor being used and the system setting necessary to maximize its operation.

INTEL PROCESSORS

When IBM was designing the first PC, it chose the Intel 8088 microprocessor and its supporting chipset as the standard CPU for its design. This was a natural decision because one of IBM's major competitors (Apple) was using the Motorola microprocessors for its designs. The choice to use the Intel microprocessor still impacts the design of PC-compatible systems. As a matter of fact, the microprocessors used in the vast majority of all PC-compatible microcomputers include the Intel 8088/86, 80286, 80386, 80486, and Pentium (80586 and 80686) devices.

The popularity of the original PCs, PC-XTs, and PC-ATs (and the software developed for them) has caused limitations to be built in to the newer microprocessors to maintain compatibility with the microprocessors used in these systems. The popularity of these processors has been so high that it has created a microprocessor clone market that designs processors to mimic the Intel design.

For the most part, the previous generations of microprocessors have disappeared from the marketplace, leaving the Pentium as the only processor type that needs to be discussed in detail. Therefore, the microprocessor material that follows builds on the earlier Intel models described in Chapter 1. This discussion first focuses on the Intel Pentium microprocessors that have set the trends in PC design and then explores the clone versions of these processors to see how they differ.

The Pentium Processor

The Pentium processor succeeded the 80486 microprocessor and maintained compatibility with the other 80X86 microprocessors. When Intel introduced the Pentium, it discontinued the 80x86 naming convention it had previously used for its microprocessors. This was done so that Intel could copyright the name (numbers cannot be copyrighted) and prevent clone microprocessor manufacturers from using the same convention. Therefore, the 80586 became the Pentium.

The original Pentium was a 32/64-bit microprocessor contained in a ceramic-pin, grid-array package. Figure 4.28 shows the internal architecture of the Pentium. The registers for the microprocessor and floating-point sections of the Pentium are identical to those of the 80486. It has a 64-bit data bus that allows it to handle Quad Word (or QWord) data transfers. The Pentium also contains two separate 8KB caches, compared to only one in the 80486. One of the caches is used for instructions or code, and the other is used for data. The internal architecture of the Pentium resembles an 80486 in expanded form. The floating-point section operates up to five times faster than that of the FPU in the 80486.

The Pentium is referred to as a superscalar microprocessor because its architecture allows multiple instructions to be executed simultaneously. This is achieved through a pipelining process that uses multiple stages to speed up instruction execution. Each stage in the pipeline performs a part of the overall instruction execution, with all operations being completed at one stage before moving on to another stage. This technique allows streamlined circuitry to perform a specific function at each stage of the pipeline, thereby improving execution time. When an instruction moves from one stage to the next, a new instruction moves into the vacated stage. The Pentium contains two separate pipelines that can operate simultaneously. The first is called the U-pipe and the second the V-pipe.

FIGURE 4.28
Inside the Pentium microprocessor.

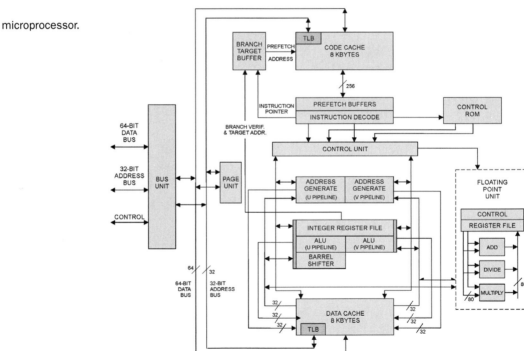

The original Pentium processor architecture has appeared in three generations. The first-generation design, code named the P5, came in a 273-pin PGA package and operated at 60 or 66MHz speeds. It used a single +5V DC operating voltage, which caused it to consume a large amount of power and generate a large amount of heat.

The Pentium processor generated so much heat during normal operation that an additional *CPU cooling fan* was usually required.

The second-generation Pentiums, referred to as P54Cs, came in a 296-pin *Staggered Pin Grid Array* (SPGA) package and operated at 75, 90, 100, 120, 133, 150m and 166MHz in different versions. For these devices, Intel reduced the power-supply voltage level to +3.3V DC to consume less power and provide faster operating speeds. Reducing the power-supply level in effect moves the processor's high- and low-logic levels closer together, requiring less time to switch back and forth between them. The SPGA packaging made the second generation of Pentium devices incompatible with the first-generation system boards.

The second-generation devices also employed internal clock multipliers to increase performance. In this scenario, the system's buses run at the same speed as the clock signal introduced to the microprocessor. However, the internal clock multiplier causes the microprocessor to operate internally at some multiple of the external clock speed. (That is, a Pentium operating from a 50MHz external clock and a 2× internal multiplier is actually running internally at 100MHz.)

Basically, all Pentium microprocessors use 50, 60, or 66MHz external clock frequencies to generate their internal operating frequencies. The value of the internal multiplier is controlled by external hardware jumper settings on the system board.

The third generation of Pentium designs, designated as P55C, use a 296-pin SPGA arrangement. This package adheres to the 321-pin Socket 7 specification designed by Intel. The P55C has been produced in versions that operate at 166, 180, 200, and 233MHz. This generation of Pentium devices operate at voltages below the +3.3 level established in the second generation of devices. The P55C is known as the Pentium MMX (Multimedia Extension) processor and is described in greater detail later in this chapter. Figure 4.29 shows a pin-out for the first-generation Pentium processor.

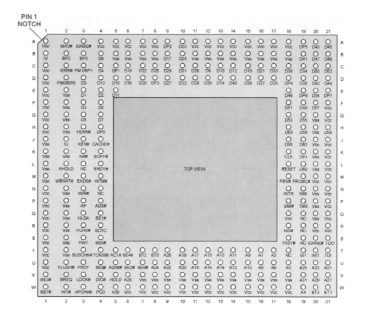

FIGURE 4.29
The pins of the Pentium microprocessor.

Advanced Pentium Architectures

Intel has continued to advance its Pentium line of microprocessors by introducing additional specifications, including the *Pentium MMX, Pentium Pro, Pentium II,* and *Pentium III* processors.

At the same time, Intel's competitors have developed clone designs that equal or surpass the capabilities of the Intel versions. The following sections look at the advancements Intel has produced and then focus on the clone processors that compete with them.

Pentium MMX

In the Pentium MMX processor, the communications-processing and multimedia capabilities of the original Pentium device were extended by the addition of 57 multimedia-specific instructions to the instruction set.

Intel also increased the onboard L1 cache size to 32KB. The cache has been divided into two separate 16KB caches: the instruction cache, and the data cache. The typical L2 cache used with the MMX was 256KB or 512KB.

The MMX added an additional multimedia-specific stage to the integer pipeline. This integrated stage-handled MMX and integer instructions quickly. Improved branching prediction circuitry also was implemented to offer higher prediction accuracy and, thereby, provide higher processing speeds. The four prefetch buffers in the MMX could hold up to four successive streams of code. The four write buffers were shared between the two pipelines to improve the memory write performance of the MMX.

The Pentium MMX processor was available in 166, 200, and 233MHz versions and used a 321-pin, SPGA Socket 7 format. It required two separate operating voltages. One source was used to drive the Pentium processor core; the other was used to power the processor's I/O pins. The pin-out of the Pentium MMX processor is shown in Figures 4.32.

Compare Figures 4.29 and 4.30. Notice the staggered pin arrangement of the MMX device compared to the uniform row and column arrangement of the original Pentium devices. Also, identify the new signals added to the Pentium architecture for later versions. Some of these additional signals were used to implement the VRM and internal clock multiplier functions for the advanced Pentiums.

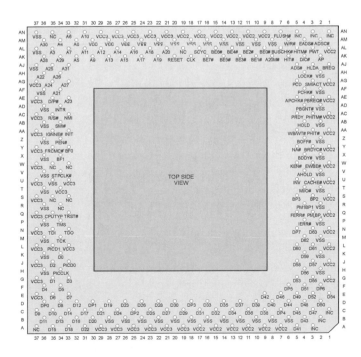

FIGURE 4.30
The pins of the Pentium MMX microprocessor.

Pentium Pro

Intel departed from just increasing the speed of its Pentium processor line by introducing the Pentium Pro processor. Although compatible with all the previous software written for the Intel processor line, the Pentium Pro is optimized to run 32-bit software.

However, the Pentium Pro did not remain pin compatible with the previous Pentium processors. Instead, Intel adopted a 2.46" × 2.66", 387-pin PGA configuration to house a Pentium Pro processor core, and an onboard 256KB (or 512KB) L2 cache. The L2 cache complements the 16KB L1 cache in the Pentium core. Figure 4.31 illustrates this arrangement. Notice that although they are on the same PGA device, the two components are not integrated into the same IC. The unit is covered by a gold-plated, copper/tungsten heat spreader.

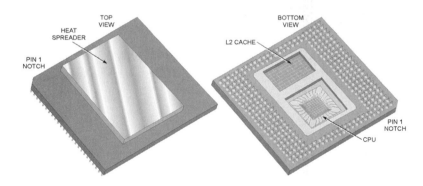

FIGURE 4.31
The Pentium Pro microprocessor.

The L2 onboard cache stores the most frequently used data not found in the processor's internal L1 cache, as close to the processor core as it can be without being integrated directly into the IC. A high-bandwidth cache bus connects the processor and cache unit together. The bus (0.5 inches in length) allows the processor and external cache to communicate at a rate of 1.2GBps.

The Pentium Pro is designed in a manner so that it can be used in typical, single-microprocessor applications or in multiprocessor environments, such as high-speed, high-volume file servers and workstations. Several dual-processor system boards have been designed for twin Pentium Pro processors. These boards, such as the one described in Figure 4.32, are created with two Pentium Pro sockets so that they can operate with either a single processor or

with dual processors. When dual processors are installed, logic circuitry in the Pentium Pro's core manages the requests for access to
the system's memory and 64-bit buses.

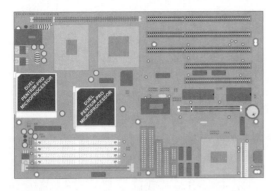

FIGURE 4.32
A dual-processor system board.

Pentium II

Intel radically changed the form factor of the Pentium processors by
housing the Pentium II processor in a new, single-edge contact
(SEC) cartridge, depicted in Figure 4.33. This cartridge uses a special retention mechanism built in to the system board to hold the
device in place.

The proprietary 242-contact socket design is referred to as the *Slot 1*
specification and is designed to enable the microprocessor to operate
at bus speeds in excess of 300MHz.

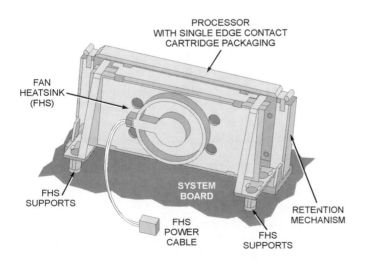

FIGURE 4.33
The Pentium II cartridge.

Remember which components Intel included in the SEC cartridge.

NOTE

Pentium II   The Pentium II includes all the multimedia enhancements from the MMX processor, and retains the power of the Pentium Pro's dynamic execution and 512KB L2 cache features. The L1 cache is increased to 32KB; the L2 cache operates with a half-speed bus.

FIGURE 4.34
Inside the Pentium II cartridge.

The cartridge also requires a special fan heat sink (FHS) module and fan. Like the SEC cartridge, the FHS module requires special support mechanisms to hold it in place. The fan draws power from a special power connector on the system board, or from one of the system's options power connectors.

Inside the cartridge, there is a substrate material on which the processor and related components are mounted. The components consist of the Pentium II processor core, a *tag RAM*, and an L2 burst SRAM. Tag RAM is used to track the attributes (read, modified, and so on) of data stored in the cache memory.

Figure 4.34 depicts the contents of the Pentium II cartridge.

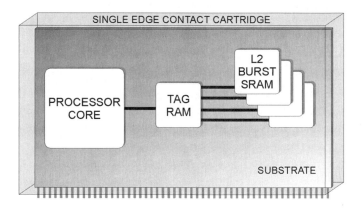

A second cartridge type, called the single-edged processor package (SEPP), has been developed for use with the Slot 1 design. In this design, the boxed processor is not completely covered by the plastic housing as it is in the SECC design. Instead, the SEPP circuit board is accessible from the back side.

The operation of Pentium Pro and Pentium II processors can be modified by uploading processor update information into BIOS that have Application Programming Interfaces (API) capabilities built in to them. The microprocessor manufacturer places update information on its Web site that can be downloaded onto a floppy disk by customers. The user transfers the update information from the update disk to the system's BIOS via the API. If the updated data is relevant (as indicated by checking its processor stepping code), the API writes the updated microcode into the BIOS. This information will, in turn, be loaded into the processor each time the system is booted.

Pentium III

Intel followed the Pentium II processor with a new Slot 1–compatible design it called the Pentium III. The original Pentium III processor (code named Katmai) was designed around the Pentium II core, but increased the L2 cache size to 512KB. It also increased the speed of the processor to 600MHz, including a 100MHz front-side bus speed.

Intel followed the Pentium III design with a less-expensive version that it named the Pentium Celeron. Unlike the original Pentium III, the Celeron version featured a 66MHz bus speed and only 128KB of L2 cache. Initially, the Celeron Mendocino was packaged in the SECC cartridge.

Later versions of the Pentium III and Celeron processors were developed for the Intel Socket 370 specification. This design returned to a 370-pin, ZIF socket/SPGA package arrangement.

The first pin grid array versions of the Pentium III and Celeron processors conformed to a standard called the Plastic Pin Grid Array (PPGA) 370 specification. Intel repackaged its processors into a PGA package to fit this specification. The PPGA design was introduced to produce inexpensive, moderate-performance Pentium systems. The design topped out at 533MHz with a 66MHz bus speed.

Intel upgraded the Socket 370 specification by introducing a variation called the Flip Chip Pin Grid Array (FC-PGA) 370 design. Intel made small modifications to the wiring of the socket to accommodate the Pentium III processor design. In addition, they employed a new 0.18 micron IC manufacturing technology to produce faster processor speeds (up to 1.12 GHz) and front-side bus speeds (100MHz and 133MHz). However, the new design provides only 256KB of L2 cache.

Pentium III and Celeron processors designed with the 0.18 micron technology are referred to as Coppermine and Coppermine 128 processors, respectively. (The L2 cache in the Coppermine 128 is only 128KB.) Future Coppermine versions should employ 0.13 micron IC technology to achieve 1.4GHz operating speeds.

Intel also has introduced an edge-connector-based Slot 2 specification that extends the Slot 1, boxed-processor scheme to a 330-contact design. For the Slot 2 design, Intel has produced three

TEST TIP

Be able to state the difference between Pentium II and Pentium III processors.

special versions of the Pentium III that they have named the Pentium Xeon. Each version features a different level of L2 cache (512KB, 1MB, 2MB). The Xeon designs were produced to fill different, high-end server needs.

Table 4.4 summarizes the characteristics of the Intel Pentium microprocessors.

TABLE 4.4

CHARACTERISTICS OF THE INTEL PENTIUM MICROPROCESSORS

Type	Address Bus Width	Space	Internal Clock Speed (MHz)	Data Bus Width	Math Coprocessor	Main Use
Pentium	32	4GB	50–100	64	Onboard	AT compatible
Pentium MMX	32	4GB	166–233	64	Onboard	AT-compatible
Pentium Pro	36	4GB × 4	150–200	64	Onboard	AT-compatible
Pentium II	36	64GB	233–450	64	Onboard	AT-compatible
Pentium III	36	64GB	450MHz–1GHz	64	Onboard	AT compatible
Celeron	36	64GB	266–766	64	Onboard	AT compatible

Pentium Clones

As mentioned earlier in this chapter, Intel abandoned the 80x86 nomenclature in favor of names that could be copyrighted in an effort to distance themselves from the clone microprocessor manufacturers. When this occurred, the other manufacturers largely followed the 80x86 path, but eventually moved toward alternative numbering schemes as well.

AMD Processors

Advanced Micro Devices (AMD) offers several clone microprocessors: the 5x86 (X5), the 5x86 (K5), the K6, the K6PLUS-3D, and K7 microprocessors. The X5 offers operational and pin compatibility with the DX4. Its performance equals that of the Pentium and MMX processors. The K5 processor is compatible with the Pentium, and the K6 is compatible with the MMX. Both the K5 and K6 models are Socket 7 compatible, enabling them to be used in conventional Pentium and Pentium MMX system board designs (with some small modifications). The K6 employs an extended 64KB L1 cache that doubles the internal cache size of the Pentium II.

The K6PLUS-3D is operationally and performance compatible with the Pentium Pro, and the K7 is operationally and performance compatible with the Pentium II. However, neither of these units has a pin-out compatibility with another processor.

NextGen produced three processors that can perform at the same level as the P5 (Nx586) and P54C (Nx686) Pentium devices. These devices use proprietary pin-outs, however, so they are not compatible with other processors. Although the performance levels compete with the Pentium, the devices offer compatibility with 80386/87 operation only. Eventually, NextGen was purchased by AMD and its designs were incorporated in the K6 design.

AMD continues to produce clone versions of Pentium processors. In some cases, the functions and performance of the AMD devices go beyond the Intel design they are cloning. Two notable AMD clone processors are the Athlon and the Duron.

The Athlon is a Pentium III clone processor. It is available in a Slot 1 cartridge clone, called the Slot A specification. Figure 4.35 depicts the cartridge version of the Athlon processor along with a Slot A connector.

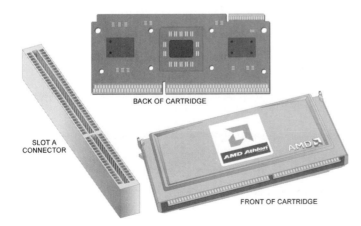

BACK OF CARTRIDGE

SLOT A
CONNECTOR

FRONT OF CARTRIDGE

FIGURE 4.35
The Slot A Athlon processor.

The Athlon also is available in a proprietary SPGA Socket A design that mimics the Intel Socket 370 specification. The Socket A specification employs a 462-pin ZIF socket and is supported only by two available chipsets.

Three versions of the Athlon processor have been introduced so far. The first version was the K7 version that ran between 500MHz and 700MHz, provided a 128KB L1 cache and a 512KB L2 cache, and employed a 100MHz system bus.

Subsequent Athlon versions have included the K75 and Thunderbird versions. Both versions are constructed using the 0.18 micron manufacturing technology. The K75 processors ran between 750MHz and 1GHz. Like the K7 version, it provided a 128KB L1 cache and a 512KB L2 cache, and employed a 100MHz system bus. The Thunderbird version ran between 750MHz and 1.2GHz, provided a 128KB L1 cache and a 256KB L2 cache, and employed a 133MHz system bus.

The Duron processor is a Celeron clone processor that conforms to the AMD Socket A specification. The Duron features processor speeds between 600MHz and 800MHZ. It includes a 128KB L1 cache and a 64KB L2 cache. Like the newer Celerons, the Duron is constructed using 0.18 micron IC manufacturing technology.

Cyrix Processors

Cyrix uses an M*x* numbering system in addition to the 5x/6x86 numbers. The M5/M6/M7 devices are compatible with their Intel counterparts in performance, compatibility, and pin-out. The 5x86 device is compatible with the 80486DX4 in performance, compatibility, and pin-out. The M1 (6x86) and M2 (6x86MX) processors are compatible with the Intel P54C and P55C units in performance and pin-out. The M1 unit is operationally compatible with the 80486DX4, and the M2 processor is operationally compatible with the Pentium MMX and Pentium Pro processors.

The 6x86 design uses a 16KB dual-ported cache for instructions and data and a 256-byte instruction cache. The 6x86MX version includes a 64KB L1 cache that competes with the K6 AMD design.

Like AMD, Cyrix has continued to develop clones of the various Pentium products. These clones include the Socket 370–compatible Celeron clone processor called the Cyrix III (originally called the Joshua Processor). The Cyrix III, depicted in Figure 4.36, can be used in system boards designed for Celeron processors. However, the system's BIOS will need to be upgraded to work with the Cyrix clock multipliers. The latest version of the processor (the Samuel version) runs at 533MHz but supports a very fast 133MHz front-side bus. It also possesses a large (128KB) L1 cache but has no support for an L2 cache.

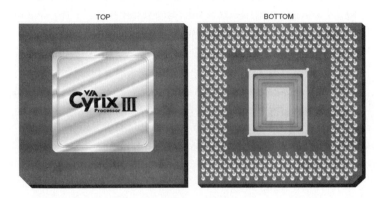

FIGURE 4.36
Cyrix III processor.

Properly installing both the AMD and Cyrix devices requires that their power-supply levels and clock multipliers be set correctly. These settings are discussed in the "Configuring Microprocessors" section in this chapter.

Table 4.5 shows the relationship between the various numbering systems. In addition to the 80x86 numbering system, Intel used a P*x* identification up to the Pentium II. The Pentium II is identified as the Klamath processor. Subsequent improved versions have been dubbed Deschutes, Covington, Mendocino, Katmai, Willamette, Flagstaff (P7), Merced, and Tahoe.

TABLE 4.5

CLONE PROCESSORS

Intel	Cyrix	AMD	NextGen
Pentium (P5/P54C)	M1 (6X86)	-K5(5X86)	NX586/686
Pentium MMX (P55C)	M2 (6X86MX)	-K6	
Pentium Pro (P6)	MXi	-K6PLUS-3D	
Pentium II	M3	-K7	
Pentium III	N/A	K75/Thunderbird	
Pentium Celeron	Cyrix III	Duron	

Socket Specifications

In addition to the clone processors, Intel has developed a line of upgrade microprocessors for their original units. These are referred to as OverDrive processors. The OverDrive unit may just be the same type of microprocessor running at a higher clock speed, or it may be an advanced architecture microprocessor designed to operate from the same socket/pin configuration as the original. To accommodate this option, Intel has created specifications for eight socket designs, designated *Socket 1 through Socket 8*.

The specifications for Socket 1 through Socket 3 were developed for 80486SX, 80486DX, and 80486 OverDrive versions that use different pin numbers and power-supply requirements. Likewise, Socket 4 through Socket 6 deal with various Pentium and OverDrive units that use different speeds and power-supply requirements. The Socket 7 design works with the fastest Pentium units and includes provisions for a *voltage-regulator module* (VRM) to allow various power settings to be implemented through the socket. The Socket 7 specification corresponds to the second generation of Pentium devices that employ SPGA packaging. It is compatible with the Socket 5, straight-row PGA specification that the first-generation Pentium processors employed. The Socket 8 specification is specific to the Pentium Pro processor.

The Socket 7 specification has been upgraded to include a new standard called Super Socket 7. This standard extends the use of the Socket 7 physical connector by adding support signal required for implementing AGP slots and the 100MHz front-side bus (FSB) specification. Microprocessors designed to use the Super Socket 7 specification include AMD's K6-2, K6-2+, and K6-III, along with Intel's Pentium MMX and Pentium Pro.

Although the Intel Slot 1 design was originally developed for the Pentium II, it also serves its Celeron and Pentium III processor designs. Like Socket 7, the Slot 1 specification provides for variable processor core voltages (2.8 to 3.3) that permit faster operation and reduced power consumption. In addition, some suppliers have created daughter boards containing the Pentium Pro processor that can be plugged into the Slot 1 connector. This combination Socket 8/Slot 1 device is referred to as a slotket processor.

The Slot 2 specification from Intel expands the Slot 1 SECC technology to a 330-contact cartridge (SECC-2) used with the Intel Xeon processor.

AMD produced a reversed version of the Slot 1 specification for its Athalon processor by turning the contacts of the Slot 1 design around. They titled the new design Slot A. Although serving the same ends as the Slot 1 design, the Slot A and Slot 1 microprocessor cartridges are not compatible.

In a departure from its proprietary slot connector development, Intel introduced a new ZIF socket standard, called Socket 370, for use with its Celeron processor. There are actually two versions of the Socket 370 specification. The first is the PPGA 370 variation intended for use with Plastic Pin Grid Array (PPGA) version of the Celeron CPUs. The other is the Flip Chip Pin Grid Array (FC-PGA) version.

The term *flip chip* is used to describe a group of microprocessors that have provisions for attaching a heat sink directly to the microprocessor die. The processors in this category include the Cyrix III, Celeron, and Pentium III. Although the PPGA and FC-PGA processors will both plug into the 370 socket, that does not mean they will work in system boards designed for the other specification.

Likewise, AMD produced a 462-pin ZIF socket specification for the PGA versions of its Athalon and Duron processors. No other processors have been designed for this specification, and only two chipsets have been produced to support it.

Table 4.6 summarizes the attributes of the various industry socket and slot specifications.

TABLE 4.6

INDUSTRY SOCKET/SLOT SPECIFICATIONS

Number	Pins	Voltages	Microprocessors
Socket 1	169 PGA	5	80486 SX/DXx, DX4 OverDrive
Socket 2	238 PGA	5	80486 SX/DXx, Pentium OverDrive
Socket 3	237 PGA	5/3.3	80486 SX/DXx, Pentium OverDrive

continues

TABLE 4.6	*continued*		

INDUSTRY SOCKET/SLOT SPECIFICATIONS

Number	*Pins*	*Voltages*	*Microprocessors*
SSocket 4	237 PGA	5	Pentium 60/66, 60/66 OverDrive
Socket 5	320 SPGA	3.3	Pentium 75–133, Pentium OverDrive
Socket 6	235 PGA	3.3	Never Implemented
Socket 7	321 SPGA	VRM	Pentium 75–200, Pentium OverDrive
Socket 8	387 SPGA	VRM	Pentium Pro
Slot 1	242 SECC/ SEPP		Celeron, Pentium II, Pentium III
Slot 2	330 SECC-2		Xeon
Super Socket 7	321 SPGA	VRM	AMD K6-2, K6-2+, K6-III, K6-III+, Pentium MMX, Pentium Pro
Socket 370	370 SPGA		Cyrix III, Celeron, Pentium III
Slot A	242 Slot A		AMD Athlon
Socket A	462 SPGA		AMD Athlon, Duron

TEST TIP

Know which processors can be used with Slot 1 and Socket 370 connections. Also know which processors can be used in Slot A.

Clock Speeds, Power Supplies, and Fans

It should be apparent that there are three compatibility issues to consider when dealing with clone processors: performance, operation, and pin-out compatibility. In addition to these three issues, it is important to be aware of the power-supply requirements for the various types of microprocessors.

The Socket 7 specification includes pins that enable the system board to be configured for microprocessors using different operating speeds. It also allows two speed settings to be established for the microprocessor: one speed for its internal core operations, and a second speed for its external bus transfers.

In the Pentium processor, the two speeds are tied together by an internal clock multiplier. Advanced Pentium designs have additional pins that work with the Socket 7 specification to determine the operating speed of the microprocessor.

Beginning with the Pentium MMX, Intel adopted dual-voltage supply levels for the overall IC and for its core. Common Intel voltage supplies are +5/+5 for older units, and +3.3/+3.3, +3.3/+2.8, +3.3/+1.8 for newer units. Clone processors may use compatible voltages (especially if they are pin compatible), or may use a completely different voltage levels.

Common voltages for clone microprocessors include +5, +3.3, +2.5, and +2.2. The additional voltage levels are typically generated by special regulator circuits on the system board. In each case, consult the system board's User Guide any time the microprocessor is being replaced or upgraded.

The Pentium processor requires the presence of a heat-sinking device and a microprocessor fan unit for cooling purposes. These devices come in many forms, including simple passive heat sinks and fan-cooled, active heat sinks. Figure 4.37 shows both types of cooling systems.

Passive heat sinks are metal slabs with fins that can be clipped onto the microprocessor or glued on the top of the processor with a heat-transmitting adhesive. The fins increase the surface area of the heat sink, allowing it to dissipate heat more rapidly. Active heat sinks include a fan unit to move air across the heat sink. The fan moves the heat away from the heat sink and the microprocessor more rapidly.

ATX-style systems use a power supply that employs a reverse-flow fan that blows cool air from the back of the unit onto the microprocessor. Of course, for this to work properly, the system board must adhere to the ATX form factor and place the microprocessor in the correct position on the system board. Theoretically, this design eliminates the need for special microprocessor cooling fans.

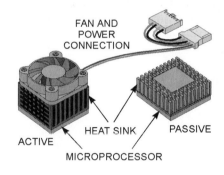

FIGURE 4.37
Microprocessor cooling systems.

Configuring Microprocessors

Most Pentium system boards are designed so that they support a number of different microprocessor types and operating speeds. Table 4.7 gives an example of the types of processors known to operate with a particular Socket 7 system board design. This example supports Pentium and Pentium clone processors from AMD, Cyrix, IBM, and Intel. Two hardware jumpers, labeled J10 and J13, are used to identify the processor type to the system board.

Two other jumpers, labeled J14 and J15, are used to establish the *core-to-bus speed ratio* for the selected processor type. For example, both jumpers must be installed (shorted) to establish the Intel Pentium's 166MHz, 2.5× internal clock multiplier. This setting is necessary to convert the system board's 66MHz clock signal into a 166MHz internal operating signal. These jumpers work in conjunction with the *bus frequency* setting determined by jumper J22. If pins 1/2 and 3/4 are shorted, the bus frequency is set at 50MHz. If pins 3/4 are open, the frequency is shifted to 60MHz. Finally, if pins 1 and 2 are open and 3 and 4 are shorted, the bus frequency is set at 66MHz.

TABLE 4.7

CONFIGURING A SOCKET 7 MICROPROCESSOR

"♦" are the CPUs with Heat Pipe Solution					JP15	JP14	JP13	JP22		JP10
					CORE/BUS Ratio		CPU Type	CPU (BUS) Freq.		CPU Type
CPU Model	Freq.	Freq.	Voltage	Ratio				1,2	3,4	
AMD-SSA/5-75 ABR	75MHz	50MHz	3.52V	1.5x	Open	Open	Open	Short	Short	1,2
AMD-K5-PR90ABQ	90MHz	60MHz	3.52V	1.5x	Open	Open	Open	Short	Open	1,2
AMD-K5-PR100ABR	100MHz	50MHz	3.52V	2x	Open	Short	Open	Short	Short	1,2
♦ AMD-K5-PR133ABQ	133MHz	66MHz	3.52V	2x	Open	Short	Open	Open	Short	1,2
♦ AMD-K5-PR166ABR	166MHz	66MHz	3.52V	2.5x	Short	Short	Open	Open	Short	1,2
♦ AMD-K6-166ALR(1) ●	166MHz	66MHz	2.9/3.3	2.5x	Short	Short	Open	Open	Short	1,2
♦ AMD-K6-200ALR(1) ●	200MHz	66MHz	2.9/3.3	3x	Short	Open	Open	Open	Short	1,2
♦ IBM26 6x86-2V2100GB	100MHz	50MHz	3.3V	2x	Short	Short	Short	Short	Short	2,3
♦ Cyrix 6x86-P150+	120MHz	60MHz	3.52V	2x	Open	Short	Short	Short	Open	2,3
Cyrix 6x86L-P150+(1)	120MHz	60MHz	2.8/3.3	2x	Open	Short	Short	Short	Open	2,3
♦ Cyrix 6x86-P166+	133MHz	66MHz	3.52V	2x	Open	Short	Short	Open	Short	2,3
♦ Cyrix 6x86 MX-PR166(1)●	133MHz	66MHz	2.9/3.3	2x	Open	Short	Open	Open	Short	2,3
♦ Cyrix 6x86 MX-PR200(1)●	166MHz	66MHz	2.9/3.3	2.5x	Short	Short	Open	Open	Short	2,3
Intel Pentium	100MHz	50MHz	3.3V	2x	Open	Short	Open	Short	Short	1,2
Intel Pentium	120MHz	60MHz	3.3V	2x	Open	Short	Open	Short	Open	1,2
Intel Pentium	133MHz	66MHz	3.3V	2x	Open	Short	Open	Open	Short	1,2
♦ Intel Pentium	166MHz	66MHz	3.3V	2.5x	Short	Short	Open	Open	Short	1,2
♦ Intel Pentium	200MHz	66MHz	3.3V	3x	Short	Open	Open	Open	Short	1,2
♦ Intel Pentium-MMX	166MHz	66MHz	3.3V	2.5x	Short	Short	Open	Open	Short	1,2
♦ Intel Pentium-MMX(1)	200MHz	66MHz	2.8/3.3	3x	Short	Open	Open	Open	Short	1,2
♦ Intel Pentium-MMX(1) ●	233MHz	66MHz	2.8/3.3	3.5x	Open	Open	Open	Open	Short	1,2

(1) Dual Supply (split rail) Devices
(2) OMD 11 only supports 50 MHz, 60 MHz and 66 MHz CLK Rate
(3) CPUs with "●" remark will be supported in "L" Ver BIOS

As mentioned earlier, the original Pentium processors ran on 50, 60, or 66MHz external clocks and used internal clock multiplier circuits to operate the microprocessor core at a much faster pace. Newer Pentium versions employ 100, 133, and 200MHz microprocessor/front-side bus clocks. Table 4.8 lists the various Pentium class microprocessors along with their associated microprocessor bus speeds.

TABLE 4.8

PENTIUM CLOCK SPEEDS

Processor Speed	*Microprocessor/Front-Side Bus Clock*
Pentium 75, 100	50MHz
Pentium 90, 120, 150	60MHz
Pentium 100, 133, 166, 200	66MHz
Pentium MMX 166, 200, 233	66MHz
Pentium Pro	66MHz
Celeron	66MHz
Pentium II/233, 333	66MHz
Pentium II/333, 450	100MHz
Pentium III	100MHz
Pentium IIIB/IIIEB	133MHz
Pentium 4	133MHz
K6-2	66MHz
K6-III	100MHz
Duron	200MHz
Athlon	200MHz

In the table, the B notation used with the Pentium III indicates that it is a 133MHz bus version of the microprocessor. Likewise, the EB notation indicates that the device is a Coppermine Pentium version using a 133MHz front-side bus.

Socket 7 systems use a voltage-regulator module to supply special voltage levels for the microprocessor. The module may be designed as a plug-in module so that it can be replaced easily in case of component failure. This is a somewhat common occurrence with voltage-regulator devices. It also allows the system board to be upgraded when a new Pentium device is developed that requires a different voltage level, or a different voltage pairing.

Typically a hardware jumper, identified as JP23 in this example, is used to establish the processor's *core voltage* level, as described in Table 4.9. The default value for the example's core voltage is 3.3V. The group of jumpers labeled JP9 is set to select between single- and dual-processor voltage levels. If pins 1/2 and 3/4 are shorted together, with pins 5/6 and 7/8 open, a single power-supply voltage is produced. Conversely, opening pins 1/2 and 3/4, while pins 5/6 and 7/8 are shorted together, establishes a dual-voltage situation for those microprocessors that require it.

TABLE 4.9

MICROPROCESSOR CORE VOLTAGE LEVELS

JP23 CPU VCORE Voltage Selector					
VOUT	**1-2**	**3-4**	**5-6**	**7-8**	
2.2V	Open	Short	Open	Open	
2.6V	Open	Short	Short	Open	
2.7V	Short	Short	Short	Open	
2.8V	Open	Open	Open	Short	
2.9V	Short	Open	Open	Short	
3.2V	Open	Open	Short	Short	
3.3V	Short	Open	Short	Short	* default
3.5V	Short	Short	Short	Short	

JP9 CPU 3V Selector					
Power	**1-2**	**3-4**	**5-6**	**7-8**	
Single	Short	Short	Open	Open	* default
Dual	Open	Open	Short	Short	

It should be obvious that these variables must be configured correctly for the type of microprocessor actually installed in the system. If the core voltage level is set too high, the microprocessor will probably overheat slowly, or burn out, depending on the amount of overvoltage applied. Conversely, if the voltage level is configured too low for the installed processor, the system will most likely refuse to start.

Likewise, setting the speed-selection jumpers incorrectly can cause the system to think that a different processor is installed in the system. As an example, setting the Core/Bus Ratio (JP15/14), CPU Type (JP13), and Bus Frequency (JP22) jumpers in Table 4.8 to Short/Short/Open/Open/Short would cause the system's BIOS to believe that an AMD K5 – 166 processor is installed. If an AMD K6 – 200 processor were actually installed, the system would still think of it, and report it, as a K5 – 166 processor.

> **TEST TIP**
>
> Be aware of how the system determines what type of microprocessor is installed and what its capabilities are.

RANDOM ACCESS MEMORY

▶ 4.2 Identify the categories of RAM (Random Access Memory) terminology, their locations, and physical characteristics.

The A+ Core Hardware objective 4.2 states that the test taker should be able to "identify the categories of RAM (random access memory) terminology, their locations, and physical characteristics."

Memory Systems

As mentioned in Chapter 1, normally three types of semiconductor memory are found on a typical system board. These include the system's ROM BIOS ICs, the system's RAM memory, and the second-level cache memory unit.

A typical PC system board uses one, or two, 256KB/128KB × 8 ROM chips to hold the system's BIOS firmware. The system's memory map reserves memory locations from F0000h to FFFFFh. These chips contain the firmware routines to handle startup of the system, the change over to disk-based operations, video, and printer output functions, as well as the Power-On Self-Test.

There are basically two types of semiconductor RAM used on system boards: *static RAM* (SRAM) and *dynamic RAM* (DRAM). Although they both perform the same types of functions, the methods they use differ completely. Static RAM stores bits in such a manner that they will remain as long as power to the chip is not interrupted. Dynamic RAM requires periodic refreshing to maintain data, even if electrical power is applied to the chip.

Dynamic RAM stores data bits on rows and columns of IC capacitors. Capacitors lose their charge over time. This is why dynamic RAM devices require data-refreshing operations. Static RAM uses IC transistors to store data and maintain it as long as power is supplied to the chip. Its transistor structure makes SRAM memory much faster than ordinary DRAM. However, it can store only about 25% as much data in a given size as a DRAM device. Therefore, it tends to be more expensive to create large memories with SRAM.

Whether the RAM is made up of static or dynamic RAM devices, all RAM systems have the disadvantage of being volatile. This means that any data stored in RAM will be lost if power to the computer is disrupted for any reason. On the other hand, both types of RAM have the advantage of being fast, with the capability to be written to and read from with equal ease.

Generally, static RAM is used in smaller memory systems, such as cache and video memories, where the added cost of refresh circuitry would increase the cost-per-bit of storage. Cache memory is a special memory structure that works directly with the microprocessor, and video memory is a specialized area that holds information to be displayed onscreen. On the other hand, DRAM is used in larger memory systems, such as the system's main memory, where the extra cost of refresh circuitry is distributed over a greater number of bits and is offset by the reduced operating cost associated with DRAM chips.

Advanced DRAM

Both types of RAM are brought together to create an improved DRAM, referred to as *enhanced DRAM* (EDRAM). By integrating an SRAM component into a DRAM device, a performance improvement of 40% can be gained. An independent write path allows the system to input new data without affecting the operation of the rest of the chip. These devices are used primarily in L2 cache memories.

Another modified DRAM type, referred to as *synchronous DRAM* (SDRAM), employs special internal registers and clock signals to organize data requests from memory. Unlike asynchronous memory modules, SDRAM devices operate in sync with the system clock. After an initial read or write access has been performed on the memory device, additional accesses can be conducted in a high-speed burst mode that operates at one access per clock cycle. This enables the microprocessor to perform other tasks while the data is being organized.

Special internal configurations also speed up the operation of the SDRAM memory. The SDRAM device employs internal interleaving that permits one side of the memory to be accessed while the other half is completing an operation. Because there are two versions of SDRAM (2-clock and 4-clock), you must make certain that the SDRAM type you are using is supported by the system board's chipset.

Extended data out (EDO) memory increases the speed at which RAM operations are conducted by cutting out the 10-nanosecond wait time normally required between issuing memory addresses. This is accomplished by not disabling the data bus pins between bus cycles. EDO is an advanced type of *fast page-mode DRAM* also referred to as *hyper page-mode DRAM*. The advantage of EDO DRAM is encountered when multiple sequential memory accesses are performed. By not turning off the data pin, each successive access after the first access is accomplished in two clock cycles rather than three.

> **TEST TIP**
>
> Know the difference between EDO and fast page-mode DRAM.

Special memory devices also have been designed to optimize video memory–related activities. Among these are *video RAM* (VRAM) and *Windows RAM* (WRAM). In typical DRAM devices, access to the data stored inside is shared between the system microprocessor and the video controller. The microprocessor accesses the RAM to update the data in it and to keep it refreshed. The video controller moves data out of the memory to become screen information. Normally, both devices must access the data through the same data bus. VRAM employs a special dual-port access system to speed up video operations. WRAM, a special version of VRAM, is optimized to transfer blocks of data at a time. This allows it to operate at speeds of up to 150% of typical VRAM and costs up to 20% less.

T E S T   TIP

Remember what type of applications VRAM and WRAM are used in.

A company named Rambus has designed a proprietary DRAM memory technology that promises very high data delivery speeds. The technology has been given a variety of different names that include Rambus DRAM (RDRAM), direct Rambus DRAM (DRDRAM), and Rambus inline memory module (RIMM). The RIMM reference applies to a special 184-pin memory module designed to hold the Rambus devices. Figure 4.38 shows that RIMMs look similar to DIMMS. However, their high-speed transfer modes generate considerably more heat than normal DIMMs. Therefore, RIMM modules include an aluminum heat shield, referred to as a heat spreader, to protect the chips from overheating.

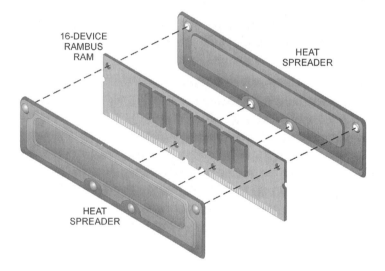

FIGURE 4.38
RIMM modules.

The Rambus technology employs a special, internal 16-bit data channel that operates in conjunction with a 400MHz clock. The 16-bit channel permits the device to operate at much higher speeds than more conventional 64-bit buses. Although Intel had expressed some interest in exploring the technology for its future system board designs, the fact that it is a proprietary standard may hinder its acceptance in the market.

RIMMs look similar to DIMMs, but have a different pin count. RIMMs transfer data in 16-bit chunks. The faster access and transfer speed generates more heat.

SRAM

Like DRAM, SRAM is available in a number of different types. Many of the memory organization techniques described for DRAM also are implemented in SRAM.

◆ **Asynchronous SRAM** is standard SRAM and delivers data from the memory to the microprocessor and returns it to the cache in one clock cycle.

◆ **Synchronous SRAM** uses special clock signals and buffer storage to deliver data to the CPU in one clock cycle after the first cycle. The first address is stored and used to retrieve the data while the next address is on its way to the cache.

◆ **Pipeline SRAM** uses three clock cycles to fetch the first data and then accesses addresses within the selected page on each clock cycle.

◆ **Burst-mode SRAM** loads a number of consecutive data locations from the cache, over several clock cycles, based on a single address from the microprocessor.

In digital electronics terms, a buffer is a holding area for data shared by devices that operate at different speeds or have different priorities. These devices permit a memory module to operate without the delays that other devices impose. Some types of SDRAM memory modules contain buffer registers directly on the module. The buffer registers hold and retransmit the data signals through the memory chips.

The holding aspect permits the module to coordinate transfers with the outside system. The retransmission factor lowers the signal drain on the host system and enables the memory module to hold more memory chips. Registered and unbuffered memory modules cannot be mixed. The design of the chipset's memory controller dictates which types of memory the computer can use.

Memory Overhead

It has already been mentioned that the DRAM devices, commonly used for the system's RAM, require periodic refreshing of their data. Some refreshing is performed just by regular reading and writing of the memory by the system. Additional circuitry must be used, however, to ensure that every bit in the memory is refreshed within the allotted timeframe. In addition to the circuitry, the reading and writing times used for refreshing must be taken into account when designing the system.

Another design factor associated with RAM is data error detection. A single, incorrect bit can shut down the entire system instantly. With bits constantly moving in and out of RAM, it is crucial that all the bits be transferred correctly. The most popular form of error detection in PC compatibles is *parity checking*. In this methodology, an extra bit is added to each word in RAM and checked each time it is used. Like refreshing, parity checking requires additional circuitry and memory overhead to operate.

DRAM Refresh

Dynamic RAM devices require that data stored in them be refreshed, or rewritten, periodically to keep it from fading away. As a matter of fact, each bit in the DRAM must be refreshed at least once every two milliseconds or the data will dissipate. Because it cannot be assumed that each bit in the memory will be accessed during the normal operation of the system (within the timeframe allotted), the need to constantly refresh the data in the DRAM requires special circuitry to perform this function.

The extra circuitry and inconvenience associated with refreshing may initially make DRAM memory seem like a distant second choice behind static RAM. Because of the simplicity of DRAM's internal structure, however, the bit-storage capacity of a DRAM chip is much greater than that of a similar static RAM chip, and it offers a much lower rate of power consumption. Both of these factors contribute to making DRAM memory the economical choice in certain RAM memory systems—even in light of the extra circuitry necessary for refreshing.

Parity Checking

Parity checking is a simple self-test used to detect RAM read-back errors. When a data byte is being stored in memory, the occurrences of logic 1s in the byte are added together by the parity generator/ checker circuit. The circuit produces a parity bit that is added to, and stored along with, the data byte. Therefore, the data byte becomes a 9-bit word. Whenever the data word is read back from the memory, the parity bit is reapplied to the parity generator and recalculated.

The recalculated parity value is then compared to the original parity value stored in memory. If the values do not match, a parity-error condition occurs and an error message is generated. Traditionally, there are two approaches to generating parity bits: The parity bit may be generated so that the total number of 1 bits equals an even number (even parity), or equals an odd number (odd parity).

To enable parity checking, an additional ninth bit is added to each byte stored in DRAM. On older systems, an extra memory chip was included with each bank of DRAM. In newer units, the extra storage is built in to the SIMM and DIMM modules. Whether a particular system employs parity check depends on its chipset. Many newer chipsets have moved away from using parity checking altogether. In these cases, SIMMs and DIMMs with parity capability can be used, but the parity function will not function. In Pentium systems, the system board's User Guide or the BIOS' Extended CMOS Setup screen should be consulted to determine whether parity is supported. If so, the parity function can be enabled through this screen.

Figure 4.39 illustrates how the system's RAM and parity checking circuits work together.

> **TEST TIP**
>
> Know that parity is a method of checking stored data for errors by adding an additional bit to it when it is read from memory.

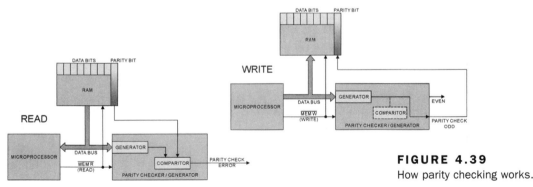

FIGURE 4.39
How parity checking works.

When a parity error occurs, a non-maskable interrupt (NMI) signal is co-generated in the system, causing the BIOS to execute its NMI handler routine. This routine normally places a parity error message onscreen, along with an option to shut down the system, or continue.

> **TEST TIP**
>
> Be aware of the types of problems that can create an NMI error and what the consequences of these errors are.

Advanced Memory Structures

As the operating speeds of microcomputers have continued to increase, it has become increasingly necessary to develop new memory strategies to keep pace with the other parts of the system. Some of these methods, such as developing faster DRAM chips, or including wait states in the memory-access cycles, are very fundamental in nature. However, these methods do not allow the entire system to operate at its full potential. Other, more elaborate memory-management schemes have been employed on faster computers to maximize their overall performance.

Cache Memory

One way to increase the memory-access speed of a computer is called *caching*. This memory-management method assumes that most memory accesses are made within a limited block of addresses. Therefore, if the contents of these addresses are relocated into a special section of high-speed SRAM, the microprocessor could access these locations without requiring any wait states.

Cache memory is normally small to keep the cost of the system as low as possible. It also is very fast, however, even in comparison to fast DRAM devices.

Cache memory operations require a great deal of intelligent circuitry to operate and monitor the cache effectively. The cache controller circuitry must monitor the microprocessor's memory-access instructions to determine whether the specified data is stored in the cache. If the information is in the cache, the control circuitry can present it to the microprocessor without incurring any wait states. This is referred to as a hit. If the information is not located in the cache, the access is passed on to the system's RAM and it is declared a miss.

The primary objective of the cache memory's control system is to maximize the ratio of hits to total accesses (hit rate), so that the majority of memory accesses are performed without wait states. One way to do this is to make the cache memory area as large as possible (thus raising the possibility of the desired information being in the cache). However, the relative cost, energy consumption, and physical size of SRAM devices work against this technique. Practical sizes for cache memories run between 16KB–512KB.

There are two basic ways to write updated information into the cache. The first is to write data into the cache and the main memory at the same time. This is referred to as write-thru cache. This method tends to be slow because the microprocessor has to wait for the slow DRAM access to be completed. The second method is known as write-back cache. A write-back cache holds the data in the cache until the system has a quiet time and then writes it into the main memory.

The Intel Pentium has a built-in first-level cache that can be used for both instructions and data. The internal cache is divided into four 2KB blocks containing 128 sets of 16-byte lines each. Control of the internal cache is handled directly by the microprocessor. The first-level cache also is known as an *L1 cache*. However, many system boards extend the caching capability of the microprocessor by adding an external, second-level 256KB/512KB memory cache. Like the L1 cache, the second-level cache also may be referred to as an *L2 cache*. Figure 4.40 depicts an external L2 cache memory system.

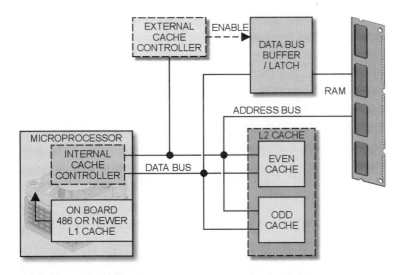

FIGURE 4.40
Controlling an external cache.

Memory Paging and Interleaving

There are also other commonly used ways to organize RAM memory so that it can be accessed more efficiently. Typically, memory accesses occur in two fashions: instruction fetches (which are generally sequential), and operand accesses (which tend to be random). Paging and interleaving memory schemes are designed to take advantage of the sequential nature of instruction fetches from memory.

Figure 4.41 illustrates the basic idea of paged-mode DRAM operations. Special memory devices called page-mode (or static-column) RAM are required for memory-paging structures. In these memory devices, data is organized into groups of rows and columns called pages. When a row access is made in the device, it is possible to access other column addresses within the same row without precharging its row address strobe (RAS) line. This feature produces access times that are half that of normal DRAM memories. Fast page-mode RAM is a quicker version of page-mode RAM, having improved column address strobe (CAS) access speed.

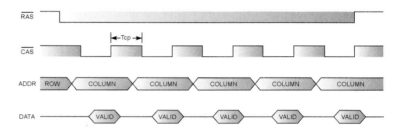

FIGURE 4.41
Page-mode DRAM operation.

Figure 4.42 depicts the operating principal behind memory interleaving. Typical interleaving schemes divide the memory into two banks of RAM with one bank storing even addresses and the other storing odd addresses.

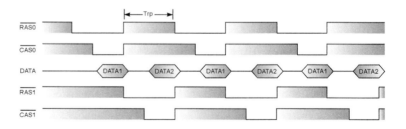

FIGURE 4.42
Memory interleaving.

The RAS signals of the two banks overlap so that the time required to precharge one bank's RAS line is used for the active RAS time of the other bank. Therefore, there should never be a precharge time for either bank, so long as the accesses continue to be sequential. If a nonsequential access occurs, a miss is encountered and a wait state must be inserted in the timing. If the memory is organized into two banks, the operation is referred to as two-way interleaving. It also is common to organize the memory into four equal-sized banks. This organization effectively doubles the average 0-wait state hit space in the memory.

SIMMs, DIMMs, and Banks

As mentioned in Chapter 1, older system boards employed banks of discrete RAM ICs in dual in-line pin (DIP) sockets. Most of these system boards arranged nine pieces of $1 \times 256KB$ DRAM chips in the first two banks (0 and 1) and nine pieces of $1 \times 64KB$ chips in banks two and three. The two banks of 256KB chips provided a total of 512KB of storage. (The ninth chip of each bank supplied a parity bit for error checking.)

The two banks of 64KB chips extended the RAM memory capacity out to the full 640KB. As with the 256KB chips, the ninth bit was for parity.

Some system boards used two $4 \times 256KB$ chips with a $1 \times 256KB$ chip to create each of the first two banks. In any event, the system would typically run with one bank installed, two banks installed, or all the banks installed. Bank 0 had to be filled first, followed by bank 1, and then all four.

Early AT-clone system boards moved the system's RAM to 30-pin single in-line pin (SIP) modules, and further refinements produced snap-in *single in-line memory modules* (SIMMs) and *dual in-line memory modules* (DIMMs). Like the SIP, the SIMM and DIMM units mount vertically on the system board. Instead of using a pin-and-socket arrangement, however, both use special snap-in sockets that support the module firmly. SIMMs and DIMMs also are keyed so that they cannot be plugged in backward. SIMMs are available in 30-pin and 72-pin versions; DIMMs are larger 168-pin boards.

> **TEST TIP**
>
> Know how many pins SIMMs and DIMMS have.

SIMM and DIMM sockets are quite distinctive in that they are normally arranged side by side. However, they can be located anywhere on the system board. SIMMs typically come in 8-bit or 32-bit bit data-storage configurations. The 8-bit modules must be arranged in banks to match the data bus size of the system's microprocessor. To work effectively with a 32-bit microprocessor, a bank of four 8-bit SIMMs would need to be used. Conversely, a single 32-bit SIMM could do the same job.

DIMMs, on the other hand, typically come in 32-bit and 64-bit bus widths to service more powerful microprocessors. Like the SIMMs, they must be arranged properly to fit the size of the system's data bus. In both cases, the modules can be accessed in smaller 8- and 16-bit segments. SIMMs and DIMMs also come in 9-, 36-, and 72-bit versions that include parity checking bits for each byte of storage.

(For example, a 36-bit SIMM provides 32 data bits and 4 parity bits—one for each byte of data.)

PCs are typically sold with less than their full RAM capacity. This enables users to purchase a less-expensive computer to fit their individual needs and yet retain the option to install more RAM if future applications call for it. SIMM and DIMM sizes are typically specified in an a-by-b format. For example, a 2×32 SIMM specification indicates that it is a dual, nonparity, 32-bit (4-byte) device. In this scheme, the capacity is derived by multiplying the two numbers and then dividing by 8 (or 9 for parity chips). Figure 4.43 depicts typical upgrade strategies using SIMM and DIMM modules to increase the memory capabilities of a system board.

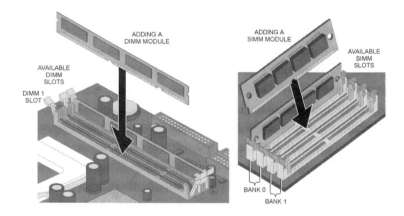

FIGURE 4.43
DIP, SIP, SIMM, and DIMM memory modules.

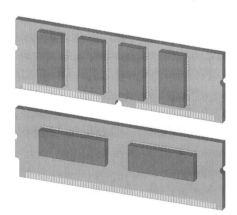

FIGURE 4.44
Small outline DIMMs.

A special form factor DIMM, called the small outline DIMM (SO DIMM) has been developed for use in notebook computers. The basic difference between SO DIMMs and regular DIMMs is that the SO DIMM is significantly smaller than the standard DIMM so that it takes up less space in notebook computers. Figure 4.44 depicts a 72-pin and a 144-pin SO DIMM. The 72-pin SO DIMM has a 32-bit data bus while the 144-pin version is 64 bits wide.

Another important factor to consider when dealing with RAM is its speed. Manufacturers mark RAM devices with speed information. DRAM modules are marked with a numbering system that indicates the number of clock cycles required for the initial read operation, followed by information about the number of reads and cycles required to move a burst of data. As an example, a fast page-mode DRAM marked as 6-3-3-3 requires 6 cycles for the initial read and 3 cycles for each of 3 successive reads. This moves an entire 4-byte block of data. EDO and FPM can operate with bus speeds up to 66MHz.

SDRAM devices are marked a little differently. Because they are designed to run synchronously with the system clock and use no wit states, a marking of 3:3:3 at 100MHz on an SDRAM module specifies the following:

◆ The CAS signal setup time is 3 bus cycles.

◆ The RAS to CAS change over time is 3 cycles.

◆ The RAS signal setup time is 3 clock cycles.

The bus speed is specified in MHz. These memory modules have been produced in six common specifications so far:

◆ PC66 (66MHz or 15 nanoseconds)

◆ PC83 (83MHz or 12 nanoseconds)

◆ PC100 (100MHz or 10 nanoseconds)

◆ PC133 (133MHz or 8 nanoseconds)

◆ PC150 (150MHz or 4.5 nanoseconds)

◆ PC166 (166MHz or 4 nanoseconds)

The PC66 and PC83 specification were the first versions produced using this system. However, they never really gained widespread acceptance. On the other hand, the PC100 and PC133 versions did gain acceptance and are widely available today. The PC150 and PC166 versions also are common.

Continued advancements in memory module design have made the MHz and CAS setup time ratings obsolete. Onboard buffering and advanced access strategies have made these measurements inconsequential. Instead, memory performance is being measured by total data throughput (also referred to as bandwidth) and is being measured in terms of gigabytes per second (GBps). As an example, some of the new standard specifications include the following:

◆ PC1600 (1.6GBps/200MHz/2:2:2)

◆ PC2100 (2.1GBps/266MHz/2:3:3)

◆ PC2600 (2.6GBps/333MHz/3:3:3)

◆ PC3200 (3.2GBps/400MHz/3:3:3)

The system board's documentation will provide information about the types of devices it can use and their speed ratings. It is important to install RAM that is compatible with the bus speed the system is running. Normally, installing RAM that is rated faster than the bus speed will not cause problems. However, installing slower RAM or mixing RAM speed ratings in a system will cause the system to not start or to periodically lock up.

CMOS RAM

▶ 4.4 Identify the purpose of CMOS (complementary metal-oxide semiconductor), what it contains, and how to change its basic parameters.

The A+ Core Hardware objective 4.4 states that the test taker should be able to "identify the purpose of CMOS (complementary metal-oxide semiconductor), what it contains, and how to change its basic parameters."

CMOS Setup Utilities

During the POST process, the BIOS Setup routines can be entered by pressing the Del key. In other BIOS types, the Ctrl+Alt+Esc key combination also can be used to access the Setup utilities. The CMOS Setup utility's Main Menu screen, similar to the one depicted in Figure 4.45, appears whenever the CMOS Setup utility is engaged. This menu enables the user to select setup functions and exit choices. The most used entries include the *Standard CMOS Setup*, BIOS Features Setup, and Chipset Features Setup options. Selecting these, or any of the other Main Menu options, will lead into a corresponding submenu.

Other typical menu items include Power Management, PnP/PCI Configuration, Integrated Peripherals Control, and Password Maintenance Services. A given CMOS Setup utility may contain the same options as those listed in the sample, options that perform the same functions under a different name, or it may not contain some options at all. This example also offers two IDE HDD-related utilities, two options for starting with default system values, and two exit options.

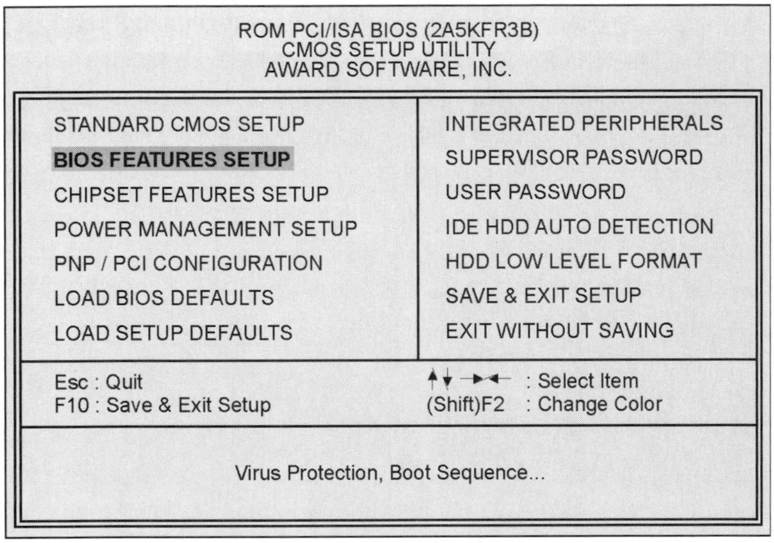

```
            ROM PCI/ISA BIOS (2A5KFR3B)
               CMOS SETUP UTILITY
              AWARD SOFTWARE, INC.

  STANDARD CMOS SETUP          INTEGRATED PERIPHERALS

  BIOS FEATURES SETUP          SUPERVISOR PASSWORD

  CHIPSET FEATURES SETUP       USER PASSWORD

  POWER MANAGEMENT SETUP       IDE HDD AUTO DETECTION

  PNP / PCI CONFIGURATION      HDD LOW LEVEL FORMAT

  LOAD BIOS DEFAULTS           SAVE & EXIT SETUP

  LOAD SETUP DEFAULTS          EXIT WITHOUT SAVING

  Esc : Quit                   ↑↓ →←   : Select Item
  F10 : Save & Exit Setup      (Shift)F2 : Change Color

            Virus Protection, Boot Sequence...
```

FIGURE 4.45
CMOS Main Menu screen.

Standard CMOS Setup Functions

Figure 4.46 depicts standard CMOS Setup screens from various manufacturers. They all provide the same basic information. They can be used to set the system clock/calendar, establish disk drive parameters and video display type, and specify which types of errors will halt the system during the POST.

> **WARNING**
>
> **Set Values with Caution**   The settings in these menus allow the system to be configured and optimized for specific functions and devices. The default values are generally recommended for normal operation. Because incorrect setup values can cause the system to fail, you should only change setup values that really need to be changed. If changes are made that disable the system, pressing the Insert key on reset will override the settings and start the system with default values.

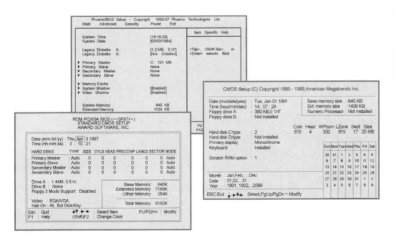

FIGURE 4.46
Standard CMOS Setup screens.

The BIOS uses military time settings (that is 13:00:00 = 1 p.m.). The PgUp and PgDn keys are used to change the setting after it has been selected using the arrow keys. This BIOS version supports daylight savings time by adding an hour when daylight saving time begins and subtracts it when standard time returns.

Current BIOSs typically support 360KB, 720KB, 1.2MB, 1.44MB, and 2.88MB floppy drive formats. The other area in this screen that may require some effort to set up is the HDD Parameters section. All BIOSs come with a list of hard drive types that they can support directly. However, they also provide a position for user-definable drive settings. Historically, this has been referred to as the "Type 47" entry, but this entry may be located at any number in the list.

Newer BIOSs possess *Auto Detect* options to detect the type of hard drives installed in the system and automatically load their parameters into CMOS. Systems with Enhanced IDE capabilities support up to four IDE drives. However, the CMOS does not typically display information about CD-ROM drives, or SCSI devices.

When the Auto Detect selection is chosen, the BIOS attempts to detect IDE devices in the system during the POST process and to determine the specifications and optimum operating mode for those devices. The drive specifications also can be selected from a built-in list of drive parameters, or they can be entered directly using the User option at the end of the list.

Four translation modes can be selected for each drive type: auto, normal, large, and LBA. In auto mode, the BIOS determines the best operating mode for the drive. In normal mode, the BIOS supports a maximum Cyl/Hds/Sec (CHS) setting of 1024/16/63. For larger drives (above 1,024 cylinders or 528MB), the large and LBA modes are used. The Large option can be used with large drives that do not support logical block addressing (LBA) techniques. For those drives that do, the LBA mode should be selected. In this mode, the IDE controller converts the sector/head/cylinder address into a physical block address that improves data throughput. Care should be taken when changing this BIOS setting because data loss may occur.

Similarly, this BIOS supports standard EGA/VGA formats, as well as older 40- and 80-column CGA and monochrome formats. In the case of errors detected during the POST process, the BIOS can be

TEST TIP

Know that the LBA mode for SCSI and IDE disk drives must be enabled in the CMOS to support hard drive sizes over 528MB.

TEST TIP

Be aware that changing the translation mode setting for an existing drive may result in the loss of all data.

set up to halt on different types of errors, or to ignore them and continue the boot-up process. These settings include the following:

◆ **No Errors.** The POST does not stop for any errors.

◆ **All Errors.** The POST stops for all detected errors and prompts the user for corrective action.

◆ **A series of "All But" options.** The POST stops for all errors except those selected (such as all but disk or keyboard errors).

Finally, the screen displays the system's memory usage. The values displayed are derived from the POST process and cannot be changed through the menu. The BIOS displays the system's total detected RAM, base memory, extended memory, and other memory (between the 640KB and 1MB marks). In most CMOS displays, the total memory does not equal the summation of the base and extended memory. This is because the BIOS reserves 384KB for shadowing purposes.

The BIOS Features Setup Screen

The BIOS Features Setup screen, shown in Figure 4.47, provides access to options that extend the standard ISA BIOS functions. This BIOS example includes a built-in virus warning utility that produces a warning message whenever a program tries to write to the boot sector of an HDD partition table. This function should be enabled for normal operations. However, it should be turned off when conducting an upgrade to the operating system. The built-in virus warning utility checks the drive's boot sector for changes. The changes that the new operating system will attempt to make to the boot sector will be interpreted as a virus and the utility will act to prevent the upgrade from occurring. If a warning message is displayed under normal circumstances, a full-feature anti-virus utility should be run on the system.

TEST TIP

Be aware that you should turn off any BIOS antivirus protection settings when changing operating systems.

The Feature Setup screen is used to configure different boot-up options. These options include establishing the system's boot-up sequence. The sequence can be set so that the system checks the floppy drive for a boot sector first, or so that it checks the hard drive without checking the floppy drive.

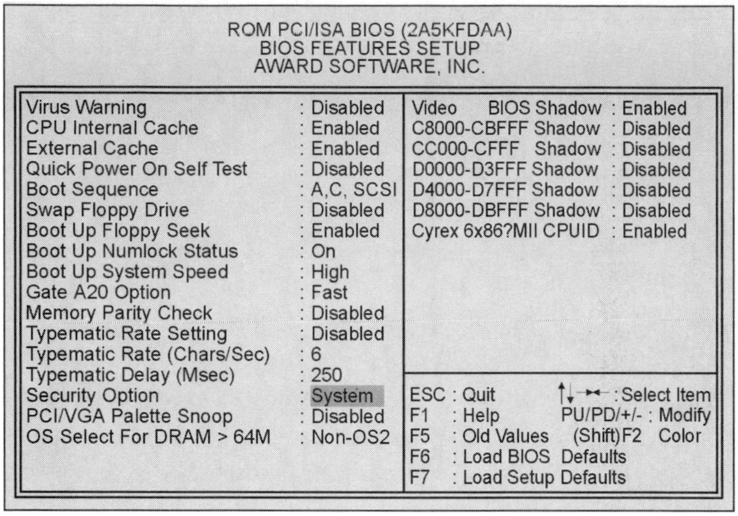

FIGURE 4.47
BIOS Features screen.

```
                    ROM PCI/ISA BIOS (2A5KFDAA)
                        BIOS FEATURES SETUP
                       AWARD SOFTWARE, INC.

 Virus Warning              : Disabled    Video    BIOS Shadow : Enabled
 CPU Internal Cache         : Enabled     C8000-CBFFF Shadow  : Disabled
 External Cache             : Enabled     CC000-CFFF  Shadow  : Disabled
 Quick Power On Self Test   : Disabled    D0000-D3FFF Shadow  : Disabled
 Boot Sequence              : A,C, SCSI   D4000-D7FFF Shadow  : Disabled
 Swap Floppy Drive          : Disabled    D8000-DBFFF Shadow  : Disabled
 Boot Up Floppy Seek        : Enabled     Cyrex 6x86?MII CPUID : Enabled
 Boot Up Numlock Status     : On
 Boot Up System Speed       : High
 Gate A20 Option            : Fast
 Memory Parity Check        : Disabled
 Typematic Rate Setting     : Disabled
 Typematic Rate (Chars/Sec) : 6
 Typematic Delay (Msec)     : 250
 Security Option            : System     ESC : Quit        ↑↓←→ : Select Item
 PCI/VGA Palette Snoop      : Disabled   F1  : Help        PU/PD/+/- : Modify
 OS Select For DRAM > 64M   : Non-OS2    F5  : Old Values   (Shift)F2  Color
                                         F6  : Load BIOS  Defaults
                                         F7  : Load Setup Defaults
```

Other boot-up options include Floppy Drive Seek, Numlock Status, and System Speed settings. The Swap Floppy Drive option can be enabled to route commands for logical drive A: to physical drive B:. This option can be used to isolate FDD problems in dual-drive units. Likewise, the Drive A: option should be enabled if the system cannot boot to the hard-disk drive.

The system board's cache memory organization is displayed in the screen's External Cache Memory field. The CMOS provides options for controlling the system's A20 line and parity checking functions. The operation of the A20 line is connected to the system's change-over from real mode to protected mode and back. When set to the Fast Mode, the chipset controls the operation of the system's A20 line. If the Normal Mode setting is selected, the keyboard controller circuitry controls the Gate A20 function, which the operating system uses to enable the real-mode changeover. The system's parity checking function is used to check for corruption in the contents of data read from DRAM memory.

The operation of the keyboard can be modified from this screen. Typematic Action refers to the keyboard's capability to reproduce characters when a key is held down for a period of time. This action is governed by two parameters set in the BIOS Features screen: Typematic Rate and Typematic Delay. Typematic Rate refers to the rate at which characters will be repeated when the key is held down; Typematic Delay defines the amount of time between the initial pressing of the key and when the repeating action begins. Typematic Action is normally enabled and values of 6 characters/second and 250 milliseconds are typical for these settings.

The system's Shadow feature is controlled through the BIOS Features screen. Shadowing can be used to copy various system firmware routines into high memory. This allows the system to read firmware from a 16-bit or 32-bit data bus rather than the normal 8-bit PC-compatible X-bus. This technique speeds up firmware read operations but reduces the high-memory space available for loading device drivers. Shadowing should be enabled for individual sections of memory as needed.

Chipset Features Setup Functions

The Chipset Features screen, depicted in Figure 4.48, contains advanced setting information that system designers and service personnel use to optimize the chipset.

```
                   ROM PCI/ISA BIOS (2A5KFR3B)
                     CHIPSET FEATURES SETUP
                      AWARD SOFTWARE, INC.

 Auto Configuration       : Enabled    Word Merge           : Enabled
 AT Bus Clock             : CLK2/4     Byte Merge           : Disabled
 Asysc. SRAM Write WS     : X-3-3-3    Fast Back-to-Back    : Disabled
 Asysc. SRAM Read WS      : X-3-3-3    PCI Write Burst      : Enabled
 EDO Read WS              : X-3-3-3    SDRAM Access Timing  : Normal
 Page Mode Read WS        : X-3-3-3    SDRAM CAS Latency    : 3
 DRAM Write WS            : X-2-2-2    TAG [10-8] Config    : Default
 CPU to DRAM Page Mode    : Disabled
 DRAM Refresh Period      : 60 us
 DRAM Data Integrity Mode : Parity
 Pipelined Function       : Disabled
 16 Bit ISA I/O Command WS  : 2 Wait
 16 Bit ISA Mem Command WS: 2 Wait
 Local Memory 15-16M      : Enabled
 Passive Release          : Enabled
 ISA Line Buffer          : Enabled   ESC : Quit       ↑↓→←: Select Item
 Delay Transaction        : Enabled   F1  : Help       PU/PD/+/- : Modify
 Primary Frame Buffer     : 2 MB      F5  : Old Values    (Shift)F2 : Color
 VGA Frame Buffer         : Enabled   F6  : Load BIOS Defaults
 Linear Merge             : Enabled   F7  : Load Setup Defaults
```

FIGURE 4.48
Chipset Features Setup screen.

The Auto Configuration option selects predetermined optimal values for the chipset to start with. When this feature is enabled, many of the screen's fields are not available to the user. When this setting is disabled, the chipset's setup parameters are obtained from the system's CMOS RAM. Many of the system's memory configuration parameters are established in this screen.

These parameters include wait-state timing for asynchronous SRAM read and writes, as well as EDO and page-mode RAM reads. Wait-state settings for slower ISA I/O and memory devices also can be configured in this screen (16-bit ISA Memory and I/O Command WS options). The Local Memory 15-16M option sets up mapping in the chipset to shift slower ISA device memory into faster local bus memory to increase system performance.

Special DRAM paging operations can be enabled in the Chipset Features screen. When this option is disabled, the chipset's memory controller closes the DRAM page after each access. When enabled, it holds the page open until the next access occurs. DRAM Refresh period and Data Integrity functions also are established here. This particular chipset features both parity-error checking and *error-checking and -correcting* (ECC) error-handling modes. ECC is a way to check data that employs a mathematical algorithm that is used to not only detect errors, but also to regenerate the correct data in case of a failure.

Access to the system buses is also controlled through the Chipset Features screen. The sample chipset uses internal buffers to control the flow of information between the system's different buses. The ISA line buffer, primary frame buffer, and VGA frame buffer are manipulated by the chipset for speed-matching purposes. When the Passive Release option is enabled, the system's microprocessor can access the DRAM during passive release periods. If not, only a PCI bus master can access the local memory.

Other options allow bytes on the data bus to be merged. Merge options include Linear Merge, Word Merge, and Byte Merge. The chipset's memory controller checks the system's address bus enable lines to determine whether items on the data bus can be used as a single unit.

Finally, the Chipset Features screen supports three fast write modes. These are the Fast Back-to-Back Write, PCI Write Burst, and M1 Linear Burst modes. When enabled, these modes allow the system to conduct consecutive PCI write cycles in fast or burst fashions.

The sample BIOS features PnP capability that makes adding options to the system more automatic. PCI devices feature PnP operation. They are questioned by the system during boot up, or when they are plugged into the system, to determine what their system resource requirements are. These requirements are compared to a listing of devices already in the systems and necessary system resources such as IRQ and DMA channels are allocated for them.

PnP/PCI Configuration Functions

The BIOS holds information about the system's resource allocations and supplies it to the operating system as required. Figure 4.49 shows the PCI Configuration screen from the sample CMOS Setup utility. The operating system must be PnP-compatible to achieve the full benefits of the PnP BIOS. In most newer PCs, the standard operating system is Windows 9x or Windows 2000, which are both PnP compliant.

```
                    ROM PCI/ISA BIOS (P155TVP4)
                         PNP AND PCI SETUP
                       AWARD SOFTWARE, INC.

Slot 1 (Right) IRQ   : Auto       DMA 1 Used By ISA      : No/ICU
Slot 2 IRQ           : Auto       DMA 3 Used By ISA      : No/ICU
Slot 3 IRQ           : Auto       DMA 5 Used By ISA      : No/ICU
Slot 4 IRQ           : Auto
PCI Latency Timer    : 32 PCI Clock   ISA MEM Block BASE : No/ICU

                                  NCR SCSI BIOS          : Auto
IRQ 3  Used By ISA  : No/ICU      USB Function           : Disabled
IRQ 4  Used By ISA  : No/ICU
IRQ 5  Used By ISA  : No/ICU
IRQ 6  Used By ISA  : No/ICU
IRQ 7  Used By ISA  : No/ICU
IRQ 8  Used By ISA  : No/ICU
IRQ 9  Used By ISA  : No/ICU
IRQ 10 Used By ISA  : No/ICU
IRQ 11 Used By ISA  : No/ICU
IRQ 12 Used By ISA  : No/ICU      ESC  : Quit      ↑↓←→      : Select Item
IRQ 13 Used By ISA  : No/ICU      F1   : Help      PU/PD/+/- : Modify
IRQ 14 Used By ISA  : No/ICU      F5   : Old Values  (Shift) F2 : Color
IRQ 15 Used By ISA  : No/ICU      F6   : Load BIOS Defaults
                                  F7   : Load Setup Defaults
```

FIGURE 4.49
PnP/PCI Configuration Options screen.

This CMOS utility can automatically configure all PnP devices if the auto mode is enabled. Under this condition, the system's IRQ and DMA assignment fields disappear as the BIOS assigns them to installed devices. When the configuration process is performed manually, each resource can be assigned as either a legacy device or a PnP/PCI device. The legacy device is one that is compatible with the original ISA slot and requires specific resource settings. The PnP/PCI device must be compliant with the PnP specification.

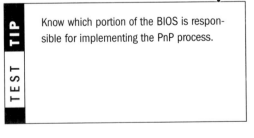

TEST TIP

Know which portion of the BIOS is responsible for implementing the PnP process.

With this chipset, the system board's IDE channels are coordinated with the operation of the PCI bus. The PCI IRQ Map To function enables the user to establish the PCI IRQ mapping for the system. Because the PCI interface in the sample chipset has two channels, it requires two interrupt services. The primary and secondary IDE interrupt fields default to values appropriate for two PCI IDE channels. The primary channel has a lower interrupt number than the secondary channel. Normally, ISA interrupts reserved for IDE channels are IRQ14 for the primary channel and IRQ15 for the secondary channel.

The secondary IDE channel can be deactivated through the PCI IDE Second Channel option. This setting is usually disabled so that an add-on IDE host adapter card can be added to the system. Only the secondary onboard IDE channel is disabled by this setting. The type of action required to trigger the interrupt also can be established in this screen. The PCI IRQ Activated By option is normally set to Level unless a device that requires an ISA-compatible, edge-triggered interrupt is added to the system.

Integrated Peripherals Setup Functions

In most Pentium-based systems, the standard I/O functions of the multi-I/O card have been integrated into the system board. In these systems, the BIOS' Integrated Peripherals screen, depicted in Figure 4.50, provides configuration and enabling settings for the system board's IDE drive connections, floppy disk drive controller, onboard UARTs, and onboard parallel port.

The Integrated Peripherals screen is used to enable the onboard IDE controller. As mentioned earlier, the second IDE channel can be enabled or disabled independently of the first channel, provided that the controller has been enabled. Any of the four possible devices attached to the interface can be configured for master or slave operation.

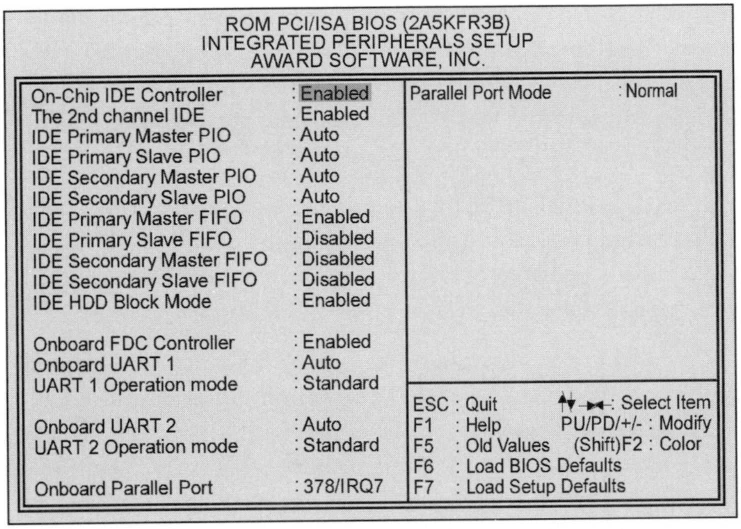

```
        ROM PCI/ISA BIOS (2A5KFR3B)
       INTEGRATED PERIPHERALS SETUP
           AWARD SOFTWARE, INC.

On-Chip IDE Controller    : Enabled   Parallel Port Mode       : Normal
The 2nd channel IDE       : Enabled
IDE Primary Master PIO    : Auto
IDE Primary Slave PIO     : Auto
IDE Secondary Master PIO  : Auto
IDE Secondary Slave PIO   : Auto
IDE Primary Master FIFO   : Enabled
IDE Primary Slave FIFO    : Disabled
IDE Secondary Master FIFO : Disabled
IDE Secondary Slave FIFO  : Disabled
IDE HDD Block Mode        : Enabled

Onboard FDC Controller    : Enabled
Onboard UART 1            : Auto
UART 1 Operation mode     : Standard
                                     ESC : Quit        ↑↓ ←→: Select Item
Onboard UART 2            : Auto     F1  : Help       PU/PD/+/- : Modify
UART 2 Operation mode     : Standard F5  : Old Values  (Shift)F2 : Color
                                     F6  : Load BIOS Defaults
Onboard Parallel Port     : 378/IRQ7 F7  : Load Setup Defaults
```

FIGURE 4.50
Integrated Peripherals screen.

Each IDE device also can be enabled for *programmed input/output* (PIO) modes. The PIO field enables the user to select any of four PIO modes (0–4) for each device. The PIO mode determines how fast data will be transferred between the drive and the system. The performance level of the device typically increases with each higher mode value.

In mode 0, the transfer rate is set at 3.3MBps with a 600-nanosecond (ns) cycle time. Mode 1 steps up to 5.2MBps with a 3.3ns cycle time. Mode 2 improves to 8.3MBps using a 240ns cycle time. Most of the faster drives support PIO modes 3 and 4 through the ATA-2 specification. These modes use 11.1MBps with a 180ns cycle time and 16.6MBps using a 120ns cycle time, respectively. These modes require that the IDE port be located on a local bus, such as a PCI bus.

If the Auto Mode option is selected, the system determines which mode is best suited for each device. If FIFO operation is selected, the system establishes special FIFO buffers for each device to speed up data flow between the device and the system.

The IDE HDD Block Mode selection should be set to Enabled for most new hard drives. This setting, also referred to as Large Block Transfer, Multiple Command, and Multiple-Sector Read/Write mode, supports LBA disk drive operations so that partitions larger than 528MB can be used on the drive.

The other MI/O functions supported through the CMOS utility include enabling the FDD controller, selecting the logical COM port addressing and operating modes for the system's two built-in UARTs, and selecting logical addressing and operating modes for the parallel port.

The UARTs can be configured to support half-duplex or full-duplex transmission modes through an infrared port, provided the system board is equipped with one. This allows wireless communications with serial peripheral devices over short distances.

The parallel printer port can be configured for normal PC-AT-compatible *standard parallel port* (SPP) operation, for extended bidirectional operation (*extended parallel port*, or EPP), for fast, buffered, bidirectional operation (*extended capabilities port*, or ECP), or for combined ECP+EPP operation. The normal setting should be selected unless both the port hardware and driver software support EPP and/or ECP operation.

> **TEST TIP**
>
> Remember that ECP and EPP modes for the parallel port must be enabled through the CMOS Setup utility.

Enhanced Parallel Port Operations

When EPP mode is selected in the port's configuration register, the standard and bidirectional modes are enabled. The functions of the port's pins are redefined under the EPP specification. Table 4.10 provides the EPP pin definitions.

TABLE 4.10

EPP PIN DEFINITIONS

HOST CONNECTOR	PIN NO.	STANDARD	EPP	ECP
1	77	Strobe	Write	Strobe
2-9	71-68, 66-63	Data <0:7>	Data <0:7>	Data <0:7>
10	62	Ack	Intr	Ack
11	61	Busy	Wait	Busy, PeriphAck
12	60	PE	Not Used	PError nAckReverse
13	59	Select	Not Used	Select
14	76	Autofd	DSTRB	AutoFd HostAck
15	75	Error	Not Used	Fault PeriphRequest
16	74	Init	Not Used	Init ReverseRqst
17	73	Selectin	Astrb	Selectin

When the EPP mode is enabled, the port can operate either as a standard, bidirectional parallel port or as a bidirectional EPP port. The software controlling the port will specify which type of operation is required. If no EPP read, write, or address cycle is being executed, the port and its control signals function as an SPP port. When the software calls for an EPP read, write, or address cycle, however, all the port's registers are enabled and the signal lines take on the functions defined by the selected EPP standard.

There are actually two EPP specifications to be aware of: EPP 1.7 and EPP 1.9. The EPP port type should be selected in the Integrated Peripherals section (or its equivalent) of the CMOS Setup utility.

ECP Mode

The ECP mode provides a number of advantages over the SPP and EPP modes. The ECP mode offers higher performance than either of the other modes. As with the EPP mode, the pins of the interface are redefined when ECP mode is selected in the system's BIOS. Table 4.11. lists the ECP definitions for the port's pins.

In ECP mode, the parallel port operates in forward (host-to-peripheral) and reverse (peripheral-to-host) directions. It employs interlocked handshaking for reliable, half-duplex transfers through the port. The capabilities of the ECP port enable it to be used in peer-to-peer applications.

The ECP port is compatible with the standard LPT port and is used in the same manner when no ECP read or write operations are called for. However, it also supports high-throughput DMA operations for both forward- and reverse-direction transfers.

Prior to ECP operation, the system examines the peripheral device attached to the port to determine that it can perform ECP operations. This operation is carried out in SPP mode. Afterward, the system initializes the port's registers for operation. In particular, it sets a direction bit in the port controller to enable the ECP drivers and sets the port's mode to ECP.

TABLE 4.11

ECP PIN DEFINITIONS

EPP SIGNAL	EPP NAME	TYPE	EPP DESCRIPTION
WRITEJ	WriteJ	O	This signal is active low. It denotes a write operation.
PD<0:7>	Address/ Data	I/O	Bi-directional EPP byte wide address and data bus.
INTR	Interrupt	I	This signal is active high and positive edge triggered. (Pass through with no inversion. Same as SPP.)
WAIT	WaitJ	I	This signal is active low. It is driven inactive as a positive acknowledgement from the device that the transfer of data is completed. It is driven active as an indication that the device is ready for the next transfer.
DATASTB	DATA StrobeJ	O	This signal is active low. It is used to denote data read or write operation.
RESET	ResetJ	O	This signal is active low. When driven active, the EPP device is reset to its initial operational mode.
ADDRSTB	Address StrobeJ	O	This signal is active low. It is used to denote address read or write operation.
PE	Paper End	I	Same as SPP mode.
SLCT	Printer Select Status	I	Same as SPP mode.
ERRJ	Error	I	Same as SPP mode.
PDIR	Parallel Port Direction	O	This output shows the direction of the data transfer on the parallel ports bus. A low means an output/write condition and a high means an input/read condition. This signal is normally low (output/write) unless PCD of the control register is set or if an EPP read cycle is in progress.

Note 1: SPP and EPP can use 1 common register.
Note 2: WriteJ is the only EPP output that can be over-ridden by SPP control port during an EPP cycle. For correct EPP read cycles, PCD is required to be a low.

The host computer may switch the direction of the port's operation by changing the mode value in the controller and then negotiating for the forward/reverse channel setting. Afterward, the mode is set back to ECP. During normal operation, commands and data may be passed through the port.

ECP transfers may be conducted in DMA or programmed I/O modes. DMA transfers use standard PC DMA services. To use this method, the host must set the port direction and program its DMA controller with the desired byte count and memory-address information.

TEST TIP

Remember that the ECP specification employs DMA operations to provide the highest data throughput for a parallel port.

Power-Management Functions

The Power Management fields enable the user to select from three power-saving modes: doze, standby, and suspend. These are Green PC–compatible power-saving modes that cause the system to step down from maximum power usage. The doze mode causes the microprocessor clock to slow down after a defined period of inactivity. The standby mode causes the hard drive and video to shut down after a period of inactivity. Finally, everything in the system except the microprocessor shuts down in suspend mode. Certain system events, such as IRQ and DRQ activities, cause the system to wake up from these modes and resume normal operation.

The Password Setting options, depicted in Figure 4.51, permit the user to enter and modify password settings. Password protection can be established for the system so that a password must be entered each time the system boots up or when the Setup utility is entered, or it can just be set up so that it is required only to access the Setup utility.

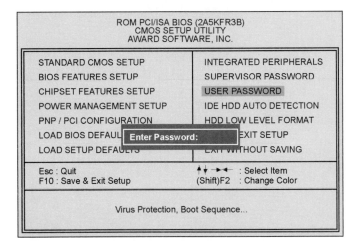

FIGURE 4.51
Password-setting options.

CHAPTER SUMMARY

The system board is the main component of any personal computer system. This chapter has examined the major components that make up typical PC-compatible system boards. These items include microprocessors, memory types, microprocessor support systems, and expansion buses.

The chapter did not move directly into the A+ 4.1 objective. Instead, it began with objective 4.3 (motherboards: components and architecture). This action allowed the discussion of all the objectives

continues

CHAPTER SUMMARY

KEY TERMS

- Asynchronous SRAM
- AT bus
- ATX form factor
- ATX system board
- Auto Detect
- Baby AT form factor
- Burst-mode SRAM
- Bus frequency
- Caching
- Core voltage
- Core-to-bus speed ratio
- CPU cooling fan
- Cyclic redundancy check (CRC)
- Dual in-line memory modules (DIMMs)
- Dynamic RAM (DRAM)
- Enhanced DRAM (EDRAM)
- Error checking and correcting (ECC)
- Extended capabilities port (ECP)
- Extended data out (EDO) DRAM
- Extended Industry Standard Architecture (EISA)
- Extended ISA (EISA) bus
- Extended parallel port (EPP)
- Fast page-mode RAM

to flow better. After completing this section, you should be able to describe the major architectural differences between system board types.

After completing the overall discussion of motherboard fundamentals, the chapter keyed in on its main component: the microprocessor. After examining this section, you should be able to describe the basic characteristics of popular microprocessors.

Following the microprocessors section, the chapter moved into an extended discussion of system memory structures. This section should enable you to describe the different categories of RAM and identify their normal system board locations and physical characteristics.

Finally, the chapter explored CMOS Setup utilities in detail. After completing this section, you should be able to describe the purpose of CMOS RAM, discuss what a typical CMOS utility contains, and explain how to change basic parameters.

- Host controller
- Hubs
- Hyper page-mode RAM
- Industry Standard Architecture (ISA)
- L1 cache
- L2 cache
- Low-profile system (LTX)
- Micro Channel Architecture (MCA)
- Mini-ATX system boards
- Parity checking
- PC-AT system board
- PC-bus
- PC-XT system boards
- Pentium II
- Pentium III

- Pentium MMX
- Pentium Pro
- Peripheral component inter-connect (PCI)
- Pipeline SRAM
- PnP registry
- Programmed input/output (PIO)
- Radio frequency interference (RFI)
- Resource conflicts
- Root hub
- Single in-line memory mod-ules (SIMMs)
- Slot 1
- Socket 1 through Socket 8
- Staggered Pin Grid Array (SPGA)

- Standard CMOS Setup
- Standard parallel port (SPP)
- Static RAM (SRAM)
- Synchronous DRAM (SDRAM)
- Tag RAM
- Universal Serial Bus (USB)
- USB devices
- USB host
- VESA (Video Electronics Standards Association)
- Video RAM (VRAM)
- VL bus
- Voltage-regulator module (VRM)
- Windows RAM (WRAM)

RESOURCE URLs

www.intel.com/design/motherbd/atx.htm

http://developer.intel.com/design/chipsets/linecard.htm

www.usb.org/developers/docs.html

www.vesa.org

www.intel.com/design/chipsets/applnots/273011.htm

www.intel.com/design/motherbd/atx.htm

www.fortron-source.com/products.htm

www.teleport.com/~ffsupport/spec/atxspecs.htm

continues

RESOURCE URLs

www.sandpile.org

www.sandpile.org/arch/cpuid.htm

www.sandpile.org/impl/p55.htm

www.cyrix.com

www.viatech.com/products/cyrindex.htm

http://developer.intel.com/sites/developer/contents.htm

www.kingston.com/tools/umg/umg1.asp#top

www.kingston.com/tools/umg/umg4.asp

www.sysopt.com/compex.html#TheBIOS

www.megatrends.com/

www.award.com/

www.fapo.com/eppmode.htm

www.fapo.com/ecpmode.htm

http://developer.intel.com/design/flash/

APPLY YOUR KNOWLEDGE

Review Questions

1. Referring to the sample core-to-bus ratio configurations listed in Table 4.5, what is the fastest Pentium device that can be installed in the sample system?

2. Refer to the example system board settings in the chapter and describe the jumper arrangements that would have to be in place to install an AMD K6-200ALR(1) microprocessor in the sample system.

3. Where are the basic I/O functions located in a typical Pentium system?

4. What system board device does PnP apply to?

5. Why do Pentium system boards employ VRMs?

6. How many hardware interrupt channels are available in an AT-compatible system?

7. Which interrupts are used with PC-compatible parallel ports?

8. What function does IRQ2 serve in an AT-compatible system?

9. Which IRQ channel services the FDD in PC-compatible systems?

10. Can a Pentium MMX processor be used to upgrade a system board that has a Pentium 66 installed?

11. Can an AMD K6 processor be used to upgrade a system board that has a Pentium 75 installed?

12. To install an Intel Pentium 166 in the sample system board from this chapter, operating with an external clock frequency of 66MHz, what conditions must be established at JP14 and JP15?

13. How do local buses differ from other expansion buses?

14. Can a Pentium MMX processor be used to upgrade a Pentium 100 system?

15. Name two advantages of using chipsets to design circuit boards.

Exam Questions

1. Which 32-bit bus can accept cards from PC and ISA buses?

   A. The ISA bus

   B. The EISA bus

   C. The MCA bus

   D. The PCI bus

2. How many hardware interrupt channels are there in a PC- or XT-compatible system?

   A. 16

   B. 2

   C. 4

   D. 8

3. What clock frequency should be applied to an Intel Pentium 166 microprocessor with a 2.5× multiplier setting?

   A. 50MHz

   B. 60MHz

   C. 66MHz

   D. 166MHz

APPLY YOUR KNOWLEDGE

4. Where can interrupt request number 1 be found in a PC-compatible system?

    A. At the keyboard's encoder chip

    B. At the system board's keyboard controller chip

    C. At the system's DRAM refresh controller chip

    D. At the system's FDD controller chip

5. Which expansion bus type will not accept an ISA card?

    A. A VESA bus slot

    B. An EISA bus slot

    C. An ISA slot

    D. A PCI slot

6. What function does IRQ0 play in a PC-compatible system?

    A. It drives the system's DRAM refresh signal.

    B. It drives the system's time-of-day clock.

    C. It drives the system's FDD interrupt.

    D. It drives the system's keyboard interrupt.

7. How many DMA channels are included in a PC- or XT-compatible system?

    A. 8

    B. 16

    C. 1

    D. 4

8. What function does DMA channel 2 serve in a PC-compatible system?

    A. It provides the system's HDD DMA channel.

    B. It provides the system's keyboard DMA channel.

    C. It provides the system's FDD DMA channel.

    D. It provides the system's video DMA channel.

9. How many devices can be attached to a USB host?

    A. 63

    B. 127

    C. 255

    D. 511

10. Which function is not typically found in a standard CMOS Setup screen?

    A. Date

    B. Floppy disk drive

    C. Hard disk drive

    D. Virus warning

Answers to Review Questions

1. An Intel Pentium MMX running at 233MHz. For more information, see the section "Configuring Microprocessors."

2. JP15=Short, JP14=Open, JP13=Open, JP22=pins 1 and 2 Open, pins 3 and 4 shorted, JP10= pins 1 and 2 shorted. For more information, see the section "Configuring Microprocessors."

3. On the system board itself. For more information, see the section "I/O Connections."

4. The BIOS. Other key PnP components include the system software, the expansion bus standard used in the system, and the I/O cards used. For more information, see the section "PCI Configuration."

APPLY YOUR KNOWLEDGE

5. To allow microprocessors that use different core and processor voltages to be used with the system board design. For more information, see the section "Socket Specifications."

6. 15. (One of the 16 channels is used to cascade the first controller to the second). For more information, see the section "Major Components."

7. IRQ5 and IRQ7. For more information, see the section "Major Components."

8. It is unused in PC- and PC/XT-compatible systems. In AT-compatible systems, it is the cascaded IRQ input for the secondary PIC device. For more information, see the section "System Board Evolution."

9. IRQ6 is dedicated to the FDD. For more information, see the section "System Board Evolution."

10. No. The Pentium 66 is a first-generation Pentium device. The socket specifications for these devices were not compatible with the second- and third-generation Pentiums. For more information, see the section "The Pentium Processor."

11. Yes. Both the Pentium 75 (a second-generation Pentium device) and the K6 are Socket 7–compatible devices. For more information, see the section "Pentium Clones."

12. Both JP14 and JP15 must be shorted. For more information, see the section "Configuring Microprocessors."

13. The local bus is designed to run directly between the I/O device and the microprocessor and operate at speeds compatible with the microprocessor. For more information, see the section "Local Bus Designs."

14. Yes. Both the Pentium 100 and Pentium MMX are Socket 7–compatible devices. For more information, see the section "Configuring Microprocessors."

15. Decreased size and decreased production costs. For more information, see the section "Chipsets."

Answers to Exam Questions

1. **B.** The EISA bus is the 32-bit extension of the ISA bus, which, in turn, is an extension of the PC bus specification. The MCA and PCI buses are proprietary designs that have no compatibility with the original PC/PC-XT/PC-AT buses. For more information, see the section "System Board Compatibility."

2. **D.** The PC and PC-XT employed an 8259 programmable interrupt controller. This device provided eight channels of programmable interrupt service. For more information, see the section "System Board Evolution."

3. **C.** 66MHz × 2.5 = 166. For more information, see the section "Configuring Microprocessors."

4. **B.** IRQ1 has always been used for keyboard interrupt functions in PC-compatible systems. The keyboard controller circuitry uses this line to notify the system's interrupt controller that it has received a complete scan-code character from the keyboard and requires service from the microprocessor. For more information, see the section "Major Components."

5. **D.** The ISA and EISA slots were designed explicitly to use ISA cards. The VESA bus was designed to be mounted in-line with an ISA expansion slot (as illustrated in Figure 4.18) and to accept its

APPLY YOUR KNOWLEDGE

cards. The PCI bus normally exists on system boards that contain ISA slots, but they are mounted away from those slots and there is no specification for any card to blend the two connectors. For more information, see the section "System Board Compatibility."

6. **B.** IRQ0 has always been used for time-of-day clock tick functions in PC-compatible systems. For more information, see the section "System Board Evolution."

7. **D.** The PC and PC-XT employed an 8237 programmable DMA controller. This device provided four high-speed DMA channels for the system. For more information, see the section "System Board Evolution."

8. **C.** DRQ2 has always been used to service the floppy disk drive in a PC-compatible system. For more information, see the section "System Board Evolution."

9. **B.** The specification allows 127 devices (128 − 1) to be attached to the USB host. The host accounts for one of the 128 possible USB addresses. For more information, see the section "Universal Serial Bus."

10. **D.** Although many new BIOS versions provide a virus warning option, it is not a standard option and does not show up in the main screen. The date, HDD, and FDD information do. For more information, see the section "Standard CMOS Setup Screens."

This chapter helps you to prepare for the Core Hardware module of the A+ Certification examination by covering the following objectives within the "Domain 5.0: Printers" section.

5.1 Identify basic concepts, printer operations and printer components.

Content may include the following:

- **Paper-feeder mechanisms**

- **Types of printers**
  - **Laser**
  - **Inkjet**
  - **Dot matrix**

Types of printer connections and configurations.

- **Parallel**
- **Network**
- **USB**

▶ Because printers are one of the most common peripheral systems used with computers, PC technicians should understand how the different types of printers operate, what their typical components are, and which ones can be serviced in the field.

▶ The connection method between the printer and the host computer affects many of the trouble-shooting steps necessary to isolate problems. Likewise, connecting a printer to a computer that is on a network will affect how the technician approaches its configuration and troubleshooting.

CHAPTER 5

5.0 Printers

5.2 Identify care and service techniques and common problems with primary printer types.

Content may include the following:

- **Feed and output**
- **Errors**
- **Paper jam**
- **Print quality**
- **Safety precautions**
- **Preventive maintenance**

▶ The technician should be familiar with common printer problems and be able to demonstrate current service techniques.

STUDY STRATEGIES

To prepare for Printers objective of the Core Hardware exam:

▶ Read the objectives at the beginning of this chapter.

▶ Study the information in this chapter.

▶ Review the objectives listed earlier in this chapter.

▶ Perform any step-by-step procedures in the text.

▶ Answer the Review and Exam Questions at the end of the chapter and check your results.

▶ Use the ExamGear test engine on the CD-ROM that accompanies this book for additional Review and Exam Questions concerning this material

▶ Review the Test Tip items scattered throughout the chapter and make certain that you are comfortable with each point.

INTRODUCTION

This domain requires knowledge of basic types of printers, basic concepts, printer components, how they work, how they print onto a page, paper path, care and service techniques, and common problems. Questions from this domain account for 10% of the Core Hardware test.

BASIC PRINTER CONCEPTS

▶ 5.1 Identify basic concepts, printer operations, and printer components.

The A+ Core Hardware objective 5.1 states that the test taker should be able to "identify basic concepts, printer operations, and printer components."

Printers are the second most common output peripheral used with PCs. As this A+ objective indicates, computer technicians must understand how the different types of printers operate, what their typical components are, and what printer components can be serviced in the field. The following sections of this chapter introduce basic printer-related terminology as well as the operation and organization of the most common printer types.

There are many instances in which a permanent copy of a computer's output may be desired. The leading hard-copy *output device* is the *character printer* (that is, letters, numbers, and graphic images). Printers can be classified in a number of ways:

- ◆ Their method of placing characters on a page (impact or nonimpact)

- ◆ Their speed of printing (low speed or high speed)

- ◆ The quality of the characters they produce (letter quality, near-letter quality, or draft quality)

- ◆ Or, how they form the character on the page (fully formed or dot matrix)

Printing Methods

The first way to differentiate printers is by how they deliver ink to the page. *Impact printers* produce the character by causing the print mechanism, or its ink ribbon, to impact the page. Conversely, non-impact printers deliver ink to the page without the print mechanism making contact with the page.

Impact Printers

Impact printers place characters on the page by causing a hammer device to strike an inked ribbon. The ribbon, in turn, strikes the printing surface (paper).

The print mechanism may have the image of the character carved on its face, or it may be made up of a group of small print wires, arranged in a matrix pattern. In this case, the print mechanism is used to create the character on the page by printing a pattern of dots resembling it.

Generally, the quality—and therefore the readability—of a fully formed character is better than that of a dot-matrix character. However, dot-matrix printers tend to be less expensive than their fully formed character counterparts. In either case, the majority of the printers in use today are of the impact variety. Figure 5.1 depicts both fully formed and dot-matrix type characters.

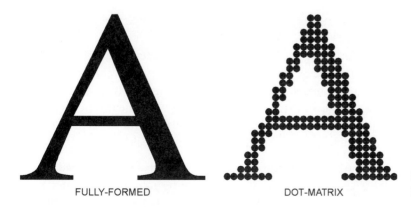

FULLY-FORMED   DOT-MATRIX

FIGURE 5.1
Fully formed and dot-matrix characters.

Nonimpact Printers

Several nonimpact ways to print are used in computer printers.

Older, nonimpact printers relied on special heat-sensitive or *chemically reactive paper* to form characters on the page. Newer methods of nonimpact printing use ink droplets squirted from a jet-nozzle device (inkjet printers), or a combination of laser/xerographic print technologies (laser printers) to place characters on a page. Currently, the most popular nonimpact printers use the inkjet or laser technologies to deliver ink to the page.

In general, nonimpact printers are less mechanical than impact counterparts. Therefore, they tend to be more dependable. Also, to their advantage, nonimpact printers tend to be quiet and faster than comparable impact printers. The major disadvantage of nonimpact printers is their inability to produce carbon copies.

Character Types

Basically, there are two ways to create characters on a page. One way places a character on the page that is fully shaped, and fully filled-in. This type of character is called a fully formed character. The other way involves placing dots on the page in strategic patterns to fool the eye into seeing a character. This type of character is referred to as a dot-matrix character.

A fully formed impact print mechanism is depicted in Figure 5.2. The quality of *fully formed characters* is excellent. However, creative choices in print *fonts* and sizes tend to be somewhat limited. To change the size or shape of a character, the print mechanism would need to be replaced. Conversely, the flexibility of using dots to create characters allows them to be altered as the document is being created. The quality of *dot-matrix characters* runs from extremely poor to extremely good, depending on the print mechanism.

Dot-matrix characters are not fully formed characters. Instead, dot-matrix characters are produced by printing a dot pattern representing the character, as illustrated in Figure 5.3. The reader's eye fills in the gaps between the dots. Today's dot-matrix printers offer good-speed, high-quality characters that approach those created by good typewriters, and nearly limitless printing flexibility.

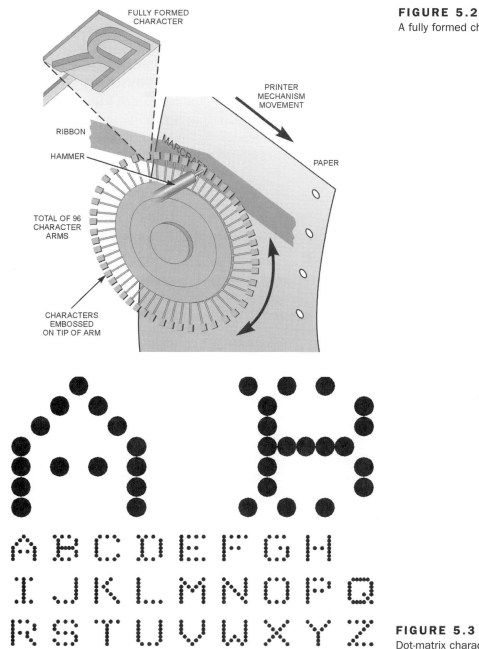

FIGURE 5.2
A fully formed character mechanism.

FULLY FORMED
CHARACTER

PRINTER
MECHANISM
MOVEMENT

RIBBON

HAMMER

MARCRATH

PAPER

TOTAL OF 96
CHARACTER
ARMS

CHARACTERS
EMBOSSED
ON TIP OF ARM

FIGURE 5.3
Dot-matrix characters.

Basically, the *printhead* in a dot-matrix printer is a vertical column of print wires controlled by electromagnets, as depicted in Figure 5.4. Dots are created on the paper by energizing selected electromagnets, which extend the desired print wires from the printhead. The print wires impact an ink ribbon, which impacts the paper. It's important to note that the entire character is not printed in a single instant of time. A typical printhead may contain 9, 18, or 24 print wires. The number of print wires used in the printhead is a major determining factor when discussing a printer's character quality.

The matrix portion of this printer's name is derived from the manner in which the page is subdivided for printing. The page is divided into a number of horizontal rows, or text lines. Each row is divided into groups of columns, called *character cells*. Character cells define the area in which a single character is printed. The size of the character cell is expressed in terms of pitch, or the number of characters printed per inch. Within the print cell, the matrix dimensions of the character are defined.

The density of the dots within the character cell determines the quality of the character printed. Common matrix sizes are 5×7, 24×9, and 36×18, to mention only a few of those available. The more dots that the printhead produces within the character cell, the better the character looks. Because the dots are closer together, the character appears more fully formed and easier to read.

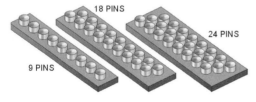

FIGURE 5.4
Dot-matrix printer pinheads.

Fonts

The term *font* refers to variations in the size and style of characters. With true fully formed characters, there is typically only one font available without changing the physical printing element. With all other printing methods, however, it is possible to include a wide variety of font types and sizes.

There are three common ways to generate character fonts: bitmapped (or *raster-scanned fonts*), *vector-based fonts*, and *TrueType outline fonts*.

Bitmapped fonts store dot patterns for all the possible size and style variations of the characters in the set. Because a complete set of dots must be stored for each character and size that may be needed, this type of font tends to take up large amounts of memory. For this reason, the number of character sizes offered by bitmapped fonts is typically limited. Font styles refer to the characteristics of the font, such as normal, bold, and italic styles. Font size refers to the physical measurement of the character. Type is measured in increments of 1/72 of an inch. Each increment is referred to as a point. Common text sizes are 10-point and 12-point type.

Vector-based fonts store the outlines of the character styles and sizes as sets of starting points and mathematical formulas. Each character is composed of a set of reference points and connecting lines between them. When a particular character is needed, the character generator sets the starting point for the character in the print cell and generates its outline from the formula. These types of fonts can be scaled up and down to achieve various sizes.

The vector-based approach requires much less storage space to store a character set and all of its variations than would be necessary for an equivalent bitmapped character set. In addition, vector-based fonts can be scaled and rotated; bitmapped fonts typically cannot be scaled and rotated. Conversely, bitmapped characters can be printed out directly and quickly, but vector-based characters must be generated when called for.

TrueType fonts are a newer type of outline fonts commonly used with Microsoft Windows. These fonts are stored as a set of points and outlines used to generate a set of bitmaps. Special algorithms adjust the bitmaps so that they look best at the specified resolution. After the bitmaps have been created, Windows stores them in a RAM cache that it creates. In this manner, the font is only generated once when it is first selected. Afterward, the fonts are just called out of memory, thus speeding up the process of delivering them to the printer. Each TrueType character set requires an FOT and a TTF file to create all of its sizes and resolutions.

> **TEST TIP**
> Be aware of the benefits and drawbacks of bitmapped characters.

> **TEST TIP**
> Know which font types are generated by establishing starting points and then calculating mathematical formulas.

Print Quality

The last criteria for comparing printers is the quality of the characters they produce. This is largely a function of how the characters are produced on the page. Printers using techniques that produce fully formed characters are described as *letter-quality* (LQ) printers. All elements of the character appear to be fully connected when printed. On the other hand, those using techniques that produce characters by forming a dot pattern are just referred to as matrix printers. On close inspection of a character, one can see the dot patterns. The characters produced on some matrix printers are difficult to distinguish from those of fully formed characters. These printers have been labeled *correspondence quality* (CQ) or *near-letter-quality* (NLQ) printers. Often, dot-matrix printers will have two printing modes, one being standard dot-matrix (sometimes called *utility* or *draft mode*) and the other a near-letter-quality mode.

Printer Mechanics

By the nature of their operation, printers tend to be extremely mechanical peripherals. During the printing operation, the print mechanism must be properly positioned over each character cell, in sequence.

Loss of synchronization in impact printers can lead to *paper jams*, tearing, smudged characters, and/or printhead damage. *Nonimpact printers* may produce totally illegible characters if synchronization is lost. The positioning action may be produced by moving the paper under a stationary printhead assembly or by holding the paper stationary and stepping the printhead carriage across the page. In the latter operation, the printhead carriage rides on rods extending across the front of the page, as shown in Figure 5.5.

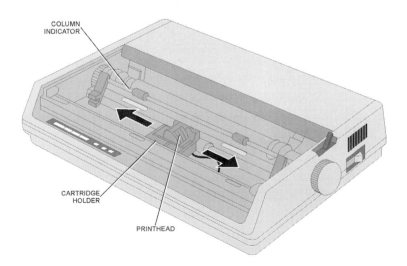

FIGURE 5.5
The printhead carriage.

Depending on the type of print mechanism used, the carriage can be stepped across the page at a rate of one character cell at a time (fully formed characters) or in sub-character-cell steps (dot-matrix characters). Printing may occur in only one direction unidirectional) or in both directions (bidirectional). In bidirectional printers, the second line of characters is stored in the printer's buffer memory and printed in the opposite direction, saving the time that would normally be used to return the carriage to the start of the second line.

The *printhead carriage assembly* is stepped across the page by a carriage-motor/timing-belt arrangement. With many printer models, the number of character columns across the page is selectable, producing variable characters spacing (expressed in characters per inch, or cpi), which must be controlled by the *carriage-position motor*. Dot-matrix printers may also incorporate variable dot densities (expressed as *dot-pitches*). Dot-pitch also is a function of the carriage-motor control circuitry. Obviously, this discussion excludes continuous-stream, inkjet printers, where printing is done by electromagnetic deflection of the ink drops, and laser printers, where the beam is reflected by a revolving mirror.

Paper Handling

In addition to positioning the print mechanism for printing, all printer types must feed paper through the print area. The type of *paper-handling mechanism* in a printer depends somewhat on the type of form intended to be used with the printer, and its speed.

Paper forms fall into two general categories: *continuous forms*, which come in folded stacks, and have holes along their edges; and *single-sheet forms*, such as common typing paper.

There are two common methods of moving paper through the printer:

◆ **Friction feed.** Uses friction to hold the paper against the printer's platen. The paper advances through the printer as the platen turns.

◆ **Pin feed.** Pulls the paper through the printer by a set of pins that fit into the holes along the edge of the form, as shown in Figure 5.6. The pins can be an integral part of the platen, or mounted on a separate, motor-driven tractor.

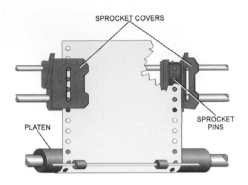

FIGURE 5.6
A pin-feed tractor mechanism.

> **TEST TIP**
> Know the major purpose of a tractor-feed mechanism and where it is most commonly used.

Friction feed is normally associated with single-sheet printers. The sheet-feeding system can be manual or automatic. *Platen* pin-feed and pin tractors are usually employed with continuous and multi-layer forms. These mechanisms can control paper slippage and misalignment created by the extra weight imposed by continuous forms. Platen pin-feed units can handle only one width of paper; tractors can be adjusted to handle various paper widths. *Tractor feeds* are used with very heavy forms, such as multiple part, continuous forms, and are most commonly found on dot-matrix printers. Most inkjet and laser printers use single-sheet feeder systems.

The gear trains involved in the paper-handling function can be treated as an field-replaceable unit (FRU) item in some printers. Although it is possible to replace the gears, or gear packs, in dot-matrix and inkjet printers (if they can be obtained from the manufacturer as separate items), it is not usually economical to do so. Laser printers, on the other hand, are normally expensive enough to warrant replacing the gear trains and clutch assemblies that handle the paper movement through the printer.

Printer Controls

Although printers vary considerably from type to type and model to model, some elements are common to all printers. Figure 5.7 depicts these common elements.

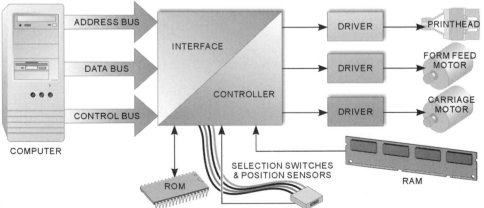

FIGURE 5.7
Common printer components.

Like most other peripherals, the heart of a character printer is its interface/controller circuitry. The interface circuitry accepts data and instructions from the computer's bus systems and provides the necessary interfacing (serial or parallel) between the computer and the printer's control circuitry.

This includes decoding the computer's instructions to the printer, converting signal logic levels between the two, and passing data to the printer's controller.

Parallel port connections are most efficient when the printer is located in close proximity to the computer. If the printer must be located remotely, the serial interface becomes more appropriate. Many manufacturers offer both connections as standard equipment. Others offer the serial connection as an option. More is said about these two interfaces later in this section. A third, less-common method of connecting printers to computers uses the SCSI interface as the connection port. As with other SCSI devices, the printer must be set up as a unique SCSI device and observe proper connection and termination procedures.

The controller section receives the data and control signals from the interface section and produces all the signals necessary to select, or generate, the proper character to be printed. It also advances the print mechanism to the next print position and feeds the paper at the proper times. In addition, the controller generates status and control signals that tell the computer what is happening in the printer.

Due to the complexity of most character printers, a dedicated micro-controller is commonly used to oversee the operation of the printer. The presence of the onboard microprocessor provides greater flexibility and additional options for the printer.

Along with the dedicated processor, the printer normally contains onboard memory in the form of RAM, ROM, or both. A speed mismatch exists, between the computer and the printer, because the computer can normally generate characters at a much higher rate than the printer can print them. To minimize this speed differential, printers typically carry onboard RAM memory buffers to hold characters coming from the computer. In this way, the transfer of data between the computer and the printer occurs at a rate compatible with the computer's operating speed. The printer obtains its character information from the onboard buffer.

NOTE
> **Printer FRU Modules** In some printers, the microcontroller, RAM chips or modules, and the ROM/EPROM devices can be treated as FRU components.

In addition to character print information, the host computer also can store printer instructions in the buffer for use by the dedicated processor. The printer also may contain onboard ROM in the form of character generators or printer-initialization programs for startup. Some printers contain EPROM rather than ROM, to provide a greater variety of options for the printer, such as *downloadable type fonts* and variable print modes.

Many laser printers come with a preset amount of RAM onboard, but allow the memory to be upgraded if needed. Many high-speed laser printers require additional RAM to be installed to handle printing of complex documents, such as desktop published documents containing large *Encapsulated PostScript* (EPS) graphics files. Similarly, ROM and EPROM devices that contain BIOS or character sets are often socketed so that they can be replaced or upgraded easily.

As with the gears and gear trains discussed earlier in this chapter, the replaceability of these units depends on the ability to source them from a supplier. In most cases, the question is not one of "Can the device be exchanged?", it's one of whether it makes economic sense to do so. For a given printer type and model, the manufacturer's service center can provide information about the availability of replacement parts.

Basically, the controller must produce signals to drive the print mechanism, the *paper-feed motor*, the *carriage motor*, and possibly optional devices, such as single-sheet feeders and add-on tractors. Most of these functions are actually performed by precision stepper motors. There are usually hardware driver circuits between the motors and the controller to provide current levels high enough to activate the motors.

The controller also gathers information from the printer through a variety of sensing devices. These include position-sensing switches, and user-operated, front-panel-mounted, mode-control switches. Some of the more common sensing switches include the *home-position sensor*, *end-of-paper sensor*, and the carriage-position sensor. The controller also responds to manual input command switches, such as On/Off Line, *Form Feed* (FF), and *Line Feed* (LF).

The sensors and switches can be treated as FRUs in many printers. This is particularly true with more expensive laser printers. In most printers, the entire *operator control panel* can be exchanged for another unit. This effectively changes all the user-operated input switches at one time.

Dot-Matrix Printers

The stalwarts of microcomputer printing have been the dot-matrix impact printers.

Figure 5.8 depicts the components of a typical dot-matrix printer. They consist of a power-supply board, a main control board, a printhead assembly, a *ribbon cartridge*, a paper-feed motor (along with its mechanical drive gears), and a *printhead-positioning motor* and mechanisms.

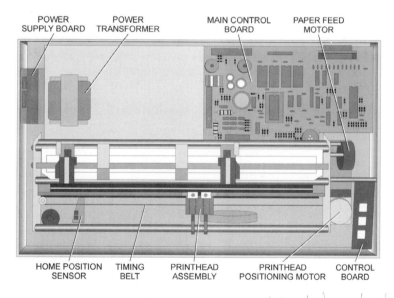

POWER SUPPLY BOARD   POWER TRANSFORMER   MAIN CONTROL BOARD   PAPER FEED MOTOR

HOME POSITION SENSOR   TIMING BELT   PRINTHEAD ASSEMBLY   PRINTHEAD POSITIONING MOTOR   CONTROL BOARD

FIGURE 5.8
Parts of a dot-matrix printer.

The Power Supply

The power-supply board provides various voltages to power the electronics on the control board. It also drives both the printhead-positioning and paper-feed motors, and energizes the wires of the printhead so that they will strike the ribbon as directed by the control board.

The Main Control Board

The control board is typically divided into four functional sections, as described in Figure 5.9. These functional blocks include the following:

◆ The interface circuitry

◆ The character-generation circuitry

◆ The printer-controller circuitry

◆ The motor-control circuitry

FIGURE 5.9

Logical parts of the control board.

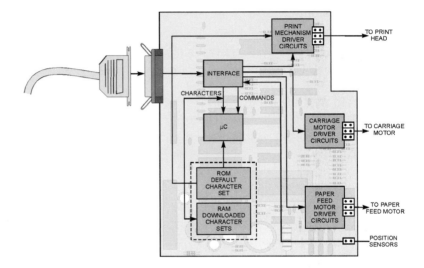

The control board contains the logic circuitry required to convert the signals received from the computer's adapter card into character patterns, as well as to generate the proper control signals to position the printhead properly on the page, fire the correct combination of printhead wires to create the character, and to advance the paper properly. The onboard microcontroller, character generators, and RAM and ROM are found on the control board.

The status of the printer's operation is monitored by the control board through a number of sensors. These sensors typically include the following:

◆ Paper out

◆ Printhead position

◆ Home position (for the printhead carriage)

Input from the printer's operator panel is also routed to the control board. Operator panel information includes the following:

◆ Online

◆ Form feed

◆ Line feed

◆ Power/Paper out

The control panel may contain a number of other buttons and indicator lights whose functions are specific to that particular printer. Always consult the printer's User Manual for information about the control panel buttons and indicators.

The printer's interface may contain circuitry to handle serial data, parallel data, or a combination of the two interface types. At the printer end of a Centronics parallel port, a 36-pin connector, such as the one depicted in Figure 5.10, is used. Of course, the computer end of the cable should have a DB-25M connector to plug into the system's DB-25F LPT port.

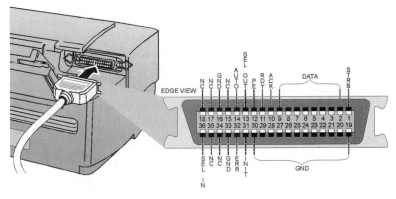

FIGURE 5.10
A parallel connection at the printer.

Dot-matrix printers process bit patterns in much the same way that CRT controllers do. The dot patterns are accessed from a character-generator ROM. In addition to the standard ASCII character set, many printers feature preprogrammed sets of block-graphics characters that can be used to create non-text images on a page. Most manufacturers use EPROM (erasable-programmable ROM) character generators rather than the older ROM type. This allows their units to accept downloadable fonts from software.

> **TEST TIP**
> Remember the types of connectors used at both the computer and the printer ends of a parallel printer cable.

Used with a high-quality printhead, a variety of typefaces—such as Roman Gothic, Italic, and foreign-language characters—can be loaded into the programmable character-generator from software. In addition, it is possible for the user to create his own character sets, typefaces, and graphic symbols. Some manufacturers even offer standard, bar-code graphics software sets for their machines.

Printhead Mechanisms

The printhead is a collection of print wires set in an electromagnetic head unit. The printhead assembly is made up of a permanent magnet, a group of electromagnets, and a housing. In the printhead, the permanent magnet keeps the wires pulled in until electromagnets are energized, causing them to move forward.

The printhead is mounted in the printhead carriage assembly. The carriage assembly rides on a bar that passes along the front of the platen. The printhead carriage assembly is attached to the printhead-positioning motor by a *timing belt*.

The printhead-positioning motor is responsible for moving the printhead mechanism across the page, and stopping it in just the right places to print. The printhead rides back and forth across the printer on a pair of carriage rods. A timing belt runs between the printhead assembly and the printhead-positioning motor, and converts the rotation of the motor into linear movement of the printhead assembly. The printhead must stop each time the print wires strike the paper. If this timing is off, the characters will be smeared on the page and the paper may be damaged. The motor steps a predetermined number of steps to create a character within a character cell. Figure 5.11 illustrates a dot-matrix printhead delivering print to a page.

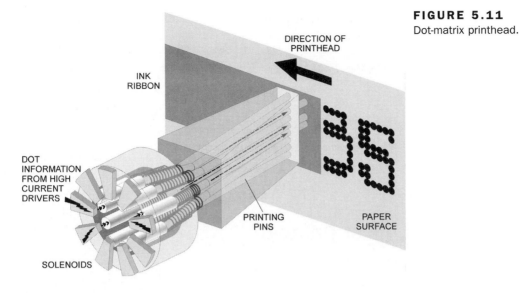

FIGURE 5.11
Dot-matrix printhead.

Paper Handling

The paper-feed motor and gear train move the paper through the printer. This can be accomplished by driving the platen assembly. The platen can be used in two different ways to move the paper through the printer. After the paper is wrapped half way around the platen, a set of rollers pins the paper to the platen as it turns. This is friction-feed paper handling. As described earlier, the platen may have small pins that drag the paper through the printer as the platen turns. In either case, the paper-feed motor drives the platen to move the paper.

The feed motor's gear train can also be used to drive the extended gear train of a tractor assembly, when it is installed. The gears of the feed motor mesh with those of the tractor, causing it to pull, or push, the paper through the printer. To use a tractor, the friction-feed feature of the platen must be released. Otherwise, the tractor and the platen may not turn at the same rate and the paper will rip or jam. Figure 5.12 depicts the installation of a tractor assembly.

FIGURE 5.12
Installing a tractor assembly.

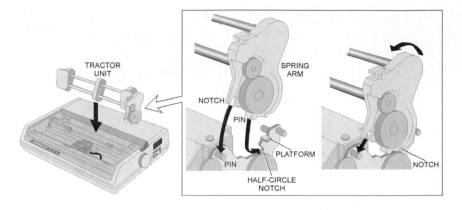

Inkjet Printers

Inkjet printers produce characters by squirting a precisely controlled stream of ink drops onto the paper, as described in Figure 5.13. The drops must be controlled very precisely in terms of their aerodynamics, size, and shape; otherwise, the drop placement on the page becomes inexact and the print quality falters.

FIGURE 5.13
Inkjet printers.

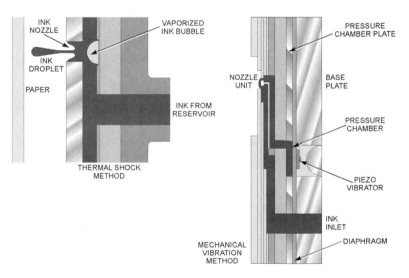

The drops are formed by one of two methods:

- ◆ **Thermal shock.** Heats the ink in a capillary tube just behind the nozzle. This increases the pressure of the ink in the tube and causes it to explode through the opening.

- ◆ **Mechanical vibration.** Uses vibrations from a piezo-electric crystal to force ink through a nozzle.

The inkjet nozzle is designed to provide the proper shape and trajectory for the ink drops so that they can be directed precisely toward the page. The nozzles are also designed so that the surface tension of the ink keeps it from running out of the nozzle uncontrollably.

Inkjet printers use two methods to deliver the drops to the page: the interrupted-stream (drop-on-demand) method, and the continuous-stream method. The drop-on-demand system forms characters on the page in much the same manner as a dot-matrix printer does. As the printhead mechanism moves across the character cells of the page, the controller causes a drop to be sprayed, only where necessary, to form the dot pattern of a character. Figure 5.14 depicts drop-on-demand printing.

Continuous-stream systems, such as the one described in Figure 5.15, produce characters that more closely resemble fully formed characters. In these systems, the printhead does not travel across the page. Instead, the drops are given a negative charge in an ion chamber, and passed through a set of deflection plates, similar to the electron beam in a CRT tube. The plates deflect the drops to their proper placement on the page, while unused drops are deflected off the page and into an ink recirculation system.

Although capable of delivering very high-quality characters at high speeds, continuous-stream systems tend to be expensive, and therefore are not normally found in printers for the consumer market. Instead, they are reserved for high-volume commercial printing applications. The inkjet printers in the general consumer market use drop-on-demand techniques to deliver ink to the page.

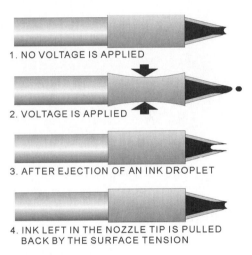

1. NO VOLTAGE IS APPLIED

2. VOLTAGE IS APPLIED

3. AFTER EJECTION OF AN INK DROPLET

4. INK LEFT IN THE NOZZLE TIP IS PULLED BACK BY THE SURFACE TENSION

FIGURE 5.14
Drop-on-demand printing.

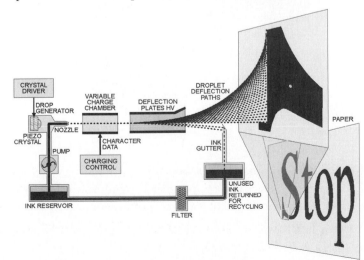

FIGURE 5.15
Continuous-stream printing.

Some inkjet printers incorporate multiple jets to permit color printing. Four basic colors can be mixed to create a veritable palate of colors, by firing the inkjets in different combinations.

Inkjet Printer Components

Aside from the printing mechanism, the components of a typical inkjet printer are very similar to those of a dot-matrix printer. Its primary components are as follows:

◆ The printhead assembly

◆ The power board

◆ The control board

◆ The printhead-positioning motor and timing belt

◆ The paper-feed motor and gear train

◆ The printer's sensors

Figure 5.16 illustrates these components.

FIGURE 5.16
Inkjet printer components.

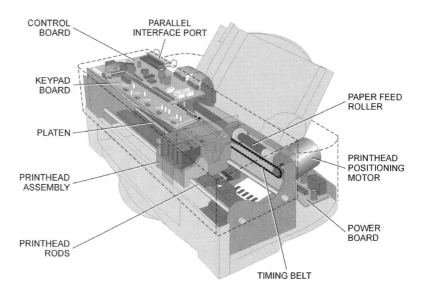

The Printhead Assembly

The *ink cartridge* snaps into the printhead assembly, which rides in front of the platen on a rail or rod. The printhead assembly is positioned by a timing belt that runs between it and the positioning motor. A flexible cable carries inkjet firing information between the control board and the printhead. This cable folds out of the way as the printhead assembly moves across the printer.

Paper Handling

The paper-feed motor turns a gear train that ultimately drives the platen, as depicted in Figure 5.17. The paper is friction fed through the printer, between the platen and the pressure rollers. Almost all *inkjet printers* used with microcomputer systems are single-sheet, friction-feed systems. The control board, power-supply board, and sensors perform the same functions in an inkjet printer that they did in the dot-matrix printer.

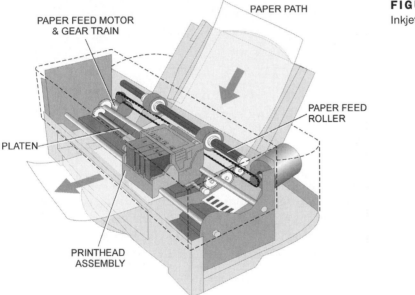

FIGURE 5.17
Inkjet paper handling.

Laser Printers

The laser printer modulates a highly focused laser beam to produce CRT-like raster-scan images on a rotating drum, as depicted in Figure 5.18.

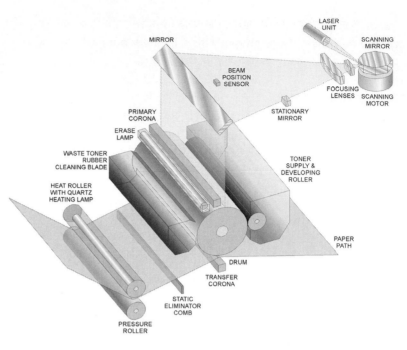

FIGURE 5.18
A typical laser printer.

The drum is coated with a photosensitive plastic, which is given a negative electrical charge over its surface. The modulated laser beam creates spots on the rotating drum. The spots written by the laser take on a positive electrical charge. A negatively charged toner material is attracted to the positively charged, written areas of the drum. The paper is fed past the rotating drum and the toner is transferred to the paper. A pair of *compression rollers* and a high-temperature lamp fuse the toner to the paper. Thus, the image, written on the drum by the laser, is transferred to the paper.

The laser beam scans the drum so rapidly that it is not practical to do the scanning mechanically. Instead, the beam is bounced off a rotating, polygonal (many-sided) mirror. The faces of the mirror cause the reflected beam to scan across the face of the drum as the mirror revolves. Using the highest dot densities available, these printers produce characters that rival typeset text. Larger laser printers produce characters at a rate of 20,000 lines per minute. Laser printers intended for the personal computer market generate 6 to 45 pages per minute.

Laser-Printer Components

From manufacturer to manufacturer, and model to model, the exact arrangement and combinations of components may vary in laser printers. However, the order of operations is always the same. The six stages of operation in a laser printer include the following:

◆ Cleaning

◆ Conditioning

◆ Writing

◆ Developing

◆ Transferring

◆ Fusing

To accomplish these objectives, all laser printers possess the following logical blocks:

◆ Power supply

◆ Control board

◆ Laser-writing unit

◆ Drum unit

◆ Fusing asscmbly

◆ Paper-feed motor and gear train

◆ System's sensors

◆ Control panel board

Figure 5.19 depicts the blocks of the typical laser printer.

The laser printer's power-supply unit is the most complex found in any type of printer. It must deliver AC power to the *fuser unit*. This unit requires power for its fusing heaters and image-erase lamps. The power supply also delivers a high-voltage DC supply (+1000V DC) to the toner-transfer mechanisms in the drum arca. The high voltages are used to create the static charges required to move toner from one component to another (that is, from the drum to the paper). Finally, the power-supply unit must deliver *DC operating voltages* to the scanning and paper-handling motors, as well as to the digital electronic circuitry on the control board.

FIGURE 5.19
Block diagram of a laser printer.

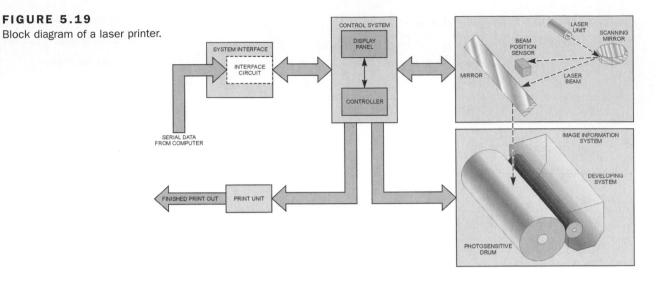

The control board contains all the circuitry required to operate the printer and to control its many parts. It receives control signals from the computer and formats the data to be printed. The control board also monitors the conditions within the printer and responds to input from the its various sensors.

When data is received from the host computer, the control board generates all the enabling signals to place the information on the page as directed. The character information is converted into a serial bit stream, which can be applied to the scanning laser. The photo-sensitive drum rotates as the laser beam is scanned across it. The laser creates a copy of the image on the photosensitive drum in the form of a relatively positive-charged drawing. This operation is referred to as registration.

Laser-Printing Operations

Before the laser writes on the drum, a set of erase lamps shine on the drum to remove any residual traces of the preceding image. This leaves the complete drum with a neutral electrical charge. A high voltage, applied to the *primary corona wire*, creates a highly charged negative field that conditions the drum to be written on, by applying a uniform negative charge (–1000V) to it. As the drum is written on by the laser, it turns through the *toner powder*, which is attracted to the more positively charged image on the drum.

Toner is a very fine powder, bonded to iron particles that are attracted to the charges written on the drum. The developer roller, in the *toner cartridge*, turns as the drum turns, and expels a measured amount of toner past a restricting blade, as illustrated in Figure 5.20. A regulating AC voltage assists the toner in leaving the cartridge, but also pulls back some excess toner from the drum. Excess toner is recycled within the toner cartridge so that it can be used again.

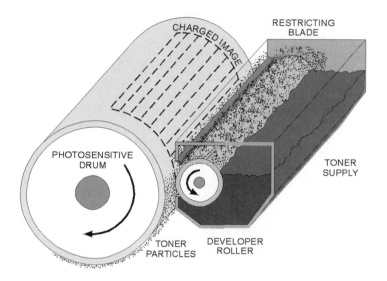

FIGURE 5.20
The developer roller.

Take great care when installing a new drum unit. Exposing the drum to light, for more than a few minutes, may damage it. Never touch the drum; this too, can ruin its surface. Keep the unit away from dust and dirt, as well as away from humidity and high-temperature areas.

The *transfer corona wire* (transfer roller) is responsible for transferring the toner from the drum to the paper. The toner is transferred to the paper because of the highly positive charge the transfer corona wire applies to the paper. The positive charge attracts the more negative toner particles away from the drum and onto the page. A special static-eliminator comb acts to prevent the positively charged paper from sticking to the negatively charged drum.

After the image has been transferred to the paper, a pair of compression rollers in the fusing unit act to press the toner particles into the paper while they melt them to it. The top compression roller, known as the *fusing roller*, is heated by a quartz lamp. This roller melts the toner to the paper as it exits the unit; the lower roller applies

TEST TIP
Know that you should never expose the drum of a laser printer to sunlight or any other strong light source.

TEST TIP
Know the functions of the two corona wires in a laser printer.

pressure to the paper. A cleaning pad removes excess particles and applies a silicon lubricant to the roller to prevent toner from sticking to the Teflon-coated fusing roller. Figure 5.21 illustrates the complete transfer process.

FIGURE 5.21
The transfer process.

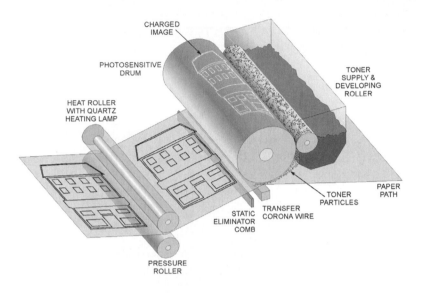

Component Variations

In Hewlett-Packard printers, the main portion of the printing system is contained in the *electrophotographic cartridge*. This cartridge contains the toner supply, the corona wire, the *drum assembly*, and the *developing roller*. Figure 5.22 depicts the H-P configuration.

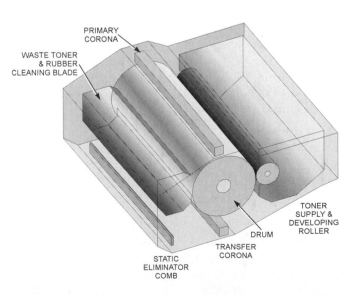

FIGURE 5.22
The H-P cartridge configuration.

In other laser printers, such as the one depicted in Figure 5.23, the basic components are combined so that the printer consists of a developer unit, a toner cartridge, a drum unit, a fuser unit, and a cleaning pad. In this case, the developer unit and toner cartridge are separate units. With this configuration, changing the toner does not involve changing some of the other wear-prone components. Although it is less expensive to change toner, attention must be paid to how much the other units are wearing. Notice that the photosensitive drum also is a separate component.

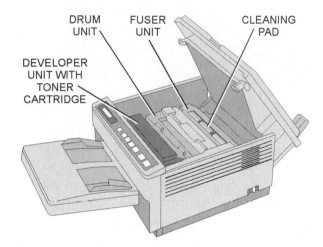

FIGURE 5.23
Basic components of a laser printer.

Paper Handling

Laser printers are very mechanical in nature. The paper-handling motor and the gear-train assembly perform a tremendous number of operations to process a single sheet of paper. The *paper-transport mechanics* must pick up a page from the paper tray and move it into the printer's *registration area*. After the drum has been written with the image, the paper-handling mechanism moves the paper into registration. A roller system moves the page past the drum and into the fusing unit. When the page exits through the fusing rollers, the printer senses that the page has exited and resets itself to wait for another page to print.

In addition to the motor and gear train, the printer uses a number of sensors and solenoid-actuated clutches to control the paper movement. It uses solenoids to engage and disengage different gear sets and clutches at appropriate times during the printing process.

> **NOTE**
>
> **Laser-Printer Sensors**   A typical laser printer has sensors to determine what paper trays are installed, what size paper is in them, and whether the tray is empty. It also uses sensors to track the movement of the paper through each stage of the printer. This allows the controller to know where the page is at all times and to sequence the activities of the solenoids and clutches properly.

Figure 5.24 summarizes the sensors found in a typical laser printer.

FIGURE 5.24
Sensor summary.

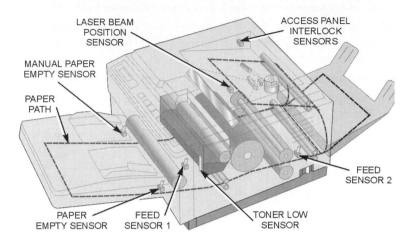

If the page does not show up at the next sensor at the appropriate time, the printer knows that a paper jam has occurred and creates an error message that indicates the area of the printer where it is. When a paper jam occurs, you must remove the paper from the inside of the printer and reset the print operation. Gaining access to the area of the jammed area of the printer requires direction from the printer's User Manual. Always allow the printer to cool and always turn it off before reaching inside the unit.

Another set of sensor switches monitor the printer's access doors to protect personnel from potentially dangerous conditions inside the printer. The *interlock switch* blocks the laser beam as a vision-protection measure. Likewise, the high-voltage supplies to various printer components also are shut down. To observe the operation of the printer, you must locate, and bypass, these interlocks. You should always be aware that these interlocks are present for protection, however, and take great care when working with them defeated.

Still other sensors are used to monitor the temperatures within different sections of the printer. A thermal sensor in the fusing unit monitors the temperature of the unit. This information is applied to the control circuitry so that it can control the fuser temperature between 140°C and 230°C. If the temperature of the fuser is not controlled correctly, it may cause severe damage to the printer and also may present a potential fire hazard.

A *thermal fuse* protects the fuser assembly from overheating and damaging the printer. The thermal fuse should normally snap back after the temperature condition is cleared. If the switch is open under cool conditions, it will need to be replaced. This is normally an indication that the thermal sensor has failed or that the fuser assembly has been installed improperly.

When the laser beam is turned on, a beam-detector sensor in the writing unit alerts the control circuitry that the writing process has begun. This signal synchronizes the beginning of the laser-modulating data with the beginning of the scan line.

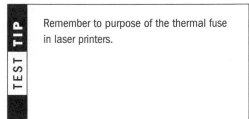

TEST TIP
Remember to purpose of the thermal fuse in laser printers.

Paper Specifications

Another reason for faint printing is that the paper-thickness lever is set to the wrong position for the weight of paper being used.

The thickness setting also causes smudged characters when the paper is too thick for the actual setting. In this case, adjust the thickness lever one or two notches away from the paper.

NOTE
Paper Weight   Paper is specified in terms of its weight per 500 sheets at 22" × 17". (That is, 500 sheets of 22" × 17"21-pound bond paper weigh 21 pounds.)

PRINTER CONNECTIONS AND CONFIGURATIONS

▶ 5.1 (subobjective) Identify the types of printer connections and configurations.

The A+ Core Hardware 5.1 subobjective states that the test taker should be able to "identify the types of printer connections and configurations."

Printers used with personal computers are available in many types and use various connection schemes. As this A+ objective points out, the computer technician must be able to connect a brand-*x* printer to a brand-*y* computer and configure them for operation.

The connection method between the printer and the computer will affect many of the troubleshooting steps necessary to isolate printing problems. Likewise, connecting a printer to a network will affect how the technician approaches the configuration and troubleshooting. The following sections concentrate on the various printer connection methods commonly found in personal computer environments.

TEST TIP
Know how paper weight is specified and how many sheets are involved.

Printer Installation

Generally speaking, one of the least difficult I/O devices to add to a microcomputer system is a parallel printer. This is largely because from the beginning of the PC era, a parallel printer has been one of the most standard pieces of equipment to add to the system.

This standardization has led to fairly direct installation procedures for most printers. Obtain an IBM Centronics printer cable, plug it into the appropriate LPT port on the back of the computer, connect the Centronic-compatible end to the printer, plug the power cord into the printer, load a device driver to configure the software for the correct printer, and print.

One note of caution concerning parallel printer cables: The IEEE has established specifications for bidirectional parallel-printer cables (IEEE 1284). These cables affect the operation of EPP and ECP parallel devices. Refer to the "Enhanced Parallel Port Operations" section of Chapter 4, "4.0 Motherboard/Processors/Memory," for additional information about these ports. Using an older, noncompliant unidirectional cable with a bidirectional parallel device will prevent the device from communicating properly with the system and may prevent it from operating.

Some failures produce error messages, such as `Printer Not Ready`; others just leave the data in the computer's print spooler. The symptom normally associated with this condition is that the parallel device just refuses to operate. If an ECP or EPP device successfully runs a self-test, but will not communicate with the host system, check the Advanced BIOS Setup screens to make certain that bidirectional printing has been enabled for the parallel port. If so, check the printer cable by substituting a known, 1284-compliant cable for it.

Regardless of the type of printer being installed, the steps for adding a printer to a system are basically the same. Connect the printer to the correct I/O port at the computer system. Make sure the port is enabled. Set up the appropriate *printer drivers*. Configure the port's communication parameters, if a serial printer is being installed. Install the paper. Run the printer's self-test, and then print a document. Figure 5.25 summarizes these steps.

TEST TIP

Setting Up Serial Printers   Serial printers are slightly more difficult to set up because the communication definition must be configured between the computer and the printer. The serial port needs to be configured for speed, parity type, character frame, and protocol.

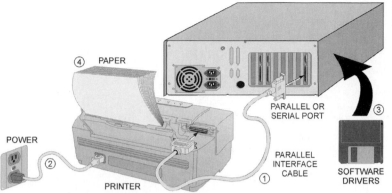

FIGURE 5.25
Printer installation steps.

Printer Drivers

Like mice, printers require device-driver programs to oversee their operation.

For example, a software developer writing a word-processing program will not have any way of knowing what type of printers will be used.

Although most printers use the same codes for alphanumeric data, they may use widely different control and special-feature codes to produce special text and to govern the printer's operation. Therefore, software producers often develop the core hardware of a program, and then offer a disk full of printer drivers to translate between the software package and different standard printers.

The user normally selects the driver program needed to operate the system through a configuration program that comes with the software. This function is usually performed the first time the software is loaded into the system. Figure 5.26 illustrates the functional position of a printer driver in the system.

Driver programs may be supplied by the software developer as part of the package or by the hardware developer. It is often in the best interests of a hardware developer to offer drivers that make the hardware compatible with popular pieces of application software. Conversely, if a software developer introduces a new piece of software, the developer often offers drivers that make the software compatible with as many hardware variants as possible.

FIGURE 5.26
Printer driver position.

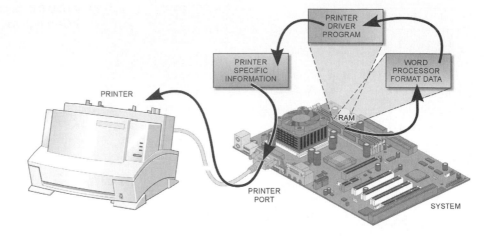

Serial Printer Considerations

In some applications, it is just impossible to locate the printer close enough to the host computer to use the parallel connection. In these cases, serially interfaced printers come into play. Printers using a serial interface connection add an extra level of complexity to the system. Unlike the parallel-printer interface that basically plugs and plays on most systems, serial interface connections require additional hardware and software configuration steps. Serial printer problems basically fall into three categories:

◆ Cabling problems

◆ Configuration problems

◆ Printer problems

Cabling Problems

Not all serial cables are created equal. In the PC world, RS-232 serial cables can take on several configurations. First of all, they may use either 9-pin or 25-pin D-shell connectors. The cable for a particular serial connection need to have the correct type of connector at each end. Likewise, the connection scheme inside the cable can vary from printer to printer. Normally, the transmit data line (TXD - pin 2) from the computer is connected to the receive data line (RXD - pin 3) of the printer. Also, the data set ready (DSR - pin 6) is typically connected to the printer's data terminal ready (DTR - pin 20) pin. These connections are used as one method to control the flow of information between the system and the printer. If the printer's character buffer becomes full, it signals the computer to hold up sending characters by deactivating this line.

Different or additional pin interconnections can be required for other printer models. The actual implementation of the RS-232 connection is solely up to the printer manufacturer. Figure 5.27 depicts typical connection schemes for both 9-pin and 25-pin connections to a typical printer. The connection scheme for a given serial printer model is normally provided in its User Manual.

> **TEST TIP**
>
> Remember the types of connectors used at both the computer and the printer end of an RS-232 serial printer cable.

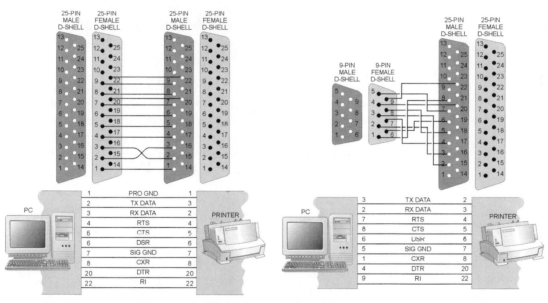

FIGURE 5.27
Serial printer connection schemes.

The other limiting factor for printer cables, both serial and parallel, is length. Although cables purchased from reputable suppliers are typically correct in length and contain all the shielding and connections required, cheaper cables and homemade cables often lack in one of these areas or the other. The recommended signal cable lengths associated with parallel and serial printers are as follows:

◆ **Standard parallel printers.** 0–10 feet (3 meters), although some equipment manufacturers specify 6 feet (1.8 meters) maximums for their cables. You should believe these recommendations when you see them.

TEST TIP

Know the recommended maximum length of a standard parallel printer cable and an RS-232 cable.

◆ **RS-232 serial printers.** 10–50 feet (15.25 meters). However, some references use 100 feet as the acceptable length of an RS-232C serial cable. Serial connections are tricky enough without problems generated by the cable being too long. Make the cable as short as possible.

Configuration Problems

After the correct connector and cabling scheme has been implemented, the printer configuration must be established at both the computer and at the printer. The information in both locations must match for communications to go on. On the system side of the serial port connection, the software printer driver must be set up to match the setting of the printer's receiving section.

First, the driver must be directed toward the correct serial port. In a Windows-based system, this is typically COM2. Second, the selected serial port must be configured for the proper character framing. The number of start, stop, data, and parity bits must be set to match what the printer is expecting to receive. These values are often established through hardware configuration switches located on the printer.

The printer driver must also be set up to correctly handle the flow of data between the system and the printer. Incorrect flow-control settings can result in slow response, lost characters, or continuous errors and retries. Flow control can be established through software or *hardware handshaking*. In a hardware-handshaking mode, the printer tells the port that it is not prepared to receive data by deactivating a control line, such as the DTR line. Conversely, in a software-handshaking environment, control codes are sent back and forth between the printer and the computer to enable and disable data flow.

NOTE

Software-Data Flow Control   Two popular methods of implementing software flow control are Xon/Xoff and ETX/ACK. In the Xon/Xoff method, special ASCII control characters are exchanged between the printer and the computer to turn the data flow on and off. In an ETX/ACK protocol, ASCII characters for End-of-Text (ETX) and ACKnowledge (ACK) are used to control the movement of data from the port to the printer.

Basically, the computer attaches the ETX character to the end of a data transmission. When the printer receives the ETX character, it checks the incoming data, and when ready, returns an ACK character to the port. This notifies the system that the printer can receive additional characters. Figure 5.28 illustrates this concept. In any event, the devices at both ends of the interface connection must be set to use the same flow-control method.

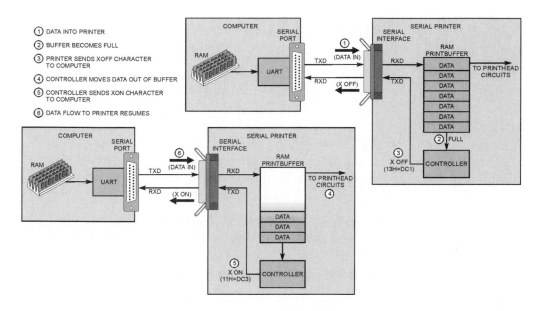

FIGURE 5.28
Software flow control.

Printer baud rate is usually designated by a set of DIP switches in the printer. Common baud rates used with serial printers are 300, 1,200, 2,400, and 9,600 bits per second. One of the most common problems associated with getting a serial interface to work interface to work is mismatched baud rates.

Serial communications standards and procedures are covered in greater detail in the section titled "Peripherals and Ports" in Chapter 1 "1.0 Installation, Configuration, and Upgrading." Consult that section for more information about character framing, error-detection and -correction methods, and serial transmission protocols.

Serial Printer Problems

Problems associated with serial printers differ from those of parallel printer only in the area of the serial interface configuration. As mentioned in the preceding section the protocol, character framing, and baud rate of the printer must match that of the system's interface. After ensuring that the interface settings match, and that the interface is working, the steps for troubleshooting a serial printer are identical to those given for parallel-interfaced printers. Therefore, the only steps that need to be added to the troubleshooting sections later in this chapter are those needed to validate the operation of the serial interface.

Networked Printers

If a printer is installed in a computer system that is part of a network, any other computer on the network can send work to the printer. Historically, the local computer is attached to the printer through one of the normal printing interfaces (that is, parallel, serial, or USB) and also is connected to the other remote computers through its network connection. In addition to the signal cable, the local computer's operating system must be configured to permit the remote stations on the network to print through it to its printer. This relationship is known as *print sharing*.

Newer printers, referred to as network-ready printers, or just as network printers, come with built-in network interfacing that enables them to be connected directly into the local area network. Most network printers contain an integrated network controller and Ethernet LAN adapter that enables it to work on the LAN without a supporting host computer.

Other printers may be connected directly to the LAN through a device called a print server port. This device resembles a network hub in appearance and can be used to connect up to three printers directly into the network.

Whereas some older network printers used coaxial cable connections, newer network printers feature RJ-45 jacks for connection to twisted-pair Ethernet networks. It is relatively easy to determine whether a printer is networked by the presence of a coaxial or a twisted-pair network signal cable connected directly to the printer. The presence of the RJ-45 jacks on the back of the printer also indicate that the printer is network capable, even if it is not being used in that manner. These cables are covered in the section titled "Basic Networking Concepts" in Chapter 6, "6.0 Basic Networking." In Windows, you can determine that a printer is networked by the appearance of its icon in the Printers folder. The icon will graphically illustrate the network connection. You also can check the Details tab of the printer in the its Windows Properties page.

Although parallel printers are easy to set up and check, and serial printers require a little more effort to set up, networked printers add another set of variables to the configuration and troubleshooting processes. To avoid dealing directly with the complexity of the network, it is normal to handle printer configuration and troubleshooting at the local level first. After the operation of the local

TEST TIP

Know how to determine whether a printer is networked.

computer/printer interface has been established, or verified, the network portion of the system can be examined. Chapter 6 deals with typical network troubleshooting procedures; Windows-related network printing problems are covered extensively in Chapter 9, "3.0 Diagnosing and Troubleshooting."

TEST TIP

Know how to identify the presence of a network-ready printer.

SERVICING PRINTERS

▶ 5.2 Identify care and service techniques and common problems with primary printer types.

The A+ Core Hardware objective 5.2 states that the test taker should be able to "identify care and service techniques and common problems with primary printer types."

Printers are connected to personal computers and they break down. Therefore, the computer technician should be familiar with common printer problems and be able to demonstrate current service techniques. The following sections deal with typical problems encountered with dot-matrix, inkjet, and *laser printers*. They also include troubleshooting methods associated with each type of printer.

Troubleshooting Dot-Matrix Printers

The classical first step in determining the cause of any printer problem is to determine which part of the printer-related system is at fault—the host computer, the signal cable, or the printer.

Nearly every printer is equipped with a built-in self-test. The easiest way to determine whether the printer is at fault is to run its self-test. Consult the printer's User Manual for instructions on running its self-test. Some printers produce audible tones to indicate the nature of an internal problem. Refer to the printer's User Manual for the definitions of the coded, beep tones, if they are available.

If the printer runs the self-test, and prints clean pages, most of the printer has been eliminated as a possible cause of problems. The problem could be in the computer, the cabling, or the interface portion of the printer. If the printer fails the self-test, however, you

TEST TIP

Know what it means if the printer produces a satisfactory self-test print out but will not print from the computer.

must diagnose the printer's problem. The following section presents typical problems encountered with dot-matrix printers.

The following are symptoms for dot-matrix printer problems:

- ◆ No lights or noise from printer
- ◆ Light or uneven print being produced
- ◆ Printhead moving, but not printing
- ◆ Dots missing from characters
- ◆ Printhead printing, but does not move
- ◆ Paper not advancing

Dot-Matrix Printer Configuration Checks

The presence of onboard microcontrollers allows modern printers to be very flexible. Like other peripheral devices, printers can be configured to operate in different modes. Operating configuration information can be stored in CMOS RAM on the control board. Some configuration settings may be made through DIP switches mounted inside the printer. These switches are read by the printer's microcontroller at startup.

In the case of dot-matrix printers, the configuration settings are normally entered into the printer through the buttons of its control panel. Typical dot-matrix configuration information includes the following:

- ◆ Printer mode
- ◆ Perforation skip (for continuous forms)
- ◆ Automatic line feed at the bottom of the page
- ◆ Paper-handling type
- ◆ ASCII character codes (7 bit or 8 bit)
- ◆ Basic character sets

Other quantities that can be set up include the following:

- ◆ Print font
- ◆ Character pitch
- ◆ Form length

Most dot-matrix printers contain two or three onboard fonts (character styles) that can be selected through the printer's configuration routines. Typical fonts included in dot-matrix printers are as follows:

- ◆ Draft
- ◆ Courier
- ◆ Prestige
- ◆ Bold prestige

In many dot-matrix printer models, however, it is also possible to download other fonts from the computer. The character pitch refers to the number of characters printed per inch. Common pitch settings include 10, 11, 12, and 14 dots per inch. Consult the printer's User Manual to find the definitions of such settings.

Dot-Matrix Printer Hardware Checks

To perform work inside the printer, you must disassemble its case. Begin by removing any add-on pieces, such as dust covers and paper feeders. Next, remove the paper-advancement knob located on the right side of most dot-matrix printers. Turn the printer over and remove the screws that hold the two halves of the case together. These screws are sometimes hidden beneath rubber feet, and compliance stickers. Finally, it may be necessary to disconnect the printer's front-panel connections from the main board to complete the separation of the two case halves. Figure 5.29 depicts this procedure.

Dot-Matrix Printer Power-Supply Problems

If the printer will not function and displays no lights, no sounds, and no actions, the power supply is generally involved. Troubleshoot printer power-supply problems in the same manner as a computer power supply. As a matter of fact, the power-supply troubleshooting routine is the same.

Check the *online* light. If the printer is *offline*, no print action will occur. A missing or improperly installed ribbon cartridge will also prevent the unit from printing. Install the ribbon correctly. Check the power outlet to make certain that it is live. Plug a lamp or other device in the outlet to verify that it is operative. Check to see that the power cord is plugged securely into the printer and the socket. Make sure the power switch is turned on.

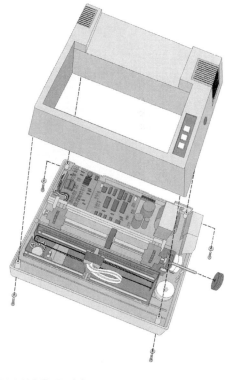

FIGURE 5.29
Disassembling the printer.

If everything is plugged in and in the on position, but still not working, turn off the power and unplug the printer from the outlet. Remove the top of the printer's case and find the power-supply board. Check the power supply's fuse to make sure that it is good. If the fuse is blown, replace it with a fuse of the same type and rating. Do not replace a blown fuse with a conductor or a slow-blow fuse. Doing so could lead to more extensive damage to the printer, and possible unsafe conditions.

Also, check the power-supply and control boards, as well as the paper-feed and printhead-positioning motors for burnt components or signs of defect. Fuses do not usually blow unless another component fails. The other possible cause of excessive current occurs when a motor (or its gear train) binds and cannot move. Check the drive mechanisms and motors for signs of binding. If the gear train or positioning mechanisms does not move, you may need to adjust them before replacing the fuse.

If none of the printer sections work, when everything is connected and power is applied, you must exchange the power-supply board for a new unit. Unlike the computer's power supply, the typical printer power supply is not enclosed in a protective housing and therefore presents a shock hazard anytime it is exposed.

To exchange the power-supply board, disconnect the power cord from the printer. Disconnect, and mark, the cabling from the control board, and any other components directly connected to the power supply. Remove any screws, or clips, that secure the power-supply board to the case. Lift the board out of the cabinet. Install the new board and reconnect the various wire bundles to it.

Ribbon Cartridges

The single item in a dot-matrix printer that requires the most attention is the ribbon cartridge. It is considered a consumable part of the printer and must be changed often. The ink ribbon is stored in a controlled wad inside the cartridge, and moves across the face of the platen, as depicted in Figure 5.30. A take-up wheel draws new ribbon out of the wad as it is used. As the ribbon wears out, the printing will become faint, and uneven. When the print becomes noticeably faint, the cartridge should be replaced. Most dot-matrix printers use a snap-in ribbon cartridge.

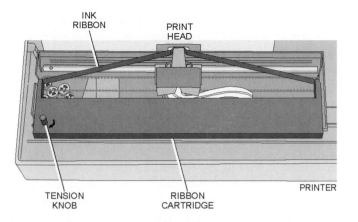

FIGURE 5.30
The printer cartridge.

To replace a typical ribbon cartridge, move the printhead carriage assembly to the center of the printer. Remove the old cartridge by freeing it from its clips, or holders, and then lifting it out of the printer.

Tighten the ribbon tension by advancing the tension knob on the cartridge in a counter-clockwise direction until the ribbon is taut. Snap the cartridge into place, making certain that the ribbon slides between the printhead and the ribbon mask. Slide the printhead assembly back and forth on the rod to check for proper ribbon movement.

Printhead Not Printing

If the printhead is moving, but not printing, begin by checking the printer's *head-gap lever* to make sure that the printhead is not too far back from the paper. If the printhead does not operate, components involved include the following:

◆ The printhead

◆ The flexible signal cable between the control board and the printhead

◆ The control board

◆ Possibly the power-supply board

Run the printer's self-test to see whether the printhead will print from the onboard test. Check the flexible signal cable to make sure that it is firmly plugged into the control board, and that it is not damaged or worn through. If none of the print wires are being energized, the first step should be to exchange the control board for a known good one of the same type. If the new control board does not correct the problem, replace the printhead. A power-supply problem could also cause the printhead to not print.

A related problem occurs when one or more of the print wires does not fire. If this is the case, check the printhead for physical damage. Also check the flexible signal cable for a broken conductor. If the control board is delivering any of the other print-wire signals, the problem is most likely associated with the printhead mechanism. Replace the printhead as a first step. If the problem continues after replacing the printhead, however, exchange the control board for a new one.

If the tops of characters are missing, the printhead is misaligned with the platen. It may need to be reseated in the printhead carriage, or the carriage assembly may need to be adjusted to the proper height and angle.

To exchange the printhead assembly, make sure that the printhead assembly is cool enough to be handled. These units can get hot enough to cause a serious burn. Unplug the printhead assembly from the control board. Slide the printhead assembly to the center of the printer and rotate the head-locking lever to release the printhead from the assembly. Remove the printhead by lifting it straight up. Install the new printhead by following the disassembly procedure in reverse. Adjust the new printhead for proper printing. In some printers, the printheads are held in the printhead assembly with screws. To remove the printhead from these units, you must remove the screws so that the printhead can be exchanged. Refer to the printer's documentation for directions concerning exchanging the printhead mechanism.

If the output of the printer gets lighter as it moves from left to right across the page, it may become necessary to adjust the printhead mechanism to obtain proper printing. Figure 5.31 illustrates this procedure. To print correctly, the printhead should be approximately 0.6mm from the platen when the head-position lever is in the center position. Move the printhead to the center of the printer. Adjusting this setting requires that the nut at the left end of the rear carriage shaft be loosened. Using a feeler gauge, set the distance between the

TEST TIP

Know what causes tops of characters to be missing from dot-matrix characters and how to correct the problem.

TEST TIP

Remember that the printhead of dot-matrix printers generate a great deal of heat and can be a burn hazard when working on these units.

platen and printhead (not the ribbon mask). Tighten the nut and check the spacing between the printhead and platen at both ends of the printhead travel.

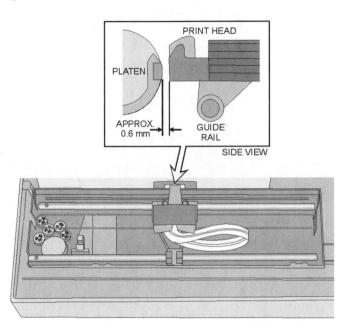

FIGURE 5.31
Adjusting the printhead spacing.

Finally, check the distance between the platen and the ribbon mask. This spacing should be 0.3mm. If not, loosen the screws that hold the ribbon mask to the printhead assembly and adjust the gap with feeler gauges. There should also be a 0.1mm space between the printhead and the ribbon mask. After setting the various gaps, run the printer's self-test to check for print quality.

Printhead Not Moving

If the printhead is printing, but not moving across the page, a single block of print will be generated on the page. When this type of problem occurs, the related components include the printhead-positioning motor, the timing belt, the home-position and *timing sensors*, the control board, and possibly the power-supply board.

With the power off, manually move the printhead to the center of the printer. Turn the printer on to see whether the printhead seeks the home position at the far-left side of the printer. If it moves to the left side of the printer, and does not shut off, or does not return to the center of the printer, the home-position sensor is malfunctioning and should be replaced. If the printhead moves on startup, but does not move during normal printing, the control board should be replaced. In the event that the printhead assembly does not move at any time, the printhead-positioning motor should be replaced. If the print is skewed from left to right as it moves down the page, the printer's bidirectional mode settings may be faulty, or the home-position/end-of-line sensors may be defective.

Testing the timing sensor would require test equipment, in the form of a logic probe or an oscilloscope, to look for pulses produced as the printhead is manually moved across the printer.

Figure 5.32 depicts the components associated with the printhead's timing belt. Replacing the timing belt requires that it be removed from the printhead assembly. In many cases, the belt is secured to the printhead assembly with adhesive cement. In such cases, removing it requires that the adhesive seal be cut with a single-edged razor blade or a hobby knife.

After the seal has been broken, it should be possible to shove the belt out of the clips that secure it to the printhead assembly. Next, remove the belt from the drive-pulley assembly at the positioning motor. It may be necessary to remove the positioning motor from the case to gain access to the pulley.

FIGURE 5.32
Printhead timing.

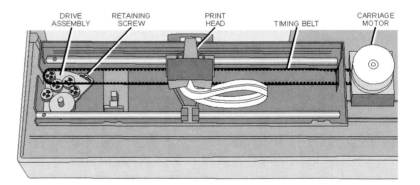

To reinstall the timing belt, apply a small drop of adhesive to the belt and reattach it to the printhead assembly. Wrap the belt around the positioning motor's drive pulley and reinstall the motor. Following this, you must adjust the tension on the belt. To set the tension on the belt, loosen the adjustment screw on the belt-tension adjustment plate. Tighten the timing belt until it will not move more than 1/4" when the printhead is at either end of the carriage shaft and the belt is pressed inward. Tighten the retaining screw to lock the tension plate in place. Run the printer's self-test and check the distance between the characters. If the intercharacter spacing is not uniform, replace the belt and perform the check again.

Paper Not Advancing

When the paper does not advance, the output is normally one line of dark blocks across the page. Examine the printer's *paper-feed selector lever* to make sure that it is set properly for the type of paper feed selected (that is, *friction feed, pin feed,* or tractor feed). If the paper feed is set correctly, the printer is online, and the paper does not move, it is necessary to troubleshoot the paper-handling motor and gear train. Check the motor and gear train by setting the printer to the offline mode and holding down the Form Feed (FF) button.

If the feed motor and gear train work from this point, the problem must exist on the control board, with the interface cable, the printer's configuration, or in the computer system. If the motor and/or gear train does not respond, unplug the paper-feed motor cable and check the resistance of the motor windings. If the windings are open, replace the paper-feed motor.

To replace the paper-feed motor and/or gear train, remove the screws that hold the paper-feed motor to the frame of the printer. Create a wiring diagram that describes the routing of the feed motor's wiring harness. Disconnect the wiring harness from the control board.

Prepare a drawing that outlines the arrangement of the gear train (if multiple gears are used). Remove the gears from the shafts, taking care not to lose any washers or springs that may be located behind the gears. After reinstalling the gears and new motor, adjust the motor and gear relationships to minimize the gear lash so that they do not bind or lock up. Use the printer's self-test to check the operation of the motor and gears.

Troubleshooting Inkjet Printers

As with the dot-matrix printer, the first step in determining the cause of an inkjet printer problem is to determine which part of the printer system is at fault—the host computer, the signal cable, or the printer.

Inkjet printers are equipped with built-in self-tests. The easiest way to determine whether the printer is at fault is to run its self-tests. Consult the printer's User Manual for instructions in running its self-tests.

If the printer runs the self-tests and prints clean pages, most of the printer has been eliminated as a possible cause of problems. The problem could be in the computer, the cabling, or the interface portion of the printer. If the printer fails the self-tests, however, you must diagnose the printer problem. The following section presents typical problems encountered with inkjet printers.

The following are symptoms of inkjet printer problems:

◆ No lights or noise from printer

◆ Light, or uneven, print being produced

◆ Printhead moving, but not printing, or printing erratically

◆ Lines on the page

◆ Printhead printing, but does not move

◆ Paper not advancing

Inkjet Printer Configuration Checks

The presence of the printer's onboard microcontroller allows modern printers to be flexible. Like other peripheral devices, printers can be configured to operate in different modes. Operating configuration information can be stored in RAM on the control board.

In the case of inkjet printers, the configuration settings are normally entered into the printer through software. Typical configuration information includes the following:

◆ Page orientation (landscape or portrait)

◆ Paper size

◆ Collation

◆ Print quality

Landscape printing is specified when the width of the page is greater than the length of the page. Portrait printing is specified when the length of the page is greater than the width. In an inkjet printer, the quality of the printout is specified in the number of dots per inch (dpi) produced. Typical inkjet resolutions run from 180×180dpi to 720×720dpi. Inkjet printers can download additional fonts from the host computer.

You also can configure the basic appearance of color and *grayscale* images produced by the inkjet printer. A color inkjet printer uses four ink colors to produce color images. These are cyan, magenta, yellow and black (referred to as *CMYK color*). To create other colors, the printer prints a predetermined percentage of the basic colors in close proximity to each other.

The different percentages determine what the new color will be. The eye does not differentiate the space between them and perceives only the combined color. This is referred to as *halftone* color. Typical color configurations include setting up the brightness, the contrast, and the saturation settings of images.

Inkjet-Printer Hardware Checks

To perform work on the printer's hardware, you must disassemble the printer's case. Begin by removing all the add-on pieces, such as dust covers and paper feeders. Remove the screws that hold the outer panels of the case to the printer frame. Figure 5.33 depicts removing the access panels of a typical inkjet printer. The retaining screws are sometimes hidden beneath rubber feet, and compliance stickers. Finally, it may be necessary to disconnect the printer's front-panel connections from the control board to complete the disassembly of the case.

Power-Supply Problems

If the printer does not function and displays no lights, no sounds and no actions, the power supply is generally involved. Check the online light. If the printer is offline, no print action will occur. A missing or improperly installed ink cartridge prevents the unit from printing. Install the ink cartridge correctly. Check the power outlet to make certain that it is live. Plug a lamp or other device in the outlet to verify that it is operative. Check to see that the power cord is plugged securely into the printer and the socket. Make sure the power switch is turned on.

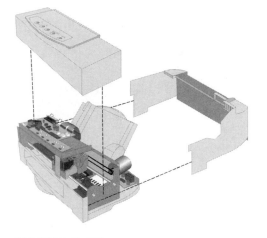

FIGURE 5.33
Printer case.

If the unit is plugged in and turned on but still not working, turn it off and unplug it. Remove the top of the printer's case and locate the power-supply board. Check the power supply's fuse to make sure that it is good. If the fuse is blown, replace it with a fuse of the same type and rating. Do not replace a blown fuse with a conductor or a slow-blow fuse. To do so could lead to more extensive damage to the printer, and possible unsafe conditions.

Also, check the power-supply and control boards, as well as the paper-feed and printhead-positioning motors for burnt components or signs of defect. Fuses do not usually blow unless another component fails. The other possible cause of over-current occurs when a motor (or its gear train) binds and cannot move. Check the drive mechanisms and motors for signs of binding. If the gear train or positioning mechanisms will not move, you may need to adjust or replace them before replacing the fuse.

If none of the printer sections work, everything is connected, and power is applied, you must exchange the power-supply board for a new unit. Unlike the computer's power supply, the typical power supply in a printer is not enclosed in a protective housing and, therefore, presents a shock hazard any time it is exposed.

To exchange the power-supply board, disconnect the power cord from the printer. Disconnect, and mark, the cabling from the control board, and any other components directly connected to the power supply. Remove any screws or clips that secure the power-supply board to the case. Lift the board out of the cabinet. Install the new board and reconnect the various wire bundles to it.

Ink Cartridges

The single item in an inkjet printer that requires the most attention is the ink cartridge (or cartridges). As the ink cartridge empties, the printing eventually becomes faint and uneven, and the resolution of the print on the page diminishes.

The density of the printout from an inkjet printer can be adjusted through its printing software. When the print becomes noticeably faint or the resolution becomes unacceptable, however, you must replace the cartridge. Most inkjet printers use a self-contained, snap-in ink cartridge, like the one shown in Figure 5.34. Some models have combined ink cartridges that replace all three colors and the black ink at the same time. Other models use individual cartridges for each color. In this way, only the colors that are running low are replaced.

You can pop an ink cartridge out of the printhead assembly and thereby inspect the inkjets. If any, or all of the jets, are clogged, it is normally possible to clear them by gently wiping the face of the cartridge with a swab. A gentle squeeze of the ink reservoir can also help to unblock a clogged jet. Using solvents to clear blockages in the jets can dilute the ink and allow it to flow uncontrollably through the jet.

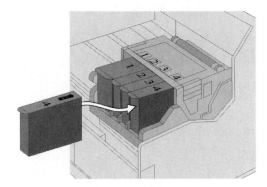

FIGURE 5.34
Self-contained, snap-in ink cartridge.

To replace a typical ink cartridge, move the printhead carriage assembly to the center of the printer. Remove the old cartridge by freeing it from its clips or holders and lifting it out of the printer.

After replacing the ink cartridge, you should cycle the printer on so that it goes through its normal warm-up procedures. During these procedures, the printer does a thorough cleaning of the inkjet nozzles and gets the ink flowing correctly from the nozzles. Afterward, print a test page to verify the output of the new ink cartridge.

Printhead Not Printing

If the printhead is moving, but not printing, begin by checking the ink supply in the print cartridge. The reservoir does not have to be completely empty to fail. Replace the cartridge(s) that appear(s) to be low. Some or all the jets may be clogged. This is particularly common if the printer has not been used for a while. If cleaning instructions are in the user manual, clean the jets and attempt to print from the self-test.

If the printer does not print from the self-tests, the components involved include the following:

- ◆ The printhead
- ◆ The flexible signal cable (between the control board and the printhead)
- ◆ The control board
- ◆ Possibly the power-supply board

Check the flexible signal cable to make sure that it is firmly plugged into the control board and that it is not damaged or worn through. If none of the inkjets are firing, the first step should be to exchange the ink cartridges for new ones. If a single inkjet is not firing, replace the cartridge that is not working.

Next, use the ohmmeter function of a multimeter to check the continuity of the conductors in the flexible-wiring harness that supplies the printhead assembly. If one of the conductors is broken, a single jet will normally be disabled. If the broken conductor is a ground or common connection, all the jets should be disabled. Exchange the control board for a known good one of the same type. If the new control board does not correct the problem, replace the printhead. A power-supply problem also can cause the printhead to not print.

If a single jet is not functioning, the output appears as a white line on the page. If one of the jets is activated all the time, black or colored lines are produced on the page. Use the preceding steps to isolate the cause of these problems—replace the print cartridge, check the flexible cabling for continuity and for short-circuits between adjacent conductors, exchange the control board for a known good one, and finally, check the power supply.

Printhead Not Moving

If the printhead is printing, but not moving across the page, a single block of print is normally be generated on the page. When this type of problem occurs, the related components include the printhead-positioning motor, the timing belt, the home-position sensor, the control board, and possibly the power supply. Figure 5.35 depicts these components.

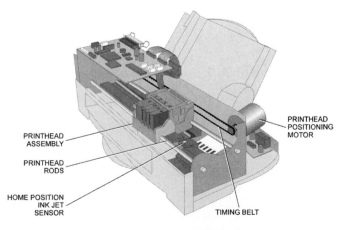

FIGURE 5.35
Printhead-positioning components.

With the power off, manually move the printhead to the center of the printer. Turn the printer on to see whether the printhead seeks the home position at the far end of the printer. If the printhead moves to the end of the printer and does not shut off, or does not return to the center of the printer, the home-position sensor is malfunctioning and should be replaced. If the printhead moves on startup, but will not move during normal printing, the control board should be replaced. In the event that the printhead assembly will not move at any time, check to see whether the printer is in maintenance mode. In this mode, the printer typically keeps the printhead assembly in the home position. If no mode problems are present, you should replace the printhead-positioning motor.

If characters are unevenly spaced across the page, the timing sensor may be failing. To test the timing sensor requires test equipment, in the form of a logic probe or an oscilloscope, to look for pulses produced as the printhead is manually moved across the printer.

Replacing the timing belt requires that the belt be removed from the printhead assembly. In many cases, the belt will be secured to the printhead assembly with adhesive cement. In such case, you must cut the adhesive seal with a single-edged razor blade or a hobby knife. After the seal has been broken, it should be possible to shove the belt out of the clips that secure it to the printhead assembly. Next, remove the belt from the drive-pulley assembly at the positioning motor. You may need to remove the positioning motor from the case to gain access to the pulley.

Paper Not Advancing

When the paper does not advance, the output is normally a thick, dark line across the page. Check the control panel to see that the printer is online. If the printer is online and the paper does not move, you must troubleshoot the paper-handling motor and gear train. Check the motor, and gear train by setting the printer to the offline mode and holding down the Form Feed button.

If the printer's paper thickness selector is set improperly, or the rollers in its paper-feed system becomes worn, the paper can slip as it moves through the printer and cause wavy graphics to be produced. Check the printer's paper thickness settings. If they are correct and the print output is disfigured, you need to replace the paper feed rollers.

If the feed motor and gear train work from this point, the problem must exist on the control board, the interface cable, the printer configuration, or the computer system. If the motor and/or gear train does not respond, unplug the paper-feed motor cable and check the resistance of the motor windings. If the windings are open, replace the paper-feed motor.

To replace the paper-feed motor and/or gear train, remove the screws that hold the paper-feed motor to the frame of the printer. Create a wiring diagram that describes the routing of the feed motor's wiring harness. Disconnect the wiring harness from the control board.

Draw an outline of the gear-train arrangement (if multiple gears are used). Remove the gears from their shafts, taking care not to lose any washers or springs that may be located behind the gears. After reinstalling the gears and new motor, adjust the motor and gear relationships to minimize the gear lash so that they do not bind or lock up. Use the printer's self-tests to check the operation of the motor and gears.

Troubleshooting Laser Printers

Many of the problems encountered in laser printers are similar to those found in other printer types. For example, most of the symptoms listed in the following section relate to the printer not printing, or not printing correctly, or not moving paper through the printer.

Due to the extreme complexity of the laser printer's paper-handling system, paper jams are a common problem. This problem tends to increase in frequency as the printer's components wear from use. Basically, paper jams occur in all three of the following main sections of the printer:

- ◆ The pickup area
- ◆ The registration area
- ◆ The fusing area

If the rubber separation pad in the *pickup area* is worn excessively, more than one sheet of paper may be drawn into the printer, causing it to jam.

If additional, optional paper-handling features—such as duplexers (for double-sided copying) and *collators* (for sorting)—can contribute to the possibility of jams as they wear. Paper problems can also cause jams to occur. Using paper that is too heavy or too thick can result in jams, as can overloading paper trays. Similarly, using the wrong type of paper can defeat the separation pad and allow multiple pages to be drawn into the printer. In this case, the multiple sheets may move through the printer together, or they may result in a jam. Using coated paper stock can be hazardous because the coating may melt or catch fire.

The following are symptoms of laser-printer problems:

◆ Printer dead, power on, but no printing.

◆ The print on the page is faint or washed out.

◆ A blank page is produced.

◆ Stains or black dust on paper.

◆ Vertical lines on paper.

◆ The printer will not load paper.

◆ Paper jams in printer.

◆ A paper jam has been cleared, but the unit still indicates a jam is present.

Laser-Printer Configuration Checks

Like other complex peripheral equipment, laser printers must be configured for the desired operational characteristics. The printer is an extension of the computer system and therefore must be part of the overall configuration. To make the system function as a unit, configure the computer, configure the printer, and configure the software. Review and record the computer's configuration information for use in setting up the printer and software. Configure the printer with the parameters that you want it to use, record these settings, and then set up the software to match. Consult the printer's user manual for configuration information specific to setting up that particular printer.

TEST TIP

Remember that paper jams in a laser printer can be caused by incorrect paper settings.

WARNING

Laser-Printer Dangers Unlike other printer types, the laser printer tends to have several high-voltage and high-temperature hazards inside it. To get the laser printer into a position where you can observe its operation, you must defeat some interlock sensors. This action places you in potential contact with the high-voltage, high-temperature areas. Take great care when working inside the laser printer.

TEST TIP

Be aware that laser printers can be a source of electrocution, eye damage (from the laser), and burns (from the fuser assembly).

Laser-Printer Hardware Checks

Variations in the hardware organization of different laser printers make it impossible to write a general troubleshooting routine that can be applied to all them without being specific to one model. The following troubleshooting discussions are general and require that the user do some interpretation to apply them to a specific laser printer.

Fortunately, laser-printer hardware has become highly modularized, as described in Figures 5.22 and 5.23. This allows entire sections of hardware to be checked by changing a single module. Unfortunately, the mechanical gear train and sensor systems are not usually parts included in the modules. Therefore, their operation needs to be checked individually.

Printer Is Dead or Partially Disabled

As usual, when the printer appears to be dead, the power supply is suspected. Again, as usual, the power supply can affect the operation of basically every section of the printer. In the laser printer, this is particularly complicated because there are three types of power being delivered to the various printer components.

If the printer does not start up, check all the normal, power-supply-related checkpoints (that is, power cord, power outlet, internal fuses, and so on). If the printer's fans and lights are working, other components associated with a defective power supply include the following:

- Main motor and gear train

- High-voltage corona wires

- Drum assembly

- Fusing rollers

The main motor may not run when the printer is supposed to print because of one (or more) of the following four basic reasons:

- The portion of the power supply that supplies the motor is defective.

- The control circuitry is not sending the enabling signals to turn the motor on.

- The motor is dead.

- The gear train is bound up and will not let the motor turn.

In the latter case, there should be sounds from the fan running and lights on the control panel. Isolate the failure and troubleshoot the components involved in that section.

If the high-voltage portion of the power supply that serves the corona wires and drum sections is defective, the image delivered to the page will be affected. If the high-voltage section of the power supply fails, the transfers of toner to the drum, and then to the paper, cannot occur. The contrast control will not be operational either.

In cases of partial failure, the image produced will have a washed-out appearance. Replace the high-voltage section of the power supply and/or the drum unit. If a separate corona wire is used, let the printer cool off sufficiently and replace the wire. Never reach into the high-voltage, high-temperature corona area while power is applied to the printer. Also, avoid placing conductive instruments in this area.

If the DC portion of the power supply fails, the laser beam will not be produced, creating a "Missing Beam" error message. The components involved in this error are the *laser/scanning module*, the control board, and the DC portion of the power supply. Replace the L/S module, the DC portion of the power supply, and the main control board.

When the heating element or lamp in the fusing area does not receive adequate AC power from the power supply, the toner will not affix to the page as it should. This condition will result in smudged output.

If the printer remains in a constant state of starting up, this is equivalent to the computer not passing the POST-tests portion of the boot-up process. If the printer starts up to an offline condition, there is likely a problem between the printer and the host computer's interface. Disconnect the interface cable and check to see whether the printer starts up to a ready state. If so, the problem is in the host computer, its interface, its configuration, or its signal cable. Troubleshoot the system in this direction.

If the printer still does not start up, note the error message produced and check the sections of the printer related to that section. Check to see whether the printer is connected to the system through a print-sharing device. If so, connect the printer directly to the system, and try it. It is not a good practice to use laser printers with these types of devices.

A better arrangement is to install, or just use, an LPT2 port to attach an additional printer to the system. Beyond two printers, it would be better to network the printers to the system.

Print on Page Is Missing or Bad

Many of the problems encountered in laser printers are associated with missing or defective print on the page. Normal print delivery problems fall into the following eight categories:

◆ Black pages

◆ White (blank) pages

◆ Faint print

◆ Random specks on the page

◆ Faulty print at regular intervals on the page

◆ White lines along the page

◆ Print missing from some portion of the page

◆ Smudged print

A black page indicates that toner has been attracted to the entire page. This condition could be caused by a failure of the primary corona, the laser-scanning module, or the main control board. If the laser is in a continuous on condition, the entire drum will attract toner. Likewise, if the primary corona is defective, the uniform negative charge will not be developed on the drum to repel toner. Replace the primary corona and/or *drum assembly*. If the problem continues, replace the laser-scanning module and the main control board.

On the other end of the spectrum, a white page indicates that no information is being written on the drum. This condition basically involves the laser-scanning module, the control board, and the power supply. Another white-page fault occurs when the corona wire becomes broken, contaminated, or corroded, so that the attracting charge between the drum and paper is severely reduced.

Specks and stains on the page may be caused by a worn-out cleaning pad or a defective corona wire. If the cleaning pad is worn, it will not remove excess toner from the page during the fusing process. If the corona wire's grid does not regulate the charge level on the

TEST TIP

Know what types of problems produce blank pages from a laser printer.

drum, dark spots will appear in the print. To correct these situations, replace the corona assembly by exchanging the toner cartridge or drum unit. Also, replace the cleaning pad in the fusing unit. If the page still contains specks after changing the cartridge, run several pages through the printer to clear excess toner that may have collected in the printer.

White lines along the length of the page are generally caused by poorly distributed toner. Try removing the toner cartridge and gently shaking it to redistribute the toner in the cartridge. Other causes of white lines include damaged or weakened corona wires. Check and clean the corona wires, if accessible, or replace the module containing the corona wires.

Faint print in a laser printer can be caused by a number of different things. If the contrast control is set too low, or the toner level in the cartridge is low, empty, or poorly distributed, print quality can appear washed-out. Correcting these symptoms is fairly easy; adjust the contrast control, remove the toner cartridge, inspect it, shake it gently (if it is a sealed unit), and retry it. If the print does not improve, try replacing the toner cartridge. Other causes of faint print include a weakened corona wire or a weakened high-voltage power supply that drives it. Replace the unit that contains the corona wire. Replace the high-voltage power supply. Make sure that latent voltages have been drained off the high-voltage power supply before working with it.

Faults in the print that occur at regular intervals along the page are normally caused by mechanical problems. When roller and transport mechanisms begin to wear in the printer, bad registration and print appear in cyclic form. This can be attributed to the dimensions of cyclic components such as the drum, developing roller in the toner cartridge, or fusing rollers. Examine the various mechanical components for wear or defects.

Missing print is normally attributed to a bad or misaligned laser-scanning module. If this module is not correctly installed, it cannot deliver lines of print to the correct areas of the page. Likewise, if the scanning mirror has a defect or is dirty, portions of the print will not be scanned on the drum. Another cause of missing print involves the toner cartridge, and low, or poorly distributed, toner. If the toner does not come out of the cartridge uniformly, areas of missing print can be created. A damaged or worn drum can also be a cause of repeated missing print. If areas of the drum will not hold the charge properly, toner will not transfer to it, or the page, correctly.

Smudged print is normally a sign of a failure in the fusing section. If the fusing roller's temperature, or pressure, is not sufficient to bond the toner to the page, the print smudges when touched. Examine the fuser unit, the power supply, and the fusing roller's heating unit.

Paper Will Not Feed, or Is Jammed

If the paper will not feed at all, the place to begin checking is the paper-tray area. The paper trays have a complex set of sensors and pickup mechanisms that must all be functioning properly to begin the paper handling. Due to the complexity of the paper-pickup operation, jams are most likely to occur in this area.

Check the paper tray to make sure that there is paper in it, and that it has the correct size of paper in it. Each tray in a laser printer has a set of tabs that contact sensor switches to tell the control circuitry that the tray is installed and what size paper is in it. A mechanical arm and photo detector are used to sense the presence of paper in the tray. If these switches are set incorrectly, the printer could print a page that was sized incorrectly for the actual *paper size*. Figure 5.36 depicts the various paper-tray sensors.

TEST TIP

Be aware of the consequences of incorrectly setting the paper tray switches in a laser printer.

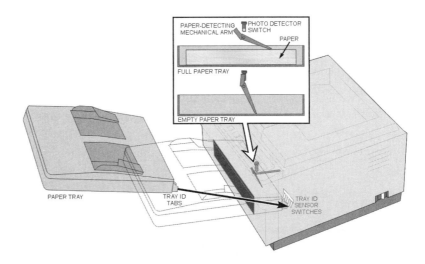

FIGURE 5.36
Paper-tray sensors.

If the printer's display panel indicates a *Paper Out error* message, locate and actuate the paper detector by hand (lift it up). While holding the paper sensor, check the sensor switches by pressing each one individually. If the message does not go out when any of the individual switches is pressed, replace that switch. If none of the switches show good, replace the paper sensor and arm. Also, check the spring-loaded plate in the bottom of the tray to make sure that it is forcing paper up to the *pickup roller* when the tray is installed in the printer.

The pickup roller must pull the top sheet of paper off of the paper stack in the tray. The controller actuates a solenoid that engages the pickup roller's gear train. The pickup roller moves the paper into position against the registration rollers. If the printer's display panel shows a jam in the pickup area, check to make sure that the paper tray is functional, and then begin troubleshooting the pickup roller and main gear train. If none of the gear train is moving, check the main motor and controller board. The power-supply board also may be a cause of the problem.

If the paper feeds into the printer, but jams after the process has begun, troubleshoot the particular section of the printer where the jam is occurring—pickup, registration, fusing area, and output devices (collators and *duplexers*). This information is generally presented by the laser printer's display panel. Figure 5.37 describes the paper path through a typical laser printer.

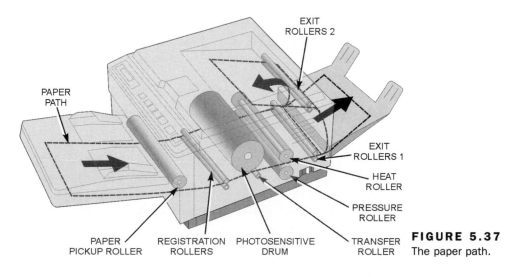

FIGURE 5.37
The paper path.

In each stage, you need to check the action of the gear train in the area. Also, inspect the various rollers in that stage for wear or damage. If the motor and gear train operate, but no action occurs in the pickup roller or registration rollers, check the solenoid and clutches for these units.

Another cause for jams is the presence of some obstruction in the paper path. Check for pieces of paper that have torn loose and lodged in the printer's paper path. In most laser printers, mechanical components are part of a replaceable module (that is, the drum unit, the developing unit, or the fusing unit). If the motor and all the exposed gears are working, replace these units one at a time.

Many times, a paper jam error remains even after the paper has been removed from the laser printer. This is typically caused by an interlock error. Just opening the printer's main access door should clear the error.

PREVENTIVE MAINTENANCE AND SAFETY ISSUES

Because printers tend to be much more mechanical than other types of computer peripherals, they require more effort to maintain. Printers generate pollutants, such as paper dust and ink droplets, in everyday operation. These pollutants can build up on mechanical parts and cause them to wear. As the parts wear, the performance of the printer diminishes. Therefore, printers require periodic cleaning and adjustments to maintain good performance.

Dot-Matrix Printers

Adjust the printhead spacing, as described in Chapter 7, "1.0 Operating System Fundamentals." If the printhead is too far away from the platen, the print should appear washed-out. The tension on the printhead-positioning belt should be checked periodically. If the belt is loose, the printer's dot positioning becomes erratic. Reset the printhead for proper tension.

Clean the printer's roller surfaces. Use a damp, soft cloth to clean the surface of the platen. Rotate the platen through several revolutions. Do not use detergents or solvents on the rollers.

Use a nonfibrous swab, dipped in alcohol, to clean the face of the dot-matrix printhead. This should loosen up paper fibers and ink that may cause the print wires to stick. Apply a small amount of oil to the face of the printhead.

Clean the paper-handling motor's gear train. Use a swab to remove build-up from the teeth of the gear train. If the gear train has been lubricated before, apply a light oil to the gears, using a swab. Turn the platen to make sure that the oil gets distributed throughout the gear train. Apply a light coating of oil to the rails that the head-positioning carriage rides on. Move the carriage assembly across the rails several times to spread the lubricant evenly.

Step by Step 5.1 describes the steps to cleaning a dot-matrix printer.

STEP BY STEP

5.1   Cleaning a Dot-Matrix Printer

1. Adjust the printhead spacing.

2. Check the tension on the printhead-positioning belt.

3. Clean the printer and its mechanisms.

4. Clean the printer's roller surfaces.

5. Clean the surface of the platen.

6. Clean the surface of the dot-matrix printhead.

7. Clean the paper-handling motor's gear train.

8. Apply light oil to the gears using a swab.

9. Turn the platen to distribute the oil.

10. Apply light coating of oil to the rails.

11. Move the carriage assembly to distribute the oil.

Inkjet Printers

The spacing of the printheads in some inkjet printers require cleaning adjustment similar to those described for dot-matrix printers.

Clean the paper-handling motor's gear train. Use a swab to remove build-up from the teeth of the gear train. If the gear train has been lubricated before, apply a light oil to the gears using a swab. Turn the platen to make sure the oil gets distributed throughout the gear train. Apply a light coating of oil to the rails on which the print-head-positioning carriage rides. Move the carriage assembly across the rails several times to spread the lubricant evenly.

Step by Step 5.2 provides the steps to clean an inkjet printer.

STEP BY STEP

5.2   Cleaning an Inkjet Printer

1. Adjust the printhead spacing.

2. Check the tension on the printhead-positioning belt.

3. Clean the printer and its mechanisms.

4. Clean the printer's roller surfaces.

5. Clean the surface of the platen.

6. Clean the surface of the inkjet printhead.

7. Clean the paper-handling motor's gear train.

8. Apply light oil to the gears using a swab.

9. Turn the platen to distribute the oil.

10. Apply light coating of oil to the rails.

11. Move the carriage assembly to distribute the oil.

Laser Printers

Use a vacuum cleaner to remove dust build-up and excess toner from the interior of the laser printer. Care should be taken to remove all excess toner from the unit. Vacuum the printer's ozone filter. Because water can mix with the toner particles in the printer, using wet sponges or towels to clean up toner inside the laser printer can create a bigger mess than the original one you were cleaning up. Remove the toner cartridge before vacuuming.

Clean the laser printer's rollers using a damp cloth, or denatured alcohol. Also, clean the paper-handling motor's gear train. Use a swab to remove build-up from the teeth of the gear train. If the gear train has been lubricated before, use a swab to apply a light oil to the gears. Make sure the oil gets distributed throughout the gear train.

Clean the writing mechanism thoroughly. Use compressed air to blow out dust and paper particles that may collect on the lenses and shutters. If possible, wipe the laser lens with lint-free wipes to remove stains and fingerprints.

If accessible, use a swab, dipped in alcohol, to clean the corona wires. Rub the swab across the entire length of the wires. Take extra care to not break the strands that wrap around the corona. If these wires are broken, the printer will be rendered useless until new, monofilament wires can be reinstalled.

Step by Step 5.3 describes the steps to cleaning a laser printer.

STEP BY STEP

5.3   Cleaning a Laser Printer

1. Remove dust build-up and excess toner from the interior.

2. Clean the laser printer's rollers.

3. Clean the paper-handling motor's gear train.

4. Apply light oil to the gears, using a swab.

5. Distribute the oil throughout the gear train.

6. Clean the corona wires.

TEST TIP

Remember acceptable ways to clean laser printers.

In some laser-printer models, the toner cartridges are designed so that they can be refilled. At this time, the third-party refill cartridges are not typically as good as those from the manufacturer. However, they tend to be much cheaper than original equipment cartridges. If the output from the printer does not have to be very high quality, refilled toner cartridges might be an interesting topic to examine. To date, no regulations govern the disposal of laser-printer cartridges.

CHAPTER SUMMARY

KEY TERMS

- Bitmapped fonts
- Carriage motor/timing belt
- Carriage-position sensor
- Character cells
- Character printer
- Chemically reactive paper
- CMYK color
- Collators
- Compression rollers
- Continuous forms
- Corona wire
- Correspondence quality (CQ)
- DC operating voltages
- Developing roller
- Dot-pitch
- Dot-matrix characters
- Downloadable type fonts
- Draft mode
- Drum assembly
- Duplexers
- Electrophotographic cartridge
- Encapsulated PostScript (EPS)
- End-of-paper sensor
- Font
- Form Feed (FF)

The focus of this chapter has been printers. The opening section presented an introduction to the different types of printers and provided a fundamental course in general printer structure and organization.

Following the general discussions of dot-matrix, inkjet, and laser-printer operations, this chapter focused on common types of printer connections and configurations.

The largest portion of this chapter presented troubleshooting procedures for each type of printer. Each procedure was divided into logical areas associated with typical printer symptoms.

The final section of this chapter featured preventative maintenance procedures that apply to the different printer types.

At this point, review the objectives listed at the beginning of this chapter to be certain that you understand each point and can perform each task listed there. Afterward, answer the Review and Exam Questions that follow to verify your knowledge of the information.

- Friction feed
- Fully formed characters
- Fuser unit
- Fusing roller
- Grayscale
- Halftone
- Hardware handshaking
- Head-gap lever
- Home-position sensor
- Impact printer
- Ink cartridge
- Inkjet printers
- Interlock switch
- Laser printer
- Laser/scanning module
- Letter quality (LQ)
- Line Feed (LF)
- Near-letter quality (NLQ)
- Nonimpact printer

- On/Offline
- Operator control panel
- Output devices
- Paper jams
- Paper Out error
- Paper size
- Paper-transport mechanics
- Paper weight
- Paper-feed motor
- Paper-feed selector lever
- Paper-handling mechanism
- Pickup area
- Pickup roller
- Pin feed
- Platen
- Primary corona wire
- Print sharing
- Printer drivers
- Printhead

- Printhead carriage assembly
- Printhead-positioning motor
- Raster-scanned fonts
- Registration area
- Ribbon cartridge
- Single-sheet forms
- Thermal fuse
- Thermal shock
- Timing belt
- Timing sensors
- Toner cartridge
- Toner powder
- Tractor feed
- Transfer corona wire
- TrueType outline fonts
- Utility mode
- Vector-based fonts

URL Resources

http://webopedia.internet.com/Hardware/Output_Devices/Printers/

http:// Aplusforum.virtualave.net/aplus/printer.html#begin

http://webopedia.internet.com/TERM/d/dot_matrix_printer.html

http://webopedia.internet.com/TERM/i/ink_jet_printer.html

www.pctechguide.com/13inkjets.htm

www.pctechguide.com/12lasers.htm

continues

URL RESOURCES

http://Aplusforum.virtualave.net/aplus/impactprinter.html#begin

http://webopedia.internet.com/TERM/d/driver.html

http://webopedia.internet.com/TERM/h/handshaking.htm/

www.pcguide.com/ts/x/comp/io.htm

http://Aplusforum.virtualave.net/aplus/inkprinter.html#begin

www.anselm.edu/homepage/ptaglini/inkjet.html

http://Aplusforum.virtualave.net/aplus/laserprinter.html#begin

APPLY YOUR KNOWLEDGE

Review Questions

1. With regard to dot-matrix, inkjet, and laser printers, describe three general types of problems common to all printers and the additional type of problem that dot-matrix and inkjet printers have.

2. What are the common transmission parameters that must be set up for a serial printer interface?

3. Describe the purpose for using pin-feed mechanisms to move paper through the printer.

4. Describe the reason for using tractor-feed paper handling.

5. If the resolution of an inkjet printer becomes unacceptable, what action should be taken?

6. Describe the function of the fuser assembly in a laser printer.

7. Describe the function of the primary corona (conditioning roller) in a laser printer.

8. If a laser printer continues to show a paper jam problem after the paper has been cleared, what type of problem is indicated, and what action should be taken?

9. List the three primary areas where paper jams occur in a laser printer, as well as any other areas where jams are likely to occur.

10. Describe two methods used by inkjet printers to put ink on the page.

11. Does a successful self-test indicate that the printer is not the cause of the problem? List the parts of the system that can still be problem causes if the self-test runs successfully.

12. How does a dot-matrix printer actually deliver ink to a page?

13. What functions do the printer's controller typically perform?

14. List four things that can be damaging to the photosensitive surface of the laser printer's drum.

15. List the basic components of an inkjet printer.

Exam Questions

1. List three common pin configurations for dot-matrix printers.

   A. 10, 20, and 30 pins

   B. 5, 10, and 15 pins

   C. 9, 18, and 24 pins

   D. 3, 6, and 9 pins

2. Name the four basic components of a Hewlett-Packard laser-printer cartridge.

   A. Laser, toner supply, drum, and fuser

   B. Toner supply, corona wire, drum assembly, and developing roller

   C. Laser, toner supply, corona wire, and drum

   D. Toner supply, corona wire, drum assembly, and fuser

3. What is the purpose of the primary corona wire in a laser printer?

   A. It cleans the paper as it enters the printer.

   B. It conditions the drum for printing.

   C. It transfers toner from the drum to the paper.

   D. It fuses the toner to the paper.

APPLY YOUR KNOWLEDGE

4. What is the first action that should be taken if the print generated by a dot-matrix printer becomes faded or uneven?

   A. Change the ribbon cartridge.

   B. Add ink.

   C. Adjust the print carriage.

   D. Add toner.

5. What is the first action that should be taken if the print generated by a laser printer becomes faded or uneven?

   A. Adjust the contrast control.

   B. Change the ink cartridge.

   C. Check the toner cartridge.

   D. Adjust the print mechanism.

6. What type of electrical charge must be placed on the corona wire to transfer toner from the drum to the paper?

   A. Negative

   B. None

   C. Neutral

   D. Positive

7. List the six stages of a typical laser printer.

   A. Pick up, registration, transfer, printing, fusing, finishing

   B. Pick up, conditioning, transfer, developing, fusing, and finishing

   C. Cleaning, conditioning, writing, developing, transferring, and fusing

   D. Cleaning, registration, writing, transferring, fusing, finishing

8. List the fundamental parts of a dot-matrix printer.

   A. Power supply, microprocessor, tractor-feed motor, printhead mechanism, and printhead-positioning motor

   B. Power supply, interface board, paper-feed motor, printhead mechanism, printhead-positioning motor, and sensors

   C. Interface board, ink cartridge, printhead mechanism, printhead-positioning motor, sensors.

   D. Controller, paper-feed motor, ribbon cartridge, and printhead-positioning motor.

9. What type of ink delivery system is normally found in inkjet printers built for the personal computers?

   A. Drop-on-demand ink delivery

   B. Continuous-stream ink delivery

   C. Impact ink delivery

   D. Compact-spray ink delivery

10. Describe what the specification for 60-pound bond paper means.

    A. 100 22" × 17" sheets weigh 60 pounds.

    B. 500 8.5" × 11" sheets weigh 60 pounds.

    C. 100 11" × 17" sheets weigh 60 pounds.

    D. 500 22" × 17" sheets weigh 60 pounds.

APPLY YOUR KNOWLEDGE

Answers to Review Questions

1. Power-supply problems, not printing problems, and paper not advancing problems. The dot-matrix and inkjet printers may also suffer from printhead not moving problems. For more information, see the sections "Troubleshooting Dot-Matrix Printers," "Troubleshooting Inkjet Printers," and "Troubleshooting Laser Printers."

2. Speed, parity type, character frame, and control protocol. For more information, see the section "Printer Installation."

3. The pin-feed method allows heavier grades of paper to be pulled through the printer. This makes it less likely to slip or become misaligned than with friction-feed paper-handling techniques. For more information, see the section "Paper Handling."

4. A tractor feed pulls paper through the printer using the pins in the tractor. The gearing of the tractor makes it especially useful in handling heavy-duty, continuous-form paper that tends to be very heavy. For more information, see the section "Paper Handling."

5. Replace the ink cartridge. For more information, see the section "Ink Cartridges."

6. The fuser melts the toner on the paper and then presses it into the paper. For more information, see the section "Laser-Printing Operations."

7. The conditioning roller applies a uniform charge to the surface of the drum to prepare it to receive the next image from the laser. For more information, see the section "Laser-Printing Operations."

8. An interlock problem has occurred. It will be necessary to open the unit to clear the interlock error. For more information, see the section "Paper Will Not Feed, or Is Jammed."

9. The pickup area, the registration area, and the fusing area. If optional output devices are included, such as collators and duplexers, jams can occur there as well. For more information, see the section "Troubleshooting Laser Printers."

10. Drop—on-demand and continuous stream. For more information, see the section "Inkjet Printers."

11. No. The computer, the printer cable, and the printer's interface circuitry. For more information, see the section "Troubleshooting Dot-Matrix Printers."

12. The designated pins of the printhead are extended from the face of the printhead due to an electrical charge. The pins strike an inked ribbon that, in turn, impacts the paper. For more information, see the section "Printhead Mechanisms."

13. It receives data and control signals from the host computer through the interface circuit and generates all the control signals necessary to carry out the operation of the printer as directed. For more information, see the section "Printer Controls."

14. Light, dust and other particles, high temperature, and high humidity. For more information, see the section "Laser-Printing Operations."

15. The power supply, the interface/controller board, the paper-feed motor and gear set, the printhead mechanism, the printhead-positioning motor and belt, and the sensors. For more information, see the section "Inkjet Printer Components."

APPLY YOUR KNOWLEDGE

Answers to Exam Questions

1. **C.** Dot-matrix printers have commonly been produced in 9-pin, 18-pin, and 24-pin versions. Currently, most dot-matrix printers use 24-pin printheads. For more information, see the section "Character Types."

2. **B.** A Hewlett-Packard laser cartridge contains the toner supply, a corona wire, the drum assembly, and the developing roller. Toner cartridges for other makes of laser printers may contain other components, or variations of these components. For more information, see the section "Component Variations."

3. **B.** The primary corona wire conditions the photosensitive drum by applying a uniform electrical charge to it after it has been cleaned. For more information, see the section "Laser-Printing Operations."

4. **A.** The printing process in a dot-matrix printer is mechanical and therefore, many things wear. The ink ribbon is the first place to look when print begins to degrade. This is the cheapest, easiest, and usually the only part that needs to be replaced when print quality diminishes. For more information, see the section "Ribbon Cartridges."

5. **A.** Adjusting the contrast control is the cheapest and easiest check to make when print quality diminishes in a laser printer. The toner supply is the second choice to check when print quality comes into question. For more information, see the section "Print on Page Is Missing or Bad."

6. **D.** The Transfer corona wire applies a relatively positive charge to the paper so that it attracts the negatively charged toner particles. For more information, see the section "Laser-Printing Operations."

7. **C.** The six stages of the laser printing process, in order, are cleaning, conditioning, writing, developing, transferring, and fusing. For more information, see the section "Laser-Printer Components."

8. **B.** All dot-matrix printers consist of a power supply, an interface board, a paper-feed motor, a printhead mechanism, a printhead-positioning motor, and various sensors. They do not necessarily possess a tractor feed and they do not use ink cartridges. For more information, see the section "Dot-Matrix Printers."

9. **A.** Drop-on-demand ink delivery is used in consumer-oriented inkjet printers. This is used for the relatively low cost (when compared to the cost of continuous-stream ink-delivery systems). For more information, see the section "Inkjet Printers."

10. **D.** ALL paper is specified by weight expressed in terms of 500 22" × 17" sheets. (Envision four, standard 8.5" × 11" sheets organized to create the standard-weight sheet.) For more information, see the section "Paper Specifications."

This chapter helps you to prepare for the Core Hardware module of the A+ Certification examination by covering the following objectives within the "Domain 6.0: Basic Networking" section.

6.1 Identify basic networking concepts, including how a network works and the ramifications of repairs on the network.

Content may include the following:

- **Installing and configuring network cards**
- **Network access**
- **Full-duplex, half-duplex**
- **Cabling (twisted pair, coaxial, fiber optic, RS-232)**
- **Ways to network a PC**
- **Physical network topologies**
- **Increasing bandwidth**
- **Loss of data**
- **Network slowdown**
- **Infrared**
- **Hardware protocols**
- **Network interface cards**

▶ Because networks have become such an integral part of computer systems in the workplace, the PC technician must understand how networks function.

▶ The PC technician is normally responsible for maintaining the portion of the network that attaches to the computer. This usually includes a network adapter card and cable.

▶ Because work in one area of a network can affect the overall operation of the network, the technician must be aware of how actions taken locally will affect the global operation of the system.

CHAPTER 6

6.0 Basic Networking

STUDY STRATEGIES

To prepare for the Basic Networking objective of the Core Hardware exam:

▶ Read the objectives at the beginning of this chapter.

▶ Study the information in this chapter.

▶ Review the objectives listed earlier in this chapter.

▶ Perform any step-by-step procedures in the text.

▶ Answer the Review and Exam Questions at the end of the chapter and check your results.

▶ Use the ExamGear test engine on the CD that accompanies this book for additional review and exam questions concerning this material

▶ Review the Test Tips scattered throughout the chapter and make certain that you are comfortable with each point.

INTRODUCTION

This section requires the test taker to demonstrate knowledge of basic network concepts and terminology, ability to determine whether a computer is networked, knowledge of procedures for swapping and configuring network interface cards (NICs), and knowledge of the ramifications of repairs when a computer is networked. The scope of this topic is specific to hardware issues on the desktop and connecting to a network. Questions from this domain account for 10% of the Core Hardware test.

BASIC NETWORKING CONCEPTS

▶ 6.1 Identify basic networking concepts, including how a network works and the ramifications of repairs on the network.

The A+ Core Hardware objective 6.1 states that the test taker should be able to "identify basic networking concepts, including how a network works and the ramifications of repairs on the network."

Within a very short time span, the use of local area networks has grown immensely. Because they have become such an integral part of commercial computer systems, as the A+ objective points out, the PC technician must understand how they function. The following sections present basic local area networking concepts and practices.

LOCAL AREA NETWORKS

Local area networks (LANs) are systems designed to connect computers together in a relatively close proximity. These connections enable users attached to the network to share resources such as printers and modems. LAN connections also enable users to communicate with each other and share data among their computers.

When discussing LANs, there are two basic topics to consider: the LAN's *topology* (hardware connection method), and its protocol (communication control method). In concept, a minimum of three stations must be connected to have a true LAN. If only two units are connected, point-to-point communications software and a simple null modem could be employed.

LAN Topologies

Network topologies are physical connection/configuration strategies. LAN topologies fall into four types of configurations:

◆ Bus

◆ Ring

◆ Star

◆ Mesh

Figure 6.1 illustrates all four topologies. In the *bus topology*, the *stations*, or *nodes*, of the network connect to a central communications link. Each node has a unique address along the bus that differentiates it from the other users on the network. Information can be placed on the bus by any node. The information must contain network address information about the node, or nodes, for which the information is intended. Other nodes along the bus will ignore the information.

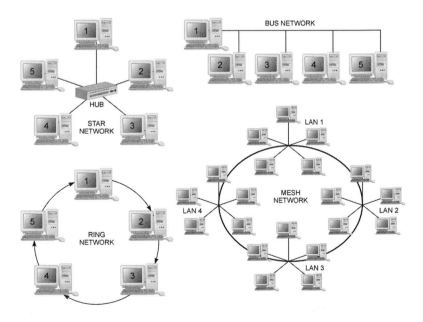

FIGURE 6.1
Star, bus, ring, and mesh configurations.

In a *ring* network configuration, the communication bus is formed into a closed loop. Each node inspects the information on the LAN as it passes by. A repeater, built in to each ring LAN card, regenerates every message not directed to it and sends it to the next appointed node. The originating node eventually receives the message back and removes it from the ring.

Ring topologies tend to offer very high data-transfer rates but require additional management overhead. The additional management is required for dependability. If a node in a ring network fails, the entire network should fail. To overcome this, ring designers have developed rings with primary and secondary data paths, as depicted in Figure 6.2. If a break occurs in a primary link, the network controller can reroute the data onto the secondary link to avoid the break.

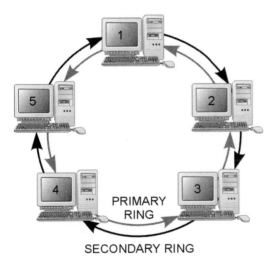

PRIMARY
RING

SECONDARY RING

FIGURE 6.2
Primary/secondary ring topologies.

In a *star topology*, the logical layout of the network resembles the branches of a tree. All the nodes are connected, in branches that eventually lead back to a central unit. Nodes communicate with each other through the central unit. The central station coordinates the network's activity by polling the nodes, one by one, to determine whether they have any information to transfer. If so, the central station gives that node a predetermined slice of time to transmit. If the message is longer than the time allotted, the transmissions are chopped into small *packets* of information that are transmitted over several polling cycles.

The *mesh design* offers the most basic network connection scheme. In this design, each node has a direct physical connection to all the other nodes in the network. Although the overhead for connecting a mesh network topology together in a LAN environment is prohibitive, this topology is employed in two very large network environments: the public telephone system and the Internet.

Logical Topologies

It should be easy to visualize the connections of the physical topologies just described if the nodes just connected to each other. However, this is typically not the case in newer LAN arrangements. This is due to the fact that most LAN installations employ connection devices (such as *hubs* and *routers*) that alter the appearance of the actual connection scheme. Therefore, the logical topology will not match the appearance of the physical topology. The particulars of the connection scheme are hidden inside the connecting device. As an illustration, Figure 6.3 shows a typical network connection scheme using a router. The physical topology appears as a star; however, the internal wiring of the connecting router provides a logical bus topology.

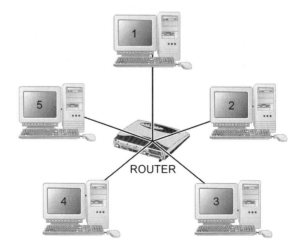

FIGURE 6.3
Logical topologies.

It is not uncommon for a logical ring or mesh topology to be implemented in a physical star topology.

Network Control Strategies

When you begin to connect computers to other computers and devices so that they can share resources and data, the issue of how and who will control the network comes up very quickly. In some applications, such as developing a book like this one, it is good for the author, artists, and pagination people to be able to share access to text and graphics files, as well as access to devices such as printers. In a business network, however, companies must have control over who can have access to sensitive information and company resources, as well as when and how much.

Control of the network can be implemented in two ways: as *peer-to-peer networks*, where each computer attached to the network is basically equal to the other units on the network; or as *client/server networks*, where dependent *workstations* (referred to as clients) operate in conjunction with a dedicated, master computer called a *file server*.

Figure 6.4 illustrates a typical peer-to-peer network arrangement. In this arrangement, the users connected to the network can share access to different *network resources*, such as each other's hard drives and printers. However, control of the local unit is fairly autonomous. The nodes in this type of network configuration usually contain local hard drives and printers that the local computer has control of. These resources can be shared at the discretion of the individual user. A common definition of a peer-to-peer network is one where all the nodes can act as both clients and servers of the other nodes under different conditions.

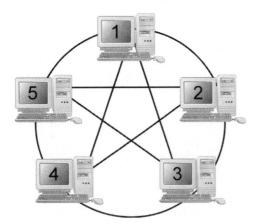

FIGURE 6.4
A peer-to-peer network.

Figure 6.5 depicts a typical client/server LAN configuration. In this type of LAN, control tends to be very centralized. The server typically holds the programs and data for its client computers. It also provides security and network policy enforcement.

FIGURE 6.5
A client/server network.

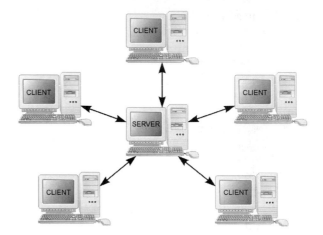

In some cases, the client units do not even include a local hard drive or floppy drive unit. Boot up is performed through an onboard BIOS, and no data is stored at the client machine. This type of client is referred to as a workstation.

The major advantages of the client/server networking arrangement include the following:

◆ Centralized administration

◆ Data and resource security

TEST TIP

Know the characteristic differences between peer-to-peer and client/server networks.

Network Cabling

Basically, the following four media are used to transmit data between computers:

◆ Copper cabling

◆ Fiber-optic cabling

◆ Infrared light

◆ Wireless radio frequency (RF) signals

Under the heading of copper cabling, there are basically two categories to consider: twisted-pair cabling and coaxial cabling. Twisted-pair cabling consists of two or more pairs of wires twisted together to provide noise reduction. The twist in the wires causes induced noise signals to tend to cancel each other out. In this type of cabling, the number of twists in each foot of wire indicates its relative noise-immunity level.

When discussing twisted-pair cabling with data networks, there are two basic types to consider: *unshielded twisted-pair* (UTP) and *shielded twisted-pair* (STP). UTP networking cable contains four pairs of individually insulated wires, as illustrated in Figure 6.6. STP cable is similar, with the exception that it contains an additional foil shield that surrounds the four-pair wire bundle. The shield provides extended protection from induced electrical noise and cross-talk by supplying a grounded path to carry the induced electrical signals away from the conductors in the cable.

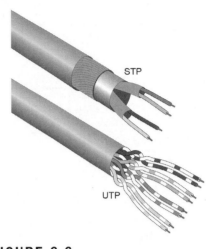

FIGURE 6.6
UTP and STP cabling.

UTP Cable

UTP cable specifications have been established jointly by two groups: the Electronic Industry Association (EIA) and the Telecommunications Industry Association (TIA). They have categorized different grades of cable along with connector, distance, and installation specifications to produce the EIA/TIA UTP wiring category (Cat) ratings for the industry (for instance, Cat3 and Cat5 cabling). Table 6.1 lists the industry's various Cat cable ratings that apply to UTP data-communications cabling. Cat5 cabling is currently the most widely used specification for data-communications wiring.

TEST TIP
Know what type of cabling is involved in the Cat5 cable rating.

TABLE 6.1

UTP CABLE CATEGORY RATINGS

Category	Maximum Bandwidth	Wiring Types	Applications
3	16MHz	100W UTP Rated Category 3	10Mbps Ethernet 4Mbps Token Ring
4	20MHz	100W UTP Rated Category 4	10Mbps Ethernet 16Mbps Token Ring
5	100MHz	100W UTP Rated Category 5	100Mbps TPDDI 155Mbps ATM
5E	160MHz	100W UTP Rated Category 5E	1.2Gbps 1000BASE-T High-Speed ATM
6 Proposed	200-250MHz	100W UTP Rated Category 6	1.2Gbps 1000BASE-T High-Speed ATM and beyond
7 Proposed	600-862MHz	100W UTP Rated Category 7	1.2Gbps 1000BASE-T High-Speed ATM and beyond

The connector and color-coded connection schemes specified for 4-pair, Cat5 UTP network cabling is illustrated in Figure 6.7. UTP cabling is terminated in an 8-pin *RJ-45* plug. The color code for attaching the connector to the cable also is shown in the figure.

FIGURE 6.7
UTP cable connections.

Coaxial cable

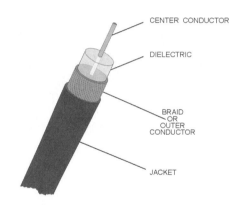

FIGURE 6.8
Coaxial cable.

Coaxial cable is familiar to most people as the conductor that carries cable TV into their homes. Coax has a single copper conductor in its center, and a protective braided copper shield around it, as illustrated in Figure 6.8.

Fiber-Optic Cable

Fiber-optic cable is plastic or glass cable designed to carry voice or digital data in the form of light pulses. The signals are introduced into the cable by a laser diode and bounce along its interior until it reaches the end of the cable, as illustrated in Figure 6.9. At the end, a light-detecting circuit receives the light signals and converts them back into usable information. This type of cabling offers potential signaling rates in excess of 200,000Mbps. However, use with current access protocols still limits fiber-optic LAN speeds to 100Mbps.

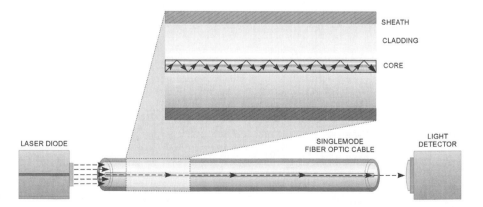

FIGURE 6.9
Transmitting over fiber-optic cable.

Because light moving through a fiber-optic cable does not attenuate (lose energy) as quickly as electrical signals moving along a copper conductor, segment lengths between transmitters and receivers can be much longer with fiber-optic cabling. In some fiber-optic applications, the maximum cable length can range up to 2 kilometers.

Fiber-optic cable also provides a much more secure data-transmission medium than copper cable because it cannot be tapped without physically breaking the conductor. Basically, light introduced into the cable at one end does not leave the cable except through the other end. In addition, it electrically isolates the transmitter and receiver so that no signal-level matching normally needs to be performed between the two ends.

As a matter of fact, getting the light out of the cable without significant attenuation is the key to making fiber-optic connections. The end of the cable must be perfectly aligned with the receiver and be free from scratches, film, or dust that would distort or filter the light.

FIGURE 6.10
Fiber optic cable connectors.

Figure 6.10 depicts two types of fiber-optic connectors. The connection on the top is an SC connector, whereas the one on the bottom is a Straight Tip (ST) connector. The SC connector is the dominant connector for fiber-optic Ethernet networks. In both cases, the connectors are designed so that they correctly align the end of the cable with the receiver.

Network Access Protocols

In a network, some method must be used to determine which node has use of the network's communications paths, and for how long it can have it. The network's protocol handles these functions, and is necessary to prevent more than one user from accessing the bus at any given time.

If two sets of data are placed on the network at the same time, a data collision occurs and data is lost. Basically, there are two de facto networking protocols in use: Ethernet and Token Ring.

Ethernet

Xerox developed Ethernet in 1976. The standard specification for Ethernet has been published by the International Electrical and Electronic Association (IEEE) as the IEEE-802.3 Ethernet protocol. Its methodology for control is referred to as *carrier sense multiple access with collision detection* (CSMA/CD). Using this protocol, a node that wants to transfer data over the network first listens to the LAN to determine whether it is in use. If the LAN is not in use, the node begins transmitting its data. If the network is busy, the node waits for the LAN to clear for a predetermined time and then takes control of the LAN.

If two nodes are waiting to use the LAN, they periodically attempt to access the LAN at the same time. When this happens, a data collision occurs, and the data from both nodes is rendered useless. The receiver portion of the Ethernet controller monitors the transmission to detect collisions.

When it senses the data bits overlapping, it halts the transmission, as does the other node. The transmitting controller generates an abort pattern code that is transmitted to all the nodes on the LAN, telling them that a collision has occurred. This alerts any nodes that might be waiting to access the LAN that there is a problem.

The receiving node (or nodes) dump any data that it might have received before the collision occurred. Other nodes waiting to send data generate a random timing number and go into a holding pattern. The timing number is a waiting time that the node sits out before it tries to transmit. Because the number is randomly generated, the odds against two of the nodes trying to transmit again at the same time are very low.

The first node to time out listens to the LAN to determine whether any activity is still occurring. Because it almost always finds a clear LAN, it begins transmitting. If two of the nodes do time out at the same time, another collision happens and the abort pattern/number generation/time-out sequence begins again. Eventually, one of the nodes gains clear access to the network and successfully transmits its data.

NOTE

Ethernet Limitations The Ethernet strategy allows for up to 1,024 users to share the LAN. From the description of its collision-recovery technique, however, it should be clear that with more users on an Ethernet LAN, more collisions are likely to occur, and the average time to complete an actual data transfer will be longer.

The Ethernet Frame

Under the Ethernet standard, information is collected into a package called a frame. Figure 6.11 depicts a typical Ethernet frame. The frame carries the following six sections of information:

◆ A preamble

◆ A destination address

◆ An originating address

◆ A type field

◆ The data field

◆ The frame-check error-detection and error-correction information

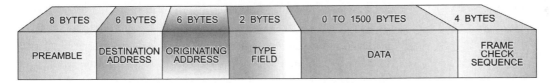

FIGURE 6.11
A typical Ethernet frame.

This organizational structure is very similar to that of a sector on a hard disk. The preamble synchronizes the receiver's operation to that of the transmitter. This action also tells the other nodes that a transmission is under way. The Ethernet preamble is a 64-bit string, made up of alternating 1s and 0s, ending in two consecutive 1s.

The destination address field is 6 bytes long, and is used to define one of three address locations. This number can represent the individual node address of the intended receiver, the address of a grouping of nodes around the LAN, or it can be a broadcast code that allows the node to send a message to everyone on the LAN.

The originating address field contains the identification address for the transmitting node. The type field is a 2-byte field that identifies the user protocol of the frame.

The data field is a variable-length field that contains the actual information. Because it is sent in a synchronous mode, the data field can be as long as necessary. The Ethernet standard does not allow for data fields less than 46 bytes, however, or longer than 1500 bytes.

The frame-check block contains an error-detection and error-correction word. Like parity and other error-detection schemes, the receiver regenerates the error code from the received data (actually the data, the address bytes, and the type field), and compares it to the received code. If a mismatch occurs, an error signal is generated from the LAN card to the system.

Ethernet Specifications

Ethernet is classified as a bus topology. The original Ethernet scheme was classified as a 10Mbps transmission protocol. The maximum length specified for Ethernet is 1.55 miles (2.5km), with a maximum segment length between nodes of 500 meters. This type of LAN is referred to as a *10BASE-5* LAN by the IEEE organization.

The *xxBASE-yy* IEEE nomenclature designates that the maximum data rate across the LAN is 10Mbps, that it is a baseband LAN (verses broadband), and that its maximum segment length is 500 meters. One exception to this method is the *10BASE-2* implementation. The maximum segment length for this specification is 185 meters (almost 200).

Newer Ethernet implementations are producing LAN speeds of up to 100Mbsp using unshielded twisted-pair (UTP) copper cabling. For these networks, the IEEE adopted *10BASE-T, 100BASE-T*, and *100BASE-TX* designations, indicating that they are operating on twisted-pair cabling and depend on its specifications for the maximum segment length. The 100BASE designation is referred to as *Fast Ethernet.* The TX version of the Fast Ethernet specification employs two pairs of twisted cable to conduct high-speed, full-duplex transmissions. The cables used with the TX version can be Cat5 UTP or STP. There is also a *100BASE-FX* Fast Ethernet designation that indicates the network is using fiber-optic cabling. This specification is described later in this chapter.

Network cards capable of supporting both transmission rates are classified as 10/100 Ethernet cards. The recommended maximum length of a 10/100BASE-T segment is 100 meters.

Ethernet Connections

Ethernet connections can be made through 50ohm, coaxial cable (10BASE-5), *thinnet* coaxial cable (10BASE-2), or UTP cabling (10BASE-T).

TEST TIP

Be aware that the 10BASE-*xx* system roughly uses the *xx* value to represent the distance (in meters) that a network segment can be. (The noticeable dissenter is the 185 meter BASE-2 value; it is *almost* 200 meter.)

NOTE

Know what type of cable 10BASE-T and 100BASE-T use.

The UTP specifications are based on telephone cable, and is normally used to connect a small number of PCs together. The twisted pairing of the cables uses magnetic-field principles to minimize induced noise in the lines. The original UTP LAN specification had a transmission rate that was stated as 1Mbps. Using UTP cable, a LAN containing up to 64 nodes can be constructed with the maximum distance between nodes set at 250 meters. Figure 6.12 depicts typical coaxial and UTP connections.

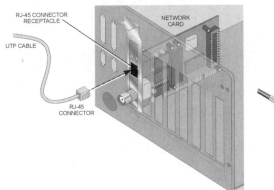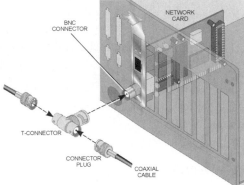

The original 10BASE-5 connection scheme required that special transceiver units be clamped to the cable. A pin in the transceiver pierced the cable to establish electrical contact with its conductor. An additional length of cable, called the drop cable, was then connected between the LAN adapter card and the transceiver. The 10BASE-2 Ethernet LAN uses thinner, industry-standard RG-58 coaxial cable, and has a maximum segment length of 185 meters.

FIGURE 6.12
Typical UTP and coax connections.

Coaxial cables are attached to equipment through *British Naval Connectors* (BNC) connectors. In a 10BASE-2 LAN, the node's LAN adapter card is usually connected directly to the LAN cabling, using a *T-connector* (for peer-to-peer networks) or by a BNC connector (in a client/server LAN).

UTP LAN connections are made through modular RJ-45 registered jacks and plugs. RJ-45 connectors are very similar in appearance to the RJ-11 connectors used with telephones and modems. However, the RJ-45 connectors are considerably larger than the RJ-11 connectors. Some Ethernet adapters include 15-pin sockets that allow special systems, such as fiber-optic cabling, to be interfaced to them. Other cards provide specialized ST connectors for fiber-optic connections.

UTP systems normally employ concentrators, or hubs, like the one in Figure 6.13, for connection purposes. Both coaxial connection methods require that a terminating resistor be installed at each end of the transmission line. Ethernet systems use 52ohm terminators.

FIGURE 6.13

UTP between a computer and a concentrator.

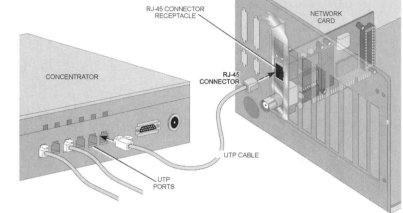

Table 6.2 summarizes the different Ethernet specifications. Other CSMA/CD-based protocols exist in the market. Some are actually Ethernet compatible. However, these systems may or may not achieve the performance levels of a true Ethernet system. Some may actually perform better.

TABLE 6.2

ETHERNET SPECIFICATIONS

Classification	Conductor	Max. Segment Length	Nodes	Max. Length	Trans. Rate
10BASE-2	RG-58	185m	30/1,024	250m	10Mbps
10BASE-5	RG-8	500m	100/1,024	2.5km	10Mbps
10BASE-T	UTP/STP	100m/200m	2/1,024	2.5km	10Mbps
100BASE-T	UTP	100m	2/1,024	2.5km	100Mbps
100BASE–FX	FO	412m	1,024	5km	100Mbps

A completely different 100Mbps standard has been developed jointly by Hewlett Packard and AT&T. This standard is referred to as the 100VG (Voice Grade)AnyLAN. The 100VG AnyLAN runs on UTP cabling. It simultaneously employs four pairs of cable strands for transfers. Instead of using CSMA/CD for collision avoidance, the 100VG AnyLAN employs an access protocol called demand priority. This scenario requires that the network nodes request and be granted permission before they can send data across the LAN. The overwhelming popularity of the Fast Ethernet specification has caused 100VG AnyLAN to nearly disappear from the market.

Token Ring

In 1985, IBM developed a token-passing LAN protocol called the *Token Ring*. As its name implies, Token Ring is a token-passing protocol operating on a ring topology. The token is a small frame that all nodes can recognize instantly. This access protocol standard specification is referred to as the IEEE-802.5 Token Ring Protocol.

In a token-passing system, contention for use of the LAN between different nodes is handled by passing an electronic enabling code, called a token, from node to node. Only the node possessing the token can have control of the LAN. Figure 6.14 illustrates this concept.

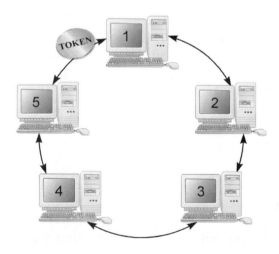

FIGURE 6.14
A token-passing scheme.

The token is passed from node to node along the LAN. Each node is allowed to hold the token a prescribed amount of time. After sending its message, or after its time runs out, the node must transfer the token to the next node. If the next node has no message, it just passes the token along to the next designated node. Nodes do not have to be in numeric sequence; their sequences are programmed in the network-management software. All nodes listen to the LAN during the token-passing time.

In a token-passing network, new or removed nodes must be added to, or deleted from, the rotational list in the network-management software. If not, the LAN will never grant access to the new nodes. Token Ring management software and cards are built so that each device attached to the LAN is interrogated when the LAN is started up. In this way, the rotational file is verified each time that the network is started.

New nodes that start up after the LAN has been initialized transmit a reconfiguration burst that can be heard by all the nodes. This burst grabs the attention of all the installed nodes, and erases their token destination addresses. Each node goes into a wait state determined by its station number. The node with the highest station number times out first and tries to access the LAN.

The highest numbered node is responsible for starting the token-passing action, after a new unit is added to the LAN. This is accomplished by broadcasting a signal to all nodes telling them what it believes is the lowest numbered node in the LAN, and asking whether it will accept the token. If no response is given, the node moves to the next known address in the LAN management software's roster and repeats the request. This action continues until an enabled node responds. At this point, the token is passed to the new node and the forwarding address is stored in the LAN Manager's list. Each successive node goes through the same process until all the nodes have been accessed.

The node passing the token must always monitor the LAN. This is done to prevent the loss of the token during its passage. If the node remains inactive for a predetermined amount of time, the transmitting node must reclaim the token and search for the next active node to pass it to. In this case, the transmitting node just increments its next node address by one and attempts to make contact with a node at that address. If not, it increments the count by one again, and retries, until it reaches an enabled node. This new node number is stored in the transmitting node and is the pass-to number for that node, until the system is shut down or reconfigured.

When the ring is idle, the token just passes counter-clockwise, from station to station. A station can transmit information on the ring any time that it receives the token. This is accomplished by turning the token packet into the start of a data packet and adding its data to it.

At the intended receiver, the packet is copied into a buffer memory, serially, where it is stored. The receiver also places the packet back on the ring so that the transmitter can get it back. Upon doing so, the transmitter reconstructs the token and places it back on the ring. Figure 6.15 depicts this concept.

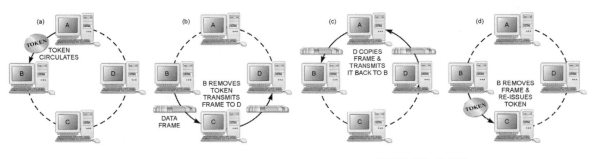

FIGURE 6.15
Token Ring concept.

The Token Ring cabling is a two-pair, shielded twisted-pair cable. The main cable is called the *trunk cable*, and the individual drops are referred to as the interface cable. The cables are grouped together in hardware units called concentrators. Internally, the concentrator's ports are connected into a ring configuration. In this manner, the concentrator can be placed in a convenient area and have nodes positioned where they are needed. Some Token Ring adapters provide 9-pin connectors for shielded twisted-pair (STP) cables as well.

The data-transfer rate stated for Token Ring systems is 4 to 16Mbps. Token passing is less efficient than other protocols when the load on the network is light. It evenly divides the network's usage among nodes, however, when traffic is heavy. It can also be extremely vulnerable to node crashes when that node has the token. LAN adapter cards are typically designed to monitor the LAN for such occurrences so that they can be corrected without shutting down the entire network.

The IEEE specifications for both Ethernet (802.3) and Token Ring (802.5) make provisions for a high-speed, full-duplexing mode (two-way simultaneous communication). This mode is normally encountered in large networks that have multiple servers. Its primary use is to perform backup functions between the large system servers where lots of data must be moved through the network. In full-duplex mode, the standard Ethernet transfer rate of 10Mbps is boosted to 20Mbps; the Token Ring rate is raised to 32Mbps. This mode is rarely encountered on desktop client units. These units tend to operate in half-duplex (two-way communication, but in only one direction at a time) mode.

Fiber-Optic LANs

As indicated earlier in this chapter, fiber-optic cabling offers the prospect of very high performance links for LAN implementation. It can handle much higher data-transfer rates than copper conductors and can use longer distances between stations before signal deterioration becomes a problem. In addition, fiber-optic cable offers a high degree of security for data communications: Because it does not radiate EMI signal information that can be detected outside the conductor, it does not tap easily and it shows a decided signal loss when it is tapped into.

Fiber-Ethernet Standards

The IEEE organization has created several fiber-optic variations of the Ethernet protocol. They classify these variations under the IEEE-803 standard. These standards are referenced as the 10/100BASE-F specification. Variations of this standard include the following:

◆ **10BASE-FP.** This specification is used for passive star networks running at 10Mbps. It employs a special hub the uses mirrors to channel the light signals to the desired node.

◆ **10BASE-FL.** This specification is used between devices on the network. It operates in full-duplex mode and runs at 10Mbps. Cable lengths under this specification can range up to 2 kilometers.

◆ **100BASE-FX**. This protocol is identical to the 10BASE-FL specification with the exception that it runs at 100Mbps. This particular version of the specification is referred to as Fast Ethernet because it can easily run at the 100Mbps rate.

The FDDI Ring Standard

There is a Token Ring–like network standard that has been developed around fiber-optic cabling. This standard is the Fiber Distributed Data Interface (FDDI) specification. The FDDI network was designed to work almost exactly like a Token Ring network, with the exception that it works on two counter-rotating rings of fiber-optic cable, as illustrated in Figure 6.16. All other differences in the two specifications are associated with their speed differences.

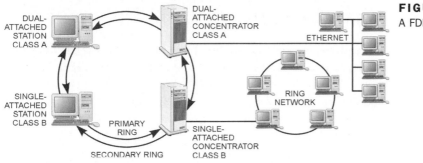

FIGURE 6.16
A FDDI network.

FDDI employs token-passing access control and provides data-transfer rates of 100Mbps. Using the second ring, FDDI can easily handle multiple frames of data moving across the network at any given time. Of course, the dual-ring implementation provides additional network dependability because it can shift over to a single-ring operation if the network controller senses that a break has occurred in one of the rings.

Infrared LANs

The IrDA infrared transmission specification makes provisions for multiple IrDA devices to be attached to a computer so that it can have multiple, simultaneous links to multiple IrDA devices. Figure 6.17 shows how IrDA links can be used to share computers and devices through a normal Ethernet hub. In these scenarios, the IrDA link provides the high-speed transmission media between the Ethernet devices.

FIGURE 6.17
IrDA networking.

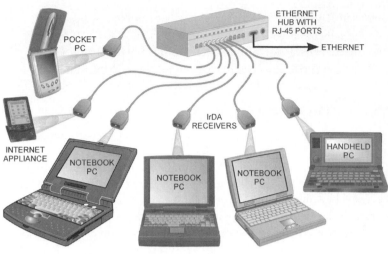

Wireless LANs

Recently, a variety of wireless local area networking (WLAN or LAWN) specifications has been introduced into the market. These networks connect computer nodes together using high-frequency radio waves. The IEEE organization has presented a specification titled IEEE-802.11 to describe its wireless networking standard.

The wireless networking community is working with two spread-spectrum technologies as the basis of their transmission method. In spread-spectrum transmissions, the frequency of the radio signal hops in a random, defined sequence that is known to the receiving device. These technologies are referred to as frequency-hopping spread spectrum (FHSS) and direct-sequence spread spectrum (DSSS). The FHSS method spreads the signal across the time spectrum using time division multiplexing (TDM) techniques. The DSSS method combines the data with a faster carrier signal according to a predetermined frequency-spreading ratio for transmission.

Time division multiple access (TDMA) technology employs TDM to divide a radio carrier signal into time-slices, called cells, and then funnels data from different sources into the cells. This technique enables a single frequency signal to serve a number of different customers simultaneously. A similar technology known as code division multiple access (CDMA) does not assign users a specific frequency. Instead, it spreads the user's data across a range of frequencies in a random digital sequence.

Another interesting wireless networking specification is known as bluetooth. This specification was originally put forth by a consortium made up of Ericsson, IBM, Intel, Nokia, and Toshiba as a short range, wireless radio technology designed to coordinate communications between network devices and the Internet. The meshing together of personal computers, cell phones, Web devices, LAN devices, and other intelligent devices in a common forum is referred to as convergence. The bluetooth specification is intended to promote convergence of these systems.

A typical wireless LAN, depicted in Figure 6.18, consists of a wireless LAN adapter card with an RF antenna. The WLAN adapter cards in the various systems of the LAN communicate with each other and a host system through an access point device. Current wireless LANs operate in the range of 1Mbps transfer rates. Wireless LAN adapters are typically available in the form of PCI and PCMCIA cards.

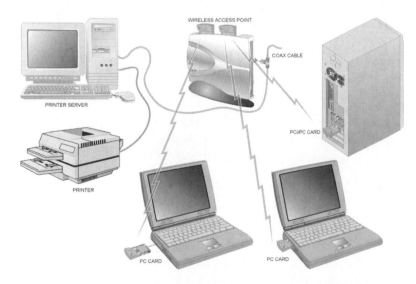

FIGURE 6.18
A wireless LAN.

INSTALLING AND CONFIGURING LANs

A portion of the A+ Core Hardware objective 6.1 states that the test taker should be able to "identify procedures for swapping and configuring network interface cards."

Because PC technicians are typically responsible for maintaining the portion of the network that attaches to the computer, they must be able to install, configure, and service the *network adapter card* and cable. The following sections deal with installing and configuring LAN cards.

LAN Adapter Cards

In a LAN, each computer on the network requires a network adapter card (also referred to as a network interface card or NIC), and every unit is connected to the network by some type of cabling. These cables are typically either twisted-pair wires, thick or thin coaxial cable, or fiber-optic cable.

LAN adapter cards must have connectors compatible with the type of LAN cabling being used. Many Ethernet LAN cards come with both an RJ-45 and a BNC connector, so the cards can be used in any type of Ethernet configuration.

Figure 6.19 depicts a typical LAN card. In addition to its LAN connectors, the LAN card may have a number of configuration jumpers that must be set up.

FIGURE 6.19
A typical LAN card.

> **WARNING**
>
> **Use the User Guide** Although some cards may have jumper instructions printed directly on themselves, the card's User Manual is normally required to configure it for operation. Great care should be taken with the User Manual, because its loss might render the card useless. At the very least, the manufacturer would have to be contacted to get a replacement.

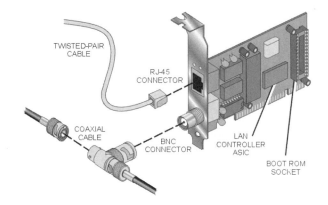

Another item that can be found on many LAN cards is a vacant ROM socket. This socket is included so that it can be used to install a boot-up ROM that will enable the unit to be used as a *diskless workstation*. One or more activity lights also may be included on the card's back plate. These lights can play a very important part in diagnosing problems with the LAN connection. Check the card's User Manual for definitions of its activity lights.

Each adapter must have an *adapter driver* program loaded in its host computer to handle communications between the system and the adapter. These are the *Ethernet*, ARCnet, and Token Ring drivers loaded to control specific types of LAN adapter cards.

In addition to the adapter drivers, the network computer must have a *network protocol driver* loaded. This program may be referred to as the *transport protocol*, or just as the protocol. It operates between the adapter and the initial layer of network software to package and unpackage data for the LAN. In many cases, the computer may have several different protocol drivers loaded so that the unit can communicate with computers that use other types of protocols.

Typical protocol drivers include the *Internetworking Packet Exchange/Sequential Packet Exchange* (IPX/SPX) model produced by Novell, and the standard *Transmission Control Protocol/Internet Protocol* (TCP/IP) developed by the U.S. military for its ARPA network. Figure 6.20 illustrates the various LAN drivers necessary to transmit, or receive, data on a network. More specific protocol information is provided in the section titled "Setting Up Internet Access" in Chapter 13, "5.0 Networks."

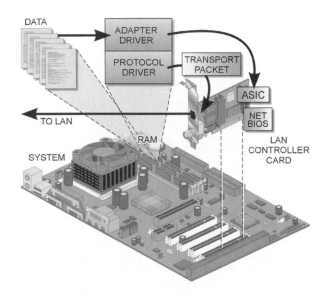

FIGURE 6.20
Various LAN drivers.

Installing LANs

Installing a LAN card in a PC follows the basic steps of installing most peripheral cards. Check the system for currently installed drivers and system settings. Consult the LAN card's Installation Guide for default settings information and compare them to those of the devices already installed in the system. If there are no apparent conflicts between the default settings and those already used by the system, place the adapter card in a vacant expansion slot and secure it to the system unit's back plate.

Connect the LAN card to the network as directed by the manufacturer's Installation Guide and load the proper software drivers for the installed adapter (see Table 6.3). Figure 6.21 illustrates connecting the computer to the LAN, using UTP or coaxial cable. If UTP is being used, the line drop to the computer would come from a concentrator like the one depicted.

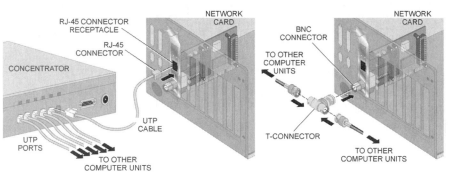

FIGURE 6.21
Connecting the computer to the LAN.

The following three important pieces of information are required to configure the LAN adapter card for use:

◆ The interrupt request (IRQ) setting the adapter will use to communicate with the system.

◆ The base I/O port address the adapter will use to exchange information with the system.

◆ The base memory address that the adapter will use as a starting point in memory for DMA transfers.

Some adapters may require that a DMA channel be defined.

Typical configuration settings for the network card's IRQ, I/O port address, and base memory are as follows:

IRQ=5
Port Address=300h
Base Memory=D8000h

If a configuration conflict appears, reset the conflicting settings so that they do not share the same value. Which component's configuration gets changed is determined by examining the options for changing the cards involved in the conflict. A sound card may have many more IRQ options available than a given network card. In that case, it would be easier to change sound card settings than network card settings.

TABLE 6.3

LAN Card Configuration Settings

I/O Address Options	Interrupt Request Channels	Extended Memory Addressing
240h	IRQ2	C000h
280h	IRQ3	C400h
2C0h	IRQ4	C800h
320h	IRQ10	CC00h
340h	IRQ11	D000h
360h	IRQ12	D400h
	IRQ15	DC00h

TEST TIP

Know the system resources normally required by network adapter cards.

Network Repair

A portion of the A+ Core Hardware objective 6.1 states that the test taker should be able to "identify the ramifications of repairs on the network."

Normally, you should begin troubleshooting a general network problem by determining what has changed since it was running last. If the installation is new, it will need to be inspected as a setup problem.

Check to determine whether any new hardware, or new software, has been added. Has any of the cabling been changed? Have any new protocols been added? Has a network adapter been replaced or moved? If any of these events have occurred, begin by checking them specifically.

Troubleshooting LANs

If the system has not been changed and has operated correctly in the past, the next step is to make certain that it functions properly as a standalone unit. Begin by disconnecting the unit from the network and testing its operation. Run diagnostics on the system to check whether any problems show up. If a hardware problem is encountered at the standalone level, troubleshoot the indicated portion of the system using the procedures already discussed.

If the problem does not appear in, or is not related to, the standalone operation of the unit, it will be necessary to check the portions of the system that are specific to the network. These elements include the network adapter card, the network-specific portions of the operating system, and the *network drop cabling*. Figure 6.22 depicts the network-specific portions of a computer system.

FIGURE 6.22
Network-related components.

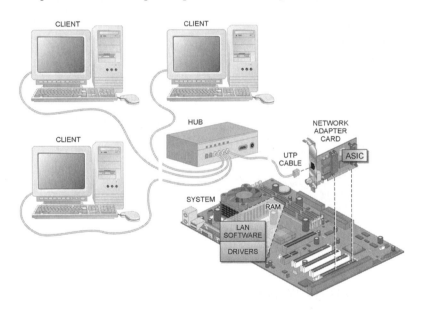

Be aware that in a network environment, no unit really functions alone. Unlike working on a standalone unit, the steps performed on a network computer may affect the operation of other units on the network.

Disconnecting a unit from a network that uses coaxial cable, for example, creates an unterminated condition in the network. A bad cable or connector can also cause this condition to exist. As a matter of fact, the majority of all network failures involve bad cabling, connectors, and connections. The open connection condition can cause several different types of problems to appear in the network:

◆ Data moving through the network can be lost.

◆ A general slowdown of data movement across the network can occur because of reduced bandwidth.

◆ Nodes may not be able to "see" or connect to each other.

If a unit must be removed from the network, it is a good practice to place a terminator in the empty connector where the unit was attached. This should allow the other units to function without the problems associated with an open connection. Take care to ensure that the proper value of terminating resistor is used. Substituting a terminator from an obsolete ARCnet network into an Ethernet system may create as many problems as the open connection would have. However, they may be harder to track down. Systems that use concentrators have fewer connection problems when a unit needs to be removed for servicing.

Even if the unit does not need to be removed from the network, diagnostic efforts and tests run across the network can use a lot of the network's bandwidth. This reduced bandwidth causes the operation of all the units on the network to slow down. This is due just to the added usage of the network.

Because performing work on the network can affect so many users, it is good practice to involve the *network administrator* in any such work being performed. This person can run interference for any work that must be performed that could disable the network or cause users to lose data.

LAN Configuration Checks

As with any peripheral device, its configuration must be correct for the software that is driving the peripheral and for the adapter card it is communicating through. An improperly configured network adapter card can prevent the system from gaining access to the network. Many newer network cards possess Plug and Play (PnP) capabilities. With other non-PnP network cards, such as most ISA NIC cards, it is necessary to configure the card manually through hardware jumpers, or through logical configuration switches in the BIOS Extension EPROM.

TEST TIP

Be aware of the affects of a missing terminator or bad cable/connector can have on an Ethernet network.

TEST TIP

Be aware of the effects that running applications across the network can have on its performance.

Check the adapter card's hardware settings to see whether they are set according to the manufacturer's default settings, or whether they have been changed to some new setting. If they have been changed, refer to the system information from the software diagnostic tool to see whether there is some good explanation for the change. If not, record the settings as they are and reset them to their default values.

Also, check the software's configuration settings and change them to match as necessary. If a defective card is being replaced with an identical unit, just transfer the configuration settings to the new card.

Use a software diagnostic package to check the system's interrupt request allocations. Try to use a package that can check the system's I/O port addresses and shadow RAM and ROM allocations. Finally, check the physical IRQ settings of any other adapter cards in the system.

Basic LAN Checks

It is at the LAN system software level that troubleshooting activities diverge. The differences between *Novell NetWare*, Microsoft's Windows NT, Windows 9x, and Windows 2000 are significant enough that there are internationally recognized certifications just for NetWare and NT. Novell NetWare and Windows NT/2000 are client/server types of network management software, whereas Windows 9x is basically a peer-to-peer networking environment.

Security Access Problems

One of the major concerns in most network environments is *data security*. Because all the data around the network is potentially available to anyone else attached to the network, all LAN administration software employs different levels of security. *Passwords* are typically used at all software levels to lock people out of hardware systems, as well as out of programs and data files.

Logon passwords and scripts are designed to keep unauthorized personnel from accessing the system or its contents. Additional passwording may be used to provide access to some parts of the system, and not others. (That is, lower-level accounting personnel may be allowed access to accounts receivable and payable sections of the business management software package, but not allowed into the payroll section.) A series of passwords also may be used to deny access to this area.

In other LAN management packages, *access and privileges* to programs and data can be established by the network administrator, through the software's security system. These settings can be established to completely deny access to certain information, or to allow limited access rights to it. An example of limited rights would be the ability to read data from a file, but not be able to manipulate it (write, delete, print, or move it) in any way.

The reason for discussing security at this point is because established security settings can prevent the technician from using any, or all, of the system's resources. In addition, having limited access to programs can give them the appearance of being defective. Because of this, the service technician must work with the network administrator when checking a networked machine. The administrator can provide the access, and the security relief, needed to repair the system. The administrator also can keep you away from data that may not be any of your business.

Section 4.2 of Chapter 10, "4.0 Networks," covers the Operating System Technologies module and offers in-depth network software troubleshooting information.

LAN Hardware Checks

Some LAN adapters come with software diagnostic programs that can be used to isolate problems with the adapter. If this type of software is included, use it to test the card. The diagnostic software can also be used to change the adapter's configuration, if necessary.

If the card fails any of the diagnostic tests, check it by exchanging it with a known good one of the same type. Set the replacement card's station address so that it is unique (usually the same as the card being removed). Depending on the type of system being tested, the file server may need to be cycled off, and then back on, to detect the presence of the new LAN card.

Check the activity light on the back plate of the LAN card (if available) to see whether it is being recognized by the network. If the lights are active, the connection is alive. If not, check the adapter in another node. Check the cabling to make sure that it is the correct type and that the connector is properly attached. A LAN cable tester is an excellent device to have in this situation.

If the operation of the local computer unit appears normal, it will be necessary to troubleshoot the network from the node out. As mentioned earlier, always consult the network administrator before performing any work on a network, beyond a standalone unit.

Check the system for concentrators, routers, and *bridges* that may not be functioning properly. Check the frame settings being used to make sure that they are compatible from device to device, or that they are represented on the file server. The operation of these devices will have to be verified as separate units.

Testing Cable

As mentioned earlier in this chapter, the most frequent hardware-related cause of network problems involves bad cabling and connectors. There are several specialized handheld devices designed for testing the various types of data-communications cabling. These devices range from inexpensive continuity testers, to moderately priced data-cabling testers, to somewhat expensive time domain reflectometry (TDR) devices.

The inexpensive continuity testers can be used to check for broken cables. This function also can be performed by the simple DMM described in Chapter 2, "2.0 Diagnosing and Troubleshooting." Data-cabling testers are designed to perform a number of different types of tests on twisted-pair and coaxial cables. These wiring testers normally consist of two units: a master test unit, and a separate load unit (as illustrated in Figure 6.23).

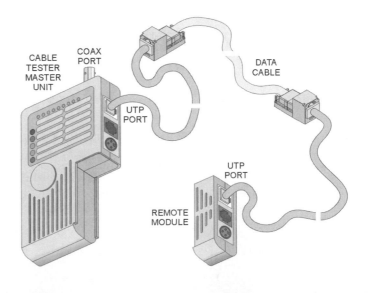

FIGURE 6.23
Cable tester.

The master unit is attached to one end of the cable, and the load unit is attached at the other. The master unit sends patterns of test signals through the cable and reads them back from the load unit. Many of these testers feature both RJ-45 and BNC connectors for testing different types of cabling. When testing twisted-pair cabling, these devices can normally detect such problems as broken wires, crossed-over wiring, shorted connections, and improperly paired connections.

TDRs are sophisticated testers that can be used to pinpoint the distance to a break in a cable. These devices send signals along the cable and wait for them to be reflected. The time between sending the signal and receiving it back is converted into a distance measurement. The TDR function is normally packaged along with the other cable-testing functions just described. TDRs used to test fiber-optic cables are known as optical time domain reflectometers (OTDRs).

Network Printing Problems

As described in the Chapter 5, "5.0 Printers," transferring data from the system to the printer over a parallel port and cable is largely a matter of connecting the cable and installing the proper printer driver for the selected printer. The protocol for sending data consists largely of a simple hardware handshake routine. Even in a serial printer, the protocol is only slightly more complex. When a network is involved, however, the complexity becomes that much greater again, because of the addition of the network drivers.

The first step in troubleshooting network printer problems is to verify that the local computer and the remote printer are set up for remote printing. Check the operating system to see that the printer is configured to be a shared resource for other computers on the network. If the local computer cannot see files and printers at the remote print server station, file and print sharing may not be enabled there. Section 4.2 of Chapter 10 covers the Operating System Technologies portion of the networking material and provides additional solutions to Windows-related network printing problems.

The first step in troubleshooting network printer problems is to verify that the local computer and the remote printer are set up for remote printing. Check the operating system to see that the printer is configured to be a *shared resource* for other computers on the network. If the remote computer cannot see files and printers at the print server station, file and print sharing may not be enabled there. Section 4.2 of Chapter 10 covers the Operating System Technologies portion of the networking material and provides additional solutions to Windows-related network printing problems.

The next step is to verify the operation of the printer. As described in Chapter 5, run a self-test on the printer to make certain that it is working correctly. Turn the printer off and allow a few seconds for its buffer memory to clear. Try to run a test page to verify the operation of the printer's hardware.

If the test page does not print, there is obviously a problem with the printer. Troubleshoot the printer using the information from Chapter 5, until the self-test works correctly. With the printer working, attempt to print across the network again.

The third step is to determine whether the print server (computer actually connected to the network printer) can print to the printer. Try to open a document on the print server and print it. If the local printing operation is unsuccessful, move to the command prompt, create a small batch file, and copy it to the local LPT port. If the file prints, there are a few possible causes of printing problems. The first possibility is that a problem exists with the printer configuration at the print server. Check the print server's drivers.

Another common problem is that there may not be enough memory or hard-drive space available in the print server. Use the Windows utility programs to determine the amount of hard drive and memory space available in the system and to optimize the system for further use. These utility programs are covered in detail in Chapter 9, "3.0 Diagnosing and Troubleshooting."

The fourth step is to verify the operation of the network. This can be accomplished by trying other network functions, such as transferring a file from the remote unit to the print sever. If the other network functions work, examine the printer driver configuration of the remote unit.

If the print drivers appear to be correct, install a generic or text-only printer driver and try to print to the print server. Also, move to the command prompt in the remote unit and create a batch text file. Attempt to copy this file to the network printer. If the generic driver or the DOS file works, reinstall the printer driver or install new drivers for the designated printer.

In the event that other network functions are operational, the final step is to verify the printer operation of the local computer. If possible, connect a printer directly to the local unit and set its print driver up to print to the local printer port. If the file prints to the local printer, a network/printer driver problem still exists. Reload the printer driver and check the network print path. Check the network cabling for good connections.

If the printer operation stalls or crashes during the printing process, a different type of problem is indicated. In this case, the remote printer was functioning, the print server was operational, and the network was transferring data. Some critical condition must have been reached to stop the printing process. Check the print spooler or print manager in the print server to see whether an error has occurred. Also, check the hard disk space and memory usage in the print server. Figure 6.24 illustrates the process of isolating network printing problems.

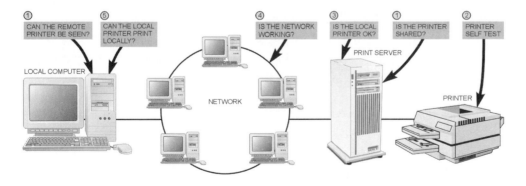

FIGURE 6.24
Isolating network printing problems.

CHAPTER SUMMARY

KEY TERMS

- 100BASE-T
- 10BASE-2
- 10BASE-5
- 10BASE-T
- 100BASE-FX
- 100BASE-TX
- Access and privileges
- Adapter driver
- British Naval Connector (BNC)
- Bridges
- Bus topology
- Carrier sense multiple access with collision detection (CSMA/CD)
- Client/server networks
- Coaxial cable
- Data security
- Diskless workstation
- Ethernet
- Fast Ethernet
- Fiber-optic cable
- File server
- Hub
- Internetworking Packet Exchange/Sequential Packet Exchange (IPX/SPX)
- Local area networks (LANs)

Local area networks have become a very common part of the computer system, particularly in the workplace. This chapter has presented basic networking in three parts: "Basic Networking Concepts," "Installing and Configuring LANs," and "Network Repair."

The "Basic Networking Concepts" section presented basic networking terminology and concepts. Major topics of this section included network topologies, types of networks, and connection schemes. The second portion of the chapter dealt with installing and configuring basic network hardware.

The final section of the chapter concerned network troubleshooting and the possible complications of performing repair work on an operational network.

At this point, review the objectives listed at the beginning of the chapter to be certain that you understand each point and that you can perform each task listed there. Afterward, answer the Review and Exam Questions that follow to verify your knowledge of the information.

- Mesh design
- Network adapter card
- Network administrator
- Network drop cabling
- Network protocol driver
- Network resources
- Network interface card (NIC)
- Nodes
- Novell NetWare
- Packet

- Passwords
- Peer-to-peer networks
- Ring topology
- RJ-45
- Routers
- Shared resource
- Shielded twisted-pair (STP)
- Star topology
- Stations
- T-connector

- Thinnet
- Token Ring
- Topology
- Transmission Control Protocol/Internet Protocol (TCP/IP)
- Transport protocol
- Trunk cable
- Unshielded twisted pair (UTP)
- Workstation

RESOURCE URLs

www.cs.herts.ac.uk/~simon/nwtworks1/node11.html

http://academic.emporia.edu/pheattch/cs410f97/CD-ROM/subjindx/page032.htm

www.otex.org/manual/chap10.htm

www.cse.bris.ac.uk/pcs/kb/3comcfg.htm

www.cit.rcc.on.ca/nm210/netcards.htm

www.personal.kent.edu/~dbarker1/ethernet_problems.htm

www.cse.bris.ac.uk/pcs/kb/3comcfg.htm

http://wwwhost.ots.utexas.edu/ethernet/descript-troubleshoot.html

www.cisco.com/warp/public/779/smbiz/service/troubleshooting/

This last entry has a lot of good information in it, but you'll need to look around for it. Also check out the /knowledge and /pin-outs sections of this site.

APPLY YOUR KNOWLEDGE

Review Questions

1. Does the network protocol driver (or transport protocol driver) replace the LAN card's adapter driver?

2. Logon passwords and scripts are designed to _____.

3. What is the primary difference between a client/server type of network and a peer-to-peer network?

4. Describe the three important configuration settings associated with a network adapter card.

5. What element determines the active unit in a Token Ring network?

6. In a LAN environment, access and privileges to programs and data can be established by the _____.

7. Describe three possible symptoms produced by an unterminated connection in a LAN.

8. What is TCP/IP, and what does it mean?

9. What do the lights on the back of a NIC card indicate if they are not active?

10. How does a Token Ring network keep a single unit from dominating the network after it receives the token? What is this called?

11. What is the first step in checking a networked computer?

12. What type of LAN is identified by the terminology 100BASE-FX?

13. Which item is usually considered the key to setting the configuration of a LAN card properly?

14. Describe two actions that should be taken if a networked printer stalls during a remote printing operation.

15. What is the likely function of a vacant socket on a LAN card?

Exam Questions

1. What is the minimum number of PCs that need to be connected together before a true network is formed?

   A. Three

   B. Two

   C. One

   D. Five

2. What type of topology is Ethernet?

   A. A token-passing topology

   B. A star topology

   C. A ring topology

   D. A bus topology

3. To which topology does FDDI belong?

   A. A CSMA/CD topology

   B. A star topology

   C. A ring topology

   D. A bus topology

4. State the maximum segment length of a 10BASE-2 Ethernet network.

   A. 100 feet

   B. 185 meters

   C. 185 feet

   D. 100 meters

APPLY YOUR KNOWLEDGE

5. What does the designation 100BASE-T tell you about a network?

   A. Its maximum cable segment length is 100 feet and it uses BNC T-connectors.

   B. Its maximum data rate is 100Mbps and it uses UTP cabling.

   C. Its maximum data rate is 100MHz and it uses BNC T-connectors.

   D. Its maximum cable segment length is 100 feet and it uses UTP cabling.

6. Define the word *protocol.*

   A. A hardware handshaking method

   B. An error-correction code

   C. An agreed-upon method of doing things

   D. A software handshaking method

7. In a client/server network, _____.

   A. At least one unit is reserved just to serve the other units.

   B. At least one unit depends on the other units for its information.

   C. Each unit has its own information and can serve as either client or server.

   D. Each unit handles some information for the network.

8. An RJ-45 connector is most commonly used with _____.

   A. Disk-drive units

   B. Fiber-optic cabling

   C. Coaxial cabling

   D. Unshielded twisted-pair cabling

9. Which type of network lets its clients transmit data only when they have a turn?

   A. Ethernet

   B. Token Ring

   C. Peer-to-peer

   D. Fiber optic

10. The maximum segment length of a 10BASE-5 network connection is _____.

    A. 15 meters

    B. 185 meters

    C. 500 meters

    D. 1000 meters

Answers to Review Questions

1. No. The transport protocol driver is added to the adapter driver to form the information into packets for the network. For more information, see the section "LAN Adapter Cards."

2. Keep unauthorized personnel from accessing the system, or its contents. For more information, see the section "Security Access Problems."

3. Client/server systems use centrally located computers to handle programs and data for the entire system. Peer-to-peer networks connect otherwise autonomous stations together so that they can share information and resources. For more information, see the section "LAN Topologies."

4. IRQ channel, base I/O port address, and base memory address settings. For more information, see the section "Installing LANs."

APPLY YOUR KNOWLEDGE

5. Possession of the network's token. For more information, see the section "Token Ring."

6. The network administrator, through the software's security system. For more information, see the section "Security Access Problems."

7. This condition can cause several different types of problems, including data moving through the network can be lost; a general slowdown of data movement across the network can occur because of reduced bandwidth; and nodes may not be able to "see" or connect to, each other. For more information, see the section "Troubleshooting LANs."

8. Transport Control Protocol/Internet Protocol is a network protocol driver that operates between the adapter and the initial layer of network software, to package and unpackage data for the LAN. For more information, see the section "LAN Adapter Cards."

9. If the lights are active, the connection is alive. If not, check the adapter in another node because it is not being recognized by the system. For more information, see the section "LAN Hardware Checks."

10. The protocol allows only one node in the network to control the packet (token) at a time. Even then, the node can hold onto the packet only for a predetermined amount of time. This concept is referred to as token passing. For more information, see the section "Token Ring."

11. Determine what has changed since the system was run last. If the unit is a new installation, treat it as a setup problem. For more information, see the section "Troubleshooting LANs."

12. A fast Ethernet LAN running on fiber-optic cabling. For more information, see the section "Fiber-Ethernet Standards."

13. The LAN card's User Manual is normally a requirement for properly setting it up. For more information, see the section "LAN Adapter Cards."

14. Check the print spooler, or print manager, in the print server to see whether an error has occurred and check the hard disk space and memory usage in the print server. For more information, see the section "Network Printing Problems."

15. It can be used to install a boot-up ROM to enable the unit to be used as a diskless workstation. For more information, see the section "LAN Adapter Cards."

Answers to Exam Questions

1. **A.** In some resources, the answer is two. With only two nodes communicating, however, you have a point-to-point communication link that could be accomplished through a simple null modem connection. This is hardly a network. When the third unit is added to the system, an entirely new control method is required to get information to the intended recipient and control access to the communication links. This is a network. (Be aware that CompTIA may ask about this and the only acceptable answer will be two.) For more information, see the section "Local Area Networks."

2. **D.** Ethernet is a bus topology. Token Ring is a token-passing topology. For more information, see the section "Ethernet Specifications."

APPLY YOUR KNOWLEDGE

3. **C.** FDDI is actually a redundant ring topology. For more information, see the section "The FDDI Ring Standard."

4. **B.** The BASE-2 designation implies 200 meters. For this one IEEE standard, however, the length is slightly off—185 meters (nearly 200: They must have taken equipment drop lengths at each end into account when they rolled out this designation.) For more information, see the section "Ethernet Specifications."

5. **B.** For more information, see the section "Ethernet Specifications."

6. **C.** A protocol is an agreed-upon way to do things, whether in a government scenario or in a network-control scenario. Although both hardware and software handshaking are classes of protocols, they do not define a protocol. For more information, see the section "LAN Topologies."

7. **A.** In client/server networks, at least one unit is reserved to be the master (server) of the other units on the network. Part of the server's responsibilities is to answer service requests from the client units for programs, data, and security. For more information, see the section "LAN Topologies."

8. **D.** The standard connector for UTP cable is a modular RJ-45 registered jack. Coaxial cables use BNC connectors, and fiber-optic cable uses special connectors designed for fiber. Disk-drive cables use BERG pin or edge connectors for connections. For more information, see the section "Ethernet Specifications."

9. **B.** In a Token Ring architecture, only the unit that has captured the token can use the network to move data. All other units are prohibited from accessing the communications link until it is their turn to hold the token. In other topologies, such as Ethernet, nodes listen for an opportunity to put information on the communication link while it is quiet. For more information, see the section "Token Ring."

10. **C.** The BASE-5 nomenclature indicates that the maximum segment length is limited to 500 meters. For more information, see the section "Ethernet Specifications."

OPERATING SYSTEM TECHNOLOGIES

This chapter helps you to prepare for the Operating System Technologies module of the A+ Certification examination by covering the following objectives within the "Domain 1.0: Operating System Fundamentals" section.

1.1 Identify the operating system's functions, structure, and major system files to navigate the operating system and how to get needed technical information.

Content may include the following:

- **Major Operating System functions**

- **Create folders**

- **Checking OS Version**

- **Major Operating System components**

- **Explorer**

- **My Computer**

- **Control Panel**

- **Contrasts between Windows 9x and Windows 2000**

- **Major system files—what they are, where they are located, how they are used, and what they contain.**

- **System, Configuration, and User Interface files**

  - **IO.SYS**

  - **BOOT.INI**

  - **WIN.COM**

  - **MSDOS.SYS**

  - **AUTOEXEC.BAT**

  - **CONFIG.SYS**

  - **COMMAND LINE PROMPT**

CHAPTER 7

1.0 Operating System Fundamentals

Memory management

- Conventional
- Extended/upper memory
- High memory
- Virtual memory
- HIMEM.SYS
- EMM386.EXE

Windows 9x

- IO.SYS
- WIN.INI
- USER.DAT
- SYSEDIT
- SYSTEM.INI
- MSCONFIG(98)
- COMMAND.COM
- REGEDIT.EXE
- SYSTEM.DAT
- RUN COMMAND
- MSCOMMAND LINE PROMPT.SYS

Windows 2000

- Computer Management
- BOOT.INI
- REGEDT32
- REGEDIT
- RUN CMD
- NTLDR
- NTDECT.COM
- NTBOOTDD.SYS

Command Prompt Procedures (Command Syntax)

- DIR
- ATTRIB
- VER
- MEM
- SCANDISK
- DEFRAG
- EDIT
- XCOPY
- COPY
- SETVER
- SCANREG

▶ The computer technician must be familiar with the functions and structure of operating systems that may be encountered in the field. The major operating systems associated with personal computers are Windows 9x and Windows 2000. Both operating systems provide a DOS-based command-line interface that works separate from their GUIs. The technician will often need to use this interface to isolate and correct problems within the operating system.

1.2   Identify basic concepts and procedures for creating, viewing, and managing files and directories, including procedures for changing file attributes and the ramifications of those changes (for example, security issues).

Content may include the following:

- File attributes – Read Only, Hidden, System, and Archive attributes

- File-naming conventions (Most common extensions)

- Windows 2000 COMPRESS, ENCRYPT

- **IDE/SCSI**
- **Internal/External**
- **Backup/Restore**

▶ The operating systems of disk-based computers handle information in the form of files. Therefore, the computer technician must be aware of the methods different operating systems use to create and manipulate files.

1.3 Identify the procedures for basic disk management.

Content may include the following:

- **ScanDisk**
- **IDE/SCSI**
- **Internal/External**
- **Backup/Restore**
- **Defragmenting**
- **Using Disk Management utilities**
- **Partitioning/Formatting/File System**
- **FAT**

- **FAT16**
- **FAT32**
- **NTFS4**
- **NTFS5**
- **HPFS**

▶ The components in a computer system that require the most attention from a computer technician are its disk drives. These devices fill up and slow down the operation of the system. They also fail more often than less-mechanical parts of the system. Therefore, the technician must be able to perform typical disk-management procedures.

Author's Note: A later revision of the A+ Objectives moved the Operating System Technologies 1.2 objective listed above into the 1.1 objective and moved a substantial amount of information about Windows-based utilities to Operating System Technologies objective 1.2. Although we have attempted to track directly with the order and scope of the Λ+ objectives, the material mentioned can be found in its original position under Operating System Technologies objective 3.2. This original location more accurately positions the material where it is used.

OUTLINE

To prepare for the Operating System Fundamentals objective of the Operating System Technology exam:

▶ Read the objectives at the beginning of this chapter.

▶ Study the information in this chapter.

▶ Review the objectives listed earlier in this chapter.

▶ Perform any step-by-step procedures in the text.

▶ Answer the Review and Exam Questions at the end of the chapter and check your results.

▶ Use the *ExamGear* test engine on the CD that accompanies this book for additional Review and Exam Questions concerning this material.

▶ Review the Test Tips scattered throughout the chapter and make certain that you are comfortable with each point.

INTRODUCTION

This domain of the exam challenges the test taker to demonstrate knowledge of underlying DOS (command-prompt functions) in Windows 9x and Windows 2000 operating systems in terms of its functions and structure, for managing files and directories, and for running programs. It also includes navigating through the operating system from command-line prompts and Windows procedures for accessing and retrieving information. Questions from this domain account for 30% of the Operating System Technologies exam.

OPERATING SYSTEM FUNDAMENTALS

▶ 1.1 Identify the operating system's functions, structures, and major file systems.

The A+ Operating System Technologies objective 1.1 states that the test taker should be able to "identify the operating system's functions, structures and major file systems."

In days past, the computer technician's major concern centered on the system's hardware and configuration. DOS was either working or it wasn't. Those days are well past, however, and as this A+ objective points out, the computer technician must be familiar with the functions and structure of various operating systems that may be encountered in the field.

The major operating systems that CompTIA associates with personal computers are DOS, Windows 9x, and Windows 2000. Although UNIX and Linux exist in the market, along with lots of Windows NT 4.0, the A+ examination deals primarily with these desktop operating systems.

OPERATING SYSTEMS

The general responsibilities of an operating system were described in Chapter 1, "1.0 Installation, Configuration, and Upgrading." This chapter investigates operating systems in much greater depth.

Literally thousands of different operating systems are in use with microcomputers. The complexity of each operating system typically depends on the complexity of the application the microcomputer is designed to fill.

The operating system for a fuel mixture controller in an automobile is relatively simple, but an operating system for a multiuser computer system that controls many terminals is relatively complex.

The complete operating system for the fuel controller could be stored in a single, small ROM device. It would likely take control of the unit as soon as power is applied, reset the system, and test it. During normal operation, the operating system monitors the sensor inputs for accelerator setting, humidity, and so on, and adjusts the air/fuel mixing valves according to predetermined values stored in ROM. Figure 7.1 depicts a fuel mixture controller.

FIGURE 7.1

A simple fuel/air mixture controller.

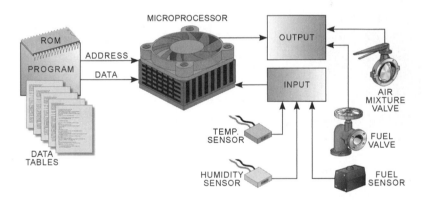

In the large, multiuser system, the operating system is likely to be stored on disk and have sections loaded into RAM when needed. As illustrated in Figure 7.2, this type of operating system must control several pieces of hardware, manage files created and used by various users, provide security for each user's information, and manage communications between different stations. The operating system also would be responsible for presenting each station with a user interface that can accept commands and data from the user. This interface can be a command-line interpreter or a graphical user interface.

DISKLESS WORK STATIONS

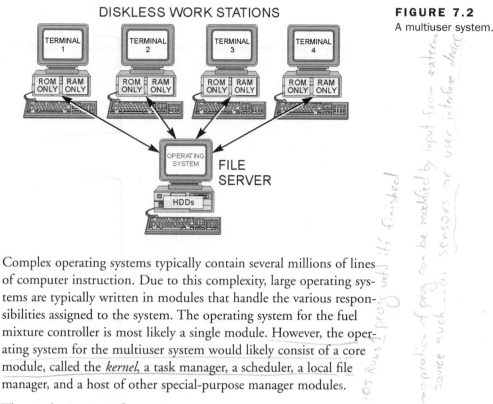

FIGURE 7.2
A multiuser system.

Complex operating systems typically contain several millions of lines of computer instruction. Due to this complexity, large operating systems are typically written in modules that handle the various responsibilities assigned to the system. The operating system for the fuel mixture controller is most likely a single module. However, the operating system for the multiuser system would likely consist of a core module, called the *kernel*, a task manager, a scheduler, a local file manager, and a host of other special-purpose manager modules.

The two basic types of operating systems are

- Single-process systems
- Multiprocess systems

In a *single-process system*, the operating system works with a single task only. These operating systems can operate in batch mode or interactive mode. In batch mode, the operating system runs one program until it is finished. In interactive mode, the operation of the program can be modified by input from external sources, such as sensors, or a user interface device.

In *multiprocess systems*, the operating system is designed so that it can appear to work on several tasks simultaneously. A task is a portion of a program under execution. Computer programs are made up of several tasks that may work alone or as a unit. Tasks, in turn, can be made up of several threads that can be worked on separately. A thread is a section of programming that can be time sliced by the operating system to run at the same time that other threads are being executed.

The multiprocess system breaks the tasks associated with a process into its various *threads* for execution. Typically, one thread may handle video output, another would handle mouse input, and another output from the printer.

Multiprocess operations can be organized in the following three different ways:

◆ Multiuser

◆ Multitasking

◆ Multiprocessor

Figure 7.3 depicts these three types of operating systems.

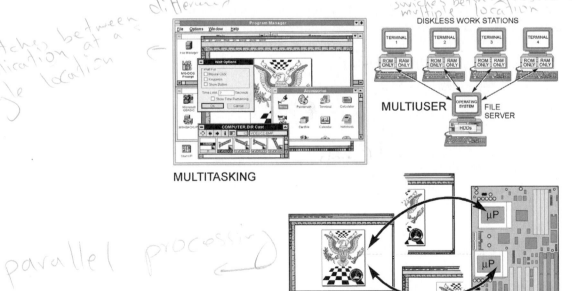

FIGURE 7.3
Multiple process operating systems.

In *multiuser* and *multitasking* operations, the appearance of simultaneous operation is accomplished by switching between different tasks in a predetermined order. The multiuser system switches between different users at multiple locations, and multitasking systems switch between different applications at a single location.

In both cases, the information concerning the first task must be stored and information about the new task loaded each time a task switch occurs. The operating system's scheduler module is responsible for overseeing the switching function.

In a *multiprocessor* operating system, tasks are divided among multiple microprocessors. This type of operation is referred to as *parallel processing*.

Although simple microcomputers store the entire operating system in ROM, most microcomputers use a bootstrapping process to load the operating system into RAM. Bootstrapping describes an arrangement where the operating system is loaded into memory by a smaller program called the *Bootstrap Loader*. The operating system can be loaded from a ROM chip, a floppy disk, a hard disk drive, or from another computer. The term bootstrap refers to the system pulling itself up by its own bootstraps, because, in loading the more-powerful operating system files from the disk, it has increased its onboard intelligence considerably. In personal computers, the bootstrap operation is one of the functions of the ROM BIOS.

Microsoft Disk Operating Systems

The bootstrap process is primarily used in disk drive–based systems to load an operating system that can control such a system. MS-DOS is a disk operating system for IBM PC–compatible computers. In its day, it was easily the most popular operating system in the world. It also is the basis from which Windows 9x derives its underlying organization.

As with any other operating system, its function is to oversee the operation of the system by providing support for executing programs, controlling I/O devices, handling errors, and providing the user interface. MS-DOS is a disk-based, single-user, single-task operating system. These qualities make it one of the easiest disk operating systems to understand.

Although the concept of MS-DOS has largely disappeared from the consumer computer market, it has not gone away for the technician. In many diagnostic and troubleshooting situations, the technician must have a firm understanding of DOS structures and commands.

MS-DOS Structure

The main portions of MS-DOS are the *IO.SYS*, *MSDOS.SYS*, and *COMMAND.COM* files. IO.SYS and MSDOS.SYS are special, hidden system files that do not show up in a normal directory listing. The IO.SYS file moves the system's basic I/O functions into memory and then implements the MS-DOS default control programs, referred to as device drivers, for various hardware components. These include the following:

◆ The boot disk drive

◆ The console display and keyboard

◆ The system's time-of-day clock

◆ The parallel and serial communications port

Conversely, the MSDOS.SYS file provides default support features for software applications. These features include the following:

◆ Memory management

◆ Character input and output

◆ Real-time clock access

◆ File and record management

◆ Execution of other programs

There is a little-known DOS system requirement that the MSDOS.SYS file must maintain a size in excess of 1KB.

The COMMAND.COM command interpreter contains the operating system's most frequently used commands. When a command is entered at the command-line prompt, the COMMAND.COM program examines it to see whether it is an internal DOS command or an external DOS command. Internal commands are understood directly by COMMAND.COM; external commands are stored in a directory called DOS. If it is one of the internal commands, the

COMMAND.COM file can execute it immediately. If not, COM-MAND.COM looks in the \DOS directory for the command program.

Likewise, when DOS runs an application, COMMAND.COM finds the program, loads it into memory, and then gives it control of the system. When the program is shut down, it passes control back to the command interpreter.

The remainder of the operating system is comprised of utility programs to carry out DOS operations, such as *formatting* disks (FORMAT), printing files (PRINT), and copying files (XCOPY).

DOS Configuration Files

System software has a subclass of configuration files that can be used to optimize the system for operations in particular functions or with different options. Although MS-DOS and Windows 3.x are not part of the A+ examination outline, certain portions of those operating systems, such as their configuration files, remain relevant because they still appear in the Windows 9x and Windows 2000 environments. For the most part, these files exist to retain some level of compatibility with older applications and hardware devices. However, the technician must understand them in order to deal with problems they may create or be a part of.

In the DOS operating system, two of these utilities, called the *CONFIG.SYS* and *AUTOEXEC.BAT* files, can be included in the DOS boot-up process. As the system moves through the boot-up procedure, the BIOS checks in the *root directory* of the boot disk for the presence of the CONFIG.SYS file. Afterward, it searches for the COMMAND.COM interpreter, and finally looks in the root directory for the AUTOEXEC.BAT file. Both the CONFIG.SYS and AUTOEXEC.BAT files play key roles in optimizing the system's memory and disk drive usage. This operation can be summarized as follows:

1. BIOS performs INT19 to search drives for Master Boot Record.

2. Primary Bootstrap Loader moves Master Boot Record into memory.

3. System executes Secondary Bootstrap Loader from Master Boot Record.

4. Secondary Bootstrap Loader moves IO.SYS and MSDOS.SYS into memory.

5. IO.SYS runs the MSDOS.SYS file to load memory and file management functions.

6. IO.SYS checks for CONFIG.SYS file in root directory.

7. If CONFIG.SYS is found, IO.SYS uses it to reconfigure the system in three read sequences (device, install, and shell).

8. IO.SYS loads COMMAND.COM.

9. COMMAND.COM checks for the AUTOEXEC.BAT file in the root directory.

10. If the AUTOEXEC.BAT file is found, COMMAND.COM carries out the commands found in the file.

11. If no AUTOEXEC.BAT file is found, COMMAND.COM displays the DOS Time and Date prompt on the display.

CONFIG.SYS (responsibilit)

During installation, DOS versions from 5.0 forward create a system file called CONFIG.SYS. DOS reserves this particular filename for use with a special file that contains setup (configuration) instructions for the system. When DOS is loaded into the system, a portion of the boot-up program automatically searches in the default drive for a file named CONFIG.SYS. The commands in this file configure the DOS program for use with options devices and applications programs in the system.

The CONFIG.SYS program is responsible for the following:

1. Setting up any memory managers being used.

2. Configuring the DOS program for use with options devices and application programs.

3. Loading device-driver software and installing memory-resident programs.

These activities are illustrated by the sample CONFIG.SYS file:

```
1 Device=C:\DOS\HIMEM.SYS
  Device=C:\DOS\EMM386.EXE 1024 RAM
```

2   FILES=30
    BUFFERS=15
    STACKS=9,256

    DEVICE=C:\DOS\SMARTDRV.SYS 1024
    DOS=HIGH,UMB

3   DEVICEHIGH=C:\MOUSE\MOUSE.SYS
    DEVICEHIGH=C:\DOS\RAMDRIVE.SYS 4096/a

4   INSTALL=C:\DOS\SHARE.EXE

Memory Managers

In the first section, the system's memory-manager programs are loaded. In this case, the *HIMEM.SYS* command loads the DOS *extended memory driver* (XMS). This driver manages the use of extended memory installed in the system so that no two applications use the same memory locations at the same time. This memory manager should normally be listed in the CONFIG.SYS file before any other memory managers or devices drivers.

HIMEM.SYS also creates a 64KB area of memory just above the 1MB address space called the *high memory area* (HMA). With this, the DOS=HIGH statement is used to shift portions of DOS from conventional memory into the HMA.

The *EMM386.EXE* program provides the system's microprocessor with access to the *upper memory area* (UMA) of RAM. Operating together with the HIMEM.SYS program, this program enables the system to conserve conventional memory by moving device drivers and memory-resident programs into the UMA. Figure 7.4 depicts this concept.

The EMM386.EXE command also can be used to simulate expanded memory–mode operations in RAM above the 1MB mark. In this case, the 1024 RAM switch in the command directs the EMM386 driver provide upper memory access and establish a 1024 byte area above the 1MB mark to simulate expanded memory operations.

FIGURE 7.4
Loading memory managers.

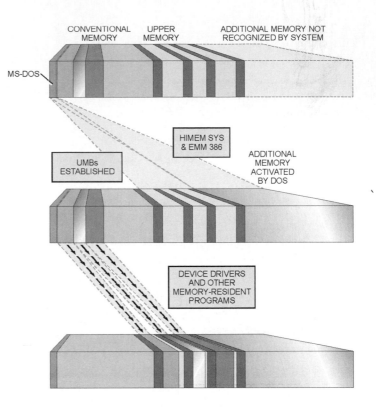

Another expanded memory manager, named LIM EMS 4.0, could be encountered in a CONFIG.SYS file set up for expanded memory operations. If the CONFIG.SYS file contains commands to load another expanded memory manager, the presence of a *NOEMS* switch in the EMM386.EXE line will prevent it from implementing expanded-mode operation when the line is encountered. When this switch is used, the command provides access to the upper memory area, but prevents access to expanded memory. A number of other switches can be used with the EMM386.EXE command. Consult an MS-DOS or Windows User Manual for further information on these switches and their usage.

Most computers use additional RAM in extended mode rather than in expanded mode. Both modes are explained in greater detail in the section "Basic Memory Management" later in this chapter.

Files, Buffers, and Stacks

In the second section of the CONFIG.SYS file are the commands that define DOS for operation with optional devices and applications. The **FILES** command causes the DOS program to establish the number of files that DOS can handle at any one time at 30. This just happens to be the minimum number required to load Windows for operation. The **BUFFERS** command sets aside 15 blocks of RAM memory space for storing data being transferred to and from disks. Similarly, the **STACKS** command establishes the number and length of some special RAM memory storage operations at 9 memory stacks, with each being 256 bytes long.

Device Drivers

Device drivers are loaded in the third part of the file. Device drivers are programs that tell DOS how to control specific devices. **DEVICEHIGH=C:\MOUSE\MOUSE.SYS** is a command that loads a third-party device driver supporting the particular mouse being used with the system.

Some device manufacturers include software installation utilities with the device that will automatically install its device drivers into the CONFIG.SYS (or AUTOEXEC.BAT) files during the installation process. With other devices, the device drivers must be installed by manually updating the CONFIG.SYS and AUTOEXEC.BAT files. The device's installation instructions will identify which method must be used to install its drivers.

The order in which device drivers appear in the CONFIG.SYS file is important. The recommended order for listing device drivers is (1) HIMEM.SYS, (2) the expanded memory manager if installed, (3) the EMM386.EXE command, and (4) then any other device drivers being used.

The *SMARTDRV.SYS* driver establishes a *disk cache* in an area of extended memory as a storage space for information read from the hard disk drive. A cache is a special area of memory reserved to hold data and instructions recently accessed from another location. A disk cache holds information recently accessed from the hard disk drive. Information stored in RAM is much quicker to access than if it were on the hard drive. When a program or DOS operation requests more data, the SMARTDRV program redirects the request to check in the cache memory area to see whether the requested data is there. If SMARTDRV finds the information in the cache, it operates on it from there. If the requested information is not in the cache, the system accesses the hard drive for it.

Using this technique, the overall operating speed of the system is improved. When the system is shut down, SMARTDRV copies the most current information onto the hard drive. Therefore, no data is lost due to it being stored in RAM. Figure 7.5 illustrates the idea behind SMARTDRV operations.

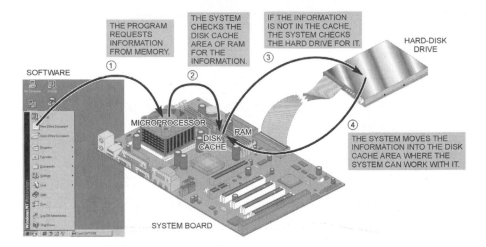

FIGURE 7.5
How SMARTDRV works.

The 1024 modifier establishes a memory cache size of 1MB (1024KB of memory) in extended memory. This is a typical cache size for SMARTDRV; however, 2MB (2048KB) is probably the most efficient size for the cache because the larger the cache size, the greater the chance that the requested information will be in the cache. So there is no need to go to the hard drive for the information. If the command is modified further by an **/A** extension, the cache is established under an expanded memory operation rather than extended memory. Extended memory is the default for SMARTDRV operations.

A number of switches can be added to the SMARTDRV statement to modify the operation of the cache. These switches are summarized as follows:

◆ **/C** writes all current cache information to the hard disk.

◆ **/F** writes cached data before the command prompt returns.

◆ **/L** prevents SMARTDRV from loading into upper memory.

◆ **/N** won't write cached data until the command prompt returns.

◆ **/Q** does not display SMARTDRV status information.

◆ **/R** clears the cache and restarts SMARTDRV.

◆ **/S** displays additional information about SMARTDRV.

◆ **/U** will not load CD-ROM caching.

◆ **/V** displays SMARTDRV status messages when loading.

◆ **/X** disables write-behind caching for all drives.

Other common SMARTDRV entries include the following:

◆ **InitCacheSize** specifies the amount of XMS memory for the cache (in KB).

◆ **WinCacheSize** specifies the amount of XMS memory for the cache with Windows (in KB).

◆ **/E:ElementSize** specifies how many bytes of information to move per transfer.

◆ **/B:BufferSize** establishes the size of the read-ahead buffer.

The RAMDRIVE.SYS driver simulates the organization of a hard disk drive in RAM memory. This type of drive is called a *virtual disk*. In this case, the **DEVICEHIGH=** command loads the RAM-DRV into the upper memory area rather than the base memory area, where a simple **DEVICE=** command would run it. Likewise, the **DOS=HIGH,UMB** command shifts the operation of DOS into the high memory area, and gives the application access to the upper memory area.

The operation of both the SMARTDRV.SYS and RAMDRIVE.SYS device drivers is governed by the HIMEM.SYS memory manager. This is normal only because both programs involve the use of memory beyond the 1MB conventional-memory level. Likewise, the **DEVICEHIGH=** and **DOS=HIGH** commands that move programs into the upper memory area perform under the guidance of the HIMEM.SYS manager.

The fourth portion of the file sets the system up to use the DOS **INSTALL** command. This command is placed in the CONFIG.SYS file to load memory-resident files into memory when the operating system starts up.

Memory-resident programs, also known as *terminate-and-stay-resident* (TSR) programs, are programs that run in the background of other programs. These files remain in memory as long as the system is on and can typically be reactivated by a predetermined keystroke combination.

instal command

A common install command is **INSTALL=C:\DOS\SHARE.EXE**. The *SHARE.EXE* program provides the capability to share files in a networked, or multitasking, environment.

Other common CONFIG.SYS commands include the following:

◆ **BREAK**. Sets or clears extended Ctrl+C checking.

◆ **COUNTRY**. Enables DOS to use international time, dates, currency, case conversions, and decimal separators.

◆ **DRIVPARM**. Defines parameters for block devices when MS-DOS is started.

◆ **LASTDRIVE**. Specifies the maximum number of drives the system can access.

◆ **NUMLOCK**. Specifies whether the NUMLOCK setting on the numeric keypad is set to on or off.

◆ **REM**. Enables the user to include comments (remarks) in a batch file or in the CONFIG.SYS file.

◆ **SET**. Displays, sets, or removes MS-DOS environment variables.

◆ **SHELL**. Specifies the name and location of the command interpreter to be used by the operating system.

◆ **INCLUDE**. Incorporates the contents of one configuration block within another.

◆ **MENUCOLOR**. Sets the text and background colors for the startup menu.

◆ **MENUDEFAULT**. Specifies the default menu item on the startup menu and sets a timeout value if desired.

◆ **SUBMENU**. Defines an item on a startup menu that, when selected, displays another set of choices.

The definitions and usage of these commands are covered in detail in the MS-DOS User Guide. The DOS-installable device drivers also are defined in that publication.

DOS comes with several other standard device driver programs. These drivers can normally be found in the C:\DOS directory and include the following:

- ◆ KEYBOARD.SYS
- ◆ DISPLAY.SYS
- ◆ ANSI.SYS
- ◆ DRIVER.SYS
- ◆ PRINTER.SYS

[handwritten annotation: other device driver program]

KEYBOARD.SYS is the DOS default keyboard definition file. The DISPLAY.SYS driver supports code-page switching for the monitor type in use by the system. A code page is the set of 256 characters that DOS can handle at one time, when displaying, printing, and manipulating text. ANSI.SYS supports ANSI escape-code sequences used to modify the function of the system's display and keyboard. This file also is required to display colors on the monitor in DOS. DRIVER.SYS creates the logical drive assignments for the system's floppy drives (that is, A: and B:). Finally, the PRINTER.SYS driver supports code-page switching for parallel ports. All these drivers are normally found in the DOS directory.

> **TEST TIP**
> Know which driver assigns logical drive letters to the system's floppy drives.

A special, power-saving program called *POWER.EXE* is designed for use in notebook computers. When it is loaded in the last line of the CONFIG.SYS file, and the system hardware meets the *Advanced Power Management* (APM) specification, the power savings can be as high as 25%. If you are using battery power, this can be a significant savings. You can realize up to 25% more operation before you need to recharge the battery. The POWER.EXE file must be available in the C:\DOS directory.

> **TEST TIP**
> Know which statements and commands are normally located in the CONFIG.SYS file.

AUTOEXEC.BAT

After completing the CONFIG.SYS operation, DOS searches for the presence of a file called the AUTOEXEC.BAT file. This file contains a batch of DOS commands that will automatically be carried out when DOS is loaded into the system.

This file also can be re-executed from the DOS prompt by just typing the command **AUTOEXEC**. This is not true of the CONFIG.SYS file, however. To perform the commands in this file, the system must be restarted.

Refer to the following sample AUTOEXEC.BAT file:

```
DATE
TIME
PROMPT=$P$G
SET TEMP=C:\TEMP
PATH=C:\;C:\DOS;C:\MOUSE
DOSKEY
SMARTDRV.EXE 2048 1024
CD\
DIR
```

keep temporarily data

The first two commands cause DOS to prompt you for the date and time (because DOS does not automatically do this when an AUTOEXEC.BAT file is present). The **PROMPT=PG** command causes the active drive and directory *path* to be displayed on the command line. The **SET TEMP=** line sets up an area for holding data temporarily in a directory named TEMP.

The **PATH** command creates a specific set of paths that DOS will use to search for executable (EXE, COM, and BAT) files. In this example, DOS will search for these files first in the root directory (C:\), followed by the DOS directory (C:\DOS), and finally through the Mouse directory (C:\MOUSE).

This statement effectively lets a MOUSE.COM or MOUSE.EXE driver program—normally located in the Mouse directory—to be executed from anywhere in the system. Upon receiving the **MOUSE** command, the operating system looks through all the *directories* in the path until it finds the specified filename.

The syntax (punctuation and organization) of the **PATH** command is very important. Each entry must be complete from the root directory and must be separated from the preceding entry by a semi-colon. There should be no spaces in the **PATH** command.

The **DOSKEY** command loads the Doskey program into memory. Following this, the SMARTDRV.EXE 2048 1024 command configures the system for a 2MB disk cache in DOS, and a 1MB cache for Windows. After the cache has been established, the **CD** command causes the DOS default directory to change to the root directory. The last line causes a DOS **DIR** command to be performed automatically at the end of the operation.

The execution of the AUTOEXEC.BAT file can be interrupted by pressing the Pause key on the keyboard. The program can be restarted by pressing any key. With DOS version 6.2, the F8 interactive bypass procedure, described for use with the CONFIG.SYS file, was extended to include the AUTOEXEC.BAT file.

You can use the DOS batch file commands to construct elaborate startup procedures. Other programs designed to test ports and peripherals can be constructed using these commands. These test files can be named using the DOS filename conventions. They must be stored with a .BAT extension to be executable from the DOS prompt, but the extension does not need to be entered to run the program.

Neither of these two special files are required for normal operation of the computer with DOS. They can prove to be very useful in tailoring the operation of the system to your personal use, however, or to the requirements of different software applications packages. To determine whether either of these files already exist on your DOS disk, just type the **DIR** command at the DOS prompt for the designated drive.

To fully understand how the CONFIG.SYS and AUTOEXEC.BAT files improve the performance of the system, you must understand how DOS views memory. This is explained in greater detail in Chapter 8. Also, refer to the MS-DOS User Guide for more information about the creation and use of the CONFIG.SYS and AUTOEXEC.BAT files.

> **TEST TIP**
> Know which commands are normally located in the AUTOEXEC.BAT file.

Windows Initialization Files

When Microsoft added the Windows 3.x operating environment to the DOS structure, it did so by creating several *initialization* (INI) files that established and controlled the parameters of the various Windows components. These files were installed in the \Windows directory with a file extension of .INI. The INI files carried the default, or current, startup settings for various Windows components.

The major Windows 3.x initialization files were as follows:

◆ WIN.INI

◆ CONTROL.INI

◆ WINFILE.INI

◆ PROGMAN.INI

◆ SYSTEM.INI

[handwritten annotations: "are text file & can be altered by text editor"]

Current versions of Windows 9x and Windows 2000 continue to include these files for compatibility reasons. The \Windows directory may also contain several other INI files. In fact, when a new Windows application is installed, it may very well install its own INI file at that time. These files can be modified to customize, or optimize, the program's execution.

Parameters in INI files are typically modified through normal Windows menus, or through pop-up dialog boxes. Others can be changed only by modifying the INI files directly. The files are broken into sections that contain the individual parameters that can be altered. Changes to the files are automatically updated whenever Windows is exited.

[handwritten annotation: "changed or modify"] *[handwritten annotation: "limiting factor"]*

Normal system functions that alter INI settings include changing *Control Panel*, *desktop*, or *Windows Explorer* entries. However, INI files are basically text files that users can alter with a standard text editor utility such as SysEdit. This utility also can be used to modify the SYSTEM.INI, WIN.INI, CONFIG.SYS, and AUTOEXEC.BAT files. The SysEdit utility can be accessed by just typing **SysEdit** in the Windows Start/Run dialog box.

The format of all the INI files is consistent. Each INI file is divided into logical sections. Each section consists of a list of entries in the format of *keyname=value*. Each section has a name enclosed in brackets. The keyname is just a name that describes the function of the entry and is normally followed by an equals sign. It can be any combination of characters and numbers. The value entry can be any integer or string. Typical enabling entries include On, True, Yes, and 1. Conversely, disabling entries are Off, False, No, and 0.

BASIC MEMORY MANAGEMENT

▶ 1.1 Memory Management

The A+ Operating System Technologies objective 1.1 states that the test taker should be able to "identify the operating system's functions, structure, and major system files to navigate the operating system and how to get needed technical information." One of its major subobjectives indicates that the content will deal with memory-management topics, such as conventional memory, extended/upper memory, high memory, expanded memory, and virtual memory, as well as the files HIMEM.SYS and EMM386.EXE.

Decisions were made in the original IBM PC design, and thereby, the MS-DOS operating system that ran it, that still affect the design of PCs and operating systems. Technicians who work on PC-compatible systems must understand how they allocate memory and how that memory can be manipulated to provide the best system performance. The following sections of this chapter describe how historical operating system developments have shaped memory usage in PC-compatible systems. They also provide ways to optimize these memory structures using a given operating system.

DOS Memory

The original DOS version was constructed in two sections. The first 640KB of memory was reserved for use by DOS and its programs. The remaining section was reserved for use by the BIOS and the system's peripherals (that is, the video card, the hard drive controller card, and so on). This arrangement used the entire 1MB addressing range of the 8088 microprocessor.

As more powerful microprocessors entered the market (80286 microprocessors can access up to 16MB of memory; the 80386 and 80486 can handle up to 4GB of memory), DOS retained the limitations imposed on it by the original version to remain compatible with older machines and software.

Special add-on programs called memory managers have been created to enable DOS to access and use the additional memory capabilities available with more powerful microprocessors.

Basic Memory Organization

Every computer has a memory organization plan called a memory map. Figure 7.6 shows a simplified memory map, showing RAM, ROM, and I/O address allocations.

FIGURE 7.6
A computer memory map.

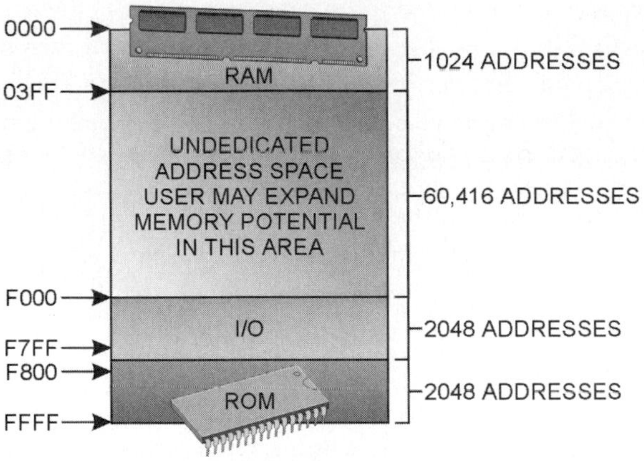
0000
03FF
F000
F7FF
F800
FFFF
RAM
UNDEDICATED ADDRESS SPACE USER MAY EXPAND MEMORY POTENTIAL IN THIS AREA
I/O
ROM
1024 ADDRESSES
60,416 ADDRESSES
2048 ADDRESSES
2048 ADDRESSES

When the original PC was designed, certain decisions were made in dividing up the 8088's 1MB of memory address space. These decisions were implemented by the original PC-DOS and MS-DOS operating systems. Because of compatibility issues, these decisions have carried over into the address allocations of all DOS-based PC compatible's, as described in Figure 7.7.

FIGURE 7.7
PC memory allocations.

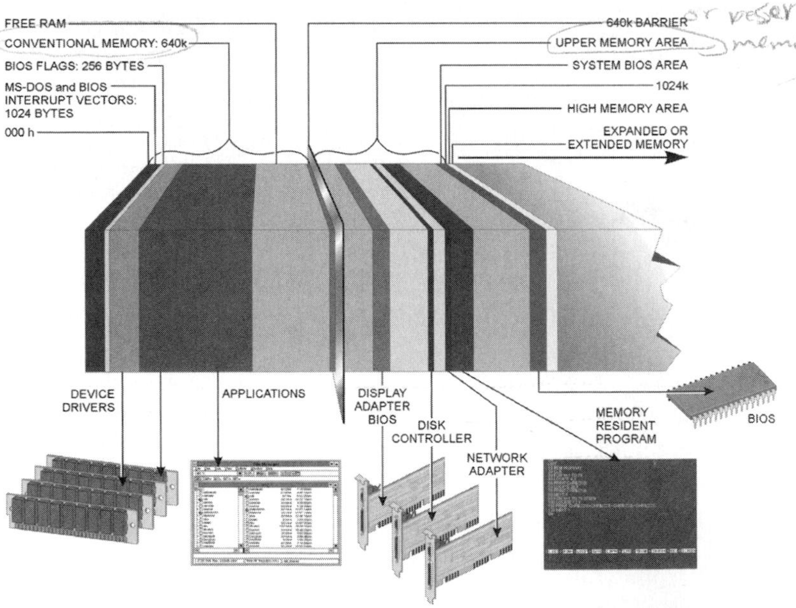
FREE RAM
CONVENTIONAL MEMORY: 640k
BIOS FLAGS: 256 BYTES
MS-DOS and BIOS INTERRUPT VECTORS: 1024 BYTES
000 h
640k BARRIER
UPPER MEMORY AREA
SYSTEM BIOS AREA
1024k
HIGH MEMORY AREA
EXPANDED OR EXTENDED MEMORY
DEVICE DRIVERS
APPLICATIONS
DISPLAY ADAPTER BIOS
DISK CONTROLLER
NETWORK ADAPTER
MEMORY RESIDENT PROGRAM
BIOS

> **NOTE**
>
> **DOS Memory** Basically, DOS can recognize the following classifications of memory: conventional memory, upper memory blocks, high memory area, expanded memory, extended memory and virtual memory.

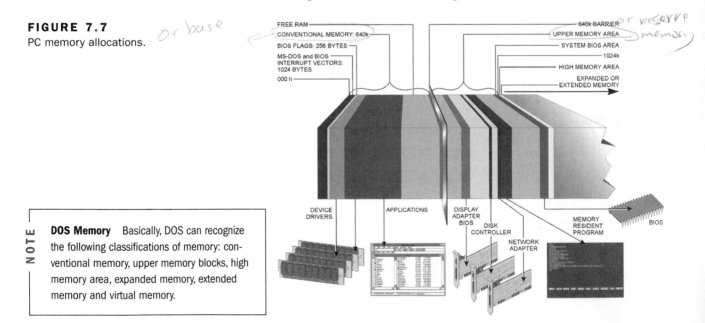

[handwritten margin notes: "or upper memory", "1 MB", "A 0000 h 384 KB Reserve memory use for display –video display –hold system Rom & Bios –extended hardware adapted Bios", "00000h 640KB", "Base memory", "or conventional mem", "for intrupt vectors –data storage –program execution"]

The Intel microprocessors have a separate memory map for I/O addresses.

PC Memory Allocations

In the original PC, the 1MB memory range was divided into two sections: base memory and reserved memory. The base memory area started at address 00000h and extended for 640KB. It was primarily used for interrupt vectors, data storage, and program execution. The reserved memory area began at address A0000h and occupied the remaining 384KB of the 1MB address map. This area was set aside for use as video display memory areas and to hold the system's ROM BIOS as well as any extended hardware adapter BIOS. Figure 7.8 depicts this organizational structure.

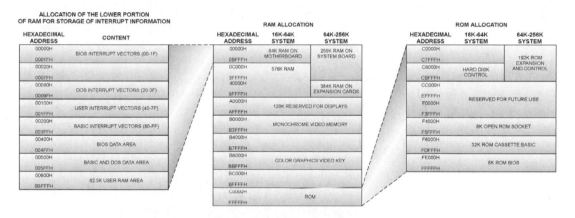

FIGURE 7.8
Original PC RAM allocations.

As systems became capable of accessing memory in excess of the 8088's 1MB range, Microsoft, Intel, software companies, and memory board manufacturers began to redefine the PC's memory allocation strategies. Two strategies were put forward to deal with the additional memory available and still service existing DOS-based programs: the extended memory specification (XMS) and the expanded memory specification (EMS). Both of these specifications were established as guidelines for hardware and software to use the additional memory capabilities.

Conventional Memory

In the process of redefining the PC's memory allocations, the base memory area began to be referred to as conventional memory and the reserved memory area became the upper memory area (UMA).

Figure 7.9 depicts these sections. Conventional memory occupies the first 640KB of addresses, and the remaining 384KB is referred to as upper memory.

FIGURE 7.9
Conventional memory.

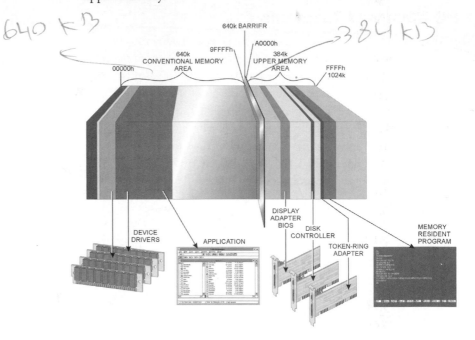

Conventional memory (locations 00000h through 9FFFFh) is the standard memory area for all PC-compatible systems. It traditionally holds DOS, interrupt vector tables, and relocated ROM BIOS tables. The remaining space in the conventional memory area is referred to as DOS program memory. Programs written to operate under PC-DOS or MS-DOS use this area for program storage and execution.

The Upper Memory Area

The UMA occupies the 384KB portion of the PC's address space from A0000h to FFFFFh. This space is not normally considered as part of the computer's total address space because programs cannot store information in this area. Instead, the area is reserved to run segments of the system's hardware. Address spaces from A0000h through BFFFFh are dedicated addresses set aside for the system's video display memory. The system's ROM BIOS occupies the address space between locations FE000h and FFFFFh.

Between the video memory and system BIOS areas, addresses are reserved to hold BIOS extension programs for add-on hardware adapters. Typical BIOS *extensions* include those for hard drive adapters, advanced video adapters, and network adapters. BIOS extensions are discussed in greater detail in Chapter 8, "2.0 Installation, Configuration, and Upgrading" in the section titled "BIOS Extensions."

After the BIOS extensions are in place, the typical UMA still has many unused memory areas that can have information mapped (copied) into them. This space is segmented into 64KB sections called upper memory blocks (UMBs), as illustrated in Figure 7.10. The primary use for these blocks is to hold installable device drivers and other memory-resident programs moved out of the conventional memory area. By moving these programs out of the conventional memory area, more space is made available there for use by application programs.

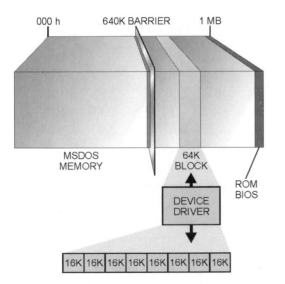

FIGURE 7.10
Upper memory blocks of the UMA.

PCs also use this area to incorporate a memory-usage scheme called shadow RAM to improve their overall performance. With this feature, the contents of the system BIOS and/or adapter BIOS are rewritten (shadowed) into faster extended memory RAM locations. The operating system then remaps the ROM addresses to the corresponding RAM locations through unused portions of the UMA.

Shadowing enables the system to operate faster when application software makes use of any of the BIOS' CALL routines. Instead of accessing an 8-bit IC ROM device, which takes up to four wait states to complete, BIOS calls are redirected by the shadow feature to the same information located in 16-bit, 32-bit, or 64-bit, 0-wait state DRAM devices. Some benchmark tests have shown performance increases between 300 and 400% in systems where the shadow feature is used.

Extended Memory

With the advent of the 80286 microprocessor and its protected operating mode, it became possible to access physical memory locations beyond the 1MB limit of the 8088. Memory above this address is generally referred to as *extended memory*. With the 80286 microprocessor, this could add up to an additional 15MB of RAM for a total of 16MB (24-bit address). Figure 7.11 depicts extended memory.

FIGURE 7.11
Extended memory.

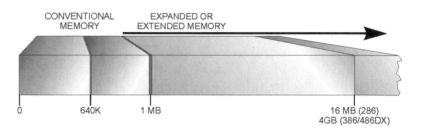

Even though the 80286 could physically access this type of memory using its protected addressing mode, it was impossible for application programs to access it at the time. This was due to the 640KB DOS limit imposed by earlier architectures. With the 32-bit address bus size of 80386-based and 80486-based computers, extended memory could range up to a total of 4GB. It was not that software could not access memory at these addresses, it was just a matter of DOS not having the capability to do so.

Applications programs can be written to specifically take advantage of these memory locations, but few are. Operating systems, such as Microsoft DOS versions beyond 4.0 and Windows versions beyond 3.0, as well as IBM's OS/2 operating system, can take full advantage of extended memory through the Protected Addressing modes of the more advanced microprocessors. This capability to manage higher memory allows the system to free up more of the base memory area for use by applications programs.

The DOS versions above 4.0 contain a memory-management program called HIMEM.SYS that manages extended memory above the
1024KB level. This utility operates under the Microsoft extended
memory specification (XMS). When the utility is loaded into memory, it shifts most of the operating system functions into the high
memory area (HMA) of extended memory. The HMA takes up the
first 64KB of addresses above the 1MB boundary and is a result of a
quirk in the segmented addressing design of the advanced Intel
microprocessors.

The HIMEM function is activated by adding a line of instruction to
the system's CONFIG.SYS file so that it is executed when the computer is booted. When the HIMEM utility is encountered, the program assumes control of the system's A20 Interrupt Handler routine.
This function is part of the BIOS program and takes control of the
system's A20 address line when activated.

The A20 Interrupt Handler is located at BIOS interrupt 15
(INT15) and is used to transfer data blocks of up to 64KB in length
between the system and extended memory. The INT15 function
also supplies entries for the various microprocessor tables required
for protected virtual addressing mode.

Expanded Memory

Some publications may refer to memory above the 1MB limit as
expanded memory. However, the term *expanded memory* is generally
reserved to describe another special memory option. In 1985, three
companies (Lotus, Intel, and Microsoft) joined together to define a
method of expanding the 8088's memory-usage capabilities by
switching banks of memory from outside of the DOS memory area
into the usable address ranges of the 8088. This method became
known as the LIM EMS (for Lotus, Intel, and Microsoft Expanded
Memory Specification) standard.

This idea of bank switching was not exactly new; it had been used
with older computer systems before the advent of the IBM line. The
LIM EMS standard just defined how this technique should be
applied to IBM PCs and their compatibles. The original standard
defined specifications for both hardware and software elements of
the EMS system. Figure 7.12 illustrates the basic principal behind
the EMS standard.

FIGURE 7.12
Expanded memory (EMS) operations.

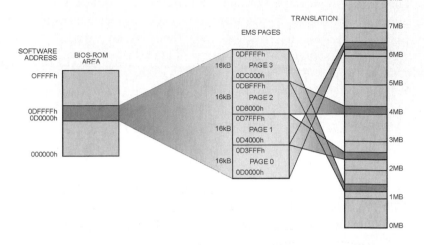

The specification allowed four 16KB areas of memory between C0000h and EFFFFh, referred to as pages, to be used as windows into predefined RAM locations above the 1MB address limit. Originally, these RAM addresses were located on special EMS RAM cards that plugged into one of the system board's expansion slot connectors. Newer system boards, based on the 80486 and Pentium microprocessors, can use their advanced virtual memory paging capabilities to handle the EMS function directly on the board.

Figure 7.12 depicts hex locations D0000h through DFFFFh being used as windows through which the expanded memory addresses are translated. In reality, the four 16KB windows can be selected from anywhere within the LIM EMS-defined address range, and can be relocated to anywhere within the 32MB physical address range.

The EMS software specifications consist of predetermined programs called Expanded Memory Manager (EMM) drivers that work with application software to control the bank-switching operations. These drivers contain special function calls that application programs can use to manipulate the expanded memory. Note, however, that the application software must be written to take advantage of the EMS function calls. EMS versions before 4.0 made provision only for the expanded memory to be used as data storage areas. Programs could not actually be executed in these areas. Versions 4.0, and later, support much larger bank-switching operations as well as program execution and multitasking.

Virtual Memory

The term *virtual memory* is used to describe memory that isn't what it appears to be. Virtual memory is actually disk drive space that is manipulated to seem like RAM. Software creates virtual memory by swapping files between RAM and the disk drive, as illustrated in Figure 7.13. This memory-management technique effectively creates more total memory for the system's applications to use. Because there is a major transfer of information that involves the hard disk drive, however, an overall reduction in speed is encountered with virtual memory operations.

Most operating systems since Windows 3.x (Windows 9x, Windows NT, Windows 2000, UNIX, and Linux) feature virtual memory operations. Within these systems, there are three types of swap files used (temporary, permanent, and variable). Some operating systems permit either a permanent or a temporary swap file to be established on the system's hard drive. A permanent swap file is always present and is a constant size. It is composed of contiguous *clusters* on the drive and cannot be established in fragmented drive space. It also cannot be established on a compressed partition. The following list shows the types of swap files supported by the various Microsoft operating systems:

◆ **Temporary.** Windows 3.x

◆ **Permanent.** Windows 3.x, NT, 2000

◆ **Variable.** Windows 9x

A compressed partition (or drive) is a special type of logical drive established by a disk-compression utility, such as DoubleSpace or DriveSpace. These drives exist as a compressed volume file (CVF) in the root directory of a normal, uncompressed host drive. The advantage of a compressed drive is that it can hold far more data than a noncompressed drive. (10MB of data may be stored in a 5MB space on the host drive.) This reduction is the result of the compression program's data-compacting techniques.

A temporary swap file is created when Windows starts. The size of this type of swap file is variable and can be created in fragmented space.

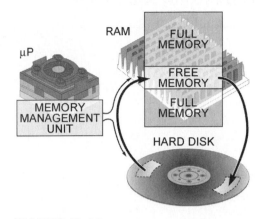

FIGURE 7.13
Virtual memory operations.

The permanent swap file option offers more efficient access to data, but it reserves disk space that may not be used. Conversely, the temporary swap file is more flexible and only uses disk space it needs. However, its space can be limited on a crowded drive. Also, its non-standard location and possibly segmented nature takes more time to find and access.

Windows 9x swap drives do not require contiguous drive space and can be established on compressed drives that use virtual device drivers. The size of the Windows 9x swap file is variable and is dynamically assigned. The Windows 9x swap file is WIN386.SWP.

Control of Windows 9x virtual memory operations is established through the Control Panel's System\Performance tab. Clicking the Virtual Memory button produces the Virtual Memory options screen depicted in Figure 7.14. The default and recommended setting is Let Windows Manage My Virtual Memory Settings.

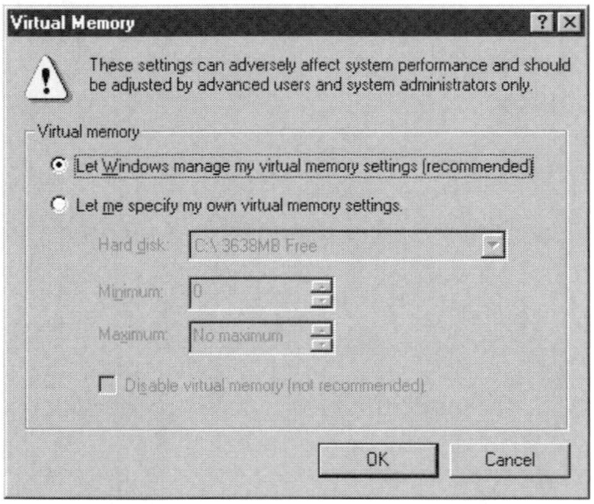

Although the default option usually provides the best performance, the swap file parameters can be manually set to optimize specific applications. Generally, this involves setting the swap file location to the fastest or least-used drive in the system. The Maximum setting, specified in kilobytes, should normally be set to the amount of free space currently available on the drive. The virtual memory manager interprets this as a sign that it can dynamically alter the size of the swap file if more space becomes available.

FIGURE 7.14
The Windows 9x Virtual Memory dialog box.

Entering a minimum file size setting for the swap file in effect creates a permanent swap file. However, the file can grow in size to the maximum available space, or maximum setting size.

This dialog box also offers an option for disabling the virtual memory feature altogether. Doing so can cause the system to crash and not start again.

Although Windows 9x allows swap files to be used with compressed drives, it does have some limitations. The swap file can be located only on the compressed drive if it has a protected-mode driver (DRVSPACE.VXD). The driver must mark the file as uncompressed and place the file in an area where it can expand. If the swap file was created with a real-mode driver and is located on a compressed drive, it should be moved to another drive.

If the DoubleSpace drive compression utility in Windows 9x will not run properly, check to see whether the swap file is compressed, whether there is a permanent swap drive on the host drive, and that there is enough space on the uncompressed portion of the drive to hold the swap file.

In Windows 2000, the virtual memory functions are located under the Control Panel's *System icon.* Just click its Advanced tab followed by the Performance Options button to view the dialog window depicted in Figure 7.15.

Pressing the Change button in the dialog window produces the Virtual Memory dialog window shown in Figure 7.16. Through this dialog window, you can establish and configure an individual swap file for each drive in the system. By highlighting a drive, you can check its virtual memory capabilities and settings. The values for the highlighted drive can be changed by entering new values in the dialog windows and clicking the Set button.

The Windows 2000 pagefile (named PAGEFILE.SYS) is created when the operating system is installed. Its default size is typically set at 1.5 times the amount of RAM installed in the system. It is possible to optimize the system's performance by distributing the swap file space between multiple drives. It also can be helpful to relocate it away from slower or heavily used derives. The swap file should not be placed on mirrored or striped *volumes.* Also, do not create multiple swap files on logical disks that exist on the same physical drive.

Flat Memory Models

Unlike MS-DOS, Windows 3.x, or Windows 9x, other operating systems (such as Windows NT, Windows 2000, UNIX, and Linux) do not employ the address-segmentation features of the Intel microprocessors to divide up the computer's memory allocations. Because segments can overlap, memory usage errors can occur when an application attempts to write data into a space being used by the operating system, or by another application.

Using the flat memory model, the memory manager sections map each application's memory space into contiguous pages of physical memory. Using this method, each application is mapped into a truly unique address space that cannot overlap any other address space. The lack of segment overlap reduces the chances of applications

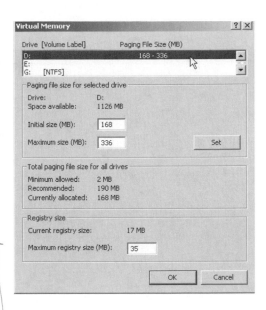

FIGURE 7.15
The System Icon Performance tab.

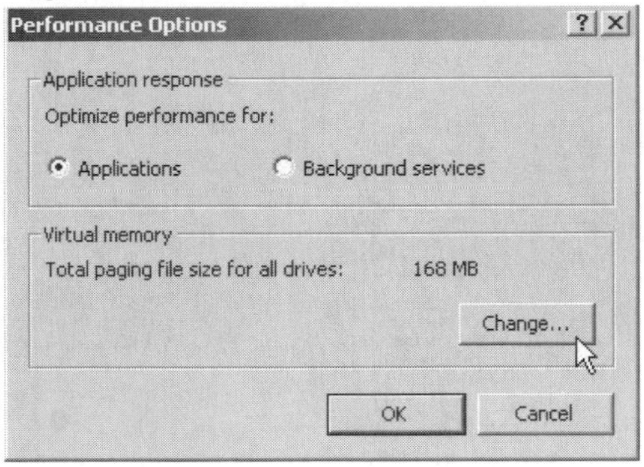

FIGURE 7.16
The Virtual Memory Dialog Window

> **TEST TIP**
> Memorize the filenames of the virtual memory swap files used in each operating system.

interfering with each other and helps to ensure data integrity by providing the operating system and other processes with their own memory spaces.

Figure 7.17 illustrates the flat memory model concept. In this example, the 32-bit address produced by the microprocessor contains three parts dictated by the operating system. The highest 10 bits of the address point to the Page Table Directory. This table sets the address boundaries for each page of memory in the memory. This guarantees that there is only one method of entering the page space (through this table). Therefore, there is no chance for poorly written software to stray into a page it has not been assigned. The lower 22 bits of the address are used to access a particular page within the block of addresses specified in the Page Table Directory (bits 12–21), and then select a particular physical address within the page (bits 0–11).

FIGURE 7.17
Flat Memory Model.

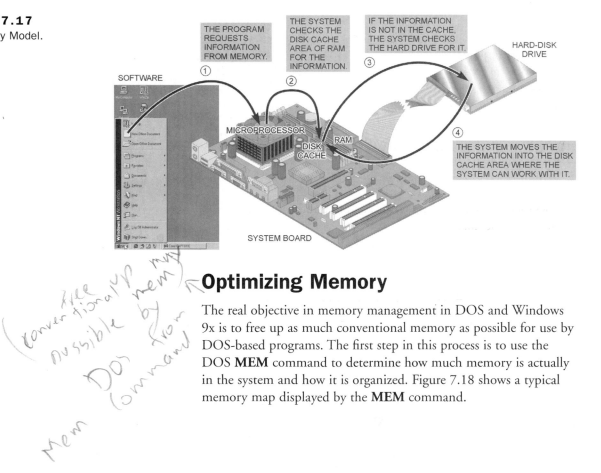

Optimizing Memory

The real objective in memory management in DOS and Windows 9x is to free up as much conventional memory as possible for use by DOS-based programs. The first step in this process is to use the DOS **MEM** command to determine how much memory is actually in the system and how it is organized. Figure 7.18 shows a typical memory map displayed by the **MEM** command.

FIGURE 7.18
The MEM display.

```
C:\>

C:\>mem
Memory Type         Total  =  Used  +  Free

Conventional         640K       47K      593K
Upper                  0K        0K        0K
Reserved             384K      384K        0K
Extended (XMS)     7,168K    2,112K    5,056K

Total memory       8,192K    2,559K    5,633K

Total under 1 MB     640K       47K      593K

Largest executable program size        593K  (607,312 bytes)
Largest free upper memory block          0K       (0 bytes)
MS-DOS is resident in the high memory area.
```

When the **MEM** command is executed without any modifying switches, the system's free and used memory is displayed. Adding a page (**/P**) switch to the line causes the output to stop at the end of each screen full of information. In versions of MS-DOS before release 6.0, the **/P** switch produced a program function that displayed the status of programs currently loaded into memory. Likewise, using a debug (**/D**) switch with the **MEM** command will show the status of currently loaded programs and internal drivers. Another switch, called the classify (**/C**) switch, displays the status of programs in conventional memory and the UMA. In addition, it provides each program's size in decimal and hex notation, along with a summary of memory usage and the largest memory blocks available. The **MEM** command can be used only with one switch at a time.

The Total Memory value is the amount of memory installed in the computer up to 640KB. Conversely, the Available to MS-DOS entry indicates the amount of conventional memory available to operate the system. The Largest Executable Program Size value describes the size of the largest contiguous section of conventional memory available.

The descriptions of the extended memory are similar to those provided for conventional memory. Total Contiguous Extended Memory applies to the amount of memory installed beyond the 1MB mark. The Available Extended Memory value applies to

make free conventional mem as long as possible by moving them to UMA

extended memory not controlled by memory managers, such as HIMEM.SYS, and Available XMS Memory does apply to this type of extended memory. Similar values display when the system is operating with an expanded memory manager, such as EMM386.

One of the keys to good memory management is in making the free conventional memory value as large as possible. This is primarily accomplished by moving as many programs into the UMA as possible. Earlier in this chapter, a typical CONFIG.SYS file structure was discussed. Recall that the first line of the file should be the **DEVICE=HIMEM.SYS** line that loads the DOS extended memory driver from a specified directory.

The second line is typically the **DEVICE=EMM386.EXE** line that loads the DOS expanded memory driver and establishes the system's upper memory blocks. This line must be loaded after the HIMEM.SYS line. Also, remember that the **EMM386** command simulates expanded memory in extended memory if it is not modified by a switch, such as **/NOEMS** (no EMS). This switch cancels the EMS function of the command and provides the maximum amount of available UMA memory to running device drivers and programs.

Conversely, modifying the **EMM386** command with a **/RAM** switch enables it to run device drivers and programs in upper memory blocks and simulate EMS as well. The amount of memory available for UMBs will be reduced using this switch. However, it will enable Windows to run applications that require EMS.

ADD DOS=High will to config.sys to free up more conventional mem

After the upper memory blocks have been established, several commands can be added to the CONFIG.SYS file to free up conventional memory. The first is the **DOS=HIGH** command that relocates a major portion of the DOS into the HMA, as illustrated in Figure 7.19. Similarly, the **DOS=UMB** command enables DOS to access the upper memory blocks established by the **EMM386** command. These two lines are typically combined into a single command expressed as **DOS=HIGH,UMB**.

After the UMBs have been established and access has been provided to them, two commands can be employed to use them: The **DEVICEHIGH=** and **LOADHIGH** commands.

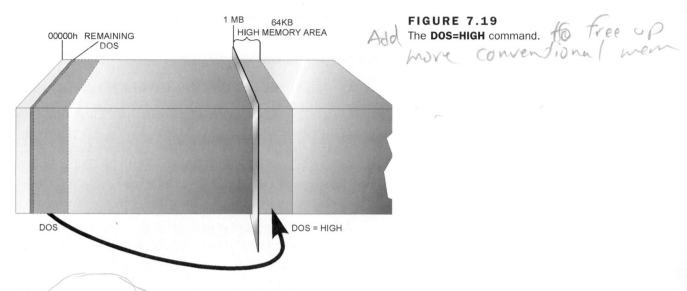

FIGURE 7.19
The **DOS=HIGH** command.

[handwritten: Add to free up more conventional mem]

The **DEVICEHIGH=** command is used to load drivers into the upper memory area instead of loading them into conventional memory as the **DEVICE=** command does. For example, the command **DEVICEHIGH=DRIVER*X*.SYS** attempts to load the device driver Driver*X* into the upper memory area. If the file is too large to fit in the buffer space available in a block of the UMA, the system may lock up. If this happens, the **DEVICE=** command loads the driver into conventional memory. Run the **MEM /D** command to determine the hexadecimal size of the file. Finally, modify the CONFIG.SYS file again using a hexadecimal size limit (expressed in bytes) to modify the **DEVICEHIGH=** line (that is, **DEVICEHIGH size=hexsize**). This modifies the **DEVICEHIGH** line to use only the buffer size actually needed.

Similarly, the **LOADHIGH** (**LH**) command loads a program into the UMA. The **LH** command can be used in either the AUTOEXEC.BAT file or it can be executed from the DOS command line. To use it, the **DOS=UMB** command must have been previously loaded in the CONFIG.SYS file. If the program is too large for the available blocks of the UMA, DOS will loads the program into conventional memory instead.

The following Step by Step shows you how to optimize the operation of the system at the DOS level.

STEP BY STEP

7.1 Optimizing at the DOS Level

1. Use a **DOS=HIGH** or **DOS=HIGH,UMB** command in the CONFIG.SYS file to load DOS into the HMA.

2. Check the CONFIG.SYS and AUTOEXEC.BAT files for lines that load the HIMEM.SYS, EMM386.EXE, SMARTDRV.EXE, and RAMDRIVE.SYS drivers. In each case, make certain that the latest version of the driver is located in the specified directory.

3. Check the order of commands in the CONFIG.SYS file to make certain that the HIMEM.SYS driver is loaded before any other extended memory application or driver. If not, move the command closer to the beginning of the file.

4. Set the memory cache size for the SMARTDRV.EXE command in the AUTOEXEC.BAT file to the largest size possible.

5. Optimize the CONFIG.SYS lines for buffers and files. Set files equal to 30 unless a currently installed application requires more handles. This step also should be used if DOS or Windows 3.x operations return a Too Many Files Are Open message. Set the number of buffers to 10 if SMARTDRV is being used and 20 if not. Using more than 10 buffers with SMARTDRV decreases efficiency, and using more than 20 buffers without SMARTDRV uses more of the system's conventional memory area.

6. Set up the RAM Drive to use the TEMP environment. This will improve printing performance and the operation of other applications that use TMP files.

7. Load EMM386.EXE to allocate upper memory blocks for TSRs and device drivers.

Even using the setup steps just listed, the system's performance will deteriorate over time. Most of this deterioration results from unnecessary file clutter and segmentation on the system's hard disk drive. To periodically tune up the performance of the system, follow these steps:

1. Periodically remove unnecessary TMP and BAK files from the system.

2. Check for and remove lost file chains and clusters using the DOS **CHKDSK** and **CHKDSK /F** commands.

3. Use the DOS *Defrag* utility to realign files on the drive that may have become fragmented after being moved back and forth between the drive and the system.

Optimizing Windows 9x

In a purely 32-bit Windows 9x environment, very little memory management is needed. In these systems, new 32-bit virtual device drivers (VxDs) are automatically loaded into extended memory during the boot-up process. This eliminates the need for **DEVICE=** and **LOADHIGH** commands for devices that have VxDs and Windows 9x application programs. When 16-bit device drivers or DOS applications are being used, however, Windows 9x must create a real-mode DOS environment for them. For this reason, Windows 9x executes a CONFIG.SYS and/or AUTOEXEC.BAT file it encounters during boot up.

If no DOS-based drivers or applications are in the system, the CONFIG.SYS and AUTOEXEC.BAT files are not necessary. However, the Windows 9x version of the IO.SYS file will automatically load the Windows 9x version of the HIMEM.SYS file during boot up. This file must be present for Windows 9x to boot up. Even though Windows loads a version of HIMEM.SYS, a **DEVICE=HIMEM.SYS** line must be present in a CONFIG.SYS file if a **DEVICE=EMM386** line, or a 16-bit device driver is required. There are likely to be multiple versions of the HIMEM.SYS file in a Windows 9x system. (There could be three or more versions.) Booting up Windows 9x and VxDs are examined in greater detail in Chapter 8.

If the System Rvn slowly

If a Windows 9x system has a CONFIG.SYS and AUTOEXEC.BAT file that has been held over from previous operating systems, be aware that any unneeded commands in these files have the potential to reduce system performance. In particular, the SMARTDRV function from older operating systems will inhibit dynamic *VCACHE* operation and slow the system down.

If the system runs slowly, check the CONFIG.SYS and AUTOEXEC.BAT files for SMARTDRV and any other disk cache software settings. Remove these commands from both files to improve performance. Also, remove any **Share** commands from the AUTOEXEC.BAT file.

The most obvious cure for most Windows 9x memory errors is to install extra RAM for extended memory. RAM has become very inexpensive to add to most systems and the Windows 9x memory-management system is very stable. If the system has troublesome DLL and/or TSR programs installed, remove them and reinstall them one by one until the offending files have been identified. Check with the application manufacturer for update versions of these files.

> **TEST TIP**
>
> Be aware of the affect that active commands in a CONFIG.SYS, AUTOEXEC.BAT, or INI file can have on the operation of an advanced Windows operating system.

STEP BY STEP

7.2 Setting Up Supplemental Cache

The overall operation of the Windows 9x system can be enhanced by establishing a supplemental cache for the CD-ROM drive. This cache enables data to be paged between the CD and the system (or hard disk). The supplemental cache is established through the Control Panel's System icon:

1. Under the System icon, click the Performance tab and select File System button.

2. Set the Supplemental Cache Size slider to the desired cache size.

3. Set the Optimize Access Pattern for setting to the Quad-speed or higher option (unless you have an old single- or double-speed drive). This will establish a 1238KB supplemental cache (provided the system's RAM size is larger than 12MB).

> **TEST TIP**
>
> Know how to optimize the operation of a CD-ROM drive.

4. Click the OK button and restart the system to create the cache.

WINDOWS 9X FUNCTIONS, STRUCTURES, AND MAJOR FILES

▶ 1.1 The A+ Operating System Technologies objective 1.1 states that the test taker should be able to "identify the operating system's functions, structures and major file systems." A portion of this objective is directed toward the Windows 9x (95 and 98) operating systems.

Windows Evolution

In April 1983, Microsoft demonstrated a graphical interface manager that would later become Windows. It gave the appearance of overlapping windowpanes, with various programs running in each window. In November of the same year, Microsoft formally announced Windows and set a release date of April 1984. Interestingly, IBM passed on the opportunity to market Windows with its units three different times. They were busy developing a GUI called TopView for their systems.

Microsoft announced Windows 1.0 in June 1985 and began shipping in November. It found a PC market that was steeped in command-line operations. Many industry analysts predicted it would come and go and "real computer users" would hold on to their DOS disks.

Version 2.0 was announced in April 1987 and actually hit the market in October, along with a version called Windows/386. By December of that year, Microsoft had shipped more than 1 million copies of Windows. Two versions of Windows 2.1 shipped in June 1988 under the titles Windows/286 and /386.

Windows 3.0 did not make it to the market until May 1990. However, it opened with a $3 million, first-day advertising campaign. In March 1992, Microsoft produced its first television advertising campaign for the upcoming Windows 3.1 version. The new version began shipping in April and had reached a level of 1 million copies shipped by June.

The 3.1 version migrated into Windows for Workgroups (WfW) in November 1992. This version integrated peer-to-peer networking directly into the operating environment. It was quick and easy to install and set up a workgroup network to share information and resources among different computers. These were terms that were not usually associated with networking computers together. By April 1993 the number of licensed copies of Windows sold had risen to 25 million. By October, Microsoft had begun shipping 3.11, the final 3.x version of Windows.

In September 1994, Microsoft announced the next version of Windows. They called it Windows 95. The first version was released in August 1995 and sold 1 million copies during the first week on the market. Within a month, the sales of Windows 95 climbed to more than 7 million copies, and by March 1996 it had topped 30 million copies.

Due to the huge installed base of Windows 3.x and Windows 95 products, every technician needs to be familiar with these operating systems for the immediate future (see Table 7.1).

TABLE 7.1

WINDOWS DEVELOPMENT TIME LINE

Year	Version	Features
1983	Graphical interface manager demonstrated.	
1985	V1.0	First official Windows release.
1987	V2.0	Task switching of applications.
	Windows/286	Use of all the extended memory for applications.
	Windows/386	Cooperative multitasking of applications.

Year	Version	Features
1990	V3.0	Preemptive multitasking of applications, enhanced memory support, use of icons, Program Manager interface.
1992	V3.1	(Windows for Workgroups) Integrated peer-to-peer networking directly in to the operating environment.
1993	V3.11	Upgraded 32-bit software and disk capabilities, BIOS calls removed from file accesses.
1995	Windows 95	Improved multimedia support, Plug and Play hardware support, 32-bit advanced multitasking function, improved email and fax capabilities, WAN usage.
1998	Windows 98	Upgraded Windows 95 and integrated Internet Explorer into the Windows interface
1999	Windows 98SE	The second edition of Windows 98. It was a simple cleanup of the original Windows 98 version.
2000	Windows ME Millennium	Extended the Windows 98 interface and features and cleaned up additional Windows 98 bugs.

Windows 9x Versions

As you can see from the table, the 9x version of Windows has been produced as four distinct products:

◆ Windows 95

◆ Windows 95 OSR2

◆ Windows 98

◆ Windows 98SE

◆ Windows Millennium Edition

The following sections describe each of these products and explain some of their key differences.

Windows 95

In 1995, Microsoft released a radically different-looking Windows environment called *Windows 95*. This Windows featured many new and improved features over previous versions. Windows 95 offered improved multimedia support for video and sound file applications, Plug and Play hardware support, 32-bit advanced multitasking functions, improved email and fax capabilities through Microsoft Exchange, and the Microsoft Network for easy *wide area network* (WAN) usage.

Even though Windows 95 is optimized for running 32-bit applications, it is still fully compatible with 16-bit Windows 3.x and DOS applications. As a matter of fact, it can be installed over either of these operating system versions as a direct upgrade. The only real concern when installing Windows 95 over either of these operating systems is that the existing system has the hardware resources needed to run Windows 95.

Windows 95 offers full built-in PnP capability. When Windows 95 is combined with a hardware system that implements PnP BIOS, expansion slots, adapter support, and that is supported with PnP adapter drivers, fully automated configuration and reconfiguration can take place.

Windows OSR2

Windows 95 OSR2, also known as *Windows 95b*, is an upgrade of the original Windows 95 package and includes patches and fixes for version 1, along with Microsoft Internet Explorer 3.0 and Personal Web Server. It also includes an enhanced file allocation table system referred to as FAT32.

In addition to the FAT32 system, *OSR2* offers advanced power management (APM) functions, bus-mastering support, MMX multimedia support, and enhanced PCMCIA functions over version 1 (which is referred to as OSR1, or Service Pack 1).

Also new in OSR2 is HDD/CD-ROM DMA access support. This feature is located in the Control Panel/System/Device Manager/Disk Drives window. At this point, choose the desired drive, select

Properties, and click the Settings tab. Check the DMA box and reboot the system. Perform the same procedure for the CD-ROM drive as well. This box appears only for IDE drives, and only when using properly installed and configured OSR2 bus-mastering drivers for the drive.

Windows 98

Microsoft's *Windows 98* replaced the Windows 95 operating system. Although many of its features remained basically the same as those of Windows 95, Windows 98 did bring certain new items to the system. Most notably, it extended the desktop to the Internet, creating a Web-based desktop environment. This feature was designed to make Internet (or intranet) access as seamless as possible for the user. It also enabled Windows 98 to perform unattended, self-upgrades directly from the Microsoft Web site when new items or repairs were released.

Windows Millennium

Windows Millennium Edition (ME) is the latest variation of the Windows 9x line of consumer operating systems. However, although it operates in a manner similar to Windows 98, it incorporates more of the look and feel of the Windows 2000 commercial operating system discussed in Chapter 8.

Windows ME minimizes the user's access to the command-prompt functions. It also includes a number of new self-repairing capabilities that perform some of the technician's repair functions automatically.

Many of the items discussed in this chapter, and in Chapter 9, have been moved to new (Windows 2000-like) locations in Windows ME. The integration of the Windows Internet Explorer is even tighter in Windows ME than it was in the Windows 98 package. All these additional features and functionality ultimately have produced an operating system whose memory footprint (requirements) is much larger than the Windows 98 operating system that it is replacing. This can be a major consideration when considering whether to upgrade a system with marginal capacity to the new operating system.

WINDOWS 9X STRUCTURE

The Windows program is loaded when the startup routine locates and executes the file named *WIN.COM*. This file resides in the Windows folder. When Windows 9x starts, several major files are loaded into the system, including the following:

handwritten note: has 9x core & load its drive driver

- ◆ The KERNEL32.DLL and KERNEL386.EXE files
- ◆ The GDI.EXE and GDI32.EXE files   *handwritten note: provides base of GUI*
- ◆ The USER.EXE and USER32.EXE files
- ◆ All fonts and other associated resources
- ◆ The WIN.INI file
- ◆ The Windows 9x shell and desktop files

The KERNEL32.DLL and KERNEL386.EXE files contain the Windows 9x core and load its device drivers. The GDI files provide the base of the graphical device interface; the USER files provide the user interface. The GDI files graphically represent and manage the system's hardware devices.

Any WIN.INI, SYSTEM.INI, and WINFILE.INI files that previously existed are included in the Windows directory to maintain compatibility functions with older software. These files are retained for use with older 16-bit applications and are not necessary for the operation of Windows 9x applications. These files need to be checked, however, if the Windows 9x system has conflicts with any 16-bit applications.

The Windows 9x shell program is normally the Windows 9x desktop. If the operating system has been configured to employ *passwords* for users, when the shell and desktop components are loaded, it displays a prompt onscreen for the user to log on. Similar to the logon process associated with networked systems, the Windows 9x logon enables the operating system to configure itself for specific users. Normal logon involves entering a username and password. If no logon information is entered, default values are loaded into the system. The logon screen appears only if the system has been configured to use a password, or when there are settings that the user can customize.

2 password   *1-for system*
2 - Network

It is possible for the system to require two password logons, one for the system and the second for the network. However, most administrators just combine these two elements into the network logon, as depicted in Figure 7.20.

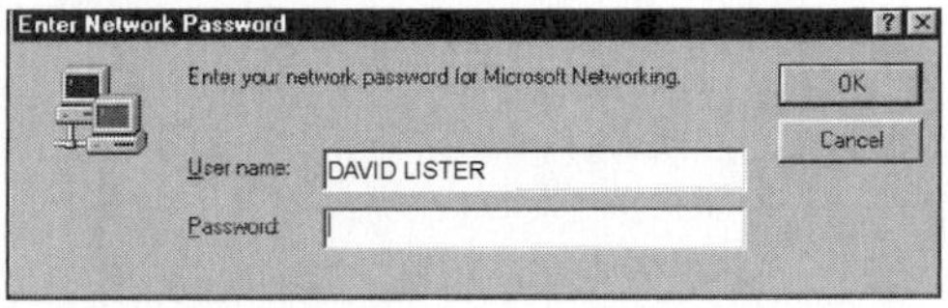

Windows 9x possesses system boot-up files that replace the DOS files described earlier in this chapter. The Windows 9x version of IO.SYS is a real-mode operating system that replaces the DOS version. It also takes over many of the functions associated with the CONFIG.SYS file. An MSDOS.SYS file is created to retain compatibility with older applications. However, the Windows 9x VMM32 and VxD files take over control of the system from the IO.SYS file during the startup process. Windows 9x supplies its own version of COMMAND.COM as well.

No CONFIG.SYS or AUTOEXEC.BAT files are created when Windows 9x is installed in a new system. These files also are not required by Windows 9x to start up or to run. Even so, both files will be retained from the previous operating system in upgraded systems, to maintain compatibility with older applications. However, entries in the CONFIG.SYS file override the values in the Windows 9x IO.SYS file. The Windows 9x IO.SYS file also handles some of the AUTOEXEC.BAT commands. In both cases, the system uses REM statements to deactivate those CONFIG.SYS and AUTOEXEC.BAT functions implemented in the IO.SYS file. Similarly, the functions of the SYSTEM.INI and WIN.INI files have been moved to the Windows 9x Registry.

The Windows 9x Setup routine stores existing MS-DOS files under .DOS extensions when it is installed as an upgrade over a previous operating system. In particular, the AUTOEXEC.BAT, COMMAND.COM, CONFIG.SYS, IO.SYS, and MSDOS.SYS files are stored with this extension. This enables an option known as dual booting to be established. In a dual-booting system, Windows 9x establishes a Startup menu that can be used to boot up the system into different operating systems. To accomplish this, Windows swaps versions of the boot-up files back and forth between their standard names and a designated set of backup names. Depending on which OS option the user selects at the start of boot up, Windows will retrieve the correct set of files, change their names, and then use them to boot the system.

FIGURE 7.20
The Windows 9x Logon dialog box.

IO.SYS → replace DOS version & takes over the functions
Config.SYS & MSDOS.SYS

} dual booting

If the system is started with the other operating system (see the "Dual-Boot Configuration" heading in Chapter 8, "2.0 Installation, Configuration, and Upgrading," for more information), the Windows 9x versions of AUTOEXEC.BAT, COMMAND.COM, CONFIG.SYS, IO.SYS, and MSDOS.SYS are stored under .W40 extensions and the renamed DOS versions of the files are returned to their normal extensions.

As mentioned earlier, the SYSTEM.INI, WIN.INI, PROTOCOL.INI, CONFIG.SYS and AUTOEXEC.BAT files can be modified through the System Editor (SysEdit) in Windows 9x. The SysEdit utility can be accessed by typing the **SysEdit** command in the Start/Run dialog box.

Windows 9x allows programs to be started automatically whenever Windows starts by adding them to the system's Startup folder. This is accomplished by accessing the Start Menu Programs tab and selecting Add. Browse until the desired program is found, and then double-click it. Finish the addition by clicking Next, and then double-clicking the Startup folder. These programs can be bypassed for troubleshooting purposes by pressing the left-Shift key during startup.

When fully installed, the Windows 9x structure is as depicted in Figure 7.21. The Windows Registry, *Configuration Manager*, Virtual Machine Manager, and Installable File System (IFS) Manager operate between the Windows 9x core and the device drivers that service the system's hardware. On the other side of the Windows 9x core, applications running on the system are accessed through the new 32-bit Shell and User Interface tools.

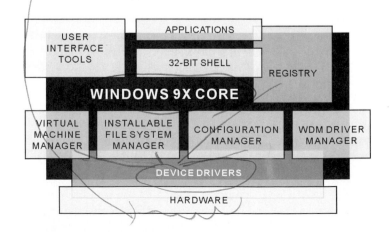

FIGURE 7.21
The Windows 9x organizational structure.

The 32-bit Windows 98 structure basically builds on the Windows 95 structure. However, Windows 98 did add enhanced video display support, power-management functions, and additional hardware support. It also featured built-in Internet Explorer functions.

The other major feature that Windows 98 added was support for a new driver model that permitted devices to operate under Windows 98 and future versions of Windows NT. This feature is referred to as the Win32 Driver Model (WDM) and exists in the Windows structure on the same level as the Virtual Machine, IFS, and Configuration Managers.

Windows 9x Core Components

The Windows 9x core consists of three components: the kernel, the GDI, and the USER files, as illustrated in Figure 7.22. Each component contains two DLL files (one 16-bit version and one 32-bit version) that facilitate applications running on the system. Their functions are basically the same for both Windows 95 and Windows 98 architectures.

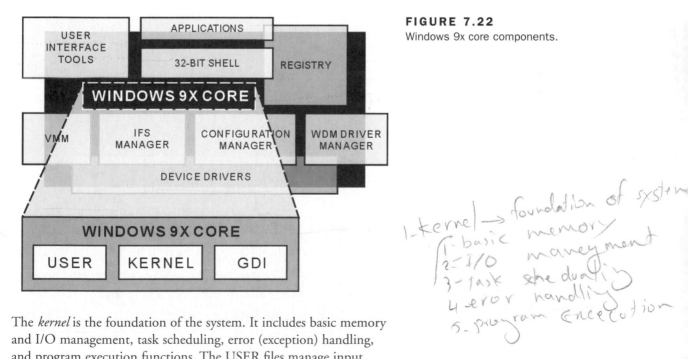

FIGURE 7.22
Windows 9x core components.

The *kernel* is the foundation of the system. It includes basic memory and I/O management, task scheduling, error (exception) handling, and program execution functions. The USER files manage input from hardware devices and output to the user interface components (that is, to the icons and screen structures). The GDI components control what appears on the display. It includes two main subsystems: The Graphics subsystem and the Printing subsystem.

The Windows 9x Registries

Under Windows 9x, the system's configuration information is held in a large hierarchical database called the *Registry*. This includes local hardware configuration information, the network environment information, file associations, and user configurations.

Many of Windows 3.1's SYSTEM.INI, CONTROL.INI, PROG-MAN.INI, and WIN.INI management functions have been relocated to the Registry. When applications were removed from the system in earlier Windows versions, the configuration information distributed between the various INI files remained, unless the user, or a special Windows Uninstall program, looked them up and removed them individually. With Windows 9x, their headings and the associated configuration information are all removed from the Registry, unlike the old INI method of tracking this information.

The contents of the Windows 9x Registry are located in two files located in the Windows directory. These are the *USER.DAT* and *SYSTEM.DAT* files. The USER.DAT file contains user-specific information; the SYSTEM.DAT file holds hardware- and computer-specific profiles and setting information.

Each time Windows 95 boots up successfully, these files are backed up with a .DA0 extension. The contents of the Registry can be viewed and altered through the *Registry Editor* (REGEDIT.EXE) utility, as depicted in Figure 7.23. If the system experiences a Registry corruption problem, the USER.DA0 and SYSTEM.DA0 files can be renamed to DAT files and used to restore the Registry to its preceding working configuration.

The contents of the Registry are not backed up in the same way under Windows 98 that they were in Windows 95. The Windows 98 system makes up to five backup copies of the Registry structure each time it successfully starts Windows. The backed up contents of

---

TEST TIP

Know where the Windows 9x Registry files are stored and what they are called.

TEST TIP

Know which two files make up the Windows 9x Registry and where they are located in the system.

the Registry are stored in the Windows\Sysbckup directory in the form of cabinet (CAB) files (not as .DA0 files). These files contain the following Registry-related files:

◆ SYSTEM.DAT

◆ SYSTEM.INI

◆ USER.DAT

◆ WIN.INI

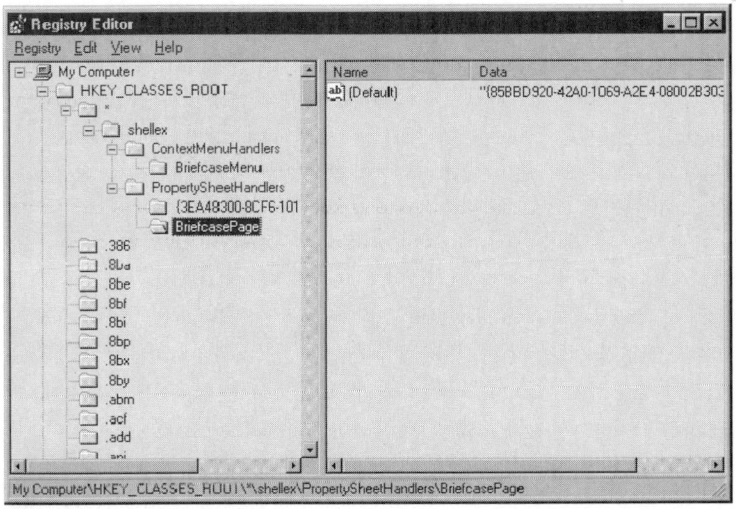

[handwritten: sybckup dir (folder (they are hidden)]

FIGURE 7.23
The Windows 9x Registry Edit window.

The Sysbckup folder is a hidden folder. To examine its contents, you must remove the hidden attribute from it. Inside the folder, the backup files are stored under an RB0*XX*.CAB format, where *XX* is a sequential backup number given to the file when it is created. Running the **Scanreg /Restore** command also produces a list of the available backup files to select from for troubleshooting purposes.

The Registry uses English-language descriptions and a hierarchical organization strategy. The hierarchy is divided into headkeys, keys, subkeys, and values. Keys are descriptive section headers that appear at the left side of the RegEdit window. Values, on the other hand, are definitions of topics organized under the keys. This organization can be thought of in the same terms as the organization of any book; the headkeys are similar to chapter titles, the keys and subkeys are equivalent to the major and minor headings of the chapters; values are equal to the sentences that convey information.

[handwritten: keys—descriptive section header, subkeys—, values]

Values can contain a wide variety of information types. They can contain interrupt and port address information for a peripheral system, or just information about an installed application program. The information can be encoded into binary, DWORDS, or strings. Values are always located at the right side of the RegEdit window.

If you examine the My Computer heading using the RegEdit option, you will find six categories listed. The headkeys all start with an HKEY_ notation.

Under My Computer the categories are as follows:

- HKEY_CLASSES_ROOT
- HKEY_CURRENT_USER
- HKEY_LOCAL_MACHINE
- HKEY_USERS
- HKEY_CURRENT_CONFIG
- HKEY_DYN_DATA

Most of the HKEY titles should appear very descriptive of their contents. The CLASSES_ROOT key divides the system's files into two *groups* by file-extension type and by association. This key also holds data about icons associated with the file.

The CURRENT_USER key holds the data about the user-specific configuration settings of the system, including color, keyboard, desktop, and start settings. The values in the CURRENT_USER key reflect those established by the user who is currently logged on to the system. If a different user logs on, the contents of the Users key is moved into the CURRENT_USER key.

The LOCAL_MACHINE key contains information about the system's hardware. This key contains all the hardware drivers and configuration information. The system will not be able to use peripheral devices that are not properly documented in the LOCAL_MACHINE key.

The Users key contains the information about the various users who have been defined to log on to the system. The information from the CURRENT_USER key is copied into this section whenever a user logs off the system, or when the system is shut down.

The DYN_DATA key and CURRENT_CONFIG keys work with the LOCAL_MACHINE key. The DYN_DATA key works with the branch of the LOCAL_MACHINE key that holds PnP dynamic status information for various system devices including current status and problems. The CURRENT_CONFIG key works with the LOCAL_MACHINE branch containing current information about hardware devices.

The Windows 9x Registry structure is primarily used to hold information about system hardware that has been identified by the enumeration or detection processes of the PnP system. When a device is installed in the system, Windows 9x detects it, either directly or through the system's bus managers, and searches the Registry and installed media sources for an appropriate driver. When the driver is found, it is recorded in the Registry along with its selected settings.

Some devices, such as PCMCIA devices, can be inserted and removed under hot conditions (while power is on). The system will detect the removal or insertion of the device and adjust its Registry configuration on-the-fly. Legacy, or PnP ISA, devices must be installed in the system before startup and must go through the PnP process.

PCMCA device

The Registry also holds information that enables the system to serve and track multiple users. It does this by retaining user- and configuration-specific information that can be used to customize the system to different users, or to different configuration situations.

Windows 98 offers remote access to Win32-based Registry APIs through a procedure called a Remote Procedure Call (RPC). This enables system management tools to be used on remote units across a network.

(RPC) (Remote procedure call)

Windows 9x System Policies

Because Windows 9x provides multiuser operations, operational system policies are necessary to govern the rights and privileges of different users. Windows 9x system policies establish guidelines to restrict user access to the options in the Control Panel and desktop. They also enable an administrator to customize the desktop and configure network settings.

When a user logs on to the system, Windows 9x checks that user's configuration information. When found, the policy information associated with that user is moved into the Registry and replaces the

for log in system

existing settings. This information is held in the CONFIG.POL file. Policies can be established for individual users, for defined groups of users, for a specific computer, for a network environment, or for default settings.

The system policies that govern these functions are established and modified using an editor similar to the Registry Editor, called the *System Policy Editor* (PolEdit). The Policy Editor is another tool that can be used to access the information in the Registry. Unlike the RegEdit utility, the Policy Editor can access only subsets of keys. The Registry Editor can access the entire Registry.

Normally, the use of the PolEdit tool is restricted to the Network administrator. Therefore, it is not normally installed on users' computers. The utility is located on the Windows 9x CD, under the Admin folder so that only the keeper of the CD can adjust the system's policies. The path to access the Policy Editor on the CD is Admin\Apptools\Poledit. Once located, it can be executed by entering **PolEdit** in the Run box. This causes the Policy Editor screen to display, as depicted in Figure 7.24.

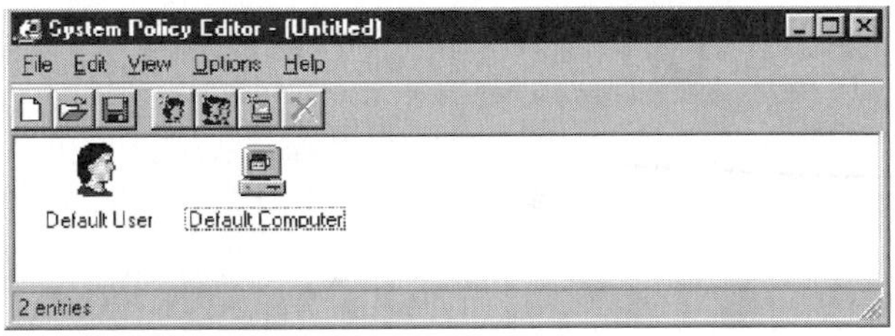

FIGURE 7.24
The Windows 9x Policy Editor.

With any multiuser system, it may be necessary to establish various working environments for different users. Some users are entrusted with access to more of the system than other users. As described earlier, this is the purpose of logon procedures. The Windows 9x policy file tracks policies for different users in a file named CONFIG.POL. The contents of this file are moved into the USER.DAT and SYS-TEM.DAT files when a user logs on.

The editor enables system administrators to configure the Windows desktop differently for different users. For some users, it may not be necessary for them to have access to certain system options, such as printers or Registry-editing tools. Through the Policy Editor, access to these options can be removed from the desktop for a given user.

The window in the figure contains an icon for a default user and a default computer. When the user logs on to the system, Windows searches for a user profile that matches to user logging on. If none is found, the default policies are copied into the new user's profile and used until modified by a system administrator. The editing screen used to modify the Default User's policies is depicted in Figure 7.25.

Like the Registry Editor, the branches of the Policy Editor can be expanded or contracted by clicking on the plus (+) and minus (–) signs in the nodes of the tree. Three options can be selected for each setting: checked, cleared, or dimmed (grayed out). When a policy is checked, it is being implemented. If it is cleared (open), the policy is not implemented. When the policy is grayed out, the policy has not been changed since the last time the user logged on and Windows will not make any related changes to the system configuration and users can make changes to the setting.

As an example of the effects of these settings, consider the system's Wallpaper setting in the Control Panel. If the setting is checked, the designated wallpaper will be displayed. If the setting is cleared, no wallpaper will be displayed. Finally, if the setting is grayed out, Windows will not enforce the policy and the user can select his or her own wallpaper pattern through the Control Panel.

FIGURE 7.25
Inside the Policy Editor.

Windows 9x Managers

sits between win98 core/Reg & system devic drivs

The Windows managers sit between the Windows 9x core/Registry and the system's device drivers. These components gather information about the system and store it in the Registry. Both Windows 95 and Windows 98 versions of the operating system provide basic services for classes of devices, so that the device's driver software need only contain device-specific information.

Configuration Manager

The Configuration Manager oversees the complete PnP configuration process for Windows 9x. Its primary purpose is to ensure that each device in the system can access an interrupt request channel without conflict and that it has a unique I/O port address. The I/O port address is a location where the system communicates with an intelligent programmable device. It constantly tracks the number and location of devices in the system and reconfigures them when required.

The Configuration Manager charts a hardware tree for the system similar to the one illustrated in Figure 7.26. The tree represents all the buses and intelligent devices in the system. Information about the buses and devices is collected by the Configuration Manager's bus enumerators. The information can be obtained from the BIOS interrupt services used by the devices, device drivers installed for the devices, and directly from the hardware.

FIGURE 7.26

The Configuration Manager's tree structure.

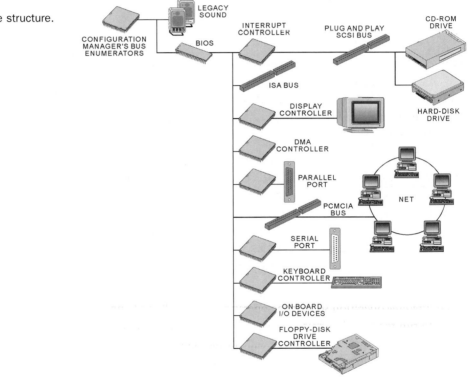

The Configuration Manager recognizes, configures, and allocates the system's resources to its installed devices. It uses resource-arbitrator routines to provide interrupts, DMA channels, I/O addressing, and memory allocations for all the systems devices. The arbitrators resolve any conflicts between the devices, and then inform each device driver about its particular resource allocations.

Virtual Machine Manager

Windows brought multitasking to the personal computer with version 3.0. The system would work its way around all the open applications, allowing them to run for a period of time before resetting and moving to the next application. One of the simplest forms of multitasking is *task switching*. In a task-switching operation, several applications can be running at the same time. When you have multiple applications open in Windows, the window currently being accessed is called the active window and appears in the foreground (over the top of the other windows). The activity of the other open windows is suspended, as denoted by their gray color, and they run in the background.

Special key combinations enable the user to move between tasks easily. By pressing the Alt and Tab keys together, you can move quickly through the open applications. The Alt+Esc key combination enables the user to cycle through open application windows.

In 386 enhanced mode, Windows 3.x operated under a *cooperative multitasking* system. In these operations, some applications gained control of the system and used the resources until they were finished. Some Windows 3.x applications took up more than their share of the system's resources. When an application crashed under this type of multitasking, a general-purpose fault was created and Windows would lock up or become too unstable to use.

When Microsoft designed Windows 9x, they designed it for *preemptive multitasking* operation so that the operating system allowed applications to run for a predetermined amount of time only, based on how critical its task is in the overall scheme of the system. More time was allotted to high-priority tasks than to low-priority tasks. However, the operating system remained the controlling force. When the application's time was up, the operating system just cut it off.

Under cooperative multitasking, the system is tied up with a single application whenever Windows is displaying an hourglass onscreen. With preemptive multitasking, a new task can be opened, or switched to, while the hourglass is being displayed onscreen. Work can be performed under that task window while the other task is being worked on by the system. More importantly, if the system locks up while working on a specific task in Windows 9x, you can just end the task instead of restarting the machine.

The components of the Windows 9x Virtual Machine Manager (VMM) are depicted in Figure 7.27. It consists of a Process Scheduler, a Memory Pager, and an MS-DOS protected-mode interface.

FIGURE 7.27
Windows 9X VM Manager.

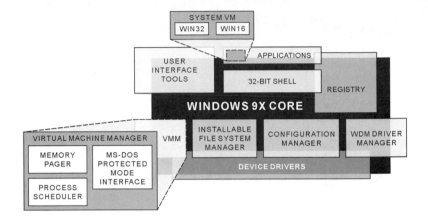

Both Windows 95 and Windows 98 are primarily designed for preemptive multitasking operations. It conducts preemptive multitasking with Win32-based applications, but reverts to cooperative multitasking with Win16-based applications to maintain compatibility with older operating systems. The Process Scheduler manages the system's multitasking operations for both types of applications. It also provides a separate virtual machine environment for each DOS-based application running in the system.

The VMM's Memory Pager allocates to each application a virtual memory space of 4GB. The first 2GB is private to the application, whereas the next 2GB is shared. The entire linear address range is divided into equal-size blocks, referred to as pages. These pages are moved between memory and disk as demanded by the application. Consecutive pages may or may not reside in a linear fashion in memory. The Pager tracks the location of all the pages in use.

Most MS-DOS-based application will run smoothly in Windows 9x. However, some MS-DOS-based applications require exclusive access to the system's resources. For these applications that will not run normally under Windows 9x, these operating systems provide the MS-DOS mode interface that establishes a special MS-DOS environment when called for. In MS-DOS mode, the application retains complete control of the system resources, and no other applications

can compete for them. Before running this type of application,
Windows 9x ends all of its active tasks, calls up a real-mode version
of MS-DOS, and executes special versions of CONFIG.SYS and
AUTOEXEC.BAT to support the application. When the MS-DOS
application is finished, the system reloads the Windows operating
system and returns to normal service. Microsoft included this mode
just to handle MS-DOS applications that do not work under
Windows.

Installable File System Manager

When a file or disk access request is received by Windows 9x, a subsection of the interface known as *the Installable File System* (IFS)
Manager processes the request by passing it to the proper file system
driver (FSD). Figure 7.28 depicts the Windows 9x IFS system. The
FSDs communicate with the IFS Manager and the drivers that work
directly with the hardware device controllers. These device-specific
drivers work within the I/O Supervisor (IOS) layer. The IOS layer
handles I/O systems that transmit and receive data in multiple-byte
transfers. Devices in this category include hard disk drives, CD-
ROM drives, tape drives, and network controllers.

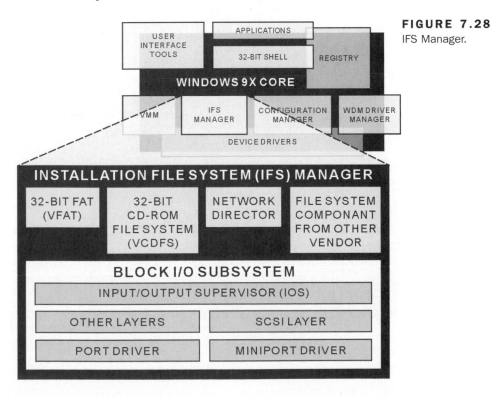

FIGURE 7.28
IFS Manager.

The major file system drivers supported by the Windows 9x IFS are the 32-bit *VFAT* driver, a 32-bit protected-mode CD-ROM File System (CDFS) driver, a 32-bit Universal Disk Format (UDF) driver, and a 32-bit network redirector. The Windows 9x VFAT works with the 32-bit VCACHE protected-mode cache driver. Unlike the SMARTDRV utility, the size of the cache under VCACHE is dynamic and depends on the needs of the system. Likewise, the 32-bit, protected-mode CDFS driver provides a dynamic cache for CD-ROM operations. The UDF file system is implemented in Windows 98 to satisfy the Optical Storage Technology Association (OSTA) specification for devices such as DVD discs. Disk caching under UDF is a function of VCACHE, and is dynamic.

Win32 Driver Model Manager

The Win32 Driver Model (WDM) Manager was introduced in Windows 98. Its main function is to support WDM drivers. This model permits hardware manufacturers to develop device drivers that will work on both Windows 98 and future Windows NT machines. The WDM manager does this by simulating the Windows NT kernel in a new layer of the VxD driver architecture.

The WDM layered architecture is depicted in Figure 7.29. This layered arrangement allows the same device drivers to be used in multiple types of operating systems.

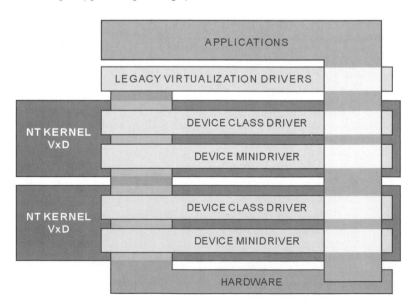

FIGURE 7.29
Win32 Driver Model layers.

Windows 2000 Functions, Structures, and Major Files

▶ 1.1 The A+ Operating System Technologies objective 1.1 states that the test taker should be able to "identify the operating system's functions, structures and major file systems." A portion of this objective is directed at the Windows NT and Windows 2000 operating systems.

Windows NT/2000

Although Microsoft developed and improved the Windows 3.x and Windows 9x products for desktop use by the general population, it also developed a more robust and complicated operating system for corporate client/server networking installations. This new windowed operating system was introduced as Windows New Technology, or Windows NT.

From the beginning, the Windows NT design departed from the mainstream Windows development path. It was built around a new operating system kernel that focused on enhanced reliability, scalability, and security elements required for corporate applications, while retaining the strengths of the Windows operating system.

Instead of being designed to operate on a single type of computer, the Windows NT operating system was designed to be portable between system using different microprocessor architectures. By exchanging a single component, the Windows NT kernel can be used to exploit advances in PC hardware including 32-bit microprocessors, Reduced Instruction Set Computer (RISC) architectures, and multiprocessor (parallel processing) systems, as well as high-capacity RAM and disk storage for the purposes of creating advanced line-of-business platforms.

The Windows NT operating system actally exists as three distinct products:

◆ A Workstation operating system

◆ A Server operating system

◆ An Extended Server operating systems to manage large enterprise networks

Although all three Windows NT product types are referenced in this chapter, the scope of the A+ examination deals with the Workstation versions of the software. Therefore, the discussions in this chapter primarily focus on these portions of the Windows NT platform. When aspects of the Server side of the package must be mentioned, this is pointed out.

Although there have been several versions of the Windows NT operating system, the A+ examination has limited its involvement to the two most rescent versions: Windows NT 4.0; and the the newest version of NT, called Windows 2000. In most parts of the chapter, these two versions are referenced as a single topic. Differences between the two versions are pointed out as necessary.

Windows NT Evolution

In the spring of 1992, Microsoft introduced the Windows NT operating system, designed for corporate business networking environments. Unlike the mainstream Windows 3.x and 9x packages that include a peer-to-peer networking function, Windows NT was designed from the beginning to perform in a client/server networking environment. Consequently, the Windows NT package was originally developed in two parts: the NT Workstation and the NT Server operating systems. The server software has just been known as NT Server. With the advent of Windows 2000, Microsoft changed the name of the workstation software to Windows 2000 Professional.

Recall that a client/server network is one in which standalone computers, called clients, are connected to, and administered by, a master computer called a server. Collectively, the members of the group make up a body called a domain. Figure 7.30 depicts a typical domain-based network arrangement. The members of the domain share a common directory database and are organized in levels. Every domain is identified by a unique name and is administered as a single unit having common rules and procedures.

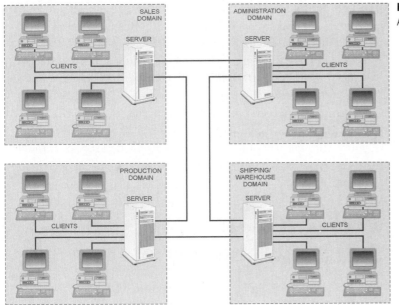

FIGURE 7.30
A client/server or domain-based network.

Although earlier Windows operating systems attempted to retain compatibility with the original MS-DOS platform, Windows NT made no such attempts. Instead, Windows NT offers a fairly specific set of software and hardware requirements that must be met for proper operation. Fortunately, more Windows NT-compatible hardware and software systems have become available over time. With Windows 2000, Microsoft opened an even wider range of compatible hardware and software options for the Windows NT platform. Even so, Windows 2000 still does not support nearly as many hardware and software options as Windows 95/98.

Windows NT Workstation

The Windows NT Workstation operating system can be employed as a client workstation in a client/server network, or it can be used as an operating system for a standalone computer that is not connected to anything. However, Windows NT was designed to work in a strong network environment. As such, many of the features that make Windows 9x packages easier to use are not located in Windows NT Workstation.

Windows NT 4.0 Workstation supports advanced multitasking and multiprocessor operations. It can maintain different hardware profiles for multiple configurations within the same system. The Windows NT memory-management system does a much better job of protecting applications from violating each other's space than the Windows 9x products do. Finally, Windows NT Workstation provides a much higher level of file, folder, and resource security than the 9x versions do. Windows NT can control access to these resources through passwords and logons on the desktop, or through a the central network controller called a server in a client/server relationship.

Windows NT Server

The Windows NT 4.0 Server package provides the same features and functions found in the Windows NT Workstation. However, the Server package also provides the tools necessary to administer and control a network from its central location.

Recall that in a peer-to-peer workgroup setting, all the nodes may act as servers for some processes and clients for others. In a domain-based network, the network is controlled from a centralized server (domain controller). In a Windows NT network, this concept is embodied by the location where the Administration and Security databases are kept. In the workgroup, each machine maintains its own security and administration databases. In a domain environment, the server is responsible for keeping the centralized user account and security databases.

With some network operating systems, servers cannot function as active workstations in the network. With the Windows NT operating system, however, both the Workstation and Server versions can be used as nodes in peer-to-peer (workgroup) networks, and as workstations in domain-based, client/server networks. Although Windows NT Server can operate as a workstation, doing so would be a very expensive waste of its capabilities. There are actually three types of workstation operating systems supported in a Windows NT domain. These include Windows 9x, Windows NT Workstation, and Windows NT Server (set up for standalone use). However, servers are not normally used as workstations so as not to slow down network operations or interrupt them with local tasks.

In the Windows NT client/server environment, two types of domain controllers exist: Primary domain controllers (PDCs) and backup domain controllers (BDC). The PDC contains the directory database for the network. This database contains information about user accounts, group accounts, and computer accounts. You also may find this database referred to as the Security Accounts Manager (SAM). BDCs are servers within the network that are used to hold read-only backup copies of the directory database. As illustrated in Figure 7.31, a network may contain one or more BCDs. These servers are used to authenticate user logons. Authentication is the process of identifying an individual as who they claim to be. This process is normally based on usernames and passwords.

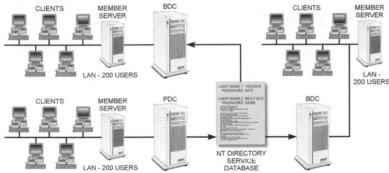

FIGURE 7.31
A PDC/BDC arrangement in a network.

As mentioned in the introduction, Windows NT 4.0 is sold in two different versions, a Standard NT Server version and an extended Enterprise Server package. Enterprise networks are those networks designed to facilitate business-to-business, or business-to-customer operations. Because monetary transactions and customers' personal information travels across the network in these environments, enterprise networks feature facilities for additional, highly protective security functions. An enterprise network consists of multiple domains (called trusted domains) where the domains are linked together, but managed independently.

Intranets

Most enterprise networks are actually intranets. An intranet is a network built on the TCP/IP protocol that belongs to a single organization. It is in essence a private Internet. Like the Internet, intranets are designed to share information and are accessible only to the organization's members, with authorization. A firewall blocks unauthorized outside users from accessing the intranet site. A relatively new term, called extranet, is being used to describe intranets that grant limited access to authorized outside users such as corporate business partners.

Microsoft continues to improve its Windows NT packages with intentions of being a major force in the Internet/corporate intranet markets that are currently dominated by UNIX and Novell NetWare operating systems. This is the major reason for the extended Enterprise Server version of the Windows NT package.

Windows 2000

Windows 2000 is the successor of the Windows NT 4 operating system. As a matter of fact, it was originally titled Windows NT 5. This operating system brings together the stability and security of Windows NT 4.0 and the PnP capabilities of Windows 98. Windows 2000 also includes built-in support for many new technologies including DVD drives, USB devices, accelerated graphics ports, multifunction adapter cards, and a full line of PC Cards. Finally, Windows 2000 provides a new, distributed directory service for managing resources across an enterprise, FAT32 support, and the Internet Explorer 5 Web browser.

Like previous NT versions, Windows 2000 comes in two basic variations: The corporate workstation version, titled Windows 2000 Professional; and the network server version, called Windows 2000 Server. The server product also is available in two extended enterprise versions: Windows 2000 Advanced Server and Windows 2000 Datacenter Server.

Windows 2000 Professional

The workstation side of Windows 2000 has been named Windows 2000 Professional. This operating system is designed to be the reliable, powerful desktop for the corporate computing world. It has been designed to be easier to set up and configure than previous Windows NT platforms. Windows 2000 Professional employs several wizards, such as the New Hardware Wizard and the Network

Connection Wizard, to make installation and configuration processes easier for users.

Windows 2000 Professional extends and improves the Windows 9x user interface. It also brings PnP to the NT workstation. The hardware supported by Windows 2000 Professional has been upgraded to include those items commonly found in newer systems.

Although it offers many improvements over previous Windows NT versions, Windows 2000 Professional may still be too complex for general consumer usage. For this reason, Microsoft has decided to continue with at least one additional upgrade version of the Windows 9x product for the general consumer market with its release of Windows ME.

Windows 2000 Server

On the server side, Windows 2000 offers a more scalable and flexible server platform than its Windows NT predecessors. Windows 2000 Server actually comes in three versions that correspond to the size and complexity of the network environment in which they are used. These versions include the Standard Server edition, the Advanced Server edition, and the Windows 2000 Datacenter Server edition.

The Standard Server edition offers a more scalable and flexible file server platform. It also functions as an application server that handles large data sets. It can be used to implement a standards-based, secured Internet/intranet* server. The standard Windows 2000 Server package can manage up to 4GB of RAM and is capable of distributing work between two microprocessors at a time. This type of operation is referred to as symmetrical microprocessing (SMP). If Windows 2000 Server has been installed as an upgrade to an existing Windows NT 4.0 Server, it can support up to four different microprocessors simultaneously.

> **NOTE**
>
> ***Intranet***   Recall that an intranet is just a private, Web-based network, typically established by an organization for the purpose of running an exclusive Web site not open to the public (for example, company Web sites for internal company use only). Intranets can be based on local or wide area networks, or constructed as combinations of the two.

The Advanced Server edition can support up to 8 symmetrical processors and up to 8GB of memory. These features enable it to function well in medium-size networks running between 100 and 500 concurrent users. In other respects, the Advanced Server product is the same as the Standard Server version. However, some enterprise versions of applications will run only on the Enterprise version of the operating system.

Datacenter
64GB of RAM
32 processor

The Windows 2000 Datacenter Server edition can handle up to 64GB of RAM and 32 processors. This enables it to support up to 1,000 simultaneous users with heavy-processing demands.

Both the Advanced and Datacenter Server editions employ a pair of high-availability features that allow them to effectively handle the traffic levels found on medium and large Web sites. These features are Network Load Balancing (NLB) and Microsoft Cluster Server (MSCS). The load-balancing feature enables the operating system to distribute IP requests to the most available Web server in a cluster of up to 32 Web servers.

With the Cluster Service feature, when one server in a cluster is taken down (crashes or goes offline), another server takes over its processing duties. This is referred to as failover and is described in Figure 7.32. In the Advanced version, the failover function is performed by one other processor, whereas the Datacenter version supports four-server failover clusters. This feature also allows servers in the system to be swapped out without interrupting service on the network.

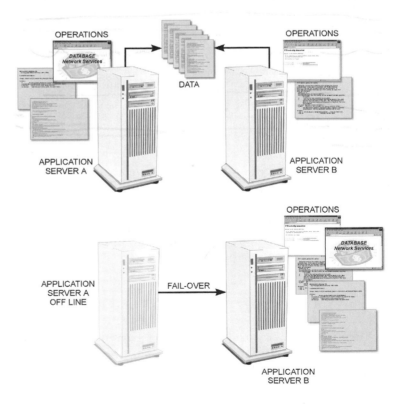

FIGURE 7.32
Failover operations.

Windows NT/2000 Structure

[handwritten: → exist in 2 layes mode]

[handwritten: 2 layer of OS mode { - kernel mode (supervise) - user mode]

When fully installed, the Windows NT logical structure exists as depicted in Figure 7.33. It is a modular operating system that allows for advances in computing technology to be integrated into the system. The operating system exists in two basic layers referred to as modes. These two levels are the kernel mode and the user mode. The kernel mode also may be referred to as the supervisor mode or protected mode.

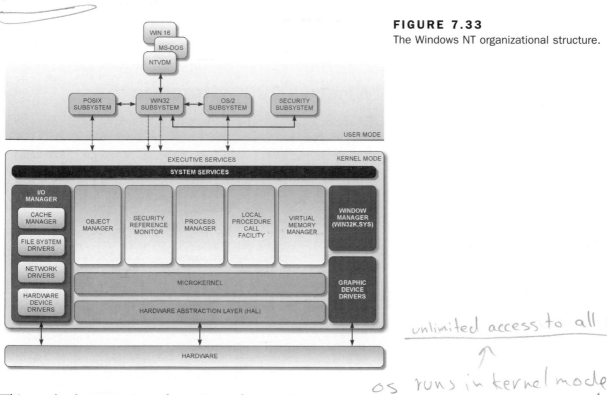

FIGURE 7.33
The Windows NT organizational structure.

[handwritten: unlimited access to all memory]

[handwritten: OS runs in kernel mode]

[handwritten: Apps runs in user mode — more restrictive — No access permitted hardware]

This two-level structure is used to separate the operating system from applications packages. Basically, the operating system runs in the kernel mode while applications run in user mode. The user mode is a more restrictive operating mode where there is no direct access of hardware permitted.

Only system code can run in the most privileged Executive Services section of the kernel mode. To switch between user mode and kernel mode, applications must use highly defined Application Program Interfaces (APIs) to pass threads between the two modes.

APIs are routines, protocols, and tools built in to the operating system and provide application designers with consistent building blocks with which to design their applications. For the user, these building blocks lead to consistent interfaces being designed for all applications.

The design of the APIs in the Windows NT kernel/user arrangement guarantees that no process can dominate the system to interfere with the operating system, or with another process. This protects the operating system from software bugs and unauthorized accesses by preventing a failing application from interfering with the operating system.

Windows 2000 Structure

It should be apparent that the organizational structure of Windows 2000, depicted in Figure 7.34, is very similar to the Windows NT structure depicted in Figure 7.33. However, Windows 2000 adds two additional managers to the Executive section: The Plug and Play Manager and the Power Management Manager.

FIGURE 7.34

Windows 2000 organizational structure.

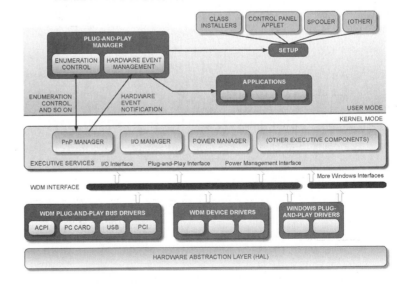

The PnP Manager employs the enumeration process to discover PnP devices installed in the system. Afterward, it loads appropriate drivers and creates Registry entries for those devices. These drivers and entries are based on information (INF) scripts developed by

Microsoft and the hardware vendors for the device being configured. The PnP Manager then allocates the system's resources (IRQ settings, DMA channels, and I/O addresses) between the devices that require them.

The Power Manager interacts with key system components to conserve energy (especially useful for portable computers) and reduce wear on system devices. Both managers depend on PnP-compliant system components as well as the APM and ACPI power-management standards.

Kernel Mode

The kernel mode is an operating mode in which the program has unlimited access to all memory, including those of system hardware, the user-mode applications, and other processes (such as I/O operations). As mentioned earlier, no application can directly access hardware or memory in the Windows NT kernel mode. Even though the operating system is highly protected, it is the responsibility of the microprocessor to enforce the protection strategy.

[handwritten: app / NT kernel has no access to hardware or memory, user mode App / win 2000 "does"]

The kernel mode consists of three major blocks: The Win32k Executive Service module, the Hardware Abstraction Layer (HAL), and the microkernel. Together, these blocks make up the Windows NT Executive.

[handwritten: 3 blocks of kernel — Win 32k eac serric module — the hardwar abst layer (HAL) — micro kernel]

In the Windows NT environment, kernel mode should not be confused with the term *kernel*, or *microkernel*. In this environment, kernel refers to the complete Windows NT Executive, whereas microkernel pertains to a functional block of the Windows NT Executive, and kernel mode is a highly privileged processing mode.

The Hardware Abstraction Layer

The Windows NT HAL is a library of hardware drivers that operate between the actual hardware and the rest of the system. These software routines act to make every architecture look the same to the operating system.

The HAL occupies the logical space directly between the system's hardware and the rest of the operating system's Executive Services. In Windows NT 4.0, the HAL enables the operating system to work with different types of microprocessors. The Windows NT 4.0 Installation disk actually contains three different HALs for use on

Intel and RISC processors. A different HAL exists for each type of microprocessor architecture with which the operating system might be used. Although Windows 2000 originally included support for RISC alpha processors in its beta copies, the first full production version provides only a HAL to work with Intel x86 processors.

The HAL accomplishes its tasks by providing a standard access port for all system hardware operations. In this manner, the rest of the operating system never "sees" or deals with the hardware, only the HAL. Its device driver routines are accessed by the other components of the Windows NT Executive, as well as by higher level device drivers.

The Windows NT Microkernel

The microkernel works closely with the HAL to keep the system's microprocessor as busy as possible. It does this by scheduling threads for introduction to the microprocessor on a priority basis. This includes preempting lower priority threads for those with higher priorities. NT code is written to be re-entrant. This means that it can be interrupted and restarted efficiently.

The microkernel also synchronizes the activities of the Executive Services blocks, such as the I/O and process managers. The Windows NT design employs preemptive multitasking to schedule processes. It also uses an asynchronous input/output system to control data flow between the system hardware and the operating system. These two elements put the user and the operating system in control of the system rather than the applications.

The operating system automatically assigns applications running in the foreground high priority and also gives priority to processes receiving input or completing I/O operations. Windows NT makes it impossible for a single application to lock up the keyboard or mouse even when the application is loading. Therefore, the system is always available to the user.

The preemptive task scheduler also can support tasks, such as communications packages, requiring constant processing availability. The scheduler allocates processing time to threads based on priority and can preempt any thread at any time. It allows very high priority tasks to run and maintain control until an equal or higher priority task takes over.

Symmetric Multiprocessing

The microkernel's task-scheduling capabilities extend to controlling multiple microprocessors. In the case of hardware with multiple microprocessors, the Windows NT microkernel provides synchronization between the different processors.

The microkernel's symmetric multiprocessing function enables threads of any process to be applied to any available processor in the system. The SMP function also enables microprocessors within a system to share memory space and assign threads to the next available microprocessor.

Windows 2000 Professional supports dual (2×) processor operations, whereas Windows 2000 Server can support up to 4 (4×) simultaneous processors. The Advanced and Datacenter versions of the Server package support 8× and 16× SMP, respectively (or 32 processors using a special OEM version of Windows 2000 Datacenter). With versions of the Server running more than 4 processors, the hardware manufacturer must supply a special, proprietary version of the Windows 2000 HAL.DLL file for their machines.

Windows NT Managers

The Win32k Executive Services block provides all the basic operating system functions for the NT environment. It is made up of a number of managers, include the following:

- ◆ I/O Manager
- ◆ Object Manager
- ◆ Security Reference Manager
- ◆ Process Manager
- ◆ Virtual Memory Manager
- ◆ Window Manager
- ◆ Graphic Device Interface
- ◆ Graphic Device Drivers

These managers support the activities of the user mode's protected subsystems, depicted in Figure 7.35. Together, these subsystems implement functions, such as basic operating system services, application environments, and APIs for the various types of applications that the Windows NT system can handle. The Executive Services block consists of a set of common API services available to all the operating system's components.

FIGURE 7.35
The protected subsystems.

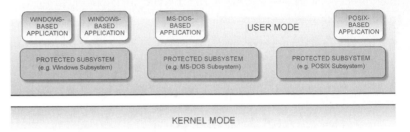

As its name indicates, the Windows NT *I/O Manager* manages all input and output functions for the operating system. Its major function involves controlling communications between file system drivers, hardware device drivers, and network drivers and the system. These drivers communicate with each other through data structures called I/O request packets (IRPs). The I/O Manager passes these packets from higher level drivers to device drivers that actually access the physical device for the manager. This translation feature is what enables Windows NT to have multiple file systems and devices active simultaneously.

The Object Manager provides specifications for naming, retaining, and setting security levels for objects. In Windows NT, objects are defined as software components made up of a data type, attributes, and a set of operations that the object performs. Each object in Windows NT is given an object handle that provides access control and a pointer to the object that processes can use to manipulate them. Windows NT 4.0 objects include the following:

◆ Directory objects

◆ File objects

◆ Port objects

◆ Process and thread objects

◆ Symbolic link objects

◆ Event objects

The Windows NT Process Manager creates and deletes processes and tracks both process and thread objects. A process is a modular part of an application that the operating system sees as a set of objects and threads. The process object is a specification that describes the virtual memory space mapping for the threads that make up the object. A thread, as you may recall, is the smallest schedulable block in the system. Each thread in a process is assigned its own set of registers in the microprocessor, its own kernel stack, an environment section, and its own user stack in its associated process' address space.

The Window Manager is the functional block responsible for creating and tracking the user interface GUI. The User Window Manager and Graphics Device Interface (GDI) functions are combined in a single component in the WIN32K.SYS file. In previous versions of Windows NT, the GDI was a part of the Win32 subsystem and ran in user mode. In Windows NT 4.0, the GDI was moved to the Executive and runs in kernel mode to speed up graphics and memory communications for the system.

The Window Manager notifies applications when a user interacts with the graphical interface (such as clicking an icon or moving a window). The GDI interprets requests from applications for graphic output to a display or printer and sends them to the appropriate driver. The driver then administers the request on the hardware.

Windows NT/2000 Memory Management

The Windows NT memory-management scheme employs a full 32-bit architecture with a flat memory model. In the Windows NT model, the Virtual Memory Manager (VMM) section of the Executive Services block assigns unique memory spaces to every active 32-bit and 16-bit DOS/Windows 3.x application. The VMM works with the environmental subsystems of the user mode to establish special environments for the 16-bit applications to run in. These environments are discussed in greater detail later in this chapter.

Unlike MS-DOS, Windows 3.x, and Windows 9x, Windows NT does not employ the address-segmentation features of the Intel microprocessors. Because memory segments can overlap in this model, memory-usage errors can occur when an application attempts to write data into a memory space allocated to the operating system or another application.

In Windows NT/2000, the VMM section maps each application's memory space into contiguous, 4KB pages of physical memory. Using this method, each application is mapped into a truly unique address space that cannot overlap any other address space. The lack of segment overlap reduces the chances of applications interfering with each other and helps to ensure data integrity by providing the operating system and other processes with their own memory spaces.

Because the flat memory model employs consecutive, unique addresses, the 32-bit addressing model enables the VMM to directly access up to 4GB of memory. As Figure 7.36 illustrates, the VMM allocates this memory in virtual memory pages so that each process appears to have its own 2GB storage area, with an additional 2GB reserved for use by the system. The VMM hides the actual organization of physical and disk memory from the system processes.

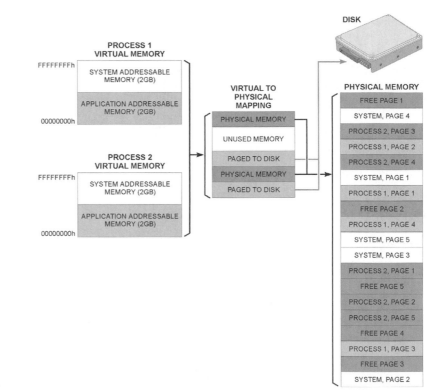

FIGURE 7.36
The Windows NT virtual memory system.

Windows NT Virtual Memory

When the VMM has exhausted the physical RAM locations available, it maps memory pages into virtual memory addresses, as described in Figure 7.37. Windows NT establishes virtual memory by creating a PAGEFILE.SYS file on the disk. The VMM shifts data between RAM memory and the disk in 4KB pages. This theoretically provides the operating system with a total memory space that equals the sum of the system's physical RAM and the capacity of the hard disk drive.

To take advantage of high RAM capacity, Windows NT automatically tunes itself to take advantage of any available RAM. The VMM dynamically balances RAM between paged memory and the virtual memory disk cache.

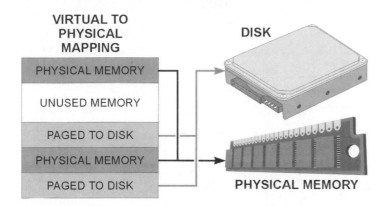

FIGURE 7.37
Virtual memory in Windows NT.

User Mode

The other basic Windows NT layer is referred to as the user mode. This mode is a collection of subsystems that interact with users and applications. As mentioned earlier, user mode is a less privileged mode that has no direct access to the system's hardware.

The Windows NT package supports programs based on 16- and 32-bit Windows, MS-DOS, POSIX, and character-based OS/2 structures through protected subsystems in this layer. POSIX, or Portable Operating System Interface for UNIX, is a set of standards that UNIX programmers go by to ensure that their applications can be ported to operating systems, such as UNIX and Windows NT, that feature POSIX compatibility. OS/2 is the GUI-based Operating System 2 that IBM developed in conjunction with Microsoft for its PS/2 line of personal computers. Although the PS/2 line was not a very successful group of products, the operating system remains in fairly wide usage with IBM products.

Running applications in user mode protects the operating system by forcing the applications to run in their own address spaces. This is accomplished through the user-mode subsystem structure depicted in Figure 7.38. Each subsystem employs well-defined APIs that enable the application to request services from the system. The APIs are responsible for the interaction with the applications and users.

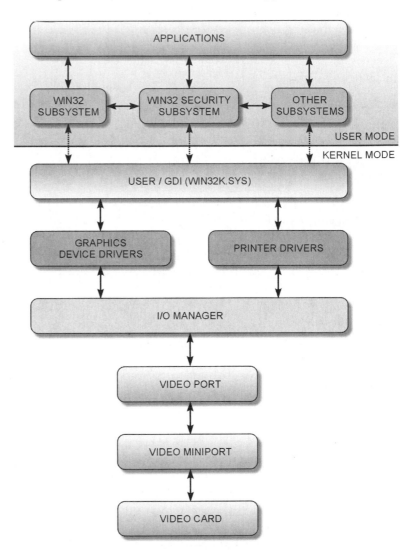

FIGURE 7.38
The user-mode subsystems.

The Win32 subsystem is the most noteworthy of the subsystems because it manages all 32-bit, protected-mode applications and also supplies the Windows user interfaces. The Security subsystem provides the system's basic security functions, such as logon and user privileges. Other subsystems include those environmental subsystems designed to work with MS-DOS, Win16, OS/2, and POSIX applications, which may or may not be running at any given time. These subsystems are designed to emulate other operating systems so that their applications can run successfully in the Windows NT environment. They are loaded when their services are required by an application.

In the Windows NT environment, applications are not allowed to directly access physical memory. It is the responsibility of the environmental subsystems in the user mode to deliver addresses to the applications in the Windows NT memory-management strategy. Notice in the Figure 7.38 that each environment is under the control of the Win32 subsystem. All communications between the kernel mode and the different types of applications must pass through this subsystem.

Whereas 32-bit applications run in protected mode and can contact the Win32 subsection directly, 16-bit DOS and Win16 applications must be housed in a protective memory-management scheme called an NT Virtual DOS Machine (NTVDM) environment. This environment protects the other parts of the system from the application. These applications can contact the Win32 subsystem only through a single thread. In the case of 32-bit applications, multithread communications can be conducted directly between the application and the Win32 subsystem.

If a 16-bit DOS application is executed, the user mode must create an isolated NTVDM environment for it to run in. The NTVDM provides an emulation of the IO.SYS/MSDOS.SYS/COMMAND.COM environment of MS-DOS. The Windows NT emulation files are named NTIO.SYS and NTDOS.SYS. Each DOS application runs all by itself in the system with full access to all the system's resources through the APIs in the Win32 subsystem. However, the application also is shut off from the rest of the system so that it cannot exchange data with applications outside the NTVDM. This prevents the 16-bit application from interfering with other applications running in the system.

In the case of 16-bit Windows 3.x applications, a special environment called Win16-on-Win32 (WOW) can be established to allow multiple Win16 applications to run in the same NTVDM. This environment emulates the Windows 3.x (KRNL386, GDI, and USER) kernel for these applications. In this scenario, the VMM relies on the applications to manage their own memory usage within the WOW environment.

The applications can exchange information within the WOW. As with the DOS environment, the applications within the WOW cannot exchange data with applications outside the immediate NTVDM. Conversely, if these applications were each loaded into separate NTVDMs, they would have full access to all system resources, but they would not be able to exchange information with each other. Figure 7.39 shows the relationship of NTVDMs and WOWs and the WIN32 subsystem.

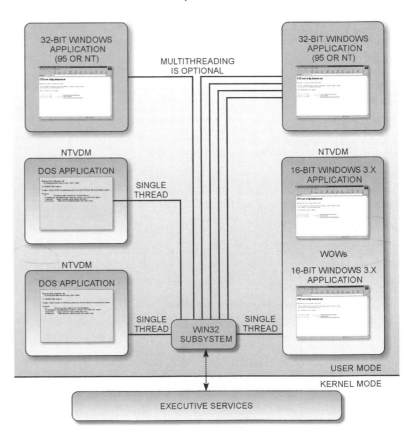

FIGURE 7.39
The NTVDMs and WOWs.

Figure 7.40 illustrates a typical interaction between an application and the video display, as it applies to the Windows NT structure. This particular discussion concerns the movement of information from the application to the hardware. From the double-headed arrows in the drawing, it should be apparent that data also can move in the reverse direction.

The application communicates with the Windows NT system through the user mode's Win32 subsystem. In turn, the Win32 subsystem communicates with the kernel mode's WIN32K.SYS Window Manager. In the case of the video information, it is processed and passed through the high-level graphics device driver and is presented to the IO Manager. Finally, the IO Manager processes the data through a miniport and applies it to the video card through the video port. The term *miniport* refers to hardware manipulating drivers supplied by the device manufacturer.

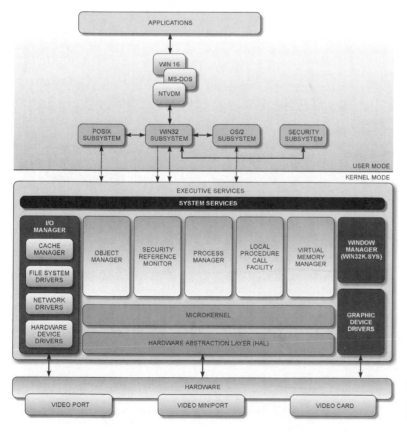

FIGURE 7.40
Interaction between an application and video display.

To hold system and user configuration infor

The Windows NT Registries

NT reg. is organized into Headkeys, subkeys & values

Like Windows 9x, Windows NT and Windows 2000 use multipart databases, called the Registry, to hold system and user configuration information. However, the Windows NT Registry is not compatible with the Windows 9x Registries. The Windows NT/2000 Registry is depicted in Figure 7.41. As with the Windows 9x Regsitry discussed in the preceding chapter, the Windows NT Registry is organized into headkeys, subkeys and values. Comparing Figure 7.41 to Figure 7.23, you should notice that both Registries contain the same HKEYs, except that no HKEY_DYN_DATA key is present in the Windows NT Registry.

FIGURE 7.41
The Windows NT/2000 Registry.

5 files (hives)

represent division of all Registry keys

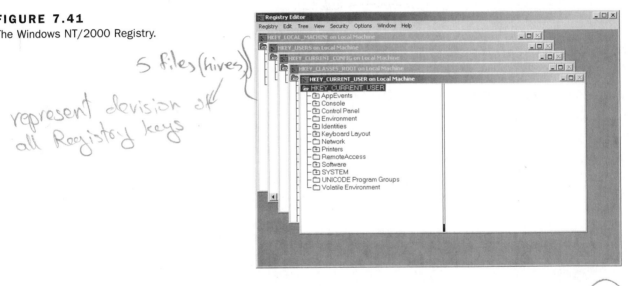

In the Windows NT world, the HKEYs also are referred to as subtrees, whereas the Registry itself is referred to as the tree. Under each subtree are one or more subkeys, which, in turn, will have one or more values assigned to them.

The contents of the Registry are physically stored in five files, referred to as *hives*. Hives represent the major divisions of all the Registry's keys, subkeys, subtrees, and values. The hives of the Windows NT Registry are as follows:

◆ The SAM hive

◆ The Security hive

- ◆ The Software hive
- ◆ The System hive
- ◆ The Default hive

These files are stored in the Winnt\System32\Config directory along with a backup copy and log file for each hive. Configuration information about every user who has logged on to the system is maintained in a named subfolder of the Winnt\Profiles directory. The actual user configuration file is named NTUSER.DAT (that is, Winnt\Profiles\Charles\NTUSER.DAT).

The major Windows NT hives and their files are as follows:

Subtree/Key	File	Log File
HKEY_LOCAL_MACHINE\SOFTWARE	Software	SOFTWARE.LOG
HKEY_LOCAL_MACHINE\SECURITY	Security	SECURITY.LOG
HKEY_LOCAL_MACHINE\SYSTEM	System	SYSTEM.LOG
HKEY_LOCAL_MACHINE\SAM	SAM	SAM.LOG
HKEY_CURRENT_USER	Userxxx	USERxxx.LOG
	Adminxxx	ADMINxxx.LOG
HKEY_USERS\DEFAULT	Default	DEFAULT.LOG

The HKEY_LOCAL_MACHINE subtree is the Registry's major branch. It contains five major keys. The SAM and Security keys hold information such as user rights, user and group information for domain or workgroup organization, and password information. The Hardware key is a database built by device drivers and applications during boot up. The database is updated each time the system is rebooted. The System key contains basic information about startup including the device drivers loaded and which services are in use. The Last Known Good configuration settings are stored here. Finally, the Software key holds information about locally loaded software, including file associations, OLE information, and configuration data.

The second most important subtree is HKEY_USERS. It contains a subkey for each local user that accesses the system. These subkeys hold desktop settings and user profiles. When a server logs on across a domain, the subkey is stored on the domain controller.

[handwritten: ...tain copy of Hkey user & Hkey-local]

The HKEY_CURRENT_USER and HKEY_CLASSES_ROOT keys contain partial copies of the HKEY_USERS and HKEY_LOCAL_MACHINE keys.

The contents of the Registry can be edited directly using the Windows NT RegEdit utility (REGEDT32.EXE). This file is located in the Winnt\System32 folder. As with the Windows 9x packages, most changes to the Registry should be accomplished through the wizards in the Windows NT Control Panel.

The Control Panel wizards are designed to correctly make changes to the Registry in a manner that the operating system can understand. Editing the Registry directly opens the possibility of changing an entry in a manner that Windows NT cannot accept, and thereby, crashing the system. In either event, it is a good practice to back up the contents of the Registry before installing new hardware or software, or modifying the Registry directly. The RDISK.EXE utility, located in the Winnt\System32 folder can be used to create a backup copy of the Registry in the Winnt\Repair folder.

Windows 2000 relies on the same Registry structure used in previous Windows NT versions. For this reason, it is not compatible with Windows 9x Registries. As with Windows NT 4.0, the user settings portion of the Registry are stored in the NTUSER.DAT file located in the Winnt\Profiles*userxxx* folder. The System portions of the Registry are stored in the Software, System, Security, and SAM hives. These files are stored in the Winnt\System32\Config folder.

Although there is a RegEdit tool in Windows 2000, this tool was designed to work with Windows 9x clients. The editor used to manage the Windows 2000 Registry is RegEdt32. However, in some instances, such as Registry searches, the RegEdit utility offers superior operation, even in Windows 2000.

[handwritten: NT registry is not compatible with win 98 key]

Active Directory

The central feature of the Windows 2000 architecture is the Active Directory (AD) structure. Active Directory is a distributed database of user and resource information that describes the makeup of the network (that is, users and application settings). It also is a method of implementing a distributed authentication process. The Active Directory replaces the domain structure used in Windows NT 4.0. This feature helps to centralize system and user configurations, as well as data backups on the server in the Windows 2000 network.

Windows 2000 remains a domain-dependent operating system. It uses domains as boundaries for administration, security, and replication purposes. Each domain must be represented by at least one domain controller. Recall that a domain controller is a server set up to track the names of all the objects and requests for resources within a domain.

In Windows 2000, the primary and backup domain controller structure from Windows NT has been replaced by a peer model where individual servers can be converted to Active Directory domain controllers without shutting down the system to reinstall the operating system.

The Active Directory structure employs two common Internet standards: The Lightweight Directory Access Protocol (LDAP) and Domain Name Service (DNS). The LDAP protocol is used to define how directory information is accessed and exchanged. DNS is the Internet standard for resolving domain names to actual IP addresses. It also is the standard for exchanging directory information with clients and other directories.

The Active Directory arranges domains in a hierarchy and establishes trust relationships among all the domains in a tree-like structure, as illustrated in Figure 7.42.

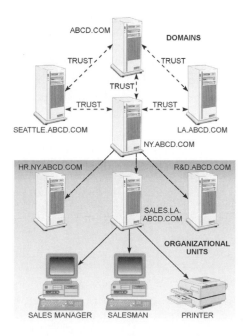

FIGURE 7.42
Basic Active Directory structure.

A *tree* is a collection of objects that share the same DNS name. Active directory can subdivide domains into organizational units (for example, Sales or Admin) that contain other units, or leaf objects, such as printers, users, and so on. Conversely, Windows 2000 can create an organizational structure containing more than one tree. This structure is referred to as a forest. Figure 7.43 expands the AD structure to demonstrate these relationships.

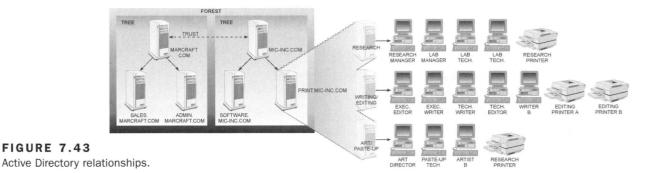

FIGURE 7.43
Active Directory relationships.

Windows 2000 automatically joins all the domains within a tree through two-way trusts. Trusts are relationships that enable users to move between domains and perform prescribed types of operations. If a trust relationship is established between the Sales and Marketing domains in the example and a similar trust exists between the Sales and Admin domains, a trust relationship also exists between the Marketing and Admin domains.

Trusts enable administrators to provide user and group rights to objects. Rights are the permission settings that control user's (or groups of users') authority to access objects and perform operations (such as reading or writing a file). Administrative rights provide authority to users down to the organizational unit level. However, they do not cross boundaries established at the domain level but can be inherited by other OUs having subordinate positions within the same tree. On the other hand, user rights must be established for individual users or for members of groups. Using groups allows common rights to be assigned to multiple users with a single administrative action (as opposed to setting up and maintaining rights for each individual in, say, a 150-person accounting staff).

In a network supported by Windows 2000 servers, the network administrator can assign applications to users so that they appear on their Start menus. When the application is selected for the first time, it is installed on the local machine. The administrator also can place optional applications on the Add/Remove Programs dialog box in the Control Panel. The user can install these applications from this location at any time.

The network administrator also can cause the contents of the local My Documents folder to reside on the server rather than on the local desktop. This option provides safe, centralized storage for user files. The server security and backup functions safeguard the data.

In Windows 2000, application software can be installed remotely across the network. This enables the network administrator to control user application software across the network and keep it uniform throughout an enterprise.

The primary tool for working with the Active Directory is the Active Directory Users and Computers, depicted in Figure 7.44. The organizational units of a domain contain users, groups, and resources. The Active Directory Manager tool is used to add users, groups, and organizational units (OUs) to the directory.

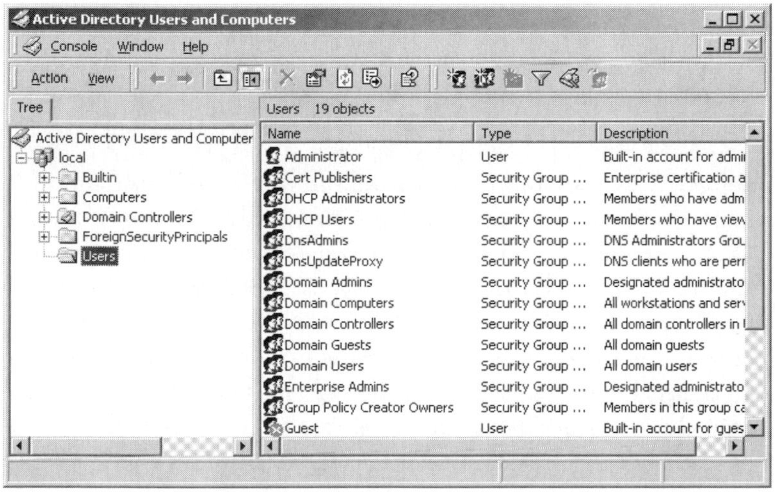

FIGURE 7.44
Active Directory Users and Computers.

Although the Active Directory structure is designed primarily to help manage a network, it also can be a valuable desktop tool. The Active Directory service running on a Windows 2000 server enables Windows 2000 Professional installations to locate printers, disk drives, and other network devices across the network.

Administering Windows 2000

Windows NT and 2000 are designed to be used in an administrated LAN environment. As such, it must provide network administrators with the tools necessary to control users and data within the network. To empower the network administrator, Windows 2000 furnishes five powerful administrative tools:

◆ System policies

◆ User profiles

◆ Groups

◆ Network shares

◆ NTFS rights

Each of these tools is designed to enable administrators to limit, or grant, users access to files, folders, services, and administrator-level services.

Computer Management Consoles

Windows 2000 concentrates many of the system's administration tools in a single location, under the Control Panel's Administrative Tools icon. The tools are combined in the Windows 2000 Computer Management Console, depicted in Figure 7.45. The Management Console can be accessed by clicking the My Computer icon and selecting the Manage option from the pop-up menu. As Figure 7.45 illustrates, the console includes three primary Microsoft Management Consoles (MMCs):

◆ System Tools

◆ Storage

◆ Services and Applications

The System Tools console provides a collection of tools that can be used to view and manage system objects. They also can be used to track and configure all the system's hardware and software. It also can be used to configure network options and view system events.

Likewise, the Storage console provides a standard set of tools for maintaining the system's disk drives. These tools include the Disk Management tool, the Disk Defragmentor utility, and a Logical Drives utility. The Disk Management tool enables the user to create and manage disk partitions and volumes. The Disk Defragmentor is used to optimize file operations on disks by rearranging their data into the most effective storage pattern for reading and writing. Finally, the Logical Drives tool shows a listing of all the logical drives in the system, including remote drives that have been mapped to the local system.

The final entry, Services and Applications, includes an advanced set of system management tools. These tools include the Windows Management Instrumentation (WMI) tools, a listing of all the system's available services, and access to the Windows 2000 indexing functions. The WMI tools are used to establish administrative controls with another computer, provide logging services, view user security settings, and enable the Windows 2000 advanced scripting services.

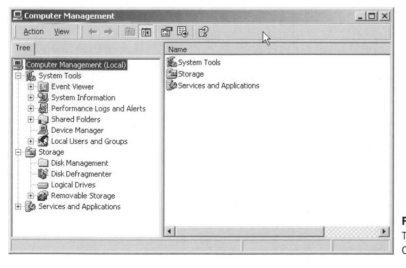

FIGURE 7.45
The Windows 2000 Computer Management Console.

Some of the Windows 2000 management consoles are not loaded when the operating system is installed. However, they are available for installation from the Windows 2000 CD. These consoles are referred to as snap-ins. In addition to the Control Panel path, all the installed MMCs can be accessed under the Start/Programs/Administrative Tools path. Extended discussions of these tools are presented throughout the remainder of the text as they apply to managing and troubleshooting the operating system.

Thin and Fat Clients

In most Windows 2000 installations, the administrative architecture is set up to store some information, such as user configurations and backup data, on the server, while leaving applications and some data on the client. However, Windows 2000 networks can be configured to operate within a range between two administration levels known as thin client and fat client.

The term *thin client* describes installation strategies that place a limited amount of information on the workstation and most of the applications on the server. The local workstation has very little control over its own operation. This enables the network administrator to exercise a very high level of control over what users do and have access to.

Conversely, a fat client installation strategy places much of the operating system and applications on the client and the processing is done locally, not on the server. Fat clients are more likely to be able to operate in a standalone manner. Currently, they also represent the more widely used strategy. Bare in mind, however, that the thin/fat client arrangement is a Server feature rather than a Windows 2000 Professional feature.

Windows 2000 Device Manager

Windows 2000 employs the Windows 9x-like *Device Manager* illustrated in Figure 7.46. The Device Manager replaces the Windows NT Diagnostic utility found in Windows NT 4.0. As with Windows 9x, the Windows 2000 Device Manager plays a major role in modifying hardware configurations and for troubleshooting hardware problems encountered in Windows 2000.

The Windows 2000 Device Manager utility can be accessed by clicking its button located under the Hardware tab of the Control Panel's *System Properties* page. In Windows 2000, however, the Device Manager is usually accessed through the Computer Management Console. Operation of the Device Manager is very similar to its Windows 9x counterparts. It can be used to identify installed ports, update device drivers, and change I/O settings for hardware installed in the system.

Even though entries in the Registry can be altered through the RegEdt32 and RegEdit utilities, the safest way to change hardware settings is to change their values through the Device Manager. Chapter 9, "3.0 Diagnosing and Troubleshooting" discusses ways to use Device Manager.

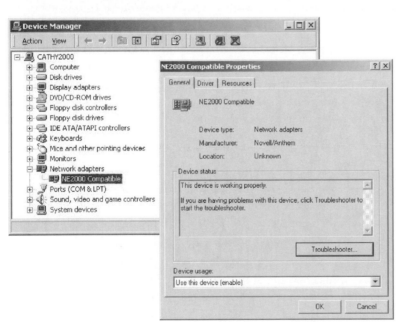

FIGURE 7.46
The Windows 2000 Device Manager.

Windows NT/2000 Group Policies

As with other Windows versions, the overall operation of Windows 2000 is governed by system policies. Basically, policies give administrators control over users. Using system policies, the network administrator can give or limit users' access to local resources, such as drives and network connections. Administrators can establish policies that force certain users to log on during specified times and lock them out of the system at all other times. System policies also allow the administrator to send updates and configure desktops for network clients. Fundamentally, any item found in the Control Panel can be regulated through system policies.

All Windows NT users are assigned a profile directory under their username the first time they log on to a given Windows NT/2000 system. This profile contains system information and settings that become particular to the user and is stored under the Documents and Settings directory. Inside the directory, the system creates the NTUSER.DAT file, along with various other data files. As discussed previously, this file contains the User portion of the Windows NT Registry. This file contains the user-specific settings that have been established for this user. When the user logs on to the system, the User and System hive portions of the Registry are used to construct the user-specific environment in the system.

The first time a user logs on to a system, the Default User profile directory is copied into the directory established under the user's name. When the user makes changes to the desktop, Start menu, My Documents, and so on, the data is stored in the appropriate files under the username. Both Windows NT and Windows 2000 provide ways to store user profiles on the server in a networked environment. This prevents the user's profile directories from being re-created at each machine the user logs on to. Instead, these operating systems provide roaming profiles that are downloaded from the server to the client when the user logs on. Changes made during sessions are uploaded to the server when the user logs off.

As with previous versions of Windows NT, Windows 2000 uses profiles to provide customized operating environments for its users. These profiles are stored in different locations, hold more information, and are more customizable than previous Windows NT versions, but they peform the same functions. However, Windows 2000 policies work very differently under the Active Directory structure from how they worked in the Windows NT domain structure.

In Windows 2000, policies are established through the Group Policy Editor (GPE), depicted in Figure 7.47. Administrators use this editor to establish which applications different users have access to; they also use it to control applications on the user's desktop.

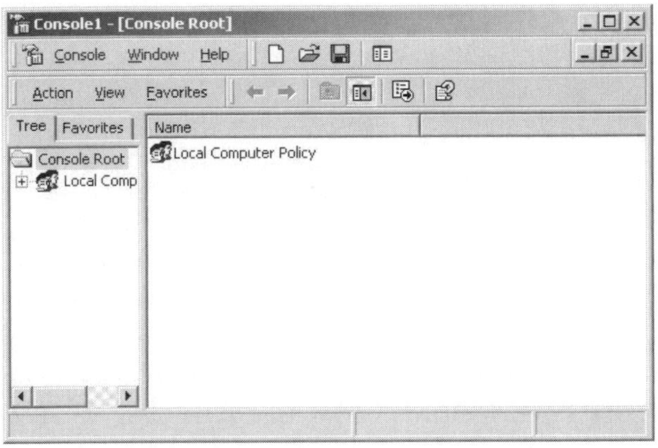

FIGURE 7.47
The Windows 2000 Group Policy Editor.

Many of Windows NT administration features have been moved to the Control Panel in Windows 2000. Whereas Windows NT used system policies, the Windows 2000 environment functions on Group Policy objects (GPOs). Group Policies are the Windows 2000 tool for implementing changes for computers and users throughout an enterprise. The Windows 2000 Group Policies can be applied to individual users, domains, organizational units and sites. In addition, the Windows 2000 policies are highly secure.

With Group Policies, administrators can institute a large number of detailed settings for users throughout an enterprise, without establishing each setting manually.

GPOs can be used to apply a large number of changes to machines and users through the Active Directory. These changes appear in the GPE under three headings:

◆ Software Installation Settings

◆ Windows Settings

◆ Administrative Templates

Each heading appears in two places: The first version is listed under Computer Configuration; the second copy is found under User Configuration. Values normally differ between the versions of the headings because the user and computer settings will differ.

The Software Installation Settings heading can be used to install, update, repair, and remove applications. The Designed for Windows 2000 logo program requires that all applications designed for Windows 2000 use the Microsoft Installer (MSI) technology. This program replaces the traditional SETUP.EXE program used for installing applications in previous Windows versions. The MSI is created by the software application developer and contains all the information that the system needs to interact with it.

The MSI is aware of the files the application requires to operate properly, where they should be installed, their sizes, and their version numbers. The administrator has the ability to customize this information to fit the needs of the installation. Examples of customized settings might include language-support selections and logical drive locations. The customized information is referred to as a transform and is used by the installer to ensure that the appropriate files are installed and configured properly.

The MSI technology also provides the operating system with the capability to self-repair applications. If one or more of a compliant application's *core files* are damaged or removed, the icon used to start the application checks with the MSI to see that no critical data is missing. If any material is missing, the MSI copies the data to the correct locations and starts the application. This same technology can be used to auto-install applications on machines that attempt to open files with MSI-recognized extensions. The MSI also can be employed to automatically deploy applications when a user logs on or accesses the Active Directory looking for the application.

The Windows Settings portion of the GPO contains startup and shutdown scripts as well as security settings. The Security Setting portion of this heading covers such topics as Account Policies, Password Policies, and User Right Assignments, to name a few. User Rights are special capabilities granted to accounts or operating systems to perform tasks, such as determining whether an acoount can add workstations to a domain or manipulate devices at a lower level.

The Administrative Template portion of the GPO stores changes to the Registry settings that pertain to the HKEY_LOCAL_ MACHINE. Figure 7.48 depicts the hierarchy of items in the Computer Administrative Templates window of the Group Policy Editor.

FIGURE 7.48
Computer Administrative Templates.

NAVIGATING OPERATING SYSTEMS

▶ 1.2 Identify basic concepts and procedures for creating, viewing, and managing files and directories, including procedures for changing file attributes and the ramifications of changes (for example, security issues).

Working in DOS

It is important to consider that MS-DOS is a disk operating system. Therefore, you must understand how DOS organizes disks. The DOS organizational structure is typically described as being like a common office file cabinet, similar to the one depicted in Figure 7.49. Think of DOS as the filing cabinet structure. This example has four drawers that can be opened. Think of these as disk drives labeled A, B, C/D, and E. Inside each drawer are hanging folders that can hold different types of items. Think of these as directories. The hanging folders may contain different types of items or other individual folders. Think of these individual folders as *subdirectories.* For organizational purposes, each hanging folder and each individual folder must have a unique label on it.

Inside each hanging folder, or individual folder, are the items being stored. In a real filing cabinet, these items in the folders are usually documents of different types. However, pictures and tapes and other items related to the folder also can be stored in them.

FIGURE 7.49
DOS organization.

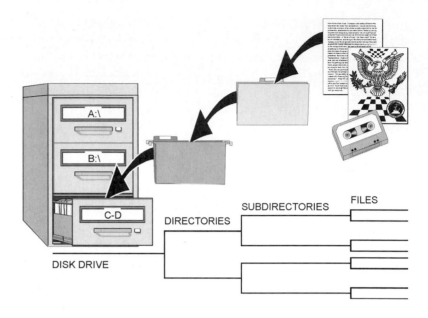

Think of the items inside the folders as files. Disk-based systems manage data blocks by giving them *filenames*. Recall that a file is just a block of logically related data, given a single name, and treated as a single unit. Like the contents of the *folders*, files can be programs, documents, drawings or other illustrations, sound files, and so on.

To find an item in the cabinet, you just need to know which drawer, hanging folder, and folder it is located in. This concept can be translated directly to the computer system. To locate a particular file, you just need to know which drive, directory, and subdirectory it is located in. In MS-DOS, the path to any file in the system can be written as a direction to the computer so that it will know where the file is that it is being directed toward. This format for specifying a path is as follows:

```
C:\directory name\subdirectory name\filename
```

In this example, the C: specifies the C: disk drive. The directory, subdirectory, and filenames would naturally be replaced by their real names. The back slashes (\) after each item indicate the presence of a directory or subdirectory. The first slash indicates a special directory, called the root directory, which is present on all DOS disks.

If the direction is to a file, the filename is always placed at the end of the path. MS-DOS allows for a basic filename of up to eight characters. It also allows for an extension of up to three characters. The extension is separated from the main portion of the filename by a period and is normally used to identify what type of file it is. (For example, the filename FILE1.LTR could be used to identify a letter created by a word processor.)

The Command Line

The operating system is responsible for providing the system's user interface. The main user interface for DOS is the command line. The command line is the space immediately following the DOS prompt on the screen. All DOS commands are typed in this space. They are executed by pressing the Enter key on the keyboard.

The *MS-DOS prompt* for using the C: hard disk drive as the active directory is displayed in Figure 7.50.

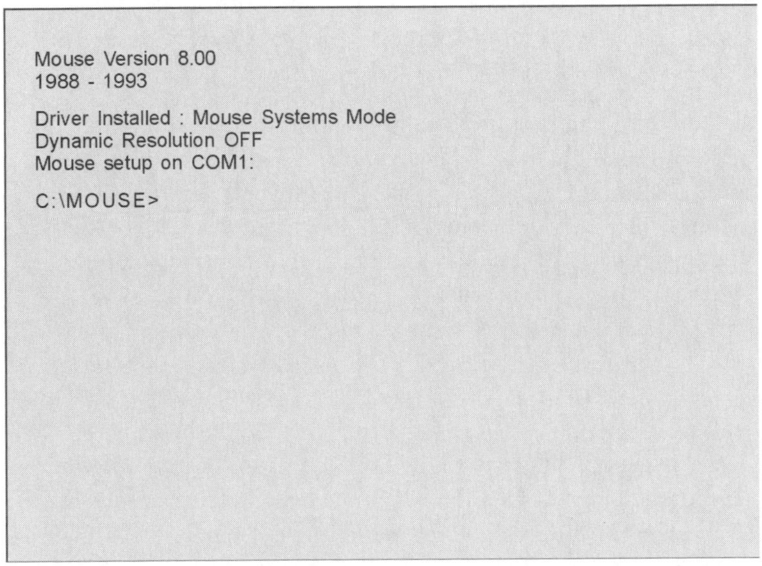

> **NOTE**
>
> **Filename Extensions**   Filename extensions are not actually required for most files. However, they become helpful in sorting between files in a congested system. You should be aware that the operating system reserves some three-letter combinations, such as COM and SYS, for its own use. More information about filenames and extensions is presented in the subsequent section concerning file-level DOS commands.

```
Mouse Version 8.00
1988 - 1993

Driver Installed : Mouse Systems Mode
Dynamic Resolution OFF
Mouse setup on COM1:

C:\MOUSE>
```

FIGURE 7.50
The DOS prompt.

From the DOS prompt, all DOS functions can be entered and executed. DOS application programs also are started from this prompt. These files can be discerned by their filename extensions. Files with .COM, .EXE, or .BAT extensions can be started directly from the prompt. The .COM and .EXE file extensions are reserved by DOS

TEST TIP

Know which file types can be executed directly from the command-line prompt.

---

and can be generated only by programs that can correctly configure them. BAT files are just ASCII text files that have been generated using DOS functions. Because they contain DOS commands mixed with COM and EXE files, DOS can execute BAT files from the command line.

Programs with other types of extensions must be associated with one of these three file types to be operated. The user can operate application software packages such as graphical user interfaces, word processors, business packages, data communications packages, and user programming languages (that is, QBasic and Debug). As an example, the core component of a word processor could be a file called WORDPRO.EXE. Document files produced by word processors are normally given filename extensions of .DOC (for document) or .TXT (for text file).

To view one of the documents electronically, you first need to run the executable file and then use its features to load up, format, and display the document. Likewise, a BASIC file normally has an extension of .BAS assigned to it. To execute a file with this extension, it is necessary to run a BASIC interpreter, such as QBASIC.EXE, and then use it to load the BAS file and run it.

The user also can type DOS commands on the command line to perform DOS functions. These commands can be grouped into drive-level commands, directory-level commands, and file-level commands. The format for using DOS commands is as follows:

```
COMMAND (space) SOURCE location (space) DESTINATION
location
```

```
COMMAND (space) location
```

```
COMMAND
```

The first example illustrates how DOS operations that involve a source and a final destination, such as moving a file from one place to another, are entered. The second example illustrates how single-location DOS operations, such as formatting a disk in a particular disk drive, are specified. The final example applies to DOS commands that occur in a default location, such as obtaining a listing of the files on the current disk drive.

DOS Comm   Can be modified.

Many DOS commands can be modified by placing one or more software switches at the end of the basic command. A switch is added to the command by adding a space, a fore-slash (/), and a single letter:

```
COMMAND (space) option /switch
```

> **N O T E**
>
> **DOS Command Switches**   Common DOS command switches include **/P** for page, **/W** for wide format, and **/S** for system. Different switches are used to modify different DOS commands. In each case, the DOS User Guide should be consulted for switch definitions available with each command.

Drives and Disks

Each disk drive in the system is identified by DOS with a single-letter name (such as A:). This name must be specified when giving the system commands so that they are carried out using the proper drive. The format for specifying which drive will perform a DOS operation calls for the presence of the drive's identifier letter in the command, followed by a colon (that is, A: or C:).

Figure 7.51 illustrates how the various disk drives are seen by a typical, standalone system. DOS reserves the letters A: and B: for the first and second floppy drives. Multiple hard disk drive units can be installed in the system unit, along with the floppy drives. DOS recognizes a single hard disk unit in the system as the C: drive. DOS utilities can be used to partition a single, physical hard disk drive into two or more volumes that the system recognizes as logical drives C:, D:, and so on.

FIGURE 7.51
The system's disk drives.

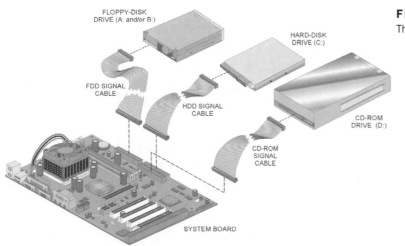

FLOPPY-DISK
DRIVE (A: and/or B:)

HARD-DISK
DRIVE (C:)

FDD SIGNAL
CABLE

HDD SIGNAL
CABLE

CD-ROM
DRIVE (D:)

CD-ROM
SIGNAL
CABLE

SYSTEM BOARD

NOTE

Drive Letters Figure 7.51 shows a CD-ROM drive as the D: drive, because this is becoming the most common PC configuration. In the case of networked systems, logical drive letters may be extended to define up to Z drives. These drives are actually the hard drives located in remote computers. The operating system in the local machine treats them as additional logical drives (that is, F, G, and so on).

Conversely, a second hard disk drive can be added to the system and set up as logical D: drive. It also may be partitioned into smaller logical drives that the system recognizes as drives E:, F:, and so on. Logical drives and disk *partitioning* are covered in Chapter 1, "1.0 Installation, Configuration, and Upgrading" and later in this chapter.

Some DOS operations are simplified by allowing the system to choose the location for the command to be carried out through the use of default settings (special predetermined settings that are automatically used by the system when no specific directions are given to change the setting). These settings are remembered in DOS and are used by the system when the operator does not specify a particular location for events to happen. The default setting in your system is the A: drive. In systems with two or more drives, it is imperative that the user specify exactly where the action called for is to occur.

Drive-Level Operations

The following DOS commands pertain to drive-level operations. They must be typed at the command prompt, and carry out the instruction along with any drive modifiers given.

- **FORMAT.** This command is used to prepare a new disk for use. Actual data locations are marked off on the disk for the tracks and sectors, and bad sectors are marked. In addition, the directory is established on the disk. New disks must be formatted before they can be used.

- **C:\>FORMAT A:.** This command is used even in a single-drive system. The system issues prompts to insert the proper disks at the correct times. A self-booting disk can be created by using an **/S** modifier (for System files) at the end of the normal **Format** command.

- **C:\>FORMAT A:/S.** This command causes three System files (boot files—IO.SYS, MSDOS.SYS, and COMMAND.COM) to be copied into the root directory of the disk after it has been formatted. The new disk will now boot up without a DOS disk.

- **C:\>FORMAT A:/Q.** This command causes the system to perform a quick format operation on the disk. This amounts to removing the FAT and root directory from the disk.

◆ **SETVER.** This command sets the DOS version number that the system reports to an application. Programs designed for previous DOS versions may not operate correctly under newer versions unless the version has been set correctly.

◆ **C:\>SETVER C:.** This entry causes all the files on the C: drive to be listed in the DOS version table. Note, however, that the **SETVER** command must be enabled by loading it in the CONFIG.SYS file before it can be used from the command line.

If the current DOS version is not known, typing **VER** at the DOS prompt will display it onscreen. These commands are particularly useful in networking operations where multiple computers are connected together to share information. In these applications, several versions of DOS may exist on different machines attached to the network.

Directories

As mentioned earlier, in hard drive–based systems, it is common to organize related programs and data into areas called directories. This makes them easier to find and work with, because modern hard drives can hold large amounts of information. MS-DOS directories can hold up to 512 directory or filename entries.

It would be difficult to work with directories if you could not know which one you were working in. The DOS prompt can be set up to display which directory is being used. This particular directory is referred to as the current, or working directory. (That is, C:\DOS\forms indicates that you are working with programs located in a subdirectory of the DOS directory named forms.) The first back slash represents the root directory on the C: hard drive.

The following DOS commands are used for directory-based operations. The format for using them is identical to disk-related commands discussed earlier.

◆ **DIR.** The **Directory** command gives a listing of the files on the disk that are in the drive indicated by the drive specifier.

C:\>**DIR** or **DIR B:** (If DIR is used without any drive specifier, the contents of the drive indicated by the prompt display.) The command also may be used with modifiers to alter the way in which the directory displays.

[handwritten: → show Dir on width]

[handwritten: page by page]

C:\>DIR/W displays the entire directory at one time across the width of the display.

C:\>DIR/P displays the contents of the directory one page at a time. You must press a key to advance to the next display page.

◆ **MKDIR (MD).** Creates a new directory in an indicated spot in the directory tree structure.

C:\>MD C:\DOS*XXX* creates a new subdirectory named *XXX* in the path that includes the root directory (C:\) and the DOS directory.

◆ **CHDIR (CD).** Changes the location of the active directory to a position specified with the command.

C:\>CD C:\DOS changes the working directory from the C: root directory to the C:\DOS directory.

◆ **RMDIR (RD).** The **Remove Directory** command erases the directory specified in the command. You cannot remove a directory until it is empty, and you cannot remove the directory if it is currently active.

C:\>RD C:\DOS\FORMS removes the DOS subdirectory forms, provided it is empty.

◆ **PROMPT.** Changes the appearance of the DOS prompt.

C:\>PROMPT PG causes the form of the prompt to change from just C: to C:\ and causes the complete path from the main directory to the current directory to display at the DOS prompt (that is, C:\DOS>).

◆ **TREE.** Lists all the directory and subdirectory names on a specified disk.

C:\>TREE C: displays a graphical representation of the organization of the C: hard drive.

◆ **DELTREE.** Removes a selected directory and all the files and subdirectories below it.

C:\>DELTREE C:\DOS\DRIVER\MOUSE deletes the subdirectory MOUSE and any subdirectories it may have.

NAVIGATING WINDOWS 9x

When Windows 95 or 98 is started, it produces the basic desktop screen depicted in Figure 7.52. The desktop is the primary graphical user interface for Windows 9x. As with previous Windows products, it uses icons to quickly locate and run applications. In Windows 9x, however, the *Start button* provides the starting point for most functions.

ICONS

MENU

START BUTTON   TOOL BAR   DESKTOP

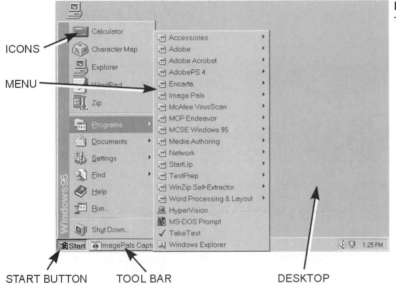

FIGURE 7.52
The Windows 9x desktop screen.

Windows 95 Desktop

The desktop interface provides an easy way to start tasks and make resource connections. Desktop icons are referred to as shortcuts (because the primary way to access applications is through the Start menu). Applying a traditional double-click to the icon starts the application or brings up its window.

In addition to the normal Windows left-click and double-click functions, Windows 95 and Windows 98 both employ the right mouse button for some activities. This is referred to as *right-clicking*, or as *alternate-clicking* for right handers, and is used to pop up a menu of functions onscreen. The right-click menus in Windows 9x are context sensitive, so the information they contain applies to the item being clicked.

Right-clicking an icon produces a pop-up menu, similar to the left-hand menu in Figure 7.53. These menus enable the user to Open, Cut, or Copy a folder (an icon that represents a directory), create a shortcut, delete or rename a folder, or examine *properties* of the folder. In the case of clicking one of the system's hardware devices, the menu permits you to perform such functions as sharing the device or checking its properties. These menus may have additional items inserted in their lists by applications that they serve. Right-clicking in an open area of the desktop produces a pop-up menu, similar to the one displayed in right side of the figure. This menu enables the user to arrange icons on the desktop, create new folders and shortcuts, and see the properties of the system's video display.

FIGURE 7.53
Right-click menus.

TEST TIP

Memorize the common options found in the My Computer right-click menu.

Windows 98 Desktop

In its basic form, the Windows 98 desktop is very similar to that of the Windows 95 desktop. The basic icons are located along the left border of the screen, the *taskbar* runs across the bottom of the screen, and the Start menu pops up from the Start button on the taskbar. However, some additional features of the new desktop, depicted in Figure 7.54, enable the user to quickly access a wide variety of resources.

ACTIVE DESKTOP ITEM   CHANNEL BAR   **FIGURE 7.54**
Windows 98 desktop.

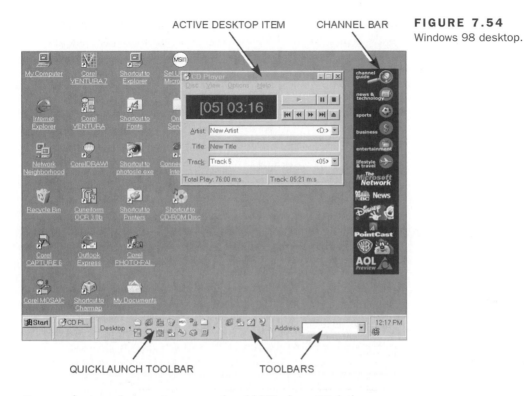

QUICKLAUNCH TOOLBAR   TOOLBARS

Because the new desktop integrates the old Windows 95 desktop functions with the Internet Explorer (IE) browser, it can display the icons and windows typically found on the desktop, as well as HTML-based documents. This feature effectively places the desktop online and creates an Active Desktop.

As a matter of fact, Web pages can be loaded into the desktop and automatically updated from the Web. This type of operation is referred to as an Active Channel. On the desktop, the system displays icons representing the Web links to these channels on the Channel Bar. The Web sites listed on the Channel Bar can be located on an intranet or on the Internet (external organization), and are updated automatically from the server. This enables the user to always have access to the most recent information directly from the desktop.

The other items of interest on the Windows 98 desktop include an extended icon system, a QuickLaunch toolbar, user-defined toolbars, and Active Desktop elements.

Windows 98 enables the user to establish toolbars for easy access to user-specific files. This can be done in any of three ways, as illustrated in Figure 7.55. The user can customize the QuickLaunch toolbar, customize the Windows 98 taskbar, or create a new toolbar. The new toolbar can be a traditional toolbar that displays on the taskbar, or it can be a floating toolbar that displays on the Active Desktop.

FIGURE 7.55
Windows 98 toolbars.

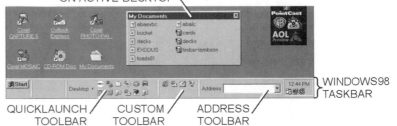

Active desktop elements can be HTML files, JPEG files, GIF files, or an Explorer window. These resources can be used to provide dynamic visual information, such as activity levels of various operations, to the user. Microsoft provides an Active Desktop Gallery Web site at www.microsoft.com/Windows/ie/ie40/gallery/. This Web site provides a variety of free Active Desktop elements that you can download.

Some of the items that appear on the desktop are a function of what the system finds as it looks for user profiles at the end of the boot-up process. As mentioned earlier, the Windows folder holds the system's default USER.DAT file. In a multiple-user system, however, the Windows\Profiles directory contains a folder for each user who logs on to the system. These folders contain the individual user's USER.DAT files, along with a number of the user's desktop-related folders. These include each user's:

◆ Internet Explorer Cookies folder

◆ Desktop folder

◆ Favorites folder

◆ History folder

◆ My Documents folder

◆ NetHood folder

◆ Recent folder

◆ Start Menu folder

◆ Temporary Internet Files folder

N O T E   **Cookie Info**   Cookies are collections of information samples from different users' visits to a Web site.

Locating, Accessing, and Retrieving Information in Windows 9x

As previously mentioned, the portion of the operating system that immediately greets the user when Windows 9x and Windows NT/2000 load up is the desktop. In its most basic form, the Windows 9x desktop features three standard icons: *My Computer*, *Network Neighborhood*, and the *Recycle Bin*. From this screen the user can have access to the full power and resources of the system.

The major user interfaces in Windows 9x include the following:

◆ My Computer

◆ Pop-up dialog boxes

◆ The Start menu

◆ Windows Explorer

◆ Internet Explorer

◆ Network Neighborhood

My Computer

The My Computer icon is the major user interface for Windows 9x. It enables the user to see the local system's contents and manage its files. Double-clicking the My Computer icon produces the My Computer window, depicted in Figure 7.56. This window displays all the system's disk drives as icons, and represents the Control Panel and system printers as folders.

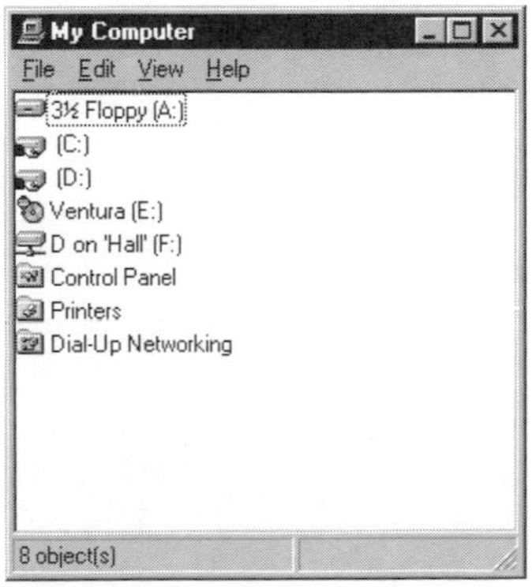

Double-clicking one of the drive icons produces a display of its contents onscreen. This information also can be displayed in several different formats using the View option. Selecting the Options entry in the View menu produces the Options window displayed in Figure 7.57. This window consists of three tabs (screens): Folders, View, and File Types.

FIGURE 7.56
My Computer window.

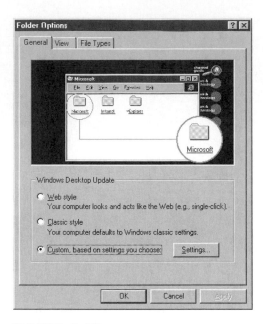

FIGURE 7.57
The View\Options window.

The Folders tab supplies information about how the desktop will display windows as the user browses through multiple windows. The View window is used to define how the folders and files in the selected window will display onscreen. This screen also determines which types of files will display. To see Hidden and System files, select the View tab and click Show Hidden Files button. Files with selected extensions will be hidden. The File Types screen lists the types of files that the system can recognize. New file types can be registered in this window.

The Control Panel and Printers folders under My Computer contain information about the system and its printers. The Windows 95 Control Panel is the user interface employed to manage hardware devices attached to the system. The Windows 98 Control Panel is explored in greater detail in a later section of this chapter.

The *Printers folder* displays the computer's installed printer types. As with other icons in the My Computer window, the printers can be displayed as small icons, large icons, in a simple list, or in a list with details. Details include such items as printer type, number of documents to print, current status, and any comments generated by the print controller.

The My Computer window is a typical Windows 9x window. Its title bar uses button icons to provide Minimize, Restore, and Close functions for the window, as described in Figure 7.58. When a program is minimized, its button appears on the taskbar at the bottom of the screen. To restore the application, just click its button.

Clicking the X in the Close box closes the window and stops any applications running in it. In Windows 9x, windows can be moved and resized, and items can be moved from one window to another, using drag-and-drop techniques.

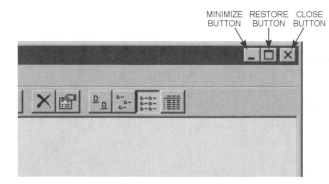

FIGURE 7.58
Windows 9x Minimize, Restore, and Close functions.

Windows 9x Pop-Up Menus

Most Windows 9x windows have menu bars that provide pop-up menus on the screen when they are accessed by clicking their titles, or by pressing the Alt key and their underlined character. (For example, the Alt+F combination pops up the File menu.) Typical menu bar options include File, Edit, View, and Help. Options that apply to the current window display as dark text. Options that are not applicable to the window are grayed out.

The File option on the My Computer menu bar can be used to perform many disk maintenance procedures. When a disk drive icon is selected, clicking the File option produces a menu that includes provisions for formatting the disk, sharing a drive with the network community, backing up the contents of the drive, or displaying its properties.

The File menu's Properties option displays general information about the drive, such as FAT type, capacity, free space, and used space. This option also provides a notice of how much time has elapsed since the last error-checking, backup, and defragmentation operations were performed on the selected drive.

The Windows 95 View menu option, depicted in Figure 7.59, is one of the most used features of the menu bar. It can be used to alter the manner in which the contents of the window display. The drives and folders in Figure 7.56 are displayed as large icons. However, they can be reduced to small icons, displayed as a list, or displayed with name, type, size, and free-space details. Other options in the menu can be used to organize the icons within the window.

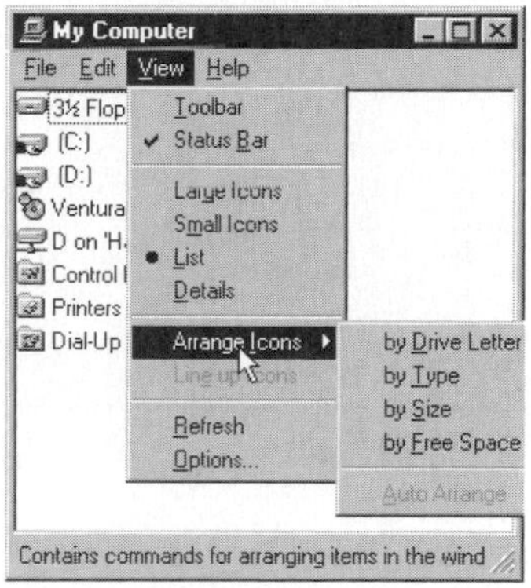

A check mark located next to the menu option indicates that the item is currently in use. The large dot next to the item indicates that it is the currently selected option.

Right-clicking the My Computer icon produces a menu listing similar to the one depicted in the left side of Figure 7.53. This menu provides options for opening the My Computer window, exploring the system drives and files through the Windows Explorer, working with network drives, creating shortcuts, renaming the selected folders and files, and accessing the properties of the system's installed devices.

FIGURE 7.59
The View menu.

In Windows 98, the My Computer options have been rearranged slightly from those of the Windows 95 My Computer window. In particular, the Options entry under the View menu has been replaced by Folder Options. The tabs in this window are titled General, View and File Types. As with the Windows 95 version, the View/Folder Options/View window is used to define how folders and files display and to determine which types of files display.

Network Neighborhood

The Network Neighborhood icon provides quick information about the world around the system, when used in a networked environment. Double-clicking this icon produces the Network Neighborhood window illustrated in Figure 7.60. Small computer icons represent the various computers attached to the network. They enable the user to browse through the network. Double-clicking any of the icons produces a listing of the resources the selected computer offers, such as disk drives and printers.

FIGURE 7.60
Network Neighborhood window.

The Recycle Bin

The Recycle Bin is a storage area for deleted files, and enables you to retrieve such files if they are deleted by mistake. When you delete a folder or file from the Windows system, it removes the first three letters of its name from the drive's FAT so that it is invisible to the system. However, the system records its presence in the Recycle Bin. The system is free to reuse the space on the drive because it does not know that anything is there. So long as it has not been over written with new data, or it has not been removed from the Recycle Bin, it can be restored from the information in the Recycle Bin. If it has been thrown out of the bin but has not been overwritten, it can be recovered using a third-party software utility for recovering deleted files.

The Recycle Bin icon should always be present on the desktop. It can be removed only through the Registry. If its icon is missing, there are two alternatives to restoring it: Establish a shortcut to the Recycle Bin using a new icon; or just reinstall Windows 9x. This action always places the Recycle Bin on the desktop.

The Taskbar

The Start button, located at the bottom of the screen, is used to accomplish several different tasks, depending on the context of the operation. For example, the Start button is used to start programs, alter system settings, and open documents. Clicking the Start button produces a Start menu onscreen.

Just to the right of the Start button is an area called the taskbar. This area is used to display all the applications currently open. Each time a program is started, or a window is opened, a corresponding button appears on the taskbar. To switch between applications, just click the desired program button to make it the active window. The button disappears from the taskbar if the program is closed.

Right-clicking the taskbar at the bottom of the screen produces a menu that can be used to control the appearance of the taskbar and open windows onscreen.

You can move the taskbar around the display by clicking and dragging it to the left, right, or top of the screen. It can be hidden just off screen by clicking its edge and then dragging it toward the edge of the display. If the taskbar is hidden, you can retrieve it by pressing the Ctrl+Esc key combination. This pops up the Start menu along with the taskbar. Enter the Start/Settings/Taskbar & Start Menu option to change the taskbar settings so that it will not be hidden. You also can locate an absent taskbar by moving the mouse around the edges of the screen until the shape of the cursor changes.

Likewise, pressing the Tab key cycles control between the Start menu, the QuickLaunch icons, the taskbar, and the desktop icons. This key also can be helpful in navigating the system if the mouse fails.

> **TEST TIP**
>
> Know how to move around the desktop, Start menu, and taskbar using the keyboard.

The Start Menu

All operations begin from the Start button. When you click the button, a pop-up menu of options appears, as illustrated in Figure 7.61. This menu normally contains the options Programs, Documents, Settings, Find, Help, Run, and Shut Down.

FIGURE 7.61
The Start Button menu.

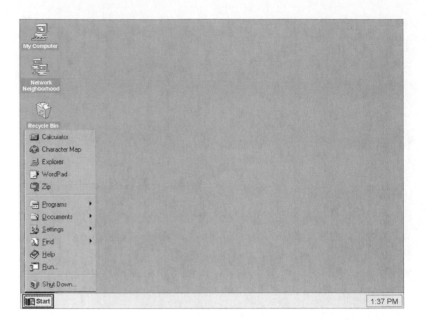

Placing the cursor over designated menu items causes any submenus associated with that option to pop up onscreen. An arrow to the right of the option indicates a submenu is available. To open the selected item, just left-click on it and its window will appear on the desktop.

The Programs submenu, depicted in Figure 7.62, has several options, including Accessories, On-line Services, Start Up, Windows 9x Training, MS-DOS Prompt, and Windows Explorer.

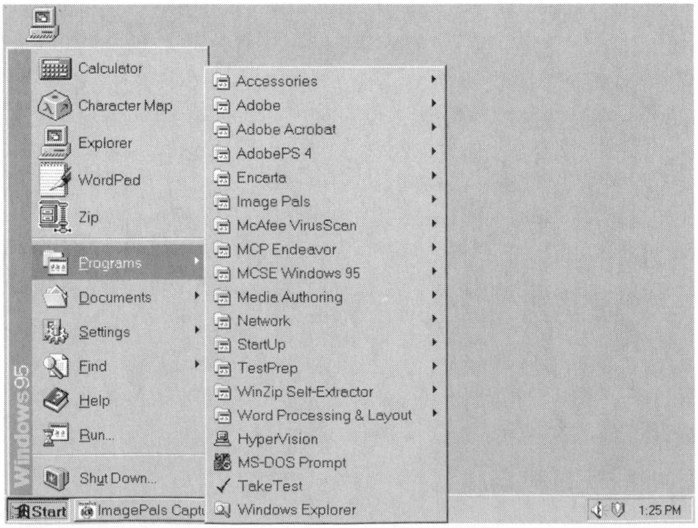

FIGURE 7.62
The Programs submenu.

The MS-DOS prompt also is accessed through the Programs option. The Start menu's Documents entry displays a list of documents previously opened.

The Settings option displays values for the system's configurable components. It combines previous Windows functions, such as copies of the Control Panel and *Print Manager* folders, as well as access to the Windows 9x taskbar.

The Find utility is used to locate folders, files, mail messages, and shared computers. The Find function can be accessed directly from the Start menu, or it can be reached by right-clicking the My Computer icon. The selection from the Start menu enables you to search for files, folders, and computers. The My Computer version searches only for files and folders. To locate a file, just type its name in the Named window, tell the system which drive or drive to look in, and click Find. Standard DOS *wildcard characters* can be included in the search name.

The Help file system provides extensive information about many Windows 9x functions and operations. It also supplies an exhaustive list of guided troubleshooting routines for typical system components and peripherals.

The Run option is used to start programs or open folders from a command-line dialog box. You can start executable files by typing their filename in the box and clicking the OK button. You can use the Browse button to locate the desired file by looking through the system's file structure.

The Start button also is used to correctly shut down Windows 9x. The Shut Down option from the Start menu shuts down the system, restarts the computer, or logs the user off. It must be used to avoid damaging files and to ensure that your work is properly saved. When it is clicked, the Shut Down Windows dialog box depicted in Figure 7.63 appears. After you select an option from the dialog box, the unit tells you to wait, and then you receive a screen message telling you that it is okay to turn off the system.

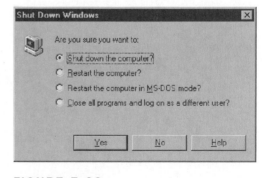

FIGURE 7.63
The Shut Down dialog box.

Windows 98 Start Menu

The Windows 98 Start button remains on the taskbar at the bottom of the screen. Clicking the button produces the Start menu, similar to the one depicted in Figure 7.64. Whereas most of the entries are carryovers from 95, the Log Off User and Favorites entries are new.

FIGURE 7.64
Windows 98 Start menu.

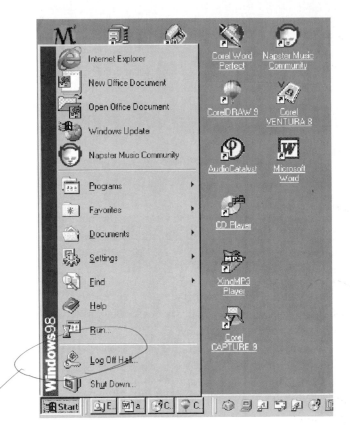

Windows 98 enables individuals in multiuser systems to log on to, and operate in, Windows 98 environments that have been specifically configured to their work needs. The Log Off User option is used to return the system to its natural setup. The Log Off entry may not appear in some installations, such as standalone machines that are not connected to a network environment.

The Favorites entry is included to enable the user to store locations of often-used files. These files can be local to the machine, located on a local area network, or remotely located on the Internet. The Internet Explorer checks Web sites specified in the Favorites folder regularly for updated information.

The Shut Down option from the menu has been changed so that there are only three possible methods listed for shutting down the session. They are Shut Down, Restart (warm boot), and Restart in MS-DOS mode. Windows 98 also includes a Standby option in the Shut Down menu. This option enables the user to put the system in a power-conservation mode when it will not be active for some time. Standby keeps Windows ready to go when an event happens, but does not keep the system I/O devices awake.

Additional items can be added to the Start menu so that they can be used directly from this menu. In doing so, the normal method of clicking Start, pointing to the Program option, and moving through submenus can be avoided. To move a frequently used item to the top of the Start menu, just drag its icon to the Start button on the taskbar.

In Windows 98, you also can move all your frequently used programs to the Programs submenu. Frequently used items can be moved to the Windows 98 taskbar, the QuickLaunch toolbar, or user-created toolbars for easy access.

> **TEST TIP**
>
> Know how to navigate to various parts of Windows 9x through the Start menus.

Windows 95 Control Panel

The Control Panel in Windows 95 can be accessed from multiple locations within the system. One Control Panel folder is located under the My Computer icon; another copy can be found under the Start\Settings path. Both folders access the Control Panel window, depicted in Figure 7.65. This window contains icons for every device attached to he system. The Control Panel icon provides access to the configuration information for each the system's installed devices specific to its type.

Double-clicking any of the device icons produces a Properties dialog box for that device. Each box differs in that they contain information specific to the selected device. These dialog boxes may have a number of different folder tabs along their tops. Each tab is labeled with the type of information it holds. Clicking a tab displays additional information for that dialog page.

FIGURE 7.65
The Windows 95 Control Panel.

The most important uses of the Control Panel are as follows:

◆ Adding or removing new hardware or software components to the system

◆ Modifying system device settings

◆ Modifying desktop items

The Control Panel is the primary user interface for assigning ports for printers and mice, as well as for specifying how various peripheral devices respond. The *Add New Hardware* and *Add/Remove Programs* icons are used to establish interrupt and port assignments for new hardware devices and to install device drivers to support the hardware.

The Windows 98 Control Panel

The Windows 98 Control Panel remains the user's primary interface for configuring system components. It has been enlarged to control a number of new functions, as illustrated in Figure 7.66. In addition to the Windows 95 configuration icons, Windows 98 adds Infrared Device Control options, an Internet Configuration tool, a Power Management utility, support for Scanners/Digital cameras, and additional modem and communication control functions in the form of a Telephony utility. The final addition to the Control Panel is the Users icon that provides tools to establish and manage profiles for multiple users on the system.

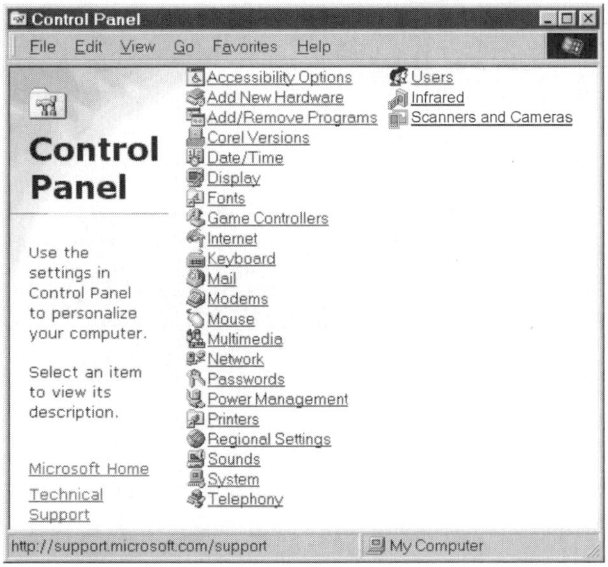

FIGURE 7.66
Windows 98 Control Panel icons.

The Control Panel can be accessed through the My Computer icon on the Desktop, or through the Settings entry in the Start menu.

Installation Wizards

The Add New Hardware icon brings the Hardware Installation Wizard into action. It immediately asks the user whether Windows should search for the new hardware through a PnP-style detection process. Clicking the Next option causes Windows to conduct the hardware-detection operation. If the device is not PnP, or if it must be installed manually because Windows 9x could not detect it, selecting the No option and clicking Next produces a hardware component list similar to the one shown in Figure 7.67. The Hardware Wizard guides the manual installation process from this point and prompts the user for any necessary configuration information. If Windows 9x does not support the device, you must click the Have Disk button and load drivers supplied by the device's manufacturer.

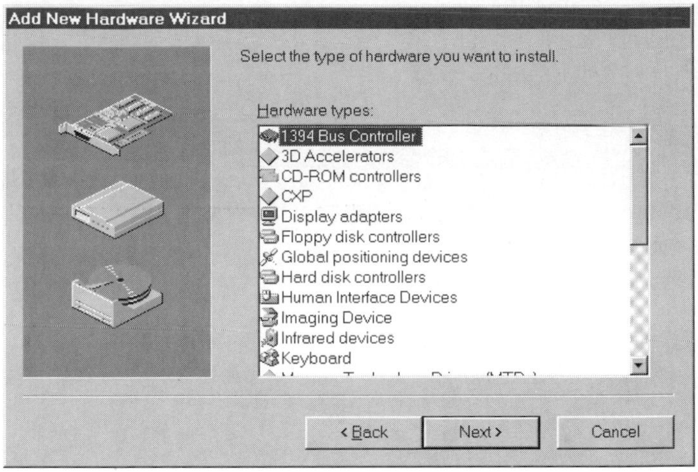

FIGURE 7.67
The Hardware Wizard's Device Selection page.

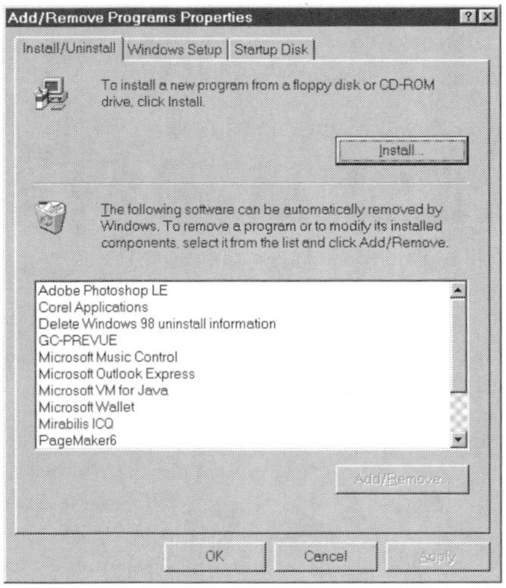

FIGURE 7.68
The Install/Uninstall Wizard tab.

The Add/Remove Programs icon leads to the Install/Uninstall screen illustrated in Figure 7.68. This page can be used to install new programs from floppy disks or CDs by just clicking the Install button. Conversely, programs listed in the Programs window can be removed from the system by highlighting their title and clicking the Add/Remove button.

The Windows Setup tab is used to add or remove selected Windows 9x components, such as communications packages or additional system tools. The Windows Startup Disk tab is used to create a clean startup disk for emergency start purposes after a crash. This disk can be used to boot the system to the command prompt (not the Windows desktop) so that you can begin troubleshooting failed startups. The Windows 98 start disk provides CD-ROM support that is not available with the Windows 95 start disk.

> **TEST TIP**
>
> Remember the location of the Control Panel screen that is used to create a Windows start disk.

The System Icon

One of the main Control Panel icons is the System icon. Clicking this icon produces the System Properties window displayed in Figure 7.69. This window features tabs for General information, the Device Manager, Hardware Profiles, and system Performance.

The General tab supplies information about the system's microprocessor type and RAM capacity, as well as its ownership and registration.

Device Manager

The Device Manager utility, depicted in Figure 7.70, provides a graphical representation of the devices configured in the system. This interface can be used to identify installed ports, update device drivers, and change I/O settings. It also can be used to manually isolate hardware and configuration conflicts. The problem device can be examined to see where the conflict is occurring. In Windows 9x, the Device Manager can be accessed through the Start/Settings/Control Panel/System path.

The Device Manager page contains a set of buttons that permit its various functions to be accessed. These buttons include Properties, Refresh, Remove, and Print.

Typical Device Manager Properties pages provide tabs that can be used to access General information, device Settings, device Drivers information, and device Resources requirements and usage. Each device may have some or all these tabs available depending on the type of device it is and what its requirements are.

The information under the tabs can be used to change the properties associated with the selected device. This often becomes necessary when resource conflicts occur in a system that has legacy devices installed. The Device Manager can be used to identify possible causes of these IRQ, DMA, I/O, and memory-settings conflicts. Use of the Device Manager to isolate problems is discussed in Chapter 9.

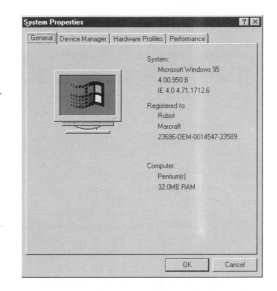

FIGURE 7.69
The System Properties window.

TEST TIP

Memorize the pathway to the Device Manager's Properties screens.

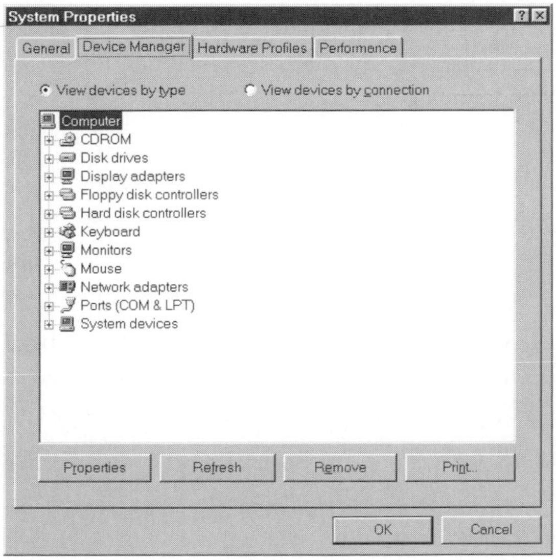

FIGURE 7.70
The Windows 9x Device Manager.

Hardware Profiles

The System icon's Hardware Profiles tab provides a window that can be used to establish different hardware configuration profiles to be implemented at startup. Most systems do not require any additional profiles. The System icon's Performance tab displays information about the system's installed RAM, system resource usage, virtual memory settings, and disk FAT type.

The final major Control Panel function is to enable users to customize the Windows 9x desktop. This customization includes such things as setting screen colors, changing the Windows wallpaper, and selecting screen savers.

Wallpaper is the pattern that shows behind the various application windows. Screen savers are screen displays that remain in motion while the system is setting idle. This utility prevents a single display from remaining onscreen for a prolonged time. This keeps the image from being "burned into" the screen. When this happens, the image becomes a permanent ghost on the screen and the monitor is ruined.

NAVIGATING WINDOWS NT/2000

Many of the Windows NT/2000 structures and navigation methods should appear very familiar after reading the Windows 9x material. With Version 4.0, Microsoft introduced a Windows 9x-like user interface to the Windows NT operating system. This includes the desktop with its icons, the pop-up Start menu, and the toolbar.

Windows NT/2000 Desktops

The Windows NT/2000 desktops include most of the same features found in their Windows 9x counterpart. The standard desktop icons in Windows NT 4.0 are the same as those mentioned for Windows 9x (that is, My Computer, Network Neighborhood, Inbox, and the Recycle Bin). If the operating system is installed on a standalone unit that does not have a network card installed, the Network Neighborhood icon will not be present on the desktop. The functions of these icons are identical to those described for the Windows 9x versions.

Figure 7.71 depicts the Windows 2000 desktop with the Start menu expanded. Notice that the standard desktop icons from Windows 2000 include My Computer, My Network Places, and the Recycle Bin.

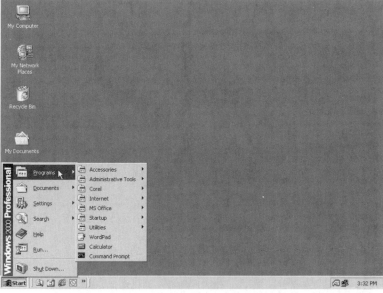

FIGURE 7.71
Windows 2000 desktop.

Windows 2000 operations typically begin from the Start menu that pops up when the Start button is clicked. The Windows NT/2000 Start menu contains Programs, Documents, Settings, Find, Help, Run, and Shut Down options. Selecting one of these options from the menu causes a pop up submenu or dialog box to display. As with the desktop icons, the operations of the Windows NT/2000 Start menu options are identical to the descriptions of their Windows 9x counterparts.

The Windows 2000 taskbar is located at the bottom of the display by default. The taskbar displays icons that represent programs running in the system. Even though the taskbar is normally located at the bottom of the screen, it can be moved to either side of the screen, or to the top of the display. When moved to the top of the screen, the Start menu drops down from above instead of popping up from the bottom.

Windows 2000 features an intelligent, personalized Programs menu. It monitors the user's program usage, and after the first six accesses, arranges the menu options according to those most frequently used. The menu options displayed change based on their usage. Less frequently used programs are not displayed in the list, but can be accessed by clicking the double arrow at the bottom of the list. The hidden portion of the list appears after a short delay. When this occurs, the six most frequently used applications are highlighted. This reduces screen clutter and makes it easier for users to access their most used items.

You can easily rename Start menu items in Windows 2000. To do so, just right-click the menu item and choose the Rename option from the context-sensitive pop-up menu. Then type the new name in the text entry box. You can accomplish all of this without opening the Start menu.

The contents of the Windows 2000 Control Panel can be cascaded as a submenu of the Start button for quick access. The My Documents menu also can be cascaded off the Start menu for fast access to documents.

The My Documents concept has been expanded to include a My Pictures folder that acts as the default location to hold graphic files. The Windows 2000 dialog boxes include an image preview function that enables the user to locate graphic files efficiently. The dialog box View menu option enables the user to toggle between Large and Small Icons, Details, and Thumbnail views. The dialog boxes can be resized to accommodate as many thumbnail images as desired.

The My Network Places folder replaces the Network Neighborhood folder employed in previous Windows NT and 9x versions. This utility enables the user to create shortcut icons to network shares on the desktop. A network share is an existing shared resource (for instance, printer, drive, modem, or folder) located on a remote system. The new icon acts as an alias to link the system to the share point on the remote unit.

Locating, Accessing, and Retrieving Information in Windows NT/2000

Locating, accessing, and retrieving information in Windows NT and Windows 2000 is virtually the same as with the Windows 9x operating systems. The major Windows NT/2000 user interfaces are as follows:

◆ My Computer

◆ Start menu

◆ Windows Explorer

◆ Internet Explorer (must be added on in Windows NT)

◆ Network Neighborhood (My Network Places in Windows 2000)

◆ Windows NT/2000 dialog boxes (windows)

These interfaces provide user access to all the major areas of the system. The My Computer window enables users to access every hardware device in the system. The Start menu provides the user with access to the system regardless of what else is occurring in the system. In doing so, it provides access to the system's installed applications, a search engine for finding data in the system, and the operating system's Help file structure. The Windows NT Windows Explorer graphically displays the entire computer system in a hierarchical tree structure. This enables the user to manipulate all the system's software and hardware. Similarly, the Network Neighborhood window extends the Windows Explorer structure to include network and domain structures. The Internet Explorer supplies the system with a tightly linked Web connection.

Alternate-clicking, (right-clicking) also is employed in the Windows NT platform to access context-sensitive options through pop-up menus on the screen. Alternate-clicking an icon produces a pop-up menu, similar to the one depicted in Figure 7.72. As with Windows 9x operating systems, these Windows NT menus enable the user to Copy a File, Create a Shortcut, Close a Folder, or examine properties of the system's installed devices. Right-click menus also may contain additional items that have been inserted by applications that they serve.

Right-clicking over an open area of the desktop produces a pop-up menu that enables the user to arrange icons on the desktop, create new folders and shortcuts, and see the properties of the system's video display.

FIGURE 7.72
Windows NT right-click menus.

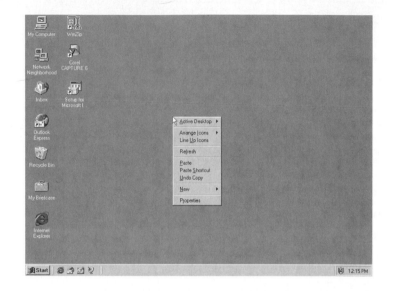

Windows 2000 offers extended common dialog boxes for File/Open, File/Print, and File/Save options. These dialog boxes provide easy organization and navigation of the system's hard drives and also provide navigation columns that grant quick access to frequently used folders, such as the My Documents and My Pictures folders. Figure 7.73 depicts the File/Open common dialog box. The navigation column also provides easy access to the My Network Places folder.

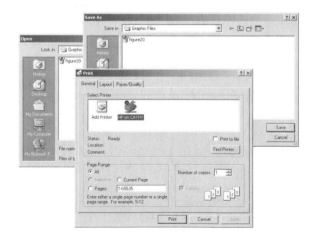

FIGURE 7.73
Windows 2000 common dialog boxes.

Windows 2000 folders include a customizable toolbar with Windows 98-like navigation buttons. The Explorer toolbar, depicted in Figure 7.74, comes with a collection of about 20 add-on buttons that you can use to customize its available options. To modify the toolbar, right-click the toolbar and then select the Customize option from the pop-up menu. Additional buttons include Move To, Copy To, Search, Map Drive, Favorites, and Full Screen. The Full Screen option is new and can be used to toggle between maximized and normal window sizes.

FIGURE 7.74
Windows 2000 Explorer toolbar.

Windows 2000 also includes powerful new search capabilities for searching the local hard drive and the Web. The new HTML-like Search function in Windows 2000 replaces the Start menu's Find option from previous Windows desktops. The Search feature provides three distinct search options:

◆ For Files and Folders

◆ On the Internet

◆ For People

The For Files and Folders option opens a dual-page version of the Windows 98/NT4 Find Files and Folders dialog window. This window provides all the old Windows search functions and adds powerful new ones, such as case-sensitive searches. These options are available through the Advanced button.

Selecting the On the Internet option brings up a search bar that establishes a link to a predetermined Internet search engine such as Yahoo! or AOL.

The Search for People option opens a Lightweight Directory Access Protocol (LDAP) dialog window that resembles the one in Windows 98 or Internet Explorer 4.0.

Enabling the Microsoft Index Server function produces particularly fast searches. The Indexing service runs in the background to provide content indexing on the local hard drive. Windows 2000 Professional includes a local version of the Indexing service that operates with the local hard drive. In a network environment that uses Windows 2000 servers, the Content Indexing service can be performed by the server. The Index Service Management tools are located in the Start/Programs/Administrative Tools path.

Searching with the Context Indexing feature enables the user to write Boolean logic expressions (such as AND, OR, and NOT) to find specific content quickly.

WINDOWS NT SECURITY

Since its creation, one of the main features of the Windows NT operating system has been its security capabilities. As an operating system designed to work in business networks, data security is one of its most important functions. Windows NT provides security in four forms:

◆ User security in the form of user logon and passwords required to access the system

◆ User security between users of the same computer to control access to local data

◆ Identification of attempted security breaches through audit trails

◆ Memory-usage protection between applications running on the same hardware

In a Windows NT system, a user must have a user account on a particular computer to gain access to its operation. In a workgroup setting, this account must be set up on each computer. In a domain environment, however, the account can be established on the domain server.

When Windows NT is first installed, a master Administrator account is established. The administrator has rights and permissions to all the system's hardware and software resources. The administrator in turn grants rights and permissions to other users as necessary.

The administrator can deal with users on an individual basis, or may gather users into groups that can be administered uniformly. In doing so, the administrator can assign permissions or restrictions on an individual or an entire group. The value of using groups lies in the time saved by being able to apply common rights to several users instead of applying them one by one.

Each user and group in the NT environment has a profile that describes the resources and desktop configurations created for him or her. Settings in the profile can be used to limit the actions users can perform, such as installing, removing, configuring, adjusting, or copying resources. When users log on to the system, it checks their profile and adjusts the system according to their information. This information is stored in the WINNT*login_name*\NTUSER.DAT file.

The Windows NT Server operating system can be used to establish profiles for the entire network from a central location. Its administration package also can be used to establish roaming profiles that enable users to log on to any workstation on the network and work under their own profile settings.

The Windows NT User Manager utility can be accessed through the Start button's Start\Programs\Administrative Tools path. Clicking the User Manager entry produces the User Manager window displayed in Figure 7.75. To create a new user, select the New User option from the User pull-down menu. Enter the necessary user information in the New User dialog box. The user's username and password must be supplied at least the first time the user logs on. If the User Must Change Password option is selected, the user can change the password to something more personal as soon as he or she logs on.

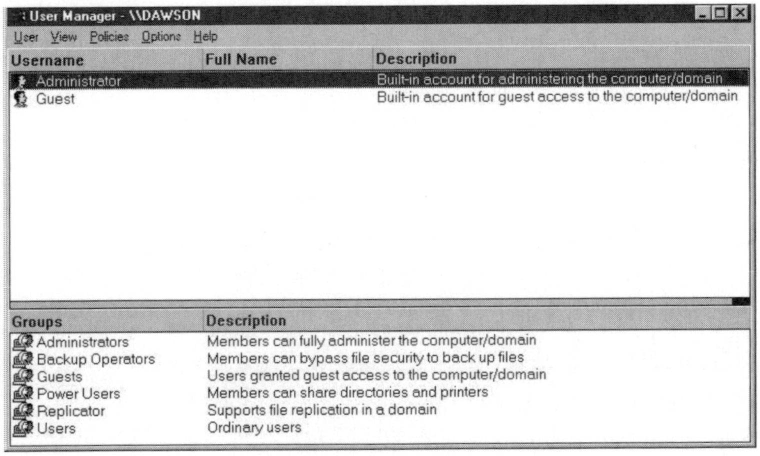

FIGURE 7.75
The User Manager window.

Selecting the Groups icon at the bottom of the screen brings up the Group Memberships dialog box depicted in Figure 7.76. Groups that the designated user is a part of are listed in the left window. Groups that the user is not a part of are listed in the right window. To add the user to a group, just highlight the desired group in the right window and click the Add button.

FIGURE 7.76
The Group Memberships dialog box.

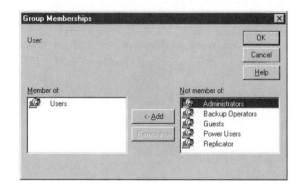

Windows 2000 Security

Windows 2000 offers a much improved security structure over previous Windows versions. The new security features apply to both LAN and wide area communications. The main security improvement is the adoption of the Kerberos authentication protocol.

Authentication is a process that determines that users on the network are who they say they are. The Kerberos protocol is used to enable users to authenticate without sending a password over the network. Instead, the user acquires a unique key from the network's central security authority at logon. The security authority is provided by the domain controller referred to as the Key Distribution Center (KDC).

When a client makes a request to access a network resource or program, it authenticates itself with the KDC as described in Figure 7.77. The KDC responds by returning a session ticket to the client that is used to establish a connection to the requested resource. The ticket can be used only to authenticate the client's access to services and resources for a limited amount of time. During that time, the client presents the ticket to the application server that verifies the user and provides access to the requested program.

The key is cached on the local machine so that the user can reuse the key at a later time to access the resource. Keys are typically good for about eight hours, so there is no need for repeated interaction between the user and the KDC. This reduces the number of interactions that must be made across the network and, thereby, reduces the traffic load on the network in general. In addition, no passwords are circulated during the process, so there is no chance of compromising them.

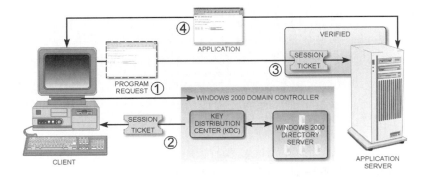

FIGURE 7.77
Kerberos protocol operations.

Digital Certificates are another major security feature in Windows 2000. Digital certificates are password-protected, encrypted data files that include data that identifies the transmitting system and can be used to authenticate external users to the network through virtual private networks (VPNs). VPNs use message encryption and other security techniques to ensure that only authorized users can intercept and access the message as it passes through public transmission media. In particular, VPNs provide secure Internet communications by establishing encrypted data tunnels across the WAN that cannot be penetrated by others.

When the certificates are combined with security standards such as the IP Security protocol (IPSec), secure and encrypted TCP/IP data can be passed across public networks, such as the Internet. IPSec is a secure, encrypted version of the IP protocol. IPSec client software connects remote users to a VPN server by creating an encrypted tunnel across the Internet to the remote user, as illustrates in Figure 7.78.

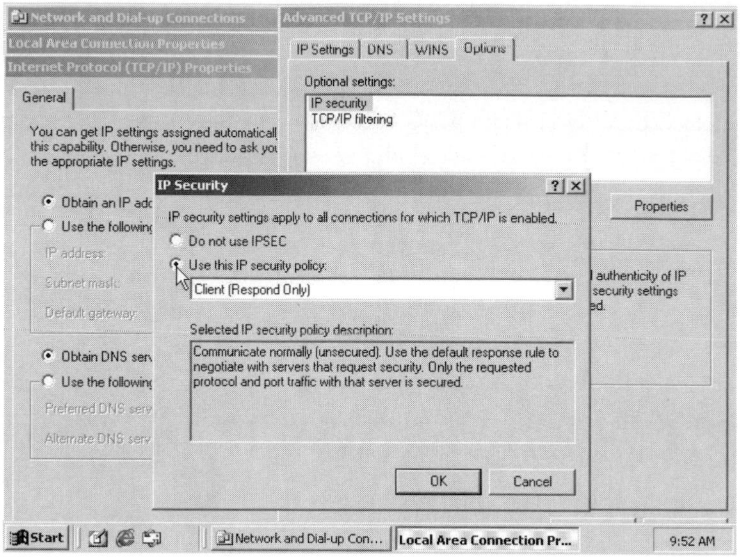

FIGURE 7.78
IP Security protocol operations.

In addition to IPSec, Windows 2000 continues to offer Point-to-Point Tunneling Protocol (PPTP) and Layer 2 Tunneling Protocol (L2TP) as alternative security technologies for VPNs. L2TP can be used in conjunction with IPSec to pass the IPSec packets through routers that perform network address translation.

In addition to the outstanding network security features, Windows 2000 provides effective local hard drive security through its Encrypting File System (EFS) feature. EFS enables the user to encrypt files stored on the drive using keys only the designated user (or an authorized recovery agent) can decode. This prevents theft of data by those who do not have the password or a decoding tool. EFS is simple to use because it is actually an attribute that can be established for file or folders.

Portable Design

The Windows 2000 operating system brings many new features for portable computers to the Windows NT line. In addition to furnishing the power-management and PnP features discussed earlier, Windows 2000 provides increased data security functions and greater administrator control over mobile PCs.

Portable computer users in the business world typically spend some time connected to a company network and other times traveling away from the network connection. The Windows 2000 Synchronization Manager enables the user to select network files and folders to travel without an active connection to a server.

When the client wants to take files, the files are moved from the server to the portable and the Synchronization Manager synchronizes the time and date version information concerning the files. While the portable client is offline, the user can continue to use the files under his network name. When the user returns to the network environment, the client resynchronizes the files with the server versions and the newer copy overwrites the older version. The synchronization process is described in Figure 7.79.

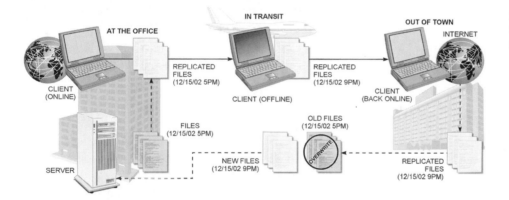

FIGURE 7.79
Windows 2000 Synchronization Manager.

The Windows 2000 EFS feature further enhances the security of files on portable computers by enabling users to designate files and folders so that they can be accessed only by using the proper encryption key. Public key encryption techniques employ two keys to ensure the security of the encrypted data: A public key and a private key. The public key (known to everyone) is used to encrypt the data, whereas the private or secret key (known only to the specified recipient) is used to decrypt it. The public and private keys are related in such a way that the private key cannot be decoded just by possessing the public key.

Windows 2000 portability features are not limited to mobile computers. Many organizations have mobile employees who work at different computers within a given location. To accommodate this type of mobility, Windows 2000 uses roaming profiles that store each user's desktop, Start menu setup, and My Document folder on the server and redirects them to the local client where the user logs on. Windows 2000 also can install applications the user requires on the local client when that user logs on.

CREATING AND MANAGING FILES

▶ 1.2 Identify basic concepts and procedures for creating, viewing, and managing files and directories, including procedures for changing file attributes and the ramifications of those changes (for example, security issues).

The A+ Operating System Technology objective 1.2 states that the test taker should be able to "identify basic concepts and procedures for creating, viewing, and managing files and directories, including procedures for changing file attributes and the ramifications of changes (for example, security issues)."

Disk-based computers handle information in the form of files. The computer technician must be to create and manipulate files in the major operating system versions. The following sections cover file handling and conventions in DOS, Windows 9x, and Windows NT/2000.

DOS Files

Disk-based systems store and handle related pieces of information in groups called files. The system recognizes and keeps track of the different files in the system by their filenames. Therefore, each file in the system is required to have a filename that differs from that of any other file in the directory. If two files having the same name were present within the same directory of the system, the computer would become confused and fail to operate properly. This is because it would not be able tell which version of the file is supposed to be worked on. Each time a new file of information is created, it is necessary to give it a unique filename by which DOS can identify and store it.

Files and Filenames

Files are created through programming packages, or by applications. When they are created, they must be assigned a filename. In an MS-DOS environment, you must remember a few rules when creating new filenames. As described earlier in this chapter, the filename consists of two parts: A name and an extension. The filename is a combination of alphanumeric characters and is between one and eight characters in length. The extension is an optional addition to the name that begins with a period, and is followed by between one and three characters.

Extensions are not required on filenames, but they often prove useful in describing the contents of a file, or in identifying different versions of the same file. If a filename that already exists is used to store another file, the computer writes the information in the new file over that of the old file, assuming that they are both the same. Therefore, only the new file will still exist. The information in the old file will be lost.

Many software packages automatically generate filename extensions for files they create. The software does this so that other parts of the program, which may work with the same file, can identify where the file came from, or what form it is in.

In any event, remember the following seven items when assigning and using filenames:

1. All files must have a filename.

2. All filenames must be different from any other filename in the system, or on the disk presently in use.

3. DOS filenames are up to eight characters long with an optional three-character extension (separated from the basic filename by a period).

4. When using a filename in a command, you must also use its extension, if one exists.

5. Some special characters are not allowed in filenames. These are: [,], :, ;, +, =, \, /, and ,.

6. When telling DOS where to carry out a command, you must tell it on which disk drive the operation is to be performed. The drive must be specified by its letter name followed by a colon (that is, A:, B:, C:, and so on).

7. The complete and proper way to specify a file call is the drive specifier, the filename, and the filename extension, in that order (that is, B:FILENAME.EXT).

The following DOS commands are used to carry out file-level operations. The format for using them is identical to the disk- and directory-related commands discussed earlier. However, the command must include the filename and its extension at the end of the directory path. Depending on the operation, the complete path may be required, or a default to the currently active drive will be assumed.

◆ **COPY.** The file **COPY** command copies a specified file from one place (disk or directory) to another:

```
C:\>COPY A:FILENAME.EXT B:FILENAME.EXT
```

C:\>COPY A:Filename.Ext B: is used if the file is to have the same name in its new location; the second filename specifier can be omitted.

In a single-drive system, you must switch disks in the middle of the operation. (Notice that the drive B: specifier is used even though only drive A: is present.) Fortunately, the DOS produces a message to tell you when to put the target disk in the drive. This is not required in a two-drive system and no prompt is given. The transfer can be specified in any direction desired:

```
C:\>COPY B:FILENAME.EXT A:
```

The only thing to keep in mind in this situation is to place the source disk in drive B: and the target disk in drive A: before entering the command.

◆ **XCOPY.** This command copies all the files in a directory, along with any subdirectories and their files. This command is particularly useful in copying files and directories between disks with different formats (that is, from a 1.2MB disk to a 1.44MB disk):

```
C:\>XCOPY A: B: /S
```

This command copies all the files and directories from the disk in drive A: (except hidden and System files) to the disk in drive B:. The **/S** switch instructs the **XCOPY** command to copy directories and subdirectories.

◆ **DEL** or **ERASE.** This command enables the user to remove unwanted files from the disk when typed in at the DOS prompt:

```
C:\>DEL FILENAME.EXT
C:\>ERASE B:FILENAME.EXT
```

Take a great deal of care when using this command. If a file is erased accidentally, it may not be retrievable.

◆ **REN.** This command enables the user to change the name or extension of a filename:

```
C:\>REN A:FILENAME.EXT NEWNAME.EXT
```

Using this command does not change the contents of the file, only its name. The original filename (but not the file) is deleted. If you want to retain the original file and filename, a **COPY** command, using different filenames, can be used:

```
C:\>COPY A:FILENAME.EXT B:NEWNAME.EXT
```

◆ **TYPE.** This command shows the contents of a designated file on the monitor screen.

C:\>TYPE AUTOEXEC.BAT displays the contents of the AUTOEXEC.BAT file.

◆ **FC.** This file-compare command compares two files to see whether they are the same. This operation is normally performed after a file **COPY** has been performed to ensure that the file was duplicated and located correctly:

```
C:\>FC A:FILENAME.EXT B:
```

If the filename is changed during the copy operation, the command must be typed as follows:

```
C:\>FC A:FILENAME.EXT B:NEWNAME.EXT
```

◆ **ATTRIB.** This command changes file attributes such as read-only (+R or –R), archive (+A or –A), system (+S or –S), and hidden (+H or –H). The + and – signs are to add or subtract the attribute from the file.

```
C:\>ATTRIB +R C:\DOS\MEMOS.DOC
```

This command sets the file MEMOS.DOC as a read-only file. Read-only attributes protect the file from accidentally being overwritten. Similarly, one of the main reasons for giving a file a hidden attribute is to prevent it from accidentally being erased. The system attribute is reserved for use by the operating system and marks the file as a system file.

TEST TIP:

Memorize the different DOS file attributes and be able to use the various attribute switch settings.

A common error message encountered when working with command-line operations is the Bad Command or Filename error message. This type of error message generally occurs when the path specified to the location of a file is incorrect, or when the file is missing or misspelled.

DOS Shortcuts

DOS provides some command-line shortcuts through the keyboard's function keys. Some of the most notable are the F1 and F3 function keys. The F1 key brings the preceding command back from the command-line buffer, one character at a time. Likewise, the F3 key brings back the entire preceding command, through a single keystroke.

When using filenames in DOS command-line operations, the filename appears at the end of the directory path in the source and destination locations. The * notation is called a wildcard and allows operations to be performed with only partial source or destination information. Using the notation as *.* tells the software to perform the designated command on any file found on the disk using any filename and extension.

TEST TIP:

Memorize the DOS wildcard characters and be able to use their variations.

You can use a question mark (?) as a wildcard, to represent a single character in a DOS name or extension. You can use multiple question marks to represent multiple characters in a filename or extension.

Data from a DOS command can be modified to fit a prescribed output format, through the use of filter commands. The main filter commands are **MORE**, **FIND**, and **SORT**. The filter command is preceded by a pipe symbol (|) on the command line, when output from another DOS command is to be modified. To view the contents of a batch file that is longer than the screen display can present at one time, for example, type **Type C:\XXX.BAT|MORE**. If the information to be modified is derived from another file, the less than (<) symbol is used.

The **FIND** command searches through files and commands for specified characters. Likewise, the **SORT** command presents files in alphabetic order.

Windows 9x Files

The Windows 9x file system does away with the 8.3 character file-name system implemented under DOS. In Windows 95, *long file-names* of up to 255 characters can be used, meaning that they can be more descriptive in nature. When these filenames are displayed in non-Windows 9x systems, they are truncated (shortened) to fit the 8.3 DOS character format and identified by a tilde character (~) followed by a single-digit number.

The tilde character is placed in the seventh character position of the filename, to show that the filename is being displayed in a shortened manner, as an alias for the full-length filename. The number following the mark will have a value of one assigned to it, unless another file has already been assigned the alias with a one value. Customers with older operating systems may overlook files because they are saved in this manner.

The tilde character is inserted into the seventh character space for up to nine iterations of similar filenames. After that, Windows replaces the sixth character for iterations up to 99. Windows 95 applies this same convention to the naming of directories as well. To change a long directory name from the command line requires that quotation marks be placed around the name. Consider the following examples:

◆ OLDLONGFILE.TXT = OLDLON~1.TXT

◆ OLDLONGTABLE.TXT = OLDLON~2.TXT

◆ OLDLONGGRAPHIC.TXT = OLDLO~63.TXT

You can use additional characters in the Windows 95 long filenames. These characters include + , : = [and]. Blank spaces also can be used in long filenames.

> **TEST TIP**
>
> Know how Windows 9x handles similar long filenames in a DOS format.

Windows NT/2000 Files

From Windows NT 4.0 forward, the NT operating system has been able to handle long filenames. Filenames in Windows NT can be up to 256 characters long. Windows NT uses a proprietary method for reducing long filenames to MS-DOS-compatible 8.3 filenames. Instead of just truncating the filename, inserting a tilde, and then assigning a number to the end of the filename, Windows NT performs a mathematical operation on the long name to generate a truly unique MS-DOS-compatible filename.

Filenames in Windows 2000 can be up to 215 characters long including spaces. Windows 2000 uses a proprietary method for reducing long filenames to MS-DOS-compatible 8.3 filenames. Instead of just truncating the filename, inserting a tilde, and then assigning a number to the end of the filename, Windows 2000 performs a mathematical operation on the long name to generate a truly unique MS-DOS-compatible filename. Windows 2000 filenames cannot contain the following characters: /\:*?"<>|.

Basically, the Windows 2000 algorithm employed to produce DOS-compatible filenames removes any characters that are illegal under DOS, removes any extra periods from the filename, truncates the filename to six characters, inserts a tilde, and adds an ID number to the end of the name. When five or more names are generated that would result in duplicate short names, however, Windows NT changes its truncation method. Beginning with the sixth filename, the first two characters of the name are retained, the next four characters are generated through the mathematical algorithm, and, finally, a tilde with an ID number are attached to the end of the name. This method is used to create DOS-compliant short filenames for MS-DOS-, Windows 3.x-, and Windows 9x-compliant FAT systems, as well as the proprietary Windows NT File System (NTFS).

Windows 2000 creates properties sheets for each file and folder in the system. These sheets contain information about the file (or folder) such as its size, location, and creation date. When you view the file's properties, you also can see its attributes, file type, the program that is designed to open it, and when the file was last opened or modified.

The NTFS file system employed in Windows 2000 provides two new file types that technicians must deal with: Encrypted files and compressed files. The Windows 2000 NTFS system provides an Encrypting File System (EFS) utility that is the basis of storing encrypted files on NTFS volumes. After a file or folder has been encrypted, only the user who encrypted it can access it. The original user can work with the file or folder just as he or should would a regular file. However, other users cannot open or share the file. (They can delete it, however.)

For other users to be able to access the file or folder, it must first be decrypted. The encryption protection disappears when the file or folder is moved to a non-NTFS partition. Only files on NTFS volumes can be encrypted. Conversely, System files and compressed files cannot be encrypted.

Files and folders can be encrypted from the command line using the **Cipher** command. Information about the **Cipher** command and its many switches can be obtained by typing **Cipher /?** at the command prompt. Files also can be encrypted through the Windows Explorer. Encryption is treated as a file attribute in Windows 2000. Therefore, to encrypt a file you just need to access its properties page by right-clicking it and selecting the Properties option from the pop-up menu. Move to the Advanced screen under the General tab and click the Encrypt Contents to Secure Data check box, as illustrated in Figure 7.80. Decrypting a file is a simple matter of clearing the check box.

The Windows Explorer also can be used to compress files and folders on NTFS volumes. Like encryption, Windows 2000 treats NTFS compression as a file attribute. To compress a particular file or folder, right-click it in the Windows Explorer and then select the Properties option, followed by the Advanced button to access its Advanced Properties screen, as illustrated in Figure 7.81. Click the Compress Contents to Save Disk Space check box to compress the file or folder.

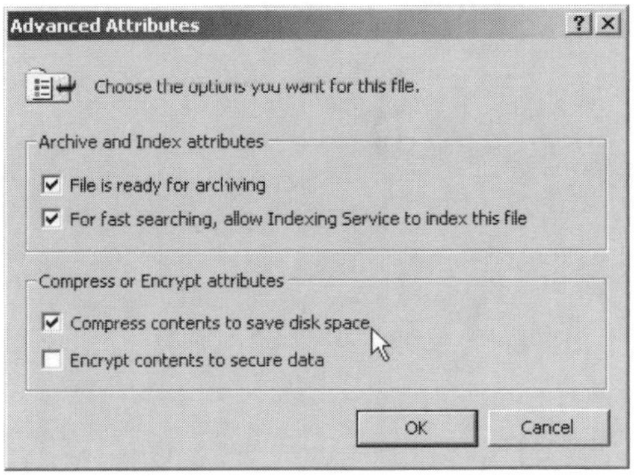

Likewise, an entire drive can be compressed through the My Computer icon. From the File menu, select the Properties option and click the Compress Drive to Save Disk Space check box.

As with the encrypting function, Windows 2000 files and folders can be compressed only on NTFS volumes. If you move a file into a compressed folder, the file is compressed automatically. These files cannot be encrypted while they are compressed. Compressed files can be marked so that they are displayed in a second color for easy identification. This is accomplished through the Folder Options setting in the Control Panel. From this page, select the View tab and click the Display Compressed Files and Folder with Alternate Color check box. The only other indication that you will have concerning a compressed or encrypted file or folder is an attribute listing when the view setting is configured to display in Web style.

FIGURE 7.80
Encrypting a file.

FIGURE 7.81
Compressing a file.

Windows Explorer

The file-management functions in Windows 9x and NT/2000 are performed through the Windows Explorer interface. This manager is located under the Start/Programs path from the desktop. By clicking the Windows Explorer entry, the system's directory structure appears, as shown in Figure 7.82. The Windows Explorer also can be accessed by right-clicking the Start button or the My Computer icon and then selecting the Explore option.

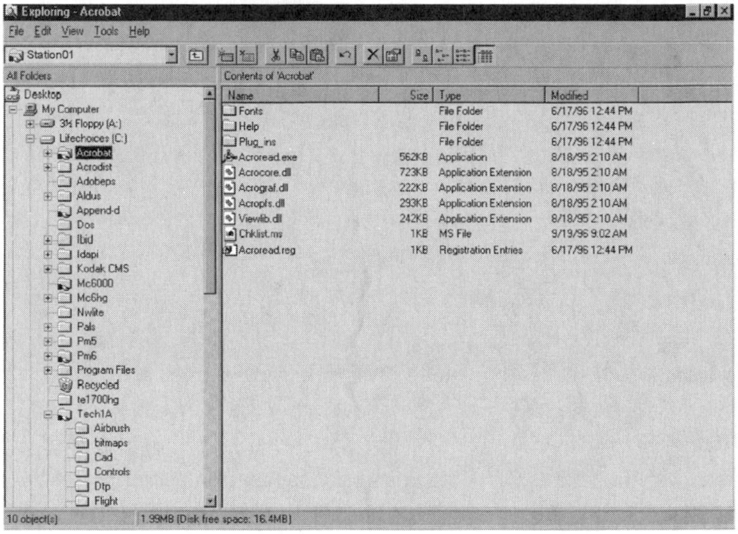

FIGURE 7.82
The Windows 9x Explorer screen.

The Windows Explorer enables the user to copy, move, and erase files on any of the system's drives. Its screen is divided into two parts. The left side displays the system's *directory tree*, showing all the directories and subdirectories of its available drives. The right side of the Windows Explorer screen displays the files of the selected directory.

In Windows, directories and subdirectories are referred to, and depicted as, folders (and subfolders). Any drive or directory can be selected by clicking its icon or folder. The contents of the folder can be expanded by clicking on the plus (+) sign beside the folder. Conversely, the same folder can be contracted by clicking on the minus (–) sign in the same box.

Windows 9x is not limited to just showing the directories, subdirectories, and files on local drives. It also displays drives and folders from throughout the network environment. The contents of the local drives are displayed at the top of the directory tree. If the system is connected to a network, the additional resources available through the network are displayed below those of the local system, as a continuation of its tree structure. One noticeable difference exists between the Windows 9x and Windows 2000 main tree structures in Windows Explorer: The Printers folder has been removed from the main tree and placed as a sub-branch of the Control Panel folder.

diff between Win 2000 & Win 98

As mentioned previously, the right side of the Windows Explorer screen displays the files of the selected directory. The status bar at the bottom of the screen provides information about the number and size of the files in the selected directory. The View menu on the Explorer menu bar can be used to set the display for large or small icons, as well as simple or detailed lists. The Explorer's View functions are the same as those described for the My Computer menu bar, shown earlier in Figure 7.59.

You can display multiple directories on the Explorer screen. This feature makes it easy to perform file operations by just opening another window. Like Windows 3.x, Windows 9x provides drag-and-drop file copies and moves for single and multiple files, as well as drag-and-drop printing capabilities.

The Windows Explorer also is used to perform DOS-like functions such as formatting and copying disks. Right-clicking a folder icon produces a menu that includes a Send To option, as described in Figure 7.83. Moving the mouse to this entry produces a submenu that you can use to send a selected folder or file to a floppy disk drive or to the desktop. Several files or folders can be selected for copying using the Shift key.

The contents of the right-click menu change in the Explorer, depending on the item that is selected. Because the right-click function is context sensitive, the menu produced for a folder differs from the one displayed for a document file. Each menu has options that apply to the selected item.

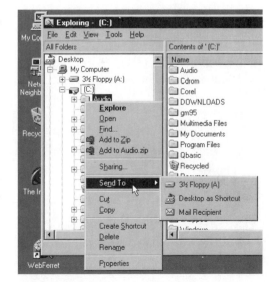

FIGURE 7.83
The Send To option.

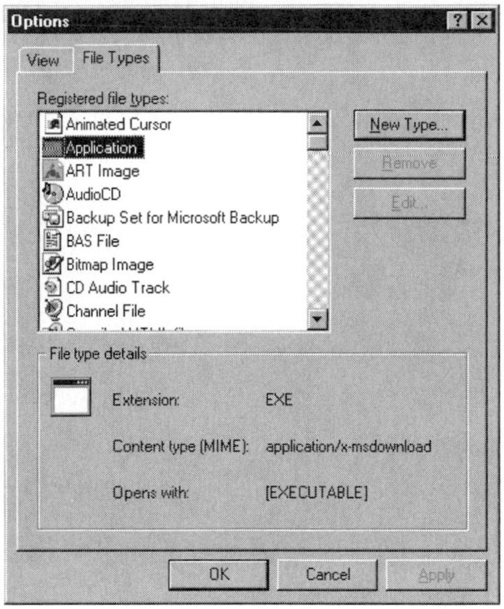

Right-clicking a document file produces options that enable the user to copy, cut, rename, open, or print the document from the Windows Explorer. This menu also provides options to create a shortcut for the document as well as to change its attributes. By default, Windows Explorer does not show SYS, INI, or DAT files. To change file attributes from the Explorer, right-click the desired file, select the Properties option from the pop-up list, move to the General page, and click the desired attribute boxes. To see hidden and system files in Windows Explorer, click the View menu option, select the Folder Options entry, click the View tab, and check the Show All Files box. If you experience difficulty with this operation from the Windows environment, you can always access the file from the command prompt and change its attributes with the **ATTRIB** command.

Selecting the Open option from the pop-up list causes Windows to examine the document to determine what type of file it is. After this has been established, Windows attempts to start the appropriate application and open the file.

If Windows cannot identify the application associated with the selected file, the operator needs to start the application and then manually open the file. However, the user also can register the file's extension type under the View/Folders option from the menu bar. This produces the Register File Types dialog box depicted in Figure 7.84.

FIGURE 7.84
The Register File Types window.

> **TEST TIP**
> Know how to navigate to various parts of Windows 9x through the Windows Explorer.

The Windows 9x File Menu

The Windows 9x Explorer's File menu performs the functions discussed in the Windows 3.x File menu. However, it includes an entry at the top of the menu titled New. Clicking this option produces the New options submenu depicted in Figure 7.85. This menu is used to create new folders, shortcuts, and files.

To create a new folder in Explorer, select a parent directory by highlighting it in the left window. Then click the File menu button, move the cursor to the New entry, slide across to the Folder option, and click it. A new unnamed folder icon appears in the right Explorer window.

The same process is used to create new files. A file icon can be produced for any of the file types registered. Right-clicking the new icon produces the menu with options to rename the icon, create a shortcut for it, and establish its properties (including its attributes).

Shortcut icons are identified by a small arrow in the lower-left corner of the icon. When a shortcut is created, Windows does not place a copy of the file or application in every location that references it. Instead, it creates an icon in each location and defines it with a link to the actual location of the program in the system. This reduces the amount of disk space required to reference the file from multiple locations.

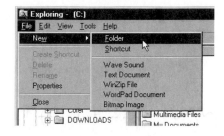

FIGURE 7.85
The New option.

DISK MANAGEMENT

▶ 1.3 Identify the procedures for basic disk management.

The A+ Operating System Technologies objective 1.3 states that the test taker should be able to "identify the procedures for basic disk management." Among other things, this objective requires the technician to be familiar with the *ScanDisk* utility, backup and restore operations, defragmentation, disk-management utilities, and file system partitioning and formatting.

DOS Disk Structure

It is important to understand how DOS sees disks. When the disk is created, its surface is electronically blank. To prepare the disk for use by the system, the following three levels of preparation that must take place, in order:

1. The low-level format (below DOS)

2. The partition (DOS **FDISK** command)

3. The high-level format (DOS **Format** command)   → *high level Format*

In the PC world, floppy disks basically come in four accepted formats: 360KB, 720KB, 1.2MB, 1.44MB, and 2.88MB. When they are formatted to one of these standards, the system performs the low- and *high-level formats* in the same operation. Floppy disks cannot be partitioned into logical disks; therefore, no partition operation needs to be performed. However, hard disk drives are created in a wide variety of physical specifications and storage capacities and, therefore, need to be partitioned so that the operating system knows how they are organized.

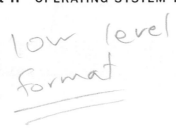

A *low-level format* is very similar to a land developer sectioning off a field for a new housing development. The process begins with surveying the property and placing markers for key structures such as roads, water lines, and electrical service. The low-level format routine is similar in that it marks off the disk into cylinders and sectors and defines their placement on the disk.

In older device-level drive types (such as ST-506 and ESDI drives), the user was required to perform the low-level format. This procedure could be accomplished through the DOS Debug program or through software diagnostic packages that came with a low-level formatter program.

Drive Partitioning

Physical hard disk drives can be divided into multiple logical drives. This operation is referred to as partitioning the drive. With earlier versions of DOS, partitioning became necessary because the capacity of hard drives exceeded the capability of the existing DOS structure to track all the possible sectors.

By creating a second logical drive on the hard disk, another complete file tracking structure is created on the drive. The operating system sees this new structure on the hard drive as a completely new disk. Therefore, it must have a new, unique drive letter assigned to it.

Figure 7.86 illustrates the concept of creating multiple logical drives on a single hard drive. This is normally done for purposes of organization and increased access speeds.

The partitioning program for MS-DOS, Windows, UNIX, and Linux is named *FDISK*. This program creates the disk's boot sector and establishes partition parameters (partition table) for the system's use.

Basically, DOS provides for two partitions on an HDD unit. The first, or the *primary partition*, must exist as the C: drive. After the primary partition has been established and properly configured, an additional partition, referred to as an *extended partition*, also is permitted. However, the extended partition may be subdivided into 23 logical drives. The extended partition cannot be deleted if logical drives have been defined within it. The active partition is the logical drive that the system will boot to. The System files must be located in this partition, and the partition must be set to Active for the system to boot up from the drive.

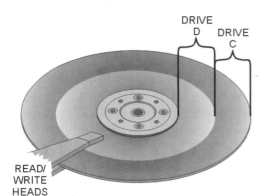

DRIVE D   DRIVE C

READ/ WRITE HEADS

FIGURE 7.86
HDD partitions.

In local and wide area networks (LANs and WANs), the concept of logical drives is carried a step further. A particular hard disk drive may be a logical drive in a large system of drives along a peer-to-peer network. On the other hand, a very large, centralized drive may be used to create several logical drives for a client/server type of network. This is accomplished by creating a logical mapping between the operating system and the desired drive, so that the local system handles the mapped drive as one of its own drives.

In some applications, partitioning is used to permit multiple operating systems to exist on the same physical drive. Because each partition on the drive contains its own boot sector, FAT and root directory, each partition can be set up to hold and boot up to a different operating system.

On a partitioned drive, a special table, called the partition table, is created in the boot sector at the very beginning of the disk. This table holds information about the location and starting point of each logical drive on the disk, along with the information about which partition has been marked as active and a Master Boot Record.

The partition table is located at the beginning of the disk because this is the point where the system looks for boot-up information. When the system checks the MBR of the physical disk during the boot process, it also checks to see which partition on the disk has been marked as active. It then jumps to that location, reads the information in that partition boot record, and boots to the operating system in that logical drive.

> **TEST TIP**
>
> Be aware of how the primary partition, extended partitions, and the active partition are related.

High-Level Formatting

The high-level format procedure is performed by the **Format** command in the MS-DOS program. This command creates two blank *file allocation tables* (FATs) and a root directory on the disk.

These elements tell the system what files are on the disk and where they can be found. Modifying the **Format** command with an **/S** switch after the drive letter designation causes the DOS System files to be moved to the drive.

Never format a disk with an older version of DOS than is currently installed on the disk. The disk can actually be damaged from this action. Before reformatting a disk, use the DOS **VER** command to determine what version of DOS is currently in use.

ver / → what version of DOS ?

Figure 7.87 describes the organization of a DOS disk and illustrates the position of the boot sector, file allocation tables, and the root directory. The remainder of the disk is dedicated to data storage. In the Chapter 1 section on booting up, it was mentioned that the first area on each logical DOS disk, or partition, is the boot sector. Although all formatted partitions have this sector, they do not all have the optional Master Boot Record located in the sector. Only those disks created to be bootable disks have this record.

FIGURE 7.87
DOS disk organization.

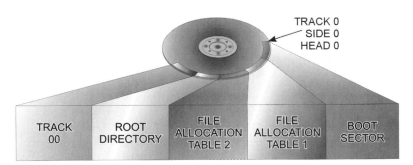

File Allocation Tables

The second section of a DOS disk is occupied by the disk's file allocation tables. This area is a table of information about how the disk is organized. Basically, the system logs the use of the space on the disk in this table.

In older versions of DOS, the amount of space dedicated to tracking the sectors on the disk was 16 bits. Therefore, only 65,536 sectors could be accounted for. This parameter limited the size of a DOS partition to 32MB (33,554,432 bytes).

To more effectively manage the space on the disk, newer versions of DOS divide the disk into groups of logically related sectors, called *allocation units*, or clusters. In a DOS system, the cluster is the smallest piece of manageable information.

The sectors on a DOS disk hold 512 bytes each. On the other hand, files can be of any length. Therefore, a single file may occupy several sectors on the disk. The DOS disk routine breaks the file into sector-sized chunks and stores it in a cluster of sectors. In this manner, DOS uses the cluster to track files rather than sectors. Because the file allocation table has to handle information for a cluster only, rather than for each sector, the number of files that can be tracked in a given-length table is greatly increased.

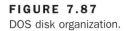

TEST TIP

Know what the smallest unit of storage in a disk-based system is.

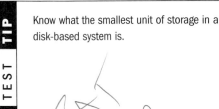

Table 7.2 describes the organization of a typical FAT. The first two entries are reserved for DOS information. Each cluster after that holds a value. Each value may represent one of three conditions. A value of 0 indicates that the cluster is available and can be used for storage. Any number besides 0 or FFFh indicates that the cluster contains data and the number provides the location of the next cluster in a chain of clusters. Finally, a value of FFFh (or FFFFh in a 16-bit entry) indicates the end of a cluster chain.

TEST TIP

Know the size of sectors in an IBM PC-compatible disk.

TABLE 7.2

FILE ALLOCATION TABLE STRUCTURE

Cluster Number	Contents
Cluster 0	Reserved for DOS
Cluster 1	Reserved for DOS
Cluster 2	3 (contains data, go to cluster 3)
Cluster 3	4 (contains data, go to cluster 4)
Cluster 4	7 (contains data, go to cluster 7)
Cluster 5	0 (free space)
Cluster 6	0 (free space)
Cluster 7	8 (contains data, go to cluster 8)
Cluster 8	FFFh (end cluster chain)
Cluster 9	0 (free)
**	
Cluster x	0 (free)
Cluster y	0 (free)
Cluster z	0 (free)

On floppy disks, common cluster sizes are one or two sectors long. With hard disks, the cluster size may vary from 1 to 16 sectors in length. The FAT keeps track of which clusters are used and which ones are free. It contains a 12- or 16-bit entry for each cluster on the disk. The 12-bit entries are used with floppy disks and hard disks that are smaller than 17MB. The 16-bit entries are employed with hard disk drives larger than 17MB. Obviously, the larger entries allow the FAT to manage more clusters.

In version b of Windows 95, also referred to as OSR2, Microsoft supplied a 32-bit file allocation table system called FAT32 to make efficient use of large hard drives (larger than 2GB). Under the previous FAT structure, large drives used large partitions, which, in turn, required large cluster sizes and wasted a lot of disk space.

The FAT32 format in OSR2 supports hard drives up to 2 terabytes (TB) in size. FAT32 uses 4KB cluster sizes for partitions up to 8GB in size.

In free clusters, a value of zero is recorded. In used clusters, the cluster number is stored. In cases where the file requires multiple clusters, the FAT entry for the first cluster holds the cluster number for the next cluster used to store the file. Each subsequent cluster entry has the number of the next cluster used by the file. The final cluster entry contains an end-of-file marker code that tells the system that the end of the file has been reached.

These *cluster links* enable the operating system to store and retrieve virtually any size file that will fit on the disk. However, the loss of any link makes it impossible to retrieve the file and use it. If the FAT becomes corrupted, chained files can become cross-linked with each other, making them useless. For this reason, two complete copies of the FAT are stored consecutively on the disk under the DOS disk structure. The first copy is the normal working copy; the second FAT is used as a backup measure in case the contents of the first FAT become corrupted.

The Root Directory

The next section following the FAT is the disk's root directory. This is a special directory present on every DOS disk. It is the main directory of every logical disk and serves as the starting point for organizing information on the disk.

The location of every directory, subdirectory, and file on the disk is recorded in this table.

Each directory and subdirectory (including the root directory) can hold up to 512, 32-byte entries that describe each of the files in them. The first 8 bytes contain the file's name, followed by 3 bytes for its filename extension.

The next 11 bytes define the file's attributes. Attributes for DOS files include the following:

- Read-only
- System file
- Volume label
- Subdirectory entry
- Archive (backup) status

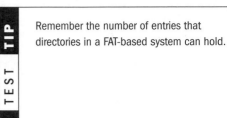

TEST TIP

Remember the number of entries that directories in a FAT-based system can hold.

To record the time the file was created or last modified, 2 bytes are used. This is followed by 2 additional bytes that record the date the file was created or last modified.

The final 4 bytes are divided equally between the value for the starting cluster number and a byte count number for the file. Unlike the previous information in the directory, the information associated with the last 4 bytes is not displayed when a directory listing displays onscreen.

Because each root directory entry is 32 bytes long, each disk sector can hold 16 entries. Consequently, the number of files or directories that can be listed in the root directory depends on how many disk sectors are allocated to it. On a hard disk drive, normally 32 sectors are set aside for the root directory. Therefore, the root directory for such a disk can accommodate up to 512 entries. A typical 3.5" 1.44MB floppy disk has 16 sectors reserved for the root directory and can hold up to 224 entries.

On a floppy disk, the logical structure normally has a group of files located under the root directory. Directory structures can be created on a floppy, but due to their relatively small capacity, this is not normally done. However, a hard drive is another matter. With hard drives, it is normal to organize the disk into directories and sub-directories, as described earlier in this chapter.

Technically, every directory on a disk is a subdirectory of the root directory. All additional directories branch out from the root directory in a tree-like fashion. Therefore, a graphical representation of the disk drive's directory organization is called a directory tree. Figure 7.88 depicts the directory organization of a typical hard drive.

FIGURE 7.88

The DOS directory tree structure.

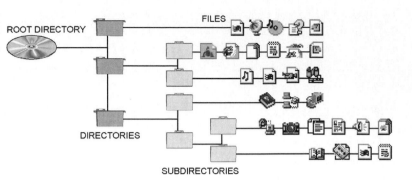

FAT32

Earlier versions of DOS and Windows supported what is now termed as *FAT16* (or *FAT12*). The OSR2 version of Windows 95 introduced the FAT32 file allocation table. As described earlier, the size of the operating system's FAT determines the size of the clusters for a given-size disk partition. Of course, smaller cluster sizes are better because even a single byte stored in a cluster will remove the entire cluster from the available storage space on the drive. This can add up to a lot of wasted storage space on larger drives. Table 7.3 describes the relationships between clusters and maximum partition sizes for various FAT entry sizes.

TABLE 7.3

FAT RELATIONSHIPS

FAT Type	*Partition Size*	*Cluster Size (In Bytes)*
FAT12	16MB	4096
FAT16	32MB	2048
FAT16	128MB	2048
FAT16	256MB	4096
FAT16	512MB	8192
FAT16	1GB	16384
FAT16	2GB	32768
FAT32	<260MB	512
FAT32	8GB	4096
FAT32	16GB	8192
FAT32	32GB	16384
FAT32	>32GB	32768

To use the FAT32 system, the hard drive must be formatted using the FDISK/Format functions in OSR2. This makes FAT32 incompatible with older versions of Windows (even Windows 95a and Windows NT) and with disk utilities and troubleshooting packages designed for FAT12/16 systems.

To use the FAT32 FDISK function in OSR2, you must enable the *Large Disk Support option.* After completing the FDISK function and exiting, it is necessary to manually reboot the system. After this, it is usually a simple matter of performing a Format operation using the OSR2 CD, or start disk, to install the FAT32 drive. Failure to reboot between the FDISK and Format operations produces an error.

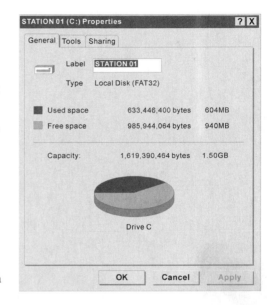

To verify that the hard drive is formatted with FAT32, select the My Computer option from the desktop and right-click the C: drive icon. This produces the [C:] Properties window displayed in Figure 7.89. The Type entry should read Local Disk [FAT 32]. The hard disk usage pie chart will not work correctly with drives larger than 2GB. It will show the drive as empty until at least 2GB of space is used

OSR2 does not require that FAT32 be used. It operates just as well, if not better, using the FAT16 format. Depending on the application of the system, it may run slower with FAT32. Remember that FAT32 is designed to optimize storage space, not performance. The simple fact that FAT32 offers the potential for more clusters makes it slower than a drive with fewer clusters. With this in mind, the decision to use FAT32 or FAT16, or to use different cluster sizes in FAT32, usually depends on the balance the user establishes between performance and storage. The default cluster size set by Microsoft for FAT32 is 4KB.

FIGURE 7.89
Showing FAT32 in the hard disk drive Properties window.

In Windows 9x, you can convert partitions created on a FAT16 drive into a FAT32 file system using the CVT.EXE utility. The main drawback to doing this is that there is some possibility of data corruption and loss. Not surprisingly, there is no utility for converting FAT32 partitions to FAT16.

Virtual File Allocation Tables

Windows 9x streamlines the 32-bit file and disk-access operations by removing both the DOS and the BIOS from the access equation, as illustrated in Figure 7.90. This allows Windows 9x to always run in protected memory mode so that no mode switching need occur.

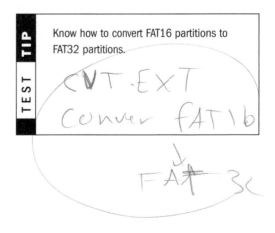

TEST TIP

Know how to convert FAT16 partitions to FAT32 partitions.

FIGURE 7.90

32-bit access in Windows 9x.

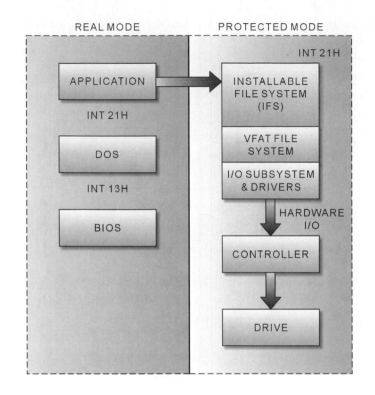

Microsoft refers to this portion of the system as the protected-mode FAT file system, or VFAT. As its full name implies, the VFAT provides a protected-mode way to interact with the file system on the disk drive. VFAT operates in 32-bit mode; however, the actual FAT structure of the disk remains as 12-bit or 16-bit allocations. Because the system does not normally have to exit and reenter protected mode, performance is increased considerably. Figure 7.91 shows the logical blocks of the VFAT.

The VFAT system replaces the SMARTDRV disk-caching utility with a protected-mode driver named VCACHE. Under VCACHE, the size of the cache data pool is based on the amount of free memory in the system rather than a fixed amount. The program automatically allocates blocks of free memory to caching operations as needed. Under Windows 9x, the VCACHE driver controls the cache for the system's CD-ROM drive, as well as for hard disk and file operations.

When a file or disk-access request is received by Windows 9x, a sub-section of the interface known as the installable file system (IFS) processes the request by passing it to the proper file system driver (FSD). The FSDs communicate with the IFS Manager and the drivers that work directly with the hardware device controllers. These device-specific drivers work within the I/O supervisor layer (IOS). The IOS layer handles I/O systems that transmit and receive data in multiple-byte transfers. Devices in this category include hard disk drives, CD-ROM drives, tape drives, and network controllers.

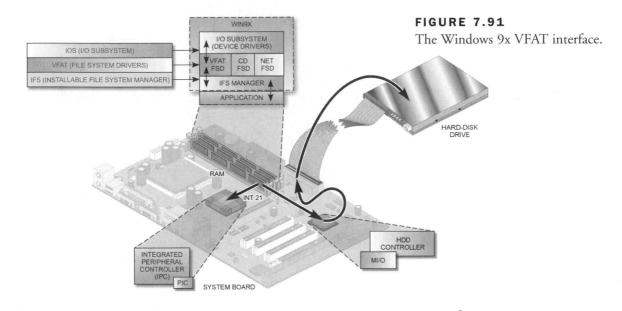

FIGURE 7.91
The Windows 9x VFAT interface.

Windows NT File System

Windows NT can function in two very different disk organizational structures. Like MS-DOS, Windows 3.x, and Windows 9x, it can employ the MS-DOS FAT system. In addition, Windows NT offers its own proprietary Windows NT File System (NTFS). The NTFS structure is designed to provide better data security and to operate more efficiently with larger hard drives than FAT systems do.

The NTFS structure uses 64-bit entries to keep track of storage on the disk (as opposed to the 16- and 32-bit entries used in FAT and FAT32 systems). The core component of the NTFS system is the Master File Table (MFT). This table replaces the FAT in an

MS-DOS compatible system and contains information about each file being stored on the disk. In order of occurrence, this information includes the following:

◆ Header information

◆ Standard information

◆ Filename

◆ Security information

◆ Data

When a volume is formatted in an NTFS system, several system files and the MFT are created on the disk. These files contain the information required to implement the file system structure on the disk. The System files produced during the NTFS formatting process include the following:

1. A pair of MFT files (the real one and a shorter backup version)

2. A log file to maintain transaction steps for recovery purposes

3. A volume file that includes the volume name, NTFS version, and other key volume information

4. An attribute definition table file

5. A root filename file that serves as the drive's root folder

6. A cluster bitmap that represents the volume and shows which clusters are in use

7. The partition boot sector file

8. A bad cluster file containing the locations of all bad sectors identified on the disk

9. A quota table for tracking allowable storage space on the disk for each user

10. An uppercase table for lowercase characters-to-Unicode uppercase characters

Unicode is a 16-bit character code standard, similar to 8-bit ASCII, used to represent characters as integer numbers. The 16-bit format allows it to represent more than 65,000 different characters. This proves particularly useful for languages that have very large character sets.

Figure 7.92 illustrates the organization of an NTFS disk volume. The first information in the NTFS volume is the 16-sector partition boot sector. The sector starts at physical sector-0 and is made up of two segments: The BIOS Parameter Block and the Code section. The BIOS Parameter Block holds information about the structures of the volume and disk file system. The Code section describes the method to be used to locate and load the startup files for the specified operating system. This code loads the Windows NT Bootstrap Loader file NTLDR in Intel-based computers running Windows NT.

FIGURE 7.92
The organization of an NTFS disk volume.

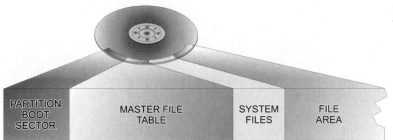

The MFT contains information about each folder and file on the volume. The NTFS system relates to folders and files as a collection of attributes. All the folder's, or file's, elements (that is, filename, security information, and data) are considered to be attributes. The system allocates space in the MFT for each file or folder based on the cluster size being used the disk.

Figure 7.93 shows a typical MFT record. The first section of the record contains standard information about the file or folder, such as its date and time stamp and number of links. The second section contains the file or folder's name. The next section contains the file, or folder's, security descriptor (which holds information about who can access it, who owns it, and what they may do with it).

The next section of the MFT record is the Data (or Index) area. The information for smaller files and folders are stored in the MFT itself. The Data area is 2KB long on smaller drives, but can be bigger on larger drives. When the data fits within the MFT record, the various portions of the file are referred to as resident attributes.

FIGURE 7.93
Basic NTFS Master File Table record.

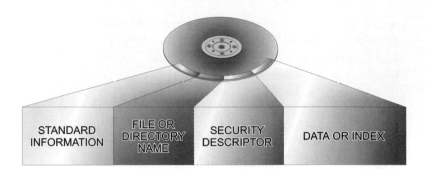

For larger files and folders that cannot be stored in a single MFT, the NTFS may resort to two other methods of using the MFT. For medium-size folders and files, the system stores standard information about the folder or file, such as its name and time information, in the MFT and then establishes index links to external cluster locations to store the rest of the data. The external clusters are referred to as data runs and are identified by 64-bit virtual cluster numbers (VCNs) assigned to them. The attributes stored outside the MFT are referred to as nonresident attributes. An Attribute List attribute, which contains the locations of all the file or folder's nonresident attributes, is created in the Data area of the MFT record. This arrangement is depicted in Figure 7.94.

FIGURE 7.94
Extended MFT record organization.

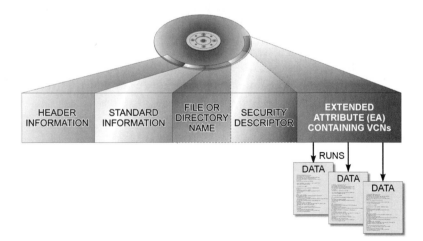

For extremely large files that cannot be identified by a single MFT record, multiple MFT records are employed. The first record contains a pointer to additional MFT records. The original MFT record contains the file or folder's standard information, followed by index links to other MFT records that, in turn have index links to the actual data runs. In these cases, the data is stored outside the table and can theoretically range up to 16EB (exabytes, 2^{60}).

All entries in the MFT are stored in alphabetic order by filename. Like FAT systems, NTFS systems use the cluster as the basic unit of disk storage. In Windows 4.0, NTFS clusters can range between 512 bytes and 64KB, depending on the size of the drive and how the disk was prepared. Clusters can range up to 64KB when established using the **Format** command from the command prompt. However, cluster sizes are limited to a maximum of 4KB when using the Windows NT Disk Manager to handle the disk organization. Clusters are numbered sequentially on the disk from start to end. These numbers are referred to as logical cluster numbers (LCNs). The default cluster size is determined by the volume size and can be specified in the Disk Administrator utility. Table 7.4 lists the default cluster sizes for NTFS systems in Windows 4.0 environments.

TABLE 7.4

NTFS CLUSTER SIZES

Partition Size	Sectors/Cluster	Cluster Size
<512 MB	1	512 bytes
512MB–1GB	2	1KB
1GB–2GB	4	2KB
2GB–4GB	8	4KB
4GB–8GB	16	8KB
8GB–16GB	32	16KB
16GB–32GB	64	32KB
>32GB	128	64KB

The smaller cluster size of the NTFS format makes it more efficient than FAT formats for storing smaller files. It also supports larger drives (over 1GB) much more efficiently than FAT16 or FAT32 structures. The NTFS system is more complex than the FAT systems and, therefore, is not as efficient for smaller drives.

The NTFS structure provides recoverable file system capabilities, including a hot-fix function and a full recovery system to quickly restore file integrity. The NTFS system maintains a copy of the critical file system information. If the file system fails, the NTFS system automatically recovers the system from the backup information as soon as the disk is accessed again. In addition, NTFS maintains a transaction log to ensure the integrity of the disk structure even if the system fails unexpectedly.

Security is a very big issue in large business networks. The Windows NT file system provides security for each file in the system, and also supplies complete file access auditing information to the system administrator. NTFS files and folders can have permissions assigned to them whether they are shared or not.

Data security also is improved by Windows NT's capability to support mirrored drives. Mirroring is a technique of storing separate copies of data on two different drives. This protects the data from loss due to hard drive failures. This is a very important consideration when dealing with server applications.

Additional fault-tolerance capabilities such as disk mirroring, drive duplexing, striping, RAID, and support for UPS are provided with the Windows NT LAN Manager.

NTFS Permissions

The NTFS system includes security features that enable permission levels to be assigned to files and folders on the disk. These permissions set parameters for activities that users can conduct with the designated file or folder.

Standard NTFS permissions include the following:

◆ **Read (R).** This permission enables users to display the file or folder along with its attributes and permissions.

◆ **Write (W).** This permission enables users to add files or folders, change file and folder attributes, add data to an existing file, and change display attributes.

◆ **Execute (X).** The execute permission enables users to make changes to subfolders, display attributes and permissions, and to run executable file types.

◆ **Delete (D).** The delete permission enables users to remove files and folders.

◆ **Change permission (P).** This permission enables users to change permission assignments of files and folders.

◆ **Take ownership (O).** This permission enables users to take ownership of the file or folder.

Some of these permission settings apply only to file-level objects, whereas others apply to both files and folders. Some combinations of the permissions are woven together in standard NTFS file and folder permissions. These include the following:

◆ **No access.** None (file and folder level)

◆ **Read.** RX (file and folder level)

◆ **Change.** RWXD (file and folder level)

◆ **Add.** WX (folder level only)

◆ **Add & Read.** RWX (folder level); RX (file level)

◆ **LIST.** RX (folder level only)

◆ **Full Control.** RWXDPO (file and folder level)

Whereas the NTFS system provides permission-level security for files and folders, other operating systems under Windows NT do not. When a file is moved from an NTFS partition to a FAT partition, for example, the NTFS-specific attributes are discarded. However, NTFS permissions do apply over a network connection.

Permissions can be assigned directly by the administrator, or they can be inherited through group settings. If a user only has Read permissions to a particular file, but is assigned to a group that has wider permissions, that individual gains those additional rights through the group.

In a server environment, the default permission setting for files is No Access.

Windows NT Partitions

Windows NT can be used to partition hard drive so that different operating systems can be used in each partition (and in extended partitions). The NTFS format lacks compatibility with other operating systems. Therefore, it will not allow other operating systems to access files on the NTFS drive. This can be a problem on partitioned drives that support multiple operating systems.

Windows NT employs very difficult terminology when referring to types of disk partitions. The disk partition where the BIOS looks for the Master Boot Record is called the system partition, whereas the partition containing the Windows NT operating system is called the boot partition. These partitions are described in Figure 7.95. Either, or both, types of partitions can be formatted as FAT or NTFS file systems. In practice, both partition types can be assigned to a single partition, or they can exist as separate partitions.

FIGURE 7.95
Windows NT partitions.

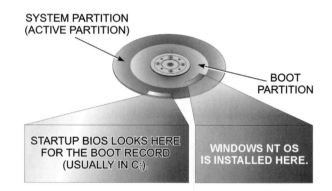

SYSTEM PARTITION
(ACTIVE PARTITION)

BOOT
PARTITION

STARTUP BIOS LOOKS HERE
FOR THE BOOT RECORD
(USUALLY IN C:).

WINDOWS NT OS
IS INSTALLED HERE.

Windows 2000 NTFS

Windows 2000 features an improved NTFS. This version enables administrators to establish user hard disk quotas limiting the amount of hard drive space to which users can have access.

The new NTFS system also offers enhanced system security. Windows 2000 NTFS provides an Encrypting File System and secure network protocol and authentication standards.

Windows NT 4.0 provides directory-level access and use controls. User rights to individual files cannot be manipulated in Windows NT 4.0. In Windows 2000, however, the administrator can limit what the user can do to any given file or directory.

Windows 2000 includes a Hierarchical Storage Management (HSM) system that enables the system to shift seldom-used data to selected backup media. When a user requests a file from a server, the server checks to see whether the file is still in residence, or if it has been offloaded to a storage device. If the file has been offloaded, the server brings it back to the server and delivers it to the requestor, as illustrated in Figure 7.96. The Windows 2000 HSM system provides drivers for DAT and DLT devices to perform this function.

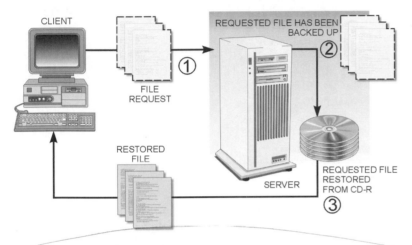

FIGURE 7.96
Windows 2000 Hierarchical Storage Management.

Windows 2000 is based on NTFS version 5.0. This version of NTFS enables the user to establish disk space quotas for users and to locate files by owner.

The new NTFS system provides the tools for the administrator to manage user access and usage rights to individual files and directories. File-level control was not possible in earlier NT versions. The Access Control List (ACL) is used to view the files to which a user can have access. This feature is new to the NT world, but it has been available in the Novell NetWare products for a long time.

The Windows 2000 Disk Management utility contains a Dynamic Volume Management feature that permits the capacity of an existing volume to be extended without rebooting or reformatting. The Disk Management utility also features a new user interface that enables administrators to configure drives and volumes located in remote computers.

Disk Management is a graphical tool that handles two distinctive types of disks: basic disks and dynamic disks. This tool also enables it to handle dynamic volumes created on dynamic disks.

A basic disk is a physical disk that contains partitions, drives, or volumes created with Windows NT 4.0 or earlier operating systems. Dynamic disks are physical disks created through the Windows 2000 Disk Management utility. These disks can hold only dynamic volumes (not partitions, volumes, or logical drives). With dynamic disks, however, the four-volume limit inherent with other Microsoft operating systems has been removed.

There are five different types of dynamic volumes:

◆ Simple

◆ Spanned

◆ Mirrored

◆ Striped

◆ RAID 5

Only systems running Windows 2000 can access dynamic volumes. Therefore, basic volumes should be established on drives that Windows 9x or Windows NT 4.0 systems need to access. To install Windows 2000 on a dynamic volume, it must be either a simple or a mirrored volume and it must be a volume that has been upgraded from a basic volume. Installing Windows 2000 on the volume requires that it has a partition table, which dynamic volumes do not have unless they have been upgraded from a basic volume. Basic volumes are upgraded by upgrading a basic disk to a dynamic disk. Windows 2000 will not support dynamic volumes on portable computers. Mirrored and RAID-5 volumes are supported only on Windows 2000 servers.

Dynamic volumes are managed through the Windows 2000 Disk Management snap-in tool, depicted in Figure 7.97, located under the Computer Management console. To access the Disk Manager, follow the Start/Settings/Control Panel/Administrative Tools path. Double-click the Computer Management icon and click the Disk Management entry. Because working with dynamic volumes is a major administrative task, you must be logged on as an administrator or as a member of Windows 2000's Administrators group to carry out the procedure. Also, system and boot volumes cannot be formatted as dynamic volumes.

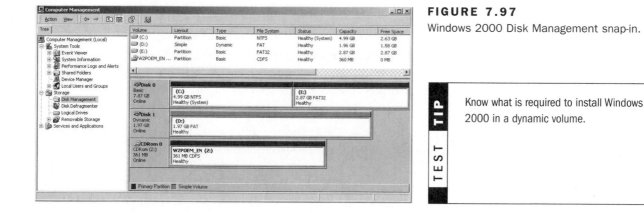

FIGURE 7.97
Windows 2000 Disk Management snap-in.

> **TEST TIP**
>
> Know what is required to install Windows 2000 in a dynamic volume.

NTFS Advantages

In most situations, the NTFS system offers better performance and features than a FAT16 or FAT32 system does. The exceptions to this occur when smaller drives are being used, other file systems are being used on the same drive, or when the operating system crashes.

In most other situations, the NTFS system offers the following:

◆ More efficient drive management due to its smaller cluster size capabilities

◆ Support for very large drives made possible by its 64-bit clustering arrangement

◆ Increased folder and file-security capabilities

◆ Recoverable file system capabilities

◆ Built-in RAID support

High Performance File System

IBM followed their successful PC-AT system with a line of personal computers called PS/2 (Personal System 2). The line was advertised around a proprietary 32-bit bus, called Micro Channel Architecture (MCA), and a new GUI-based operating system called OS/2 (Operating System 2). The PS/2 line has long since faded into the background of PC hardware, but the OS/2 software continues in some circles.

At the heart of the OS/2 operating system is the High Performance File System (HPFS). It provides a very robust file system for its time. The HPFS structure retains the FAT directory structure, but features long filenames (up to 254 characters) and volume sizes up to 8GB. Under HPFS, the unit of management was changed to physical sectors rather than clusters.

Its other attributes include good performance when directories contain several files, built-in fault tolerance, *fragmentation* resistance, and good effectiveness when working with large partitions.

HPFS employs banding to organize the disk efficiently. Using this arrangement, HPFS segments the drive into 8MB bands with 2KB allocation bitmaps between each band. The bitmaps are used to record which sectors have been used within a band. Whenever possible, the operating system tries to retain files within a single band. In doing so, the drive's R/W head does not have to return to track-0 for reference.

The HPFS file system is accessible only under the OS/2 and Windows NT 3.51 operating systems.

HDD Utilities

The operation of hard drives can slow down with general use. Files stored on the drive may be erased, and moved, causing parts of them to be scattered around the drive. This causes the drive to reposition the R/W heads more often during read and write operations, thereby requiring more time to complete the process.

Five important utilities can be used to optimize and maintain the operation of the hard disk drive. These are the CHKDSK, ScanDisk, defrag, backup, and antivirus utilities. With the exception of ScanDisk, which is a Windows utility, all these utilities have been available since early MS-DOS versions.

In Windows 9x, these functions are located in several areas of the system. The icons for backup, ScanDisk, and defrag are located in the Programs\Accessories\System Tools path. The executable file for ScanDisk can be found in C:\Windows\Command; the defrag icon is just under C:\Windows. The backup file is located in C:\Prgram Files\Accessories. The built-in antivirus function is missing from Windows 9x. An add-on program from a second party should be used. The MSAV and MWAV programs from DOS and Windows 3.x, respectively, can be found in the C:\DOS directory if Windows 9x was installed as an upgrade.

CHKDSK

The DOS **CHKDSK** (Check Disk) command is a command-line utility that has remained in use with Windows 3.x, 9x, NT, and 2000 and is used to recover *lost allocation units* from the hard drive. These lost units occur when an application terminates unexpectedly.

Over a period of time, lost units can pile up and occupy large amounts of disk space. To remove these lost units from the drive, an **/F** modifier is added to the command so that the lost units will be converted into files that can be investigated, and removed if necessary. In some cases, the converted file is a usable data file that can be rebuilt for use with an application. The **CHKDSK /F** command is often used before running a drive-defragmentation program.

ScanDisk

A similar program, called ScanDisk, is available in DOS 6.x and Windows 9x. ScanDisk searches the disk drive for disconnected file clusters and converts them into a form that can be checked and manipulated. This enables the user to determine whether there is any information in the lost clusters that can be restored. ScanDisk also detects, and deletes if necessary, *cross-linked files*. Cross-linked files occur when information from two or more files is mistakenly stored in the same sector of a disk.

The standard ScanDisk operation examines the system's directory and file structure. However, a Thorough option can be selected to examine the physical disk surface as well as its files and directories. If potential defects exist on the surface, ScanDisk can be used to recover data stored in these areas.

DOS and Windows offer a number of utility programs that enable the user to periodically clean up the drive and ensure its top performance. Among these programs are the defrag, backup, and antivirus utilities.

TEST TIP

Remember where the HDD utility programs are located in the Windows 9x environments.

Backup

Backup utilities enable the user to quickly create extended copies of files, groups of files, or an entire disk drive. This operation is normally performed to create backup copies of important information, for use if the drive crashes or the disk becomes corrupt.

The **Backup** and **Restore** commands can be used to back up and retrieve one or more files to another disk.

Because a backup of related files is typically much larger than a single floppy disk, serious backup programs allow information to be backed up to a series of disks; they also provide file-compression techniques to reduce the size of the files stored on the disk. Of course, it is impossible to read or use the compressed backup files in this format. To be usable, the files must be decompressed (expanded) and restored to the DOS file format.

Backup Types

Most backup utilities allow backups to be performed in a number of ways. Typically, backups fall into four categories:

- ◆ Full or total
- ◆ Incremental
- ◆ Selective
- ◆ Differential (or modified only)

In a full, or total backup, the entire contents of the designated disk is backed up. This includes directory and subdirectory listings and their contents. This backup method requires the most time each day to back up, but also requires the least time to restore the system after a failure. Only the most recent backup copy is required to restore the system.

Three partial backup techniques are used to store data, but yet conserve space on the storage media: incremental backups, selective backups, and differential backups.

In an incremental backup operation, the system backs up those files that have been created or changed since the last backup. Restoring the system from an incremental backup requires the use of the last full backup and each incremental backup taken since then. However, this method requires the least amount of time to back up the system but the most amount of time to restore it.

To conduct a selective backup, the operator moves through the tree structure of the disk marking, or tagging, directories and files to be backed up. After all the desired directories/files have been marked, they are backed up in a single operation.

Specifying a differential backup causes the backup utility to examine each file to determine whether it has changed since the last full backup was performed. If not, it is bypassed. If the file has been altered, however, it is backed up. This option is a valuable time-saving feature in a periodic backup strategy. To restore the system, you need a copy of the last full backup and the last differential backup.

In DOS, the basic **Backup** command can be modified through command switches. An **/S** switch causes all files and subdirectories to be backed up. The **/M** switch modifies the command so that only those files that have changed are backed up. The **/D** and **/T** switches examine the date and time stamps of each file and back up only those files modified after a specified date or time. Other switches can be used to format the backup media and to maintain a backup log on the disk.

> **TEST TIP**
>
> Know which backup type requires the least amount of time to perform and the least amount of effort to restore the system.

Data Backup

Use the **CHKDSK/F** command to clean up lost file clusters. Instruct the program to convert any lost chains into files that can be checked later. The operation of the Microsoft Windows 98 Backup utility is described in the following paragraphs.

Start the Backup program. Click Start, point to Programs/ Accessories/System Tools. If you do not see the Backup entry in the Accessories menu, it has not been installed.

Add the Backup utility to the System Tools menu through the Windows Setup tab. Click the Start button, point to Settings, click Control Panel, and double-click the Add/Remove Programs icon. This action opens the Add/Remove Programs Properties screen. Click the Windows Setup tab to access the list of available utilities. If you used a compact disc to install Windows, you receive a prompt to insert it into your computer.

Select the Backup option from the System Tools menu to start the Backup program and display the Backup Welcome screen, depicted in Figure 7.98. If you select the Create a New Backup Job option, the Windows Backup Wizard displays to guide you through the Backup setup process. The wizard asks you questions about which items to back up (entire computer or selected folder and files), what to back up (selected files or only new/changed files), and where to back up to. It also asks you to supply a name for the backup job.

FIGURE 7.98
Welcome to Backup.

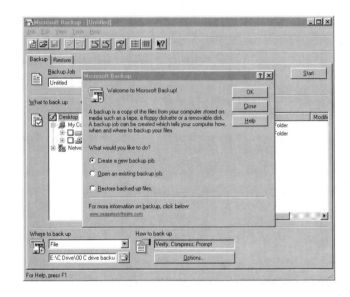

To set New Backup parameter

If you select the Open an Existing Backup Job option, you are asked to select the name of the existing backup job from a pop-up dialog box. Select a job and the Backup screen, similar to that shown in Figure 7.99, displays. Under this option, you can accept the parameters of the existing job or change them to new values.

To set new backup parameters, follow these steps:

1. Click the desired radio button in the What to Backup area (that is, All Selected Files or New and Changed Files).

2. Select the desired drive in the left pane by clicking its icon. Expand or contract the branches of the directory tree to gain access to any particular folders or files that you want to back up. Checking an object marks all of its subfolders and files. To unmark any selected files or folders, you must click the check box next to it.

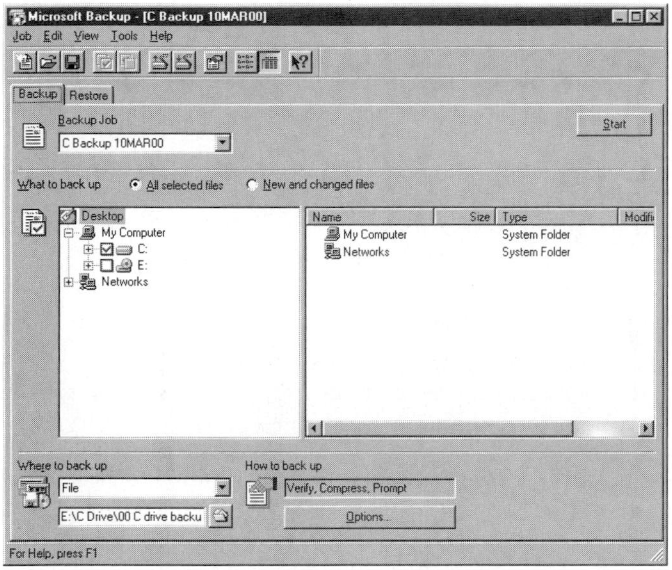

FIGURE 7.99
The Windows Backup screen.

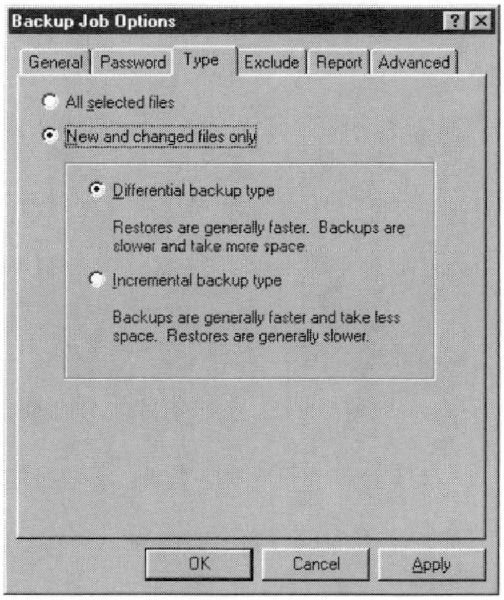

3. Identify where to back up by specifying that the backup will be a file and the path to the location where it should be stored. Select the backup options by clicking the Options button. This action provides access to the Backup Job Options screen depicted in Figure 7.100. Select the desired backup options from the window by clicking the radio button next to each option. Under the Type tab, verify the All Selected Files or New and Changed Files Only option. Click the OK button to accept the new options.

4. Click the Job option on the menu bar and select the appropriate Save As or Save option. If you select the Save As option, you must supply a new name for the job. If you select Save, the job, along with any new parameters, will be saved under its existing name.

5. Click the Start button to begin the backup operation.

Restoring Data

To restore data in Windows 98, start the Backup utility by selecting it from the System Tools submenu.

1. From the Backup Welcome screen, select the Restore option by checking its radio button and then clicking the OK button.

FIGURE 7.100
The Backup Options screen.

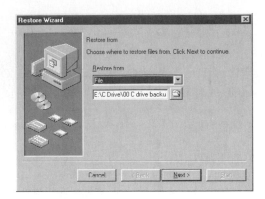

FIGURE 7.101
The Restore Wizard.

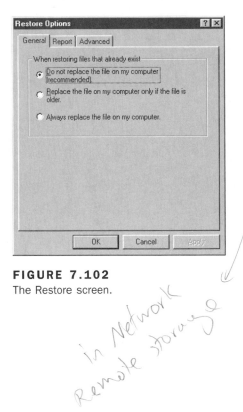

FIGURE 7.102
The Restore screen.

in Network
Remote storage

2. The Restore Wizard appears, as shown in Figure 7.101. Supply the file and path of where the restore should come from in the dialog boxes. Click the Next button to continue with the restore operation.

3. Check the parameters of the backup job. Make any changes to the job by manually check marking any items that you do not want to restore.

4. In the Where to Restore dialog box, you can select to use the Original location for the restore, or you can select an Alternate location option for the restored folders and files. If you select this option, you need to specify the new location in the drop-down dialog window.

5. Under the How to Restore option, click the Options button to access the Restore Options screen depicted in Figure 7.102. Select the restore options from the window by checking the box next to each option. Click the OK button to return to the Restore screen.

7. Click the Start button to restore the specified directories and files from the backup location.

Other Backup Methods

In a network environment, the Remote Storage Service function of the Windows 2000 Server's HSM system can be set up to move infrequently used programs and data to slower storage devices, such as tape or CD-R, while still maintaining the appearance of the data being present. The operation of the HSM system is illustrated in Figure 7.103. When the server receives a request from a user for a file that has been offloaded, it retrieves the data from the storage device and ships it to the user. This frees up space on the server without creating an inconvenience when users need to access these files.

The RSS function is an MMC snap-in that is available only with the Windows 2000 Server packages, not the Professional version. As with the other Windows 2000 Microsoft Management Consoles, the RSS console is accessed through the Start/Programs/Administrative Tools path.

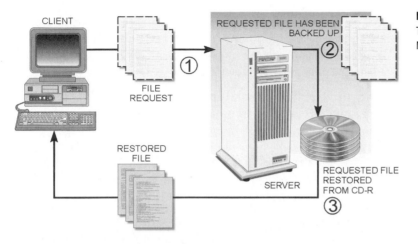

FIGURE 7.103
The Microsoft Hierarchical Storage Management system.

Windows 2000 includes an improved RAID controller utility. This built-in backup utility provides control of levels 0 through 5 RAID structures and provides changes between levels without needing to rebuild the array.

HDD Defragmentation

In the normal use of the hard disk drive, files become fragmented on the drive, as illustrated in Figure 7.104. This file fragmentation creates conditions that cause the drive to operate more slowly. Fragmentation occurs when files are stored in noncontiguous locations on the drive. This happens when files are stored, retrieved, modified, and rewritten due to differences in the sizes of the "before" and "after" files.

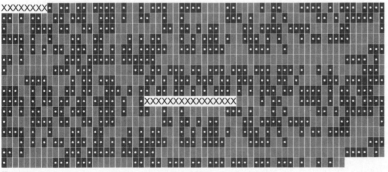

FRAGMENTED HARD DISK DRIVE

■ – USED
▨ – UNUSED
X – UNMOVABLE
1 BLOCK = 53 CLUSTERS

FIGURE 7.104
Data sectors.

Because the fragmented files do not allow efficient reading by the drive, it takes longer to complete multisector read operations. The defragmentation program realigns the positioning of related file clusters, to speed up the operation of the drive.

Some portions of files may become lost on the drive when a program is unexpectedly interrupted (such as when software crashes, for example, or during a power failure). These lost allocation units (chains) also cause the drive to operate slowly. Therefore, it is customary to use the DOS **CHKDSK** command to find these chains and remove them before performing a defrag operation.

It also may be necessary to remove some data from the drive to defragment it. If the system is producing Out of Disk Space error messages, the defragmentation utility will not have enough room on the drive to realign clusters. When this happens, some of the contents of the drive will need to be transferred to a backup media (or discarded) to free up some disk space for the realignment process to occur.

The defrag utility has been available since the later versions of MS-DOS (with the exception of Windows NT). In Windows 9x and Windows 2000, the defragmenter utility is located under the Start/Program/Accessories/System Tools path.

In Windows 2000, the defragmenter can be accessed through the Start/Settings/Control Panel/Computer Management path. To use the defrag tool from this point, follow these steps:

1. Click the Disk Defragmenter option.

2. Click the desired drive to highlight it.

3. Click the Defragment button to begin the operation.

4. The Defrag main screen displays, similar to that shown in Figure 7.105.

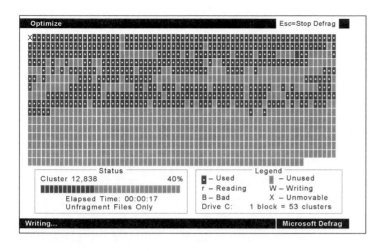

FIGURE 7.105
The Defrag main screen.

CHAPTER SUMMARY

This chapter has looked at basic operating systems in depth. It has concentrated in particular on the ROM BIOS and MS-DOS disk operating systems.

The initial section introduced the various types of operating systems. Items covered in this section included, single- and multiprocess, multiuser, and multitasking systems.

The second section of the chapter focused on the function, structure, and major system files of MS-DOS, Windows 9x, and Windows NT/2000.

The third section concentrated on disk and directory architectures, and how to navigate through MS-DOS, Windows 9x, and Windows 2000 environments. The section also included a guide to DOS commands and usage, as well as ways to work in the major user interfaces of Windows 9x and Windows 2000.

The next section of the chapter dealt with file and directory manipulation in the three operating systems/environments.

The chapter's final section was dedicated to basic disk management. This section began with an explanation of how disks are organized and then the discussion moved to standard disk-management utilities.

KEY TERMS

- Add New Hardware
- Add/Remove Programs
- Advanced Power Management (APM)
- Allocation units
- ATTRIB command
- AUTOEXEC.BAT
- BACKUP
- Bootstrap Loader
- CHKDSK (Check Disk)
- Cluster links
- Clusters
- COMMAND.COM
- CONFIG.SYS

CHAPTER SUMMARY

- Configuration Manager
- Control Panel
- Cooperative multitasking
- Core files
- Cross-linked files
- DEFRAG
- Desktop
- Device drivers
- Device Manager
- Directories
- Directory tree
- Disk cache
- EMM386.EXE
- Expanded memory
- Extended memory
- Extended memory driver (XMS)
- Extended partition
- Extensions
- FAT12
- FAT16
- FDISK
- File allocation tables (FATs)
- Filename
- FILES command
- Folders
- Formatting

At this point, review the objectives listed at the beginning of the chapter to be certain that you understand and can perform each item listed there. Afterward, answer the Review Questions that follow to verify your knowledge of the information.

- Groups
- High memory area (HMA)
- High-level format
- HIMEM.SYS
- Icon
- Initialization (INI) files
- Installable File System (IFS) Manager
- IO.SYS
- Kernel
- Large Disk Support option
- Long filenames
- Lost allocation units
- Low-level format
- MS-DOS prompt
- MSDOS.SYS
- Multiprocess systems
- Multiprocessor
- Multitasking
- Multiuser
- My Computer
- Network Neighborhood
- NOEMS
- OSR2

- Parallel processing
- Partitioning
- Password
- POWER.EXE
- Preemptive multitasking
- Primary partition
- Print Manager
- Printers folder
- PROMPT=PG
- Properties
- Recycle Bin
- Registry
- Registry Edit (REGEDIT.EXE)
- Right-clicking (alternate-clicking)
- Root directory
- ScanDisk
- SETVER command
- SHARE.EXE
- Single-process systems
- SMARTDRV.SYS
- Start button
- Subdirectories
- System Editor (SysEdit)

- System icon
- System Policy Editor (PolEdit)
- System Properties
- SYSTEM.DAT
- Taskbar
- Task switching
- Terminate-and-stay-resident (TSR)
- Threads
- Upper memory area (UMA)
- USER.DAT
- VCACHE
- VFAT
- Virtual disk
- Virtual memory
- Volumes
- Wide area network (WAN)
- Wildcard characters
- WIN.COM
- Windows 95
- Windows 95 (b) OSR2
- Windows 98
- Windows Explorer
- Windows Millennium Edition (ME)

RESOURCE URLs

www.okc.cc.ok.us/pweaver/1353lec1.htm

www.cit.rcc.on.ca/os100/os01.htm

www.cit.rcc.on.ca/os100/msdos08.htm

www.okc.cc.ok.us/pweaver/1353wn31.htm

www.execpc.com/~iniman/ex_1.html

http://aol.pcwebopedia.com/TERM/_/_INI_file.html

http://webopedia.com/TERM/D/DLL.html

www.cit.rcc.on.ca/os100/win9501.htm

http://webopedia.internet.com/TERM/R/Registry.html

www.pctusa.com/tips.html

www.okc.cc.ok.us/pweaver/1353lec1.htm

www.cit.rcc.on.ca/os100/msdos11.htm

www.pctusa.com/pcdos.htm

www.okc.cc.ok.us/pweaver/1353wn31.htm

www.pctusa.com/pc02001.htm

www.cit.rcc.on.ca/os100/win9503.htm

www.bus.msu.edu/nrc/class/95/desktop.html

www.pctusa.com/tips.html

www.okc.cc.ok.us/pweaver/1353lec1.htm

www.cit.rcc.on.ca/os100/win9508.htm

www.bus.msu.edu/nrc/class/95/explorer.html

www.pctusa.com/tips.html

www.cit.rcc.on.ca/os100/msdos22.htm

www.pctusa.com/win95/win95_12.html

www.pctusa.com/pcdos.htm

webopedia.internet.com/TERM/S/ScanDisk.html

www.codemicro.com/badsector.htm

APPLY YOUR KNOWLEDGE	

Review Questions

1. Where is the PATH statement located?

2. What is the significance of placing items in the Windows 9x Startup folder?

3. What type of operating system breaks the tasks associated with a process into its various threads for execution?

4. Which Windows NT 4.0 utility can be used to create a backup copy of the Registry? Where is the utility located and where will the backup copy be stored?

5. _____ are the Windows 2000 tool for implementing changes for computers and users throughout an enterprise.

6. Which memory manager should always be listed before any other memory managers or device drivers?

7. Describe the steps required to change a file's attributes in Windows 9x Explorer?

8. What action must be taken to see hidden files in Windows 9x?

9. What is the core component of the NTFS system, and what is its counterpart in a FAT system?

10. What does the asterisk character (*) stand for when used in a DOS filename?

11. How does the XCOPY command differ from the COPY or DISKCOPY command?

12. Where should changes to Windows 2000 Registry items be made?

13. Name three advantages of the Windows NT file system over FAT16 and FAT32 file-management structures.

14. Where are the Windows NT Hive files stored?

15. Which file contains the user-related configuration information for Windows NT?

Exam Questions

1. Which DOS command prepares a disk to function as a self-booting disk?

   A. BOOT /S

   B. FDISK /S

   C. Format /S

   D. MEM /S

2. In the Windows NT environment, which types of applications can communicate directly with the Win32 Services block?

   A. 16-bit DOS applications

   B. 16-bit Windows 3.x applications

   C. 32-bit Windows 98 applications

   D. 64-bit POSIX applications

3. What is the maximum length of a Windows NT 4.0 filename?

   A. 8 characters

   B. 16 characters

   C. 256 characters

   D. 1,024 characters

APPLY YOUR KNOWLEDGE

4. Before running the defragmentation utility, what other DOS utility should be used to eliminate file chaining on a hard disk drive?

   A. The Restore utility

   B. The MSAV utility

   C. The CHKDSK or ScanDisk utilities

   D. The Backup utility

5. What is the purpose of placing a SMARTDRV.EXE command in the CONFIG.SYS file?

   A. To establish a disk cache in conventional memory

   B. To establish a disk cache in extended memory

   C. To establish a disk cache in base memory

   D. To establish a RAM disk in extended memory

6. Where would you find the system's memory managers listed?

   A. In the CONFIG.SYS file

   B. In the boot record

   C. In the AUTOEXEC.BAT file

   D. In the COMMAND.COM file

7. Which of the following items is located in the root directory of a hard disk drive?

   A. The drive letter

   B. The file attributes

   C. The MBR

   D. The IO.SYS file

8. Which filename extensions allow programs to be started directly from the DOS prompt?

   A. .TXT, .BAT, and .DOC

   B. .EXE, .COM, and .BAT

   C. .EXE, .DOC, and .BAT

   D. .BAT, .EXE, and .BAS

9. What does HIMEM.SYS do?

   A. It governs the use of shadow RAM.

   B. It governs the use of conventional memory.

   C. It governs the use of extended memory.

   D. It governs the use of base memory.

10. The portion of the Windows NT structure that communicates directly with the system hardware is _____.

    A. The Win32 Executive

    B. The user mode

    C. The Hardware subsystem

    D. The HAL

Answers to Review Questions

1. The PATH statement is an AUTOEXEC.BAT statement that instructs the operating system where to look for the executable version of a filename entered at the command prompt. For more information, see the section "AUTOEXEC.BAT."

2. A program can be set up to automatically start along with Windows by placing its icon in the Startup folder. For more information, see the section "Windows 9x Structures."

3. Multiprocess operating systems. For more information, see the section "Operating Systems."

4. The RDISK.EXE utility. It is located in the WINNT\System32 folder and will create a backup copy of the Registry in the WINNT\Repair folder. For more information, see the section "The Windows NT Registries."

5. With Group Policies, administrators can institute a large number of detailed settings for users throughout an enterprise, without establishing each setting manually. For more information, see the section "Windows NT/2000 Group Policies."

6. The HIMEM.SYS command. For more information, see the section "Memory Managers."

7. From the Windows Explorer window, right-click the file, select the Properties option from the list, move to the General page, and click the boxes to create check marks in the desired boxes. For more information, see the section "Windows Explorer."

8. Click the View option on the menu bar, select the Folders option from the list, select the View tab, and click the Show Hidden Files button. For more information, see the section "My Computer."

9. The Master File Table (MFT) is the centerpiece of the NTFS system. Its DOS counterpart is the FAT. For more information, see the section "Windows NT File System."

10. The asterisk symbol is used as wildcard character that can be substituted for an unknown character or character string in DOS commands. For more information, see the section "DOS Shortcuts."

11. The XCOPY command copies all the files in a directory, along with any subdirectories and their files; the file COPY command copies a specified file from one place (disk or directory) to another. For more information, see the section "Files and Filenames."

12. Registry changes should be made through the wizards located in the Control Panel. For more information, see the section "The Windows NT Registries."

13. NTFS provides more efficient drive management due to its smaller cluster size capabilities, support for very large drives made possible by its 64-bit clustering arrangement, increased folder and file security capabilities, recoverable file system capabilities, and built-in RAID support. For more information, see the section "NTFS Advantages."

14. The Registry hive files are stored in the \WINNT\SYSTEM32\CONFIG folder. For more information, see the section "The Windows NT Registries."

15. Under Windows NT, the file that contains the user-related configuration information is NTUSER.DAT. For more information, see the section "The Windows NT Registries."

Answers to Exam Questions

1. **C.** The Format command used with the /S (System) switch creates a self-booting disk by moving the IO.SYS, MSDOS.SYS, COMMAND.COM to the disk. For more information, see the section "Drive-Level Operations."

APPLY YOUR KNOWLEDGE

2. **C.** Whereas 32-bit applications run in protected mode and can contact the Win32 subsection directly, 16-bit DOS and Win16 applications must be housed in a protective memory-management scheme called an NT Virtual DOS Machine environment. This environment protects the other parts of the system from the application. These applications can contact the Win32 subsystem only through a single thread. For more information, see the section "User Mode."

3. **C.** Windows NT 4.0 can handle long filenames up to 256 characters. Interestingly, Windows 2000 filenames are limited to 215 characters. For more information, see the section "Windows NT/2000 Files."

4. **C.** Before defragmenting the drive, the CHKDSK /F or ScanDisk operation should be performed to find/repair/remove these damaged files from the system. Locating and removing them after the defragmentation operation would just create new fragmentation on the drive. For more information, see the section "HDD Defragmentation."

5. **B.** SMARTDRV creates a disk cache in extended memory. The operating system uses this cache to swap information back and forth between the system's disk drive and RAM so that the rest of the system sees a large RAM area, even though no additional physical RAM has been added to the system. For more information, see the section "Device Drivers."

6. **A.** The system's memory managers must be listed in the CONFIG.SYS file to be functional. The first memory manager is typically HIMEM.SYS, followed by an EMM386 statement. For more information, see the section "CONFIG.SYS."

7. **D.** The root directory typically contains the IO.SYS, MSDOS.SYS, and COMMAND.COM files. The IO.SYS and MSDOS.SYS files are hidden, read-only System files that will not normally show up in a directory listing of the root. For more information, see the section "The Root Directory."

8. **B.** Files that have been created as executable (EXE), command (COM), or batch (BAT) files can be executed directly from the command line. This is not due to their extensions, but the way that they are created. For more information, see the section "The Command Line."

9. **C.** HIMEM.SYS is the extended memory manager for Microsoft operating systems. It must be installed at the top of the CONFIG.SYS file and oversees the operation of any other memory managers loaded into the system—including expanded memory managers. For more information, see the section "Memory Managers."

10. **D.** The HAL communicates directly with the system hardware in the Windows NT/2000 environment. For more information, see the section "The Hardware Abstraction Layer."

This chapter helps you to prepare for the Operating System Technologies module of the A+ Certification examination by covering the following objectives within the "Domain 2.0: Installation, Configuration, and Upgrading" section.

2.1 Identify the procedures for installing Windows 9x and Windows 2000 and bringing the software to a basic operational level.

Content may include the following:

- **Start Up**

- **Partition**

- **Format drive**

- **Loading drivers**

- **Run appropriate setup utility**

▶ Computers do not run without operating systems. Ergo, technicians must be able to install operating systems on new machines, repaired machines, and upgraded machines.

2.2 Identify steps to perform an operating system upgrade.

Content may include the following:

- **Upgrading Windows 9x**

- **Upgrading Windows 2000**

▶ Operating system versions change at a rapid pace. Technicians must be able to upgrade hardware platforms from one operating system to another to successfully service their customers.

CHAPTER 8

2.0 Installation, Configuration, and Upgrading

2.3 Identify the basic system boot sequences and boot methods, including steps to create an emergency boot disk with utilities installed for Windows 9x, Windows NT, and Windows 2000.

Content may include the following:

- **Startup disk**

- **Safe Mode**

- **DOS mode**

- **NTLDR (NT Loader)**

- **Files required to boot**

- **Creating an Emergency Repair Disk (ERD)**

▶ The technician must be able to observe a boot-up sequence and determine where problems occur. Therefore, technicians must be familiar with typical boot-up sequences, know how to alter them, and be prepared to handle problems that arise when systems do not boot up correctly.

2.4 Identify procedures for loading/adding and configuring device drivers, applications, and the necessary software for certain devices.

Content may include the following:

- **Windows 9x Plug and Play and Windows 2000**

- **Identify the procedures for installing and launching typical Windows and non-Windows applications**

Procedures for set up and configuration of the Windows printing subsystem

- **Setting Default printer**

- **Installing/Spool setting**

- **Network printing (with help of LAN admin)**

▶ The flexibility of the PC system has always rested on the capability to add third-party items to the system as desired. The operating system handles these additions through software device drivers. Therefore, the technician must be able to install and configure device drivers for the operating system being used.

▶ Like operating system versions and printers, users add and update application software packages frequently. The technician must be able to install these packages, both Windows- and DOS-based, and be able to bring them to a fully functional level.

▶ Printers are the second most-used output devices for the PC. As with other software and hardware components, users add and change these items often. Therefore, the technician must be able to add new printers to the system and make them functional. This includes setting up their parameters in the operating system.

STUDY STRATEGIES

To prepare for the Installation, Configuration, and Upgrading objectives of the Operating System Technologies exam:

▶ Read the objectives at the beginning of this chapter.

▶ Study the information in this chapter.

▶ Review the objectives listed earlier in this chapter.

▶ Perform any step-by-step procedures in the text.

▶ Answer the Review and Exam Questions at the end of the chapter and check your results.

▶ Use the ExamGear test engine on the CD-ROM that accompanies this book for additional Review and Exam Questions concerning this material

▶ Review the Test Tips scattered throughout the chapter and make certain that you are comfortable with each point.

INTRODUCTION

This section requires the test taker to demonstrate knowledge of installation, configuration, and upgrading of Windows 9x and Windows 2000. This includes knowledge of system boot sequences. Questions from this domain account for 15% of the Operating System Technologies test.

INSTALLING OPERATING SYSTEMS

▶ 2.1 Identify the procedures for installing Windows 9x and Windows 2000 and bringing the software to a basic operational level.

The A+ Operating System Technologies objective 2.1 states that the test taker should be able to "identify the procedures for installing Windows 9x and Windows 2000 and bringing the software to a basic operational level."

Operating systems must be loaded on to new computers and most computers will have their operating system upgraded at least once in their lifetime. Therefore, technicians must be able to install operating systems on new machines, repair operating system problems, and upgrade operating systems to new versions. The opening sections of this chapter deal with installing DOS, Windows 9x, and Windows 2000 systems and getting them to a functional level.

Disk Preparation

As mentioned in Chapter 1, "1.0 Installation, Configuration, and Upgrading," when a magnetic disk is created, it is for all practical purposes blank. In the earliest versions of PC DOS and MS-DOS, the complete operating system was contained on two uncompressed disks: the *system disk* and the *supplemental disk*.

When PCs were floppy drive-based, the main portion of the disk operating system was loaded into the system from a system disk during the boot-up process. The most used DOS functions were loaded into RAM during the boot-up process.

Complex operating system functions required that external DOS commands be temporarily loaded into the system from the supplemental disk. Programs and data were stored on data disks, or work disks. Control of the floppy disk system was built directly into the system's BIOS.

When the PCs moved to hard drive–based operations, the main DOS files were placed in the *root directory* on the hard disk as a part of its formatting process. Recall that these files included *IO.SYS*, *MSDOS.SYS*, and *COMMAND.COM*. This function is typically the result of using a */S* switch on a **FORMAT** command. These files can be replaced or upgraded to a new version level through the use of the DOS **SYS** command. The other DOS files were typically copied into a C:\DOS directory when the unit was set up.

Installing the operating system directly on the hard disk meant that disks did not need to be exchanged for every different function the user wanted to perform. Programs and data also were stored directly on the drive. Who could ever fill up those huge 10MB drives that came with the PC-XTs?

Installing the operating system on a new hard drive has evolved into the four basic steps outlined in this A+ objective:

1. Partition the drive for use with the operating system.

2. Format the drive with the basic operating system files.

3. Run the appropriate setup utility to install the complete operating system.

4. Load all the drivers necessary to enable the operating system to work with the system's installed hardware devices.

The disk partition and format processes were described in Chapter 1, as well as in Chapter 7, "1.0 Operating System Fundamentals."

Installing Windows 9x

Windows 9x versions must be installed over an existing operating system, such as MS-DOS. In particular, the Windows 9x installation program must find a recognizable MS-DOS FAT16 partition on the drive. This prevents it from being installed over some other type of operating system, such as Windows NT or Novell NetWare OS.

TEST TIP

Remember that Windows 9x requires that a FAT16 partition exist on the drive where it is being installed.

The system must be at least an 80386DX or higher machine, operating with at least 4MB of RAM (8MB is recommended). Although the 80386DX is the listed minimum microprocessor for running Windows 9x, the recommended processor is the 80486DX; the Pentium processors are actually the preferred microprocessor for running Windows 9x. Likewise, 4MB may be the minimum RAM option, with 8MB being the recommended option, but 16MB, 32MB, or 64MB are preferred for running Windows 9x.

The system also should possess a mouse and a VGA or better monitor. The system's hard drive should have at least 20MB of free space available to successfully install Windows 9x.

The actual requirements to successfully install Windows 9x depend on the type of installation being conducted and from what level it is being conducted. As already mentioned, Windows 9x versions must be installed on a hard drive that already has a FAT16 structure in place.

In addition, the Windows 9x setup routine provides for different types of installations to be established, including Typical, Portable, Compact, and Custom. All these options install different combinations of the possible Windows 9x system. Therefore, they all have different system requirements for proper installation.

To perform a Typical installation in a DOS system requires a minimum of 40MB of free drive space. Conversely, conducting a Compact installation on the same system requires only 30MB. When the installation is being conducted from a Windows 3.1 or Windows for Workgroup environment, the free space requirements drop to 30MB Typical/20MB Compact for Windows 3.1 and 20MB Typical/10MB Compact for Windows for Workgroups. The total required free space can range up to 85MB when a Custom install is conducted using all the Windows 95 options.

When Windows 9x is installed over the existing operating system files on the disk, new versions of some files, such as IO.SYS, MSDOS.SYS, and COMMAND.COM, are created. The Windows 9x versions of these files are not compatible with the older versions. Therefore, if the system crashes during the Windows 9x installation process, it may not be able to reboot to the hard drive. Consequently, having a *backup* of the old system on disk is definitely recommended before installing Windows 9x to a system.

TEST TIP

Memorize the minimum, recommended, and preferred CPU specifications for running Windows 9x.

TEST TIP

Memorize the minimum and recommended amounts of memory specified to start Windows 95.

The system also can be configured for a Dual Boot option between the existing operating system and the Windows 9x installation. This option is accomplished by renaming the old operating system's Core files and then swapping back and forth between the old versions and the Windows 9x versions, depending on which operating system is selected for boot up. This option is easiest to establish during the setup process. Ways to establish dual booting are discussed in detail later in this chapter.

Installing Windows 98

Unlike Windows 95, Windows 98 does not need to be installed over an existing operating system. Only the Upgrade version of Windows 98 requires an existing operating system such as MS-DOS, Windows 3.1x, or Windows 95. The distribution CD for the full version of Windows 98 can be used to boot the system and provide options to partition and format the drive. To install Windows 98, the system hardware must be at least an 80486DX/66 or higher machine, operating with at least 16MB of RAM. The system also should possess a modem, a mouse, and a 16-color VGA or better monitor. The system's hard drive should have between 120 and 355MB of free space available to successfully install Windows 98. The actual amount of disk space used depends on the type of installation being performed (Typical, Custom, Portable, Compact, New, Upgrade, and so on). Typical installations use between 170 and 225MB of disk space.

Several possible circumstances will determine how Windows 98 should be installed. The primary concern is which operating system it will be replacing. Is the system a new installation, or is it being upgraded from DOS, Windows 3.x, or Windows 95? The second concern is the type of system on which the installation is being conducted. Is the system a standalone unit, or is it a networked unit?

If Windows 98 is being installed in a new unit, or to a disk drive that has been reformatted, you must boot the system from the Windows distribution CD or run the *SETUP.EXE* program from the DOS prompt. This method also is employed when Windows 98 is being used to upgrade a system from Windows 95 using new settings.

Using this approach, the Windows 98 Setup program runs a real-mode version of the ScanDisk utility on the drive. This requires that the CD-ROM or network drive's real-mode driver be present and loaded. This ScanDisk version performs FAT, directory, and file checks on the drive and creates a ScanDisk log file. If an error is detected, the program displays an *error message* indicating that the log file should be checked. The file can be accessed through the ScanDisk screen's View Log selection.

After the ScanDisk inspection has been completed, the Setup program initializes the system and begins copying installation files to the drive. The installation is carried out in the five-step procedure, as follows:

1. Preparing to Run Windows 98 Setup

   During this part of the procedure, Setup performs the following steps to prepare the Windows 98 Setup Wizard to guide the user through the installation process:

   a. Creates a SETUPLOG.TXT file in the drive's root directory

   b. Identifies the source and destination drive locations for the Windows 98 files

   c. Copies a minimal Windows 98 Setup cabinet file, called MINI.CAB, into the Wininst0.400 directory it creates at C:\

   d. Extracts the major Setup files PRECOPY1.CAB and PRECOPY2.CAB into the Wininst0.400 directory

2. Collecting Information About Your Computer

   After the Setup files have been extracted to the hard drive, the Setup Wizard begins operation by presenting the Microsoft Licensing Agreement and asking the user to enter the Product Key number, as illustrated in Figure 8.1. The product key can be found on the software's Certificate of Authenticity, or on the CD cover. On standalone machines, this number must be entered correctly to continue the installation. Conversely, there will not be any Product Key request when Windows 98 is being installed across a network.

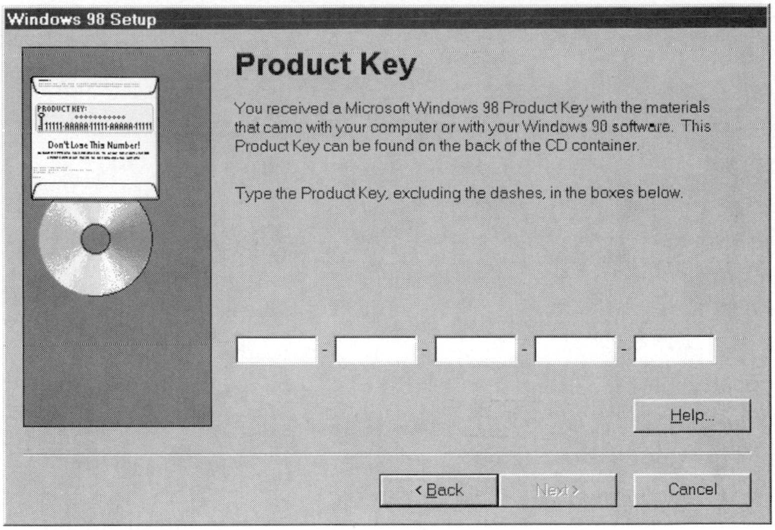

FIGURE 8.1

The Windows Product Key window.

After the registration information has been gathered, Setup begins to collect information concerning the system. This information includes the following:

a. The location of the installation directory where Windows 98 files should be moved into

b. Verification that the selected drive has enough space to hold the Windows 98 installation

c. The type of installation desired (that is, Typical, Portable, Compact, and Custom)

d. The user's company and usernames

e. Windows 98 components that should be installed

f. The computer's network identification (if installing in a network environment)

g. The Internet location where the system can receive regional update information from the Internet

After gathering this information, the Setup routine stops to prompt the installer to create an emergency start disk and then begins installing Windows 98 files to the selected drive.

3. Copying Windows 98 Files to Your Computer

   This portion of the operation begins when the Start Copying Files dialog box appears onscreen. The complete operation of this phase is automated so that no external input is required. However, any interruption of the Setup operation during this period may prevent the system from starting up again. In this event, you must rerun the Setup routine from the beginning.

4. Restarting Your Computer

   Once Setup has copied the Windows 98 files into their proper locations, it presents a prompt to restart the system. Doing so allows the newly installed Windows 98 functions to become active. The restart is conducted automatically if no entry is detected within 15 seconds.

5. Setting Up Hardware and Finalizing Settings

   After the system has been restarted, Setup finalizes the installation of the following items:

   a. The Control Panel

   b. The contents of the Start menu

   c. The basic Windows 98 Help functions

   d. Settings for DOS programs

   e. Application Start functions

   f. Time-zone information

   g. The system's configuration information

Upon completion of these steps, Setup again restarts the system and presents a log-on prompt. After the log-on process, Setup establishes a database of system driver information, updates the system's settings, establishes personalized system options, and presents a Welcome to Windows 98 page onscreen.

[handwritten margin note: need Advance planning]

[handwritten margin note: 1st — chck the hardware compatibility with NT]

[handwritten margin note: 2nd which file mangmnt should be use (Typical FAT file sys or NTFS)]

Installing Windows NT/2000

The installation process for Windows NT versions, including Windows 2000, can be a little more difficult than that of the Windows 9x versions. In particular, the lack of extensive hardware and software compatibility requires some advanced planning before installing or upgrading to Windows NT.

The first issue to deal with is hardware compatibility. Windows NT makes no claim to maintaining compatibility with a wide variety of hardware devices. Is the hardware being used supported by the intended version of Windows NT? If the current hardware does not appear in the Microsoft Hardware Compatibility List (HCL) of the new version, you are on your own for technical support.

The second factor to sort out is which file management system should be used. Windows NT can be configured to use either a typical FAT-based file system or its own proprietary NTFS file system. Review the NTFS advantages section in Chapter 7 to determine which file system is better suited to the particular situation.

Installing Windows 2000 Professional

The minimum hardware requirements for installing Windows 2000 Professional on a PC-compatible system are as follows:

◆ Microprocessor: 166MHz Pentium (P5 equivalent or better)

◆ RAM: 32MB (64MB recommended, 4GB maximum)

◆ HDD space: 650MB or more free on a 2GB drive

◆ VGA monitor

For installation from a CD-ROM, a 12× drive is required. If the CD-ROM drive is not bootable, a high-density 3.5-inch floppy drive also is required.

Before installing Windows 2000 Professional from the CD, it is recommended that the file CHECKUPGRADEONLY be run. This file is located on the installation CD under \i386\winnt32 and checks the system for possible hardware compatibility problems. The program generates a text file report named UPGRADE.TXT that can be found under the Windows folder. It contains Windows 2000 compatibility information about the system along with a list of potential complications.

If your system has hardware devices that are not on the Windows 2000 HCL, contact the manufacturer of the device to determine whether it has new, updated Windows 2000 drivers for its device. Many peripheral makers have become very proactive in supplying updated drivers for their devices—often, posting their latest drivers and product compatibility information on their Internet Web sites, where they can be downloaded by customers. This is a good place to begin looking for needed drivers. The second alternative is to try the device with Windows NT or Windows 9x drivers to see whether it will work. The final option is to get a device that is listed on the Windows 2000 HCL.

If Windows Professional is to be installed across a network, a Windows 2000 Professional-compatible NIC is required. A list of Microsoft verified network cards can be read from the HCL.TXT file on the Windows 2000 Professional distribution CD. The system also must have access to the network share that contains the Setup files.

If several machines in a given organization are being upgraded to the same status, the Windows 2000 scripting capabilities can be put to good use. This feature can be used to create installation routines that require no user interaction. Microsoft also has added increased support for third-party disk copy and imaging utilities that perform multiple installs within a networked system.

To conduct a new Windows 2000 Professional installation, you need the Windows 2000 Professional distribution CD. If the installation is being performed on a system that cannot boot to the CD-ROM drive, you also need Windows 2000 Professional Setup disks. Just follow the instructions in Step by Steps 8.1 and 8.2.

TEST TIP

Know what to do if you encounter hardware devices not listed on the Windows 2000 HCL.

STEP BY STEP

8.1 Conducting a New Windows 2000 Professional Installation from a Floppy Disk

1. Turn the system off, place the Windows 2000 Professional Startup Disk #1 in the floppy drive, and turn on the system.

continues

continued

When the Setup program starts, it brings the Windows 2000 Setup Wizard to the screen (see Figure 8.2). The Setup Wizard collects information including Names, Passwords, and Regional Settings and writes the information to files on the hard drive. Afterward, the wizard checks the system's hardware and properly configures the installation.

FIGURE 8.2
Windows 2000 Setup Wizard.

2. Choose whether the installation is a New Install or an Upgrade. If a new installation is being performed, the Setup program installs the Windows 2000 files in the WINNT folder.

3. Follow the wizard's instructions, entering any information required. The choice made concerning the type of setup being performed and user-provided input determines the exact path the installation process will take.

STEP BY STEP

8.2 Conducting a New Windows 2000 Professional Installation from a CD-ROM

1. Boot the system to the existing operating system and then insert the Windows 2000 Professional distribution CD in the CD-ROM drive.

2. If the system detects the CD in the drive, just click the Install Windows 2000 option. If not, start Setup through the **Run** command. In Windows 9x and NT 4.0, click Start and then Run. In Windows 3.x and NT 3.51 click File and then Run.

3. At the prompt, enter the location on the Windows 2000 start file (WINNT.EXE or WINNT32.EXE) on the distribution CD (for instance, **d:\i386\WINNT32.EXE**). In the case of Windows 3.x, use the WINNT.EXE option.

4. Choose whether the installation is a New Install or an Upgrade.

5. Follow the wizard's instructions, entering any information required.

To install Windows 2000 Professional across a network, you must establish a shared connection between the local unit and the system containing the Windows 2000 Professional Setup files. Follow the instructions in Step by Step 8.3.

STEP BY STEP

8.3 Conducting a New Windows 2000 Professional Installation Across a Network

1. Boot the local unit to the existing operating system and establish a connection with the remote unit.

2. At the command prompt, enter the path to the remote WINNT32.EXE file. (Use the WINNT.EXE file if an older 16-bit operating system is being used on the local unit.)

3. Choose whether the installation is a New Install or an Upgrade.

4. Follow the wizard's instructions, entering any information required.

The Windows 2000 Setup Wizard collects information about the system and the user during the installation process. The most important information that must be provided includes the type of file management system that will be used (FAT or NTFS), computer name and administrator password, network settings, and workgroup or domain operations.

OPERATING SYSTEM UPGRADING

▶ 2.2 Identify steps to perform an operating system upgrade.

The A+ Operating System Technologies objective 2.2 states that the test taker should be able to "identify steps to perform an operating system upgrade."

As mentioned earlier, it is not uncommon for a computer to have its operating system upgraded, possibly several times, during its life span. The following sections of this chapter cover upgrading from DOS or Windows 9x environments to the Windows 9x or Windows 2000 operating systems.

Upgrading to Windows 95

With the Windows 95 Setup disk, or CD-ROM in the drive, the Windows 95 Setup routine can be executed from the *DOS command line*, from the Windows 3.x Program Manager's Run box, or from the File Manager window. The preferred method is to run the Setup program from Windows 3.x. As already mentioned, with any major system change, all important data should be backed up on some acceptable media before attempting to upgrade the operating system.

Step by Step 8.4 explains how to run the Setup program from Windows 3.x.

STEP BY STEP

8.4   Running the Windows 95 Setup Program from Windows 3.x

   1. Boot the computer and start Windows.

2. Insert the Windows 95 Start disk (Disk 1) in drive A:, or place the Windows 95 CD in the CD-ROM drive.

3. Open the File Manager and select the proper drive.

4. Double-click the SETUP.EXE file entry.

5. Follow the directions from the screen and enter the information requested by the program for the type of installation being performed.

Step by Step 8.5 shows you how to run the Setup program from DOS.

STEP BY STEP

8.5 Running the Windows 95 Setup Program from DOS

1. Boot the computer.

2. Insert the Windows 95 Start disk (Disk 1) in drive A:, or place the Windows 95 CD in the CD-ROM drive.

3. Move to the drive that contains the Windows 95 Installation files.

4. At the DOS prompt, type **Setup** and press the Enter key.

5. Follow the directions from the screen and enter the information requested by the program for the type of installation being performed.

The Setup program provides options for performing Typical (default), Portable, Compact, and Custom installations. Figure 8.3 depicts the Windows 95 Setup Wizard's Setup Options screen.

The Typical process normally installs most of the Windows 95 files to the C:\Windows directory without intervention from the user. However, this option does provide the user with the opportunity to install the operating system in another drive or directory. It also prompts the user to provide user and computer identification, and also enables the user to decide whether to create an *emergency start disk.* All other aspects of the installation are carried out by the Windows 95 Setup utility.

The Portable option installs those options most closely associated with portable computer systems. The Compact option is a minimal installation for those units with limited disk space available. The Custom option enables the user to make customized selections for most device configurations. This method may be required for installations that are using non-PnP-compliant adapter cards.

If Setup detects the presence of a Windows 3.x operating system, it

FIGURE 8.3
The Windows 95 Setup Options screen.

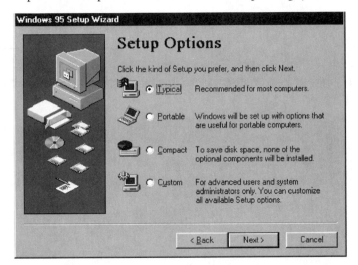

asks whether it should install its files in the same directory. If the prompt is answered with Yes, Windows 95 acts as an upgrade over the existing Windows structure. It obtains existing configuration information from the SYSTEM.INI, WIN.INI, and PROTOCOL.INI files and moves it into the Windows 95 *Registry.* This enables these settings to work automatically when Windows 95 is first started.

Windows 95 also migrates the contents of the existing Windows 3.x Group (GRP) files into the Registry during installation. Because Windows 95 rummages around in these files, both the INI and GRP files from the original Windows 3.x setup should be backed up before installing Windows 95.

Upgrading to Windows 98

To upgrade to Windows 98 from an existing Windows version, and retain the current system settings, execute the Setup program from the Windows 95 user interface. Windows 98 Setup executes the same basic five-step procedure described earlier from either interface. However, the events that occur within each step depend on the operating system information that is already available.

Although Windows 95 to Windows 98 upgrades are convenient, they also can be unstable afterward. Therefore, if you do not need to retain any specific settings, you may want to just back up the system's data, FDISK the disk, and perform a clean Windows 98 installation.

{ uninstall windows & Back up Disk }

When Windows 98 is installed on a current Windows 95 machine, using the existing settings, the Setup program acquires information about the system's hardware, applications, and utilities from the existing Registry entries. The existing information is just migrated into the new Windows 98 structure. In this manner, a lot of time is saved because the system does not have to run a full hardware-detection routine, or configure the system's hardware. The Setup routine also skips the option of selecting a Setup type (for instance Custom or Typical).

During Phase 1 of the Windows 98 upgrade, the system checks for the presence of antivirus software in the system. The Setup routine may fail if CMOS Antivirus is enabled. If this occurs, check the SETUPLOG.TXT file for information about the antivirus test. In some cases, the Setup program may ask that the antivirus software be disabled so that it can have access to the Master Boot Record. Setup also modifies the AUTOEXEC.BAT file, causing it to run a file called SUWARN.BAT. This file reboots the system in case of a failure, and presents an explanation of why the setup failed.

In Phase 2 of the upgrade, the real-mode ScanDisk operation is carried out, and Setup runs the SCANREGW.EXE file to check the existing Registry for corruption. The Setup routine also provides a prompt that permits the current DOS or Windows System files to be saved in case an uninstall operation is required for Windows 98 at some future time.

The Setup routine copies the Windows 98 files to the computer during Phase 3. This segment of the process begins with the appearance of the Start Copying Files dialog box on the screen. The complete operation of this phase is automated and requires no external intervention. However, any interruption of the Setup operation during this period may prevent the system from starting up again. In this event, you must repeat the entire Setup routine from the beginning.

In Phase 4, the Restart operation includes a step where the Setup routine modifies the WIN.INI, SYSTEM.INI, and Registry files to include the appropriate Windows 98 entries. Likewise, an existing *AUTOEXEC.BAT* or *CONFIG.SYS* file will be examined for device drivers and terminate-and-stay-resident (TSR) programs that may be incompatible with the upgraded installation. TSR programs can be quite problematic and should be deactivated before conducting any operating system upgrade. The results of this check are logged in a hidden file at C:\Windows\Inf_folder\SETUPC.INF. The Setup routine disables the questionable entries in these files by using **REM** statements.

Be aware that active antivirus software may prevent Windows 98 from installing to a system. These utilities see the changes to the new operating system's Core files as a virus activity and will work to prevent them from occurring. Disable any antivirus programs prior to running Windows 98 Setup. The program can be re-enabled after the setup process has been completed.

When it is desirable to install Windows 98 into some directory other than the C:\Windows directory, click the Other Directory button in the Select Directory dialog box, depicted in Figure 8.4, and select the Next option. This action produces the Change Directory dialog box. Type the new directory name in the dialog box and click the Next option. The new directory will be created automatically, if it does not already exist.

If Windows 98 is installed in a new directory, you must reinstall any Windows-based applications in the system. This is required for the applications to function properly. The applications' support DLLs will not be able to automatically access the Windows 98 structure in the new directory. Likewise, existing GRP and INI files will not work unless Windows 98 has been installed in the Windows directory.

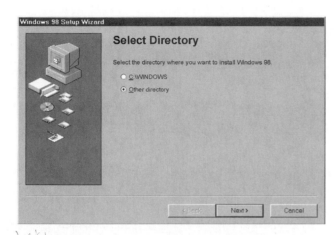

FIGURE 8.4
The Select Directory dialog box.

Upgrading to Windows 2000

Systems can be upgraded to Windows 2000 Professional from Windows 3.x and 9x, as well as Windows NT 3.5 and 4.0 workstations. This includes older NTFS, FAT16, and FAT32 installations. When you install Windows 2000, it can recognize all three of these file system types.

The process of upgrading to Windows 2000 can be performed in incremental steps. This enables network administrators to bring network machines up to Windows 2000 status over time. During the system upgrade process, the Windows NT 4.0 units can interact with the Windows 2000 units because they see them as NT 4 systems.

Upgrading Windows 2000 from a Windows NT 4 or Windows 9x base is quicker than performing a new installation.

When a system is upgraded to Windows 2000 Professional, the Setup utility replaces any existing Windows files with Windows 2000 Professional versions. However, existing settings and applications will be preserved in the new environment. As with previous Windows NT products, Windows 2000 does not attempt to remain compatible with older hardware and software. Therefore, some applications may not be compatible with Windows 2000 and may run poorly or fail completely after an upgrade.

Upgrading to Windows 2000 is suggested for those using an existing Windows operating system that is compatible with Windows 2000 who want to maintain their existing data and preference settings.

STEP BY STEP

8.6 Upgrading to Windows 2000

1. To upgrade a system to Windows 2000 from a previous operating system using a CD-ROM install, boot the system to the existing operating system and then insert the Windows 2000 Professional distribution CD in the CD-ROM drive.

2. If the system detects the CD in the drive, just click the Install Windows 2000 option. If not, start Setup through the **Run** command. In Windows 9x and NT 4.0, click Start and then Run. In Windows 3.x and NT 3.51 click File and then Run.

3. At the prompt, enter the location on the Windows 2000 start file (WINNT.EXE or WINNT32.EXE) on the distribution CD (for instance, **d:\i386\WINNT32.EXE**). In the case of Windows 3.x, use the WINNT.EXE option.

4. Choose whether the installation is a New Install or an Upgrade.

5. Follow the wizard's instructions, entering any information required.

To upgrade Windows 2000 Professional from a previous operating system across a network, you must establish a shared connection between the local unit and the system containing the Windows 2000 Professional Setup files.

STEP BY STEP

8.7 Upgrading Windows 2000 Professional Across a Network

1. Boot the local unit to the existing operating system and establish a connection with the remote unit.

2. At the command prompt, enter the path to the remote WINNT32.EXE file. (Use the WINNT.EXE file if an older operating system is being used on the local unit.) The **WINNT** command is used with 16-bit operating systems such as DOS or Windows 3x. The WINNT32 version is used with 32-bit operating systems including Windows 95, 98, NT 3.5, NT 4.0.

3. Choose the Upgrade Your Computer to Windows 2000 option.

4. Follow the Setup Wizard's instructions, entering any information required.

During the installation process, the Windows 2000 Setup Wizard collects information about users and the system. Most of this information is collected automatically. However, some information must be provided by the user/technician.

The most important information required during the setup process is the file management system to be used, the computer name and administrator password, network settings, and workgroup/domain selection.

Dual Booting

By establishing a *dual-boot configuration*, it is possible to install Windows 9x or some other operating system on an existing system and still retain the original operating system. The first step in establishing a dual-boot system is to install the Windows 9x operating system into a new directory.

To dual boot with DOS, or DOS/Windows 3.x, the system must have a copy of MS-DOS 5.0 or higher already running. If the Windows 9x installation is a new setup, the dual-boot option can be configured during the installation process. When prompted by the Setup utility to use the C:\Windows directory or specify another directory for the Windows files, choose a new directory for the Windows 9x installation. The Windows 9x Setup program will automatically adjust the existing DOS, CONFIG.SYS, and AUTOEXEC.BAT files for the new operating system.

The original IO.SYS, MSDOS.SYS, COMMAND.COM, CONFIG.SYS, and AUTOEXEC.BAT files are stored in the root directory using a .DOS extension. If Windows 3.x was originally installed on the drive, those files will remain in the C:\Windows directory and can be used if the system is booted to the original DOS operating system.

In addition, the setting for the Windows 9x MSDOS.SYS file's BOOTMULTI= entry must be set to a value of 1. To do so, bring the file into a text editor, such as Notepad, and change the setting to the desired value. After rebooting the system, you can boot into the old DOS/Windows 3.x environment by pressing the F4 function key when the Starting Windows message appears during boot up. Pressing the F8 function key reveals that the previous version of MS-DOS option has been added to the *Startup menu*.

If Windows 9x is already installed in the system, it is still possible to set up the system to dual boot with a DOS environment. You must copy the IO.SYS, MSDOS.SYS, and COMMAND.COM files from the DOS disk to a bootable floppy. Afterward, rename these files to *IO.DOS*, *MSDOS.DOS*, and *COMMAND.DOS*, and then copy them into the root directory of the boot drive.

The boot-up system files must be handled as any other hidden, read-only, system files. Use the **ATTRIB** command to read and copy them (that is, **ATTRIB -H -S -R IO.SYS**). You must perform the same copy/rename/copy operations to create CONFIG.DOS and AUTOEXEC.DOS files that are appropriate for the version of DOS you are using in the system.

Just restart the system and make the necessary steps to start and run the DOS or Windows 9x operating system.

Windows NT can be set up to dual-boot with DOS or Windows 9x operating systems. This provides the option for the system to boot up into a Windows NT environment, or into a DOS/Windows 9x environment. In such cases, a Startup menu appears and asks which operating system should be used. Establishing either of these dual-boot conditions with Windows NT requires that the DOS or Windows 9x operating system be installed first.

The major drawback of dual-booting with Windows NT is that the other operating system cannot use applications installed in the other operating system's partition. Therefore, software to be used by both operating systems must be installed in the system twice (once for each operating system partition).

Take care when formatting a logical drive in a Windows NT dual-boot system. The file-management formats of Windows NT and the other operating systems are not compatible. If the disk is formatted with NTFS, the DOS or Windows 9x operating systems cannot read the files in the NTFS partition. However, Windows NT can operate with the FAT file systems used by DOS and Windows 3.x/9x. As a matter of fact, Windows 2000 can be installed on FAT16, FAT32, or NTFS partitions. Windows 2000 also supports the CDFS file system used with CD-ROM drives in PCs. Therefore, it is recommended that logical drives in a dual-boot system be formatted with the FAT system.

BOOTING THE SYSTEM

▶ 2.3 Identify the basic system boot sequences and boot methods, including the steps to create an emergency boot disk with utilities installed for Windows 9x, Windows NT, and Windows 2000.

The A+ Operating System Technologies objective 2.3 states that the test taker should be able to "identify the basic system boot sequences and boot methods, including the steps to create an emergency boot disk with utilities installed for Windows 9x, Windows NT, and Windows 2000."

Booting up the disk operating system is one of the most critical times in the operation of the computer. A technician must know the general sequence of events that should occur during this process. By knowing this information, the technician can observe the process and watch for telltale symptoms of operation system startup problems. Therefore, the following sections of the chapter deal with booting up the operating system.

The Boot Process

PC system boards use one or two IC chips to hold the system's BIOS firmware. The system's memory map reserves memory locations from E0000h to FFFFFh for the system board BIOS routines. These chips contain the programs that handle startup of the system, the changeover to disk-based operations, video and printer output functions, and a *Power-On Self-Test*.

POST Tests and Initialization

The POST test is actually a series of tests performed each time the system is turned on. The different tests check the operation of the microprocessor, the keyboard, the video display, the floppy and hard disk drive units, as well as both the RAM and ROM memory units.

When the system board is reset, or when power is removed from it, the system begins generating clock pulses when power is restored. This action applies a Reset pulse to the microprocessor, causing it to clear most of its registers to 0. However, it sets the Instruction Pointer (IP) register to 0FFF0h and the Code Segment (CS) register to F0000h. The first instruction is taken from location FFFF0h. Notice that this address is located in the ROM BIOS program. This is not coincidental. When the system is started up, the microprocessor must begin taking instructions from this ROM location to initialize the system for operation.

Initial POST Checks

The first instruction that the microprocessor executes causes it to jump to the POST tests where it performs standard tests such as the ROM BIOS checksum test (that verifies that the BIOS program is accurate), and the system's various DRAM tests (that verify the bits of the memory). It also tests the system's CMOS RAM (to make certain that its contents have not changed because of a battery failure). During the memory tests, the POST displays a running memory count to show that it is testing and verifying the individual memory locations.

Sequentially, the system's interrupts are disabled, the bits of the microprocessor's flag register are set, and a read/write test is performed on each of its internal registers. The test program just writes a predetermined bit pattern into each register and then reads it back to verify the register's operation. After verifying the operation of the microprocessor's registers, the BIOS program begins testing and initializing the rest of the system. It moves forward by inspecting the ROM BIOS chip itself. It does this by performing a checksum test of certain locations on the chip and comparing the answer with a known value stored in another location.

A checksum test involves adding the values stored in the key locations together. The result is a rounded-off sum of the values. When the checksum test is performed, the sum of the locations is recalculated and compared to the stored value. If they match, no error is assumed to have occurred. If they do not match, an error condition exists and an error message or *beep code* is produced.

At this point, the program checks to see whether the system is being started from an off condition, or being reset from some other state. When the system is started from an off condition, a *cold boot* is being performed. However, simultaneously pressing Ctrl+Alt+Del while the system is in operation generates a reset signal in the system and causes it to perform a shortened boot-up routine. This operation is referred to as a *warm boot* and allows the system to be shut down and restarted without turning it off. This function also allows the computer's operation to be switched to another operating system.

If power was applied to the system prior to the occurrence of the reset signal, some of the POST's memory tests are skipped.

If a cold boot is indicated, the program tests the first 16KB of RAM memory by writing five different bit patterns into the memory and reading them back, to establish the validity of each location. Figure 8.5 shows the BIOS startup steps.

FIGURE 8.5
The startup sequence.

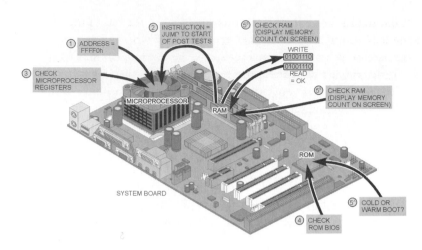

System Initialization

If the first 16KB of RAM successfully passes all five of the bit-pattern tests, the BIOS routine initializes the system's intelligent devices. During this part of the program, startup values stored in the ROM chip are moved into the system's programmable devices, to make them functional.

The BIOS loads starting information into all the system's standard AT-compatible components, such as the interrupt, DMA, keyboard, and video controllers, as well as its timer/counter circuits. The program checks the DMA controller by performing an R/W test on each of the its internal registers and then initializes them with startup values.

The program continues by setting up the system's interrupt controller. This includes moving the system's interrupt vectors into address locations 00000h through 003FFh. In addition, an R/W test is performed on each of the interrupt controller's internal registers. The routine then causes the controller to mask (disable) all of its interrupt inputs, and tests each one to ensure that no interrupts occur.

The programming of the interrupt controller is significant because most of the events in a PC-compatible system are interrupt driven. Its operation affects the operation of the computer in every phase from this point forward. Every peripheral or software routine that needs to get special services from the system makes use of the interrupt controller.

Following the initialization of the interrupt controller, the program checks the output of the system's timer/counter channels. It does this by counting pulses from the counters for a given period of time to verify that the proper frequencies are being produced.

If the timer/counter frequencies are correct, the routine initializes and starts the video controller. The program obtains information about the type of display (monochrome, color, or both) being used with the system by reading configuration information from registers in the system's CMOS RAM. After this has been established, the program conducts R/W tests on the video adapter's RAM memory. If the video adapter passes all these tests, the program causes a cursor symbol to display on the monitor. Figure 8.6 shows the steps of the initialization process.

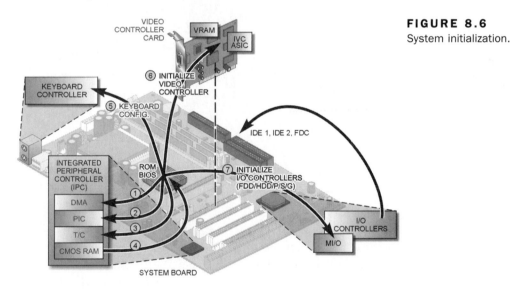

FIGURE 8.6
System initialization.

Additional POST Checks

After the display adapter has been checked, the BIOS routine resumes testing the system's onboard memory. First, R/W testing is performed on all the additional RAM on the system board (beyond the first 16KB). In addition, the BIOS executes the system's built-in Setup program to configure its day/time setting, its hard disk and floppy disk drive types, and the amount of memory actually available to the system.

Following the final memory test, the remaining I/O devices and adapters are tested. The program begins by enabling the keyboard circuitry and checking for a scan code from the keyboard. No scan code indicates that no key has been depressed. The program then proceeds to test the system's parallel printer and RS-232C serial ports. In each case, the test consists of performing R/W tests on each of the port's registers, storing the addresses of functional ports (some ports may not be installed, or in use), and storing time limitations for each port's operation. Figure 8.7 shows the steps of the POST process.

FIGURE 8.7
Completion of the POST test.

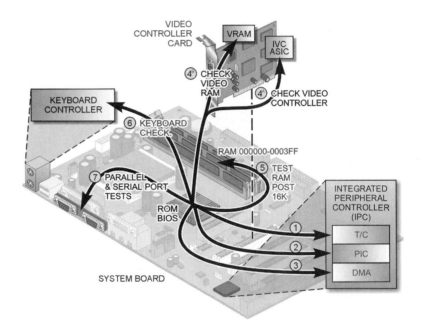

BIOS Extensions

After the initialization and POST tests are completed, the BIOS checks the area of memory between C0000h and DFFFFh for *BIOS extension* programs.

IBM system designers created this memory area so that new or non-standard BIOS routines could be added to the basic BIOS structure. These extended firmware routines match software commands from the system to the hardware they support. Therefore, the software running on the system does not have to be directly compatible with the hardware.

BIOS extensions are created in 512-byte blocks that must begin at a 2KB marker (that is, C8000h, C8200h, C8400h, C8800h, and so on), as illustrated in Figure 8.8. A single extension can occupy multiple blocks; however, it can start only at one of the markers. When the main BIOS encounters the special 2-byte extension code at one of the 2KB markers, it tests the block of code and then turns control over to the extension. Upon completion of the extension code, control is passed back to the main BIOS, which then checks for an extension marker at the next 2KB marker.

Although the extension addresses are memory addresses, the extension code may be located anywhere in the system. In particular, BIOS extensions are often located on expansion cards. The system just accesses them through the expansion bus.

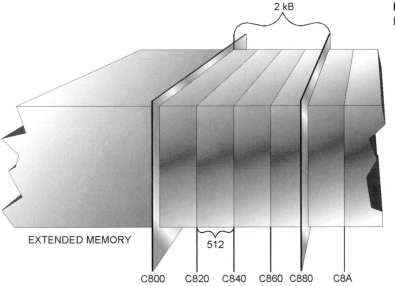

FIGURE 8.8
BIOS extension blocks.

Advanced video cards contain video BIOS code, either in a ROM IC or built directly into the video controller ASIC. The IBM EGA and VGA standards allow for onboard ROM that uses addresses between C0000h and C7FFFh.

Likewise, different types of HDD controller cards contain a BIOS extension IC. The HDD controllers in old XT units had BIOS extensions that used the address space between C8000h and C9FFFh. Some current HDD controllers, such as ESDI and SCSI adapters, reserve memory blocks between C8000h and CBFFFh.

Another type of device that commonly uses the C000h–D000h blocks are network adapter cards. These cards allow the computer to be connected to other computers in the local area. The BIOS extension code on a network card may contain an Initial Program Load (IPL) routine that will cause the local computer to load up and operate from the operating system of a remote computer.

The system can accommodate as many extensions as will mathematically fit within the allotted memory area. However, two extension programs cannot be located in the same range of addresses. With this in mind, peripheral manufacturers typically include some method of switching the starting addresses of their BIOS extensions so that they can be set to various markers.

Plug and Play

In the case of *Plug and Play* (PnP) systems, the BIOS also must communicate with the adapter cards located in the expansion slots to determine what their characteristics are. Even in a system using a PnP-compliant operating system, such as Windows 9x, the BIOS also must be PnP-compatible before the system can recognize and manipulate system resources. When the system is turned on, the PnP devices involved in the boot-up process become active in their default configuration. Other logical devices, not required for boot up, start up in an inactive mode.

Before starting the boot-up sequence, the PnP BIOS checks the devices installed in the expansion slots to see what types they are, how they are configured, and which slots they are in. It then assigns each adapter a software handle (name) and stores their names and configuration information in a special section of CMOS RAM called the Extended System Configuration Data (ESCD) area. The BIOS and operating system both access the ESCD area each time the system is restarted to see if any information has changed. This enables the BIOS and operating system to work together in sorting out the needs of the installed devices and assigning them needed system resources. Next, the BIOS checks the adapter information against the system's basic configuration for *resource conflicts*. If no conflicts are detected, all the devices required for boot up are activated.

Devices not required for boot up can be configured and activated by the BIOS or they may just be configured and left in an inactive state. In either event, the operating system is left with the task of activating the remaining intelligent devices and resolving any resource conflicts that the BIOS detected and could not resolve. If the PnP option is not working for a particular device, or the operating system cannot resolve the remaining resource conflicts, use the manufacturer's setup instructions to perform manual configurations.

The Windows 9x PnP process can be examined by printing out its *DETLOG.TXT* file. The printout of this file is located under the C:\ root directory and provides a step-by-step listing of the operating system's hardware-detection process. It demonstrates the order of resource allocation as well as the process of detecting and assigning resources to the system's various hardware devices. A partial listing of a sample DETLOG file is presented in Chapter 9, "3.0 Diagnosing and Troubleshooting."

Boot Up

If the option to enter the setup routine is bypassed, or if the routine has been exited, the BIOS begins the process of booting up to the operating system. A simple single-operating system, single-disk boot-up process is described in Figure 8.9. As you can see, it is a multiple-access operation that uses two different bootstrap routines to locate and load two different boot records.

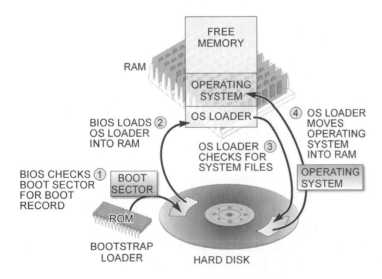

FIGURE 8.9
The bootstrap operation.

The very first section on any logical DOS disk is called the *boot sector*. This section contains information about how the disk is organized. It also may contain the small, optional Master Boot Record that can access a larger, more powerful Bootstrap Loader program located in the root directory.

NOTE

Starting the Boot-Up Process   The boot-up process starts when the BIOS begins looking through the system for a *Master Boot Record* (MBR). This record can reside on drive A: or C:, or at any other location.

In most systems, the Master Boot Record is found at sector 1, head 0, and track 0 of the first logical hard drive. Some texts may refer to the first sector as sector 0, keeping with the idea that the first one of anything in a digital system is 0. If the disk possesses a Master Boot Record, it can boot up the hardware system to the operating system. The disk is then referred to as a *bootable disk*, or a system disk. If not, the disk is just a data disk that can be used for storing information.

The usage of the term *system disk* has changed somewhat over time. In the old days, when MS-DOS came on two disks labeled System Disk and Supplemental Disk, the system disk was the one that contained the files necessary to boot the system. Now, the term is used generally to specify any floppy disk that has a Master Boot Record so that it can boot the system—regardless of the type of operating system it carries.

Traditionally, BIOS programs will search for the Master Boot Record in floppy disk drive A: first. If a bootable disk is in the floppy disk drive, the BIOS executes the *Primary Bootstrap Loader* routine to move the Master Boot Record into RAM and then begins the process of loading the operating system. In the original IBM PC, the BIOS searched in the floppy disk drive for the boot record. If it was not located there, the BIOS routine turned over control to a BASIC program located in the PC's ROM BIOS IC.

In the PC-XT, the BIOS looked first in the floppy drive, or drives, and then in the hard disk drive. If neither location contained the boot record, the system loaded up the ROM BASIC program. In clone systems, there was no ROM BIOS present to default to when no boot record was found. If the BIOS did not locate the boot record in the floppy or hard drive, it just displayed a Non-System Disk or Disk Error or ROM BASIC Interpreter Not Found message onscreen.

In newer systems, the order in which the BIOS searches drives for the boot record is governed by information stored in the system's CMOS configuration RAM. The order can be set to check the floppy drive first and then the hard drive, or to check the hard drive first, or to check the hard drive only.

In a networked system, a Bootstrap Loader routine also can be located in the ROM extension of a network card as described earlier. When the system checks the BIOS extensions, the bootstrap routine redirects the boot-up process to look for a boot record on the disk drive of another computer. Any boot record on the local drive will be bypassed.

To accomplish the boot up, the BIOS enables the system's nonmaskable interrupts and causes a single, short tone to be produced by the speaker circuitry. The single beep indicates that the POST portion of the boot up has successfully completed.

The next BIOS instruction executes an Interrupt19 Disk Drive service routine. This interrupt routine carries out the Primary Bootstrap Loader program, which looks for the Master Boot Record in the first section of the floppy and hard disks. When located, it moves the Master Boot Record into system RAM to be executed.

The Master Boot Record contains the Secondary Bootstrap Loader, also called the *Operating System Loader*. This routine looks for an operating system boot record, typically located on the disk. When found, it loads the bigger boot record into RAM and begins executing it. This boot record brings special operating system files into memory so that they can control the operation of the system (that is, the operating system). In the case of Microsoft DOS, the special files in the OS boot record are the IO.SYS and MSDOS.SYS files.

The Operating System Loader looks for a command processor file. The command processor can belong to any operating system, such as Microsoft MS-DOS, UNIX, IBM PC DOS, Novell NetWare, and so on. The default command processor for DOS is a system file called COMMAND.COM. This file interprets the input entered at the DOS prompt. When the bootstrap program finds the command processor, it moves it into system RAM along with the operating system support files. In DOS systems, the command processor provides the basic user interface, called the command line.

In the original PC DOS from IBM, the files were titled IBMBIO.COM, IBMDOS.COM, and COMMAND.COM. This step marks the end of the BIOS routine. The three system files must be found in the root directory (the starting point for any disk-based operations) to successfully boot DOS. Figure 8.10 depicts the total boot-up process.

FIGURE 8.10
The boot-up process.

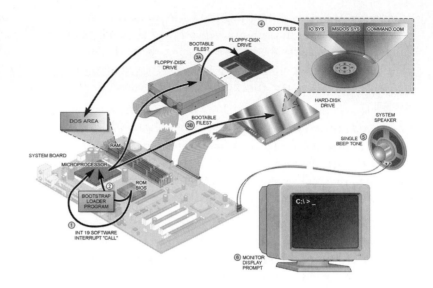

If the system has performed a standard DOS boot up, without any modifications, it should print date and time prompts on the monitor screen, followed by the DOS command-line prompt (A:\>> or C:\>>). The prompt indicates that DOS is operational and that the currently active drive is the A: floppy drive or the C:\ hard drive. Now the DOS software will control the movement of data and the overall operation of the system. DOS allows the basic boot up to be modified through two special configuration files, called CONFIG.SYS and AUTOEXEC.BAT, discussed later in this chapter.

The following list summarizes the files and their execution order required for boot up in an MS-DOS system:

- ◆ IO.SYS
- ◆ MSDOS.SYS
- ◆ CONFIG.SYS
- ◆ COMMAND.COM
- ◆ AUTOEXEC.BAT

In a DOS system, the operation of the system is now in the control of the operator and whatever software is being used with the system. The system is waiting for the user to do something, such as enter commands and instructions or run programs from the other two

TEST TIP

Remember the files involved in the DOS boot-up process and the order of their execution.

software categories. The user hasn't had anything to do with the operation of the system yet. This is why this type of software is referred to as system software.

Altering CONFIG.SYS Steps

The operation of the CONFIG.SYS file can be altered or bypassed by pressing selected keys during the boot-up process. Holding the Shift key or pressing the F5 key while the MS-DOS message Starting DOS is onscreen causes the boot-up process to skip all the commands in the CONFIG.SYS file. This action also bypasses all the steps of the AUTOEXEC.BAT file.

When this option is used, the system will boot up with a complete set of default settings. No installable device drivers will be installed, the current directory will be set to C:\DOS, and you may receive a *Bad or Missing Command Interpreter* message. If this message is received, the system asks you to manually enter the path to the COMMAND.COM file.

Similarly, pressing the F8 function key while the Starting DOS message is onscreen causes the system to stop between each CONFIG.SYS command and ask for verification before proceeding. This is referred to as a single-step startup option and can be very helpful in troubleshooting configuration and boot-up problems. This action also causes the system to ask the user whether the AUTOEXEC.BAT file should be run or skipped. Placing a question mark after a CONFIG.SYS command (before the = sign) causes the system to automatically seek verification whenever the system is booted up.

The special function keys available during the DOS startup are summarized as follows:

- ◆ **F5 (also left Shift key).** Skips CONFIG.SYS and AUTOEXEC.BAT files.

- ◆ **F8.** Proceeds through the CONFIG.SYS and AUTOEXEC.BAT files one step at a time waiting for confirmation from the user.

> **TEST TIP**
>
> Know which function keys can be used during the boot-up process to alter it.

Windows 9x Startup

Unlike previous versions of Windows, the Windows 9x structure does not overlay a separate DOS structure. Instead, Windows 9x takes over the complete boot-up function as a normal part of its operation. This seamless boot up may be convenient but can offer some interesting problems when the system will not boot up—there's no DOS level to fall back to for troubleshooting purposes.

Basically, the Windows 9x boot-up sequence occurs in five phases:

> Phase 1: Bootstrap with the BIOS
>
> Phase 2: Loading DOS drivers and TSR files
>
> Phase 3: Real-mode initialization of static virtual device drivers (VxDs)
>
> Phase 4: Protected-mode switchover
>
> Phase 5: Loading of any remaining VxDs

VxDs are protected-mode drivers that allow multiple applications to access a system hardware or software resource. The x in the abbreviation represents a particular type of driver (that is, VDD is a display driver, VPD is a printer driver, and so forth).

There are two types of VxDs: those that must be statically loaded, and those that may be dynamically loaded. Static VxDs are loaded into memory and stay there while the system is operating. All *virtual device drivers* were loaded this way in older Windows versions. The problem with loading drivers in this manner is that they use a lot of memory. Windows 9x dynamically loads some drivers into memory while they are needed. Windows 9x VxDs files have an extension of .VXD; older Windows drivers retain the .386 extension.

Phase 1: The Bootstrap Process

During the bootstrap process, the BIOS is in control of the system and functions as described in Chapter 1. However, most newer BIOS contain PnP features designed to work with the Windows 9x architecture. In particular, the BIOS passes configuration information about the system to the Windows 9x Configuration Manager.

During the bootstrap process, the PnP BIOS checks the system's CMOS RAM to determine which PnP devices should be activated, and where their PnP information should be stored. Each device's DMA, IRQ, and I/O addressing assignments also are collected. This period is referred to as the hardware-detection phase.

After all the configuration information has been gathered, the BIOS configures the PnP cards and the intelligent system board devices. It then performs the traditional POST and initialization functions for the rest of the system. These functions are illustrated in Figures 8.11, 8.12, and 8.13.

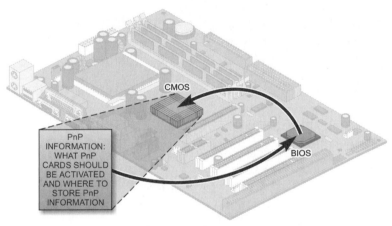

FIGURE 8.11
Reading PnP information from CMOS.

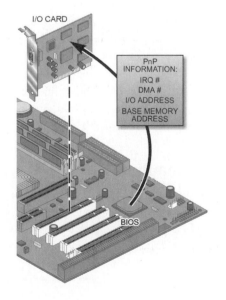

FIGURE 8.12
Initializing PnP devices.

FIGURE 8.13
Programming the onboard devices.

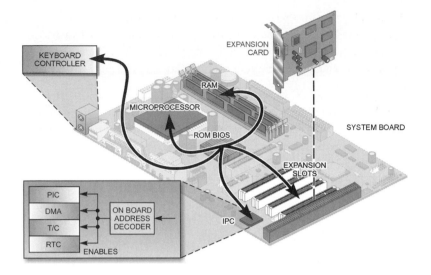

Upon completion of the configuration-check operation, the BIOS configures the PnP cards and the intelligent system board devices. The BIOS then performs the traditional POST and initialization functions for the rest of the system.

The BIOS then moves into the boot-up process. The Bootstrap Loader routine searches for the Master Boot Record as it does with every other operating system. When the MBR is found, the system loads the IO.SYS and MSDOS.SYS files from the disk into memory and turns over control to the IO.SYS file.

At this point, IO.SYS has the capability to display the Windows 9x Startup menu, described later in this chapter. The menu can be displayed each time the system boots by setting the BootMenu=1 option in the MSDOS.SYS file. The same menu can be retrieved by pressing the left Ctrl key during boot up. When using this key, the Starting Windows 9x message will not appear onscreen. The F8 function key will still perform this function as well.

Phase 2: Loading DOS Drivers and TSR Files

After the disk boot, IO.SYS checks the system's hardware profile to determine its actual configuration. This profile is a function of the BIOS' detection process during the initialization phase.

IO.SYS begins loading default drivers that were previously taken care of by the CONFIG.SYS file. These files include HIMEM.SYS, IFSHLP.SYS, SETVER.EXE, and DBLSPACE.BIN, as well as files=, buffers=, stacks=, and DOS=HIGH settings.

If the F8 option for step-by-step startup has been selected, the system begins to generate a *BOOTLOG.TXT* file. This file tracks the Windows 9x components and drivers that successfully load and initialize during the startup process. The BOOTLOG.TXT file is described in greater detail in Chapter 9.

At this point, IO.SYS begins looking for a CONFIG.SYS file. If found, the lines of the file are executed and any values that differ from those loaded by the IO.SYS file are used instead. The CONFIG.SYS values for buffers, files, and stacks must be set to at least equal the default values in the IO.SYS file. The EMM386.EXE function must be initiated from the CONFIG.SYS file for any programs that require this memory manager.

Next, IO.SYS checks the MSDOS.SYS file for paths to find other Windows directories and files. These include such items as the selected location of the Windows 9x directory and startup files, including the Registry. The [Options] section of the file permits selected boot-up events to be altered. This section can contain items to automatically display the Boot menu and to enable or disable key boot-up features.

This is followed by executing the COMMAND.COM file. As with previous Microsoft operating systems, the Windows 9x COMMAND.COM extends the I/O functions of the system, supplies the command interface for the system, and looks for the AUTOEXEC.BAT file. If found, the AUTOEXEC.BAT commands are executed, loading device drivers and TSR programs in real mode.

In the Windows 9x environment, the CONFIG.SYS and AUTOEXEC.BAT files primarily exist to maintain compatibility with applications written for earlier operating systems and environments. If neither of these files are present, the system will start and run fine.

Phase 3: Initializing Static VxDs

The system next checks the SYSTEM.DAT file for the first part of the Registry file and processes it. SYSTEM.DAT is a hidden file that contains all the system's hardware configuration information, including the PnP and application settings. It is always located under the Windows directory. If a Windows 95 system does not find the SYSTEM.DAT file, it will refer to the SYSTEM.DA0 file created as a backup during the previous boot-up sequence. However, in a Windows 98 system, the Registry Backup files (RB000X.CAB) stored in the C:\Windows\Sysbackup directory are checked.

Afterward, IO.SYS loads the *WIN.COM* file to control the loading and testing of the Windows 9x core components. This is followed by loading the *VMM32.VXD virtual machine manager* and, finally, the SYSTEM.INI file. SYSTEM.INI is loaded so that its information can be used to maintain compatibility with nondynamic VxDs

The VMM32.VXD file creates the virtual environment and loads the VxD files. It contains a list of all the VxD files the system requires. These files are stored in the Hkey_Local_Machine\System\CurrentControlSet\Services\VxD branch of the Windows 9x Registry. The Registry is a centralized, improved replacement for the old Window 3.x "INI" initialization files. The virtual machine manager searches this branch of the Registry looking for static drivers. If the value in the listing is represented by a STATICVXD= statement, the VMM32.VXD file loads and initializes it in real mode. It also statically loads any VxDs that have a DEVICE=XXXVXD entry. The dynamic VxD files are not loaded by the VMM32.VXD file.

VMM32 also checks the [386Enh] section of the SYSTEM.INI file for static VxDs (DEVICE=XXXVXD). If it finds a VxD in the SYSTEM.INI file, that version will be used rather than any version that is found in the Registry. Any device that does not possess a virtual driver must be run in MS-DOS compatibility (virtual 86) mode, using real-mode drivers.

Phase 4: Protected-Mode Changeover

After loading all the static VxDs, the VMM32.VXD file shifts the microprocessor into protected-mode operation and begins loading the protected-mode components of the system.

The Configuration Manager is loaded and initialized with configuration information from the PnP BIOS' earlier detection efforts. If no PnP information is available, the Configuration Manager develops a PnP tree by loading dynamically loadable drivers. After the tree is in place, the Configuration Manager reconciles the configuration information for each device, resolves any conflicts, and then reconfigures any necessary devices.

The Windows 9x VxD configuration process can be examined by printing out its BOOTLOG.TXT file. This file is located under the C:\ root directory and provides a step-by-step listing of the operating system's real-mode and VxD-driver loading process. It demonstrates the order of loading as well as the process of initializing the drivers for these various hardware devices. A partial listing of a sample BOOTLOG file is presented in Chapter 9.

Phase 5: Loading Remaining Components

Following the initialization process, the final Windows 9x components are loaded into the system. During this period, the following occurs:

◆ The KERNEL32.DLL and KERNEL386.EXE files are executed.

◆ The GDI.EXE and GDI32.EXE files are executed.

◆ The USER.EXE and USER32.EXE files are executed.

◆ All fonts and other associated resources are loaded.

◆ The WIN.INI file values are checked.

◆ The Windows 9x shell and machine policies are loaded.

◆ The desktop components are loaded.

Each pair of Core files provides a 16-bit and a 32-bit version to provide services for the various applications run on the system. As mentioned in Chapter 7, the Kernel files provide the basic operating system functions, including task scheduling, virtual memory management, and file I/O services. The *KERNEL32.DLL* file contains the Windows 9x core components while the KERNEL386 file loads the Windows 9x device drivers.

The user components manage input from the system's installed input devices, and the GDI components manage what appears on the display screen. The GDI also supplies basic support for printer graphics drivers.

The WIN.INI and SYSTEM.INI files are included in the Windows directory to maintain compatibility functions with older software. These files are retained for use with older 16-bit applications and are not necessary for the operation of Windows 9x applications. These files need to be checked, however, if the Windows 9x system has conflicts with any 16-bit applications.

When the shell and desktop components are loaded, the system may display a logon prompt onscreen. This logon process enables the operating system to configure itself for specific users. Normal logon involves entering a username and password. If no logon information is entered, default values are loaded into the system. The logon screen appears only if the system is in use with a network, or when there are settings that the user can customize.

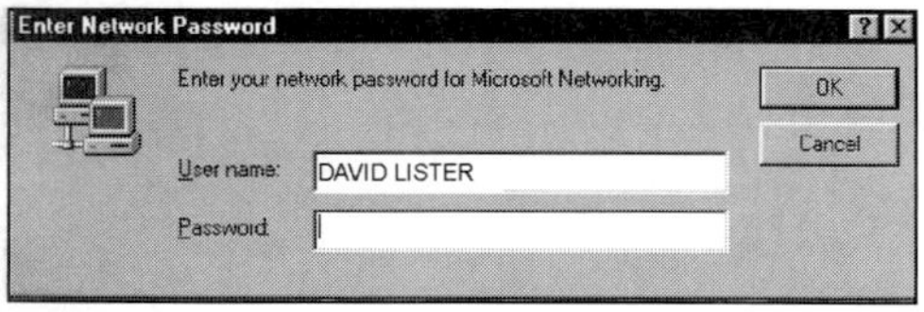

FIGURE 8.14
Windows 9x Network Logon dialog box.

If the system is connected to a network, the network logon screen appears, as depicted in Figure 8.14. Logging on to a network is becoming more common every day. Therefore, one of the most common startup actions for Windows 9x users is entering their information into the logon window. After the user logs on, the system's user-specific setup instructions are carried out.

Windows 9x searches the Hkey_Local_Machine key, and the user's home directory, for user profile information. Windows 9x creates a folder for each user who logs on to the system. This profile is held in the Windows\Profiles subdirectory. Each profile contains a USER.DAT file (the second half of the Registry) that holds the Registry information for that user. It also contains a number of other files that customize the desktop just for that user. As with the SYS-TEM.DAT file, the USER.DAT file is backed up as USER.DA0 each time the Windows 95 system is rebooted. Under Windows 98, the USER.DAT backup is part of the RB000X.CAB files.

The preceding chapter mentioned that the USER.DAT and SYS-TEM.DAT files were located in the Windows folder. The difference between that statement and the one here is that for single-user systems, these files are located in the Windows folder. In multiple-user systems, however, Windows keeps profile information about all of its users and keeps the information in the Windows\Profiles folder.

The Windows 9x startup sequence can be summarized as follows:

1. POST tests.

2. PnP configuration.

3. Operating system boot up looks for MBR.

4. System loads IO.SYS.

5. IO.SYS loads and executes CONFIG.SYS.

6. IO.SYS loads MSDOS.SYS.

7. IO.SYS loads and executes COMMAND.COM.

8. COMMAND.COM looks for and executes (loads) AUTOEXEC.BAT.

9. Windows 9x Core files are loaded.

10. Windows 9x checks the Startup folder.

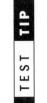

T E S T   T I P

Remember the files involved in the Windows startup process and the order of their execution.

Self-Booting DOS Disks

It is always good to have a *clean boot disk* to start the system. This tool provides a well-defined point to begin troubleshooting operating system problems.

STEP BY STEP

8.8 Creating a Self-Booting DOS Disk

1. To create a self-booting DOS disk, place a new disk in the floppy drive and enter the following lines at the DOS prompt:

```
Format A:/s
MD C:\DOS
CD \DOS
```

2. To make the disk truly useful, the following files should be copied to the boot disk, under the DOS directory:

```
FDISK
FORMAT
```

continues

continued

TEST TIP

Know which files should be included on a boot disk.

continued

```
SYS
EDIT
CHKDSK
MSD
```

3. New minimum configuration CONFIG.SYS and AUTOEXEC.BAT files should be created for the startup disk. The files should include the following entries:

```
CONFIG.SYS
FILES=40
BUFFERS=40
SHELL=COMMAND.COM C:\DOS /p /e:256
AUTOEXEC.BAT
PATH=c:\;C:DOS
PROMPT $P$G
SET COMSPEC=C:\DOS
```

Creating a Windows 95 Emergency Start Disk

Because Windows 95 does not start up through DOS, it is very difficult to gain access to the system if Windows becomes disabled. Therefore, it is helpful to have an emergency start disk to troubleshoot Windows 95-related problems. In the event that the Windows program becomes nonfunctional, you must use the start disk to gain access to the system so that you can restore it to proper operation.

The Windows 95 Startup disk boots the system only up to the command prompt. From this point, you need to be familiar with command-line operations so that you can employ tools and utilities that will get the system up and running again.

During the Windows setup operation, the software provides an option for creating an emergency start disk. Use this option for every Windows 95 installation. Setup copies the operating system files to the disk along with utilities for troubleshooting startup problems. The disk can then be used to boot up the system in *safe mode* and display a DOS command-line prompt. The emergency start disk also can be used to replace lost or damaged system files on the hard disk.

An emergency start disk also can be created through the Control Panel's Add/Remove Programs icon. This option is normally used to create a new startup disk after new hardware has been installed, or when configuration information has been changed.

In addition to creating a startup floppy disk, Windows 95 transfers a number of diagnostic files to the disk, including the following:

- ◆ IO.SYS
- ◆ MSDOS.SYS
- ◆ COMMAND.COM
- ◆ SYS.COM
- ◆ FDISK.EXE
- ◆ FORMAT.COM
- ◆ EDIT.COM
- ◆ REGEDIT.EXE
- ◆ ATTRIB.EXE
- ◆ SCANDISK.EXE and SCANDISK.INI

These utilities are particularly helpful in getting a Windows 95 machine operational again. This disk provides one of the few tools for the technician to service a down machine with this operating system. The steps involved in creating the boot disk are as follows:

TEST TIP

Be aware of the two ways to create emergency start disks in Windows 9x and know when these disks should be employed.

TEST TIP

Know which files should be included on a Windows Startup disk.

STEP BY STEP

8.9   Create the Emergency Start Disk

1. Click the Start button.
2. Move to Settings option in the Start menu.
3. Select the Control Panel from the list.
4. Double-click the Add/Remove Programs icon.

continues

continued

> **5.** Select the Startup Disk tab.
>
> **6.** Click the Create Disk button.
>
> **7.** Place the Windows 95 CD in the CD-ROM drive when prompted.
>
> **8.** Follow the menu items as directed.
>
> **9.** Place a blank disk in the A: drive when prompted.
>
> **10.** Remove the Windows 95 CD from the drive when the operation is complete.

Next, you can examine the startup disk by following these steps.

STEP BY STEP

8.10 Examine the Start Disk

> **1.** Close the Control Panel window.
>
> **2.** Select the Windows Explorer option from the Start/Programs menu.
>
> **3.** Click the 3.5" Floppy A: option from the list in the All Folders window and take note of the files that the disk contains. These files and utilities are the tools you will have at your disposal if the system crashes. Because many of these files are special System files, you need to remove their hidden attributes to see them.
>
> **4.** Remove the floppy disk from the drive, label it as an emergency start disk, and store it in a convenient location so that you can find it easily.

You also can examine the CONFIG.SYS file if you want to.

STEP BY STEP

8.11 Examining the New CONFIG.SYS File on the Boot Disk

1. Select the Notepad utility in the Start/Programs/ Accessories menu.

2. Click the File and Open options in the Notepad window.

3. Select the 3.5" Floppy (A:) option in the Look In window.

4. Select the All File (*.*) option from the Files of Type window.

5. Double-click the CONFIG.SYS entry in the window.

Several files also can come in handy when on the startup disk. The next Step by Step shows you how to add them.

STEP BY STEP

8.12 Adding Helpful Files to the Start Disk

1. Close the Notepad utility.

2. Select the Windows Explorer option from the Start/Programs menu.

3. Click the File and Open options in the Notepad window.

4. Select the 3.5" Floppy (A:) option in the Look In window.

5. Select the Folder option from the File/New menu.

6. Type your three initials in the box for the new subdirectory.

7. Select the (C:) option in the Look In window.

8. Locate the AUTOEXEC.BAT file in the Contents of C:\ window.

9. Click, hold, and drag the file to the 3.5" Floppy (A:) option on the Look In window and release.

continues

continued

10. Repeat steps 4–9 for the SYSTEM.DAT, CONFIG.SYS, WIN.INI, and SYSTEM.INI files.

11. Exit the Windows Explorer.

You also can examine the AUTOEXEC.BAT file if you want to.

STEP BY STEP

8.13 Examining the New AUTOEXEC.BAT File on the Boot Disk

1. Select the Notepad utility in the Start/Programs/Accessories menu.

2. Click the File and Open options in the Notepad window.

3. Select the 3.5" Floppy (A:) option in the Look In window.

4. Select the All File (*.*) option from the Files of Type window.

5. Double-click the AUTOEXEC.BAT entry in the window.

Because the system settings are basically contained in the two Registry files, SYSTEM.DAT and USER.DAT, it is not uncommon to back them up on the emergency start disk. This operation is performed with the RegEdit utility's Export function. The Export function can be used to save a selected branch or the entire Registry as a REG text file.

The following Step by Step explains how to export the Registry.

STEP BY STEP

8.14 Exporting the Registry

1. Start the RegEdit function.

2. Select the Run option from the Start menu.

3. Type **REGEDIT** in the Filename dialog box and click OK.

4. From the RegEdit toolbar, select the Registry menu.

5. Choose the Export Registry file option from the drop-down menu.

6. In the Export window, click the All button.

7. Type the filename **REGBACK** in the Filename window.

8. Select the 3.5" Floppy (A:) entry from the Save In window.

9. Click the Save button

10. Check the contents of the A: drive to make certain that the REGBACK.REG file is there.

The Registry backup file can be used to restore the Registry to the system after a crash. Once again, this involves using the RegEdit Import function to restore the Registry for use. The RegEdit Import function can be performed using the Windows-based version, or it can be conducted from the command line using the real-mode version located on the emergency start disk. For the purposes of this text, this discussion focuses on the version needed in a troubleshooting-and-repair scenario.

STEP BY STEP

8.15   Using the Start Disk to Restore the Registry

1. Restart the system.

2. Place the emergency start disk in the A: drive.

3. Turn the computer on.

4. Import the original Registry into Windows 95 to return it to its original condition.

5. Place the disk containing the REGBACK.REG file in the floppy drive.

continues

Registry Restoration Caveat The **REGEDIT /C** command should not be used except for cases where the Registry is heavily corrupted. It must have a complete image of the Registry to be used in this manner. Also realize that Windows 9x backs up the Registry files each time it is started. There should be several iterations of the Registry files that could be renamed and copied over the existing Registry files to repair them.

TEST TIP

Know where to make emergency start disks in Windows 9x.

continued

6. From the RegEdit toolbar, select the Registry menu.

7. At the A:\> prompt, type **REGEDIT /C REGBACK**.

8. Wait for the file to be imported.

9. Remove the floppy disk from the A: drive.

10. Turn the system off and then back on again.

The system should be restored to the same operating parameters that it had when the Registry backup file was created.

Store the Windows 95 emergency start disk in a convenient place and label it clearly so that it is easy to find when you need it.

The Windows 98 Emergency Start Disk

As with any other operating system, one of the most important tools to have on hand is the emergency start disk. In the event that the system software becomes corrupt, or that an option hangs Windows up and doesn't let it restart, the Windows 98 emergency start disk will provide access to the system and allow repair steps to be taken.

The emergency start disk is basically a DOS disk, with key utilities included, to assist in restarting the system when Windows 98 doesn't boot. This disk can be created during the installation process, or by accessing the Startup disk tab in the Control Panel's Add/Remove Programs window. From this point, creating the emergency disk is just a matter of inserting a blank disk in the floppy drive and clicking the Create Disk button. As always, store the start disk in an obvious, but safe location.

In addition to the necessary system files required to start the system in a minimal, real-mode condition, the Windows 98 Startup disk provides a number of diagnostic programs, and a pair of real-mode CD-ROM drivers, to allow the CD-ROM drive to operate from safe mode. One driver is a generic ATAPI driver called OAKCDROM.SYS. Of course this driver is incompatible with SCSI drives. However, the Startup disk does include real-mode SCSI CD-ROM support. Along with these drivers, the disk provides a RAMDrive and a new **Extract** command (EXTRACT.EXE). The **Extract** command is used to pull necessary files from the cabinet (CAB) files on the Windows 98 CD-ROM.

If the CD-ROM drive uses a sound card for its interface, you must include a copy of the correct real-mode driver on the emergency start disk. You also must edit the startup disk's CONFIG.SYS file to load the driver from the disk.

Be aware that Windows 98 will not run if the system is started with an emergency start disk from another Windows version. The machine can be started on the older versions of the start disk, and some repair operations can be carried out, but the new version will not be able to be started and some items could become corrupted with the older operating system.

> **TEST TIP**
>
> Know which files should be present on an emergency start disk.

Windows 9x Startup Modes

The Windows 9x Startup menu (not to be confused with the desktop's Start menu), depicted in Figure 8.15, can be obtained on a nonstarting system by holding down the F8 function key when the Starting Windows 9x message is onscreen. The menu offers several startup options, including Normal, Logged, Safe, Step-by-Step Confirmation, and DOS modes.

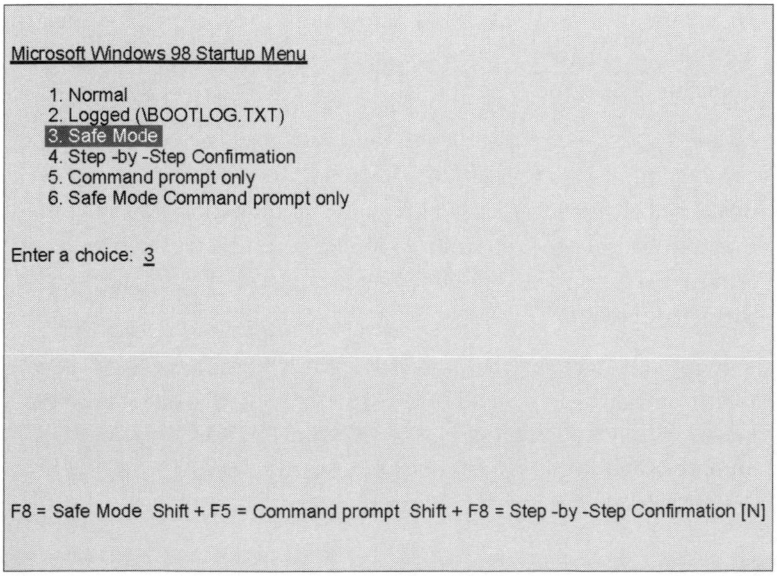

FIGURE 8.15
The Startup menu.

```
Microsoft Windows 98 Startup Menu

   1. Normal
   2. Logged (\BOOTLOG.TXT)
   3. Safe Mode
   4. Step -by -Step Confirmation
   5. Command prompt only
   6. Safe Mode Command prompt only


Enter a choice: 3




F8 = Safe Mode  Shift + F5 = Command prompt  Shift + F8 = Step -by -Step Confirmation [N]
```

If the *Normal Mode* option is selected, the system just tries to restart as it normally would, loading all of its normal startup and Registry files. The *Logged Mode* option also attempts to start the system in normal mode, but keeps an error log file that contains the steps performed and outcome. This text file (BOOTLOG.TXT) can be read with any text editor or printed out on a working system.

Safe Mode

If Windows 9x determines that a problem has occurred that prevented the system from starting, it attempts to restart the system in safe mode. This mode bypasses several startup files to provide access to the system's configuration files. In particular, the CONFIG.SYS and AUTOEXEC.BAT files are bypassed, along with the Windows 9x Registry and the SYSTEM.INI [Boot] and [386Enh] sections. This startup mode also can be accessed by pressing the F5 function key when the Starting Windows 9x message is onscreen.

The Windows 95 Startup menu provided a Safe Mode with Network Support option (F6). Selecting this option bypassed the startup files in the same manner as the normal Safe Mode option and it supplied basic network support drivers. Windows 98 offers no such option on its boot menu. However, pressing the F6 key during startup brings this option to the screen. (I suppose that Microsoft forgot to take it out of the actual programming.)

Unless modified, the Safe Mode screen appears as depicted in Figure 8.16. Active functions appear onscreen along with the Safe Mode notice in each corner.

In *step-by-step confirmation mode*, the system displays each startup command line by line and waits for a confirmation from the keyboard before moving ahead. This allows an offending startup command to be isolated and avoided, so that it can be replaced or removed. This option is obtained by pressing the F8 function key at the Startup menu.

Windows 9x maintains a number of log files that track system performance and that can be used to assess system failures. These log files are SETUPLOG.TXT, DETLOG.TXT, and BOOTUPLOG.TXT and are stored in the drive's root directory. All three are text files that can be viewed with any text editor package. Unlike the other log files, the BOOTLOG.TXT file is not created when Windows is installed. Instead, it is generated in response to the Logged Mode selection in the Startup menu.

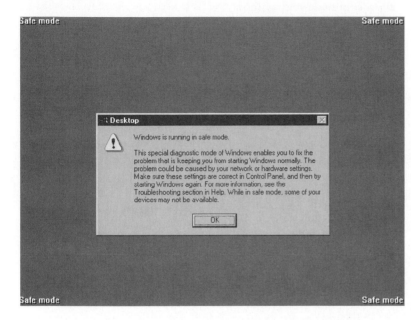

FIGURE 8.16
The Safe Mode startup screen.

Their filenames are indicative of the types of information they log. As described earlier, the BOOTUPLOG.TXT file tracks the events of the startup procedure. Likewise, SETUPLOG.TXT tracks the events of the setup process. The DETLOG.TXT file monitors the presence of detected hardware devices and identifies the parameters for them. This file just happens to be a very good description of the system's PnP operations.

Know which log file is not generated during the Windows installation process.

DOS Modes

Other startup options also may be available from the menu, depending on the configuration of the system. Some options start the system and bring it to a DOS command-line prompt.

Selecting the *Command Prompt Only* mode option causes the system to boot up to the command line, using the startup files and the Registry. If this option will not start the system, reboot the computer and select the *Safe Mode Command Prompt Only* option from the Startup menu. This option performs the same function as pressing the Shift and F5 keys simultaneously (Shift+F5) during the boot-up process. The system will start in safe mode with minimal drivers (while not executing any of the startup files) and will produce the DOS command-line prompt.

The special function keys available during the Windows 9x startup are summarized as follows:

F5	Safe Mode
F6	Safe Mode with Network Support
F8	Step-by-Step Confirmation
Shift+F5	Safe Mode Command Prompt Only

Windows NT/2000 Startup

Unlike the Windows 9x products, Windows NT 4.0 provides very few options when it starts up. The user is normally offered two options. The NTLDR file causes the system to display a selection menu of which operating system to boot from, along with an option to start the system in VGA mode. The menu listing is based on what NTLDR finds in the BOOT.INI file. If the VGA option is selected, the system will start up as normal, with the exception that it will load only the standard VGA driver to drive the display.

The second option presented is the Last Known Good Hardware Configuration mode option. Selecting this option causes the system to start up using the configuration information that it recorded the last time a user successfully logged on to the system. The option appears onscreen for a few seconds after the operating system selection has been made. You must press the Spacebar while the option is displayed on the screen to select this startup mode. If no selection is made, the system continues on with a normal startup as previously outlined, using the existing hardware configuration information.

Windows NT/2000 Startup Modes

The sequence of steps in the Windows NT/2000 boot-up and startup processes is similar to those presented in the previous chapters for DOS and Windows 9x systems. The main differences relate to terminology and the names of the files that Windows NT/2000 employs.

Like any other PC system, the Windows NT-based PC starts up by running a series of POST tests, performing an initialization of its intelligent system devices, and performing a system boot process. It is in the boot process that the descriptions of the two operating systems diverge.

When the BIOS executes the Master Boot Record on the hard drive, the MBR examines the disk's partition table to locate the active partition. The boot process then moves to the boot sector of that partition (referred to as the partition boot sector) located in the first sector of the active partition. Here the MBR finds the code to begin loading the Secondary Bootstrap Loader from the root directory of the boot drive.

In the case of a Windows NT partition, the Bootstrap Loader is the NT Loader file named NTLDR. This file is the Windows NT equivalent of the DOS IO.SYS file and is responsible for loading the NT operating system into memory. Afterward, NTLDR passes control of the system over to the Windows NT operating system.

When Windows NT gains control of the system, its first action is to initialize the video hardware and switch the microprocessor into protected mode. In the Windows NT system, the microprocessor is switched into the 32-bit, flat memory mode described earlier in this chapter.

Next, a temporary, miniature file system that can read both FAT and NTFS file structures is loaded to aid NTLDR in reading the rest of the system. Recall that Windows NT has the capability to work in either FAT or proprietary NTFS partitions. At this stage of the boot process, however, the operating system is still uncertain as to which system it will be using.

With the minifile system in place, the NTLDR can locate and read a special, hidden boot loader menu file named BOOT.INI. NTLDR uses this text file to generate the Boot Loader menu that is displayed onscreen. If no selection is made after a given time delay, the default value is selected.

If Windows NT is the designated operating system to be used, the NTLDR program executes a hardware detection file called NTDE-TECT.COM. This file is responsible for collecting information about the system's installed hardware devices and passing it to the NTLDR program. This information is later used to upgrade the Windows NT Registry files.

If a different operating system is to be loaded, as directed by the Boot Loader menu entry, the NTLDR program loads a file called BOOTSECT.DOS from the root directory of the system partition and passes control to it. From this point, the BOOTSECT file is responsible for loading the desired operating system.

Finally, the NTLDR program examines the partition for a pair of files named NTOSKRNL.EXE and HAL.DLL. NTOSKRNL.EXE is the Windows NT Kernel file that contains the Windows NT core and loads its device drivers. HAL.DLL is the Hardware Abstraction Layer driver that holds the information specific to the CPU with which the system is being used.

Even though NTLDR reads the NTOSKRNL and HAL files at this time, it does not load or execute them. Instead, it uses a file named NTDETECT.COM to gather information about the hardware devices present and passes it to the NTLDR. Note that this should not be confused with the PnP enumeration process that occurs later in the Windows 2000 boot-up process. The information gathered by NTDETECT is stored to be used later for updating the Hardware Registry hive.

In particular, the NTDETECT program checks for information concerning the following:

◆ Machine ID

◆ Bus types

◆ Keyboard

◆ Mouse

◆ Video type

◆ Floppy drives

◆ Parallel ports

◆ COMM Ports

After the information has been passed back to NTLDR, it opens the System Hive portion of the Registry to find the current control set. At this point, the system displays the Starting Windows NT logo on the display along with a sliding progress bar that shows the degree of progress being made in loading the drivers. After the drivers have been loaded, the NTLDR program passes control to the NTOSKRNL file to complete the boot-up sequence.

When NTOSKRNL gains control of the system, it initializes the HAL.DLL file (along with the BOOTVID.DLL file in Windows 2000) and shifts the video display to graphics mode. It then initializes the drivers prepared by NTLDR and uses the NTDETECT information to create a temporary Hardware Hive in memory. Finally, NTOSKRNL executes a Session Manager file titled SMSS.EXE to carry out prestart functions such as running a boot-time version of *CHKDSK* called AUTOCHK. It also establishes parameters concerning the Windows NT paging file (PAGEFILE.SYS) to hold RAM memory swap pages.

After these tasks have been performed, the Session Manager loads the console logon service file (WINLOGON.EXE) to begin the authentication verification process. WINLOGON starts the Local Security Authority Subsystem (LSASS.EXE) and the *print spooler* (SPOOLS.EXE) along with their supporting files. Finally, WINLOGON loads the Service Controller (SCREG.EXE) that completes the loading process by bringing in the remaining devices and services.

When Windows NT/2000 starts, several major files are loaded into the system, including the following:

1. The NTOSKRNL.EXE file is loaded.

2. The HAL.DLL file is loaded.

3. The BOOTVID.DLL file is loaded.

4. The NETDETECT.COM file is loaded.

5. The System Hive portions of the Registry are loaded.

6. The Starting Windows NT message displays.

7. The Temporary Hardware Hive is created.

8. The Session Manager starts along with a memory-paging function.

9. WINLOGON loads LSASS and the Logon screen displays.

10. WINLOGON loads SCREG, which loads the Windows NT shell and desktop files.

> **TEST TIP**
> Know what the swap file in Windows NT/2000 is called.

FIGURE 8.17
The Windows 2000 Logon dialog box.

FIGURE 8.18
Windows 2000 Advanced Options menu.

As with Windows 9x, the Windows NT/2000 shell program is the Windows desktop. When the shell and desktop components are loaded, the system displays a prompt onscreen for the user to log on, as depicted in Figure 8.17. The Windows NT logon allows the operating system to configure itself for specific users. Normal logon involves entering a username and password. If no logon information is entered, default values are loaded into the system. In Windows NT/2000 systems, the logon screen always appears even if the system is not being use with a network.

Windows 2000 Startup Modes

The Windows 2000 operating system incorporates a number of Windows 9x-like startup options that can be engaged to get the system up and running in a given state to provide a starting point for troubleshooting operations.

The Windows 2000 Advanced Options menu, depicted in Figure 8.18, contains several options that can be of assistance when troubleshooting startup failures. To display this menu, press F8 at the beginning of the Windows 2000 startup process.

```
Windows 2000 Advanced Options Menu
Please select an option:

    Safe Mode
    Safe Mode with Networking
    Safe Mode with Command Prompt

    Enable Boot Logging
    Enable VGA Mode
    Last Known Good Configuration
    Directory Services Restore Mode (Windows 2000 domain controllers only)
    Debugging Mode

    Boot Normally
    Return to OS Choices Menu


Use ↑ and ↓ to move the highlight to your choice.
Press Enter to choose.
```

The Windows 2000 Startup menu basically provides the same safe-mode options as the Windows 9x operating systems do (for instance, Boot Normally, Safe Mode, Safe Mode with Networking, and Safe Mode with Command Prompt).

However, the Windows 2000 menu also provides a number of Windows NT-like options, including the following:

◆ **Enable Boot Logging.** This creates a log file called NTBT-LOG.TXT in the root folder. This log is very similar to the BOOTLOG.TXT file described earlier in that it contains a listing of all the drivers and services that the system attempts to load during startup and can be useful when trying to determine what service or driver is causing the system to fail.

◆ **Enable VGA Mode.** When selected, this option boots the system normally, but uses only the standard VGA driver. If you have configured the display incorrectly and cannot see the desktop, booting into VGA mode will enable you to reconfigure those settings.

◆ **Last Known Good Configuration.** This starts Windows 2000 with the settings that existed the last time a successful user logon occurred. All system setting changes made since the last successful startup are lost. This is a very useful option if you have added or reconfigured a device driver that is causing the system to fail.

◆ **Debugging Mode.** This starts Windows 2000 in a kernel debug mode that enables debugger utilities to access the kernel for troubleshooting and analysis. This is a very advanced function.

Windows NT/2000 Emergency Repair Disks

In the Windows 2000 arena, the user should have on hand the following two different types of troubleshooting-related disks:

◆ The setup disks

◆ The Emergency Repair Disk

Setup disks are the equivalent of the Windows 9x Startup disk. Windows NT 4.0 generates a three-disk set, whereas Windows 2000 creates a four-disk set. Unlike the Windows 9x Start disk, the setup disks do not bring the system to a command prompt. Instead, they initiate the Windows Setup process.

Both Windows NT 4.0 and Windows 2000 provide for an Emergency Repair Disk (ERD) to be produced. The ERD differs from the setup disks in that it is intended for use with an operational system when it crashes. It is not a bootable disk and must be used with the setup disks or the CD. Whereas the setup disks are uniform for a given version of Windows NT, the ERD is specific to the machine from which it is created. It contains a copy of the SAM in Windows NT and the Registry in Windows 2000. When dealing with the NT ERD, it is necessary to manually copy the Registry files to the disk.

Windows NT/2000 Setup Disks

The Windows NT setup disks basically perform three functions. They load a miniature file system into the system, initialize its drives, and start the installation process. All Windows NT setup disks are the same for all machines running that version of Windows NT.

Under Windows NT 4.0, you must install the NT distribution CD in the system and type **WINNT /ox** at the command prompt.

Under Windows 2000, you must place the distribution CD in the drive and launch the MakeBootDisk utility to create the four disk images for its Windows 2000 setup disks. You also can create setup disks from the command prompt using the MAKEBT32.EXE file for Windows 2000. These disks also can be made from the Start/ Run/Browse/CD-ROM path. From the CD, select the BOOTDISK option followed by the MAKEBT32.EXE command.

Windows NT 4.0 ERD

During the installation process, Windows NT Setup asks whether you want to create an Emergency Repair Disk. You also can create an ERD later using the Repair Disk program (RDISK.EXE). To do so, select the Run option from the Start menu, enter the **CMD** command in the Run box, and then type **RDISK** at the command prompt.

When Windows NT is installed, the Setup routine stores Registry information in the %Systemroot%\System32\Config folder and creates a %Systemroot%\Repair folder to hold key files.

Creating a Windows 2000 Emergency Repair Disk

The Windows 2000 Setup routine prompts you to create an ERD during the installation process. The ERD also can be created using the Windows 2000 Backup utility located under the Programs/ Accessories/System Tools path. Choosing this option activates the Windows 2000 ERD Creation Wizard, depicted in Figure 8.19. The Windows 2000 ERD disk contains configuration information specific to the computer that will be required during the emergency repair process.

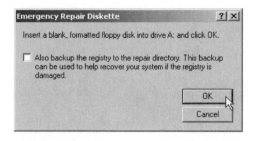

FIGURE 8.19
Windows 2000 ERD Creation Wizard.

LOADING AND ADDING DEVICE DRIVERS

▶ 2.4 Identify procedures for loading/adding device drivers and the necessary software for certain devices.

The portion of the A+ Operating System Technologies objective 2.4 states that the test taker should be able to "identify procedures for loading/adding device drivers and the necessary software for certain devices."

One of the reasons for the success of the PC-compatible system is its open architecture and its versatility. This versatility is the result of an architecture that allows all types of devices to be added to it. In the PC world, this is accomplished through the use of software device drivers that interface diverse equipment to the basic system. Although the process for installing equipment and their drivers in a PC has become increasingly easy, the technician must still be able to install whatever drivers are necessary. Therefore, the following sections of this chapter are dedicated to device-driver installations.

> **TEST TIP**
> Know where ERDs are created in Windows NT 4.0 and in Windows 2000.

Windows 9x Device Drivers

The PnP-compliant design of Windows 9x makes installing most new hardware nearly automatic (as long as the new device also is PnP-compatible). The PnP function automatically detects new PnP-compliant hardware when it is started. If the device is not PnP-compliant, or the system just cannot detect it for some reason, use the Windows 9x *Add New Hardware Wizard.*

> **NOTE**
>
> **Setting Up New Hardware** Windows 9x is designed to assist the user in setting up any new hardware components that may be added to the system. The Add New Hardware icon can be found under the Control Panel option of the Settings menu.

Double-clicking this icon activates the Windows 9x Hardware Wizard, depicted in Figure 8.20. The wizard program is designed to guide you through hardware setup steps. The new card or device should already be installed in the system before running this procedure.

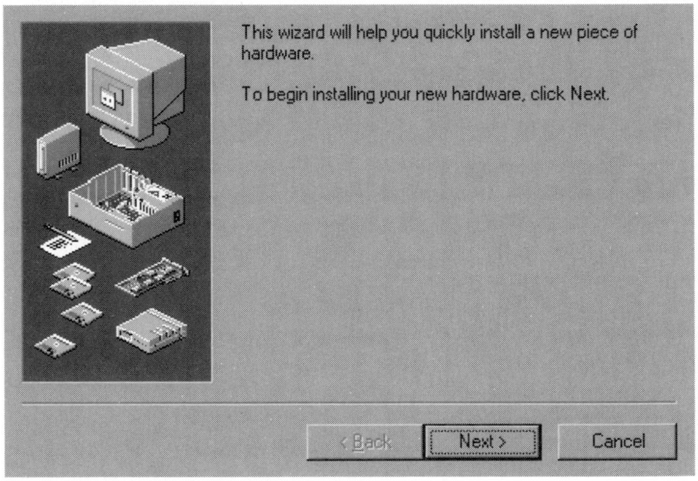

FIGURE 8.20
The Windows 9x Hardware Wizard.

The Hardware Wizard is a series of screens that will guide the installation process for the new device. The first user-selectable option is to use the AutoDetect function, described in Figure 8.21. The progress indicator bar at the bottom of the page displays the progress of the detection operation in bar-chart format. When it has filled the opening, Windows will indicate what hardware it has found that can be installed. Clicking the Details button will show which hardware it found.

If the wizard does not detect the hardware, the user can attempt to locate the device in the wizard's list of supported devices, as shown in Figure 8.22. The only other option for installing hardware devices is to obtain an OEM disk or CD for the device that has Windows 9x drivers. If the driver disk does not have an AutoStart function, click the Have Disk button and supply the file's location to complete the installation process.

The installation process can be concluded by clicking the Finish button. This causes Windows to install the drivers for the new hardware in the system. It also may request configuration information from the user before finishing. Afterward, reboot the system for the configuration changes to take effect.

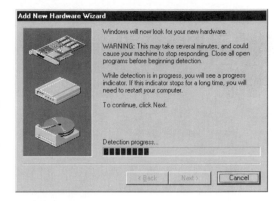

FIGURE 8.21
Windows 9x detecting new hardware.

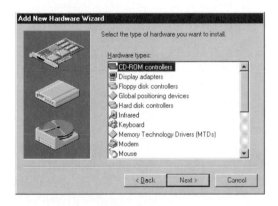

FIGURE 8.22
Windows 9x-supported hardware listing.

Windows NT/2000 Device Drivers

As mentioned earlier in the chapter, Windows NT does not support as many hardware devices as the Windows 9x platforms do. However, Windows NT still offers support for a fairly wide range of disk drive types, VGA video cards, network interface cards, tape drives, and printers. To determine what components Windows NT supports, consult the Hardware Compatibility List for the version of Windows NT/2000 being used (see Note).

Windows 2000 supports a wide array of newer hardware devices. These devices include DVD, USB, and IEEE 1394 devices. Microsoft works with hardware vendors to certify their drivers. These drivers are digitally signed so that they can be loaded automatically by the system.

NOTE

Hardware Compatibility List   This information can be obtained from the Microsoft web site, depicted in Figure 8.23.

FIGURE 8.23

Microsoft 2000 driver page.

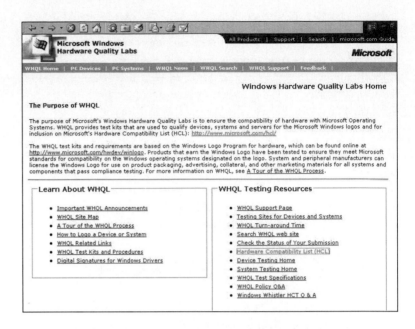

Windows 2000 brings PnP capabilities to the Windows NT environment. The Windows NT PnP manager can assign and reallocate system resources as needed.

If drivers for the device being installed are not listed at this location, there is a good chance the device will not operate, or will not operate well in the Windows NT environment. If this is the case, the only recourse is to contact the device's manufacturer for Windows NT drivers.

Adding new devices to Windows 2000 is accomplished through the Add New Hardware icon located in the Control Panel. Figure 8.24 depicts the Windows 2000 Control Panel icons. As with Windows 9x systems, the Windows 2000 Control Panel is used to add or remove new hardware and software components to the system and modify device settings and desktop items.

Double-clicking a device icon in the Control Panel produces a Properties dialog box for that device. The dialog box holds configuration information specific to that device. The tabs located along the tops of the dialog box can be used to review and change settings and drivers for the device.

from here

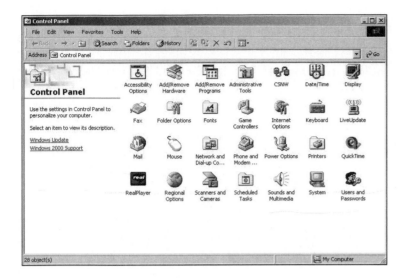

FIGURE 8.24
Windows 2000 Control Panel icons.

Windows NT 4.0 does not possess PnP, although it does feature some autodetection capabilities. It also provided no Add New Hardware Wizard. Devices had to be installed manually under Windows NT 4.0 through the icons in the Control Panel, or through installation routines provided by the equipment manufacturer.

software

WORKING WITH APPLICATIONS

▶ 2.4 Identify the procedures for installing and launching typical Windows and non-Windows applications.

A portion of the A+ Operating System Technologies objective 2.4 states that the test taker should be able to "identify the procedures for installing and launching typical Windows and non-Windows applications."

The other factor that makes PC-compatible systems so widely accepted is the fact that so many software applications are available for them. Because these applications are, at least for the most part, not installed by the computer maker, the technician must be able to successfully install application software and configure it according to the customer's specifications. The following sections deal with application installations under Windows 9x.

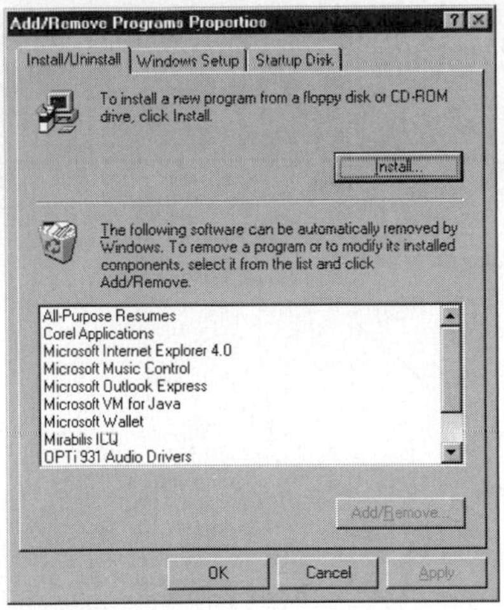

FIGURE 8.25

The Windows 9x Add/Remove Programs window.

Windows Applications

Like the Hardware Wizard, Windows offers the user assistance in installing new programs. The *Add/Remove New Programs* icon under the Control Panel is used to install new programs automatically. Figure 8.25 shows the Add/Remove Programs screen.

In DOS, adding a program to the system was normally a simple process of copying it to the hard drive. Removing the program was also simple—just delete its directory and files. In older Windows versions, removing a program would normally leave several INI and DLL files scattered around the hard drive. Not only did these files take up disk space, they also could become a source of conflict with new software added to the system.

The main page of the Add/Remove window is the Install/Uninstall page used to add and remove the desired software package. The upper half of the page contains the Install button that is clicked to start the software installation process.

The lower half of the page lists the Windows 9x software packages that are already installed in the system. However, non-Windows 9x-compliant software packages will not appear in the list. Only those programs that the Windows 9x Install/Uninstall utility can uninstall appear here.

Some Windows 9x applications may share support files with other applications. In these instances, the Uninstall utility will produce a dialog box asking about deleting the shared files. The best response is to keep the file to avoid disabling the other application. If the files are to be deleted, a backup should be made before running the Uninstall utility so that the files can be replaced if needed.

Windows Setup

The Windows 9x Setup tab, depicted in Figure 8.26, also is located under the Control Panel's Add/Remove Programs icon. This utility allows different Windows 9x components to be added to or removed from the system. Windows configuration settings can be changed through its dialog boxes. The window in the center of the Setup page provides a list of the standard Windows 9x groups, along with their total sizes.

An empty box beside the option indicates that it has not been installed. Conversely, a check mark inside the box indicates that the complete group has been installed in the system. Finally, a gray check mark indicates that some of the files in the group have been installed.

Highlighting a group title with the cursor and then clicking the Details button causes a listing of the group's files to appear. Items in this list may be added to the system by checking on the box next to them. After the options to be added have been checked, the system needs to be restarted for the new options to become active.

Most software manufacturers include a proprietary setup program for their Windows 9x applications. These programs normally run directly from the CD-ROM when they are inserted into the drive for the first time (unless the AutoPlay function is disabled). For applications that do not feature the automatic installation function, or if the AutoPlay function is disabled, the software needs to be installed manually. This is accomplished through the Have Disk button. Click this button to produce a dialog box asking for the name and location of the application's installation file. Most software suppliers provide a SETUP.EXE or INSTALL.EXE file to handle the actual installation and configuration process for their software.

One of the optional groups that you may typically leave out is the Accessibility option. This group contains programs that modify the operations of the Windows keyboard and audio and video output for use by those who have physical conditions that inhibit their use of the computer. If you require visual warning messages for hearing disabilities or special color controls for visual difficulties, install this component and select the options that you need access to.

When the Accessibility option is installed, its icon appears in the Control Panel and when it is removed, it disappears. This option uses 4.6MB of space when it is installed.

Launching Windows Applications

In the DOS environment, starting, or launching, an application was a simple matter of typing the name of its executable file at the DOS prompt of the directory in which it was installed. Special startup batch files could also be used. In the Windows environment, however, starting an application is as simple as double-clicking its icon.

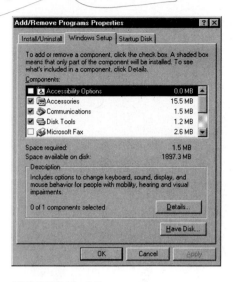

FIGURE 8.26
The Windows 9x Setup page.

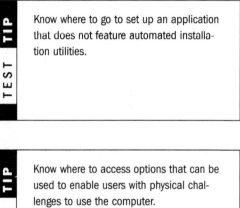

TEST TIP

Know where to go to set up an application that does not feature automated installation utilities.

TEST TIP

Know where to access options that can be used to enable users with physical challenges to use the computer.

T E S T   T I P

Be aware of the various ways to launch an application in the Windows environment.

lurch Appli
from start

from Run (by
Typing file name
path)

click on my
computer icon

click from file
menue option

In Windows, several acceptable ways enable you to launch an application, including the following:

◆ From the Start menu, select the applications entry, click the folder where the desired application is, and double-click its filename.

◆ From the Start menu, select the Run entry, and then enter the full path and filename for the desired executable file.

◆ Double-click the application's filename in Windows Explorer or in My Computer.

◆ Click the File menu option from the menu bar in My Computer or Windows Explorer, and select the Open option. (You also can right-click on the application and choose Open.)

◆ Create a shortcut icon on the desktop for the application, so that it can be started directly from the desktop by just double-clicking its icon.

In Windows 9x, NT, and 2000, an application can be set up to run by association. Using this method, the application is called into action any time that an associated file (such as a document and its related word processor) is double-clicked. This is accomplished by defining the file's type in the Registry.

Because the Registry is a delicate place to operate, you also can associate an application program with a given file.

STEP BY STEP

8.16   Associate an Application Program with a Given File

1. Click the Folder Options entry in the My Computer (or Windows Explorer) View menu.

2. Click the File Types tab.

3. Select the file type you want to change from the list.

4. Click the Edit button.

5. In the Actions dialog box, click the Open option.

6. Click the Edit button.

7. In the Application Used to Perform Action dialog window, enter the name of the program you want to use to open files that have the designated extension

8. Click the OK button to complete the association process. The settings for selected file types are shown in File Type Details.

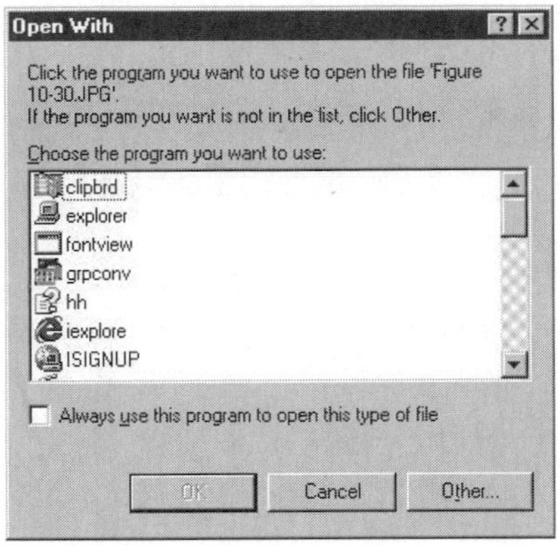

In Windows NT/2000, this is accomplished by defining the file's type in the Open With dialog box. The first time you attempt to open an application, the Open With dialog box, depicted in Figure 8.27, appears. The Open With dialog box also can be accessed by clicking the file's Properties/General tab and then selecting the Change option.

FIGURE 8.27
The Windows NT Open With dialog box.

Non-Windows Applications

Even though Windows 9x and NT/2000 all provide mechanisms for simulating an MS-DOS command-line environment, in many instances, it is desirable to run a DOS application from within the Windows environment.

Prior to the Windows 3.1 operating system, a simple request for a hard disk access while running in protected mode would result in Windows, DOS, and the BIOS handing the request back and forth a number of times (that is, application-to-Windows-to-DOS-to-Windows-to-BIOS-to-Windows-to-DOS-to-Windows-to-application). Figure 8.28 depicts this operation.

Windows 3.x introduced 32-bit access to the Windows package. Contrary to the sound of its name, 32-bit access had nothing to do with moving data in 32-bit blocks. Instead, it was a way to reduce the need to move back-and-forth between real and protected memory modes when an access request was made.

The new access method reduced the work associated with disk and file operations by removing the BIOS completely from the loop. A protected-mode device driver called FastDisk emulated the BIOS routines in Windows. The upgraded software capabilities sped up the operation of the system by eliminating the changes between real and protected modes that occurred each time Windows had to hand over control to the DOS or BIOS. Figure 8.29 demonstrates the advanced access process using FastDisk.

FIGURE 8.28
The Windows/DOS/BIOS relationship.

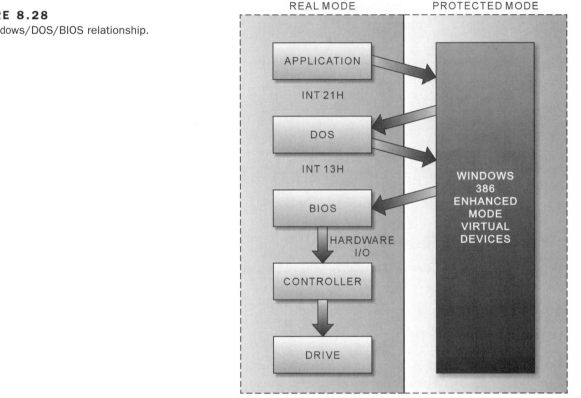

Windows 3.x also added 32-bit capabilities to file accesses as well as disk accesses. This further increased the system's overall operating speed by removing BIOS calls from file accesses as well.

As mentioned in Chapter 7, Windows 9x streamlined the 32-bit file and disk-access operations further by removing both the DOS and the BIOS from the access equation, as illustrated in Figure 8.30. The Windows 9x VFAT module enables the operating system to always remain in protected memory mode so that no mode switching needs to occur.

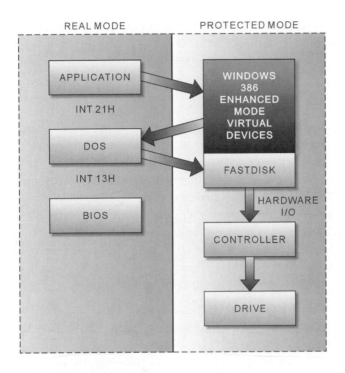

FIGURE 8.29
32-bit access with FastDisk.

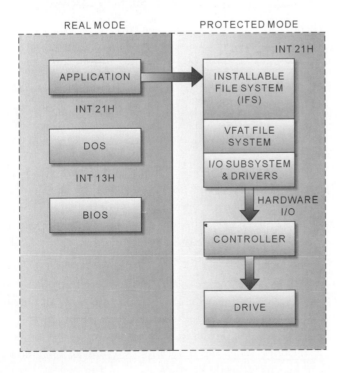

FIGURE 8.30
32-bit access in Windows 9x.

From this discussion of how Windows, DOS, and the BIOS interact, it should be apparent that running a DOS program from within Windows can be a difficult undertaking.

DOS and Windows 9x

DOS-based applications are installed in Windows 9x by just running their executable file from the Run dialog box, or from the Windows 9x Explorer. If the file has never been run under Windows 9x, the operating system creates a default entry in its APPS.INF file for that program. A copy of the new entry also is used to create a *program information file* (PIF) for the application. A PIF file is a file created to serve as a bridge between a DOS-based application and the Windows environment in older versions of Windows. These files contain information about how much memory the application requires and which system resources it needs.

After the APPS.INF entry has been created, it can be accessed and modified through the Properties window for that application. These Properties windows replace the *PIF editor* used in previous versions of Windows. The Properties window contains the following six tabs that enable the operation of the application to be modified:

- ◆ General
- ◆ Program
- ◆ Font
- ◆ Memory
- ◆ Screen
- ◆ Misc

The Program tab enables the user to define where the DOS program is located, what it is called, and how it should be displayed. The tab's Run entry is used to establish the initial window-size setting for the application. Options for this setting include Normal Window, Maximized Window, and Minimized Window.

Nearly every DOS-based program should run successfully in Windows 9x. Even DOS programs that require access to all the system's resources can run successfully in the Windows 9x *MS-DOS mode.* In this mode, basically all but a small portion of Windows exits from memory. When the application is terminated, Windows restarts and returns to the desktop screen.

MS-DOS mode is established for the application by configuring its properties in the Advanced dialog box under the My Computer/ Properties/Program tab, as illustrated in Figure 8.31. Just right-click the application's executable filename in the My Computer window and select the MS-DOS Mode setting in the Advanced screen.

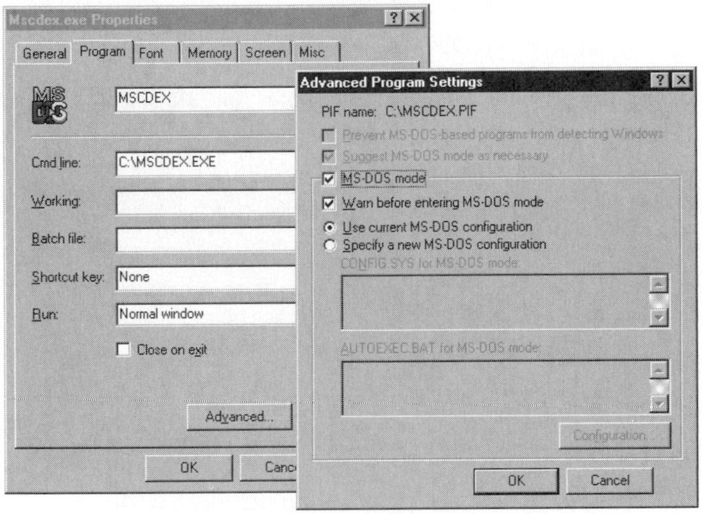

FIGURE 8.31
Establishing MS-DOS mode in Windows 9x.

It also is possible to adjust the memory allocated to the program through the My Computer/Properties/Memory tab. This function is accessed by right-clicking its executable filename, moving to the Memory window, and increasing or decreasing the memory available, as illustrated in Figure 8.32.

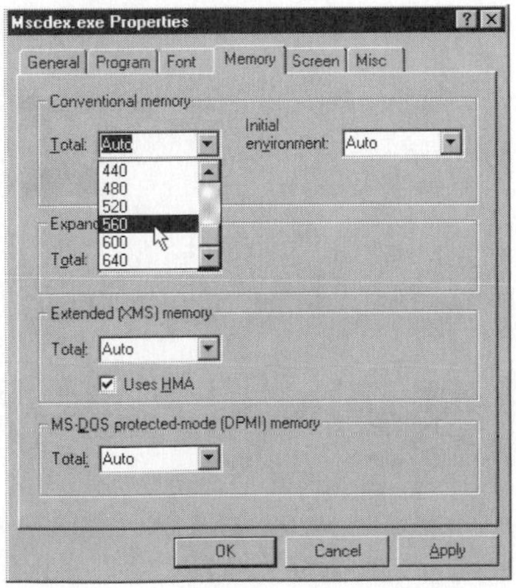

FIGURE 8.32
Adjusting DOS-mode memory.

The Memory tab enables the user to establish memory-allocation properties for the application. Values can be selected for Conventional, Extended, and Expanded memory usage, as well as for configuring HMA and UMB operations. These settings are still dependent on the information that may exist in the CONFIG.SYS file. In particular, check the CONFIG.SYS file for NOEMS parameters in the EMM386.EXE statement. If present, replace them with an appropriate RAM or X=MMMM-NNNN parameter.

The Screen tab provides several options for how the application will be presented onscreen. It is possible to set the window size that the application will run in. These options include full screen, a user-definable window size, and a default window size based on the graphic mode the application is using.

This tab also permits the Windows 9x *toolbar* to be displayed on the bottom of the screen. This feature can be valuable if the application becomes unstable or has trouble running in Windows.

Finally, the Screen tab allows the application to use the Windows 9x fast ROM emulation and dynamic memory-allocation features. These functions are selected to speed up video output operations.

If a DOS application takes up the entire screen in Windows 9x, you must press the Alt+Enter key combination to switch the application into a window. The Alt+Tab key combination switches the screen to another application. Some applications may grab the entire screen and cover the toolbar and Start menu button when maximized. When this occurs, resize the application's window through the Screen tab to access the toolbar. The Start menu can be accessed just by pressing Ctrl+Esc.

The Windows NT/2000 environment employs an Add/Remove Programs wizard to assist users in installing new applications. The Windows NT Add/Remove Programs icon is located in the main Control Panel, as illustrated in Figure 8.33. As you can see, it is very similar to the Windows 9x Control Panel.

Double-clicking the Add/Remove Programs icon produces the Add/Remove Programs dialog box. Any application that employs a SETUP.EXE or INSTALL.EXE installation routine can be installed through this window. Clicking the Install button causes the system to request the location of the installation program.

TEST TIP

Know the consequences of running DOS utilities from a Widows environment and how to solve problems associated with DOS applications running in the Windows environment.

FIGURE 8.33
Windows NT Add/Remove Programs icon.

In addition to third-party applications, the Add/Remove Programs Wizard can be used to install or remove optional components of the Windows NT operating system. Clicking the Windows NT Setup tab under the Properties box produces a list of Windows NT components that can be selected for inclusion or removal from the Windows NT system.

Windows 2000 Application Installer

As already mentioned, Windows 2000 features a new, more versatile MSI application installer called the Windows 2000 Application Installer. This program is designed to better handle DLL files in the Windows 2000 environment. In previous versions of Windows, applications would copy similar versions of shared DLL files, and other support files, into the Windows folder. When a new application overwrites a particular DLL file that another application needs to operate properly, a problem is likely to occur with the original software package.

The Windows 2000 Application Installer enables applications to check the system before introducing new DLLs to the system. Software designers who want their products to carry the Windows 2000 logo must write code that does not place proprietary support files in the Windows directory (including DLL files). Instead, the DLL files are located in the application's folder.

Windows Installer–compatible applications can repair themselves if they become corrupted. When the application is started, the operating system checks the properties of its key files. If a key file is missing, or appears to be damaged, it will invoke the Installer and prompt the user to insert the application distribution CD. When the CD has been inserted, the Installer automatically reinstalls the file in question.

This Installer enables applications to be installed on demand, or in a partial manner. Most major applications packages contain features that many users will never need. To avoid installing unnecessary functions and options, the Windows 2000 Installer allows a service called Install on Demand. If the application is written to take advantage of this feature, the program's installable modules will appear on the toolbar. The Installer will automatically load the option the first time the application calls for it. Likewise, the partial application installation can be updated as desired.

Windows 9x and Windows NT

Microsoft did not intend for the Windows NT and Windows 9x systems to be compatible with each other. There is no direct pathway between the two and no direct upgrade path from Windows 9x to Windows NT. Because both rely on Registry structures and because those structures are incompatible with each other, there is no way to bring them together.

Hardware support is another difference that prevents the two Windows operating systems from working with each other. Although some Windows 9x device drivers require direct access to system hardware, the Windows NT/2000 HAL cannot tolerate such operations. Therefore, the Windows 9x drivers just will not work in Windows NT and neither will the devices they support. Windows NT also lacks support for the virtual device drivers (VxDs) employed by Windows 9x.

For these reasons, Microsoft does not recommend or support dual-booting operation of the two operating systems. However, the Windows 2000 design does allow for upgrading from Windows 9x platforms.

DOS and Windows NT/2000

Like Windows 9x, Windows NT and Windows 2000 provide a Command Prompt window. Unlike Windows 9x, however, when this feature is engaged in Windows NT, no separate DOS version is being accessed. Windows NT just provides a DOS-like interface that enables users to perform some DOS functions. There is no MS-DOS icon in the Windows NT system. To access the DOS emulator, select the Run option from the Start menu and type the command **CMD** into the dialog box.

As mentioned earlier in this chapter, under Windows NT, 16-bit DOS applications run in special NTVDM environments. Likewise, Win16 applications run in special Win16-on-Win32 NTVDMs. These environments prevent the 16-bit applications from interacting with any other applications while providing full access to all of the system's resources through the APIs in the Win32 subsystem.

After placing a 16-bit application on the system's hard drive, the next step in establishing an NTVDM environment for it is to create a shortcut for the program on the desktop. This is accomplished through the Windows Explorer utility. Start the Explorer and then click-and-drag the application's executable filename to the desktop to create the shortcut icon. Click the shortcut text box to edit its name.

The Properties of the shortcut must be edited through the shortcut icon. Click the icon, select Properties from the floating menu, click the Program tab, and click the Windows NT button. This should produce the Windows NT PIF Settings dialog box depicted in Figure 8.34.

FIGURE 8.34
Windows NT PIF Settings dialog box.

Notice that an AUTOEXEC.NT and CONFIG.NT initialization file exists to support DOS applications. These files mimic the functions of the AUTOEXEC.BAT and CONFIG.SYS files found in MS-DOS and Windows 3.x environments. Although it is possible to establish separate initialization files for each DOS application, normally all such applications use the default files. The DOS commands inside the files are executed by the NTVDM when it is first loaded.

The next step in setting up DOS applications to run in Windows NT is to configure memory for them. This is accomplished by clicking the Memory tab in the DOS Properties page. This produces the

Memory Usage screen depicted in Figure 8.35. The Auto Mode settings are normally selected so that Windows NT retains control over memory usage.

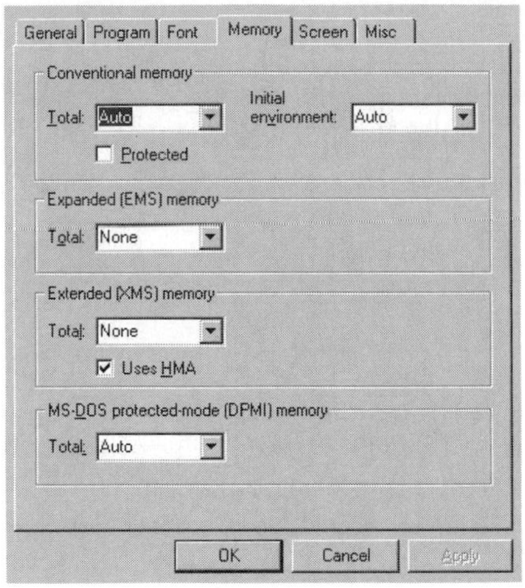

FIGURE 8.35
Windows NT Memory Usage screen.

In the case of 16-bit Windows applications, select the Shortcut tab from the Shortcut Properties window. To run the application in its own NTVDM, click the Run option and select the Run in Separate Memory Space box.

PRINTING IN WINDOWS

▶ 2.4 Identify procedures for setup and configuration of the Windows printing subsystem.

A portion of the A+ Operating System Technologies objective 2.4 states that the test taker should be able to "identify the procedures for changing options, configuring, and using the Windows printing subsystem."

The Windows environment supplies the printing function for all its applications. Instead of having a printer driver for each application to deal directly with whatever printer is installed, Windows applications need to communicate only with the environment. The drivers are built in to, or added to, the Windows package. Printing from nearly any Windows package is as simple as choosing the Print option from the application's File menu.

In both, Windows 9x and Windows 2000, all printing activities are controlled by the Windows *Print Manager*. In both Windows types, the Print Manager can be found in the My Computer folder, or it can be accessed through the Start/Settings path.

Printing in Windows 9x

Printing is significantly improved in Windows 9x. The Print Manager function and its support components have been integrated into a single print-processing architecture, referred to as the print spooler. This integration provides smooth printing in a background mode and quick return-to-application time. The key to this operation is in how the print spooler sends data to the printer. Data is moved to the printer only when it is ready. Therefore, the system is never waiting for the printer to digest data that has been sent to it.

To print an open file in Windows 9x, just move to the application's File menu as normal and click the Print option. If the file is not open, it is still possible to print files in Windows 9x. Under the My Computer icon, right-click a selected file to produce a Print option in a pop-up menu. From the Windows Explorer screen, files can be printed by following the same right-click menu method. The document also can be dragged-and-dropped onto a printer icon in the Printers folder, in the Network Neighborhood listing, or on the desktop. Obviously, this option can be performed with both local and remote networked printers.

The settings for any printer can be changed through the My Computer icon on the desktop or through the Printers option under the Start menu's Settings entry. The process is the same for both routes, just double-click the Printers folder, right-click the desired printer, and select its Properties entry from the menu, as illustrated in Figure 8.36.

To view documents waiting to be printed from the print spooler, double-click on the desired printer's icon in the Printers folder. This action displays the existing print *queue*, as illustrated in Figure 8.37. Unlike earlier Windows Print Managers, closing the Print window does not interrupt the print queue in Windows 9x. The fact that the print spooler runs in its own 32-bit virtual environment means that printer hang-ups will not lock up the system. The print jobs in the queue will be completed unless they are deleted from the list.

FIGURE 8.36
Printer right-click pop-up menu.

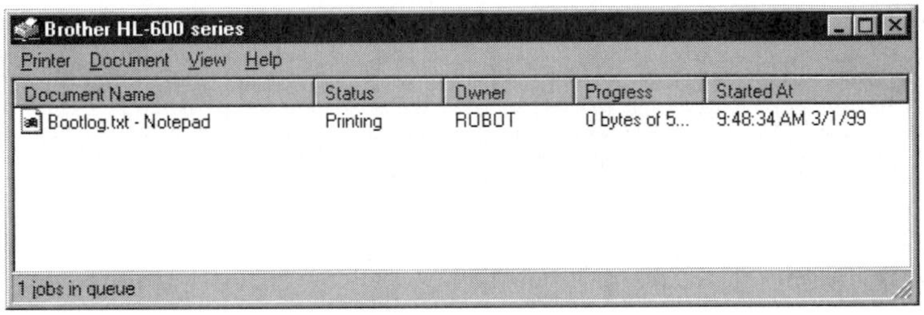

FIGURE 8.37
Windows 9x Print Queue display.

The Print Spooler window's menu bar items permit printing to be paused and resumed. They also can be used to delete print jobs from the queue. Right-clicking a printer icon produces a pop-up menu that also can be used to control printing operations being performed by that printer. Both options offer a Properties option that can be used to access the printer's configuration and connection information. One of the most important Printer Properties tabs is the Details page depicted in Figure 8.38.

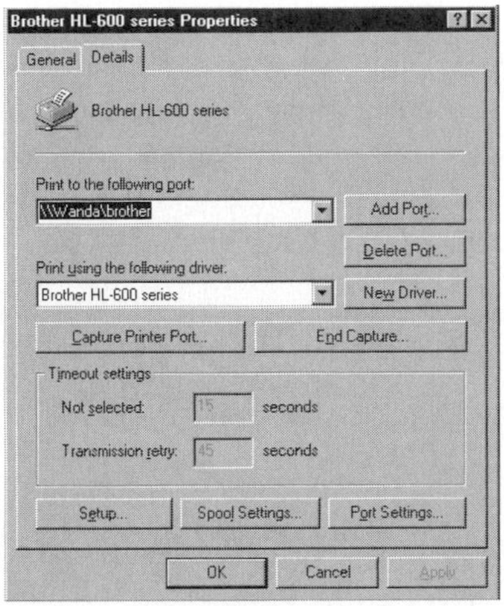

FIGURE 8.38
Windows 9x Printer Properties/Details
page.

Installing Printers in Windows 9x

Windows 9x automatically adopts any printers that have been established prior to its installation. If no printers are already installed, the
Setup program runs the new *Add Printer Wizard* to allow a printer
to be installed. Each printer in the system has its own print window
and icon to work from. The wizard can be accessed at any time
through the Windows 9x My Computer icon or Start menu. In the
Start menu, move to the Settings entry and click Printers. Likewise,
through the My Computer icon, or the Control Panel window,
double-click the Printers folder or icon.

To install a printer, open the Printers folder and double-click the
Add Printers icon. From this point, the Printer Wizard guides the
installation process. Because Windows 9x has built-in networking
support, the printer can be a local unit (connected to the computer)
or a remote unit located somewhere on the network. If the physical
printer is connected to a remote computer, referred to as a *print
server*, the remote unit must supply the printer drivers and settings
to control the printer. Likewise, the print server must be set up to
share the printer with the other users on the network.

To install the network printer, access the Network Neighborhood icon on the desktop, select the remote computer's *network name*, the remote unit's printer name, and right-click the Install option, as illustrated in Figure 8.39. After the remote printer has been installed, the local computer can access it through the Network Neighborhood icon.

FIGURE 8.39

Installing a Network Printer in Windows 9x.

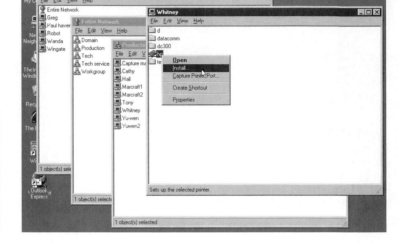

Memorize the procedure for installing a network printer in Windows 9x.

Know how to install Printer drivers in Windows 9x if the particular device is not listed in the standard Windows driver listings.

If the printer is not recognized as a model supported by the Windows 9x driver list, OEM drivers can be installed from a disk containing the OEMSETUP.INF file.

Printing in Windows 2000

To print an open file in Windows 2000, just move to the application's File menu as normal and click the Print option. If the file is not open, you can still print files in Windows 2000. Under the My Computer icon, right-click a selected file to produce a print option in a pop-up menu like the one in Figure 8.40. Files can be printed from the Windows Explorer screen by employing the same right-click menu method. The document also can be dragged-and-dropped onto a printer icon in the Printers folder, in the My Network Places listing, or on the desktop. Obviously, this option can be performed with both local and remote networked printers.

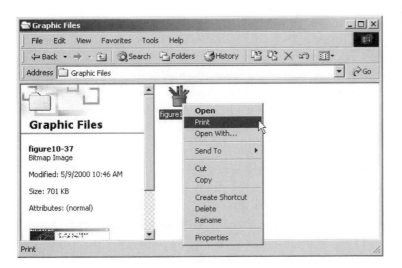

FIGURE 8.40
My Computer right-click pop-up menu.

The settings for any printer can be changed through the My Computer icon on the desktop or through the Printers option under the Start menu's Settings entry. The process is the same for both routes: Just double-click the Printers folder, click the desired printer, and select its Properties entry from the menu.

To view documents waiting to be printed from the print spooler, double-click the desired printer's icon in the Printers folder. This action displays the existing print queue, as illustrated in Figure 8.41. Closing the print window does not interrupt the print queue in Windows 2000.

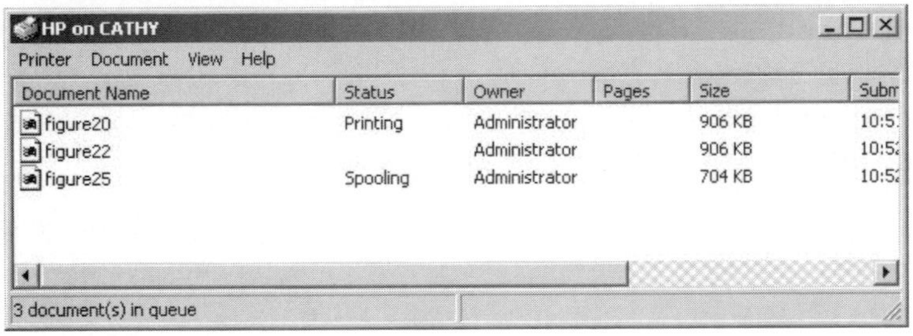

FIGURE 8.41
Windows 2000 print queue.

The fact that the print spooler runs in its own 32-bit virtual environment means that printer stalls will not lock up the system. The print jobs in the queue will be completed unless they are deleted from the list.

The Print Spooler window's menu bar contains the same basic tool set described for the Windows 9x print spooler. The menu items allow printing to be paused and resumed. They also can be used to delete print jobs from the queue. Right-clicking a printer icon produces a pop-up menu that also can be used to control printing operations being performed by that printer. Both options offer a Properties option that can be used to access the printer's configuration and connection information.

The Windows 2000 Printers dialog box enables users to sort between different printers based on their attributes. Windows 2000 Professional possesses the capability of printing across the Internet using the new standards-based Internet Printing Protocol (IPP). Using this protocol Windows 2000 Professional can print to a URL, view the print queue status using an Internet browser, and install print drivers across the Internet.

Windows 2000 Professional also supports a new universal font format called OpenType. This font type combines the best features of TrueType and Type 1 fonts. OpenType is supported by subsetting and compression technology that makes it efficient for transmission over the Internet.

Establishing Printers in Windows 2000

Like Windows 9x, Windows 2000 will automatically adopt any printers that have been established prior to its installation in the system. If no printers have been installed, the Setup routine runs the new Add Printer Wizard, depicted in Figure 8.42, enabling you to install a new printer. Each printer in the system possesses its own print window and icon to work from. The wizard can be accessed at any time through the Start menu.

To use the Start menu, move to the Settings entry and click Printers. To install a printer, open the Printers folder and double-click the Add Printer icon. From this point, the Printer Wizard guides the installation process. Because Windows 2000 has built-in networking support, the printer can be a local unit (connected to the computer), or a remote unit located somewhere on the network.

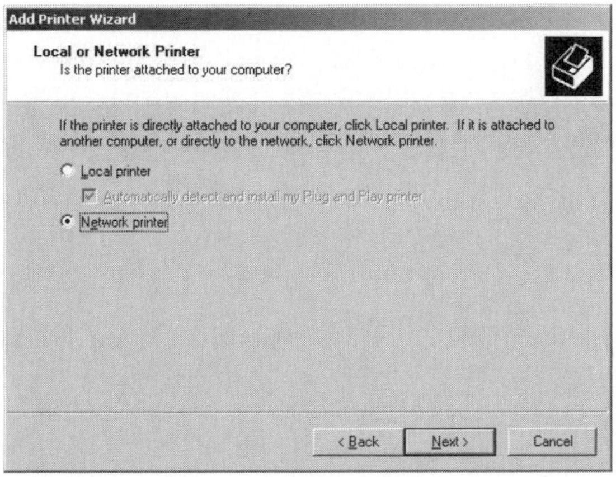

FIGURE 8.42
The Windows 2000 Add Printer Wizard.

To install local printers, choose the Local Printer option and click the Next button. Normally, the LPT1 options should be selected from the list of port options. Next, the Add Printer Wizard produces a list of manufacturers and models to choose from. This list will be similar to the one depicted in Figure 8.43. Just select the correct manufacturer and then the desired model from the list and inform the wizard about the location of the \i386 directory to fetch the driver from. If the \i386 directory has been copied to the hard drive, it will be faster to access the driver there. If not, the Windows 2000 distribution CD will be required.

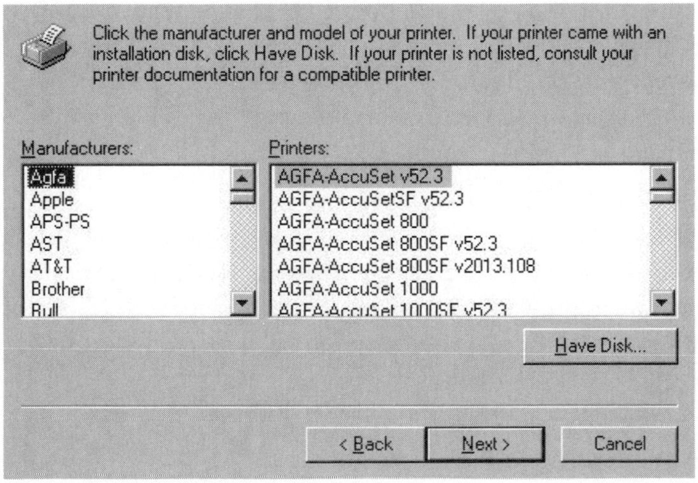

FIGURE 8.43
A list of printer manufacturers and models.

If the printer is not recognized as a model supported by the Windows 2000 driver list, OEM drivers can be installed from a disk containing the OEMSETUP.INF file. Select the Have Disk option from the Add Printer Wizard screen.

After loading the driver, the wizard will request a name for the printer to identify it to the network system. Enter a unique name or choose to use the default name supplied by Windows and continue.

Finally, the Add Printer Wizard will ask whether the printer is to be shared with other units on the network. If so, the printer must have a unique name to identify it to others on the network and must be set as Shared. The shared printer also must be set up for the different types of operating systems that may want to use it. The wizard will display a list of OS types on the network. Any, or all, of the OS types may be selected. The installation process is completed when the Finish button is clicked.

The Add printer Wizard also can be accessed through the My Computer icon, the Control Panel, or by double-clicking the Printers folder or icon.

Printer Properties

Printer properties are all the defining features about a selected printer, including information that ranges from which port it should use to what security features have been implemented with it. To examine or change the properties of a printer in Windows NT, select the Printers option from the Start button menu. Inside the printer window, click the desired printer to select it. From the File menu option, select the Properties entry to display the printer's properties sheet, as depicted in Figure 8.44.

The General tab provides general information about the printer. This includes such information as its description, physical location, and its installed driver name. The Ports tab lists the system's physical ports; whereas the Job Scheduling tab displays the printer's availability, priority level, and spooling options. The Sharing tab shows the printer's share status and share name.

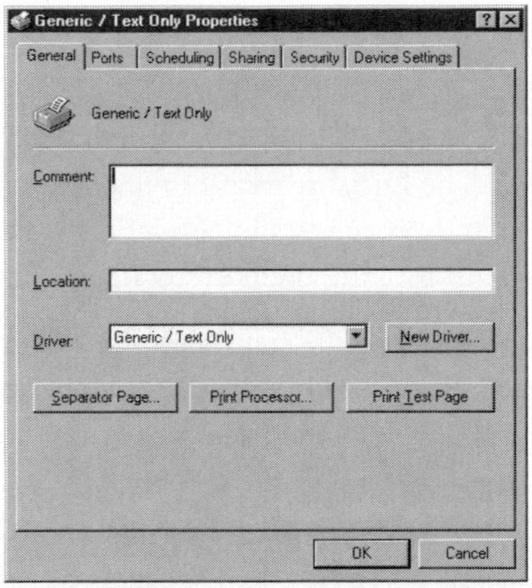

FIGURE 8.44
Printer Properties sheet.

The Security tab provides access to three major components. These are the Permissions button, the Auditing button, and the Ownership button. The Permissions button enables the system administrator to establish the level of access for different users in the system. The Auditing button provides user and event-tracking capabilities for the administrator. Finally, the Ownership button displays the name of the printer's owner.

The Device Settings tab provides a wide array of information about the printer, including such items as paper tray sizes and its font substitution tables. This feature is used to import downloadable font sets, install font cartridges, and increase the printer's virtual memory settings. The Device Settings tab, depicted in Figure 8.45, is one of the most important tabs in the Printer Properties page.

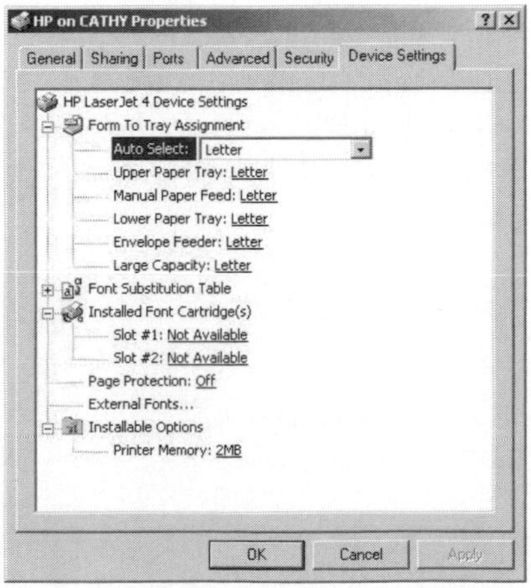

FIGURE 8.45
Windows 2000 Printer Properties/
Device Settings tab.

CHAPTER SUMMARY

KEY TERMS

- Add New Hardware Wizard
- Add Printer Wizard
- Add/Remove New Programs
- AUTOEXEC.BAT
- Backup
- Bad or Missing Command Interpreter
- Beep code
- BIOS extension
- Boot sector
- Bootable disk
- BOOTLOG.TXT
- CHKDSK (Check Disk)
- Clean boot disk
- Cold boot
- Command Prompt Only
- COMMAND.COM
- COMMAND.DOS
- CONFIG.SYS
- Default printer
- DETLOG.TXT
- DOS command line
- Dual-boot configuration
- Emergency start disk
- Error message

This chapter has focused on installing, configuring, and upgrading operating systems. The initial section of the chapter presented system requirements and procedures for installing Windows 9x and Windows 2000, and bringing them up to a basic operating level.

The second section covered the steps required to perform system upgrades from previous operating system versions to the Windows 9x or Windows 2000 operating systems.

The third section of the chapter presented the basic boot-up sequences for DOS and Windows systems in detail. Alternative boot-up methods and reasons were also described. This section also included step-by-step procedures to create a Windows 9x emergency start disk with utilities installed and a Windows 2000 Emergency Repair Disk.

Procedures for loading/adding device drivers to the system were described in the fourth section of the chapter for Windows 9x and Windows 2000.

The fifth section presented procedures for installing and running Windows and non-Windows applications in both Windows 9x and Windows 2000 systems.

The final section of the chapter identified procedures for installing printers in the Windows 9x and Windows 2000 environments. It also dealt with changing options, configuring, and using the Windows 9x and Windows 2000 printing subsystems.

At this point, review the objectives listed at the beginning of the chapter to be certain that you understand each point and can perform each task listed there. Afterward, answer the Review and Exam Questions that follow to verify your knowledge of the information.

- GDI.EXE
- GDI32.EXE
- IO.DOS
- IO.SYS
- KERNEL32.DLL
- KERNEL386.EXE
- Logged mode
- Master Boot Record (MBR)
- MS-DOS mode
- MSDOS.DOS
- MSDOS.SYS
- Network name
- Normal mode
- Operating System Loader
- PIF editor
- Plug and Play
- Power-On Self-Test
- Primary Bootstrap Loader
- Print Manager
- Print server
- Print spooler
- Printer name
- Printers folder
- Program information file (PIF)
- Queue
- Registry
- Resource conflicts
- Root directory
- Safe mode
- Safe Mode Command Prompt Only
- SETUP.EXE
- SETUPLOG.TXT
- Startup menu
- Step-by-step confirmation mode
- Supplemental disk
- System disk
- Toolbar
- USER.EXE
- USER32.EXE
- Virtual device drivers (VxDs)
- VMM32.VXD virtual machine manager
- Warm boot
- WIN.COM

RESOURCE URLS

www.fixwindows.com/charts/95/95sphng.htm

http://webopedia.internet.com/TERM/P/PIF_file.html

http://webopedia.internet.com/TERM/c/configuration.html

www.bus.msu.edu/nrc/class/95/upgrade.html

www.windrivers.com/tech/troubleshoot/winexceptions.htm

http://pclt.cis.yale.edu/pclt/BOOT/Chicago.htm

http://rama.bl.pg.gda.pl/~slawcok/mirror/pcmech/pnp.htm

www.cit.rcc.on.ca/os100/msdos06.htm

www.codemicro.com/windows.htm

continues

continued

http://webopedia.internet.com/TERM/k/kernel32_dll.html

www.pcguide.com/ref/mbsys/res/pnp.htm

www.pcguide.com/ref/mbsys/res/confl.htm

www.drivershq.com/mainhome.html

http://webopedia.internet.com/TERM/s/spooling.html

http://webopedia.internet.com/TERM/s/server.html

www.cit.rcc.on.ca/os100/win9505.htm

www.bus.msu.edu/nrc/class/95/startapp.html

APPLY YOUR KNOWLEDGE

Review Questions

1. Describe the sequence of events required to upgrade a Windows 95 Registry HKEY to a Windows 2000 HKEY.

2. What is a PIF file and what does it do?

3. Pressing the F8 key while the Starting Windows 9x message is onscreen will have what effect on the system?

4. From the system startup point of view, how do cold and warm boots differ?

5. How much memory is required to install Windows 2000 Professional?

6. Which operating systems can be upgraded to Windows 2000 Professional?

7. What type of FAT must be located on the partition that Windows 9x will be installed in?

8. List the minimum hardware resources required to install Windows 2000 Professional.

9. How is the MS-DOS command line accessed in Windows NT?

10. Which devices are loaded in a standard safe-mode startup?

11. List two ways to perform a safe-mode startup in Windows 9x.

12. What prevents printer hang-ups in Windows 9x from locking up the system?

13. Why would a step-by-step confirmation mode startup be performed?

14. What is the function of the BOOT.INI file in a Windows NT system?

15. Name two factors that must be taken into account when considering upgrading a Windows 9x system to the Windows NT or Windows 2000 operating system.

Exam Questions

1. Which file starts the Windows 9x program?

   A. WIN.BAT

   B. WIN.COM

   C. WIN.EXE

   D. WIN32.EXE

2. Which Windows NT/2000 file contains the Windows NT core and loads its device drivers?

   A. NTLDR

   B. NTDETECT.COM

   C. NTOSKRNL.EXE

   D. BOOT.INI

3. What types of file systems cannot be used under Windows 2000 Professional?

   A. NTFS 4.0

   B. HPFS

   C. FAT16

   D. FAT32

4. Which of the following is the first step in preparing a hard drive for operation?

   A. Load all the drivers necessary to enable the operating system to work with the system's installed hardware devices.

APPLY YOUR KNOWLEDGE

B. High-level format the drive with the basic operating system files.

C. Run the appropriate setup utility to install the complete operating system.

D. Partition the drive for use with the operating system.

5. What function does the BOOTLOG.TXT file serve?

A. It tracks the events of the Startup procedure.

B. It carries out the steps of the Startup procedure.

C. It tracks the events of the Shut Down procedure.

D. It tracks the events of the POST sequence.

6. Which file is the Operating System Loader looking for during the boot-up process?

A. An OS Loader

B. A Primary Bootstrap Loader

C. A Master Boot Record

D. The root directory

7. What file loads the Windows NT operating system kernel?

A. NTLDR

B. NTDETECT.COM

C. NTOSKRNL.EXE

D. BOOT.INI

8. Which Windows NT file is responsible for providing the NT Boot menu?

A. NTLDR

B. NTDETECT.COM

C. NTOSKRNL.EXE

D. BOOT.INI

9. Where will the Windows NT Setup utility install the Windows NT files in a typical installation?

A. The \Windows directory

B. The \i386 folder

C. The \Windows\System folder

D. The \WINNT folder

10. List the three files that must be located in the root directory to successfully boot MS-DOS.

A. MSDOS.SYS, IO.SYS, and COMMAND.COM.

B. CONFIG.SYS, COMMAND.COM, and AUTOEXEC.BAT

C. Files, stacks, and buffers

D. HIMEM.SYS, EMM386.EXE, and COMMAND.COM

Answers to Review Questions

1. There is no way to upgrade any part of the Windows 9x Registry to a Windows 2000 Registry. They are incompatible structures. For more information, see the section "Windows 9x and Windows NT."

2. PIFs are program information files created for any DOS-based files Setup finds in the system. For more information, see the section "DOS and Windows 9x."

3. The Windows 9x Startup menu can be accessed by holding down the F8 function key when the Starting Windows 9x display is onscreen. The

APPLY YOUR KNOWLEDGE

menu offers several startup options, including Normal, Logged, Safe, Step-by-Step Confirmation, and DOS modes. For more information, see the section "Windows 9x Startup Modes."

4. In a cold boot situation, the system executes the entire BIOS startup routine. In a warm boot, only some of the POST tests are performed on the system. This makes a warm boot much quicker. For more information, see the section "Initial POST Checks."

5. The minimum amount of RAM required to install Windows 2000 Professional is 32MB (64MB recommended, 4GB maximum). For more information, see the section "Installing Windows 2000 Professional."

6. Systems that can be upgraded to Windows 2000 Professional include Windows 3.x and 9x, as well as Windows NT 3.5 and 4.0 workstations. For more information, see the section "Upgrading to Windows 2000."

7. The Windows 9x installation program must find a recognizable MS-DOS FAT16 partition on the drive. This prevents it from being installed over some other type of operating system, such as Windows NT or Novell NetWare. For more information, see the section "Installing Windows 9x."

8. The minimum requirements for installing Windows 2000 Professional are microprocessor—166MHz Pentium or better; RAM—32MB; HDD space—650MB or more free on a 2GB drive; and a VGA monitor. For more information, see the section "Installing Windows 2000 Professional."

9. There is no MS-DOS icon in the Windows NT system. To access the DOS emulator, select the Run option from the Start menu and type the command **CMD** into the Run dialog box. For more information, see the section "DOS and Windows NT/2000."

10. In safe mode, the keyboard, mouse, and standard-mode VGA drivers are active. For more information, see the section "Safe Mode."

11. Safe mode can be accessed by typing **WIN /D:M** at the DOS prompt, or by pressing the F5 function key during startup. For more information, see the section "Safe-Mode."

12. The fact that the Windows print spooler runs in its own 32-bit virtual environment means that printer hang-ups will not lock up the system. For more information, see the section "Printing in Windows 9x"

13. The step-by-step confirmation mode displays each startup command line by line and waits for a confirmation from the keyboard before moving ahead. This allows an offending startup command to be isolated and avoided, so that it can be replaced or removed. For more information, see the section "Safe Mode."

14. It generates the Boot Loader menu. For more information, see the section "Windows NT/2000 Startup."

15. You must take into account its compatibility with current hardware and determine which file-management system to use. For more information, see the section "Upgrading to Windows 2000."

862   Part II   OPERATING SYSTEM TECHNOLOGIES

APPLY YOUR KNOWLEDGE

Answers to Exam Questions

1. **B.** The file that actually starts the Windows program is WIN.COM. For more information, see the section "Phase 3: Initializing Static VxDs."

2. **C.** NTOSKRNL.EXE is the Windows NT Kernel file that contains the Windows NT core and loads its device drivers. For more information, see the section "Windows NT/2000 Startup."

3. **B.** Systems can be upgraded to Windows 2000 Professional from Windows 3.x and 9x, as well as Windows NT 3.5 and 4.0 workstations. This includes older NTFS, FAT16, and FAT32 installations. When you install Windows 2000, it can recognize all three of these file system types. For more information, see the section "Upgrading to Windows 2000."

4. **D.** The first step in preparing a modern hard drive for operation is to partition the drive. In pre-IDE and SCSI drives, the first step involved placing a low-level format on the disk. For more information, see the section "Disk Preparation."

5. **A.** When logged-mode startup is activated, the system will create the BOOTLOG file. The BOOTLOG.TXT file tracks the events of the startup procedure and can show which step of the boot-up process caused problems. For more information, see the section "Safe Mode."

6. **C.** The system searches for a Master Boot Record that it can execute. This file can be located on one of the system's disk drives or in a remote computer connected by a communications path. For more information, see the section "Boot Up."

7. **A.** In the case of a Windows NT partition, the Bootstrap Loader is the NT Loader file named NTLDR. This file is the Windows NT equivalent of the DOS IO.SYS file and is responsible for loading the NT operating system into memory. Afterward, NTLDR passes control of the system over to the Windows NT operating system. For more information, see the section "Windows NT/2000 Startup."

8. **D.** With the minifile system in place, the NTLDR can locate and read a special, hidden Boot Loader menu file named BOOT.INI. NTLDR uses this text file to generate the Boot Loader menu that is displayed on the screen. If no selection is made after a given time delay, the default value is selected. For more information, see the section "Windows NT/2000 Startup."

9. **D.** If a new installation is being performed, the Setup program will install the Windows 2000 files in the \WINNT folder. For more information, see the section "Installing Windows 2000 Professional."

10. **A.** The files IO.SYS, MSDOS.SYS, and COMMAND.COM must be in the root directory to boot DOS (or Windows for that matter). For more information, see the section "Boot Up."

This chapter helps you to prepare for the Operating System Technologies module of the A+ Certification examination by covering the following objectives within the "Domain 3.0: Diagnosing and Troubleshooting" section.

3.1 Recognize and interpret the meaning of common error codes and startup messages from the boot sequence, and identify steps to correct the problem.

- **Safe mode**
- **No operating system found**
- **Error in CONFIG.SYS line XX**
- **Bad or missing COMMAND.COM**
- **HIMEM.SYS not loaded**
- **Missing or corrupt HIMEM.SYS**
- **SCSI**
- **Swap file**
- **NT boot issues**
- **Dr. Watson**
- **Failure to start GUI**
- **Windows protection error**
- **Event Viewer – event log is full**
- **A device referenced in SYSTEM.INI, WIN.INI, Registry not found**

▶ The startup process is one of the most common times when personal computers fail. Therefore, to be successful, the technician must be able to identify and correct problems associated with the startup process.

3.2 Recognize common problems and determine how to resolve them.

- **Eliciting problem symptoms from customers**
- **Having customer reproduce error as part of the diagnostic process**

CHAPTER 9

3.0 Diagnosing and Troubleshooting

- **Identifying recent changes to the computer environment from the user**
- **Troubleshooting Windows-specific printing problems**
  - **Print spool is stalled**
  - **Incorrect/incompatible driver for print**
  - **Incorrect parameter**

Other common problems

- **General protection faults**
- **Illegal operation**
- **Invalid working directory**
- **System lock up**
- **Option (sound card, modem, input device) will not function**
- **Application will not start or load**
- **Cannot log on to network (option – NIC not functioning)**
- **TSR (Terminate-and-Stay Resident) programs and viruses**
- **Applications don't install**

Windows-based utilities

- **ScanDisk**
- **Device Manager**
- **System Manager**
- **Computer Manager**
- **MSCONFIG.EXE**
- **REGEDIT.EXE (view information/backup Registry)**
- **REGEDIT32.EXE**
- **ATTRIB.EXE**
- **DEFRAG.EXE**
- **EXTRACT.EXE**

- **EDIT.COM**
- **FDISK.EXE**
- **SYSEDIT.EXE**
- **SCANREG**
- **WSCRIPT.EXE**
- **HWINFO.EXE**
- **ASD.EXE (automatic skip driver)**
- **CVT1.EXE (drive converter FAT16 to FAT32)**

Viruses and virus types

- **What they are**
- **Sources (floppy, email, and so on)**
- **How to determine their presence**

▶ As with hardware problems, every technician should be able to effectively acquire information from the customer concerning the nature of a software problem and then involve the user in the troubleshooting process as required.

▶ The Windows operating environment and operating system provide the printing functions for all the applications in a Windows system. The successful technician must be able to recognize and correct printing problems related to the Windows environment.

▶ After the operating system has started up and is functional, another set of problems can exist. As with startup problems, the technician must be able to identify and correct operational problems associated with the operating system.

▶ Viruses have become a major cause of problems in the personal computer environment. The technician must be aware of how typical viruses work, how they are contracted, and how to deal with them.

To prepare for the Diagnosing and Troubleshooting objective of the Operating System Technologies exam:

▶ Read the objectives at the beginning of this chapter.

▶ Study the information in this chapter.

▶ Review the objectives listed earlier in this chapter.

▶ Perform any step-by-step procedures in the text.

▶ Answer the Review and Exam Questions at the end of the chapter and check your results.

▶ Use the *ExamGear* test engine on the CD that accompanies this book for additional Review and Exam Questions concerning this material.

▶ Review the Test Tips scattered throughout the chapter and make certain that you are comfortable with each point.

INTRODUCTION

This domain requires the test taker to apply knowledge to diagnose and troubleshoot common problems relating to Windows 9x and Windows 2000. This includes understanding normal operation and symptoms relating to common problems. Questions from this domain account for 40% of the Operating System Technologies test.

OPERATING SYSTEM
TROUBLESHOOTING BASICS

▶ 3.1 Recognize and interpret the meaning of common error codes and startup messages from the boot sequence and identify steps to correct the problem.

The A+ Operating System Technologies objective 3.1 states that the test taker should be able to "recognize and interpret the meaning of common error codes and startup messages from the boot sequence and identify steps to correct the problem."

Troubleshooting operating system problems involves the same steps as any other logical troubleshooting procedure. The steps are just adapted to fit the structure of the operating system. Analyze the symptoms displayed, isolate the error conditions, correct the problem, and test the repair.

After the installation process has been successfully completed, operating system problems can be divided into three basic categories: setup problems, startup problems, and *operating problems.*

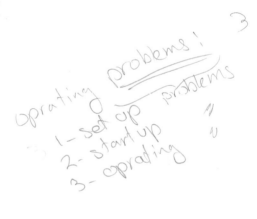

As you have seen in previous chapters, operating systems are tremendous collections of complex programming code brought together to control every operation of the computer hardware and link it to the software applications that users want to employ. As with anything so complex, operating systems fail from time to time—some more than others—and although potentially millions of things can go wrong with complex software systems, you should be happy to know that you can group operating system problems into three basic areas:

◆ Setup problems (those that occur during installation or upgrading)

◆ Startup problems (those that occur when the system is booting up)

◆ Operational problems (those that occur during the normal course of operations)

By isolating a particular software problem to one of these areas, the troubleshooting process becomes less complex.

Setup problems typically involve failure to complete an OS install or upgrade operation. In some cases, this can leave the system stranded between an older OS version and a newer OS version, making the system unusable.

Startup problems usually produce conditions that prevent the system hardware and software from coming up and running correctly. These problems fall into two major groups:

◆ Hardware configuration problems

◆ Operating system boot-up problems

Operational problems are problems that occur after the system has booted up and started running. These problems fall into three main categories:

◆ When performing normal application and file operations

◆ When printing

◆ When performing network functions

TROUBLESHOOTING SETUP PROBLEMS

Setup problems are those errors that occur during the process of installing the operating system on the hard disk drive. With early DOS versions, installation was a simple matter of making a \DOS directory on the hard drive and copying the contents of the DOS disks into it. For operating system versions from MS-DOS 5.0 forward, however, the installation procedure became an automated process requiring an Install or Setup program to be run.

One of the most common OS setup problems involves situations in which the system's hard drive does not have enough free space to carry out the installation process. When this occurs, you must remove files from the disk until you have cleared enough room to perform the installation. Unless you can remove enough obsolete files from the drive to make room for the new operating system, it is recommended that the files be backed up to some other media before erasing them from the drive.

Setup problems also occur when the system's hardware will not support the operating system that is being installed. These errors can include the following:

◆ Memory speed mismatches

◆ Insufficient memory problems

◆ Incompatible device drivers

The memory speed mismatch or mixed RAM-type problem produces a Windows *Protection Error* message during the installation process. This error indicates that the operating system is having timing problems that originate from the RAM memory used in the system. Correcting this problem involves swapping the system's RAM for devices that meet the system's timing requirements.

It is not uncommon for mouse or video drivers to fail during the installation of an operating system. If the video driver fails, you must normally turn off the system and attempt to reinstall the operating system from scratch. Conversely, if the mouse driver fails during the install, it is possible to continue the process using the keyboard. This problem is normally self-correcting after the system reboots. A similar problem occurs when the operating system is looking for a PS/2 mouse and the system is using a serial mouse. It will not detect the serial mouse, and you will need to complete the installation process using the keyboard. Afterward, you can check the CMOS Port Settings for the serial port the mouse is connected to and install the correct driver for the serial mouse if necessary.

The best way to avoid hardware-compatibility problems is to consult Microsoft's Web site to see that the hardware you are using is compatible with the operating system version you are installing.

Most error messages produced during an operating system installation stop the system. However, some errors offer to continue the process. It is our experience that continuing the installation rarely works out. Instead, just shut down the system, attempt to clear the problem, and then reinstall the operating system.

Windows 9x Setup Problems

Windows 9x draws from the existing FAT structure when it is being installed. Therefore, an interruption, or a crash during the installation process may leave the system with no workable operating system in place. If this occurs, you must boot the system from a bootable floppy disk and reinstall Windows 9x from that point. If the FAT version that Setup detects on the hard drive is older than MS-DOS 3.1, it presents an Incorrect MS-DOS Version message onscreen. If so, you must reformat the hard drive with a more current version of DOS.

If the system crashes during the hardware detection phase of a Windows 9x install, Microsoft recommends that you just reboot the system until the installation process is successful. The Windows Setup Wizard will mark startup steps that have failed and will bypass those steps the next time you attempt to install the operating system. The failed steps are recorded in the SETUPLOG text file, described later in this chapter. This process is known as safe recovery.

The Windows 9x installation files are stored on the installation disk in a compressed *cabinet* (CAB) file format. Therefore, they cannot just be copied over to the hard drive to repair files damaged in an aborted installation. The best recovery method for this situation is to boot the system to a floppy disk, run *FDISK* to repartition the drive, format the drive, and run the Windows 9x Setup utility (provided your data was backed up beforehand).

If some programs or hardware options fail to run properly after a system has been upgraded to a Windows 9x operating system, you must determine whether they require specific real-mode drivers to be retained in the CONFIG.SYS and AUTOEXEC.BAT files. Recall that during the Restart phase of the installation process, Windows 9x deactivates files that it perceives as incompatible, or unnecessary by placing a Remark (REM) statement at the beginning of the line. This may cause different applications or hardware to fail if they require these specific entries for operation.

This condition can be detected by removing the REM comment and retrying the program or hardware. Be aware that restoring the driver can cause other problems within Windows 9x. The best choice is always to contact the software or hardware manufacturer for a Windows 9x driver.

Windows NT/2000 Setup Problems

When an attempt to install Windows NT or Windows 2000 fails, a Stop screen error will normally result. Stop errors occur when Windows NT or Windows 2000 detects a condition from which it cannot recover. The system stops responding, and a screen of information with a blue or black background displays, as illustrated in Figure 9.1. Stop errors are also known as Blue Screen errors, or the *Blue Screen of Death* (BSOD). Troubleshooting these types of errors is discussed in more detail later in the chapter.

```
*** STOP:0x0000001A   (0x00000000, 0x00000000, 0x00000000, 0x00000000)
KMODE_EXCEPTION_NOT_HANDLED

*** Address 00000000 base at 00000000, DateStamp 0000000000 - driver.sys

If this is the first time you've seen this Stop error screen, restart your
computer. If this screen appears again, follow these steps:

Check to be sure you have adequate disk space. If a driver is identified in
the Stop message, disable the driver or check with the manufacturer for
driver updates. Try changing video adapters.

Check with your hardware vendor for any BIOS updates. Disable BIOS memory
options such as caching or shadowing. If you need to use Safe Mode to
remove or disable components, restart your computer, press F8 to select
Advanced Startup Options, and then select Safe Mode.

Refer to your Getting Started manual for more information on troubleshooting
Stop errors.

Kernel Debugger Using: COM1 (Port 0x3F8, Baud Rate 19200)
Beginning dump of physical memory...
```

FIGURE 9.1
Stop error or Blue Screen error.

Some other problems can typically occur during the Windows 2000 installation process. These problems include items such as the following:

Problems during Installation [handwritten]

- ◆ Noncompliant hardware failures.
- ◆ Insufficient resources.
- ◆ File system type choices.
- ◆ The installation process starts over after rebooting.
- ◆ WINNT32.EXE will not run from the command-line errors.

You can correct these particular installation-related problems as follows:

- ◆ **Verify hardware compatibility.** The hardware-compatibility requirements of Windows NT and Windows 2000 are more stringent than those of the Windows 9x platform. When either of these operating systems encounters hardware that is not compatible during the setup phase, they fail. In some cases, the system incorrectly detects the hardware, whereas in other cases the system produces a *Blue Screen* error.

  Make certain to check the Hardware Compatibility List to ensure that your hardware is compatible with Windows 2000. If the hardware is not listed, contact the hardware vendor to determine whether it supports Windows 2000 before starting the installation.

- ◆ **Verify minimum system resource requirements.** Make certain that your hardware meets the minimum hardware requirements, including the memory, free disk space, and video requirements. When the Windows NT or Windows 2000 Setup routines detect insufficient resources (that is, processor, memory, or disk space), it either informs you that an error has occurred and halts or it just hangs up and refuses to continue the install.

- ◆ **Establish the file system type.** During the installation process, you must decide which file system you are going to use. If you are going to dual-boot to Windows 98, and have a drive that is larger than 2GB, you must choose FAT32. Choosing NTFS for a dual-boot system renders the NTFS partition unavailable when you boot to Windows 98. FAT16

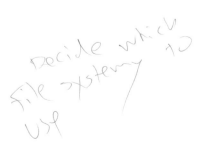

Decide which file system to use [handwritten]

does not support drives larger than 2GB. You can upgrade from FAT16 to FAT32 or from FAT32 to NTFS; however, you can never revert to the older file system after you have converted it. Be aware that Windows NT does not support FAT32 partitions. Therefore, Windows NT 4.0 or earlier cannot be used on a Windows 9x drive. Consider using the lowest common file system during installation and upgrade later.

◆ **Installation process reboots.** If you discover after the initial installation of Windows 2000 and the subsequent rebooting of the system to finish the installation, that the installation program seems to start over again, check the CD-ROM drive for the installation disc. Leaving the bootable CD-ROM in the CD player normally causes this condition because the BIOS settings instruct the computer to check for a bootable CD-ROM before looking on the hard drive for an operating system. To correct this problem, remove the Windows 2000 CD from the player, or change the System Setup configuration to not check the CD player during boot up.

◆ **WINNT32 will not run from the command prompt.** The WINNT32.EXE program is designed to run under a 32-bit operating system and will not run from the command line. It is used to initiate upgrades from Windows 9x or Windows NT to Windows 2000. From a 16-bit operating system, such as DOS or Windows 95, you must run the WINNT.EXE program from the command line to initiate the installation of Windows 2000.

In most cases, a failure during the Windows 2000 setup process produces an unusable system. When this occurs, you usually must reformat the disks and reinstall the system files from the Windows 2000 Setup (boot) disks.

Upgrade Problems

You will encounter many of the same problems performing an operating system upgrade that you do when performing a clean install. To review, these problems are normally related to the following:

◆ Insufficient hard drive or partition sizes

◆ Memory speed mismatches

◆ Insufficient memory problems

◆ Incompatible device drivers

In addition to these basic installation problems, upgrade operations can encounter problems created by version incompatibilities. New versions of operating systems are typically produced in two styles: full versions and upgrade versions. In some cases, you cannot use a full version of the operating system to upgrade an existing operating system. Doing so will produce an Incompatible Version error message telling you that you cannot use this version to upgrade. You must either obtain an upgrade version of the operating system, or partition the drive and perform a new installation (losing your existing data).

You also must have the appropriate version of the upgrade for the existing operating system. (That is, Windows 98SE comes in two versions—one upgrades both Windows 95 and Windows 98, whereas the other version upgrades only Windows 98.)

To determine the current version of a Windows operating system running on a computer, click the My Computer icon, select the Properties option from the pop-up menu, and select the General tab of the System Properties window.

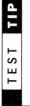

> **TEST TIP**
>
> Know how to display the current version of Windows information for a system.

TROUBLESHOOTING STARTUP PROBLEMS

Fortunately, only a few problems can occur during the startup process of a disk-based computer. These problems include the following:

◆ Hardware problems

◆ Configuration problems

◆ Boot-up (or OS-startup) problems

All three of these problem types can result in startup failures. Some prevent any activity from appearing in the system, others produce symptoms that can be tracked to a cause, and yet others produce error messages that can be tracked to a source.

As described in Chapter 2, "2.0 Diagnosing and Troubleshooting," an interesting troubleshooting point occurs at the single beep in the boot-up process of most computers. If the system produces an error message, or a beep-coded error signal, before the beep, the problem is hardware-related.

[handwritten margin note: — Beep in Boot up process) is hardware problem.]

On the other hand, if the error message or beep code is produced after the single beep occurs, the problem is likely to be associated with starting up the operating system. At this point, the problem becomes an operating system startup problem.

When dealing with a disk operating system, the following four things can prove very useful to help you isolate the cause of startup problems:

◆ Error messages and beep codes

◆ System log files

◆ Clean boot disks (Emergency Start Disks)

◆ Single-step startup procedures

The following Step by Step identifies the preliminary ways to troubleshoot startup problems.

STEP BY STEP

9.1 Troubleshooting Startup Problems

1. Try to reboot the system.

2. Check system log files if available to determine where the process was interrupted.

3. Perform a clean boot with minimal configuration settings to remove nonessential elements from the process.

4. Perform a single-step boot up to isolate any driver problems that are preventing boot up from taking place.

Error Codes and Startup Messages

Error messages that occur during the boot-up process indicate that a problem exists that must be sorted out before the system can boot up and operate correctly.

If the system will not boot up correctly, you need to boot the system to a minimum configuration and establish a point to begin troubleshooting the problem. This startup method enables you to bypass any unnecessary configuration and normally involves using a clean boot disk or the *Emergency Start Disk* to start the system.

If the system boots up from the minimal condition, the problem exists in the bypassed files. Restart the system and select a startup mode that single-steps through the configuration and startup file sequence.

The *single-step startup procedure* enables you to isolate the problem command. If the system crashes while trying to execute a particular command, restart the boot-up process and skip the offending command. Repeat the process until the system reaches boot up. Track all offending commands so that you can correct them individually. Check the syntax (spelling, punctuation, and usage) of any offending lines.

When the system will boot to the clean boot disk, but will not boot up to the hard drive, and has no configuration or startup file errors, a problem exists in the operating system's boot files. These errors typically return some type of `Bad or Missing Command Interpreter` message, or a `Disk Boot Failure` message. Basically, three conditions produce these types of error messages:

◆ The Master Boot Record or Command Interpreter file cannot be found on the hard drive, and no bootable disk is present in the A: drive.

◆ The Master Boot Record or operating system's Command Interpreter file is not located in the partition's root directory. This message is likely when installing a new hard drive or a new operating system version.

◆ The user has inadvertently erased the Master Boot Record or operating system Command Interpreter file from the hard drive, possibly during the process of establishing a dual-boot disk or when setting up a multiple operating system environment.

You can repair a Missing Command Interpreter error by restoring the boot record and operating system files to the hard disk. To do so, you normally copy or extract the files from the clean boot disk to the hard drive. Similarly, if the boot disk contains a copy of the **FDISK** command, you can use the **FDISK /MBR** command to restore the hard drive's Master Boot Record, along with its partition information.

WINDOWS 9X STARTUP PROBLEMS

Windows 9x offers many improved features over previous operating systems. However, it can suffer many of the same problems as any other operating system. To overcome some of the typical system problems, Windows 9x includes several built-in troubleshooting tools. These tools include several *safe-mode startup options*, a trio of *system log files*, and an extensive *interactive troubleshooting Help file* system.

As with previous operating systems, you can use three important tools when a Windows 9x system is having startup problems: the Emergency Start (clean boot) Disk, safe modes, and the step-by-step startup sequence. With Windows 9x, the clean boot disk is referred to as an Emergency Start Disk. To access the safe modes and the single-step with confirmation startup process, press the Shift and F8 function keys simultaneously when the Starting Windows 9x message appears onscreen.

The special function keys available during the Windows 9x startup are as follows:

◆ **F5.** Safe mode

◆ **F6.** Safe mode with network support

◆ **F8.** Step-by-step confirmation mode

◆ **Shift+F5.** Safe mode command prompt only

Typical Windows 9x startup error messages include the following:

◆ HIMEM.SYS not loaded.

◆ Unable to initialize display adapter.

> **TEST TIP**
> Memorize the shortcut keys used to skip startup sections and to single-step through the boot-up process.

◆ Device referenced in WIN.INI could not be found.

◆ Bad or missing COMMAND.COM.

◆ Swap file corrupt.

◆ Damaged or missing Core files.

◆ Device referenced in SYSTEM.INI could not be found.

These and other Windows 9x-related startup messages indicate the presence of problems that must be corrected before the system can boot up and run correctly.

The generic process for isolating the cause of a Windows 9x startup problem is as follows:

1. Use the Emergency Start Disk to gain access to the system and the hard drive.

2. If necessary, repair the System files and Command Interpreter files as described earlier in this chapter.

3. Attempt to boot up into safe mode to see whether the problem is driver related.

4. Reboot the system into the step-by-step confirmation startup mode to isolate configuration and driver problems. Continue single-stepping through the startup process until all offending steps have been identified and corrected.

5. Review the Windows 9x log files for problem steps.

Be aware that the MSDOS.SYS file in Windows 9x is used to provide startup options, load some drivers, and establish paths for certain system files. You should check these entries if Windows 9x does not start properly.

In the case of the HIMEM.SYS error, use the *System Editor* to check the syntax and correctness of the entry in the CONFIG.SYS file if present. With Windows 9x, the HIMEM.SYS statement must be present and correct for the operating system to run. Also check the HIMEM.SYS file to make sure it is the correct version and in the correct location. In the case of a Windows 9x upgrade, as many as three versions of HIMEM.SYS may be present in the system. The Unable to Initialize Display Adapter error message is indicative of errors that occur during the hardware-detection phase of the

Windows 9x PnP boot-up routine. These errors normally occur either because the Windows 9x PnP function cannot detect the hardware component, or because it cannot reconcile the adapter's needs to the available system resources. However, do not assume that just because Windows 9x is running that PnP is in effect and running. The system's BIOS and the peripheral device also must be PnP-compliant for the autodetection function to work.

You should be able to sort-out problems that occur during the detection phase by starting the system in *step-by-step confirmation mode* (pressing F8 during the boot up) and then single-step through the driver loading process to sort out the display driver/hardware problem. You must use the Control Panel's Add New Hardware Wizard to install device drivers when the PnP detection function does not work. Key Windows 9x files prevent the system from starting up if they become corrupted. These files include those associated with the Master Boot Record, the boot sector, the FATs, and the Windows Core files. Errors that occur between the single beep that marks the end of the POST and the appearance of the Starting Windows 9x message on the screen are associated with the boot sector. Problems that show up between the Starting Windows message and the appearance of the desktop involve the Windows Core files. In any event, if disk corruption is detected, you must rebuild the corrupted file structures.

When IO.SYS is corrupted in Windows 9x, the system hangs up before the Starting Windows message appears and produces a System Disk Invalid error message onscreen. If the MSDOS.SYS file is missing or corrupted, Windows displays a blue screen with an Invalid VxD Dynamic Link message and fails to start up.

Other MSDOS.SYS-related problems relate to the Registry, the *Extended Memory Manager* (XMS), and the *Installable File System Manager* (IFSMGR). These problems produce errors that appear during startup and are caused by syntax errors in the [Paths] section of the file.

Likewise, the COMMAND.COM problem produces an error message onscreen and fails to start up Windows. You can repair the missing COMMAND.COM error by using the DOS *COPY* and *SYS* commands, as described in Chapter 2. These commands copy the COMMAND.COM and system files from the clean boot disk to the hard drive. Similarly, if the boot disk contains a copy of the

FDISK command, you can use the **FDISK/MBR** command to restore the hard drive's Master Boot Record, along with its partition information.

As mentioned in Chapter 2, the following conditions produce a Bad or Missing COMMAND.COM error message:

◆ The COMMAND.COM file cannot be found on the hard drive, and no bootable disk is present in the A: drive.

◆ The COMMAND.COM file is not located in the hard drive's root directory. This message is likely when installing a new hard drive or a new DOS version.

◆ The user inadvertently erases the COMMAND.COM file from the hard drive.

To correct these problems, start the system using the Emergency Start Disk. At the command prompt, type **SYS C:** to copy the IO.SYS, MSDOS.SYS, and COMMAND.COM files onto the hard disk. You can use the DOS **Attribute** command to verify that the hidden system files have been successfully copied to the disk (that is, **Attrib -r -s -h c:\IO.SYS** and **Attrib –r –s –h C:\MSDOS.SYS** to make them visible and to remove their read-only and system status).

The COMMAND.COM file can also be restored from the command line, or through the Windows Explorer. To restore the COMMAND.COM file from the command line, start the system from the startup disk and use the **Copy** command to transfer the file manually.

The COMMAND.COM file can also be dragged from the startup disk to the root directory of the hard drive using the Windows 9x My Computer or Windows Explorer functions. As with the manual copy procedure, the COMMAND.COM file's read-only, system, and hidden attributes must be removed so that it can be manipulated within the system.

To locate and correct the Missing Core File problem cited earlier, check for corrupted files on the disk drive. To accomplish this, start the system in safe mode using the Command Prompt Only option. When the command prompt appears, move to the Windows Command directory and run the *ScanDisk* utility. If ScanDisk detects corrupted files, you must replace them. The ScanDisk utility can locate and fix several types of problems on the hard drive. These problems include corrupted FATs, long filenames, lost clusters and cross-linked files, tree structure problems, and bad sectors on the drive.

You can use the Windows 9x Setup function to verify or repair damaged Windows operating system files. To accomplish this, run the Setup utility and select the Verify option when presented by the Setup procedure. You then can repair damaged system files without running a complete reinstall operation.

It is also possible to extract Windows 9x components from the installation disk using the **Extract** command. Windows 9x stores its files in a compressed *cabinet* (CAB) format on the distribution CD. If corrupted Windows 9x files are found in the system, it is not possible to just copy new ones onto the drive from the CD. Instead, you must run Setup using the distribution CD and the Validate/Restore option.

You also can run the *EXTRACT.EXE* command from the Windows Command directory to extract selected compressed files from the CD. The preferable method is the Setup option. In most cases, however, it is simpler to reinstall Windows than to search for individual files and structures.

The Windows 9x swap file is controlled through the System icon in the Control Panel. From this point, enter the Performance page and click its Virtual Memory button. Typically, the Let Windows Manage Virtual Memory option should be selected. If the system locks up and does not start, the swap file may have become corrupted, or the Virtual Memory setting may have been changed to Disabled. In either case, you must reinstall Windows 9x to correct the problem.

The device or driver files referenced in the Missing INI Files error messages should be checked to make certain that they have been properly identified, and that their location and path are correct. If they are not, use the System Editor to make the necessary changes by installing the specified device driver in the designated INI file. If the path and syntax are correct for the indicated files, you should reload them from the Emergency Start Disk to correct the offending lines.

> **WARNING**
>
> **Check the Versions** The ScanDisk version used with a Windows 9x system must be the one specifically designed for that operating system (i.e., Windows 95 ScanDisk version should not be used on a Windows 98 system). Using other versions may not work correctly and could result in data loss. When using ScanDisk to isolate startup problems, the Windows 9x version used should be the version that is located on the particular computer's Emergency Start Disk and it should be the version that runs from the command prompt.

If a DOS-based application is causing the system to stall during Windows 9x startup, you should reboot the computer. When the Starting Windows 9x message appears onscreen, press the F8 key to bring up the Startup menu. Select the Restart in MS-DOS mode option from the list. From this point, you must edit the AUTOEXEC.BAT and CONFIG.SYS files to disable selected lines. In the AUTOEXEC.BAT file, place Remark (REM) statements at the beginning of the following lines:

◆ \Windows\command

◆ \call c:\windows\command***

◆ \windows\win.com/wx

Also REM the dos=single line in the CONFIG.SYS file.

After making these corrections, shut the system down and restart it. The system should boot up and run correctly with these lines removed.

Errors in the CONFIG.SYS and AUTOEXEC.BAT files will produce the Error in CONFIG.SYS Line *XX* or Error in AUTOEXEC.BAT Line *XX* messages described in the A+ objectives. The line specified by the *XX* in the error message contains a syntax (spelling, punctuation, or usage) error that prevents it from running. Syntax errors also can produce an Unrecognized Command in CONFIG.SYS message. These errors also can be caused by missing or corrupted files specified in the CONFIG.SYS or AUTOEXEC.BAT files. To correct these errors, correct the line in the file, reload the indicated file, and restart the computer. One of the final problems that could affect startup in Windows 9x is the *password*. Normally, when a user forgets his local Windows logon password, he can click the Cancel option and gain access to most of the local resources. However, the user will not be able to see any network resources, or access resources restricted through the System Policy setting. The system declares network resources "Unavailable" to the user. The most direct way to get around a local logon password is to access the local machine and delete the *username*.PWL file in the C:\Windows directory. You also could create a new user account in Windows 9x to establish another password.

To get around a forgotten network password, remove the Client for Microsoft Networks protocol from the Network Components window and then reinstall it. When you restart the system, it asks you to establish a new user who will have a new password.

Windows 9x Startup Modes

The Windows 9x Startup menu (not to be confused with the desktop's Start menu), depicted in Figure 9.2, can be obtained on a non-starting system by holding down the F8 function key when the Starting Windows 9x is displaying onscreen. The menu offers several startup options including Normal, Logged, Safe, Step-by-Step Confirmation, and DOS Modes. These startup modes play an important role in getting the Windows 9x operating system up and running when it fails to start.

FIGURE 9.2
The Startup menu.

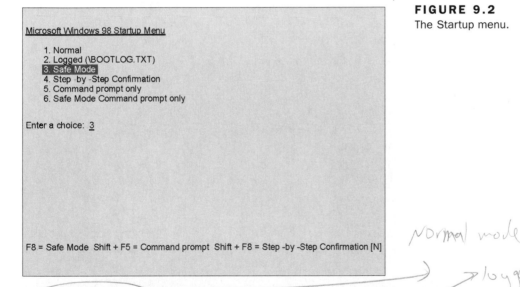

```
Microsoft Windows 98 Startup Menu

    1. Normal
    2. Logged (\BOOTLOG.TXT)
    3. Safe Mode
    4. Step -by -Step Confirmation
    5. Command prompt only
    6. Safe Mode Command prompt only

Enter a choice: 3




F8 = Safe Mode  Shift + F5 = Command prompt  Shift + F8 = Step -by -Step Confirmation [N]
```

In normal mode, the system just tries to restart as it normally would, loading all of its normal startup and Registry files. The *logged-mode* option also attempts to start the system in normal mode, but keeps an error log file that contains the steps performed and outcome. You can read this text file (BOOTLOG.TXT) with any text editor, or you can print it out on a working system.

TEST TIP

Be aware that the BOOTLOG.TXT file is not normally created during startup. It has to be initiated with the logged mode.

Safe Mode

> **What's Active In Safe Mode?** In safe mode, the minimal device driver's (keyboard, mouse, and standard-mode VGA drivers) are active to start the system. However, the CD-ROM drive will not be active in safe mode.

If Windows determines that a problem that prevents the system from starting has occurred, or if it senses that the Registry is corrupt, it automatically attempts to restart the system in safe mode. This mode bypasses several startup files to provide access to the system's configuration settings. In particular, any existing CONFIG.SYS and AUTOEXEC.BAT files are bypassed, along with the Windows 9x Registry and the [Boot] and [386enh] sections of the SYSTEM.INI file. The contents of these files are employed to retain compatibility with older hardware and applications.

You also can access safe mode by pressing the F5 function key while the Starting Windows 9x message is displaying onscreen. Windows 9x also reverts to this mode if an application requests it.

Unless modified, the safe-mode screen appears as depicted in Figure 9.3. Active functions appear onscreen along with the safe-mode notice in each corner. However, there is no taskbar in safe mode.

FIGURE 9.3
The safe-mode startup screen.

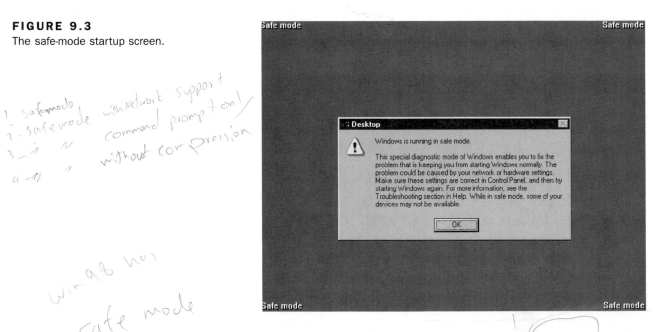

Windows 9x has four safe-mode startup options: *Safe Mode, Safe Mode with Network Support* (Windows 98 does not officially support safe mode with network support. However, it can be accessed by pressing the F6 function key during boot up), *Safe Mode Command Prompt Only,* and *Safe Mode Without Compression.* Each option is customized for specific situations and disables selected portions of the system to prevent them from interfering with the startup process.

The standard safe-mode startup is used when the system

◆ Will not start after the Starting Windows9x message appears onscreen

◆ Stalls repeatedly or for long periods of time

◆ Cannot print to a local printer after a complete troubleshooting sequence

◆ Has video display problems

◆ Slows down noticeably, or does not work correctly

In standard safe-mode startup, Windows bypasses certain startup and configuration files and loads a standard set of device drivers to start the system. The bypassed files include the following:

◆ The Registry

◆ The CONFIG.SYS and AUTOEXEC.BAT files

◆ The [Boot] and [386Enh] sections of the SYSTEM.INI file

The only device drivers loaded in safe mode are the mouse driver, the standard keyboard driver, and the standard VGA driver. This should enable enough of the Windows structure to operate so that the offending portions can be isolated and repaired using step-by-step checking procedures.

The Step-by-Step Confirmation option enables you to check each line of the startup procedure individually. In doing so, the Step-by-Step option enables you to verify which drivers are being loaded, temporarily disable any offending drivers, and check other startup errors that may be indicated through error messages. You should use this option when the system

◆ Fails while loading the startup files

◆ Needs to load real-mode drivers

◆ Displays a Registry Failure error message

As the startup process moves forward, the system asks whether each line is correct. Press the Enter key to confirm the line, or press the Esc key to skip a line. Keep track of any skipped lines so that you can check them individually. If the system crashes after a line has been confirmed, mark it as a problem and restart the system using the Step-by-Step option. Bypass the offending line on the next attempt to reach boot up. Record all lines that prevent the boot-up process and troubleshoot them one by one.

The sequence of the step-by-step prompts is as follows:

1. Load the DoubleSpace/DriveSpace driver (if present)?

2. Process the Registry?

3. Create a startup log file?

4. Process the CONFIG.SYS file?

5. Process the AUTOEXEC.BAT file?

6. Run WIN.COM to start Windows 9x?

7. Load all Windows drivers?

As the list illustrates, the Step-by-Step option provides an opportunity to create a startup log file called BOOTLOG.TXT. This file helps you isolate startup problems—such as real-mode, 16-bit adapter drivers that refuse to load and prevent the system from booting. You can check the contents of the log file for offending entries that stop the system. More information is provided concerning the BOOTLOG.TXT file later in this chapter.

Responses for the CONFIG.SYS and AUTOEXEC.BAT prompts are Y and N for individual lines. You can use the Tab key to accept the entire file. An N answer to the Load All Windows Drivers prompt results in Windows operating in safe mode. Otherwise, answering Y to all the prompts starts Windows 9x as normal, with the exception that the Windows logo does not appear at startup.

The Safe Mode with Network Support option typically bypasses the CONFIG.SYS and AUTOEXEC.BAT files and loads the COMMAND.COM processor. It then loads HIMEM.SYS and

IFSHLP.SYS, followed by any drive-compression drivers, the Windows 9x files Core and Registry files, and the basic network driver files.

This mode is used in networked environments when the system

◆ Stops responding when a remote network is accessed

◆ Cannot print to a remote printer

◆ Stalls during startup and cannot be started using a normal safe mode startup

Because this mode loads the Windows Registry, it cannot be used if the Registry has been corrupted. If the system will load Windows in standard safe mode, but not with the Network Support option, check the network configuration settings.

Also be aware that Windows 9x uses the MSDOS.SYS file to establish paths for some options. In the case of real-mode networking, the [Paths] entry, WINDIR=, must be defined for the NET-START.BAT file used to start the network. If this file does not run, Windows will fail to load.

DOS Modes

The Safe Mode Command Prompt Only option loads only COMMAND.COM and the disk-compression utility files (DriveSpace or DoubleSpace), if present. It does not load any of the Windows 9x files, HIMEM.SYS, or IFSHLP.SYS. This option should be chosen when the system fails to start in safe mode. You can enter this mode directly during the startup process by pressing the Shift and F5 keys simultaneously (Shift+F5) when the Starting Windows9x message is onscreen. You also can use it to:

◆ Employ command-line switches, such as **WIN D/X**

◆ Employ command-line tools, such as DOS editors

◆ Avoid loading HIMEM.SYS or IFSHLP.SYS

The Safe Mode Without Compression option appears only in systems using compressed drives. In operation, it is similar to the Command Prompt Only option with the exception that no compression drivers are loaded. The following list provides reasons for selecting this option:

◆ The system stops responding when a compressed drive is accessed.

◆ A *Corrupt CVF* (Compressed Volume File) error displays during startup.

◆ When Safe Mode and Safe Mode Command Prompt Only options fail to start the system.

If the **BootMulti=** option was set to 1 during the Windows 9x setup, the menu will contain an option to Start Using the Previous Version of MS-DOS. As its name indicates, this option starts the system with the version of DOS that was on the hard drive before Windows 9x was installed. Dual-booting must be enabled in the MSDOS.SYS file for this option to function.

WIN Switches

When Windows 9x refuses to start up, a number of options are available for starting it from the command line. Starting Windows using a **/D** switch is often helpful in isolating possible areas of the operating system as problem sources (that is, **WIN /D**). You can modify the **/D** switch to start Windows in a number of different configurations:

◆ Using an **/D:F** switch disables 32-bit disk access.

◆ The **/D:M** and **/D:N** switches start Windows in safe mode, or safe with networking mode.

◆ An **/D:S** switch inhibits Windows from using address space between F0000h and FFFFFh.

◆ The **/D:V** switch prevents Windows from controlling disk transfers. Instead, HDD interrupt requests are handled by the BIOS.

◆ The **/D:X** switch prevents Windows from using the area of memory between A000h and FFFFh.

Other switches can be used with the **WIN** command. The **WIN /B** switch causes Windows to start in logged mode and to produce a BOOTLOG.TXT file during startup. This option enables you to determine whether specific device drivers are stalling the system. Logged mode can also be selected by pressing the F8 key while the Starting Windows 9x message is onscreen. After selecting the Logged option, restart the system using the Safe Mode Command Prompt Only option. Then, use a text editor to examine the contents of the BOOTLOG.TXT file and determine which driver has failed to load.

Using a question mark as a switch with the **WIN** command (that is, **WIN /?**) shows a listing of all the switches associated with the command. You can use these switches to start Windows with various portions of the operating system disabled. If the system runs with a particular section disabled, at least some portion of the problem can be linked to that area.

Windows 9x Log Files

Windows 9x maintains four log files: *BOOTLOG.TXT*, *SETUPLOG.TXT*, *DETLOG.TXT*, and *DETCRASH.LOG*. These files maintain a log of different system operations and enable you to see what events occurred leading up to a failure. The TXT files can be read with Notepad, DOS Editor, or any other text editor.

BOOTLOG.TXT

The BOOTLOG.TXT file contains the sequence of events conducted during the startup of the system. The original BOOTLOG.TXT file is created during the Windows 9x setup process. You can update the file by pressing the F8 key during Startup, or by starting Windows 9x with a **WIN /b** switch. It is not updated automatically each time the system is started. The log information is recorded in five basic sections.

The log information is recorded in five basic sections.

1. Loading real-mode drivers

   This section records a two-part loading report during the boot-up process. In the example section that follows, the system successfully loads the HIMEM.SYS and EMM386.EXE memory managers. Afterward, a list of other real-mode drivers is loaded. In the case of an unsuccessful load operation, the report returns a LoadFailed= entry.

```
[000E3FDC] Loading Device = C:\WINDOWS\HIMEM.SYS
[000E3FE0] LoadSuccess    = C:\WINDOWS\HIMEM.SYS
[000E3FE0] Loading Device = C:\WINDOWS\EMM386.EXE
[000E3FEC] LoadSuccess    = C:\WINDOWS\EMM386.EXE
*
*
```

2. Loading VxDs

   In the second section, the system loads the VxD drivers. The
   following list includes a sample of various VxDs that have
   been loaded. The asterisks in the sample listing are included to
   indicate sections of omitted lines. This is done to shorten the
   length of the file for illustration purposes.

```
*
[000E41F3] Loading Vxd = int13
[000E41F3] LoadSuccess = int13
[000E41F3] Loading Vxd = vmouse
[000E41F4] LoadSuccess = vmouse
[000E41F6] Loading Vxd = msmouse.vxd
[000E41F9] LoadSuccess = msmouse.vxd
[000E41F9] Loading Vxd = vshare
[000E41F9] LoadFailed  = vshare
*
```

3. Initialization of critical VxDs

   Check this section to verify that system-critical VxDs have
   been initialized.

```
[000E420A] SYSCRITINIT  = VMM
[000E420A] SYSCRITINITSUCCESS  = VMM
[000E420A] SYSCRITINIT  = VCACHE
[000E420A] SYSCRITINITSUCCESS  = VCACHE
*
*
```

4. Device initialization of VxDs

   This section of the log shows the VxDs that have been successfully initialized. In each cycle, the system attempts to initialize
   a VxD, and then reports its success or failure.

```
[000E420D] DEVICEINIT  = VMM
[000E420D] DEVICEINITSUCCESS  = VMM
*
[000E421F] Dynamic load device  isapnp.vxd
[000E4225] Dynamic init device  ISAPNP
[000E4226] Dynamic init success ISAPNP
[000E4226] Dynamic load success isapnp.vxd
*
*
```

The bold information in the listing points out the dynamic loading and initialization of the PnP driver for the ISA bus.

5. Successful initialization of VxDs

   The entries in this section verify the successful completion of the initialization of the system's VxDs. A partial listing of these activities follows:

```
[000E4430] INITCOMPLETE = VMM
[000E4430] INITCOMPLETESUCCESS = VMM
[000E4430] INITCOMPLETE = VCACHE
[000E4430] INITCOMPLETESUCCESS = VCACHE
*
*
```

SETUPLOG.TXT

The *SETUPLOG.TXT* file holds setup information that was established during the installation process. The file is stored on the system's root directory and is used in *safe recovery* situations.

The log file exists in seven basic sections, as described in the following sample sections. Entries are added to the file as they occur in the setup process. Therefore, the file can be read to determine what action was being taken when a setup failure occurred.

```
[OptionalComponents]
"Accessories"=1
"Communications"=1
*
"Monitor"="(Unknown Monitor)"
"Mouse"="Standard Serial Mouse"
"Power"="No_APM"
"Locale"="L0409"
*
[Setup]
InstallType=1
Customise=0
Express=0
ChangeDir=1
Network=1
*
CleanBoot=0
Win31FileSystem=-8531
CopyFiles=1
*
[Started]
version=262144,950
OldLogFile
*
```

```
Display_InitDevice:Checking display driver. No PNP registry
➥found.
Mouse_InitDevice:Checking mouse driver. No PNP registry
➥found.
```

The bold text in the sample section shows the system's response to not finding a PnP Registry entry for different devices.

```
[FileQueue]
CacheFile() C:\WINDOWS\win.ini returns=0
CacheFile() C:\WINDOWS\exchng32.ini returns=0
CacheFile() C:\WINDOWS\control.ini returns=0
CacheFile() C:\WINDOWS\qtw.ini returns=0
CacheFile() C:\WINDOWS\system.cb returns=0
SrcLdid:(11)skyeagle.cpl
CacheFile() C:\WINDOWS\msoffice.ini returns=0
*
[FileCopy]
VcpClose:About to close
VcpClose:Delete 1514
VcpClose:Rename 4
VcpClose:Copy 827
CAB-No volume name for LDID 2, local copy - path
C:\WININST0.400
*
diskdrv.inf=17,,7915,20032
drvspace.bin=13,,7915,20032
*
[Restart]
*
Resolve Conflict:C:\DBLSPACE.BIN ConflictType: 240
drvspace.bin=31,DBLSPACE.BIN,7915,20032
Resolve Conflict:C:\drvspace.bin ConflictType: 240
drvspace.bin=31,,7915,20032
drvspace.sys=13,dblspace.sys,7915,20032
*
*
```

The bold lines in the example demonstrate the capability of the PnP system to resolve conflicts between programs and devices. In this case, a conflict exists between a driver named DBLSPACE and another named DRVSPACE.

DETCRASH.LOG

This *Detect Crash log* file is created when the system crashes during the hardware detection portion of the startup procedure. It contains information about the detection module that was running when the crash occurred. This file is a binary file and cannot be read directly. However, a text version of the file, named DETLOG.TXT, is available under the root directory of the drive.

DETLOG.TXT

The DETLOG.TXT file holds the text equivalent of the information in the DETCRASH.LOG file. This file can be read with a text editor to determine which of the system's hardware components have been detected and what their parameters are. This printout is really a detailed explanation of the hardware-detection phase of the system's PnP operation.

The following section of a sample DETLOG.TXT file demonstrates the type of information logged in this file:

```
[System Detection: 11/07/97 - 12:05:11]
Parameters "", InfParams "", Flags=01004233
SDMVer=0400.950, WinVer=0700030a, Build=00.00.0,
➥WinFlags=00000419
LogCrash: crash log not found or invalid
SetVar: CDROM_Any=
Checking for: Programmable Interrupt Controller
QueryIOMem: Caller=DETECTPIC, rcQuery=0
     IO=20-21,a0-a1
Detected: *PNP0000\0000 = [1] Programmable interrupt
➥controller
     IO=20-21,a0-a1
     IRQ=2
Checking for: Direct Memory Access Controller
QueryIOMem: Caller=DETECTDMA, rcQuery=0
     IO=0-f,81-83,87-87,89-8b,8f-8f,c0-df
Detected: *PNP0200\0000 = [2] Direct memory access
➥controller
     IO=0-f,81-83,87-87,89-8b,8f-8f,c0-df
     DMA=4
*
Checking for: Standard Floppy Controller
QueryIOMem: Caller=DETECTFLOPPY, rcQuery=0
     IO=3f2-3f5
QueryIOMem: Caller=DETECTFLOPPY, rcQuery=0
     IO=372-375
Detected: *PNP0700\0000 = [11] Standard Floppy Disk
➥Controller
     IO=3f2-3f5
     IRQ=6
     DMA=2
Checking for: Serial Communication Port
QueryIOMem: Caller=DETECTCOM, rcQuery=0
     IO=3f8-3ff
GetCOMIRQ: IIR=1
Detected: *PNP0500\0000 = [12] Communications Port
     IO=3f8-3ff
     IRQ=4
SetVar: COMIRQ3f8=4,0
SetVar: COMIRQ2f8=3,0
Checking for: Serial Mouse
QueryIOMem: Caller=DETECTSERIALMOUSE, rcQuery=2
```

```
      IO=3f8-3ff
Serial mouse ID: M (004d)
Detected: *PNP0F0C\0000 = [14] Standard Serial Mouse
SetVar: COMIRQ3f8=4,0
*
```

Referring to the information in the sample file, it should be easy to see the type of information that is logged about the system. The detection routine cycles through a three-part process; first, it identifies the activity it is about to perform (that is, `Checking for: Serial Mouse`), and then it queries the system at addresses normally allocated to that type of device (`IO=3f8-3ff`), and finally verifies that it was detected (or not). Some entries also include a listing of the IRQ and DMA resources allocated to the device. The sample list includes information about many of the system and I/O devices found in a typical PC system.

In each case, the PnP system inquires about particular system devices and logs the parameters of the device it detects. The sample also shows that, at least in this case, no crash log has been created. To use the file for crash-detection purposes, just check the last entry created in the log. To determine exactly where a problem has occurred, it may be necessary to compare this information to the listing in a file named DETLOG.OLD. This file is the old version of the DET-LOG file that was renamed before the latest detection phase began.

Using the Windows 9x Startup Disk

If the system will not make it to the Startup menu, you must boot the system with the Startup disk and begin checking the operating system on the boot drive. When the system is booted from a Windows 98 Startup disk, a menu such as the following displays:

Microsoft Windows 98 Startup menu:

1. Start the computer with CD-ROM support.

2. Start the computer without CD-ROM support.

3. View the Help file.

If the CD-ROM support option is selected, the system will execute the portion of the CONFIG.SYS file that loads the CD-ROM driver, and will set up a 2MB RAMDrive.

Use the Startup disk to boot the system and gain access to the operating system's files. After gaining access to the system, you can use the built-in troubleshooting aids on the Windows 9x and Windows 2000 startup disks to isolate the cause of the problem.

Using Windows 98 System Tools on Startup Problems

In addition to the clean-boot, safe mode, and log file functions previously described, Windows 98 contains a wealth of other troubleshooting tools that you can use to isolate and correct problems.

If a startup problem disappears when the system is started using any of the safe modes, use the *System Configuration* utility (MSCONFIG.EXE) to isolate the conflicting items. Of course, you may need to enter this command from the command line.

Select the Diagnostic Startup option to interactively load device drivers and software options from the General tab screen. When the Startup menu appears, select the Step-by-Step option. Begin by starting the system with only the CONFIG.SYS and AUTOEXEC.BAT files disabled. If the system starts, move into those tabs and step through those files, one line at a time, using the Selective Startup option. The step-by-step process is used to systematically enable/disable items, until all the problem items are identified. If an entry is marked with a Microsoft Windows logo, it is used when the Selective Startup option is disabled.

If the problem does not go away, you can use the Advanced button from the General tab to inspect lower-level configuration settings, such as real-mode disk accesses, and VGA standard video settings. You also can start the *Device Manager* from the MSCONFIG View option. This will allow the protected-mode device drivers to be inspected. The MSINFO-Problem Devices section also should be examined to check for possible problem-causing devices. Other items to check include missing or corrupted system files (using the System File Checker utility), corrupted Registry entries (using the Registry Checker), viruses (using a virus checker program), and hardware conflicts using the CMOS Configuration screens.

irrelevant

When a potential problem setting has been identified in the CON-FIG.SYS, AUTOEXEC.BAT, or Registry, use the Automatic Skip Driver utility to automatically isolate and disable the suspect line. Just select the ASD option from the System Information's Tools menu. Select the operation that has failed by marking it in the Hardware Troubleshooting Agent dialog box, and then select the Details option. This action should cause the Enumerating a Device dialog box to provide recommendations for correcting any problems. This normally involves replacing the driver disabled by the ASD utility. This series of automated tests basically replaces the manual isolation method performed with the Step-by-Step Startup option.

The system may contain up to five backup copies of the Registry structure. If the system fails to start up after installing some new software or hardware component, run the Registry Checker utility using the **/Restore** option (**ScanReg /Restore**) to return the Registry to its previous condition. Just type **ScanReg /Restore** at the MS-DOS prompt to view a list of available backup copies. Generally, the most recent version should be selected for use. These tools are discussed in greater detail later in this chapter.

WINDOWS 2000 STARTUP PROBLEMS

For Windows 2000, you can build on the operating system troubleshooting methodology previously discussed. If Windows 2000 fails to boot, the first troubleshooting step is to determine whether the computer is failing before or after the operating system takes control.

If the startup process makes it to the beep that indicates the end of the POST, but you do not see the operating system *Boot Selection menu*, the problem is probably due to one of the following:

◆ System partition problems

◆ Master Boot Record problems

◆ Partition boot sector problems

These types of problems are usually the result of hard disk media failure, or a virus, and must be repaired before the operating system can function. Typical symptoms associated with these failures include the following:

◆ Blue Screen or Stop message appears.

◆ Boot up stops after the POST.

◆ The Boot Selection menu is never reached.

◆ An error message is produced.

Windows 2000 displays a number of error messages related to these problems, including the following:

◆ Missing Operating System

◆ Disk Read Error

◆ Invalid Partition Table

◆ Hard Disk Error (or Absent/Failed)

◆ Insert System Disk

◆ Error Loading Operating System

The BOOT.INI file allows Windows 2000 to boot to separate operating systems. If this file is missing or corrupt, you will not be able to boot to the previous version of Windows; the computer will just boot to Windows 2000. To correct this, copy the BOOT.INI file from a backup or from another machine running the same setup with the same installation directories.

The NTDETECT.COM or NTLDR files also might be missing or might have become corrupted. If you receive the message `NTLDR is missing` or `NTDETECT failed`, the partition boot sector is okay, but the NTLDR or NTDETECT.COM file is missing or corrupt. You need to reinstall Windows 2000 or boot to the Recovery Console and copy the missing or corrupt file from a backup.

The `Missing Operating System` and `Invalid Partition Table` error messages indicate a problem with the Master Boot Record. Use the FIXMBR command in the Recovery Console to replace the Master Boot Record. Although this works well on a standalone drive, it does not work with disks that contain partitions or logical drives that are part of striped or volume sets.

You also should not perform this procedure on drives that use third-party translation, partitioning, or dual-boot programs.

If the startup problem occurs at some point after the screen clears and the operating system selection menu appears, or after selecting Windows 2000 from the boot menu, the issue is probably with the operating system. Most likely, necessary files are missing or corrupt.

Windows 2000 provides a wealth of tools for recovering from a startup problem, including the following:

◆ Windows 2000 safe-mode options

◆ Windows 2000 Recovery Console

◆ Windows 2000 Emergency Repair Disk

The following sections describe these tools and their use in detail.

Windows 2000 Startup Modes

The Windows 2000 operating system incorporates a number of Windows 9x-like startup options that can be engaged to get the system up and running in a given state to provide a starting point for troubleshooting operations.

The Advanced Options menu, depicted in Figure 9.4, contains several options that can be of assistance when troubleshooting startup failures. To display this menu, press F8 at the beginning of the Windows 2000 startup process.

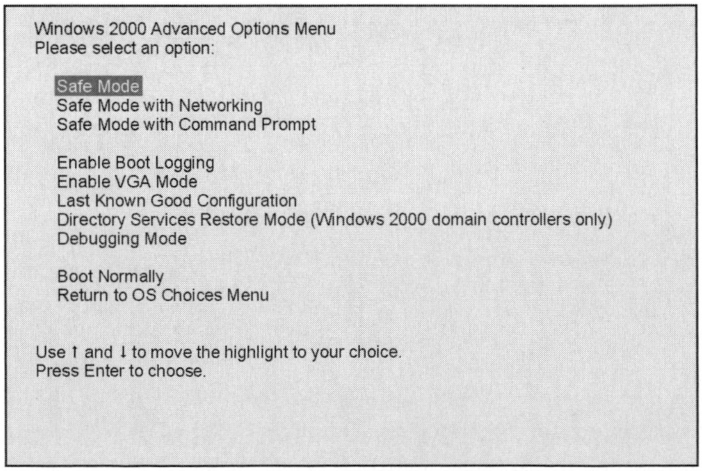

```
Windows 2000 Advanced Options Menu
Please select an option:

   Safe Mode
   Safe Mode with Networking
   Safe Mode with Command Prompt

   Enable Boot Logging
   Enable VGA Mode
   Last Known Good Configuration
   Directory Services Restore Mode (Windows 2000 domain controllers only)
   Debugging Mode

   Boot Normally
   Return to OS Choices Menu


Use ↑ and ↓ to move the highlight to your choice.
Press Enter to choose.
```

FIGURE 9.4
The Advanced Options menu.

The following startup options are available on the Windows 2000 Advanced Options Menu. As you can see, they include typical Windows 9x safe-mode and command-prompt options as well as several Windows 2000-specific modes.

- ◆ **Safe Mode.** Launches Windows 2000 with only the basic devices and drivers (such as the mouse, keyboard, video, hard disks) and basic system services. A log file is created, as described in the Enable Boot Logging menu option. Display settings are dropped to standard VGA with 640 × 480 resolution. Safe mode is very useful in the event that you have a faulty device driver, or have loaded a system service or automatically loading application that is causing the operating system to fail. Safe mode permits you to disable, remove, or reconfigure drivers, services, and applications.

- ◆ **Safe Mode with Networking.** The same as safe mode, but with the addition of networking services. This is useful if you need to connect to another computer across the network to reinstall an application, driver, or service. There is the potential that one of the network services is causing the system to fail, in which case this option will not be effective.

- ◆ **Safe Mode with Command Prompt**. The same as Safe Mode, but the GUI is not started and the user is left at a command prompt. This option is generally used when the GUI will not load in safe mode, and you want access to command-line utilities or just want to explore the hard disks in search of the problem. The option executes the CMD.EXE file and brings the user to the command prompt.

- ◆ **Enable Boot Logging.** Creates a log file called NTBTLOG. TXT in the system_root folder. This log file contains a listing of all the drivers and services that the system attempts to load during startup, and can prove useful when trying to determine what service or driver is causing the system to fail.

- ◆ **Enable VGA Mode.** When selected, this option boots the system normally, but only loads the basic VGA driver. If you have configured the display incorrectly and are unable to see the desktop, booting into VGA mode will enable you to reconfigure those settings. All forms of safe mode include VGA mode.

◆ **Last Known Good Configuration.** Will start Windows 2000 with the settings that were in existence the last time the system booted successfully. (Remember that a successful boot occurs only after a user has logged on.) All system setting changes that have occurred since the last successful startup will be lost. This proves very useful if you have added or reconfigured a device driver that has caused the system to fail. This option may permit you to work around the failure so that you can try again with a different configuration or driver. However, it will be of no use in the event that drivers or files are missing or corrupted.

◆ **Directory Service Restore Mode.** Enables restores of Active Directory on a domain controller. It will not be present on computers that are running Windows 2000 Professional or on member servers.

◆ **Debugging Mode.** Starts Windows 2000 in kernel debug mode. This is a very advanced function that enables a debugger to access the kernel for troubleshooting and analysis.

◆ **Boot Normally.** Starts the system normally, loading all startup files and Registry values.

NOTE

Safe-Mode Caveat The Safe Mode and Safe Mode with Command Prompt options will not function properly on domain controllers. If the network services are not started on a domain controller, you will be unable to log on.

Windows 2000 Recovery Console

The *Recovery Console* is a command-line interface that provides you with access to the hard disks and many command-line utilities when the operating system will not boot. The Recovery Console can access all volumes on the drive, regardless of the file system type. If you have not added the Recovery Console option prior to a failure, however, you will not be able to employ it and will need to use the Windows 2000 Setup disks instead. You can use the Recovery Console to perform tasks such as the following:

◆ Copy files from a floppy disk, CD, or another hard disk to the hard disk used for boot up, enabling you to replace or remove files that may be affecting the boot process. Because of the security features in Windows 2000, you are granted only limited access to certain files on the hard drive. You cannot copy files from the hard drive to a floppy or other storage device under these conditions.

◆ Control the startup state of services, enabling you to disable a service that could potentially be causing the operating system to crash.

◆ Add, remove, and format volumes on the hard disk.

◆ Repair the MBR or boot sector of a hard disk or volume.

◆ Restore the Registry.

The Recovery Console can be permanently installed on a system and be made accessible from the Advanced Options menu. It also can be started at any time by booting from the Windows 2000 Setup disks or CD, choosing to repair an installation, and selecting Recovery Console from the repair options.

To install the Recovery Console onto a computer, follow these steps:

1. Put the Windows 2000 CD in the drive, or connect to an installation share on the network.

2. Run **Winnt32 /cmdcons**. Windows 2000 Setup will launch, as illustrated in Figure 9.5, and install the Recovery Console.

3. The Recovery Console will be added to the Advanced Options menu automatically.

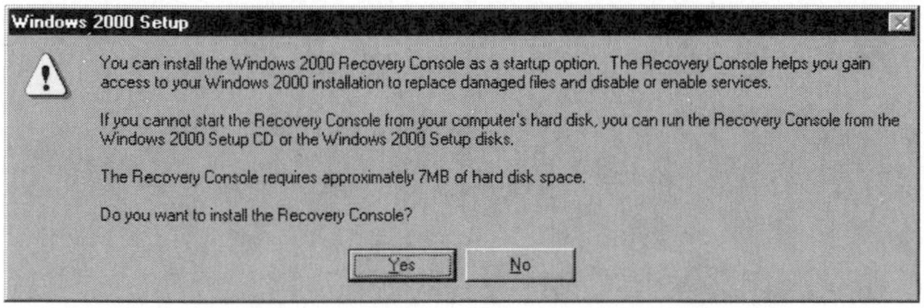

Windows 2000 Setup

⚠ You can install the Windows 2000 Recovery Console as a startup option. The Recovery Console helps you gain access to your Windows 2000 installation to replace damaged files and disable or enable services.

If you cannot start the Recovery Console from your computer's hard disk, you can run the Recovery Console from the Windows 2000 Setup CD or the Windows 2000 Setup disks.

The Recovery Console requires approximately 7MB of hard disk space.

Do you want to install the Recovery Console?

[Yes] [No]

FIGURE 9.5
Installing the Recovery Console using **Winnt32 /cmdcons**.

You can use the Recovery Console to restore the Registry. Every time you back up the system state data with Windows 2000 backup, a copy of the Registry is placed in the Repair\RegBack folder. If you copy the entire contents of this folder or only particular files to \System32\Config (which is the folder where the working copy of the Registry is stored), you can restore the Registry to the same condition as last time you performed a system state data backup. It is recommended that you create a copy of the files in System32\Config prior to restoring the other files from backup so that you can restore the Registry to the original condition if necessary.

> **NOTE**
>
> **Calling for Help** When you start the Recovery Console, you are prompted to choose the folder that contains the Windows 2000 installation that you are trying to repair, and then to log on as Administrator. When logged on, type **HELP** to get a list of available commands.

Troubleshooting Stop Errors

Stop errors occur most frequently when new hardware or device drivers have been installed, or when the system is running low on disk space. Also, Stop errors can occur on a system that has been running without a problem for months, but for whatever reason experiences a hardware error of some sort that causes the system to crash. You need to be aware that they can happen for a variety of other reasons and can be very difficult to troubleshoot.

There is no set procedure for resolving Stop errors, but you can do many things to potentially eliminate the error, or to gain additional information about what caused the error.

Use the following steps to troubleshoot Stop errors:

◆ Restart the computer to see whether the error repeats. In many cases, an odd series of circumstances within the system can cause the error, and just restarting will correct the condition and the system will function normally. If the Stop error appears again, however, you need to take further action.

◆ If you have recently installed new hardware in the system, verify that it has been installed correctly and that you are using the most current version of the device drivers.

◆ Check the HCL to verify that any newly installed hardware and device drivers are compatible with Windows 2000.

◆ Remove any newly installed hardware to see whether that relieves the Stop error and Windows 2000 starts. If Windows 2000 does start, immediately use Event Viewer to view any additional error messages that were generated before the Stop error occurred to get further information as to why the hardware caused the system to crash.

◆ Try to start Windows 2000 in safe mode. If you can start the system in safe mode, you can remove any newly installed software that could be causing the Stop error, and remove or update device drivers that could be causing the Stop error.

◆ Attempt to start the system using the Last Known Good configuration. This resets the system configuration to whatever the hardware configuration was the last time you were able to successfully boot the system, and gives you the opportunity to try to install or configure a new hardware device again.

◆ Verify that the system has the latest Windows 2000 service pack installed.

◆ Use TechNet or visit the Microsoft Support Center Web site and search on the particular Stop error number to see whether you can get any further information. The Stop error number is noted in the upper-left corner of the Stop screen. In Figure 9.1 the Stop error number is 0x0000001A.

◆ Disable caching or shadowing memory options in the system BIOS.

◆ Run diagnostic software on the system to check for memory errors.

◆ Use a virus-checker utility to check for viruses using the procedures outlined by its Users Guide, and eliminate any viruses if found.

◆ Verify that the system BIOS is the latest revision. If not, contact the manufacturer of your system to determine how to update the BIOS.

latest version of system BIOS

One of these steps should enable you to resolve the error, or pinpoint it to a particular component that you can eliminate from the system to clear up the symptom.

Performing an Emergency Repair

The Emergency Repair Disk provides another option if safe mode and the Recovery Console do not enable you to repair the system. If you have already created an ERD, you can start the system with the Windows 2000 Setup CD or the Setup floppy disks, and then use the ERD to restore core system files.

The emergency repair process enables you to do the following:

◆ Repair the boot sector

◆ Repair the startup files

◆ Replace the system files

> **NOTE**
> **Limited to OS Repair** The emergency repair process is designed to repair the operating system only, and cannot be of assistance in repairing application or data problems.

To perform an emergency repair, follow these steps:

1. Boot the system from the Window 2000 CD. If the system will not boot from CD, you must boot with the Setup Boot Disk, which is the first of four Setup floppy disks that are required. You create the Setup floppy disks with MAKE-BOOT.EXE, which is in the BOOTDISK folder in the Windows 2000 CD root directory.

2. When the text-mode portion of setup begins, follow the initial prompts. When you reach the Welcome to Setup screen, as shown in Figure 9.6, follow the onscreen instructions.

FIGURE 9.6

Repairing a Windows 2000 installation.

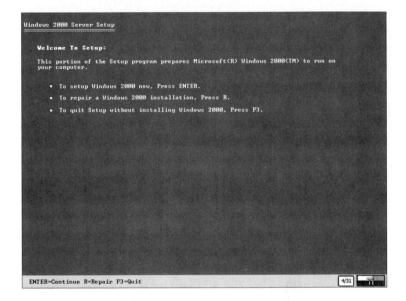

3. When prompted, choose the emergency repair process by pressing R.

4. When prompted, press F for fast repair.

5. Follow the instructions, and insert the Emergency Repair Disk into the floppy disk drive when prompted.

Logon Problems

One last problem that can occur during startup (even though it is not actually a startup problem) is a logon problem. Basically, users cannot log on to systems when they have the proper authorization to do so. These problems tend to be very common in secure environments such as those that use Windows 2000.

The most common logon problem is the forgotten or invalid username and password. Invalid usernames and passwords typically result from poor typing, or from having the Caps Lock function turned on.

Users also can be prevented from logging on due to station or time restrictions imposed. Check with the network administrator to see whether the user's rights to the system have been restricted.

COMMON OPERATING SYSTEM OPERATIONAL PROBLEMS

▶ 3.2 Recognize common problems and determine how to resolve them.

A portion of the A+ Operating System Technologies objective 3.2 states that the test taker should be able to "recognize common problems and determine how to resolve them."

After the operating system has been started up and is functional, particular types of problems come into play. Many of these problems are documented in this A+ objective. It indicates that the technician must be able to identify and correct operational problems associated with the operating system. To this end, the following sections deal specifically with OS operational symptoms and problems, including the following:

◆ Memory usage

◆ Application

◆ Printing

◆ Networking

Memory Usage Problems

Memory usage problems occur when the operating system, or one of its applications, attempts to access an unallocated memory location. When these memory conflicts occur, the data in the violated memory locations is corrupted and may crash the system. In Windows 3.x, these types of problems were labeled general protection faults (GPF) and were generally the product of data protection errors induced by poorly written programs. These programs typically use stray pointers or illegal instructions that access areas of memory that have been protected.

Although the Windows 9x structure provides a much better multitasking environment than its predecessor did, applications can still attempt to access unallocated memory locations, or attempt to use another application's space. When these memory conflicts occur, the system can either return an error message or just stop processing. Due to the severity of the GPF problems in Windows 3.x, Microsoft chose to provide memory usage error messages in Windows 9x that say This Operation Has Performed an Illegal Operation and Is About to Be Shut Down.

Some memory usage errors are nonfatal and provide an option to ignore the fault and continue working, or to just close the application. These errors are generally caused by Windows applications and can sometimes be tracked to *dynamic link library* (DLL) files associated with a particular application. Although the application may continue to operate, it is generally not stable enough to continue working on an extended basis. It is recommended that the application be used only long enough to save any existing work.

On the other hand, some memory usage errors affect the Windows Core files (KRNL*XXX*.EXE, GDI.EXE, or USER.EXE). If a kernel file is damaged, you need to restart the Windows program. Any work that was not saved prior to the error will be lost. If the error is in the GDI or User files, it may be linked to a display driver, or to an I/O device driver.

Windows NT and Windows 2000 employ a flat memory management scheme that does not use the segmented memory mapping features associated with the Intel microprocessors. Therefore, these operating systems have very few memory usage problems.

General Protection Faults

A general protection fault occurs when Windows 3.x, or one of its applications, attempts to access an unallocated memory location. When these memory conflicts occur, the data in the violated memory locations is corrupted and may crash the system. GPFs are generally the product of data protection errors induced by poorly written programs that use stray pointers or illegal instructions that access areas of memory that have been protected.

In Windows 3.0, a GPF usually required that Windows be exited and the system be rebooted. Version 3.1 provided improved control of GPFs. In this version, the error notice, depicted in Figure 9.7, includes information about where the error occurred and which application caused the error. In addition, Windows 3.1 remains stable enough after a GPF to allow the work in progress to be saved before exiting the program.

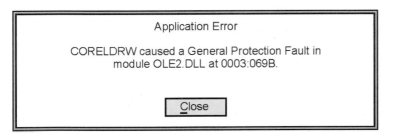

FIGURE 9.7
A typical GPF message.

Typical causes of GPFs include the following:

◆ Running applications written specifically for a different Windows version.

◆ Selecting an incorrect machine or network during the installation process.

◆ The CONFIG.SYS or AUTOEXEC.BAT files contain incompatible or unsupported TSR programs or network drivers.

◆ An incorrect version of DOS is being used in the system.

NOTE

Windows 9X and GPFs   The Windows 9x structure provides a much improved multitasking environment over its predecessor (Windows 3.x). Applications can still attempt to access unallocated memory locations, however, or attempt to use another application's space. When these memory conflicts occur, the system can either return an error message or just stop processing.

If the GPF error occurs in random locations, follow these steps:

1. Check the DOS version to see that it is correct for the system.

2. Check the HIMEM.SYS version to see that it is 3.01 or higher.

3. Check the device drivers in the CONFIG.SYS file.

4. Perform a **CHKDSK /F** operation from the DOS prompt to check for cross-linked files.

5. Start Windows using the **WIN /D:XSV** switch.

   If the GPF continues, you must reinstall the operating system.

   If the GPF disappears, reduce the switch to **WIN /D:XS**.

   If the GP fault does not return, reduce the switch to **WIN /D:X.**

General Windows 9x Operating Problems

Aside from the application, printing and networking problem categories listed earlier, if the Windows 9x operating system starts up properly, only a limited number of things can go wrong afterward. The disk drive can run out of space, files can become corrupt, or the system can lock up due to software exception errors. When these problems occur, the system can either return an error message or just stop processing.

The *System Information* utility in the Programs\Accessories\System_Tools path can be used to view the disk drive's space parameters. You also can check the drive's used/available space information by performing a *Check Disk* operation on it.

If the system produces an Out of Memory error in Windows 9x, it is very unlikely that the system is running out of RAM, unless you are running DOS-based applications. In Windows 9x, this error indicates that the system is running out of memory space altogether (RAM and virtual).

Run the Windows System Monitor utility described later in this chapter to observe system memory usage and determine the nature of the error. If you are running DOS-based applications, you can optimize the system's use of conventional memory by running the old DOS MEMMAKER utility from the Tools\Oldmsdos directory on the Windows distribution CD. You can view the drive's swap file settings through the Control Panel's System/Performance/Virtual Memory option or through the System Tool's System Information utility. As always, any lost clusters taking up space on the drive can be identified and eliminated using the ScanDisk utility. A heavily used, heavily fragmented hard drive can affect the system's virtual memory and produce memory shortages as well. Run the Defrag utility to optimize the storage patterns on the drive.

If the system is running a FAT16 drive, you can free up additional space by converting it to a FAT32 drive. The DOS utility for this is CVT1.EXE. The smaller sector clustering available through FAT32 frees up wasted space on the drive. The drawbacks of performing this upgrade are that you run some risk of losing data if a failure occurs in the conversion process, and that larger files will have slightly slower read/write times than they did under FAT16.

If these corrective actions do not clear the memory error, you need to remove unnecessary files from the drive or install a larger drive.

If the system begins to run out of hard disk space, remember that there may be up to five backup copies of the Registry on the drive. This is a function of using the SCANREGW utility to check out the Registry structure for corruption. Each backup can be up to 2MB in size and can be removed to free up additional disk drive space.

The Windows 9x structure provides a much better multitasking environment than its predecessors. However, applications can still attempt to access unallocated memory areas, or attempt to access another application's designated memory areas. These actions create a software exception error in the system. Windows 9x typically responds to these errors by placing a This Program Has Committed an Illegal Operation and Is About To Be Shut Down message onscreen. When this happens, Windows may take care of the error and allow you to continue operating by just pressing a specific key.

TEST TIP

Be aware of the part that the disk drive plays in Windows 9x memory management and how to optimize its use.

If the system locks up, or an application stalls, it is often possible to regain access to the Close Program Dialog box by pressing the Ctrl+Alt+Del key combination. Once the Close Program dialog box is onscreen, you can close the offending application and continue operating the system without rebooting.

As an example, in Windows 9x the Windows Explorer shell (EXPLORER.EXE) may crash and leave the system without a Start button or taskbar. To recover from this condition, use the Ctrl+Alt+Del combination to access the Close Programs dialog box and shut down the system in a proper manner. The Alt+F4 key combination also can be used to close active windows. Pressing this key combination in an application stops the application and moves to the next active application in the task list. If the Alt+F4 combination is pressed when no applications are active, the Windows Shut Down menu appears on the display. This enables you to conduct an orderly shutdown or restart of the system.

If the application repeatedly locks up the system, you must reinstall the application and check its configuration settings. The Dr. Watson utility also proves very useful in detecting application faults. When activated, Dr. Watson intercepts the software actions, detects the failure, identifies the application, and provides a detailed description of the failure. The information is automatically transferred to the disk drive and stored in the Windows\Drwatson*.WLG file. You can view and print the information stored in the file from a word processor.

If a DOS-based program is running and the system locks up, you must restore Windows 9x. To accomplish this, attempt to restart the system from a cold boot. If the system starts in Windows 9x, check the *properties* of the DOS application. This information can be obtained by locating the program through My Computer or through the Windows Explorer interfaces, right-clicking its filename, and selecting the Properties option from the pop-up menu. From the Properties window, select the Programs tab and then click the Advanced button to view the file's settings, as depicted in Figure 9.8. If the application is not already set for MS-DOS-mode operation, click the box to select it. Also select the Prevent MS-DOS-based programs from detecting Windows option. Return to the failing application to see whether it will run correctly in this environment.

Windows 98 occasionally produces an error message that says you are *running out of resources.* This message indicates that the operating system believes that it has exhausted all the system's real and virtual memory. Although the message tells you to correct the problem by shutting down applications, and it provides an endless series of application shutdown dialog windows, this process almost never works. Even shutting the applications down through the Close Program dialog box will not restore the system. Therefore, you should shut down the system and restart it. This action normally clears the problem.

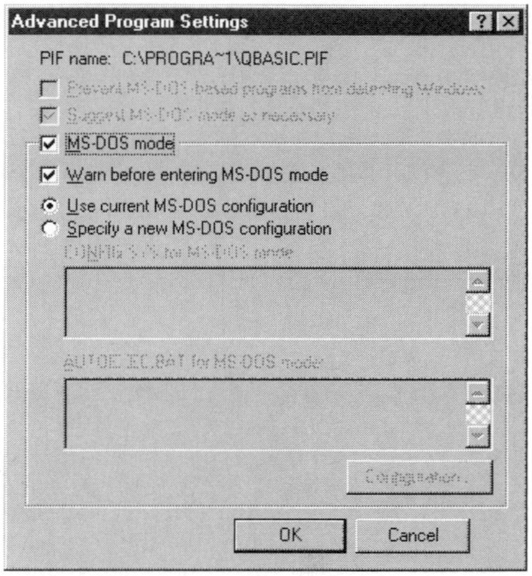

Windows 2000 Operating Problems

Be aware of some typical symptoms that can pop up during the normal operation of the Windows 2000 operating system, including the following:

◆ User cannot log on.

◆ You cannot recover an item that was deleted by another user.

◆ You cannot recover any items deleted.

◆ The video adapter supports higher resolution than the monitor does.

◆ Personalized menus are not working.

The first time you log on to the Windows 2000 system, the only usable account is the *Administrator* account; the Guest account is disabled. If a user cannot log on, check the user's password. The password is case sensitive, so verify that the Caps Lock key is not an issue. If you have forgotten the Administrator password and you have not created any other accounts with Administrator privileges, you must reinstall Windows 2000. Some third-party utilities may be able to help you recover the Administrator password, but you will usually find it easier to just reinstall the operating system at this point.

You cannot recover an item that was deleted by another user because the Recycle Bin is maintained on a user-by-user basis. If one user deletes something, only that user can recover it. You must log on as the user who deleted the items.

FIGURE 9.8
DOS Program Properties.

Files and folders deleted from a floppy disk or network drive are permanently deleted and cannot be recovered. Once the Recycle Bin fills to capacity, any newly deleted file or folder added causes older deleted items to be automatically deleted from the Recycle Bin.

Many video cards can display very high resolution at high refresh rates. However, some monitors do not have the same capabilities. When you configure the video card with settings that the monitor cannot display, symptoms may range from a simple blank screen, to several ghost images being displayed onscreen. To correct this problem, start Windows 2000 in safe mode. This action causes Windows 2000 to load a basic VGA video driver, enabling you to then change the display properties of the video card.

If the personalized menus are not working, the Personalized Menu feature may be turned off. To turn this feature on, click Start, point to Settings, click Taskbar & Start Menu, and then select Use Personalized Menus on the General tab.

By default, Windows 2000 hides known filename extensions. If you cannot see filename extensions, open the Windows Explorer, click Tools, click Folder Options, click the View tab, and locate and deselect the Hide File Extensions for Known Files option.

Likewise, Windows 2000 by default does not display hidden or system files in Explorer. To see hidden or system files, open the Windows Explorer, click Tools, click Folder Options, click the View tab, and locate and select the Show Hidden Files and Folders option.

Troubleshooting Application Problems

One of the other major operational problems that affect operating systems involves the application programs running in the system. In the Microsoft world, if the application is a BAT, EXE, or COM file, it should start when its name is properly entered on the command line. If such an application will not start in a command-line environment, you have a few basic possibilities to consider: It has been improperly identified; it is not located where it is supposed to be; or the application program is corrupted.

Check the spelling of the filename and reenter it at the command prompt. Also, verify that the path to the program has been presented correctly and thoroughly. If the path and filename are correct, the application may be corrupted. Reinstall it and try to start it again.

Other possible reasons for application programs not starting in a command-line environment include low conventional memory or disk space, and file attributes that will not let the program start. In client/server networks, permission settings may not permit a user to access a particular file or folder.

Windows 9x Application Problems

If an application will not start in Windows 9x, you have four basic possibilities to consider: The application is missing; part or all of the application is corrupted; the application's executable file is incorrectly identified; or its attributes are locked.

As with other GUI-based environments, Windows 9x applications hide behind icons. The properties of each icon must correctly identify the filename and path of the application's executable file; otherwise, Windows will not be able to start it. Likewise, when a folder, or file, accessed by the icon, or by the shortcut from the Windows 9x Start menu, is moved, renamed, or removed, Windows will again not be able to find it when asked to start the application. Check the application's properties to verify that the filename, path, and syntax are correct.

Some applications require Registry entries to run. If these entries are missing or corrupt, the application will not start. In addition, Windows 9x retains the DLL structure of its Windows 3.x predecessor under the Windows\System directory. Corrupted or *conflicting DLL files* prevent applications from starting. To recover from these types of errors, you must reinstall the application.

Windows 2000 Application Problems

Windows 2000 may suffer the same types of application problems described for the Windows 9x versions.

◆ Incorrect application properties (filename, path, and syntax)

◆ Missing or corrupt Registry entries

◆ Conflicting DLL files

Because Windows NT and Windows 2000 are typically used in client/server networks, however, some typical administrative problems associated with files, folders, and printers can pop up during their normal operations. These problems include such things as the following:

◆ Users cannot gain access to folders.

◆ Users send a print job to the printer but cannot locate the documents.

◆ Users have Read permissions to a folder, but they can still make changes to files inside the folder.

◆ Users complain that they can see files in a folder but cannot access any of the files.

◆ Users complain that they cannot set any NTFS permissions.

The following paragraphs identify ways that you can correct these particular administrative problems.

A user's inability to gain access to folders can come from many places. Check the effective permissions; remember that permissions combine, giving the user the highest level permission, except when the Deny permission is set. Also remember that lesser and included permissions will be denied.

If the print job is not still in the local spooler or the print server, but print pooling is enabled, check all the printers in the pool. You cannot dictate which printer receives the print job. If the print job is visible in the spooler but does not print, this can be caused by the printer availability hours being set for times other than when you submitted the print job.

For users who have Read permission for a folder, but can still make changes to files inside the folder, their file permissions must be set to Full Control, Write, or Modify. These permissions are set directly to the file and override the folder permissions of Read. You can correct this by changing the permissions on the individual files or at the folder level and allow the permissions to propagate to files within the folder.

When users complain that they can see files in a folder but cannot access any of the files, they have most likely been assigned the List permission at the folder level. The List permission allows users to view the contents of the folder only, denying them all other permissions, including Read and Execute.

With users who complain that they cannot set any NTFS permissions, the first item to check is that the file or folder is on an NTFS partition. FAT16 and FAT32 have no security options that can be assigned. If the partition is NTFS, the user must have Full Control permission to set any security permissions to a file or folder.

Windows 2000 Task Manager

In Windows NT and Windows 2000, the Close Program dialog window is referred to as the Task Manager. This utility can be used to determine which applications in the system are running or stopped, as well as which resources are being used. You also can determine what the general microprocessor and memory usage levels are.

When an application hangs up in these operating systems, you can access the Task Manager window depicted in Figure 9.9 and remove it from the list of tasks. The Task Manager can be accessed by pressing Ctrl+Alt+Del or Ctrl+Shift+Esc.

To use the Task Manager, select the application from the Applications tab and press the End Task button. If prompted, press the End Task button again to confirm the selection. The Performance tab provides a graphical summary of the system's CPU and memory usage. The Process tab provides information that can be helpful in tracking problems associated with slow system operation.

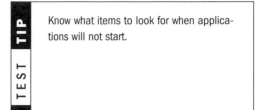

TEST TIP

Know what items to look for when applications will not start.

able to determin which APP is running or stoped and which recources is used

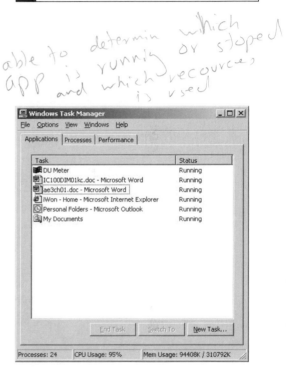

FIGURE 9.9
Task Manager.

WINDOWS-RELATED PRINTING PROBLEMS

▶ 3.2 Recognize Windows-specific printing problems and identify the procedures for correcting them.

A portion of the A+ Operating System Technologies objective 3.2 states that the test taker should be able to "recognize Windows-specific printing problems and identify the procedures for correcting them."

Troubleshooting Printing Problems

In operating systems, there are two lines of thought when it comes to applications printing information to a printer: Let the application control the printer; or have the application communicate with the operating system's printer mechanisms. Older operating systems tended to turn over control of printing operations to the application. However, most newer operating systems reserve the right to control printing operations themselves.

In a Windows-based system, the Windows environment controls the printing function through its drivers. When an application presents a particular font type for printing, Windows must locate or create the font codes. If the code is a TrueType code, it just creates the bitmaps required and sends them to the printer. If the printer code is some other font style, however, Windows must attempt to locate that font in the system.

If the requested font is not available or is not supported by the selected printer, Windows must substitute a font for it. In these cases, the Windows Font Map is used to decide the most appropriate font to use. Windows bases this choice on several factors including the character set, family, typeface, height, and width of the possible substitute font.

When Windows is forced to substitute fonts other than the one called for by the application, printing problems can occur. The printer can lock up or just produce print that is not correct or that is out of place. (That is, the substituted font may be the wrong size or may have undesired attributes that shove the text onto a following page or wrap it around a frame within the page.)

If font-related printing problems are suspected, check to see that TrueType fonts are selected. Some font converters do not work properly with Windows. Therefore, their output is corrupted and will not drive the printer correctly. This should produce a GPF message.

Other factors that can cause font problems include low system RAM and third-party video or printer drivers. Check the video driver setting in the Windows Setup window to determine which video driver is being used. Substitute the standard VGA driver and try to print a document. Check the printer driver using the Control Panel's Print icon to make certain that the correct driver is installed.

Some types of drivers are known to conflict with the Windows
TrueType fonts. These include the Adobe Type Manager, Bitstream
FaceLift, and Hewlett Packard's Intellifont. If any of these font managers are present, they should be disabled and/or removed from the
system for troubleshooting purposes.

If printer problems continue, try printing a sample file from a non-
Windows environment. The easiest check of this type involves trying
to use the Print Screen key on the keyboard to print from a DOS
environment. Another good example of this type of test is to copy
the AUTOEXEC.BAT or CONFIG.SYS files to the LPT1 port. If
this does not work from the DOS level, a hardware or configuration
problem is indicated.

Is there a printer switch box between the computer and the printer?
If so, remove the print sharing equipment, connect the computer
directly to the printer, and try to print from the DOS level as previously described.

Determine whether the Print option from the application's File menu
is unavailable (gray). If so, check the Windows Control Panel/
Printers window for correct parallel port settings. Make certain that
the correct printer driver is selected for the printer being used.

If no printer type, or the wrong printer type is selected, just set the
desired printer as the default printer.

Windows Printing Problems

If a printer is not producing anything in a Windows 9x/NT/2000
environment, even though print jobs have been sent to it, check
the Print Spooler to see whether any particular type of error has
occurred. To view documents waiting to be printed, double-click the
desired printer's icon. Return to the Printer folder, right-click the
printer's icon, click Properties, and then select Details. From this
point, select *Spool Settings* and select the Print Directly to the Printer
option. If the print job goes through, there is a spooler problem. If
not, the hardware and printer driver are suspect.

To check spooler problems, examine the system for adequate hard
disk space and memory. If the *Enhanced Metafile* (EMF) Spooling
option is selected, disable it, clear the spooler, and try to print.
To check the printer driver, right-click the printer's icon, select
Properties, and click the Details option. Reload or upgrade the
driver if necessary.

If a Windows printer operation stalls, or crashes, during the printing process, some critical condition must have been reached to stop the printing process. The system was running but stopped. Restart the system in safe mode and try to print again. If the system still will not print, check the print driver, the video driver, and the amount of space on the hard disk drive. Delete backed up spool files (SPL and TMP) in the System/Spool/Printers directory.

DOS-based applications should have no trouble printing in the different Windows environments. Windows has enhanced DOS printing capabilities that can take part in the new spooling function and usually result in quicker printing of DOS documents. If a particular DOS application has trouble printing, check other DOS applications to see whether they share the problem. If so, use the normal Windows 9x troubleshooting steps previously outlined to locate and correct the problem. If the second DOS application prints correctly, check the print settings of the original malfunctioning application.

Troubleshooting Network Printing Problems

The complexity of conducting printer operations over a network is much greater, because of the addition of the network drivers and protocols. Many of the problems encountered when printing over the network involve components of the operating system. Therefore, its networking and printing functions must both be checked.

When printing cannot be carried out across the network, verify that the local computer and the network printer are set up for remote printing. In the Windows operating systems, this involves sharing the printer with the network users. The local computer that the printer is connected to, referred to as the print server, should appear in the Windows 9x Network Neighborhood window of the remote computer. If the local computer cannot see files and printers at the print server station, file and print sharing may not be enabled there.

In Windows 9x, file and printer sharing can be accomplished at the print server in a number of ways. First, double-click the printer's icon in the My Computer window, or the Windows Explorer screen. Select the Printer/Properties/Sharing option and then choose the desired configuration. The second method uses a right-click on the printer's icon, followed by selecting Share in the Context menu, and choosing the desired configuration. The final method is similar except that you right-click the printer's icon and click Properties, Sharing, and then choose the configuration.

Run a printer's self-test to verify that its hardware is working correctly. If it will not print a test page, there is obviously a problem with the printer hardware. Next, troubleshoot the printer hardware. When the operation of the hardware is working, attempt to print across the network again.

Next, determine whether the print server can print directly to the printer. Open a document on the print server and attempt to print it. If the local printing operation is unsuccessful, move to the MS-DOS prompt, create a small batch file, and copy it to the local LPT port. If the file prints, there is a possibility that a problem exists with the printer's configuration at the print server. Check the print server's printer drivers.

The print server may not have enough memory or hard drive space available. In Windows 9x, check the spool settings, shown in Figure 9.10, under the Details entry of the Control Panel/Printers/Properties path. If the spooler is set to EMF, set it to RAW spooling. If the print spool is set to RAW, turn the spool off and click the 2 button. If the unit prints the test page, use the ScanDisk utility to check the disk space. Clear the contents of the \Temp directory.

If the file will not print directly to the local printer, there is a problem in the local hardware. Troubleshoot the problem as a local, standalone printing problem.

Next, verify the operation of the network by attempting to perform other network functions, such as transferring a file from the remote unit to the print server. If other network functions work, examine the printer driver configuration of the remote computer. In Windows 9x, open the Control Panel's Printer folder and select the Properties entry in the drop-down File menu. Check the information under the Details and Sharing tabs.

If the print drivers appear to be correct, install a generic or text-only printer driver and try to print to the print server. Next, move to the command prompt in the remote computer and create a batch text file. Attempt to copy this file to the network printer. If the generic driver or the DOS file works, reinstall the printer driver or install new drivers for the designated printer.

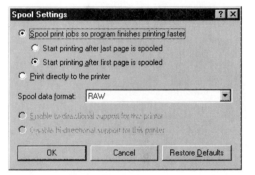

FIGURE 9.10
Windows 9x Spool Settings.

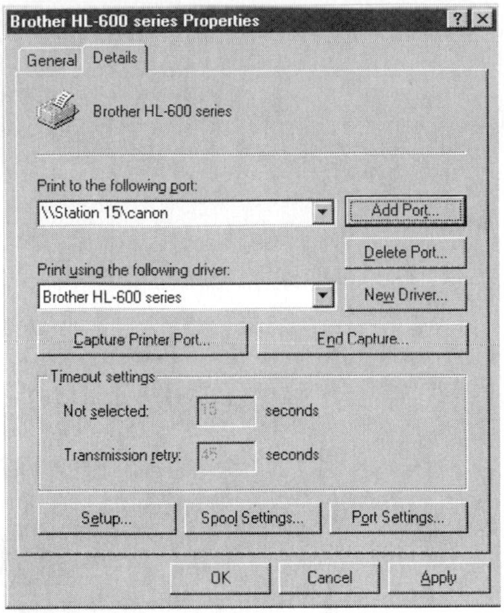

Brother HL-600 series Properties

General | Details

Brother HL-600 series

Print to the following port:
\\Station 15\canon

Add Port...

Delete Port...

Print using the following driver:
Brother HL-600 series

New Driver...

Capture Printer Port... End Capture...

Timeout settings

Not selected: 15 seconds

Transmission retry: 45 seconds

Setup... Spool Settings... Port Settings...

OK Cancel Apply

FIGURE 9.11
Checking the printer path.

> **TEST TIP**
>
> Know how to create a UNC path from a local computer to a remote printer, or a directory located on a remote computer.

In the event that other network functions are operational, verify the printer operation of the local computer. If possible, connect a printer directly to the local unit and set its print driver up to print to the local printer port. If the file prints to the local printer, a network/printer driver problem still exists. Reload the printer driver and check the network print path, as depicted in Figure 9.11. The correct format for the UNC network path name is \\computer_name\shared device_name.

If the printer operation stalls, or crashes, during the printing process, a different type of problem is indicated. In this case, the remote printer was functioning, the print server was operational, and the network was transferring data. Some critical condition must have been reached to stop the printing process. Check the print spooler in the print server to see whether an error has occurred. Also, check the hard disk space and memory usage in the print server.

WINDOWS UTILITIES

▶ 3.2 Windows-based utilities.

A portion of the A+ Operating System Technologies objective 3.2 states that the test taker should be able to "recognize common problems and determine how to resolve them."

Successful troubleshooting of operating systems requires tools. In addition to the startup tools already described (*clean boot disks* and single-step boot-up utilities), a number of other utilities are available through the Windows operating systems to isolate and correct operating system problems.

Many of these utilities can be added directly to the startup disk so that they will be readily available in emergency situations. Some of the utilities that should be added to the startup disk include the following:

♦ **SCANDISK.EXE.** Checks the disk for lost clusters and cross-linked files and can examine disks and their contents for errors.

♦ **DEFRAG.EXE.** Realigns the file structure on the disk to optimize its operation.

◆ **MEM.EXE.** Used to view system memory organization.

◆ **SYSEDIT.EXE/REGEDIT.EXE.** These utilities can be used to edit Windows 9x system structures such as CONFIG.SYS, AUTOEXEC.BAT, and INI files, as well as the Windows 9x Registry structure.

◆ **FDISK.EXE.** Used to create, view, and manage partitions on a hard disk.

◆ **ATTRIB.EXE.** Can be employed to change the attribute of files (such as hidden, read-only, and system files) so that they can be seen and manipulated for troubleshooting purposes.

◆ **FORMAT.COM.** Used to establish the high-level format on disk drives.

◆ **SYS.COM.** Used to copy key system files to a disk so that it will be self-booting.

In the case of Windows 9x, the *Create Startup Disk* option under the Add/Remove Programs tab includes most of these utilities on the Emergency Start Disk when it is created. Other utilities that can be very helpful in troubleshooting operating system problems include the Microsoft Diagnostic program and the Windows 9x Device Manager.

Windows 98 Troubleshooting Tools

The Windows operating system has become quite complex, both in structure and operation. The Windows 98 Resource Kit, from Microsoft Press, is nearly 1,800 pages and growing. This is considerably larger than the combined MS-DOS and Windows 3.1x manuals that supported DOS and Windows 3.1x. To help contend with these complexities, Microsoft has included an extensive set of troubleshooting system tools in Windows 98. It has also expanded the built-in Troubleshooting menu located in the Windows 98 Help functions. Both of these items are included to assist in the location and correction of many problems.

The System Tools

The following list identifies the Windows 98 troubleshooting tools:

Microsoft System Information

Windows Report Tool

MS-DOS Report Tool

Dr. Watson

System File Checker

Registry Checker

System Configuration Utility

Automatic Skip Driver Agent

Version Conflict Manager

Scheduling Tasks

Maintenance Wizard

Microsoft Backup

Microsoft System Recovery

Digital Signal Check

Signature Verification Tool

Windows Update

The *Microsoft System Information* tool (MSINFO32.EXE) is located at Program Files\Common Files\Microsoft Shared\MSINFO. You can use this utility to view system hardware resources, installed devices, and drivers. It can also be used to view reports generated by Web-based Windows and MS-DOS Report Tools. This enables remote service providers to inspect MSINFO information from local units across a LAN or WAN.

MSINFO is typically started by clicking the System Information option in the Programs\Accessories\SystemTools path from the Start menu. If Windows 98 does not run, the program can be executed by typing **MSINFO32** at the DOS command prompt. When the utility starts, the System Information screen depicted in Figure 9.12 appears.

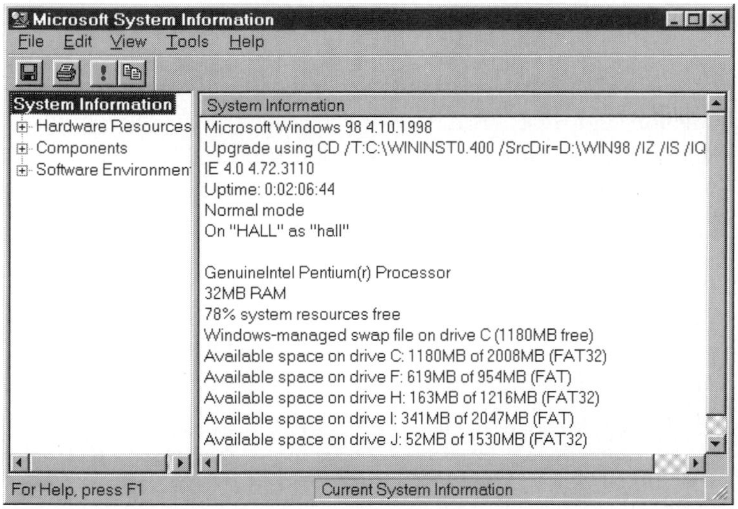

FIGURE 9.12
System Information screen.

The information is divided into a four-part arrangement. The main System Information screen displays general system information. The Hardware Resources entry provides information about system hardware settings, including IRQ, DMA, I/O, and memory addresses. The Components entry shows information about multimedia-related software, networking software, and device drivers. The final entry, Software Environment, lists the software loaded into the system's memory.

The *Windows Report Tool* (WINREP.EXE) is located in the Windows directory and provides a copy of the MSINFO information in HTML format. The *MS-DOS Report Tool* (DOSREP.EXE), also located in the Windows directory, provides a snapshot of the system files and can upload it to an FTP site when Windows is not working.

The *Dr. Watson* function from Windows 3.1x is alive and well in the Windows 98 version. As before, it is used to trace problems that appear under certain conditions, such as starting, or using a certain application. When Dr. Watson is started, it runs in the background with only an icon appearing on the taskbar to signify that it is present. When a system error occurs, Dr. Watson logs the events that were going on up to the time of the failure. In many cases, the program will describe the nature of the error, and possibly suggest a fix. However, Dr. Watson is less than perfect. In some cases, the utility will completely miss the failing event.

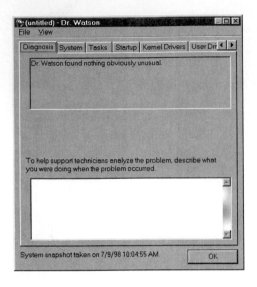

FIGURE 9.13
Dr. Watson main screen.

FIGURE 9.14
System File Checker main menu.

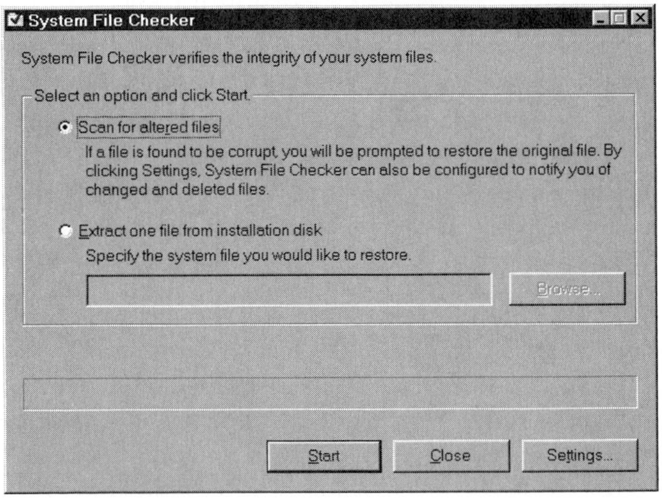

The Dr. Watson utility is not located in any of the Windows 98 menus. To use the utility, it is necessary to execute the program from the Start menu's Run option. Just type the name **drwatson** in the dialog box, and click OK to start the log file. The Dr. Watson icon should appear on the taskbar. Dr. Watson also can be started through the Tools menu in the System Information screen. This option is located in the Programs\Accessories\System Tools path.

To see the resulting log file, click the icon. This action produces the Dr. Watson main screen, depicted in Figure 9.13. From this screen, select the System tab. This information also can be viewed from the System Information section of the System Tools menu.

The *System File Checker* utility (SFC.EXE) checks the system files for changed, deleted, or possibly corrupt files. If it finds such files, it attempts to extract the original version of the file from Windows files. This file can be found at Windows\System.

The System File Checker is activated by clicking the System File Checker entry in the System Information Tools menu. When it is activated, the utility's main screen, depicted in Figure 9.14, appears. This provides two options: scanning for altered system files, or extracting a file from the Windows 98 distribution CD.

Windows 98 also includes a pair of Registry checker utilities
(SCANREG.EXE and SCANREGW.EXE) to scan, fix, back up, and
restore Registry files. The SCANREG file is a DOS-based program,
whereas SCANREGW is a Windows-based version. The DOS version is located in the Windows\Command directory, whereas the
Windows version is just in the Windows directory.

Windows 98 has a collection of configuration-related troubleshooting tools. These utilities include the *System Configuration Utility*
(MSCONFIG.EXE), the *Automatic Skip Driver Agent* (ASD.EXE),
and the *Version Conflict Manager* (VCMUI.EXE).

The System Configuration Utility enables you to examine the system's configuration through a check-box system. By turning different
configuration settings on and off, problem settings can be isolated,
and corrected, by a process of elimination. You can access this utility
through the System Information screen. From the Tools menu, select
the System Configuration Utility. This action brings up the System
Configuration Utility's main screen, depicted in Figure 9.15.

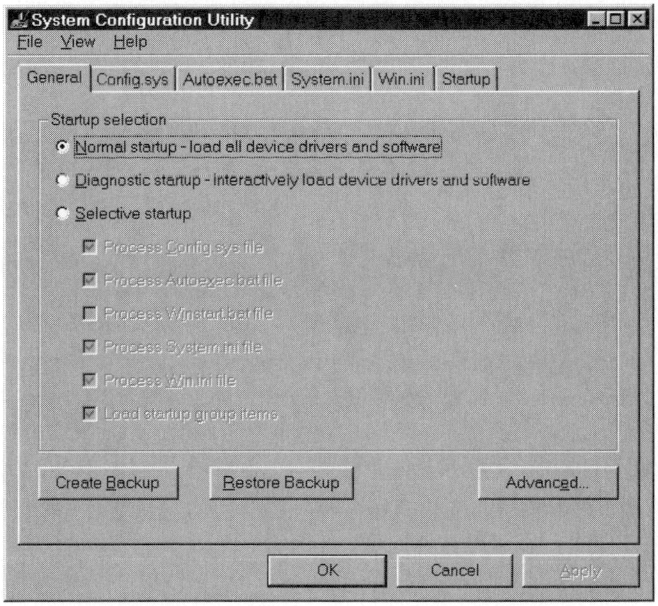

FIGURE 9.15
System Configuration Utility main screen.

The screen is divided into six tabs that correspond to the files that run during the startup process. The information under the General tab enables you to select the type of startup. For most troubleshooting efforts, the Diagnostic Startup is selected first to provide a clean environment. When the Selective Startup option is chosen, complete sections of the boot-up sequence can be disabled. Once an offending section has been isolated, you can use the individual tabs to enter that section and selectively disable individual lines within the file.

In cases in which the configuration problem is more severe, you can use the Automatic Skip Driver Agent. This utility senses, and skips, configuration steps that prevent Windows 98 from starting.

Finally, the Version Conflict Manager automatically installs Windows 98 drivers over other drivers that it finds, even if these drivers are newer. The System Configuration Manager is located in the Windows\System directory, whereas the other two utilities are found under the Windows directory.

Windows 98 offers two utilities that you can use to automate the operation of important preventive maintenance utilities such as Backup, ScanDisk, *Defrag*, and so on. The *Scheduling Tasks* (MSTASK.EXE) program allows these utilities to be run at preset time intervals, such as every 24 hours, or each week. On the other hand, the Windows 98 *Maintenance Wizard* (TUNEUP.EXE) allows the operation of the housekeeping utilities to be independently scheduled. The Schedule Tasks utility is located in the Windows\ System directory, whereas the Maintenance Wizard can be found under the \Windows directory.

The Windows 98 Backup and Recovery utilities (*MSBACKUP.EXE* and *PCRESTOR.BAT*) are invaluable tools for protecting against application and data loss due to hardware crashes. The Recovery utility has been updated to operate completely in protected mode. It is located on the Windows 98 CD, and provides a step-by-step process for recovering MSBACKUP files. The Backup utility is located in the Program Files\Accessories\System Tools\Backup directory.

The Windows 98 Backup screen is depicted in Figure 9.16. As with previous Microsoft Backup utilities, the process of backing up is fairly straightforward. Start the Backup utility, select the type of backup to perform, what items to back up, where to back them up to, select any desired backup options, and then click Start.

Windows 98 Backup supports a variety of backup media. These include removable media (such as floppy disks, JAZ, and SyQuest cartridges, as well as tape drives—including QIC-80, 3010, 3020, and DC-6000 formats). This version of Backup is compatible with Windows 95 backup files, but not with DOS or Windows 3.x backups.

Both Backup and Restore can be run with or without the help of their wizards. The wizards provide step-by-step guidance through each procedure. Without the wizards, the processes are roughly equal to older Microsoft backup and restore operations.

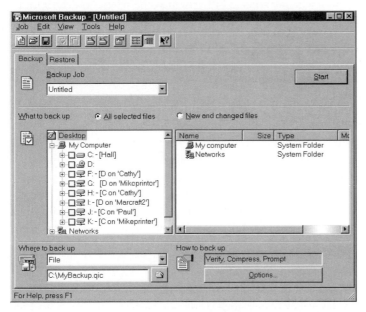

FIGURE 9.16
Windows Backup utility screen.

The Backup utility is not installed as a default item when Windows 98 is installed. It must be set up using the Add/Remove Programs icon in the Control Panel. From the Add/Remove Programs screen, select the Windows Setup tab and double-click the System Tools entry. Check the box next to the Backup entry, click OK, select the Apply box, and click OK. These actions copy the Backup utility files into the System Tools menu in the Start menu's Programs\Accessories path.

The final tools covered here deal with Microsoft-approved drivers and files. Microsoft works with hardware suppliers and *signs* (certifies) its drivers for Windows 98 compatibility by adding special digital codes to them. The Digital Signal Check function is enabled through the Windows 98 Policy Editor in the Hkey_Local_Machine\Software\Microsoft Registry subkey. This check verifies that driver files have been signed by Microsoft. This Driver Signing tool is valuable to administrators who do not want users to introduce questionable devices and drivers into the system.

The *Signature Verification Tool* (SIGVERIF.EXE) checks files to determine whether Microsoft has signed them. It also determines whether the files have been modified since they were signed.

Finally, the Windows *Update utility* (WUPDMGR.EXE) is a Windows 98 extension located on the Microsoft Web site (www.microsoft.com/windowsupdate). It enables you to update the system's files and drivers with new or improved versions over the Web.

Two other valuable utilities in Windows 9x are the System Monitor and the System Resource Meter programs. The System Monitor can be used to track the performance of key system resources for both evaluation and troubleshooting purposes. If system performance is suspect but there is no clear indication of what might be slowing it down, the System Monitor can be used to determine which resource is operating at capacity (and thereby limiting the performance of the system).

Typical resources that the System Monitor can track include those associated with processor usage and memory management. Results can be displayed in real-time using statistical mode, line chart mode, or bar chart mode. Figure 9.17 illustrates the monitor operating in line chart mode. The System Monitor can be set up to run on top of other applications so that it can be used to see what effect they are having on the system.

The Resource Meter depicted in Figure 9.18 is a simple bar chart display that shows the percent usage of the system resources, user resources, and GDI resources. When activated, the meter normally resides as an icon on the extreme right side of the taskbar, at the bottom of the desktop. Double-clicking the icon brings the bar chart display to the desktop. As with the System Monitor, the Resource Meter can be used to evaluate hardware and software performance.

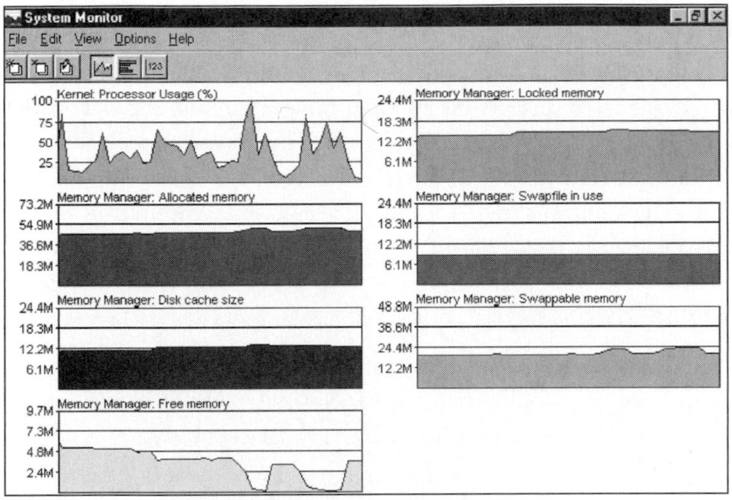

FIGURE 9.17
Using the System Monitor.

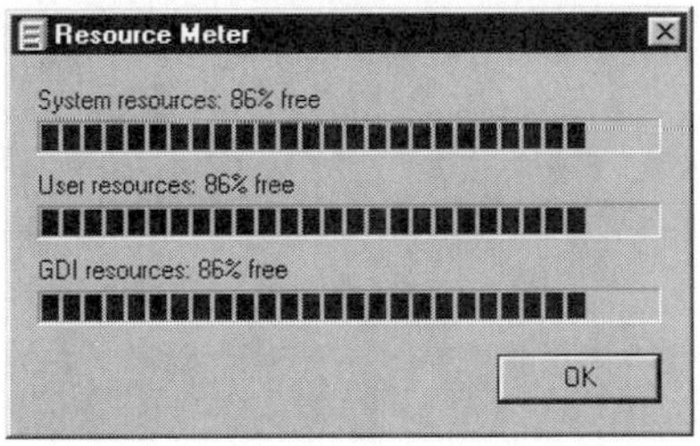

FIGURE 9.18
Using the Resource Meter.

Both the System Monitor and the Resource Meter are installed through the Setup tab under the Control Panel's Add/Remove Programs applet. From the Setup tab, highlight the System Tools entry and click the Details button. Select the utilities and click the Apply button.

Windows 2000 System Tools

As mentioned earlier, Windows 2000 clusters a number of administrative, diagnostic, and troubleshooting tools under the Control Panel's Microsoft Management Console.

Event Viewer

In Windows 2000, significant events (such as system events, application events, and security events) are routinely monitored and stored. These events can be viewed through the *Event Viewer* utility depicted in Figure 9.19. As described earlier, this tool is located under the Control Panel/Administrative Tools/Computer Management path.

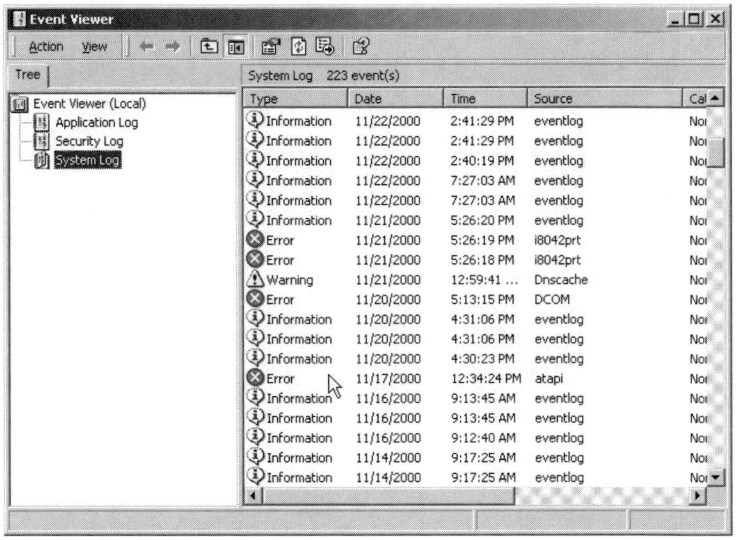

FIGURE 9.19
Windows 2000 Event Viewer.

System events include items such as successful and failed Windows component startups, as well as successful loading of device drivers. Likewise, application events include information about how the system's applications are performing. Not all Windows applications generate events that the Event Viewer will log. Finally, security events are produced by user actions such as logons and logoffs, file and folder accesses, and creation of new Active Directory accounts.

Three default event logs track and record the events just mentioned. The system log records events generated by the operating system and its components. The application log tracks events generated by high-end applications. Likewise, the security log contains information generated by audit policies that have been enacted in the operating system. If no audit policies are configured, the security log will remain empty.

In addition to the default logs, some special systems such as domain controllers and DNS systems will have specialized logs to track events specifically related to the function of the system.

The Event Viewer produces three categories of system and application events:

◆ **Information events.** Events that indicate an application, service, or driver has loaded successfully. These events require no intervention.

◆ **Warning events.** Events that have no immediate impact, but that could have future significance. These events should be investigated.

◆ **Error events.** Events that indicate an application, service, or driver has failed to loaded successfully. These events require immediate intervention.

Figure 9.20 depicts the Windows 2000 Event Viewer displaying these types of events. Notice that the information events are denoted by a small "i" in a cloud, whereas the warning and error events are identified by an exclamation mark (!) and an X, respectively.

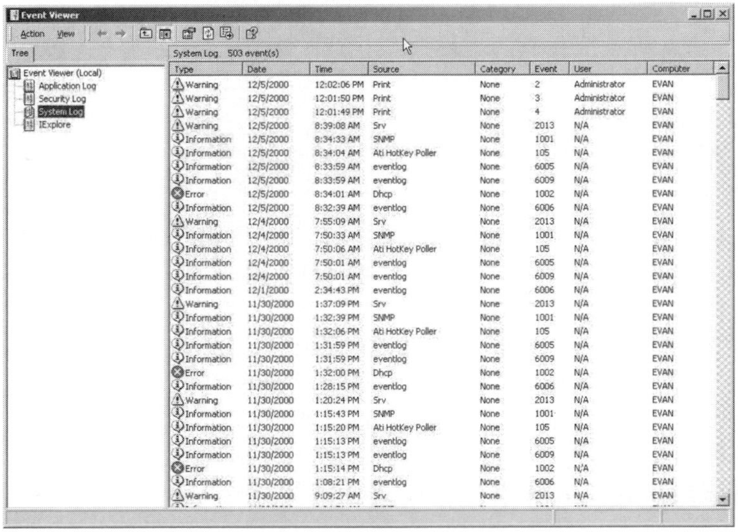

FIGURE 9.20
Viewing event types.

System Information

The Windows 2000 *System Information* utility, depicted in Figure 9.21, provides five subfolders of information about the system. These folders include a system summary, a list of hardware resources being used, a list of I/O components in the system, a description of the system's current software environment, and a description of the Windows Internet Explorer.

FIGURE 9.21
The System Information tool.

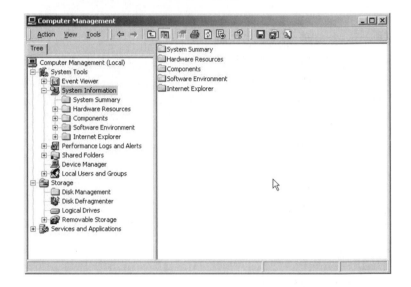

As with the Windows 98 System Information tool, the Windows 2000 version can be used to enable remote service providers to inspect the system's information across a LAN environment.

To save system information to a file, right-click the System Information entry and select the Save As option from the resulting menu. Saving this information enables you to document events and conditions when errors occur. You can use the results of different system information files to compare situations and perhaps determine what changes may have occurred to cause the problem.

Using Device Manager

Hardware and configuration conflicts also can be isolated manually using the Windows 9x Device Manager from the Control Panel's System icon. This utility is basically an easy-to-use interface for the Windows 9x and Windows 2000 Registries.

You can use the Device Manager, depicted in Figure 9.22, to identify installed ports, update device drivers, and change I/O settings. From this window, the problem device can be examined to see where the conflict is occurring.

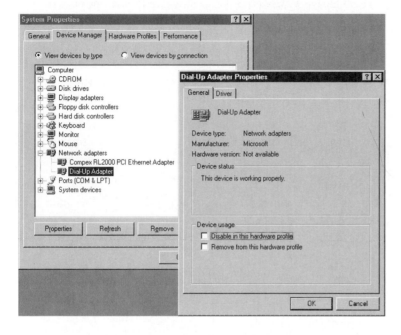

FIGURE 9.22
The Device Manager display.

Two radio buttons on the Device Manager page can be used to alter the way it displays the devices installed in the system. Clicking the left button (the page's default setting), displays the system's devices alphabetically by device type. The rightmost radio button shows the devices by their connection to the system. As with the Registry and Policy Editors, the presence of plus (+) and (–) signs in the nodes of the devices indicates expandable and collapsible information branches at those nodes.

The Device Manager will display an exclamation point (!) inside a yellow circle whenever a device is experiencing a direct hardware conflict with another device. The nature of the problem is described in the device's Properties dialog box. Similarly, when a red X appears at the device's icon, the device has been disabled due to a *user-selection conflict*.

TEST TIP

Memorize symbols used by the Windows Device Manager.

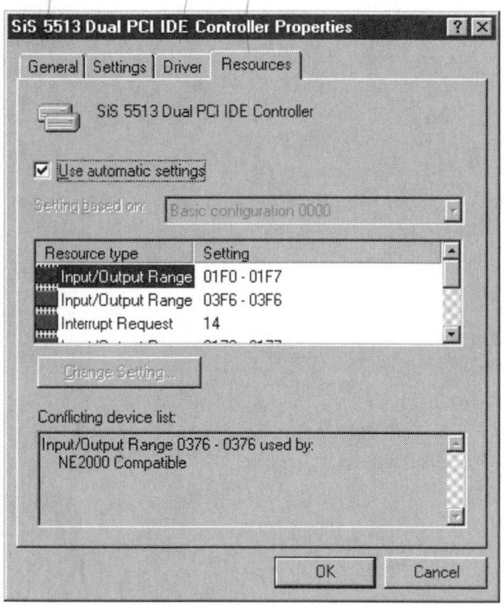

FIGURE 9.23
The Device Manager Resource page.

TEST TIP

Know how to find conflicts using the Windows Device Manager.

This situation can occur when a user wants to disable a selected device without removing it. For example, a user that travels and uses a notebook computer may want to temporarily disable device drivers for options not used in travel. This can be accomplished through the Device Manager's Disable in This Hardware Profile option. This will keep the driver from loading up until it is re-activated.

Clicking the Properties button at the bottom of the Device Manager screen produces the selected device's Properties sheet. The three tabs at the top of the page provide access to the device's general information, Driver specifications, and system resource assignments.

When a device conflict is suspected, just click the offending device in the listing, make sure that the selected device is the current device, and then click the Resources tab to examine the conflicting device's list, as depicted in Figure 9.23.

To change the resources allocated to a device, click the resource to be changed, remove the check mark from the Use Automatic Settings box, click the Change Settings button, and scroll through the resource options. Take care when changing resource settings. The Resource Settings window displays all the available resources in the system, even those that are already spoken for by another device. You must know which resources are acceptable for a given type of device and which ones are already in use.

To determine what resources the system already has in use, click the Computer icon at the top of the Device Manager display. The *Computer Properties* page, depicted in Figure 9.24, provides ways to view and reserve system resources.

Through this page, you can click radio buttons to display the system's usage of four key resources: IRQ channels, DMA channels, I/O addresses, and memory addresses. The Reserve Resources page is used to set aside key resources to avoid conflicts with the PnP configuration operations. If a resource is reserved and Windows detects it as already in use, a warning dialog box displays onscreen and asks for a confirmation.

Normal causes for conflict include devices sharing IRQ settings, I/O address settings, DMA channels, or base memory settings. The most common conflicts are those dealing with the IRQ channels. Nonessential peripherals, such as sound and network adapters, are most likely to produce this type of conflict.

When a device conflict is reported through the Resource tab's *Conflicting Devices* list, record the current settings for each device, refer to the documentation for each device to determine what other settings might be used, and change the settings for the most flexible device. If either device continues to exhibit problems, reset the configurations to their original positions and change the settings for the other device.

Make sure that the device has not been installed twice. When this occurs, it is normally impossible to determine which driver is correct. Therefore, it will be necessary to remove both drivers and allow the PnP process to redetect the device. If multiple drivers are present for a given device, remove the drivers that are not specific to the particular device installed in the system.

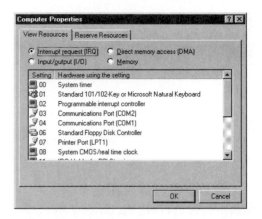

FIGURE 9.24
The Device Manager Computer Properties page.

System Editors

The Windows operating systems contain three important editors: the *System Editor* (SysEdit), the *Registry Editor* (RegEdit and RegEdt32), and the *Policy Editor* (PolEdit). Windows 2000 also includes a very powerful *Group Policy Editor* (GPE) .

Later versions of DOS contain a small, text editor program (EDIT.COM) that enables users to easily modify text files. This package is started by typing **EDIT** along with the filename at the DOS prompt. The DOS Editor's working screen is depicted in Figure 9.25.

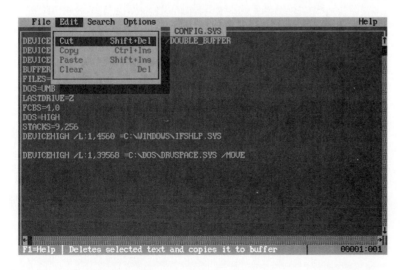

FIGURE 9.25
The DOS Editor screen.

The editor is particularly useful in modifying the CONFIG.SYS and AUTOEXEC.BAT files. The DOS Editor is an unformatted text file editor. It does not introduce formatting codes, such as underlining and italic, into the text in the manner that more powerful word processors do. This is an important consideration when dealing with DOS utility files. Formatting codes can introduce errors in these files, because DOS cannot recognize them.

In Windows, this editor is the System Editor (SYSEDIT.EXE), depicted in Figure 9.26.

FIGURE 9.26

The Windows System Editor screen.

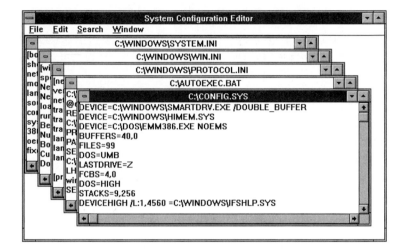

To start the SysEdit function, select the Run option from the Start menu. Type **SYSEDIT** in the Run dialog box and click the OK button. The SysEdit commands are similar to those of other Windows-based text editing programs, such as Notepad or Write.

Windows 9x contains three important editors: the System Editor (SysEdit), the Registry Editor (RegEdit), and the Policy Editor (PolEdit). The Windows 9x SysEdit function is used to modify text files, such as any INI files in the system, as well as the CONFIG.SYS and AUTOEXEC.BAT files.

Windows 2000 includes two Registry editors: *RegEdit* and RegEdt32. Both utilities enable you to add, edit, and remove Registry entries and to perform other basic functions. However, specific functions can be performed only in one editor or the other.

RegEdt32 is the Registry editor that has historically been used with Windows NT. It presents each subtree as an individual entity, in a separate window. RegEdit is the Registry editor that was introduced with Windows 95, and also was included with Windows NT 4.0. The subtrees are presented as being part of the same entity in a single window, as illustrated in Figure 9.27.

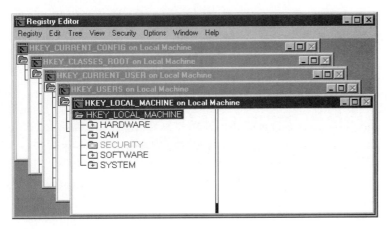

FIGURE 9.27
RegEdt32 Registry editor.

The Registry has a permissions system that is similar to NTFS permissions, which enables you to control access to the keys and assigned values. RegEdt32 enables you to view and set permissions through the Security menu. RegEdit does not allow you to access the permissions system.

The Find capabilities of RegEdt32 are accessed from the View menu, and are very limited. You can search only for keys, not assigned values or their corresponding data. This is the equivalent of being able to search for folders in the file system, but not for files. Also, you can initiate a search in only one subtree at a time. The Find capabilities of RegEdit are accessed through the Edit menu, and are very strong. You have the option to search for keys and assigned values, and you can search all subtrees at once.

RegEdit also enables you to save frequently accessed Registry l ocations as favorites to enable quicker access.

WARNING

Warning   Editing the Registry with RegEdit or RegEdt32 should be done only when you have no other alternative. These editors bypass all the safeguards provided by the standard utilities, and allow you to enter values that are invalid or that conflict with other settings. Incorrect editing of the Registry can cause Windows 2000 to stop functioning correctly, prompting a significant amount of troubleshooting or a reinstall of the operating system.

Using Dr. Watson

In an earlier section of this chapter, you learned what GPFs are and how they occur. They are memory-usage faults that occur when one application tries to use memory that has been set aside for another application. The main tool for isolating and correcting GPFs is the Dr. Watson utility provided in all Windows versions.

If the GPF cannot be directly attributed to the Windows operating software, an application program may be the source of the problem. This information is typically part of the GPF error message onscreen. In these cases, the Dr. Watson utility should be set up to run in the background as the system operates.

As the system operates, the Dr. Watson utility monitors its operation and logs its key events in the DRWATSON.LOG file. This log provides a detailed listing of the events that led up to a failure, such as a GPF. The information is automatically stored in the log file.

If a GPF error occurs in the same program each time it is run, the application probably contains defective code that requires repair before it can run under Windows. Programmers and application developers can use the Dr. Watson logs to debug their software and provide patches (software fixes) to their users. They should ask for a copy of the Dr. Watson log file if they are not already aware of the problem.

Using Windows HDD Utilities

Even with normal usage, every system's performance deteriorates over time. Most of the deterioration is due to unnecessary file clutter and segmentation on the system's hard disk drive. Each disk operating system possesses a set of disk utilities that you can use to perform housekeeping functions on the system's disk drives. In Windows 9x and Windows 2000, the most important disk utilities are still Check Disk/ScanDisk and Defrag and FDISK.

In Windows 9x, they are located in several areas of the system. The icons for ScanDisk and Defrag are located in the Start/Program/ Accessories/System Tools navigation path. The executable file for ScanDisk can be found in the C:\Windows\Command directory, whereas the Defrag icon is just under C:\Windows.

You should use these HDD utilities periodically to tune-up the performance of the system. To do so, follow these steps:

1. Periodically remove unnecessary TMP and BAK files from the system.

2. Check for and remove lost file chains and clusters using the Check Disk or ScanDisk utilities.

3. Use the Defrag utility to realign files on the drive that may have become fragmented after being moved back and forth between the drive and the system.

The Check Disk and ScanDisk utilities are used to search the system's drives for lost allocation units and corrupted files that may have been cross-linked in the FAT. The Check Disk (CHKDSK) utility was used with early MS-DOS systems; the ScanDisk version is associated with the MS-DOS 6.x and Windows 9x operating systems. Both programs are used to optimize disk storage by locating and removing files that have been corrupted. Figure 9.28 depicts a typical CHKDSK display. CHKDSK just locates lost clusters and, when used with an **/F** switch, converts them into files that can be viewed with a text editor.

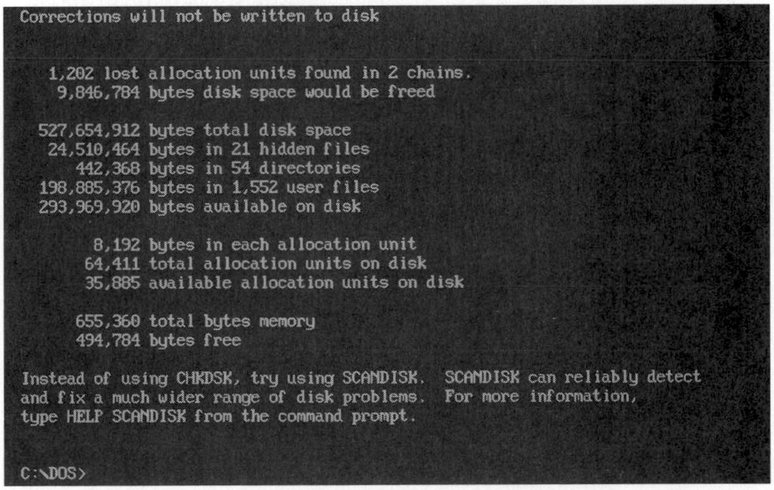

```
Corrections will not be written to disk

   1,202 lost allocation units found in 2 chains.
   9,846,784 bytes disk space would be freed

527,654,912 bytes total disk space
 24,510,464 bytes in 21 hidden files
    442,368 bytes in 54 directories
198,885,376 bytes in 1,552 user files
293,969,920 bytes available on disk

      8,192 bytes in each allocation unit
     64,411 total allocation units on disk
     35,885 available allocation units on disk

    655,360 total bytes memory
    494,784 bytes free

Instead of using CHKDSK, try using SCANDISK.  SCANDISK can reliably detect
and fix a much wider range of disk problems.  For more information,
type HELP SCANDISK from the command prompt.

C:\DOS>
```

FIGURE 9.28
A CheckDisk display.

TEST TIP

Be aware of what events will cause ScanDisk to run automatically.

In addition to locating and converting lost clusters on the disk drive, the *ScanDisk* utility can detect and delete cross-linked files from the drive. It also can make corrections to file and disk errors that it detects. ScanDisk can be run from the DOS command line or as a Windows utility program. As with other disk utilities, only a Windows version of ScanDisk should be used on a Windows system. Using a command-line-based version of ScanDisk may cause data loss rather than optimization, because the command-line version does not lock out the system when the file structure is being modified. By default, the command-line version of ScanDisk runs automatically during startup whenever the operating system detects that the system has not been shut down correctly.

Windows 9x actually provides two ScanDisk utilities: an MS-DOS-based version that remains on the Windows 9x Startup disk, and a Windows-compatible graphics-based version (ScanDskw) that can be run from the Windows 9x environment. The MS-DOS version (ScanDisk) is designed to be run from the Startup disk's command line in emergency recovery operations.

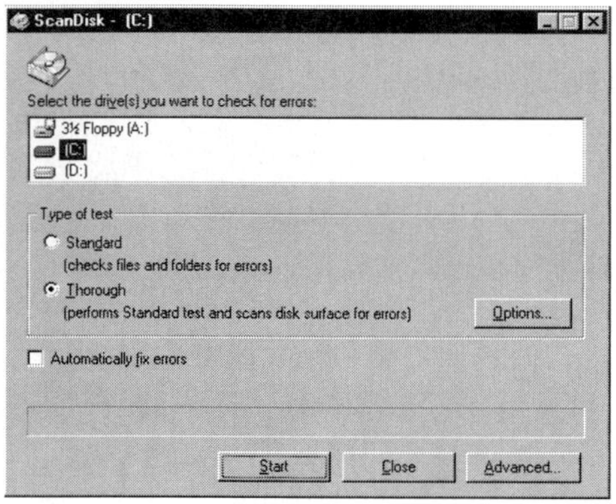

FIGURE 9.29
A ScanDisk display.

The Windows version of ScanDisk is located in the Start/Programs/Accessories/System_Tools directory. It can be run from the System Tools location, or it can be started through the Start/Run dialog box by typing **ScanDisk**. The Windows version repairs long filenames and is the recommended version for repairing disks. Figure 9.29 shows a typical Windows ScanDisk main page.

In the ScanDisk main window, select the drive to be examined, choose the type of test to be performed (Standard or Thorough), and set ScanDisk so that it will automatically attempt to fix errors it finds. The Standard test checks the folders and files on the drive for errors; the Thorough test also examines the disk's physical surface for problems.

TEST TIP

Know the difference between the Standard and Thorough ScanDisk operations.

Selecting the *Thorough* option will pop up the Surface Scan Options page depicted in Figure 9.30. This page is used to control the scope of the surface scan, and therefore the time involved in checking it. The entire disk may be checked, or the test can be limited to only the data or system areas of the disk.

Clicking the Advanced button on the ScanDisk main page produces another options page, shown in Figure 9.31. The Advanced Options page is used to determine how ScanDisk will deal with errors it finds. Its options include what to do with lost and cross-linked clusters, how to handle the log file, and how to display its results.

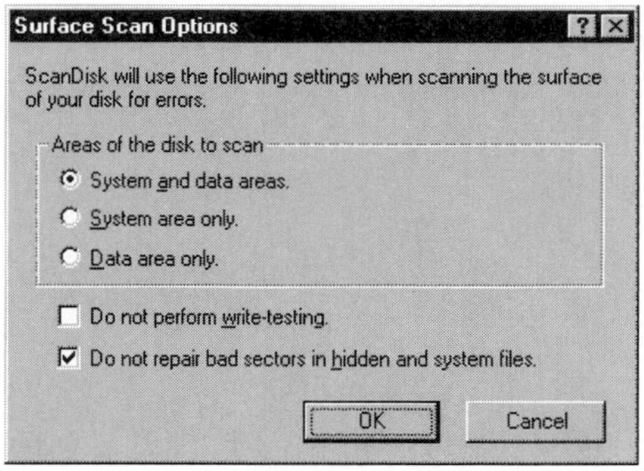

The Defrag utility also is used to optimize the operation of the system's disk drives. It does this by reorganizing data on the disk into logically contiguous blocks. With data arranged in this manner, the system does not need to reposition the drive's read/write heads as many times to read a given piece of data.

The operation of the command-line Defrag program also is described in Chapter 7. Although the operation of the Windows 9x version of Defrag is identical, its usage is not. To start the Windows 9x version, click the Start button on the desktop, select the Run option, and enter **Defrag** in the Run dialog box. Specify the drive to be defragmented in the Select Drive dialog box, and click the OK button.

The Advanced button on the Select Drive page produces the Defragmentation Advanced Options page displayed in Figure 9.32. You can use this page to specify a defragmentation method, error checking, and the time when these options should be used.

Viewing the defragmentation operation is possible through the My Computer window. Just right-click the drive icon and select the Properties option. From this point, click the Tools option and select Defrag. However, viewing the operation of the defragmentation process makes the operation longer. It is better to run this utility in a minimized condition.

Another important disk management utility is the Backup and Restore utility found in both Windows 9x and Windows 2000. This utility is not automatically installed when Windows is set up. If the user decides to install this feature, the actual Backup file (BACKUP.EXE) is placed in the C:\Program_Files\Accessories directory. Windows also creates a shortcut icon for the Backup utility in the C:\Windows\Start Menu\Programs\Accessories\System Tools directory.

FIGURE 9.30
Surface ScanDisk options.

FIGURE 9.31
ScanDisk Advanced Options page.

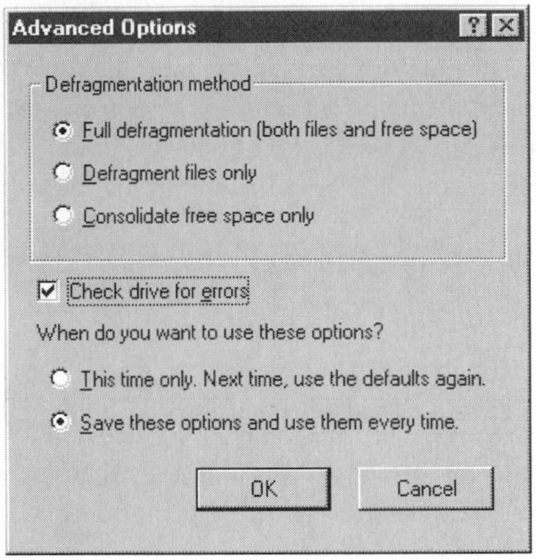

FIGURE 9.32
The Defrag Advanced Options page.

Windows Help Files

Windows 9x, NT 4.0, and 2000 come with built-in *troubleshooting Help file systems*. This feature includes troubleshooting assistance for a number of different Windows problems. The Windows 9x and Windows 2000 troubleshooters are much more expansive than the Windows NT troubleshooters.

In all three systems, the troubleshooter utilities can be accessed from the Start menu, or from the Help menu entry on the taskbar. In either case, the Help Topic window appears, as depicted in Figure 9.33.

FIGURE 9.33
The Windows 9x Help Topics window.

Double-clicking the Troubleshooting entry accesses the Troubleshooting Help section. This section contains a list of several entries with information about common Windows problems and situations. Clicking a topic produces a Help window with information about the troubleshooting process associated with that particular problem (for instance, Hardware Conflict Troubleshooting). This window is depicted in Figure 9.34. The interactive text contains a step-by-step procedure for isolating the problem listed.

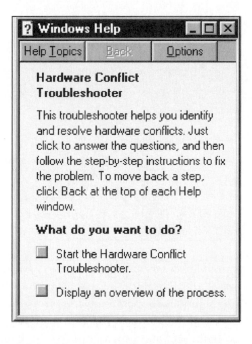

FIGURE 9.34
Hardware Conflict Troubleshooting window.

Windows Troubleshooting Help Files

Along with the additional troubleshooting tools, the Windows 98 Help file system has been upgraded to provide extended troubleshooting topics. The new Windows 98 Help function includes both the local help, such as that supplied by Windows 95, as well as online help through a built-in Web browser. The online help allows the system to access Microsoft's significant online help resources. The updated Windows 98 Help file system can be accessed through the Start menu.

Selecting the Help entry from the Start menu produces the main Help window, depicted in Figure 9.35. The local Help screens are manipulated by making a selection from the electronic Contents list. In the Troubleshooting entry, just follow the questions and suggestion schemes provided.

FIGURE 9.35
Windows 98 Help window.

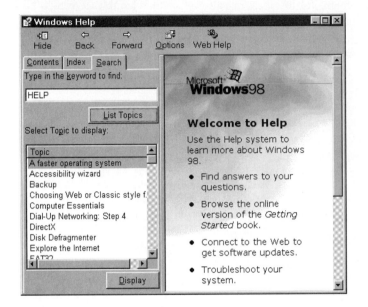

The Windows troubleshooters are a special type of help available in Windows 9x and 2000. These utilities enable you to pinpoint problems and identify solutions to those problems. Troubleshooters ask a series of questions and then provide you with detailed troubleshooting information based on your responses to those questions.

There are troubleshooters to help you diagnose and solve problems in the following areas, to name a few:

◆ Hardware

◆ Display

◆ Modems

◆ Printing

◆ Sound/multimedia/games

◆ TCP/IP networking

◆ Internet connections

◆ DHCP

◆ DNS

◆ WINS

◆ Active Directory and Group Policy

◆ CSNW

◆ Startup and shutdown

◆ Stop errors

You can access the troubleshooters in many ways, including through context-sensitive Help, through the Help option on the Start menu, and through the Device Manager.

Other Information and Troubleshooting Resources

You can turn to many resources outside of the operating system for information and troubleshooting assistance, such as Windows Resource Kits, the Internet, and Microsoft TechNet. The following sections discuss these additional resources.

Windows Resource Kits

The Windows 95, 98, NT 4.0, and 2000 Resource Kits provide thousands of pages of in-depth technical information on these Windows operating systems, as well as hundreds of additional utilities that you can use to enhance deployment, maintenance, and troubleshooting of your Windows network. The Resource Kit is an excellent printed reference for Windows 2000, and also comes with searchable electronic versions.

There are two different versions of the Resource Kit for each NT operating system: one for Windows NT Workstation, and one for Windows NT Server (as well as one for Windows 2000 Professional, and one for Windows 2000 Server). The Resource Kits are published by Microsoft Press and are available from major book retailers.

Internet Help

The Windows 98 and Windows 2000 online Help functions are activated by selecting a topic from the menu and then clicking the Web Help button. This must be followed by clicking the Support On-line at the lower right of the Help window. This action brings up the Internet Sign-In dialog box, if the system is not already logged on to the Internet. After signing in, the Microsoft technical support page appears, as shown in Figure 9.36.

FIGURE 9.36
Microsoft Online Help window.

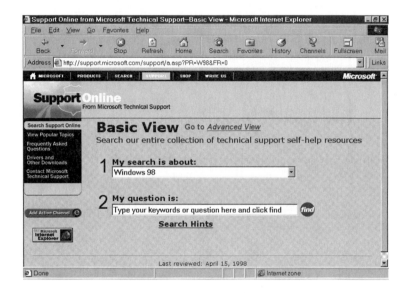

Microsoft's online Product Support Services can provide a wealth of information about Microsoft products, including their operating systems. The Web address for Product Support Services is www.Microsoft.com/support. Features of Microsoft Product Support include the following:

◆ Microsoft Knowledge Base, which is a searchable database of information and self-help tools. The Knowledge Base is used by Microsoft Technical Support to support its customers and is made available to you free of charge.

◆ Download Center, which enables you to search all available downloads for any Microsoft product, including service packs, patches, and updates.

- ◆ Facts by Product, which enables you to browse for information by product, and includes a list of most frequently asked questions about each product.

- ◆ Listing of support phone numbers (in case you want to speak to a "real" person). A charge applies for phone support.

- ◆ Online Support Requests, which enable you to submit questions to Microsoft support personnel. A charge applies for online support.

Microsoft TechNet

Microsoft's TechNet Web site is designed to support IT professionals. The URL for this site is www.Microsoft.com/technet. This is an excellent site for getting the latest information about Windows 2000 (and all other Microsoft products and technologies).

TechNet features include the following:

- ◆ Search capabilities for the Technical Information database and the Knowledge Base.

- ◆ What's New section that highlights new issues every month.

- ◆ Access to the Product Support Services Web site.

- ◆ Information categorized by product to help you troubleshoot, maintain, and deploy software.

- ◆ Chats, user groups, and Feedback Central for communicating with your peers and with Microsoft.

Microsoft also provides a TechNet subscription service. For an annual fee, the Technical Information database, Knowledge Base, service packs, patches, fixes, software utilities, product enhancements, Resource Kits, beta versions of future Microsoft products, training information, and many other useful items will be shipped to you each month in CD format. A TechNet subscription can be purchased at the TechNet Web site.

Viruses

▶ 3.2 Identify concepts relating to viruses and virus types: their danger, their symptoms, sources of viruses, how they infect, how to protect against them, and how to identify/ remove them.

A portion of the A+ Operating System Technologies objective 3.2 states that the test taker should be able to "identify concepts relating to viruses and virus types: their danger, their symptoms, sources of viruses, how they infect, how to protect against them, and how to identify/remove them."

Computer Viruses

Computer viruses are destructive programs designed to replicate and spread on their own. Viruses are created to sneak into personal computers. Sometimes these programs take control of a machine to leave a humorous message, and sometimes they destroy data. After they infiltrate one machine, they can spread into other computers through infected disks that friends and coworkers pass around, or through local and wide area network connections.

Researchers at the National Computer Security Association estimate that between 200 and 300 new viruses are being introduced into the computer community every month. However, the top-10 viruses in the United States account for about 80% of virus infections.

There are basically three types of viruses, based on how they infect a computer system:

◆ **A boot-sector virus.** This type of virus copies itself onto the boot sector of floppy and hard disks. The virus replaces the disk's original boot-sector code with its own code. This allows it to be loaded into memory before anything else is loaded. Once in memory, the virus can spread to other disks.

◆ **A file infector.** File infectors are viruses that add their virus code to executable files. After the file with the virus is executed, it spreads to other executable files.

macro virus (handwritten)

A similar type of virus, called a *macro virus*, hides in the macro programs of word processing document files. These files can be designed to load when the document is opened or when a certain key combination is entered. In addition, these types of viruses can be designed to stay resident in memory after the host program has been exited (similar to a TSR program), or may just stop working when the infected file is terminated.

◆ **A Trojan horse.** This type of virus appears to be a legitimate program that may be found on any system. Trojan horse viruses are more likely to do damage by destroying files, and can cause physical damage to disks.

legitimate prog (handwritten)

A number of different viruses have been created from these three virus types. They have several different names, but they all inflict basically the same damage. After the virus file has become active in the computer, it basically resides in memory when the system is running. From this point, it may perform a number of different types of operations that can be as complex and damaging as the author designs them to be.

As an example, a strain of boot-sector virus known as *CMOS virus* infects the hard drive's Master Boot Record and becomes memory-resident. When activated, the virus writes over the system's configuration information in the CMOS area. Part of what gets overwritten is the HDD and FDD information. Therefore, the system cannot boot up properly. The initial infection comes from booting from an infected floppy disk. The virus overwrites the CMOS once in every 60 boot ups.

A similar boot-sector virus, referred to as the FAT virus, becomes memory-resident in the area of system memory where the IO.SYS and MSDOS.SYS files are located. This allows it to spread to any non-write-protected disks inserted into the computer. In addition, the virus moves the system pointers for the disk's executable files to an unused cluster and rewrites the pointers in the FAT to point to the sector where the virus is located. The result is improper disk copies, inability to back up files, large numbers of lost clusters, and all executable files being cross-linked with each other.

TEST TIP

Know how the different types of viruses attack the system.

In another example, a file infector virus strain, called the *FAT table virus*, infects EXE files but does not become memory-resident. When the infected file is executed, the virus rewrites another EXE file.

Virus Symptoms

Because virus programs tend to operate in the background, it is sometimes difficult to realize that the computer has been infected. Typical virus symptoms include the following:

- ◆ Hard disk controller failures.
- ◆ Disks continue to be full even when files have been deleted.
- ◆ System cannot read write-protected disks.
- ◆ The hard disk stops booting and files are corrupted.
- ◆ The system will boot to floppy disk, but will not access the HDD. An `Invalid Drive Specification` message usually displays when attempting to access the C: drive.
- ◆ CMOS settings continually revert to default even though the system board battery is good.
- ◆ Files change size for no apparent reason.
- ◆ System operation slows down noticeably.
- ◆ Blank screen when booting (flashing cursor).
- ◆ Windows crashes.
- ◆ The hard drive is set to DOS compatibility and 32-bit file access suddenly stops working.
- ◆ Network data transfers and print jobs slow down dramatically.

TEST TIP

Know how viruses are spread.

A few practices increase the odds of a machine being infected by a virus. These include use of shareware software, software of unknown origin, or bulletin board software. One of the most effective ways to reduce these avenues of infection is to buy shrink-wrapped products from a reputable source.

Another means of virus protection involves installing a virus-scanning program that checks disks and files before using them in the computer. MS-DOS provided a minimal antivirus scanner called *VSafe* that could be installed as a TSR program to continuously monitor the system for viruses. DOS also included an *MSAV* utility that could be run from the DOS prompt to scan for and remove viruses.

Several other companies offer third-party virus-protection software that can be configured to operate in various ways. If the computer is a standalone unit, it may be nonproductive to have the antivirus software run each time the system is booted up. It would be much more practical to have the program check floppy disks only, because this is the only possible entryway into the computer.

A networked or online computer has more opportunity to contract a virus than a standalone unit, however, because viruses may enter the unit over the network or through the modem. In these cases, setting the software to run at each boot up is more desirable. Most modern antivirus software includes utilities to check files downloaded to the computer through dial-up connections, such as from the Internet.

Antivirus Programs

Later versions of MS-DOS included an antivirus utility called MSAV. Windows 3.x included an updated version known as MWAV. With Windows 95, Microsoft abandoned integrated antivirus protection. Therefore, you must use third-party antivirus programs with Windows 9x and Windows 2000.

CHAPTER SUMMARY

KEY TERMS

- Boot-sector virus
- BOOTLOG.TXT
- Cabinet (CAB) file
- Check Disk
- Clean boot disks
- CMOS virus
- Computer Properties
- Computer viruses
- Conflicting Devices list
- Conflicting DLL files
- Corrupt CVF (Compressed Volume File)
- Create Startup Disk
- Defrag
- Detect Crash log (DETCRASH.LOG)
- DETLOG.TXT
- Device Manager
- Disk Boot Failure
- Dynamic link library (DLL)
- Emergency Start Disk
- Enhanced Metafile (EMF)
- EXTRACT.EXE
- FAT table virus
- FDISK
- File infectors

This chapter has focused on diagnosing and troubleshooting operating system problems. The first section of the chapter examined installation and startup problems associated with Windows 9x and Windows 2000 systems. Typical startup error messages were related to probable causes for each type of system. Full discussions of safe-mode startups and Windows log files were also presented in this section.

The second section of the chapter contained the material that pertains to typical operational problems associated with Microsoft operating systems. Once again, Windows 9x and Windows 2000 systems were discussed, and typical error messages and symptoms were related to probable causes for each type of system. An extended discussion of Windows utilities was presented in this section as well.

The third section of the chapter was dedicated to printing problems associated with the Windows operating systems. Specific types of printing problems were presented, along with procedures for correcting them.

The final topic of the chapter dealt with computer viruses. Different types of viruses were described along with ways to protect computer systems against them.

At this point, review the objectives listed at the beginning of the chapter to be certain that you understand each point and can perform each task listed there. Afterward, answer the Review Questions that follow to verify your knowledge of the information.

- Macro virus
- PolEdit
- Properties
- RegEdit
- Safe mode
- Safe Mode Command Prompt Only
- Safe Mode with Network Support
- Safe Mode Without Compression
- Safe Recovery
- Safe-mode startup options
- ScanDisk
- SETUPLOG.TXT
- Single-step startup procedure
- Spool settings
- Step-by-step confirmation mode
- System Editor (SYSEDIT.EXE)
- System log files
- Terminate-and-stay-resident (TSR) programs
- Trojan horse
- Troubleshooting Help file system
- User-selection conflict

RESOURCE URLs

http://www.troubleshooters.com/tuni.htm

http://pclt.cis.yale.edu/pclt/BOOT/DOS.HTM

www.fixwindows.com/win95/index.htm

www.fixwindows.com/win98/index.htm

www.fixwindows.com/nt40/index.htm

www.fixwindows.com/win2000/index.htm

www.fixwindows.com/winME/index.htm

www.globetrotting.com/windows95/troubles.htm

www.windrivers.com/tech/troubleshoot/winexceptions.htm

http://w3.one.net/~alward/gpf.html

www.globetrotting.com/windows95/utilitie.htm

www.windrivers.com/tech/troubleshoot/registry.htm

www.windrivers.com/tech/troubleshoot/winexceptions.htm

http://pclt.cis.yale.edu/pclt/BOOT/fat.htm

www.fixwindows.com/charts/95/95print.htm

www.globetrotting.com/windows95/printers.htm

APPLY YOUR KNOWLEDGE

Review Questions

1. Where is the Dr. Watson log file saved?

2. Describe the main reason why DLL files become corrupted.

3. If a Windows 9x system locks up while running a DOS application, what item should be checked first?

4. List the four preliminary steps used to troubleshoot operating system startup problems.

5. Which devices are loaded in a standard safe-mode startup?

6. What type of error is indicated by a `This Program Has Performed an Illegal Operation` message?

7. List three types of computer viruses, and describe how they differ.

8. Why are defragmentation programs run on computers?

9. What is the purpose of running a CHKDSK operation before performing a backup or defragmentation operation on the hard drive?

10. List three possible causes for receiving a Bad or Missing Command Interpreter message.

11. Which Windows utility can be used to examine and change ASCII text files such as CONFIG.SYS and the Windows INI files?

12. Why would a step-by-step confirmation mode startup be performed?

13. If an application will not start in Windows when its icon is clicked, what action should be taken?

14. How can the print spooler be isolated as a cause of printing problems in Windows?

15. Name six tasks that the Windows 2000 Recovery Console enables you to perform.

Exam Questions

1. Which command is used to move selected files from the Windows 9x distribution disk to the system's hard drive?

   A. Copy

   B. Extract

   C. Setup

   D. Install

2. Do viruses normally attack the system's CMOS settings?

   A. Yes; this is how a virus attacks most computers.

   B. No; viruses do not normally attack CMOS settings.

   C. Yes; this is how viruses attack all computers.

   D. No; viruses never attack CMOS settings.

3. Starting the Windows system in _____ mode will bypass real-mode drivers and load a protected-mode version of Windows.

   A. Normal

   B. Logged

   C. Safe

   D. Step-by-Step Confirmation

APPLY YOUR KNOWLEDGE

4. How are most computer viruses spread from computer to computer?

   A. By downloading programs from networks

   B. By passing infected disks among individuals

   C. By not formatting disks before use

   D. By transferring files over modems

5. What action occurs if the HIMEM.SYS file is missing in Windows 9x?

   A. Windows will not start.

   B. Windows will start in DOS mode.

   C. Windows will start in standard mode.

   D. Windows will start in safe mode.

6. Which utility can be used to detect and repair corrupted files in a Windows system?

   A. ScanDisk

   B. Check Disk

   C. System Monitor

   D. Defrag

7. When the system will not start in standard safe mode, what is the next alternative?

   A. Use the **SYS** command to copy files to the hard drive.

   B. Use Safe Mode with Network Support.

   C. Use Safe Mode Command Prompt Only.

   D. Use the **Copy** command to restore the MBR on the hard drive.

8. What Windows utility can be used to change Registry entry values?

   A. SysEdit

   B. PolEdit

   C. Device Manager

   D. ResourcEdit

9. If an exclamation point inside a yellow circle appears by an entry in the Windows Device Manager, what is indicated?

   A. The device has been disabled by a user-selection conflict.

   B. The device is experiencing a direct hardware conflict with another device.

   C. The device's real-mode driver is not being loaded.

   D. The device's virtual-mode driver is not being loaded.

10. If an X appears by an entry in the Windows Device Manager, what is indicated?

   A. The device has been disabled by a user-selection conflict.

   B. The device is experiencing a direct hardware conflict with another device.

   C. The device's real-mode driver is not being loaded.

   D. The device's virtual-mode driver is not being loaded.

APPLY YOUR KNOWLEDGE

Answers to Review Questions

1. When activated, Dr. Watson intercepts the software actions, detects the failure, identifies the application, and provides a detailed description of the failure. The information is automatically transferred to the disk drive and stored in the Windows\Drwatson*.WLG file. The information stored in the file can be viewed and printed from a word processor. For more information, see the section "General Windows 9x Operating Problems."

2. When a new application is installed in Windows 3.x or 95, it may update certain DLLs used by other applications. When the old applications are activated, they may not be able to use the updated version of the DLL and fail to start. For more information, see the section " General Windows 9x Operating Problems."

3. Check the application's properties to see whether it is set to run in MS-DOS mode. For more information, see the section "General Windows 9x Operating Problems."

4. (1) Try to reboot the system. (2) Check system log files, if available, to determine where the process was interrupted. (3) Perform a clean boot with minimal configuration settings to remove nonessential elements from the process. (4) Perform a single-step boot up to isolate any driver problems that are preventing boot up from taking place. For more information, see the section "Troubleshooting Startup Problems."

5. The mouse driver, keyboard driver, and the standard VGA video driver. For more information, see the section "Safe Mode."

6. A memory-management conflict has occurred in the Windows 9x environment and the application should be saved and restarted. For more information, see the section "General Windows 9x Operating Problems."

7. Boot-sector viruses, file infectors, and Trojan horses. These viruses differ in how they infect the system. For more information, see the section "Viruses."

8. To rearrange information on the disk in a logical sequence so that it is quicker to read and write. For more information, see the section "Using Windows HDD Utilities."

9. To locate and remove lost allocation units (clusters) that slow down the operation of the drive. For more information, see the section "Using Windows HDD Utilities."

10. Reasons for this message include (1) the COMMAND.COM file cannot be found on the hard drive, and no bootable disk is present in the A: floppy disk drive; or (2), the COMMAND.COM file is not located in the hard drive's root directory. This message is likely when installing a new hard drive or a new operating system version. The third cause is that the user inadvertently erased the COMMAND.COM file from the hard drive. For more information, see the section "Windows 9x Startup Problems."

11. Windows includes the SysEdit utility for this function. For more information, see the section "System Editors."

12. This safe-mode option permits each line of the startup procedure to be checked individually to verify which drivers are being loaded. It enables

you to temporarily disable any offending drivers and to check other startup errors that may be indicated through error messages. This option should be employed when the system fails while loading the startup files, needs to load real-mode drivers, or displays a Registry Failure error message. For more information, see the section "Safe Mode."

13. Right-click the icon and select the Properties option from the menu. Review the filename, path, and syntax that link the icon to the application. For more information, see the section "General Windows 9x Operating Problems."

14. Set up the system so that it prints directly to the printer. For more information, see the section "Windows Printing Problems."

15. The Windows 2000 Recovery Console can be used to: (1) copy files to and from the hard disk, enabling you to replace or remove files that may be affecting the boot process; (2) control the startup state of services, enabling you to disable a service that could potentially be causing the operating system to crash; (3) add, remove, and format volumes on the hard disk; and (4), repair the MBR or boot sector of a hard disk or volume, and restore the Registry. For more information, see the section "Windows 2000 Recovery Console."

Answers to Exam Questions

1. **B.** The **Extract** command is required to move files from the Windows 9x CD to a hard drive. These files are stored on the distribution disc in a compressed CAB format that cannot be accessed through a **Copy** command. For more information, see the section "Windows 9x Startup Problems."

2. **B.** Most viruses attack files on disk drives and hang out in memory when the system is running. Only one type of virus attacks the information stored in the CMOS area. For more information, see the section "Antivirus Programs."

3. **C.** Selecting the Safe Mode option will bypass real-mode drivers and load a protected-mode version of Windows. For more information, see the sections "Windows 9x Startup Modes" and "Windows 2000 Startup Modes."

4. **B.** Although viruses can be passed on through any of the answers listed, the primary method of transmitting viruses is through third-party disks shared among individuals. For more information, see the section "Antivirus Programs."

5. **A.** Windows will not start without a correct and proper HIMEM.SYS entry. For more information, see the section "Windows 9x Startup Problems."

6. **A.** The utility for detecting and repairing corrupted or cross-linked files in a Windows 95 system is ScanDisk. In Windows 9x, there are utilities for both DOS and Windows operation. For more information, see the section "Windows

x to here

> ## APPLY YOUR KNOWLEDGE

9x Startup Problems."

7. **C.** If the system will not start in safe mode, the only step left is to try to boot the system to the command line. Using the SYS or /MBR options only does anything if the Master Boot Record has been corrupted. Otherwise, they will have no affect on the problem. For more information, see the section "Safe-Mode Startups."

8. **C.** Although the Registry can be altered through the RegEdit function, the safest way to change Registry settings is to change values through the Device Manager. For more information, see the section "Using Device Manager."

9. **A.** This icon indicates that the specified component has a problem caused by the user selecting an inappropriate resource setting. For more information, see the section "Using Device Manager."

10. **B.** When an X appears next to an entry in the Device Manager, the device is experiencing a conflict with another device. For more information, see the section "Using Device Manager."

This chapter helps you to prepare for the Operating System Technologies module of the A+ Certification examination by covering the following objectives within the "Domain 4.0: Networks" section.

4.1 Identify the networking capabilities of Windows including procedures for connecting to the network.

Content may include the following:

- **Protocols**
- **IPCONFIG.EXE**
- **WINIPCFG.EXE**
- **Sharing disk drives**
- **Sharing print and file services**
- **Network type and network card**
- **Installing and configuring browsers**

▶ Local area networks are becoming a major part of the personal computer market. Therefore, a PC technician must know how to install and maintain LAN equipment and software.

4.2 Identify concepts and capabilities relating to the Internet and basic procedures for setting up a system for Internet access.

Content may include the following:

Concepts and terminology

- **ISP**
- **TCP/IP**
- **Email**
- **PING**
- **HTML**
- **HTTP://**
- **FTP**
- **Domain names (Web sites)**
- **Dial-up access**

CHAPTER 10

4.0 Networks

▶ The Internet is the most famous example of wide area networking. With so many people going online, the technician must understand how the Internet is organized. The successful technician also must be able to establish and maintain Internet connections using the major operating systems and Dial-Up Networking software.

STUDY STRATEGIES

To prepare for the "Networks" section of the Operating System Technologies exam:

▶ Read the objectives at the beginning of this chapter.

▶ Study the information in this chapter.

▶ Review the objectives listed earlier in this chapter.

▶ Perform any step-by-step procedures in the text.

▶ Answer the Review and Exam Questions at the end of the chapter and check your results.

▶ Use the *ExamGear Test Engine* on the CD that accompanies this book for additional review and exam questions concerning this material.

▶ Review the Test Tips scattered throughout the chapter and make certain that you are comfortable with each point.

INTRODUCTION

This section requires the test taker to demonstrate knowledge of the network capabilities of Windows, and how to connect to networks on the client side, including what the *Internet* is about, its capabilities, basic concepts relating to Internet access, and generic procedures for system setup.

Questions from this domain account for 15% of the Operating System Technologies test.

NETWORKING WITH WINDOWS

▶ 4.1 Identify the networking capabilities of Windows including procedures for connecting to the network.

The A+ Operating System Technologies objective 4.1 states that the test taker should be able to "identify the networking capabilities of Windows including procedures for connecting to the network."

The prevalence of local area networks (LANs) in businesses requires that PC technicians know how to install and maintain LAN equipment and software. This is evident by the increased weight of the "Networking" domain in the new A+ exams. The following sections of this chapter deal with the software side of local area networking. LAN hardware installation and troubleshooting were discussed in Chapter 6, "6.0 Basic Networking." Taken together, these two chapters provide a comprehensive study of desktop networking.

Network Hardware

Networking PCs begins with the network type and card. Although the hardware side of networking was covered in Chapter 6, some information about the network type and the network card must be obtained before the software side of the network can be addressed. The type of network determines which transfer protocol you need to load, and the network card determines which adapter driver you can install. You can find the network card's information in its User Manual or Installation Guide. You also can find the network type information that the network adapter can support in these guides.

You should configure network interface cards (NICs) to communicate with the system software before installing them in the system. On older network cards, you accomplish this by setting hardware jumpers to a specified pattern on the card. With software-configured ISA and PCI cards, you accomplish this through configuration software that downloads information to a configuration EEPROM on the card. The typical parameters that must be established for the NIC include the following:

IRQ level (**IRQ5**/10/11/15)

Base I/O port address (**300h**/210h/220h)

Base memory address (**D000h**/C800h)

Typical values used for these parameters in a PC are presented in parentheses, with the typical default values in bold. The address values presented in literature may drop the last zero. You also might have to find alternative settings for one or more of the parameters if those default values are already being used in the system. Record the hardware setting so that there is less chance for mix-ups when setting the corresponding software parameters.

Some network cards do not provide a user-definable base memory address because they do not use system RAM to exchange information between the local and remote units. For those cards that do use a base memory address, it should be apparent that the address given falls within the Upper Memory Blocks used by the EMM386 line of the CONFIG.SYS file. To avoid Upper Memory Block conflicts in a networked system, use the X= switch to modify the EMM386 line so that it excludes the UMB used by the network adapter. (For instance, DEVICE=EMM386.EXE X=C800–CEFFh excludes addresses between C8000h and CEFF0h from being used for anything except the network adapter.)

Resource Sharing

The concept of sharing directories, files, and hardware resources is central to the design of any *network operating system* (NOS). The overriding features that distinguish a NOS system from a DOS system are the sharing and security features of the NOS. These features are typically manifested in *passwords*, *permission levels*, and *access rights* for the system's users.

Initially, MS-DOS made no provision for sharing resources across LANs. The only computer-to-computer communications practiced in the early days of the PC were point-to-point communications between two units. This could be performed through a direct, null-modem connection between the serial ports of the two systems, or through a pair of modems.

In later versions of DOS, however, Microsoft added the the *SHARE.EXE* command to provide file-sharing and -locking capabilities for files on a local hard disk drive. These capabilities enabled multiple users to access the same file at the same time in a networked or multitasking environment. The *SHARE* command had to be loaded in the CONFIG.SYS file using an **INSTALL=** statement (that is, **INSTALL=SHARE /F:4096 /l:25**).

With version 3.11, the Windows operating system added built-in, peer-to-peer networking capabilities to the operating environment and titled it *Windows for Workgroups* (*WfW*).

In a network environment, only shared directories and resources can be accessed across the network. The sharing function is instituted at the remote computer. In Windows, the presence of a hand under the folder or device icon notifies other potential users that this resource or directory has been shared and can be accessed.

To access a shared remote resource, the local operating system must first connect to it. When the connection is established with a remote drive or folder, the local operating system creates a new logical drive on the local machine to handle the shared directory. Normally, the local file management system assigns the directory the next available drive letter in the local system.

The path to the shared resource contains a little more information than the path to a local directory. The remote path must include the remote computer's name and shared resource name (directory or printer). It also must be expressed using the *universal naming convention* (UNC) format. This format begins with a pair of back slashes followed by the computer name and the resource name. Each name in the path is separated by a single backslash. Therefore, the format of a shared path is \\computer name\directory name.

creates logical drive on local machine to handle shared dir

Valid computer names in Windows 9x can be up to 15 characters in length and cannot contain any blank spaces. In Windows 2000 using the TCP/IP protocol, computer names can range up to 63 characters in length and should be made up of the letters A through Z, numbers 0 through 9, and hyphens.

> **TEST TIP**
>
> Know the specifications for setting up computer names in a given operating system.

Networking with Windows 9x

In Windows 9x, the peer-to-peer local area networking function is an integral part of the system. The heart of the Windows 9x networking system is contained in the desktop's *Network Neighborhood* icon and the Control Panel's Network icon.

Network Neighborhood

The Network Neighborhood display, depicted in Figure 10.1, is the primary network user interface for Windows 9x. This screen is used to browse and access shared resources on the LAN, in a method similar to that used with the Windows Explorer for a local hard drive. As a matter of fact, most directory- and file-level activities, such as opening and saving files, can be performed through the Network Neighborhood screen.

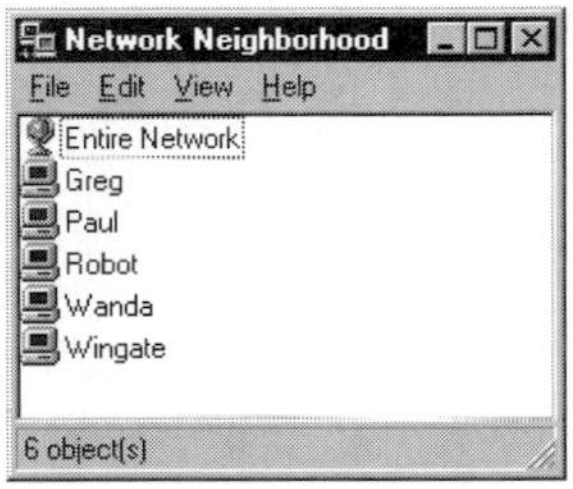

Microsoft networks group logically related computers together in *workgroups* for convenient browsing of resources. The local computer is a part of a workgroup. Double-clicking the Network Neighborhood icon displays the printers and folders available in the workgroup, in either a list or an icon format. As with the Windows Explorer, you can change the format through the View menu options.

If the desired computer does not display, double-click the Entire Network icon. This action produces any other workgroups in the system and displays additional printers and folders that are available.

If the Network Neighborhood window is empty, or if its icon is missing, networking connections have not been established. If this is the case, you must correctly configure networking on the local unit to connect to any other computers on the network. This is done through the Control Panel's Network icon. After you locate the desired computer, double-click its icon (or entry) to view its resources.

FIGURE 10.1
The Network Neighborhood window.

The Network Neighborhood also provides an easy way to connect to and use other network resources. If the local computer is connected to the network, double-click any remote computer in the list to connect to it. This action displays its contents in the neighborhood. In this condition, it is possible to copy files between the local and remote computers.

Mapping a Drive

It is possible for the local system to assign a logical drive letter to the remote unit, or folder. This is referred to as mapping the drive letter to the resource. This mapping allows non-Windows 9x applications running on the local computer to use the resources across the network.

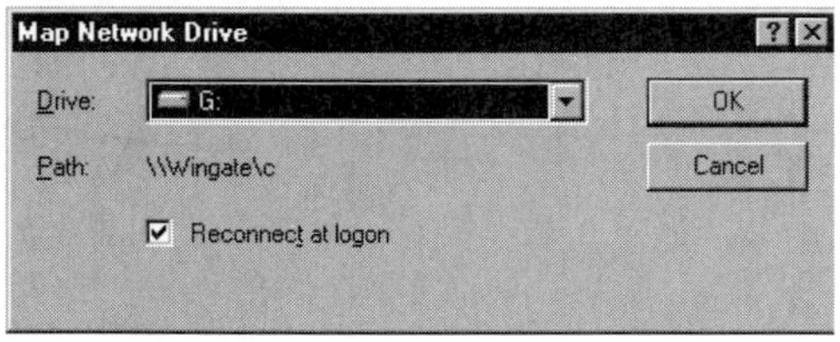

To *map* (assign) a drive letter to a remote network computer, or folder, open the Windows Explorer. From the Tools menu, select the *Map Network Drive* option. The Map Network Drive dialog box displays (see Figure 10.2).

Windows attempts to assign the next available drive letter to the computer or folder indicated in the Path dialog box. Establishing the map to the resource is a simple matter of entering the required path and share name in the dialog box, using the UNC format (\\Path\Remote_Name\Folder_Name).

Windows produces a prompt for a password if the remote unit requires one. You can map a computer or a folder that has been used recently by clicking the down arrow beside the Path window and then choosing the desired resource from the pop-up list.

The Reconnect at Logon option must be selected in the Map Network Drive page for the drive mapping to become a permanent part of the system. If the option is not selected when the user logs off, the mapped drive information disappears and needs to be remapped for any further use. If a red X appears on the icon of a properly mapped drive, this indicates that the drive is no longer available. Its host computer may be turned off, the drive may have been removed, or it may no longer be on the same path. If the drive was mapped to a particular folder and the folder name has been changed, the red X also will appear.

FIGURE 10.2
Map Network Drive dialog box.

> **TEST TIP**
> Know what will cause a mapped drive to disappear from a system when it is shut down and restarted.

The Windows 9x Network Control Panel

The Control Panel's Network screen, shown in Figure 10.3, provides configuration and properties information about the system's networks. The system's installed *network components* are listed under the Network Configuration tab.

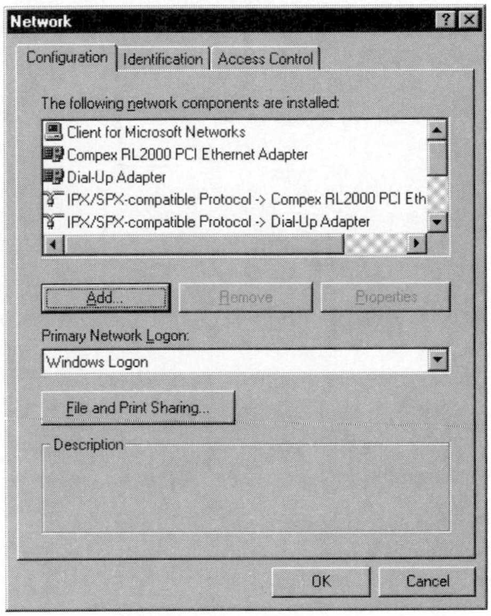

FIGURE 10.3
The Network Control Panel screen.

Double-clicking an installed adapter's driver, or clicking the Properties button when the driver is highlighted, produces its Configuration information page. The Add and Remove buttons on this page are used to install and remove network drivers from the system.

The *Primary Network Logon* window is used to establish which type of network Windows 9x will enter when it starts up. This proves particularly helpful on systems that may be working in multiple network environments (such as a computer that may need to access Microsoft network resources in some situations and Novell network resources at other times).

The *File and Print Sharing* button is used to select the first level of resource sharing for the local unit. Sharing can be individually enabled/disabled for file and printer accesses from remote computers.

The page's Identification tab is used to establish a network identity for the local computer, as illustrated in Figure 10.4. This page establishes the local computer's share name and workgroup association.

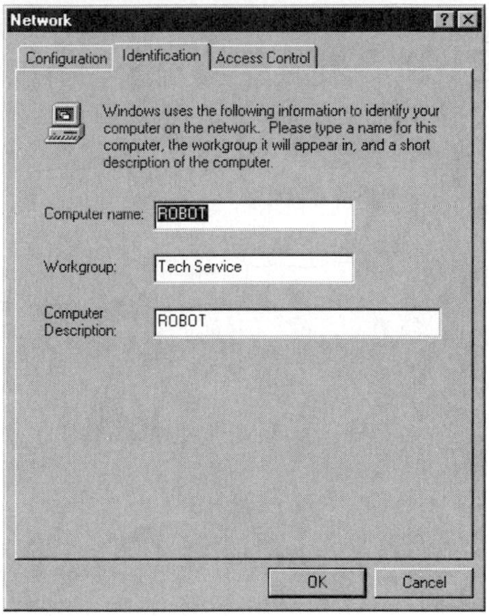

FIGURE 10.4
Network Identification tab.

Similarly, the Access Control tab enables the local user to set the level of access control that is applied to remote accesses. The possible options are similar to those of the Windows 3.11 network: Assign a password requirement for each access, or grant access to selected groups or users.

As mentioned earlier, double-clicking a driver in the Configuration tab opens a series of pages describing its properties. The Resources section of an NE-2000-compatible network adapter's configuration (common in Ethernet installations) is depicted in Figure 10.5.

This page shows the adapter's current system resource allocations (using IRQ5, I/O addresses 280h–29Fh, and memory addresses D8000h–DBFFFh).

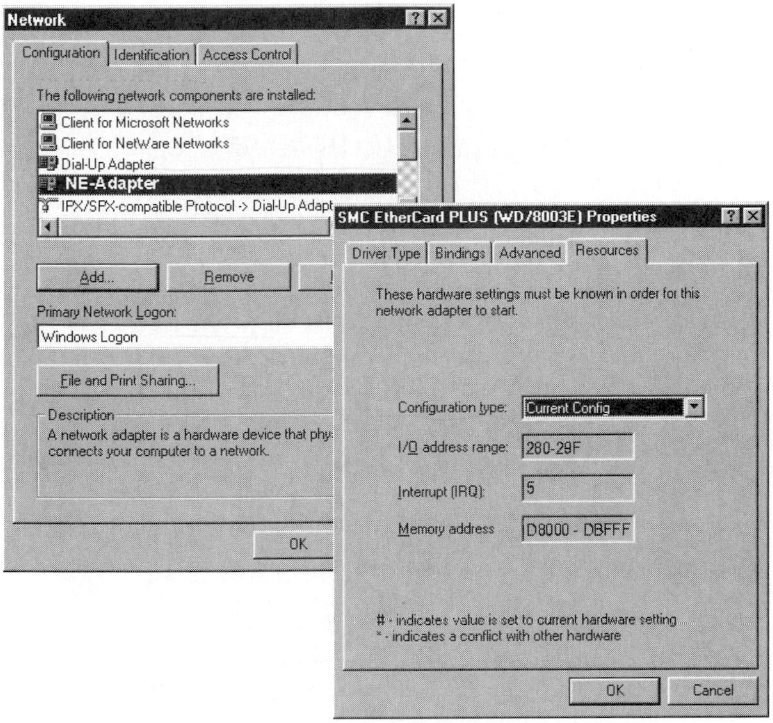

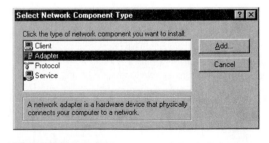

FIGURE 10.5
NE-2000-compatible Resources screen.

Installing Network Components

After the network adapter card has been configured and installed, the next step in setting up the computer on the network is to load its drivers, protocols, and services. In most Windows 9x and Windows 2000 installations, the majority of these steps are accomplished by just rebooting the computer and allowing Windows to detect the network adapter.

The Windows 9x networking utilities should produce an adapter driver, a *Microsoft Client protocol*, and a *Novell NetWare Client protocol* in the Network Configuration window in a typical installation. A default set of file and print sharing services also are loaded.

The only items that must be installed manually are the protocols for the particular type of network in which the computer is being used. Click the Add button in the Network Configuration page to bring up the Select Network Component Type screen shown in Figure 10.6.

FIGURE 10.6
The Select Network Component Type screen.

Networking components include four categories:

◆ **Client.** Software that enables the system to use files and printers shared on other computers

◆ **Adapter**. Drivers that control the physical hardware connected to the network

◆ **Protocol**. Rules that the computers use to govern the exchange of information across the network

◆ **Service**. Utilities that enable resource sharing and provide support services, such as automated backup, remote Registry, and network-monitoring facilities

Each entry contains a list of primary and alternative drivers, protocols, and configuration settings that can be viewed by clicking the title in the window. These alternatives are included because there are many non-Microsoft networks in use, and Windows 9x attempts to support the most common ones.

If a particular network type is not supported in the standard listings, the Components page features a Have Disk button that permit the system to upload Windows-compatible drivers and protocols.

Because the boot-up detection process loads the adapter driver, two types of clients to choose from, and a set of sharing parameters, most installation procedures require only that the appropriate protocols be loaded for the network type. In a Microsoft network application, these usually include the *NetBEUI* and *IPX/SPX* protocols for the LAN. An additional *TCP/IP* protocol can be added for Internet support.

In a Windows network, the set of rules that govern the exchange of data between computers is the *NetBIOS Extended User Interface* (NetBEUI) protocol. This protocol works in most purely Windows networks, so another protocol is rarely called for. If an additional protocol is required, choose the Add Protocol option in the Network Components dialog box to add another protocol. Network adapters can typically handle up to four different protocols. The key to protocol selection is that the devices on the network must use the same protocol to be able to talk with each other.

Although NetBEUI is easy to implement, it is a non-routable proto-col. Because NetBEUI uses broadcast techniques to find other nodes on the network, it has no inherent capabilities to access nodes out-side of the immediate physical network segment. Therefore, it is not used in wide area networking applications. However, NetBEUI is required to support dial-up Remote Access Services (RAS) through a modem. The RAS service uses the NetBEUI protocol to navigate through a network after you have dialed in to it. Both the calling client and the receiving server in the LAN must be running NetBEUI. If either computer does not have this protocol active, the client will be able to connect with the LAN, but will not be able to navigate through it.

IPX/SPX is a Novell network protocol for LANs, and TCP/IP is the Internet protocol supported by Windows 9x and *Windows NT*/2000.

> **TEST TIP**
>
> Be aware that NetBEUI is required to navi-gate a dial-up connection to a local area network.

without BEUI, can contact LAN But not able to Navigate though it

Network Printing with Windows 9x

Network printing in Windows 9x is a matter of creating and linking an icon on the local unit with a shared physical device attached to a remote computer.

The standard way to install a printer in Windows 9x is to activate the Add Printer Wizard through the Printers folder. This folder pro-vides a central location for adding and managing printer operations. The Printers folder can be accessed from the following:

◆ Start/Settings/Printers

◆ My Computer/Printers

◆ Control Panel/Printers

To install a network printer on the local computer, access the local Printers folder and double-click the Add Printer option. This action starts the Windows 9x Add Printer Wizard depicted in Figure 10.7. This wizard asks a number of questions about how the printer will be used. Because you are installing a remote network printer, you need to supply the complete path to the printer, or browse for the network to find its location.

You also can use the Network Neighborhood icon to browse the network until you locate the desired computer. Then double-click it so that its designated printer displays. A hand under the icon indicates a shared printer.

You also can install the desired remote printer by clicking and dragging its icon to the local Printers window and then dropping it anywhere inside the window.

FIGURE 10.7
The Add Printer Wizard.

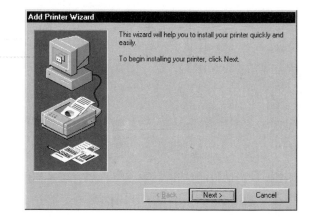

The Add Printer Wizard performs three basic tasks in setting up the local unit to use the remote printer. First, it establishes the printing path for DOS-based applications. Because these programs do not handle UNC-based paths, a logical *port name*, such as LPT2, must be established for them.

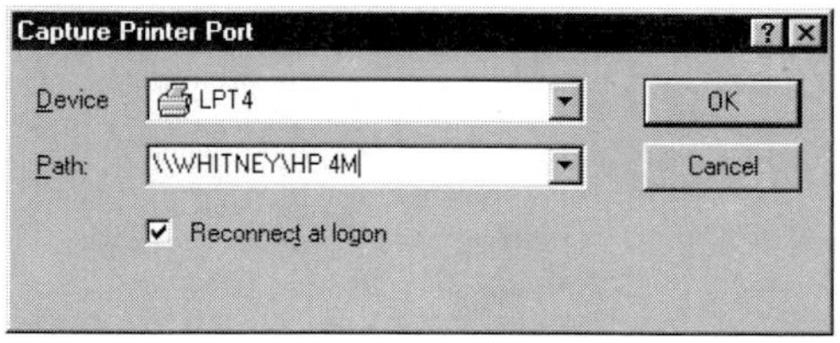

FIGURE 10.8
The Capture Printer Port dialog box.

If the Yes option is selected, Windows captures a local port for those applications to use. Clicking the Capture Printer Port button produces the Capture Printer Port dialog box depicted in Figure 10.8. This is a logical port designation and does not need to actually be installed in the system. As a matter of fact, any actual port in the local unit that has been assigned that handle will be disabled.

The next step in setting up the remote printer is to assign it a unique printer name. In a network environment, this name should have some relevance to what type of printer it is, or what relationship it has to the local unit.

The final step in setting up the printer is to configure its icon properties as if it were a local printer. Right-click the printer icon and select Properties. Enter all the information required to bring the printer to operation.

Networking with Windows 2000

During the Windows 2000 setup process, the system must be configured to function as a workgroup node, or as part of a domain. A workgroup is a collection of networked computers assigned the same workgroup name. Any user can become a member of a workgroup by specifying the particular workgroup's name during the setup process.

Conversely, a domain is a collection of networked computers established and controlled by a network administrator. As mentioned in Chapter 7, "1.0 Operating System Fundamentals," domains are established for security and administration purposes.

The Setup routine requires that a computer account be established before a computer can be included in the domain. This account is not the same as the user accounts that the system uses to identify individual users.

If the system has been upgraded from an existing Windows NT version, Windows 2000 adopts the current computer account information. If the installation is new, the Setup utility requests that a new computer account be established. This account is normally assigned by the network administrator prior to running Setup. Joining the domain during setup requires a username and password.

My Network Places

In the Windows 2000 system, the Network Neighborhood folder has been replaced with a more powerful *My Network Places* folder, depicted in Figure 10.9. The new folder includes new Recently Visited Places and Computers Near Me views. The Add Network Places options enable you to more easily establish connections to other servers on the network. The user can establish shortcuts to virtually every server on the network.

FIGURE 10.9
My Network Places.

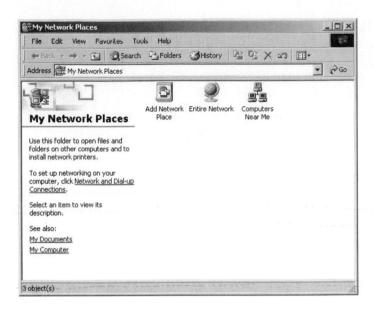

Mapping a Drive

As illustrated in Chapter 8, a drive map is an important tool in a network environment. It allows a single computer to act as though it possesses all the hard drives that reside in the network. The Network File Service (NFS) portion of the operating system coordinates the systems so that drives located on other physical machines show up as logical drives on the local machine. This shows up in the Windows Explorer and My Computer screens, as illustrated in Figure 10.10. It also makes the additional drives available through the command-line prompt.

FIGURE 10.10
A mapped drive display.

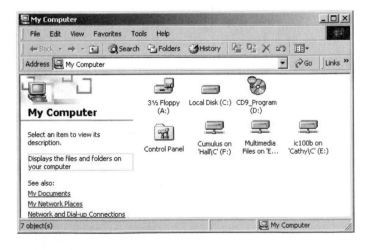

The primary reason to map a drive in a network environment is because some applications cannot recognize volume names. They can see only drive letters. In Windows, the number of recognizable drive letters is 26 (A–Z). Some network operating systems can recognize an extended number of drive letters (for example, A–Z and AA–ZZ). By using unique volume names to identify drives, however, the system is capable of recognizing a vast number of network drives.

For a local system to access a remote resource, the resource must be shared, and the local user must have a valid network user ID and password. The user's assigned rights and permissions are tied to his or her password throughout the network, either through individual settings or through group settings.

The Windows 2000 Network Control Panel

The Network icon under the Windows 2000 Control Panel provides access to the Network and Dial-Up Connections window depicted in Figure 10.11. This window provides several key functions associated with local and wide area networking. It is used to install new network adapter cards and change their settings, change network component settings, and to install TCP/IP. → internet protocols

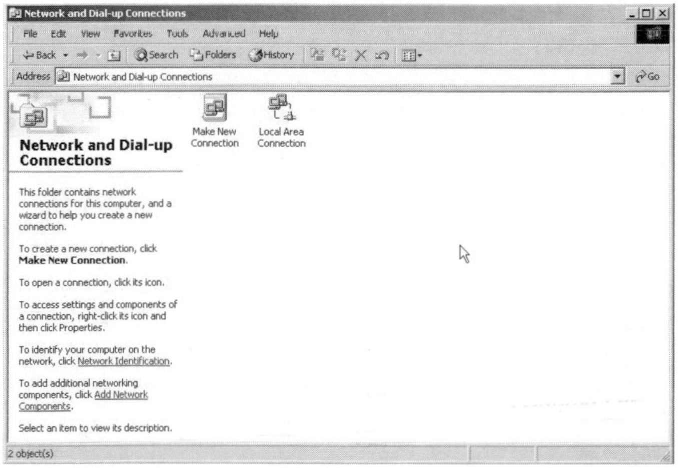

FIGURE 10.11
The Network and Dial-Up Connections window.

The organization of the Windows 2000 Network Control Panel differs somewhat from the one in Windows 9x. The Windows 2000 version features five tabs.

The functions associated with the Windows 2000 Local Area Connections Properties (see figure 10.12) include the following:

◆ **Services.** Used to add, remove, or configure network services such as DNS, WINS, and DHCP functions.

◆ **Protocols.** Used to add, remove, or configure network protocols for specific types of network environments.

◆ **Adapters.** Used to add, remove, or configure NIC cards for operation with the system. This includes loading drivers and assigning system resources to the adapter.

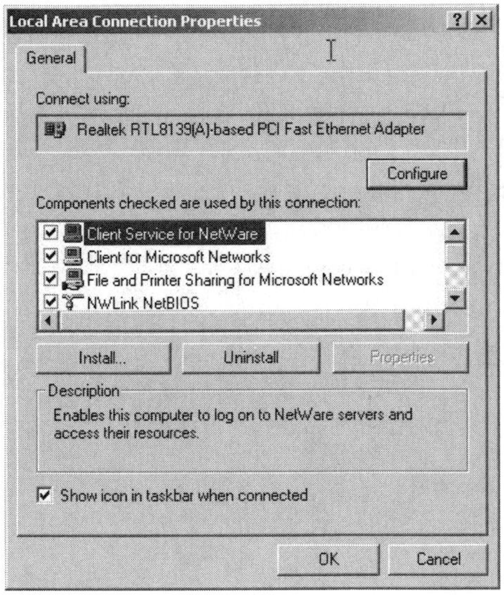

FIGURE 10.12

Windows 2000 Local Area Connections dialog box.

To configure any of these functions for a given component, access the Local Area Connection Properties page, highlight the desired component, and click the Install button. Other functions affecting the Networking and Dial-Up connections in Windows 2000 include the following:

◆ **Network Identification.** Specifies the computer name and the workgroup or domain name to which it belongs. This option is located under the System icon in the Control Panel.

◆ **Bindings.** Sets a potential pathway between a given network service, a network protocol, and a given network adapter. The order of the bindings can affect the efficiency of the system's networking operations. To establish bindings, access the Network and Dial-Up Connections page and click the Advanced entry on its drop-down menu bar. Then select the Advanced Settings option from the menu.

Although the organization of the Network Control Panel is different in Windows 2000, the sequence of events involved in installing network components is identical to that used in the Windows 9x environment.

Network Printing with Windows 2000

As with the Windows 9x operating systems, Windows NT 4 and Windows 2000 provide installation wizards to guide the network printer installation.

If the physical printer is connected to a remote computer, referred to as a print server, the remote unit must supply the printer drivers and settings to control the printer. Likewise, the print server must be set up to share the printer with the other users on the network.

To install the network printer, access the My Network Places icon on the desktop, navigate the network to locate and open the remote computer's network name, right-click the remote unit's printer name, select the Connect option from the pop-up menu, and follow the directions provided by the Windows Add Printer Wizard. When the wizard produces a dialog box asking whether to install the selected printer, click the OK button. The Add Printer Wizard driver selection dialog box appears, as depicted in Figure 10.13. After the remote printer is installed, the local computer can access it through the My Network Places icon.

Windows 2000 includes a printing feature called *Autopublish* (or Point and Print). This feature enables the user to install a printer driver on a client PC from any application. The Active Directory also enables the user to browse the network for a specific printer type or location.

FIGURE 10.13

Installing a network printer in Windows 2000.

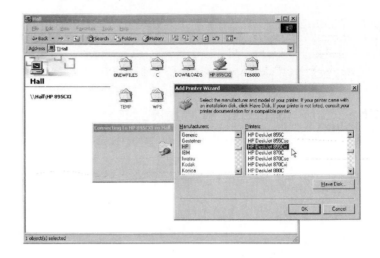

Internet print / works like fax machin

Windows 2000 features Internet printing capabilities. This function enables the user to print to a remotely located printer using the Internet as the network. Microsoft designed this feature to compete with document faxing. Instead of faxing a document to a remote fax machine, just print it out on a printer at that location. Any standard printer can be used for this operation, as long as it is being hosted by a Windows 2000 Server.

The File/Print window, depicted in Figure 10.14, includes a Find Printer button that you can use to search for printers locally, connected to the LAN, or connected across the Internet. After a printer is located, Windows 2000 automatically installs the driver for that printer on the client PC.

FIGURE 10.14

The Windows 2000 File/Print window.

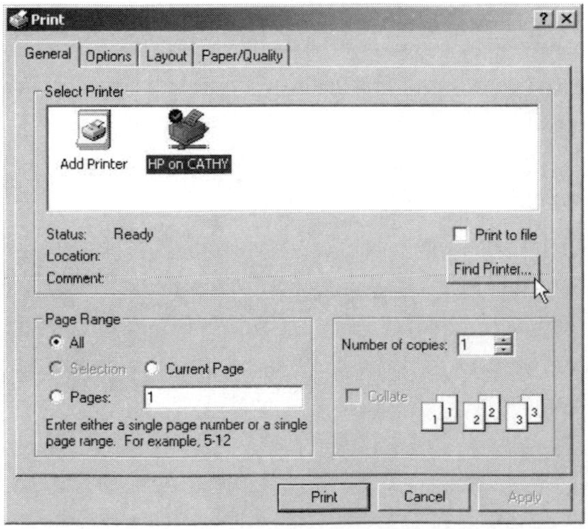

Windows 2000 includes a library of more than 2,500 printer drivers. If the local unit is not set up for the type of printer selected, it is possible to add these files and initiate the print job without leaving the Print dialog box.

Sharing Printers in Windows 2000

Shared printers, also referred to as networked printers, receive data from computers throughout the network and direct it to a local printer. As in other networks, these printers must be selected as shared printers in the Windows 2000 environment in order for remote computers to be able to access them.

To share a printer under Windows 2000, select the Printers option from the Start/Settings path. Alternate-click the printer to be shared and select the *Sharing* option. This action produces the Sharing tab depicted in Figure 10.15. From this page, click the *Shared As* option, enter a share name for the printer, and click the OK button to complete the sharing process. Unlike the Windows 9x systems, you must have administrative rights to make these changes in Windows 2000.

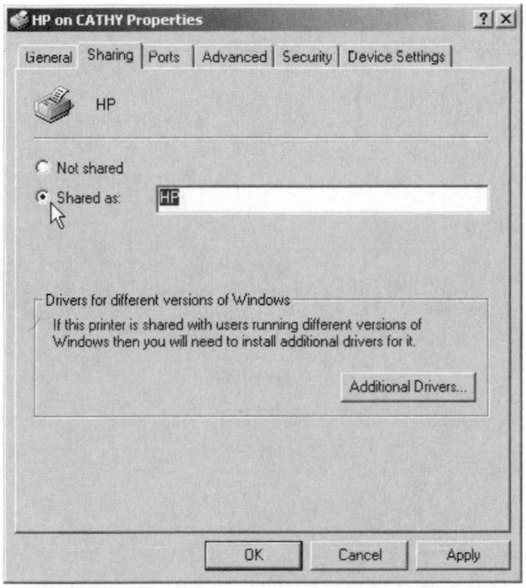

FIGURE 10.15
Sharing a printer in Windows 2000.

To connect to a printer on the network, select the Printers option from the Start/Settings path and double-click the Add Printer icon. The Welcome to the Add Printer Wizard page displays. Click the Next button to move forward in the connection process. In the

Local or Network Printer page, select the Network Printer option, click the Next button, and then enter the network printer name. Use the UNC format to specify the path to the printer being connected to (that is, \\computer_name\share_name). If the printer's name is not known, click the Type the Printer Name option or click the Next to Browse for a Printer option.

To link up with a printer over the Internet (or the company intranet), select the Connect to Printer on the Internet or on Your Intranet option and enter the URL address of the printer. The URL must be expressed in standard HTTP addressing format (that is, http://*servername/ printer/*). The connection wizard guides the connection from this point.

Troubleshooting Local Area Networking Problems

Figure 10.16 depicts the system components associated with LAN troubleshooting. Generally, the order of isolating LAN problems is as follows:

1. Check the local networking software.

2. Check the cabling and connectors.

3. Check the NIC adapter.

FIGURE 10.16
LAN hardware components.

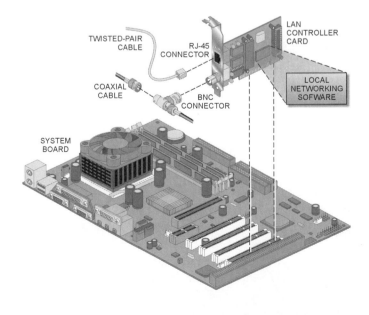

The order of checking is based on convenience and speed of isolating problems. The configuration checks performed on the operating system do not require that any hardware be disassembled. Likewise, cables and connectors are easier and faster to check than internal hardware.

Most network adapter cards come from the manufacturer with a disk, or CD-ROM, of drivers and diagnostic utilities for that particular card. You can run these diagnostic utilities to verify that the LAN hardware is functioning properly. However, it may be easier to run the Windows PING utility from the command prompt and attempt to connect to the network. In a LAN environment, you need to know the IP address or the name of a computer in the network to which you can direct the PING.

Cabling is one of the biggest problems encountered in a network installation. Is it connected? Are all the connections good? Is the cable type correct? Has there been any termination, and if so, has it been done correctly? The most efficient way to test network cable is to use a *line tester* to check its functionality.

With UTP cabling, just unplug the cable from the adapter card and plug it into the tester. If coaxial cable is used, you must unplug both ends of the cable from the network, install a terminating resistor at one end of the cable, and plug the other end into the tester. The tester performs the tests required to analyze the cable and connection.

Troubleshooting Windows 9x Networking Problems

There are several possible reasons why users cannot log on to a network in Windows 9x. Some of these reasons are hardware related. Running the Add New Hardware Wizard and allowing it to detect the network hardware should point out these types of problems. However, also click the Network icon in the Control Panel to review the NIC settings. Use the Advanced tab under the Properties window to confirm that the Transceiver Type value is correct for the type of physical network being used. Also, check under the Resources tab to confirm the adapter card's settings. Use the *Detected Config* option, illustrated in Figure 10.17, if the NIC settings are unknown.

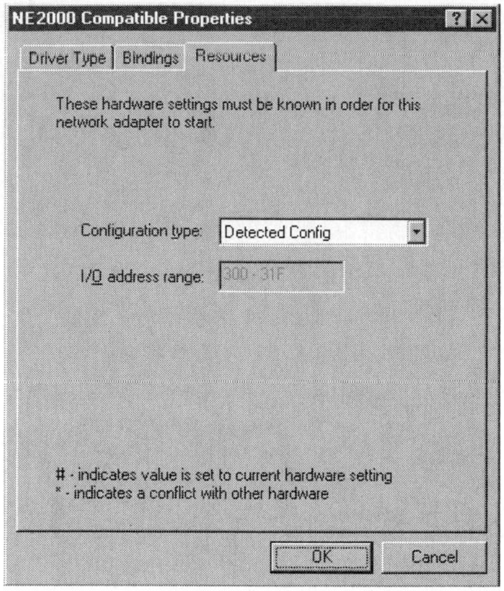

FIGURE 10.17
The Detected Config option.

If the network adapter card is installed in the system and the cabling is connected correctly, the operating system's network support must be checked. The most obvious items to check are those found in the Properties pages of the Network Neighborhood window. Possible reasons for not being able to log on to the network include the following:

- ◆ Incorrect services settings (Configuration page)
- ◆ Incorrect protocol settings (Configuration page)
- ◆ Incorrect adapter settings (Configuration page)
- ◆ Incorrect Primary Network Logon settings (Configuration page)
- ◆ Missing computer name (Identification page)
- ◆ Missing workgroup name (Identification page)

Right-click the Network Neighborhood icon and select the Properties option from the pop-up list. The information that could prevent network logon is found under the Configuration and Identification tabs. Review each setting for correctness and reload if necessary.

In Windows 9x, begin by checking the system for resource conflicts that might involve the network adapter card. You can obtain this information by accessing the Control Panel's Device Manager. If a conflict exists, an exclamation point (!) should appear beside the network adapter card in the listing. If Windows thinks the card is working properly, the Device Manager displays a normal listing.

If a conflict is detected, move into the network adapter's Properties page, depicted in Figure 10.18, and check the adapter's resources against those indicated by the card's diagnostic utility. The conflict must be resolved between the network adapter and whatever device is using its resources.

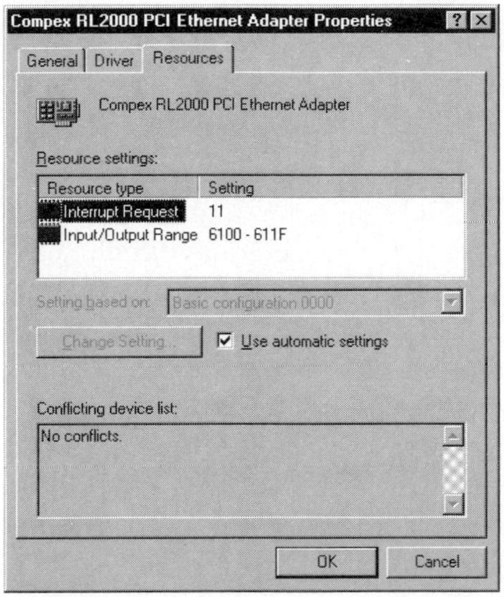

FIGURE 10.18
Network Adapter Properties page.

If the adapter resources are okay, the next step depends on the type of symptom being encountered:

◆ Can any units be seen on the network?

◆ Can other units be seen but not used? If the network cannot be seen in the Network Neighborhood, or the network cannot be browsed from this utility, the network protocols and drivers should be checked.

Network adapters and protocols are checked through the Control Panel's Network icon. Check the protocols listed in the Configuration tab's Installed Components window. Compare these to those listed on working units in the workgroup. Each machine must have all the clients and protocols other machines are using; otherwise, it will not be possible to browse the network. The local computer and the Entire Network icon should be present, but the other units will not be visible.

Other reasons for not being able to browse the network include the Primary Network Logon setting is incorrect for the type of network being used, and the local computer is not listed in the correct workgroup under the Identification tab.

If you can browse the network but cannot use certain resources in other locations, sharing is not turned on in the remote unit, or the local unit does not have proper access rights to that resource.

To use the remote resource across the network, the system's File and Print functions must be turned on, and its Share function must be enabled. Turning on the File and Print functions place the local resources in the network's Browse listing. However, this does not enable the Share function. The Share function is established by supplying the system with a valid share name. In addition, the computer must be running Client for Microsoft Networks for File and Print to be available on a Microsoft network. If this client service is not installed, the File and Print functions are unavailable for use (grayed out). The Client for Microsoft Networks services component must be installed in the Select Network Component Type screen.

Troubleshooting Windows 2000 Networking Problems

In most respects, the process for troubleshooting Windows 2000 LAN problems are the same as those described for the Windows 9x system. In a client/server system such as a Windows 2000 system, however, the computer professional's main responsibility is to get the local station to boot up to the network's *login prompt.* At this point, the network administrator, or network engineer, becomes responsible for directing the troubleshooting process.

Some typical networking problems can occur during normal Windows 2000 operations, including the following:

◆ The user cannot see any other computers on the local network.

◆ The user cannot see other computers on different networks.

◆ The clients cannot see the DHCP server, but do have an IP address.

◆ The clients cannot obtain an IP address from a DHCP server that is on the other side of a router.

If a client cannot see any other computers on the network, improper IP addressing may be occurring. This is one of the most common problems associated with TCP/IP. Users must have a valid IP address and subnet to communicate with other computers. If the IP address is incorrect, invalid, or conflicting with another computer in the network, you will be able to see your local computer, but will not be able to see others on the network.

One reason for an incorrect IP address problem would be that the local system in a TCP/IP network is looking for a DHCP Server that is present. In some LANs, a special server called a DHCP Server is used to dynamically assign IP addresses to its clients in the network. In large networks, each segment of the network would require its own DHCP Server to assign IP addresses for that segment. If the DHCP Server were missing, or not functioning, none of the clients in that segment would be able to see the network.

Likewise, if a DHCP client computer were installed in a network segment that did not use DHCP, it would need to be reconfigured manually with a static IP address. The DHCP settings are administered through the TCP/IP Properties' window. This window is located under the Start/Settings/Networking and Dial-Up Connections option. From this point, open the desired Local Area or Dial-Up Connection and click the Properties button. DHCP operations are covered in more detail later in this chapter.

[handwritten margin notes: IPConfig /All; Ping => sent test packets; physical layer => chek to see computer is physically connected; if proplem is routing check NET View to check/ remote computer it display available shares]

Begin the troubleshooting process for this type of problem by checking the TCP/IP Properties under the Network icon. Next, check the current TCP/IP settings using the command line **IPCONFIG/ALL** (or the **WINIPCFG**) utility. They will display the current IP settings and offer a starting point for troubleshooting. Afterward, use the **PING** utility to send test packets to other local computers you find. The results of this action indicate whether the network is working.

As mentioned earlier, another area that can cause connectivity problems is the physical layer. Check to see that the computer is physically connected to the network and that the status light is glowing (normally green). The presence of the light indicates whether the NIC sees any network traffic.

If users can see other local computers in a TCP/IP network, but cannot see remote systems on other networks, the problem may be routing. Check to see that the address for the default gateway listed in the TCP/IP properties is valid. Use the **NET VIEW** command to see whether the remote computer is available. If the user is relying on the My Network Places feature to see other computers, a delay in updating the Browse list may cause remote systems to not be listed. The **NET VIEW** command directly communicates with the remote systems and displays available shares.

If the clients have an IP address of 169.254.xxx.xxx, it is because they cannot communicate with the DHCP server. Windows 2000 automatically assigns the computer an IP address in the 169.254 range if it cannot be assigned one from a DHCP server. Check the previously discussed procedures to determine what the problem may be.

Many *routers* do not pass the broadcast traffic generated by DHCP clients. If clients cannot obtain an IP address from a DHCP server that is on the other side of a router, the network administrator must enable the forwarding of DHCP packets, or place a DHCP server on each side of a router.

Networking with Novell NetWare

In a client/server system, such as a *Novell NetWare* or Windows NT/2000 system, the technician's main responsibility is to get the local station to boot up to the network's login prompt. At this point, the network administrator, or network engineer, becomes responsible for directing the troubleshooting process.

In a Novell system, check the root directory of the workstation for the NETBIOS and IPX.COM files. Check the AUTOEXEC.BAT file on the local drive for command lines to run the NETBIOS, load the IPX file, and load the ODI (or NETx) files.

The NETBIOS file is an emulation of IBM's *Network Basic Input/Output System* (NetBIOS), and represents the basic interface between the operating system and the LAN hardware. This function is implemented through ROM ICs, located on the network card. The *Internetworking Packet Exchange* (IPX) file passes commands across the network to the file server. The NETBIOS and IPX protocols must be bound together to navigate the Novell network from a computer using a Windows operating system. This is accomplished by enabling the NETBIOS bindings in the IPX protocol Properties in the Network Properties window.

The *Open Datalink Interface* (ODI) file is the network shell that communicates between the adapter and the system's applications. Older versions of NetWare used a shell program called NETx. These files should be referenced in the AUTOEXEC.BAT or NET.BAT files.

> **TEST TIP**
>
> Be aware of the elements required to navigate through a Novell network from a computer running a Microsoft operating system.

INTERNET CONCEPTS

▶ 4.2 Identify concepts and capabilities relating to the Internet and basic procedures for setting up a system for Internet access.

The A+ Operating System Technologies objective 4.2 states that the test taker should be able to "identify concepts and capabilities relating to the Internet and basic procedures for setting up a system for Internet access."

The tremendous popularity of the Internet, and its heavy concentration on PC platforms, requires that the PC technician understand how the Internet is organized and how the PC relates to it. The successful technician must be able to establish and maintain Internet connections for customers, using the major operating systems and *dial-up networking* software. The remainder of this chapter focuses on wide area networking and Internet concepts.

WIDE AREA NETWORKS

The fastest-growing segment of the personal computer world is in the area of wide area networks (WANs).

A typical WAN is a local city- or countywide network, like the one in Figure 10.19. This network links network members together through a *bulletin board service* (BBS). Users can access the bulletin board's server with a simple telephone call.

FIGURE 10.19
Countywide network.

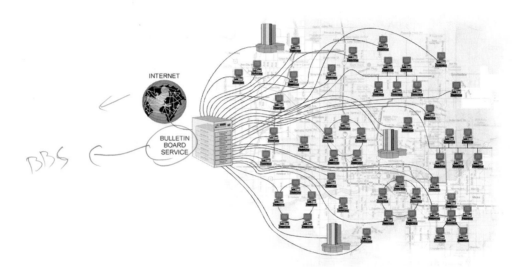

BBS

WANs are connected by several different types of communication systems. These communication paths are referred to as *links*. Most users connect to the network via standard telephone lines, using dial-up modems. *Dial-up connections* are generally the slowest way to connect to a network, but they are inexpensive to establish and use.

Dial-Up

Other users, who require quicker data transfers, contract with the telephone company to use special, high-speed *Integrated Service Digital Network* (ISDN) lines. These types of links require a *digital modem* to conduct data transfers. Because the modem is digital, no analog conversion is required.

– Integrated service Digital Network

ISDN

Users who require very high volumes will lease dedicated *T1 and T3 lines* from the telephone company. These applications generally serve businesses that put several of their computers or networks online.

– T1, T3 lines

[handwritten: Fiber optic satellite up, down link UHF microwave transmission sys]

After the information is transmitted, it can be carried over many types of communications links on its way to its destination. These interconnecting links can include fiber-optic cables, satellite up and down links, UHF, and microwave transmission systems. Figure 10.20 illustrates different ways to access WANs.

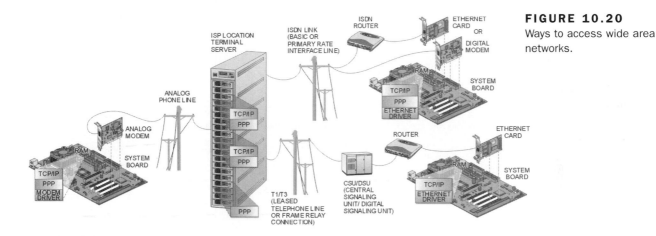

FIGURE 10.20
Ways to access wide area networks.

In some areas, high-speed intermediate-sized networks, referred to as *metropolitan area networks* (MANs), are popping up. These networks typically cover areas up to 30 miles (50 kilometers) in diameter and are operated to provide access to regional resources. They are like LANs in speed and operation, but use special high-speed connections and protocols to increase the geographic span of the network, like a WAN.

The Internet   *[handwritten: → is WAN]*

The most famous WAN is the Internet. The Internet is actually a network of networks, working together. The main communication path for the Internet is a series of networks, established by the U.S. government, to link supercomputers together at key research sites.

This pathway is referred to as the *backbone*, and is affiliated with the *National Science Foundation* (NSF). Since the original backbone was established, the Internet has expanded around the world and now offers access to computer users in every part of the globe.

TCP/IP

The language of the Internet *is Transport Control Protocol/Internet Protocol* (TCP/IP). No matter what type of computer platform or software is being used, the information must move across the Internet in this format. This protocol calls for data to be grouped together, in bundles, called *network packets.*

The U.S. Department of Defense originally developed the TCP/IP protocol as a hacker-resistant, secure protocol for transmitting data on a network. It is considered to be one of the most secure of the network protocols. Because it was developed by the U.S. government, no one actually owns the TCP/IP protocol. It was adopted as the transmission standard for the Internet.

The TCP/IP packet is designed primarily to permit message fragmentation and reassembly. It exists through two header fields: the IP header and the TCP header, followed by the data field, as illustrated in Figure 10.21.

FIGURE 10.21
TCP/IP packet.

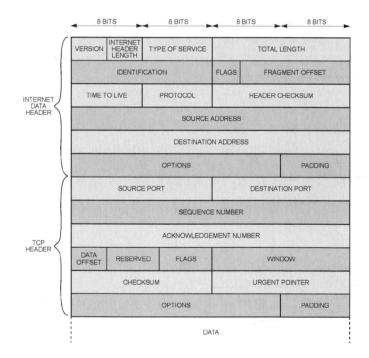

The TCP/IP protocol was so widely accepted by the Internet community that virtually every network operating system supports it, including Apple, MS-DOS/Windows, UNIX, Linux, OS/2, and even networked printers. It also can be used on any topology (for instance, Ethernet and Token Ring). Therefore, all these computer types can exchange data across a network using the TCP/IP protocol.

In the Windows operating systems, the TCP/IP settings are established through the Start/Settings/Control Panel/Network/TCP-IP Adapter/Properties. In this location, you can click the IP Address tab to establish the method of obtaining an IP address (for instance, automatically from a DHCP Server, or manually, by specifying a static IP address). If you choose the option to Specify an IP Address, you need to enter the IP address and subnet mask settings.

Internet Service Providers

Connecting all the users and individual networks together are *Internet service providers* (ISPs). ISPs are companies that provide the technical gateway to the Internet. These companies own blocks of access addresses that they assign to their customers, to give the customer an identity on the network. Service that most ISPs deliver to their customers include the following:

- ◆ Internet identity through IP addresses
- ◆ Email services through POP3 and SMTP servers
- ◆ Internet news service through Usenet archive servers
- ◆ Internet routing through DNS servers

All these services are described in greater detail later in this chapter.

IP Addresses

The blocks of Internet access addresses that ISPs provide to their customers are called the *Internet Protocol addresses*, or *IP addresses*. The IP address makes each site a valid member of the Internet. This is how individual users are identified to receive file transfers, email, and file requests.

TEST TIP

Know what TCP/IP is and what it does.

TEST TIP

Know the advantages of using the TCP/IP protocol.

TEST TIP

Be able to describe the pathway that should be used to manually establish IP address and subnet mask settings.

TEST TIP

Be aware of common services that ISPs provide their Internet customers.

IP addresses exist in the numeric format of xxx.yyy.zzz.aaa. Each address consists of four 8-bit fields (*octets*) separated by dots (.). This format of specifying addresses is referred to as *dotted-decimal notation*. The decimal numbers are derived from the binary address that the hardware understands. For example, a binary network address of

10000111.10001011.01001001.00110110 (binary)

corresponds to

135.139.073.054 (decimal)

Each IP address consists of two parts: the network address and the host address. The network address identifies the entire network; the host address identifies an intelligent member within the network (router, a server, or a workstation).

Three classes of standard IP addresses are supported for LANs: Class A, Class B, and Class C. These addresses occur in four-octet fields like the example.

NOTE

Where's 127?   The 127.x.x.x address range is a special block of addresses reserved for testing network systems. The U.S. government owns some of these addresses for testing the Internet backbone. The 127.0.0.1 address is reserved for testing the bus on the local system.

◆ **Class A addresses** are reserved for large networks and use the last 24 bits (the last three octets, or fields, of the address) of the address for the host address. The first octet always begins with a 0, followed by a 7-bit number. Therefore, valid Class A addresses range between 001.x.x.x and 126.x.x.x. This allows a Class A network to support 126 different networks with nearly 17 million hosts (nodes) per network.

◆ **Class B addresses** are assigned to medium-sized networks. The first two octets can range between 128.x.x.x and 191.254.0.0. The last two octets contain the host addresses. This enables Class B networks to include up to 16,384 different networks with approximately 65,534 hosts per network.

◆ **Class C addresses** are normally used with smaller LANs. In a Class C address, only the last octet is used for host addresses. The first three octets can range between 192.x.x.x and 223.254.254.0. Therefore, the Class C address can support approximately 2 million networks with 254 hosts each.

Within this context, sections of the network can be grouped together into subnets that share a range of IP addresses. These groups are referred to as *intranets*. (Actually, a true intranet requires that the segment have a protective *gateway* to act as an entry and exit point for the segment.) In most cases, the gateway is a device called a *router*. A router is an intelligent device that receives data and directs it toward a designated IP address.

Some networks employ a firewall as a gateway to the outside. A firewall is a combination of hardware and software components that provide a protective barrier between networks with different security levels. The firewall is configured by an administrator to pass only data to and from designated IP addresses and TCP/IP ports.

One reason for creating subnets is to isolate one segment of the network from all the others. Suppose, for example, that a large organization has 1,000 computers, all of which are connected to the network. Without segmentation, data from all 1,000 units would run through every other network node. The effect of this would be that everyone else in the network would have access to all the data on the network, and the operation of the network would be slowed considerably by the uncontrolled traffic.

Another reason to use subnets is to efficiently use IP addresses. Because the IP addressing scheme is defined as a 32-bit code, there are only a certain number of possible addresses. Although 126 networks with 17 million customers may seem like a lot, in the scheme of a worldwide network system, that's not a lot of addresses to go around. In this worldwide context, IP addresses are purchased from a governing body (the Network Information Center, or NIC). Therefore, there are only so many to go around. There are no more Class A addresses to be obtained. They have all been accounted for. Likewise, Class B and Class C addresses are becoming scarce due to the popularity of the Internet.

A third reason for subnetting is to utilize a single IP address across physically divided locations, such as remotely located areas of a campus. By subnetting a Class C address, half of the 253 possible addresses can be allocated to one campus location, and the other half can be allocated to hosts at the second location. In this manner, both locations can operate using a single Class C address.

Suppose, for example, that a school has two physically separated campuses and that they have purchased a single Class C address. If one campus has 60 hosts and the other has 100 hosts, you need to divide the Class C's 256 possible addresses between the campuses (by subnetting them), or purchase another Class C address for the second campus. In the process, 156 addresses are wasted at each location.

Subnets are created by masking off (hiding) the network address portion of the IP address on the units within the subnet. This, in effect, limits the mobility of the data to those nodes within the subnet, because they can reconcile only addresses from within their masked range.

Internet Domains

The IP addresses of all the computers attached to the Internet are tracked using a listing system called the *Domain Name System* (DNS). This system evolved as a way to organize the members of the Internet into a hierarchical management structure.

The DNS structure consists of various levels of computer groups called *domains*. Each computer on the Internet is assigned a domain name, such as mic-inc.com. The mic-inc is the user-friendly domain name assigned to the Marcraft site.

In the example, the .com notation at the end of the address is a top-level domain that defines the type of organization, or country of origin associated with the address. In this case, the .com designation identifies the user as a commercial site. The following list identifies the Internet's top-level domain codes:

* .com = Commercial businesses
* .edu = Educational institutions
* .gov = Government agencies
* .int = International organizations
* .mil = Military establishments
* .net = Networking organizations
* .org = Nonprofit organizations

Fully qualified domain name)

On the Internet, domain names are specified in terms of their fully qualified domain names (FQDNs). An FQDN is a human-readable address that describes the location of the site on the Internet. It contains the host name, the domain name, and the top-level domain name. For example, the name www.oneworld.owt.com is an FQDN.

The letters www represent the *host name.* The host name specifies the name of the computer that provides services and handles requests for specific Internet addresses. In this case, the host is the World Wide Web. Other types of hosts include FTP and HTTP sites.

The .owt extension indicates that the organization is a domain listed under the top level domain heading. Likewise, the .oneworld entry is a subdomain of the .owt domain. It is likely one of multiple networks supported by the .owt domain.

At each domain level, the members of the domain are responsible for tracking the addresses of the domains on the next-lower level. The lower domain is then responsible for tracking the addresses of domains, or end users, on the next level below it.

In addition to its domain name tracking function, the DNS system resolves (links) individual domain names of computers to their current IP address listings. Some IP addresses are permanently assigned to a particular domain name so that whenever the domain name is issued on the Internet it always accesses the same IP address. This is referred to as *static IP addressing.* However, most ISPs use a *dynamic IP addressing* scheme for allocating IP addresses.

If an ISP wants to service 10,000 customers within its service area, using static IP addressing, it needs to purchase and maintain 10,000 IP addresses. Because most Internet customers are not online all the time, however, their IPs are not always in use. Therefore, the ISP can purchase a reasonable number of IP addresses that it can hold in a bank and dynamically assign to its users as they log on to their service. When the user logs off, the IP address returns to the bank for other users.

The Internet software communicates with the service provider by embedding the TCP/IP information in a *Point-to-Point Protocol* (PPP) shell for transmission through the modem in analog format. The communications equipment, at the service provider's site, converts the signal back to the digital TCP/IP format. Older units running *UNIX* used a connection protocol called *Serial Line Internet Protocol* (SLIP) for dial-up services.

Some service providers, such as America Online (AOL) and CompuServe, have become very well known. However, there are thousands of lesser known, dedicated Internet access provider companies offering services around the world. Figure 10.22 illustrates the service provider's position in the Internet scheme, and shows the various connection methods used to access the Internet.

FIGURE 10.22
Service provider's position.

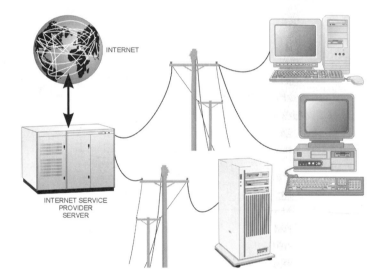

When you connect to a service provider, you are connecting to its computer system, which, in turn, is connected to the Internet through devices called *routers*. A router is a device that intercepts network transmissions and determines for which part of the Internet they are intended. It then determines what the best routing scheme is for delivering the message to its intended address. The routing schedule is devised on the known, available links through the Internet and the amount of traffic detected on various segments. The router then transfers the message to a *network access point* (NAP).

Internet Transmissions

The TCP/IP protocol divides the transmission into packets of information suitable for retransmission across the Internet. Along the way, the information passes through different networks that are organized at different levels. Depending on the routing scheme, the packets may move through the Internet using different routes to get to the intended address. At the destination, however, the packets are reassembled into the original transmission. Figure 10.23 illustrates this concept.

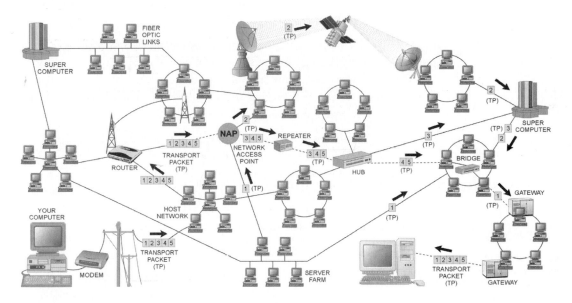

As the message moves from the originating address to its destination, it may pass through LANs, mid-level networks, routers, repeaters, hubs, bridges, and gateways. A mid-level network is just another network that does not require an Internet connection to carry out communications.

As mentioned previously, a router is a device that receives messages, amplifies them, and retransmits them, to keep the messages from deteriorating as they travel. Hubs are used to link networks together so that nodes within them can communicate with each other. Bridges connect networks together so that data can pass through them as it moves from one network to the next. A special type of bridge, called a gateway, translates the message as it passes through so that it can be used by different types of networks.

FIGURE 10.23
Packets moving through the Internet.

ISDN

ISDN service offers high-speed access to the public telephone system. However, ISDN service requires digital modems (also referred to as terminal adapters, or TAs). Not only does the end user require a digital modem, the telephone company's switch gear equipment must be updated to handle digital switching. This fact has slowed implementation of ISDN services until recently.

Three levels of ISDN service are available: *Basic Rate Interface* (BRI) services, *Primary Rate Interface* (PRI) services, and *Broadband ISDN* (BISDN) services.

BRI services are designed to provide residential users with basic digital service through the existing telephone system. The cost of this service is relatively low, although it is more expensive than regular analog service. BRI service is not available in all areas of the country, but it is expanding rapidly.

Typical residential telephone wiring consists of a four-wire cable. Up to seven devices can be connected to these wires. Under the BRI specification, the telephone company delivers three information channels to the residence over a two-wire cable. The two-wire system is expanded into the four-wire system at the residence through a network terminator. Figure 10.24 depicts the ISDN organization structure.

FIGURE 10.24
ISDN organizational structure.

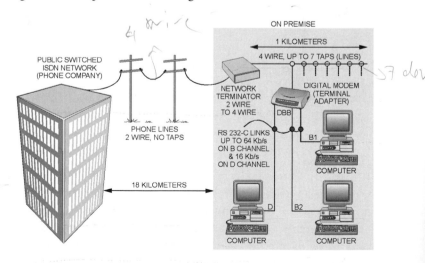

The BRI information channels exist as a pair of 64Kbps channels and a 16Kbps control channel. The two 64Kbps channels, called bearer, or B channels, can be used to transmit and receive voice and data information. The 16Kbps D channel is used to implement advanced control features such as call waiting, call forwarding, caller ID, and others. The D channel also can be used to conduct packet-transfer operations.

PRI services are more elaborate ISDN services that support very high data rates needed for live video transmissions. This is accomplished using the telephone company's existing wiring and advanced ISDN devices. The operating cost of PRI service is considerably more expensive than BRI services. The higher costs of PRI tend to limit its usage to larger businesses.

The fastest, most expensive ISDN service is Broadband ISDN. This level of service provides extremely high transfer rates (up to 622Mbps) over coaxial or fiber-optic cabling. Advanced transmission protocols are also used to implement B ISDN.

Digital modems are available in both internal and external formats. In the case of external devices, the analog link between the computer and the modem requires a D-to-A and A-to-D conversion process at the computer's serial port and then again at the modem. Of course, with an internal digital modem these conversion processes are not required.

File Transfer Protocol

A special application, called the *File Transfer Protocol* (FTP), is used to upload and download information to, and from, the Internet.

FTP is a client/server type of software application. The server version runs on the host computer, and the client version runs on the user's station. To access an FTP site, the user must move into an FTP application and enter the address of the site to be accessed. After the physical connection has been made, the user must log on to the FTP site by supplying an account number and password. When the host receives a valid password, a communication path opens between the host and the user site, and an FTP session begins.

[handwritten: Archie - list of specific FTP sites]

[handwritten: SMTP - Simple mail transfer protocol]

Around the world, thousands of FTP host sites contain millions of pages of information that can be downloaded free of charge. However, most FTP sites are used for file transfers of things such as driver updates and large file transfers that are too large for email operations.

Special servers, called *Archie servers* (archival servers), contain listings to assist users in locating specific topics stored at FTP sites around the world.

Email

One of the most widely used functions of WANs is the *electronic mail* (email) feature. This feature enables Internet users to send and receive electronic messages to each other over the Internet.

As with the regular postal service, email is sent to an address, from an address. With email, however, you can send the same message to several addresses at the same time, using a mailing list.

Several email programs are available to provide this function. Email is normally written as ASCII text files. These files can be created using an ordinary word processing package. An email mailer program is then used to drop the text file into an electronic mailbox. Email messages also can have graphics, audio, and files from other applications attached to them. However, the intended user must have the same application packages that were originally used to create the files to run them or conversion or translation add-ins for the email application that may allow the user to view or open the files.

On the Internet, the message is distributed in packets, as with any other TCP/IP file. At the receiving end, the email message is reassembled, and stored, in the recipient's mailbox. When the designated user boots up on the system, the email program delivers the message and notifies the user that it has arrived. The user can activate the email reader portion of the program to view the information.

The default email reader supported by the Windows 9x Outlook Express applet is the *POP3* standard. Likewise, it includes a standard *Simple Mail Transfer Protocol* (SMTP) email utility for outgoing email. These utilities must be accessed through the Tools option of the Outlook Express applet. From the Tools option on the Outlook Express menu bar, select the Accounts entry, highlight an account name, and click the Properties tab. Finally, click the Servers tab to access the email account configuration, as depicted in Figure 10.25.

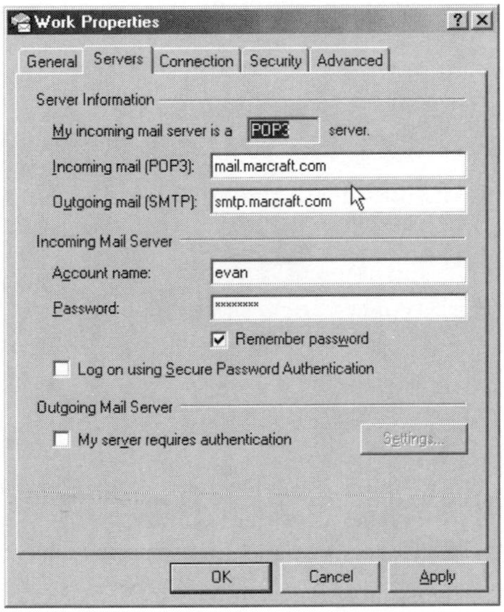

FIGURE 10.25
Email account configurations.

When setting up an email account, you must supply the following configuration information:

◆ Account name

◆ Password

◆ POP3 server address

◆ SMTP server address

 → for incoming & read email
→ simple mail transfer protocol for outgoing email

The order that this information is entered into the email client software varies from program to program. However, you are basically prompted to enter a account name and password of your choice, followed by POP3 and SMTP server addresses provided by the network administrator or the ISP.

The World Wide Web

The *World Wide Web* (WWW) is a menu system that ties together Internet resources from around the world. These resources are scattered across computer systems everywhere. *Web servers* inventory the Web's resource, and store address pointers, referred to as links, to them.

These links are used to create *hypermedia* documents that can contain information from computer sites around the world.

Inside a hypermedia document, the links enable the user to move around the document in a nonlinear manner. In an online encyclopedia, for example, the user can move around the encyclopedia to review all the entries concerning a single topic, without reading through every entry looking for them. The contents of the document can be mixed as well. A hypermedia document can contain text, graphics, and animation, as well as audio and video sequences.

Each Web site has a unique address called its *Universal Resource Locator* (URL). URLs have a format similar to a DOS command line. To access a Web site, the user must place the desired URL on the network. Each URL begins with *http://*. These letters stand for *Hypertext Transfer Protocol,* and identify the address as a Web site. The rest of the address is the name of the site being accessed (that is, http://www.mic-inc.com is the *home page* of Marcraft, located on a server at One World Telecommunications). Each Web site begins with a home page. The home page is the menu to the available contents of the site.

Web Browsers

As the Internet network grows, service providers continue to provide more user-friendly software for exploring the World Wide Web. These software packages are called browsers and are based on *hypertext links.*

Browsers use hypertext links to interconnect the various computing sites in a way that resembles a spider's web—hence the name, Web.

Browsers are to the Internet what Windows is to operating environments. Graphical browsers such as *Netscape Navigator* and *Microsoft Internet Explorer* enable users to move around the Internet and make selections from graphically designed pages and menus, instead of operating from a command line. The original Internet operating environment was a command-line program called UNIX. Fortunately, the UNIX structure and many of its commands were the basis used to create MS-DOS. Therefore, users who are DOS literate do not require extensive training to begin using UNIX. With the advent of a variety of browsers, however, it is unlikely that most users will become involved with UNIX.

The *National Center for Supercomputing Applications* introduced the first graphical browser in 1993. This program was known as *Mosaic*. As its name implies, Mosaic allowed graphical pages to be created using a mixture of text, graphics, audio, and video files. It translated the *Hypertext Markup Language* (HTML) files that were used to create the Web, and that ultimately link the various types of files together. These files can be recognized in older systems by their abbreviated .HTM file extension.

Mosaic was soon followed by Netscape Navigator and the Microsoft Internet Explorer. Figure 10.26 depicts the home page (presentation screen) for the Netscape Navigator from Netscape Communications Corporation.

TEST TIP

Be aware of different file types used with the Internet.

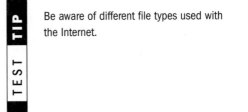

FIGURE 10.26
Netscape Navigator home page.

Figure 10.27 illustrates the Microsoft Internet Explorer. Its features are similar to those of the Netscape Navigator. Both provide a graphical interface for viewing Web pages. Links to *search engines* are useful for finding information on the Internet. Both have links to built-in email facilities and to their respective creator's home page.

In the Netscape Navigator, searches look at Netscape-recommended sites; the Explorer, on the other hand, first checks out Microsoft sites. Operating either browser in Windows versions before Windows 9x requires an external Windows socket program to be loaded before running the browser. With Windows 9x, the socket was integrated directly in to the operating environment.

FIGURE 10.27

Internet Explorer home page.

Several software packages enable users to generate their own Web pages. Programs such as word processors and desktop publishers have included provisions for creating and saving HTML files, called applets, that can be used as home pages. Internet browsers, such as Netscape and Internet Explorer, include facilities for generating home page documents. *Scripting languages*, such as *Java*, also are used to create HTML applets.

WIDE AREA NETWORKING WITH WINDOWS 9X

The Internet is the most famous example of wide area networking. The primary way to connect to the Internet with Windows 9x is through a dial-up networking connection (using a modem). The dial-up communications system in Windows 9x offers many improvements over previous operating systems. Under Windows 9x, applications can cooperatively share the dial-up connections through its *Telephony Application Programming Interface* (TAPI). This interface provides a universal set of drivers for modems and COM ports to control and arbitrate telephony operations for data, faxes, and voice.

TEST TIP

Know what the Telephony Application Programming Interface (TAPI) is and what it does.

TAPI
Telephone Application
Programing interface -

The Windows 9x Internet Connection

To establish dial-up Internet connection using the Windows 9x operating systems, follow the steps in Step by Step 10.1.

STEP BY STEP

10.1   Establishing a Dial-Up Internet Connection

1. Configure the Windows 9x Dial-Up Networking feature.

2. Establish the Windows 9x modem configuration.

3. Set up the ISP dial-up connection information.

4. Establish the server address for the connection (if required by the ISP).

5. Set up the Internet Explorer (or other browser).

6. Connect to the Internet.

The following sections discuss each of these steps in more detail.

Configuring the Dial-Up Networking Feature

To set up Dial-Up Networking to connect to the Internet, turn on the computer, double-click the My Computer icon on the desktop and click the Dial-Up Networking icon. You also can reach this icon through the Start button. Choose the Programs option from the Start menu, point at the Accessories entry, and click the Dial-Up Networking entry.

If this option has never been set up before, a Welcome to Dial-Up Networking message comes up. Press the Next button to advance into the Make New Connection screen, illustrated in Figure 10.28. At this point, enter the name of the *Internet service provider* in the Type window.

FIGURE 10.28
The Make New Connection window.

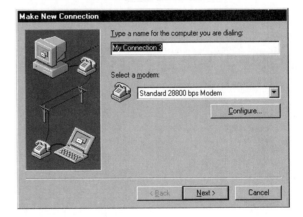

Establishing the Windows 9x Modem Configuration

Click the Configure button and set the maximum speed value to its fastest available setting, to allow compression and smoother connection. Next, click the Connection tab to see the modem *Connection Preferences* information, as illustrated in Figure 10.29.

Click the *Port Settings* button and set the Receive Buffer speed setting to 75%. Also, set the Transmit Buffer speed setting to 100%. You must set the Receive Buffer speed below the Transmit Buffer speed, otherwise the modem will try to receive as fast as it sends and will end up filling the buffer, slowing the operation of the connection.

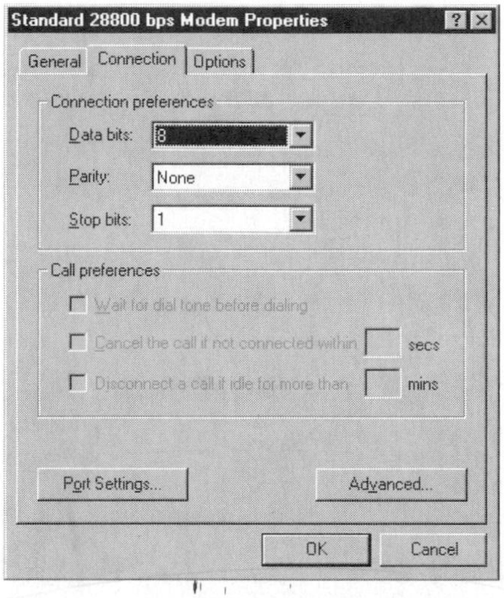

FIGURE 10.29
The Connection Preferences window.

Click the OK button to return to the Connection Preference window. Select the Advanced button and add any extra settings desired for the installed modem. For example, an M0 setting should turn the volume on your modem off so that it is quiet when connecting to the Internet. Click the OK button to return to the Modem Preferences window.

Setting Up the ISP Dial-Up Connection Information

From the Modem Preferences window, click the OK button to move into the Make New Connection entry. Click the Next button to advance to the phone number entry page illustrated in Figure 10.30.

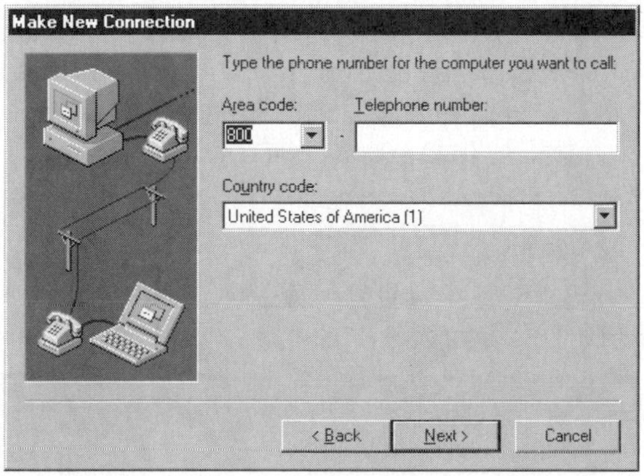

FIGURE 10.30
ISP Connection window.

FIGURE 10.31
The Dial-Up Networking window.

Type in the dial-in phone number of your ISP, area code and local number. If a dialing prefix is required, such as 9, set this up as well. If the number is a long-distance number, Windows detects this during dialing and automatically enters the appropriate long-distance prefix (for instance, a 1 in the United States). Click the Next button to record the information and click Finish. Then an icon displays in the Dial-Up Networking window, similar to the one depicted in Figure 10.31.

Establishing the IP and Server Addresses

As described earlier in this chapter, most ISPs use dynamic IP address assignments for their customers. The *Dynamic Host Configuration Protocol* (DHCP) service makes this possible by dynamically assigning IP addresses to the server's clients. This service is available in both Windows 9x and Windows NT/2000 and must be located on both the server and the client computers.

The ISP also will have one or more *name server* computers to route traffic on to and off of the Internet and to reconcile IP addresses to domain names. These are the computers that users dial in to, to establish and conduct their Internet communications. Each name server has a DNS number/name, just as every other Internet computer does. Like IP addresses, the domain *server address* can be static or dynamic. If the ISP has several servers, the ISP may allow traffic to be routed to the servers with the lightest workload, instead of waiting for a particular server to become free.

With some ISPs, it may be necessary to manually enter server address and IP information that they supply. Some users require that their IP address not be changed. Therefore, they purchase an IP address from the ISP that is always assigned to them. Of course, this removes an assignable address from the ISP's bank of addresses, but the customer normally pays a great deal more for the constant address. In these situations, it may be necessary to enter the IP address information into the Internet connection's TCP/IP configuration.

Likewise, some ISPs may assign static server addresses that must be entered manually; others assign their server addresses dynamically and, therefore, do not require that this information be entered into the TCP/IP configuration.

In both cases, Windows 9x allows for the local unit to assign values to IP and server addresses, or for the server to assign those values after the connection has been made. In dial-up situations, the ISP typically determines which option is used.

In those situations in which the ISP requires a server and/or IP address to be supplied, just move into the Dial-Up Networking window and right-click the Internet Connection icon. Select the Properties option from the list and move into the Server Types page, depicted in Figure 10.32. From this page, verify the *Dial-Up Server type*—usually PPP for Windows 9x, Windows NT, and Windows 2000—and click the *TCP/IP Settings* button. Set the TCP/IP settings as directed by the ISP's instructions. If specific values are entered into this page, the ISP connects the system to the Internet through a specific server address.

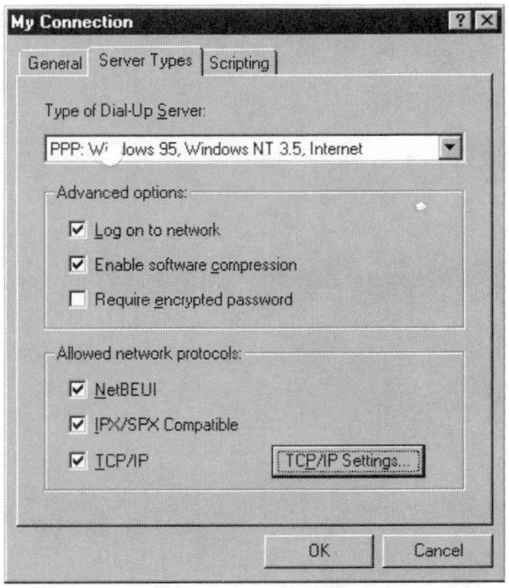

Click the Specify Name Server Address button and enter the *Primary DNS* and *Secondary DNS* addresses provided to you by the ISP. The screen should be similar to the one depicted in Figure 10.33. Return to the Dial-Up Networking window.

Although DNS is the naming service used by the Internet, it is not the only name-resolution service used with PCs. In the case of Windows LANs, the Microsoft-preferred naming system is the *Windows Internet Naming Service* (WINS). This service can be used to translate IP addresses to NetBIOS names within a Windows LAN environment. The LAN must include a *Windows name server* running the WINS server software that maintains the IP address/NetBIOS name database for the LAN.

Each client in the WINS LAN must contain the WINS client software and be WINS enabled. In Windows 9x, you can establish the WINS client service through the Control Panel's Network icon. On the Network page, select the TCP/IP LAN adapter from the list and click the Properties button. Select the *WINS Configuration* tab to obtain the page shown in Figure 10.34, and enable the WINS resolution function. Then, enter the IP address of the WINS server.

FIGURE 10.32
The Server Types page.

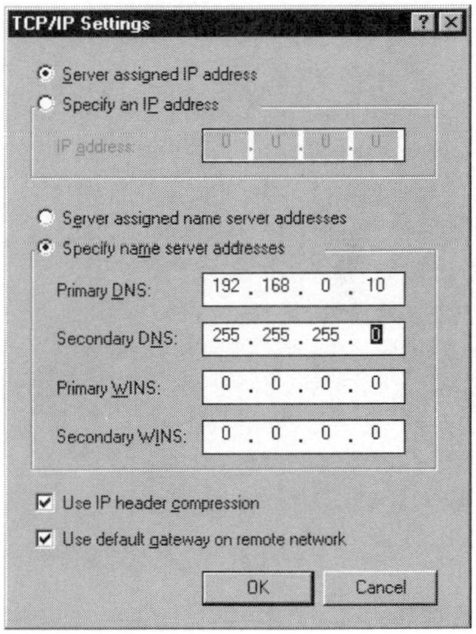

FIGURE 10.33
TCP/IP Settings numbers.

<table>
<tr><td>TEST TIP</td><td>Know what DNS and WINS are, what they do, and how they are different.</td></tr>
</table>

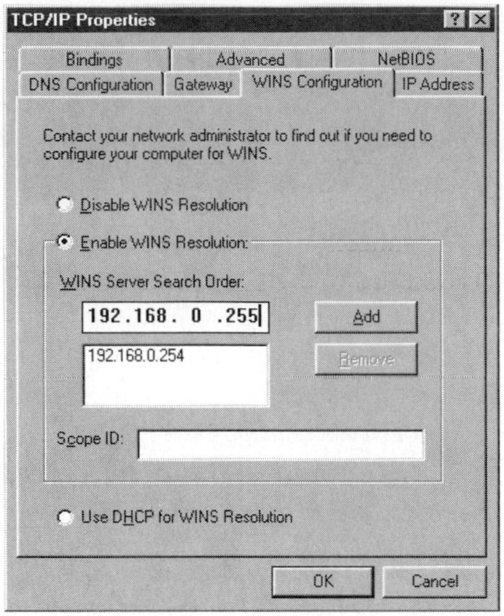

FIGURE 10.34
WINS enabling.

Setting Up the Internet Explorer Browser

As mentioned previously in this chapter, Internet browsers make the Internet much easier to navigate. Nearly every Internet connection is made through a browser of some type. Windows 9x includes a default browser called Internet Explorer (IE). Unless a different browser is installed, Windows 9x places the IE icon on the desktop and automatically refers to this browser for Internet access.

To browse the Internet using the IE, you must configure it for use. You can do so in three different ways:

◆ From the IE View menu, select the Internet Options entry.

◆ Right-click the desktop Internet icon and click the Properties tab.

◆ Click the Internet icon under the Start/Settings/Control Panel path.

Selecting one of these options leads to an Internet Options page or Internet Properties page. From either page, choose the Connection tab and click the Connect button to bring up Windows *Internet*

Connection Wizard and feature the Get Connected page. Pressing the Next button provides three possible options for setting up the Internet connection and the browser:

◆ I want to choose an Internet service provider and set up an Internet account. (MSN is the default.)

◆ I want a new connection on this computer to my existing Internet account using my phone line or local area network (LAN).

◆ I already have an Internet connection set up on this computer and I do not want to change it.

If you choose the first option, the Internet Wizard asks for the first three digits of the local phone number and tries to dial the MSN Web page. It is suggesting that the Microsoft Network be selected using the Microsoft Internet Explorer.

Unless the default is acceptable, select the "I want a new connection on this computer to my existing Internet account using my phone line or local area network (LAN)" statement. Selecting this option produces the Internet Connection Wizard window page, similar to the one in Figure 10.35.

FIGURE 10.35
The Internet Connection Wizard.

The first page of the wizard asks whether the connection will be made through a phone line or a local area network. Most home-use and small-business connections are of the dial-up modem type. Small, medium, and large businesses typically use LAN-based connections.

In a dial-up situation, click the Connect Using My Phone Line option and advance to the next page. The Dial-Up Connection page displays, as depicted in Figure 10.36.

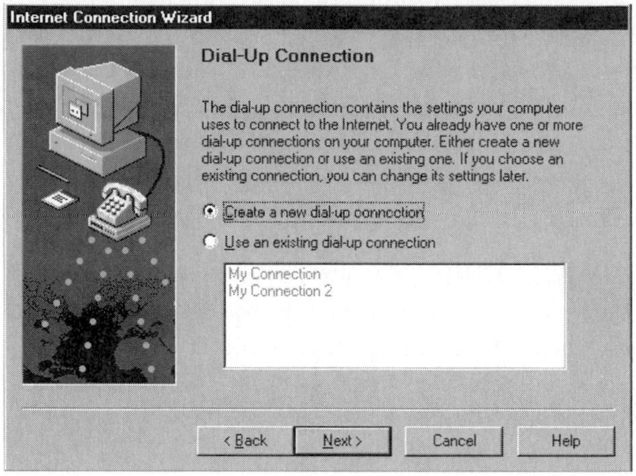

FIGURE 10.36
The Windows 9x Dial-Up Connection screen.

If the dial-up connection scheme has already been entered, a connection will already exist in the dialog box. Highlight the desired connection in the window, select the Use an Existing Dial-Up Connection option, and click the Next button to establish this connection for use.

If the desired connection is not present in the list, or if a new connection is being established, select the Create a New Dial-Up Connection option and click Next. A guided setup sequence for the new connection displays.

Choosing the I Already Have a Connection to the Internet option and clicking the Next button brings up the installed browser.

Installing Other Browsers

Although Windows 9x includes the Microsoft Internet Explorer, the public may prefer to use other browsers. To use another browser in the system, it is necessary to install it in the system. This is typically a function of the browser's Windows 9x Install Wizard.

If the install process detects an existing Dial-Up Networking configuration in Windows, it normally imports those values into its structure. If not, the Windows 9x Dial-Up Connection Wizard runs as a part of the third-party installation process. The User Manual for the browser normally provides exact instructions for installing its software in a Windows 9x system.

Connecting to the Internet

Double-click the icon of the new connection. Enter the username and password supplied by your ISP. Click the Connect option. You should hear the modem dialing at this point (unless the M0 parameter was specified in the Modem Properties/Extra Settings dialog windows to silence the modem's volume). A Connecting To window should appear on the screen, displaying the status of the modem. When it comes up, the Connected To window should minimize to the taskbar. The system is now connected to the Internet.

quiet dialing up

Setting Up Internet Email

Windows systems that run Microsoft Internet Explorer 4.0 or newer have a built-in email manager called Outlook Express that resides on the desktop taskbar. To set up an email account, open Outlook Express and click on the drop-down Tools menu. From the menu, choose the Account option, click the Add button, and select the Mail entry.

On successive screens, you need to enter the following:

- Your display name (the name that will be displayed to those receiving emails from you)

- Email address

- Internet Mail Server information (POP3 and SMTP) for incoming and outgoing mail

- The ISP-supplied Mail Account name and password

At the end of the setup process, you simply click the Finish button to complete the email setup.

All email managers require these pieces of information. If you are using a different email manager (for example, Eudora, Netscape Mail, and so forth), you will need to enter this information in the appropriate spaces provided by the particular manager.

Accessing the Internet Explorer

After the hardware has been installed and the Internet connection has been arranged, click the desktop Internet icon to access the Internet. In the Connect To window, click the Connect button. You should hear the modem communications sounds again. The Internet Explorer main screen displays, as depicted in Figure 10.37.

FIGURE 10.37

Internet Explorer main screen.

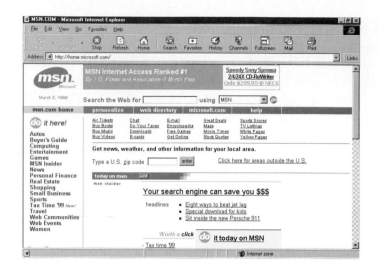

Remote Access Service
(R A S)

WIDE AREA NETWORKING WITH WINDOWS 2000

Older versions of Windows NT refer to all aspects of the dial-up networking function as Remote Access Services (RAS). With Windows NT 4.0, however, Microsoft changed the nomenclature to Dial-Up Networking on its client side elements. Microsoft did so to maintain compatibility with Windows 9x descriptions. The server side elements are still referred to as RAS. This same convention continues in the Windows 2000 product.

Windows NT Workstation provides all the software tools required to establish an Internet connection. These include a TCP/IP network protocol and the Windows NT Workstation Dial-Up Networking component. The Dial-Up Networking component is used to establish a link with the ISP over the public telephone system. This link also can be established over an ISDN line. Windows NT versions from 4.0 forward feature the built-in Microsoft Internet Explorer Web browser and a personal Web Server.

The Windows 2000 Internet Infrastructure

Windows 2000 replaces the Network Settings item from the Windows NT 4.0 Control Panel with a New Network Connections folder, located in the My Computer window. To create a dial-up connection in Windows 2000, click the Make New Connection icon in the My Computer Network Connections folder. This action opens the Windows 2000 Network Connection Wizard that guides the connection process. The wizard requires information about the type of connection, modem type, and the phone number to be dialed. The connection types offered by the wizard include private networks, virtual private networks, and other computers.

The Network Connection Wizard enables users to employ the same device to access multiple networks that may be configured differently. This is accomplished by enabling users to create connection types based on who they are connecting to, rather than how they are making the connection.

Establishing the Windows 2000 Modem Configuration

Under Windows 2000, the operating system should detect, or offer to detect, the modem through its Plug and Play facilities. It may also enable you to select the modem drivers manually from a list in the Control Panel.

After the modem has been detected, or selected, it appears in the Windows 2000 Modem list. The settings for the modem can be examined or reconfigured by selecting it from the list and clicking its Properties tab. In most cases, the device's default configuration settings should be used.

Configuring the modem to operate properly with an ISP is much easier in Windows 2000 than it was in Windows NT 4.0. The Connection Settings tab from the Windows NT 4.0 Modem Properties dialog window has been replaced by the Advanced tab with space to enter the initialization string received from the ISP.

[handwritten notes in margin: "Win 2000 / Dialing Rules / Control panel / phone & modem"]

Establishing Dialing Rules

For Windows 2000 to connect to a network or dial-up connection, it must know what rules to follow in establishing the communication link. These rules are known as the Dialing Rules. In Windows 2000, the Dialing Rules are configured through the Start/Settings/ Control Panel/Phone and Modem Options path. If the connection is new, a Location Information dialog window displays, enabling you to supply the area code and telephone system information.

To create a new location, click the New button and move through the General, Area Code Rules, and Calling Card tabs, depicted in Figure 10.38, to add information as required. The default rules for dialing local, long-distance, and international calls are established under the General tab. These rules are based on the country or region identified on this page. Ways to reach an outside line (such as dialing 8 or 9 to get an outside line in a hotel or office building) are established here. Similarly, the Area Code Rules information modifies the default information located under the General tab. As its name implies, the information under the Calling Cards tab pertains to numbers dialed using a specific calling card or long-distance company.

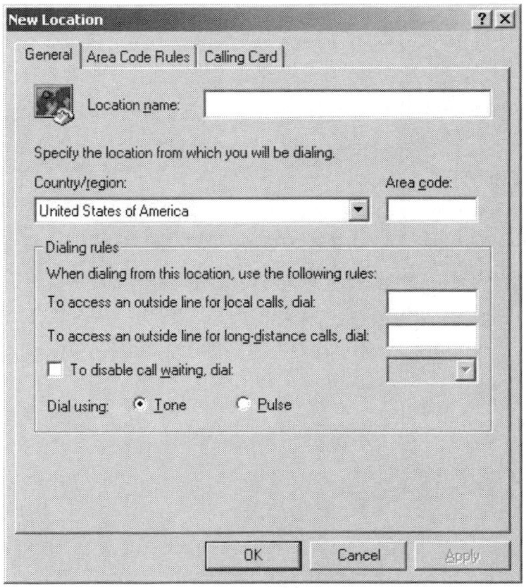

FIGURE 10.38

The Windows 2000 Phone and Modem Options/New dialog window.

Establishing Dial-Up Internet Connections

The Windows 2000 Internet Connection Wizard, depicted in Figure 10.39, provides an efficient way to establish Internet connectivity. You can use the Internet Connection Wizard to set up the Web browser, the Internet email account, and the newsgroup reader. To create the Internet connection to an existing account with an ISP, you need to know the following:

- The ISP's name

- The username and password

- The ISP's dial-in access number

If the system is equipped with a cable modem or an Asymmetrical Digital Subscriber Line (ADSL), the ISP will need to furnish any additional connection instructions. The cable modem is a device that transmits and receives data through cable television connections. Conversely, ADSL is a special, high-speed ADSL modem technology that transmits data over existing telephone lines. The Internet Connection Wizard collects this information and then creates the Internet connection.

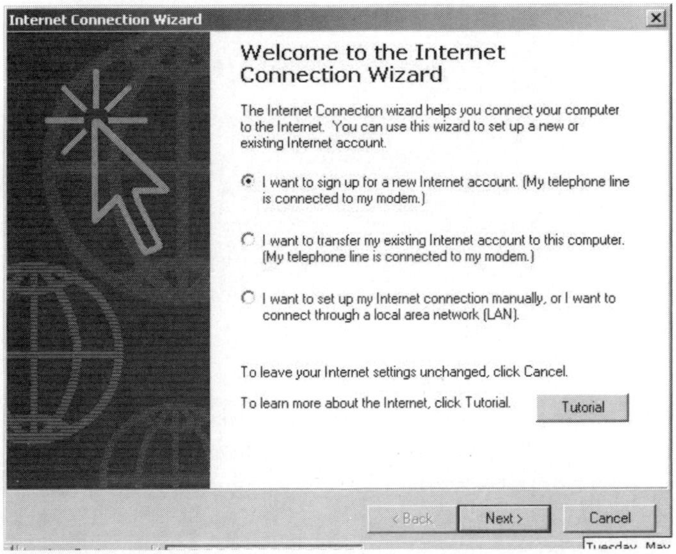

FIGURE 10.39
The Internet Connection Wizard.

To connect to the Internet, select the Internet Connection Wizard option from the Start/Programs/Accessories/Communications path. If the connection is new, the Location Information dialog box displays, as depicted in Figure 10.40, along with the Dialing Rules defined in the preceding section. You also need to click the I Want to Sign Up for a New Internet Account option, click the Next button, and follow the wizard's instructions.

FIGURE 10.40
The Location Information dialog box.

Establishing Internet Connection Sharing

Windows 2000 makes it possible to share resources such as printers and folders and Internet connections across a network. Sharing an Internet connection allows several computers to be connected to the Internet through a single dial-up connection. These connections can be made individually, or simultaneously, with each user maintaining the ability to use the same services it did when it was connected directly to the Internet.

To establish Internet connection sharing, you must log on to the computer using an account that has Administrator rights. Afterward, click Start/Settings and select the Network and Dial-Up Connections option. Alternate-click the connection to be shared and select the Properties option. The Internet Connection Sharing screen displays, as depicted in Figure 10.41.

Under the Internet Connection-Sharing tab, select the Enable Internet Connection Sharing for This Connection check box. If the connecting computer is supposed to dial in to the Internet automatically, click the Enable on Demand Dialing check box. Clicking the OK button causes protocols, services, interfaces, and routes to be configured automatically.

Troubleshooting WAN Problems

Unless you work for an Internet service provider, most of the work at an Internet site involves the components, and software, of the local computer. In most single-user situations, this is confined to the system, a modem, and the dial-up communications software. In some business settings, the range of components is increased to include network cards, concentrators, routers, and LAN servers. The information that follows pertains to typical dial-up Internet access applications.

The quickest items to check in a WAN application are the dial-up network software settings. Check the spelling of fully qualified domain names to make sure they are spelled exactly as they should be. If the spelling is wrong, no communications will take place. The major difference in checking WAN problems occurs in checking the Internet-specific software, such as the browser.

Most of the WAN troubleshooting steps from the local computer level involve the modem. The modem hardware should be examined as described in Chapter 2, "2.0 Diagnosing and Troubleshooting." If the hardware is functional, the operating system's driver and resource configuration settings must be checked.

In Windows 9x, you can find the modem configuration information in the Control Panel under the Modems icon. This icon has two tabs: the General tab and the Diagnostics tab. The Properties button in the General window provides Port and Maximum Speed settings.

The Connection tab provides character-framing information, as illustrated in Figure 10.42. The Connection tab's Advanced button provides Error and Flow Control settings, as well as Modulation Type.

FIGURE 10.42
The Connection tab.

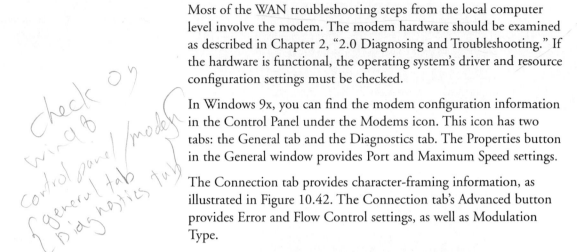

The Diagnostics tab's dialog box, depicted in Figure 10.43, provides access to the modem's driver and additional information. The PnP feature reads the modem card and returns its information to the screen, as demonstrated in the depiction.

FIGURE 10.43
The Diagnostics tab.

Each user should have received a packet of information from his or her ISP when the service was purchased. These documents normally contain all the ISP-specific configuration information needed to set up the user's site. This information should be consulted when installing, and configuring, any Internet-related software.

The ISP establishes an Internet access account for each user. These accounts are based on the user's account name and password that are asked for each time the user logs on to the account. Forgetting or misspelling either item will result in the ISP rejecting access to the Internet. Most accounts are paid for on a monthly schedule. If the account isn't paid up, the ISP may cancel the account and deny access to the user. In either of these situations, if the user attempts to log on to the account, the user will repeatedly be asked to enter his or her account name and password until a predetermined number of failed attempts has been reached.

Checking the modem, or network card, is the major hardware-related activity normally involved with Internet sites. However, you may be required to work with the customer's local Internet service provider to solve some types of problems.

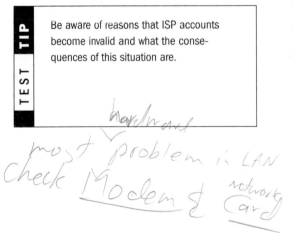

TEST TIP

Be aware of reasons that ISP accounts become invalid and what the consequences of this situation are.

The most common communication error is the Disconnected message. This message occurs for a number of reasons, including a noisy phone line or random transmission errors. You can normally overcome this type of error by just retrying the connection. Other typical error messages include the following:

◆ **No Dial Tone.** This error indicates a bad or improper phone-line connection, such as the phone line plugged into the modem's line jack rather than the phone jack.

◆ **Port in Use.** This error indicates a busy signal or an improper configuration parameter.

◆ **Can't Find Modem.** This error indicates that the PnP process did not detect the modem, or that it has not been correctly configured to communicate with the system.

If the system cannot find the modem, the first step is to reboot the system and allow Windows 9x to redetect the modem. If rebooting does not detect the modem, run any diagnostics available for the modem. In particular, use the utility disk, or CD-ROM, that comes with the modem to run tests on the hardware. Check any hardware configuration settings for the modem and compare them to the settings in the Control Panel's Device Manager. These values can be checked through the Control Panel's Modems/Properties page, but the Device Manager must be used to make changes.

If the modem is present, move into the Device Manager and check the modem for resource conflicts. If there is a conflict with the modem, an exclamation point (!) should appear beside the modem listing.

If you detect a conflict, move into the *Modems Properties* page and check the modem's resources. Also, record the Connection Preferences from the Connection page and make certain the character-framing configuration is correct. The conflict must be resolved between the modem and whatever device is using its resources.

If no conflict is indicated, move into the Diagnostics page and highlight the installed device. Click the More Info button. This action causes Windows to communicate with the modem hardware. If no problems are detected by this test, Windows 9x displays the modem's port information, along with a listing of the AT commands that it used to test the hardware, as illustrated in Figure 10.44. If an error is detected during the Windows testing, an error message displays onscreen. These messages are similar to those previously listed.

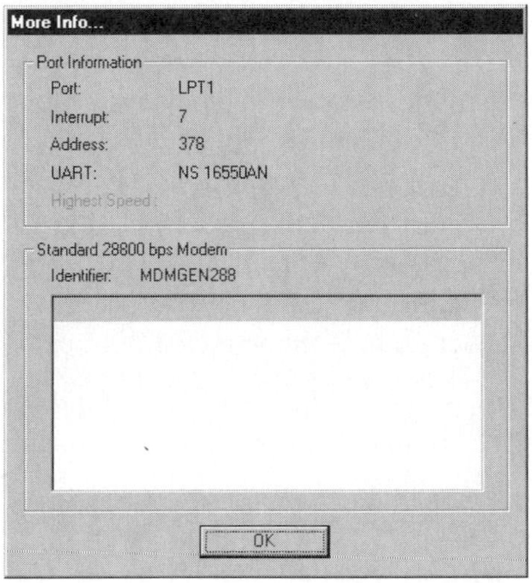

FIGURE 10.44
Modem Properties More Info response.

If the modem tests are okay, check the User Name and Password settings. This can be accomplished through the My Computer/Dial-Up Networking path, or through the Start/Programs/Accessories/ Communications/Dial-Up Networking path in Windows 98.

In the Dialup Networking window, right-click the desired connection icon and select the Properties option from the list. Check the phone number and modem type on the General page. Next move into the Server Types page and check Type of Dial-Up Server installed. For Windows Internet dial-up service, this is typically a "PPP, Internet, Windows NT, Windows 98" connection. Also, disable the NetBEUI and IPX/SPX settings from the page and make certain that the TCP/IP setting is enabled.

Click the TCP/IP Settings button to examine these settings. Most ISPs use DHCP to assign IP, DNS, and gateway addresses to clients for dial-up accounts. Therefore, in a dial-up situation, the Server Assigns IP Address option and the Server Assigns Name Server Address option are normally enabled. Check the ISP-supplied package to make sure that these settings do not need to be set manually.

If they are, set up the page to match the ISP-specified settings. In the case of intranets with "in-house" clients, the network administrator determines how the values are assigned (statically or via DHCP).

Network Troubleshooting Tools

Windows provides fundamental troubleshooting information for wide area networking through its system of Help screens. Just select Help from the Control Panel's toolbar and click the topics related to the problem. Also use a word processing package to read the Windows 9x SETUPLOG.TXT and BOOTLOG.TXT files. These files record where setup and booting errors occur. Use the F8 function key during boot up to examine each driver being loaded.

When TCP/IP is installed in Windows 9x or Windows 2000, a number of TCP/IP troubleshooting tools are automatically installed with it. All TCP/IP utilities are controlled by commands entered and run from the command prompt. These TCP/IP tools include the following:

◆ **Address Resolution Protocol (ARP).** This utility enables you to modify IP-to-Ethernet address-translation tables.

◆ **FTP.** This utility enables you to transfer files to and from FTP servers.

◆ **PING.** This utility enables you to verify connections to remote hosts.

◆ **NETSTAT.** This utility enables you to display the current TCP/IP network connections and protocol statistics. A similar command, called **NBTSTAT**, performs the same function using NetBIOS over the TCP/IP connection.

◆ **Trace Route (TRACERT).** This utility enables you to display the route, and a hop count, taken to a given destination. The route taken to a particular address can be set manually using the **ROUTE** command.

◆ **IPCONFIG** This command-line utility enables you to determine the current TCP/IP configuration (MAC address, IP address, and subnet mask) of the local computer. It also can be used to request a new TCP/IP address from a DHCP server. **IPCONFIG** is available in both Windows 98 and Windows 2000. Windows 95 did not support **IPCONFIG**.

TEST TIP

Know from where TCP/IP utilities are run.

The **IPCONFIG** utility can be started with two important option switches: **/RENEW** and **/RELEASE**. These switches are used to release and update IP settings received from a DHCP server. Use the **/ALL** switch to view the TCP/IP settings for all the adapter cards to which the local station is connected.

win 98, 2000 *only in win 95*

◆ **WINIPCFG.** This is a GUI version of the **IPCONFIG** command available only in Windows 95. The various command-line switches available with the **IPCONFIG** command are implemented in graphical buttons. Like **IPCONFIG**, **WINIPCFG** can be used to release and renew IP addresses leased from a DHCP server.

Although all of these utilities are useful in isolating different TCP/IP problems, the most widely used commands are PING and TRACERT.

The **PING** utility sends *Internet Control Message Packets* (ICMP) to a remote location and then waits for echoed response packets to be returned. The command waits for up to one second for each packet sent and then displays the number of transmitted and received packets. You can use the command to test both the name and IP address of the remote unit. A number of switches can be used to set parameters for the ping operation. Figure 10.45 depicts the information displayed by a typical ping operation.

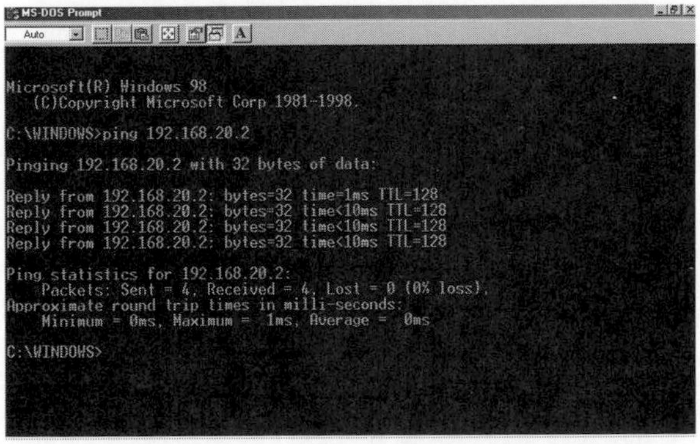

ping → send → ICMP

TEST TIP

Know which TCP/IP utilities can be used to release and renew IP address information from a DHCP server.

FIGURE 10.45
A ping operation.

TEST TIP

Know which Windows tools to use to check out network-related problems.

Most Internet servers do not respond to ICMP requests created by pinging. However, you can use the **PING** utility to access `www.somewebsitename.com`. By doing so, you can get a reply that will verify that TCP/IP, DNS, and gateway are working. The **TRACERT** utility traces the route taken by ICMP packets sent across the network, as described in Figure 10.46. Routers along the path return information to the inquiring system and the utility displays the host name, IP address, and round-trip time for each hop in the path.

Because the **TRACERT** report shows how much time is spent at each router along the path, it can be used to help determine where network slowdowns are occurring.

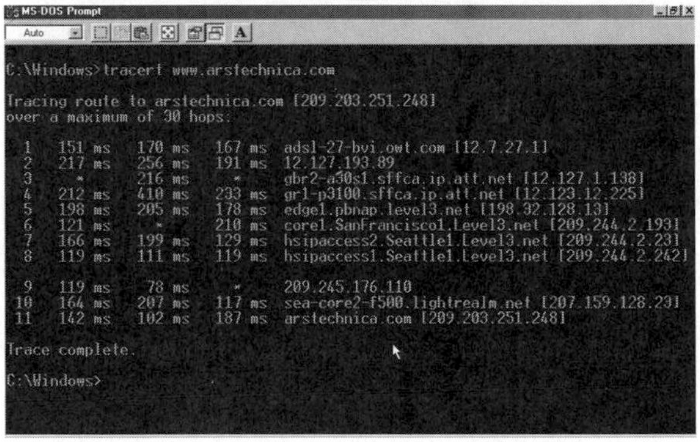

FIGURE 10.46
A TRACERT operation.

CHAPTER SUMMARY

KEY TERMS

- Access rights
- Backbone
- Basic Rate Interface (BRI)
- Bridges
- Broadband ISDN (BISDN)
- Bulletin board service (BBS)
- Connection Preferences

This chapter focused on the software side of networking, concentrating on the major operating systems. Both local and wide area networking concerns were addressed.

The first half of the chapter dealt with local area networking under Windows 9x and Windows NT/2000. The steps for establishing and using a networked printer were described in detail. The final part of the section provided step-by-step instructions for troubleshooting LAN problems.

The last half of the chapter handled wide area networking aspects under Windows 9x and Windows 2000. This section included Internet basics, as ways to configure and use a dial-up network configuration to access the Internet. The final part of this section provided instructions for troubleshooting Internet access problems.

At this point, review the objectives listed at the beginning of the chapter to be certain that you understand each point and can perform each task listed there. Afterward, answer the Review Questions that follow to verify your knowledge of the information.

- Diagnostic server
- Dial-Up Connection
- Dial-up networking
- Domain Name Service (DNS)
- Dotted-decimal notation
- Dynamic Host Configuration Protocol (DHCP)
- Dynamic IP addressing
- Electronic mail (email)
- File and Print Sharing
- File Transfer Protocol (FTP)
- Gateway
- Hubs
- Hypertext links
- Hypertext Markup Language (HTML)
- Hypertext Transfer Protocol (HTTP)
- Integrated Service Digital Network (ISDN)
- Internet
- Internet Connection Wizard
- Internet Mail Server
- Internet Protocol addresses (IP addresses)
- Internet service provider (ISP)
- Internetworking Packet Exchange (IPX)

continues

continues

- IPX/SPX
- Login prompt
- Map Network Drive
- Metropolitan area networks (MANs)
- Microsoft Client protocol
- Microsoft Internet Explorer
- Modems Properties
- My Network Places
- Name server
- National Center for Supercomputing Applications
- National Science Foundation (NSF)
- NetBEUI
- Netscape Navigator
- Network access point (NAP)
- Network Basic Input/Output System (NetBIOS)

- Network drivers
- Network Neighborhood
- Network operating system (NOS)
- Novell NetWare
- Novell NetWare Client protocol
- Open Datalink Interface (ODI)
- Passwords
- Permission levels
- Point-to-Point Protocol (PPP)
- Port name
- Primary DNS
- Primary Network Logon
- Primary Rate Interface (PRI)
- Routers
- Search engines

- Secondary DNS
- Serial Line Internet Protocol (SLIP)
- SHARE.EXE
- Static IP addressing
- TCP/IP
- TCP/IP Settings
- Universal naming convention (UNC)
- Universal Resource Locator (URL)
- Web servers
- Wide area networks (WANs)
- Windows Naming Service (WINS)
- WINS Configuration
- Workgroups
- World Wide Web (WWW)

RESOURCE URLS

www.otex.org/manual/chap13.htm

www.otex.org/manual/chap12.htm#C1211

www.cit.rcc.on.ca/win311/win311a.htm

www.otex.org/manual/chap12.htm#C1211

www.cit.rcc.on.ca/nm210/default.htm

www.cit.rcc.on.ca/winnt/default.htm

www.globetrotting.com/windows95/networks.htm

www.cit.rcc.on.ca/internet/instart.htm

www.cit.rcc.on.ca/internet/inet3.htm#ftp

http://geocities.com/~anderberg/ant/history

www.cit.rcc.on.ca/internet/default.htm

www.cisco.com/warp/public/779/smbiz/service/knowledge/wan/ppp_auth.htm

www.cisco.com/warp/public/779/smbiz/service/troubleshooting/ts_wan.htm

www.cisco.com/warp/public/779/smbiz/service/knowledge/tcpip/dhcp.htm

APPLY YOUR KNOWLEDGE

Review Questions

1. Describe the function of the World Wide Web.

2. What is the PING utility used for?

3. Why are drives mapped in Windows 9x?

4. Describe the function of the IPCONFIG command?

5. If a resource cannot be seen in the Network Neighborhood, what problem likely exists?

6. What Windows 9x tool is used to determine the configuration settings of a network card?

7. What is the purpose of a router in a network?

8. What is TCP/IP, and what does it mean?

9. What function does a browser perform?

10. Describe the function of a hub in a network system.

11. Write a UNC path statement to access a remote printer named lasrprn1 that is attached to a computer named Marcraft1.

12. Identify the network utility that displays the current TCP/IP network connection and protocol statistics?

13. Describe the function of the DNS.

14. Define the acronym URL and describe what it is used for.

15. Describe the function of an Internet service provider.

Exam Questions

1. Which networking component is not normally loaded as a part of the Windows 9x detection process?

   A. Client

   B. Adapter

   C. Protocol

   D. Service

2. If one computer cannot see another computer on the network, what might the most logical problem be?

   A. The Device Manager does not recognize the adapter.

   B. A matching protocol is not installed.

   C. The Network Control Panel has not been enabled.

   D. The Networking Services have not been installed.

3. What is the purpose of NetBEUI?

   A. Novell LAN protocol

   B. Windows Internet protocol

   C. Novell Internet protocol

   D. Windows LAN protocol

4. What is the function of IPX/SPX?

   A. Novell LAN protocol

   B. Windows Internet protocol

   C. Novell Internet protocol

   D. Windows LAN protocol

APPLY YOUR KNOWLEDGE

5. Which utility displays the route and a hop count, taken to a given network destination?

   A. PING

   B. NETSTAT

   — C. TRACERT

   D. IPGONFIG

6. Describe the steps to connect to a remote shared printer in Windows 9x.

   A. Browse the Network Control Panel, locate remote computer, double-click it to show printers, access the local Printers folder, click and drag the remote printer icon into the Control Panel and drop it, and answer Printer Wizard questions about the printer.

   B. Browse the Network Neighborhood, locate remote computer, double-click it to show printers, access the local Printers folder, click and drag the remote printer icon into the local Printers window and drop it, and answer Printer Wizard questions about the printer.

   C. Browse the Print Manager, locate remote computer, double-click it to show printers, access the local Printers folder, click and drag the remote printer icon into the Print Manager window and drop it, and answer Printer Wizard questions about the printer.

   D. Browse the Print Spooler, locate remote computer, double-click it to show printers, access the local Printers folder, click and drag the remote printer icon into the local Print Spooler window and drop it, and answer Printer Wizard questions about the printer.

7. What type of device is used to implement an ISDN connection?

   — A. A digital modem

   B. A router

   C. A hub

   D. A bridge

8. In Windows 9x, what tool will provide the network card's type information?

   A. Internet Explorer

   B. Control Panel

   C. Windows Explorer

   — D. Device Manager

9. Which file format is used to send files over the Internet?

   A. IPX

   B. NetBEUI

   — C. FTP

   D. WWW

10. What language is used to create documents for the World Wide Web?

   — A. Hypertext Markup Language

   B. QBASIC Language

   C. FTP Language

   D. Mosaic Language

APPLY YOUR KNOWLEDGE

Answers to Review Questions

1. A menu system that ties together the resources of the Internet. For more information, see the section "The World Wide Web."

2. The PING command sends Internet Control Message Packets (ICMP) to a remote location and then waits for echoed response packets to be returned. The command waits for up to one second for each packet sent and then display the number of transmitted and received packets. The command can be used to test both the name and IP address of the remote unit. For more information, see the section "Network Troubleshooting Tools."

3. Mapping a drive letter to a resource enables non-Windows 9x applications running on the local computer to use the resources across the network. For more information, see the section "Network Neighborhood."

4. This IPCONFIG command is used to determine the current TCP/IP configuration of the local computer. It also may be used to request a new TCP/IP address from a DHCP server. For more information, see the section "Network Troubleshooting Tools."

5. A needed driver or protocol match is not loaded. If the network cannot be seen or browsed from the Network Neighborhood, the network protocols and drivers should be checked. For more information, see the section "Troubleshooting Local Area Networks."

6. Device Manager. For more information, see the section "Troubleshooting Local Area Networks."

7. Receives network traffic, amplifies it, and then resends it so that it does not deteriorate during transmission. For more information, see the section "Internet Domains."

8. Transport Control Protocol/Internet Protocol is the language of the Internet. For more information, see the section "TCP/IP."

9. Browsers enable users to move around the Internet and make selections from graphically designed pages and menus, instead of operating from a command line. For more information, see the section "Web Browsers."

10. Hubs are used to link networks together so that nodes within them can communicate with each other. For more information, see the section "Internet Transmissions."

11. \\Marcraft1\lasrprn1. For more information, see the section "Network Printing with Windows 2000."

12. The NETSTAT command displays the current TCP/IP network connections and protocol statistics. A similar command, called NBTSTAT, performs the same function using NetBIOS over the TCP/IP connection. For more information, see the section "Network Troubleshooting Tools."

13. The Domain Name System tracks IP addresses of all the computers attached to the Internet. This system is a method of organizing the members of the Internet into a hierarchical management structure. For more information, see the section "Internet Domains."

14. The Universal Resource Locator (URL), that is the address assigned to a Web site on the Internet. For more information, see the section "The World Wide Web."

APPLY YOUR KNOWLEDGE

15. Organizations that provide the technical gateway to the Internet. For more information, see the section "Internet Service Providers (ISPs)."

Answers to Exam Questions

1. **C.** The Windows 9x detection process does not load the networking protocol. For more information, see the section "Installing Network Components."

2. **B.** The most common reason for not being able to see another node on the network is the use of different protocols between the units. To communicate on a network, everyone in the conversation must be using the same protocol. For more information, see the section "Troubleshooting Local Area Networks."

3. **D.** NetBEUI is the Microsoft Windows local area network protocol. It is nonroutable and therefore not used for wide area network applications. For more information, see the section "Installing Network Components."

4. **A.** IPX/SPX is the Novell NetWare LAN transport protocol. For more information, see the section "Installing Network Components."

5. **C.** TRACERT. For more information, see the section "Network Troubleshooting Tools."

6. **B.** Browse the Network Neighborhood, locate the remote computer, double-click it to show printers, access the local Printers folder, click and drag the remote printer icon into the local Printers window and drop it, and answer Printer Wizard questions about the printer being connected to. For more information, see the section "Network Printing with Windows 9x."

7. **A.** ISDN connections are special digital communications links that use digital-signal processing equipment. Historically, modems have been analog devices. ISDN communications require digital modems to carry out communications and are therefore not compatible with normal dial-up telephone lines. For more information, see the section "Wide Area Networks."

8. **D.** In Windows 9x, the Device Manager displays the resource and configuration information assigned to all the hardware devices in the system. For more information, see the section "Troubleshooting Local Area Networks."

9. **C.** FTP is the TCP/IP File Transfer Protocol and it is used to send files across the Internet. For more information, see the section "File Transfer Protocol."

10. **A.** Web documents are created as HTML (Hypertext Markup Language) files. These documents can be identified in the system by their .HTM extensions. For more information, see the section "Web Browsers."

Final Review

Fast Facts: Core Hardware Service Technician Exam

Fast Facts: Operating System Technologies Exam

Study and Exam Prep Tips

Practice Exam: Core Hardware Service Technician

Practice Exam: Operating System Technologies

The Fast Facts listed in this and the following chapter are designed as a refresher of key points and topics required to succeed on the A+ Certification exam. By using these summaries of key points, you can spend an hour prior to your exam to refresh key topics and ensure that you have a solid understanding of the objectives and information required for you to succeed in each major area of the exam.

CompTIA has established two modules for the A+ examination: the Core Hardware Service Technician module, and the Operating System Technologies module. The information here is organized like the Core Hardware Service Technician test objectives, and each domain that follows includes the key points from each chapter. If you have a thorough understanding of the key points here, chances are good that you will pass the exam.

Chapters 1 through 6 are dedicated to the six domains covered in the Core Hardware Service Technician module. Now that you have read those chapters, answered all the Review and Exam Questions at the ends of the chapters, and explored the *ExamGear* test engine on the CD that accompanies the book, you are ready to take the exam.

Albert Einstein supposedly said, "Everything should be as simple as possible, but not simpler." These Fast Facts are designed as a quick (less than an hour) study aid that you can use just prior to taking the exam. It cannot serve as a substitute for knowing the material supplied in these chapters. However, its key points should refresh your memory on critical topics. In addition to the information located here, remember to review the Glossary terms. (They intentionally are not covered here.)

Fast Facts

CORE HARDWARE SERVICE TECHNICIAN EXAM

The following are the domains that CompTIA uses to arrange the objectives for the Core Hardware Service Technician module:

◆ 1.0 Installation, Configuration, and Upgrading

◆ 2.0 Diagnosing and Troubleshooting

◆ 3.0 Preventive Maintenance

◆ 4.0 Motherboard/Processors/Memory

◆ 5.0 Printers

◆ 6.0 Basic Networking

1.0 Installation, Configuration, and Upgrading

This domain requires the knowledge and skills required to identify, install, configure, and upgrade microcomputer modules and peripherals. The main points follow:

◆ The tremendous popularity of the original IBM PC-XT and AT systems created a set of pseudo standards for hardware and software compatibility. The AT architecture became so popular that it has become the Industry Standard Architecture (ISA). The majority of microcomputers are both hardware and software compatible with the original AT design.

◆ The system unit is the main portion of the microcomputer system and is the basis of any PC system arrangement.

◆ The system board is the center of the system. It contains the portions of the system that define its computing power and speed.

◆ The system's power-supply unit provides electrical power for every component inside the system unit, and also supplies AC power to the video display monitor.

◆ The system board communicates with various optional input/output (I/O) and memory systems through adapter boards that plug into its expansion slots. These connectors are normally located along the left-rear portion of the system board so that the external devices they serve can access them through openings at the rear of the case.

◆ The microprocessor is the major component of any system board. It executes software instructions and carries out arithmetic operations for the system.

◆ Microprocessor manufacturers produce microprocessor-support chipsets that provide auxiliary services for the microprocessor.

◆ Each time the system is turned on, or reset, the BIOS program checks the system's configuration settings to determine what types of optional devices may be included in the system.

◆ Newer microcomputers can automatically reconfigure themselves for newly installed options. This feature is referred to as Plug and Play (PnP) capability.

◆ Most personal computers use standardized expansion slot connectors that enable users to attach various types of peripheral devices to the system. Optional I/O devices, or their interface boards, may be plugged into these slots to connect the devices to the system's address, data, and control buses.

◆ The video adapter card provides the interface between the system board and the display monitor.

◆ A CRT is an evacuated glass tube with one or more electron guns in its neck, and a fluorescent-coated surface opposite the electron gun. When activated, the electron gun emits a stream of electrons that strikes the fluorescent coating on the inside of the screen, causing an illuminated dot to be produced.

◆ Video information is introduced to the picture by varying the voltage applied to the electron gun as it scans the screen.

◆ The color CRT uses a combination of three-color phosphors—red, blue, and green—arranged in adjacent trios of dots or bars, called picture elements, pixels, or PELS. By using a different electron gun for each element of the trio, the individual elements can be made to glow at different levels to produce almost any color desired.

◆ In designing the VGA standard, IBM departed from the signal formats found in its previous display standards. To accommodate a wide range of onscreen color possibilities, the VGA standard resorted to the use of analog video signals.

◆ From the beginning, most secondary memory systems have involved storing binary information in the form of magnetic charges on moving magnetic surfaces.

◆ The system unit normally comes from the manufacturer with a floppy disk drive, a hard disk drive, and a CD-ROM drive installed.

◆ A single ribbon cable is used to connect the system's floppy drive(s) to the disk drive controller card. Generally, the cable has two edge connectors, and two 34-pin, two-row BERG headers along its length.

◆ The most common drive arrays are redundant arrays of inexpensive disks (RAID) systems. There are five levels of RAID technology specifications given by the RAID Advisory Board.

◆ Soon after the compact disc became popular for storing audio signals on optical material, the benefits of storing computer information in this manner became apparent.

◆ The information on a compact disc is stored in one continuous spiral track, unlike floppy disks, on which the data is stored in multiple concentric tracks.

◆ Another popular type of information-storage system is the tape drive unit. These systems can store large amounts of data on small tape cartridges.

◆ Tape drives are generally used to store large amounts of information that will not need to be accessed often or quickly. Such applications include making backup copies of programs and data.

◆ Peripherals are devices and systems added to the basic computer system to extend its capabilities. These devices and systems can be divided into three general categories: input systems, output systems, and memory systems.

◆ Generally, the most difficult aspect of connecting peripheral equipment to a computer is obtaining the proper interfacing and cabling.

◆ In its simplest form, a modem consists of a modulator and a demodulator. The modulator is a transmitter that converts the digital/parallel computer data into a serial/analog format for transmission. The demodulator is the receiver that accepts the serial/analog transmission format and converts it into a digital/parallel format usable by the computer or peripheral. A device called a UART is actually responsible for the parallel/serial conversions, whereas the modulator and demodulator take care of the digital/analog conversions.

◆ All modems require software to control the communication session. At the fundamental instruction level, most modems use a set of commands known as the Hayes-compatible AT command set.

◆ To maintain an orderly flow of information between the computer and the modem, and between the modem and another modem, a protocol, or set of rules governing the transfer of information, must be in place.

◆ In addition to modulation techniques, advanced modems use data-compression techniques to reduce the volume of data that must be transmitted.

◆ The sound card takes samples of the analog waveform at predetermined intervals and converts them into corresponding digital values. Therefore, the digital values approximate the instantaneous values of the sound wave.

◆ A system's BIOS program is one of the keys to its compatibility. To be IBM PC-compatible, for example, the computer's BIOS must perform the same basic functions that the IBM PC's BIOS does.

◆ While the system is operating, the BIOS continues to perform several important functions. It contains routines that the operating system calls on to carry out basic services. These services include providing BIOS interrupt calls (software interrupt routines) for such operations as printing, video, and disk drive accesses.

◆ Operating systems are programs designed to control the operation of a computer system. Every portion of the system must be controlled and coordinated so that the millions of operations that occur every second are carried out correctly and on time. The operating system should also hide the complexity of the personal computer from the user.

◆ On Pentium-based system boards, the configuration jumpers and switches for enabling functions have been replaced by BIOS-enabling settings. These settings usually include the disk drives, keyboard, and video options, as well as onboard serial and parallel ports.

◆ Most sound cards support microphones through stereo RCA jacks. A very similar speaker jack also is normally present on the back of the card. Depending on the card, the jack may be designed for mono or stereo output.

◆ Scanners convert pictures, line art, and photographs into electronic signals that can be processed by software packages.

◆ Hard disk drives are created in a wide variety of storage capacities. To prepare the hard disk for use by the system, three levels of preparation must take place: the installation of the hardware, the partition of the drive, and the high-level format of the drive.

◆ Before a high-level format can be performed, the drive must be partitioned. The partition establishes the size and number of logical drives on the physical drive.

◆ The high-level format procedure is performed by the **FORMAT** command in the MS-DOS program. This format program creates the blank file allocation table and root directory on the disk.

◆ In Windows 9x, an advanced CD-ROM driver called CDFS (CD-ROM file system) has been implemented to provide protected-mode operation of the drive.

◆ In addition to the millions of possible memory locations in a PC, thousands of addresses are typically set aside for input and output devices in a system.

◆ The alphanumeric keyboard is one of the most widely used input devices for microcomputers. It provides a simple, finger-operated way to enter numbers, letters, symbols, and special control characters into the computer.

◆ A mouse is a handheld pointing device that produces input data by being moved across a surface. Basically, the mouse is an x-y positioning device that enables the user to move a cursor, or some other screen image, around the display screen.

◆ Parallel ports have been a staple of the PC system since the original PCs were introduced. They are most widely used to connect printers to the computer.

◆ The Centronics standard interface allows the computer to pass information to the printer, eight bits at a time, across the eight data lines. The other lines in the connection carry handshaking signals back and forth between the computer and the printer.

◆ DOS keeps track of the system's installed printer ports by assigning them the logical device names (handles) LPT1, LPT2, and LPT3. Whenever the system is booted up, DOS searches the hardware for parallel ports installed at hex addresses 3BCh, 378h, and 278h, consecutively.

◆ Newer specifications for the operation of the parallel printer port, called EPP and ECP, improve the functionality of the port by offering two-way communications. The ECP port employs DMA transfer techniques to gain a speed advantage over the EPP specification.

◆ Two methods are used to provide timing for serial transfers: the data may be sent synchronously (in conjunction with a synchronizing clock pulse) or asynchronously (without an accompanying clock pulse).

◆ Notable advanced UART versions include the 16450 and 16550. The 16450 is the 16-bit improvement of the 8250; the 16550 is a high-performance UART, with an onboard 16-byte buffer.

◆ As with parallel ports, DOS assigns COM port designations to the system's serial ports during boot up. COM port designations are normally COM1 and COM2, but they can be extended to COM3 and COM4 in advanced systems.

◆ Notebook computer designers work constantly to decrease the size and power consumption of all the computer's components.

◆ The drawback of portable computers from a service point of view is that conventions and compatibility disappear. Therefore, interchangeability of parts with other machines or makers goes by the wayside.

◆ The PCMCIA bus was developed to accommodate the space-conscious notebook and subnotebook computer market.

◆ Three types of PCMCIA adapters currently exist: the PCMCIA Type I cards are 3.3mm thick and work as memory-expansion units.

◆ PCMCIA Type II cards are 5mm thick and support virtually any traditional expansion function, except removable hard drive units. Type II slots are backward compatible, so Type I cards will work in them.

◆ PCMCIA Type III cards are 10.5mm thick and are intended primarily for use with removable hard drives. Both Type I and Type II cards can be used in a Type III slot.

◆ The most common type of the flat-panel displays used for the smaller PCs are liquid-crystal displays (LCDs). They are flat, lightweight, and require very little power to operate.

◆ The internal PC boards of the portable computer are designed to fit around the nuances of the portable case and its components rather than to match a standard design with standard spacing and connections. Therefore, interchangeability of parts with other machines goes by the wayside. The only source of most portable computer parts, with the exception of PC Cards and disk drive units, is the original manufacturer.

◆ Access to the notebook's internal components is normally challenging. Each case design has different methods for assembly and disassembly of the unit. Even the simplest upgrade task can be difficult with a notebook computer.

◆ There are two ideal characteristics for portable computers: compact and lightweight. Portable computer designers work constantly to decrease the size and power consumption of all the computer's components.

◆ One of the biggest problems for portable computers is heat buildup inside the case. The closeness of the portable's components and the small amount of free air space inside their cases add to heat-related design problems.

◆ The PC Card interface is designed so that cards can be inserted into the unit while it is turned on (hot insertion).

◆ External CD-ROM drives typically connect to a SCSI host adapter or to an enhanced parallel port. The latter connection requires a fully functional, bidirectional parallel port and a special software device driver.

◆ A single USB port can be used to connect up to 127 peripheral devices, such as scanners, printers, mice, modems, and keyboards.

◆ USB devices are "hot swappable." This means that you can connect and disconnect devices without any potential for causing damage to your computer.

◆ IEEE-1394 cables are limited to 4.5 meters (14ft) between devices before signal distortion begins to occur.

◆ With IEEE 1394, you can connect up to 63 devices together. When the IEEE-1394.1 bus bridges become available, it will be possible to connect more than 60,000 devices together using this bus.

◆ A standard ATA connection can accommodate two devices: one master and one slave device.

◆ Apple Computers created a derivation of the SCSI-3 standard called FireWire. To avoid licensing issues, most OEMs started using the technical specification name IEEE 1394.

◆ FireWire, IEEE 1394, and I-Link are the same specification. FireWire is optimized for digital multimedia devices.

◆ The maximum length of a SCSI daisy chain is 19.67 feet (6 meters) for a single-ended connection. If you allow 3 feet for internal cabling, most computers can support a daisy chain of just more than 16 feet.

◆ A maximum of eight devices can be attached to a standard SCSI connection. The SCSI controller is usually SCSI-7 and the first hard drive is usually SCSI-0.

◆ A standard SCSI connector has 50 contacts/pins. Apple Computer also uses a small 25-pin D-shell connector for SCSI-1.

◆ Typically, the range of an IrDA device is 0–2 meters, but the IrDA standard requires the capability to transmit from at least 1 meter.

◆ IrDA is the protocol used for infrared network connections.

◆ Each FireWire connection can support 63 devices, and up to 1,023 buses can be interconnected.

◆ The ATX power supply is controlled by an electronic switch produced on the motherboard. Other differences include the monitor—power passthrough is gone, and the ATX supply provides +3.3V through its new, keyed motherboard connector. Also, its fan blows air into the case rather than out.

◆ The IrLAN protocol was designed to be used in wireless infrared networks.

◆ After an infrared device is installed, the Wireless Link icon appears in the Control Panel. When another IrDA transceiver comes in range, the Wireless Link icon appears on the desktop and on the taskbar.

◆ When you plug a printer into a USB port on a Windows 98 machine for the first time, the system's Add New Hardware Wizard comes up and prompts you to insert vendor-specific software.

2.0 DIAGNOSING AND TROUBLESHOOTING

This domain requires the ability to apply knowledge relating to diagnosing and troubleshooting common module problems and system malfunctions. This includes knowledge of the symptoms relating to common problems. The main points follow:

◆ It is normal practice to first set the digital meter to its highest voltage range to make certain that the voltage level being measured does not damage the meter.

◆ Unlike the voltage check, resistance checks are always made with power removed from the system.

◆ One of the first things to do if you are not personally familiar with the system is to eliminate the user as a possible source of the problem.

◆ If an error or setup mismatch is encountered, the BIOS issues an error code, either in message form on the display screen or in beep-coded form through the system's speaker.

◆ Field replaceable units (FRUs) are the portions of the system that can be conveniently replaced in the field (for instance, keyboards, disk drives, monitors, and mice).

◆ After you have isolated the problem, and the computer boots up and runs correctly, work backward through the troubleshooting routines, reinstalling any original boards and other components removed during the troubleshooting process.

◆ With Pentium systems, you must check the Advanced CMOS Setup to determine whether a port has been enabled, and, if so, whether it has been enabled correctly.

◆ Typically, if the boot-up process reaches the point where the system's CMOS configuration information is displayed onscreen, you can assume that no hardware configuration conflicts exist in the system's basic components. If an error occurs after this point and before the single-beep boot-up tone, you must clean-boot the system and single-step through the remainder of the boot-up sequence.

◆ An interesting troubleshooting point occurs at the single beep in the boot-up process. If the system produces an error message or beep-code signal before the beep that indicates the end of the POST, the problem is hardware related.

Conversely, if the error message or beep code is produced after the beep, the problem is likely to be associated with the operating system.

◆ Normally, configuration problems occur when the system is being set up for the first time or when a new option is installed. The other condition that causes a configuration problem involves the system board's CMOS backup battery.

◆ A number of things can cause improper floppy disk drive operation or disk drive failure. These items include the use of unformatted disks, incorrectly inserted disks, damaged disks, erased disks, loose cables, drive failure, adapter failure, system board failure, or a bad or loose power cord.

◆ Modems can actually perform three different kinds of self-diagnostic possessive tests. These include the local digital loopback, local analog loopback, and remote digital loopback tests.

◆ With an external modem, the front-panel lights can be used as diagnostic tools to monitor its operation. The progress of a call, and its handling, can be monitored along with any errors that may occur.

◆ Every COM port on a PC requires an IRQ line to signal the processor for attention. In most PC systems, two COM ports share the same IRQ line. The IRQ4 line works for COM1 and COM3, and the IRQ3 line works for COM2 and COM4.

◆ Every LPT port in a PC requires an IRQ line to signal the processor for attention. In most PC systems, LPT1 uses IRQ7 and LPT2 typically employs IRQ5.

◆ The components involved in the audio output of most computer systems are very simple. There is a sound card, some speakers, the audio-related software, and the host computer system.

◆ The first step in isolating the monitor as the cause of the problem is to exchange it for a known good one. If the replacement works, the problem must be located in the monitor.

◆ Great caution must be used when opening or working inside the monitor. The voltage levels present during operation are lethal. Electrical potentials as high as 25,000 volts are present inside the unit when it is operating.

◆ To avoid conflicts with other devices attempting to use COM2, disable this port in CMOS before installing an internal modem.

◆ If one device stops working whenever another device is installed or activated (sound, modem, NIC, I/O controller, and so on), it is usually caused by a resource conflict of some sort (IRQ, I/O address).

3.0 PREVENTIVE MAINTENANCE

This domain requires the knowledge of safety and preventive maintenance. With regard to safety, it includes the potential hazards to personnel and equipment when working with high-voltage equipment and items that require special disposal procedures that comply with environmental guidelines. With regard to preventive maintenance, this includes knowledge of preventive maintenance products, procedures, environmental hazards, and precautions when working on microcomputer systems. The main points follow:

◆ Most IBM compatibles have only two potentially dangerous areas. One of these is inside the display monitor; the other is inside the power-supply unit. Both of these areas contain lethal voltage levels.

◆ Laser printers contain many hazardous areas. The laser light can be very damaging to the human eye. In addition, the typical laser printer has multiple high-voltage areas and a high-temperature area to contend with.

◆ Most computer components contain some level of hazardous substances. Printed circuit boards consist of plastics, precious metals, fiberglass, arsenic, silicon, gallium, and lead. CRTs contain glass, metal, plastics, lead, barium, and rare earth metals. Batteries from portable systems can contain lead, cadmium, lithium, alkaline manganese, and mercury.

◆ Cleaning is a major part of keeping a computer system healthy. Therefore, the technician's tool kit should also contain a collection of cleaning supplies.

◆ The human body can build up static charges that range up to 25,000 volts. These buildups can discharge very rapidly into an electrically grounded body or device. Placing a 25,000V surge through any electronic device is potentially damaging to it.

◆ In general, MOS devices are sensitive to voltage spikes and static electricity discharges. This can cause many problems when you have to replace MOS devices. The level of static electricity present in your body is high enough to destroy the inputs of a CMOS device.

◆ The term *ground* is often a source of confusion for the novice, because it actually encompasses a collection of terms. Generically, ground is just any point from which electrical measurements are referenced.

◆ Digital systems tend to be sensitive to power variations and losses. Even a very short loss of electrical power can shut a digital computer down, resulting in a loss of any information that has not been saved to a mass storage device.

◆ Uninterruptible power supplies are battery-based systems that monitor the incoming power and kick in when unacceptable variations occur in the power source.

◆ The environment around a computer system, and the manner in which the computer is used, greatly determines how many problems it will have. Occasionally dedicating a few moments of care to the computer can extend its mean time between failures (MTBF) considerably. This activity, involving maintenance not normally associated with a breakdown, is called preventive maintenance.

◆ Unlike hard disk drives, floppy drives are at least partially open to the atmosphere, and the disks may be handled on a regular basis. This opens the floppy disk drive to a number of maintenance concerns not found in hard disk drives. Smoke, dust, and other airborne contaminates have access to the internal components of the floppy drive and cause them to wear. In addition, the R/W heads ride directly on the disk surface in a floppy drive. This produces a small amount of dust and causes both the disk and the heads to wear. To this end, the heads and other components of the drive (especially the R/W heads) should be cleaned periodically with alcohol and a lint-free swab to lengthen the drive's life.

◆ Input peripherals generally require very little in the way of preventive maintenance. An occasional dusting and cleaning should be all that's really required.

◆ Because printers tend to be much more mechanical than other types of computer peripherals, they require more effort to maintain. Printers generate pollutants, such as paper dust and ink droplets, in everyday operation. These pollutants can build up on mechanical parts and cause them to wear.

◆ The dangers of the high-voltage and glass tubes associated with the CRT monitor requires that replacement/repair of these devices be conducted in a proper workshop rather than in the field.

4.0 MOTHERBOARD/ PROCESSORS/MEMORY

This domain requires knowledge of specific terminology and facts, along with ways and means of dealing with classifications, categories, and principles of motherboards, processors, and memory in microcomputer systems. The main points follow:

◆ System boards fundamentally change for three reasons: new microprocessors, new expansion slot types, and reduced chip counts. Reduced chip counts typically result from improved microprocessor-support chipsets. Chipsets combine PC- and AT-compatible structures into larger ICs.

◆ One of the items that makes computers PC compatibles is their adherence to standards established by the original IBM PC and PC-AT systems. Tables 1 and 2 contain information about how these systems allocate their interrupt and direct memory access (DMA) resources.

TABLE 1
SYSTEM INTERRUPT LEVELS

Interrupt	Description
NMI	I/O Channel Check or Parity Check error
	INTC1
IRQ0	Time-of-Day Tick
IRQ1	Keyboard Buffer Full
IRQ2	Cascade from INTC2
IRQ3	Serial Port 2
IRQ4	Serial Port 1
IRQ5	Parallel Port 2
IRQ6	FDD Controller
IRQ7	Parallel Port 1
	INTC2
IRQ8	Real-Time Clock
IRQ9	Cascade to INTC1
IRQ10	Spare
IRQ11	Spare
IRQ12	Spare
IRQ13	Coprocessor
IRQ14	Primary IDE Controller
IRQ15	Secondary IDE Controller

TABLE 2
STANDARD DMA CHANNEL USAGE IN PCs

Channel	Function
CH0	Spare
CH1	SDLC (network)
CH2	FDD controller
CH3	Spare
CH4	Cascade to controller
CH5	Spare
CH6	Spare
CH7	Spare

◆ The microprocessors used in the vast majority of all PC-compatible microcomputers include the 8088/86, the 80286, 80386, 80486, and Pentium (80586 and 80686) microprocessors.

◆ In protected mode, address bits A20 and higher are enabled, and the microprocessor can access physical memory addresses above the 1MB limit. Protected mode also can be used to perform virtual memory operations. In these operations, the system treats an area of disk space as an extension of RAM memory.

◆ Beginning with the 80386, Intel microprocessors offered an improved protected-addressing mode, referred to as virtual 86 mode. This mode enabled the 80386 to simulate several 8086 microprocessors running at the same time.

◆ The Pentium is called a superscalar microprocessor because its architecture allows multiple instructions to be executed simultaneously. This is achieved by a pipelining process that uses multiple stages to speed up instruction execution.

◆ In the Pentium MMX processor, the multimedia and communications processing capabilities of the Pentium device are extended by the addition of 57 multimedia-specific instructions to the instruction set.

◆ Intel departed from just increasing the speed of its Pentium processor line by introducing the Pentium Pro processor.

◆ The Pentium II includes all the multimedia enhancements from the MMX processor, and yet still retains the power of the Pentium Pro's dynamic execution and L2 cache features.

◆ The original Pentium III processor (code-named Katmai) was designed around the Pentium II core, but increased the L2 cache size to 512KB. It also increased the speed of the processor to 600MHz, including a 100MHz front-side bus speed.

TABLE 3
INDUSTRY SOCKET SPECIFICATIONS

Number	Pins	Voltages	Microprocessors
Socket 1	169 PGA	5	80486 SX/DXx, DX4 OverDrive
Socket 2	238 PGA	5	80486 SX/DXx, Pent OverDrive
Socket 3	237 PGA	5/3.3	80486 SX/DXx, Pent OverDrive
Socket 4	237 PGA	5	Pentium 60/66, 60/66 OverDrive
Socket 5	320 SPGA	3.3	Pentium 75–133, Pent OverDrive
Socket 6	235 PGA	3.3	Never Implemented
Socket 7	321 SPGA	VRM	Pentium 75–200, Pent OverDrive
Socket 8	387 SPGA	VRM	Pentium Pro
Slot 1	242 SECC/SEPP		Celeron, Pentium II, Pentium III
Slot 2	330 SECC-2		Xeon
Super Socket 7	321 SPGA	VRM	AMD K6-2, K6-2+, K6-III, K6-III+, Pentium MMX, Pentium Pro

continues

TABLE 3   CONTINUED
INDUSTRY SOCKET SPECIFICATIONS

Number	Pins	Voltages	Microprocessors
Socket 370	370 SPGA		Cyrix III, Celeron, Pentium III
Slot A	242 Slot A		AMD Athlon
Socket A	462 SPGA		AMD Athlon, Duron

◆ Normally, three types of semiconductor memory are found on a typical system board: the system's ROM BIOS ICs, the system's RAM memory, and the second-level cache memory unit.

◆ Caching is a memory-management method that assumes that most memory accesses are made within a limited block of addresses. Therefore, if the contents of these addresses are relocated into a special section of high-speed SRAM, the microprocessor can access these locations without requiring any wait states.

◆ The system's expansion slots provide the connecting point for most of its I/O devices. Interface cards communicate with the system through the extended microprocessor buses in these slots.

◆ The local bus connects special peripherals to the system board (and the microprocessor) through a proprietary expansion slot connector and allows the peripheral to operate at speeds compatible with the front-side bus speed of the microprocessor.

◆ The main component in the PCI bus is the PCI bus controller, called the host bridge. This device monitors the microprocessor's address bus to determine whether addresses are intended for devices in a PCI slot or one of the system board's other types of expansion slots.

◆ Like the PCI bus, the VL-bus controller monitors the microprocessor's control signals and addresses to determine what type of operation is being performed and where it is located in the system.

◆ The microprocessor, the RAM modules, and the cache memory can be exchanged to increase the performance of the system. These devices are normally mounted in sockets to make replacing or upgrading them an easy task.

◆ The video RAM is normally implemented through dynamic RAM devices. However, newer memory types are beginning to offer improved video memory. These memory types include extended data out DRAM (EDO RAM), synchronous DRAM (SDRAM), and video RAM (VRAM).

◆ A new serial interface scheme, called the Universal Serial Bus, (USB) has been developed to provide a fast, flexible method of attaching peripheral devices to the computer.

◆ Enhanced parallel port (EPP) and enhanced Centronics parallel (ECP) ports can be converted between unidirectional and bidirectional operation through the CMOS Setup screen.

◆ The Accelerated Graphics Port (AGP) was created by Intel based on the PCI slot, but is designed especially for the throughput demands of contemporary 3-D graphics adapters.

◆ The standard AGP channel is 32 bits wide and runs at 66MHz. This translates into a total bandwidth of 266MBps, as opposed to the PCI bandwidth of 133MBps. AGP 2× supports throughputs of 533MBps. AGP 4× supports throughputs of 1.07GBps.

◆ Low-speed USB devices support a data transfer rate of 1.5MBps. High-speed USB devices support a data transfer rate of 12MBps.

◆ The USB 1.1 specification prescribes a maximum high-power unit load of 500 mA. The maximum low-power unit load is 100 mA.

◆ The maximum transmission distance of the USB 1.1 specification is 5 meters without additional equipment.

◆ Intel Pentium III processors are designed to work in Socket 370 FC-PGA or Slot 1 connections.

◆ The AMD version of Slot 1 is called Slot A. It was designed for the Athlon processor.

◆ The Cyrix III processor is designed to fit Socket 370.

◆ The Communications and Networking Riser (CNR) was designed to support software-controlled devices such as modems, NICs, and sound cards.

◆ The host computer must have a USB host controller and USB root hub installed and properly configured in the Windows Device Manager to make a USB device work.

◆ A 168-pin DIMM uses a 64-bit memory bus.

◆ An ATA/IDE can have only two devices: a master and a slave. To install more IDE devices, you must install an ATA/IDE controller card in one of the system's expansion slots.

◆ High-speed USB supports a maximum cable length between devices of 5 meters. Low-speed USB supports a maximum cable length between devices of 3 meters.

◆ The CMOS virus-warning routine is designed to prevent boot sector viruses from making your computer unusable. However, they also can prevent upgrading software from writing to the boot sector of the hard drive. You should disable this feature before upgrading.

5.0 PRINTERS

This domain requires knowledge of basic types of printers, basic concepts, printer components, how they work, how they print onto a page, paper path, care and service techniques, and common problems. The main points follow:

◆ Impact printers place characters on the page by causing a hammer device to strike an inked ribbon. The ribbon, in turn, strikes the paper.

◆ Older, nonimpact printers relied on special heat-sensitive, or chemically reactive paper to form characters on the page. Newer methods use ink droplets, squirted from a jet-nozzle device, or a combination of laser/xerographic print technologies, to place characters on a page.

◆ Basically, there are two ways to create characters on a page. One method places a character on the page that is fully shaped, and fully filled-in. This type of character is called a fully formed character. The other method involves placing dots on the page in strategic patterns to fool the eye into seeing a character. This type of character is referred to as a dot-matrix character.

◆ The term font refers to variations in the size and style of characters. With true fully formed characters, typically only one font is available without changing the physical printing element. There are three common methods of generating character fonts: as bitmapped (or raster-scanned fonts), as vector-based fonts, and as TrueType outline fonts.

◆ In addition to positioning the print mechanism for printing, all printer types must feed paper through the print area. The type of paper-handling mechanism in a printer depends somewhat on the type of form that is going to be used with the printer, and the printer's speed.

◆ Like most other peripherals, the heart of a character printer is the interface/controller that accepts data and instructions from the computer's bus systems and provides the necessary interfacing between the computer and the printer's control circuitry.

◆ One of the least difficult I/O devices to add to a microcomputer system is a parallel printer. From the beginning of the PC era, the parallel printer has been one of the most standard pieces of equipment to add to the system.

◆ Serial printers are slightly more difficult to set up, because the communication definition must be configured between the computer and the printer. The serial port must be configured for speed, parity type, character frame, and protocol.

◆ Not all serial cables are created equal. In the PC world, RS-232 serial cables can take on several configurations. First of all, they may use either 9-pin or 25-pin D-shell connectors. The cable for a particular serial connection will need to have the correct type of connector at each end. Likewise, the connection scheme inside the cable can vary from printer to printer.

◆ Like mice, printers require device-driver programs to oversee their operation.

◆ The components of a typical dot-matrix printer include a power-supply board, a main control board, a printhead assembly, a ribbon cartridge, a paper-feed motor (along with its mechanical drive gears), and a printhead-positioning motor and mechanisms.

◆ The printhead is a collection of print wires set in an electromagnetic head unit. The printhead assembly is made up of a permanent magnet, a group of electromagnets, and a housing.

◆ Paper is specified in terms of its weight per 500 sheets at 22" × 17". (That is, 500 sheets of 22" × 17", 21-pound bond paper weigh 21 pounds.)

◆ Inkjet printers produce characters by squirting a precisely controlled stream of ink drops onto the paper. The drops must be controlled very precisely in terms of their aerodynamics, size, and shape; otherwise, the drop placement on the page becomes inexact.

◆ A color inkjet printer uses four ink colors to produce color images. These are cyan, magenta, yellow, and black (referred to as CMYK color). To create other colors, the printer prints a predetermined percentage of the basic colors in close proximity to each other.

◆ The single item in an inkjet printer that requires the most attention are the ink cartridge or cartridges.

◆ The laser printer modulates a highly focused laser beam to produce CRT-like raster-scan images on a rotating drum.

◆ As the drum is written on by the laser, it turns through the toner powder, which is attracted to the charged image on the drum.

◆ A typical laser printer has sensors to determine what paper trays are installed, what size paper is in them, and whether the tray is empty. It also uses sensors to track the movement of the paper through each stage of the printer.

◆ The laser printer tends to have several high-voltage and high-temperature hazards inside it. It may be necessary to defeat some interlock sensors. This action will place you in potential contact with the printer's high-voltage, high-temperature areas. Take great care when working inside the laser printer.

6.0 BASIC NETWORKING

This domain requires knowledge of basic network concepts and terminology, ability to determine whether a computer is networked, knowledge of procedures for swapping and configuring network interface cards, and knowledge of the ramifications of repairs when a computer is networked. The main points follow:

◆ LANs are systems designed to connect computers together in a relatively close proximity. These connections enable users attached to the network to share resources. LAN connections also enable users to communicate with each other and to share data between their computers.

◆ Control of the network can be implemented in two ways: as peer-to-peer networks, where each computer is attached to the network in a star, ring, or bus fashion; and client/server networks, where client workstations operate in conjunction with a dedicated file server.

◆ In a network, some method must be used to determine which node has use of the network's communications paths, and for how long it can have it. The network's protocol handles these functions, and it is necessary to prevent more than one user from accessing the bus at any given time.

◆ The Ethernet strategy allows for up to 1,024 users to share the LAN. From the description of its collision-recovery technique, however, it should be clear that with more users on an Ethernet LAN, more collisions are likely to occur and the average time to complete an actual data transfer will be longer.

◆ Ethernet is classified as a bus topology. The original Ethernet scheme was classified as a 10MHz transmission protocol. The maximum length specified for Ethernet is 1.55 miles (2.5km), with a maximum segment length between nodes of 500 meters. This type of LAN is referred to as a 10BASE-5 LAN by the IEEE organization.

◆ In 1985, IBM developed a token-passing LAN protocol it called the Token Ring. As its name implies, Token Ring is a token-passing protocol operating on a ring topology. Table 4 lists the Ethernet/ Token Ring specifications.

TABLE 4
ETHERNET SPECIFICATIONS

Classification	Conductor	Max. Segment Length	Nodes	Max. Length	Trans. Rate
10BASE-2	RG-58	185m	30/1,024	250m	10Mbps
10BASE-5	RG-8	500m	100/1,024	2.5km	10Mbps
10BASE-T	UTP/STP	100m/200m	2/1,024	2.5km	10Mbps
100BASE-T	UTP	100m	2/1,024	2.5km	100Mbps
100BASE–FX	FO	412m	1,024	5km	100Mbps

◆ In a LAN, each computer on the network requires a network adapter card, and every unit is connected to the network by some type of cabling. These cables are typically either twisted-pair copper wires, thick or thin coaxial cable, or fiber-optic cable.

◆ Begin troubleshooting a general network problem by determining what has changed since it was running last. If the installation is new, inspect it as a potential setup problem.

◆ Be aware that in a network environment, no unit really functions alone. Unlike working on a standalone unit, the steps performed on a network computer may affect the operation of other units on the network.

◆ One of the major concerns in most network environments is data security. Passwords are typically used at all software levels to lock people out of hardware resources, as well as out of programs and data files.

◆ When a computer is networked to another computer, a certain amount of security is lost. Because a physical path has been established into the computer, data stored in the system is now potentially available to anyone on the network. Therefore, all networking software includes some type of data-security system.

◆ In a client/server system, the technician's main responsibility is to get the local station to boot up to the network's login prompt.

◆ The most common network problems involve cabling. Bad connections account for more problems than any other network-related component.

The Fast Facts listed in this and the preceding chapter are designed as a refresher of key points and topics required to succeed on the A+ Certification exam. By using these summaries of key points, you can spend an hour prior to your exam to refresh key topics and ensure that you have a solid understanding of the objectives and information required for you to succeed in each major area of the exam.

CompTIA has established two modules for the A+ examination: the Core Hardware Service Technician module, and the Operating System Technologies (or operating system) module. The information here is organized to follow the sequence of the Operating System Technologies test objectives, and each domain that follows includes the key points from each chapter. If you have a thorough understanding of the key points here, chances are good that you will pass the exam.

Chapters 7 through 10 are dedicated to the four domains covered in the A+ Operating System Technologies module. Now that you have read those chapters, answered all the Review and Exam Questions at the ends of the chapters, and explored the *ExamGear* test engine on the CD that accompanies the book, you are ready to take the exam.

This chapter is designed as a quick (less than an hour) study aid that you can use just before taking the exam. Its key points should jog your memory in critical areas. In addition to the information located in this chapter, remember to review the Glossary terms. (They intentionally are not covered here.)

Fast Facts

OPERATING SYSTEM TECHNOLOGIES EXAM

CompTIA uses the following domains to arrange the objectives for the Operating System Technologies module:

◆ 1.0 Operating System Fundamentals

◆ 2.0 Installation, Configuration, and Upgrading

◆ 3.0 Diagnosing and Troubleshooting

◆ 4.0 Networks

1.0 OPERATING SYSTEM FUNDAMENTALS

This domain requires knowledge of underlying DOS (command-prompt functions), Windows 9x, and Windows 2000 operating systems in terms of its functions and structure for managing files and directories and running programs. It also includes navigating through the operating system from the command-line prompts and Windows procedures for accessing and retrieving information. The main points are as follows:

◆ In multiuser and multitasking operations, the appearance of simultaneous operations is accomplished by switching between different tasks in a predetermined order. The multiuser system switches between different users at multiple locations; multitasking systems switch between different applications at a single location. Both Windows 9x and Windows 2000 provide these capabilities.

◆ The operating system is responsible for providing the user interface. The main user interface for DOS is the command line. The command line is the space immediately following the DOS prompt onscreen.

◆ MS-DOS is a disk operating system for IBM PC–compatible computers. As with any other operating system, its function is to oversee operation of the system by providing support for executing programs, controlling I/O devices, handling errors, and providing the user interface. MS-DOS is a disk-based, single-user, single-task operating system.

◆ The WIN.INI file contains parameters that can be altered to change the Windows environment to suit the user's preferences. This is one of the largest INI files installed by Windows. The major sections of the WIN.INI file are Windows, Desktop, Extensions, and Colors.

◆ The SYSTEM.INI file contains hardware-setting information for the drivers and modules that Windows uses to configure itself when started.

◆ The contents of the Windows 95 Registry are located in two files located in the Windows directory. These are the USER.DAT and SYSTEM.DAT files. In Windows 95, these files are backed up using a .DA0 extension. These files can be used to rebuild the Registry if it becomes corrupt.

◆ The second section of a DOS disk is an area referred to as the file allocation table (FAT). This area is a table of information about how the disk is organized. Basically, the system logs the use of the space on the disk as shown in the following table.

TABLE 1
FAT SIZE RELATIONSHIPS

FAT Type	Partition Size	Cluster Size (in bytes)
FAT12	16MB	4096
FAT16	32MB	2048
FAT16	128MB	2048
FAT16	256MB	4096
FAT16	512MB	8192
FAT16	1GB	16384
FAT16	2GB	32768
FAT32	< 260MB	512
FAT32	8GB	4096
FAT32	16GB	8192
FAT32	32GB	16384
FAT32	> 32GB	32768

◆ The next section following the FAT tables is the disk's root directory. This is a special directory present on every DOS disk. It is the main directory of every logical disk, and serves as the starting point for organizing information on the disk. The root directory can hold up to 512 entries.

◆ DOS systems offer a number of commands that can be used to maintain, and optimize the performance of the hard drive. The **CHKDSK** command is used to recover lost allocation units from the hard drive.

◆ Backup utilities enable the user to quickly create extended copies of files, groups of files or an entire disk drive. Backup operations are normally performed to back up important information in case the drive crashes or the disk becomes corrupt.

◆ File fragmentation creates conditions that cause the drive to operate slower. Fragmentation occurs when files are stored, retrieved, modified, and rewritten due to differences in the sizes of the before and after files.

◆ The My Computer icon is the major user interface for Windows 95. It enables the user to see the local system's contents and manage its files.

◆ The Network Neighborhood icon provides quick information about the world around the system when it is used in a networked environment.

◆ One of the main Control Panel icons is the System icon. Clicking this icon produces the System Properties window. This window features tabs for General information, the Device Manager, Hardware Profiles, and System Performance.

◆ The Device Manager utility provides a graphical representation of the devices configured in the system. This interface can be used to identify installed ports, update device drivers, and change I/O settings. It also can be used to manually isolate hardware and configuration conflicts. The problem device can be examined to see where the conflict is occurring.

◆ Disk-based systems store and handle related pieces of information in groups called files. The system recognizes and keeps track of the different files in the system by their filenames. Therefore, each file in the system is required to have a filename that differs from that of any other file in the directory.

◆ The Windows 9x and Windows 2000 file systems do away with the 8.3 character filename system implemented under DOS. In Windows 95, long filenames of up to 255 characters can be used; so they can be more descriptive in nature. When these filenames are displayed in non-Windows systems, they are truncated (shortened) to fit the 8.3 DOS character format and identified by a tilde character (~) followed by a single-digit number.

◆ The Windows 9x file management system will number subsequent copies of the same file with the number incremented each time. Up to 99 iterations of the same 8.3 filename can be saved this way in Windows 95.

◆ The partitioning program for MS-DOS and Windows is named FDISK. This program creates the disk's Master Boot Record and establishes partition parameters for the system's use. The Windows FDISK utility provides upgraded support for very large hard drives. The original version of Windows 95 set a size limit for logical drives at 2GB. The FDISK version in the upgraded OSR2 version extended the maximum disk partition size to 8GB.

◆ Basically, DOS can recognize the following classifications of memory: conventional memory, upper memory blocks, high memory area, expanded memory, extended memory, and virtual memory.

◆ Conventional memory slots (locations 00000h through 9FFFFh) are the standard memory area for all PC-compatible systems. It traditionally holds DOS, interrupt vector tables, and relocated ROM BIOS tables. The remaining space in the conventional memory area is referred to as DOS program memory. Programs written to operate under PC DOS or MS-DOS use this area for program storage and execution.

◆ The upper memory area occupies the 384KB portion of the PC's address space from A0000h to FFFFFh. This space is not normally considered as part of the computer's total address space

because programs cannot store information in this area. Instead, the area is reserved to run segments of the system's hardware. Address spaces from A0000h through BFFFFh are dedicated addresses set aside for the system's video display memory. The system's ROM BIOS occupies the address space between locations FE000h and FFFFFh.

◆ With the advent of the 80286 microprocessor and its protected operating mode, it became possible to access physical memory locations beyond the 1MB limit of the 8088. Memory above this address is generally referred to as extended memory.

◆ The term virtual memory is used to describe memory that isn't what it appears to be. Virtual memory is actually disk drive space manipulated to seem like RAM. Software creates virtual memory by swapping files between RAM and the disk drive. Because there is a major transfer of information that involves the hard disk drive, an overall reduction in speed is encountered with virtual memory operations.

◆ The CONFIG.SYS program is responsible for: (1) setting up any memory managers being used; (2) configuring the DOS program for use with options devices and application programs; (3) loading up device-driver software; and (4) installing memory-resident programs.

◆ After completing the CONFIG.SYS operation, DOS searches for the AUTOEXEC.BAT file. This file contains a batch of DOS commands that will be carried out automatically when DOS is loaded into the system.

◆ The real objective in memory management in DOS or Windows 9x is to free up as much conventional memory as possible for use by DOS-based programs. The first step in this process is to use the DOS **MEM** command to determine how much memory is actually in the system and how it is organized.

◆ Pressing the Alt+F4 key combination in Windows 9x brings up the Shut Down Windows dialog box. Pressing the Enter key next either shuts down or reboots the machine. You can then enter safe mode and fix the display properties without losing any data.

◆ The Windows Disk Defrag utility arranges the files on a drive to give the fastest access to those used most recently. This utility can be used to speed up a heavily used drive.

◆ The Windows Registry is a hierarchical database used to hold system information concerning its installed hardware, software, and user configurations.

◆ In the Windows environment, a check mark next to an option in a drop-down menu indicates that the interface is using that item. For example, a check mark next to Status Bar in the View menu means that it will display the status of the Explorer on the bottom border of the window.

◆ When a file is deleted and removed from the Recycle Bin, the first three letters of its name are removed from the FAT. This permits the system to use its clusters on the drive to store new information. The data for the file is still on the drive until the operating system writes another file over it. Until this occurs, you can use a recover tool, such as Norton Utilities, to recover the file after it has been removed it from the Recycle Bin.

◆ The virtual memory file in Windows 98 is WIN386.SWP.

◆ To recover a hidden taskbar, move the mouse pointer to the edge of the screen. The taskbar can be resized to be at the edge of the screen. If so, the cursor changes shape when over the taskbar. Likewise, pressing the Ctrl+Esc key combination opens the Start menu, enabling you to see where the taskbar is located. You can then change the setting of the taskbar so that it is not hidden.

◆ In Windows 2000, the Add/Remove Hardware Wizard is used to add, remove, unplug, or troubleshoot hardware devices when Plug and Play is not working. This includes adding new device drivers.

◆ In Windows 2000, the **CMD** command starts a new instance of the Windows 2000 command interpreter and provides the command-line prompt.

◆ In Windows 2000, the **COMPACT** command is used to display or alter the compression of files on NTFS partitions. It can be used to compress or decompress selected files on an NTFS partition.

◆ In Windows 2000, the **CONVERT** command converts FAT volumes to NTFS volumes. Always back up the information on the drive before converting it.

◆ In Windows 2000, the **RECOVER** command recovers readable information from a bad or defective disk. This command reads a file sector by sector and recovers data from the good sectors. However, data located in bad sectors is lost.

◆ PAGEFILE.SYS is the swap filename used in Windows NT or 2000. When the system is running low on memory, Windows NT or 2000 uses this file on the hard drive to simulate RAM.

◆ NTFS5 is the file system used in Windows 2000. Windows NT 4.0 employed NTFS4. NTFS5 includes encryption capabilities and administrative enhancements that NTFS4 did not have.

◆ Under Windows 2000 NTFS, drives can be established as basic or dynamic disks. Dynamic drives (striped and mirrored) are created by converting basic disks.

◆ The CVRT1.EXE file can be used to convert FAT16 drives into FAT32 drives.

◆ Pressing the Ctrl+Alt+Del key combination in Windows 9x and 2000 produces the Task Manager utility. Running applications, processes, and system performance can be viewed from this window. This includes a graphical representation of your CPU and memory usage history.

◆ In Windows 98 and Windows 2000, the keys of the Registry can be edited using the RegEdit or RegEdit32 utilities.

◆ The Windows 2000 Computer Management tool combines many of the operating system's administrative tools, including System Information, Performance Logs, Shared Folders, Local Users, Disk Management and Defragmenter, Logical Drives, and Services and Applications, in a single location.

◆ The main reason to encrypt a file is to secure it for transmitting. You can encrypt files using different cipher strengths. The user can decrypt the contents of the files after they have been received.

◆ In Windows 2000, User Registry files are stored under Documents and Settings. Other Registry files are stored in C:\WINNT\System32\Config folder.

◆ To view hidden files in Windows 2000, run Explorer, click the Tools menu, select Folder Options, click the View tab, and change to the appropriate setting.

◆ Disk Defragmenter in Windows 2000 can defragment NTFS, FAT, and FAT32 volumes.

◆ In Windows 2000, the MSINFO32.EXE command can be used to display various components of the hardware and software environment and to show conflicting resources.

◆ In Windows 2000, the Administrators group has complete and unrestricted access to the computer/domain.

◆ Even in Windows 9x and Windows 2000, many applications maintain INI files that contain their configuration information. This enables the program to run properly based on the user's needs.

2.0 INSTALLATION, CONFIGURATION, AND UPGRADING

This domain requires knowledge of installing, configuring, and upgrading DOS, Windows 3.x, and Windows 95. This includes knowledge of system boot sequences. The main points are as follows:

◆ Windows 9x must be installed over an existing operating system, such as MS-DOS or Windows 3.x. The system must be at least an 80386DX or higher machine, operating with at least 4MB of RAM (8MB is recommended).

◆ By establishing a dual-boot configuration, it is possible to install Windows 9x or Windows NT/2000 on an existing system and still retain the original operating system.

◆ Windows 9x is designed to assist the user in setting up any new hardware components that may be added to the system. An icon named Add New Hardware can be found under the Control Panel option of the Settings menu.

◆ The POST test is actually a series of tests performed each time the system is turned on. The different tests check the operation of the microprocessor, the keyboard, the video display, the floppy and hard disk drive units, as well as both the RAM and ROM memory units.

◆ If the first 16KB of RAM successfully passes all five of the bit-pattern tests, the BIOS routine initializes the system's intelligent devices. During this part of the program, startup values stored in the ROM chip are moved into the system's programmable devices to make them functional.

◆ After the initialization and POST tests are completed, the BIOS checks the area of memory between C0000h and DFFFFh for BIOS extension programs.

◆ The boot-up process starts when the BIOS begins looking through the system for a Master Boot Record. This record can reside on drive A: or C:, or at any other location.

◆ Because there is no separate DOS level present in the Windows 9x/NT/2000 startup routine, special precautions and procedures must be used to protect the system in case of startup problems. Two very good tools to use in these situations are an Emergency Start Disk and the Startup menu.

◆ In safe mode, only the keyboard, mouse, and standard-mode VGA drivers are active. Safe mode is accessed by pressing the F5 function key during the boot-up process.

◆ The standard safe mode startup is used when the system

  • Will not start after the Starting Windows message appears onscreen.

  • Stalls repeatedly or for long periods of time.

  • Cannot print to a local printer after a complete troubleshooting sequence.

  • Has video display problems.

  • Slows down noticeably, or doesn't work correctly.

◆ The Step-by-Step Confirmation startup option allows each line of the startup procedure to be checked individually. In doing so, this option makes it possible to verify which drivers are being loaded, temporarily disable any offending drivers, and check other startup errors that may be indicated through error messages.

◆ The Plug and Play–compliant design of Windows 9x and Windows 2000 makes installing most new hardware nearly automatic (as long as the new device is also PnP compatible). The PnP function automatically detects new PnP-compliant hardware when it is started. If the device is not PnP compliant, or if the system just cannot detect it for some reason, it will be necessary to use the Windows 9x Add New Hardware Wizard. For PnP to work, there must be (1) a PnP BIOS, (2) PnP devices, and (3) a PnP operating system.

◆ The Windows environment supplies the printing function for all its applications. Instead of each application having printer drivers to deal directly with whatever printer is installed, Windows applications need to communicate only with the environment.

◆ Printing is significantly improved in Windows 9x and 2000. The Print Management function and its support components have been integrated into a single print-processing architecture, referred to as the print spooler. This integration provides smooth printing in a background mode and quick return-to-application time. The key to this operation is in how the print spooler sends data to the printer. Data is moved to the printer only when it is ready. Therefore, the system is never waiting for the printer to digest data that has been sent to it.

◆ Windows 9x automatically adopts any printers that have been established prior to its installation. If no printers are already installed, the Setup program runs the new Add Printer Wizard to allow a printer to be installed.

◆ Like the Hardware Wizard, Windows 9x and 2000 offer the user assistance in installing new programs. The Add/Remove New Programs icon under the Control Panel is used to install new programs automatically.

◆ DOS-based applications are installed in Windows 9x and 2000 by just running their executable file from the Run dialog box or from Windows Explorer. If the file has never been run under Windows 9x, the operating system creates a default entry in its APPS.INF file for that program. A copy of the new entry is also used to create a PIF file for the application.

◆ The minimum requirements for installing Windows 98 are a 80486DX/66MHz system with 24MB of RAM installed.

◆ The largest disk partition allowed under FAT32 is 2 terabytes. Windows 95b (OSR2), Windows 98, and Windows ME are all capable of working with FAT32.

◆ The proper order for preparing a hard disk drive for use in a Windows 9x system is partition, reboot, and format. After you partition the hard drive, you must reboot the computer for it to recognize the FAT table changes. After rebooting, you can format the partition with the operating system and it will be bootable and usable. A final reboot is not necessary but usually occurs after an operating system has been installed.

◆ The minimum requirements to install Windows 2000 Professional are a 133MHz Pentium processor with 32MB (64MB recommended) of RAM

installed, with a HDD having 650MB or more of free space on a 2GB drive. It also requires at least a VGA monitor.

◆ When Windows 2000 is started, the sequence of events is NTLDR, NTDETECT.COM, BOOT.INI. The BOOT.INI file turns control of the boot process over to the OSLOADER.EXE file.

◆ During the Windows 2000 startup, you can enter boot-logging mode by pressing the F8 function key. This action displays the Bootup Options screen, which includes startup options such as safe mode.

◆ To install a network printer from Windows 2000, you can (1) select Add Printer from Control Panel and select Network Printer when prompted; (2) open My Network Places, browse for the printer, and double-click it; or (3) click Start/Settings/Printers/Add New Printer and type the path of the network printer.

◆ Windows 2000 is typically installed in the C:\WINNT folder.

◆ If Windows 2000 has an invalid BOOT.INI file, it will notify the user of the invalid file and then boot normally from the C:\WINNT installation directory without it.

◆ The Windows 2000 Print Spooler service loads files to be printed into memory and then forwards them to the printer as required.

◆ The Windows 2000 Plug and Play service manages device installation and configuration and notifies programs of device changes. The Plug and Play service will auto detect new devices and enable programs to use them. However, Windows 2000 doesn't always prompt the user that it is installing the new device.

- In Windows 2000, the Windows Installer service manages all the software installed in the system.

- When converting a partition from FAT to NTFS, you should always back up the contents of the partition because there is the potential to lose the data from the drive during the conversion.

- To connect to a network printer with the name MYPRINTER on SERVER1 in Window 2000, you should access the Start/Settings/Printers/Add Printer option and then connect to Network Printer at \\SERVER1\MYPRINTER.

- Windows 2000 can be installed into FAT, FAT32, or NTFS partitions.

3.0 DIAGNOSING AND TROUBLESHOOTING

This domain requires the ability to apply knowledge to diagnose and troubleshoot common problems relating to DOS, Windows 3.x, and Windows 95/NT/2000. The main points are as follows:

- It is always good to have a clean boot disk to start the system. This tool provides a well-defined point to begin troubleshooting operating system problems.

- One of the best tools to have when troubleshooting Windows problems is an Emergency Start Disk. When the Windows 9x or NT/2000 program becomes nonfunctional, you must use the Start disk to boot the system, and then use its utilities to restore the system to proper operation. You should be aware that the Start or Setup disk restores the system just to the command prompt. Therefore, you must know how to operate from the command line to repair the system.

- Normally, if the system will not start in standard mode, some program or device is taking up too much memory. If the system has enough physical memory to run Windows, you must free up additional extended memory for use.

- Windows 9x offers many improved features over previous operating systems. However, it can suffer many of the same problems as any other operating system. To overcome some of the typical system problems, Windows 95 includes several built-in troubleshooting tools. These tools include several safe-mode startup options, a trio of system log files, and an extensive interactive troubleshooting Help file system.

- Windows 9x maintains four log files named BOOTLOG.TXT, SETUPLOG.TXT, DET-LOG.TXT, and DETCRASH.LOG. These files maintain a log of different system operations and can be used to determine that events that led up to a failure.

- Windows 9x and Windows 2000 comes with a built-in troubleshooting Help file system. This feature includes troubleshooting assistance for a number of different Windows-related problems.

- When Windows fails to start properly, no separate underlying DOS platform can be accessed to separate boot-up/configuration problems from operating-environment problems. Windows 9x and Windows 2000 provide the safe-mode Startup utility, however, which can be employed to isolate and repair startup problems.

- When Windows 9x refuses to start, a number of options are available for starting it from the command line. Starting Window using a **/D:x** switch is often helpful in isolating possible areas of the operating system as problem sources (that is, **WIN /D:**). The **/D:** switch can be modified to start Windows in a number of different configurations.

◆ The BOOTLOG.TXT file contains the sequence of events conducted during the startup of the system. A boot log can be created by pressing the F8 key during startup or by starting Windows 9x with a **WIN /B** switch.

◆ The SETUPLOG.TXT file holds setup information that was established during the installation process. The file is stored on the system's root directory and is used in Safe Recovery situations.

◆ The DETLOG.TXT file holds the text equivalent of the information in the DETCRASH.LOG file. This file can be read with a text editor to determine which hardware components have been detected by the system and what their parameters are.

◆ Windows 9x produces a `This Program Has Performed an Illegal Operation and Is About to Shut Down` message when a memory conflict occurs.

◆ When Windows is forced to substitute fonts other than the one called for by the application, printing problems can occur. The printer can lock up or just produce print that is not correct or that is out of place.

◆ If nothing is being produced by the printer, even though print jobs have been sent to it, check the print spooler to see whether any particular type of error has occurred. To view documents waiting to be printed, double-click the desired printer's icon. Return to the Printer folder, right-click the printer's icon, click Properties, and then select Details. From this point, select Spool Settings and select the Print Directly to the Printer option. If the print job goes through, there is a spooler problem. If not, the hardware and printer driver are suspect.

◆ The complexity of conducting printer operations over a network becomes much greater due to the addition of the network drivers and protocols. Many of the problems encountered when printing over the network involve components of the operating system. Therefore, its networking and printing functions must both be checked.

◆ Computer viruses are destructive software programs designed to replicate and spread on their own. Sometimes these programs take control of a machine to leave a humorous message, and sometimes they destroy data.

◆ Using the **FDISK /MBR** command replaces the Master Boot Record on the hard drive, leaving the rest of the files in tact. In the case of repairing boot-sector viruses, it would replace the Master Boot Record and temporarily remove the virus from that record. As soon as the system runs a virus-infected file on the hard drive, however, the virus is back. Therefore, the best thing to do for boot-sector virus infections is to run a virus-scanner utility immediately after booting the system with a clean boot disk.

◆ If a user's Internet account has been cancelled, the Internet would keep requesting the user to log on to the ISP. Likewise, if the user enters an incorrect spelling for the username or password, the ISP will not be able to find a match for it. This is the same as not having a valid account setup. Both of these situations result in an Internet connection message constantly reappearing requesting a username and password.

◆ The Event Viewer is a Windows NT/2000 administrative tool used to view and manage logs of system, program, and security events on the computer.

◆ By default, the ScanDisk utility will run in a Windows 2000 system whenever it has been shut down improperly.

◆ In Windows 4.0, the **RDISK** command can be executed to create a new Emergency Repair Disk.

4.0 NETWORKS

This domain requires knowledge of network capabilities of DOS and Windows, and how to connect to networks, including what the Internet is about, its capabilities, basic concepts relating to Internet access, and generic procedures for system setup. The main points are as follows:

◆ After the network card has been configured and installed, the next step in establishing the Windows 3.x network is to install the network adapter driver. This is accomplished through the Program Manager's Network program group.

◆ In Windows 9x, the local area networking function is an integral part of the system. The heart of the Windows 9x networking system is contained in the desktop's Network Neighborhood icon and the Control Panel's Network icon.

◆ The Network Neighborhood display is the primary network user interface for Windows 9x. It is used to browse and access shared resources on the LAN, in a method similar to that used with the Windows Explorer for a local hard drive.

◆ It is possible for the local system to assign a logical drive letter to the remote unit or folder. This is referred to as mapping the drive letter to the resource. This will enable non-Windows 95 applications running on the local computer to use the resources across the network.

◆ The Control Panel's Network screen provides configuration and properties information about the system's networks.

◆ After the network adapter card has been configured and installed, the next step in setting up the computer on the network is to load its drivers, protocols, and services. In most Windows 95 installations, the majority of these steps are accomplished just by rebooting the computer and allowing Windows to detect the network adapter.

◆ In a wide area network, computers are typically separated by distances that must be serviced via modems rather than through local area network cards.

◆ The most famous wide area network is the Internet. It is actually a network of networks, working together.

◆ Connecting all the users and individual networks together are Internet service providers. ISPs are companies that provide the technical gateway to the Internet.

◆ The IP addresses of all the computers attached to the Internet are tracked using a listing system called the Domain Name Service (DNS).

◆ The TCP/IP protocol divides the transmission into packets of information, suitable for retransmission across the Internet. Along the way, the information passes through different networks organized at different levels.

◆ ISDN service offers high-speed access to the public telephone system. However, ISDN service requires digital modems.

◆ A special application, called FTP, is used to upload and download information to, and from, the network.

◆ One of the most widely used functions of wide area networks is email. This feature enables network users to send and receive electronic messages to each other over the network.

◆ The World Wide Web is a menu system that ties together Internet resources from around the world. These resources are scattered across computer systems everywhere.

◆ As the Internet network has grown, service providers have continued to provide more user-friendly software for exploring the World Wide Web. These software packages are called browsers and are based on hypertext links.

◆ The NBTSTAT (NetBIOS over TCP STATistics) utility shows the Windows NetBIOS names for the connected computers and lists their IP address and the status of the connection.

◆ The **NET VIEW** command lists all the computers currently connected to your local area network (LAN). It also can display all the shared devices associated with a particular network host.

◆ The command **TRACERT** *hostname*, where *hostname* is the IP address or DNS name of a host, traces the path of a network connection to that remote host.

◆ The **PING** command causes a data packet to be sent to a specified IP address and returned to your machine. If the IP address is not currently active, you receive a message stating that the transaction has timed out.

◆ All TCP/IP utilities are controlled by commands entered at the MS-DOS command prompt (that is, C:>).

◆ The Address Resolution Protocol (ARP) utility can be used to identify address information by examining the contents of the ARP caches on either the client or the server. It is primarily used to map IP addresses to physical MAC addresses.

◆ The **NETSTAT** command is used to display statistics about the current session.

◆ The IPCONFIG utility enables you to see your current IP address and other useful network configuration information.

◆ The WINIPCFG utility provides all the network configuration features of IPCONFIG. Due to its graphical interface, it tends to be more user friendlier.

◆ IPX/SPX is a protocol created by Novell for NetWare networks.

◆ NetBIOS Enhanced User Interface (NetBEUI) is a Windows network-specific protocol.

◆ The TCP/IP protocol uses an ID system that assigns a unique number to every node on the network. This number is known as the node's IP address.

◆ Remote Access Service (RAS) allows remote hosts to access a local network server.

◆ Domain Name Service (DNS) associates host and domain names to the associated IP addresses.

◆ Dynamic Host Configuration Protocol (DHCP) enables the host server to automatically assign IP addresses and subnet masks every time a client computer begins a network session.

◆ Windows Internet Name Service (WINS) provides name registration, renewal, release, and resolution of NetBIOS names.

◆ The IP address tab, in the TCP/IP Properties feature of the Network Control Panel, is used to administer DHCP.

◆ The IP Address tab in the TCP/IP Properties window is used to manually set the IP address and subnet mask.

◆ The WINIPCFG interface enables the user to release or renew an IP address leased from a DHCP server.

◆ The TCP/IP protocol is associated with peer-to-peer Ethernet networks and large WANs such as the Internet.

◆ The IPX/SPX network protocol was designed to be used with Novell NetWare networks.

◆ The NetBEUI protocol is a Microsoft version of the IBM NetBIOS protocol for small LANs.

◆ The **IPCONFIG/ALL** command displays all current network parameters including DHCP status, IP address and subnet mask, physical MAC address, default gateway, DNS server address, and IP lease information.

◆ Most ISPs provide email service via POP3 and SMTP servers, provide Internet news service via Usenet archive servers, and provide Internet routing service via DNS servers. However, they do not normally provide and maintain a phone, cable, or satellite connection to the Internet.

◆ Hypertext Transfer Protocol (HTTP) defines how messages are formatted and transmitted and what actions Web servers and browsers should take in response to various commands.

◆ A user using DHCP to connect to a DHCP server leases an IP address for a length of time. Therefore, the user's IP address changes periodically.

◆ File Transfer Protocol (FTP) is an older communications protocol used to transfer files over a remote network connection.

These "Study and Exam Prep Tips" provide you with some general guidelines to help prepare for the exams. The information is organized into two sections. The first section addresses your pre-exam preparation activities and covers general study tips. Following this are some tips and hints for the actual test-taking situation. Before tackling those areas, however, think a little bit about how you learn.

LEARNING AS A PROCESS

To better understand the nature of preparation for the exams, it is important to understand learning as a process. You probably are aware of how you best learn new material. You may find that outlining works best for you, or you may need to "see" things as a visual learner. Whatever your learning style, test preparation takes place over time. Obviously, you cannot start studying for these exams the night before you take them; it is very important to understand that learning is a developmental process. And as part of that process, you need to focus on what you know and what you have yet to learn.

Learning takes place when we match new information to old. You have some previous experience with computers, and now you are preparing for these certification exams. Using this book, software, and supplementary materials will not just add incrementally to what you know; as you study, you will actually change the organization of your knowledge as you integrate this new information into your existing knowledge base. This will lead you to a more comprehensive understanding of the tasks and concepts outlined in the objectives and of computing in general. Again, this happens as a repetitive process rather than a singular event. Keep this model of learning in mind as you prepare for the exam, and you will make better decisions concerning what to study and how much more studying you need to do.

Study and Exam Prep Tips

STUDY TIPS

There are many ways to approach studying, just as there are many different types of material to study. The following tips, however, should work well for the type of material covered on the certification exams.

Study Strategies

Although individuals vary in the ways they learn, some basic principles apply to everyone. You should adopt some study strategies that take advantage of these principles. One of these principles is that learning can be broken into various depths. Recognition (of terms, for example) exemplifies a more surface level of learning in which you rely on a prompt of some sort to elicit recall. Comprehension or understanding (of the concepts behind the terms, for example) represents a deeper level of learning. The ability to analyze a concept and apply your understanding of it in a new way represents an even deeper level of learning.

Your learning strategy should enable you to know the material at a level or two deeper than mere recognition. This will help you do well on the exams. You will know the material so thoroughly that you can easily handle the recognition-level types of questions used in multiple-choice testing. You also will be able to apply your knowledge to solve new problems.

Macro and Micro Study Strategies

One strategy that can lead to this deeper learning includes preparing an outline that covers all the objectives and subobjectives for the particular exam you are working on. You should delve a bit further into the material and include a level or two of detail beyond the stated objectives and subobjectives for the exam. Then expand the outline by coming up with a statement of definition or a summary for each point in the outline.

An outline provides two approaches to studying. First, you can study the outline by focusing on the organization of the material. Work your way through the points and subpoints of your outline with the goal of learning how they relate to one another. Be certain, for example, that you understand how each of the main objective areas is similar to and different from the others. Then do the same thing with the subobjectives; be sure you know which subobjectives pertain to each objective area and how they relate to one another.

Next, you can work through the outline, focusing on learning the details. Memorize and understand terms and their definitions, facts, rules and strategies, advantages and disadvantages, and so on. In this pass through the outline, attempt to learn detail rather than the big picture (the organizational information that you worked on in the first pass through the outline).

Research has shown that attempting to assimilate both types of information at the same time seems to interfere with the overall learning process. To better perform on the exam, separate your studying into these two approaches.

Active-Study Strategies

Develop and exercise an active-study strategy. Write down and define objectives, subobjectives, terms, facts, and definitions. In human information-processing terms, writing forces you to engage in more active encoding of the information. Just reading over it exemplifies more passive processing.

Next, determine whether you can apply the information you have learned by attempting to create examples and scenarios on your own. Think about how or where you could apply the concepts you are learning. Again, write down this information to process the facts and concepts in a more active fashion.

Common-Sense Strategies

Finally, you also should follow common-sense practices when studying. Study when you are alert, reduce or eliminate distractions, take breaks when you become fatigued, and so on.

Pre-Testing Yourself

Pre-testing enables you to assess how well you are learning. One of the most important aspects of learning is what has been called meta-learning. Meta-learning has to do with realizing when you know something well or when you need to study some more. In other words, you recognize how well or how poorly you have learned the material you are studying.

For most people, this can be difficult to assess objectively on their own. Practice tests are useful in that they reveal more objectively what you have learned and what you have not learned. You should use this information to guide review and further study. Developmental learning takes place as you cycle through studying, assessing how well you have learned, reviewing, and assessing again until you feel you arc ready to take the exam.

You may have noticed the practice exams included in this book. Use them as part of the learning process. The ExamGear software on the CD-ROM also provides a variety of ways to test yourself before you take the actual exam. By using the practice exams, you can take an entire timed, practice test quite similar in nature to that of the actual Core Hardware Service Technician or Operating System Technologies exams. The ExamGear Adaptive Exam option can be used to take the same test in an adaptive testing environment. This mode monitors your progress as you are taking the test to offer you more difficult questions as you succeed. By using the Study Mode option, you can set your own time limit, focus only on a particular objective domain (such as Diagnosing and Troubleshooting

or Basic Networking) and also receive instant feedback on your answers.

You should set a goal for your pre-testing. A reasonable goal would be to score consistently in the 90% range.

See Appendix D, "Using the ExamGear, Training Guide Edition Software," for a more detailed explanation of the test engine.

EXAM PREP TIPS

A+ Certification exams start out as standardized, computerized, fixed-form exams that reflect the knowledge domains established by CompTIA. After being in use for some period of time, the questions in the test banks become stable and CompTIA converts their tests to an adaptive delivery mode.

An original fixed-form, computerized exam is based on a fixed set of exam questions. The individual questions are presented in random order during a test session. If you take the same exam more than once, you will see the same number of questions, but you won't necessarily see the exact same questions. This is because two or three final forms are typically assembled for such exams. These are usually labeled Forms A, B, and C.

As suggested previously, the final forms of a fixed-form exam are identical in terms of content coverage, number of questions, and allotted time, but the questions differ. You may notice, however, that some of the same questions appear on, or rather are shared among, different final forms. When questions are shared among multiple final forms of an exam, the percentage of sharing is generally small. Many final forms share no questions, but some older exams may have a 10% to 15% duplication of exam questions on the final exam forms.

Fixed-form exams also have a fixed time limit in which you must complete the exam. The ExamGear test engine on the CD-ROM that accompanies this book provides fixed-form exams.

Finally, the score you achieve on a fixed-form exam is based on the number of questions you answer correctly. The exam's passing score is the same for all final forms of a given fixed-form exam.

Table 1 shows the formats for the exams.

TABLE 1

TIME AND NUMBER OF QUESTIONS BY EXAM

Exam	Time Limit in Minutes	Number of Questions
Core Hardware Service Technician	90	70
Operating System Technologies	90	70

This may seem like ample time for each question, but remember that many of the scenario questions are lengthy word problems, which can ramble on for paragraphs and/or include several exhibits. Your 90 minutes of exam time can be consumed very quickly.

Keep in mind that to pass the Core Hardware Service Technician exam, a score of at least 683 on a scale of 100 to 900 is required. To pass the Operating System Technologies exam, a score of at least 614 on the same scale is required.

When CompTIA converts the exams to an adaptive-delivery format (as discussed previously), the number of questions you will be asked will decrease. The adaptive test engine measures your performance as you move through the test and adjusts the difficulty level of the questions you receive. If you answer introductory questions correctly, you will be shifted to more difficult questions until you have achieved enough points to pass the test. Therefore, you should see only between 20 and 25 questions under the adaptive exam, versus the 69/70 question in the fixed length tests. The adaptive engine also will end the exam when it detects that you have mathematically been eliminated from passing the test. The main point to remember when preparing for the exam is that the fixed-length and adaptive tests all use the same question pools.

Putting It All Together

Given all these different pieces of information, the task now is to assemble a set of tips that will help you successfully tackle the A+ Certification exams.

More Pre-Exam Prep Tips

Generic exam-preparation advice is always useful. Tips include the following:

◆ Become familiar with PCs and the operating systems. Hands-on experience is one of the keys to success. Review the exercises and the Step by Steps in the book.

◆ Review the current exam-preparation guide on the CompTIA Web site.

◆ Memorize foundational technical detail, but remember that you need to be able to think your way through questions as well.

◆ Take any of the available practice tests. We recommend the ones included in this book and the ones you can create using the ExamGear software on the CD-ROM.

◆ Look on the CompTIA Web site for samples and demonstration items.

During the Exam Session

The following generic exam-taking advice that you have heard for years applies when taking an A+ Certification exams:

◆ Take a deep breath and try to relax when you first sit down for your exam session. It is very important to control the pressure you may (naturally) feel when taking exams.

◆ You will be provided scratch paper. Take a moment to write down any factual information and technical detail that you committed to short-term memory.

◆ Carefully read all information and instruction screens. These displays have been put together to give you information relevant to the exam you are taking.

◆ Read the exam questions carefully. Reread each question to identify all relevant detail.

◆ Tackle the questions in the order they are presented. Skipping around will not build your confidence; the clock is always counting down.

◆ Do not rush, but also do not linger on difficult questions. The questions vary in degree of difficulty. Don't let yourself be flustered by a particularly difficult or verbose question.

◆ Note the time allotted and the number of questions appearing on the exam you are taking. Make a rough calculation of how many minutes you can spend on each question and use this to pace yourself through the exam.

◆ Take advantage of the fact that you can return to and review skipped or previously answered questions. Record the questions you cannot answer confidently, noting the relative difficulty of each question, on the scratch paper provided. After you have made it to the end of the exam, return to the more difficult questions.

◆ If session time remains after you have completed all questions (and if you aren't too fatigued!), review your answers. Pay particular attention to questions that seem to have a lot of detail or that involved graphics.

◆ As for changing your answers, the general rule of thumb here is *don't*! If you read the question carefully and completely and you felt like you knew the right answer, you probably did. Do not second-guess yourself. If as you check your answers, one clearly stands out as incorrectly marked, of course you should change it. If you are at all unsure, however, go with your first impression.

If you have done your studying and follow the preceding suggestions, you should do well. Good luck!

This exam simulates the CompTIA A+ Core Hardware Service Technician exam. It is representative of what you should expect on the actual exam. The answers and explanations for them follow the questions. It is strongly suggested that when you take this exam, you treat it just as you would the actual exam. Time yourself, read carefully, and answer all the questions as best you can. There are 69 questions, just as on the actual exam. Set yourself a 90-minute time limit. This is the amount of time you are given to take the real thing. The questions also reflect the amount of coverage given each domain in the exam.

1.0 Installation, Configuration, and Upgrading - 30% = 21 Questions

2.0 Diagnosing and Troubleshooting - 30% = 21 Questions

3.0 Preventive Maintenance - 5% = 3 Questions

4.0 Motherboards, Processors, Memory - 15% = 10 Questions

5.0 Printers - 10% = 7 Questions

6.0 Basic Networking - 10% = 7 Questions

Run through the exam, and if you score less than 75%, try rereading the chapters on the domains in which you had trouble.

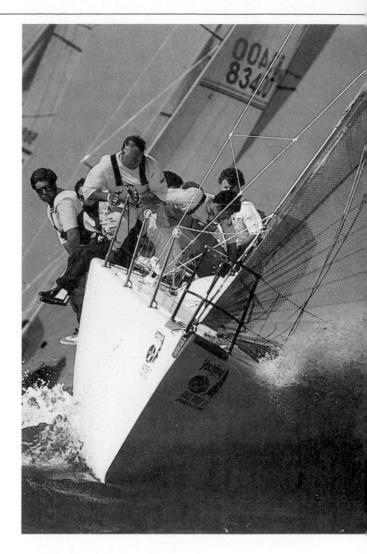

Practice Exam: Core Hardware Service Technician

EXAM QUESTIONS

1. The POST program can be found in _____.

   A. the BIOS chips

   B. the DOS disk

   C. the Windows program

   D. the CMOS RAM chip

2. An AT-compatible system has _____ DMA channels.

   A. 2

   B. 4

   C. 8

   D. 16

3. AGP stands for _____.

   A. Another Graphics Port

   B. Apple Graphics Port

   C. Advanced Graphics Port

   D. Accelerated Graphics Port

4. The purpose of the rechargeable battery on a system board is _____.

   A. to back up the contents of RAM memory, in case of a power fluctuation

   B. to keep the microprocessor's registers alive, in the case of a power fluctuation

   C. to maintain the contents of CMOS RAM, in the case of a power fluctuation

   D. to maintain the system's time-of-day chip, in the event of a power fluctuation

5. IRQ 4 is normally assigned to _____.

   A. COM1

   B. COM2

   C. LPT1

   D. LPT2

6. IRQ 7 is generally assigned to _____.

   A. COM1

   B. COM2

   C. LPT1

   D. LPT2

7. A USB device can be located a maximum distance of _____ from the host.

   A. 10 feet (3 meters)

   B. 15 feet (5 meters)

   C. 20 feet (7 meters)

   D. 30 feet (10 meters)

8. The recommended maximum length of an RS-232 serial connection is _____.

   A. 10 feet (3 meters)

   B. 25 feet (8.5 meters)

   C. 50 feet (15 meters)

   D. 100 feet (33 meters)

9. The recommended maximum length of a Centronics parallel connection is _____.

   A. 10 feet (3 meters)

   B. 25 feet (8.5 meters)

   C. 50 feet (15 meters)

   D. 100 feet (33 meters)

10. What type of connector is used with IBM-compatible versions of the parallel printer port?

   A. 36-pin, D-shell connectors

   B. 9-pin, D-shell connectors

   C. 25-pin, D-shell connectors

   D. 25-pin, edge connectors

11. Serial ports transmit data _____.

   A. 1 bit at a time

   B. 1 byte at a time

   C. when a clock pulse is applied to them

   D. in one direction only

12. Parallel ports transmit data _____.

   A. 1 bit at a time

   B. 1 byte at a time

   C. when a clock pulse is applied to them

   D. in one direction only

13. A 25-pin, female D-shell connector, located on the back of a PC, is used as _____.

   A. the COM1 serial port

   B. the COM2 serial port

   C. the LPT1 parallel port

   D. the game port

14. _____ transmissions are conducted at irregular intervals, using start, stop, and parity bits.

   A. Serial

   B. Parallel

   C. Synchronous

   D. Asynchronous

15. The COM2 and COM4 serial port settings are normally assigned to _____.

   A. IRQ1

   B. IRQ2

   C. IRQ3

   D. IRQ4

16. A .28 dot pitch monitor has _____.

   A. .28 inches between dots on the screen

   B. .28mm between dots on the screen

   C. .28 inches between characters on the screen

   D. .28mm between characters on the screen

17. A IEEE-1394 FireWire port can support a maximum of _____ devices.

   A. 8

   B. 23

   C. 58

   D. 63

18. How many pins does a Wide Ultra2 SCSI connector have?

   A. 68

   B. 50

   C. 25

   D. 9

19. How many logical drives can be created using Microsoft operating systems?

   A. 8

   B. 23

   C. 38

   D. 44

20. An IDE hard drive interface on a system board that docs not contain an enhanced BIOS has a maximum disk partition size of _____.

    A. 528MB

    B. 1GB

    C. 2GB

    D. 32MB

21. A 15-pin D-shell connector would probably be used as a _____.

    A. SCSI port

    B. printer port

    C. serial port

    D. joystick port

22. What system component can cause problems to appear in all the system's other components?

    A. The system board

    B. The expansion slots

    C. The power supply

    D. The hard disk drive

23. When using the ohmmeter function of a DMM to perform tests, you must always _____.

    A. Connect the meter in series with the device being tested

    B. Connect the meter in parallel with the device being tested

    C. Remove the device being tested from the circuit board

    D. Open the circuit that contains the device being tested

24. The majority of all problems encountered with PCs occur _____.

    A. On the system board

    B. With hard drives

    C. In peripheral cards

    D. In software and configuration settings

25. What is the major difference between AT and ATX power supplies?

    A. ATX power supplies require 240V AC input.

    B. The ATX power supply is controlled by a software switch on the system board.

    C. ATX power supplies deliver more power to the system.

    D. AT power supplies blow air onto the system board rather than out through the back of the unit.

26. If the power supply's fan runs and the hard drive spins up, but the system appears dead, what is the most likely cause of the problem?

    A. The monitor is just turned off.

    B. An I/O card is defective and has the system buses disabled.

    C. The floppy disk drive is defective.

    D. The system board is bad.

27. Cyrix III CPUs can be used in which of the following slots or sockets?

    A. Socket A

    B. Slot 1

    C. Slot A

    D. Socket 370

28. What type of cabling is used in a 100Base-TX system?

    A. CAT-5 STP

    B. CAT-5 UTP

    C. CAT-6 STP

    D. CAT-3 UTP

29. What item in your system's CMOS settings can prevent you from upgrading your operating system software?

    A. The hard disk drive Type setting

    B. The USB Enable setting

    C. The Virus Warning function

    D. The Auto-Detect hard drive's setting

30. You have been asked by a customer to install an additional hard drive in an older AT-style computer that has only one IDE controller. The system already has a hard drive and a CD-ROM drive installed. How can you handle the request?

    A. Add a SCSI controller to the system.

    B. Install a new IDE cable with an additional connector on it.

    C. Connect the hard drive to the B: floppy disk drive connector.

    D. Install an IDE host adapter card in the system.

31. What action should logically be taken as a first step if a `Disk Boot Failure` error message is received during boot up?

    A. Replace the hard disk drive.

    B. Replace the disk drive controller.

    C. Boot the system from a boot floppy, and type **SYS C:**.

    D. Replace the floppy disk drive.

32. What is the transmission range of an IrDA device?

    A. 1 meter

    B. 5 meters

    C. 10 meters

    D. 20 meters

33. If a functioning system fails to boot up after installing a new sound card, what is the most likely cause of the problem?

    A. The sound card is bad.

    B. The system board does not have enough RAM to accommodate the new card.

    C. An interrupt-level conflict exists between the sound card and some other device in the system.

    D. The sound card has a DMA conflict with another system device.

34. An ATA interface can provide for how many drive connections?

    A. 7

    B. 4

    C. 15

    D. 2

35. Which of the following device types are supported by CNR slots? (Choose two answers.)

    A. Memory devices

    B. Modems

    C. Sound cards

    D. Advanced-configuration power interfaces

36. The best way to transport a PC board is
    _____.

    A. in an antistatic bag

    B. in a shielded box

    C. in a Styrofoam container

    D. inside aluminum foil

37. You should not wear a wrist grounding strap
    when _____.

    A. repairing a CRT

    B. replacing an adapter card

    C. repairing a motherboard

    D. adding or replacing RAM

38. ESD can become more of a problem in condi-
    tions that are _____.

    A. hot and dry

    B. cool and dry

    C. hot and humid

    D. cool and humid

39. When disposing of a CRT, you should first
    _____.

    A. pack it in its original container

    B. discharge the HV anode

    C. check applicable local ordinances

    D. smash the CRT's glass envelope with a
       hammer

40. When replacing the fuser assembly in a laser
    printer, be careful because _____.

    A. it has sharp edges

    B. it may leak toner

    C. it may be hot

    D. it may be broken

41. When the system comes back on following a
    power outage, the primary concern is _____.

    A. to print the remaining jobs in the queue

    B. to recover any lost data

    C. to reestablish Internet connections

    D. to guard against power surges to the system

42. To protect a computer system from the effects of
    sudden power loss, _____.

    A. use a battery backup for CMOS

    B. use an uninterruptable power supply

    C. save your work frequently

    D. employ all the listed actions

43. Most ATX Pentium system boards use which
    combination of extension bus types?

    A. VESA, ISA, and PCI

    B. ISA, AGP, and MCA

    C. ISA, PCI, and VESA

    D. ISA, AGP, and PCI

44. Cache memory is used to _____.

    A. increase the speed of data accesses

    B. increase the size of memory available to
       programs

    C. store data in nonvolatile memory

    D. augment the memory used for the operating
       system kernel

45. The Pentium MMX CPU will fit into which of
    the following slots or sockets?

    A. Socket 8

    B. Socket A

    C. Socket 370

    D. Super Socket 7

46. In a Pentium MMX-based system board, the L2 cache is located _____.

    A. on an expansion card

    B. in the microprocessor cartridge

    C. on the system board

    D. on the microprocessor

47. In a Pentium II-based system board, the L2 cache is located _____.

    A. on an expansion card

    B. in the microprocessor cartridge

    C. on the system board

    D. on the microprocessor

48. An ATX-type system board supports a _____.

    A. soft power switch

    B. total of 16 expansion slots

    C. universal expansion slots

    D. RAM memory capacity of 256MB

49. A 72-pin memory module is known as a _____.

    A. SIMM

    B. DIMM

    C. DRAM

    D. PRAM

50. Where is WRAM used in a PC system?

    A. System RAM

    B. Video RAM

    C. Cache RAM

    D. Flash RAM

51. What is the most likely condition indicated by light printout of a dot-matrix type of printer?

    A. Printhead misalignment

    B. Worn platen

    C. Spent ribbon

    D. Incorrect printer setup

52. The first item to check when a laser printer produces blank pages is _____.

    A. the fuser assembly

    B. the toner cartridge

    C. the transfer corona

    D. the conditioning roller

53. Paper weight is specified in terms of _____.

    A. pounds

    B. pounds per 8.5" × 11" sheets

    C. pounds per 17" × 22" sheets

    D. pounds per 11" × 17" sheets

54. The flow of operations in a laser printer can be summarized as _____.

    A. condition, clean, transfer, fuse, write, develop

    B. condition, transfer, fuse, clean, write, develop

    C. clean, condition, transfer, fuse, develop, write

    D. clean, condition, write, develop, transfer, fuse

55. Paper jams are most likely to occur in which laser printer operation?

    A. Paper pickup

    B. Cooling

    C. Fusing

    D. Registration

56. A customer calls with a CD stuck in a nonfunctioning drive and wants to know how to get it out. What do you tell the customer?

    A. Remove the top of the drive housing from the drive unit.

    B. Push a paper clip into the hole near the activity light.

    C. Use a small knife to pry the drawer open just enough to get the disc out.

    D. Apply 110V AC directly to the power supply connections on the back of the drive to eject the disc.

57. Which function can be performed by a Type III PCMCIA card, but not by Type I or Type II cards?

    A. Removable HDD functions

    B. Memory expansion functions

    C. Serial port functions

    D. Parallel port functions

58. Notebook computers do not have _____.

    A. RAM memory

    B. power connections

    C. floppy drives

    D. ISA expansion slots

59. What must occur for a PCMCIA card to work properly?

    A. The TCP/IP protocol must be active.

    B. A COM3 port must be added to the system.

    C. A special jumper must be set on the motherboard.

    D. A software enabler must be loaded.

60. Which system can be classified as a bus topology?

    A. Ethernet

    B. FDDI

    C. Token Ring

    D. PS/2

61. An RJ-45 connector is most commonly used with _____.

    A. disk drive units

    B. fiber-optic cabling

    C. coaxial cabling

    D. unshielded twisted-pair cabling

62. The maximum length of a 10BASE-2 Ethernet network segment is _____.

    A. 15 meters

    B. 185 meters

    C. 520 meters

    D. 1,050 meters

63. If all the drives in an IDE system stop working when a new drive is installed, what is the most likely cause?

    A. The new drive has not been partitioned.

    B. The CMOS settings for the new drive have not been enabled in the BIOS.

    C. The old drive is not compatible with the new drive type.

    D. The master/slave settings of the two drives are conflicting.

64. In a peer-to-peer network _____.

    A. each node contains a security database of users

    B. all nodes can only be clients

    C. all nodes must act as servers

    D. all nodes can act as servers or clients under different circumstances

65. Your system will not boot to the hard drive, so you try to start it with a boot disk in the A: drive. However, the system still refuses to boot up. What should you do next?

    A. Change the Boot Sequence setting in the CMOS Setup utility to check A: drive first.

    B. Replace the floppy drive and signal cable and then restart the system.

    C. Replace the hard drive and signal cable and then reinstall the operating system and applications.

    D. Replace the boot disk with a working disk.

66. When you start a Windows-based system in safe mode with standard VGA drivers, at what resolution will the monitor operate?

    A. 640 × 480

    B. 800 × 600

    C. 1024 × 768

    D. 800 × 400

67. Which I/O connections in an ATX system can be confusing?

    A. The COM1 And COM2 serial ports

    B. The mouse and keyboard ports

    C. The VGA video and game ports

    D. The modem and LAN ports

68. What items are found in an SEC cartridge?

    A. Toner, primary corona, and drum

    B. Microprocessor and L2 cache

    C. Fan and heat sink module

    D. A sealed disk drive unit

69. The accounting department manager complains that each time their backup tape drive runs, the system's sound card fails. What should you do about this problem?

    A. Tell the manager to run backups at night or during off-hours to avoid conflicts with other devices and systems.

    B. Install a new power supply with a higher wattage rating so that the drive does not spike the sound card when it runs.

    C. Install an external tape drive that has its own power supply.

    D. Check for conflicting IRQ and DMA settings.

Answers to Exam Questions

1. **A.** The POST program is one of the three primary components of the ROM BIOS firmware. This program is located in the BIOS chip (or chips) on the system board.

2. **C.** The AT system uses the equivalent of two 8,237 4-channel DMA controllers to complete the 8-channel AT-compatible DMA function. However, one of the channels in the primary DMA controller is used to funnel all the secondary channels through. Therefore, only 7 channels are actually available for use by the system.

3. **D.** The Accelerated Graphics Port (AGP) was created by Intel based on the PCI slot, but is designed especially for the throughput demands of 3-D graphics adapters.

4. **C.** The system board uses the rechargeable battery to maintain power to the system's CMOS RAM area. This area has been used to hold the system's configuration information since the early days of the 80286 AT systems. Because this area is actually RAM, even a short loss of power results in the loss of the configuration information.

5. **A.** In a PC-compatible system, IRQ4 is generally assigned to the COM1 serial port. The COM2 port is assigned IRQ3. For these two ports, it may be easy to remember that there is an even/odd reversal between the IRQ and COM values.

6. **C.** In a PC-compatible system, IRQ7 is generally assigned to the LPT1 parallel port. The LPT2 port is typically assigned IRQ5.

7. **B.** The limit of the USB 1.1 connection is 15 feet (5 meters) without additional equipment.

8. **C.** The recommended maximum RS-232 cable length, as recognized by CompTIA, is 50 feet (15 meters). The maximum length for a standard RS-232C connection is actually 100 feet (33 meters).

9. **A.** The stated maximum length of a Centronics parallel printer cable is 10 feet (3 meters). Some manufacturers will call for a maximum of 6 feet (2 meters) in their documentation. These distances should be taken seriously.

10. **C.** At the back of the computer, the connector specified for the IBM printer port is a 25-pin female D-shell connector. The original Centronics specification called for a 36-pin D-shell but that was not used in the PC. However, the 36-pin Centronics connector is still used at the printer end of the cable.

11. **A.** Serial ports pass data back and forth as a string of single bits. The UARTS in serial ports enable the port to both transmit and receive data. In asynchronous mode, the timing of the data through the port is controlled by start and stop bits placed at the beginning and end of each character.

12. **B.** Parallel ports pass a complete byte of data through the port at one time. The transmission of the data is synchronized by a control signal handshaking sequence that goes on between the port and the peripheral device. Currently, two types of bidirectional parallel printer ports are on the market.

13. **C.** A 25-pin female D-shell connector is almost always the LPT1 parallel port connector. In cases where there are two such connectors, one should be LPT1 and the other would be LPT2. The game port uses a 15-pin female D-shell connector; serial ports use 9-pin and 25-pin male D-shells.

14. **D.** Asynchronous (meaning without timing) transmissions are conducted at irregular intervals. They use start and stop bits to define the data character sandwiched between them.

15. **C.** The COM2 and COM4 (both even numbers) are assigned to IRQ3 (an odd number) in the PC-compatible environment.

16. **B.** The .28 dot pitch monitor has .28mm between the centers of each triad of color spots on the face of a color monitor.

17. **D.** With an IEEE-1394 bus, you can connect up to 63 devices together. When IEEE-1394.1 bus bridges become available, it will become possible to connect more than 60,000 devices using an IEEE-1394 bus.

18. **A.** An advanced SCSI connector, such as those used with Wide Ultra2 SCSI, has 68 contacts/pins.

19. **B.** The drive can be partitioned into a primary partition and an extended partition. The extended partition can be subdivided into 23 logical drives (labeled D through Z).

20. **A.** Without large drive support from the BIOS, the IDE drive specification can handle only drives up to 528MB (very small by current standards).

21. **D.** There are two possibilities for the purpose of a 15-pin female D-shell connector on the back of the computer. The first is a 3-row version used with the VGA video standard; the second is a 2-row version used for game ports, to which joysticks and other game devices can be connected.

22. **C.** The power supply must deliver power to every portion of the basic system. Even the adapter cards receive power from the power supply through the system board's expansion slots. Therefore, a problem with the power supply could be manifested in any part of the system.

23. **D.** The ohmmeter function uses an internal battery within the meter to control the environment being checked. Therefore, it is very important that power in the circuit under test be removed. In addition, at least one end of the component being tested must be disconnected from the system. This prevents any of the control current from the battery from being directed away through other circuits to which the device may be connected. This would cause the reading taken to be inaccurate.

24. **D.** In a PC system, most problems occur in the area of software setup and system configuration. This is due to the great flexibility and openness of the PC system. Wide varieties and types of both hardware and software have been developed for these systems due to their flexibility. The drawback is that these optional devices and programs must be configured for operation with the rest of the system. Other types of computers control add-on options to their units just so such problems do not occur.

25. **B.** The ATX power supply is controlled by an electronic switch from the system board. Other differences between the ATX and AT power supplies include the monitor power passthrough is gone from the ATX design, ATX power supplies provide +3.3V, AXT uses a new, keyed system board connector, and its fan blows into the system unit rather than out.

26. **D.** Under the conditions cited, the power supply is clearly receiving power (fan running and lights on) and is providing power to the disk drive unit. Otherwise, the system appears dead. The system board is the logical next choice because the problem does not appear to be confined to a particular part of the system (such as just the disk drive or monitor boot-up actions).

27. **D.** The Cyrix III processor was designed specifically to fit in a Socket 370 system.

28. **B.** 100Base-TX local area network systems are connected together by Category 5 UTP cable.

29. **C.** The BIOS Anti Virus setting is designed to prevent boot-sector viruses from infecting the system and making the computer unusable. However, this same utility also prevents the upgrading software from writing to the boot sector of the hard drive. Therefore, it is necessary to disable this feature before upgrading.

30. **D.** A standard ATA/IDE interface can have only two devices attached to it (master and slave). To install more devices, you must install an ATA2/EIDE host adapter card in one of the system's PCI slots.

31. **C.**   When a `Disk Boot Failure` error message displays, it means that the system could not find the boot record it was looking for on the drive. This record could be missing or corrupted. If it is missing, the drive may not have been formatted. If it is corrupted, the boot record will need to be restored. Booting to a floppy disk enables you to attempt to access the hard drive. If it cannot be accessed, repartition and reformat the drive. If the drive can be seen but not booted, install the system files to it from the floppy disk using the SYS command.

32. **A.**   Typically the transmission range of an IrDA device is specified as 0-2 meters, but the IrDA standard requires that the device have the ability to communicate from at least 1 meter.

33. **C.**   If the system refuses to boot up after a new option has been installed, it is a good guess that it has detected a conflict between the new device and one of the other system devices, and that it wants you to get the conflict straightened out before it will go back to work.

34. **D.**   A standard ATA connection can support a maximum of one master and one slave device.

35. **B, C.**   The Communications and Networking Riser (CNR) was designed to support software-controlled devices such as modems, NICs, and sound cards.

36. **A.**   Printed circuit boards are typically shipped in antistatic bags, if they are not already installed in a system. They also are typically shipped with an antistatic foam sheet along the solder side of the board. This scenario has been designed and refined by the PC board manufacturers for shipping their products around the world safely. This is also the best method for transporting PC boards.

37. **A.**   A wrist strap is a conductor designed to carry electrical charges away from your body. In high-voltage environments such as those found inside a power-supply unit or a monitor, however, this safety device becomes a potential path for electrocution.

38. **A.**   ESD tends to form when conditions are hot and dry. These conditions provide the low humidity that ESD requires to form.

39. **C.**   Although there are not any national requirements for disposing of computer equipment, there may be local requirements in your area. Check the dumpsite regulations before disposing of computer equipment of any kind.

40. **C.**   The fuser assembly in a laser printer is a burn hazard. It is one of the three types of hazards present in laser printers: burn, vision damage, and shock.

41. **D.**   When power is restored after an outage, every piece of equipment that has a power switch in the On position draws maximum power. This places a very high initial load on the power-supply system and results in short-term fluctuations—power surges and sags. These fluctuations can cause havoc and damage with a digital system.

42. **D.**   All the items listed in the question are valid methods for protecting the computer from data loss and damage. Each method listed represents a different level of protection for the system.

43. **D.**   Historically, the vast majority of all Pentium system boards have uses a combination of ISA and PCI slots to service the system. With the advent of ATX-compliant system boards, the AGP slot for video graphics adapters became a common addition.

44. **A.**   Cache memory of any type—and there are several applications for caching—is used to speed up the system's access to data. It is volatile memory and it always operates in parallel with some other memory type (for instance, RAM or disk).

45. **D.**   The Super 7 PPGA socket is a derivation of the Socket 7 specification. It had the addition of support for a 100MHz Front Side Bus specification.

46. **C.**   In the Pentium and Pentium MMX, the second-level cache is located on the system board. In the Pentium Pro and Pentium II designs, the L2 cache migrates from the system board to the same substrate that the microprocessor is constructed on.

47. **B.**   In the Pentium Pro and Pentium II microprocessor designs, the L2 cache has been migrated from the system board to the same substrate that the microprocessor is constructed on. This provides extremely fast access of the cache by the processor core.

48. **A.**   One of the features of the ATX specification is the addition of a software On/Off switch that is activated by a single key. This is not a new idea; it has been available in the Apple Macintosh design for some time.

49. **A.**   The 72-pin memory module is the larger sized single in-line memory module (SIMM). The smaller, original module is a 30-pin version. DIMMs, on the other hand, are physically larger, physically different, and have 168 pins.

50. **B.**   Windows RAM or WRAM is designed specifically for use as video memory. It is a special version of VRAM that has been optimized to transfer blocks of video data at a time. This enables WRAM to operate at speeds up to 150% of typical VRAM devices.

51. **C.**   Light print produced by any type of printer typically indicates that the primary printing element is wearing out or running low. In the case of a dot-matrix printer, this is the ink ribbon.

52. **B.**   The first item to check when a laser printer produces blank pages is the toner supply. Without toner, the printer cannot put anything on the page. If toner is present, another major problem, such as the transfer corona, may be indicated.

53. **C.**   The page size for determining paper weight is the equivalent of four standard 8.5" × 11" sheets.

54. **D.**   In the laser printer, the drum is *cleaned* to remove and excess toner, *conditioned* by applying a uniform charge to its surface, *written* on with the new information to be printed. The image on the drum is *developed* by attracting toner to the electronic image, and then it is *transferred* to the paper. Finally, the toner image is *fused* to the paper.

55. **A.**   Picking up something as thin as a piece of paper without wrinkling it is difficult enough for humans. It also is a difficult undertaking for the mechanical laser printer. This is the leading place for paper jams to occur in the laser printer.

56. **B.**   Pushing a straightened paper clip into the small opening on the front panel of the drive mechanically releases the CD tray from the drive and lets it open. This is the only nondestructive way to remove a disc from a nonfunctioning CD-ROM drive.

57. **A.**   The Type III PCMCIA (PC Card) specification was designed specifically to enable them to handle removable disk drive systems. Of course, this specification remains compatible with the memory usage specification for Type I and the general I/O functions of Type II cards.

58. **D.** There is not enough room in a portable computer case for traditional expansion slots. This is one of the traditional drawbacks of portable computers and the basic reason that PC Cards exist.

59. **D.** The PCMCIA specification allows for hot insertion of PC Cards in the system. However, the system's PC Card–enabling drivers must be loaded and running so that it can interrogate the card and configure it for use when it is added to the system.

60. **A.** Ethernet runs as a bus topology. ARCnet and Token Ring networks operate as ring topologies.

61. **D.** The RJ-45 Registered Jack is the connector specified for use with the unshielded twisted-pair (UTP) cabling world. Coaxial cables use BNC connectors, and fiber cabling uses ST connectors.

62. **B.** The 10BASE-2 specification is a misuse of the naming methodology because it is not 200 meters. I suppose that 185 meters is close to 200, and it may compensate for the equipment links that must be used at the end of the network to connect to the user.

63. **D.** If the original drive was working but stopped when the new drive was installed, a device conflict is indicated. (Recall that installing a new device is one of those times when a configuration conflict is likely to occur.) In the case of IDE devices, the most common device conflicts occur due to master/slave settings. If these settings are wrong, the system cannot differentiate between the devices to communicate with them; therefore, no boot or drive recognition is possible with these devices.

64. **D.** In a peer-to-peer network, all nodes can act as servers or clients under different circumstances. They can access files and folders on other nodes if they are shared and can make their resources available to other members of the network by marking them as shared.

65. **A.** With newer CMOS configuration options, it is common to set up the system boot sequence to skip checking the A: floppy disk drive. This makes the boot-up process a couple of seconds faster. However, when a boot-up problem occurs, the system has no reason to check the A: drive. Therefore, the technician must go into the CMOS settings to direct the system toward the A: drive during boot up.

66. **A.** Under the VGA video specification, the standard resolution setting is 640×480 pixels.

67. **B.** Because the ATX specification employs a 6-pin PS/2 mini-DIN connector for both the keyboard and mouse connections, it is very easy to confuse the two when installing the system's peripherals. This is a particularly interesting choice of connectors considering past connectivity choices (such as video and COM port connections) that have been confusing to users and technicians.

68. **B.** The SEC cartridge is the container that Intel designed to hold its Pentium II microprocessor and its L2 cache. The package was designed to plug into the proprietary Intel Slot-1 design.

69. **D.** If two devices attempt to use the same system resources at the same time, they will have conflicts. The resources they are sharing (such as IRQ and DMA channels) will attempt to refer to different service routines that were never written for them, or to incorrect memory locations. Therefore, at least one of the devices is doomed to fail due to improper service support.

This exam simulates the CompTIA A+ Operating System Technologies exam. It is representative of what you should expect on the actual exam. The answers and explanations for them follow the questions. It is strongly suggested that when you take this exam, you treat it just as you would the actual exam. Time yourself, read carefully, and answer all the questions as best you can. There are 70 questions, just as on the actual exam. Set yourself a 90-minute time limit. This is the amount of time you are given to take the real thing. The questions also reflect the amount of coverage given each domain in the exam.

1.0 Operating System Fundamentals - 30% = 22 Questions

2.0 Installation, Configuration, and Upgrading - 15% = 10 Questions

3.0 Diagnosing and Troubleshooting - 40% = 28 Questions

4.0 Networks - 15% = 10 Questions

Run through the exam, and if you score less than 75%, try rereading the chapters on the domains in which you had trouble.

Practice Exam: Operating System Technologies

EXAM QUESTIONS

1. Which statement is not normally a part of the CONFIG.SYS file?

   A. FILES=20

   B. BUFFERS=20

   C. STACKS=65,000

   D. PATH=C:\WINDOWS;C:\DOS

2. The purpose of a device driver is to _____.

   A. Tell DOS how to interface with an external

   B. Provide more useful memory by moving device control data to extended memory

   C. Improve performance of installed devices by optimizing access patterns

   D. Modify application programs to work correctly with devices attached to the system

3. Which of the following commands is not proper for use in the AUTOEXEC.BAT file?

   A. Echo

   B. Pause

   C. Loadhigh

   D. Files

4. Memory-manager programs are loaded from the _____.

   A. AUTOEXEC.BAT file

   B. BIOS

   C. CONFIG.SYS file

   D. CMOS

5. Which of the following file types cannot be run from the DOS prompt?

   A. BAT

   B. EXE

   C. RUN

   D. COM

6. _____ interprets input from the DOS prompt.

   A. IO.SYS

   B. MSDOS.SYS

   C. COMMAND.COM

   D. BIO.COM

7. In Windows 2000, which utility you use to rewrite scattered parts of files into contiguous sectors on a hard disk?

   A. The Add/Remove Hardware applet

   B. The Disk Defrag utility

   C. The Disk Cleanup utility

   D. The Backup utility

8. The MYFILE.EXE file is located in the C:\Test Directory. To execute the file from anywhere, _____.

   A. Add C:\Test to the Path statement.

   B. Add the line C:\Test\MYFILE.EXE to the CONFIG.SYS file.

   C. Add the line DEVICE=MYFILE.EXE to the AUTOEXEC.BAT file.

   D. Add ;C:\TEST to the Path statement.

9. To configure the file MYFILE.TXT as read-only, use the _____ DOS command.

    A. ATTRIB +A MYFILE.TXT

    B. ATTRIB –A MYFILE.TXT

    C. ATTRIB +R MYFILE.TXT

    D. ATTRIB–R MYFILE.TXT

10. What is the primary user interface for Windows 9x?

    A. The monitor

    B. The desktop GUI

    C. The command prompt

    D. The keyboard

11. You are installing new hardware in a Windows 2000 system that does not use Plug and Play. From where can you install the drivers for the new devices?

    A. The Add/Remove Hardware Wizard

    B. The System Properties icon

    C. The Device Manager utility

    D. The Add New Programs Wizard

12. In Windows 9x, a filename can be up to _____ characters long.

    A. 8

    B. 16

    C. 32

    D. 255

13. When Windows 95 boots up successfully, the Registry files are backed up with the _____ extension.

    A. .DAT

    B. .DOC

    C. .DA0

    D. .DMM

14. By default, ScanDisk runs in a Windows 2000 system _____.

    A. each time the system is shut down

    B. once a week

    C. according to the schedule established in the Computer Management Console

    D. whenever Windows is shut down incorrectly

15. In Windows 9x, the command used to edit the Registry is _____.

    A. SysEdit

    B. RegEdit

    C. AutoEdit

    D. WinEdit

16. Where can a startup disk be created in the Windows 9x environment?

    A. In the Add/Remove Programs Wizard

    B. In the \System Tools directory

    C. In the Windows Explorer

    D. In the Start Menu's Run dialog box

17. If an application hangs up in Windows 2000, you should _____.

    A. press Alt+Tab, click Applications, and close applications that are not responding

    B. press Ctrl+Alt+Del, click Task Manager, click Applications, and close applications that are not responding

    C. press Ctrl+Esc, click Applications, and select the appropriate application to close

    D. turn the power off to the system unit and restart

18. A customer cannot find the file QUESTION-POOL.DOC while searching in MS-DOS mode. The customer should _____.

   A. look for a abbreviated name for the file, such as QUESTI~1.DOC

   B. consider the file deleted

   C. look for the file in Windows 95 instead

   D. look for an abbreviated name for the file, such as QUESTION.DOC

19. ScanDisk does all the following except _____.

   A. relocate data into sequential sectors

   B. check the FAT

   C. review the filenames

   D. locate cross-referenced sectors

20. Which Windows 2000 command starts a new instance of the Windows 2000 command-prompt interpreter?

   A. Run

   B. Command

   C. Start

   D. CMD

21. Which Windows 2000 command converts FAT volumes to NTFS?

   A. FattoNTFS

   B. Convert

   C. Changevol

   D. Switch

22. PAGEFILE.SYS is _____.

   A. the Windows 98 virtual memory swap file

   B. the Windows 98 expanded memory manager

   C. the Windows 2000 virtual memory swap file

   D. the Windows 2000 expanded memory manager

23. Which file is responsible for loading Windows 2000?

   A. BOOT.INI

   B. KERNEL32.EXE

   C. WIN.COM

   D. NTLDR

24. Windows 2000 is based on which new file system?

   A. NTFS 3

   B. NTFS 4

   C. NTFS 5

   D. HPFS

25. How do upper memory and high memory differ?

   A. There is no difference.

   B. Upper memory is any memory above 1MB.

   C. High memory is the memory between 640KB and 1MB.

   D. High memory is the first 64KB area of memory above 1MB.

26. The Windows 9x System Monitor can be used to _____.

   A. view monochrome graphics in color

   B. input TV signals directly

   C. reproduce U.S. currency

   D. detect major system bottlenecks

27. What is the purpose of HIMEM.SYS?

    A. Control the shadow RAM operations

    B. Load programs into expanded memory

    C. Load the ROM BIOS into the high memory area

    D. Load programs into extended memory

28. Memory from 0–640KB is called _____.

    A. enhanced

    B. conventional

    C. expanded

    D. extended

29. What are the minimum hardware requirements for installing Windows 2000 Professional?

    A. 133MHz Pentium processor with 64MB RAM installed

    B. 150MHz Pentium processor with 32MB RAM installed

    C. 166MHz Pentium processor with 24MB RAM installed

    D. 266MHz Pentium processor with 32MB RAM installed

30. To install Windows 9x on the system's D: drive, _____.

    A. disconnect the C: drive from the system before installing Windows

    B. just copy the Windows directory to the D: drive after Windows has been installed

    C. click the Other Directory option during the Setup routine and change the Install path

    D. Use the Move function in Windows Explorer to move the Windows directory to the D: drive after Windows has been installed

31. To install a network printer from Windows 9x, you would _____.

    A. click File/Print from the application, and click the Printer button and select the printer

    B. click Start/Settings/Printers, and select the printer to install

    C. click the My Computer icon, click the Printers folder, and select the printer

    D. click the Network Neighborhood icon, computer name, printer name, and right-click Install

32. Which startup mode is not a Window 9x mode?

    A. Normal mode

    B. Safe mode

    C. Standard mode

    D. MS-DOS mode

33. Identify the correct sequence of events that occur when Windows 2000 is started?

    A. NTLDR, NTDETECT.COM, BOOT.INI

    B. BOOT.INI, NTDETECT.COM, NTLDR

    C. NTDETECT.COM, NTLDR, BOOT.INI

    D. NTLDR, BOOT.INI, NTDETECT.COM

34. The purpose of safe mode in Windows is _____.

    A. to start Windows with minimal drivers loaded

    B. to single-step through the Windows startup process

    C. to skip all the Windows configuration steps

    D. to start Windows with an MS-DOS command line

35. A/an _____ partition must be on the hard disk drive to install Windows 95.

    A. CDFS

    B. NTFS

    C. FAT

    D. HPFS

36. The boot sequence for Windows 9x is _____.

    A. POST, Bootstrap Loader, IO.SYS, MSDOS.SYS, COMMAND.COM, CONFIG.SYS

    B. POST, Bootstrap Loader, IO.SYS, CONFIG.SYS, COMMAND.COM, MSDOS.SYS, AUTOEXEC.BAT

    C. POST, Bootstrap Loader, IO.SYS, CONFIG.SYS, MSDOS.SYS, COMMAND.COM, AUTOEXEC.BAT

    D. POST, Bootstrap Loader, IO.SYS, CONFIG.SYS, MSDOS.SYS, AUTOEXEC.BAT, COMMAND.COM

37. Which Windows 2000 administrative tool can you use to view several administrative tools, such as Event Viewer and Device Manager, in one window?

    A. Tool Viewer

    B. Services and Applications

    C. Computer Management Console

    D. Performance Meter

38. To single-step through the Windows 9x boot process, press _____ while the Starting Windows message is onscreen.

    A. F3

    B. F4

    C. F5

    D. F8

39. To boot directly into safe mode, press _____ while the Starting Windows 9x message is onscreen.

    A. F3

    B. F4

    C. F5

    D. F8

40. If Plug and Play is not working in Windows, where can a device driver be installed from?

    A. The Start menu

    B. The My Computer window

    C. The Add/Remove Programs Wizard

    D. The Add New Hardware Wizard

41. Which is *not* an acceptable way to install a device driver in Windows 9x?

    A. Let the PnP function install it.

    B. Use the Device Manager to install it.

    C. Use the Add New Hardware Wizard to install it.

    D. Use the Add/Remove Programs Wizard to install it.

42. You suspect a program is causing errors in a Windows 2000 system, but the system is not reporting any errors. What tool will you use to view errors in the system?

    A. Event Viewer

    B. Local Security Policy

    C. Services

    D. Component Services

43. The main reason to encrypt a file is to _____.

    A. reduce its size

    B. secure it for transmission

    C. prepare it for backup

    D. include it in the startup sequence

44. Which of the following is not true regarding the boot sector?

    A. It contains the Master Boot Record (MBR).

    B. It contains the disk's partition table.

    C. It resides on each disk partition.

    D. It contains information about the drive and disk.

45. You can enter boot logging mode by pressing ___ at Windows 2000 startup.

    A. F1

    B. Ctrl

    C. F8

    D. ESC+F4

46. Which of the following protocols was designed to be used with a Novell network?

    A. TCP/IP

    B. IrLAN

    C. IPX/SPX

    D. NetBEUI

47. VxD drivers for Windows 9x are designed for _____ operation.

    A. 8-bit

    B. 16-bit

    C. 32-bit

    D. 64-bit

48. What type of networking is included as the default in Windows 9x?

    A. None

    B. Peer to peer

    C. Client based

    D. Workstation

49. A customer has asked you to install a 5GB hard drive in his Windows 95b machine. He wants to use the entire drive, but does not want to change his operating system. What's the minimum number of partitions you must have to utilize the whole drive?

    A. 1

    B. 2

    C. 3

    D. 4

50. Which protocol enables a network server to assign IP address to a network node?

    A. RAS

    B. DNS

    C. DHCP

    D. WINS

51. Which of the following presents the least likely cause of computer virus infections?

    A. Shareware programs

    B. Bulletin board software

    C. User-copied software

    D. Shrink-wrapped original software

52. To locate and install a missing or corrupt Windows 9x file from the Windows 9x CD, use _____.

    A. the SUBTRACT.EXE program

    B. the COMPACT.EXE program

    C. the EXTRACT.EXE program

    D. the LOCATE.EXE program

53. The system is running in Windows 9x and then stops. Restarting the system is unsuccessful. What is the problem?

    A. The power supply is bad.

    B. The Virtual Memory function is enabled.

    C. The Virtual Memory function is disabled.

    D. The hard drive controller is defective.

54. If an application freezes in Windows 9x, press _____ to remove the offending task.

    A. Alt+Tab

    B. Ctrl+Alt+Del

    C. Esc

    D. Alt+Esc

55. What TCP/IP utility is commonly used to test a remote network node to see whether it is active?

    A. IPCONFIG

    B. ARP

    C. PING

    D. WinIPCFG

56. When comparing Thorough ScanDisk operation with Standard ScanDisk operation, _____.

    A. Thorough operation checks the files and folders on the drive that you specify

    B. Standard operation checks the disk surface on the drive that you specify

    C. Thorough operation checks the disk surface, files, and folders on the drive that you specify

    D. Standard operation checks the disk surface, files, and folders on the drive that you specify

57. To share a printer in Windows 9x, _____.

    A. double-click its icon, select Printer/Properties/ Sharing, and choose the configuration

    B. right-click its icon, select Sharing, and choose the configuration

    C. right-click its icon, select Properties/Sharing, and choose the configuration

    D. perform any of the first three choices

58. In Windows 9x, if one DOS application prints fine but another does not, _____.

    A. check the print settings in the malfunctioning application

    B. print the job using the DOS application that works

    C. use only applications that are written for Windows 95 to do printing

    D. select a printer that will work with both DOS programs

59. Device Manager can do all the following except _____.

    A. update drivers

    B. change peripheral I/O settings

    C. check for viruses

    D. identify installed ports

60. The Device Manager displays a red X symbol when _____.

    A. a device is disabled due to some type of user selection conflict

    B. a device is experiencing a direct hardware conflict with another device

    C. the selected device is not present on the system

    D. the selected device is not operating properly and requires repair

61. In Windows 9x, where do you go to correct any conflicting IRQs?

    A. Print Manager

    B. Device Manager

    C. File Manager

    D. System Manager

62. Which of the following is the correct UNC network path name?

    A. \\server_name\computer_name\user_name

    B. \\computer_name\share_name

    C. \\user_name\computer_name\share_name

    D. \\computer_name\user_name\share_name

63. How can you see hidden files in Windows 2000?

    A. Edit the appropriate Registry entry.

    B. Right-click My Computer, select Properties, click the View tab, and change to the appropriate setting.

    C. Run Explorer, click the Tools menu, select Folder Options, click the View tab, and change to the appropriate setting.

    D. Right-click the desktop, click Properties, click the View tab, and change to the appropriate setting.

64. Internet Service providers _____.

    A. install modems

    B. provide Internet addresses

    C. install cable

    D. create Internet browsers

65. A customer wants to use an installed modem for Internet operation. You should _____.

    A. install another modem, and get the ISP information

    B. get the ISP information

    C. install Dial-Up Networking and enter the ISP information

    D. install Dial-Up Networking

66. In Windows 2000 Professional, from where are TCP/IP utility programs run?

    A. At the MS-DOS command prompt

    B. At the TCP/IP Properties window

    C. At the window that appears when you double-click the file TCPIP.COM

    D. At the Run window, accessed via the Start menu

67. What condition causes other network users to not be able to see any files on your local machine?

   A. You have not enabled any file or print sharing functions on the local computer.

   B. The remote computers have not enabled a file- or print-sharing function for your computer.

   C. The local computer is password protected, and they have not entered the correct password to gain access.

   D. The remote computers do not have their directories shared.

68. What file type is not associated with the Internet?

   A. HTML

   B. FTP

   C. X.40

   D. POP3

69. What could cause a properly mapped drive to disappear when the system is rebooted?

   A. The installed network protocol has been corrupted.

   B. The network interface card is bad.

   C. The Reconnect at Logon option has not been selected.

   D. Mapped drives must always be reentered when the system is rebooted.

70. Which TCP/IP utility traces the connection path from your terminal to a remote Internet address?

   A. NBTSTAT

   B. NET VIEW

   C. Tracert

   D. PING

Answers to Exam Questions

1. **D.** The PATH command is associated and properly used in the AUTOEXEC.BAT file. The other options are all valid CONFIG.SYS files.

2. **A.** The device driver is a piece of interfacing software that tells the system how to communicate with and manage an external device. Applications use the driver, through the operating system, to address devices, but the driver does not alter the application. They also have no effect on where they are stored.

3. **D.** The Files statement is properly used in the CONFIG.SYS file. The other options are legitimate AUTOEXEC.BAT statements.

4. **C.** The CONFIG.SYS file's statements are responsible for loading the system's memory managers. This normally involves the HIMEM.SYS and EMM386 lines.

5. **C.** There is no system extension called .RUN. All the other file types can be executed directly from the DOS command line.

6. **C.** The COMMAND.COM command interpreter is responsible for accepting input from the DOS command line and interpreting it for the system.

7. **B.** The Defrag utility rearranges files and unused space on the hard disk into contiguous blocks so that the drive can operate more efficiently.

8. **D.** The Path statement in the AUTOEXEC.BAT file sets the system up with an automatic search order for executing files. To make a file, such as MYFILE.EXE, so that it can be executed from anywhere, it must be added to the Path statement (set off by the semicolon).

9. **C.** The +R switch modifies the ATTRIB command to mark the specified file as read-only. The –R switch would be used to remove such a specification from the file.

10. **B.** The desktop is the primary user interface for Windows 9x. Within the desktop, the My Computer icon is the primary navigation tool for the system and Windows Explorer serves as the primary file-management tool. The Start menu is the secondary user interface for navigation.

11. **A.** The Add/Remove Hardware Wizard is used to install and configure hardware devices.

12. **D.** The file-management system in Windows 9x can accommodate filenames up to 255 characters in length. This allows for very descriptive filenames to be used to represent the contents of the file.

13. **C.** The Windows 95 startup procedure produces a backup copy of SYSTEM.DAT and USER.DAT each time the system successfully boots up. Before storing them, the system renames the old SYSTEM and USER file with a .DA0 extension and saves it.

14. **D.** ScanDisk is scheduled to run only when Windows 2000 does not shut down correctly. It runs in DOS mode before Windows boots up.

15. **B.** The utility for directly modifying the Windows 9x Registry is RegEdit. This utility is started from the command line by executing the REGEDIT.EXE file.

16. **A.** The emergency start disk for Windows 9x can be created from the setup process during installation. Alternatively, it can be created at any time from the Add/Remove Programs utility.

17. **B.** Press Ctrl+Alt+Del, click the Task Manager, click Applications, and close the applications that are not responding. These are the steps for entering Task Manager, which you can use to view applications, processes, system performance, and to shut down anything that is not responding.

18. **A.** If the file was saved with a Windows 9x long filename, a directory listing would not display the name in its entirety. Instead, the name is truncated (shortened) and displayed with a tilde character (~) in the seventh position of the filename. A numeric character, beginning with 1, is inserted into the eighth character position to show that it is the first iteration of the truncated filename. If other filenames are created with the same first six characters, they are labeled as the second, third, and so on iteration.

19. **A.** The ScanDisk utility does not relocate blocks of data into sequential sectors. This is the function of the Defrag utility.

20. **D.** The CMD command is used to start the Windows 2000 command interpreter. It can be used to set the environment variables of the new interpreter.

21. **B.** The Convert command can be used to convert drive file systems. Always back up all important information on the drive before converting file systems.

22. **C.** This is a swap filename used in Windows NT or 2000. When the computer is running low on memory, Windows (NT or 2000) can use hard drive space, PAGEFILE.SYS, to simulate RAM.

23. **D.** The NTLDR file, along with NTDETECT, loads the NT/2000 operating system into memory.

24. **C.** The newest NTFS file system (NTFS 5) is included in Windows 2000. It brings with it some encryption and administrative enhancements over its predecessors.

25. **D.** Upper memory is the area of RAM in the PC memory map between 640KB and 1MB. It has existed since the original PC design. High memory is the 64KB area just above the 1MB mark that is created by the segmented offset addressing style of the Intel microprocessor. The HMA comes into existence when the HIMEM.SYS driver is loaded in the CONFIG.SYS file.

26. **D.** The Windows 9x System Monitor is designed to monitor the operation of key system resources and graphically identify processing bottlenecks that occur.

27. **D.** HIMEM.SYS has two functions. It is the memory manager responsible for controlling any other memory managers in the system. It provides access to the extended memory area and creates the high memory area.

28. **B.** Memory between 0 and 640KB was originally referred to as base memory in the original PC. When additional memory became available in the PC-AT, however, in the form of expanded and then extended memory, this area of memory began to be called conventional memory.

29. **A.** 133MHz processor with 64 MB RAM installed. These are the requirements set by Microsoft for installation of the Windows 2000 Professional operating system.

30. **D.** Even if the Typical option is selected for the installation, the Windows 9x Setup utility enables the user to specify a new directory for the Windows 9x files to be placed. This new directory can be located on a different drive.

31. **D.** A network printer is installed in Windows 9x by accessing the Network Neighborhood through its desktop icon, selecting the remote computer's network name, and then selecting the remote printer's name. From this point, right-click the Install option to install the printer in the local system.

32. **C.** There is no standard mode in the Windows 9x world. Normal mode is just the normal Windows 9x startup. Safe mode is a special troubleshooting mode that loads only the minimum number of device drivers required to get the basic parts of the system operational. MS-DOS mode is a command-prompt-only mode that simulates the DOS environment.

33. **A.** NTLDR, NTDETECT.COM, BOOT.INI. This is the correct sequence; BOOT.INI next passes control to OSLOADER.EXE.

34. **A.** Safe mode is a special troubleshooting mode that loads only the minimum number of device drivers required to get the basic parts of the system operational. This includes a reduced version of the Windows GUI environment. If the system will not function in this mode, a command-prompt-only mode is available that removes even these few drivers. Safe mode startup also provides a step-by-step boot-up mode that you can use to single-step through the boot-up process and identify steps that cause the system to crash.

35. **C.** The Windows 95 Setup routine must find a copy of a FAT16 partition running on the intended drive where it is supposed to install Windows 95.

36. **C.** When Windows 9x boots, the sequence of events is the system initialization and POST tests are performed. The Bootstrap Loader finds the MBR and loads the Windows version of the IO.SYS file. IO.SYS checks the CONFIG.SYS file for system configuration parameters. It then loads the MSDOS.SYS file and checks its information. It then looks for and executes the COMMAND.COM file, which in turn looks for and executes the AUTOEXEC.BAT file if it finds one. Be aware that in a pure Windows 9x installation, no CONFIG.SYS or AUTOEXEC.BAT files will be present. The order of events for all other possible answers is incorrect.

37. **C.** The Computer Management Console combines many of the tools including System Information, Performance Logs, Shared Folders, Local Users, Disk Management and Defragmenter, Logical Drives, and Services and Applications.

38. **D.** The Step-by-Step Startup option can be accessed by pressing the F8 key while the Starting Windows message is onscreen. This action brings up the Start menu, from which you can select any of the various Windows startup modes from menu setting.

39. **C.** Pressing the F5 key while the system is starting up boots the system directly into safe mode. The system also defaults to this mode if it detects a configuration problem that the PnP function cannot sort out.

40. **D.** From the options given in this list, the Control Panel's Add New Hardware Wizard must be used to manually install a device driver in the Windows system.

41. **D.** The Add/Remove Programs Wizard cannot be used to install device drivers. All the other methods can be used to install the device driver.

42. **A.** The Event Viewer administrative tool is used to view and manage logs of system, program, and security events that occur in the computer.

43. **B.** You can encrypt files using different cipher strengths. The files can be decrypted after they are sent to the user.

44. **B.** The boot sector does not contain information about the size and layout of the disk. This is the function of the partition table.

45. **C.** Pressing the F8 key during startup causes Windows 2000 to display the Bootup Options menu, which includes options such as Safe Mode.

46. **C.** The IPX/SPX protocol was designed for use with Novell NetWare networks.

47. **C.** Virtual drivers (VxDs) are designed for 32-bit virtual-mode operations under Windows 9x.

48. **B.** By default, Windows 9x provides easy-to-use peer-to-peer networking software. It can be set up as a client or workstation for Windows NT, 2000, UNIX, or Novell NetWare networks, but this is not its default networking scheme.

49. **A.** Windows 95b allows the use of the FAT32 file system. FAT32 allows partitions of up to 2 terabytes in size.

50. **C.** Dynamic Host Configuration Protocol (DHCP) enables the host server to automatically assign IP addresses and subnet masks every time a client computer begins a network session.

51. **D.** The least likely (but not foolproof) source of virus infections is original manufacturer, shrink-wrapped software. Most reputable software manufacturers test their software and systems for viruses before placing them in the marketplace. All the other sources of software listed provide a much higher possibility for viruses to have been attached to the software.

52. **C.** In Windows 9x, the installation files are stored on the distribution disks, or disc, in a compressed Cabinet (CAB) format. These files can be moved and expanded into the system using the Windows Extract command in MS-DOS mode.

53. **C.** If the Virtual Memory function is disabled in Windows 9x, the system will stop running at some point and you will be unable to restart it.

54. **B.** Because Windows 9x employs preemptive multitasking, it is possible to exit to the Windows task list, remove the offending task, and continue processing. The Windows 9x task list is accessed by pressing the Ctrl+Alt+Del key combination.

55. **C.** The PING command is one of the key tools for troubleshooting TCP/IP. PING causes a data packet to be sent to a specified IP address and returned to your machine.

56. **C.** The Thorough ScanDisk option not only checks the system's files and folders for cross-linked files to repair, it also examines the disk surface for physical defects.

57. **D.** All the options provided for this question can be used to share a printer with the system.

58. **A.** In the DOS environment, the applications were responsible for handling their own printing chores. In the Windows 9x setting, each DOS application runs as if it were in its own little 8086 world. Therefore, a printing problem with one DOS application may not show up in any other application. Because the problem in this question does not affect other applications, troubleshoot the printer-related settings of the affected DOS application.

59. **C.** There is no virus-checking function in the Device Manager. In Windows 9x, there is no integrated virus detection or correction. This feature must be added from a third-party supplier.

60. **A.** An X associated with a device listed in the Device Manager indicates that the device has been disabled by a user-selection conflict.

61. **B.** The Device Manger lists all the hardware installed in the system along with the resources the hardware has been allotted. By selecting the device from the list and clicking its driver, you can enter the device's Resources tab and change its IRQ settings.

62. **B.** The correct UNC path begins with two slashes and has both the computer name and the share name for the device.

63. **C.** In Windows 2000, the appearance of file extension is controlled through the View tab in Folder Options.

64. **B.** ISPs provide Internet addresses for their users. The ISPs have purchased blocks of IP addresses that they rent to their customers so that they can have access to the Internet and an identity on the Web.

65. **C.** If a working modem is already installed in the system, only two things need to occur. Windows needs to have its Dial-Up Networking feature operational, and it needs to be loaded with the service provider's contact and configuration information.

66. **A.** All TCP/IP utilities are controlled by commands entered at the MS-DOS command prompt (for instance, C:>).

67. **A.** The file- and print-sharing functions on the local computer must be enabled for other network locations to see these resources on your system. If they were not enabled, you would not be able to see, or to access, their resources.

68. **C.** There is no X40 file format. The HTML file is the format used to create Internet documents and pages. The FTP file format is used to transfer files across the Internet, and POP3 is an email protocol format.

69. **C.** The Reconnect at Logon box is often overlooked when mapping a drive. When the user logs off, the drive map disappears and must be reentered at the next logon.

70. **C.** The command Tracert *host name*, where *host name* is the IP address or DNS name of a host, traces the path of a network connection to that remote host.

APPENDIXES

Glossary

A

A: drive   The commonly understood term designating the first floppy disk drive in Microsoft's DOS microcomputer operating system.

Accelerated Graphics Port (AGP)   A newer 32-bit video interface specification based on the PCI bus design. Instead of using the PCI bus for video data, the AGP system provides a dedicated point-to-point path between the video graphics controller and system memory. The AGP bus was designed specifically to handle the high data-transfer demands associated with 3-D graphic operations.

ACK (ACKnowledge)   A data communications code used by the receiver to tell the transmitter it is ready to accept data. During a data transfer, this signal is continually used to indicate successful receipt of the last data character or block and to request more.

Active Directory (AD)   The central feature of the Windows 2000 architecture. It is a distributed database of user and resource information that describes the makeup of the network (that is, users and application settings). It also is a way to implement a distributed authentication process. The Active Directory replaces the domain structure used in Windows NT 4.0. This feature helps to centralize system and user configurations, as well as data backups on the server in the Windows 2000 network.

active partition   The disk partition that possesses the system files required to boot the system. This is the logical drive that the system reads at boot up.

adapter   A device that permits one system to work with and connect to another. Many I/O device adapters interface with the microcomputer by plugging into the expansion slots on the system board. These specialized circuit boards are often called adapter cards.

Add New Hardware Wizard   Windows 9x/2000 applet designed to guide the installation process for non-PnP hardware. When installing Plug and Play devices, the Add New Hardware Wizard should not be used. Instead, the Windows PnP function should be allowed to detect the new hardware. The new hardware must be installed in the computer before running the wizard.

Add/Remove Programs Wizard   Windows 9x/2000 applet designed to guide the installation or removal of application programs. This utility also can be used to install or remove optional Windows components, such as Accessibility options, or to create a Windows Start disk.

add/remove windows components   Windows 9x/2000 utilities that can be used to change optional hardware (Add New Hardware) and software (Add/Remove Programs) components installed in the system. These utilities are located in the Windows Control Panel.

address   The unique location number of a particular memory storage area, such as a byte of primary memory, a sector of disk memory, or of a peripheral device itself.

address bus   A unidirectional pathway that carries address data generated by the microprocessor to the various memory and I/O elements of the computer. The size of this bus determines the amount of memory a particular computer can use and therefore is a direct indication of the computer's power.

American Standard Code for Information Interchange (ASCII) The 7-bit binary data code used in all personal computers, many minicomputers, and also in communications services. Of the 128 possible character combinations, the first 32 are used for printing and transmission control. Because of the 8-bit byte used in digital computers, the extra bit can be used either for parity checking or for the extended ASCII set of characters, which includes foreign language characters and line-draw graphic symbols.

Application Specific Integrated Circuit (ASIC) A very large scale device designed to replace a large block of standardized PC circuitry. After the parameters of the device achieve a pseudo standard usage status, IC manufacturers tend to combine all the circuitry for that function into a large IC custom designed to carry out that function. Examples include integrated VGA controllers, integrated MI/O controllers, and integrated peripheral controllers.

asynchronous transmission A method of serial data transmission in which the receiving system is not synchronized, by a common clock signal, with the transmitting system.

AT Attachment (ATA) Also known also as IDE. A system-level interface specification that integrates the disk drive controller on the drive itself. The original ATA specification supports one or two hard drives through a 16-bit interface using Programmed I/O (PIO) modes. The ATA-2 specification, also known as EIDE or Fast ATA, supports faster PIO and DMA transfer modes, as well as logical block addressing (LBA) strategies.

AT bus Also referred to as ISA (Industry Standard Architecture) bus. The 16-bit data bus introduced in the AT class personal computer that became the industry standard for 16-bit system.

ATTRIB The DOS command used to change attributes assigned to files (for instance, system, read-only, and hidden status).

attribute Properties of DOS files. Special file attributes include system, read-only, and hidden status. These conditions can be altered using the external DOS command **ATTRIB**.

ATX form factor A newer system board form factor that improves on the previous Baby AT form factor standard by reorienting the system board by 90 degrees. This makes for a more efficient design, placing the IDE connectors nearer to the system unit's drive bays and positioning the microprocessor in line with the output of the power supply's cooling fan.

AUTOEXEC.BAT An optional DOS program that the system's command interpreter uses to carry out customized startup commands at boot up.

B

backup An operation normally performed to create backup copies of important information in case the drive crashes or the disk becomes corrupt. Backup utilities enable the user to quickly create extended copies of files, groups of files, or an entire disk drive.

backup domain controller (BDC) Backup domain controllers are servers within the network that are used to hold read-only backup copies of the directory database. A network can contain one or more BCDs. These servers are used to authenticate user logons.

Backup Wizard An automated software routine in Windows 2000 designed to lead users through a step-by-step process of configuring and scheduling a backup job.

BAT file (Batch file)   A filename extension used to identify a batch file in Microsoft DOS versions. A batch file, created by a word processor, contains a list of DOS commands that are executed as if each were typed and entered one at a time.

baud rate   The number of electrical-state changes per second on a data communications line. At lower speeds, the baud rate and the bits-per-second rate are identical. At higher speeds, the baud rate is some fraction of the bits-per-second rate.

binary   This means two. In conjunction with digital computers, all data is processed only after being converted into binary numbers consisting of the two digits, 0 and 1.

Basic Input Output System (BIOS)   See *ROM BIOS.*

bit (binary digit)   One digit of a binary number (0 or 1). Groups of bits are manipulated together by a computer into various storage units called nibbles, bytes, words, or characters.

bitmap   A term used in computer graphic to describe a memory area containing a video image. One bit in the map represents one pixel on a monochrome screen; whereas in color or grayscale monitors, several bits in the map can represent one pixel.

Blue Screen   A kernel-mode stop that indicates a failure of a core operating system function. Also known as the Blue Screen of Death because the system stops processing and produces a blue screen, instead of risking catastrophic memory and file corruption.

boot   To start the computer. It refers to the word bootstrap, because the straps help in pulling boots on, just as the bootable disk helps the computer to get its first instructions.

Boot menu   The Startup options screen menu displayed during the Windows 2000 boot-up process. This menu is produced when the F8 function key is depressed while the Starting Windows message is onscreen. This menu is generated by the BOOT.INI boot loader menu file. Options in this menu include the variety of operating systems installed on the computer. If no selection is made from this menu after a given time, the default value is selected.

boot partition   The disk partition that possesses the system files required to load the operating system into memory. Also referred to as the active partition.

boot sector   The first sector on a disk (or partition). On bootable disks or partitions, this sector holds the code (called the boot record) that causes the system to move the operating system files into memory and begin executing them.

bootable disk   A disk that starts the operating system. Normally refers to a floppy disk containing the computer operating system.

BOOT.INI   BOOT.INI is a special, hidden boot loader menu file used by the NTLDR during the boot-up process to generate the Boot Loader menu that is displayed onscreen. If no selection is made from this menu after a given time, the default value is selected.

BOOTSECT.DOS   A Windows NT file used to load operating systems other than Windows NT. If an entry from the boot loader menu indicates an operating system other than Windows NT is to be loaded, the NTLDR program loads the BOOTSECT.DOS file from the root directory of the system partition and passes control to it. From this point, the BOOTSECT file is responsible for loading the desired operating system.

Bootstrap Loader   A term used to refer to two different software routines involved in starting a system and loading the operating system. The Primary Bootstrap Loader is a firmware routine that locates the boot record required to load the operating system into memory. The OS loader takes over from the primary bootstrap loader and moves the operating system into memory (known as booting the OS).

bits per second (bps)   A term used to measure the speed of data being transferred in a communications system.

bus   A parallel collection of conductors that carry data or control signals from one unit to another.

bus master   Any class of intelligent devices that can take control of the system buses of a computer.

byte   The most common word size used by digital computers. It is an 8-bit pattern consisting of both a high- and a low-order nibble. Computers of any size are frequently described in terms of how many bytes of data can be manipulated in one operation or cycle.

C

C: drive   This is the commonly understood term designating the system or first hard disk drive in the DOS and OS/2 microcomputer operating systems.

cache   An area of high-speed memory reserved for improving system performance. Blocks of often used data are copied into the cache area to permit faster access times. A disk cache memory is an area of RAM used to hold data from a disk drive that the system may logically want to access, thereby speeding up access.

cache controller   A highly automated memory controller assigned the specific task of managing a sophisticated cache memory system.

carriage   The part in a printer or typewriter that handles the feeding of the paper forms.

cartridge   A removable data-storage module, containing disks, magnetic tape or memory chips, and inserted into the slots of disk drives, printers, or computers.

cathode ray tube (CRT)   The vacuum tube used as the display screen for both TVs and computer terminals. Sometimes, the term is used to mean the terminal itself.

central processing unit (CPU)   The part of the computer that does the thinking. It consists of the control unit and the arithmetic logic unit. In personal computers, the CPU is contained on a single chip, whereas on a minicomputer, it occupies one or several printed circuit boards. On mainframes, a CPU is contained on many printed circuit boards. Its power comes from the fact that it can execute many millions of instructions in a fraction of a second.

Centronics interface   The 36-pin standard for interfacing parallel printers, and other devices, to a computer. The plug, socket, and signals are defined.

Certificate   A security service used to authenticate the origin of a public key to a user possessing a matching private key.

character printer   Any printer that prints one character at a time, such as a dot-matrix printer of a daisy wheel.

chip   The common name for an integrated circuit (IC). Preceded by the development of the transistor, ICs can contain from several dozen to several million electronic components (resistors, diodes, transistors, and so forth) on a square of silicon approximately 1/16th- to 1/2-inch wide and around 1/30th of an inch in thickness. The IC can be packaged in many different styles depending on the specific use for which it is intended.

chipset   A group of specifically engineered ICs designed to perform a function interactively.

CHKDSK   A DOS disk-maintenance utility used to recover lost allocation units from a hard drive. These lost units occur when an application terminates unexpectedly. Over a period of time, lost units can pile up and occupy large amounts of disk space.

Clear To Send (CTS)   An RS-232 handshaking signal sent from the receiver to the transmitter indicating readiness to accept data.

client   Workstation that operates in conjunction with a master server computer that controls the operation of the network.

client/server network   Workstations or clients operate in conjunction with a master server computer to control the network.

clock   An internal timing device. Several varieties of clocks are used in computer systems. Among them are the CPU clock, the real-time clock, a timesharing clock, and a communications clock.

cluster   Clusters are organizational units used with disk drives to represent one or more sectors of data. These structures constitute the smallest unit of storage space on the disk.

CMOS Setup   A software setup program used to provide the system with information about what options are installed. The configuration information is stored in special CMOS registers that are read each time the system boots up. Battery backup prevents the information from being lost when power to the system is removed.

Complementary Metal-Oxide Semiconductor (CMOS)   A MOS technology used to fabricate IC devices. It is traditionally slower than other IC technologies, but it possesses higher circuit-packing density than other technologies. CMOS ICs are sensitive to voltage spikes and static discharges and must be protected from static shock.

cold boot   Booting a computer by turning the power on.

color monitor   Also known as RGB monitors, these display types allow the user to run text and/or color-based applications such as graphics drawing and CAD programs. There are two basic RGB type monitors: digital (TTL) and analog. Analog RGB monitors allow the use of many more colors than digital RGB monitors.

color printer   Any printer capable of printing in color, using thermal-transfer, dot-matrix, electro-photographic, electrostatic, inkjet, or laser-printing techniques.

COM1   The label used in Microsoft DOS versions assigned to serial port #1.

COMMAND.COM   The DOS command interpreter that is loaded at the end of the boot-up process. It accepts commands issued through the keyboard, or other input devices, and carries them out according to the command's definition. These definitions can be altered by adding switches to the command.

command prompt   A screen symbol that indicates to the user that the system is ready for a command. It usually consists of the current drive letter, followed by a colon and a blinking cursor.

compatible   A reference to any piece of computer equipment that works like, or looks like a more widely known standard or model. A PC-compatible, or clone, is a PC that, although physically differing somewhat from the IBM-PC, runs software developed for the IBM-PC and accepts its hardware options.

Computer Management Console   A Windows 2000 management console that enables the user to track and configure all the system's hardware and software. It also can be used to configure network options and view system events.

computer names   A name created for a computer by a network administrator. This name identifies the computer to other members of the network. It is generally recommended that computer names be 15 characters or less. If the computer has the TCP/IP networking protocol installed, however, its name can range up to 63 characters long but should contain only the numbers 0–9, the letters A–Z and a–z, and hyphens. It is possible to use other characters, but doing so may prevent other users from finding your computer on the network.

CONFIG.SYS   A Microsoft operating system configuration file that, upon startup, is used to customize the system's hardware environment. The required peripheral device drivers (with .SYS file extensions) are initialized.

configuration   A customized computer system or communications network composed of a particular number and type of interrelated components. The configuration varies from system to system, requiring that some means be established to inform the system software about what options are currently installed.

Configuration Manager   A component of the Windows PnP system that coordinates the configuration process for all devices in the system.

continuous forms   Paper sheets that are joined together along perforated edges and used in printers that move them through the printing area with motorized sprockets. Sprockets may fit into holes on both sides of the paper.

control bus   A pathway between the microprocessor and the various memory, programmable and I/O elements of the system. Control bus signals are not necessarily related to each other and can be unidirectional or bidirectional.

control character   A special type of character that causes some event to occur on a printer, display, or communications path such as a line feed, a carriage return, or an escape.

control panels   The Windows components used to customize the operation and appearance of Windows functions. In Windows 9x and Windows NT/2000, the control panels can be accessed through the Start button/Settings route, or under the My Computer icon on the desktop.

control protocols   Protocols that configure the communication interface to the networking protocols employed by the system. Each network transport supported under Windows 2000 has a corresponding control protocol.

cursor   The movable, display screen symbol that indicates to the user where the action is taking place. The text cursor is usually a blinking underline or rectangle, while the graphics cursor can change into any predetermined shape at different parts of the screen.

cursor keys   Special keyboard keys that can be used to move the cursor around the display screen. Enhanced keyboards have two clusters of cursor keys so that the numeric keypad portion of the keyboard can be used separately.

cyclic redundancy check (CRC)   The error-checking technique that ensures communications-channel integrity by utilizing division to determine a remainder. If the transmitter and receiver do not agree on what the remainder should be, an error is detected.

cylinder   The combination of all tracks, normally on multiple-platter disk drives, that reside at the same track number location on each surface.

D

data Information assembled in small units of raw facts and figures.

data bus A bidirectional pathway linking the microprocessor to memory and I/O devices, the size of which usually corresponds to the word size of the computer.

Data Communications Equipment (DCE) A communications device, usually a modem, that establishes, maintains, and terminates a data-transfer session. It also serves as a data converter when interfacing different transmission media.

data compression Most compression algorithms use complex mathematical formulas to remove redundant bits, such as successive 0s or 1s from the data stream. When the modified word is played back through the decompression circuitry, the formula reinserts the missing bits to return the data stream to its original state.

Data Encryption Standard (DES) A U.S. standard method of encrypting data into a secret code. Down-level clients employ the DES standard to encrypt user passwords.

Data Set Ready (DSR) An RS-232 handshaking signal sent from the modem to its own computer to indicate its ability to accept data.

Data Terminal Ready (DTR) An RS-232 handshaking signal that is sent to a modem by its own computer to indicate a readiness to accept data.

default The normal action taken, or setting used, by the hardware or software when the user does not otherwise specify.

defragmentation Disk maintenance operation performed to optimize the use of disk space by moving scattered file fragments into continuous chains to speed up data retrieval from the drive.

demodulator A device that removes the data from the carrier frequency and converts it to its originally unmodulated form.

DEVICE= CONFIG.SYS commands used to load specified device drivers into memory at boot up. For instance, the statement **DEVICE=C:\MOUSE\MOUSE.SYS** loads a mouse driver from the MOUSE directory. Used as **DEVICEHIGH=**, the command will load the specified device driver into the upper memory blocks, thereby freeing up conventional memory space.

device driver Special memory-resident program that tells the operating system how to communicate with a particular type of I/O device, such as a printer or a mouse.

Device Manager A Windows 95/98/2000 Control Panel utility that provides a graphical representation of devices in the system. It can be used to view resource allocations and set hardware configurations properties for these devices. This utility also can be used to identify and resolve resource conflicts between system devices. The Device Manager is located under the Control Panel's System icon.

diagnostics Software programs specifically designed to test the operational capability of the computer memory, disk drives, and other peripherals. The routines are available on disks or on ROM chips. Errors may be indicated by beep codes or visual reports. They can normally point to a board-level problem, but not down to a particular component, unless the routine has been written for a particular board being used in the system under test. A complete system failure would require a ROM-based diagnostic program as opposed to a disk-based routine.

dial-up networking Methods of accessing the public telephone system to carry on data-networking operations. These methods include modem, ISDN, and DSL accesses.

DIMMs   Dual in-line memory modules. DIMMs are 168-pin plug-in memory modules similar to SIMMs.

direct I/O   An I/O addressing method that uses no address allocations, but requires extra control lines.

Direct Memory Access (DMA)   The ability of certain intelligent, high-speed I/O devices to perform data transfers themselves, with the help of a special IC device called a DMA controller.

directory   A hierarchical collection of disk files organized under one heading and simulating the concept of a drawer in a file cabinet. In the structure of a disk drive system, the directory is the organizational table that holds information about all files stored under its location. This information includes filename, size, time and date of when it was last changed, and its beginning location on the disk.

disk   A term usually applied to a removable, floppy disk memory-storage device.

disk arrays   A collection of multiple disk drives operating under the direction of a single controller for the purpose of providing fault tolerance and performance. Data files are written on the disks in ways that improve the performance and reliability of the disk drive subsystem, as well as to provide detection and corrective actions for damaged files. Redundant Array of Inexpensive Disks (RAID) 5 in Windows 2000.

disk drive   The peripheral storage device that reads and writes data to spinning magnetic or optical disks. The drive can either hold removable disks or contain permanent platters.

Disk Operating System (DOS)   Can be a generic term, but in most cases, it refers to the Microsoft family of computer operating systems (PC-DOS for IBM equipment or MS-DOS for compatibles).

docking station   Special platforms designed to work with portable computers to provide additional I/O capacity. The docking station is designed so that the portable computer is inserted into it to that it can have access to the docking station's expansion slots, additional storage devices, and other peripheral devices, such as full size keyboards and monitors. No standards exist for docking stations, so they must be purchased for specific types of portable computers.

domain   Collectively, a domain is a group of members that share a common directory database and are organized in levels. Every domain is identified by a unique name and is administered as a single unit having common rules and procedures.

domain name   A unique name that identifies a host computer site on the Internet.

Domain Name Service (DNS)   A database organizational structure whereby higher level Internet servers keep track of assigned domain names and their corresponding IP addresses for systems on levels under them. The IP addresses of all the computers attached to the Internet are tracked by this listing system. DNS evolved as a way to organize the members of the Internet into a hierarchical management structure that consists of various levels of computer groups called domains. Each computer on the Internet is assigned a domain name, which corresponds to an additional domain level.

dot-matrix printer   A type of printer that forms its images out of one or more columns of dot hammers. Higher resolutions require a greater number of dot hammers to be used.

dot pitch   A measurement of the resolution of a dot matrix. The width of an individual dot in millimeters describes a display's resolution, with the smaller number representing the higher resolution. The number of dots per linear inch describes a printer's resolution, with the higher number representing the higher resolution.

drive   (1) An electromechanical device that moves disks, discs, or tapes at high speeds so that data can be recorded on the media, or read back from it. (2) In the organizational structure of a DOS system, a drive can be thought of as the equivalent of a file drawer that holds folders and documents. (3) In electronic terms, it is a signal output of a device used to activate the input of another device.

dual booting   A condition that can be established on a hard disk drive that holds two or more operating systems. A preboot option is created that enables the system to be booted from one of the designated operating systems (for instance, Windows 98 or Windows 2000 Professional).

Dynamic Host Configuration Protocol (DHCP) Software protocol that dynamically assigns IP addresses to a server's clients. This software is available in both Windows 9x and Windows NT/2000 and *must be* located on both the server and the client computers (installed on servers and activated on clients). This enables ISPs to provide dynamic IP address assignments for their customers.

dynamic link library (DLL) files   Windows library files that contain small pieces of executable code that can be shared between Windows programs. These files are used to minimize redundant programming common to certain types of Windows applications.

Dynamic Random Access Memory (DRAM)   A type of RAM that will lose its data, regardless of power considerations, unless it is refreshed at least once every 2 milliseconds.

E

edge connector   The often double-sided row of etched lines on the edge of an adapter card that plugs into one of the computer's expansion slots.

Electrically Erasable Programmable Read-Only Memory (EEPROM)   A type of nonvolatile semiconductor memory device that allows erasure and reprogramming from within a computer using special circuitry. These devices allow specific memory cells to be manipulated, instead of requiring a complete reprogramming procedure (as in the case of EPROMs).

electromagnetic interference (EMI)   A system-disrupting electronic radiation created by some other electronic device. The FCC sets allowable limits for EMI, in Part 5 of its Rules and Regulations. Part A systems are designed for office and plant environments, and Part B systems are designed for home use.

electron gun   The device by which the fine beam of electrons is created that sweeps across the phosphor screen in a CRT.

Electronics Industries Association (EIA)   An organization, founded in 1924, made up of electronic parts and systems manufacturers. It sets electrical and electronic interface standards such as the RS-232C.

electrostatic discharge (ESD)   As it applies to computer systems, a rapid discharge of static electricity from a human to the computer, due to a difference of electrical potential between the two. Such discharges usually involve thousands of volts of energy and can damage the IC circuits used to construct computer and communications equipment.

Emergency Repair Disk (ERD)   A disk created to repair the Windows NT/2000 system when its boot disk fails. ERD provides another option if safe mode and the Recovery Console do not provide a successful solution to a system crash. If you have already created an ERD, you can start the system with the Windows NT/2000 Setup CD, or the Setup floppy disks, and then use the ERD to restore core system files.

Enhanced Cylinder Head Sector (ECHS) format
BIOS translation mode used to configure large hard drives (more than 504MB) for operation. This mode is an extended CHS mode and is identical to Large and LBA modes. However, reconfiguring drives to other configration settings risks the prospects of losing data.

Enhanced IDE (EIDE)   An improved version of the Integrated Drive Electronics interface standard. The new standard supports data transfer rates up to four times that of the original IDE standard. It also makes provisions for supporting storage devices of up to 8.4GB in size, as opposed to the old standard's limit of 528MB. The new standard is sometimes referred to as Fast ATA or Fast IDE.

enterprise networks   Enterprise networks are those networks designed to facilitate business-to-business or business-to-customer operations. Because monetary transactions and customers' personal information travels across the network in these environments, enterprise networks feature facilities for additional highly protective security functions.

Erasable Programmable Read-Only Memory (EPROM)   A type of nonvolatile semiconductor memory device that can be programmed more than once. Selected cells are charged using a comparatively high voltage. EPROMs can be erased by exposure to a source of strong ultraviolet light, at which point they must be completely reprogrammed.

ergonomics   The study of people-to-machine relationships. A device is considered to be ergonomic when it blends smoothly with a person's body actions.

error checking   The act of testing the data transfer in a computer system or network for accuracy.

Esc key (Escape key)   This keyboard key is used to cancel an application operation or to exit some routine.

Ethernet   A popular network topology that uses Carrier Sense Multiple Access with Collision Detection (CSMA/CD) for collision detection and avoidance. Ethernet can be physically implemented as either a bus or a star network organization.

expanded memory (EMS)   A memory-management strategy for handling memory beyond of the 1MB of conventional memory. Using this strategy, the additional memory is accessed in 16K pages, through a window established in the upper memory area.

Expanded Memory Manager (EMM)   Any software driver that permits and manages the use of expanded memory in 80386 and higher machines.

Expanded Memory Specification (EMS)   A method of using memory above one megabyte on computers using DOS. Co-developed by Lotus, Intel, and Microsoft, each upgrade has allowed for more memory to be used. EMS is dictated by the specific application using it. In 286 machines, EMS is installed on an adapter card and managed by an EMS driver. See *Expanded Memory Manager (EMM)*.

expansion slot   The receptacle mounted on the system board into which adapter cards are plugged to achieve system expansion. The receptacle interfaces with the I/O channel and system bus; therefore, the number of slots available determines the expansion potential of the system.

Extended Industry Standard Architecture (EISA)   A PC bus standard that extends the AT bus architecture to 32 bits and allows older PC and AT boards to plug into its slot. It was announced in 1988 as an alternative to the IBM Micro Channel.

extended memory   The memory above 1 megabyte in Intel 286 and higher computers, and used for RAM disks, disk-caching routines, and for locating the operating system files in recent versions of Microsoft DOS.

extended memory (XMS) A memory-management strategy for handling memory beyond of the 1MB of conventional memory. Using this strategy, Windows and Windows-based programs directly access memory above the 1MB marker. Extended memory requires that the HIMEM.SYS memory manager be loaded in the DOS CONFIG.SYS.

extended partition Secondary partitions that can be created after the drive's primary partition has been established. It is the only other partition allowed on a disk after the primary partition is made using FDISK. However, an extended partition can be subdivided into up to 23 logical drives.

Extended System Configuration Data (ESCD) A portion of CMOS memory that holds PnP configuration information.

F

FDISK command The disk utility program that permits the partitioning of the hard disk into several independent disks.

field replaceable unit (FRU) The components of the system that can be conveniently replaced in the field.

file Any program, record, table, or document stored under its own filename.

file allocation table (FAT) A special table located on a formatted DOS disk that tracks where each file is located on the disk.

file menu A drop-down menu attached to Windows graphical interfaces whose options enable users to open, move, copy and delete selected folders, files, or applications.

file systems File-management systems. The organizational structures that operating systems employ to organize and track files. Windows 2000 employs the NTFS5 file system to perform these functions. It is a hierarchical directory system that employs directories to organize files into a tree-like structure.

File Transfer Protocol (FTP) An application layer protocol that copies files from one FTP host site to another.

filenames Names assigned to files in a disk-based system. These systems store and handle related pieces of information in groups called files. The system recognizes and keeps track of the different files in the system through their names. Therefore, each file in the system is required to have a filename that differs from that of any other file in the directory.

FireWire Also known as IEEE 1394, FireWire is a very fast I/O bus standard designed to support the high-bandwidth requirements of real-time audio/visual equipment. The IEEE-1394 standard employs streaming data-transfer techniques to support data transfer rates up to 400Mbps. A single FireWire connection can be used to connect up 63 external devices.

firmware A term used to describe the situation in which programs (software) are stored in ROM ICs (hardware) on a permanent basis.

floppy disk Also called a diskette, a removable secondary storage medium for computers, composed of flexible magnetic material and contained in a square envelope or cartridge. A floppy disk can be recorded and erased hundreds of times.

flow control A method of controlling the flow of data between computers. The receiving system signals the sending PC when it can and cannot receive data. Flow control can be implemented through hardware or software protocols. Using the software method, the receiving PC sends special code characters to the sending system to stop or start data flow. XON/XOFF is an example of a software flow-control protocol.

folders Icons that represent directories. In Windows 9X/NT/2000, directories and subdirectories are referred to and depicted as folders.

Folder Options Options that enable the user to change the appearance of their desktops and folder content, and to specify how their folders will open. Users can select whether they want a single window to open, as opposed to cascading windows, and they can designate whether folders will open with a single-click or double-click. This option also can be used to turn on the Active Desktop, change the application used to open certain types of files, or make files available when they are not online with the network. Changes made in Folder Options apply to the appearance of the contents of Windows Explorer (including My Computer, My Network Places, My Documents, and Control Panel) windows.

font One set of alphanumeric characters possessing matching design characteristics such as typeface, orientation, spacing, pitch, point size, style, and stroke weight.

forests A group of one or more Active Directory domain trees that trust each other. Unlike directory trees, forests do not share a contiguous namespace. This permits multiple namespaces to be supported within a single forest. In the forest, all domains share a common schema, configuration, and global catalog.

form feed The moving of the next paper form into the proper printing position, accomplished either by pressing the Form Feed (FF) button on the printer or by sending the printer the ASCII form-feed character.

FORMAT command A Microsoft DOS utility that prepares a disk for use by the system. Track and sector information is placed on the disk while bad areas are marked so that no data will be recorded on them.

formatting The act of preparing a hard or floppy disk for use with an operating system. This operation places operating system-specific data tracking tables on the media and tests its storage locations (sectors or blocks) to make certain they are reliable for holding data.

fragmentation A condition that exists on hard disk drives after files are deleted, or moved, where areas of free disk space are scattered around the disk. These areas of disk space cause slower performance because the drive's read/write heads have to be moved more often to find the pieces of a single file.

frame (1) A memory window that applications and the operating system exchange data through, such as the EMS frame in upper memory that expanded memory managers use to move data between conventional memory and additional memory beyond the 1MB mark. (2) The construction of a complete package of data with all overhead (headers) for transferring it to another location (that is, an Ethernet frame). (3) One screen of computer graphics data, or the amount of memory required to store it.

full duplex A method of data transmission that allows data flow in both directions simultaneously.

fully qualified domain name (FQDN) A name that consists of the host name and the domain name, including the top-level domain name (for instance, www.mic-inc.com; where www is the host name, mic-inc is the second-level domain name, and com is the top-level domain name).

function keys A special set of keyboard keys used to give the computer special commands. They are frequently used in combination with other keys, and can have different uses depending on the software application being run.

G

GDI.EXE   A Windows core component responsible for managing the operating system's/environment's graphical user interface.

General Protection Fault (GPF)   A Windows memory usage error that typically occurs when a program attempts to access memory currently in use by another program.

GHz (Giga Hertz)   One billion hertz or cycles per second.

graphical user interface (GUI)   A form of operating environment that uses a graphical display to represent procedures and programs that can be executed by the computer.

graphics   The creation and management of pictures using a computer.

ground   (1) Any point from which electrical measurements are referenced. (2) *Earth* ground is considered to be an electrical reference point of absolute zero, and is used as the electrical return path for modern power transmission systems. This ground, often incorporated by electronic devices to guard against fatal shock, is called *chassis* or *protective* ground. (3) An actual conductor in an electronic circuit being used as a return path, alternately called a *signal* ground.

Group Policies   Administrators use these tools to institute large numbers of detailed settings for users thorughout an enterprise, without establishing each setting manually.

Group Policy Editor   Utility employed to establish policies in Windows 2000. Administrators use this editor to establish which applications different users have access to, as well as to control applications on the user's desktop.

groups   The administrative gathering of users that can be administered uniformly. In establishing groups, the administrator can assign permissions or restrictions to the entire body. The value of using groups lies in the time saved by being able to apply common rights to several users instead of applying them one by one.

H

HAL.DLL   HAL.DLL is the Hardware Abstraction Layer driver that holds the information specific to the CPU that the system is being used with.

half-duplex communication   Communications that occur in both directions, but can only occur in one direction at a time. Most, older networking strategies were based on half-duplex operations.

handshaking   A system of signal exchanges conducted between the computer system and a peripheral device during the data-transfer process. The purpose of these signals is to produce as orderly a flow of data as possible.

hard disk   A metal disk for external storage purposes, coated with ferromagnetic coating and available in both fixed and removable format.

hardware   Any aspect of the computer operation that can be physically touched. This includes IC chips, circuit boards, cables, connectors, and peripherals.

Hardware Abstraction Layer (HAL)   The Windows NT HAL is a library of hardware drivers that operate between the actual hardware and the rest of the system. These software routines act to make every architecture look the same to the operating system. The HAL occupies the logical space directly between the system's hardware and the rest of the operating system's Executive Services. In Windows NT 4.0, the HAL enables the operating system to work with different types of microprocessors.

Hardware Compatibility List (HCL) The list of Microsoft-certified compatible hardware devices associated with Windows 2000 Professional and Windows 2000 Server products.

HIMEM.SYS The DOS memory manager that enables expanded and extended memory strategies for memory operations above the 1MB conventional memory range.

hives The five files that hold the contents of the Windows NT Registry. Hives represent the major divisions of all the Registry's keys, subkeys, subtrees, and values. The hives of the Windows NT Registry are the SAM hive, the Security hive, the Software hive, the System hive, and the Default hive. These files are stored in the \WINNT\System32\Config directory along with a backup copy and log file for each hive.

host Any device that communicates over the network using TCP/IP. The term refers to a device that has an assigned (dedicated) IP address.

I

icons Graphical symbols used to represent commands. These symbols are used to start and manipulate programs without knowing where that program is, or how it is configured.

impact printer Any printer that produces a character image by hammering onto a combination of embossed character, ribbon, and paper.

Industry Standard Architecture (ISA) A term that refers to the bus structures used in the IBM PC series of personal computers. The PC and XT uses an 8-bit bus, whereas the AT uses a 16-bit bus.

Infrared Data Association (IrDA) A data-transmission standard for using infrared light. IrDA ports provide wireless data transfers between devices.

These ports support data-transfer rates roughly equivalent to traditional parallel ports. The only downside to using IrDA ports for data communications is that the two devices must be within one or two meters of each other and have a clear line of sight between them.

INI files Windows initialization text files that hold configuration settings that are used to initialize the system for Windows operation. Originally, these files form the basis of the Windows 3.x operating environments. They were mostly replaced in Windows 9x and NT/2000 by the Registry structure. However, some parts of the INI files still exist in these products.

initialization The process of supplying startup information to an intelligent device or peripheral (for instance, the system board's DMA controller or a modem), or to a software application, or applet.

inkjet printer A high-resolution-type printer that produces its image by spraying a specially treated ink onto the paper.

input device Any computer input-generating peripheral device such as keyboard, mouse, light pen, scanner, or digitizer.

instruction word A class of binary coded data word that tells the computer what operation to perform and where to find any data needed to perform the operation.

integrated circuit (IC) The technical name for a chip. See *chip*.

Integrated Drive Electronics (IDE) A method of disk drive manufacturing that locates all the required controller circuitry on the drive itself, rather than on a separate adapter card. Also known as AT Attachment interface.

Integrated Services Digital Network (ISDN) A digital communications standard that can carry digital data over special telephone lines, at speeds much higher than those possible with regular analog phone lines.

intelligent controller   Usually an IC, or series of ICs, with built-in microprocessor capabilities dedicated to the controlling of some peripheral unit or process. Single-chip controllers are sometimes referred to as smart chips.

interface   The joining of dissimilar devices so that they function in a compatible and complementary manner.

interlaced   The method of rewriting the monitor screen repeatedly by alternately scanning every other line and then scanning the previously unscanned lines.

Internet   The most famous wide area network is actually a network of networks working together. The main communication path is a series of networks established by the U.S. government that has expanded around the world and offers access to computers in every part of the globe.

Internet Printing Protocol (IPP)   A protocol included with Windows 2000 that enables users to sort between different printers based on their attributes. This standards-based Internet protocol provides Windows users with the capability of printing across the Internet. With IPP, the user can print to a URL, view the print queue status using an Internet browser, and install print drivers across the Internet.

Internet Protocol (IP)   The network layer protocol where logical addresses are assigned. IP is one of the protocols that make up the TCP/IP stack.

Internet Protocol (IP) address   A 32-bit network address consisting of four dotted-decimal numbers, separated by periods, that uniquely identifies a device on the network. Each IP address consists of two parts: the network address and the host address. The network address identifies the entire network, whereas the host address identifies an intelligent member within the network (router, a server, or a workstation).

Internet service provider (ISP)   Companies that provide the technical gateway to the Internet. It connects all the users and individual networks together.

interrupt   A signal sent to the microprocessor from the interrupt controller, or generated by a software instruction, which is capable of interrupting the microprocessor during program execution. An interrupt is usually generated when an input or output operation is required.

interrupt controller   A special programmable IC responsible for coordinating and prioritizing interrupt requests from I/O devices and sending the microprocessor the starting addresses of the interrupt service routines so that the microprocessor can service the interrupting device and then continue executing the active program.

interrupt request (IRQ)   Hardware interrupt request lines in a PC-compatible system. System hardware devices use these lines to request service from the microprocessor as required. The microprocessor responds to the IRQ by stopping what it is doing, storing its environment, jumping to a service routine, servicing the device, and then returning to its original task.

intranet   An intranet is a network built on the TCP/IP protocol that belongs to a single organization. It is, in essence, a private Internet. Like the Internet, intranets are designed to share information and are accessible only to the organization's members, with authorization.

I/O (input/output)   A type of data transfer occurring between a microprocessor and a peripheral device. Whenever any data transfer occurs, output from one device becomes an input to another.

I/O port   The external window or connector on a computer, used to effect an interface with a peripheral device. The I/O port may appear as either parallel data connections or serial data connections.

IO.SYS   A special hidden, read-only boot-up file that the Bootstrap Loader finds and moves into RAM to manage the boot-up process. After the boot-up is complete, this file manages the basic input/output routines of the system. This includes communication between the system and I/O devices such as hard disks, printers, floppy disk drives, and so on.

IPCONFIG   A TCP/IP networking utility that can be used to determine the IP address of a local machine.

IPX/SPX   Internetwork Packet Exchange/Sequential Packet Exchange protocol. A proprietary transport protocol developed by Novell for the NetWare operating system. The IPX portion of the protocol is a connectionless, network layer protocol, which is responsible for routing. The SPX portion of the protocol is a connection oriented, transport layer protocol that manages error checking. These protocols are primarily found on local area networks that include NetWare servers.

J

joystick   A computer input device that offers quick, multidirectional movement of the cursor for CAD systems and video games.

jumper   Normally, a 2- or 4-pin BERG connector, located on the system board or an adapter card, which permits the attachment of a wired, hardware switch or the placement of a shorting bar to effect a particular hardware function or setting.

K

kernel   The Windows 3.x and 95 core files that are responsible for managing Windows resources and running applications.

kernel mode   The kernel mode is the operating mode in which the program has unlimited access to all memory, including those of system hardware, the user-mode applications and other processes (such as I/O operations). The kernel mode consists of three major blocks: the Win32k Executive Service module, the Hardware Abstraction Layer, and the microkernel.

keyboard   The most familiar computer input device, incorporating a standard typewriter layout with the addition of other specialized control and function keys.

L

laser printer   Any printer that utilizes the electro-photographic method of image transfer. Light dots are transferred to a photosensitive rotating drum, which picks up electrostatically charged toner before transferring it to the paper.

legacy devices   Adapter cards and devices that do not include PnP capabilities. These are typically older ISA expansion cards that are still being used for some reason.

letter quality   Refers to a print quality as good or better than that provided by an electric typewriter.

light-emitting diode (LED)   A particular type of diode that emits light when conducting, and used in computers and disk drives as active circuit indicators.

liquid-crystal display (LCD)   The type of output display created by placing liquid-crystal material between two sheets of glass. A set of electrodes is attached to each sheet of glass. Horizontal (row) electrodes are attached to one glass plate, whereas vertical (column) electrodes are fitted to the other plate. These electrodes are transparent and let light pass through. A pixel is created in the liquid-crystal material at each spot where a row and a column electrode intersect. When the pixel is energized, the liquid-crystal material bends and prevents light from passing through the display.

local area network (LAN)   A collection of local computers and devices that can share information. A LAN is normally thought of as encompassing a campus setting, room, or collection of buildings.

logical block addressing (LBA)   A hard disk drive organizational strategy that permits the operating system to access larger drive sizes than older BIOS/DOS FAT-management schemes could support.

logon   The process of identifying ones self to the network. Normally accomplished by entering a valid username and password that the system recognizes.

loopback   A modem test procedure that allows a transmitted signal to be returned to its source for comparison with the original data.

lost allocation units   Also referred to as lost clusters. File segments that do not currently belong to any file in the file allocation table. The DOS command **CHKDSK/F** can be used to locate and free these segments for future use.

LPT1   The label used in Microsoft DOS versions assigned to parallel port #1, usually reserved for printer operation.

M

magnetic disk   The most popular form of secondary data storage for computers. Shaped like a platter and coated with an electromagnetic material, magnetic disks provide direct access to large amounts of stored data and can be erased and rerecorded many times.

magnetic tape   Traditionally, one of the most popular forms of secondary data storage backup for computers. However, Windows 2000 offers a number of other backup capabilities that may render tape an undesirable backup media in the future. Because access to data is sequential in nature, magnetic tape is primarily used to restore a system that has suffered a catastrophic loss of data from its hard disk drive.

mapped drives   A technique employed to enable a local system to assign a logical drive letter to the remote disk drive, or folder. This is referred to as mapping the drive letter to the resource. This will enable applications running on the local computer to use the resources across the network.

Master Boot Record (MBR)   Also referred to as the Master Partition Boot Sector. This file is located at the first sector of the disk. It contains a Master Partition Table that describes how the hard disk is organized. This table includes information about the disk's size, as well as the number and locations of all partitions on the disk. The MBR also contains the Master Boot Code that loads the operating system from the disk's active partition.

Master File Table (MFT)   The core component of the NTFS system, this table replaces the FAT in an MS-DOS-compatible system and contains information about each file being stored on the disk.

MEM.EXE   The DOS command that can be used to examine the total and used memory of the system.

memory   Computer components that store information for future use. In a PC, memory can be divided into two categories: primary and secondary (that is, semiconductor RAM and ROM and other devices). Primary memory can be divided into ROM, RAM, and cache groups. Likewise, secondary memory contains many types of storage devices such as floppy drives, hard disk drives, CD-ROM drives, DVD drives, tape drives, and so on.

memory management   Methodology used in handling a computer's memory resources, including bank switching, memory protection, and virtual memory.

memory map   A layout of the memory and/or I/O device addressing scheme used by a particular computer system.

memory-mapped I/O   An I/O addressing method where I/O devices are granted a portion of the available address allocations, thus requiring no additional control lines to implement.

menu   A screen display of available program options or commands that can be selected through keyboard or mouse action.

metal-oxide semiconductor (MOS)   A category of logic and memory chip design that derives its name from the use of metal, oxide, and semiconductor layers. Among the various families of MOS devices are PMOS (P-Type semiconductor material), NMOS (N-Type semiconductor material), and CMOS (Complimentary/Symmetry MOS material). The first letter of each family denotes the type of construction used to fabricate the chip's circuits. MOS families do not require a highly regulated +5V DC power supply, like TTL devices.

MHz (Mega Hertz)   One million hertz, or cycles per second.

microcomputer   The same thing as a personal computer, or a computer using an microprocessor as its CPU.

Microsoft Management Console (MMC)   A collection of manageability features that accompanies Windows 2000. These features exist as "snap-in" applets that can be added to the operating system through the MMC.

mirroring   A RAID fault-tolerance method where an exact copy of all data is written to two separate disks at the same time.

modem (modulator-demodulator)   Also called a DCE device, it is used to interface a computer or terminal to the telephone system for the purpose of conducting data communications between computers often located at great distances from each other.

monitor   (1) A name for a CRT computer display. (2) Any hardware device, or software program, such as the Windows 95 System Resource Monitor, that checks, reports about or automatically oversees a running program or system.

mouse   A popular computer I/O device used to point or draw on the video monitor by rolling it along a desktop as the cursor moves on the screen in a corresponding manner.

MSD (Microsoft Diagnostics)   Microsoft Diagnostic program that can be used from the command prompt to examine different aspects of a system's hardware and software configuration. The MSD utility has been included with MS-DOS 6.x, Windows 3.x, and Windows 9x.

MSDOS.SYS   One of the hidden, read-only system files required to boot the system. It is loaded by the IO.SYS file during the boot-up process. It handles program and file-management functions for MS-DOS systems. In Windows 95, its function is changed to that of providing pathways to other Windows files and supporting selected startup options.

multimedia   A term applied to a range of applications that bring together text, graphics, video, audio, and animation to provide interactivity between the computer and its human operator.

Multimedia Extensions (MMX) technology   An advanced Pentium microprocessor that includes specialized circuitry designed to manage multimedia operations. Its additional multimedia instructions speed up high-volume input/output needed for graphics, motion video, animation, and sound.

multitasking   The capability of a computer system to run two or more programs simultaneously.

N

National Television Standards Committee (NTSC)
This organization created the television standards in the United States, and is administered by the FCC.

near letter quality (NLQ)   A quality of printing nearly as good as an electric typewriter. The very best dot-matrix printers can produce NLQ.

Negative ACKnowledge (NAK)   A data communications code used by a receiver to tell the transmitter that the last message was not properly received.

NetBEUI (NetBIOS Extended User Interface)   The Microsoft networking protocol used with Windows-based systems.

NetBIOS   An emulation of IBM's NETwork Basic Input/Output System. NetBIOS represents the basic interface between the operating system and the LAN hardware. This function is implemented through ROM ICs, located on the network card.

NetWare   The Novell client/server network operating system.

Network Connection Wizard   Automated setup routine in Windows 2000 that can be invoked to guide the user through the process of creating a network connection.

Network Neighborhood   The Windows 95 utility used to browse and connect multiple networks, to access shared resources on a server without having to map a network drive.

nibble   A 4-bit binary pattern, which can easily be converted into a single hexadecimal digit.

nonimpact printer   Any printer that does not form its characters by using a hammer device to impact the paper, ribbon, or embossed character.

nonmaskable interrupt (NMI)   A type of interrupt which cannot be ignored by the microprocessor during program execution. Three things can cause a nonmaskable interrupt to occur: (1) a numeric coprocessor installation error; (2) A RAM parity check error; (3) an I/O channel check error.

nonvolatile memory   Memory that is not lost after the power is turned off, such as ROM.

NT File System (NTFS)   The proprietary Windows NT file system. The NTFS structure is designed to provide better data security and to operate more efficiently with larger hard drives than FAT systems do. Its structure employs 64-bit entries to keep track of storage on the disk (as opposed to the 16- and 32-bit entries used in FAT and FAT32 systems).

NTDETECT   NTDETECT.COM is the Windows NT hardware-detection file. This file is responsible for collecting information about the system's installed hardware devices and passing it to the NTLDR program. This information is later used to upgrade the Windows NT Registry files.

NTLDR   NT Loader is the Windows NT Bootstrap Loader for Intel-based computers running Windows NT. It is the Windows NT equivalent of the DOS IO.SYS file and is responsible for loading the NT operating system into memory. Afterward, NTLDR passes control of the system over to the Windows NT operating system.

NTOSKRNL   NTOSKRNL.EXE is the Windows NT kernel file that contains the Windows NT core and loads its device drivers.

NTUSER.DAT   The Windows NT/2000 file that contains the User portion of the Windows NT Registry. This file contains the user-specific settings that have been established for this user. When a user logs on to the system, the User file and System hive portions of the Registry are used to construct the user-specific environment in the system.

null modem cable   A cable meeting the RS-232C specification, used to cross-connect two computers through their serial ports by transposing the transmit and receive lines. They must be physically located close to one another, eliminating the need for a modem.

O

odd parity   The form of parity checking where the parity bit is used in order to make the total number of 1s contained in the character an odd number.

off-hook   A condition existing on a telephone line that is now capable of initiating an outgoing call, but unable to receive an incoming call.

offline   Any computer system or peripheral device that is not ready to operate, not connected, not turned on, or not properly configured.

on-hook   A condition that exists on any telephone line that is capable of receiving an incoming call.

online   Any computer system or peripheral device that is not only powered up, but also is ready to operate.

operating system   A special software program, first loaded into a computer at power up, and responsible for running it. The operating system also serves as the interface between the machine and other software applications.

optical mouse   A mouse that emits an infrared light stream to detect motion as it is moved around a special x-y matrix pad.

output device   Any peripheral device (such as a monitor, modem, or printer) that accepts computer output.

P

paging file   Also known as the swap file. The hidden file located on the hard disk that makes up half of the Windows 2000 virtual memory system. This file holds the programs and data that the operating system's virtual memory manager moves out of RAM memory and stores on to the disk as virtual memory.

parallel interface   The multiline channel through which the simultaneous transfer of one or more bytes occurs.

parallel mode   The mode of data transfer where an entire word is transferred at once, from one location to another, by a set of parallel conductors.

parallel port   The external connector on a computer that is used to effect an interface between the computer and a parallel peripheral, such as a printer.

parity bit   Used for error checking during the sending and receiving of data within a system and from one system to another. The parity bit's value depends on how many 1 bits are contained in the byte it accompanies.

parity checking   A method to check for data-transmission errors by using a ninth bit to ensure that each character sent has an even (even parity) or odd (odd parity) number of logic 1s before transfer. The parity bit is checked for each byte sent.

parity error   This error occurs when a data transfer cannot be verified for integrity. At least one data bit or the parity bit has corrupted during the transfer process.

partition   A logical section of a hard disk. Partitioning allows a single, physical disk to be divided into multiple logical drives that can each hold a different operating system. Most disks contain a single partition that holds a single operating system.

Partition Boot Sector   The boot sector of that partition located in the first sector of the active partition. Here, the MBR finds the code to begin loading the Secondary Bootstrap Loader from the root directory of the boot drive.

partitioning   Partitioning establishes the logical structure of the hard disk in a format that conforms to the operating system being used with the computer. It is a function of the operating system being used. In the case of Microsoft operating systems, the FDISK utility is used to establish and manipulate partitions.

partition table   The table present at the start of every hard disk that describes the layout of the disk, including the number and location of all partitions on the disk.

passwords   Unique code patterns associated with a user's logon account that is used to access the resources of a network.

path   The location of the file on the disk in reference to the drive's root directory. The file's full path is specified by a logical drive letter and a listing of all directories between the root directory and the file.

PC bus   Refers to the bus architectures used in the first IBM PCs, the original 8-bit bus, and the 16-bit bus extension used with the AT.

peer-to-peer network   A network that does not have a centralized point of management and where each computer is equal to all the others. In this scenario, all the members can function as both clients and servers.

Peripheral Component Interconnect (PCI) bus   A low-cost, high-performance 32-/64-bit local bus developed jointly by IBM, Intel, DEC, NCR, and Compaq.

peripherals   Also called I/O devices, these units include secondary memory devices, such as hard disk drives, floppy disk drives, magnetic tape drives, modems, monitors, mice, joysticks, light pens, scanners, and even speakers.

permissions   A feature that enables security levels to be assigned to files and folders on the disk. These settings provide parameters for activities that users can conduct with the designated file or folder.

Personal Computer Memory Card International Association (PCMCIA) card   A credit-card-sized adapter card designed for use with portable computers. These cards slide into a PCMCIA slot and are used to implement modems, networks, and CD-ROM drives.

Personal Digital Assistants (PDAs)   Handheld computing devices that typically include telephone, fax, and networking functions. A typical PDA can function as a cell phone, a fax, and a personal organizer. Most are pen-based devices that use a wand for input rather than a keyboard or mouse. PDAs are a member of the palmtop class of computers.

pin feed   A method of moving continuous forms through the print area of a printer by mounting pins on each side of a motorized platen to engage the holes on the right and left side of the paper.

PING   Network troubleshooting utility command that is used to verify connections to remote hosts. The **PING** command sends Internet Control Message Packets to a remote location and then waits for echoed response packets to be returned. The command waits for up to one second for each packet sent and then displays the number of transmitted and received packets. The command can be used to test both the name and IP address of the remote unit. A number of switches can be used to set parameters for the ping operation.

pixel   Also called a PEL, or picture element, it is the smallest unit (one dot for monochrome) into which a display image can be divided.

Plug and Play (PnP)   A specification that requires the BIOS, operating system, and adapter cards to be designed so that the system automatically configures new hardware devices to eliminate system resource conflicts.

pointing device Any input device used for the specific purpose of moving the screen cursor or drawing an image.

Point-to-Point Protocol (PPP) A connection protocol that controls the transmission of data over the wide area network. PPP is the default protocol for the Microsoft Dial-Up adapter. In a dial-up situation, Internet software communicates with the service provider by embedding the TCP/IP information in a PPP shell for transmission through the modem in analog format. The communications equipment, at the ISP site, converts the signal back to the digital TCP/IP format. PPP has become the standard for remote access.

Point-to-Point Tunneling Protocol (PPTP) The de facto industry standard tunneling protocol first supported in Windows NT 4.0. PPTP is an extension of the Point-to-Point Protocol (PPP) and takes advantage of the authentication, compression, and encryption mechanisms of PPP. PPTP is installed with the Routing and Remote Access service. By default, PPTP is configured for five PPTP ports that can be enabled for inbound remote access and demand-dial routing connections through the Windows 2000 Routing and Remote Access Wizard. PPTP and Microsoft Point-to-Point Encryption (MPPE) provide the primary security technology to implement Virtual Private Network services of encapsulation and encryption of private data.

polarizer An optical device that either blocks or allows the passage of light through it, depending on the polarity of an electrical charge applied to it.

policies Network administrative settings that govern the rights and privileges of different users in multiuser operations.

PolEdit The system Policy Editor, used to establish or modify system policies, that governs user rights and privileges. The Policy Editor is another tool that can be used to access the information in the Registry. Unlike the RegEdit utility, however, PolEdit can access only subsets of keys. The Registry Editor can access the entire Registry.

polling A system of initiating data transfer between a computer system and a peripheral, in which the status of all the peripherals is examined periodically under software program control by having the microprocessor check the ready line. When it is activated by one of the peripherals, the processor begins the data transfer using the corresponding I/O port.

Power-On Self-Tests (POST) A group of ROM BIOS-based diagnostic tests performed on the system each time it is powered up. These tests check the PC's standard hardware devices, including the microprocessor, memory, interrupts, DMA, and video.

power supply The component in the system that converts the AC voltage from the wall outlet to the DC voltages required by the computer circuitry.

preventive maintenance Any regularly scheduled checking and testing of hardware and software with the goal of avoiding future failure or breakdown.

primary domain controller (PDC) Primary domain controllers contain the directory databases for the network. These databases contain information about user accounts, group accounts, and computer accounts. PDCs also are also referred to as Security Accounts Managers.

primary partitions Bootable partitions created from unallocated disk space. Under Windows 2000, up to four primary partitions can be created on a basic disk. The disk also can contain three primary partitions and an extended partition. The primary partition becomes the system's boot volume by being marked as Active. The free space in the extended partition can be subdivided into up to 23 logical drives.

printer A peripheral device for the printing of computer text or graphics output.

printer font   A prescribed character set properly formatted for use by the printer.

profiles   Information about each user and group defined in the system that describes the resources and desktop configurations created for them. Settings in the profiles can be used to limit the actions users can perform, such as installing, removing, configuring, adjusting, or copying resources. When users log on to the system, it checks their profile and adjusts the system according to their information. This information is stored in the \WINNT*login_name*\NTUSER.DAT file.

program   Any group of instructions designed to command a computer system through the performance of a specific task. Also called software.

Program Information Files (PIF)   Windows 3.x information files used to identify resources required for DOS-based applications.

programmed I/O   A system of initiating data transfer between a computer system and a peripheral, in which the microprocessor alerts the specific device by using an address call. The I/O device can signal its readiness to accept the data transfer by using its busy line. If busy is active, the microprocessor can perform other tasks until the busy line is deactivated, at which time the transfer can begin.

prompt   A software-supplied message to the user, requiring some specific action or providing some important information. It also can be a simple symbol, indicating that the program is successfully loaded and waiting for a command from the user.

protected mode   An operational state that allows an 80286 or higher computer to address all of its memory, including that memory beyond the 1MB MS-DOS limit.

protocol   A set of rules that govern the transmitting and receiving of data communications.

Q

queue   A special and temporary storage (RAM or registers) area for data in printing or internal program execution operations.

quotas   Windows 2000 security settings that enables administrators to limit the amount of hard drive space users can have access to.

QWERTY keyboard   A keyboard layout that was originally designed to prevent typists from jamming old-style mechanical typewriters, it is still the standard English language keyboard. The name spells out the first six leftmost letters in the first alphabetic row of keys.

R

RAM disk   An area of memory that has been set aside and assigned a drive letter to simulate the organization of a hard disk drive in RAM memory. Also referred to as a virtual disk.

random-access memory (RAM)   A type of semiconductor memory device that holds data on a temporary or volatile basis. Any address location in the RAM memory section can be accessed as fast as any other location.

raster graphics   A graphics representation method that uses a dot matrix to compose the image.

raster scan   The display of a video image, line by line, by an electron beam deflection system.

read only   (1) A file parameter setting that prevents a file from being altered. (2) Refers to data permanently stored on the media or to such media itself.

read-only memory (ROM)   A type of semiconductor memory device that holds data on a permanent or nonvolatile basis.

read/write head   Usually abbreviated R/W head, the device by which a disk or tape drive senses and records digital data on the magnetic medium.

real mode   A mode of operation in 80286 and higher machines in which the computer functions under the same command and addressing restrictions as an 8086 or 8088.

reboot   To restart the computer or to reload the operating system.

Redundant Array of Inexpensive Disks (RAID)   A set of specifications for configuring multiple hard drives to store data to increase storage capacity and improve performance. Some variations configure the drives in a manner to improve performance, whereas others levels concentrate on data security.

refresh   A required way to re-energize a memory cell or display pixel so that its data is continually held.

Registry   A multipart, hierarchical database established to hold system and user configuration information in Windows 9x, NT, and 2000.

Registry keys   The Registries in Windows 9X, NT, and 2000 are organized into headkeys, subkeys, and values.

RegEdit   The editing utility used to directly edit the contents of the Registry (REGEDIT.EXE and REGEDIT32.EXE). This file is located in the WINNT\System32 folder.

RESET   A control bus signal, activated either by a soft or hard switch, which sets the system microprocessor and all programmable system devices to their startup, or initialization, values. This allows the computer to begin operation following the application of the RESET input signal.

resolution   A measurement of the sharpness of an image or character, either of a printer or a display monitor. For a monitor, resolution consists of the number of dots per scan line, times the number of

scans per picture. For a printer, resolution consists of the number of dots present per linear inch of print space.

ROM BIOS   A collection of special programs (native intelligence) permanently stored in one or two ROM ICs installed on the system board. These programs are available to the system as soon as it is powered up, providing for initialization of smart chips, POST tests, and data-transfer control.

root directory   The main directory of every logical disk. It follows the FAT tables and serves as the starting point for organizing information on the disk. The location of every directory, subdirectory, and file on the disk is recorded in this directory.

RS-232C   The most widely used serial interface standard, it calls for a 25-pin D-type connector. Specific pins are designated for data transmission and receiving, as well as a number of handshaking and control lines. Logic voltage levels also are established for the data and the control signals on the pins of the connector.

RS-422   An enhancement to the original RS-232C interface standard and adopted by the EIA, it uses twisted-pair transmission lines and differential line voltage signals resulting in higher immunity for the transmitted data.

RS-423   Another enhancement to the original RS-232C interface standard and adopted by the EIA, it uses coaxial cable to provide extended transmission distances and higher data-transfer rates.

S

safe mode   A special Windows 95/98/2000 startup mode that starts the system by loading minimum configuration drivers. This mode is used to allow the correction of system errors when the system will not boot up normally. Safe mode is entered by pressing F5 or F8 when the Starting Windows message is displayed during boot up.

scan rate   The total number of times per second that a video raster is horizontally scanned by the CRT's electron beam.

sector   One of many individual data-holding areas into which each track of a disk is divided during the format process.

serial interface   A channel through which serial digital data transfer occurs. Although multiple lines can be used, only one of these will actually carry the data. The most popular serial interface standard is the EIA RS-232C.

Serial Line Internet Protocol (SLIP)   Older units running UNIX employ this Internet connection protocol for dial-up services. The protocol wraps the TCP/IP packet in a shell for transmission through the modem in analog format. The communications equipment, at the service provider's site, converts the signal back to the digital TCP/IP format.

serial mode   The mode of data transfer in which the word bits are transferred one bit at a time, along a single conductor.

serial mouse   A type of mouse that plugs into a serial port rather than an adapter card.

serial port   The external connector on a computer that is used to effect an interface between the computer and a serial device such as a modem. A typical serial port uses a DB-25 or a DB-9 connector.

servers   Powerful network computers (or devices) that contain the network operating system and manage network resources for other computers (clients). Some servers take on special management functions for the network. Some of these functions include print servers, Web servers, file servers, database servers, and so on.

setup disks   Disks created to get a failed Windows NT/2000 system restarted. These disks are created by the Windows 2000 Backup utility and contain information about the system's current Windows configuration settings.

shadow RAM   An area of RAM used for copying the system's BIOS routines from ROM. Making BIOS calls from the RAM area improves the operating speed of the system. Video ROM routines are often stored in shadow RAM also.

shared resources   A system resource (device or directory) that has been identified as being available for use by multiple individuals throughout the network environment.

shares   Resources, such as printers and folders, that are made available for use by other network users.

simplex communications   Communications that occur only in one direction. A public address system is an example of simplex communications.

single in-line memory module (SIMM)   A memory chip, circuit board module, containing eight (without parity) or nine (with parity) memory chips, and designed to plug into special sockets.

Small Computer System Interface (SCSI) bus   A system-level interface standard used to connect different types of peripheral equipment to the system. The standard actually exists as a group of specifications (SCSI, SCSI-2, and SCSI-3) featuring several cabling connector schemes. Even within these three specifications, there can exist major variations: Wide SCSI, Fast SCSI, and Fast/Wide SCSI. Apple was the first personal computer maker to select the SCSI interface as the bus standard for peripheral equipment that can provide high-speed data-transfer control for up to seven devices, while occupying only one expansion slot. The standard is gaining widespread support in the PC market, particularly in the area of portable PCs. See *system-level interface*.

SMARTDRV.EXE (SmartDrive)   A DOS driver program that establishes a disk cache in an area of extended memory as a storage space for information read from the hard disk drive. When a program requests more data, the SMARTDRV program redirects the request to check in the cache memory area to see whether the requested data is there.

software   Any aspect of the computer operation that cannot be physically touched. This includes bits, bytes, words, and programs.

speaker   The computer system's audio output device. Measuring 2 1/4 inches in diameter, and rated at 8 ohms, 1/2 watts, the speaker is usually used as a system prompt, and as an error indicator. It also can produce arcade sounds, speech, and music.

start bit   In asynchronous serial data transmission, this bit denotes the beginning of a character and is always a logic low pulse, or space.

static electricity   A stationary charge of electricity normally caused by friction and potentially very damaging to sensitive electronic components. It can be a serious problem in environments of low humidity.

static random-access memory (SRAM)   A type of RAM that can store its data indefinitely, as long as power to it is not interrupted.

stop bit   The bit, sent after each character in an asynchronous data-communications transmission, that signals the end of a character.

Stop errors   Errors that occur when Windows 2000 detects a condition from which it cannot recover. The system stops responding, and a screen of information with a blue, or black, background displays. Stop errors are also known as Blue Screen errors, or the Blue Screen of Death (BSOD).

subnet mask   The decimal number 255 is used to hide, or mask, the network portion of the IP address while still showing the host portions of the address.

The default subnet mask for Class A IP addresses is 255.0.0.0. Class B is 255.255.0.0, and Class C is 255.255.255.0.

swap file   A special file established on the hard drive to provide virtual memory capabilities for the operating system. Windows 3.x can work with temporary or permanent swap files. Windows 95 uses a dynamically assigned, variable-length swap file.

synchronous transmission   A method of serial data transmission in which both the transmitter and the receiver are synchronized by a common clock signal.

SYSEDIT.EXE   A special Windows text editor utility that can be used to alter ASCII text files, such as CONFIG.SYS, AUTOEXEC.BAT, WIN.INI, and SYSTEM.INI files.

system board   The large printed circuit board (motherboard) into which peripheral adapter boards (daughter boards) can plug into, depending on the number of devices working with the system. The system board is populated with 100 or more IC chips, depending on how much onboard memory is installed. Besides RAM chips, the system board contains the microprocessor, BIOS ROM, several programmable controllers, system clock circuitry, switches and various jumpers. Also, most system boards come with an empty socket into which the user can plug a compatible coprocessor chip to give the computer some high-level number-crunching capabilities.

system files   Files that possess the System attribute. These are normally hidden files used to boot the operating system.

system-level interface   An interface that allows the system to directly access the I/O device through an expansion slot without an intermediate interface circuit. The system is isolated from the peripheral device and sees only its logical configuration.

system partitions Normally the same as the boot partition. More precisely, the disk partition that contains the hardware-specific files (NTLDR, OSLOADER, BOOT.INI, and NTDETECT) required to load and start Windows 2000.

system software A class of software dedicated to the control and operation of a computer system and its various peripherals.

system unit The main computer cabinet housing containing the primary components of the system. This includes the main logic board (system- or motherboard), disk drive(s), switching power supply, and the interconnecting wires and cables.

T

tape drive The unit that actually reads, writes, and holds the tape being used for backup purposes.

task switching The changing of one program or application to another either manually by the user or under the direction of a multitasking operating system environment.

telephony In the computer world, this term is used to refer to hardware and software devices that perform functions typically performed by telephone equipment. Microsoft offers the TAPI interface for both clients and servers. see *Telephony API*.

Telephony API (TAPI, Telephony Application Programming Interface) This software interface provides a universal set of drivers that enable modems and COM ports to control and arbitrate telephony operations for data, faxes, and voice. Through this interface, applications can cooperatively share the dial-up connections functions of the system.

TCP/IP (Transfer Control Protocol/Internet Protocol) A collection of protocols developed by the U. S. Department of Defense in the early days of the network that would become the Internet. It is the standard transport protocol used by many operating systems and the Internet.

toner A form of powdered ink that accepts an electrical charge in laser printers and photocopying machines. It adheres to a rotating drum containing an image that is given an opposite charge. The image is transferred to paper during the printing process.

TRACERT A network troubleshooting utility that displays the route and a hop count taken to a given destination. The route taken to a particular address can be set manually using the **ROUTE** command. The TRACERT utility traces the route taken by ICMP packets sent across the network. Routers along the path return information to the inquiring system and the utility displays the host name, IP address, and round-trip time for each hop in the path.

track A single disk or tape data-storage channel, upon which the R/W head places the digital data in a series of flux reversals. On disks, the track is a concentric data circle; whereas on tapes, it is a parallel data line.

trackball (1) A pointing device that enables the user to control the position of the cursor on the video display screen by rotating a sphere (trackball). (2) The sphere inside certain types of mice that the mouse rides on. As the mouse moves across a surface, the trackball rolls, creating x-y movement data.

tractor feed A paper-feeding mechanism for printers that use continuous forms. The left and right edges of the forms contain holes through which the tractor pins pull the paper through the print area.

transmit Although this term usually means to send data, between a transmitter and receiver, over a specific communications line, it can also describe the transfer of data within the internal buses of a computer or between the computer and its peripheral devices.

Transport Control Protocol (TCP) TCP is a transport layer protocol used to establish reliable connections between clients and servers.

trees In Active Directory, a collection of objects that share the same DNS name. All the domains in a tree share a common security context and global catalog.

troubleshooters A special type of Help utilities available in Windows 9x and 2000. These utilities enable the user to pinpoint problems and identify solutions to those problems, by asking a series of questions and then providing detailed troubleshooting information based on the user responses.

U

Ultra DMA A burst-mode DMA data transfer protocol, used with Ultra ATA IDE devices, to support data transfer rates of 33.3MBps. Although the official name of the protocol is Ultra DMA/33, it is also referred to as UDMA, UDMA/33, and DMA mode 33.

Ultra SCSI A series of advanced SCSI specifications that include (1) Ultra SCSI, which employs an 8-bit bus and supports data rates of 20MBps; (2) SCSI-3 (also referred to as Ultra Wide SCSI), which widens the bus to 16 bits and supports data rates of 40MBps; (3) Ultra2 SCSI, which uses an 8-bit bus and supports data rates of 40MBps; and (4) Wide Ultra2 SCSI, which supports data rates of 80MBps across a 16-bit bus.

Uniform Resource Locator (URL) A unique address on the World Wide Web used to access a Web site.

uninterruptible power supply (UPS) A special power-supply unit that includes a battery to maintain power to key equipment in the event of a power failure. A typical UPS is designed to keep a computer operational after a power failure long enough for the user to save his or her current work and properly shut down the system. Many UPSs include software that

provides automatic backup and shutdown procedures when the UPS senses a power problem.

Universal Asynchronous Receiver/Transmitter (UART) A serial interface IC used to provide for the parallel-to-serial and serial-to-parallel conversions required for asynchronous serial data transmission. It also handles the parallel interface to the computer's bus, as well as the control functions associated with the transmission.

Universal Naming Convention (UNC) A standardized way to specify a path to a network computer or a device (for instance, \\Computername\Sharename).

Universal Serial Bus (USB) A specification for a high-speed, serial communication bus that can be used to link various peripheral devices to the system. The standard permits up to 127 USB-compliant devices to be connected to the system in a daisy-chained or tiered-star configuration.

Universal Synchronous Asynchronous Receiver/Transmitter (USART) A serial interface IC used to provide for the parallel-to-serial and serial-to-parallel conversions required for both asynchronous and synchronous serial data transmission. It also handles the parallel interface to the computer's bus, as well as the control functions associated with the transmission.

upgrading The process of replacing an older piece of hardware or software with a newer version of that hardware or software. Upgrading also serves as an interim solution for bugs discovered in software.

upper memory area (UMA) The area in the DOS memory map between 640KB and 1MB. This memory area was referred to as the reserved memory area in older PC and PC-XT systems. It typically contains the EMS page frame, as well as any ROM extensions and video display circuitry.

upper memory blocks (UMBs)   Special 16KB blocks of memory established in the upper memory area between the 640KB and 1MB marks.

user profiles   User profiles are records that permit each user that logs on to a computer to have a unique set of properties associated with them, such as particular desktop or Start menu configurations. In Windows 2000, user profiles are stored in C:\Documents and Settings by default. User profiles are local, meaning that they reside only on that computer. Therefore, users can have different profiles created and stored for them on each computer they log on to.

username   The public portion of the user logon name that identifies permissions and rights to network resources.

utility program   A term used to describe a program designed to help the user in the operation of the computer.

V

very large scale integration (VLSI)   IC devices containing a very large number of electronic components (from 100,000 to 1,000,000 approximately).

video adapter   Sometimes referred to as a display adapter, graphics adapter, or graphics card, it is a plug-in peripheral unit for computers, fitting in one of the system board option slots, and providing the interface between the computer and the display. The adapter usually must match the type of display (digital or analog) with which it is used.

Video Electronics Standards Association (VESA) bus   A 64-bit local bus standard developed to provide a local bus connection to a video adapter. Its operation has been defined for use by other adapter types, such as drive controllers, network interfaces, and other hardware.

Video Graphics Array (VGA)   Another video standard, developed by IBM, providing medium and high text and graphics resolution. It was originally designed for IBM's high-end PS/2 line, but other vendors have created matching boards for PC and AT machines also, making it the preferred standard at this time. Requiring an analog monitor, it originally provided 16 colors at 640 × 480 resolution. Third-party vendors have boosted that capability to 256 colors, while adding an even greater 800 × 600 resolution, calling it Super VGA.

View menu   A Windows 2000 dialog box drop-down menu option enables the user to toggle screen displays between Large and Small Icons, Details, and Thumbnail views. The dialog boxes can be resized to accommodate as many thumbnail images as desired.

virtual disk   A method of using RAM as if it were a disk.

virtual memory   A memory technique that allows several programs to run simultaneously, even though the system does not have enough actual memory installed to do this. The extra memory is simulated using disk space.

Virtual Memory Manager (VMM)   The section of the Windows 9x, NT, and 2000 structure that assigns unique memory spaces to every active 32-bit and 16-bit DOS/Windows 3.x application. The VMM works with the environmental subsystems of the user mode to establish special environments for the 16-bit applications to run in.

virtual private network (VPN)   Virtual private networks use message encryption and other security techniques to ensure that only authorized users can intercept and access the message as it passes through public transmission media. In particular, VPNs provide secure Internet communications by establishing encrypted data tunnels across the WAN that cannot be penetrated by others.

virus   A destructive program designed to replicate itself on any machine that it comes into contact with. Viruses are spread from machine to machine by attaching themselves to (infect) other files.

volatile memory   Memory (RAM) that loses its contents as soon as power is discontinued.

volumes   Portions of disks signified by single drive designators. In the Microsoft environment, a volume corresponds to a partition.

volt ohm milliammeter (VOM)   A basic piece of electronic troubleshooting equipment that provides for circuit measurements of voltage, current and resistance in logarithmic analog readout form.

W

warm boot   Booting a computer that has already been powered up. This can be accomplished by pressing the Reset switch on the front of most computers or by selecting one of the Restart options from the Windows Exit Options dialog box.

Web sites   A location on the World Wide Web. Web sites typically contain a home page that displays when the site is accessed. It likely contains other pages and programs that can be accessed through the home page.

wildcards   Characters, such as * or ?, used to represent letters or words. Such characters are typically used to perform operations with multiple files.

Windows   A graphical user interface from Microsoft Corporation. It uses a graphical display to represent procedures and programs that can be executed by the computer. Multiple programs can run at the same time.

Windows Explorer   The Windows 95, Windows 98, and Windows NT/2000 utility that graphically displays the system as drives, folders, and files in a hierarchical tree structure. This enables the user to manipulate all the system's software using a mouse.

WINNT32   WINNT.EXE or WINNT32.EXE are the programs that can be run to initiate the installation of Windows 2000. The WINNT32.EXE program is designed to run under a 32-bit operating system and will not run from the command line. The WINNT.EXE program is designed to run under a 16-bit operating system and will not run from within a 32-bit operating system such as Windows NT.

WINS   A Microsoft-specific naming service that can be used to assign IP addresses to computer domain names within a LAN environment. The LAN must include a Windows NT name server running the WINS server software that maintains the IP address/domain name database for the LAN. Each client in the LAN must contain the WINS client software and be WINS enabled.

wizards   Special Windows routines designed to lead users through installation or setup operation using a menu style of selecting options. The wizards carry out these tasks in the proper sequence, requesting information from the user at key points in the process.

word   Refers to the amount of data that can be held in a computer's registers during a process, and is considered to be the computer's basic storage unit.

workgroups   A network control scenario in which all the nodes may act as servers for some processes and clients for others. In a workgroup environment, each machine maintains its own security and administration databases.

X

x-axis   (1) In a two-dimensional matrix, the horizontal row/rows such as on an oscilloscope screen. (2) The dimension of width in a graphics representation.

Xmodem   A very early and simple asynchronous data communications protocol developed for personal computers, and capable of detecting some transfer errors, but not all.

XON-XOFF   An asynchronous data communications protocol that provides for synchronization between the receiver and transmitter, requiring the receiver to indicate its capability to accept data by sending either an XON (transmit on-buffer ready) or XOFF (transmit off-buffer full) signal to the transmitter.

x-y matrix   Any two-dimensional form or image, where x represents width and y represents height.

Y

y-axis   (1) In a two-dimensional matrix, the vertical column/columns such as on an oscilloscope screen. (2) The dimension of height in a graphics representation.

Ymodem   An improvement of the Xmodem protocol that increases the data block size from 128 bytes to 1,024 bytes. An off-shoot known as Ymodem Batch includes filenames in the transmission so that multiple files can be sent in a single transmission. Another variation, labeled Ymodem G, modified the normal Ymodem flow-control method to speed up transmissions

Z

Zmodem   This dial-up protocol can be used to transmit both text and binary files (such as EXE files across telephone lines, not the Internet). It employs advanced error-checking/correcting schemes and provides Autofile Restart crash-recovery techniques.

Overview of the Certification Process

DESCRIPTION OF THE PATH TO CERTIFICATION

You must pass two certification exams to become an A+ certified technician. The Core Hardware Service Technician component is covered by exam number 220-201 and the Operating System Technologies component is covered by exam number 220-202. These closed-book exams provide a valid and reliable measure of your technical proficiency and expertise. Developed in consultation with computer-industry professionals who have on-the-job experience with multivendor hardware and software products in the workplace, the exams are conducted by the independent organization known as Vue Testing Services. VUE has more than 2,500 authorized testing centers serving more than 100 countries.

The exam prices vary depending on your CompTIA member status:

CompTIA members: $78 each

Non-CompTIA members: $132 each

To schedule an exam, call VUE at 800-837-8969. You can also contact Vue or locate a convenient testing center through their Web site at www.vue.com.

ABOUT THE A+ CERTIFICATION PROGRAM

The A+ Certification is an internationally recognized industry-standard certification designed to measure the competency of an entry-level technician. Entry-level in this case is defined as the equivalent knowledge of a technician with 6 months of experience in a support role. This certification is attained by passing the 2 tests within 90 days of each other. Each of these tests covers a separate series of objectives, as described in the Introduction to this book.

The Computing and Technology Industry Association (CompTIA) developed the A+ Certification in response to several factors, not the least of which was the growing need for computer hardware and software manufacturers to create a standard curriculum. Prior to this standard, each manufacturer created individual lower-level courses to provide a logical path to their own product offerings. This caused entry-level courses to be duplicated by various manufacturers, albeit in many different ways and with many different results.

CompTIA itself provides the following reasons for the creation of the A+ Certification:

- ◆ To set an industry-wide, nationally recognized standard of basic competency levels in the field of computer service.

- ◆ To maximize efficiency in recruiting, hiring, training, and promoting employees.

- ◆ To help meet the needs of today's information technology workforce by providing individuals with in-demand skills.

- ◆ To give job seekers identifiable career paths, transferable skills, and industry-recognized credentials.

- ◆ To give educators and trainers the standards necessary to better prepare individuals to meet today's job-skill requirements.

The A+ Certification has undergone a few changes since its inception. The most recent changes (the January 31, 2001 version) include dropping the Windows 3.x operating information from the test and upgrading the Operating System Technologies exam to include Windows 98 and Windows 2000 Professional questions. The Core Hardware Service Technician exam now includes a larger base of questions relating to newer bus systems and new hardware additions (such as the Intel Pentium III processor and its clones, as well as the IEEE-1394 FireWire bus specifications). Also, the customer satisfaction objectives have been removed from the Core Hardware Service Technician exam.

You may be asking why this exam is for you, and why now. Aside from joining the swelling ranks of A+ certified technicians (more than 260,000 members and rising), the A+ program gives you access to the CompTIA organization and to the benefits this access affords. CompTIA's Web site, for instance, identifies the following benefits for prospective A+ technicians:

- ◆ **Recognized proof of professional achievement.** A level of competence commonly accepted and valued by the industry.

- ◆ **Enhanced job opportunities.** Many employers give preference in hiring to applicants with certification. They view this as proof that a new hire knows the procedures and technologies required.

- ◆ **Opportunity for advancement.** The certification can be a plus when an employer awards job advancements and promotions.

- ◆ **Training requirement.** Certification may be required as a prerequisite to attending a vendor's training course, so employers will offer advance training to those employees who are already certified.

- ◆ **Customer confidence.** As the general public learns about certification, customers will require that only certified technicians be assigned to their accounts.

For any additional information or clarification of the CompTIA A+ Certification path and its history and benefits, consult the CompTIA home page at `www.comptia.org`.

What's on the CD-ROM

This appendix is a brief rundown of what you will find on the CD-ROM that accompanies this book. For a more detailed description of the newly developed ExamGear test engine, exclusive to New Riders Publishing, see Appendix D, "Using the ExamGear, Training Guide Edition Software."

EXAMGEAR

ExamGear is a test engine developed exclusively for New Riders Publishing. It is, we believe, the best test engine available because it closely emulates the format of the A+ exams. The CD contains 150 sample test questions provided by Marcraft International, a leader in computer service training. For an additional $50, you can unlock 650 additional questions by calling Marcraft International at 800-441-6006. Each time you run ExamGear it randomly selects a set of questions from the question database, so you never take the same exam twice.

In addition to providing a way to evaluate your knowledge of the exam material, ExamGear features several innovations that help you to improve your mastery of the subject matter. ExamGear also includes an adaptive testing feature that simulates the adaptive testing method that CompTIA eventually converts its exams into.

The practice tests enable you to check your score by exam area or category, for example, to determine which topics you need to study further. Other test preparation modes provide immediate feedback on your responses, explanations of correct answers, a Flash Card format, and even hyperlinks to the chapter in an electronic version of the book where the topic is covered. Again, for a complete description of the benefits of ExamGear, see Appendix D.

Before running the ExamGear software, be sure that AutoRun is enabled. If you prefer not to use AutoRun, you can run the application from the CD by clicking START.EXE.

EXERCISES

The CD contains 44 lab procedures. They offer a variety of presentation styles. These procedures begin with a basic assembly/disassembly lab to familiarize the user with the physical part of a computer system and how they are organized and connected. There is also a digital multimeter procedure that acquaints the reader with the use of this basic test instrument. The other procedures are divided between hardware and software explorations. Both types of procedures include installation, configuration, management, and troubleshooting labs for different hardware devices, as well as for Windows ME and Windows 2000 Professional operating systems.

Exclusive Electronic Version of Text

The CD-ROM also contains the electronic version of this book in Portable Document Format (PDF). In addition to the links to the book that are built in to ExamGear, you can use this version to help search for terms you need to study or other book elements. The electronic version comes complete with all figures as they appear in the book.

Electronic Reference Shelf

A selection of more in-depth (non-A+) material explains how different technologies such as monitors and disk drives actually work. These titles are identified at appropriate points in the text and can be accessed through the Reference Shelf menu on the CD. The materials are in PDF format and can be viewed or printed.

Copyright Information and Disclaimer

Using the ExamGear, Training Guide Edition Software

This *Training Guide* includes a special version of ExamGear—a revolutionary new test engine designed to give you the best in certification exam preparation. ExamGear offers sample and practice exams for many of today's most in-demand technical certifications. This special Training Guide Edition is included with this book as a tool to utilize in assessing your knowledge of the *Training Guide* material while also providing you with the experience of taking an electronic exam.

This appendix describes in detail what ExamGear, Training Guide Edition is, how it works, and what it can do to help you prepare for the exam. Note that although the Training Guide Edition includes nearly all the test simulation functions of the complete, retail version, the questions focus on the *Training Guide* content rather than on simulating the actual A+ exam.

EXAM SIMULATION

One of the main functions of ExamGear, Training Guide Edition is exam simulation. To prepare you to take the actual vendor certification exam, the Training Guide edition of this test engine is designed to offer the most effective exam simulation available.

Question Quality

The questions provided in the ExamGear, Training Guide Edition simulations are written to high standards of technical accuracy. The questions tap the content of the *Training Guide* chapters and help you review and assess your knowledge before you take the actual exam.

Interface Design

The ExamGear, Training Guide Edition exam simulation interface provides you with the experience of taking an electronic exam. This enables you to effectively prepare for taking the actual exam by making the test experience a familiar one. Using this test simulation can help eliminate the sense of surprise or anxiety that you might experience in the testing center, because you will already be acquainted with computerized testing.

STUDY TOOLS

ExamGear provides you with several learning tools to help prepare you for the actual certification exam.

Effective Learning Environment

The ExamGear, Training Guide Edition interface provides a learning environment that not only tests you through the computer, but also teaches the material you need to know to pass the certification exam. Each question comes with a detailed explanation of the correct answer and provides reasons why the other options were incorrect. This information helps to reinforce the knowledge you have already and also provides practical information you can use on the job.

Automatic Progress Tracking

ExamGear, Training Guide Edition automatically tracks your progress as you work through the test questions. From the Item Review tab (discussed in detail later in this appendix), you can see at a glance how well you are scoring by objective, by chapter, or on a question-by-question basis (see Figure D.1). You also can configure ExamGear to drill you on the skills you need to work on most.

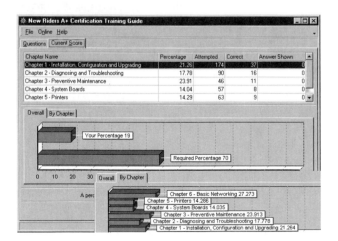

FIGURE D.1
Item review.

How EXAMGEAR, TRAINING GUIDE EDITION WORKS

ExamGear comprises two main elements: the interface and the database. The interface is the part of the program that you use to study and to run practice tests. The database stores all the question-and-answer data.

Interface

The ExamGear, Training Guide Edition interface is designed to be easy to use and provides the most effective study method available. The interface enables you to select from the following modes:

◆ **Study mode.** In this mode, you can select the number of questions you want to see and the time you want to allow for the test. You can select questions from all the chapters or from specific chapters. This enables you to reinforce your knowledge in a specific area or strengthen your knowledge in areas pertaining to a specific objective. During the exam, you can display the correct answer to each question along with an explanation of why it is correct.

◆ **Practice Exam mode.** In this mode, you take an exam designed to simulate the actual certification exam. Questions are selected from all test-objective groups. The number of questions selected and the time allowed are set to match those parameters of the actual certification exam.

◆ **Adaptive Exam mode.** In this mode, you take an exam simulation using the adaptive testing technique. Questions are taken from all test-objective groups. The questions are presented in a way that ensures your mastery of all the test objectives.

After you have a passing score or if you reach a point where it is statistically impossible for you to pass, the exam ends. This method provides a rapid assessment of your readiness for the actual exam.

Note: The current A+ exam is not adaptive and it will be some time before CompTIA settles its test pool enough to take it adaptive.

Database

The ExamGear, Training Guide Edition database stores a group of around 955 test questions and answers; 150 of them are marked as demo questions and are available free of charge. You can purchase the rest of the questions; these questions are already on the CD and merely need to be "unlocked" so that you can access them.

INSTALLING AND REGISTERING EXAMGEAR, TRAINING GUIDE EDITION

This section provides instructions for ExamGear, Training Guide Edition installation and describes the process and benefits of registering your Training Guide Edition product.

Requirements

ExamGear requires a computer with the following:

◆ Microsoft Windows 95, Windows 98, Windows NT 4.0, Windows 2000, or Windows ME.

A Pentium or later processor is recommended.

◆ 20-30MB free disk space.

◆ A minimum of 32MB of RAM.

As with any Windows application, the more memory, the better your performance.

◆ A connection to the Internet.

An Internet connection is not required for the software to work, but it is required for online registration and to download product updates.

◆ A Web browser.

A Web browser is not required for the software to work, but it is invoked from the Online, Web Sites menu option.

Installing ExamGear, Training Guide Edition

Install ExamGear, Training Guide Edition by running the setup program on the ExamGear, Training Guide Edition CD. Follow these instructions to install the Training Guide Edition on your computer:

1. Insert the CD in your CD-ROM drive. The AutoRun feature of Windows launches the software. If you have AutoRun disabled, click Start and choose Run. Go to the root directory of the CD and choose START.EXE. Click Open and then click OK.

2. Click the button in the circle. A Welcome screen appears. From here you can install ExamGear. Click the ExamGear button to begin installation.

3. The Installation Wizard appears onscreen and prompts you with instructions to complete the installation. Select a directory on which to install ExamGear, Training Guide Edition.

4. The Installation Wizard copies the ExamGear, Training Guide Edition files to your hard drive, adds ExamGear, Training Guide Edition to your Program menu, adds values to your Registry, and installs the test engine's DLLs to the appropriate

system folders. To ensure that the process was successful, the setup program finishes by running ExamGear, Training Guide Edition.

5. The Installation Wizard logs the installation process and stores this information in a file named INSTALL.LOG. This log file is used by the uninstall process in the event that you choose to remove ExamGear, Training Guide Edition from your computer. Because the ExamGear installation adds Registry keys and DLL files to your computer, it is important to uninstall the program appropriately (see the section "Removing ExamGear, Training Guide Edition from Your Computer").

Registering ExamGear, Training Guide Edition

The Product Registration Wizard appears when ExamGear, Training Guide Edition is started for the first time, and ExamGear checks at startup to see whether you are registered. If you are not registered, the main menu is hidden, and a Product Registration Wizard appears. Remember that your computer must have an Internet connection to complete the Product Registration Wizard.

The first page of the Product Registration Wizard details the benefits of registration; however, you can always elect not to register. The Show This Message at Startup Until I Register option enables you to decide whether the registration screen should appear every time ExamGear, Training Guide Edition is started. If you click the Cancel button, you return to the main menu. You can register at any time by selecting Online, Registration from the main menu.

The registration process is composed of a simple form for entering your personal information, including your name and address. You are asked for your level of experience with the product you are testing on and whether you purchased ExamGear, Training Guide Edition from a retail store or over the Internet. The information will be used by our software designers and marketing department to provide us with feedback about the usability and usefulness of this product. It takes only a few seconds to fill out and transmit the registration data. A confirmation dialog box appears when registration is complete.

After you have registered and transmitted this information to New Riders, the registration option is removed from the pull-down menus.

Registration Benefits

Registering enables New Riders to notify you of product updates and new releases.

Removing ExamGear, Training Guide Edition from Your Computer

In the event that you elect to remove the ExamGear, Training Guide Edition product from your computer, an uninstall process has been included to ensure that it is removed from your system safely and completely. Follow these instructions to remove ExamGear from your computer:

1. Click Start, Settings, Control Panel.

2. Double-click the Add/Remove Programs icon.

3. You are presented with a list of software that is installed on your computer. Select ExamGear, Training Guide Edition from the list and click the Add/Remove button. The ExamGear, Training Guide Edition software is then removed from your computer.

It is important that the INSTALL.LOG file be present in the directory where you have installed ExamGear, Training Guide Edition should you ever choose to uninstall the product. Do not delete this file. The INSTALL.LOG file is used by the uninstall process to safely remove the files and Registry settings that were added to your computer by the installation process.

USING EXAMGEAR, TRAINING GUIDE EDITION

ExamGear is designed to be user friendly and very intuitive, eliminating the need for you to learn some confusing piece of software just to practice answering questions. Because the software has a smooth learning curve, your time is maximized because you start practicing almost immediately.

General Description of How the Software Works

ExamGear has three modes of operation: study mode, practice exam mode, and adaptive exam mode (see Figure D.2). All three sections have the same easy-to-use interface. Using study mode, you can hone your knowledge as well as your test-taking abilities through the use of the Show Answers option. While you are taking the test, you can expose the answers along with a brief description of why the given answers are right or wrong. This gives you the ability to better understand the material presented.

The practice exam section has many of the same options as study mode, but you cannot reveal the answers. This way, you have a more traditional testing environment with which to practice.

The adaptive exam questions continuously monitor your expertise in each tested topic area. If you reach a point at which you either pass or fail, the software ends the examination. As in the practice exam, you cannot reveal the answers.

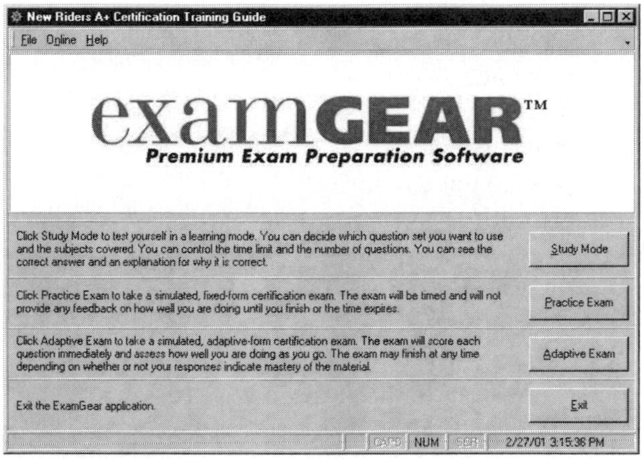

FIGURE D.2
The opening screen offers three testing modes.

Menu Options

The ExamGear, Training Guide Edition interface has an easy-to-use menu that provides the following options:

Menu	Command	Description
File	Print	Prints the current screen.
	Print Setup	Enables you to select the printer.
	Exit ExamGear	Exits the program.
Online	Registration	Starts the Registration Wizard and enables you to register online. This menu option is removed after you have successfully registered the product.

continues

Menu	Command	Description
Online	Check for Product Updates	Opens the ExamGear Web site with available updates.
	Web Sites	Opens the Web browser with either the New Riders Publishing or ExamGear home pages.
Help	Contents	Opens ExamGear, Training Guide Edition's Help file.
	About	Displays information about ExamGear, Training Guide Edition, including serial number, registered owner, and so on.

File

The File menu enables you to exit the program and configure print options.

Online

In the Online menu, you can register ExamGear, Training Guide Edition, check for product updates (update the ExamGear executable as well as check for free, updated question sets), and surf applicable Web sites. The Online menu is always available, except when you are taking a test.

Registration

Registration is free and enables you to access updates. Registration is the first task that ExamGear, Training Guide Edition asks you to perform. You will not have access to the free product updates if you do not register.

Check for Product Updates

This option takes you to ExamGear, Training Guide Edition's Web site, where you can update the software. You must be connected to the Internet to use this

option. The ExamGear Web site lists the options that have been made available since your version of ExamGear was installed on your computer.

Web Sites

This option provides a convenient way to start your Web browser and connect to either the New Riders or ExamGear home page.

Help

As it suggests, this menu option gives you access to ExamGear's Help system. It also provides important information like your serial number, software version, and so on.

Starting a Study-Mode Session

Study mode enables you to control the test in ways that actual certification exams do not allow:

◆ You can set your own time limits.

◆ You can concentrate on selected skill areas (chapters).

◆ You can reveal answers or have each response graded immediately with feedback.

◆ You can restrict the questions you see again to those missed or those answered correctly a given number of times.

◆ You can control the order in which questions are presented—random order or in order by skill area (chapter).

To begin testing in study mode, click the Study Mode button from the main Interface screen. You see the Study Mode configuration page (see Figure D.3).

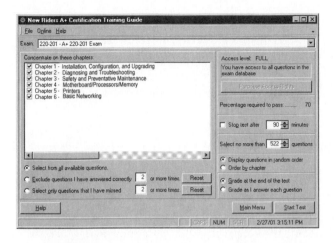

FIGURE D.3
The Study Mode configuration page.

At the top of the Study Mode configuration screen, you see the Exam drop-down list. This list shows the activated exam that you have purchased with your ExamGear, Training Guide Edition product, as well as any other exams you may have downloaded or any Preview exams that were shipped with your version of ExamGear. Select the exam with which you want to practice from the drop-down list.

Below the Exam drop-down list, you see the questions that are available for the selected exam. Each exam has at least one question set. You can select the individual question set or any combination of the question sets if more than one is available for the selected exam.

Below the Question Set list is a list of skill areas or chapters on which you can concentrate. These skill areas or chapters reflect the units of exam objectives defined by CompTIA for the exam. Within each skill area you will find several exam objectives. You can select a single skill area or chapter to focus on, or you can select any combination of the available skill areas/chapters to customize the exam to your individual needs.

In addition to specifying which question sets and skill areas you want to test yourself on, you also can define which questions are included in the test based on your previous progress working with the test. ExamGear, Training Guide Edition automatically tracks your progress with the available questions. When configuring the study-mode options, you can opt to view all the questions available within the question sets and skill areas you have selected, or you can limit the questions presented. Choose from the following options:

◆ **Select from All Available Questions.** This option causes ExamGear, Training Guide Edition to present all available questions from the selected question sets and skill areas.

◆ **Exclude Questions I Have Answered Correctly *X* or More Times.** ExamGear offers you the option to exclude questions that you have previously answered correctly. You can specify how many times you want to answer a question correctly before ExamGear considers you to have mastered it (the default is two times).

◆ **Select Only Questions That I Have Missed *X* or More Times.** This option configures ExamGear, Training Guide Edition to drill you only on questions that you have missed repeatedly. You may specify how many times you must miss a question before ExamGear determines that you have not mastered it (the default is two times).

At any time, you can reset ExamGear, Training Guide Edition's tracking information by clicking the Reset button for the feature you want to clear.

At the top-right side of the Study Mode configuration page, you can see your access level to the question sets for the selected exam. Access levels are either Full or Preview. For a detailed explanation of each of these access levels, see the section "Obtaining Updates" in this appendix.

Under your access level, you see the score required to pass the selected exam. Below the required score, you can select whether the test will be timed and how much time will be allowed to complete the exam. Select the Stop Test After 90 Minutes check box to set a time limit for the exam. Enter the number of minutes you want to allow for the test. (The default is 90 minutes.) Deselecting this check box enables you to take an exam with no time limit.

You also can configure the number of questions included in the exam. The default number of questions changes with the specific exam you have selected. Enter the number of questions you want to include in the exam in the Select No More than X Questions option.

You can configure the order in which ExamGear, Training Guide Edition presents the exam questions. Select from the following options:

◆ **Display Questions in Random Order.** This option is the default option. When selected, it causes ExamGear, Training Guide Edition to present the questions in random order throughout the exam.

◆ **Order by Skill Area.** This option causes ExamGear to group the questions presented in the exam by skill area. All questions for each selected skill area are presented in succession. The test progresses from one selected skill area to the next, until all the questions from each selected skill area have been presented.

ExamGear offers two options for scoring your exams. Select one of the following options:

◆ **Grade at the End of the Test.** This option configures ExamGear, Training Guide Edition to score your test after you have been presented with all the selected exam questions. You can reveal correct answers to a question, but if you do, that question is not scored.

◆ **Grade as I Answer Each Question.** This option configures ExamGear to grade each question as you answer it, providing you with instant feedback as you take the test. All questions are scored unless you click the Show Answer button before completing the question.

You can return to the ExamGear, Training Guide Edition main startup screen from the Study Mode configuration screen by clicking the Main Menu button. If you need assistance configuring the study-mode exam options, click the Help button for configuration instructions.

After you have finished configuring all the exam options, click the Start Test button to begin the exam.

Starting Practice Exams and Adaptive Exams

This section describes the practice and adaptive exams, defines the differences between these exam options and the study-mode option, and provides instructions for starting them.

Differences Between the Practice and Adaptive Exams and Study Mode

Question screens in the practice and adaptive exams are identical to those found in study mode, except that the Show Answer, Grade Answer, and Item Review buttons are not available while you are in the process of taking a practice or adaptive exam. The practice exam provides you with a report screen at the end of the exam. The adaptive exam gives you a brief message indicating whether you have passed or failed the exam.

When taking a practice exam, the Item Review screen is not available until you have answered all the questions. This is consistent with the behavior of most vendors' current certification exams. In study mode, Item Review is available at any time.

When the exam timer expires, or if you click the End Exam button, the Examination Score Report screen comes up.

Starting an Exam

From the ExamGear, Training Guide Edition main menu screen, select the type of exam you want to run. Click the Practice Exam or Adaptive Exam button to begin the corresponding exam type.

What Is an Adaptive Exam?

To make the certification testing process more efficient and valid and therefore make the certification itself more valuable, some vendors in the industry are using a testing technique called adaptive testing. (The current A+ exam is not adaptive at this time.) In an adaptive exam, the exam "adapts" to your abilities by varying the difficulty level of the questions presented to you.

The first question in an adaptive exam is typically an easy one. If you answer it correctly, you are presented with a slightly more difficult question. If you answer that question correctly, the next question you see is even more difficult. If you answer the question incorrectly, however, the exam "adapts" to your skill level by presenting you with another question of equal or lesser difficulty on the same subject. If you answer that question correctly, the test begins to increase the difficulty level again. You must correctly answer several questions at a predetermined difficulty level to pass the exam. After you have done this successfully, the exam is ended and scored. If you do not reach the required level of difficulty within a predetermined time (typically 30 minutes) the exam is ended and scored.

Why Do Vendors Use Adaptive Exams?

Many vendors who offer technical certifications have adopted the adaptive testing technique. They have found that it is an effective way to measure a candidate's mastery of the test material in as little time as necessary. This reduces the scheduling demands on the test taker and allows the testing center to offer more tests per test station than they could with longer, more traditional exams. In addition, test security is greater, and this increases the validity of the exam process.

Studying for Adaptive Exams

Studying for adaptive exams is no different from studying for traditional exams. You should make sure that you have thoroughly covered all the material for each of the test objectives specified by the certification exam vendor. As with any other exam, when you take an adaptive exam, either you know the material or you don't. If you are well prepared, you will be able to pass the exam. ExamGear, Training Guide Edition allows you to familiarize yourself with the adaptive exam testing technique. This will help eliminate any anxiety you might experience from this testing technique and allow you to focus on learning the actual exam material.

ExamGear's Adaptive Exam

The method used to score the Adaptive Exam requires a large pool of questions. For this reason, you cannot use this exam in preview mode. The adaptive exam is presented in much the same way as the practice exam. When you click the Start Test button, you begin answering questions. The Adaptive Exam does not allow item review, and it does not allow you to mark questions to skip and answer later. You must answer each question when it is presented.

Assumptions

This section describes the assumptions made when designing the behavior of the ExamGear, Training Guide Edition adaptive exam.

◆ You fail the test if you fail any chapter, earn a failing overall score, or reach a threshold at which it is statistically impossible for you to pass the exam.

◆ You can fail or pass a test without cycling through all the questions.

◆ The overall score for the adaptive exam is Pass or Fail. However, to evaluate user responses dynamically, percentage scores are recorded for chapters and the overall score.

Algorithm Assumptions

This section describes the assumptions used in designing the ExamGear, Training Guide Edition Adaptive Exam scoring algorithm.

Chapter Scores

You fail a chapter (and the exam) if any chapter score falls below 66%.

Overall Scores

To pass the exam, you must pass all chapters and achieve an overall score of 86% or higher.

You fail if the overall score percentage is less than or equal to 85% or if any chapter score is less than 66%.

Inconclusive Scores

If your overall score is between 6/ and 85%, it is considered to be inconclusive. Additional questions will be asked until you pass or fail or until it becomes statistically impossible to pass without asking more than the maximum number of questions allowed.

Question Types and How to Answer Them

Because certification exams from different vendors vary, you will face many types of questions on any given exam. ExamGear, Training Guide Edition presents you with different question types to enable you to become familiar with the various ways an actual exam may test your knowledge. This section describes each of the question types presented by ExamGear and provides instructions for answering each type.

Multiple Choice

Most of the questions you see on a certification exam are multiple choice (see Figure D.4). This question type asks you to select an answer from the list provided. Sometimes you must select only one answer, often indicated by answers preceded by option buttons (round selection buttons). At other times, multiple correct answers are possible, indicated by check boxes preceding the possible answer combinations.

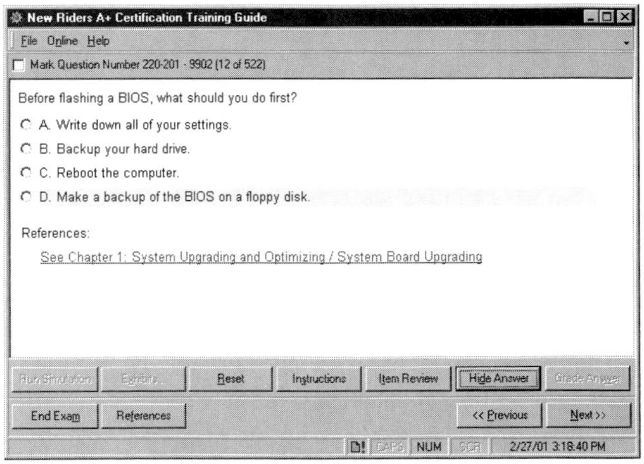

FIGURE D.4
A typical multiple-choice question.

You can use three methods to select an answer:

◆ Click the option button or check box next to the answer. If more than one correct answer to a question is possible, the answers will have check boxes next to them. If only one correct answer to a question is possible, each answer will have an option button next to it. ExamGear, Training Guide Edition prompts you with the number of answers you must select.

◆ Click the text of the answer.

◆ Press the alphabetic key that corresponds to the answer.

You can use any one of three methods to clear an option button:

◆ Click another option button.

◆ Click the text of another answer.

◆ Press the alphabetic key that corresponds to another answer.

You can use any one of three methods to clear a check box:

◆ Click the check box next to the selected answer.

◆ Click the text of the selected answer.

◆ Press the alphabetic key that corresponds to the selected answer.

To clear all answers, click the Reset button.

Remember that some of the questions have multiple answers that are correct. Do not let this throw you off. The multiple-correct questions do not have one answer that is more correct than another. In the single-correct format, only one answer is correct. ExamGear, Training Guide Edition prompts you with the number of answers you must select.

Hot Spot Questions

Hot spot questions (see Figure D.5) ask you to correctly identify an item by clicking an area of the graphic or diagram displayed. To respond to the question, position the mouse cursor over a graphic. Then press the right mouse button to indicate your selection. To select another area on the graphic, you do not need to deselect the first one. Just click another region in the image.

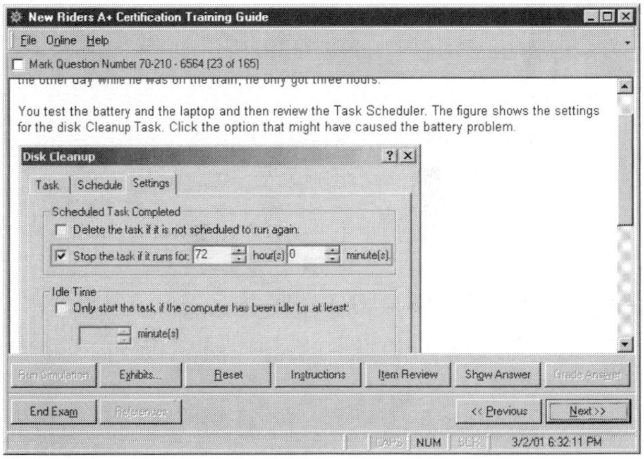

FIGURE D.5
A typical hot spot question.

Standard ExamGear, Training Guide Edition Options

Regardless of question type, a consistent set of clickable buttons enables you to navigate and interact with questions. The following list describes the function of each of the buttons you may see. Depending on the question type, some of the buttons will be grayed out and will be inaccessible. Buttons that are appropriate to the question type are active.

◆ **Run Simulation.** This button is enabled if the question supports a simulation. (It is disabled for this book.) Clicking this button begins the simulation process.

◆ **Exhibits.** This button is enabled if exhibits are provided to support the question. An exhibit is an image, video, sound, or text file that provides supplemental information needed to answer the question. If a question has more than one exhibit, a dialog box appears, listing exhibits by name. If only one exhibit exists, the file is opened immediately when you click the Exhibits button.

◆ **Reset.** This button clears any selections you have made and returns the question window to the state in which it appeared when it was first displayed.

◆ **Instructions.** This button displays instructions for interacting with the current question type.

◆ **Item Review.** This button leaves the question window and opens the Item Review screen. For a detailed explanation of the Item Review screen, see the "Item Review" section later in this appendix.

◆ **Show Answer.** This option displays the correct answer with an explanation of why it is correct. If you choose this option, the current question will not be scored.

◆ **Grade Answer.** If Grade at the End of the Test is selected as a configuration option, this button is disabled. It is enabled when Grade as I Answer Each Question is selected as a configuration option. Clicking this button grades the current question immediately. An explanation of the correct answer is provided, just as if the Show Answer button were pressed. The question is graded, however.

◆ **End Exam.** This button ends the exam and displays the Examination Score Report screen.

◆ **<< Previous.** This button displays the previous question on the exam.

◆ **Next >>.** This button displays the next question on the exam.

◆ **<< Previous Marked.** This button displays if you have opted to review questions that you have marked using the Item Review screen. This button displays the previous marked question. Marking questions is discussed in more detail later in this appendix.

◆ **<< Previous Incomplete.** This button displays if you have opted to review questions that you have not answered using the Item Review screen. This button displays the previous unanswered question.

◆ **Next Marked >>.** This button displays if you have opted to review questions that you have marked using the Item Review screen. This button displays the next marked question. Marking questions is discussed in more detail later in this appendix.

◆ **Next Incomplete>>.** This button displays if you have opted to review questions, using the Item Review screen, that you have not answered. This button displays the next unanswered question.

Mark Question and Time Remaining

ExamGear provides you with two methods to aid in dealing with the time limit of the testing process. If you find that you need to skip a question or if you want to check the time remaining to complete the test, use one of the options discussed in the following sections.

Mark Question

Check this box to mark a question so that you can return to it later using the Item Review feature. The adaptive exam does not allow questions to be marked because it does not support item review.

Time Remaining

If the test is timed, the Time Remaining indicator is enabled. It counts down minutes remaining to complete the test. The adaptive exam does not offer this feature because it is not timed.

Item Review

The Item Review screen enables you to jump to any question. ExamGear, Training Guide Edition considers an incomplete question to be any unanswered question or any multiple-choice question for which the total number of required responses has not been selected. If the question prompts for three answers and you selected only A and C, for example, ExamGear considers the question to be incomplete.

The Item Review screen enables you to review the exam questions in different ways. You can enter one of two browse sequences (series of similar records): Browse Marked Questions or Browse Incomplete Questions. You also can create a custom grouping of the exam questions for review based on a number of criteria.

When using Item Review, if Show Answer was selected for a question while you were taking the exam, the question is grayed out in item review. The question can be answered again if you use the Reset button to reset the question status.

The Item Review screen contains two tabs. The Questions tab lists questions and question information in columns. The Current Score tab provides your exam score information, presented as a percentage for each chapter and as a bar graph for your overall score.

The Item Review Questions Tab

The Questions tab on the Item Review screen (see Figure D.6) presents the exam questions and question information in a table. You can select any row you want

by clicking in the grid. The Go To button is enabled whenever a row is selected. Clicking the Go To button displays the question on the selected row. You also can display a question by double-clicking that row.

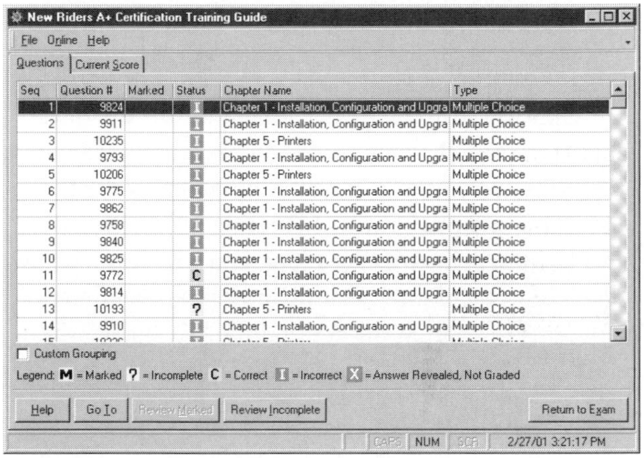

FIGURE D.6
The Questions tab on the Item Review screen.

Columns

The Questions tab contains the following six columns of information:

◆ **Seq.** Indicates the sequence number of the question as it was displayed in the exam.

◆ **Question Number.** Displays the question's identification number for easy reference.

◆ **Marked.** Indicates a question that you have marked using the Mark Question check box.

◆ **Status.** The status can be M for Marked, ? for Incomplete, C for Correct, I for Incorrect, or X for Answer Shown.

◆ **Chapter Name.** The chapter associated with each question.

◆ **Type.** The question type, which can be Multiple Choice or Hot Spot.

To resize a column, place the mouse pointer over the vertical line between column headings. When the mouse pointer changes to a set of right and left arrows, you can drag the column border to the left or right to make the column more or less wide. Just click with the left mouse button and hold that button down while you move the column border in the desired direction.

The Item Review screen enables you to sort the questions on any of the column headings. Initially, the list of questions is sorted in descending order on the sequence number column. To sort on a different column heading, click that heading. You will see an arrow appear on the column heading indicating the direction of the sort (ascending or descending). To change the direction of the sort, click the column heading again.

The Item Review screen also enables you to create a custom grouping. This feature enables you to sort the questions based on any combination of criteria you prefer. For instance, you might want to review the question items sorted first by whether they were marked, then by the chapter name, and then by sequence number. The Custom Grouping feature enables you to do this. Start by checking the Custom Grouping check box (see Figure D.7). When you do so, the entire questions table shifts down a bit onscreen, and a message appears at the top of the table that reads `Drag a Column Header Here to Group by That Column.`

Just click the column heading you want with the left mouse button, hold that button down, and move the mouse into the area directly above the Questions table (the custom grouping area). Release the left mouse button to drop the column heading into the custom grouping area. To accomplish the custom grouping previously described, first check the Custom Grouping check box. Then drag the Marked column heading into the custom grouping area above the Questions table. Next, drag the Chapter Name column heading into the custom grouping area. You will see the two column headings joined together by a line that indicates the order of the custom grouping. Finally, drag the Seq

column heading into the custom grouping area. This heading will be joined to the Chapter Name heading by another line indicating the direction of the custom grouping.

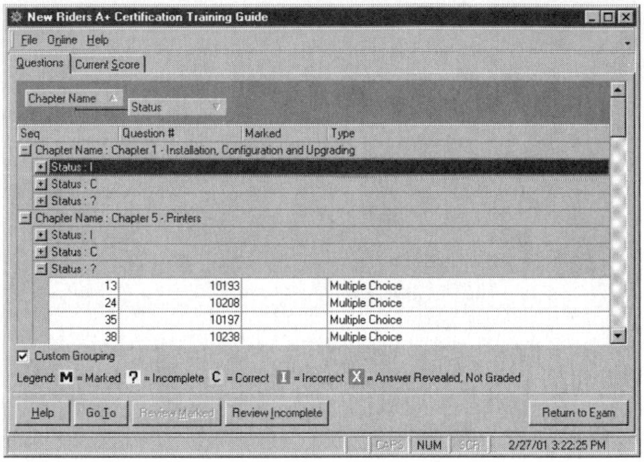

FIGURE D.7
The Custom Grouping check box enables you to create your own question sort order.

Notice that each column heading in the custom grouping area has an arrow indicating the direction in which items are sorted under that column heading. You can reverse the direction of the sort on an individual column-heading basis using these arrows. Click the column heading in the custom grouping area to change the direction of the sort for that column heading only. For example, using the custom grouping created previously, you can display the question list sorted first in descending order by whether the question was marked, in descending order by chapter name, and then in ascending order by sequence number.

The custom grouping feature of the Item Review screen gives you enormous flexibility in how you choose to review the exam questions. To remove a custom grouping and return the Item Review display to its default setting (sorted in descending order by sequence number), just uncheck the Custom Grouping check box.

The Current Score Tab

The Current Score tab of the Item Review screen (see Figure D.8) provides a real-time snapshot of your score. The top half of the screen is an expandable grid. When the grid is collapsed, scores are displayed for each chapter. Chapters can be expanded to show percentage scores for objectives and subobjectives. Information about your exam progress is presented in the following columns:

◆ **Chapter Name.** This column shows the chapter name for each objective group.

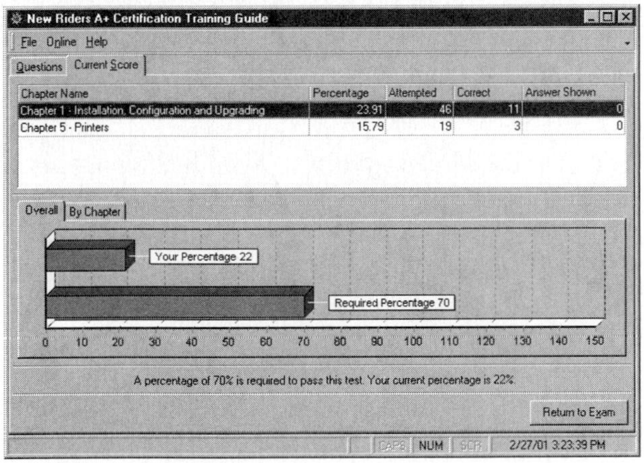

FIGURE D.8
The Current Score tab on the item review screen.

◆ **Percentage.** This column shows the percentage of questions for each objective group that you answered correctly.

◆ **Attempted.** This column lists the number of questions you answered either completely or partially for each objective group.

◆ **Correct.** This column lists the actual number of questions you answered correctly for each objective group.

◆ **Answer Shown.** This column lists the number of questions for each objective group that you chose to display the answer to using the Show Answer button.

The columns in the scoring table arc resized and sorted in the same way as those in the questions table on the Item Review Questions tab. Refer to the earlier section "The Item Review Questions Tab" for more details.

A graphical overview of the score is presented below the grid. The graph depicts two red bars: The top bar represents your current exam score; the bottom bar represents the required passing score. To the right of the bars in the graph is a legend that lists the required score and your score. Below the bar graph is a statement that describes the required passing score and your current score.

In addition, the information can be presented on an overall basis or by exam chapter. The Overall tab shows the overall score. The By Chapter tab shows the score by chapter.

Clicking the End Exam button terminates the exam and passes control to the Examination Score Report screen.

The Return to Exam button returns to the exam at the question from which the Item Review button was clicked.

Review Marked Items

The Item Review screen enables you to enter a browse sequence for marked questions. When you click the Review Marked button, questions that you have previously marked using the Mark Question check box are presented for your review. While browsing the marked questions, you will see the following changes to the buttons available:

◆ The caption of the Next button becomes Next Marked.

◆ The caption of the Previous button becomes Previous Marked.

Review Incomplete

The Item Review screen enables you to enter a browse sequence for incomplete questions. When you click the Review Incomplete button, the questions you did not answer or did not completely answer display for your review. While browsing the incomplete questions, you will see the following changes to the buttons:

◆ The caption of the Next button becomes Next Incomplete.

◆ The caption of the Previous button becomes Previous Incomplete.

Examination Score Report Screen

The Examination Score Report screen (see Figure D.9) appears when the study mode, practice exam, or adaptive exam ends—as the result of timer expiration, completion of all questions, or your decision to terminate early.

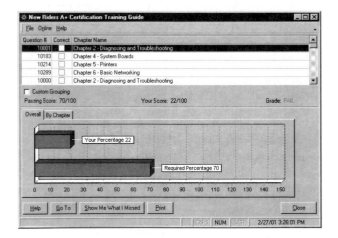

FIGURE D.9
The Examination Score Report screen.

This screen provides you with a graphical display of your test score, along with a tabular breakdown of scores by chapter. The graphical display at the top of the screen compares your overall score with the score required to pass the exam. Buttons below the graphical display allow you to open the Show Me What I Missed browse sequence, print the screen, or return to the main menu.

Show Me What I Missed Browse Sequence

The Show Me What I Missed browse sequence is invoked by clicking the Show Me What I Missed button from the Examination Score Report or from the configuration screen of an adaptive exam.

Note that the window caption is modified to indicate that you are in the Show Me What I Missed browse sequence mode. Question IDs and position within the browse sequence appear at the top of the screen, in place of the Mark Question and Time Remaining indicators. Main window contents vary, depending on the question type. The following list describes the buttons available within the Show Me What I Missed browse sequence and the functions they perform:

◆ **Return to Score Report.** Returns control to the Examination Score Report screen. In the case of an adaptive exam, this button's caption is Exit, and control returns to the adaptive exam configuration screen.

◆ **Run Simulation.** Opens a simulation in Grade mode, causing the simulation to open displaying your response and the correct answer. If the current question does not offer a simulation, this button is disabled.

◆ **Exhibits.** Opens the Exhibits window. This button is enabled if one or more exhibits are available for the question.

◆ **Instructions.** Shows how to answer the current question type.

◆ **Print.** Prints the current screen.

◆ **Previous or Next.** Displays missed questions.

CHECKING THE WEB SITE

To check the New Riders home page or the ExamGear, Training Guide Edition home page for updates or other product information, choose the desired Web site from the Web Sites option of the Online menu. You must be connected to the Internet to reach these Web sites.

Frequently Asked Questions

ExamGear FAQ can be found at http://www. newriders.com/examgear/support/faq.cfm.

OBTAINING UPDATES

The procedures for obtaining updates are outlined in this section.

The Catalog Web Site for Updates

Selecting the Check for Product Updates option from the Online menu shows you the full range of products you can either download for free or purchase from your Web browser. You must be connected to the Internet to reach these Web sites.

Types of Updates

Several types of updates may be available for download, including various free updates and additional items available for purchase.

Free Program Updates

Free program updates include changes to the ExamGear, Training Guide Edition executables and runtime libraries (DLLs). When any of these items are downloaded, ExamGear automatically installs the upgrades. ExamGear, Training Guide Edition will be reopened after the installation is complete.

Free Database Updates

Free database updates include updates to the exam or exams that you have registered. Exam updates are contained in compressed, encrypted files and include exam databases and exhibits. ExamGear, Training Guide Edition automatically decompresses these files to their proper location and updates the ExamGear software to record version changes and import new question sets.

CONTACTING NEW RIDERS PUBLISHING

At New Riders, we strive to meet and exceed the needs of our customers. We have developed ExamGear, Training Guide Edition to surpass the demands and expectations of network professionals seeking technical certifications, and we think it shows. What do you think?

If you need to contact New Riders regarding any aspect of the ExamGear, Training Guide Edition product line, feel free to do so. We look forward to hearing from you. Contact us at the following address or phone number:

New Riders Publishing
201 West 103rd Street
Indianapolis, IN 46290
800-545-5914

You can also reach us on the World Wide Web:

`http://www.newriders.com`

Technical Support

Technical support is available at the following phone number during the hours specified:

Telephone: 317-581-3833

Email: examgear@newriders.com

Monday through Friday, 10 a.m—3 p.m. Central Standard Time.

You can visit the online support Web site at `www.newriders.com/support` and submit a support request over the Internet.

Customer Service

If you have a damaged product and need a replacement or refund, please call the following phone number:

800-858-7674

Product Updates

Product updates can be obtained by choosing ExamGear, Training Guide Edition's Online pull-down menu and selecting Check For Products Updates. You will be taken to a Web site with full details.

Product Suggestions and Comments

We value your input! Please email your suggestions and comments to the following address:

`nrfeedback@newriders.com`

LICENSE AGREEMENT

YOU SHOULD CAREFULLY READ THE FOLLOWING TERMS AND CONDITIONS BEFORE BREAKING THE SEAL ON THE PACKAGE. AMONG OTHER THINGS, THIS AGREEMENT LICENSES THE ENCLOSED SOFTWARE TO YOU AND CONTAINS WARRANTY AND LIABILITY DISCLAIMERS. BY BREAKING THE SEAL ON THE PACKAGE, YOU ARE ACCEPTING AND AGREEING TO THE TERMS AND CONDITIONS OF THIS AGREEMENT. IF YOU DO NOT AGREE TO THE TERMS OF THIS AGREEMENT, DO NOT BREAK THE SEAL. YOU SHOULD PROMPTLY RETURN THE PACKAGE UNOPENED.

LICENSE

Subject to the provisions contained herein, New Riders Publishing (NRP) hereby grants to you a nonexclusive, nontransferable license to use the object-code version of the computer software product (Software) contained in the package on a single computer of the type identified on the package.

SOFTWARE AND DOCUMENTATION

NRP shall furnish the Software to you on media in machine-readable object-code form and may also provide the standard documentation (Documentation) containing instructions for operation and use of the Software.

LICENSE TERM AND CHARGES

The term of this license commences upon delivery of the Software to you and is perpetual unless earlier terminated upon default or as otherwise set forth herein.

TITLE

Title, ownership right, and intellectual property rights in and to the Software and Documentation shall remain in NRP and/or in suppliers to NRP of programs contained in the Software. The Software is provided for your own internal use under this license. This license does not include the right to sublicense and is personal to you and therefore may not be assigned (by operation of law or otherwise) or transferred without the prior written consent of NRP. You acknowledge that the Software in source code form remains a confidential trade secret of NRP and/or its suppliers and therefore you agree not to attempt to decipher or decompile, modify, disassemble, reverse engineer, or prepare derivative works of the Software or develop source code for the Software or knowingly allow others to do so. Further, you may not copy the Documentation or other written materials accompanying the Software.

UPDATES

This license does not grant you any right, license, or interest in and to any improvements, modifications, enhancements, or updates to the Software and Documentation. Updates, if available, may be obtained by you at NRP's then-current standard pricing, terms, and conditions.

LIMITED WARRANTY AND DISCLAIMER

NRP warrants that the media containing the Software, if provided by NRP, is free from defects in material and workmanship under normal use for a period of sixty (60) days from the date you purchased a license to it.

THIS IS A LIMITED WARRANTY AND IT IS THE ONLY WARRANTY MADE BY NRP. THE SOFTWARE IS PROVIDED "AS IS" AND NRP SPECIFICALLY DISCLAIMS ALL WARRANTIES OF ANY KIND, EITHER EXPRESS OR IMPLIED, INCLUDING, BUT NOT LIMITED TO, THE IMPLIED WARRANTY OF MERCHANTABILITY AND FITNESS FOR A PARTICULAR PURPOSE. FURTHER, COMPANY DOES NOT WARRANT, GUARANTEE, OR MAKE ANY REPRESENTATIONS REGARDING THE USE, OR THE RESULTS OF THE USE, OF THE SOFTWARE IN TERMS OR CORRECTNESS, ACCURACY, RELIABILITY, CURRENTNESS, OR OTHERWISE AND DOES NOT WARRANT THAT THE OPERATION OF ANY SOFTWARE WILL BE UNINTERRUPTED OR ERROR FREE. NRP EXPRESSLY DISCLAIMS ANY WARRANTIES NOT STATED HEREIN. NO ORAL OR WRITTEN INFORMATION OR ADVICE GIVEN BY NRP, OR ANY NRP

DEALER, AGENT, EMPLOYEE, OR OTHERS SHALL CREATE, MODIFY, OR EXTEND A WARRANTY OR IN ANY WAY INCREASE THE SCOPE OF THE FOREGOING WARRANTY, AND NEITHER SUBLICENSEE OR PURCHASER MAY RELY ON ANY SUCH INFORMATION OR ADVICE. If the media is subjected to accident, abuse, or improper use, or if you violate the terms of this Agreement, then this warranty shall immediately be terminated. This warranty shall not apply if the Software is used on or in conjunction with hardware or programs other than the unmodified version of hardware and programs with which the Software was designed to be used as described in the Documentation.

LIMITATION OF LIABILITY

Your sole and exclusive remedies for any damage or loss in any way connected with the Software are set forth below.

UNDER NO CIRCUMSTANCES AND UNDER NO LEGAL THEORY, TORT, CONTRACT, OR OTHERWISE, SHALL NRP BE LIABLE TO YOU OR ANY OTHER PERSON FOR ANY INDIRECT, SPECIAL, INCIDENTAL, OR CONSEQUENTIAL DAMAGES OF ANY CHARACTER INCLUDING, WITHOUT LIMITATION, DAMAGES FOR LOSS OF GOODWILL, LOSS OF PROFIT, WORK STOPPAGE, COMPUTER FAILURE OR MALFUNCTION, OR ANY AND ALL OTHER COMMERCIAL DAMAGES OR LOSSES, OR FOR ANY OTHER DAMAGES EVEN IF NRP SHALL HAVE BEEN INFORMED OF THE POSSIBILITY OF SUCH DAMAGES, OR FOR ANY CLAIM BY ANOTHER PARTY. NRP'S THIRD-PARTY PROGRAM SUPPLIERS MAKE NO WARRANTY, AND HAVE NO LIABILITY WHATSOEVER, TO YOU. NRP's sole and exclusive obligation and liability and your exclusive remedy shall be: upon NRP's election,

(i) the replacement of our defective media; or (ii) the repair or correction of your defective media if NRP is able, so that it will conform to the above warranty; or (iii) if NRP is unable to replace or repair, you may terminate this license by returning the Software. Only if you inform NRP of your problem during the applicable warranty period will NRP be obligated to honor this warranty. SOME STATES OR JURISDICTIONS DO NOT ALLOW THE EXCLUSION OF IMPLIED WARRANTIES OR LIMITATION OR EXCLUSION OF CONSEQUENTIAL DAMAGES, SO THE ABOVE LIMITATIONS OR EXCLUSIONS MAY NOT APPLY TO YOU. THIS WARRANTY GIVES YOU SPECIFIC LEGAL RIGHTS AND YOU MAY ALSO HAVE OTHER RIGHTS WHICH VARY BY STATE OR JURISDICTION.

MISCELLANEOUS

If any provision of the Agreement is held to be ineffective, unenforceable, or illegal under certain circumstances for any reason, such decision shall not affect the validity or enforceability (i) of such provision under other circumstances or (ii) of the remaining provisions hereof under all circumstances, and such provision shall be reformed to and only to the extent necessary to make it effective, enforceable, and legal under such circumstances. All headings are solely for convenience and shall not be considered in interpreting this Agreement. This Agreement shall be governed by and construed under New York law as such law applies to agreements between New York residents entered into and to be performed entirely within New York, except as required by U.S. Government rules and regulations to be governed by Federal law.

YOU ACKNOWLEDGE THAT YOU HAVE READ THIS AGREEMENT, UNDERSTAND IT, AND AGREE TO BE BOUND BY ITS TERMS AND CONDITIONS. YOU FURTHER AGREE THAT IT

IS THE COMPLETE AND EXCLUSIVE STATE-
MENT OF THE AGREEMENT BETWEEN US
THAT SUPERSEDES ANY PROPOSAL OR PRIOR
AGREEMENT, ORAL OR WRITTEN, AND ANY
OTHER COMMUNICATIONS BETWEEN US
RELATING TO THE SUBJECT MATTER OF THIS
AGREEMENT.

U.S. GOVERNMENT RESTRICTED RIGHTS

Use, duplication, or disclosure by the Government is subject to restrictions set forth in subparagraphs (a) through (d) of the Commercial Computer-Restricted Rights clause at FAR 52.227-19 when applicable, or in subparagraph (c) (1) (ii) of the Rights in Technical Data and Computer Software clause at DFARS 252.227-7013, and in similar clauses in the NASA FAR Supplement.

Index

D

M

Q-R

T

U

W

X-Z

Additional Tools for Certification Preparation

Taking the author-driven, no-nonsense approach that we pioneered with our *Landmark* books, New Riders proudly offers something unique for Windows 2000 administrators—an interesting and discriminating book on Windows 2000 Server, written by someone in the trenches who can anticipate your situation and provide answers you can trust.

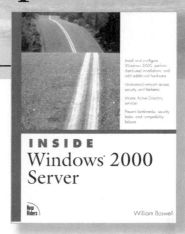

INSIDE
Windows 2000 Server

William Boswell

ISBN: 1-56205-929-7

Windows 2000
ESSENTIAL REFERENCE

Includes coverage of Server, Workstation, and Professional

Steven Tate, et al.

Architected to be the most navigable, useful, and value-packed reference for Windows 2000, this book uses a creative "telescoping" design that you can adapt to your style of learning. It's a concise, focused, and quick reference for Windows 2000, providing the kind of practical advice, tips, procedures, and additional resources that every administrator will need.

ISBN: 0-7357-0869-X

Understanding the Network is just one of several new titles from New Riders' acclaimed *Landmark Series*. This book addresses the audience in practical terminology, and describes the most essential information and tools required to build high-availability networks in a step-by-step implementation format. Each chapter could be read as a stand-alone, but the book builds progressively toward a summary of the essential concepts needed to put together a wide area network.

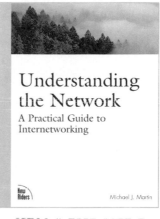

Understanding the Network
A Practical Guide to Internetworking

Michael J. Martin

ISBN: 0-7357-0977-7

New Riders
Windows 2000 Resources

Advice and Experience for the Windows 2000 Networker

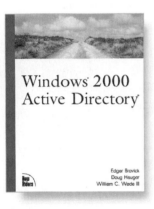

LANDMARK SERIES

We know how important it is to have access to detailed, solution-oriented information on core technologies. *Landmark* books contain the essential information you need to solve technical problems. Written by experts and subjected to rigorous peer and technical reviews, our *Landmark* books are hard-core resources for practitioners like you.

ESSENTIAL REFERENCE SERIES

The *Essential Reference* series from New Riders provides answers when you know what you want to do but need to know how to do it. Each title skips extraneous material and assumes a strong base of knowledge. These are indispensable books for the practitioner who wants to find specific features of a technology quickly and efficiently. Avoiding fluff and basic material, these books present solutions in an innovative, clean format—and at a great value.

CIRCLE SERIES

The *Circle Series* is a set of reference guides that meet the needs of the growing community of advanced, technical–level networkers who must architect, develop, and administer Windows NT/2000 systems. These books provide network designers and programmers with detailed, proven solutions to their problems.

The Road to MCSE Windows 2000

The new Microsoft Windows 2000 track is designed for information technology professionals working in a typically complex computing environment of medium to large organizations. A Windows 2000 MCSE candidate should have at least one year of experience implementing and administering a network operating system.

MCSEs in the Windows 2000 track are required to pass **five core exams and two elective exams** that provide a valid and reliable measure of technical proficiency and expertise.

See below for the exam information and the relevant New Riders title that covers that exam.

Core Exams

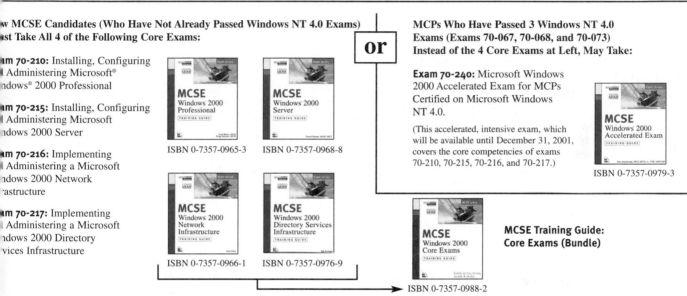

w MCSE Candidates (Who Have Not Already Passed Windows NT 4.0 Exams) st Take All 4 of the Following Core Exams:

am 70-210: Installing, Configuring Administering Microsoft® ndows® 2000 Professional

am 70-215: Installing, Configuring Administering Microsoft ndows 2000 Server

am 70-216: Implementing Administering a Microsoft ndows 2000 Network astructure

am 70-217: Implementing Administering a Microsoft ndows 2000 Directory vices Infrastructure

ISBN 0-7357-0965-3   ISBN 0-7357-0968-8

ISBN 0-7357-0966-1   ISBN 0-7357-0976-9

or

MCPs Who Have Passed 3 Windows NT 4.0 Exams (Exams 70-067, 70-068, and 70-073) Instead of the 4 Core Exams at Left, May Take:

Exam 70-240: Microsoft Windows 2000 Accelerated Exam for MCPs Certified on Microsoft Windows NT 4.0.

(This accelerated, intensive exam, which will be available until December 31, 2001, covers the core competencies of exams 70-210, 70-215, 70-216, and 70-217.)

ISBN 0-7357-0979-3

MCSE Training Guide: Core Exams (Bundle)

ISBN 0-7357-0988-2

PLUS - All Candidates - 1 of the Following Core Elective Exams Required:

am 70-219: Designing a Microsoft Windows 2000 Directory vices Infrastructure

am 70-220: Designing Security for a Microsoft Windows 2000 Network

am 70-221: Designing a Microsoft Windows 2000 work Infrastructure

ISBN 0-7357-0983-1   ISBN 0-7357-0984-X   ISBN 0-7357-0982-3

LUS - All Candidates - 2 of the Following Elective Exams Required:

y current MCSE electives (visit www.microsoft.com for a list of current electives)

ected third-party certifications that focus on interoperability will be accepted as an alternative to one tive exam. Please watch for more information on the third-party certifications that will be acceptable.)

am 70-219: Designing a Microsoft Windows 2000 Directory Services Infrastructure

am 70-220: Designing Security for a Microsoft Windows 2000 Network

am 70-221: Designing a Microsoft Windows 2000 Network Infrastructure

am 70-222: Upgrading from Microsoft Windows NT 4.0 to Microsoft Windows 2000

ISBN 0-7357-0983-1   ISBN 0-7357-0984-X   ISBN 0-7357-0982-3

re exams that can also be used as elective exams may only be counted once toward a certification; that is, if a candidate receives it for an exam as a core in one track, that candidate will not receive credit for that same exam as an elective in that same track.

New Riders

WWW.NEWRIDERS.COM

Windows 2000 Professional

By Jerry Honeycutt
350 pages, $34.99 US
ISBN: 0-7357-0950-5

Windows 2000 Professional explores the power available to the Windows workstation user on the corporate network and Internet. The book is aimed directly at the power user who values the security, stability, and networking capabilities of NT alongside the ease and familiarity of the Windows 95/98 user interface. This book covers both user and administration topics, with a dose of networking content added for connectivity.

Windows 2000 Power Toolkit

By Barry Shilmover &
Stu Sjouwerman
1st Edition
1000 pages, $49.99
ISBN: 0-7357-1061-9
Available May 2001

This book covers the analysis, tuning, optimization, automation, enhancement, maintenance, and troubleshooting of Windows 2000. This advanced title comprises a task-oriented treatment of the Windows NT/2000 environment. By concentrating on the use of new Windows features, operating system tools and utilities, resource kit elements, and selected third-party tuning, analysis, optimization, and productivity tools, this book will show you how to carry out everyday and advanced tasks.

Windows 2000 User Management

By Lori Sanders
300 pages, $34.99
ISBN: 1-56205-886-X

With the dawn of Windows 2000, it has become even more difficult to draw a clear line between managing the user and managing the user's environment and desktop. This book, written by a noted trainer and consultant, provides comprehensive, practical advice to managing users and their desktop environments with Windows 2000.

Windows 2000 Deployment & Desktop Management

By Jeffrey A. Ferris, MCSE
1st Edition
400 pages, $34.99
ISBN: 0-7357-0975-0

More than a simple overview of new features and tools, *Windows 2000 Deployment & Desktop Management* is a thorough reference to deploying Windows 2000 Professional to corporate workstations. Incorporating real-world advice and detailed exercises, this book is a one-stop resource for any system administrator, integrator, engineer, or other IT professional.

Planning for Windows 2000

By Eric K. Cone, Jon Boggs, and Sergio Perez
1st Edition
400 pages, $29.99
ISBN: 0-7357-0048-6

Windows 2000 is poised to be one of the largest and most important software releases of the next decade, and you are charged with planning, testing, and deploying it in your enterprise. Are you ready? With this book, you will be. *Planning for Windows 2000* lets you know what the upgrade hurdles will be, informs you of how to clear them, guides you through effective Active Directory design, and presents you with detailed rollout procedures. Eric K. Cone, Jon Boggs, and Sergio Perez give you the benefit of their extensive experiences as Windows 2000 Rapid Deployment Program members by sharing problems and solutions they've encountered on the job.

SQL Server System Administration

By Sean Baird, Chris Miller, et al.
1st Edition
352 pages, $29.99
ISBN: 1-56205-955-6

How often does your SQL Server go down during the day when everyone wants to access the data? Do you spend most of your time being a "report monkey" for your coworkers and bosses? *SQL Server System Administration* helps you keep data consistently available to your users. This book omits introductory information. The authors don't spend time explaining queries and how they work. Instead, they focus on the information you can't get anywhere else, like how to choose the correct replication topology and achieve high availability of information.

Inside Windows 2000 Server

By William Boswell
2nd Edition
1533 pages, $49.99
ISBN: 1-56205-929-7

Finally, a totally new edition of New Riders' best-selling *Inside Windows NT Server 4*. Taking the author-driven, no-nonsense approach pioneered with the *Landmark* books, New Riders proudly offers something unique for Windows 2000 administrators—an interesting, discriminating book on Windows 2000 Server written by someone who can anticipate your situation and give you workarounds that won't leave a system unstable or sluggish.

Internet Information Services Administration
By Kelli Adam
1st Edition,
200 pages, $29.99
ISBN: 0-7357-0022-2

Are the new Internet technologies in Internet Information Services giving you headaches? Does protecting security on the Web take up all of your time? Then this is the book for you. With hands-on configuration training, advanced study of the new protocols, the most recent version of IIS, and detailed instructions on authenticating users with the new Certificate Server and implementing and managing the new e-commerce features, *Internet Information Services Administration* gives you the real-life solutions you need. This definitive resource prepares you for upgrading to Windows 2000 by giving you detailed advice on working with Microsoft Management Console, which was first used by IIS.

SMS 2 Administration
By Michael Lubanski and Darshan Doshi
1st Edition
350 pages, $39.99
ISBN: 0-7357-0082-6

Microsoft's new version of its Systems Management Server (SMS) is starting to turn heads. Although complex, it allows administrators to lower their total cost of ownership and more efficiently manage clients, applications, and support operations. If your organization is using or implementing SMS, you'll need some expert advice. Michael Lubanski and Darshan Doshi can help you get the most bang for your buck with insight, expert tips, and real-world examples. Michael and Darshan are consultants specializing in SMS and have worked with Microsoft on one of the most complex SMS rollouts in the world, involving 32 countries, 15 languages, and thousands of clients.

SQL Server 7 Essential Reference
By Sharon Dooley
1st Edition
500 pages, $35.00 US
ISBN: 0-7357-0864-9

SQL Server 7 Essential Reference is a comprehensive reference of advanced how-tos and techniques for SQL Server 7 administrators. This book provides solid grounding in fundamental SQL Server 7 administrative tasks to help you tame your SQL Server environment. With coverage ranging from installation, monitoring, troubleshooting security, and backup and recovery plans, this book breaks down SQL Server into its key conceptual areas and functions. This easy-to-use reference is a must-have for any SQL Server administrator.

UNIX/Linux Titles

Solaris 8 Essential Reference
By John P. Mulligan
1st Edition
400 pages, $34.99
ISBN: 0-7357-1007-4

Looking for the fastest and easiest way to find the Solaris command you need? Need a few pointers on shell scripting? How about advanced administration tips and sound, practical expertise on security issues? Are you looking for trustworthy information about available third-party software packages that will enhance your operating system? Author John Mulligan—creator of the popular "Unofficial Guide to The Solaris™ Operating Environment" Web site (sun.icsnet.com)—delivers all that and more in one attractive, easy-to-use reference book. With clear and concise instructions on how to perform important administration and management tasks, and key information on powerful commands and advanced topics, *Solaris 8 Essential Reference* is the book you need when you know what you want to do and only need to know how.

Linux System Administration
By M. Carling, Stephen Degler, and James Dennis
1st Edition
450 pages, $29.99
ISBN: 1-56205-934-3

As an administrator, you probably feel that most of your time and energy is spent in endless firefighting. If your network has become a fragile quilt of temporary patches and work-arounds, this book is for you. Have you had trouble sending or receiving email lately? Are you looking for a way to keep your network running smoothly with enhanced performance? Are your users always hankering for more storage, services, and speed? *Linux System Administration* advises you on the many intricacies of maintaining a secure, stable system. In this definitive work, the authors address all the issues related to system administration, from adding users and managing file permissions, to Internet services and Web hosting, to recovery planning and security. This book fulfills the need for expert advice that will ensure a trouble-free Linux environment.

GTK+/Gnome Application Development
By Havoc Pennington
1st Edition
492 pages, $39.99
ISBN: 0-7357-0078-8

This title is for the reader who is conversant with the C programming language and UNIX/Linux development. It provides detailed and solution-oriented information designed to meet the needs of programmers and application developers using the GTK+/Gnome libraries. Coverage complements existing GTK+/Gnome documentation, going into more depth on pivotal issues such as uncovering the GTK+ object system, working with the event loop, managing the Gdk substrate, writing custom widgets, and mastering GnomeCanvas.

Developing Linux Applications with GTK+ and GDK
By Eric Harlow
1st Edition
490 pages, $34.99
ISBN: 0-7357-0021-4

We all know that Linux is one of the most powerful and solid operating systems in existence. And as the success of Linux grows, there is an increasing interest in developing applications with graphical user interfaces that take advantage of the power of Linux. In this book, software developer Eric Harlow gives you an indispensable development handbook focusing on the GTK+ toolkit. More than an overview of the elements of application or GUI design, this is a hands-on book that delves into the technology. With in-depth material on the various GUI programming tools and loads of examples, this book's unique focus will give you the information you need to design and launch professional-quality applications.

Linux Essential Reference
By Ed Petron
1st Edition
350 pages, $24.95
ISBN: 0-7357-0852-5

This book is all about getting things done as quickly and efficiently as possible by providing a structured organization for the plethora of available Linux information. We can sum it up in one word—value. This book has it all: concise instructions

on how to perform key administration tasks, advanced information on configuration, shell scripting, hardware management, systems management, data tasks, automation, and tons of other useful information. This book truly provides groundbreaking information for the growing community of advanced Linux professionals.

Lotus Notes and Domino Titles

Domino System Administration
By Rob Kirkland, CLP, CLI
1st Edition
850 pages, $49.99
ISBN: 1-56205-948-3

Your boss has just announced that you will be upgrading to the newest version of Notes and Domino when it ships. How are you supposed to get this new system installed, configured, and rolled out to all of your end users? You understand how Lotus Notes works—you've been administering it for years. What you need is a concise, practical explanation of the new features and how to make some of the advanced stuff work smoothly by someone like you, who has worked with the product for years and understands what you need to know. *Domino System Administration* is the answer—the first book on Domino that attacks the technology at the professional level with practical, hands-on assistance to get Domino running in your organization.

Lotus Notes & Domino Essential Reference

By Tim Bankes, CLP
and Dave Hatter, CLP, MCP
1st Edition
650 pages, $45.00
ISBN: 0-7357-0007-9

You're in a bind because you've been asked to design and program a new database in Notes for an important client who will keep track of and itemize myriad inventory and shipping data. The client wants a user-friendly interface that won't sacrifice speed or functionality. You are experienced (and could develop this application in your sleep), but feel you need something to facilitate your creative and technical abilities—something to perfect your programming skills. The answer is waiting for you: *Lotus Notes & Domino Essential Reference*. It's compact and simply designed. It's loaded with information. All of the objects, classes, functions, and methods are listed. It shows you the object hierarchy and the relationship between each one. It's perfect for you. Problem solved.

Networking Titles

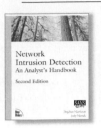

Network Intrusion Detection: An Analyst's Handbook

By Stephen Northcutt
and Judy Novak
2nd Edition
460 pages, $45.00
ISBN: 0-7357-1008-2

Get answers and solutions from someone who has been in the trenches. The author, Stephen Northcutt, original developer of the Shadow intrusion detection system and former director of the United States Navy's Information System Security Office at the Naval Security Warfare Center, gives his expertise to intrusion detection specialists, security analysts, and consultants responsible for setting up and maintaining an effective defense against network security attacks.

Understanding Data Communications, Sixth Edition

By Gilbert Held
Sixth Edition
600 pages, $39.99
ISBN: 0-7357-0036-2

Updated from the highly successful fifth edition, this book explains how data communications systems and their various hardware and software components work. More than an entry-level book, it approaches the material in textbook format, addressing the complex issues involved in internetworking today. A great reference book for the experienced networking professional that is written by the noted networking authority, Gilbert Held.

Other Books By New Riders

SECURITY

Intrusion Detection
1-57870-185-6 • $50.00 US / $74.95 CAN
Understanding Public-Key Infrastructure
1-57870-166-X • $50.00 US / $74.95 CAN
Network Intrusion Detection: An Analyst's Handbook, 2E
0-7357-1008-2 • $45.00 US / $67.95 CAN
Linux Firewalls
0-7357-0900-9 • $39.99 US / $59.95 CAN
Intrusion Signatures and Analysis
0-7357-1063-5 • $39.99 US / $59.95 CAN
Hackers Beware
0-7357-1009-0 • $45.00 US / $67.95 CAN
• Available July 2001

LOTUS NOTES/DOMINO

Domino System Administration
1-56205-948-3 • $49.99 US / $74.95 CAN
Lotus Notes & Domino Essential Reference
0-7357-0007-9 • $45.00 US / $67.95 CAN

PROFESSIONAL CERTIFICATION

TRAINING GUIDES

MCSE Training Guide: Networking Essentials, 2nd Ed.
1-56205-919-X • $49.99 US / $74.95 CAN
MCSE Training Guide: Windows NT Server 4, 2nd Ed.
1-56205-916-5 • $49.99 US / $74.95 CAN
MCSE Training Guide: Windows NT Workstation 4, 2nd Ed.
1-56205-918-1 • $49.99 US / $74.95 CAN
MCSE Training Guide: Windows NT Server 4 Enterprise, 2nd Ed.
1-56205-917-3 • $49.99 US / $74.95 CAN
MCSE Training Guide: Core Exams Bundle, 2nd Ed.
1-56205-926-2 • $149.99 US / $223.95 CAN
MCSE Training Guide: TCP/IP, 2nd Ed.
1-56205-920-3 • $49.99 US / $74.95 CAN

MCSE Training Guide: IIS 4, 2nd Ed.
0-7357-0865-7 • $49.99 US / $74.95 CAN
MCSE Training Guide: SQL Server 7 Administration
0-7357-0003-6 • $49.99 US / $74.95 CAN
MCSE Training Guide: SQL Server 7 Database Design
0-7357-0004-4 • $49.99 US / $74.95 CAN
MCSD Training Guide: Visual Basic 6 Exams
0-7357-0002-8 • $69.99 US / $104.95 CAN
MCSD Training Guide: Solution Architectures
0-7357-0026-5 • $49.99 US / $74.95 CAN
MCSD Training Guide: 4-in-1 Bundle
0-7357-0912-2 • $149.99 US / $223.95 CAN
A+ Certification Training Guide, Second Edition
0-7357-0907-6 • $49.99 US / $74.95 CAN
Network+ Certification Guide
0-7357-0077-X • $49.99 US / $74.95 CAN
Solaris 2.6 Administrator Certification Training Guide, Part I
1-57870-085-X • $40.00 US / $59.95 CAN
Solaris 2.6 Administrator Certification Training Guide, Part II
1-57870-086-8 • $40.00 US / $59.95 CAN
Solaris 7 Administrator Certification Training Guide, Part I and II
1-57870-249-6 • $49.99 US / $74.95 CAN
MCSE Training Guide: Windows 2000 Professional
0-7357-0965-3 • $49.99 US / $74.95 CAN
MCSE Training Guide: Windows 2000 Server
0-7357-0968-8 • $49.99 US / $74.95 CAN
MCSE Training Guide: Windows 2000 Network Infrastructure
0-7357-0966-1 • $49.99 US / $74.95 CAN
MCSE Training Guide: Windows 2000 Network Security Design
0-73570-984X • $49.99 US / $74.95 CAN
MCSE Training Guide: Windows 2000 Network Infrastructure Design
0-73570-982-3 • $49.99 US / $74.95 CAN
MCSE Training Guide: Windows 2000 Directory Svcs. Infrastructure
0-7357-0976-9 • $49.99 US / $74.95 CAN

MCSE Training Guide: Windows 2000 Directory Services Design
0-7357-0983-1 • $49.99 US / $74.95 CAN
MCSE Training Guide: Windows 2000 Accelerated Exam
0-7357-0979-3 • $69.99 US / $104.95 CAN
MCSE Training Guide: Windows 2000 Core Exams Bundle
0-7357-0988-2 • $149.99 US / $223.95 CAN

FAST TRACKS

CLP Fast Track: Lotus Notes/Domino 5 Application Development
0-73570-877-0 • $39.99 US / $59.95 CAN
CLP Fast Track: Lotus Notes/Domino 5 System Administration
0-7357-0878-9 • $39.99 US / $59.95 CAN
Network+ Fast Track
0-7357-0904-1 • $29.99 US / $44.95 CAN
A+ Fast Track
0-7357-0028-1 • $34.99 US / $52.95 CAN
MCSD Fast Track: Visual Basic 6, Exam #70-175
0-7357-0019-2 • $19.99 US / $29.95 CAN
MCSD FastTrack: Visual Basic 6, Exam #70-175
0-7357-0018-4 • $19.99 US / $29.95 CAN

SOFTWARE ARCHITECTURE & ENGINEERING

Designing for the User with OVID
1-57870-101-5 • $40.00 US / $59.95 CAN
Designing Flexible Object-Oriented Systems with UML
1-57870-098-1 • $40.00 US / $59.95 CAN
Constructing Superior Software
1-57870-147-3 • $40.00 US / $59.95 CAN
A UML Pattern Language
1-57870-118-X • $45.00 US / $67.95 CAN

HOW TO CONTACT US

IF YOU NEED THE LATEST UPDATES ON A TITLE THAT YOU'VE PURCHASED:

1) Visit our Web site at www.newriders.com.

2) Enter the book ISBN number, which is located on the back cover in the bottom right-hand corner, in the site search box on the left navigation bar.

3) Select your book title from the list of search results. On the book page, you'll find available updates and downloads for your title.

IF YOU ARE HAVING TECHNICAL PROBLEMS WITH THE BOOK OR THE CD THAT IS INCLUDED:

1) Check the book's information page on our Web site according to the instructions listed above, or

2) Email us at userservices@pearsoned.com, or

3) Fax us at 317-581-4663 ATTN: Tech Support.

IF YOU HAVE COMMENTS ABOUT ANY OF OUR CERTIFICATION PRODUCTS THAT ARE NON-SUPPORT RELATED:

1) Email us at nrfeedback@newriders.com, or

2) Write to us at New Riders, 201 W. 103rd St., Indianapolis, IN 46290-1097, or

3) Fax us at 317-581-4663.

IF YOU ARE OUTSIDE THE UNITED STATES AND NEED TO FIND A DISTRIBUTOR IN YOUR AREA:

Please contact our international department at international@mcp.com.

IF YOU ARE INTERESTED IN BEING AN AUTHOR OR TECHNICAL REVIEWER:

Email us at opportunities@newriders.com. Include your name, email address, phone number, and area of technical expertise.

IF YOU WISH TO PREVIEW ANY OF OUR CERTIFICATION BOOKS FOR CLASSROOM USE:

Email us at nrmedia@newriders.com. Your message should include your name, title, training company or school, department, address, phone number, office days/hours, text in use, and enrollment. Send these details along with your request for desk/examination copies and/or additional information.

IF YOU ARE A MEMBER OF THE PRESS AND WOULD LIKE TO REVIEW ONE OF OUR BOOKS:

Email us at nrmedia@newriders.com. Your message should include your name, title, publication or website you work for, mailing address, and email address.

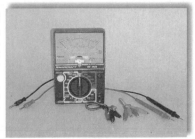

i-Net+ Certification

The i-Net+ certification program is designed specifically for any individual interested in demonstrating baseline technical knowledge that would allow him or her to pursue a variety of Internet-related careers. i-Net+ is a vendor-neutral, entry-level Internet certification program that tests baseline technical knowledge of Internet, Intranet and Extranet technologies, independent of specific Internet-related career roles. Learning objectives and domains examined include Internet basics, Internet clients, development, networking, security and business concepts.

Certification not only helps individuals enter the Internet industry, but also helps managers determine a prospective employee's knowledge and skill level.

Linux+ Certification

The Linux+ certification measures vendor-neutral Linux knowledge and skills for an individual with at least 6 months practical experience. Linux+ Potential Job Roles: Entry Level Helpdesk, Technical Sales/Marketing, Entry Level Service Technician, Technical Writers, Resellers, Application Developers, Application Customer Service Reps.

Linux+ Exam Objectives Outline: User administration, Connecting to the network, Package Management, Security Concept, Shell Scripting, Networking, Apache web server application, Drivers (installation, updating, removing), Kernel (what it does, why to rebuild), Basic printing, Basic troubleshooting.

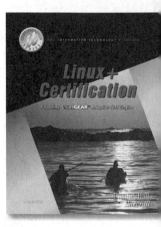

The Complete Introductory Computer Course

The Complete Introductory Computer Course is an entry-level course that helps prepare students for the more challenging A+ Computer Technician Repair course. It also helps launch their careers into the fast-growing IT industry. The 198-page, highly-illustrated manual provides over 45 hours of easy-to-understand explorations of the basic parts of a computer, computer construction, and computer operations. This introductory course helps build student confidences and basic computer literacy. The reusable MC-2300 computer course comes complete with convenient plastic storage case, text book, computer hardware, Windows 98, and integrated application software (CD-ROM) that includes: database, word processing, and spreadsheet. Best of all, it comes with a toll-free tech support line. 1-800-441-6006

ꞏꞏꞏ MARCRAFT
Your IT Training Provider
(800) 441-6006

Data Cabling Installer Certification

The Data Cabling Installer Certification provides the IT industry with an introductory, vendor-neutral certification for skilled personnel that install Category 5 copper data cabling.

The Marcraft *Enhanced Data Cabling Installer Certification Training Guide* provides students with the knowledge and skills required to pass the Data Cabling Installer Certification exam and become a certified cable installer. The DCIC is recognized nationwide and is the hiring criterion used by major communication companies. Therefore, becoming a certified data cable installer will enhance your job opportunities and career advancement potential.

Fiber Optic Cabling Certification

There is a growing demand for qualified cable installers who understand and can implement fiber optic technologies. These technologies cover terminology, techniques, tools and other products in the fiber optic industry. This text/lab book covers basics of fiber optic design discipline, installations, pulling and prepping cables, terminations, testing and safety considerations. Labs will cover ST-compatible and SC connector types, both multimedia and single mode cables and connectors. Learn about insertion loss, optical time domain reflectometry, and reflectance. Cover mechanical and fusion splices and troubleshooting cable systems. This Text/Lab covers the theory and hands-on skills needed to prepare you for fiber optic entry-level certification.

TEAMS 32 Classroom Management System

Marcraft makes classroom management complete and affordable
Classroom management just got a heck of a lot easier. Thanks to TEAMS 32 you're relieved from many of the mundane and time-consuming tasks involved in managing a classroom. It can even eliminate a lot of the paper- work -- maybe all of it!
And you get back the time to do what you actually want to do: teach.
Flexible to fit your classroom TEAMS 32 is flexible enough to fit any classroom size or style, whether traditional or a more complex rotational system. Manage your classroom the way you want! And classroom records are kept and updated automatically, including individual student test performance, attendance, class rosters and other student information.
Fully Network-Compatible TEAMS 32 takes full advantage of modern TCP/IP networked-classrooms to automate test administration. Exams are instantly sent to student computers, and immediately retrieved by the instructor's computer when completed. Multiple-choice tests are automatically graded and made available to the student for review over the network.